Fodor's 2008

FLORIDA

Where to Stay and Eat
for All Budgets

Must-See Sights
and Local Secrets

Ratings You Can Trust

Fodor's Travel Publications   New York, Toronto, London, Sydney, Auckland
www.fodors.com

FODOR'S FLORIDA 2008

Editor: Jacinta O'Halloran, Paul Eisenberg

Editorial Production: Tom Holton

Editorial Contributors: Diane Bair, Suzy Buckley, LoAnn Halden, Lynne Helm, Jennie Hess, Susan MacCallum-Whitcomb, Alicia Mandigo, Gary McKechnie, Kristin Milavec, Kerry Speckman, Rowland Stiteler, Mary Thurwachter, Jim and Cynthia Tunstall, Chelle Koster Walton, Pamela Wright

Maps & Illustrations: David Lindroth; Bob Blake and Rebecca Baer, map editors

Design: Fabrizio La Rocca, creative director; Guido Caroti, art director; Melanie Marin, senior picture editor

Cover Photo: (Florida Keys): Susan Findlay/Masterfile

Production/Manufacturing: Angela L. McLean

COPYRIGHT

ISBN: 978-1-4000-1796-6

ISSN: 0193–9556

SPECIAL SALES

This book is available at special discounts for bulk purchases for sales promotions or premiums. Special editions, including personalized covers, excerpts of existing books, and corporate imprints, can be created in large quantities for special needs. For more information, write to Special Markets/Premium Sales, 1745 Broadway, MD 6-2, New York, New York 10019, or e-mail specialmarkets@randomhouse.com.

AN IMPORTANT TIP & AN INVITATION

Although all prices, opening times, and other details in this book are based on information supplied to us at press time, changes occur all the time in the travel world, and Fodor's cannot accept responsibility for facts that become outdated or for inadvertent errors or omissions. So always confirm information when it matters, especially if you're making a detour to visit a specific place. Your experiences—positive and negative—matter to us. If we have missed or misstated something, please write to us. We follow up on all suggestions. Contact the Florida editor at editors@fodors.com or c/o Fodor's at 1745 Broadway, New York, NY 10019.

PRINTED IN THE UNITED STATES OF AMERICA

10 9 8 7 6 5 4 3 2 1

Be a Fodor's Correspondent

Your opinion matters. It matters to us. It matters to your fellow Fodor's travelers, too. And we'd like to hear it. In fact, we need to hear it.

When you share your experiences and opinions, you become an active member of the Fodor's community. That means we'll not only use your feedback to make our books better, but we'll publish your names and comments whenever possible. Throughout our guides, look for "Word of Mouth," excerpts of your unvarnished feedback.

Here's how you can help improve Fodor's for all of us.

Tell us when we're right. We rely on local writers to give you an insider's perspective. But our writers and staff editors—who are the best in the business—depend on you. Your positive feedback is a vote to renew our recommendations for the next edition.

Tell us when we're wrong. We're proud that we update most of our guides every year. But we're not perfect. Things change. Hotels cut services. Museums change hours. Charming cafés lose charm. If our writer didn't quite capture the essence of a place, tell us how you'd do it differently. If any of our descriptions are inaccurate or inadequate, we'll incorporate your changes in the next edition and will correct factual errors at fodors.com immediately.

Tell us what to include. You probably have had fantastic travel experiences that aren't yet in Fodor's. Why not share them with a community of like-minded travelers? Maybe you chanced upon a beach or bistro or B&B that you don't want to keep to yourself. Tell us why we should include it. And share your discoveries and experiences with everyone directly at fodors.com. Your input may lead us to add a new listing or highlight a place we cover with a "Highly Recommended" star or with our highest rating, "Fodor's Choice."

Give us your opinion instantly at our feedback center at www.fodors.com/feedback. You may also e-mail editors@fodors.com with the subject line "Florida Editor." Or send your nominations, comments, and complaints by mail to Florida Editor, Fodor's, 1745 Broadway, New York, NY 10019.

You and travelers like you are the heart of the Fodor's community. Make our community richer by sharing your experiences. Be a Fodor's correspondent.

Happy traveling!

Tim Jarrell, Publisher

CONTENTS

About This Book 8

When to Go 9

What's Where 10

Quintessential Florida 14

If You Like 16

Great Itineraries 18

On the Calendar 21

1 THE PANHANDLE 27

Around Pensacola Bay. 30

The Gulf Coast. 41

Inland Across the Panhandle 63

Tallahassee. 66

The Panhandle Essentials 73

2 NORTHEAST FLORIDA 76

Jacksonville 79

St. Augustine 105

Daytona & the Space Coast. 116

Inland Towns 138

Northeast Florida Essentials 148

3 WALT DISNEY WORLD & THE ORLANDO AREA 152

Exploring Walt Disney World and the Orlando area 153

Universal Orlando 170

SeaWorld & Discovery Cove 174

Away from the Parks. 178

Where to Eat 182

Where to Stay 197

Nightlife 217

Sports & the Outdoors. 220

Shopping 222

The Orlando Area Essentials. . . . 225

4 PALM BEACH & THE TREASURE COAST 228

Palm Beach 231

West Palm Beach. 243

South to Boca Raton 253

The Treasure Coast 267

Palm Beach & the Treasure Coast Essentials. 284

5 FORT LAUDERDALE & BROWARD COUNTY 288

Fort Lauderdale 293

North on Scenic A1A. 319

South Broward. 326

Fort Lauderdale & Broward Essentials. 335

6 MIAMI & MIAMI BEACH 339

Exploring Miami & Miami Beach 341

Where to Eat 366

Where to Stay 377

Nightlife 396

Beaches, Sports & the Outdoors. 402

Shopping 409

Side Trip to South Dade. 417

Miami & Miami Beach Essentials 420

7 THE FLORIDA KEYS 429

The Upper Keys 433

The Middle Keys. 458

The Lower Keys 467

Key West 475

The Florida Keys Essentials 502

8 THE EVERGLADES 510

Biscayne National Park 514

Everglades National Park. 517

Big Cypress National Preserve . . 539

The Everglades Essentials 540

9 THE LOWER GULF COAST... 545

Fort Myers Area 548

The Coastal Islands 560

Naples Area 573

The Lower Gulf Coast
Essentials. 591

10 THE TAMPA BAY AREA 594

North & West Around Tampa
Bay. 596

The Nature Coast. 627

South of Tampa Bay 632

The Tampa Bay Area Essentials. . 648

FLORIDA ESSENTIALS 652

INDEX. 674

ABOUT OUR WRITERS 688

CLOSEUPS

Perks for Disney Resort Guests. . 199

Best Disney Souvenirs. 223

Florida's Sea Turtles: The Nesting
Season. 268

Cruising for a Taxi 301

An African-American Gem 312

Swap till You Drop. 316

Close Encounters of the
Flipper Kind. 460

Hemingway Was Here 482

Bobbing for Sponges. 626

MAPS

Florida 6–7

The Panhandle. 32

Northeast Florida 80

Jacksonville 82

St. Augustine 107

Orlando Area 179

Where to Stay in the

Orlando Area. 205

Gold Coast & Treasure Coast . . . 233

**Palm Beach & West Palm
Beach 237**

Broward County. 297

Fort Lauderdale 298

Miami Beach. 345

Downtown Miami. 350

Miami, Coral Gables, Coconut
Grove & Key Biscayne. . . . 356–357

Where to Eat in the Miami
Area. 368–369

Where to Stay in the Miami
Area. 378–379

South Dade 419

The Florida Keys 437

Key West 479

Big Cypress National Preserve &
the Everglades & Biscayne
National Parks. 519

The Lower Gulf Coast 550

Naples 578

Tampa/St. Petersburg 598

Bradenton/Sarasota. 633

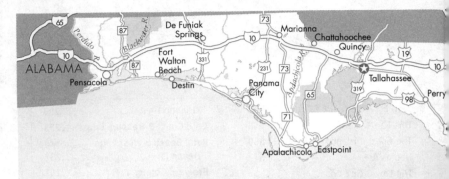

Gulf of Mexico

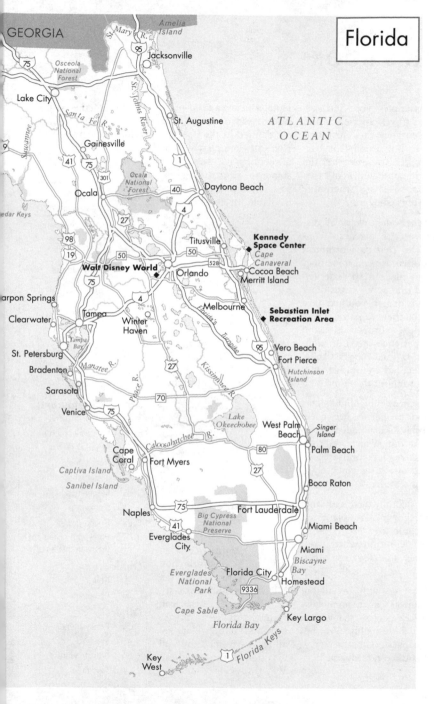

Florida

GEORGIA

Amelia Island

St. Mary R.

Jacksonville

Osceola National Forest

Lake City

Santa Fe R.

St. Johns River

St. Augustine

ATLANTIC OCEAN

Gainesville

Ocala National Forest

Ocala

Daytona Beach

edar Keys

Kennedy Space Center

Titusville

Cape Canaveral

Walt Disney World

Orlando

Cocoa Beach

Merritt Island

arpon Springs

Melbourne

Sebastian Inlet Recreation Area

Clearwater

Tampa

Winter Haven

Florida's Turnpike

Vero Beach

Fort Pierce

St. Petersburg

Tampa Bay

Manatee R.

Hutchinson Island

Bradenton

Peace R.

Kissimmee R.

Sarasota

Venice

Lake Okeechobee

West Palm Beach

Singer Island

Cape Coral

Fort Myers

Caloosahatchee R.

Palm Beach

Captiva Island

Sanibel Island

Boca Raton

Naples

Fort Lauderdale

Big Cypress National Preserve

Miami Beach

Everglades City

Miami

Biscayne Bay

Everglades National Park

Florida City

Homestead

Cape Sable

Key Largo

Florida Bay

Florida Keys

Key West

ABOUT THIS BOOK

Sometimes you find terrific travel experiences and sometimes they just find you. But usually the burden is on you to select the right combination of experiences. That's where our ratings come in.

As travelers we've all discovered a place so wonderful that its worthiness is obvious. And sometimes that place is so experiential that superlatives don't do it justice: you just have to be there to know. These sights, properties, and experiences get our highest rating, **Fodor's Choice**, indicated by orange stars throughout this book.

Black stars highlight sights and properties we deem **Highly Recommended,** places that our writers, editors, and readers praise again and again for consistency and excellence.

By default, there's another category: Any place we include in this book is by definition worth your time, unless we say otherwise. And we will.

Disagree with any of our choices? Care to nominate a place or suggest that we rate one more highly? Visit our feedback center at www. fodors.com/feedback.

Hotel and restaurant price categories from ¢ to $$$$ are defined in the opening pages of each chapter. For attractions, we always give standard adult admission fees; reductions are usually available for children, students, and senior citizens. Want to pay with plastic? AE, D, DC, MC, V following restaurant and hotel listings indicate whether American Express, Discover, Diners Club, MasterCard, and Visa are accepted.

Unless we state otherwise, restaurants are open for lunch and dinner daily. We mention dress only when there's a specific requirement and reservations only when they're essential or not accepted—it's always best to book ahead.

Hotels have private bath, phone, TV, and air-conditioning and operate on the European Plan (aka EP, meaning without meals), unless we specify that they use the Continental Plan (CP, with a continental breakfast), Breakfast Plan (BP, with a full breakfast), or Modified American Plan (MAP, with breakfast and dinner) or are all-inclusive (including all meals and most activities). We always list facilities

but not whether you'll be charged an extra fee to use them, so always ask.

Many Listings
★ Fodor's Choice
★ Highly recommended
⊠ Physical address
✛ Directions
⌖ Mailing address
☎ Telephone
🖷 Fax
⊕ On the Web
✍ E-mail
🎫 Admission fee
☉ Open/closed times
Ⓜ Metro stations
🚃 Credit cards

Hotels & Restaurants
🏨 Hotel
🛏 Number of rooms
⬥ Facilities
🍴 Meal plans
✕ Restaurant
🍽 Reservations
🚭 Smoking
🍷 BYOB
✕🏨 Hotel with restaurant that warrants a visit

Outdoors
🏌 Golf
⛺ Camping

Other
🅒 Family-friendly
⇨ See also
⊠ Branch address
☞ Take note

WHEN TO GO

Although Florida is a year-round vacation venue, it divides the calendar into regional tourism seasons. Holidays and school breaks are major factors. However, the clincher is weather, with the best months being designated as peak periods.

High season in southern Florida starts with the run-up to Christmas and extends through Easter. Snowbirds migrate down then to escape the frosty weather back home. Festivalgoers also flock in because major events are held this time of year to avoid summer's searing heat and high humidity. Moreover, winter is *the* time to visit the ever-popular Everglades: temperatures and mosquito activity are lower, as are water levels (making wildlife easier to spot).

Northern Florida, conversely, experiences the greatest influx from Memorial Day to Labor Day. Costs are highest then, but so are temperatures. (In winter, when the mercury dips into the 40s, you'll get a chilly reception on Panhandle beaches.) Specific areas—like Panama City Beach or Daytona Beach—attract throngs and thongs during spring break, too. In the latter, also expect revved-up revelers during Speed Weeks (in February) and Bike Week (in March).

Thanks to its unparalleled theme parks, Central Florida is a magnet for families. So crowds gather, logically enough, whenever class lets out. Line-ups at attractions do shrink after children return to school. Yet large numbers of international families—and increasing numbers of "kid-free" adults—keep this area hopping year-round. Spring and fall shoulder seasons are the optimal time to visit both weather-wise and price-wise.

Climate

Florida is rightly called the Sunshine State. (Areas like Tampa Bay report 361 days of sunshine a year!) But it could be dubbed the Humid State. June through September, 90% humidity levels aren't uncommon. Nor are accompanying thundershowers: in fact, more than half the state's rain falls during these months. Florida's two-sided coastline also makes it a target for tropical storms. Hurricane season officially begins June 1 and ends November 30.

Forecasts

Weather Channel Connection (⊕*www.weather.com*).

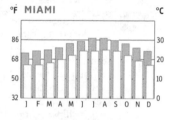

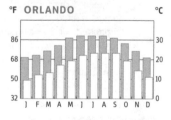

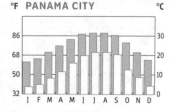

WHAT'S WHERE

THE PANHANDLE 	The underappreciated Panhandle is a colorful place. Tourism officials have dubbed it the Emerald Coast because of its green Gulf of Mexico waters. Fishermen sometimes refer to it as the Red Coast because of the abundance of red snapper. But it's the bone-white crushed-quartz sand that keeps regular folks returning. Florida's northwest shore is basically one big, beautiful beach. Large swaths of it, including the Gulf Islands National Seashore, have been carefully preserved, whereas others, particularly around Panama City Beach, are more notable for high-rise condos and kitschy seaside amusements. The Panhandle, however, promises more than a day at the beach. Pensacola, for instance, boasts almost 500 years of history, and Tallahassee (a mere 14 mi from the Georgia border) has a distinct antebellum charm. In fact, the whole area has much in common with the Deep South. So expect fragrant magnolias, deep-fried foods, and soft Southern drawls.
NORTHEAST FLORIDA 	Northeastern Florida scores points for diversity. For starters, America's oldest continually inhabited city is here. St. Augustine was founded by the Spanish in 1565, and time seems to rewind when you visit Castillo de San Marcos (the colonial-era fortress) or stroll the streets of the Old City that grew up around it. After experiencing life in the past lane, you can fast forward—literally—to the land of race cars and rocket ships. Ormond Beach is considered the "Birthplace of Speed," thanks to men like Henry Ford and Louis Chevrolet who tested their prototypical vehicles on the town's hard-packed sands. On nearby Daytona Beach (where you are still allowed to drive along the shore) Model T's have given way to bullet cars and motorbikes. Farther down the coast, past a stretch of blissful beaches, lies our launch pad to the moon: the 700,000-acre Kennedy Space Center.
WALT DISNEY WORLD & ORLANDO 	Millions of visitors equate Florida with theme parks. So it's understandable that Orlando—the state's undisputed theme park capital—would be a top tourist draw. The granddaddy of area attractions is Walt Disney World: a sprawling 47-square-mi complex that includes four separate parks, scores of hotels, and various satellite attractions. Disney has built its enviable reputation on innovative rides, dazzling Animatronics, and efficient management. But that doesn't mean it holds a monopoly on fun. SeaWorld Orlando is another established favorite, and it can be argued that Universal Orlando's two parks (Universal Studios and Islands of

Adventure) actually pack a greater punch in terms of thrills and chills. Taken together, these parks create a veritable fantasy world—one that includes enough watery options (Wet 'n Wild, Discovery Cove, Typhoon Lagoon, and Blizzard Beach among them) to make you forget that Florida's signature beaches are miles away.

PALM BEACH & THE TREASURE COAST	If money could talk, you'd hardly be able to hear above the din in Palm Beach. The upper crust started calling Palm Beach home, during the winter months at least, back in the early 1900s. And today it remains a ritzy glitzy enclave for both Old Money and the nouveau riche (a coterie led by "The Donald" himself). Simply put, Palm Beach is the sort of place where shopping is a full-time pursuit and residents don't just wear Polo—they play it. For more conspicuous consumption, continue south on the Gold Coast (an apt name given the area's golden sand and the golden bank accounts of its rich and famous residents) to Boca Raton. Those who favor the unspoiled over the spoiled can instead venture inland to Lake Okeechobee or north to the Treasure Coast, where you'll discover idyllic nature preserves, endless outdoor opportunities, and an "Old Florida" ambience.
FORT LAUDERDALE & BROWARD COUNTY	Fort Lauderdale is a master of reinvention. The classic beach blanket movie *Where the Boys Are,* filmed on-site in 1960, instantly made it a magnet for scantily clad spring breakers. After a quarter-century, however, locals tired of the swelling, swilling crowd and rolled up the welcome mat. To entice a more sophisticated clientele, the city then refashioned itself as an upscale destination complete with refurbished waterfront, plus trendy arts, entertainment, shopping, and dining districts. Now change is in the air again. In 2005 all of Broward County softened its stance on gambling, and in late 2006 the first of four regulated facilities opened with Las Vegas–style slot machines. Time will tell if this latest gamble pays off. But trend-watchers can take heart. For all the changes, the county still features 23 mi of broad beaches and 300 mi of scenic inland waterways that beg to be explored by boat.

WHAT'S WHERE

MIAMI & MIAMI BEACH 	Miami is hot and steamy—and we're not just talking about the weather. Anyone who has watched TV in the past few years is probably familiar with the images: glass-skinned sky-scrapers, towering palms, a plethora of super yachts, and a population so stylish that even crime scene investigators (or, to be more precise, the actors portraying them) look hot. On top of all that, Miami also lays claim to the country's most celebrated strand: South Beach. The Ocean Drive section, lined with trendy clubs and edgy eateries, is where the see-and-be-seen crowd tends to gather. But even if you don't aspire to über coolness, South Beach's glorious Art Deco buildings make this a must-see destination. Elsewhere in Miami, the newly minted Design District (an 18-block area crammed with showrooms and galleries) and Little Havana (the Cuban neighborhood where you can sample Latin culture) are also worth a look.
THE FLORIDA KEYS 	The 800-plus islands and islets lying off southern Florida are at once a unique landmass and a mass of contradictions. Long years of geographic isolation not only allowed the tropical flora and fauna to flourish here, but enabled locals to nurture a unique, decidedly quirky culture. Unfortunately, the increased volume of visitors traveling the 110-mi-long Overseas Highway that links the Upper, Middle, and Lower Keys has threatened both. So the Keys now have a split personality. On one hand they're a junglelike, reef-rimmed wilderness populated by free-spirited folks; on the other they're a relatively mainstream realm comprising traffic jams, shopping malls, and trailer parks. Avoiding the latter can be difficult. But you'll find that the charm of the former is ample reward—particularly if you stick to spots like Bahia Honda State Park and John Pennekamp Coral Reef State Park, or attend an authentic "Conch" celebration.
THE EVERGLADES 	Everglades National Park covers the farthest tip of the state, and no trip to southern Florida is complete without a visit to this one-of-a-kind ecosystem. The "River of Grass" is home to 2,000 species of plants, 700 fish varieties, 400 species of birds, and 100 species of mammals (including the elusive Florida panther). Oh, and there are bugs, too—lots of bugs. Although you can hike, bike, or take a tram tour here, the best way to get around is by kayak or canoe. (Amped-up modes of transport—like airboats—aren't permitted within the park, but outfitters operate them on the fringes.) Not far

away, on Florida's southeast edge, is Biscayne National Park, 95% of which is underwater. It's the nation's largest marine park and contains the northernmost extremities of Florida's coral reefs. Between the two parks is a corridor of "civilization" with motels and fast-food joints.

THE LOWER GULF COAST 	Between the southern end of Tampa Bay and the northern reaches of the Everglades, the Lower Gulf Coast serves up soft, sandy beaches and pockets of untouched beauty that range from cypress swamps to mangrove-fringed barrier islands. This may have been the last bit of Florida coastline to be settled, yet these days it is far from uncivilized. Naples, for instance, has chichi shops, chic restaurants, and a surplus of golf courses, which is why it's alternately considered to be "The Palm Beach of the Gulf Coast" and "The World's Golf Capital." Fort Meyers (the former stomping ground of Thomas Edison and Henry Ford) has its own up-market amenities, including the Barbara B. Mann Performing Arts Hall and the Florida Repertory Theatre. For a back-to-basics alternative, outdoorsy types can try tranquil Sanibel Island. Connected to the mainland by a 3-mi causeway, it's a must for beachcombers and shell collectors.
THE TAMPA BAY AREA 	As a booming city with exceptional beaches, Tampa is an ideal destination for indecisive vacationers who want to enjoy surf and sand in a semitropical climate without sacrificing urban experiences. Beyond the beach, families will love Busch Gardens: a major zoo and theme park. Football and hockey fans, moreover, will relish the chance to see the Tampa Bay Buccaneers and Tampa Bay Lightning in action. Baseball is big, too: the Devil Rays are based here, and the Yankees descend annually for spring training. Southwest of Tampa, St. Pete Beach is famous for surreally beautiful beaches, and St. Petersburg is home to the world's most comprehensive collection of Salvador Dalí's surrealist paintings. Farther south is Sarasota County. In addition to 35 mi of beaches and two impressive state parks, it has a thriving arts scene bolstered by a professional symphony, ballet and opera companies, more than 10 theaters, and dozens of galleries.

QUINTESSENTIAL FLORIDA

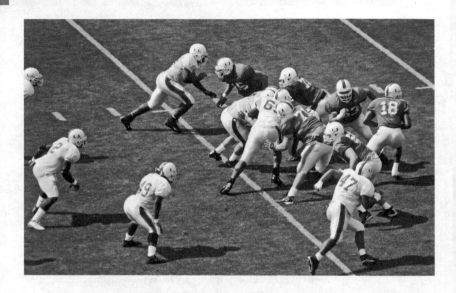

H2O

Spanish explorer Ponce de León didn't find the Fountain of Youth when he swung through Florida in 1513. But if he'd lingered longer, he could have located 7,800 lakes, 1,700 rivers and creeks, and more than 350 springs. Over the centuries, these have attracted Native Americans, immigrants, opportunists, and, of course, countless outdoor adventurers. Boaters come for navigable inland waterways and a 1,200-mi coast, and anglers are lured by some 700 species of fish. (Florida claims 700 world-record catches, too, so concocting elaborate "fish tales" is seldom necessary.) Snorkelers and divers who'd rather be under the water than on it can get face time with the marine life that thrives around the world's third-largest coral reef or bone up on maritime history by exploring nine underwater archaeological preserves. Oh, and back on dry land the beaches abutting the water are pretty impressive, too....

Theme Parks

Kids tend to think of Florida as a playland that's liberally sprinkled with pixie dust. And who can blame them? Walt Disney World opened the first of its four Floridian parks in 1971. Competitors like SeaWorld and Universal followed suit, transforming a swampy cattle-and-citrus town into "Fun Central." Today dozens of smaller Orlando venues—including a Christian park called Holy Land Experience—vie for visitors' dollars; and Busch Gardens in Tampa (85 mi southwest) scrambles for a piece of the pie with its own roundup of rides.

Superlative Sports

Panthers and Dolphins and Rays. Oh my! Florida is teeming with teams—and residents take the games they play *very* seriously. Baseball fans regularly work

Florida is synonymous with sunshine, and every year more than 83 million visitors come to revel in it. However, the people who live here—a remarkably diverse group that includes Mouseketeers, millionaires, rednecks, and rocket scientists— know that the state's fundamental appeal rests on more than those reliable rays.

themselves into a fever pitch: after all, the state has a pair of Major League franchises and hosts another 16 each spring when the Grapefruit League goes to bat. Those with a preference for pigskin might cheer for NFL teams in Jacksonville, Miami, and Tampa. But the state is also home to top-ranking college teams, and two (the Gators and 'Noles) have especially fervent followings. Basketball lovers, meanwhile, feel the "Heat" in Miami or the "Magic" in Orlando, and neophyte hockey fans (along with Snowbirds needing a hockey fix) stick around to watch the Florida Panthers and Tampa Bay Lightning. As if that wasn't enough, the ATP (Association of Tennis Professionals) and Sony Ericsson WTA (Women's Tennis Association) tours as well as the PGA (Professional Golfers Association) Tours are headquartered here.

Food, Glorious Food

Geography and gastronomy go hand in hand in Florida. Seafood, for instance, is a staple almost everywhere, yet locals will point out that the way it's prepared changes considerably as you maneuver around the state. Northern restaurants show their regional roots with Cajun classics and Dixieland dishes. (It seems any fish can be crusted with pecans and served with greens!) In southern Florida, menus highlight Floribbean cuisine, which marries Floridian, Caribbean, and Latin flavors. (Think mahimahi with mango salsa.) Inland, expect catfish, gator tails, and frogs' legs, all of which are best enjoyed at a Cracker-style fish camp with a side of hush puppies. Assorted seafoods—along with peanuts, sweet corn, watermelons, and citrus fruits—all merit their own down-home festival.

IF YOU LIKE

Beaches

Each of us defines the "perfect" beach differently. But whether you want to swim, surf, lounge, or leer, Florida has one to fit your criteria. Best of all, in this long, lean state—bounded by the Atlantic *and* Gulf of Mexico—the coast is never more than 60 mi away.

■ **Miami.** Over the past 20 years, no American beach has generated as much buzz as the one that hugs Ocean Drive, and it's easy to see why. Fringed with palms, backed by Art Deco architecture, and pulsating with urban energy, South Beach is simply the hippest place to stretch out or strut.

■ **Space Coast.** Canaveral National Seashore boasts pristine beaches, plus wetlands that attract both endangered marine animals and the people who admire them. Running from New Smyrna Beach to Titusville, the 24-mi preserve remains undeveloped, which means you can relax in the shelter of dunes, not the shadow of high-rises.

■ **Panhandle.** Although northwest Florida has a surplus of Grade-A Gulf beaches, Grayton Beach is arguably the pick of the bunch. Halfway between Panama City and Pensacola, it has shockingly white sand and aqua-green water that's as clear as any you'd find in the Keys or the Bahamas.

■ **Lower Gulf Coast.** Sanibel's beaches are justifiably famous for seashells. Conchs, cockles, clams: they're all here. But if you'd rather construct sand castles than do the "Sanibel Stoop," cross the causeway to Fort Myers Beach. It has the finest building material.

The Call of the Wild

Florida ranks third in the nation with more than 1,200 kinds of critters.

■ **Birds.** Strategically located on two major migratory routes, Florida draws more than 470 species of birds—and the 2,000-mi Great Florida Birding Trail helps you find them. Through detailed guides and highway signs, it identifies sites where you might spy anything from bald eagles and burrowing owls to bubblegum-pink flamingos.

■ **Manatees.** They're nicknamed sea cows and resemble walruses. But Florida's official marine mammals are most closely related to elephants, which may account for their slow pace and hefty frames. In winter, scan the water for a telltale glassy patch (or "footprint") that indicates a manatee swimming below.

■ **Sea Turtles.** Ready for a late-night rendezvous with the massive leatherbacks and loggerheads that lumber onto Floridian beaches between May and October to lay their eggs? Archie Carr National Wildlife Refuge, the world's second-largest sea turtle nesting site, organizes free guided turtle watches in June and July.

■ **Alligators.** Florida has more than 1.5 million resident alligators. You can see them do tricks at places like Gatorland, but "gator spotting" in swamps or roadside waterways is itself a favorite pastime. Eating the official state reptile in deep-fried nugget form is pretty popular, too. Mmm …

Life in the Fast Lane

The Sunshine State has been satisfying visitors' need for speed ever since Henry Ford and his snowbird buddies started using Ormond Beach as a test track. Today roller coasters, stock cars, supersonic jets, and spaceships rule.

- **Tampa.** If you think the pursuit of happiness is a high-speed activity, head for Busch Gardens: Florida's premier roller-coaster location. SheiKra is the tallest dive coaster in the world, Kumba features one of the world's largest vertical loops, and Montu (a gut-churning inverted coaster) delivers a G-force of 3.85.

- **Daytona.** Daytona 500, NASCAR's most prestigious event, pulls in legions of fans every February. But any time of year you can slip into a driving suit, then into the driver's seat of a Winston Cup–style stock car by signing up for the Richard Petty Driving Experience at Daytona International Speedway.

- **Pensacola.** The National Museum of Naval Aviation displays more than 140 military aircraft and has motion-based simulators that let you "fly" an F/A-18. Better yet, the U.S. Navy Precision Flight Team (familiar to most of us as the Blue Angels) is based here, so you might see them in action.

- **Kennedy Space Center.** This working spaceport has the right stuff. Witness a shuttle launch, check out the rockets, or take your own "giant leap" with the Astronaut Training Experience. The daylong program consists of realistic training exercises culminating in a simulated mission.

Something Old, Something New

Amid the skyscrapers and sprawling suburbs of "New Florida" are reminders of the state's rich past.

- **St. Augustine.** Fortify yourself with a trip to Castillo de San Marcos. Built by the Spanish to defend "La Florida," this formidable 17th-century structure qualifies as America's oldest masonry fort. Even kids will be impressed by the Castillo's turrets, moat, and double drawbridge.

- **Apalachicola.** A booming cotton-and-lumber industry turned this Panhandle town into a bustling port during the 19th century. Now it's part of the Forgotten Coast. The hundreds of preserved buildings, ranging from antebellum warehouses to gracious Victorian-style homes, give it a time-warped appeal.

- **Coral Gables.** You can soak up 1920s architecture in Miami Beach. But in nearby Coral Gables, you can soak *in* it at the Venetian Pool: a vintage municipal "lagoon" fashioned out of a quarry. Mediterranean-inspired fountains, loggias, and a sigh-worthy bridge earned it a spot on the National Register of Historic Places.

- **Cross Creek.** The backwoods scrub immortalized by Marjorie Kinnan Rawlings in the Dirty Thirties hasn't changed much. Nor has the Cracker-style house where the Pulitzer Prize winner wrote *The Yearling.* You can tour it October through July and visit the surrounding farm and grove, both in Marjorie Kinnan Rawlings Historic State Park, year-round.

GREAT ITINERARIES

3 to 4 Days: Orlando

Visitors of any age can easily spend a week "doing the attractions." (Remember, Walt Disney World alone is roughly the size of San Francisco!) But unless you're a die-hard ride hound, a few days will let you sample select attractions and still enjoy some of Orlando's other amenities. The hard part is deciding where to start. The Magic Kingdom has the greatest concentration of classic sites, and Epcot proves this really is "a small world." Film buffs can experience "reel life" at MGM or Universal Studios, and thrill seekers can gravitate to the wild rides at Islands of Adventure. As for wildlife, you can also get up close and personal with animals at Disney's Animal Kingdom or SeaWorld. In Orlando itself, the collection of modern paintings at the Orlando Museum of Art is worth visiting; and flower fans can stop to smell the roses at the 50-acre Harry P. Leu Gardens botanical preserve. Boaters, moreover, can take advantage of the area's numerous lakes, and golfers can link up at some of the state's best courses.

2 to 3 Days: Panhandle

Let's be honest: people come to Florida's Panhandle primarily for those award-winning, sugar-white beaches. But it's possible to work on a tan and still work in some sightseeing. At the Gulf Islands National Seashore, for instance, you can soak up the sun, cast a fishing net, take a hike, tour centuries-old forts, and have enough time left for a quick trip into nearby Pensacola. Similarly, after beach time around Apalachicola Bay, you can stop for oysters at a local raw bar (90% of Florida's haul comes from here); head north through the canopied roads around Apalachicola National Forest; then get a true taste of the South in moss-draped Tallahassee. Yet another day could be devoted to glorious Grayton Beach, where scuba diving and kayaking can be followed up with a relaxing drive along Route 30A to cute (and controversial) communities like WaterColor and Seaside. When planning your trip, bear in mind that the Panhandle not only has its own time zone, but its own tourism season, and summer is prime time for beach going.

2 to 3 Days: Space Coast

Although there are enough wide open expanses to justify the region's moniker, it was actually the National Aeronautics and Space Administration that put the "space" in Space Coast—and the Kennedy Space Center remains its star attraction. Space memorabilia and aeronautic antiques that range from early Redstone rockets to the *Apollo XIV* command module turn a visit here into a trip back in time for anyone who lived through the Space Race. Yet for today's kids the center opens up a "brave new world" filled with interactive bells and whistles. Down-to-earth types can visit Merritt Island National Wildlife Refuge, which serves as a buffer for the space program and a sanctuary for flora and fauna (including 330 species of birds). Adjacent to it is Canaveral National Seashore: the longest stretch of undeveloped beach on Florida's Atlantic coast. For a change of pace, try surfing at Cocoa Beach Pier or make the trek up the coast to St. Augustine. They may seem centuries removed, but the futuristic spaceport and the country's oldest continuously inhabited city are less than two hours apart.

2 to 3 Days: Gold Coast & Treasure Coast

The opulent mansions of Palm Beach's Ocean Boulevard give you a glimpse of how the richer half lives. For exclusive boutique shopping, art-gallery browsing, and glittery sightseeing, stroll down "The Avenue" (that's Worth Avenue to non–Palm Beachers). The sporty set will find dozens of places to tee up in the area (hardly surprising given that the PGA is based here), along with top-ranking tennis courts, polo clubs, and even a croquet center. Those who'd like to explore more of the Gold Coast can continue traveling south through Boca Raton to Fort Lauderdale (aka "the Yachting Capital of the World"). But to balance the highbrow with the low-key, consider heading northward for a tour of the Treasure Coast. It was named for the booty spilled by a fleet of Spanish galleons wrecked here in 1715, and for centuries treasure kept washing ashore south of the Sebastian Inlet. These days you're more likely to find manatees, golden surfing opportunities, and the sea turtles that lay their own little treasures in the sands from May through August.

2 to 3 Days: Miami Area

Seeing the Art Deco and Mediterranean Revival architecture in South Beach National Historic District tops most tourists' itineraries. After checking out the candy-colored buildings, park yourself on the sand or a café

2 to 3 Days: Florida Keys

You'll need a couple of days to devote to the Keys—and not just because of the persistent traffic problems. Vacations here are as much about lifestyle as locale, so it's important to have time to decompress properly. Key West, alternately known as the Conch Republic and "the end of the road," is a good place to get initiated. The Old Town has a funky, laid-back feel. So take a leisurely walk; then—assuming you haven't imbibed too much at one of "Margaritaville's" fabled watering holes—rent a moped to tour the rest of the island. Clear waters and abundant marine life make snorkeling or diving here another must. After scoping out the parrot fish, you can always head back into town and join local "Parrott-heads" in a Jimmy Buffett sing-along. When retracing your route to the mainland, plan a stop at Bahia Honda State Park (it has ranger-led activities plus the Keys' best beach) and John Pennekamp Coral Reef State Park, which contains 40 species of coral and hundreds more of fish.

2 to 3 Days: Tampa Bay Area

Whether you bypassed Orlando's theme parks or simply want to add another one to your "I did it" list, Busch Gardens is a logical starting point. With hair-raising rides and more than 2,700 animals, it appeals to adrenaline junkies and 'fraidy cats alike. Later you can catch a pro game (Tampa has Major League baseball, football, and hockey teams) or catch an act in the Ybor City entertainment district. If you're more interested in catching some rays, try Caladesi Island State Park (to the west of the city) or Fort DeSoto Park (at

GREAT ITINERARIES

the mouth of Tampa Bay). Aside from offering loads of water-based activities, both routinely make the list of "America's Best Beaches" issued annually by Stephen Leatherman—otherwise known as Dr. Beach. From there, culture lovers can visit St. Petersburg's museums; then move south to Sarasota for a show at the Van Wezel Performing Arts Hall. Nature lovers, conversely, can proceed north to Crystal River to see—or even snorkel with—the manatees that congregate in the warm waters from November through March.

TIPS

■ If you have a single week to experience Florida, plan on flying into Orlando: it's centrally located and, because of the volume of direct flights, easy to reach.

■ Break up a visit to Walt Disney World with an overnight excursion to the Space Coast. Located less than an hour east, it has the beaches inland Orlando lacks (72 mi worth to be exact), plus boundless eco-opportunities and top-flight attractions such as the Kennedy Space Center.

■ If you don't have time to access the Glades from the east, try taking a tour out of Naples or Marco Island. Marco, which has great beaches and beachfront hotels, makes a good overnight stop because of a "shortcut" to Key West—a three-hour ferry ride as opposed to a six-hour drive.

■ When visiting national or state parks and preserves, be sure to inquire about scheduled activities. Many run free or low-cost ranger-led nature programs.

ON THE CALENDAR

	Florida actually does have seasons, and each has its own festivals and special events. Just remember to plan ahead if you hope to attend any of the following celebrations.
WINTER Dec.	Launched in 2002, **Art Basel Miami Beach** (☎305/674–1292 ⊕www.artbaselmiamibeach.com) is now one of the world's hippest art fairs. Rising and renowned artists exhibit at Miami Beach Convention Center and satellite locations in early December. During the **Winterfest Boat Parade** (☎954/767–0686 ⊕www.winterfestparade.com) in mid-December, 100-plus vessels decked out with festive decorations light up the Intracoastal Waterway in Fort Lauderdale.
Late Dec.–early Jan.	Orlando football fans prep for two big college games—the **Champs Sports Bowl** (Dec. 29) and **Capital One Bowl** (Jan. 1)— at **Bowl-a-Palooza** (☎407/423–2476 ⊕www.bowlapalooza.com). Think of it as a weeklong tailgate party. Also kicking off on New Year's Day: the **Gator Bowl** (☎904/798–1700 ⊕www.gatorbowl.com) in Jacksonville and the **Outback Bowl** (☎813/874–2695 ⊕www.outbackbowl.com) in Tampa. Miami's **Orange Bowl** (☎305/341–4700 ⊕www.orangebowl.org) is about more than football. Related events include the **Junior Orange Bowl Parade** (☎305/662–1210 ⊕www.jrorangebowl.com) and the **King Mango Strut** (☎305/401–1171 ⊕www.kingmangostrut.org), which parodies it.
Jan.	A well-heeled crowd gathers early in the month to watch mallet-wielding men mount up for the start of **Polo Season** (☎561/798–7000 ⊕www.palmbeachpolo.com) at the Palm Beach Polo and Country Club in West Palm Beach. Sarasota struts its stuff on **Arts Day** (☎941/365–5118 ⊕www.sarasota-arts.org). Local performers take to the stage, local craftspeople demonstrate their work, and local arts organizations showcase their programs with performances and previews. Midmonth, **Art Deco Weekend** (☎305/672–2014 ⊕www.mdpl.org) spotlights Miami Beach's famed architecture with walking tours, lectures, and a street fair on Ocean Drive. About half a million people take part in the 85-plus events. The **Florida Citrus Festival and Polk County Fair** (☎863/292–9810 ⊕www.citrusfestival.com), held dur-

ON THE CALENDAR

.	ing the second half of the month in Winter Haven, marks the annual citrus harvest with juicy displays and entertainment. Birders flock to the **Space Coast Birding & Wildlife Festival** (☎ *321/268–5224* ⊕ *www.nbbd.com/fly*) in Titusville for five days of field trips, seminars, and workshops conducted by leading ornithologists. Ahoy, mateys! On the last Saturday in January, more than 1,000 pirates sail into Tampa Bay. A swashbuckling parade and themed street festival follow during the **Gasparilla Festival** (☎ *813/353–8108* ⊕ *www. gasparillapiratefest.com*)
Late Jan.–mid-Feb.	Daytona pulls out all the stops with **Speed Weeks.** (☎ *386/255–0981* ⊕ *www.daytonachamber.com*). This auto extravaganza starts with the Rolex 24-Hour Race and culminates in the famed Daytona 500 at Daytona International Speedway.
Feb.	The promise of stone crabs, crawfish, catfish, and frogs' legs attracts hungry souls to Everglades City's **Everglades Seafood Festival** (☎ *239/695–4100* ⊕ *www.evergladesseafoodfestival. com*) the first full weekend in February. About 300 artists and 300,000 visitors pack the quaint, usually quiet streets of Mount Dora for the **Mount Dora Arts Festival** (☎ *352/383–0880* ⊕ *www.mountdoracenterfor-thearts.com*) the first full weekend in February. The **Miami International Film Festival** (☎ *305/237–3456* ⊕ *www.miami-filmfestival.com*) sponsors 10 days of international, domestic, and local films. Related events—like panel discussions and seminars—leave film fans reeling. The **Florida State Fair** (☎ *813/621–7821* ⊕ *www.floridastatefair.com*) has been a Tampa tradition since 1904. Expect cotton candy, 4-H shows, down-home crafts, and a massive midway. The North and the South go at it again during the **Olustee Battle Festival** (☎ *386/758–0400* ⊕ *www.olusteefestival.com*) in Lake City. It includes a memorial service, Blue/Grey square dance, and reenactment of Florida's only major Civil War Battle. Attention, shoppers. On Presidents' Day Weekend, juried artisans sell millions of dollars' worth of work in every imaginable medium during the **Coconut Grove Arts Festival** (☎ *305/447–0401* ⊕ *www.coconutgroveartsfest.com*).
SPRING Mid-Feb.–early Mar.	Spread over five weekends, the **Florida Renaissance Festival** (☎ *954/776–1642* ⊕ *www.ren-fest.com*) in Deerfield Beach

	features minstrels, magicians, and jousting knights, along with hundreds of authentic-looking festivalgoers. Strawberry shortcake, strawberry sundaes, strawberry cobbler...**Florida Strawberry Festival** (☎813/752–9194 ⊕*www.flstrawberry-festival.com*) in Plant City.
Mar.	It's hog heaven! **Bike Week** (☎386/255–0981 ⊕*www.officialbikeweek.com*), one of Daytona's biggest events, draws more than 600,000 riders from across the United States for 10 days of races, plus demo rides, parades, and even coleslaw wrestling. Go fore it! Each March, the **PGA Tour** (☎561/624–8400 ⊕*www.pga.com*) swings through Florida with the **Ford Championship at Doral** (Miami), **Honda Classic** (Palm Beach Gardens), and **Arnold Palmer Invitational** (Orlando). Beachcombers descend on the "Shell Capital of the World" for the **Sanibel Shell Fair** (☎239/472–2155 ⊕*www.sanibelcommunityhouse.com/ShellFair.htm*) in early March. Rest assured: seashells are indeed shown—and sold—by the seashore. **Carnaval Miami** (☎305/644–8888 ⊕*www.carnavalmiami.com*) offers 10 days of irresistible hip-swiveling, salsa-spiced action. A sea of human bodies forms the world's longest conga along Calle Ocho during the frenetic finale. The prestigious **Winter Park Sidewalk Arts Festival** (☎407/672–6390 ⊕*www.wpsaf.org*) spotlights internationally known artists in mid-March. Student work is also exhibited and artsy kids create their own masterpieces at special workshops. Get jazzed up at the **Sarasota Jazz Festival** (☎941/336–1552 ⊕*www.jazzclubsarasota.com*), one of the nation's premier jazz events. Past headliners have included the Count Basie Orchestra and Eartha Kitt. Vintage Chris-Crafts, Hackers, Garwoods, and more vie for your attention at Mount Dora's **Antique Boat Festival** (☎904/221–9290 ⊕*www.acbs-sunnyland.com*), held the fourth weekend in March.
Late Mar.–early Apr.	**Springtime Tallahassee** (☎850/224–5012 ⊕*www.springtimetallahassee.com*) is the capital city's major cultural event. A "Jubilee in the Park" and crowd-pleasing parade are on the agenda.
Apr.	Nationally recognized performers and local talent entertain blues lovers during the three-day **Springing the Blues Festival** (⊕*www.springingtheblues.com*) at the Jacksonville Beach

ON THE
CALENDAR

	pavilion the first full weekend of April. Gyrate to the sounds of America's indigenous musical form during the annual **Pensacola Jazz Fest** (☎850/433–8382 ⊕*jazzpensacola.com*) in Seville Square. Still wondering where the beef is? You'll find it—along with the pork and chicken—when the country's champion barbecuers fire up the grill at St. Augustine's **Rhythm and Ribs Festival** (☎904/819–9089 ⊕*www.rhythman-dribs.net*). Fibbers large and small gather in mid-April for the Liar's Contest at the **Ocala Storytelling Festival** (☎352/629–1785 ⊕*www.ocalastorytellingfestival.com*). Honest folks are invited to listen. The **Delray Affair** (☎561/278–0424 ⊕*www.delrayaffair.com*), held the weekend after Easter, is Delray Beach's biggest event and includes juried arts and crafts, along with continuous local entertainment.
Late Apr.–early May	The "island nation" of Key West asserts its sovereignty during the **Conch Republic Celebration** (☎305/296–0213 ⊕*www.conchrepublic.com*). Highlights are the Royal Family Investiture and a Great Battle involving water cannons and assorted edibles.
May	Seafood reigns supreme as Fernandina Beach—the "birthplace of the modern shrimping industry"—hosts the **Isle of Eight Flags Seafood Festival** (☎904/261–3248 ⊕*www.shrimpfestival.com*) on the first weekend in May. Some 275,000 people celebrate everything under the sun at **Sunfest** (☎561/837–8065 ⊕*www.sunfest.org*), Florida's largest music, art, and waterfront festival, in West Palm Beach during the first weekend in May. A case of the blues hits St. Petersburg early in the month when the annual **Tampa Bay Blues Festival** (☎727/502–5000 ⊕*www.tampabaybluesfest.com*) brings big-name acts to Vinoy Waterfront Park. More than 2 million people look skyward to see flyovers, demonstrations, and aerobatic shows performed by top military and civilian aviators at the **Air & Sea Show** (☎954/467–3555 ⊕*www.nationalsalute.com*) in Fort Lauderdale. The Stephen Foster Folk Culture Center State Park, on the legendary Suwannee River near White Springs, sponsors the **Florida Folk Festival** (☎386/397–2733 ⊕*www.floridafolkfestival.com*) each year on Memorial Day weekend.
SUMMER June	The **Miami-Bahamas Goombay Festival** (☎800/891–7811) in Coconut Grove recognizes the city's Bahamian heritage

		the first weekend of June with bands, food stands, and street dancing.
	July	Cities statewide mark **Independence Day** with a bang. Orlando's **Fireworks over the Fountain** (☎407/246–2121 ⊕*www.cityoforlando.net*) is a picnic and pyrotechnic display for traditionalists.
		Over at **Walt Disney World** (☎407/824–4321 ⊕*www.disneyworld.com*) the Magic Kingdom, Epcot, and MGM all schedule their own fireworks shows. You'll see the rockets red (and white and blue) glare, as well as glaringly large crowds. Gentlemen, stop your engines. Music supersedes motors at the **Florida International Festival** (☎386/257–7790 ⊕*www.fif-lso.org*) in Daytona Beach. The London Symphony Orchestra is a star attraction at this biennial event, held in odd-numbered years. Participants in **Hemingway Days** (☎305/296–1552 ⊕*www.fla-keys.com*), held each July in Key West, understand the importance of being Ernest. Be prepared for marlin tournaments, mock bull running, and bushy-bearded Papa clones.
FALL	Sept.	Fans of contemporary Christian music have their prayers answered during **Night of Joy** at the Magic Kingdom (☎407/824–4321 ⊕*www.disneyworld.com*) and **Rock the Universe** (☎866/788–4636 ⊕*www.rocktheuniverse.com*) at Universal Studios. As if "fruits of the seas" fried, broiled, battered, and grilled weren't appealing enough, the **Pensacola Seafood Festival** (☎850/433–6512 ⊕*www.fiestaoffiveflags.org*) throws in some gourmet options. Anyone for crawfish éé
	Oct.	Destin proves it is the "World's Luckiest Fishing Village" by playing host to the **Destin Fishing Rodeo** (☎850/837–6734 ⊕*www.destinfishingrodeo.org*). Anglers young and old compete throughout the month in both in- and off-shore categories.
		The **Fort Lauderdale International Boat Show** (☎954/764–7642 ⊕*www.flibs.net*), billed as the world's largest, displays more than $1.6 billion worth of boats in every size, shape, and price range at the Bahia Mar marina and five other venues. Motorcycles rule at **Biketoberfest** (☎386/255–0415 ⊕*www.biketoberfest.org*). Championship races take place at the

ON THE CALENDAR

	Daytona International Speedway, and rallies, concerts, contests, and swap meets round out the agenda. Key West's 10-day **Fantasy Fest** (☎*305/296–1817* ⊕*www.fantasyfest. net*) is an over-the-top Halloween party and town fair that attracts more than 70,000 hedonistic revelers. Timid types need not apply. Theme parks get into the spirit of things throughout October. Kids love **Mickey's Not-So-Scary Halloween Party** (☎*407/824–4321* ⊕*www.disneyworld.com*) in the Magic Kingdom, whereas fearmongers prefer **Halloween Horror Nights** (☎*407/363–8000* ⊕*www.universalorlando.com*) at Universal Studios. **SeaWorld Orlando** (☎*407/351–3600* ⊕*www.seaworldorlando.com*) and **Busch Gardens Tampa Bay** (☎*888/800–5447* ⊕*www.buschgardens.com*) dole out their own seasonal tricks and treats.
Mid-Oct.–mid-Nov.	Independent cinema from around the globe is the focus of the **Fort Lauderdale International Film Festival** (☎*954/760–9898* ⊕*www.fliff.com*). From mid-October to mid-November, parties and popcorn are guaranteed.
Nov.	The **Florida Seafood Festival** (☎*888/653–8011* ⊕*www.floridaseafoodfestival.com*) in Apalachicola celebrates the oyster harvest, with oyster-shucking contests, oyster-eating competitions, and a blessing of the fleet.
	Paging all bibliophiles! **Miami Book Fair International** (☎*305/237–3940* ⊕*www.miamibookfair.com*), one of the largest book fairs in the United States, has an eight-day program that includes readings, a rare-books showcase, and a Congress of Authors. St. Augustine unwraps Christmas early with **Nights of Lights** (☎*904/829–1711* ⊕*www.nightsoflights.com*). More than 2 million white lights illuminate the city mid-November through January, and nighttime tours, cruises, and concerts are organized. Starting mid-November Disney's Magic Kingdom celebrates at **Mickey's Very Merry Christmas Party** (☎*407/824–4321* ⊕*www.disneyworld.com*). The after-hours event features themed parades, shows, and even a nightly smattering of "snow."

The Panhandle

WORD OF MOUTH

"I've lived in the Panhandle most of my life. The Forgotten Coast is suddenly being remembered. Come quickly. The Panhandle, as we know it, will soon be gone."

—Sunshinesue

"We just got back from St. George Island. It's near Apalachicola, which is a pretty town, well worth walking through with a lot of cute shops, more for looking than buying, unless money is not a concern. Apalachicola is very popular with fishermen. The oysters there are famous, so I ate a lot of them, and they were good. Of course this is March, but it didn't seem crowded or especially touristy. I came home feeling very relaxed."

—ebgibbs

By Gary
McKechnie

FLORIDA'S THIN, GREEN NORTH-WEST CORNER snuggles up between the Gulf of Mexico and the Alabama and Georgia state lines. Known as the Panhandle, it's sometimes called "the other Florida," since in addition to palm trees what thrives here are the magnolias, live oaks, and loblolly pines common in the rest of the Deep South. As south Florida's season is winding down in May, action in the northwest is just picking up. The area is even in a different time zone: the Apalachicola River marks the dividing line between eastern and central times.

TOP 5
■ Old and New Capitol Buildings, Tallahassee
■ Florida State Historical Museum, Tallahassee
■ Beach Stroll, Panama City Beach
■ National Museum of Naval Aviation, Pensacola
■ Grayton Beach State Park, Grayton Beach

Until World War II, when activity at the Panhandle air bases took off, this section of the state was little known and seldom visited. But by the mid-1950s, the 100-mi stretch along the coast between Pensacola and Panama City was dubbed the Miracle Strip because of a dramatic rise in property values. In the 1940s this beachfront land sold for less than $100 an acre; today that same acre can fetch hundreds of thousands of dollars. To convey the richness of the region, with its white sands and sparkling green waters, swamps, bayous, and flora, public-relations pros ditched the Redneck Riviera moniker that locals had created and coined the phrase Emerald Coast.

Politicians, developers, and community advocates haggle continuously over waterfront development, but despite unfortunate pro-growth realities, the Panhandle remains, for the time being, a land of superlatives: it has the biggest military installation in the Western Hemisphere (Eglin Air Force Base), many of Florida's most glorious white-sand beaches, and the most productive fishing waters in the world (off Destin). It has glitzy resorts, campgrounds where possums and deer invite themselves to lunch, and every kind of lodging in between. Students of the past can wander the many historic districts or visit archaeological digs. For sports enthusiasts there's a different golf course or tennis court for each day of the week, and for nature lovers there's a world of hunting, canoeing, biking, and hiking. And most anything that happens on water happens here, including scuba diving and plenty of fishing, both from deep-sea charter boats or the end of a pier.

EXPLORING THE PANHANDLE

There are sights in the Panhandle, but sightseeing is not the principal activity here. The area is better known for its rich history, military presence, ample fishing and diving spots, and for being a spot to simply relax.

Florida's westernmost city, Pensacola, with its antebellum homes and historic landmarks, is a good place to start your trek through northwest Florida. After exploring the museums and preservation districts, head east on coastal Highway 98 to Fort Walton Beach, the Emerald Coast's largest city, and on to neighboring Destin, where sportfishing is king. Continuing along the coast, there are a dozen or so family-friendly communities collectively known as the Beaches of South Walton, where sugar-white, quartz-crystal sands and emerald-green waters make for some of the finest beaches in the country. This is also where you'll find some of the Panhandle's newest, most luxurious developments, such as WaterColor, where luxury meets modern seaside chic in smartly designed vacation homes and intimate inns. The next resort center along the coast is Panama City Beach—just look for the construction cranes—whereas to the far southeast is historic Apalachicola, the Panhandle's oyster-fishing capital. Just south of Apalachicola, St. George Island, a 28-mi-long barrier island bordered by the gulf and Apalachicola Bay, has vacation homes on one end and a pristine state park on the other. Inland, a number of interesting towns and state parks lie along Interstate 10, which crosses the historic Suwannee River on its long eastward trek to the state capital, Tallahassee.

SCENIC ROUTE

Instead of Interstate 10, take Highway 90: it's the less traveled, original, two-lane back road that takes you directly through the cute communities of Quincy, Marianna, Chipley, DeFuniak Springs, Crestview, and Milton.

DINING

A staggering quantity and variety of seafood is harvested from the Panhandle's coastal waters each day, and much of it appears within hours at restaurants throughout the region. You'll find fresh oysters, crab, shrimp, scallops, and fish simply prepared at casual beachside cafés or elegantly presented at upscale resort dining rooms. Chain restaurants haven't had the effect here that they've had in other parts of the state, so you'll still find small-town seafood shacks, where you can dine "Florida Cracker"–style on deep-fried mullet, cheese grits, coleslaw, and hush puppies. Some restaurants in resort areas and beach communities close or modify their hours during off-season, so call first if visiting during winter months.

LODGING

Chain hotels and motels flank the major highways in all but the smallest towns here, but because most Panhandle visitors come to stay and play for a week or more, long-term lodging is definitely the most popular and plentiful option. Beach communities all along the coast offer short- and long-term rentals tailored to fit every lifestyle, from the simplest efficiencies to secluded bungalows to fully furnished condos and even spectacular vacation homes that peek out from between powdery dunes. Great for families and get-togethers, they let you do your own housekeeping and cooking and explore the area without tour guides. Local visitors bureaus often act as clearinghouses for these types of properties. You can also opt to stay at one of the all-inclusive resorts where everything you might need or wish to do is available on-site.

WHAT IT COSTS					
	¢	$	$$	$$$	$$$$
RESTAURANTS	under $10	$10–$15	$15–$20	$20–$30	over $30
HOTELS	under $80	$80–$100	$100–$140	$140–$220	over $220

Restaurant prices are per person for a main course at dinner. Hotel prices are for a standard double room, excluding 6% sales tax (more in some counties) and 1%–4% tourist tax.

TIMING

North Florida enjoys as much sunshine as the southern part of the state, but the climate here is more temperate than tropical. Unlike the rest of Florida, the Panhandle's high season falls roughly between Memorial Day and Labor Day, when hordes of tourists and vacationing families from neighboring states head south for the summer. (Up to 80% of Panhandle visitors drive in from Alabama, Georgia, and other cities in Florida.) Lodging prices in the region are usually based on a four-season system: spring break and summer rates are highest, winter lowest, and fall and spring are between the two extremes. (In the Tallahassee area only, hotel room prices increase during Florida State University home-game weekends, graduation week, and when the Legislature's in session around March and April.) If you prefer your beach less crowded or can't take the heat the Panhandle is famous for, plan to visit in the autumn—October and November can be the loveliest months of the year here—when warm, sunny days alternate with cool, rainy spells and there's relatively little humidity. Winter days can be both brilliant and bitterly cold, perfect for fishing or walking along miles of deserted beach.

AROUND PENSACOLA BAY

In the years since its founding, Pensacola has come under the control of five nations, earning this fine, old southern city its nickname, the City of Five Flags. Spanish conquistadors, under the command of Don Tristan de Luna, landed on the shores of Pensacola Bay in 1559, but discouraged by a succession of destructive tropical storms and dissension in the ranks, de Luna abandoned the settlement two years after its founding. In 1698 the Spanish again established a fort at the site, and during the early 18th century control jockeyed among the Spanish, the French, and the British. Finally, in 1821 Pensacola passed into U.S. hands, although during the Civil War it was governed by the Confederate States of America and flew yet another flag. The city itself has many historic sights, however. Across the bay lies Pensacola Beach on Santa Rosa Island, an area still recovering from the devastation caused by Hurricane Ivan in 2004.

PENSACOLA

1 *59 mi east of Mobile, Alabama.*

Historic Pensacola consists of three distinct districts—Seville, Palafox, and North Hill—though they are easy to explore as a unit. Stroll down streets mapped out by the British and renamed by the Spanish, such as Cervantes, Palafox, Intendencia, and Tarragona. An influx of restaurants and bars is bringing new nightlife to the historic districts, but one-way streets can make navigation a bit tricky, especially at night. In late 2004, Hurricane Ivan blew through, downing many of the town's stately oak trees, severely damaging countless homes and commercial properties, washing out bayfront roadways and a stretch of Interstate 10, and scaring the heck out of residents. The Pensacola Bay area has made great strides rebuilding paradise after Ivan's hit-and-run, and years later, recovery efforts continue. One example is the $2.3 million Plaza DeLuna, a 2-acre park with open grounds, interactive water fountains, and an amphitheater, being built in downtown Pensacola at the site of the former Bayfront Auditorium.

The best way to orient yourself is to stop at the **Pensacola Visitor Information Center,** at the foot of the Pensacola Bay Bridge. Pick up maps here of the self-guided historic-district tours. ⊠*1401 E. Gregory St.* ☎*850/434–1234 or 800/874–1234* ⊕*www.visitpensacola.com.*

Established in 1559, the **Seville Square Historic District** is the site of Pensacola's first permanent Spanish colonial settlement, which beat St. Augustine's by six years. Its center is Seville Square, a live oak–shaded park bounded by Alcaniz, Adams, Zaragoza, and Government streets. Roam these brick streets past honeymoon cottages and homes set in an oak-filled parklike setting. Many of the buildings have been converted into restaurants, commercial offices, and shops that overlook broad Pensacola Bay and coastal road Highway 98, which you'll use to access the Gulf Coast and beaches. For information on home and museum tours, contact Historic Pensacola Village.

Within the Seville district is the **Historic Pensacola Village,** a complex of several museums and historic homes whose indoor and outdoor exhibits trace the area's history back 450 years. The Museum of Industry (200 E. Zaragoza St.), in a late-19th-century warehouse, is home to permanent exhibits dedicated to the lumber, maritime, and shipping industries—once mainstays of Pensacola's economy. A reproduction of a 19th-century streetscape is displayed in the Museum of Commerce (201 E. Zaragoza St.). Also in the village are the Julee Cottage (210 E. Zaragoza St.), the "first home owned by a free woman of color," Dorr House (311 S. Adams St.), Lavalle House (205 E. Church St.), and Quina House (204 S. Alcaniz St.). Strolling through the area gives you a good look at many architectural styles, but to enter some of the buildings you must purchase an all-inclusive ticket at the Village gift shop in the Tivoli High House—which was once in the city's red-light district but now is merely a calm reflection of a restored home. Opt for the guided tour (11 AM, 1 PM, and 2:30 PM), and you'll experience the history of Pensacola as you visit the 1805 Lavalle House, the

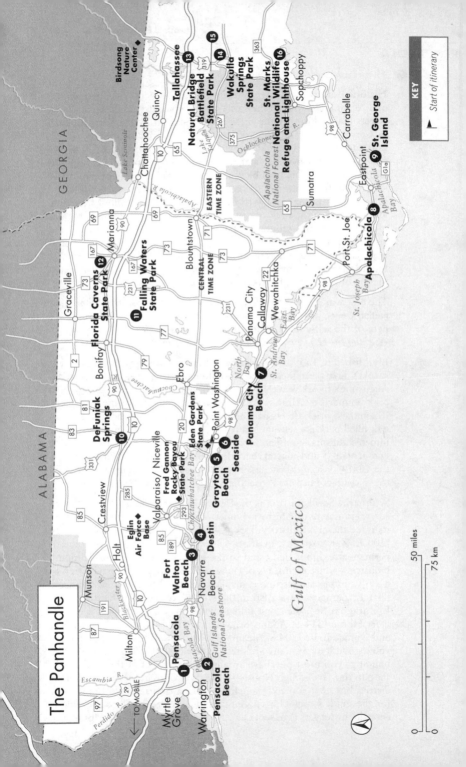

The Panhandle

KEY

▲ *Start of itinerary*

GEORGIA

ALABAMA

Gulf of Mexico

Birdsong Nature Center ◆

Tallahassee

Natural Bridge Battlefield State Park

Wakulla Springs State Park

St. Marks National Wildlife Refuge and Lighthouse

Sopchoppy

Quincy

Chattahoochee

Lake Seminole

Lake Talquin

Ochlockonee R.

Apalachicola National Forest

Carrabelle

Eastpoint

St. George Island

Apalachicola

Apalachicola Bay

Sumatra

Marianna

Florida Caverns State Park

Falling Waters State Park

Graceville

Bonifay

DeFuniak Springs

Blountstown

EASTERN TIME ZONE

CENTRAL TIME ZONE

Port St. Joe

Wewahitchka

St. Joseph Bay

Panama City

Callaway

East Bay

St. Andrew Bay

North Bay

Panama City Beach

Point Washington

Eden Gardens State Park

Seaside

Grayton Beach

Ebro

Choctawhatchee R.

Crestview

Holt

Munson

Valparaiso/ Niceville

Fred Gannon Rocky Bayou State Park

Eglin Air Force Base ◆

Destin

Fort Walton Beach

Navarre Beach

Milton

Pensacola

Pensacola Beach

Pensacola Bay

Gulf Islands National Seashore

Myrtle Grove

Warrington

Escambia R.

Perdido R.

TO MOBILE →

Blackwater R.

50 miles

75 km

GREAT ITINERARIES

Numbers in the text correspond to numbers in the margin and on the Panhandle map.

3 DAYS

History and nature are the two biggest calling cards of this part of the Sunshine State. Visit 🖬 **Grayton Beach ❺** and **Seaside ❻** ☞ and take advantage of some of Florida's finest beaches. On Day 2 drive to the capital, 🖬 **Tallahassee ⓭**, and soak up some of the state's past. On Day 3, make a trip to nearby **Wakulla Springs State Park ⓮**, where you'll find one of the world's deepest springs—perfect for sightseeing (the glass-bottom-boat ride is a must for kids) and swimming.

4 DAYS

Plant yourself in the 🖬 **Beaches of South Walton**—choose from a cabin at 🖬 **Grayton Beach State Park,** a hotel, or a beach-house rental—and use the area as a base of operation. The idyllic beach here will make it hard to pull yourself away to explore the area, but here are a few ideas for your to-do list. Enjoy a picnic on the grounds of the antebellum mansion at the **Eden Gardens State Park,** set amid moss-draped live oaks—it'll give you a feel for the history of the area, a great photo op, and a view of the intracoastal waterway. Laze away a quiet afternoon canoeing on Western Lake at **Grayton Beach State Park,** one of the most scenic spots along the Gulf

Coast. Ditch the car one day and rent a bike to explore **Seaside ❻**, a "New Urbanist" model community of shops, restaurants, and gingerbread-style, tin-roof vacation homes.

5 DAYS

Start with the state capital, Tallahassee. Check out the local sights, including the State Capitol building, the Tallahassee Historic Trail, and Maclay Gardens State Park. Take another day to head east on Interstate 10, visiting **Falling Waters State Park ⓫** in the morning and then exploring the cool, dark caves of the **Florida Caverns State Park ⓬** in the afternoon when things heat up: you'll be amazed that such an extensive cave system exists anywhere in the Sunshine State. On Day 3, head south out of town toward **Wakulla Springs State Park ⓮**, where you can explore the spectacular springs either with a mask and snorkel or from inside a glass-bottom boat. In the afternoon, head down to **St. Marks National Wildlife Refuge and Lighthouse ⓰**, to hike, swim, or have a leisurely picnic. Eventually make your way to the coast and take Highway 98 west toward Apalachicola.

In **Apalachicola ❽**, spend a day wandering around the historic downtown area and the waterfront, and spend another day on **St. George Island ❾**.

1871 Dorr House, Old Christ Church, and the 1890s Lear-Rocheblave House. Tours last approximately 90 minutes to two hours. *Tivoli High House* ✉*205 E. Zaragoza St.* ☎*850/595–5985* ⊕*www.historicpensacola.org* ☜*$6 (for adults) includes tour and Wentworth Museum* ☾*Mon.–Sat. 10–4* ☎*850/595–5993* ⊕*www.historicpensacola.org.*

☾ Even if you don't like museums, this is worth a look. The **T. T. Wentworth Jr. Florida State Museum,** housed in the elaborate, Renaissance Revival–

style former city hall, has an interesting mix of exhibits illustrating life in the Florida Panhandle over the centuries. Mr. Wentworth was quite a collector (as well as politician and salesman), and his eccentric collection includes a mummified cat (creepy) and the size 37 left shoe of Robert Wadlow, the world's tallest man (not creepy, but a really big shoe). Check out the exhibit that compares the devastating effects of 2004's Hurricane Ivan with a similarly destructive unnamed hurricane that blew through in 1926. Eerie. ⊠ *330 S. Jefferson St.* ☎ *850/595–5990* 🖃 *Free* ⊘ *Mon.–Sat. 10–4.*

Palafox Street is the main stem of historic downtown Pensacola and the center of the **Palafox Historic District.** The commercial and government hub of Old Pensacola is now an active cultural and retail district. Note the opulent Spanish Renaissance–style **Saenger Theater,** Pensacola's 1925 movie palace, which now hosts performances by the local symphony and opera, and the **Bear Block,** a former wholesale grocery with wrought-iron balconies that are a legacy from Pensacola's Creole past. On Palafox between Government and Zaragoza streets is a **statue of Andrew Jackson** that commemorates the formal transfer of Florida from Spain to the United States in 1821. While in the area, stop by Veterans Memorial Park, just off Bayfront Parkway near 9th Avenue. The ¾-scale replica of the Vietnam Memorial in Washington, D.C., honors the more than 58,000 Americans who lost their lives in the Vietnam War.

Pensacola's city jail once occupied the 1906 Spanish Revival–style building that is now the **Pensacola Museum of Art.** It provides a secure home (you can still see the actual cells with their huge iron doors) for the museum's permanent collection of paintings, sculptures, and works on paper by 20th- and 21st-century artists; traveling exhibits have focused on photography (Wegman, Leibovitz), Dutch masters, regional artists, and the occasional art-world icon, such as Andy Warhol and Salvador Dalí. ⊠ *407 S. Jefferson St.* ☎ *850/432–6247* ⊕ *www. pensacolamuseumofart.org* 🖃 *$5, free Tues.* ⊘ *Tues.–Fri. 10–5, weekends noon–5.*

Pensacola's affluent families, many made rich in the turn-of-the-20th-century timber boom, built their homes in what's known as the **North Hill Preservation District,** where British and Spanish fortresses once stood. Residents still occasionally unearth cannonballs in their gardens. North Hill occupies 50 blocks, with more than 500 homes in Queen Anne, neoclassical, Tudor Revival, and Mediterranean styles. Take a drive through this community, but remember these are private residences. Places of general interest include the 1902 Spanish mission–style **Christ Episcopal Church; Lee Square,** where a 50-foot obelisk stands as a tribute to the Confederacy; and **Fort George,** an undeveloped parcel at the site of the largest of three forts built by the British in 1778.

Locals almost unanimously suggest this as *the* must-see attraction of Pensacola. As you drive over to the **Pensacola Naval Air Station,** don't be alarmed if you're suddenly struck with the shakes—they're probably caused by the U.S. Navy's Blue Angel aerobatic squadron buzzing overhead. This is their home base, and they practice maneuvers here on Tuesday and Wednesday mornings at 8:30 from March to November. Public viewing is allowed from an area along the runway just behind the National Museum of Naval Aviation. So cover your ears as the six F/A-18s blast off in unison for 45 minutes of thrills and skill. Now that you're awake, you can fully appreciate the 300,000-square-foot **National Museum of Naval Aviation** (☎850/452–3604), with examples of more than 140 aircraft that played important roles in aviation history. Among

> ### TOP GUN
>
> The National Museum of Naval Aviation is one of only two locations nationwide that features four real F-14 military flight-training simulators with all the actual controls. Experience mock air-to-air combat, practice carrier landings, or simply cruise over Las Vegas, Iraq, Miramar, California, and other simulated sites during a 20-minute joyride. The $20 experience includes "cockpit orientation training."

them are the NC-4, which in 1919 became the first plane to cross the Atlantic; the famous World War II fighter the F6 *Hellcat*; and the Skylab Command Module. Other attractions include an atomic bomb (they assure us it's defused), *Mercury* and *Apollo* capsules, and the restored Cubi Bar Café, a very cool former airmen's club transplanted here from the Philippines. Relive the morning's maneuvers in the 14-seat motion-based simulator as well as an IMAX theater playing *The Magic of Flight* and other educational films, such as *Dolphins* and *Everest.* ⊠*1750 Radford Blvd.* ☎*850/453–2389, 800/327–5002, 850/453–2024 IMAX theater* ⊕*www.naval-air.org* ⊠*Free, IMAX film $8, two films for $12* ☉*Daily 9–5.*

Dating from the Civil War, **Fort Barrancas** has picnic areas and a ½-mi woodland nature trail on its grounds. The fort, which is just northeast of the Museum of Naval Aviation, is part of the Gulf Islands National Seashore, maintained by the National Park Service. ⊠*Taylor Rd.* ☎*850/455–5167* ⊠*Free* ☉*Nov.–Feb., daily 8:30–3:45; Mar.–Oct., daily 9:30–4:45.*

OFF THE BEATEN PATH

The ZOO. The local zoo, about 12 mi east of Pensacola, near Gulf Breeze, has more than 700 animals, including many endangered species. Kids especially enjoy the petting zoo, where they can touch most every critter on Old MacDonald's farm. Other attractions yield tigers, zebras, and such unusual creatures as African wild dogs and pygmy hippos, and there's a tall platform where you can have face-to-face meetings with giraffes. The Safari Line Limited train runs through 30 acres of free-roaming animals in their natural habitats. ⊠*5701 Gulf Breeze Pkwy., Gulf Breeze* ☎*850/932–2229* ⊠*$10.95 (safari train $3 extra)* ☉*Daily 9–5 during standard time; daily 9–4 during daylight-saving time.*

WHERE TO STAY & EAT

$$–$$$ ✕**Dharma Blue.** Geographically speaking, this trendy spot is in downtown Pensacola, on leafy Seville Square, but culinarily speaking it's all over the map. The menu roams from Asia (sushi and spring-roll

appetizers) to Italy (grilled vegetables with risotto) to Mexico
(lime-roasted chicken quesadilla)
to the American South (fried-green-
tomato club sandwich)—but just
stick close to home and you won't
be disappointed. The lunch menu
includes barbecued salmon with
lemon coleslaw and Texas toast,
focaccia BLT, or fish-and-chips. For
dinner try tomato-crusted grouper
with caper cream sauce, the fish of
the day (blackened, grilled, or tem-
pura-fried), or Guinness-marinated
sirloin with chipotle aioli. Dine

HEADS UP!

Watching the Blue Angels practice
their aerobatics is one of the
best "free" shows in all of Florida
(your tax dollars are already paying for these jets). The Naval Air
Station's bleachers hold about
1,000 people and they fill up
fast, so get here early. Then stay
late—the pilots stick around after
the show to shake hands and sign
autographs.

inside under a collection of Southern folk art, or outside under café
umbrellas and droopy oaks. ⊠ *300 S. Alcaniz St.* ☎ *850/433–1275*
⊟ *AE, MC, V* ⊘ *No lunch Sun.*

$$–$$$ ✕ **Mesquite Charlie's.** Saddle up and head on over to this Wild West
saloon, with brick walls, arched doorways, mounted game, and a second-floor balcony overlooking the lobby. All that's missing are the
swinging doors. The 32-ounce porterhouse is large enough to satisfy
a posse of cowboys and, in a publicity schtick lifted straight from a
Simpsons episode, the monster-size 76-ounce sirloin is free if you finish
it—along with your baked potato, baked beans, salad, and bread—in
less than an hour (otherwise you'll pay $49.99). All steaks are char-
broiled with 100% mesquite charcoal and seasoned with natural spices.
⊠ *5901 N. W St.* ☎ *850/434–0498* ⊟ *AE, D, MC, V.*

$–$$$ ✕ **Fish House.** Come one, come all, come hungry, and come at 11 AM
to witness the calm before the lunch storm. By noon, the Fish House
is packed with Pensacola's professionals, power players, and poseurs,
all waiting for tables and the fresh fish brought in on the docks steps
away. The wide-ranging menu of fish dishes served broiled, blackened,
or fried is the bait. The attentive service, bayfront setting, and signature
"Grits a Ya-Ya" dish (fresh gulf shrimp on a bed of smoked Gouda-
cheese grits smothered with a portobello-mushroom sauce) keeps din-
ers in the net. Steaks, delicious homemade desserts, a sushi bar, and a
full-service bar don't hurt the extraordinary popularity of this restau-
rant either. The hot-ticket table is one out on the deck at sunset. ⊠ *600
South Barracks St.* ☎ *850/470–0003* ⊟ *AE, MC, V.*

¢–$$$ ✕ **McGuire's Irish Pub.** Spend anywhere from $10 to $100 for a ham-
burger here, depending on whether you want it topped with cheddar
or served with caviar and champagne. Beer is brewed on the premises,
and the wine cellar has more than 8,500 bottles. Menu items include
corned beef and cabbage and a hickory-smoked prime rib. In an old
firehouse, the pub is replete with antiques, moose heads, Tiffany-style
lamps, and Erin-go-bragh memorabilia. As for the "richness" of the
decor, there are more than 550,000 dollar bills signed and dated by
the pub's patrons fluttering from the ceiling. ⊠ *600 E. Gregory St.*
☎ *850/433–2849 or 850/433–6789* ⊟ *AE, D, DC, MC, V.*

¢–$$ ✕**Ragtyme Grille.** Downtown's historic Economy Shoe Repair building now houses this intimate corner eatery that's become a favorite of local journalists (the *Pensacola News-Journal* offices are across the street). Choose from standard deli sandwiches (Reubens, corned beef), po'boys, and grilled fish specials; salads—with fresh fish, fruit, or chicken—and burgers round out the menu. Grab a table inside, or relax over a beer, margarita, or glass of wine on the covered patio. ⊠*201 S. Jefferson St.* ☎*850/429–9655* ☐*AE, MC, V.*

¢–$ ✕**Global Grill.** When you have an appetite that begs for variety, consider this trendy yet friendly downtown Pensacola tapas restaurant. Come hungry and fill your eyes, plate, and belly from the selection of 51 different tapas, like the high-demand quick-fried calamari with garlic squash fries, the spicy seared tuna with five-pepper jelly, or the pork empanadas with cucumber cream. Wear an elastic waistband, because you may be tempted to try the 48 others. ⊠*27 S. Palafox* ☎*850/469–9966* ☐*AE, MC, V* ⊘*No lunch Sun. and Mon.*

$$–$$$ ▦**Crowne Plaza–Pensacola Grand Hotel.** After a complete smackdown by Hurricane Ivan in 2004, it took this local institution two years to shake itself off and reopen its doors. Its rich heritage remains: the Crowne Plaza is on the site of the restored historic Louisville & Nashville (L&N) railroad passenger depot, which now houses the lobby, lounges, shops, and meeting rooms. A 15-story glass tower, attached to the train depot by a glass atrium, features guest rooms with all new furniture, and incredible views of historic Pensacola. Bi-level penthouse suites have whirlpool baths. The hotel's proximity to downtown dining and nightlife, along with its amenities, makes it a good choice for business travelers. ⊠*200 E. Gregory St., 32501* ☎*850/433–3336 or 800/348–3336* ☐*850/432–7572* ⊕*www.pensacolagrandhotel.com* ⟿*200 rooms, 10 suites* ⚲*In-hotel: restaurant, bar, pool, gym, airport shuttle* ☐*AE, D, DC, MC, V.*

$$–$$$ ▦**Residence Inn by Marriott.** In the downtown bayfront area, this immaculately kept all-suites hotel is perfect for extended stays, whether for business or pleasure. The location is ideal for exploring Pensacola's historic streets on foot—rooms in the back have views of the bay—and families will especially appreciate the fully equipped kitchens and free grocery delivery. Breakfast and evening social hour are complimentary. ⊠*601 E. Chase St., 32502* ☎*850/432–0202* ☐*850/438–7965* ⊕*www.residenceinn.com* ⟿*78 suites* ⚲*In-room: kitchen, refrigerator. In-hotel: tennis court, pool, gym, some pets allowed (fee)* ☐*AE, D, DC, MC, V.*

¢–$$ ▦**New World Inn.** If you like your inns small, warm, and cozy, with the
★   bay on one side and a short two-block walk to the downtown historic area, then this is the inn for you. Furnishings reflect the five periods of Pensacola's past: French and Spanish provincial, early American, antebellum, and Queen Anne. Several rooms have four-poster mahogany beds and the rooms are large and comfortable, but the old-style furnishings might benefit from a little new-world dusting. A complimentary breakfast consists of pastries and boxed cereals. The lobby's collection of signed portraits of famous (and formerly famous) guests is a hoot. ⊠*600 S. Palafox St., 32502* ☎*850/432–4111* ☐*850/432–*

6836 ⊕*www.newworldlanding.com* ⤴*14 rooms, 1 suite* ⊟*AE, MC,*
V ⦿⏐*CP.*

NIGHTLIFE & THE ARTS

THE ARTS   Most cultural and arts offerings in town are conveniently centered
around the historic district. The **Pensacola Little Theatre** (⊠*400 S. Jef-*
ferson St. ☎*850/432–2042* ⊕*www.pensacolalittletheatre.com*) is
a popular little venue for locals, with plays and musicals presented
year-round. **Pensacola's Symphony Orchestra** (⊠*205 E. Zaragoza St.*
☎*850/435–2533* ⊕*www.pensacolasymphony.com*) offers more than
17 concerts each season at the Saenger Theatre and other locations.
Productions at the restored 1925 **Saenger Theatre** (⊠*118 S. Palafox*
St. ☎*850/595–3880* ⊕*www.pensacolasaenger.com*) include touring
Broadway shows and three locally staged operas a year. Additional
details can be found at www.pensacolaopera.com.

NIGHTLIFE   There's almost as much to do after dark as there is during daylight
hours. **Hub Stacey's** (⊠*312 E. Government St.* ☎*850/469–1001*
⊕*www.hubstaceys.com*), on the corner by Seville Square, is the friendly
neighborhood locale with 55 types of bottled beer, sidewalk tables, and
a good vibe. **McGuire's Irish Pub** (⊠*600 E. Gregory St.* ☎*850/433–6789*
⊕*www.mcguiresirishpub.com*) is a restaurant and microbrewery that
welcomes those of Irish descent, or anyone else who enjoys cold home-
brewed ales, beers, or lagers. Their 8,500-capacity wine cellar includes
bottles ranging in price from $14 to $20,000. If you want a quiet drink,
steer clear on Friday and Saturday nights—or when Notre Dame games
are televised. **Mesquite Charlie's** (⊠*5901 N. W St.* ☎*850/434–0498*)
offers country music and all the Western trappings. **New York Nick's**
(⊠*9–11 S. Palafox St.* ☎*850/469–1984* ⊕*www.enorthshore.com/*
nyn/) is a sports bar, rock-and-roll club, shrine to Bruce Springsteen,
and popular downtown bar and grill. It's an "A+" spot for all the
best "B's" in life—beer, billiards, burgers, and the Boss. **Starbuck's Bil-**
liards (⊠*22 S. Palafox St.* ☎*850/438–9818*) is always hopping, with
players lined up at the 20 billiards tables until 2:30 AM. The **Seville**
Quarter (⊠*130 E. Government St.* ☎*850/434–6211* ⊕*www.rosies.*
com) has nine rooms, seven fabulous bars, and two courtyards, offering everything from disco to dueling pianos, Motown acts, blues bands,
and rockabilly trios—you name it. College students pack the place
on Thursday, tourists on the weekend, and military men and women
from six nearby bases are stationed here nearly all the time. In the heart
of the historic district, it's Pensacola's equivalent of New Orleans's
French Quarter.

SPORTS & THE OUTDOORS

CANOEING &   **Adventures Unlimited** (⊠*Rte. 87* ☎*850/623–6197 or 800/239–6864*
KAYAKING   ⊕*www.adventuresunlimited.com*), on Coldwater Creek, rents light
watercraft as well as campsites and cabins along the Coldwater and
Blackwater rivers in the Blackwater State Forest. Canoe season lasts
roughly from March through mid-November, but they rent year-round.
Canoe and kayak rentals for exploring the Blackwater River—the pur-
est sand-bottom river in the nation—are available from **Blackwater**
Canoe Rental (⊠*6974 Deaton Bridge Rd., Milton* ☎*850/623–0235 or*

800/967–6789 ⊕*www.blackwatercanoe.com*), northeast of Pensacola off Interstate 10 Exit 31.

It's called the "Mighty O," but it was formerly known as the **USS** *Oriskany.* (⊕*www.mbtdivers.com*)The retired aircraft carrier was sunk 24 mi off the Pensacola Pass in 2006, and now the superstructure is the world's largest artificial reef. The "island" is accessible just 67 feet down, and the flight deck can be reached at 137 feet. Visibility and water temperatures are ideal for a visit, and divers from around the world are jumping in to explore the wrecked reef.

DOG RACING   Rain or shine, year-round there's live racing at the **Pensacola Greyhound Track.** Lounge and grandstand areas are fully enclosed and air-conditioned and have instant-replay televisions throughout. ⊠*951 Dog Track Rd., West Pensacola* ☎*850/455–8595* ⊠*Free* ⊗*Racing Wed.– Sat. at 7 PM, weekends at 1.*

FISHING   For a full- or half-day deep-sea charter ($75–$100 per person) that heads 10–20 mi into the gulf, try the **Beach Marina** (⊠*655 Pensacola Beach Blvd.* ☎*850/932–8466*), which represents several charter outfits. Bottom fishing is best for amberjack and grouper, offshore trolling trips are searching for tuna, wahoo, and sailfish, and inshore charters are out to hook redfish, cobia, and pompano. For a complete list of local fishing charters, visit ⊕www.visitpensacola.com/Sports/fishresults.asp.

GOLF   There are several outstanding golf courses in and around Pensacola. **The Club at Hidden Creek** (⊠*3070 PGA Blvd., Navarre* ☎*850/939–4604*) is an 18-hole course in Santa Rosa County, 20 mi from Pensacola; green fee $15/$55 with cart. **The Moors Golf Club** (⊠*3220 Avalon Blvd., Milton* ☎*850/994–2744*) is a public, 18-hole, par-70, Scottish links–style course. Green fee $39/$49. The course was designed by John LaFoy. In Perdido, the **Perdido Bay Golf Club** (⊠*1 Doug Ford Dr.* ☎*850/492– 1223*) has a well-kept 18-hole course. Green fee $29/$69 with cart. Also in Perdido is the **Lost Key Golf Club** (⊠*625 Lost Key Dr., Perdido Key Beach* ☎*850/492–1300* ⊕*www.lostkey.com*), a public, par-71, 18-hole Arnold Palmer Signature Design Course that was the first golf course in Florida—and the world—to be certified as an Audubon International Silver Signature Sanctuary. Green fee $65/$75 with cart. **Tiger Point Golf & Country Club** (⊠*1255 Country Club Rd., Gulf Breeze* ☎*850/932–1330*) is a semiprivate 36-hole club. Green fee $35/$75 with cart.

TENNIS   There are fine public tennis courts in more than 30 locations in the Pensacola area. The **Pensacola Racquet Club** (⊠*3450 Wimbledon Dr.* ☎*850/434–2434*) has 10 rubico (soft) and 2 hard courts, plus a junior-size Olympic pool with a baby pool and restaurant.

SHOPPING

The Palafox District is an enjoyable area for browsing. The **Quayside Art Gallery** (⊠*915–17 E. Zaragossa St.* ☎*850/438–2363*), the largest co-op art gallery in the Southeast, reopened in November 2005, after Ivan's devastation, with new displays and items by local artists in a variety of media. Other shops here display art glass, wood, metal, paintings, and jewelry. Ten miles north of the historic district is the **Cordova Mall** (⊠*5100 N. 9th Ave.* ☎*850/477–5563*), anchored by three department stores, with more than 150 specialty shops and a food court. **Harbourtown Shopping Village** (⊠*913 Gulf Breeze Pkwy., Gulf Breeze*) has trendy shops and the look of a wharfside New England village.

PENSACOLA BEACH

❷ *5 mi south of Pensacola via U.S. 98 to Rte. 399 (Bob Sikes) Bridge.*

When Hurricane Opal tore across this skinny barrier island in 1995, the damaged areas were redeveloped, sand was brought in to fill the eroded beachfront, and beach facilities and parking were added to what came to be known as the "Opal Day Use Area," named in honor of the hurricane responsible for the destruction. A local bartender even invented a potent but short-lived concoction called a "Raging Opal" to commemorate the storm.

It's doubtful, however, that any public parks or cocktails will be named after Hurricane Ivan, which devastated the area in 2004. That's because this Category 4 storm, which caused a level of destruction not seen in these parts for nearly a century, wasn't an event that anyone around here cares to remember. The storm's tidal surge washed completely over the island in several places, and the obvious reminders of Ivan's visit—washed-out roads, decimated homes, uprooted lives, and erased sand dunes—are still visible and may well be for years to come.

Since the national media focused its attention on Pensacola Beach for not much longer than it took the storm to do its damage, the scope of the disaster might come as a surprise to many visitors: nearly half of the island's homes were destroyed; all of the island's hotels were closed for months (some will never reopen); and the miles of sea oat–covered, pristine dunes that protected the island from winter storms and gave the area its laid-back Florida look were leveled in hours. In short, Pensacola Beach is a city changed.

But locals here know the post-hurricane drill: dig in, dig out, and move on. Several hotels have reopened after complete renovations, homes and condos have been demolished or are being rebuilt (such as a new seaside $500 million, 700-hotel/condo unit complex), and city and state crews have made significant progress in reconnecting roads to areas of the island rendered inaccessible by the storm. Since some of our information gathered at press time is based on estimated reopening schedules, it's best to call to check on the status before paying the $1 toll to cross the bridge to reach Pensacola Beach.

Dotting the 150-mi stretch between Destin, Florida, and Gulfport, Mississippi, is **Gulf Islands National Seashore** (☎*850/934–2600* ⊕*www.nps. gov/guis*), managed by the National Park Service. The Gulf Islands National Seashore, which bookends Pensacola beach on the east and west with miles of unsullied, undeveloped beach, has reopened, and the main road—buried under 5 mi of sand after Ivan—was expected, as of this writing, to be cleared by mid-2007. Once accessible (call to verify) Fort Pickens Road will permit access to Fort Pickens (see below), a pre–Civil War–era brick fortress that once served as the jail of Apache chief Geronimo. At **Opal Beach Day Use Area** (⊠ *Rte. 399, 5 mi east of Pensacola Beach*) you'll find pristine coastline, barbecue areas, covered picnic facilities, and restrooms. At the western tip of the island and part of the Gulf Islands National Seashore, **Fort Pickens** dates to 1834. Constructed of more than 21 million locally made bricks, the fort once served as the prison of Apache chief Geronimo. A National Park Service plaque describes the complex as a "confusing jumble of fortifications," but the real attractions here are the beach, nature exhibits, a large campground, an excellent gift shop, and breathtaking views of Pensacola Bay and the lighthouse across the inlet. It's the perfect place for a picnic lunch and a bit of history, too. ⊠ *Ft. Pickens Rd.* ☎ *850/934–2635* ☜ *$8 per car* ☉ *Daily 7–sunset.*

The 1,471-foot-long **Pensacola Beach Gulf Pier** touts itself as the longest pier on the Gulf of Mexico. This peerless pier hosts serious anglers who find everything they'll need here—from pole rentals to bait—to land that big one, but those looking to catch only a beautiful sunset are welcome, too. Check the pier's Web site for the latest reports on what's biting. ⊠ *41 Ft. Pickens Rd.* ☎ *850/934–7200* ⊕ *www.fishpensacola-beachpier.com* ☜ *Observers $1, fishing $6.50.*

THE GULF COAST

On U.S. 98, several towns, each with its own personality, are strung along the shoreline from Pensacola southeast to St. George Island. The twin cities of Destin and Fort Walton Beach seemingly merge into one sprawling destination and continue to spread as more condominiums, resort developments, shopping centers, and restaurants crowd the skyline each year. The view changes drastically—and for the better—farther along the coast as you enter the quiet stretch known as the Beaches of South Walton, scattered along Route 30-A, the main coastal road. Here, building restrictions prohibit high-rise developments, and the majority of dwellings are privately owned homes, most of which are available to vacationers. A total of 19 beach communities cluster along 30-A. Many are little more than a wide spot in the road, and all are among the least known and least developed in the Gulf Coast area, even though Grayton Beach is regularly ranked among the country's top 20 beaches. Seaside, which reached its quarter-century mark in 2006, is a thriving planned community with old-fashioned Victorian architecture, brick streets, restaurants, retail stores—and a surfeit of art galleries.

Continuing southeast on U.S. 98, you'll find Panama City Beach, whose "Miracle Strip," once crammed with carnival-like amusement parks, junk-food vendors, T-shirt shops, and go-kart tracks, is in the middle of a building frenzy that will double the number of condominiums and give the area a much-needed face-lift. Farther east, past the up-and-coming sleeper cities of Port St. Joe and Mexico Beach (these days, the din of construction drowns out the sounds of surf all along this coast), you'll come to the quiet blue-collar town of Apalachicola, Florida's main oyster fishery. Watch oystermen ply their trade, using long-handled tongs to bring in their catch. Cross the Apalachicola Bay via the Bryant Patton Bridge to St. George Island. This unspoiled 28-mi-long barrier island offers some of America's most scenic beaches, including St. George Island State Park, which has the longest beachfront of any state park in Florida.

FORT WALTON BEACH

❸ *46 mi east of Pensacola.*

This coastal town dates from the Civil War but had to wait more than 75 years to come into its own. Patriots loyal to the Confederate cause organized Walton's Guard (named in honor of Colonel George Walton, onetime acting territorial governor of West Florida) and camped at a site on Santa Rosa Sound, later known as Camp Walton. In 1940 fewer than 90 people lived in Fort Walton Beach, but within a decade the city became a boomtown, thanks to New Deal money for roads and bridges and the development of Eglin Field during World War II. The military is now Fort Walton Beach's main source of income, but tourism runs a close second. Don't miss a chance to waddle out to the end of the Okaloosa Island Pier. It costs only a buck to walk the plank, $6.50 if you'd like to fish.

Encompassing 724 square mi of land, **Eglin Air Force Base** includes 10 auxiliary fields and a total of 21 runways. Jimmie Doolittle's Tokyo Raiders trained here, as did the Son Tay Raiders, a group that made a daring attempt to rescue American POWs from a North Vietnamese prison camp in 1970. Off-limits to civilians, there are private tours for ROTC and military reunion groups. ⊠ *Rte. 85* ☎ *850/882–3931* ⊕ *www.eglin.af.mil.*

★ The collection at the **Air Force Armament Museum,** just outside the Eglin Air Force Base's main gate, contains more than 5,000 armaments from World Wars I and II and the Korean and Vietnam wars. Included are uniforms, engines, weapons, aircraft, and flight simulators; larger craft such as transport planes are exhibited on the grounds outside. A 32-minute movie about Eglin's history and its role in the development of armaments plays continuously. ⊠ *Rte. 85, Eglin Air Force Base* ☎ *850/882–4062* ☜ *Free* ☉ *Mon.–Sat. 9:30–4:30.*

John C. Beasley Wayside Park is Fort Walton Beach's seaside playground on Okaloosa Island. Across the dunes, a boardwalk leads to the beach, where there are a dozen covered picnic tables, pavilions, changing rooms, and freshwater showers. Lifeguards are on duty in summer. ⊠ *Okaloosa Island* ☎ *No phone.*

It's strange that this is smack dab in the middle of a busy commercial district, but when it was built 10,000 years ago, odds are that the **National Historic Landmark Temple Mound** was in the suburbs. A ☾ few feet away at **Indian Temple Mound Museum,** you can learn all about the prehistoric peoples who inhabited northwest Florida up to 10,000 years ago. It's a small museum, but the prehistoric Native American artifacts and weaponry are particularly fascinating, as are the few hands-on exhibits that are a reminder of the area's previous inhabitants. More than a thousand years ago, local tribes built this large earthen mound as a center of religious, political, and social activity. It is now a reminder of a lost world. ✉ *139 Miracle Strip Pkwy. SE (U.S. 98)* ☎ *850/833–9595* ✑ *$2* ☉ *Weekdays 10–4, Sat. 9–4.*

☻ **Gulfarium.** Its main attraction is the Living Sea, a 60,000-gallon tank that simulates conditions on the ocean floor. See campy performances by trained porpoises, sea-lion shows, and marine-life exhibits (a multi-species act includes dolphins and sea lions in the same show). Among other species here are otters, penguins, alligators, harbor seals, and sharks. Feeding time is always a young-crowd pleaser. Don't overlook the old-fashioned Dolphin Reef gift shop, where you can buy anything from conch shells to beach toys. There's also a dolphin-interaction program, but you don't swim with them. Instead, you sit in a pool as spotted dolphins swim up to your lap. ✉ *U.S. 98 E* ☎ *850/243–9046 or 800/247–8575* ⊕ *www.gulfarium.com* ✑ *$17.50, dolphin interaction $125* ☉ *Sept.–May, daily 9–4; June–Aug., daily 9–6.*

WHERE TO STAY & EAT

$$–$$$$ ✕ **Staff's.** Sip a Tropical Depression or a rum-laced Squall Line while you peruse a menu tucked into the centerfold of a tabloid-size newspaper filled with snippets of local history, early photographs, and family memorabilia. Since 1913 folks have been coming to this garage-turned-eatery for steaks and seafood dishes like Florida lobster and char-grilled amberjack. The grand finale is a trip to the delectable dessert bar; try a generous wedge of cherry cheesecake. ✉ *24 Miracle Strip Pkwy. SE* ☎ *850/243–3482* ▭ *AE, D, MC, V.*

$$–$$$ ✕ **Pandora's Steakhouse and Lounge.** On the Emerald Coast the name ★ Pandora's is synonymous with prime rib. Steaks are cooked over a wood-burning grill, and you can order your prime rib regular or extra-cut; fish aficionados should try the char-grilled yellowfin tuna or one of the daily fish specials. Cozy up in an alcove to enjoy your meal in peace or head to the lounge, where the mood turns a bit more gregarious with live entertainment Wednesday through Saturday. ✉ *1226 Santa Rosa Blvd.* ☎ *850/244–8669* ▭ *AE, D, DC, MC, V* ☉ *Closed Mon..*

¢–$$ ✕ **Angler's.** You can't dine any closer to the beach than at this casual beachside bar and grill next to the Gulfarium and at the entrance to Okaloosa Island Pier (and within a complex of other nightclubs and restaurants). Inside, it's the requisite sports bar with a million or more televisions (in the elevators and bathrooms even) broadcasting an equal number of sports events. Outside, a volleyball net tempts diners onto the sands to work up an appetite. When you do, snack on nachos and quesadillas, or sample the fresh-catch dishes on the dinner menu. ✉ *1030 Miracle Strip Pkwy. SE* ☎ *850/796–0260* ▭ *AE, D, MC, V.*

$$–$$$ ▦ **Ramada Plaza Beach Resort.** If your family loves the water, splash down at this beachside extravaganza. Activity here revolves around a 194,000-gallon pool (allegedly the area's largest) with a separate grotto

pool and bar and spectacular swim-through waterfall that tumbles down from an island oasis; there's also a separate kiddie pool, as well as an 800-foot private beach. Standard rooms have refrigerators, coffeemakers, and two double beds (a few have kings), in-room safes, and free high-speed Internet; beachfront units come with microwaves. It's a popular spot for conventions, spring break, and families on a budget: there's no charge for additional guests under 18, and roll-away beds are only an extra $10 per night. For an extra-special evening, book an odd-numbered room between 1133 and 1143—the back door of each opens right into the pool. ⊠*1500 Miracle Strip Pkwy. SE, 32548* ☎*850/243–9161 or 800/874–8962* ≜*850/243–2391* ⊕*www.rama-dafwb.com* ⤻*309 rooms, 26 suites* ⅃*In-room: refrigerator. In-hotel: restaurant, bars, pools, gym, beachfront, no elevator in some buildings* ▤*AE, D, DC, MC, V.*

NIGHTLIFE & THE ARTS

THE ARTS   To appreciate dancing skills that go beyond your own tiptoeing on hot sands, visit the **Northwest Florida Ballet** (☎*850/664–7787* ⊕*www. nfballet.org*). Based in Fort Walton Beach, they have presented classical and contemporary dance performances to audiences along the Gulf Coast since 1969. Call for season schedule and ticket information as well as their current performance venue.

NIGHTLIFE   Dueling pianos (Wednesday through Sunday only) and a beachfront bar fuel the furious sing-alongs that make **Howl at the Moon** (⊠*1450 Miracle Strip Pkwy.* ☎*850/301–0111*), at the Boardwalk on Okaloosa Island, one of Fort Walton's most popular evening entertainment spots. The show starts at 8 PM, and rocks every night until 2, although the Comedy Zone—featuring stand-up comedians—takes over on Sundays. For a more subtle evening, **The Grape** (⊠*4107 Legendary Dr., Suite F103* ☎*850/654–7273* ⊕*www.yourgrape.com*) in Destin Commons is a chic retreat where wines are classified by taste. It's a comfortable atmosphere for novices and connoisseurs.

SPORTS & THE OUTDOORS

BIKING   **Eglin Air Force Base Reservation** is the size of Rhode Island—1,045 square mi, 463,448 acres—and has 810 mi of creeks and plenty of challenging, twisting wooded trails. Outdoor enthusiasts hunt, fish, canoe, and swim here, and for $7 you can buy a day pass to mountain bike on the Timberlake Trail, which is open from 7 AM to 4:30 PM Monday through Saturday. Permits can be obtained from the **Jackson Guard** (⊠*107 Rte. 85 N, Niceville* ☎*850/882–4164*).

FISHING   **Harbor Walk Marina** (⊠*66 U.S. 98 E, Destin 32541* ☎*850/337–8250* ⊕*www.harborwalk-destin.com*) is a rustic-looking waterfront complex where you can get bait, gas, tackle, food, and anything else you might need for a day of fishing. Party fishing-boat excursions cost as little as $40, a cheaper alternative to chartering or renting your own boat.

GOLF   The **Fort Walton Beach Golf Club** (⊠*Rte. 189* ☎*850/833–9529*) is a 36-hole municipal course whose links (Oaks and Pines) lie about 400 yards from each other. The two courses are considered by many to be one of Florida's best public layouts. Greens fee: $34 with a shared cart. **Shalimar Pointe Golf & Country Club** (⊠*302 Country Club Dr., Shalimar* ☎*850/651–1416*) has 18 holes with a pleasing mix of water and bunkers. Greens fee: $39/$45 with cart.

SCUBA DIVING Take diving lessons, arrange excursions, and rent all the necessary equipment at the **Scuba Shop** (⊠*348 Miracle Strip Pkwy.* ☎*850/243–1600*), where the specialty is wreck diving. Although visibility here isn't on par with the reefs of the Atlantic coast, local divers consider views up to 50 feet—and diving depths up to 90 feet—good enough. Closed Wednesday.

TENNIS The **Municipal Tennis Center** (⊠*45 W. Audrey Dr.* ☎*850/833–9588*) has 12 lighted hard courts, four racquetball courts, and four practice walls. **Destin City Tennis Courts** (⊠*224 Holmes Blvd.*) has two asphalt courts for daytime use.

SHOPPING

There are four department stores in the **Santa Rosa Mall** (⊠*300 Mary Esther Blvd., Mary Esther* ☎*850/244–2172*), as well as 118 other shops, 15 bistro-style eateries, and a 10-screen movie theater. If you miss the homogenization of home, you can find the usual suspects of Wal-Mart, Target, Books-A-Million, and more in new shopping plazas along Highway 98, concentrated primarily near Highway 293.

DESTIN

④ *8 mi east of Fort Walton Beach.*

Fort Walton Beach's neighbor lies on the other side of the strait that connects Choctawhatchee Bay with the Gulf of Mexico. Destin takes its name from its founder, Leonard A. Destin, a Connecticut sea captain who settled his family here sometime in the 1830s. For the next 100 years Destin remained a sleepy little fishing village until the strait, or East Pass, was bridged in 1935. Then recreational anglers discovered its white sands, blue-green waters, and abundance of some of the most sought-after sport fish in the world. More billfish are hauled in around Destin each year than from all other gulf fishing ports combined, giving credence to its nickname, the World's Luckiest Fishing Village. But you don't have to be the rod-and-reel type to love Destin. There's plenty to entertain the sand-pail set as well as senior citizens, and there are many nice restaurants, which you'll have an easier time finding if you remember that the main drag through town is referred to as both U.S. 98 and Emerald Coast Parkway. The name makes sense, but part of what makes the gulf look so emerald in these parts is the contrasting whiteness of the sand on the beach. Actually, it's not sand—it's pure, powder-soft Appalachian quartz that was dropped off by a glacier a few thousand years back. Since quartz doesn't compress (and crews clean and rake the beach each evening), your tootsies get the sole-satisfying benefit of soft, sugary "sand." Sand so pure, it squeaks.

☾ In addition to a seasonal water park, **Big Kahuna's Lost Paradise** has year-round family attractions, including 54 holes of miniature golf, two go-kart tracks, an arcade, thrill rides for kids of all ages, and an amphitheater. ⊠ *U.S. 98 E* ☎ *850/837–4061* ⊕ *www.bigkahunas.com* ☒ *Grounds free, water park $33, miniature golf $5, go-karts $5.50, combination ticket (water park, golf, and two go-kart tickets) $41* ☉ *Water park: May–Labor Day, weekends 10–5; Labor Day–mid-Sept., daily 10 AM–midnight.*

WHERE TO STAY & EAT

$$-$$$$ ✕**Marina Café.** A harbor view, impeccable service, and sophisticated
★ fare create one of the finest dining experiences on the Emerald Coast. The ocean motif is expressed in shades of aqua, green, and sand accented with marine tapestries and sea sculptures. The chef calls his creations contemporary Continental, offering diners a choice of classic creole, Mediterranean, or Pacific Rim dishes. One regional specialty is the popular black pepper–crusted yellowfin tuna with braised spinach and spicy soy sauce. The menu changes daily, and the wine list is extensive. ⊠ *404 U.S. 98 E* ☎ *850/837–7960* ☰ *AE, D, DC, MC, V* ☉ *No lunch.*

$-$$$ ✕**Louisiana Lagniappe.** In Louisiana when you say *lagniappe,* it means you're getting a little something extra—here it's the extra zing fresh local seafood gets when transformed into Cajun-style cuisine. You can't go wrong ordering Cajun standards like shrimp creole, crab bisque, and crawfish étouffée. Locals love the chef's innovations, such as grouper Cocodrie, sautéed and topped with fried crawfish, artichoke hearts, and a rich Béarnaise sauce. There's outside dining overlooking Destin Harbor, but whether you're dining inside or out, the sunset views are delicious. ⊠ *775 Gulf Shore Dr., at Sandpiper Cove* ☎ *850/837–0881* ☖ *Reservations not accepted* ☰ *AE, D, DC, MC, V* ☉ *No lunch.*

$$$$ 🏨 **Sandestin Golf and Beach Resort.** Almost a city in itself, and certainly
Fodor's Choice its own little world. Newlyweds, conventioneers, and families all find
★ their fit in this 2,400-acre resort with more than 1,400 accommodation offerings spread across five areas: Beachfront, Beachside, Village, Bayside, and Dockside. Each of the five neighborhood clusters offers a unique locale with villas, cottages, condominiums, boat slips, and an inn. All rooms have a view, either of the gulf, Choctawhatchee Bay, a golf course, a lagoon, or a natural wildlife preserve. This resort accommodates an assortment of tastes, from the simple to the extravagant (the dial-up to the Wi-Fi), but the gigantic suites at the Westwinds are a cut above the rest. Baytowne Wharf has art galleries, wine stores, and a "festival marketplace" of shops and restaurants, so once you get here, you won't need—or want—to leave. ⊠ *9300 Emerald Coast Pkwy. W, 32550* ☎ *850/267–8000 or 800/277–0800* ☎ *850/267–8222* ⊕ *www.sandestin.com* ⇥ *175 rooms, 250 condos, 275 villas* ☖ *In-room: kitchen (some), refrigerator (some), Wi-Fi. In-hotel: 10 restaurants, bars, golf courses, tennis courts, pools, gym, beachfront, public Internet* ☰ *AE, D, DC, MC, V.*

$$$-$$$$ 🏨 **Holiday Inn Destin.** Lounge on sugar-white sands, get to several golf courses with ease, and walk to some of Destin's amusement parks. Common areas jazzed up with skylights and greenery are spacious and eye-pleasing. The standard rooms are uniformly bright and well kept; prices vary depending on the view. ⊠ *1020 U.S. 98 E, 32541*

☎850/837–6181 🖷850/837–1523 ⊕*www.hidestin.com* ⇦233 *rooms* ⚒*In-room: Wi-Fi. In-hotel: restaurant, bar, pools, beachfront, laundry facilities* ▤*AE, D, DC, MC, V.*

$$-$$$$ ⚏**Bluewater Bay Resort.** Popular for its 36 holes of championship golf ★ (on courses designed by Jerry Pate and Tom Fazio), this upscale resort is 12 mi north of Destin via the Mid-Bay Bridge, on the shores of Choctawhatchee Bay. It offers vacation rentals ranging from motel rooms to villas to patio homes. Tennis courts are privately owned, but you can use them for a special rate. ✉*1940 Bluewater Blvd., Niceville 32578* ☎*850/897–3613 or 800/874–2128* 🖷*850/897–2424* ⊕*www. bwbresort.com* ⇦*23 rooms, 22 suites* ⚒*In-hotel: restaurant, bar, golf course, tennis courts, pools* ▤*AE, D, DC, MC, V.*

NIGHTLIFE

Folks come by boat and car to **AJ's Club Bimini** (✉*116 U.S. 98 E* ☎*850/837–1913*), a supercasual bar and restaurant overlooking a marina. Nightly live music means young, lively crowds pack the dance floor. **Harbor Docks** (✉*538 U.S. 98 E* ☎*850/837–2506*) is another favorite with the local seafaring set. It's famous for live music and high-quality sushi. The **Hog's Breath Saloon** (✉*541 U.S. 98 E* ☎*850/837–5991*), a chain hot spot with other locations in Key West and Destin, presents good live music Wednesday through Sunday. The food—steaks, burgers, salads—isn't bad, either. Not only does **Night Town** (✉*140 Palmetto St.* ☎*850/837–7625*) provide two clubs under one roof, but it also offers a mighty generous 14,000-square-foot lighted dance floor, a beach bar, live music, pool tables—and it stays open until almost dawn (4 AM).

SPORTS & THE OUTDOORS

FISHING   If you come to Destin and don't fish, you're missing out, since the city has the largest charter boat fishing fleet in the entire state. You can also pier-fish from the 3,000-foot-long Destin Catwalk and along the East Pass Bridge. For a charter, check with **Adventure Charters** (✉*East Pass Marina, 288 U.S. 98 E* ☎*850/654–4070*), which offers deepsea, bay-bottom, and light-tackle fishing excursions. **East Pass Bait and Tackle** (✉*East Pass Marina, 288 U.S. 98 E* ☎*850/837–2622*) sells bait, tackle, and most anything else you'd need for a day of fishing.

GOLF   The **Indian Bayou Golf & Country Club** (✉*1 Country Club Dr. E, off Airport Rd., off U.S. 98* ☎*850/650–2284* ⊕*www.indianbayougolf. com*) has a 27-hole course; green fee $55/$75 with cart. The 18-hole **Kelly Plantation Golf Club** (✉*307 Kelly Plantation Dr.* ☎*850/650–7600* ⊕*www.kellyplantationgolf.com*), designed by Fred Couples and Gene Bates, is a semiprivate course that runs along Choctawhatchee Bay. Green fee: $125 with cart. There's an 18-hole, semiprivate course at **Regatta Bay Golf & Country Club** (✉*465 Regatta Bay Blvd.* ☎*850/337– 8080* ⊕*www.regattabay.com*). The green fee is $69/$89. For sheer number of holes, the **Sandestin Golf and Beach Resort** (✉*9300 U.S. 98 W* ☎*850/267–8211* ⊕*www.sandestin.com*) tops the list, with 72. There are four courses: **Baytowne Golf Club at Sandestin**, green fee $105/$125; **Burnt Pines Course**, green fee $129/$149; **Links Course**, green fee $95/$115; and the **Raven Golf Club**, green fee $129/$149.

SCUBA DIVING Scuba-diving and snorkeling instruction and outings are available through **Emerald Coast Scuba** (✉*110 Melvin St.* ☎*850/837–0955 or 800/222–0955* ⊕*www.divedestin.com*). An appropriately named center, **The Scuba Shop** (✉*348 S.W. Miracle Strip Pkwy. #19* ☎*850/243–1600* ⊕*www.thescubashopfwb.com*), offers dives and lessons as well.

TENNIS The **Destin Athletic Club** (✉*995 Airport Rd.* ☎*850/837–7300*) has six clay courts. **Sandestin Golf and Beach Resort** (✉*9300 U.S. 98 W* ☎*850/267–7110*), one of the nation's five-star tennis resorts, has 15 courts with grass, hard, and Rubico surfaces.

SHOPPING

Don't call it a mall. **Destin Commons** (✉*Mid-Bay Bridge and Hwy. 98, Destin* ☎*850/337–8700*) is an "open-air lifestyle center." More than 70 high-end specialty shops are here, as well as a 14-screen theater, Hard Rock Cafe, a miniature train and a nautical-theme park for kids, and a 49-tap soda-pop fountain. The **Market at Sandestin** (✉*9300 Emerald Coast Pkwy. W, Sandestin* ☎*850/267–8092*) has about two dozen upscale shops that peddle such goods as expensive chocolates and designer clothes in an elegant mini-mall in a courtyard setting. **Silver Sands Factory Stores** (✉*10562 Emerald Coast Pkwy. W* ☎*850/654–9771* ⊕*www.silversandsoutlet.com*) is one of the Southeast's largest retail designer outlets. More than 100 shops sell top-name merchandise that ranges from gifts to kids' clothes to menswear.

GRAYTON BEACH

5 *18 mi east of Destin.*

The 26-mi stretch of coastline between Destin and Panama City Beach is referred to as the Beaches of South Walton. From the middle of this mostly residential stretch of the Panhandle you can see the monolithic condos of Destin and Panama City Beach in either direction, like massive bookends in the distance, flanking the area's low-slung, less imposing structures. A decidedly laid-back, refined mood prevails in these parts, where vacation homes go for millions and selecting a dinner spot is usually the day's most challenging decision. Accommodations consist primarily of private-home rentals, the majority of which are managed by local real-estate firms. Also scattered along Route 30A are a growing number of boutiques selling everything from fine art to unique hand-painted furniture, to jewelry, gifts, and clothes. Inland, pine forests and hardwoods surround the area's 14 dune lakes, giving anglers ample spots to drop a line and kayakers a peaceful refuge. Grayton Beach, the oldest community in this area, has reached its 100-year mark. You can still see some of the old weathered-cypress homes scattered along narrow, crushed gravel streets. The town has taken off with the addition of adjacent WaterColor, a high-end development of vacation homes with a stylish boutique hotel as its centerpiece. The architecture is tasteful, development is carefully regulated—no buildings taller than four stories are allowed—and bicycles and kayaks are the preferred methods of transportation. Stringent building restrictions, designed to protect the pristine beaches and dunes, ensure that Grayton maintains its small-town feel and look.

Fodor'sChoice
★

The 2,133-acre **Grayton Beach State Park** is one of the most scenic spots along the Gulf Coast. Composed primarily of untouched Florida woodlands, it also has salt marshes, rolling dunes covered with sea oats, crystal-white sand, and contrasting blue-green waters. The park has facilities for swimming, fishing, snorkeling, and camping, and there's an elevated boardwalk that winds over the dunes to the beach. Even if you are just passing by, the beach here is worth the stop. Thirty fully equipped cabins are available for rent *(see Where to Stay & Eat, below).* ⊠ *357 Main Park Rd. (off 30A)* ☎ *850/231–4210* ⌨ *$4 per vehicle, up to 8 people* ☉ *Daily 8–sunset.*

OFF THE BEATEN PATH

Eden Gardens State Park. Scarlett O'Hara might be at home here on the lawn of an antebellum mansion amid an arcade of moss-draped live oaks. Furnishings in the spacious rooms date as far back as the 17th century. The surrounding grounds—the perfect setting for a picnic lunch—are beautiful year-round, but they're nothing short of spectacular in mid-March, when the azaleas and dogwoods are in full bloom. ⊠ *Rte. 395, Point Washington* ☎ *850/231–4214* ⌨ *Gardens $3, mansion tours, $3* ☉ *Daily 8–sunset, mansion tours hourly Thurs.–Mon. 10–3.*

WHERE TO STAY & EAT

$$$–$$$$

✕ **Criollas.** Inventive, contemporary, and constantly changing fare continues to win raves for this popular spot. You might choose to experience Island Hopping—a three-course dinner focusing on a particular Caribbean region—or stick closer to home with Southern-inspired fare like crawfish callaloo soup, creole panfried oysters, or barbecue shrimp. The menu changes seasonally, so returning diners can sample a different cuisine each visit. ⊠ *170 E. Hwy. 30A* ☎ *850/267–1267* ▱ *AE, D, MC, V* ☉ *Closed Sun. and Mon. Nov.–Jan. No lunch.*

$$$–$$$$
Fodor'sChoice
★

✕ **Fish Out of Water.** Time your appetizers to arrive at sunset here and you'll witness the best of both worlds: sea oats lumbering on gold-dusted dunes outside, and a stylish interior that sets new standards of sophistication for the entire Panhandle. Colorful, handblown glass accent lighting that "grows" out of the hardwood floors, plush taupe banquettes, oversize handmade lamp shades, and a sleek bar area that screams New York (complete with a cloud-white curtain-wall) create an atmosphere worthy of the inventive cuisine. Influences range from Asian (Thai-style grouper with lobster-coconut broth) to Southern (Low Country shrimp and scallops with creamy grits) to classic Continental (porcini-crusted osso buco), but all are convincingly wrought and carefully presented. The extensive wine list keeps pace with the menu offerings. ⊠ *34 Goldenrod Circle, 2nd fl. of WaterColor Inn* ☎ *850/534–5050* ▱ *AE, D, DC, MC, V* ☉ *No lunch.*

$–$$

✕ **Picolo Restaurant & Red Bar.** You could spend weeks here just taking in all the funky-junky, eclectic toy chest memorabilia—from Marilyn Monroe posters to flags to dolls—dangling from the ceiling and tacked to every available square inch of wall. The contemporary menu is small, changes daily, and is very Floridian. A baked eggplant dish stuffed with shrimp, scallops, and grilled vegetables is a popular entrée. Blues and jazz musicians play nightly in the Red Bar. ⊠ *70 Hotz Ave.* ☎ *850/231–1008* ▭ *No credit cards.*

$$$$
Fodor's Choice
★
▢ **WaterColor Inn.** Nature meets seaside chic at this boutique property, the crown jewel of the area's latest—and largest—planned community. Rooms are done in seashell tones with sea-blue comforters and accents; stylish armoires and desks look as natural and unfinished as driftwood. Dune-level bungalows have private courtyards with outdoor showers, whereas upper rooms have huge balconies and walk-in showers with windows overlooking the gulf. Standard rooms come with a king-size bed and a queen sleeper-sofa, but consider one of the three Rotunda rooms for something larger and more spectacular. ⊠ *34 Goldenrod Circle, 32459* ☎ *850/534–5000* ▤ *850/534–5001* ⊕ *www.watercolor-vacations.com* ⇩ *60 rooms* ⛊ *In-room: safe, refrigerator, dial-up. In-hotel: restaurant, pool, beachfront, airport shuttle, no-smoking rooms, Internet, minibar.*

$$
★
▢ **Cabins at Grayton Beach State Park.** Back-to-nature enthusiasts and families like the stylish accommodations set among the sand pines and scrub oaks of this pristine state park. The two-bedroom duplexes (each named after a different species of tree found in the park) have tin roofs, white trim, and tropical wooden window louvers, and the beach is a leisurely five-minute walk away via a private boardwalk. Modern conveniences include central heat and air-conditioning and full-size kitchens complete with pots and pans. There is no daily maid service—fresh linens are provided, however—and no room phones or televisions, but gas fireplaces, barbecue grills, and screen porches add a homey touch. They're often booked solid as much as 11 months in advance, but call to check for cancellations. ⊠ *357 Main Park Rd.* ☎ *800/326–3521 for reservations* ⊕ *www.reserveamerica.com* ⇩ *30 cabins* ⛊ *In-room: no phone, kitchen, no TV* ▭ *AE, MC, V.*

NIGHTLIFE

The **Red Bar** (⊠ *70 Hotz Ave.* ☎ *850/231–1008*), the local watering hole, presents red-hot blues or jazz acts every night. On Friday and Saturday nights it's elbow-to-elbow at the bar.

THE OUTDOORS

The **Santa Rosa Golf & Beach Club** (⊠ *Rte. 30A, Santa Rosa Beach* ☎ *850/267–2229*) is a semiprivate 18-hole course that, thankfully, has little residential development beside the fairways; green fee $60–$95 with cart.

SHOPPING

Gaffrey Art Gallery (⊠ *21 Blue Gulf Dr., 3 mi west of Grayton Beach, Santa Rosa Beach* ☎ *850/267–0228* ⊕ *www.gaffreyart.com*) displays the contemporary and colorful folk art of Billie and Justin Gaffrey. **Grayton Beach House of Art** (⊠ *26 Logan La.* ☎ *850/231–9997* ⊕ *www. gordiehinds.com*) specializes in the works of Gordie Hinds, who gave up charter fishing and picked up a paintbrush in 2003. He paints what he knows best: fishing, seashores, piers, and marshes. Under the shade trees of Grayton Beach, **Magnolia House** (⊠ *2 Magnolia St.* ☎ *850/231–5859*) sells gift items, bath products, and accessories for the home.

The **Shops of Grayton** (⊠*Rte. 283 [Grayton Rd.], 2 mi south of U.S. 98* ☎*No phone*) is a colorful complex of eight Cracker-style cottages selling gifts, artwork, and antiques. At **Woodie Long Folk Art Gallery** (⊠*1066 B. North Bay Dr./Rte. 283, Santa Rosa Beach* ☎*850/231–9961*), in the living room of the artist's residence, you'll find a few of the 10,000 artworks the quirky local claims to have painted (a feature in *Smithsonian* magazine put Woodie on the art-world map). His folk paintings can be seen at the Cooperstown Museum, the Philadelphia Museum of Art, and on CD jackets and book covers.

SEASIDE & ROSEMARY BEACH

6 *2 mi east of Grayton Beach.*

This community of Victorian-style homes is so reminiscent of a storybook town that producers chose it for the set of the 1998 film *The Truman Show,* starring Jim Carrey. The brainchild of Robert Davis, **Seaside** was designed to promote a neighborly, old-fashioned lifestyle, and there's much to be said for an attractive, billboard-free village where you can park your car and walk everywhere you need to go. Pastel-color homes with white picket fences, front-porch rockers, and captain's walks are set amid redbrick streets, and all are within walking distance of the town center and its unusual cafés and shops.

The community has come into its own in the last few years, achieving a comfortable, lived-in look and feel that had escaped it since its founding in the 1970s: some of the once-shiny tin roofs are starting to rust around the edges, and the foliage has completely matured, creating pockets of privacy and shade. Still, while Seaside's popularity continues to soar, it retains a suspicious sense of *Twilight Zone* perfection that can weird out some visitors. Summer months can be crowded with the retired-CEO and prep-school-student-and-parent sets, so if you're seeking a little solitude, you might prefer visiting during the off-season—between Labor Day and Memorial Day.

Farther east down Highway 30A is **Rosemary Beach,** a fledgling development that is, like eleventy-million other new coastal communities, a variation on the theme pioneered by Seaside's founders. A few restaurants and shops have opened, and a super-luxe boutique hotel is under construction, so investors are snatching up the snazzy beach houses as fast as they're built (in many cases, even before they are built). Despite the growth, the focus here is still on preserving the local environment (the landscape is made up completely of indigenous plants) and maintaining its small-town appeal. You can already see a nascent sense of community sprouting at the Town Green, a perfect patch of manicured lawn fronting the beach, where locals gather with their wineglasses to toast the sunset.

WHERE TO STAY & EAT

$$$–$$$$ ✕ **Bud & Alley's.** This down-to-earth beachside bistro (named for a pet cat and dog) has been a local favorite since 1986. Tucked in the dunes by the gulf, the rooftop Tarpon Club bar makes a great perch for a

sunset toast (guess the exact moment the sun will disappear and win a drink). Daily salad specials are tangy introductions to such entrées as sesame-seared tuna on wild greens with rice-wine vinaigrette and soy dipping sauce. The Cuban steak frites, served with a flavorful tomato-and-avocado salsa, is a spicy local twist on a classic dish. ⊠*Rte. 30A, Santa Rosa Beach* ☎*850/231–5900* ⊕*www.budandalleys.com* ▤*MC, V* ⊘*No lunch.*

$$$–$$$$ ✕**Café Thirty-A.** In a beautiful Florida-style home with high ceilings
★ and a wide veranda, this restaurant has an elegant look—bolstered by white linen tablecloths—and impeccable service. The menu changes nightly and includes such entrées as chili-dusted wild king salmon, oven-roasted black grouper, and grilled organic free-range lamb rack. Even if you're not a Southerner, you should try the appetizer of grilled Georgia quail with creamy grits and sage fritters. With nearly 20 creative varieties, the martini menu alone is worth the trip. ⊠*3899 E. Hwy. 30A, Seagrove Beach* ☎*850/231–2166* ⊕*www.cafethirtya.com* ▤*AE, D, DC, MC, V* ⊘*No lunch.*

¢–$$ ✕**Shades Restaurant.** This is not a sports bar, so don't be fooled by the extensive (and impressive) beer list or the three televisions and the Buffalo Bills shrine in the front bar. Just grab a seat in the side room, where local artwork graces the walls, or relax on the covered patio overlooking the main square and watch the (Truman) show go by. The standout here is the seafood, from lunchtime shrimp po'boys to the always-available crab cakes, mango-and-chicken plate, and the perfectly prepared catch of the day (the tuna and grouper are both excellent), served over equally fresh garden greens and vegetables. Breakfast—including eggs any way you want 'em, French toast sticks for kids, and beignets with fresh fruit—is served every morning from 8 to 10. ⊠*83 Central Sq.* ☎*850/231–1950* ▤*AE, MC, V.*

$$$$ ⊡**Seaside Cottage Rental Agency.** When residents aren't using their
★ homes, they rent out their one- to six-bedroom, porticoed, faux-Victorian cottages furnished with fully equipped kitchens, TV-VCRs, and vacuum cleaners—a perfect option for a family vacation or a large group. Gulf breezes blowing off the water remind you of the unspoiled sugar-white beaches a short stroll away. ⊠*Rte. 30A, Box 4730, 32459* ☎*850/231–1320 or 800/277–8696* 🖷*850/231–2231* ⊕*www.seasidefl.com* ⊅*275 units* ⚲*In-room: kitchen. In-hotel: tennis courts, pools, bicycles, no elevators.* ▤*AE, D, MC, V.*

$$$–$$$$ ⊡**Josephine's Inn.** The charming rooms in this grand, Georgian-style accommodation have gulf views, four-poster beds, fireplaces, and claw-foot tubs, bringing a bit of elegance to a modern seaside spot. The daily country-style breakfast is delicious, and dinners are garnished with fresh herbs and flowers from the owners' garden. ⊠*38 Seaside Ave., 32459* ☎*850/231–1940 or 800/848–1840* 🖷*850/231–2446* ⊕*www.josephinesinn.com* ⊅*7 rooms, 2 suites* ⚲*In-room: VCR* ▤*AE, D, MC, V.*

$$–$$$ ⊡**The Pensione at Rosemary Beach.** Penny and Mark Dragonette run this spotless, eight-room inn on the town's main square, one block from the Gulf of Mexico. In keeping with the true *pensione* concept, rooms (all with queen beds) are basic, almost dorm-style, yet comfortable—those

in front have views of the gulf across the street—and thoughtful touches like chocolates, whimsical murals, and picture guides to local butterflies add a touch of homeyness. You're guaranteed peace and quiet here: children under 16, spring breakers, and overzealous wedding parties are not allowed. Continental breakfast is included in the room price, making this smart property one of the best bargains around. Onano, a "neighborhood café," occupies the inn's first floor. ⊠*78 Main St., Rosemary Beach 32461* ☎*850/231–1790* 🖷*850/231–2995* ⊕*www. thepensione.com* 🛏*8 rooms* ♨*In-room: VCR. In-hotel: no kids under 16, no-smoking rooms* ☰*AE, D, MC, V* ⏽*CP.*

NIGHTLIFE

Courtyard Wine and Cheese (⊠*66 Main St., Rosemary Beach* ☎*850/231– 1219* ⊕*www.courtyardwineandcheese.com*) is a sophisticated wine bar (with free Wi-Fi) that opens onto a Tuscan-style courtyard and stocks 150 wines, fine cheeses, and artwork, too. It's closed Monday. The upstairs, open-air bar at **Bud & Alley's** (⊠*Rte. 30A* ☎*850/231–5900*) draws a friendly crowd for sunset, and the festivities usually last until the wee hours.

THE OUTDOORS

An 8-foot-wide pathway covering 18 mi of scenic Route 30A winds past freshwater lakes, woodlands, and beaches. **Butterfly Rentals** (⊠*3657 E. Rte. 30A* ☎*850/231–2826*) rents bikes and kayaks and has free delivery and pickup. In Seaside, consult the **Cabana Man** (☎*850/231–5046*) for beach chairs, umbrellas, rafts, kayaks, and anything else you might need for a day at the beach. If there's no answer, just head to the beach and you'll find him there.

SHOPPING

Seaside's central square and open-air market, along Route 30A, offer a number of unique and whimsical boutiques carrying clothing, jewelry, and arts and crafts. **Perspicacity** (⊠*178 Market St.* ☎*850/231–5829*), an open-air market, sells simply designed women's clothing and accessories perfect for easy, carefree beach-town casualness. At **Ruskin Place Artist Colony,** in the heart of Seaside, a collection of small shops and artists' galleries has everything from toys and pottery to fine works of art.

PANAMA CITY BEACH

❼ *21 mi southeast of Seaside.*

The dizzying number of high-rises under construction on the Miracle Strip—about two dozen in total—has led to the formation of a new moniker for this stretch of the Panhandle: the "Construction Coast." But the vast majority of the new buildings are condominiums, not hotels, and many of the older mom-and-pop motels that once gave this town its beach-resort flavor have fallen victim to the wrecking ball. Invasive growth has turned the main thoroughfare, Front Beach Road, into a dense mass of traffic that peaks in spring and between June and August when college students descend en masse from neighboring states. The bright side of the changing landscape is that land values have risen so dramatically in the last few years that many of the attractions that gave parts of this area a seedy reputation (i.e., strip joints and dive bars) have been driven out, replaced by new retailers and the occasional franchise "family" restaurant or chain store.

The one constant in this sea of change, however, is the area's natural beauty that, in some areas at least, manages to excuse its gross overcommercialization. The shoreline in town is *17 mi* long, so even when a mile is packed with partying students, there are 16 more miles where you can toss a beach blanket. What's more, the beaches along the Miracle Strip, with their powder-soft sand and translucent emerald waters, are some of the finest in the state; in one sense, anyway, it's easy to understand why so many condos are being built here. Cabanas, umbrellas, sailboats, wave runners, and floats are available from any of dozens of vendors along the beach. For an aerial view, for about $30 you can strap yourself beneath a parachute and go parasailing as you're towed aloft behind a speedboat a few hundred yards offshore. And St. Andrews State Park, on the southern end of the beaches, is treasured by locals and visitors alike.

The area's incredible white sands, navigable waterways, and plentiful marine life that attracted Spanish conquistadors today draw invaders of the vacationing kind—namely families, the vast majority of whom hail from nearby Georgia and Alabama.

■TIP→When coming here, be sure to set your sights for Panama City *Beach*. Panama City is its beachless inland cousin.

☺ Once part of the now-defunct Miracle Strip Amusement Park operation, **Shipwreck Island,** a 6-acre water park, offers everything from speedy slides and tubes to the slow-moving Lazy River. ■TIP→**Oddly enough, admission is based on height: 50 inches $29; between 35 and 50 inches, $24; under 35 inches, free. Wear flats.** ✉*12000 Front Beach Rd.* ☎*850/234–0368* ⊕*www.shipwreckisland.com* ✉*$29* ☾*Mid-Apr.– May, weekends 10:30–5; June–early Sept., daily 10:30–5.*

☺ At the unique **Museum of Man in the Sea,** see rare examples of breathing apparatuses and diving equipment, some dating as far back as the 1600s, in addition to exhibits on Florida's historic shipwrecks. There are also treasures recovered from famous wrecks, including artifacts from the Spanish galleon *Atocha,* and live creatures found in the area's coastal waters. ✉*17314 Panama City Beach Pkwy.* ☎*850/235–4101* ✉*$5* ☾*Daily 10–4.*

☺ It's certainly no SeaWorld, but **Gulf World,** the resident marine park, with a tropical garden, tropical-bird theater, plus alligator and otter exhibits, is still a winner with the kids. The stingray petting pool and the shark-feeding and scuba demonstrations are big crowd pleasers, but the old favorites—performing sea lions, otters, and bottle-nosed dolphins—still hold their own. If you're really nautically minded, consider the Trainer for a Day program, which allows you to go behind the scenes to assist in food preparation and training sessions and make an on-stage appearance in the Dolphin Show. ✉15412 Front Beach Rd. ☎850/234-5271 ⊕www.gulfworldmarinepark. com ☞$24 ⊙Late May–early Sept., daily 9 AM–4 PM; call for hrs at other times of year.

At the eastern tip of Panama City Beach, **St. Andrews State Park** includes 1,260 acres of beaches, pinewoods, and marshes. Complete camping facilities are here, and a snack bar, too, as well as places to swim, pier-fish, or hike the dunes along clearly marked nature trails. Board a ferry to **Shell Island**—a 700-acre barrier island in the Gulf of Mexico with some of the best shelling north of Sanibel Island. A rock jetty creates a calm, shallow play area that is perfect for young children. Come to this spectacular park for a peek at what the entire beach area looked like before developers sank their claws into it. ✉4607 State Park La. ☎850/233-5140 ⊕www.floridastateparks.org ☞$5 per vehicle, up to 8 people ⊙Daily 8–5.

WHERE TO STAY & EAT

$–$$$$ ✕**Capt. Anderson's.** Come early to watch the boats unload the catch of the day on the docks, and to beat the long line that forms each afternoon in this noted restaurant. Here since 1953, it doesn't seem to have changed much. A nautical theme is reinforced by tables made of hatch covers in the attached bar, which attracts longtime locals. The Greek specialties aren't limited to feta cheese and shriveled olives; charcoal-broiled grouper, amberjack, and yellowfin tuna, crab-stuffed jumbo shrimp, and steaks have a prominent place on the menu as well. If you're visiting in the off-season, call to make sure they are adhering to the posted hours before venturing out. ✉5551 N. Lagoon Dr. ☎850/234-2225 ⚑Reservations not accepted ▤AE, D, DC, MC, V ⊙Closed Sun. and Nov.–Jan. No lunch.

$$–$$$ ✕**Boars Head.** An exterior that looks like an oversize thatch-roof cottage sets the mood for dining in this ersatz-rustic restaurant and tavern. Prime rib has been the number one people-pleaser since the house opened in 1978, but blackened seafood and broiled shrimp with crabmeat stuffing are popular, too. ✉17290 Front Beach Rd. ☎850/234-6628 ⊕www.boarsheadrestaurant.com ▤AE, D, DC, MC, V ⊙No lunch.

$–$$$ ✕**Schooners.** Billing itself as the "last local beach club," and more boldly, "the best place on earth," this beachfront spot is a perfect place for a casual family lunch or early dinner: kids can have burgers and play on the beach while Mom and Dad enjoy grown-up drinks and more substantial fare such as homemade gumbo, steak, or simply pre-pared seafood. Late-night crowds pile in for live music and dancing. ✉5121 Gulf Dr. ☎850/235-3555 ⊕www.schooners.com ▤AE, D, MC, V.

¢–$$$ ✕**The Boatyard.** The same folks who operate Schooners on the beach side opened this larger, more stylish establishment overlooking a marina on the Grand Lagoon. For starters, try fried peanut-crusted crab claws, or conch fritters with hot-pepper jelly and wasabi mayonnaise. For dinner, choose from the Caesar salad with Apalachicola oyster fritters, the lobster sandwich, or the aptly named Fried Shrimp You Can't Live

Without. The coconut-and-plantain-crusted grouper is a knockout, as is the pan-roasted catch with bacon, mushrooms, and grits (this is definitely the South). There are a kids' menu, an extensive wine list, and a full bar, and the upstairs deck area is a great place to get away from the beach for a long, lazy lunch or romantic sunset dinner. Be aware that the Boatyard kicks into high gear at sundown, transforming into one of the hottest nightspots in town. ⊠*5325 N. Lagoon Dr.* ☎*850/249–9273* ⊕*www.boatyardclub.com* ⊟*AE, D, DC, MC, V.*

¢–$$ ✕**Billy's Steamed Seafood Restaurant, Oyster Bar, and Crab House.** Roll up your sleeves and dig into some of the gulf's finest blue crabs and shrimp seasoned to perfection with Billy's special recipe. Homemade gumbo, crawfish, and the day's catch as well as sandwiches and burgers round out the menu. The taste here is in the food, not the surroundings, but you can eat on an outdoor patio in the cooler months. ⊠*3000 Thomas Dr.* ☎*850/235–2349* ⊟*AE, D, MC, V.*

¢–$$ ✕**Montego Bay.** A tiki-style bar is the focal point at this former beach cottage where you're guaranteed friendly service and reasonably priced seafood, chicken, and steak dishes. Appetizers include deep-fried Cajun crawfish and "gator bites" (if you've never eaten fried alligator tail, try it here: it's nowhere near as exotic as you might think), calamari, chicken wings, and coconut shrimp. Main courses range from fresh fish (fried, sautéed, or grilled) to caramelized ribs, grilled sirloin, and Jamaican jerk chicken. There's a special menu just for kids, and beer, wine, and frozen specialty drinks for adults. ⊠*4920 Thomas Dr.* ☎*850/234–8686* ⊕*www.montegobaypcb.com* ⊟*AE, D, DC, MC.*

¢ ✕**Coram's.** Don't feel slighted if you're the only one in the place the waitress doesn't know by name—she'll know it by the time you leave (and "Hon" will do in the meantime). More than a local institution, this plain-Jane, diner-style restaurant with parking-lot views makes up in taste and price for what it lacks in atmosphere. Locals flock here for hearty breakfasts—the fluffy omelets are ample enough for two—lunchtime salads and sandwiches, and a dinner menu that includes barbecued pork, fish specials, and steaks and roast beef preparations served with mashed potatoes. For solid food at criminally low prices 24/7, you just can't beat this place. ⊠*2016 Thomas Dr.* ☎*850/234–8373* ⚐*Reservations not accepted* ⊟*No credit cards.*

$$$–$$$$ ⊡**Edgewater Beach Resort.** The sticker-shock price of this resort is tem-
★ pered when you realize that you can sleep at least four and as many as eight in the luxurious one-, two-, and three-bedroom apartments in beachside towers and golf-course villas. Rooms are elegantly furnished with wicker and rattan, and the resort centerpiece is a Polynesian-style lagoon pool with waterfalls, reflecting ponds, footbridges, and more than 20,000 species of tropical plants. With plenty of swimming and sporting options, this is a good beachfront option for longer stays or family vacations. ⊠*11212 Front Beach Rd., 32407* ☎*850/235–4044 or 800/874–8686* ☐*850/233–7529* ⊕*www.edgewaterbeachresort.com* ⊅*520 apartments* ⚐*In-hotel: 2 restaurants, bars, golf course, tennis courts, spa, beachfront, Internet* ⊟*D, DC, MC, V.*

$$$–$$$$ ⊡**Legacy by the Sea.** Every room at this 14-story, pastel-peach all-suites hotel has a private balcony with commanding gulf views. Rooms are

designed with families in mind, from the fully equipped kitchens, to the two televisions and waterproof sofa cushions, to the door that conveniently separates the bedroom area from the rest of the unit. There's a gulf-front pool and hot tub area (with a kiddie pool), and freebies include continental breakfast, daily newspaper, local calls, and an airport shuttle. Shopping, dining, and attractions are within walking distance, and a variety of water-sport options, including parasailing and Jet Skiing, is offered by on-site concessionaires. The hotel's closed-circuit cable channel, airing nothing but live security camera feeds (inside the elevator, around the pool, in the common areas), makes keeping an eye on the kids a breeze—and keeping an eye on unsuspecting adults a hoot. ⌧ *15325 Front Beach Rd., 32413* ☎*850/249–8601 or 888/886–8917* 🖷*850/249–8601* ⊕*www.legacybythesea.com* ⇱*278 rooms, 78 suites* ⚭*In-room: kitchen, dial-up (some), Wi-Fi (some). In-hotel: pool, airport shuttle* ▤*AE, D, DC, MC, V.*

$$$–$$$$ 🖵**Marriott Bay Point Resort Village.** Across the Grand Lagoon from St.
Fodor'sChoice Andrews State Park, this expansive property exudes sheer elegance. The
★ tropical-chic feel starts in the light-filled lobby, with its polished marble floors, glowing chandeliers, potted palms, and colorful floral paintings. Quiet guest rooms continue the theme with light-wood furnishings and armoires, floral-print fabrics, and private balconies or patios overlooking the lush grounds and peaceful bay. Rooms on the upper floors of the main building have expansive views of the bay and the gulf beyond, and villas are a mere tee-shot away from the hotel. A meandering boardwalk (which doubles as a jogging trail) leads to a private bayside beach where an open-air bar and water sports await. ⌧*4200 Marriott Dr., 32408* ☎*850/236–6000 or 800/874–7105* 🖷*850/236–6158* ⊕*www. marriottbaypoint.com* ⇱*278 rooms, 78 suites* ⚭*In-room: refrigerator (some), dial-up. In-hotel: 5 restaurants, bars, golf courses, pools, gym, airport shuttle* ▤*AE, D, DC, MC, V.*

$–$$$$ 🖵**Holiday Inn SunSpree Resort.** The pool area at this expansive, kidney-shape beachfront resort has waterfalls, faux-rock formations, lush foliage, thatch-roof huts, and Jamon, billed as the resort's own "Polynesian Islander," who lights the poolside torches every night. You might see why this tiki schtick appeals to spring breakers, who flock to the place in huge numbers, but if peace and quiet are your thing in spring, this is the wrong place—and the wrong town. The rest of the year, though, it's a pleasant enough retreat for families: kids enjoy the myriad planned activities of the Splash Around Kids Club and the beachfront game room, and parents can simply relax at the in-pool grotto bar. All rooms have terra-cotta tile floors, tropical-print bedspreads, wicker furnishings, and private balconies with views of the gulf. If you want a decent place to plant the whole family without having to leave the grounds for food or entertainment, this is it. ⌧*11127 Front Beach Rd., 32407* ☎*850/234–1111* 🖷*850/235–1907* ⊕*www.holidayinnsunspree.com* ⇱*337 rooms, 4 suites* ⚭*In-room: safe, refrigerator, dial-up. In-hotel: restaurant, bars, pool, gym, beachfront, children's programs (ages 3–18), laundry facilities* ▤*AE, D, DC, MC, V.*

NIGHTLIFE & THE ARTS

THE ARTS   Broadway touring shows, top-name entertainers, and concert artists are booked into the **Marina Civic Center** (⊠*8 Harrison Ave., Panama City* ☎*850/769–1217 or 850/763–4696* ⊕*www.marinaciviccenter.com*). The **Martin Theatre** (⊠*409 Harrison Ave., Panama City* ☎*850/763–8080*) is host to traditional plays and concerts throughout the year.

NIGHTLIFE   **The Boatyard** (⊠*5325 North Lagoon Dr.* ☎*850/249–9273*) is a multi-level, indoor-outdoor waterfront nightclub and restaurant that presents a regular lineup of bands, ranging from blues to steel drums to classic rock and beyond (DJs round out the entertainment roster). There's never a cover for locals, so act like a local, if you dare.

Pineapple Willy's (⊠*9875 S. Thomas Dr.* ☎*850/235–0928*) is an eatery and bar geared to families and tourists—as well as sports fans.

SPORTS & THE OUTDOORS

CANOEING   Rentals for a trip down Econofina Creek, known as Florida's most beautiful canoe trail, are supplied by **Econofina Creek Canoe Livery.** Kayaks can be rented for $25, canoes for $35. (⊠*Strickland Rd., north of Rte. 20, Youngstown* ☎*850/722–9032*).

DIVING   Snorkeling and scuba diving are extremely popular in the clear waters here. If you have the proper certification, you can dive among dozens of ships sunk by the city to create artificial reefs. The **Panama City Dive Center** (⊠*4823 Thomas Dr., Panama City Beach* ☎*850/235–3390* ⊕*www.pcdivecenter.com*) offers instruction, rentals, and charters.

DOG RACING   Find pari-mutuel betting year-round and live greyhound racing five nights and two afternoons a week at the **Ebro Greyhound Park.** Simulcasts of thoroughbred racing from the Miami area are also shown throughout the year. Schedules change periodically, so call for details. ⊠*Rte. 79 and Hwy. 20, Ebro* ☎*850/234–3943* ⊠*$2, clubhouse $1 extra.*

GOLF   The **Hombre Golf Club** (⊠*120 Coyote Pass* ☎*850/234–3673* ⊕*www.hombregolfclub.com*) has a 27-hole course that occasionally hosts professional tours; green fee $55/$75 with cart. **Marriott Bay Point Resort** (⊠*4200 Marriott Dr.* ☎*850/235–6950 or 850/235–6949* ⊕*www.baypointgolf.com*) has a country club with two courses open to the public: the **Nicklaus Course** and the **Meadows Course.** Green fee $59/$99 each.

TENNIS   The tennis center at **Marriott Bay Point Resort** (⊠*4200 Marriott Dr.* ☎*850/235–6910*) has 10 Har-Tru tennis courts.

SHOPPING

Stores in the **Manufacturer's Outlet Center** (⊠*105 W. 23rd St., Panama City*) offer well-known brands at substantial discounts. The **Panama City Mall** (⊠*2150 Martin Luther King Jr. Blvd., Panama City* ☎*850/785–9587*) is the only true mall within an hour's radius, and has a mix of some 100 franchise shops and national chain stores.

APALACHICOLA

8 *65 mi southeast of Panama City Beach.*

It feels like a long haul between Panama City Beach and here. Add an odd name and a town's below-the-radar reputation to that long drive and you may be tempted to skip Apalachicola. But you shouldn't. It's a weirdly fascinating Cracker town that, for some reason, has a growing cosmopolitan veneer. And that makes it worth a visit.

Meaning "land of the friendly people" in the language of its original Native American inhabitants, Apalachicola—known in these parts as simply Apalach—lies on the Panhandle's southernmost bulge. European settlers began arriving in 1821, and by 1847 the southern terminus of the Apalachicola River steamboat route was a bustling port town. Although the town is now known as the Oyster Capital of the World, oystering became king only after the local cotton industry flagged—the city's extra-wide streets, built to accommodate bales of cotton awaiting transport, are a remnant of that trade—and the sponge industry moved down the coast after depleting local sponge colonies. But the newest industry here is tourism, and visitors have begun discovering the Forgotten Coast, as the area is known, flocking to its intimate hotels and bed-and-breakfasts, dining at excellent restaurants, and browsing in unique shops selling everything from handmade furniture to brass fixtures recovered from nearby shipwrecks. If you like oysters or want to go back in time to the Old South of Gothic churches and spooky graveyards, Apalachicola is a good place to start.

Drive by the **Raney House**, circa 1850, and **Trinity Episcopal Church**, built from prefabricated parts in 1838. The town is at a developmental turning point, pulled in one direction by well-intentioned locals who want to preserve Apalachicola's port-town roots and in the other by longtime business owners who fear preservation will inhibit commercial growth. For now, however, the city exudes a refreshing authenticity—think Key West in the early 1960s—that many others in the Sunshine State lost long ago, one that might be lost to Panama City Beach–style overdevelopment unless local government institutes an official historic-preservation committee.

Stop in at the **John Gorrie Museum State Park,** which honors the physician credited with inventing ice-making, and almost inventing air-conditioning. Although he was hampered by technology, later air-conditioning patents used Gorrie's discoveries. Exhibits of Apalachicola history are displayed here as well. ⊠ *Ave. D and 6th St.* ☎ *850/653–9347* ▱ *$1* ☉ *Thurs.–Mon. 9–5.*

WHERE TO STAY & EAT

$–$$$ ✕ **Magnolia Grill.** Chef-owner Eddie Cass has earned local and regional
★ acclaim from major food critics who have discovered the culinary pearl in this oyster town. In addition to meat dishes such as char-grilled pork tenderloin served with raspberry bordelaise sauce, Eddie pays tribute to local seafood with a broiled seafood feast that includes three of the freshest market fish served with locally harvested shrimp, scallops, and

Apalachicola Bay oysters. Dinners here tend to be leisurely events (this is the South, after all), and the stellar desserts—anything chocolate will wow you—deserve an hour of their own. The restaurant is small, so reservations are recommended. ⊠99 11th St. ☎850/653–8000 ⊕www. chefeddiesmagnoliagrill.com ⊟MC, V ⊗Closed Sun. No lunch.

$–$$$ ✕**Owl Café.** This old-fashioned, charming lunch and dinner spot pleases modern palates, both in the white-linen elegance of the dining room and in the colorful garden terrace. The food is an artful blend of old and new as well: Grandma's chicken wrap seems as much at home on the lunch menu as the crab quesadillas. Dinner seafood specials are carefully prepared, but special requests are sometimes met with resistance from the kitchen. Fine wines for adults and special menu selections for children make this a family-friendly place. At night, with a full liquor bar the mood shifts to a casual lounge setting. ⊠15 Ave. D ☎850/653–9888 ⊕www.owlcafeflorida.com ⊟AE, MC, V ⊗Closed Sun.

$–$$$
★ ✕**Tamara's Cafe Floridita.** Tamara, a native Venezuelan, brings the food and warmth of her homeland to this colorful bistro, which mixes Florida flavors with South American flair. For starters, try the creamy black-bean soup or the pleasantly spicy oyster stew; for dinner choose from seafood paella, prosciutto-wrapped salmon with mango-cilantro sauce, or margarita chicken and scallops with a tequila-lime glaze. All entrées come with black beans and rice, fresh vegetables, and focaccia bread, but if you still have room for dessert, try the fried banana split or the *tres leches* (cake soaked in three types of milk), a South American favorite. The chef, who keeps watch over the dining room from an open kitchen, is happy to accommodate most any whim. ⊠17 Ave. E ☎850/653–4111 ⊟AE, MC, V.

¢–$$$ ✕**Boss Oyster.** Eat your oysters fried, Rockefeller-style, on the half shell, or Greek, Mexican, English, with garlic, with shrimp, with crab, with hot peppers, with … oh, just eat 'em with gusto at this laid-back eatery overlooking the Apalachicola River. In addition to oysters, they lay down jumbo gulf shrimp, blue crabs, bay scallops, and fresh gulf grouper. Eat alfresco at picnic tables or inside in the busy, rustic dining room, but don't let the modest surroundings fool you—oysters aren't cheap here or anywhere in Apalach. The menu also includes such staples as steak and pizza. ⊠125 Water St. ☎850/653–9364 ⊟AE, D, DC, MC, V.

$ ✕**Avenue Sea.** Hobnob with Apalachicola aristocracy as you eat in a serene, Edwardian-style dining room at the Gibson Inn, the town's traditional hotel. A sea change came in 2006 when Chef David Carrier, an alum of The French Laundry, arrived to infuse a strong focus on fresh, local seafood and worldly wines. Entrées, though, are not your usual portions. Each is served as a 4-ounce course—much like a tapas menu—and you can order as many as you prefer. Sit at the cozy wooden bar for an after-dinner drink, a piece of key lime pie, and a taste of Apalachicola of yesteryear. ⊠51 Ave. C ☎850/653–2193 ⊟AE, MC, V.

$$$–$$$$ ▥**The Consulate.** These four elegant suites, on the second story of the former offices of the French consul, range in size from 650 to 1,650 square feet and combine a 19th-century feel with 21st-century luxury. Exposed wooden beams and brick walls, 13-foot ceilings, hardwood floors, and antique architectural details add more than a hint of charm, and custom-built kitchens, full-size washers and dryers, and cordless room phones make living easy. The two front units share an expansive balcony, where you can take in the constant parade of fishing vessels headed out the intracoastal waterway. The homelike amenities make this a popular spot for families, larger groups, and even wedding parties, and discounts are given for stays longer than two nights. The Grady Market, a locally owned art and clothing boutique, occupies the building's first floor. ⊠76 Water St., 32320 ☎850/653–1515 or 877/239–1159 ♺850/653–1516 ⊕www.consulatesuites.com ♴4 suites ⌂In-room: kitchen, VCR. In-hotel: no elevator ⊟AE, MC, V.

$–$$$$ ▨**Coombs House Inn.** Nine fireplaces and an ornate oak staircase with lead-glass windows on the landing lend authenticity to this restored 1905 mansion. No two guest rooms are alike, but all are appointed with Victorian-era settees, four-poster or sleigh beds, English chintz curtains, and Asian rugs on polished hardwood floors. A full breakfast is served in the dining room. Eighty steps away is Coombs House East, and, beyond that, a renovated carriage house. Popular for weddings and receptions, these may be the most elegant homes in Apalachicola. Free tours are offered in the afternoon if the accommodations are not in use. ⊠80 6th St., 32320 ☎850/653–9199 ♺850/653–2785 ⊕www. coombshouseinn.com ♴18 rooms ⌂In-hotel: bicycles, no-smoking rooms ⊟D, MC, V.

$–$$$ ▨**Gibson Inn.** One of a few inns on the National Register of Historic Places still operating as a full-service facility, this turn-of-the-20th-century hostelry in the heart of downtown is easily identified by its wraparound porches, intricate fretwork, and captain's watch. Large rooms are furnished with period pieces like four-poster beds, antique armoires, and pedestal lavatories. Extremely popular for weddings and special events, the inn equally impresses overnight visitors with its cleanliness, style, service, and rocking-chair-rich wraparound porch. Add chills to your thrills and ask for the haunted room. ⊠51 Ave. C, 32320 ☎850/653–2191 ♺850/653–3521 ⊕www.gibsoninn.com ♴30 rooms, 2 suites ⌂In-hotel: restaurant, bar, some pets allowed, no elevator ⊟AE, MC, V.

$–$$ ▨**Best Western Apalach Inn.** Basic but impeccably kept, this modern property 1 mi from the downtown waterfront area has everything you need for a convenient, inexpensive overnight. Standard guest rooms—each with two queens or a king bed—are done in earth tones with wicker headboards and burgundy-print curtains and bedspreads. A large swimming pool, free local calls, and a complimentary continental breakfast are unexpected bonuses. ⊠249 U.S. 98 W, 32320 ☎850/653–9131 ♺850/653–9136 ⊕www.bwapalachinn.com ♴42 rooms ⌂In-room: dial-up. In-hotel: pool, no elevator ⊟AE, D, MC, V ⏍CP.

$–$$ ▨**Rancho Inn.** This mom-and-pop operation—the owners live on-site—prides itself on its homeyness and personalized service. Rooms are spotless, if a little dated in their beige-and-brown color schemes (a few have undergone recent renovations), but 27-inch color TVs (complete with HBO and other premium channels), in-room coffeemakers, refrigerators, and microwaves make it a hard-to-beat option for those on a budget. The owners advertise "never-smoked-in rooms"—and impose fines of $100 for guests who light up in them. Trained pets can share accommodations for a fee. ⊠240 U.S. 98 W, 32320 ☎850/653–9435 ⊟850/653–9180 ⊕www.ranchoinn.com ⛱31 rooms, 1 suite ♿In-room: refrigerator. In-hotel: pool ☰AE, D, MC, V.

SHOPPING

The **Tin Shed** (⊠170 Water St. ☎850/653–3635) has an impressive collection of antiques and knickknacks, from antique brass luggage tags to 1940s nautical charts to sponge-diver wet suits to hand-glazed tiles and architectural elements salvaged from demolished buildings. Closed Sunday. The **Grady Market** (⊠76 Water St. ☎850/653–4099), on the first floor of the Consulate Inn, is a collection of more than a dozen boutiques, including several antiques dealers and the gallery of Richard Bickel, known for his stunning black-and-white photographs of local residents. **Avenue E** (⊠15 Ave. E ☎850/653–1411) is a stylish store specializing in reasonably priced antique and reproduction pieces, including furniture, lamps, artwork, and interior accessories.

ST. GEORGE ISLAND

9 *8 mi southeast of Apalachicola.*

Pristine St. George Island sits 5 mi out into the Gulf of Mexico just south of Apalachicola. Accessed via the Bryant Patton Bridge off U.S. 98, the island is bordered by both Apalachicola Bay and the gulf, offering vacationers the best of both. The rich bay is an angler's dream, whereas the snowy-white beaches and clear gulf waters satisfy even the most finicky beachgoer. Indulge in bicycling, hiking, canoeing, and snorkeling or find a secluded spot for reading, gathering shells, or bird-watching. Accommodations mostly take the form of privately owned, fully furnished condos and single-family homes, which allow for plenty of privacy.

Fodor'sChoice **St. George Island State Park** gives you Old Florida at its undisturbed
★ best. On the east end of the island are 9 mi of undeveloped beaches and dunes—the longest beachfront of any state park in Florida. Sandy coves, salt marshes, oak forests, and pines provide shelter for many species, including such birds as bald eagles and ospreys. Spotless restrooms and plentiful parking make a day at this park a joy. ☎850/927–2111 ⊕www.floridastateparks.org/stgeorgeisland ⛱$4 per vehicle, up to 8 people ⊙Daily 8–sunset.

WHERE TO STAY & EAT

$$–$$$ ✗**Blue Parrot.** You'll feel like you're sneaking in the back door as you climb the side stairs leading to an outdoor deck overlooking the gulf. Or if you can, grab a table indoors. During special-event weekends, the place is packed, and service may be a little slow. The food is hard to beat if you're not looking for anything fancy. Baskets of shrimp, oys-

ters, and crab cakes—fried or char-grilled and served with fries—are more than one person can handle. Daily specials are listed on the blackboard. ⊠ *68 W. Gorrie Dr.* ☏ *850/927–2987* ═ *AE, D, MC, V.*

$–$$$ ✕ **That Place on 98.** This place used to be as folksy and unassuming as its name suggests—that is, until the owner decided on an eye-popping turquoise-and-pink color scheme. Lucky for you, though, because now you *can't* miss it, washed up on the shores of Apalachicola Bay like a Benjamin Moore shipwreck. Nonetheless, it's one of the most authentic seafood shacks on the entire Gulf Coast, and it's *the* place to go if you're looking for fresh oysters. Get them any way you like them: on the half-shell, steamed, fried, Rockefellered, or 98'ed (baked with bacon, onions, garlic, and mozzarella). Fresh fish dishes, chicken, beef, and Greek salads round out the menu. ⊠ *500 Hwy. 98* ☏ *850/670– 9898* ☉ *Closed Sun.*

¢ ✕ **BJs.** In any other locale you might think twice before dining at a restaurant that advertises "kegs-to-go" on the menu, but this is an island, so establishments tend to wear several hats (some even sell live bait). Fear not. This simple beach shack serves solid, if predictable, sandwiches (grilled chicken, turkey club, BLT), salads (Caesar, tuna, fried chicken), and appetizers (Buffalo wings, cheese sticks, onion rings), but the pizza is definitely worth stopping for. Pies range from white pizza with chicken and bacon, to shrimp-and-mozzarella, to build-your-own personal pie (choose from 15 toppings). Beer and wine are available, and there are pool tables to pass the time while you wait for your order. ⊠ *105 W. Gulf Beach Dr.* ☏ *850/927–2805* ⚱ *Reservations not accepted* ═ *MC, V.*

¢–$$ ☖ **St. George Inn.** A little piece of Key West smack in the middle of the Panhandle, this cozy inn has tin roofs, hardwood floors, wraparound porches—even a widow's walk. Personal touches like private porches and in-room coffeemakers keep things homey. Both beach and bay are within view, and several restaurants and a convenience store are within walking distance. Two larger suites have full kitchens, and the pool is heated for year-round swimming. Specials are posted on the inn's Web site during off-season, when prices can drop by more than half. ⊠ *135 Franklin Blvd., 32320* ☏ *850/927–2903 or 800/824–0416* ⊕ *www. stgeorgeinn.com* ⤶ *15 rooms, 2 suites* ⚘ *In-room: kitchen (some), refrigerator. In-hotel: pool* ═ *MC, V.*

THE OUTDOORS

BOATING For a **boat tour** (☏ *850/697–3989*) of St. George Sound and Apalachicola Bay, call charter captain A.P. Whaley. He's famous in these parts for his uncanny ability to attract dolphins to the stern of his boat, the *Gat V.*

INLAND ACROSS THE PANHANDLE

Farther inland, where the northern reaches of the Panhandle butt up against the back porches of Alabama and Georgia, you'll find a part of Florida that goes a long way toward explaining why the state song is "Suwannee River" (and why its parenthetical title is "Old Folks at

Home"). Stephen Foster's musical genius notwithstanding, the inland Panhandle area is definitely more Dixie than Sunshine State, with few lodging options other than the chain motels that flank the Interstate 10 exits and a decidedly slower pace of life than you'll find on the tourist-heavy Gulf Coast. But the area's natural attractions—hills and farmlands, untouched small towns, pristine state parks—make for great day trips from the coast should the sky turn gray or the skin red. Explore underground caverns where eons-old rock formations create bizarre scenes, visit one of Florida's up-and-coming wineries, or poke around small-town America in DeFuniak Springs. Altogether, the inland area of the Panhandle is one of the state's most satisifyingly soothing regions.

> **PARK IT HERE**
>
> You can now buy a Florida State Park Annual Express Pass to alleviate individual park admissions. For $40 per person—or $80 for a family—you'll have entrance into any Florida state park (except Homosassa Springs and the Skyway Fishing Pier in St. Petersburg) for a full year. Even though you may not be here that long, it's worth considering if you plan to hit several state parks, which usually charge $4 per carload, and especially if you plan to return to Florida within the year. You can buy a pass at any state park, or buy one via their Web site at ⊕ *www.floridastateparks.org.*

DEFUNIAK SPRINGS

⑩ *28 mi east of Crestview.*

This scenic spot has a rather unusual claim to fame: at its center lies a nearly perfectly symmetrical spring-fed lake, one of only two such naturally circular bodies of water in the world (the other is in Switzerland). In 1848 the Knox Hill Academy was founded here, and for more than half a century it was the only institution of higher learning in northwestern Florida. In 1885 the town was chosen as the location for the New York Chautauqua educational society's winter assembly. The Chautauqua programs were discontinued in 1922, but DeFuniak Springs attempts to revive them, in spirit at least, by sponsoring a countywide Chautauqua Festival in April. Christmas is a particularly festive time, when the sprawling Victorian houses surrounding the lake are decorated to the nines. There's not a tremendous amount to see here, but if you have the good sense to travel Highway 90 to discover Old Florida, at least take the time to travel Circle Drive to see its beautiful Victorian homes.

By all accounts, the 16-by-24-foot **Walton-DeFuniak Public Library** is Florida's oldest library continuously operating in its original building. Opened in 1887, the original space has been added to over the years. The library now contains nearly 30,000 volumes, including some rare books, many older than the structure itself. The collection also includes antique musical instruments and impressive European armor. ⊠ *3 Circle Dr.* ☎ *850/892–3624* ☉ *Mon. and Wed.–Sat. 9–5, Tues. 9–8.*

The **Chautauqua Winery** opened in 1989, and its vintages have slowly won respect from oenophiles wary of what was once considered to be an oxymoron at best: "Florida wine." But the state has history on its side: according to historical records, the first wine produced by Europeans in the New World was made in Florida in 1562 by French Huguenots (obviously, this predated their little-known Siege of Napa Valley). Take a free tour to see how ancient art blends with modern technology; then retreat to the tasting room and gift shop. ⊠*I–10 and U.S. 331* ☎*850/892–5887* ⊕*www.chautauquawinery.com.*

Some of the finest examples of Victorian architecture in the state can be seen while you are walking or motoring around **Circle Drive,** the road that wraps around Circle Lake. The circumference is marked with beautiful Victorian specimens like the Walton-DeFuniak Public Library, the Dream Cottage, and the Pansy Cottage. Most of the other notable structures are private residences, but you can still admire them from the street.

WHERE TO STAY & EAT

$–$$ ✕⬚**Hotel De Funiak.** You can't miss this Depression-era two-story red-brick structure on a quiet corner a few blocks from peaceful Lake DeFuniak—just look for the two-tone 1937 Buick permanently moored out front. Each room has a different theme decor, from Oriental to Art Deco to French Country, and contains a combination of period antiques and reproductions, many of which can be purchased on the spot. In 2006, new owners turned the hotel restaurant into Bogey's (☎850/951–2233), where the dinner menu centers around fresh gulf seafood, yet also includes chicken and veal. It's an unusual find in a small town, and one of the nicer places to stay in this part of the Panhandle. ⊠*400 E. Nelson Ave., 32433* ☎*850/892–4383 or 877/333–8642* ⬚*850/892–5346* ⊕*www.hoteldefuniak.com* ⇆*7 rooms, 3 suites* ♿*In-hotel: restaurant, no-smoking rooms, Wi-Fi* ▭*AE, D, MC, V* ⦿*CP.*

FALLING WATERS STATE PARK

⓫ *35 mi east of DeFuniak Springs.*

This site of a Civil War–era whiskey distillery and, later, an exotic plant nursery—some imported species still thrive in the wild—is best known for also being the site of one of Florida's most notable geological features—the Falling Waters Sink. The 100-foot-deep cylindrical pit provides the background for a waterfall, and there's an observation deck for viewing this natural phenomenon. The water free-falls 67 feet to the bottom of the sink, but where it goes after that is a mystery. ⊠*Rte. 77A, Chipley* ☎*850/638–6130* ⊕*www.floridastateparks.org/falling-waters* ⬚*$4 per vehicle, up to 8 people* ⊙*Daily 8–sunset.*

FLORIDA CAVERNS STATE PARK

★ **⑫** *13 mi northeast of Falling Waters off I–10 on U.S. 231.*

Marianna is a cute and pristine community, and a short drive from the center of town you can see what's behind, or—more accurately—what's beneath it all. Take a ranger-led cave tour to see stalactites, stalagmites, soda straws, columns, rimstones, flowstones, and "waterfalls" of solid rock at these underground caverns where the temperature hovers at an oh-so-pleasant 68°F year-round. Some of the caverns are off-limits to the public or open for scientific study only with a permit, but you'll still see enough to fill a half day or more—and you'll be amazed that caverns of this magnitude exist anywhere in the Sunshine State. Between Memorial Day and Labor Day, rangers offer guided lantern tours on Friday and Saturday nights. There are also hiking trails, campsites, and areas for swimming, horseback riding, and canoeing on the Chipola River. ⊠*3345 Caverns Rd. (off Hwy. 90 on Rte. 166), Marianna* ☎*850/482–9598, 800/326–3521 for camping reservations* ⊕*www. floridastateparks.org/floridacaverns* ⊠*Park $4 per vehicle, up to 8 people; caverns $5* ⊙*Daily 8–sunset; cavern tours daily 9–4.*

TALLAHASSEE

⑬ *61 mi southeast of Florida Caverns.*

Tallahassee is Florida with a Southern accent, a preserved part of the past and the only Southern capital spared in the Civil War. For such an active city, the pace here seems unusually slow, perhaps because of the canopies of ancient oaks and spring bowers of azaleas that line many streets. Along with Florida State University, the perennial Seminoles football champions, and FAMU's fabled "Marching 100" band, the city also has more than a touch of the Old South. Tallahassee maintains a tranquillity quite different from the sun-and-surf hedonism of the major coastal towns. Vestiges of the city's colorful past are found throughout. For example, in the capitol complex, the turn-of-the-20th-century Old Capitol building is strikingly paired with the New Capitol skyscraper. Tallahassee's tree-lined streets are particularly memorable—among the best "canopy roads" (as they are called) are St. Augustine, Miccosukee, Meridian, Old Bainbridge, and Centerville, all dotted with country stores and antebellum plantation houses. This is easily one of Florida's most pleasing cities.

DOWNTOWN

A GOOD WALK

The downtown area is compact enough so that most sights can be seen on foot, although it's also served by a free, continuous shuttle trolley. Start at the capitol complex, which contains the **Old Capitol** ☞ and its counterpoint, the **New Capitol.** Across the street from the older structure is the restored **Union Bank Building,** and two blocks west of the new statehouse you'll find the **Museum of Florida History,** with exhibits

on many eras of the state's history and prehistory. If y
to get a feel for Old Tallahassee, walk the **Downtown Tall**
Trail as it wends its way from the capitol complex thr
the city's historic districts.

TIMING

You can't do justice to the capitol complex and downtown area in less than two hours. Allow four hours to walk the 8-mi stretch of the historic trail. If you visit between March and April, you'll find flowers in bloom and the Springtime Tallahassee festival in full swing.

WHAT TO SEE

Downtown Tallahassee Historic Trail. A route originally mapped and documented by an eager Eagle Scout as part of a merit-badge project, this trail has become a Tallahassee sightseeing staple. The starting point is the New Capitol, where you can pick up maps and descriptive brochures at the visitor center. You'll walk through the **Park Avenue and Calhoun Street historic districts,** which will take you back to Territorial days and the era of postwar reconstruction. The trail is dotted with landmark churches and cemeteries, along with outstanding examples of Greek Revival, Italianate, and prairie-style architecture. Some houses are open to the public. The **Brokaw-McDougall House** (⊠ *329 N. Meridian St.* ⊙ *Weekdays 9–3* ⊠ *Free*) is a superb example of the Greek Revival and Italianate styles. The **Meginnis-Monroe House** (⊠ *125 N. Gadsden St.* ⊠ *Free* ⊙ *Tues.–Sat. 10–5, Sun. 2–5*) served as a field hospital during the Civil War and is now an art gallery.

Museum of Florida History. If you thought Florida was founded by Walt Disney, stop here. Covering 12,000 years, the displays explain Florida's past by highlighting the unique geological and historical events that have shaped the state. Exhibits include a mammoth armadillo grazing in a savanna, the remains of a giant mastodon found in nearby Wakulla Springs, and a dugout canoe that once carried Native Americans into Florida's backwaters. Florida's history also includes settlements by the Spanish, British, French, and Confederates who fought for possession of the state. Gold bars, weapons, flags, maps, furniture, steamboats, and other artifacts underscore the fact that although most Americans date the nation to 1776, Florida's residents had been building settlements hundreds of years earlier. If this intrigues you, one floor up is the **Florida State Archives and Library,** where there's a treasure trove of government records, manuscripts, photographs, genealogical records, and other materials. ⊠ *500 S. Bronough St.* ☎ *850/245–6400, 850/245–6600 (library and archives)* ⊕ *www.flheritage.com* ⊠ *Free* ⊙ *Weekdays 9–4:30, Sat. 10–4:30, Sun. noon–4:30.*

★ **New Capitol.** In the 1960s, when there was talk of relocating the capital to a more central location like Orlando, Panhandle legislators got to work and approved the construction of a 22-story modern skyscraper that would anchor the capital right where it was. It's perfectly placed at the crest of a hill, sitting prominently behind the low-rise Old Capitol. The governor's office is on the first floor, and House and Senate chambers on the fifth floor provide viewer galleries for when the legislative sessions take place (March to May). Catch a panoramic view of Tallahassee and the surrounding countryside all the way into Georgia from the fabulous 22nd-floor observation deck. Also on this floor is the Florida Artists Hall of Fame, a tribute to Floridians such as Ray Charles, Burt Reynolds, Tennessee Williams, Ernest Hemingway, and Marjorie Kinnan Rawlings. To pick up information about the area, stop at the Florida Visitors Center, on the plaza level. There are guided tours from 9 to 3 on the hour (except at noon), booked in advance. ⊠ *400 S. Monroe St.* ☎ *850/488–6167* ⛝ *Free* ☉ *Visitor center weekdays 8–5.*

★ ⏵ **Old Capitol.** The centerpiece of the capitol complex, this 1842 structure has been added to and subtracted from several times. Having been restored, the jaunty red-and-white-stripe awnings and combination gas-electric lights make it look much as it did in 1902. Inside, it houses a must-see museum of Florida's political history as well as the old Supreme Court chambers and Senate Gallery—a very interesting peek into the past. ⊠ *S. Monroe St. at Apalachee Pkwy.* ☎ *850/487–1902* ⛝ *Free* ☉ *Self-guided or guided tours weekdays 9–4:30, Sat. 10–4:30, Sun. noon–4:30.*

Union Bank Building. Chartered in 1833, this is Florida's oldest bank building. Since it closed in 1843, it has played many roles, from ballet school to bakery. It has been restored to what is thought to be its original appearance and currently houses Florida A&M's Black Archives Extension, which depicts black history in Florida. Call ahead for hours, which are subject to change, and directions. ⊠ *Calhoun St. at Apalachee Pkwy.* ☎ *850/487–3803* ⛝ *Free* ☉ *Weekdays 9–4.*

AWAY FROM DOWNTOWN

WHAT TO SEE
Alfred Maclay Gardens State Park. Starting in December the grounds at this 1,200-acre estate are afire with azaleas, dogwood, Oriental magnolias, spring bulbs of tulips and irises, banana shrubs, honeysuckle, silverbell trees, pansies, and camellias. Allow half a day to wander past the reflecting pool into the tiny walled garden, and around the lakes and woodlands. The Maclay residence (open January through April only) is furnished as it was in the 1920s; picnic areas, gardens, and swimming and boating facilities are open to the public. ⊠ *3540 Thomasville Rd.* ☎ *850/487–4556* ⊕ *www.floridastateparks.org/maclaygardens* ⛝ *$4 per vehicle, up to 8 people; extra $4 per person for garden admission Jan.–Apr.; free rest of yr* ☉ *Daily 8–sunset.*

Lake Jackson Mounds Archaeological State Park. Here are waters to make bass anglers weep. For sightseers, Native American mounds and the ruins of an early-19th-century plantation built by Colonel Robert Butler, adjutant to General Andrew Jackson during the siege of New Orleans, are found along the shores of the lake. ⊠ *3600 Indian Mounds Rd.* ☎ *850/562–0042* ⛝ *$2* ☉ *Daily 8–sunset.*

San Luis Archaeological and Historic Site. This museum focuses on the archaeology of 17th-century Spanish mission and Apalachee Indian town sites. In its heyday, in 1675, the Apalachee village here had a population of at least 1,400, and it was near here that explorer Hernando de Soto celebrated the New World's first Christmas. Threatened by Creek Indians and British forces in 1704, the locals burned the village and fled. Take self-guided tours and watch scientists conducting digs daily (usually). The museum's popular Living History program is held on the third Saturday of the month, 10 AM–2 PM. ✉ *2020 W. Mission Rd.* ☎ *850/487-3711* ✉ *Free* ⊙ *Tues.–Sun. 10–4.*

Tallahassee Museum. About 20 minutes from downtown, this bucolic park showcases a peaceful and intriguing look at Old Florida. Although called a museum, this is really a working 1880s pioneer farm that offers daily hands-on activities for children, such as soap making and blacksmithing. A boardwalk meanders through the 52 acres of natural habitat that make up the zoo, which has such varied animals as panthers, bobcats, white-tailed deer, bald eagles, red wolves, hawks, owls, otters, and black bears—many of which were brought here injured or orphaned. Also on-site are nature trails, a one-room schoolhouse dating from 1897, and an 1840s Southern plantation manor, where you can usually find someone cooking on the weekends. It's peaceful, pleasing, and educational. ✉ *3945 Museum Dr.* ☎ *850/576-1636* ⊕ *www.tallahasseemuseum.org* ✉ *$8* ⊙ *Mon.–Sat. 9–5, Sun. 12:30–5.*

Fodor'sChoice
★
⑭

Known for having one of the deepest springs in the world, the very picturesque and highly recommended **Wakulla Springs State Park** remains relatively untouched, retaining the wild and exotic look it had in the 1930s, when the films *Tarzan* and *Creature from the Black Lagoon* were shot here. Take a glass-bottom boat deep into the lush, jungle-lined waterways to catch glimpses of alligators, snakes, nesting limpkins, and other waterfowl. It costs only $50 to rent a pontoon boat and go it alone. It may be worth it since an underground river flows into a pool so clear you can see the bottom more than 100 feet below. The park is 15 mi south of Tallahassee on Route 61. If you can't pull yourself away from this idyllic spot, spend the night in the 1930s Spanish-Mediterranean lodge (see below). ✉ *550 Wakulla Park Dr., Wakulla Springs* ☎ *850/922-3632* ✉ *$4 per vehicle, up to 8 people; boat tour $6* ⊙ *Daily 8–sunset, boat tours hourly 9:30–4:30.*

WHERE TO STAY & EAT

$$–$$$ ✕**Chez Pierre.** You'll feel as if you've entered a great-aunt's old plantation home in this restored 1920s house set back from the road in historic Lafayette Park. Since 1976, its warm, cozy rooms, gleaming hardwood floors, and large French doors separating dining areas have created an intimate place to go for authentic French cuisine. Try the tournedos of beef or one of the special lamb dishes. The Sunday brunch is one of the most popular around. ✉ *1215 Thomasville Rd.* ☎ *850/222-0936* ▭ *AE, D, MC, V.*

$-$$$ ✗**Andrew's 228.** Part of a smart complex in the heart of the political district, this two-story "urban Tuscan villa" (contradiction noted) is the latest of owner Andy Reiss's restaurant incarnations to occupy the same space (the last was Andrew's Second Act). The high-price entrées were thrown out with the old decor; instead choose from daily pastas, grilled steak or chicken dinner sandwiches, or more substantive classics like Tuscan chicken and filet mignon. It's a noisy, vivacious spot—think exposed brick with arched ceilings, dim lighting, banquettes—on one of downtown's most high-profile corners. As you might expect, the all-you-can-eat soup-and-salad lunch special is wildly popular in this college town—as is the bar menu of some 600 martinis. ⊠ *228 S. Adams St.* ☎ *850/222–3444* ▤ *AE, D, MC, V.*

¢-$ ✗**Rice-Bowl Oriental.** Bamboo woodwork and thatched-roof booths lend an air of authenticity to this Asian-hybrid spot tucked away in a Tallahassee strip mall. Chinese, Japanese, Thai, and Vietnamese favorites are all represented here, from General Tso's chicken to fresh sushi to green curry and rice noodle dishes. The all-you-can-eat lunch buffet (Sunday to Friday, $6.95), complete with entrées, salads, soups, and fresh sushi, just might be one of the best deals in town. ⊠ *3813 N. Monroe St.* ☎ *850/514–3632* ▤ *AE, D, DC, MC, V.*

¢   ✗**Decent Pizza.** The name is terribly modest—the pizza here is much more than decent, and the prices are more than reasonable. A couple of Florida State University grads opened this simple pizzeria, which became an instant hit with those on an undergraduate budget: slices and salads start at $3.25 each, and at a buck each, half-pint draft beers are cheaper than sodas. Choose from more than 30 toppings for regular red-sauce, pesto, or white pies. ⊠ *1026 N. Monroe St.* ☎ *850/222–6400* ⌲ *Reservations not accepted* ▤ *MC, V.*

¢   ✗**Hopkins' Eatery.** Locals in the know flock here for superb salads, homemade soups, and sandwiches—expect a short wait at lunchtime—via simple counter service. Kids will like the traditional peanut butter–and–jelly sandwich (with bananas and sprouts, if they dare); adults might opt for a chunky chicken melt, smothered beef, or garden vegetarian sub. The spearmint iced tea is a must-have, as is a slice of freshly baked chocolate cake. A second location on North Monroe Street offers the same menu. ⊠ *1415 Market St.* ☎ *850/668–0311* ⊠ *1840 N. Monroe St.* ☎ *850/386–1809* ▤ *AE, D, DC, MC, V* ☉ *Closed Sun. No dinner Sat.*

★ **$$$-$$$$**   ⌂ **Governors Inn.** Only a block from the capitol, this plushly restored historic warehouse is abuzz during the week with politicians, press, and lobbyists. It's a perfect location for business travelers and, on weekends, for tourists who want to visit downtown sites. Rooms are a rich blend of mahogany, brass, and classic prints. ⊠ *209 S. Adams St., 32301* ☎ *850/681–6855 or 800/342–7717* 🖷 *850/222–3105* ⊕ *www.thegovinn.com* ⌐ *29 rooms, 12 suites* ⌂ *In-hotel: laundry service, parking (fee), no elevator* ▤ *AE, D, DC, MC, V* ⏃⌐*CP.*

$-$$$$ ⌂ **DoubleTree Hotel Tallahassee.** This hotel a mere two blocks from the capitol hosts heavy hitters from the worlds of politics and media. Since it's also an easy walk from the FSU campus, it welcomes plenty of Seminoles fans during football season. Rooms, which overlook either a city park or the capitol, are basic but clean, with beige wallpaper and occasional chairs and green-and-yellow-stripe bedspreads. Most have two full-size beds, which can be pushed together to create an ersatz king. ⊠*101 S. Adams St., 32301* ☎*850/224–5000* 📠*850/513–9516* 🛏*243 rooms* ⚒*In-room: Wi-Fi. In-hotel: restaurant, bar, pool, gym* ▤*AE, D, DC, MC, V.*

¢–$ 🏨 **Super 8.** The quiet courtyard with its own pool and the darkly welcoming cantina (where a complimentary continental breakfast is served) convey the look of Old Spain. Rooms are furnished in heavy Mediterranean style—and come with two double beds or one king. Time it right: rates double on FSU football home-game weekends. ⊠*2801 N. Monroe St., 32303* ☎*850/386–8286* 📠*850/422–1074* ⊕*www.super8.com* 🛏*108 rooms, 23 suites* ⚒ *In-room: Wi-Fi. In-hotel: pool.* ▤*AE, D, MC, V* ⏐◎⏐*CP.*

NIGHTLIFE & THE ARTS

THE ARTS If you're too shy to crash a frat party, here's a more civilized evening out: **Florida State University** (☎*850/644–4774 School of Music, 850/644–6500 School of Theatre* ⊕*www.music.fsu.edu*) plays host to more than 400 concerts and recitals annually in year-round performances by its School of Music, and many productions by its School of Theatre. The **Monticello Opera House** (⊠*185 W. Washington [U.S. 90 E], Monticello* ☎*850/997–4242*) presents concerts and plays in a restored gaslight-era opera house. The **Tallahassee Little Theatre** (⊠*1861 Thomasville Rd.* ☎*850/224–8474* ⊕*www.tallahasseelittletheatre.org*) has a five-production season that runs from September through May. The season of the **Tallahassee Symphony Orchestra** (☎*850/224–0461* ⊕*www.tsolive.org*) usually runs from October through April; performances are usually held at Florida State University's Ruby Diamond Auditorium.

NIGHTLIFE There are endless options for after-dark entertainment for Tallahassee's government and university populations. When you're in town, be sure to check the college newspapers for the latest developments. **Waterworks** (⊠*1133 Thomasville Rd.* ☎*850/224–1887*), with its retro-chic tiki-bar fittings, attracts jazz fans and hipsters of all ages for cocktails and DJ-spun dance music. On Friday night there's a banjo player, a retro-cool treat. **Floyd's Music Store** (⊠*666-1 W. Tennessee St.* ☎*850/222–3506*) hosts some of the hottest local and touring acts around. Other performers, from dueling pianos to Dave Matthews cover bands to assorted DJs, round out the schedule. Don't let the name fool you: the **Late Night Library** (⊠*809 Gay St.* ☎*850/224–2429*) is the quintessential college-town party bar with dancing, drinking, cavorting—you get the picture.

SIDE TRIPS

SOUTH TO THE GULF

South of the capital and east of the Ochlockanee River are several fascinating natural and historic sites. These sites are near one another, so string several together on an excursion from Tallahassee.

⑮ **Natural Bridge Battlefield State Park** marks the spot where in 1865 Confederate soldiers stood firm against a Yankee advance on St. Marks. The Rebs held, saving Tallahassee—the only Southern capital east of the Mississippi that never fell to the Union. Ten miles southeast of Tallahassee, the site is a good place for a hike and a picnic. Visit the first week in March (call for schedule) to see a reenactment of the battle. ⊠ *Natural Bridge Rd., off Rte. 363, Woodville* ☎ *850/922–6007* 🖼 *Free* ☉ *Daily 8–sunset.*

> **BUCKS FIZZ**
>
> Roughly 10 mi west of Tallahassee on Highway 90, the tiny slow-as-molasses town of Quincy may look rough on the surface, but there are reportedly more millionaires here per capita than any area in the nation. Why? Because a little more than 100 years ago, a local banker suggested that his customers invest in an unknown soft drink a friend had created. Smart idea—and smart investors. The drink was Coca-Cola.

⑯ As its name suggests, **St. Marks National Wildlife Refuge and Lighthouse** is of both natural and historical interest. Natural salt marshes, tidal flats, and freshwater pools that nourished Paleo Indians 10,000 years ago and Apalachee Indians in the 1500s set the stage for the once-powerful Fort San Marcos de Apalache that was built nearby in 1639. Stones salvaged from the fort were used in the lighthouse, which is still in operation. In winter the 100,000-acre-plus refuge on the shores of Apalachee Bay is the resting place for thousands of migratory birds of more than 300 species, but the alligators seem to like it year-round (keep your camera ready and you're bound to get a photo op). The visitor center has information on more than 75 mi of marked trails, some of which wend through landscapes with foliage more reminiscent of North Carolina than Florida. Hardwood swamps and pine woodlands also provide habitat for wood ducks, black bears, otter, raccoons, deer, armadillo, coyotes, feral hogs, fox squirrels, gopher tortoises, and woodpeckers. Twenty-five miles south of Tallahassee, the refuge can be reached via Route 363. ⊠ *1255 Lighthouse Rd., St. Marks* ☎ *850/925–6121* ⊕ *saintmarks.fws.gov* 🖼 *$5 per vehicle* ☉ *Refuge daily sunrise–sunset; visitor center weekdays 8–4, weekends 10–5.*

Spreading north of Apalachicola and west of Tallahassee and U.S. 319 is the **Apalachicola National Forest,** with campsites, hiking trails, picnic areas, and plentiful lakes for old-fashioned swimmin'. Honor-system fees range from $3 admission to $8 camping. ☎ *850/643–2282.*

CANOEING
TNT Hideaway (⊠ *U.S. 98 at the Wakulla River, St. Marks* ☎ *850/925–6412*), 18 mi south of Tallahassee, arranges canoe trips on the spring-fed Wakulla River. An average trek takes about three hours, and a four-hour canoe rental for two costs $25.

WHERE TO STAY & EAT
¢–$ ✕🖼 **Wakulla Springs State Park and Lodge.** Built in 1937, this is a beautifully intriguing and well-preserved piece of Florida history on the grounds of Wakulla Springs State Park. There's a huge fireplace in the

lobby; broad, painted, Moorish-style beams across the ceiling; and cozy, if spartan, rooms. It's at the head of Florida's largest spring, so you can dive right in or take a $6 narrated nature cruise downriver. The dining room serves three meals a day in a sunny, simple setting that seems little changed from the 1930s. Schedule lunch here to sample the famous bean soup, home-baked muffins, and a slab of pie. In the soda shop, order a "ginger yip" (ice cream, whipped cream, and ginger ale) or buy a wind-up toy alligator as a memento of your stay. ⊠*550 Wakulla Park Dr., Wakulla Springs 32327* ☎*850/224–5950* ⎙*850/561–7251* ⟿*27 rooms* ⅛*In-hotel: restaurant, beachfront* ▤*AE, D, MC, V.*

THE PANHANDLE ESSENTIALS

To research prices, get advice from other travelers, and book travel arrangements, visit www.fodors.com.

TRANSPORTATION

BY AIR

CARRIERS

Pensacola Regional Airport (⊕*www.flypensacola.com*) is served by Air Tran, American Eagle, Continental, Delta, Northwest, and US Airways.

Okaloosa County Regional Airport (⊕*www.okaloosacountyairports. com*) is served by American Eagle, Delta Connection, Continental Express, and Northwest.

Panama City–Bay County International Airport (⊕*www.pcairport. com*) is served by Delta Connection, Northwest Airlink, and Chautauqua Airlines.

Tallahassee Regional Airport (⊕*www.talgov.com/airport*) is served by Continental, Delta, Northwest, and US Airways Express.

Contacts **AirTran** (☎*800/247-8726*). **American/American Eagle** (☎*800/433-7300*). **Continental** (☎*800/523-3273*). **Delta** (☎*800/221-1212*). **Northwest** (☎*800/225-2525*). **Northwest Airlink** (☎*800/225-2525*). **US Airways/US Airways Express** (☎*800/428-4322*).

AIRPORTS & TRANSFERS

A trip from Pensacola Regional Airport via Yellow Cab costs about $14 to downtown and $24 to Pensacola Beach. A ride from the Okaloosa County Regional Airport via Checker Cab costs $18 to Fort Walton Beach and $24 to Destin. Bluewater Car Service charges $15–$17 to Fort Walton Beach and $28 to Destin. Yellow Cab charges about $15–$27 from Panama City–Bay County International Airport to the beach area, depending on the location of your hotel. DeLuxe Coach Limo Service provides van service to downtown Panama City and to Panama City Beach for $1.25 per mile. Yellow Cab travels from Tallahassee Regional Airport to downtown for $13–$16.

Airport Contacts **Okaloosa County Regional Airport** (☎*850/651-7160* ⊕ *www.okaloosacountyairports.com*). **Panama City–Bay County International**

Airport (☎ *850/763-6751* ⊕ *www.pcairport.com*). **Pensacola Regional Airport** (☎ *850/436-5005* ⊕ *www.flypensacola.com*). **Tallahassee Regional Airport** (☎ *850/891-7800* ⊕ *talgov.com/airport*).

Airport Transportation Contacts Okaloosa County Airport: Gulf Coast Shuttle Service (☎ *850/642-1042*). **Panama City Beach: Affordable Limousine Service** (☎ *850/233-0029*). **Pensacola: All Airports Taxi and Shuttle** (☎ *850/865-5619 or 800/643-4711*).

Tallahassee: Capital Transportation There are two choices for cabs: **City Taxi** (☎ *850/562-4222*) or **Yellow Cab** (☎ *850/575-1022*).

BY BUS

Greyhound has stations in Crestview, DeFuniak Springs, Fort Walton Beach, Panama City, Pensacola, and Tallahassee. The Baytown Trolley serves Bay County, including downtown Panama City and the beaches ($1). In Pensacola, Escambia County Area Transit (ECAT) provides regular citywide bus service ($1), downtown trolley routes, tours through the historic district (25¢), and from Memorial Day to Labor Day free trolley service on Friday, Saturday, and Sunday.

Contacts Baytown Trolley (☎ *850/769-0557*). **Escambia County Area Transit** (☎ *850/595-3228*). **Greyhound Lines** (☎ *800/231-2222, 850/682-6922 in Crestview, 850/892-5566 in DeFuniak Springs, 850/243-1940 in Fort Walton Beach, 850/785-6111 in Panama City, 850/476-4800 in Pensacola, 850/222-4240 in Tallahassee*).

BY CAR

The main east–west arteries across the top of the state are Interstate 10 and U.S. 90. Pensacola is about an hour's drive east of Mobile. Tallahassee is 3½ hours west of Jacksonville. It takes about four hours to drive from Pensacola to Tallahassee. Driving along Interstate 10 can be monotonous, but U.S. 90 piques your interest by routing you along the main streets of several county seats. U.S. 98 snakes eastward along the coast, splitting into 98 and 98A at Inlet Beach before rejoining at Panama City and continuing on to Port St. Joe and Apalachicola. The view of the gulf from U.S. 98 can be breathtaking, especially at sunset, but ongoing construction projects make it slow going most of the time. If you need to get from one end of the Panhandle to the other in a timely manner, you're better off driving inland to Interstate 10, where the speed limit runs as high as 70 mph in places. Even with the extra time it takes to drive inland, you'll wind up getting where you need to go much more quickly. Route 399 between Pensacola Beach and Navarre Beach was completely destroyed by Hurricane Ivan and, as of this writing, was not open. Major north–south highways that weave through the Panhandle are (from east to west) U.S. 231, U.S. 331, Route 85, and U.S. 29. From U.S. 331, which runs over a causeway at the east end of Choctawhatchee Bay between Route 20 and U.S. 98, the panorama of barge traffic and cabin cruisers on the twinkling waters of the Intracoastal Waterway will get your attention.

1

CAR RENTAL
Contacts **Alamo** (☎ *800/462–5266*). **Avis** (☎ *800/331–1212*). **Budget** (☎ *800/527–7000*). **Hertz** (☎ *800/654–3131*). **National** (☎ *800/227–7368*).

BY TRAIN
Amtrak connects the Panhandle to the east and west coasts via the *Sunset Limited*, with stations in Pensacola, Crestview, and Tallahassee.

Contact **Amtrak** (☎ *800/872–7245*).

CONTACTS & RESOURCES

EMERGENCIES
Ambulance or Police **Emergencies** (☎ *911*).

24-Hour Medical Care Destin Urgent Care and Diagnostic Center (✉ *996 Airport Rd., Destin* ☎ *850/837–9194*). **Fort Walton Beach Medical Center** (✉ *1000 Mar-Walt Dr., Fort Walton Beach* ☎ *850/862–1111*). **Gulf Coast Medical Center** (✉ *449 W. 23rd St., Panama City* ☎ *850/769–8341*). **Tallahassee Memorial Hospital** (✉ *Magnolia Dr. and Miccosukee Rd., Tallahassee* ☎ *850/431–1155*). **West Florida Hospital** (✉ *8383 N. Davis Hwy., Pensacola* ☎ *850/494–4000*).

VISITOR INFORMATION
All local visitor information centers are open weekdays, and many are open Saturday—or all weekend—as well. In winter these hours might be curtailed, so call or check the Web sites listed below for schedules. The Panhandle is blessed with many beautiful areas that are being preserved as parks by the State of Florida. Check out the Florida Department of Environmental Protection's excellent parks Web site for hours and admission fees, as well as photos and brief histories of the parks.

Contacts Apalachicola Bay Chamber of Commerce (✉ *122 Commerce St., Apalachicola 32320* ☎ *850/653–9419* ⊕ *www.apalachicolabay.org*). **Beaches of South Walton Visitor Information Center** (✉ *U.S. 331 and U.S. 98, Santa Rosa Beach 32459* ☎ *850/267–1216 or 800/822–6877* ⊕ *www.beachesofsouthwalton. com*). **Destin Chamber of Commerce** (✉ *4484 Legendary Dr., Destin 32541* ☎ *850/837–6241* ⊕ *www.destinchamber.com*). **Emerald Coast Convention & Visitors Bureau** (✉ *1540 Miracle Strip Pkwy. SE, Fort Walton Beach 32548* ☎ *850/651–7131 or 800/322–3319* ⊕ *www.destin-fwb.com*). **Florida Department of Environmental Protection–Parks Division** (☎ *850/245–2157 Information Line* ⊕ *www.dep.state.fl.us/parks*). **Panama City Beach Convention & Visitors Bureau** (✉ *17001 Panama City Beach Pkwy., Panama City Beach 32413* ☎ *850/233–5070 or 800/722–3224* ⊕ *www.thebeachloversbeach.com*). **Pensacola Visitor Information Center** (✉ *1401 E. Gregory St., Pensacola 32502* ☎ *850/434–1234 or 800/874–1234* ⊕ *www.visitpensacola.com*). **Tallahassee Area Convention and Visitors Bureau** (✉ *106 E. Jefferson St., Tallahassee 32301* ☎ *850/413–9200 or 800/628–2866* ⊕ *www.seetallahassee.com*). **Walton County Chamber of Commerce** (✉ *95 Circle Dr., DeFuniak Springs 32433* ☎ *850/892–3191* ⊕ *www. waltoncountychamber.com*).

Northeast Florida

WORD OF MOUTH

"[In the St. Augustine historic district] there are several things you can do within easy walking distance. Shopping on St. George Street and the side streets is a must. There is a trolley tour of town that allows on/off privileges. You can also take a carriage ride tour. Flagler College, in the old Ponce de León Hotel, offers hour-long tours of its impressive buildings. For something really cool that not many people see, head through the breezeways of the Lightner Museum (the Alcazar Hotel, back in the day) and toward the right out back to the antique mall. It's actually housed in the hotel's former indoor swimming pool! Very impressive."

—xrae

2

Updated
by Kerry
Speckman

SOME OF THE OLDEST SETTLE-MENTS in the state—indeed in all of the United States—are in northeastern Florida, although the region didn't get much attention until the Union army came through during the Civil War. The soldiers' rapturous accounts of the mild climate, pristine beaches, and lush vegetation captured the imagination of folks up north. First came the specu-

TOP 5
■ Kennedy Space Center
■ Ocala National Forest
■ Daytona Beach
■ Historic St. Augustine
■ Jacksonville Zoo

lators and the curiosity seekers. Then the advent of the railroads brought more permanent settlers and the first wave of winter vacationers. Finally, the automobile transported the full rush of snowbirds, seasonal residents escaping from harsh northern winters. They still come to sop up sun on the beach, to tee up year-round, to bass-fish and bird-watch in forests and parks, and to party in the clubs and bars of Daytona, a popular spring-break destination. The region is remarkably diverse. Tortuous, towering live oaks; plantations; and antebellum-style architecture recollect the Old South. The mossy marshes of Silver Springs and the St. Johns River look as untouched and junglelike today as they did generations ago. Horse farms around Ocala resemble Kentucky's bluegrass country or the hunt clubs of Virginia. St. Augustine is a showcase of early U.S. history, and Jacksonville is a young but sophisticated metropolis. Yet these are all but light diversions from northeastern Florida's primary draw—absolutely sensational beaches. Hugging the coast are long, slender barrier islands whose entire eastern sides make up a broad band of spectacular sand. Except in the most populated areas, development has been modest, and beaches are lined with funky, appealing little towns.

EXPLORING NORTHEAST FLORIDA

The region defies any single description. Much of its tourist territory lies along the Atlantic coast, both on the mainland and on the barrier islands just offshore. A1A (mostly called Atlantic Avenue south of St. Augustine) is the main road on all the barrier islands, and it's here that you find the best beaches. Both Jacksonville, the region's only real highrise city, and the relatively remote Amelia Island, just south of the Georgia border, are in the far northeast. St. Augustine, about a 45-minute drive south of Jacksonville on Interstate 95, is the historic capital of this part of Florida. Farther south along the coast, the diversity continues among neighbors like Daytona Beach, where annual events are geared toward spring breakers, auto racers, and bikers; New Smyrna Beach, which offers quiet appeal; and Cocoa Beach, the ultimate Boogie-board beach town. Inland are charming small towns, the sprawling Ocala National Forest, and Gainesville, home of the University of Florida.

GREAT ITINERARIES

Numbers in the text correspond to numbers in the margin and on the Northeast Florida and St. Augustine maps.

3 DAYS

Spend your first night in 🏨 **Jacksonville ❶–❿** 🍴, using it as a base to explore the **Museum of Contemporary Art Jacksonville ❼** or the **Cummer Museum of Art and Gardens ❹**, as well as Fort Clinch State Park on **Amelia Island ❽**, which has one of the best-preserved brick forts in the United States. Take Interstate 95 south to **St. Augustine ❿–❷** and see the restored **Colonial Spanish Quarter ❼** and the **Castillo de San Marcos National Monument ❽** before continuing down the coast. Enjoy Canaveral National Seashore—accessible from either 🏨 **New Smyrna Beach ❸** or 🏨 **Cocoa Beach ❸**—and don't miss the Kennedy Space Center Visitor Complex in **Titusville ❸**.

5 DAYS

Before leaving **Jacksonville ❶–❿** 🍴 try to visit the three largest museums, the **Museum of Contemporary Art Jacksonville ❼**, the **Cummer Museum of Art and Gardens ❹**, and the **Museum of Science and History ❺**. Then focus your sightseeing on **Amelia Island ❽**, including its historic district and Fort Clinch State Park. Going south on Interstate 95, stop in **St. Augustine ❿–❷**. Follow the Old City Walking Tour suggested by the **Visitor Information and Preview Center ❿** and stroll through the restored **Colonial Spanish Quarter ❼**. Consider taking the slightly longer but more scenic Route A1A to **Daytona Beach ❸**; visit the Museum of Arts and Sciences and

the famous beaches. For your last night, stay in 🏨 **New Smyrna Beach ❸** or 🏨 **Cocoa Beach ❸**, both within reach of Canaveral National Seashore and Kennedy Space Center.

10 DAYS

As in the previous two itineraries, start in 🏨 **Jacksonville ❶–❿** 🍴 and visit the attractions mentioned above; by staying three nights, however, you'll have time to make the drive north to Kingsley Plantation, Florida's oldest remaining plantation, on Fort George Island, and hike or picnic in Fort Clinch State Park on **Amelia Island ❽**. Next, head to 🏨 **St. Augustine ❿–❷**. Three days here enable you to conduct a more leisurely exploration of the extensive historic district and to take in the **Lightner Museum ❷**, in what was originally one of Henry Flagler's fancy hotels. Another three-day stay, this time based at 🏨 **Daytona Beach ❸**, 🏨 **New Smyrna Beach ❸**, or 🏨 **Cocoa Beach ❸**, allows you to cover Daytona's Museum of Arts and Sciences, drive along the shoreline, spend some time at the beach, and see Canaveral National Seashore, as well as the Kennedy Space Center Visitor Complex near **Titusville ❸**. Then head inland for a day in **Ocala National Forest ❸**, a beautiful wilderness area.

ABOUT THE RESTAURANTS

The ocean, St. Johns River, and numerous lakes and smaller rivers are teeming with fish, and so, naturally, seafood dominates local menus. In coastal towns, catches are often from the restaurant's own fleet. Shrimp, snapper, swordfish, and grouper are especially prevalent.

ABOUT THE HOTELS

For the busy seasons—during summer in and around Jacksonville, and during summer holiday weekends all over Florida—always reserve well ahead for the top properties. Jacksonville's beach hotels fill up quickly for PGA's The Players Championship in mid-May. Daytona Beach presents similar lodging dilemmas during the Daytona 500 (mid-February), Bike Week (late February–early March), spring break (March), and the Pepsi 400 (early July). St. Augustine stays busy all year because of its historic character. Fall is the slowest season: rates are low and availability is high, but it is also the prime time for hurricanes.

WHAT IT COSTS					
	¢	$	$$	$$$	$$$$
RESTAURANTS	under $10	$10–$15	$15–$20	$20–$30	over $30
HOTELS	under $80	$80–$100	$100–$140	$140–$220	over $220

Restaurant prices are per person for a main course at dinner. Hotel prices are for a standard double room, excluding 6% sales tax (more in some counties) and 1%–4% tourist tax.

TIMING

Fair weather is one of the many factors drawing residents to the area. The temperature dips to the low 50s in Jacksonville and low 60s in Cocoa Beach in winter and hovers around 80 in summer throughout the area. The ocean warms up by March, when college kids on spring break often pack the beaches—but this is also the best month to see the azalea gardens in bloom. Midsummer is hot, yet breezy, as long as you stick to the beaches; inland, the heat and humidity can be stifling.

JACKSONVILLE

❶–❿ *399 mi north of Miami.*

One of Florida's oldest cities and at 730 square mi the largest city in the continental United States, Jacksonville makes for an underrated vacation spot. It offers appealing downtown riverside areas, handsome residential neighborhoods, the region's only skyscrapers, a thriving arts scene, and, for football fans, the NFL Jaguars and the NCAA Gator Bowl. Remnants of the Old South flavor the city, especially in the Riverside/Avondale historic district, where moss-draped oak trees frame prairie-style bungalows and Tudor Revival mansions, and palm trees, Spanish bayonet, and azaleas populate the landscape.

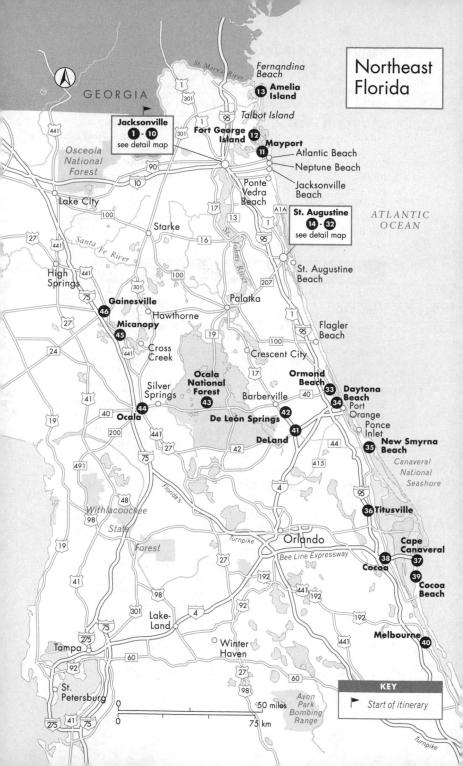

Northeast Florida

GEORGIA

St. Mary's River

Fernandina Beach

13 **Amelia Island**

Talbot Island

Jacksonville
1 - **10**
see detail map

Fort George Island

12

Mayport

11

Atlantic Beach

Neptune Beach

Jacksonville Beach

Osceola National Forest

Lake City

Ponte Vedra Beach

St. Augustine
14 - **32**
see detail map

ATLANTIC OCEAN

Starke

Santa Fe River

High Springs

St. Johns River

St. Augustine Beach

46 **Gainesville**

45 **Micanopy**

Hawthorne

Palatka

Flagler Beach

Cross Creek

Crescent City

Ocala National Forest

43

Silver Springs

Barberville

Ormond Beach

33

Daytona Beach

34

Port Orange

44 **Ocala**

42 **De León Springs**

Ponce Inlet

41

DeLand

35 **New Smyrna Beach**

Canaveral National Seashore

Withlacoochee State Forest

Florida's

36 **Titusville**

Turnpike

Orlando

Bee Line Expressway

Cape Canaveral

38 **Cocoa**

37

39 **Cocoa Beach**

Lake-Land

Winter Haven

Melbourne **40**

Tampa

St. Petersburg

Avon Park Bombing Range

50 miles

75 km

KEY

▶ *Start of itinerary*

Turnpike

EXPLORING JACKSONVILLE

Because Jacksonville was settled along both sides of the twisting St. Johns River, a number of attractions are on or near a riverbank. Both sides of the river, which is spanned by myriad bridges, have downtown areas and waterfront complexes of shops, restaurants, parks, and museums. Some attractions can be reached by water taxi or Skyway Express monorail system—scenic alternatives to driving back and forth across the bridges—but a car is generally necessary.

Numbers in the text correspond to numbers in the margin and on the Jacksonville map.

A GOOD TOUR

Start your morning at the riverfront campus of Jacksonville University, site of the **Alexander Brest Museum** ❶ ⏴. After browsing the collections, head south on University Boulevard and east on Arlington Expressway to **Kona Skatepark** ❷, where you can practice your sausage grinds or watch X-treme athletes riding the concrete wave. Even if you've just worked up a virtual sweat, you'll want to cool off, so go east on Atlantic Boulevard, over the Hart Bridge, to **Kids Kampus** ❸, a 10-acre recreational facility with a splash park. Next, head west on Gator Bowl Boulevard–Bay Street and follow the signs for Riverside to get to another riverfront landmark, the **Cummer Museum of Art and Gardens** ❹. After touring the museum and its grounds, head back on Riverside Avenue toward the Acosta Bridge and take the first exit, San Marco Boulevard. Two blocks north is the **Museum of Science and History** ❺. Walk a block south to the Automated Skyway Express station and take a monorail across the river to the **Jacksonville Landing** ❻, where you can shop and grab some lunch. Afterward, walk four blocks north to the **Museum of Contemporary Art Jacksonville** ❼. Head back to the Landing to recross the river, but for the return trip, catch a water taxi. On the road again, go back over the Acosta Bridge and stay on Broad Street to First Street, where you'll find the **Karpeles Manuscript Library Museum** ❽. Next, proceed west on State Street to Interstate 95 north, then take the Heckscher Drive exit east to Zoo Road for the **Jacksonville Zoo** ❾. Finally, head back to Interstate 95 north and exit east at Dunn Avenue, which becomes Busch Road, and visit the **Anheuser-Busch Jacksonville Brewery** ❿.

TIMING

Jacksonville's sprawl dictates a generous amount of time for reaching and touring these sights. Allow at least two days, six hours a day (including driving time), budgeting at least an hour for each attraction, more for the zoo and the contemporary art museum.

WHAT TO SEE

❶ **Alexander Brest Museum.** Boehm and Royal Copenhagen porcelain and Steuben glass are among the collections at this Jacksonville University museum. Also on display are cloisonné pieces, pre-Columbian artifacts, and one of the finest collections of ivory anywhere from the early 17th to the late 19th century. ⊠ *Jacksonville University, Phillips Fine Arts*

Alexander
Brest Museum ...**1**

Anheuser-Busch
Jacksonville
Brewery **10**

Cummer
Museum
of Art and
Gardens **4**

Jacksonville
Landing **6**

Jacksonville
Zoo **9**

Karpeles
Manuscript
Library
Museum **8**

Kids Kampus **3**

Kona
Skatepark **2**

Museum of
Contemporary Art
Jacksonville **7**

Museum of
Science and
History **5**

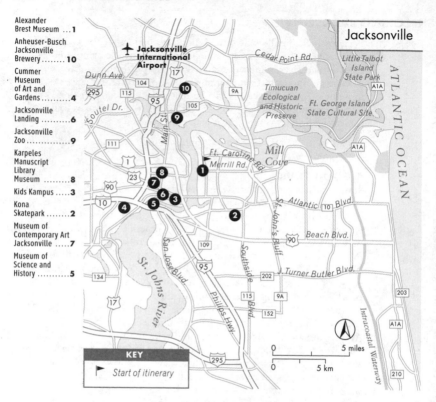

Bldg., 2800 University Blvd. N ☎904/256–7371 ⊕art.ju.edu/art.html
☞Free ⊙ Weekdays 9–4:30; Sat. noon–5.

❿ Anheuser-Busch Jacksonville Brewery. Beer lovers will appreciate this
behind-the-scenes look at how barley malt, rice, hops, and water form
the "King of Beers." Guided tours take guests through the entire brewing and bottling process. Or you can hightail it through the self-guided
tour and head straight to the free beer tastings (for those guests 21
years and older, that is). ⊠111 Busch Dr. ☎904/696–8373 ⊕www.
budweisertours.com ☞Free ⊙ Mon.–Sat. 10–4; guided tours Mon.–
Sat. 10–3 on the ½ hr.

❹ Cummer Museum of Art and Gardens. The world-famous Wark Collection
of early-18th-century Meissen porcelain is just one reason to visit this
former riverfront estate, which includes 13 permanent galleries with
more than 5,000 items spanning more than 8,000 years and 3 acres
of riverfront gardens reflecting Northeast Florida's blooming seasons
and indigenous varieties. For the kids, Art Connections allows them to
experience art through hands-on, interactive exhibits. One of the museum's latest additions, the Thomas H. Jacobsen Gallery of American
Art, focuses on works by American artists, including Max Weber, N. C.
Wyeth, and Paul Manship. ⊠829 Riverside Ave. ☎904/356–6857

⊕ *www.cummer.org* 🖼*$8 adults, $5 children over 5, free Tues. 4–9* ⊙ *Tues. and Thurs. 10–9, Wed., Fri., and Sat. 10–5, Sun. noon–5.*

❻ Jacksonville Landing. During the week, this riverfront festival marketplace caters to locals and tourists alike, with more than 40 specialty shops with home furnishings, apparel, and toys, 11 full-service restaurants—including a sushi bar, Italian bistro, and steak house—and an internationally flavored food court. On the weekends, the Landing hosts more than 250 events each year, ranging from the good clean fun of the American Cancer Society Duck Race to the just plain obnoxious Florida/Georgia game after-party, as well as live music (usually of the local cover band variety) in the courtyard. ⊠ *2 Independent Dr.* ☎*904/353–1188* ⊕*www.jacksonvillelanding.com* 🖼*Free* ⊙*Mon.– Thurs. 10–8, Fri. and Sat. 10–9, Sun. noon–5:30; some restaurants open earlier and close later.*

❾ Jacksonville Zoo and Gardens. Encompassing more than 120 acres on Jacksonville's north side, this midsize zoo is home to thousands of amphibians, birds, invertebrates, mammals, and reptiles, from barking tree frogs and Madagascar hissing cockroaches to dusky pygmy rattlesnakes and giant anteaters. Among the zoo's outstanding exhibits is its collection of rare waterfowl and the Serona Overlook, which showcases some of the world's most venomous snakes. The Florida Wetlands is a 2½-acre area with black bears, bald eagles, white-tailed deer, and other animals native to Florida. The African Veldt has alligators, elephants, and white rhinos, among other species of African birds and mammals; and the Range of the Jaguar, winner of the Association of Zoos and Aquarium's Exhibit of the Year, includes 4 acres of exotic big cats as well as 20 other species of animals. The zoo's newest addition is its Play Park, complete with a splash park, forest play area, maze, and discovery building. ⊠ *370 Zoo Pkwy., off Heckscher Dr. E* ☎*904/757–4463* ⊕*www.jaxzoo.org* 🖼*$11 adults, $7.50 children 3–12* ⊙*Daily 9–5.*

Fodor'sChoice ★

❽ Karpeles Manuscript Library Museum. File this one under "hidden treasure," because the majority of folks who live in Jacksonville have never even heard of, let alone visited, Karpeles. That's too bad, because this museum, in a 1921 neoclassical building on the outskirts of downtown, has displayed some priceless documents, such as the original draft of the Bill of Rights, the Emancipation Proclamation signed by Abraham Lincoln, handwritten manuscripts of Edgar Allan Poe and Charles Dickens, and musical scores by Beethoven and Mozart. Manuscript exhibits change every three months or so and coincide with monthly art exhibits. Also on the premises are an antique-book library, with volumes dating from the late 1800s, and a children's museum. ⊠ *101 W. 1st St.* ☎*904/356–2992* ⊕*www.rain.org/~karpeles/jax.html* 🖼*Free* ⊙*Mon.–Sat. 10–3.*

❸ Kids Kampus. Directly on the St. Johns River adjacent to Metropolitan Park, this 10-acre recreational facility, developed by local educators, encourages children's natural curiosity with climbing and sliding apparatuses, engaging playscapes, mini-representations of Jacksonville landmarks like Bay Street, Kings Road, and the main post office, and a splash park. It's not exactly Disney World, but parents looking for a way to entertain the kids for a couple of hours, especially in the sweltering Florida heat, report that it just might be the happiest place on earth. The "kampus" also has a picnic pavilion and jogging trail. ⊠ *1410 Gator Bowl Blvd.* ☎ *904/630–5437* ⊠ *Free* ⊘ *Mar.–Oct., Mon.–Sat. 8–8, Sun. 10–8; Nov.–Feb., Mon.–Sat. 8–6, Sun. 10–6.*

🐾 ❷ **Kona Skatepark.** Built back in the '70s—before most of its patrons were even born—this X-treme sport outpost still has its original bowls, plus updates like an 80-foot-wide vertical ramp, two street courses, and one of the area's few snake runs (a high-speed downhill run with banked turns). Skateboard legend Tony Hawk digs the park's retro feel so much that he named it one of his five favorite U.S. skate parks. The park, which also caters to in-line skaters, rents boards, skates, and safety equipment (required of all skaters) and offers lessons. Reduced rates are available on weekdays. And as proof that you're never too old to skate, skaters over 30 get half off every Wednesday night and those over 65 skate free every day. ⊠ *8739 Kona Ave.* ☎ *904/725–8770* ⊕ *www.konaskatepark.com* ⊠ *$10* ⊘ *Weekdays noon–10, Sat. 10–10, Sun. noon–9.*

❼ **Museum of Contemporary Art Jacksonville.** In this loftlike downtown building, the former headquarters of the Western Union Telegraph Company, a permanent collection of 20th-century art shares space with traveling exhibitions. The museum encompasses five galleries and ArtExplorium, a highly interactive educational exhibit for kids, as well as a funky gift shop and Cafe Nola, open for lunch, Sunday brunch, and dinner on Wednesday. MOCA Jacksonville (previously known as the Jacksonville Museum of Modern Art) also hosts film series, lectures, and workshops throughout the year. Big-city visitors often remark that they're impressed with the facility and exhibitions, but with MOCA Jacksonville comprising just 14,000 square feet (compared with the 630,000 at New York's Museum of Modern Art), they wonder where the rest is. Sunday is free for kids and their accompanying adults. ⊠ *Hemming Plaza, 333 N. Laura St.* ☎ *904/366–6911* ⊕ *www.mocajacksonville. org* ⊠ *$6 adults, $4 children over 2, free Wed. 5–9 and Sun.* ⊘ *Tues. and Thurs.–Sun., 10–4, Wed. 10–9; Tues. hrs subject to change.*

Fodor's Choice
★

🐾 ❺ **Museum of Science and History.** You won't find any mad scientists here, but you'll probably find lots of giggling ones. Targeted at the elementary and middle school set, MOSH aims to educate and entertain kids about science and history through a variety of interactive exhibits like the JEA Science Theatre, where they'll participate in live experiments related to electricity and electrical safety; the Florida Naturalist's Center, where they can explore Northeast Florida wildlife (like American alligators, gopher turtles, and various native snakes and birds); and the Universe of Science, where they'll learn about properties of physical science through hands-on demonstrations. Other permanent exhibits include Atlantic Tails, a hands-on exploration of whales, dolphins, and manatees; Currents of Time, chronicling 12,000 years of North-

2

east Florida history; and Prehistoric Park, featuring a life-size Allosaurus skeleton. The Alexander Brest Planetarium hosts daily shows on astronomy (request your seating pass from the front desk 30 minutes before any showing) and, on weekends, Cosmic Concerts, 3-D laser shows set to pop music. ⊠ *1025 Museum Circle* ☎ *904/396–6674* ⊕ *www.themosh.org* ☜ *$8 adults, $6 children 3–12, Cosmic Concerts $3–$6* ⊙ *Weekdays 10–5, Sat. 10–6, Sun. 1–6.*

WHERE TO STAY & EAT

$$$–$$$$
Fodor's Choice
★

✕ **Matthew's.** He doesn't have his own show on the Food Network or a cookbook on the best-seller list, but Matthew Medure is about as close to a celebrity chef as you'll find in Jacksonville. Local foodies sing his praises not only for his culinary creativity but also his dazzling presentation, made even more dramatic when compared with the restaurant's dramatically spare decor—stainless steel, polished bronze, and terrazzo flooring. The menu changes nightly but might include lemon-roasted Amish chicken with honey-truffle spaghetti squash, or herb-roasted rack of lamb with mustard pistachio crust. Complement your meal with one of 450 wines (topping out at more than $1,000 per bottle), then dive into one of the warm soufflés for dessert. And if you're lucky, Medure might even autograph your bill. ⊠ *2107 Hendricks Ave., San Marco* ☎ *904/396–9922* ⊟ *AE, D, DC, MC, V* ⊙ *Closed Sun. No lunch.*

$$–$$$$
★

✕ **Bistro Aix.** When a Jacksonville restaurant can make Angelinos feel like they haven't left home, that's saying a lot. With its slick black-leather booths, 1940s brick work, velvet drapes, and intricate marbled globes, Bistro Aix (pronounced "X") is just that place. Regulars can't get enough of the creamy onion soup, crispy calamari, and house-made potato chips with warm blue-cheese appetizers or entrées like oak-fired fish Aixoise, grilled salmon, and filet mignon. Aix's resident pastry chef ensures no sweet tooth leaves unsatisfied. For the most part, waitstaff are knowledgeable and pleasant, though some patrons find their demeanor snooty, except, of course, the ones from L.A. Call for preferred seating. ⊠ *1440 San Marco Blvd., San Marco* ☎ *904/398–1949* ☜ *Reservations not accepted* ⊟ *AE, D, DC, MC, V* ⊙ *No lunch weekends.*

$$–$$$
★

✕ **bb's.** Sleek yet cozy, this hip bistro is as popular with corporate muckety-mucks looking to close a deal as it is with thirtysomething lovebirds seemingly on the verge of popping the question (though shouting the question might be more appropriate, considering how loud the dining room gets on weekends). The modern decor, which includes concrete floors and a stainless-steel wine bar (read: no hard liquor), provides an interesting backdrop for comfort food—inspired entrées and daily specials that might include char-grilled beef tenderloin, prosciutto-wrapped pork chops, or mushroom triangoli ravioli. On the lighter side, grilled pizzas, sandwiches, and salads, especially warm goat-cheese salad, are favorites. Although a wait is practically guaranteed, you can pass the time sizing up the display of diet-destroying desserts.

✉ *1019 Hendricks Ave., San Marco* ☎ *904/306–0100* ⌕ *Reservations not accepted* ═ *AE, D, DC, MC, V* ⊘ *Closed Sun.*

$$–$$$ ✗**Crush Bistro.** Judging from its location—next door to a sketchy dive bar and across the street from a grubby self-service laundry—Crush Bistro should be serving microwaveable hamburgers and pork rinds, not "soul-satisfying French cuisine." Yet this ironic juxtaposition is what makes it all the more delicious. The menu changes seasonally but often includes customer-favorites *poisson choux chaud et lardons* (pan-seared wild striped bass, warm cabbage, and bacon salad) and *tartare de boeuf avec frites* (steak tartare with house-made fries). As to be expected with a name like "Crush," the restaurant also has an extensive wine list with a focus on French, Spanish, and American appellations. And although the owners try to promote the restaurant as being "without pretension," just try ordering a Miller Lite and see if the server can keep a straight face. Or if you really want to have some fun, take out your cell phone and make a call: they'll be all over you like almond butter on a baked pear pancake. ✉ *3630 Park St., Avondale* ☎ *904/381–0909* ═ *AE, D, DC, MC, V* ⊘ *Closed Sun. No lunch.*

$$–$$$ ✗**River City Brewing Company.** You'd think that hosting Super Bowl XXIX's Playboy Party would improve a place's mojo. Not so much for this riverfront restaurant, which still churns out the shrimp scampi, grilled New York striploin steak, and roasted double breast of chicken it's been serving for years (ditto for its microbrews). Despite its less-than-cutting-edge culinary offerings, RCBC, as it's known to locals, is still quite popular, mostly for having one of the best dining views in the city and the area's most extravagant Sunday brunch buffet. ✉ *835 Museum Circle, Southbank Riverwalk* ☎ *904/398–2299* ═ *AE, D, DC, MC, V.*

$–$$$ ✗**Biscottis.** The local artwork on the redbrick walls is a mild distraction from the jovial crowds (from yuppies to soccer moms to metrosexuals) jockeying for tables in this midsize restaurant. Elbows almost touch, but no one seems to mind. The menu offers the unexpected: wild-mushroom ravioli with a broth of corn, leek, and dried apricot; or curry-grilled swordfish with cucumber fig bordelaise. Be sure to sample from Biscottis' decadent dessert case (we hear the peanut butter ganache is illegal in three states). ✉ *3556 St. Johns Ave., Avondale* ☎ *904/387–2060* ⌕ *Reservations not accepted* ═ *AE, MC, V.*

$–$$$ ✗**Clark's Fish Camp.** It's out of the way and hard to find, but every mile and missed turn will be forgotten once you step inside this former bait shop overlooking Julington Creek. Clark's has one of the largest menus in town, with more than 160 appetizers and entrées, including the usual—shrimp, catfish, and oysters—and the unusual—ostrich, rattlesnake, and kangaroo. In keeping with the more bizarre entrées is the decor, best described as early American taxidermy: hundreds of stuffed birds and critters gaze upon you in the main dining room, and preserved lions, gazelles, baboons, even a rhino, keep a watchful eye in the bar. One person's kitschy may be another's creepy. Reservations are accepted for parties of eight or more; call-ahead service is available for everyone else. ✉ *12903 Hood Landing Rd., Mandarin* ☎ *904/268–3474* ═ *AE, D, MC, V* ⊘ *No lunch weekdays.*

$-$$ ✕**Taste of Thai.** Ravenous regulars dominate the tightly packed tables at this warm family-owned restaurant in a nondescript strip mall down the street from Memorial Medical Center (which would explain the proliferation of diners in scrubs). For 10 years, proprietress Aurathai Sellas, who might just be the most cheerful person in the entire restaurant business, has prepared the exotic dishes of her homeland, including *Pla Lad Prig* (hot and spicy fish), *Goog Thod* (crispy shrimp), and Chicken Peanut Sauce, as well as pad thai. There may be fancier Thai restaurants in town, but none have the service and loyalty of this one. Reservations are accepted for parties of six or more. ✉*4317 University Blvd. S* ☎*904/737–9009* 🖃*AE, D, MC, V* ⊘*Closed Sun. No lunch Mon.*

¢–$$ ✕**Sticky Fingers.** In the South, barbecue joints are a dime a dozen, yet this Baymeadows smokehouse manages to stand out year after year. Perhaps it's the atypical environment—meals are served on real dishes rather than paper plates, soft lighting replaces harsh fluorescents, and B. B. King plays in the background instead of Tim McGraw. Maybe it's staff who will go out of their way to make sure you're satisfied. Probably, it's the classic, Memphis-style smoked ribs, slow-cooked over aged hickory and available in five versions, including Memphis-style dry, Tennessee whiskey, and Carolina sweet. A full bar sweetens the deal. ✉*8129 Point Meadows Way, Baymeadows* ☎*904/493–7427* 🖃*AE, D, MC, V.*

¢–$ ✕**Al's Pizza.** Although it fits the criteria of a neighborhood pizza joint— cheap, casual, and frequented by locals—this funky-chic pizzeria looks more like a hipster hangout than Jacksonvillians low on dough (pardon the pun). Both in-town locations are slick, Art Deco–inspired spaces with colorful palettes, wood-and-steel accents, and original artwork throughout. As to be expected, the main draw is the pizza, particularly Al's gourmet white pie, but eggplant parmigiana, stuffed shells, and lasagna are also good. The Riverside location caters to its more upscale clientele with table service and a separate bar area, but for some reason, the folks in the kitchen don't grasp the concept of getting all of a table's orders to come out at the same time. ✉*1620 Margaret St. #201, Riverside* ☎*904/388–8384* ✉*14286 Beach Blvd., Intracoastal West* ☎*904/223–0991* ⌖*Reservations not accepted* 🖃*AE, D, MC, V.*

¢–$ ✕**Mossfire Grill.** The tongue-in-cheek name of this Southwest-inspired restaurant speaks to the sassy waitstaff and the patrons who frequent it (the city's Great Fire of 1901 was started when a mattress factory, which processed moss, ignited). Dinner entrées range from fish tacos and crab-cake salad to New York strip loin and pecan chicken. The dimly lighted upstairs lounge has a coffeehouse vibe—with a handful of cozy booths, two-tops, and leather couches—and has the city's only tequila bar. Local bands perform jazz Friday and Saturday night. ✉*1537 Margaret St., Riverside* ☎*904/355–4434* ⌖*Reservations not accepted* 🖃*AE, MC, V* ⊘*Closed Sun.*

¢ ✕**Burrito Gallery.** There are no paintings of tortillas stuffed with beef and rice adorning the walls of this downtown hot spot. Instead, original artwork, mostly by local painter Mactruque, livens up this otherwise nondescript restaurant, and tasty burritos, tacos, quesadillas, and nachos decorate your plate. Head down the narrow hallway after dinner and you'll find the hidden Urb Garden Bar with a collection of local characters and a unique view of downtown. ⌧*21 E. Adams St., Downtown* ☎*904/598–2922* ⌕*Reservations not accepted* ▤*AE, D, MC, V* ⊗*Closed Sun. No dinner Mon. and Tues.*

¢ ✕**European Street Cafe.** Wicker baskets and lofty shelves brimming ★ with European confections and groceries like Toblerone and Nutella fill practically every inch of space not occupied by café tables. The menu can be similarly overwhelming, with nearly 100 deli sandwiches and salads. Notable are raspberry almond chicken salad and the "Blue Max," with pastrami, corned beef, Swiss cheese, sauerkraut, hot mustard, and blue-cheese dressing. This spot is favored by area professionals looking for a quick lunch, as well as the under-forty set doing 23-ounce curls with one of the restaurant's 20-plus beers on tap (plus more than 100 in bottles). Entertainment-wise, the San Marco location offers live music Thursday nights, and the Riverside restaurant has corny knock-knock jokes on the bathroom stalls. ⌧*2753 Park St., Riverside* ☎*904/384–9999* ⌧*1704 San Marco Blvd., San Marco* ☎*904/398–9500* ⌧*5500 Beach Blvd., Southside* ☎*904/398–1717* ⌕*Reservations not accepted* ▤*AE, D, MC, V.*

¢ ✕**The Loop Pizza Grill.** Standing in line to place their orders, first-time diners may think this Jacksonville-based chain is just another fast-food joint. But one look at the menu, chock-full of designer salads, specialty pizzas, and upscale sandwiches, not to mention the stylish dining room complete with upholstered booths, funky light fixtures, and tiled floors, and they'll think they're in McDreamland. The big sellers here are the burgers (the Loop 'N Cheddar and Loop 'N Blue, in particular) and pizzas (both California-thin and Chicago-thick), but sandwiches like the portobello mushroom and Cajun chicken merit special mention. The salads can be a bit blah, but the onion rings and milk shakes are among the best in town. ⌧*2014 San Marco Blvd., San Marco* ☎*904/399–5667* ⌧*14444 Beach Blvd., San Pablo* ☎*904/223–6611* ⌧*9965 San Jose Blvd., Mandarin* ☎*904/262–2210* ⌧*4000 St. Johns Ave., Avondale* ☎*904/384–7301* ⌧*8221 Southside Blvd., Deerwood* ☎*904/645–7788* ⌕*Reservations not accepted* ▤*AE, D, MC, V.*

¢ ✕**Tidbits.** Hearing locals speak of Tidbits' best-selling side dish is a little like listening to Homer Simpson talk about doughnuts ("Mmm, potato salad")—dreamy and lustful. Although not every item on the menu has such a hypnotic hold on its customers, the lunch-only restaurant has a devoted customer base, mostly San Marco and downtown worker bees, who gobble up the chicken supreme pita, french dip, veggie surprise, and Tidbit Special, with seasoned chicken chunks and pasta on a bed of lettuce topped with avocado and cheddar. It's open fewer than 20 hours a week and there's almost always a line 10 deep. Don't be discouraged. It moves fast. ⌧*1076 Hendricks Ave., San Marco* ☎*904/396–0528* ⌕*Reservations not accepted* ⊗*Closed weekends. No dinner.*

$$$–$$$$ ▣**Crowne Plaza Jacksonville Riverfront.** A staple on Jacksonville's south bank for decades, the former Hilton Jacksonville Riverfront maintains its commanding presence but now as a Crowne Plaza property. Its location on the south side of the St. Johns River puts it within walking

2

distance of museums, restaurants, the Automated Skyway Express, and the water taxi; Ruth's Chris Steak House is one of the on-site restaurants. Rooms are spacious with walk-out balconies. Guests wanting to live like a king can book the San Marco (aka the Elvis Room), a premier suite with Jacuzzi tub and two balconies that Presley called home during numerous trips to Jacksonville. (For true authenticity, order a couple of fried banana and peanut butter sandwiches from room service.) Or rent out the hotel's private yacht, the *Jacksonville Princess,* for a romantic cruise down the river (public dinner cruises set sail every Saturday evening at 7). Pros: newly renovated rooms, riverfront balconies, friendly staff. Cons: small bathrooms, loud a/c units, no free parking. ⊠*1201 Riverplace Blvd., 32207* ☎*904/398–8800* 🖷*904/398–8880* 🌐*www.cpjacksonville.com* ⇆*292 rooms, 30 suites* ⚘*In-room: kitchen (some), refrigerator (some), Wi-Fi. In-hotel: 2 restaurants, room service, bars, pool, gym, laundry service, concierge, executive floor, public Internet, public Wi-Fi, parking (fee), no-smoking rooms* ☰*AE, D, DC, MC, V.*

$$$ **Embassy Suites Hotel.** As the city's only full-service, all-suites hotel, the Embassy Suites gets high marks from business travelers looking for comfortable accommodations at a reasonable price. Each two-room suite features a separate living room with sleep sofa, a refrigerator, and a microwave, as well as a spacious work table and broadband access. All rooms have a balcony and overlook the hotel's six-story atrium. The Baymeadows location makes the hotel convenient to a number of restaurants, clubs, and shops. A cooked-to-order breakfast and a two-hour cocktail reception on weekdays are included in the rate. Pros: location, shuttle service (within 7 mi), evening reception. Cons: traffic, expensive on-site restaurant, atrium can be noisy. ⊠*9300 Baymeadows Rd., 32256* ☎*904/731–3555 or 800/362–2779* 🖷*904/731–4972* 🌐*www.embassysuitesjax.com* ⇆*277 suites* ⚘*In-room: kitchen, refrigerator, Ethernet, Wi-Fi. In-hotel: restaurant, room service, bar, pool, gym, laundry facilities, laundry service, concierge, executive floor, public Wi-Fi, parking (no fee), no-smoking rooms* ☰*AE, DC, MC, V* ⦿*BP.*

$$$ **Riverdale Inn.** In the early 1900s Jacksonville's wealthiest residents built mansions along a strip of Riverside Avenue dubbed "The Row." More than a century later, the three-story Riverdale Inn is only one of two such homes remaining. Innkeepers Linda and Bob Waln took great care in preserving the home's original details, including the solid heart of pine floors, crown moldings, and original painting shingle facade. Guest rooms, some with fireplaces, are individually decorated to evoke a turn-of-the-century feel, assuming, of course, you overlook the TV, hair dryer, microwave, and Internet access. Some rooms have clawfoot tubs and shower combinations; others have only showers. The hotel, just a block off the St. Johns River, is within walking distance of numerous restaurants, the Cummer Museum of Art and Gardens, and Five Points. Or simply stumble downstairs to The Row Restaurant and Gum Bunch Pub. Pros: on-site restaurant and pub, proximity to area restaurants and shops, private bathrooms. Cons: small rooms, restaurant and pub can be noisy, limited parking. ⊠*1521 Riverside*

Ave.32204 ☎*904/354–5080* 🖨*904/354–6859* ⊕*www.riverdale-inn.com* ⇨*7 rooms, 3 suites* ⌂*In-room: kitchen (some), refrigerator (some), DVD (some), Wi-Fi. In-hotel: restaurant, bar, no elevator, public Wi-Fi, parking (no fee), some pets allowed, no-smoking rooms* ☰*AE, D, MC, V.*

$$–$$$ 🖳**Hyatt Regency Jacksonville Riverfront.** In Jacksonville, it doesn't get much more convenient than this downtown waterfront hotel. Perched on the north bank of the St. Johns River, the 19-story property is within walking distance of the Jacksonville Landing, Florida Theatre, and Times-Union Center, as well as corporate office towers and the county courthouse. The former Adam's Mark Hotel has undergone some significant changes, including the addition of the Plaza III Steakhouse and a complete room overhaul with splashy Florida-style decor, triple-sheeted beds, and sliding glass doors. Since Northeast Florida's largest hotel encompasses 110,000 square feet of meeting space, chances are pretty good you'll share an elevator with someone wearing a name tag (if you're not wearing one yourself). And during football season, don't be surprised to see face-painted fans or players themselves (supposedly, the Jacksonville Jaguars stay the night before every home game). Pros: riverfront location, newly renovated, roof-top pool and gym. Cons: not all rooms are riverfront, slow valet service, no minibars. ✉*225 E. Coastline Dr., 32202* ☎*904/588–1234* 🖨*904/633–9988* ⊕*www.jacksonville.hyatt.com* ⇨*966 rooms, 21 suites* ⌂*In-room: Ethernet. In-hotel: 3 restaurants, room service, bar, pool, gym, laundry facilities, laundry service, concierge, executive floor, public Wi-Fi, parking (fee), no-smoking rooms* ☰*AE, D, DC, MC, V.*

$$–$$$ 🖳**The Inn at Oak Street.** Built in 1902 as a private residence, the three-
★ story, 6,000-square-foot Frame Vernacular–style building was restored and reopened as a bed-and-breakfast popular for romantic weekends and girlfriend getaways. Rooms include the cozy and romantic Boudoir room, with four-poster bed and inlaid-tile fireplace, and the more modern St. John's Room, with cobalt-hue walls and a geometric bedspread. Each room has a private bath—some with whirlpool tubs and others with double-head showers—and second-story rooms offer balconies. Mornings start with a hearty breakfast in the dining room or on the enclosed porch; evenings wind down with wine and refreshments in the parlor. Pros: meticulously clean, walking distance to restaurants, private bathrooms. Cons: hardwood floors can be noisy, not for families with small children, no pool. ✉*2114 Oak St., 32204* ☎*904/379–5525* ⊕*www.innatoakstreet.com* ⇨*6 rooms, 1 suite* ⌂*In-room: kitchen (some), DVD, dial-up, Wi-Fi. In-hotel: spa, no elevator, public Wi-Fi, parking (no fee), no kids under 12, no-smoking rooms* ☰*AE, D, MC, V* ⦿*BP.*

$$–$$$ 🖳**Omni Jacksonville Hotel.** Further cementing its reputation as Jackson-
★ ville's most luxurious and glamorous hotel, the 16-story Omni underwent a multimillion-dollar makeover in 2006, including "downtown urban style" guest rooms (think neutral grays and creams, dark wood, stainless steel, and flat-screen TVs), which they claim are the largest in the city, and an expanded fitness center. The splashy marble-floor

2

lobby leads to the reception area, an upscale lounge—J Bar—and Juliette's Bistro, with cozy banquettes and tables that look up to a soaring atrium. Omni scores high marks on the family-friendly front, with Nintendo in every room, no adult films, and the Omni Kids Rule program. Bell service is also exemplary: with most porters having 10-plus years on the job, they can, and will happily, help you find just about anything. Pros: downtown location, large rooms, roof-top pool. Cons: congested valet area, pricey on-site restaurant, chaotic when there's a show at the T-U Center across the street. ⊠*245 Water St., 32202* ☎*904/355–6664 or 800/843–6664* 🖷*904/791–4812* ⊕*www.omni-jacksonville.com* ⬩*326 rooms, 28 suites* ♿*In-room: kitchen (some), Wi-Fi. In-hotel: restaurant, room service, bar, pool, gym, children's programs (ages 3–10), laundry service, concierge, public Wi-Fi, parking (fee), some pets allowed, no-smoking rooms* ⊟*AE, D, DC, MC, V.*

$$–$$$ 🏨 **Plantation Manor Inn.** Stately, yet cozy, this three-story Greek Revival plantation home has been divvied up into nine unique guest rooms, each with elegant antique furniture, chandeliers, Oriental rugs, and artwork. Authenticity aside, innkeepers Kathy and Jerry Ray understand the need for modern conveniences and equip each room with a private bath, hair dryer, iron and ironing board, and high-speed Internet access. The tranquil garden has a lap pool and hot tub. Pros: quiet, full breakfast, pool area. Cons: $25 minimum cancellation policy, single occupancy rates, closed six months of the year. ⊠*1630 Copeland St., 32204* ☎*904/384–4630* 🖷*904/387–0960* ⊕*www.plantationmanorinn.com* ⬩*9 rooms* ♿*In-room: DVD (some), ethernet. In-hotel: pool, no elevator, parking (no fee), no kids under 12, no-smoking rooms* ⊟*AE, DC, MC, V* �"⊚"*BP.*

NIGHTLIFE & THE ARTS

THE ARTS The **Alhambra Dinner Theatre** (⊠*12000 Beach Blvd.* ☎*904/641–1212*) serves up professional theater along with a menu that's often altered with each new play. Northeast Florida's major presenter of professional national and international touring attractions is the **FCCJ Artist Series** (⊠*501 W. State St.* ☎*904/632–3373*). **The Florida Theatre** (⊠*128 E. Forsyth St.* ☎*904/355–2787*) presents concerts, dance productions, and special events, as well as a classic-movie series. The **Jacksonville Symphony Orchestra** (☎*904/354–5547*) performs at the Jacoby Music Hall in the Times-Union Center for the Performing Arts and gives outdoor concerts at downtown's Metro Park. Opened in 2003, the 16,000-seat **Jacksonville Veterans Memorial Arena** (⊠*300 A. Philip Randolph Blvd.* ☎*904/630–3900*) is the latest addition to the city's entertainment complex. It hosts concerts, special events, and sporting events, and is home to the Jacksonville Barracudas hockey team. **Metropolitan Park** (⊠*1410 Gator Bowl Blvd.* ☎*904/630–0837*) is a 27-acre riverfront venue that hosts the city's major musical and cultural events, such as the Jacksonville Jazz Festival in April, and Freedom, Fanfare and Fireworks on July Fourth. Florida Community College at Jacksonville's South Campus is the site of the **Nathan H. Wilson Center for the Arts** (⊠*11901 Beach Blvd.* ☎*904/646–2222*), a performing- and visual-arts facility showcasing multidisciplinary productions by students and professional artists. Dubbed "the Harlem of the South" in the 1920s, historic La Villa is the site of the **Ritz Theatre** (⊠ *829 N. Davis St.* ☎ *904/632–5555*), which hosts musical and theatrical events of particular interest to the African-American community. One of the oldest continuously operating community theater in the United States, **Theatre Jacksonville** (⊠ *2032 San Marco Blvd.* ☎ *904/396–4425*) presents outstanding productions ranging from Shakespeare to programs for children. The **Times-Union Center for the Performing Arts** (⊠ *300 W. Water St.* ☎ *904/633–6110*) draws rock bands, musicals, and children's shows. The **University of North Florida Fine Arts Center** (⊠ *4567 St. Johns Bluff Rd. S, Bldg. 45* ☎ *904/620–2878*) presents dance and comedy troupes and other shows.

NIGHTLIFE **Buffalo Wild Wings** (⊠ *9550 Baymeadows Rd. #26* ☎ *904/448–1293*), known as "BW3" to the locals, is *the* place to watch college and pro football. Inside the Ramada Inn Mandarin, the **Comedy Zone** (⊠ *3130 Hartley Rd.* ☎ *904/292–4242*) is the area's premier comedy nightclub. Crowds head to **Dave & Buster's** (⊠ *7025 Salisbury Rd.* ☎ *904/296–1525*) for its huge video-game room and for a part in the whodunit at the mystery theater Saturday night. Stylish dress is required at **Endo Exo** (⊠ *1224 Kings Ave.* ☎ *904/396–7733*), a cozy lounge with live music on the outdoor deck. **Fuel Coffeehouse** (⊠ *1037 Park St.* ☎ *904/425–3835*) in Five Points is the hippest place to get your java on, as well as enjoy a pick-up chess game, live music, underground films, and spoken-word performances. Wine snobs, rejoice! You, too, have a place to hook up called **The Grotto** (⊠ *2012 San Marco Blvd.* ☎ *904/398–0726*). **Harmonious Monks** (⊠ *10550 Old St. Augustine Rd.* ☎ *904/880–3040*) claims to have "the world's most talented waitstaff," who perform throughout the night and encourage customers to dance on the bar. **Jack Rabbits** (⊠ *1528 Hendricks Ave.* ☎ *904/398–7496*) welcomes the latest and greatest indie bands and budding rock stars. Fans of Christian music flock to the **Murray Hill Theatre** (⊠ *932 Edgewood Ave. S* ☎ *904/388–7807*), a no-smoking, no-alcohol club. At 12,000 square feet, **Plush** (⊠ *845 University Blvd. N* ☎ *904/743–1845*) is certainly Jacksonville's largest nightclub; it's also the loudest. **Square One** (⊠ *1974 San Marco Blvd.* ☎ *904/306–9004*) hosts an upscale singles scene, with live music on weekends. The **Twisted Martini** (⊠ *Jacksonville Landing, 2 Independent Dr.* ☎ *904/353–8464*) is a glitzy meat market complete with designer martinis, chichi bar food, and a VIP area with bottle service.

SPORTS & THE OUTDOORS

⚘ **BASEBALL**

The **Jacksonville Suns** (⊠ *301 A. Phillip Randolph Blvd.* ☎ *904/358–2846*), the AA minor-league affiliate of the Los Angeles Dodgers, play at the Baseball Grounds of Jacksonville, their $25 million ballpark.

DOG RACING

Jacksonville Greyhound Racing splits its live racing season between two tracks. In town, the **Jacksonville Kennel Club** (✉ *1440 N. McDuff Ave.* ☎ *904/646–0001*) runs greyhound races from late May through early September. At the **Orange Park Kennel Club** (✉ *455 Park Ave., Orange Park ✛ ½ mi south of I–295* ☎ *904/646–0001*), the dogs hit the track from early September through late May. **The "Best Bet" at St. Johns** (✉ *6322 Race Track Rd.* ☎ *904/646–0001*) is a simulcast-only facility that includes a 14,000-square-foot poker room.

Troll the backwaters of North Florida or hit the high seas of the Atlantic Ocean with **Hammond Fishing** (☎ *904/757–7550*). **North Florida Fishing Charters** (☎ *904/346–3868*) specializes in in-shore light tackle fishing from St. Augustine to Amelia Island.

FOOTBALL

ALLTEL Stadium (✉ *1 ALLTEL Stadium Pl.*) is home to the NFL's **Jacksonville Jaguars** (☎ *904/633–6000, 904/633–2000 tickets*). Jacksonville kicks off each year with its own New Year's bowl game, the **Toyota Gator Bowl** (☎ *904/798–1700*), which usually hosts NCAA top-10 teams from the SEC, ACC, or Big East conferences. Billed as the "World's Largest Outdoor Cocktail Party," the **Florida/Georgia Game** (☎ *904/630–3690*) celebrates one of college football's most heated rivalries—between the Florida Gators and Georgia Bulldogs.

GOLF

Champions Club at Julington Creek (✉ *1111 Durbin Creek Blvd.* ☎ *904/287–4653*) is well-maintained and reasonably priced; green fee: $38–$45. The 6,891-yard course at **Cimarrone Golf Club** (✉ *2800 Cimarrone Blvd.* ☎ *904/287–2000*) features a water or marsh feature on every hole; green fee: $52–$62. **Deercreek Country Club** (✉ *7816 McLaurin Rd.* ☎ *904/363–1604*) is a semi-private, par-71 course with five different sets of tees; green fee: $44–$54. The **Eagle Harbor Golf Club** (✉ *2217 Eagle Harbor Pkwy., Orange Park* ☎ *904/269–9300*) has an 18-hole, par-72 course designed by Clyde Johnston and has a driving range, club rentals, and discount packages; green fee: $51–$62. **Magnolia Point Golf and Country Club** (✉ *3670 Clubhouse Dr., Green Cove Springs* ☎ *904/269–9276*) boasts a "player-friendly" course with beautiful scenery and wildlife; green fee: $45–$65. **Panther Creek Golf Club** (✉ *11209 Panther Creek Pkwy.* ☎ *904/783–2600*) is Northeast Florida's premier public course; green fee: $45–$60. **Windsor Parke Golf Club** (✉ *13823 Sutton Park Rd.* ☎ *904/223–4972*) has 18 holes (par 72) on tree-lined fairways and amid natural marshlands, green fee: $39–$49.

HOCKEY

The **Jacksonville Barracudas,** affiliated with the Southern Professional Hockey League, play at the **Jacksonville Veterans Memorial Arena** (✉ *300 A. Philip Randolph Blvd.* ☎ *904/367–1423*).

SKYDIVING

The city's only drop zone, **Skydive Jacksonville** (⊠*Herlong Airport, 9300 Normandy Blvd., 3 mi west of I–295* ☎*888/586–7529*), also boasts north Florida's highest tandem jump, with prices ranging from $150 to $175 per person, including equipment rental and instruction. Or get certified with accelerated freefall training (call for prices). Certified skydivers pay just $25 per jump. Video and photography services are available for an additional charge.

TENNIS

Boone Park Tennis Center (⊠*3730 Park St.* ☎*904/384–8687*) is a public tennis facility with hard and clay courts as well as picnic and restroom facilities. **Southside Tennis Complex** (⊠*1539 Hendricks Ave.* ☎*904/399–1761*) has hard and clay courts, picnic areas, and restrooms.

SHOPPING

At **Five Points** (⊠*Intersection of Park, Margaret, and Lomax Sts., Riverside*) you'll find a small but funky shopping district of new and vintage clothing boutiques, shoe stores, and antiques shops, as well as a handful of eateries and bars, not to mention some of the most colorful characters in the city. **The Shoppes of Avondale** (⊠*St. Johns Ave., between Talbot Ave. and Dancy St.*) highlight upscale clothing and accessories boutiques, art galleries, home-furnishing shops, a chocolatier, and trendy restaurants. **San Marco Square** (⊠*Intersection of San Marco and Atlantic Blvds.*) has dozens of interesting apparel, home, and jewelry stores and restaurants in 1920s Mediterranean Revival–style buildings. Northeast Florida's newest shopping destination, the **St. Johns Town Center** (⊠*4663 River City Dr., Southside* ☎*904/642–8339*), is an outdoor "lifestyle center" with shops not found anywhere else in Northeast Florida, including Anthropologie, Apple, Lucky Brand Jeans, and Sephora, as well as The Cheesecake Factory, P. F. Changs, and Maggiano's Little Italy. Traditional malls (department stores, specialty shops, food courts, and the like) include **The Avenues** (⊠*10300 Southside Blvd., Southside* ☎*904/363–3060*), **Orange Park Mall Mall** (⊠*1910 Wells Rd., Orange Park* ☎*904/269–2422*), and **Regency Square Mall** (⊠*9501 Arlington Exp., Regency* ☎*904/725–3830*).

JACKSONVILLE BEACHES

20 mi east of Jacksonville on U.S. 90 (Beach Blvd.).

Separated from the mainland by the Intracoastal Waterway, Jacksonville's main beaches run along the barrier island that includes the laidback towns of Jacksonville Beach, Neptune Beach, Atlantic Beach, and Ponte Vedra Beach. The northernmost of Jacksonville's beaches, Atlantic Beach is more subdued but a favorite with local surfers. Adjacent Neptune Beach is largely residential and draws bicyclists and in-line skaters who cruise up and down First Street. Just south is Jacksonville Beach, which has a decidedly more active shoreline, with volleyballs and Frisbees buzzing through the air and portable radios blaring everything from Kanye West to Van Halen. With multimillion-dollar homes stretching for miles, Ponte Vedra is the most difficult beach to access, but makes for a lovely drive down A1A. Lifeguards are on duty on the more populated stretches of the beaches from 10 to 6 in summer.

WHAT TO SEE

Adventure Landing and Shipwreck Island Water Park. With go-karts, two miniature-golf courses, laser tag, batting cages, kiddie rides, and arcade, Adventure Landing is more like an old-timey boardwalk than a high-tech amusement park. But when the closest theme park is more than two hours away, you make do. The largest family entertainment center in Northeast Florida also encompasses Shipwreck Island Water Park, which features a lazy river for tubing, a 500,000-gallon wave pool, and three extreme slides—the Rage, HydroHalfpipe, and Eye of the Storm. ⊠*1944 Beach Blvd., Jacksonville Beach* ☎*904/246–4386* ⊕*www. adventurelanding.com* ⊠*Adventure Landing: free (fees for rides and games), Shipwreck Island: $23.99* ☉*Adventure Landing: Mon.–Thurs. and Sun. 10 AM–11 PM, Fri. and Sat. 10 AM–midnight. Shipwreck Island: hrs vary (call for specific dates and times); Shipwreck Island closed late Sept.–late Mar.*

WHERE TO STAY & EAT

$$–$$$ ✕**Ocean 60.** Despite its location—a block from the Atlantic Ocean—this lively restaurant–wine bar–martini room has gone largely undiscovered by tourists, who might think fine dining and flip-flops don't mix. Those who do stumble upon it, however, are pleasantly surprised to find that a casual aura befits Ocean 60's eclectic seasonal menu, with signature items like walnut-grilled salmon and Mayport prawns, Kona coffee–grilled rack of lamb, and Buddha's Delight, vegetables sautéed with cellophane noodles and a Thai coconut and Kaffir lime broth. Things are anything but laid-back on Friday and Saturday nights, however, when live music and potent cocktails attract the party crowd to the martini room, where you'll be more likely to wear your martini than drink it. ⊠*60 Ocean Blvd., Atlantic Beach* ☎*904/247–0060* ☉*Closed Sun. No lunch.*

$$–$$$
Fodor'sChoice
★
✕**Restaurant Medure.** At more than 4,500 square feet, this chic Ponte Vedra restaurant is more spacious than its sister restaurant, Matthew's, in Jacksonville. And with its uplit floor-to-ceiling wine cellars, patina-stained concrete floors, overstuffed leather chairs, and room dividers constructed of oak branches and brushed aluminum, it's decidedly more urban. What is a constant, however, is Chef Matthew Medure's deliciously eclectic menu, including favorites like ahi tuna tartare, seared foie gras with huckleberry compote, and inventive variations on grouper and flounder. Although this kind of culinary genius doesn't come cheap, those looking to cut corners would be wise to dine on Monday, when bottles of wine are half price, or Wednesday, when you can enjoy hors d'oeuvres and five featured wines for just $15 a person. ⊠*818 N. A1A, Ponte Vedra Beach* ☎*904/543–3797* ⊟*AE, D, DC, MC, V* ☉*Closed Sun. No lunch.*

$–$$ ✕**Homestead.** A two-story log cabin built in 1934 and recently renovated, this down-home haunt serving classic Southern cooking is always busy. The specialty is skillet-fried chicken with rice and gravy, but newer, regional fare includes crispy Parmesan-crusted rainbow trout, panfried Georgia quail, Memphis-style barbecued duck, and low-country braised lamb shank. Sunday brunch is popular, as are predinner drinks in the Coppertop Pub. Otherworldly visits from Alpha Paynter, the building's deceased former owner, are popular with ghostbusters. Reservations are accepted for parties of eight or more. ✉ *1712 Beach Blvd., Jacksonville Beach* ☎ *904/249–9660* ☰ *AE, D, MC, V* ⊘ *No lunch Mon.*

$–$$ ✕ **Ragtime Tavern & Seafood Grill.** A New Orleans theme prevails at this
★ loud place that attracts a sophisticated young bunch in their twenties and thirties. Bayou bouillabaisse (lobster, shrimp, scallops, fish, crab, clams, and crawfish in a creole court bouillon) and ragtime shrimp (deep-fried fresh shrimp rolled in coconut) are the true specialties here, along with microbrews made on the premises. If you aren't into creole and Cajun, try a po'boy sandwich or fish sizzled on the grill. ✉ *207 Atlantic Blvd., Atlantic Beach* ☎ *904/241–7877* ⌧ *Reservations not accepted* ☰ *AE, D, DC, MC, V.*

¢–$$ ✕ **Sticky Fingers.** Like its counterpart across the ditch (beach-speak for the Intracoastal Waterway), the Atlantic Beach location of this über-popular barbecue joint is known for its inviting atmosphere, perky staff, and spectacular service. Oh, yeah, and some people really seem to like their ribs, too. Slow cooked over aged hickory, the ribs come in five versions, including Memphis-style dry, Tennessee whiskey, and Carolina sweet. The hickory-smoked chicken wings are arguably the best wings in town. ✉ *363 Atlantic Blvd. #1, Atlantic Beach* ☎ *904/241–7427* ⌧ *Reservations not accepted* ☰ *AE, D, MC, V.*

¢–$ ✕ **Al's Pizza.** The beach locations of this popular restaurant defy all expectations of a neighborhood pizza joint. Bright colors and geometric patterns accent the dining room, which also takes on an industrial feel. The menu is fairly predictable; there's pizza by the slice and by the pie, plus standbys like lasagna and ravioli. The clientele, too, is typical Beaches, with lots of twentysomething surfer dudes and dudettes and sunburned families. ✉ *303 Atlantic Blvd., Atlantic Beach* ☎ *904/249–0002* ✉ *635 A1A N, Ponte Vedra Beach* ☎ *904/543–1494* ⌧ *Reservations not accepted* ☰ *AE, D, MC, V.*

¢ ✕ **European Street Cafe.** After more than 25 years of dominance in Jacksonville, the colorful and quirky family-owned eatery finally lands at the beach with the same ambitious menu of sandwiches, salads, and soups; overflowing gourmet food section; mind-boggling beer list; and cookies big enough to knock someone unconscious. An impressive, hand-carved bar is a favorite hangout for thirsty locals who belly up for monthly beer tastings and one of the best happy hours, while the senior crowd prefer to sip their carafes of Zinfandel in the bustling dining room. ✉ *992 Beach Blvd., Jacksonville Beach* ☎ *904/249–3001* ⌧ *Reservations not accepted* ☰ *AE, D, MC, V.*

$$$$ ⌂ **The Lodge & Club.** Inspired by a Mediterranean villa, this oceanfront
FodorsChoice resort—with its white-stucco exterior and Spanish roof tiles—is luxury
★ lodging at its best. Rooms are quite spacious and have cozy window seats, appealing artwork, and private balconies overlooking the Atlan-

tic Ocean. Some units include a whirlpool tub and gas fireplace. Guests consistently praise staff for going the extra mile, whether it's accommodating special diets in the dining room or running to the drugstore for a guest who's under the weather. Relax in one of three pools or on the private beach. Guests at the Lodge have full access to sports, recreation, and spa facilities at sister property Ponte Vedra Inn & Club, less than 2 mi away. Pros: high-end accommodations, excellent service, private beach. Cons: overrated food, nonvalet parking can be a hike, most recreation facilities are off-site at the Inn & Club. ⊠607 Ponte Vedra Blvd., Ponte Vedra Beach 32082 ☎904/273–9500 or 800/243–4304 🖷904/273–0210 ⊕www.pvresorts.com ⟳42 rooms, 24 suites ⬙In-room: safe, kitchen (some), refrigerator (some), ethernet. In-hotel: 2 restaurants, room service, bars, pools, gym, beachfront, water sports, bicycles, concierge, children's programs (ages 4–12), laundry service, public Wi-Fi, airport shuttle, parking (fee), no-smoking rooms ⊟AE, D, DC, MC, V.

\$\$\$\$
Fodor's Choice
★

Ponte Vedra Inn & Club. Considered Northeast Florida's premier resort for decades, this 1928 country-club landmark continues to wow guests with its stellar service and recently renovated rooms and common areas. Accommodations are in a series of white-stucco Spanish-style buildings lining the beach; rooms are extra-large, and most have ocean views. The main house holds the registration area and some common spaces, including a big living room with fireplace. The inn's renowned full-service spa, which recently got a face-lift of its own, still attracts the rich and famous, including actors, supermodels, and former first ladies. Pros: accommodating and friendly staff, private beach, adults-only pool. Cons: small beds, charge for umbrellas and chaises on the beach, crowded pool. ⊠200 Ponte Vedra Blvd., Ponte Vedra Beach 32082 ☎904/285–1111 or 800/234–7842 🖷904/285–2111 ⊕www.pvresorts.com ⟳205 rooms, 45 suites ⬙In-room: safe, kitchen (some), refrigerator (some), DVD (some), VCR (some), Wi-Fi. In-hotel: 4 restaurants, room service, bars, golf courses, tennis courts, pool, gym, spa, beachfront, water sports, bicycles, children's programs (ages 4–12), laundry facilities, laundry service, concierge, public Wi-Fi, parking (no fee), no-smoking rooms ⊟AE, D, DC, MC, V.

\$\$\$–\$\$\$\$

Sawgrass Marriott Resort and Spa. As the second-largest golf resort in the country and home of the world-famous TPC at Sawgrass Stadium Course, the Sawgrass Marriott has plenty to offer golfers, including playing privileges at both TPC courses, the Ponte Vedra Country Club, and Marsh Landing Country Club. This is truly a full-service resort, whether you've come to laze about (the resort includes a 20,000-square-foot, full-service spa and guests also have access to the Cabana Club, a private beach club nearby) or spend some time on the courts. The lobby and some guest rooms may need an update in terms of decor (especially the villas), but the accommodations are clean and comfortable. Pros: championship golf courses, readily available shuttle, family friendly. Cons: beach not within walking distance, outdated villas, noise from frequent weddings and high school reunions. ⊠1000 PGA Tour Blvd., Ponte Vedra Beach 32082 ☎904/285–7777 or 800/457–4653 🖷904/285–0906 ⊕www.sawgrassmarriott.com ⟳508 rooms,

24 suites &In-room: kitchen (some), refrigerator, ethernet. In-hotel: 7 restaurants, room service, bars, golf, tennis, pools, gym, spa, children's programs (ages 5–12), laundry facilities, laundry service, concierge, public Wi-Fi, some pets allowed, no-smoking rooms ⊟AE, D, DC, MC, V.

$$$ **Casa Marina Hotel.** Compared with nearby oceanfront inns, it's small. But Casa Marina's creature comforts and rich history—including a stint as military housing during World War II and host to Franklin Delano Roosevelt and Al Capone in its early days—make it a big hit with tourists and locals (especially of the wedding party kind) looking for a peaceful retreat with character. Rooms are spacious, with comfy beds, and most have some view of the ocean. Unwind in the large courtyard behind the hotel with a drink from the bar, or take a stroll on the beach. Take note that Friday and Saturday night can get a little noisy with the Penthouse Lounge (and all those drunken groomsmen) in operation. ⊠*691 N. 1st St., Jacksonville Beach 32250* ☎*904/270–0025* 🖷*904/270–1159* ⊕*www.casamarinahotel.com* ⬅*7 rooms, 16 suites &In-room: refrigerator, Wi-Fi. In-hotel: 2 restaurants, room service (weekends only), bars, beachfront, public Wi-Fi, parking (no fee), no-smoking rooms ⊟AE, D, MC, V.*

$$$ **Quality Suites Oceanfront.** The Breakers it ain't, but this simple, all-suites hotel, popular with families and couples alike, atones for its lack of designer decor and gourmet dining with clean and spacious rooms (each room has a bedroom and separate sitting area with pull-out sofa, microwave, refrigerator, and private balcony) and personable and down-to-earth staff. Budget-conscious travelers will appreciate the complimentary hot breakfast and weeknight manager's reception (with free drinks and hors d'oeuvres) and rates that won't "breakers" the bank. Room service is available only between 3 and 10, and it comes from Carabba's, a popular Italian chain restaurant down the street. Pros: all rooms are oceanfront, pets allowed, clean. Cons: small pool, slow elevators, no on-site restaurant or bar. ⊠*11 N. First St., Jacksonville Beach 32410* ⊕*www.qualitysuitesjacksonvillebeach.com* ⬅*72 rooms &In room: safe, kitchen, ethernet. In hotel: room service, pool, gym, beachfront, laundry facilities, laundry service, parking (no fee), some pets allowed, no-smoking rooms.*

$$ **Sea Horse Oceanfront Inn.** Lacking the hoity-toity decor and amenities of other beachfront properties, this bright pink, '50s throwback (you check in at the motel office, not a grand lobby) caters to budget-minded guests seeking an ultracasual, laid-back vibe. Rooms are modestly decorated and equipped but feature an ocean view with a private balcony or patio. The Lemon Bar is a hot spot for locals and hotel guests. Pros: beach access with private walk-over, popular bar on-site, walking distance to restaurants and shops. Cons: no-frills decor, no room service. ⊠*120 Atlantic Blvd., Neptune Beach 32266* ☎*904/246–2175 or 800/881–2330* 🖷*904/246–4256* ⊕*www.seahorseoceanfrontinn.com* ⬅*39 rooms, 2 suites &In-room: kitchen (some), refrigerator, Wi-Fi. In-hotel: bar, pool, beachfront, no elevator, parking (no fee), no-smoking rooms ⊟AE, D, MC, V.*

NIGHTLIFE

A groovy, low-key lounge during the week, **The Atlantic** (✉*333 N. 1st St., Jacksonville Beach* ☎*904/249–3338*) becomes jam-packed with twentysomethings on weekends. **Atlantic Theatres** (✉*751 Atlantic Blvd., Atlantic Beach* ☎*904/249–7529*) hosts stand-up comedy, music concerts, theatrical productions, and special events. **Fionn MacCool's** (✉*333 N. 1st St., Jacksonville Beach* ☎*904/242–9499*) is, first and foremost, an Irish pub, but its top-notch menu is nothing to shake a shillelagh at. Hoist a pint o' Guinness and sing along with Emerald Isle troubadours at **Lynch's Irish Pub** (✉*514 N. 1st St., Jacksonville Beach* ☎*904/249–5181*). The beautiful people gather at the **Ocean Club** (✉*401 N. 1st St., Jacksonville Beach* ☎*904/242–8884*) for dancing, flirting, and drinking, not necessarily in that order. The oldest bar in Jacksonville and the beaches, **Pete's Bar** (✉*117 1st St., Neptune Beach* ☎*904/249–9158*) is notable for the cheapest drinks, cheapest pool tables, and most colorful clientele in town. Entertainment at the **Sun Dog** (✉*207 Atlantic Blvd., Neptune Beach* ☎*904/241–8221*) often includes acoustic guitarists. With nearly 80 TVs and an impressive menu (by sports-bar standards anyway), **Sneakers Sports Grille** (✉*111 Beach Blvd., Jacksonville Beach* ☎*904/482–1000*) is the go-to sports bar at the beach. If you'd rather gawk at sports stars in person than on the tube, head out to the oceanfront **Penthouse Lounge** (✉*Casa Marina Hotel, 691 N. 1st St., Jacksonville Beach* ☎*904/270–0025*), where NFL and PGA stars have been known to congregate.

SPORTS & THE OUTDOORS

BIKING **American Bicycle Company** (✉*240 S. 3rd St., Jacksonville Beach* ☎*904/246–4433*) rents beach cruisers by the hour and by the day. **Ponte Vedra Bicycles** (✉*250 Solana Rd., Ponte Vedra Beach* ☎*904/273–0199*) includes free bike maps with your rental.

MAYPORT

⑪ *20 mi northeast of Jacksonville.*

Dating back more than 300 years, this is one of the oldest fishing communities in the United States. It has several excellent and very casual seafood restaurants and a large commercial shrimp-boat fleet. It's also the home to the third-largest naval facility in the country, Naval Station Mayport.

Fodor'sChoice **Kathryn Abbey Hanna Park** is a 450-acre oceanfront property just north ★ of Atlantic Beach. It's filled with spectacular beaches, biking and hiking trails, wooded campsites, and a 60-acre freshwater lake, perfect for swimming, kayaking, and canoeing. The lake area also includes picnic tables, grills, and a quarter-acre water park with fountains and squirting hoses. Throughout the park there are restrooms, showers, and snack bars, open April through Labor Day, as well as lifeguards supervising all water activities during summer. Surfers in the know head to "the poles" for the best wave action in town. Camping fees range from $20 to $34 per day. ✉*500 Wonderwood Dr.* ☎*904/249–4700* 🖃*$1–$3 per vehicle* ⊙*Apr.–Oct., 8–8; Nov.–Mar., 8–6.*

EN ROUTE The arrival of the **St. Johns River Ferry** in 1948 represented a huge convenience to local residents, plus a fun activity to share with kids. The ferry (the *Jean Ribault*) continues to delight passengers young and old as they drive aboard the 153-foot vessel and embark on the 10-minute cruise across the river. ☎ *904/241–9969* ⊕ *www.stjohnsriverferry.com* ✉ *$2.50 per motorcycle, $3.25 per car, $3.25–$4.50 per RV, $1 for pedestrians and bicyclists* ⊙ *Daily 6 AM–10 PM, departing every ½ hr.*

FORT GEORGE ISLAND

⑫ *25 mi northeast of Jacksonville.*

One of the oldest inhabited areas of Florida, Fort George Island is lush with foliage, natural vegetation, and wildlife. A 4-mi nature and bike trail meanders through the island, revealing shell mounds dating as far back as 6,000 years.

Built in 1792 by Zephaniah Kingsley, an eccentric slave trader, the **Kingsley Plantation** is the oldest remaining cotton plantation in the state. The ruins of 23 tabby (a concretelike mixture of sand and crushed shells) slave houses, a barn, and the modest Kingsley home are open to the public and reachable by ferry or bridge. ⊠ *A1A–Hecksher Dr., north of St. Johns River Ferry, Fort George Island* ☎ *904/251–3537* ⊕ *www.nps.gov/timc* ✉ *Free* ⊙ *Daily 9–5; ranger talks daily at 2.*

AMELIA ISLAND (FERNANDINA BEACH)

⑬ *35 mi northeast of Jacksonville.*

At the northeasternmost reach of Florida, Amelia Island has beautiful beaches with enormous sand dunes along its eastern flank, a state park with a Civil War fort, sophisticated restaurants, interesting shops, and accommodations that range from B&Bs to luxury resorts. The town of Fernandina Beach is on the island's northern end; a century ago casinos and brothels thrived here, but those are gone. Today there's little reminder of the town's wild days, though one event comes close: the Isle of Eight Flags Shrimp Festival, held during the first weekend of May in Fernandina, attracts more than 150,000 people a year.

★ The **Amelia Island Historic District,** in Fernandina Beach, has more than 50 blocks of buildings listed on the National Register of Historic Places; 450 ornate structures built before 1927 offer some of the nation's finest examples of Queen Anne, Victorian, and Italianate homes. Many date to the haven's mid-19th-century glory days. Pick up a self-guided-tour map at the chamber of commerce, in the old train depot—once a stopping point on the first cross-state railroad—and take your time exploring the quaint shops, restaurants, and boutiques that populate the district, especially along Centre Street.

Founded in 1859, **St. Peter's Episcopal Church** (⊠ *801 Atlantic Ave., Fernandina Beach* ☎ *904/261–4293*) is a Gothic Revival structure with

Tiffany glass–style memorials and a turn-of-the-20th-century L.C. Harrison organ with magnificent hand-painted pipes.

★ One of the country's best-preserved and most complete brick forts is at **Fort Clinch State Park.** Fort Clinch was built to discourage further British intrusion after the War of 1812 and was occupied in 1863 by the Confederacy; a year later it was retaken by the North. During the Spanish-American War it was reactivated for a brief time but for the most part wasn't used. The 1,086-acre park has camping, nature trails, carriage rides, a swimming beach, and surf and pier fishing. Wander through restored buildings, including furnished barracks, a kitchen, and a repair shop. Scheduled periodically are living-history reenactments of Civil War garrison life. ✉ *2601 Atlantic Ave., Fernandina Beach* ☎ *904/277-7274* ⊕ *www.floridastateparks.org/fortclinch* ☞ *$5 per vehicle, up to 8 people, tours $2* ☉ *Daily 8–sunset.*

Amelia Island's eastern shore includes **Main Beach**, a 13-mi stretch of white-sand beach edged with dunes, some 40 feet high. It's one of the few beaches in Florida where horseback riding is allowed.

WHERE TO STAY & EAT

$$$$
Fodor's Choice
★
✕**Salt.** The Ritz-Carlton, Amelia Island's renowned fine dining restaurant, may have gotten a new look, a new menu, and a new name, but fortunately, inventive cuisine remains (not to mention the spectacular view of the Atlantic Ocean), ensuring that it, too, will set the culinary standard in Northeast Florida. Brighter and more contemporary in design than its predecessor, Salt also features more daring fare with a Chef's Adventure menu, a completely customized experience that changes from day to day, table to table. Chef de Cuisine Jordi Vallès focuses on seasonal products in creating dishes that might include bison rib eye accompanied by corn five ways or wild salmon with sweet potato–and–goat cheese "ravioli." The impressive wine list has more than 500 bottles, and service is nothing short of impeccable. For a unique dining experience, reserve A Seat in the Kitchen, a private dining room within the kitchen where you'll watch the chefs at work and enjoy a personalized five-course meal. Sunday brunch is a feast in itself. Collared shirts are required and reservations a necessity. ✉ *Ritz-Carlton, Amelia Island, 4750 Amelia Island Pkwy.* ☎ *904/277–1100* ⌂ *Reservations essential* ▭ *AE, D, DC, MC, V* ☉ *No lunch.*

$$$–$$$$
★
✕**Beech Street Grill.** Housed in an 1889 sea captain's house, this highly regarded Fernandina Beach restaurant caters to locals who crave its comfort-food-inspired dishes like tenderloin meat loaf with spinach, ham, and provolone cheese with shiitake-mushroom gravy and chive whipped potatoes, as well as visiting foodies who have heard its quiet buzz from miles away. Hardwood floors and marble fireplaces aside, one of Beech Street's most coveted fixtures is pianist John "If-you-can-hum-it-I-can-play-it" Springer, who has been entertaining diners for decades. A blackboard lists four or five fresh fish specials nightly. The outstanding wine list includes some coveted Californians. ✉ *801*

Beech St., Fernandina Beach ☎*904/277–3662* ⚛*Reservations essential* ▤*AE, D, DC, MC, V* ⊘*No lunch.*

$$–$$$$ ✕**Verandah Restaurant.** Despite being on Amelia Island Plantation, this family-friendly restaurant is open to nonresort guests, many of whom drive from Jacksonville to dine here. The dining room has a casual hotel-restaurant vibe to it, with floral prints and roomy booths, but the menu is all business. Fresh seafood dishes are a highlight, including red snapper with pecan, crab meunière, pasta paella, and surf and turf. And if you luck out and find she-crab soup on the menu (it's seasonal and not always available), order yourself the biggest bowl or bucketful they have. ⊠*6800 1st Coast Hwy.* ☎*904/321–5050* ⚛*Reservations not accepted* ▤*AE, D, MC, V* ⊘*No lunch.*

$$–$$$ ✕**Down Under.** Off the beaten path and underneath the A1A bridge overpass (accessible only by a very bumpy dirt road), the rustic Down Under is worth finding. Enjoy the glorious views of the tranquil Intracoastal Waterway and order baskets of fried shrimp or fried oysters; dine on stuffed tuna, shrimp scampi, or grilled tuna; or go for the seafood platter. For landlubbers, chicken and steak are available. ⊠*Intracoastal Waterway, under the Rte. A1A bridge, Fernandina Beach* ☎*904/261–1001* ⚛*Reservations not accepted* ▤*AE, D, MC, V* ⊘*No lunch.*

$$$$ ▦ **The Ritz-Carlton, Amelia Island.** Guests know what to expect from The
Fodor'sChoice Ritz-Carlton (namely, elegance, superb comfort, and excellent service),
★ and the Amelia Island location is certainly no exception. All accommodations in the eight-story building have balconies and ocean views; suites and rooms are spacious and luxurious and are furnished with heavy print draperies, plush carpet, framed prints, and beds so comfortable, you'll need a drag-out call instead of a wake-up call. Public areas are exquisitely maintained, and fine cuisine can be had at a choice of restaurants, including Salt. Room service is available 24/7. Recent additions include a 32,000-square-foot, state-of-the-art spa and Our Space, a social/recreational program for guests 12–19. Pros: fine dining restaurant, good spa, private beach access. Cons: no self-parking, lack of nightlife, a drive to sites and restaurants. ⊠*4750 Amelia Island Pkwy., 32034* ☎*904/277–1100* 🖷*904/261–9064* ⊕*www.ritzcarlton. com/resorts/amelia_island* ⇩*444 rooms, 45 suites* ⚭*In-room: safe, Wi-Fi. In-hotel: 4 restaurants, room service, bars, golf course, tennis courts, pool, gym, spa, beachfront, bicycles, children's programs (ages 5–12), laundry service, concierge, executive floor, no-smoking rooms* ▤*AE, D, DC, MC, V.*

$$$–$$$$ ▦**Amelia Island Plantation.** The first-rate golf, tennis, and spa facilities
Fodor'sChoice are big draws at this sprawling, family-oriented resort where accom-
★ modations include full-service hotel rooms as well as home and condo (or "villa") rentals. All hotel rooms are oceanfront with private balconies or patios, though first-floor rooms have a better view of the pool or golf course than the Atlantic. If the sound of waves crashing on the beach doesn't lull you to sleep, the pillow-top mattresses should do the trick. Villas are privately owned, meaning availability and amenities are inconsistent (shag carpet, anyone?). With its ancient oaks, marshes, and lagoons, the resort is also a worthy destination for hiking,

biking, and bird-watching, and is one of the few places in Northeast Florida to rent Segways (guided nature tours aboard the "human transporters" are $80). Good dining and shopping options mean you don't have to leave the property. Pros: family friendly, variety of outdoor activities, shuttle service throughout property. Cons: hotel far removed from other facilities (golf course, shops, tennis courts), quality of villas inconsistent, a hike to some hotel rooms. ⊠*6800 1st Coast Hwy., 32034* ☎*904/261–6161 or 800/874–6878* 🖷*904/277–5945* ⊕*www. aipfl.com* ⇆*249 rooms, 3 suites, 361 1-, 2-, and 3-bedroom villas* ⚫*In-room: safe, kitchen (some), refrigerator (some), ethernet. In-hotel: 10 restaurants, room service, bars, golf courses, tennis courts, pools, gym, spa, beachfront, water sports, bicycles, children's programs (ages 3–10), laundry facilities (villas only), laundry service, airport shuttle, no-smoking rooms* ▤*AE, D, MC, V.*

$$$–$$$$ ⊞**Ash Street Inn.** It's only fitting that the sunny yellow historic homes that make up this precious inn are surrounded by a white picket fence. Just a block from the heart of downtown Fernandina Beach, rooms are spacious and individually decorated with bedspreads and fabrics, and, in some cases, window treatments and antiques. Some rooms have claw-foot tubs, others have whirlpools, and one has a working fireplace. The rate includes a three-course breakfast that can be enjoyed either in the bright dining room or out on the porch. Lemonade and fresh baked cookies often appear on the porch in the afternoon. Pros: walking distance to historic district, pets allowed in certain rooms, friendly staff, complimentary bicycles and beach gear (towels, umbrellas). Cons: may be boring for kids, small pool, not within walking distance of the beach. ⊠*102 S. 7th St., 32034* ☎*904/277–6660 or 800/277–6660* 🖷*904/277–4646* ⊕*www.ashstreetinn.com* ⇆*10 rooms* ⚫*In-room: kitchen (some), VCR, dial-up, Wi-Fi. In-hotel: pool, bicycles, public Wi-Fi, parking (no fee), some pets allowed (fee), no-smoking rooms* ▤*AE, D, MC, V* ⵿*BP.*

$$$–$$$$ ⊞**Elizabeth Pointe Lodge.** Guests at this oceanfront inn, built to resemble
★ an 1890s sea captain's house, can't say enough about the impeccable personal service, beginning with its legendary gourmet breakfasts (dill scrambled eggs and French toast are among the crowd pleasers) and ending with social hour every evening with wine and hors d'oeuvres in the library. Oceanside units have great water views, albeit through disappointingly small windows, with the Tradewinds Suite deemed the most romantic. A chair-lined porch offers everyone a chance to rock in ocean breezes, and on cold nights guests can cluster around the living-room fireplace. An adjacent cottage has additional rooms and a suite. The restaurant is open for lunch only. Pros: beachfront location, hospitable staff, 24-hour desk attendant. Cons: pricey for a B&B, not all rooms are oceanfront, kids may be bored. ⊠*98 S. Fletcher Ave., 32034* ☎*904/277–4851 or 800/772–3359* 🖷*904/277–6500* ⊕*www. elizabethpointelodge.com* ⇆*24 rooms, 1 2-bedroom cottage* ⚫*In-room: Wi-Fi. In-hotel: beachfront, laundry service, concierge, parking (no fee), no-smoking rooms* ▤*AE, D, MC, V* ⵿*BP.*

$$–$$$ ⊞**Amelia Hotel & Suites.** Across the street from the beach, this mid-size inn is not only convenient but an economical and family-friendly alter-

native to the luxury resorts and romantic and kid-unfriendly B&Bs that populate the area. The beach and several restaurants are within walking distance, particularly convenient for families. Parents will also appreciate the hotel-wide no-smoking policy and continental breakfast served each morning in the lobby. Rooms are modestly furnished and have ocean views (provided you're not near-sighted) and pool views (considering the pool is practically in the parking lot, it's not much to look at). Pros: complimentary breakfast, free Wi-Fi, suites feature Tempur-Pedic mattresses. Cons: pool is small and only open seasonally, not all rooms have balconies, no onsite restaurant. ⊠ *1997 S. Fletcher Ave., 32034* ☎ *904/261–5735 or 877/263–5428* ⊞ *904/261–9480* ⊕ *www. ameliahotelandsuites.com* ⇌ *90 rooms, 18 suites* ⌂ *In-room: kitchen (some), refrigerator (some), Wi-Fi. In-hotel: pool, public Wi-Fi, parking (no fee), some pets allowed, no-smoking rooms* ☰ *AE, D, MC, V* ⫟⦿⫠*CP.*

$$–$$$ ☷**Hoyt House Bed & Breakfast.** Modeled after the Rockefeller Cottage in Jekyll Island, Georgia, this Queen Anne Victorian home is as warm and inviting today as it was when it was built a century ago. Inside, rooms show off antique and reproduction furniture, down quilts, and walls painted in rich hues, and a turn-of-the-century birdcage comes alive with colorful finches in the parlor. Relax in one of the rockers on the wide veranda, browse the fully stocked library, or tickle the ivories on the lobby piano; just don't miss the wine and cheese reception every afternoon. Pros: gourmet breakfast, pool and hot tub, walking distance to historic district. Cons: two-night stay required most weekends, some small bathrooms, rooms near the kitchen can be noisy. ⊠ *804 Atlantic Ave., 32034* ☎ *904/277–4300 or 800/432–2085* ⊞ *904/277–9626* ⊕ *www.hoythouse.com* ⇌ *10 rooms* ⌂ *In-room: DVD (some), VCR (some), Wi-Fi. In-hotel: pool, bicycles, no elevator, public Wi-Fi, parking (no fee), some pets allowed (fee), no kids under 12, no-smoking rooms* ☰ *AE, D, MC, V* ⫟⦿⫠*BP.*

HORSEBACK RIDING

Country Day Stables (☎ *904/879–9383*) in Callahan offers individual and group rides, including private picnic outings, on its 40-acre ranch. Reservations are required. **Kelly Seahorse Ranch** (⊠ *7500 1st Coast Hwy., Amelia Island* ☎ *904/491–5166*) takes guests on horseback rides on the beach.

KAYAKING

Kayak Amelia (☎ *904/251–0016*) takes adventurous types on guided tours of salt marshes and Fort George River and also rents equipment for those looking to create their own adventures. Reservations are required.

SHOPPING

Within the **Amelia Island Historic District** are numerous shops, art galleries, and boutiques, many clustered along cobblestone Centre Street.

ST. AUGUSTINE

14–**32** *35 mi south of Jacksonville.*

Founded in 1565 by Spanish explorers, St. Augustine is the nation's oldest city and has a wealth of historic buildings and attractions. In addition to the historic sites on the mainland, the city has 43 mi of beaches on two barrier islands to the east, both reachable by causeways. Several times a year St. Augustine holds historic reenactments, such as December's Grand Christmas Illumination, which commemorates the town's British occupation.

EXPLORING ST. AUGUSTINE

The core of any visit is a tour of the historic district, a showcase for more than 60 historic sites and attractions, plus 144 blocks of houses listed on the National Register of Historic Places. You could probably spend several weeks exploring these treasures, but don't neglect other, generally newer, attractions found elsewhere in town.

Numbers in the text correspond to numbers in the margin and on the St. Augustine map.

A GOOD WALK

A good place to start is the **Visitor Information and Preview Center 14** ⌐: pick up maps, brochures, and information. It's on San Marco Avenue between Castillo Drive and Orange Street. From there cross Orange Street to reach the **City Gate 15**, the entrance to the city's restored area. Walk south on St. George Street to the **Oldest Wooden Schoolhouse 16**. Directly across from it is the **Colonial Spanish Quarter 17**. Go out Fort Alley and cross San Marco Avenue to the impressive **Castillo de San Marcos National Monument 18**. Now head west on Cuna Street and turn left on Cordova Street. Walk south three blocks to Valencia Street and turn right. At the end of the block is the splendid **Flagler Memorial Presbyterian Church 19**. Head one block south on Sevilla Street and turn left on King Street to find the **Museum of Historic St. Augustine Government House 20** and three more of Henry Flagler's legacies: the **Lightner Museum 21**, **Flagler College 22**, and the Casa Monica Hotel. Continue two blocks east on King Street and turn right onto St. George Street to reach the **Ximenez-Fatio House 23**. Afterward, head a few blocks south down Aviles Street to St. Francis Street for a look at a microcosm of the city's history, the **Oldest House 24** (not to be confused with the Oldest Wooden Schoolhouse). Head back north to the Bridge of Lions, the **Plaza de la Constitución 25** and the **Basilica Cathedral of St. Augustine 26**. You have to cross the Bridge of Lions to get to Anastasia Island and the historic **St. Augustine Lighthouse & Museum 27**, but it's worth the effort.

Several attractions are beyond this walk, including two of particular historic note: the **Mission of Nombre de Dios 28**, north of the visitor center, is the site of America's first Christian mass; and well north of the city's cluster of sights is the **Fountain of Youth National Archaeological Park 29**, marking the location of the famed spring. For recreation, also consider **Vilano Beach** ❸⓪, north of the city, as well as **St. Augustine Beach** ❸① and **Anastasia State Park** ❸②, both on Anastasia Island.

TIMING

Allot eight hours for the tour, covering it in two days if possible. Though most sights keep the same hours (daytime only), a few are not open on Sunday. Weekday mornings generally have the smallest crowds.

WHAT TO SEE

❸② **Anastasia State Park.** With 1,700 protected acres of bird sanctuary, this Anastasia Island park draws families that like to hike, bike, camp, swim, and play on the beach. ✉*1340 Rte. A1A S, Anastasia Island* ☎*904/461–2033* ⊕*www.floridastateparks.org/anastasia* ☜*$5 per vehicle, up to 8 people* ☉*Daily 8–sunset.*

❷⑥ **Basilica Cathedral of St. Augustine.** The cathedral has the country's oldest written parish records, dating from 1594. Restored in the mid-1960s, the current structure (1797) had extensive changes after an 1887 fire. ✉*40 Cathedral Pl.* ☎*904/824–2806* ☜*Donation welcome* ☉*Weekdays 9–4:30.*

①⑧ **Castillo de San Marcos National Monument.** This massive structure is three
★ centuries old, and it looks every second of it. The fort was constructed of coquina, a soft limestone made of broken shells and coral. Built by the Spanish to protect St. Augustine from British raids (English pirates were handy with a torch), the fort was used as a prison during the Revolutionary and Civil wars. Park rangers provide an introductory narration, after which you're on your own to explore the moat, turrets, and 16-foot-thick walls. Garrison rooms depict the life of the era, and special cannon-firing demonstrations are held on weekends from Memorial Day to Labor Day. Children under 15 are admitted free and must be accompanied by an adult. Save the receipt since admission is valid for seven days. ✉*1 Castillo Dr.* ☎*904/829–6506* ⊕*www.nps. gov/casa* ☜*$5* ☉*Daily 8–5.*

①⑤ **City Gate.** The gate is a relic from the days when the Castillo's moat ran westward to the river, and the Cubo Defense Line (defensive wall) protected against approaches from the north. ✉*St. George St.*

①⑦ **Colonial Spanish Quarter.** Wander through the narrow streets at your own pace in this village with eight sites. Along the way you may see a blacksmith building his shop (a historic reconstruction) or artisans busy at candle-dipping, spinning, weaving, or cabinetmaking. They are all making reproductions for use within the restored area. **Triay House** (✉*29 St. George St.*) has period artifacts and an orientation center. Buy your tickets at the museum store. ✉*33 St. George St.* ☎*904/825–6830* ⊕*www.historicstaugustine.com* ☜*$6.50* ☉*Daily 9–4:45.*

②② **Flagler College.** Originally one of two posh hotels Henry Flagler built in 1888, this building—now a small liberal-arts college—is a riveting structure with towers, turrets, and arcades decorated by Louis Comfort Tiffany. Tours are offered daily through Flagler's Legacy Tours. ✉*74 King St.* ☎*904/829–6481, 904/823–3378 tour information* ⊕*www. flagler.edu* ☜*Tours $6 per person.*

Anastasia
State Park **32**

Basilica
Cathedral of
St. Augustine ..**26**

Castillo de San
Marcos National
Monument **18**

City Gate **15**

Colonial Spanish
Quarter **17**

Flagler
College **22**

Flagler Memorial
Presbyterian
Church **19**

Fountain of Youth
National
Archaeological
Park **29**

Lightner
Museum **21**

Mission of
Nombre de
Dios **28**

Museum of Historic
St. Augustine
Government
House **20**

Oldest House ..**24**

Oldest Wooden
Schoolhouse ...**16**

Plaza de la
Constitución ...**25**

St. Augustine
Beach **31**

St. Augustine
Lighthouse &
Museum **27**

Vilano
Beach **30**

Visitor Information
and Preview
Center **14**

Ximenez-Fatio
House **23**

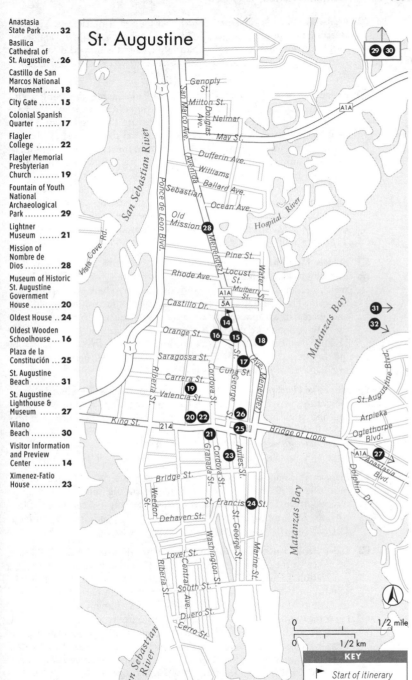

St. Augustine

KEY

► *Start of itinerary*

⑲ Flagler Memorial Presbyterian Church. To look at a marvelous Venetian Renaissance–style structure, head to this church, built by Flagler in 1889. The dome towers more than 100 feet and is topped by a 20-foot Greek cross. ✉ *Valencia and Sevilla Sts.* ☎ *904/829–6451* ☉ *Weekdays 8:30–4:30.*

㉙ Fountain of Youth National Archaeological Park. Here's the thing about "North America's first historical site": you either love it, or you hate it. Fans of the grade-A tourist trap appreciate the kitsch factor. They laugh at the cheesy costumes and educational displays. They chuckle at the tired planetarium show. They sip from the legendary Fountain of Youth, if only to mock Ponce de León and his followers for believing such foul-tasting water could hold magical powers. If you don't, however, appreciate kitsch, you'll only be disappointed in the dated exhibits and disinterested employees and wish you had spent your six bucks on a roast beef sandwich. ✉ *11 Magnolia Ave.* ☎ *904/829–3168 or 800/356–8222* ⊕ *www.fountainofyouthflorida.com* 💲 *$6.50 adults, $3.50 children 6–12* ☉ *Daily 9–5.*

㉑ Lightner Museum. In his quest to turn Florida into an American Riv-
★ iera, Henry Flagler built two fancy hotels in 1888—the Ponce de León, which became Flagler College, and the Alcazar, which now houses this museum. The building showcases three floors of furnishings, costumes, and Victorian art glass, plus ornate antique music boxes, which visitors say is not to be missed (demonstrations daily at 11 and 2). The Lightner Antiques Mall perches on three levels of what was the hotel's indoor pool. ✉ *75 King St.* ☎ *904/824–2874* ⊕ *www.lightnermuseum. org* 💲 *$8* ☉ *Museum daily 9–4:30.*

㉘ Mission of Nombre de Dios. The site, north of the historic district, commemorates where America's first Christian mass was celebrated. A 208-foot-tall stainless-steel cross marks the spot where the mission's first cross was planted. ✉ *27 Ocean Ave.* ☎ *904/824–2809 or 800/342–6529* ⊕ *www.missionandshrine.org* 💲 *Donation requested* ☉ *Weekdays 8–5, Sat. 9–5, Sun. 9:30–5.*

⑳ Museum of Historic St. Augustine Government House. With a collection of more than 300 artifacts from archaeological digs and Spanish shipwrecks off the Florida coast, this museum reflects five centuries of history. ✉ *48 King St.* ☎ *904/825–5033* 💲 *$2.50 adults, $1 students* ☉ *Daily 9–4:30.*

㉔ Oldest House. Known as the Gonzalez-Alvarez House, the Oldest House (technically, the oldest surviving Spanish Colonial dwelling in Florida), is a National Historic Landmark. The current site dates from the early 1700s, but a structure has been on this site since the early 1600s. Much of the city's history is seen in the building's changes and additions, from the coquina blocks—which came into use to replace wood soon after the town burned in 1702—to the house's enlargement during the British occupation. Most visitors can't get over how small the house is. ✉ *14 St. Francis St.* ☎ *904/824–2872* ⊕ *www.staugustinehistoricalsociety.org* 💲 *$8 adults, $4 children 6–18* ☉ *Daily 9–5.*

2

⑯ Oldest Wooden Schoolhouse. In another instance of exaggerated advertising in the Old City, the Oldest Wooden Schoolhouse is actually thought to be *one* of the nation's oldest schoolhouses. Nevertheless, the tiny 18th-century building of cypress and cedar has a fascinating history—told by automated mannequins of a teacher and students—including its serving as a guardhouse and sentry shelter during the Seminole Wars. ⊠*14 St. George St.* ☎*888/653–7245* ⊕*www.oldestwoodenschoolhouse.com* ⊠*$3* ⊙*Daily 9–5.*

㉕ Plaza de la Constitución. The central area of the original settlement was laid out in 1598 by decree of King Philip II, and little has changed since. At its center is a monument to the Spanish constitution of 1812, and at the east end is a public market dating from early American days. Just beyond is a statue of Juan Ponce de León, who "discovered" Florida in 1513. ⊠*St. George St. and Cathedral Pl.*

㉛ St. Augustine Beach. This very popular strand is the closest beach to downtown. It's on the northern end of Anastasia Island, directly east of town. ⊠*1200 Rte. A1A S* ☎*No phone* ⊠*Free.*

㉗ St. Augustine Lighthouse & Museum. Its beacon no longer guides ships to St. Augustine's shores, but the historic lighthouse continues to draw thousands of visitors each year. The 1874 structure replaced an earlier lighthouse built by the Spanish when the city was founded in 1565. The visitor center has an exhibit gallery and a store. With more than 200 steps from top to bottom, the winding staircase might be difficult for some, but those who make the journey say getting a little winded is well worth the trip. ⊠*81 Lighthouse Ave.* ☎*904/829–0745* ⊕*www.staugustinelighthouse.com* ⊠*$7.75* ⊙*Daily 9–6, last ticket sold at 5:45.*

㉚ Vilano Beach. Once-quiet Vilano Beach, just north of St. Augustine, is slowly blossoming into a bustling community with a town center, cozy restaurants and outdoor cafés, condos, and hotels. ⊠*3400 Coastal Hwy., across the St. Augustine Inlet* ☎*No phone* ⊠*Free.*

⑭ St. Johns County Visitor Information Center. An entertaining film on the founding of St. Augustine, *Struggle to Survive*, is shown hourly 9–4. ⊠*10 Castillo Dr.* ☎*904/825–1000* ⊠*Free, movie $1* ⊙*Daily 8:30–5:30.*

㉓ Ximenez-Fatio House. Built as a merchant's house and store in 1797, the place became a tourist boardinghouse in the 1800s. It's been restored to look like it did during its inn days. ⊠*20 Aviles St.* ☎*904/829–3575* ⊕*www.ximenezfatiohouse.org* ⊠*$5 adults, $4 children 6–17* ⊙*Tues.–Sat. 11–4.*

OFF THE BEATEN PATH

St. Augustine Alligator Farm Zoological Park. Founded in 1893, the Alligator Farm is one of Florida's oldest (and, at times, smelliest) zoological attractions and is credited with popularizing the alligator in the national consciousness and helping to fashion an image for the state. In addition to oddities like Maximo, a 15-foot, 1,250-pound saltwater crocodile, and a collection of rare albino alligators, the park is also home to Land of Crocodiles, the only place in the world to see all 23 species of living crocodilians. Reptiles are the main attraction, but there's also a wading bird rookery, an exotic birds and mammals exhibit, and nature trails. Educational presentations are held throughout the day, including live alligator feedings (not for the faint of heart). ⊠ *999 Anastasia Blvd.* ☎ *904/824–3337* ⊕ *www.alligatorfarm.us/* ☜ *$19.95 adults, $10.95 children 5–11* ⊙ *Daily 9–5.*

World Golf Hall of Fame. This stunning tribute to the game of golf is the centerpiece of **World Golf Village,** an extraordinary complex that includes 36 holes of golf, a golf academy, several accommodation options, a convention center, and a variety of restaurants, including Murray Bros. Caddyshack. The Hall of Fame features an adjacent IMAX theater and houses a variety of exhibits combining historical artifacts and personal memorabilia with the latest in interactive technology. Stand up to the pressures of the TV camera and crowd noise as you try to sink a final putt, take a swing on the museum's simulator, or snap a photo as you walk across a replica of St. Andrews' Swilcan Burn Bridge. ⊠ *1 World Golf Pl.* ☎ *904/940–4123* ⊕ *www.wgv.com* ☜ *$17 adults, $8.50 children 4–12 (includes one IMAX film and one round on the putting course), IMAX film $8 adults, $5 children 4–12* ⊙ *Mon.–Sat. 10–6, Sun. noon–6.*

WHERE TO STAY & EAT

$$$–$$$$ ✕ **95 Cordova.** Tucked away on the first floor of the Casa Monica Hotel,
Fodor'sChoice this restaurant serves classic cuisine with an international flair. Sup
★ in one of three dining rooms, including the main room with intricate Moroccan-themed chandeliers, wrought-iron chairs, and heavy wood columns, or the Sultan's Room, a gold-dipped space accented with potted palms and a silk-draped ceiling. The exotic furnishings are inherently romantic, but still lend an appropriate feel to dinner with friends or business associates. Innovative dishes change seasonally and highlight local seafood and produce. The tasting menu offers diners six international courses paired with the restaurant's outstanding wines. ⊠ *95 Cordova St.* ☎ *904/810–6810* ▤ *AE, D, MC, V.*

$$–$$$$ ✕ **Columbia.** Arroz con pollo, fillet *salteado* (with a spicy sauce), and a
★ fragrant seafood paella: this heir to the original Columbia, founded in Tampa in 1905 and still going strong, serves the same time-honored Cuban and Spanish dishes. Befitting its cuisine, the restaurant has a white stucco exterior and an atrium dining room full of palm trees, hand-painted tiles, and decorative arches. Sunday's Fiesta Brunch has everything from cheeses and cold meats to Belgian waffles. The wait can be off-putting, especially during summer, when the tourists are out in full force, but a glass of homemade sangria or a refreshing mojito usually manages to take the edge off. ⊠ *98 St. George St.* ☎ *904/824–3341, 800/227–1905 in Florida* ▤ *AE, D, DC, MC, V.*

$$–$$$ ✕ **Salt Water Cowboy's.** Rustic handmade twig furniture and 100-year-
★ old hardwood floors are reminders that this spot, hidden in the salt marshes flanking the Intracoastal Waterway, began as a secluded fish camp (with more "fragrant" reminders at low tide). Clam chowder, oyster stew, barbecue ribs, and crispy fried chicken are standard fare, along with blackened and broiled seafood, steamed oysters, and steak. For more adventuresome palates, the menu includes frogs' legs, alliga-

tor, and cooter (fried soft-shell turtle rolled in seasoned bread crumbs). ⊠*299 Dondanville Rd.* ☎*904/471–2332* ⌂*Reservations not accepted* ▭*AE, D, DC, MC, V* ☉*Closed Mon. and Tues. No lunch.*

$–$$$ ✕**O.C. White's Seafood & Spirits.** Don't even go inside the General Worth house, circa 1791, since the best part about dining at this bayfront eatery is being on the water. Local favorites include coconut shrimp, blue crab cakes, Caribbean jerk chicken, and Alaskan snow-crab clusters. Beef lovers may want to try the 20-ounce porterhouse or the 12-ounce New York strip. Ask for an upstairs table to admire the marina or in the courtyard when the jasmine is in bloom. ⊠*118 Avenida Menendez* ☎*904/824–0808* ⌂*Reservations not accepted on weekends* ▭*AE, D, MC, V* ☉*No lunch weekdays.*

$–$$ ✕**Harry's Seafood Bar and Grill.** Although this casual eatery calls itself a seafood bar and grill, you might think you're on Bourbon Street when you step inside and get a whiff of the spicy cooking. Red beans with rice and sausage, shrimp and crab étouffée, and jambalaya are house specialties, but the menu also includes lobster and seafood pasta, catfish Pontchartrain, and tasty desserts such as bayou brownies and bananas Foster. Tables are in several small rooms and are almost always full. Service isn't always the speediest, according to regulars, but there's always good people-watching to help pass the time. ⊠*46 Avenida Menendez* ☎*904/824–7765* ▭*AE, D, MC, V.*

$$$–$$$$ 🏨**Casa Monica Hotel.** Hand-stenciled Moorish columns and arches,
Fodor'sChoice hand-crafted chandeliers, and gilded iron tables decorate the lobby
★ of this late-1800s Flagler-era masterpiece. A retreat for the nation's wealthiest until the Great Depression put it out of business, it has returned to its perch as St. Augustine's grande dame. The turrets, towers, and wrought-iron balconies offer a hint of what's inside. Rooms— dressed in blues, greens, and whites—include wrought-iron two- and four-poster beds and mahogany writing desks and nightstands. The downtown location is within walking distance of many attractions. Guests also have access to the Serenata Beach Club, including three pools, private beach access, and beach-equipment rentals. Pros: location, architecture and decor, service. Cons: tourists clogging the lobby, parking, extra charges, small rooms. ⊠*95 Cordova St., 32084* ☎*904/827–1888 or 800/648–1888* 🖷*904/819–6065* ⊕*www.casa-monica.com* ⇆*138 rooms, 14 suites* ⌂*In-room: safe, kitchen (some), refrigerator (some), ethernet. In-hotel: restaurant, room service, bar, pool, gym, laundry service, concierge, public Wi-Fi, parking (fee), no-smoking rooms* ▭*AE, D, DC, MC, V.*

$$$–$$$$ 🏨**Casablanca Inn Bed & Breakfast on the Bay.** Breakfast comes with sce-
Fodor'sChoice nic views of the Matanzas Bay at this restored 1914 Mediterranean
★ Revival stucco-and-stone house, just north of the historic Bridge of Lions. Recently renovated rooms vary in size and shape; some have separate sitting rooms, some have views of the bay, and some have whirlpool tubs, but all are decorated with period and reproduction furniture and feature SleepNumber beds. You can enjoy breakfast on the patio or in the sunny dining room. In the evening, you can sip complimentary sherry in the cozy parlor or pay up for something stronger in the Tini Martini Bar. Pros: beds, friendly staff, complimentary

snacks and beverages. Cons: some rooms have no view, not for kids. ⊠*24 Avenida Menendez, 32084* ☎*904/829–0928 or 800/826–2626* 🖷*904/826–1892* ⊕*www.casablancainn.com* 🛏*23 rooms, 13 suites* ⚒*In-room: kitchen (some), DVD (some), Wi-Fi. In-hotel: no elevator, public Wi-Fi, parking (no fee), no kids under 12, no-smoking rooms* ⊟*AE, D, MC, V* ⦙◎⦙*BP.*

$$–$$$$ 🏠 **Carriage Way Bed and Breakfast.** The grandly restored vernacular-style mansion with Victorian details is within walking distance of the old town. Innkeepers Bill Johnson and his family see to such welcoming touches as fresh flowers, home-baked breads, and evening cordials, and are happy to dispense advice about what to see and where to eat. Special-occasion breakfasts, flowers, picnic lunches, romantic dinners, or a simple family supper can be arranged with advance notice. Younger children are permitted when guests rent the cottage, a beautifully restored late 1800s retreat several doors down from the main building. Pros: gourmet breakfast, central location, cleanliness. Cons: no pool, two-night minimum on weekends, no TV in some rooms. ⊠*70 Cuna St., 32084* ☎*800/908–9832* 🖷*904/826–1461* ⊕*www.carriageway.com* 🛏*11 rooms* ⚒*In-room: kitchen (some), DVD (some), VCR (some), no TV (some), Wi-Fi. In-hotel: bicycles, no elevator, public Wi-Fi, parking (no fee), no-smoking rooms* ⊟*D, MC, V* ⦙◎⦙*BP.*

$$–$$$$ 🏠 **Centennial House Bed & Breakfast.** Wide steps lead up to the entrance of this charming B&B in a fully restored 19th-century frame house in the heart of downtown St. Augustine. Each room is different (including more masculine options like the Gentlemen's Quarters and Safari Room), but all are painted in deep hues and have 10-foot-high ceilings and a mix of antiques and reproduction furniture. Some rooms have gas fireplaces and some have whirlpools. The brick courtyard is a peaceful outdoor space for taking a break. Pros: good breakfast, comfortable beds, thermostat in each room. Cons: traffic noise, no young children, seven-day cancellation policy. ⊠*26 Cordova St., 32084* ☎*904/810–2218 or 800/611–2880* 🖷*904/810–1930* ⊕*www.centennialhouse.com* 🛏*8 rooms* ⚒*In-room: VCR, Wi-Fi. In-hotel: no elevator, public Wi-Fi, parking (no fee), no kids under 10, no-smoking rooms* ⊟*MC, V* ⦙◎⦙*BP.*

$$–$$$$ ★ 🏨 **Renaissance Resort at World Golf Village.** If you want to be within walking distance of all World Golf Village has to offer, this full-service resort is an excellent choice. The 10-story resort is surrounding by stately palm trees and overlooks a peaceful lake. Rooms and suites surround a soaring atrium, at the bottom of which is a restaurant set amid tropical foliage and cool streams. Units are oversize and are furnished in muted pastels. The hotel is adjacent to the World Golf Hall of Fame and the St. Johns County Convention Center, and borders one of World Golf Village's championship golf courses. And if you don't know the difference between a bogey and a birdie, not to worry; the PGA TOUR Spa Laterra is but a free shuttle ride away. Guests also have privileges at the private oceanfront Serenata Beach Club. Pros: breakfast buffet, friendly staff, large bathrooms. Cons: not much to do for nongolfers, small pool. ⊠*500 S. Legacy Trail, 32092* ☎*904/940–8000 or 888/740–7020* 🖷*904/940–8008* ⊕*www.worldgolfrenaissance.com*

�300 rooms, 28 suites ⚲In-room: safe, refrigerator, Wi-Fi. In-hotel: restaurant, room service, bar, golf, tennis, pool, gym, bicycles, laundry facilities, laundry service, concierge, public Wi-Fi, airport shuttle, parking (no fee), no-smoking rooms ▤AE, D, DC, MC, V.

$–$$$$ ⛉ **Old City House Inn and Restaurant.** It's hardly noticeable amid the palatial Flagler-era architecture of the historic district, but this small two-story inn is certainly worth a visit. Touches of Paris, Venice, and India are just a few of the surprises within its coquina walls, where innkeepers Ilse and James Philcox, both avid travelers, have decorated the rooms to reflect international cities or themes. Although it's downtown and near busy attractions, the property's tall brick walls and lush foliage offer ample privacy, though some rooms are noisier than others. Friday-night wine-and-cheese parties on the porch enable guests to get to know each other and swap ghost stories (legend has it that a Spanish soldier who accidentally shot himself still patrols the hallway). Each room has its own entrance, and a second-floor deck is perfect for taking in sunsets. Pros: location, romantic, on-site restaurant. Cons: no young children allowed, thin walls, may have to share room with a ghost. ⊠115 Cordova St., 32084 ☎904/826–0113 ⊕www.oldcityhouse.com ➧7 rooms ⚲In-room: VCR (some). In-hotel: restaurant, no elevator, parking (no fee), no kids under 10, no-smoking rooms ▤AE, D, MC, V ⏁BP.

$$$ ⛉ **Hilton St. Augustine Historic Bayfront.** Travelers who want to stay in the heart of historic St. Augustine but don't want to be surrounded by antiques and chintz will find this Spanish colonial-inspired hotel (read: non-B&B) overlooking Matanzas Bay a comfortable and convenient alternative. Nineteen separate buildings make up the non-traditional Hilton property, most of which have water or city attraction views. Given its location in the thick of the Oldest City, the hotel caters to the tourist throngs with services such as in-room refrigerators, coin laundry, and cell phone rentals. Staff are knowledgeable about the local attractions and dining options and are happy to offer suggestions. Pros: location, comfortable beds, great for families. Cons: 4 PM check-in, expensive parking, noise from the road. ⊠32 Avenida Menendez, 32084 ☎904/829–2277 or 800/445–8667 ⏚904/826–2005 ➧72 rooms ⚲In room: refrigerator, ethernet. In hotel: restaurant, room service, bar, pool, laundry facilities, laundry service, concierge, public Wi-Fi, parking (fee), no-smoking rooms.

$$–$$$ ⛉ **Kenwood Inn.** For more than a century, this stately Victorian inn has welcomed wayfarers, and the Constant family continues the tradition. The decor is early American grandmother, with lots of pastel floral prints, silk flower arrangements, patchwork quilts, and doilies galore. In keeping with the theme, tea, coffee, lemonade, and cookies—just like Grandma used to make—are served every afternoon. The inn is in the historic district, making it convenient to walk to restaurants and sightseeing, but parking can be a hassle when the small lot is full. A continental buffet breakfast of home-baked cakes and breads is included. Pros: pool, friendly staff, location. Cons: no phones in rooms, limited parking, continental breakfast only. ⊠38 Marine St., 32084 ☎904/824–2116 or 800/824–8151 ⏚904/824–1689 ⊕www.

thekenwoodinn.com ⇌*14 rooms, 3 suites* ⟁*In-room: no phone, Wi-Fi. In-hotel: pool, bicycles, no elevator, public Wi-Fi, parking (no fee), no kids under 8, no-smoking rooms* ⊟*D, MC, V* ⊺◯*BP.*

$$–$$$ ⊞**St. Francis Inn Bed & Breakfast.** If the walls could whisper, this late-18th-century house in the historic district (i.e., the oldest inn in the Oldest City) would tell tales of slave uprisings, buried doubloons, and Confederate spies. The inn, a guesthouse since 1845, offers rooms, suites, a room in the former carriage house, and a five-room cottage. Furnishings are a mix of antiques and just plain old. Guests these days rave about the friendly yet quiet atmosphere, gourmet food (there's a chef on property), and thoughtful extras like free admission to the Anastasia Athletic Club, beach house access, and nightly desserts. Pros: warm hospitality, family-friendly cottage, Southern breakfast buffet. Cons: small rooms, small pool, dated decor (and not in a good way). ⊠*279 St. George St., 32084* ☎*904/824–6068 or 800/824–6062* ⊟*904/810–5525* ⊕*www.stfrancisinn.com* ⇌*13 rooms, 4 suites, 1 2-bedroom cottage* ⟁*In-room: kitchen (some), refrigerator (some), VCR (some), Wi-Fi. In-hotel: pool, bicycles, no elevator, public Wi-Fi, parking (no fee), no kids under 10 in main house, some pets allowed (fee), no-smoking rooms* ⊟*MC, V* ⊺◯*BP.*

NIGHTLIFE

Live music haven **Cafe Eleven** (⊠*501 A1A Beach Blvd., St. Augustine Beach* ☎*904/460–9311*) specializes in catch-them-before-they-get-too-big bands. The **Mill Top Tavern** (⊠*19½ St. George St.* ☎*904/829–2329*) is one of the city's hottest nightspots. If you're staying on Anastasia Island, the **Oasis Deck and Restaurant** (⊠*4000 Rte. A1A S, at Ocean Trace Rd., St. Augustine Beach* ☎*904/471–3424*) is your best bet for nightly entertainment, offering 24-ounce draft beers, beach access, and what many locals consider the best burgers in town. Something is always happening at **Scarlett O'Hara's** (⊠*70 Hypolita St.* ☎*904/824–6535*). Some nights it's blues or jazz bands; on others it might be disco, Top 40, or karaoke; and many nights the early and late-night entertainment are completely different. **Trade Winds** (⊠*124 Charlotte St.* ☎*904/829–9336*) showcases bands every night, from country and western to rock. **The White Lion** (⊠*20 Cuna St.* ☎*904/824–2388*) brings a taste of old England to this old city.

SPORTS & THE OUTDOORS

BIKING

Rent bikes to ride on the beach or in the bike lanes along A1A at **Bike Fitters at Bike America** (⊠*3936 Rte. A1A S, St. Augustine Beach* ☎*904/461–5557*). **Solano Cycle** (⊠*32 San Marco Ave.* ☎*904/825–6766*) rents bicycles, as well as single- and double-seater scooters.

2

FISHING

K-2 Sport Fishing (⊠*U.S. 1 and Rte. 207* ☎*904/824–9499*) offers 10- and 12-hour charters in addition to overnight and extended-stay trips. Charter the *Sea Love II* (⊠*250 Vilano Rd.* ☎*904/824–3328*), or sign up to join a half- or full-day fishing trip.

GOLF

Ocean Hammock (⊠*105 16th Rd., Palm Coast* ☎*386/447–4611*) at the Palm Coast Golf Resort is considered among the best open-to-the-public courses in the state. Green fee: $285. Golfers looking for a more reasonably priced round at Palm Coast can check out **Hampton Golf at Matanzas Woods** (⊠*398 Lakeview Blvd., Palm Coast* ☎*386/446–6330*); green fee: $30–$80. Like Matanzas Woods, **Pine Lakes at Hampton Golf** (⊠*400 Pine Lakes Pl., Palm Coast* ☎*386/445–0852*) was designed by Arnold Palmer and Ed Seay and is also reasonably priced; green fee: $45–$65. As part of its complex, **World Golf Village** (⊠*21 World Golf Pl.* ☎*904/940–4000*) has two 18-hole layouts named for and partially designed by golf legends Sam Snead, Gene Sarazen, Arnold Palmer, and Jack Nicklaus. The courses are the **Slammer & Squire** (☎*904/940–6088*), green fee: $104; and the **King & Bear** (☎*904/940–6200*), green fee: $134–$154.

TENNIS

Ron Parker Park (⊠*901 Pope Rd., St. Augustine Beach* ☎*904/209–0333*) has two lighted tennis courts and four paddleball courts. Public courts are available at **Treaty Park** (⊠*1595 Wildwood Dr.* ☎*904/209–0333*). It has six lighted tennis courts, eight paddleball and eight racquetball courts, and a skate park with ramps and jumps.

WATER SPORTS

Rent surfboards, skim boards, and body boards at the **Surf Station** (⊠*1020 Anastasia Blvd.* ☎*904/471–9463*). Or head off into the wild blue yonder, 1,400 feet over the ocean, with **Smile High Parasail** (⊠*111 Avenida Menendez* ☎*904/819–0980*).

SHOPPING

Just north of St. Augustine, at Exit 95 on Interstate 95, is the **St. Augustine Premium Outlets** (⊠*2700 State Rd. 16* ☎*904/825–1555* ⊕*www.premiumoutlets.com/staugustine*), with 95 designer and brand-name outlets. **Belz Factory Outlet World** (⊠*500 Belz Outlet Rd.* ☎*904/826–1311*) has 75 name-brand stores. In town, be sure to walk along car-free **St. George Street** (⊠*Between Cathedral Pl. and Orange St.*) to check out the art galleries and one-of-a-kind shops with candles, home accents, handmade jewelry, aromatherapy products, pottery, books, and clothing.

DAYTONA & THE SPACE COAST

This section of coast covers only 75 mi, but it offers considerable variety, from the unassuming bedroom community of Ormond Beach to the spring-break capital of Daytona Beach, to the world's only launch site for the space shuttle in Cape Canaveral. On the northernmost tip of the coast sits Ormond Beach, established at the turn of the 20th century as a tourist haven for the rich and famous, now catering to families and seniors seeking a quiet escape. To the south is Daytona Beach. Primarily associated with auto racing and spring break, the World's Most Famous Beach is fronted with a mixture of tall condos and apartments, hotels, low-rise motels, and flashy nightclubs. Farther south is the small town of New Smyrna Beach, its beach lined with private houses, some empty land, and an occasional taller condominium. Just below it lies the Canaveral National Seashore and the John F. Kennedy Space Center. Still farther south, the laid-back town of Cocoa Beach attracts visitors on weekends all year, as it's the closest beach to Orlando. Although the hurricanes of 2004 and 2005 caused hundreds of millions of dollars in damage to the Daytona area, most commercial properties and many smaller family-owned properties have since reopened.

ORMOND BEACH

㉝ *60 mi south of St. Augustine.*

The town got its reputation as the birthplace of speed because early car enthusiasts such as Alexander Winton, R. E. Olds, and Barney Oldfield raced their autos on the sands here. The Birthplace of Speed Antique Car Show and Swap Meet is held every Thanksgiving, attracting enthusiasts from across the nation. Ormond Beach borders the north side of Daytona Beach on both the mainland and the barrier island; nowadays you can't tell you've crossed from one to the other unless you notice the sign.

The scenic **Tomoka State Park,** 3 mi north of Ormond Beach, is perfect for fishing, camping, hiking, and boating. It is the site of a Timucuan Indian settlement discovered in 1605 by Spanish explorer Alvaro Mexia. Wooded campsites, bicycle and walking paths, and guided canoe tours on the Tomoka and Halifax rivers are the main attractions. ✉ *2099 N. Beach St.* ☎ *386/676–4050, 800/326–3521 (Reserve America) for camping reservations* 🖳 *386/676–4060* ⊕ *www.floridastateparks.org/ tomoka* 🖾 *$4 per vehicle, up to 8 people* ☉ *Daily 8–sunset.*

★ Listed on the National Register of Historic Places, the **Casements,** the restored winter retreat of John D. Rockefeller, is now a cultural center and museum. Take a tour through the period Rockefeller Room, which contains some of the family's memorabilia. The estate and its formal gardens host an annual lineup of events and exhibits; there's also a permanent exhibit of Hungarian folk art and musical instruments. ✉ *25 Riverside Dr.* ☎ *386/676–3216* 🖾 *Donations accepted* ☉ *Weekdays 8:30–5, Sat. 9–noon, tours 10–2:30.*

Take a walk through 4 acres of lush tropical gardens, past fishponds and fountains, at the **Ormond Memorial Art Museum and Gardens**. The museum has historical displays, symbolic religious paintings by Malcolm Fraser, and special exhibits by Florida artists. ⊠ *78 E. Granada Blvd.* ☎ *386/676–3347* ⊕ *www.ormondartmuseum.org* ⊠ *$2 donation suggested* ⊙ *Weekdays 10–4, weekends noon–4.*

WHERE TO STAY & EAT

$–$$$$
★

✕ **La Crepe en Haut.** Outside stairs lead up to this quiet French restaurant with several dining rooms and many window tables. Although some guests think the frilly and floral decor could use some updating, few dispute the quality of the cuisine. Consider starting with onion soup, and then try fillet of beef with burgundy sauce or roasted duck with berries. Leave room for a sweet fruit tart or a slice of creamy cheesecake. The wine list includes excellent French labels. ⊠ *142 E. Granada Blvd.* ☎ *386/673–1999* ▤ *AE, MC, V* ⊙ *Closed Mon. No lunch Sat.*

$$

▥ **Comfort Inn on the Beach.** Accommodation-wise, this beachfront hotel is nothing to write home about. The rooms, though fairly large, are nondescript and modestly furnished (they do, however, come equipped with a refrigerator and microwave). But for price-conscious travelers looking for a reliable hotel on the ocean—without the bedlam that is Daytona Beach—this may just do the trick. Complimentary continental breakfast is included. Pros: free Wi-Fi, oceanfront pool, beach access. Cons: no on-site restaurant, spotty service, no-frills decor. ⊠ *507 S. Atlantic Ave., 32176* ☎ *386/677–8550* 🖷 *386/673–6260* ♿ *In-room: safe, kitchen (some), refrigerator, Wi-Fi. In-hotel: pool, beachfront, public Wi-Fi, parking (free), some pets allowed (fee), no-smoking rooms* ▤ *AE, D, MC, V.*

DAYTONA BEACH

❸❹ *65 mi south of St. Augustine.*

Best known for the Daytona 500, Daytona has been the center of automobile racing since cars were first raced along the beach here in 1902. February is the biggest month for race enthusiasts, and there are weekly events at the International Speedway. During race weeks, bike weeks, spring-break periods, and summer holidays, expect extremely heavy traffic along the strip as well as on the beach itself, since driving on the sand is allowed; areas marked NO CAR ZONES are less frenetic and more family friendly. On the mainland, near the inland waterway, several blocks of Beach Street have been "street-scaped," and shops and restaurants open onto an inviting, broad brick sidewalk.

Daytona Lagoon. Parents looking for a nonsandy way to occupy the kids for a few hours or a whole day may find their salvation at this colorful complex that features go-karts, miniature golf, laser tag, a video arcade with more than 100 games, and a water park with 10 different slides and a 500,000-gallon tidal wave pool. More adult entertainment—in the form of pool tables, dartboards, and plasma TVs—can be found in Gilligan's Sports Bar and Grill. ⊠ *601 Earl St.* ☎ *386/254–5020* ⊕ *www.daytonalagoon.com* ⊠ *Entertainment Center: free (fees for* *rides and games), Water Park: $21.99 adults, $16.99 children under 48" tall ⊘ Family Entertainment Center: Sun.–Thurs. 10–10, Fri. and Sat. 10–midnight; Water Park: hrs vary (call for specific dates and times); Water Park closed Nov.–Feb.*

Memorabilia from the early days of beach automobile racing are on display at the **Halifax Historical Museum,** as are historic photographs, Native American artifacts, a postcard exhibit, and a video that details city history. There's a shop for gifts and antiques, too, and kids get free admission on Saturday. ⊠ *252 S. Beach St.* ☎ *386/255–6976* ⊕ *www. halifaxhistorical.org* ⊑ *$4, free Thurs.* ⊘ *Tues.–Sat. 10–4.*

☺ ★   As the "official attraction of NASCAR," **Daytona USA** lets you experience the thrill of a race from the driver's seat with its Dream Laps motion simulator. For the truly brave, Acceleration Alley puts the pedal to the metal with speeds reaching 200 mph. Participate in a pit stop on a NASCAR Winston Cup stock car or computer-design your own race car. There's also an exhibit of the history of auto racing with a rotating display of cars, an IMAX film, and track tours. ⊠ *1801 W. International Speedway Dr.* ☎ *386/947–6800* ⊕ *www.daytonausa. com* ⊑ *$24 adults, $19 children 6–12* ⊘ *Daily 9–7.*

One of only a dozen photography museums in the country, the **Southeast Museum of Photography,** at Daytona Beach Community College, has changing historical and contemporary exhibits. ⊠ *1200 W. International Speedway Blvd., Building 100* ☎ *386/506–4475* ⊕ *www.smponline.org* ⊑ *Donation welcome* ⊘ *Mon. and Wed.–Fri. 10–4, Tues. 11–7, weekends 1–5.*

The humanities section of the **Museum of Arts and Sciences,** one of the largest museums in Florida, includes displays of Chinese art, and glass, silver, gold, and porcelain examples of decorative arts. The museum also has pre-Castro Cuban art, Florida Native American items, pre-Columbian art, Indian and Persian miniature paintings, and an eye-popping complete skeleton of a giant sloth that is 13 feet long and 130,000 years old. ⊠ *352 S. Nova Rd.* ☎ *386/255–0285* ⊕ *www. moas.org* ⊑ *$12.95 adults $6.95, children 6–17* ⊘ *Daily 9–5.*

★   **Daytona Beach,** which bills itself as the World's Most Famous Beach, permits you to drive your car right up to your beach site, spread out a blanket, and have all your belongings at hand; this is especially convenient for beachgoers who are elderly or have disabilities. However, heavy traffic during summer and holidays makes it dangerous for children, and families should be extra careful or stay in the designated car-free zones. The speed limit is 10 mph. To get your car on the beach, look for signs on Route A1A indicating beach access via beach ramps. Sand traps are not limited to the golf course, though—cars can get stuck.

WHERE TO STAY & EAT

$–$$$$ ✕ **Aunt Catfish's on the River.** Don't be surprised if your server introduces herself as your cousin, though you've never seen her before in your life. You see, everybody's "cousin" at Aunt Catfish's (as in, "Can I get you another mason jar of sweet tea, Cousin?"). The silly Southern hospitality is only one of the draws at this wildly popular seafood restaurant. The main lure, of course, is the food: fried chicken, fried shrimp, fried catfish, and crab cakes. Hot cinnamon rolls and hush puppies come with every entrée and can be a meal in and of themselves. Bring your appetite and your patience—a wait is practically guaranteed. Aunt Catfish's is on the west bank of the Intracoastal Waterway (off U.S. 1, before crossing the Port Orange Causeway), just south of Daytona. ⊠ *4009 Halifax Dr., Port Orange* ☎ *386/767–4768* ⌕ *Reservations not accepted* ☰ *AE, MC, V.*

$–$$$$ ✕ **Gene's Steak House.** Quiet and intimate, this family-operated restaurant and race-car-driver hangout, a bit west of town, has long upheld its reputation as the best place for steaks in the area. Signature entrées include cooked-to-order filet mignons, sirloins, and porterhouses. Seafood is also available, and the wine list is one of the state's largest. ⊠ *3674 W. International Speedway Blvd. (U.S. 92)* ☎ *386/255–2059* ☰ *AE, DC, MC, V* ⊗ *Closed Sun. and Mon. No lunch.*

$–$$$ ✕ **Anna's Italian Trattoria.** White table linens and flowers complement delightful Italian fare at this cozy spot. Choose from a long list of delicious homemade pastas, such as spaghetti with Italian sausage and onions, angel-hair pasta with fresh chopped tomatoes and garlic, or spinach-stuffed ravioli. Or try the house specialty, risotto alla Anna. Portions are huge, so bring your appetite—or a friend. ⊠ *304 Seabreeze Blvd.* ☎ *386/239–9624* ☰ *MC, V* ⊗ *Closed Sun. and Mon. No lunch.*

$–$$$ ✕ **Chops Restaurant by Martinis.** Local beautiful people seem to flock to this trendy South Daytona Beach eatery and lounge as much for the scene as they do for the food. The bar area, done in tangerine with splashes of lime green, is a modern meeting place for the after-work crowd, and the outdoor deck and bar attract a livelier bunch (especially considering the eatery's designation, oddly enough, as "the official restaurant of Bike Week"). Those who do deign to dine will appreciate the chef's use of homegrown herbs and creative sauces in dishes such as key lime–and-ginger-marinated Atlantic salmon or seared filet mignon in Kahlua White Russian sauce, which can be enjoyed in the sleek dining room or in the garden complete with a 20-foot lighted waterfall. ⊠ *1815 S. Ridgeview Ave., South Daytona* ☎ *386/763–1090* ☰ *AE, D, MC, V* ⊗ *Closed Mon. No lunch.*

¢–$$ ✕ **McK's Dublin Station.** Crowds fill up the bar, the tables, and the cozy booths in this lively tavern. The fare is simple, hearty, and generous; cheeseburgers are thick and juicy, the chili is extra-spicy, and a big slice of homemade meat loaf comes with mashed potatoes. There's a long list of stuffed sandwiches. Onion rings are a specialty, and the Guinness is arguably a meal in itself. Plus, McK's is one of the few places in town—without a drive-thru window—that serves food after midnight. ⊠ *218 S. Beach St.* ☎ *386/238–3321* ☰ *AE, MC, V* ⊗ *Closed Sun.*

$$$$ ⚏ **The Shores Resort & Spa.** Formerly the Hilton Daytona Oceanfront, this 11-story beachfront resort underwent a $10 million face-lift in 2004. Rooms are spacious and have views of either the ocean or the Intracoastal Waterway. Rustic furniture and beds swathed in mosquito

Fodor's Choice
★

netting lend themselves to the Old Florida decor, but there's nothing primitive about the hotel's amenities, including a luxury bed and a 42-inch plasma TV in every room, the Indonesian-inspired SpaTerre, and Baleen restaurant and lounge overlooking the ocean. Pros: beachfront location, spa, friendly staff. Cons: only restaurant is expensive, pool can be crowded, not all rooms have balconies. ⊠*2637 S. Atlantic Ave., Daytona Beach Shores 32218* ☎*386/767–7350 or 866/934–7467* 🖷*386/760–3651* ⊕*www.shoresresort.com* ➟*212 rooms, 2 suites* ♨*In-room: safe, refrigerator (some), DVD, VCR, Wi-Fi. In-hotel: restaurant, room service, bars, pool, gym, spa, beachfront, laundry service, concierge, public Wi-Fi, parking (no fee), some pets allowed (fee), no-smoking rooms* ⊟*AE, D, DC, MC, V.*

$$$ 🏨 **Hilton Daytona Beach Oceanfront Resort.** Perched on the only traffic-
★ free strip of beach in Daytona, this high-rise hotel is, ironically enough, as popular with families as it is with couples. Every room has a great ocean view, and the Old Florida decor (nostalgic prints, rattan headboards, and sandy palettes) is warm and inviting. If beach bumming isn't your thing, check out the spacious sundecks, and two pools. Or take a stroll down to the pier or boardwalk, both within walking distance. The hotel is also connected to the Ocean Walk Shoppes via covered walkways. Pros: location, spacious rooms, beach access. Cons: small pool, extra charges, spotty valet service. ⊠*100 N. Atlantic Ave., 32118* ☎*386/254–8200 or 866/536–8477* 🖷*386/947–8088* ⊕*www. daytonahilton.com* ➟*744 rooms, 52 suites* ♨*In-room: refrigerators (some), Wi-Fi. In-hotel: 5 restaurants, room service, bars, pool, gym, beachfront, laundry facilities, laundry service, concierge, no-smoking rooms* ⊟*AE, D, DC, MC, V.*

$$–$$$ 🏨 **Perry's Ocean-Edge Resort.** Perhaps more than any other property in Daytona, Perry's has a die-hard fan base, many of whom started coming to the oceanfront resort as children, then returned with their children and their children's children. Parents and kids alike are kept happy with the free homemade doughnuts and coffee served in the lush solarium every morning, and the clean indoor pool surrounded by a 10,000-square-foot-atrium with a retractable roof. A complete renovation, after significant hurricane damage, added fun new features like a pool tiki bar and spa (the largest in Daytona Beach), and spiffed up the decor. Most rooms have kitchens and great ocean views. Pros: spacious rooms, helpful staff, nice pools. Cons: small bathrooms, slow elevators, limited TV channels. ⊠*2209 S. Atlantic Ave., 32118* ☎*386/255–0581 or 800/447–0002* 🖷*386/258–7315* ⊕*www.perrysoceanedge.com* ➟*200 rooms* ♨*In-room: safe, kitchen (some), refrigerator (some), ethernet. In-hotel: restaurant, bar, pools, gym, beachfront, children's programs (ages 4–12), laundry facilities, public Wi-Fi, parking (no fee), some pets allowed (fee), no-smoking rooms* ⊟*AE, D, DC, MC, V.*

NIGHTLIFE & THE ARTS

THE ARTS   Jazz, big band, blues, and folk acts perform at the outdoor, oceanfront **Daytona Beach Bandshell** (⊠*250 N. Atlantic Ave.* ☎*386/671–3420*). Internationally acclaimed orchestras and soloists appear as part of the **Daytona Beach Symphony Society** (⊠*140 S. Beach St., Suite 107* ☎*386/253–2901*). Affiliated with Bethune Cookman College, the

2,500-seat **Mary McLeod Bethune Performing Arts Center** (✉ *698 W. International Speedway Blvd.* ☎*386/481–2778*) showcases performing and visual arts productions by students and professional touring companies. The **Ocean Center at Ocean Walk Village** (✉ *101 N. Atlantic Ave.* ☎*386/254–4500 or 800/858–6444*) hosts events like boat shows and rodeos, and is home to the Daytona Thunder indoor football team. **Peabody Auditorium** (✉*600 Auditorium Blvd.* ☎*386/671–3460*) is used for concerts and programs year-round. **Seaside Music Theater** (✉*221 N. Beach St.* ☎*386/252–6200 or 800/854–5592*) presents musicals in two venues January through February and June through August.

NIGHTLIFE Despite its reputation as a biker bar, the **Boot Hill Saloon** (✉*310 Main St.* ☎*386/258–9506*) welcomes nonbikers and even nonbiker tourists! **Ocean Deck** is the only oceanfront nightclub with live reggae music (✉*127 S. Ocean Ave.* ☎*386/253–5224*). **Ocean Walk** (✉*250 N. Atlantic Ave.* ☎*386/258–9544*) is a lively, always-hopping cluster of shops, restaurants, and bars right on the ocean, including **Adobe Gila's Margarita Fajita Cantina** (☎*386/481–1000*) and the **Mai Tai Bar** (☎*386/947–2493*). Spring breakers congregate by the thousands at **The Oyster Pub** (✉*555 Seabreeze Blvd.* ☎*386/255–6348*). At **Razzles Nightclub** (✉*611 Seabreeze Blvd.* ☎*386/257–6236*), DJs play high-energy dance music from 8 PM to 3 AM.

SPORTS & THE OUTDOORS

AUTO RACING The massive **Daytona International Speedway** (✉*1801 W. International Speedway Blvd.* ☎*386/254–2700*), on Daytona's major east–west artery, has year-round auto and motorcycle racing, including the Daytona 500 in February and the Pepsi 400 in July.

DOG RACING There are more than 400 live races each year at the **Daytona Beach Kennel Club and Poker Room** (✉*2201 W. International Speedway Blvd.* ☎*386/252–6484*).

FOOTBALL The World's Most Famous Beach, more specifically, the Ocean Center at Ocean Walk Village, is home to **Daytona Beach Thunder** (☎*386/254–4545*), of the World Indoor Football League.

GOLF **Indigo Lakes Golf Club** (✉*312 Indigo Dr.* ☎*386/254–3607*) has 18 holes of golf; green fee: $30–$70. The public courses at **LPGA International** (✉*1000 Champions Dr., Daytona Beach* ☎*386/523–2001*) have 36 holes; green fee: $60–$100. **Pelican Bay South Country Club** (✉*550 Sea Duck Dr.* ☎*386/788–6496*) rents clubs and has a pro shop and a restaurant, in addition to 18 holes; green fee: $28–$40. There's an 18-hole course at **Spruce Creek Golf & Country Club** (✉*1900 Country Club Dr., Port Orange* ☎*386/756–6114*), along with practice and driving ranges, rental clubs, a pro shop, and a restaurant; green fee: $39–$49.

WATER SPORTS Catch air at **Blue Sky Parasail** (✉*2025 S. Atlantic Ave.* ☎*386/334–2191*). Rent surfboards or Boogie boards at any **Salty Dog** (✉*700 E. International Speedway Blvd.* ☎*386/258–0457* ✉*100 S. Atlantic Ave.* ☎*386/253–2755* ✉*Bellair Plaza, 2429 N. Atlantic Ave.* ☎*386/673–5277*).

SHOPPING

Daytona Flea & Farmers Market (⊠*2987 Bellevue Ave.* ☎*386/253–3330* ⊕*www.daytonafleamarket.com*) is one of the largest in the South. The **Volusia Mall** (⊠*1700 W. International Speedway Blvd.* ☎*386/253–6783*) has more than 125 stores, including JCPenney and Dillards.

NEW SMYRNA BEACH

㉟ *19 mi south of Daytona Beach.*

The long, dune-lined beach of this small town abuts the Canaveral National Seashore. Behind the dunes sit beach houses, small motels, and an occasional high-rise (except at the extreme northern tip, where none are higher than seven stories). Canal Street, on the mainland, and Flagler Avenue, with many beachside shops and restaurants, have both been "street-scaped" with wide brick sidewalks and stately palm trees. The town is also known for its internationally recognized artists' workshop.

Changing exhibits every two months, the **Atlantic Center for the Arts** has works of internationally known artists. Media include sculpture, mixed materials, video, drawings, prints, and paintings. Intensive three-week workshops are periodically run by visual, literary, and performing master artists such as Edward Albee, James Dickey, and Beverly Pepper. ⊠*1414 Art Center Ave.* ☎*386/427–6975* ⊕*www.atlanticcenterforthearts.org* ☜*Free* ☉*Weekdays 9–5.*

In a warehouse that has been converted into a stunning 5,000-square-foot, high-ceiling art gallery, **Arts on Douglas** has a new exhibit of works by a Florida artist every month. Representing more than 50 Florida artists, the gallery has hosted exhibits on the handmade jewelry of Mary Schimpff Webb and landscape and still-life oils by Barbara Tiffany. The gallery also holds an opening reception every first Saturday of the month from 4 to 7. ⊠*123 Douglas St.* ☎*386/428–1133* ⊕*www.artsondouglas.net* ☜*Free* ☉*Tues.–Fri. 11–6, Sat. 10–2, and by appointment.*

Smyrna Dunes Park is on the northern tip of its barrier island. Here 1½ mi of boardwalks crisscross sand dunes and delicate dune vegetation to lead to beaches and a fishing jetty. Botanical signs identify the flora, and there are picnic tables and an information center. It's also one of the few county parks where pets are allowed (on leashes, that is). ⊠*N. Peninsula Dr.* ☎*386/424–2935* ⊕*volusia.org/parks/smyrnadunes.htm* ☜*$3.50 per vehicle, up to 8 people* ☉*Daily sunrise—sunset, guided nature walks Sat. at 11.*

New Smyrna Beach's public beach extends 7 mi from the northernmost part of the barrier island south to the Canaveral National Seashore. It's mostly hard-packed white sand and at low tide can be stunningly wide. The beach is lined with heaps of sandy dunes, but because they're endangered, it's against the law to walk on or play in them or to pick the sea grass, which helps to stabilize the dunes. From sunrise to sunset cars are allowed on certain sections of the beach (speed limit: 10 mph). In season there's a nominal beach access fee for cars.

★ Miles of grassy, windswept dunes and a virtually empty beach await you at **Canaveral National Seashore,** a remarkable 57,000-acre park with 24 mi of undeveloped coastline spanning from New Smyrna to Titusville. Stop at any of the six parking areas and follow the wooden walkways to the beach. Ranger-led weekly programs include canoe trips and sea-turtle talks. At the northern end of the Seashore and the southernmost tip of New Smyrna Beach is **Apollo Beach** (☎386/428–3384). In addition to typical beach activities (lifeguards are on duty May 30–September 1), visitors can also ride horses here (with a permit), hike self-guided trails, and tour the historic Eldora Statehouse. ☒7611 S. Atlantic Ave. ☎321/267–1110 ⊕www.nps.gov/cana ☜$3 per person ⊙Nov.–Mar., daily 6–6, Apr.–Oct., daily 6 AM–8 PM.

WHERE TO STAY & EAT

$$–$$$ ✕**Spanish River Grill.** Michelle and Henry Salgado own this first-rate
★ restaurant, which many consider the best in New Smyrna Beach. Henry combines his Cuban grandmother's recipes with local ingredients for knockout results. Start with fried green plantains or clams tossed with garlic and avocado. For the main course, try the incredible paella, or a tender rib-eye steak stuffed with chorizo. Be sure to save room for one of Michelle's desserts. ☒737 E. 3rd Ave. ☎386/424–6991 ⚑Reservations not accepted ▤AE, MC, V ⊙Closed Mon. No lunch.

$–$$$ ✕**J.B.'s Fish Camp and Restaurant.** Better known simply as J.B.'s, this local landmark is on the eastern shore of the Indian River (i.e., the middle of nowhere). Crowds gather around the picnic-style tables covered with brown paper inside and out, or belly up to the bar to dine on mounds of spicy seafood, Cajun alligator, J.B.'s famous crab cakes, and blue crabs by the dozen. It's a great place to catch the sunset, and there's live music weekend afternoons. Five bucks says at least one person at your table says their hush puppies are the best he's ever eaten. ☒859 Pompano Ave. ☎386/427–5747 ⚑Reservations not accepted ▤AE, D, MC, V.

$–$$$ ✕**New Smyrna Steakhouse.** You *could* find a fancier place to get your steak on, but why bother? Superb steaks and ribs bring locals and visitors to this dark, busy spot. Booths are lighted by individual, low-hanging lamps that provide intimacy but enough light to read the menu. Try the 12-ounce New York strip or sirloin, the 22-ounce porterhouse, the 8-ounce filet mignon, or a rack of tender ribs. Other good choices are the Cajun pizza, shrimp Caesar salad, and mesquite chicken. ☒723 3rd Ave. ☎386/424–9696 ▤AE, D, MC, V.

$–$$$ ✕**Norwood's Seafood Restaurant.** Fresh local fish and shrimp are the specialties at this bustling New Smyrna Beach landmark, open since 1946. Built as a gas station, the building later served as a general store and piggy-bank factory, but the remodeled interior belies this back story; the place is replete with wood, from the chairs and booths to the walls and rafters. Order steak, blackened chicken breast, or pasta. Prices are reasonable, and more than 3,000 bottles of wine are on hand. Don't be fooled by the fancy wine list and linen tablecloths; you can still wear shorts (business casual, however, is the norm). ⊠*400 2nd Ave.* ☎*386/428–4621* ⚓*Reservations not accepted* ▭*AE, D, MC, V.*

$–$$ ✕**Chase's on the Beach.** Eat on the deck beneath the stars—gazing at either the ocean or the pool—or dine indoors (the latter is recommended for folks who don't want to lose their lunch, literally, watching not-so-hard bodies covered in oil and splayed out on lounge chairs). Barefoot beachgoers wander up for beverages, hamburgers, and salads during the day (shoes required inside), whereas the evening crowd comes for fried shrimp, grouper sandwiches, and weekend entertainment. A sunset menu is available weekdays from 4 to 6 with all entrées less than $13. ⊠*3401 S. Atlantic Ave.* ☎*386/423–8787* ⚓*Reservations not accepted* ▭*AE, D, MC, V.*

$$–$$$ ⌕**Riverview Hotel and Spa.** A landmark since 1885, this former bridge
★   tender's home is set back from the Intracoastal Waterway at the edge of the north causeway, which still has an operating drawbridge. Rooms open out to plant-filled verandas and balconies, and views look either through trees to the intracoastal or onto the private courtyard and pretty pool. Each room is furnished differently with charming antique touches, such as an old washbasin, a quilt, or a rocking chair. An "expanded" continental breakfast is served in your room. The inn has a full-service spa and an excellent gift shop, and is near art galleries and stores. Pros: on-site spa, hospitable staff, homey feel. Cons: small rooms, strict cancellation policy, blocks from the beach. ⊠*103 Flagler Ave., 32169* ☎*386/428–5858 or 800/945–7416* 🖷*386/423–8927* ⊕*www.riverviewhotel.com* ⌁*18 rooms, 1 suite* ♿*In-room: safe, Wi-Fi. In-hotel: restaurant, pool, spa, bicycles, no elevator, public Wi-Fi, parking (no fee)* ▭*AE, D, DC, MC, V* ⍾*CP.*

$–$$ ⌕**Coastal Waters Inn.** Popular with families, this three-story blue-and-white beachfront hotel has one- and two-bedroom suites with kitchens as well as standard rooms. Some units have excellent ocean views, and most have balconies or patios. Furnishings are spare but comfortable. Pros: oceanfront, family friendly, inexpensive. Cons: spotty service, lots of rules, no-frills decor. ⊠*3509 S. Atlantic Ave., 32169* ☎*386/428–3800 or 800/321–7882* 🖷*396/423–5002* ⊕*www.coastalwatersinn. com* ⌁*8 rooms, 32 suites* ♿*In-room: kitchen (some), refrigerator (some). In-hotel: pool, beachfront, no elevator, parking (no fee), no-smoking rooms* ▭*D, MC, V.*

THE ARTS

The **Little Theatre of New Smyrna Beach** (⊠*726 3rd Ave.* ☎*386/423–1246*) has been offering productions for more than half a century. The six productions a season vary from comedy to mystery to drama.

SHOPPING

Flagler Avenue (⊠*North Causeway*) is the major entranceway to the beach, and art galleries, gift shops, and surf shops line the street. **Arts on Douglas** (⊠*123 Douglas St.* ☎*386/428–1133*) displays works by 50 artists plus a solo exhibit, which changes monthly.

TITUSVILLE

36 *17 mi north of Cocoa.*

It's unusual that such a small, easily overlook accommodate what it does, namely the Kenne nerve center of the U.S. space program, and the Island National Wildlife Refuge.

Fodor'sChoice ★

The must-see **Kennedy Space Center Visitor Complex,** just southeast of Titusville, is one of Central Florida's most popular sights. Following the lead of the theme parks, they've switched to a one-price-covers-all admission, but there are several add-on options mentioned below that you might want to consider.

As of this writing, the $60 million Shuttle Launch Experience was scheduled to debut in May 2007: Designed by a team of astronauts, NASA experts, and renowned attraction engineers, the 44,000-square-foot structure will use a sophisticated motion-based platform, special effects seats, and high-fidelity visual and audio components to simulate the sensations experienced in an actual space shuttle launch, including MaxQ, Solid Rocker Booster separation, main engine cutoff, and External Tank separation. Call the Center or check the Web site for the attraction's fee.

Interactive programs make for the best experiences here, but if you want a low-key overview of the facility (and if the weather is foul) take the bus tour, included with admission. Buses depart every 15 minutes, and you can get on and off any bus whenever you like. Stops include the **Launch Complex 39 Observation Gantry,** which has an unparalleled view of the twin space-shuttle launchpads; the *Apollo/Saturn V* **Center,** with a don't-miss presentation at the Firing Room Theatre, where the launch of America's first lunar mission, 1968's *Apollo VIII,* is re-created with a ground-shaking, window-rattling liftoff; and the **International Space Station Center,** where NASA is building pieces of the Center; a mock-up of a "Habitation Module" is worth seeing.

Exhibits near the center's entrance include the **Early Space Exploration** display, which highlights the rudimentary yet influential *Mercury* and *Gemini* space programs; **Robot Scouts,** a walk-through exhibit of unmanned planetary probes; and the **Exploration in the New Millennium** display, which offers you the opportunity to touch a piece of Mars (it fell to the Earth in the form of meteorite). Don't miss the outdoor **Rocket Garden,** with walkways winding beside spare rockets, from early Atlas spacecraft to a *Saturn IB.* Children love the space playground, with a one-fifth-scale space shuttle and a crawl-through, multilevel tower, about right for kids three and older. Also fun for kids is a full-scale reproduction of a space shuttle, *Explorer:* you can walk through the payload bay, cockpit, and crew quarters. Within the garden there's also a museum filled with exhibits on spacecraft that have explored the last frontier, and a theater showing several short films.

The most moving exhibit is the **Astronaut Memorial,** a tribute to those who have died while in pursuit of space exploration. A 42½-foot-high by 50-foot-wide "Space Mirror" tracks the movement of the sun throughout the day, using reflected sunlight to brilliantly illuminate the names of the 24 fallen U.S. astronauts that are carved into the monument's 70,400-pound polished granite surface.

We recommend **Lunch with an Astronaut** ($60.99, includes general admission), where astronauts talk about their experiences and engage in a good-natured Q&A; the typical line of questioning from kids—"How do you eat/sleep/relieve yourself in space"—provokes awe-inspiring responses your young ones will remember for a long time. **NASA Up Close** tour ($59, general admission included) brings visitors to sights seldom accessible to the public, such as the Vehicle Assembly Building, the shuttle landing strip, and the 6-million-pound crawler that transports the shuttle to its launchpad. Or see how far the space program has come with the **Cape Canaveral: Then and Now** tour ($59, includes general admission), which visits America's first launch sites from the 1960s and the 21st century's active unmanned rocket program.

The only back-to-back twin **IMAX theater** in the world is in the complex, too. The dream of space flight comes to life on a movie screen five stories tall with dramatic footage shot by NASA astronauts during missions. Realistic 3D special effects will make you feel like you're in space with them. Films alternate throughout the year. Call for specific shows and times. ⊠*S.R. 405, Kennedy Space Center* ☎*321/449-4444* ⊕*www.kennedyspacecenter.com* ⊠*General admission includes bus tour, IMAX movies, Visitor Complex shows and exhibits, and the Astronaut Hall of Fame, $38* ☉*Space Center opens daily at 9, closing times vary according to season (call for details), last regular tour 3 hrs before closing; closed certain launch dates.*

The original *Mercury 7* team and the later *Gemini, Apollo, Skylab,* and shuttle astronauts contributed to make the **United States Astronaut Hall of Fame** the world's premium archive of astronauts' personal stories. Authentic memorabilia and equipment from their collections tell the story of human space exploration. You'll watch videotapes of historic moments in the space program and see one-of-a-kind items like Wally Schirra's relatively archaic *Sigma 7* Mercury space capsule, Gus Grissom's spacesuit (colored silver only because NASA thought silver looked more "spacey"), and a flag that made it to the moon. The exhibit **First on the Moon** focuses on crew selection for *Apollo 11* and the Soviet Union's role in the space race. Definitely don't miss the **Astronaut Adventure,** a hands-on discovery center with interactive exhibits that help you learn about space travel. One of the more challenging activities is a space-shuttle simulator that lets you try your hand at landing the craft—and afterward replays a side view of your rolling and pitching descent. If that gets your motor going, consider enrolling in **ATX (Astronaut Training Experience).** Held at the Hall of Fame, this is an intense full-day experience where you can dangle from a springy harness for a simulated moonwalk, spin in ways you never thought possible in a multi-axis trainer, and either work Mission Con-

that is) and larger than those in comparable hotels. The property also scores points for conveniences like 24/7 coffee and tea service in the lobby and complimentary hot breakfast. Pros: free shuttle, free Internet, extra-comfy beds. Cons: no coffeemakers in rooms, thin walls, no restaurant on-site. ⊠*4760 Helen Hauser Blvd., 32780* ☎*321/383–9191* 🖷*321/383–9166* ⧀*86 rooms, 4 suites* ⚒*In-room: refrigerator (some), ethernet. In-hotel: pool, gym, laundry facilities, laundry service, public Wi-Fi, parking (no fee), some pets allowed (fee), no-smoking rooms* ❏*CP.*

CAPE CANAVERAL

③⑦ *5 mi north of Cocoa Beach.*

This once-bustling commercial fishing area is still home to a small shrimping fleet, charter boats, and party fishing boats, but its main business these days is as a cruise-ship port. Cocoa Beach itself isn't the spiffiest place around, but what *is* becoming quite clean and neat is the north end of the port where the Carnival, Disney, and Royal Caribbean cruise lines set sail, as well as Sun Cruz and Sterling casino boats. **Port Canaveral** is now Florida's second-busiest cruise port, which makes this a great place to catch a glimpse of these giant ships even if you're not headed out to sea.

Jetty Park Campgrounds serves a wonderful taste of the real Florida. At Port Canaveral's south side, there are assorted restaurants and marine shops, a 4½-acre beach, more than 150 campsites for tents and RVs, picnic pavilions, and a 1,200-foot-long fishing pier that doubles as a perfect vantage point from which to watch a liftoff of the space shuttle. A jetty constructed of giant boulders adds to the landscape, and a walkway that crosses it provides access to a less-populated stretch of beach. Real and rustic, this is Florida without the theme-park varnish. ⊠*400 E. Jetty Rd., Cape Canaveral* ☎*321/783–7111* ⧀*$5 per car, $7 for RVs for fishing or beach; camping $18–$24 for basic, $22–$28 with water and electric, $25–$31 full hookup* ◷*Daily 7 AM–9 PM.* **Sterling Casino Lines** is like a mini–Las Vegas on the high seas with four casinos, five lounges, and cheesy celebrity impersonator shows, not to mention over-stimulated seniors wasting away their retirement savings one nickel slot at a time. The five-deck, 75,000-square-foot *Ambassador II,* which sets sail from Port Canaveral twice a day (afternoon cruises begin at 4, evening cruises at 7), features the standard casino table games, including blackjack, craps, and roulette, and more than 1,000 slot machines. Guests must be 21 to board. ⊠*Port Canaveral, 180 Jetty Dr., Terminal B* ☎*321/784–8558* ⊕*www.sterlingcasinolines.com* ⧀*Free* ◷*Sun.-Thurs. 11–4 and 7–midnight; Fri. and Sat. 11–4 and 7–1.*

WHERE TO STAY & EAT

¢–$$$ ✕**Rusty's Seafood & Oyster Bar.** Oysters, prepared raw, steamed, or casino-style, are just one of the draws at this casual eatery. Daily happy hour (dollar drafts and two-for-one cocktails) and waitresses sporting nylon short-shorts are undoubtedly among the others. Rusty's quick service and proximity to the cruise ships make it a favorite for those about to hit the high seas. Other menu items include seafood gumbo, spicy wings, steamed crab legs, burgers, and baskets of fish-and-chips, clam strips, or fried calamari. ⊠*628 Glen Cheek Dr., Port Canaveral* ☎*321/783–2033* ☰*AE, D, MC, V.*

$$–$$$ 🏨**Radisson Resort at the Port.** For cruise-ship passengers who can't wait to get under way, this splashy resort, done up in pink and turquoise, already feels like the Caribbean. Guest rooms have wicker furniture, hand-painted wallpaper, tropical-theme decor, and ceiling fans. The pool is lushly landscaped and features a cascading 95-foot mountain waterfall, tiki bar, and occasional appearances by the "Radisson parrots", about a dozen renegade birds who call the resort home (can you blame them?). This resort, directly across the bay from Port Canaveral, is not on the ocean, but it does provide complimentary transportation to the beach, Ron Jon Surf Shop, and the cruise-ship terminals at Port Canaveral. Pros: cruise ship convenience, pool area, free shuttle. Cons: three-day cancellation policy, rooms around the pool can be noisy, loud a/c in some rooms. ⊠*8701 Astronaut Blvd., Cape Canaveral* ☎*321/784–0000 or 888/201–1718* 🖷*321/784–3737* ⊕*www. radisson.com/capecanaveralfl* ⮐*284 rooms, 72 suites* ⌂*In-room: refrigerator (some), kitchen (some), ethernet. In-hotel: restaurant, bar, tennis court, pool, gym, laundry facilities, laundry service* ☰*AE, DC, MC, V.*

SPORTS & THE OUTDOORS

Cape Marina (⊠*800 Scallop Dr.* ☎*321/783–8410*) books 8-, 10-, and 16-hour fishing charters in search of the elusive wahoo, tuna, dolphin, mackerel, snapper, grouper, amberjack, marlin, and sailfish.

COCOA

38   *50 mi east of downtown Orlando, 60 mi east of Walt Disney World.*

Not to be confused with the seaside community of Cocoa Beach, the small town of Cocoa sits smack-dab on mainland Florida and faces the Intracoastal Waterway, known locally as the Indian River. There's a planetarium and a museum, as well as a rustic fish camp along the St. Johns River, a few miles inland.

Perhaps Cocoa's most interesting feature is restored **Cocoa Village.** Folks in a rush to get to the beach tend to overlook this Victorian-style village, but it's worth a stop. Within the cluster of restored turn-of-the-20th-century buildings and cobblestone walkways, you can enjoy several restaurants, indoor and outdoor cafés, snack and ice-cream shops, and more than 50 specialty shops and art galleries. The area hosts music performances in the gazebo, arts-and-crafts shows, and other family-friendly events throughout the year. To get to Cocoa Village, head east on Route 520—named King Street in Cocoa—and when the streets get narrow and the road curves, make a right onto Brevard Avenue; follow the signs for the free municipal parking lot. ⊠*S.R. 520 and Brevard Ave.* ☎*321/631–9075* ⊕*www.cocoavillage.com* 🎟*Free* ☽*Hours vary by store.*

As its name suggests, **Porcher House** was the home of E.P. Porcher (pronounced Por-*shay*), one of Cocoa's pioneers and the founder of the Deerfield Citrus groves. The Porcher home, built in 1916 and now a National Historic Landmark, is an example of 20th-century Classical Revival–style architecture incorporating local coquina rock. The house is open to the public for self-guided tours. ✉ *434 Delannoy Ave., Cocoa Village* ☎ *321/639–3500* ⊕ *www.cocoavillage.com/porcherhouse* ✉ *Donation welcome* ⊙ *Weekdays 9–5.*

☾ The **Brevard Community College Planetarium and Observatory,** one of the largest public-access observatories in Florida, has a 24-inch telescope through which visitors can view objects in the solar system and deep space. The on-campus planetarium has two theaters, one showing a changing roster of nature documentaries, the other hosting laser-light as well as changing planetarium shows. Science Quest Exhibit Hall has hands-on exhibits, including scales calibrated to other planets (on the moon, Vegas-era Elvis would have weighed just 62 pounds). The International Hall of Space Explorers displays exhibits on space travel. Show schedules and opening hours may vary, so it's best to call ahead. Travel 2½ mi east of Interstate 95 Exit 75 on Route 520, and take Route 501 north for 1¾ mi. ✉ *1519 Clearlake Rd.* ☎ *321/433–7373* ⊕ *www.brevardcc.edu/planet* ✉ *Observatory and exhibit hall free; film or planetarium show $7 adults, $4 children; both shows $11 adults, $7 children; laser show $7, triple combination $16* ⊙ *Call for current schedule.*

To Whom It May Concern: Whom It May Concern: see what the lay of
☾ the local land looked like in other eras, check out the **Brevard Museum of History & Science.** Hands-on activities for children are the draw here. Not to be missed is the Windover Archaeological Exhibit of 7,000-year-old artifacts indigenous to the region. In 1984, a shallow pond revealed the burial ground of more than 200 Native Americans who lived in the area about 7,000 years ago. Preserved in the muck were bones and, to the archaeologists' surprise, the brains of these ancient people. Don't overlook the hands-on discovery rooms and the collection of Victoriana. The museum's nature center has 22 acres of trails encompassing three distinct ecosystems—sand pine hills, lake lands, and marshlands. ✉ *2201 Michigan Ave.* ☎ *321/632–1830* ⊕ *www.brevardmuseum.com* ✉ *$6 adults, $4.50 children 5–16* ⊙ *Mon.–Sat. 10–4, Sun. noon–4.*

If you haven't seen the swampy, alligator-ridden waters of Florida, then you haven't really seen Florida. **Twister Airboat Rides** takes guests on a unique and thrilling wildlife tour where eagles and wading birds coexist with water moccasins and gators. The Coast Guard–certified deluxe airboats hit speeds of up to 45 mph and offer unparalleled opportunities to photograph native species. The basic tour lasts 30 minutes, but 60- and 90-minute eco tours are also available. Twister Airboat Rides is inside the Lone Cabbage Fish Camp, about 9 mi west of Cocoa's city limits, 4 mi west of Interstate 95. ✉ *8199 Rte. 520 at the St. Johns River* ☎ *321/632–4199* ⊕ *www.twisterairboatrides.com* ✉ *$20 adults, $12 children 12 and under* ⊙ *Daily 10–6.*

WHERE TO EAT

$$–$$$ ✕**Black Tulip Restaurant.** Two intimate dining rooms invite romance at
★ this Cocoa Village bistro, which takes pride in its 50-plus-label wine
menu. Appetizers include tortellini with meat sauce and crab-stuffed
mushrooms. Select such entrées as fettuccine primavera Alfredo; sautéed pork loin simmered with apples, brandy, and cream; roast duckling
with peaches and cashews; or fillet medallions with artichoke sauce.
Lighter lunch selections include sandwiches, salads, and quiches. Don't
miss the chocolate mousse pie and the warm apple strudel. ✉*207 Brevard Ave.* ☎*321/631–1133* ▤*AE, D, DC, MC, V* ☺*Closed Sun. and
Mon. No lunch.*

$$–$$$ ✕**Café Margaux.** Dine inside or out at this charming, cozy Cocoa Village
spot with its eclectic, creative mix of French and Italian cuisine. The
lunch menu includes black-sesame–coated chicken over mesclun greens,
as well as lump crab cakes over pancetta and roasted corn relish. Dinners are equally exotic, with oak-smoked Norwegian salmon rosettes
and samplers like a baked Brie coated in pecans. ✉*220 Brevard Ave.*
☎*321/639–8343* ▤*AE, DC, MC, V* ☺*Closed Sun. and Tues.*

¢–$ ✕**Lone Cabbage Fish Camp.** The word *rustic* doesn't even begin to
describe this down-home, no-nonsense restaurant (translation: you eat
off paper plates with plastic forks) housed in a weathered old clapboard shack along with a bait shop and airboat tour company. Set your
calorie counter for plates of catfish, frogs' legs, turtle, and alligator
(as well as burgers and hot dogs). Dine inside or on the outdoor deck
overlooking the St. Johns River. Who knows, you might even see your
dinner swimming by. And don't miss Lone Cabbage's world-famous
fish fry the first and third Sunday of every month. ✉*8199 Rte. 520*
☎*321/632–4199* ⚓*Reservations not accepted* ▤*AE, MC, V.*

NIGHTLIFE & THE ARTS

In 1918 this building was a Ford dealership that sold Model Ts. After
that, it evolved into the Aladdin Theater, a vaudeville house, and then
did a turn as a movie theater before being purchased by Brevard Community College. Today, the **Cocoa Village Playhouse** (✉*300 Brevard Ave.*
☎*321/636–5050*) is the area's community theater. The September-
through-June performance schedule has musicals starring local talent.
The rest of the year the stage hosts touring professional productions,
concerts, and, in summer, shows geared to children on vacation.

SHOPPING

You could spend hours browsing in the more than 50 boutiques and
shops of **Cocoa Village,** along Brevard Avenue and Harrison Street,
which has the densest concentration of shops. Although most are of
the gift and clothing variety, the Village is also home to several antiques
shops, art galleries, florists, bookstores, and even a tattoo parlor. Kids
come to a screeching halt when they catch sight of the dizzying selection of toys displayed in the storefront windows of **Annie's Toy Chest**
(✉*405 Brevard Ave.* ☎*321/632–5890*). The **Bath Cottage** (✉*425 Brevard Ave.* ☎*321/690–2284*) has fine soaps, aromatherapy candles,
plush towels, and elegant shower curtains, as well as colorful blown-
glass balls, drawer pulls, and table lamps. For some terrific sculptures

of fish, follow the brick path back to the **Harry Phillips Gallery** (⊠*116-B Harrison St.* ☏*321/636–4160*). If you like to cook, or even just like to eat, spend some time wandering through the many kitchen and cooking items—handsome ceramic bowls, colorful glassware, regional cookbooks, exotic soup mixes—and gourmet ingredients at **The Village Gourmet** (⊠*9 Stone St.* ☏*321/636–5480*). Take a break from the heat with a hand-packed ice-cream cone from the **Village Ice Cream & Sandwich Shop** (⊠*120-B Harrison St.* ☏*321/632–2311*).

THE OUTDOORS

BIKING Rent a beach-cruiser bike from **Matt's Bicycle Center** (⊠*166 N. Atlantic Ave.* ☏*321/783–1196*) and ride like the wind up and down the strand.

COCOA BEACH

39 *65 mi east of Orlando, 70 mi east of Walt Disney World.*

Named for the former astronaut, **Alan Shepard Park** (⊠*East end of S.R. 250* ☏*321/868–3274*) is a 5-acre oceanfront park that, aptly enough, provides excellent views of shuttle launches. Facilities include 10 picnic pavilions, shower and restroom facilities, and more than 300 parking spaces (parking is $5 per day). Shops and restaurants are within walking distance.

After crossing a long and high bridge just east of Cocoa Village, you'll be dropped down upon a barrier island. A few miles farther and you'll reach the Atlantic Ocean and picture-perfect **Cocoa Beach** at Route A1A. This is one of the Space Coast's nicest beaches, with many wide stretches that are excellent for biking, jogging, power walking, or strolling. In some places there are dressing rooms, showers, playgrounds, picnic areas with grills, snack shops, and surf-side parking lots. Beach vendors offer necessities, and guards are on duty in summer. Cocoa Beach is considered the capital of Florida's surfing community.

Stretching far over the Atlantic, the **Cocoa Beach Pier** (⊠*401 Meade Ave.* ☏*321/783–7549* ⊕*www.cocoabeachpier.com*) is an everyday gathering spot as well as a beachside grandstand for space-shuttle launches. There are several souvenir shops, bars, and restaurants, as well as a bait-and-tackle shop. It costs $3 to park here, and another $1 for access to the fishing part of the pier that dangles 800 feet out into the Atlantic. Don't expect pristine Disney cleanliness here; this is a weather-beaten, sandy hangout for people who love the beach.

The 10-acre oceanfront **Sidney Fischer Park** (⊠*2100 block of Rte. A1A* ☏*321/868–3252*) has showers, playgrounds, changing areas, picnic areas with grills, snack shops, and plenty of well-maintained, inexpensive surf-side parking lots. Beach vendors carry necessities for sunning and swimming. The parking fee is $5 for cars and RVs.

WHERE TO STAY & EAT

$$–$$$$ ✕**Bernard's Surf.** Since 1948 this family operation, and Cocoa Beach institution, has served astronauts, athletes, politicians, and celebrities a variety of fresh seafood entrées, from swordfish, cobia, and pompano to lobster and shrimp. The common folk also eat up the fresh catches that vary by the season and whim of the sea, but snapper under a creamy seafood sauce is the house specialty. Landlubbers can choose pork chops or steak. Try the tableside Caesar salad, and save room for the cheesecake. ⊠*2 S. Atlantic Ave.* ☎*321/783–2401* ▤*AE, D, MC, V.*

$$–$$$$ ✕**Mango Tree Restaurant.** Candles, fresh flowers, and rattan basket chairs
★   set a romantic mood in the intimate dining room, designed to evoke the feel of a South Pacific plantation (a lush entryway with a koi pond with black-neck swans add to the dramatic effect). *Lobsterocki* (Maine lobster wrapped in bacon with teriyaki cream sauce), baked Brie, or rare seared tuna are good appetizer choices. For a main course, try Indian River crab cakes, roast Long Island duckling, or filet mignon stuffed with cream cheese and chives. ⊠*118 N. Atlantic Ave.* ☎*321/799–0513* ▤*AE, MC, V* ⊘*Closed Mon. No lunch.*

$$–$$$ ✕**Heidelberg.** As the name suggests, the cuisine here is definitely German, from the sauerbraten served with potato dumplings and red cabbage to the beef Stroganoff and spaetzle to the classically prepared Wiener schnitzel. All the soups and desserts are homemade; try the Viennese-style apple strudel and the rum-zapped almond-cream tortes. Elegant interior touches include crisp linens and fresh flowers. There's live music Friday and Saturday evenings. You can also dine inside the jazz club, Heidi's, next door. ⊠*7 N. Orlando Ave., opposite City Hall* ☎*321/783–6806* ▤*AE, MC, V* ⊘*Closed Mon.*

$–$$$ ✕**Oh Shucks Seafood Bar.** At the only open-air seafood bar on the beach, at the entrance of the Cocoa Beach Pier, the main item is oysters, served on the half shell. You can also grab a burger here, and there's live entertainment on Friday and Saturday. Some diners complain that the prices don't jibe with the ultracasual atmosphere (hello, plastic chairs!), but they're also paying for the "ex-Pier-ience." ⊠*401 Meade Ave., Cocoa Beach Pier* ☎*321/783–7549* ▤*AE, D, DC, MC, V.*

¢–$$ ✕**Fischer's Bar and Grill.** This casual eatery, owned by the same family that runs the more upscale Bernard's Surf, right next door, is a perfect spot for winding down after a tough day at the beach. Although complete dinners are available, people tend to come for the salads, pasta, burgers, and platters of tasty fried shrimp. The family's fleet of fishing boats brings in fresh seafood daily. Happy hour is from 4 to 7. ⊠*2 S. Atlantic Ave.* ☎*321/783–2401* ⌨*Reservations not accepted* ▤*AE, D, MC, V.*

$$$–$$$$ ▦**Doubletree Oceanfront Hotel Cocoa Beach.** After significant hurricane damage in 2004, this oceanfront hotel underwent an $8 million top-to-bottom renovation. Guest rooms are West Indies–inspired, with dark oak furniture, colorful tropical prints, and cheerful yellow walls. Most rooms are oceanfront, with superb water views and private balconies. The five-story hotel is a favorite of families as well as Orlandoans on weekend getaways, as are the chain's famous chocolate chip cook-

ies. Pros: private beach, refrigerator and microwave in every room, comfy beds. Cons: extra charge for beach-chair rental, loud a/c in some rooms, roof views. ✉ *2080 N. Atlantic Ave., 32931* ☏ *321/783–9222* 📠 *321/799–3234* ⊕ *www.cocoabeachdoubletree.com* 🛏 *148 rooms, 12 suites* ⚘ *In-room: refrigerator, Wi-Fi. In-hotel: restaurant, room service, bar, pool, gym, beachfront, laundry service, concierge, executive floor, public Wi-Fi, no-smoking rooms* ▤ *AE, D, DC, MC, V.*

$$$ 🏨 **Hilton Cocoa Beach Oceanfront.** In 2004, the seven-story hotel sus-
★ tained considerable hurricane damage, but thanks to a $15 million renovation, it's back as one of the best hotels in Cocoa Beach. Most rooms have ocean views, but for true drama get a room on the east end, facing the water. The hotel's best feature is its location, right on the beach. In season, a band plays poolside (on the 10,000-square-foot deck) on weekends, and activities directors keep kids busy with arts and crafts and surfing lessons. Pros: beachfront, friendly staff, clean. Cons: no refrigerators in standard rooms, overpriced restaurant, small pool. ✉ *1550 N. Atlantic Ave., 32931* ☏ *321/799–0003* 📠 *321/799–0344* ⊕ *www.hiltoncocoabeach.com* 🛏 *285 rooms, 11 suites* ⚘ *In-room: refrigerator (some), Wi-Fi. In-hotel: 2 restaurants, room service, bar, pool, gym, beachfront, laundry facilities, laundry service, executive floor, public Wi-Fi, parking (no fee), no-smoking rooms* ▤ *AE, D, DC, MC, V.*

$$–$$$ 🏨 **Holiday Inn Cocoa Beach Oceanfront Resort.** When two adjacent beach hotels were redesigned and a promenade park landscaped between them, the Holiday Inn Cocoa Beach Resort was born. Hit hard by the 2004 hurricanes, the oceanfront property underwent a multimillion-dollar renovation, with a complete exterior makeover and updates to guest rooms and meeting rooms. Standard rooms are modern, and designed in bright tropical colors. Suites and villas have a Key West feel, with louvered doors and rattan ceiling fans. Lodging options include standard and king rooms; oceanfront suites, which have a living room with sleeper sofa; villas; or bi-level lofts. Kids are given the royal treatment, with specially designed KidsSuites that feature bunk beds and video games and a pirate-ship pool with water-blasting cannons. Pros: beachfront, varied lodging options, fun pool area. Cons: small bathrooms, loud a/c in some rooms. ✉ *1300 N. Atlantic Ave., 32931* ☏ *321/783–2271 or 800/206–2747* 📠 *321/784–8878* ⊕ *www. hicocoabeachhotelsite.com* 🛏 *500 rooms, 119 suites* ⚘ *In-room: safe, kitchen (some), refrigerator (some), Wi-Fi. In-hotel: restaurant, bars, tennis courts, pool, gym, beachfront, laundry facilities, laundry service, executive floor, parking (no fee)* ▤ *AE, DC, MC, V.*

$$ 🏨 **Inn at Cocoa Beach.** One of the area's best, this charming oceanfront
★ inn has spacious, individually decorated rooms with four-poster beds, upholstered chairs, and balconies or patios; most have ocean views. Deluxe rooms are much larger, with a king-size bed, sofa, and sitting area; most also have a dining table. Jacuzzi rooms are different sizes. Several have fireplaces, and all have beautiful ocean views. Included in the rate are afternoon socials in the breezeway, evening wine and cheese, and a continental breakfast. Pros: quiet, romantic, honor bar. Cons: no on-site restaurant, "forced" socializing. ✉ *4300 Ocean*

Beach Blvd., 32931 ☎*321/799–3460, 800/343–5307 outside Florida* ☎*321/784–8632* ⊕*www.theinnatcocoabeach.com* ⌁*50 rooms* ⚬*In-room: safe, VCR (some) Wi-Fi. In-hotel: pool, beachfront, public Wi-Fi, parking (no fee), no-smoking rooms* ▭*AE, D, MC, V* ⦾*CP.*

$$ **Wakulla Suites Resort.** This kitschy two-story motel in a converted
★ 1970s apartment building is clean and comfortable and just off the beach. Some rooms are a block away from the water, and a few are just a walk down the boardwalk. The bright rooms are fairly ordinary, decorated in tropical prints. Completely furnished five-room suites, designed to sleep six, are great for families; each includes two bedrooms and a living room, dining room, and fully equipped kitchen. Pros: kitchen, BBQ grills. Cons: lots of kid noise, a hike to the beach, seven-day cancellation policy. ✉*3550 N. Atlantic Ave., 32931* ☎*321/783–2230 or 800/992–5852* ☎*321/783–0980* ⊕*www.wakullasuites.com* ⌁*117 suites* ⚬*In-room: kitchen, Wi-Fi. In-hotel: restaurant, pool, no elevator, laundry facilities, laundry service, parking (no fee), no-smoking rooms* ▭*AE, D, DC, MC, V.*

NIGHTLIFE

The **Cocoa Beach Pier** (✉*401 Meade Ave.* ☎*321/783–7549*) is for locals, beach bums, surfers, and people who don't mind the weather-worn wood and sandy, watery paths. At the **Mai Tiki Bar** they claim that "No Bar Goes This Far," which is true, considering it's at the end of the 800-foot pier. Come to **The Boardwalk** Friday night for the Boardwalk Bash, with live acoustic and rock-and-roll music; drop in Saturday for more live music; and come back Wednesday evening to catch the reggae band. For great live jazz, head to **Heidi's Jazz Club** (✉*7 Orlando Ave. N.* ☎*321/783–4559* ⊕*www.heidisjazzclub.com*). Local and nationally known musicians (Boots Randolph and Mose Allison have taken the stage) play Tuesday through Sunday, with showcase acts appearing on weekends.

SPORTS & THE OUTDOORS

The **Cocoa Beach Recreation Complex** (✉*5000 Tom Warriner Blvd.* ☎*321/868–3351*) is actually an extensive public sports complex that's owned by the city and open to anyone. Facilities include an Olympic-size swimming pool; soccer, softball, and baseball fields; a restaurant and snack bar; and a riverside pavilion with picnic tables. The **Cocoa Beach Country Club** (☎*321/868–3361*) offers 27 holes of championship golf (green fee: $44–$45) with an abundance of waterfowl and other birds, with species listed and information offered at each hole. The **Racquet Club** (☎*321/868–3224*) has 10 lighted tennis courts.

BIKING   Although there are no bike trails as such in the area, cycling is allowed on the beaches and the Cocoa Beach Causeway. Bikes can be rented hourly, daily, or weekly at **Ron Jon Surf Shop** (✉*4151 N. Atlantic Ave., Rte. A1A* ☎*321/799–8888*). Locks are available.

FISHING   The **Cocoa Beach Pier** (✉*401 Meade Ave.* ☎*321/783–7549*) has a bait-and-tackle shop and a fishing area. Although most of the pier is free to walk on, there's a $1 charge to enter the fishing area at the end of the

800-foot-long boardwalk, and a $3.50 fishing fee. You can rent rods and reels here.

KAYAKING Specializing in manatee encounters, **Adventure Kayak of Cocoa Beach** (☎321/480–8632) takes guests on one- and two-person kayak tours of mangroves, channels, and islands.

SURFING If you can't tell a tri-skeg stick from a hodaddy shredding the lip on a gnarly tube, then you may want to avail yourself of the **Ron Jon Surf School** (✉*150 E. Columbia La.* ☎*321/868–1980*). They teach grommets (dudes) and gidgets (chicks) from kids to seniors. Private lessons range from $60 for a one-hour lesson to $130 for three hours. Group lessons are $70 per person for three hours. Payment is strictly by cash, check, or traveler's check. **Ron Jon Watersports** (✉*4275 N. Atlantic Ave.* ☎*321/799–8888*) rents surfboards, body boards, and wet suits, as well as kayaks and bikes. The building also houses the **East Coast Surfing Hall of Fame and Museum.**

SHOPPING

Merritt Square Mall (✉*777 E. Merritt Island Causeway, Merritt Island* ☎*321/452–3272*), the area's only major shopping mall, is about a 20-minute ride from the beach. Stores include Macy's, Dillard's, JCPenney, Sears, Bath & Body Works, Foot Locker, Island Surf and Skate, and roughly 100 others. There's a six-screen multiplex, along with a food court and several restaurant chains. It's impossible to miss the

Fodor'sChoice **Ron Jon Surf Shop** (✉*4151 N. Atlantic Ave., Rte. A1A* ☎*321/799–*
★   *8888* ⊕*www.ronjons.com*). With a giant surfboard and an aqua, teal, and pink Art Deco facade, Ron Jon takes up nearly two blocks along A1A. What started in 1963 as a small T-shirt and bathing-suit shop has evolved into a 52,000-square-foot superstore that's open every day 'round the clock. The shop has water-sports gear as well as chairs and umbrellas for rent, and sells every kind of beachwear, surf wax, plus the requisite T-shirts and flip-flops. For up-to-the-minute surfing conditions, call the store and press 3 and then 7 for the **Ron Jon Surf and Weather Report.**

MELBOURNE

40 *20 mi south of Cocoa.*

Despite its dependence on the high-tech space industry, this town is decidedly laid-back. The majority of the city is on the mainland, but a small portion trickles onto a barrier island, separated by the Indian River Lagoon and accessible by several inlets, including the Sebastian Inlet.

It took 20,000 volunteers two weeks to turn 56 acres of forest and wetlands into the **Brevard Zoo,** the only American Zoo and Aquarium Association–accredited zoo built by a community. Stroll along the shaded boardwalks and get a close-up look at alligators, crocodiles, giant anteaters, marmosets, jaguars, eagles, river otters, kangaroos, exotic birds, and kookaburras. Alligator, crocodile, and river-otter feedings are held on alternate afternoons—although the alligators do not dine on the otters. Stop by Paws-On, an interactive learning playground where kids and adults can crawl into human-size gopher burrows, beehives, and spiderwebs; get cozy with several domestic animals in Animal Encounters; have a bird hop on your shoulder in the Australian Free Flight Aviary; and step up to the Wetlands Outpost, an elevated pavilion that's a gateway to 22 acres of wetlands through which you can paddle kayaks and keep an eye open for the 4,000 species of wildlife that live in these waters and woods. Overnight Zoo Safaris for kids ages 7–14 include a nighttime safari by flashlight and marshmallows cooked over a campfire. Picnic tables, a snack bar, and a gift shop complete the daytime picture. ⊠*8225 N. Wickham Rd.* ☎*321/254–9453* ⊕*www. brevardzoo.org* ☚*$10.50 adults, $7.50 children 2–12; train ride $3* ⊙*Daily 9:30–5.*

The **King Center for the Performing Arts** is one of the premier performance centers in Central Florida. Oddly enough, top-name performers often bypass Orlando to appear in this comfortable 2,000-seat hall. Call for a performance schedule. ⊠*3865 N. Wickham Rd.* ☎*321/242–2219 box office.*

OFF THE BEATEN PATH

Satellite Beach. The beaches of this sleepy little community just south of Patrick Air Force Base, about 15 mi south of Cocoa Beach on A1A, are cradled between the balmy Atlantic Ocean and biologically diverse Indian River Lagoon. It's a popular spot for family vacations because of its slow pace and lack of crowds.

Paradise Beach. Small and scenic, this 1,600-foot stretch of sand is part of a 10-acre park north of Indialantic, about 20 mi south of Cocoa Beach on A1A. It has showers, restrooms, picnic tables, a refreshment stand, and lifeguards in summer.

SPORTS & THE OUTDOORS

BASEBALL Even though they play in our nation's capital during the regular season, the **Washington Nationals** (⊠*5800 Stadium Pkwy.Viera* ☎*321/633–4487* ⊕*www.nationals.com*), formerly the Montreal Expos, use Melbourne's Space Coast Stadium for their spring-training site. Tickets are $7–$20. For the rest of the season, the facility is home to the **Brevard County Manatees** (☎*321/633–9200*), one of the Milwaukee Brewers' minor-league teams.

GOLF **Baytree National Golf Links** (⊠*8207 National Dr.* ☎*321/259–9060*) is an 18-hole course; green fee: $39–$74. **Viera East Golf Club** (⊠*2300 Clubhouse Dr., Viera* ✛*5 mi from Melbourne* ☎*321/639–6500 or 888/843–7232*) has a public 18-hole course; green fee: $31–$51.

INLAND TOWNS

Inland, peaceful little towns are separated by miles of two-lane roads running through acres of dense forest and flat pastureland and skirting one lake after another. There's not much else to see but cattle, though you may catch a glimpse of the state's few hills. Gentle and rolling, they're hardly worth noting to folks from true hill country, but they're significant enough in Florida for much of this area to be called the "hill and lake region."

DELAND

41 *21 mi southwest of Daytona Beach.*

The quiet town is home to Stetson University, established in 1886 by hat magnate John Stetson. Several inviting state parks are nearby; as for activities, there's great manatee-watching during winter, as well as skydiving for both spectators and participants.

Soaring ceilings and neoclassical furnishings provide the backdrop at the **Duncan Gallery of Art,** on the Stetson University campus. The gallery hosts exhibits by southeastern and national artists and Stetson students. ⊠*Stetson University, Sampson Hall, Michigan and Amelia Aves.* ☎*386/822–7386* ✉*Donation welcome* ⊙*Mon.–Sat. 10–4, Sun. 1–4.*

The **DeLand Museum of Art,** in the Cultural Arts Center across from Stetson University, has nationally recognized exhibits of painting, photography, sculpture, and fine crafts. ⊠*600 N. Woodland Blvd.* ☎*386/734–4371* ⊕*www.delandmuseum.com* ✉*Donation welcome* ⊙*Tues.–Sat. 10–4, Sun. 1–4.*

One of the most historically and scientifically significant collections of gems and minerals in the world can be found in the **Gillespie Museum,** on the Stetson University campus. ⊠*Stetson University, Michigan and Amelia Aves.* ☎*386/822–7330* ⊕*www.gillespiemuseum.stetson.edu* ✉*$2* ⊙*Call for hours.*

February is the top month for sighting sea cows at this designated manatee refuge, but they begin to head here in November, as soon as the water gets cold enough (below 68°F). (Your best bet for spotting a manatee is to walk along the boardwalk.) **Blue Spring State Park,** once a river port where paddle wheelers stopped to take on cargoes of oranges, also contains a historic homestead that is open to the public. Home to the largest spring on the St. Johns River, the park offers hiking, camping, and picnicking facilities. ⊠*2100 W. French Ave., Orange City* ☎*386/775–3663* ⊕*www.floridastateparks.org/bluespring/* ✉*$5 per vehicle, up to 8 people* ⊙*Daily 8–sunset.*

WHERE TO STAY & EAT

$–$$$ ✕**Original Holiday House.** The original location ("born" in 1959) of what has become a small chain of buffet restaurants is enormously popular with senior citizens, families, and college students (it's across from the Stetson University campus). Although the main draw is the buffet—salad only, salad and vegetables only, or the full buffet for less than $10—the menu also includes a short list of sandwiches and entrées. Holiday House uses only organic vegetables, bans MSG from all foods, and offers sugarless desserts. ⊠*704 Hwy. 17* ☎*386/734–6319* ♿*Reservations not accepted* ▭*D, MC, V* ⊙*Closed Mon.*

¢–$$ ✕**Main Street Grill.** The menu at this hugely popular restaurant has an Italian slant, but it also offers a variety of chicken, beef, and seafood entrées, as well as sandwiches and salads. Dine inside the historic brick building surrounded by colorful murals depicting downtown DeLand or outside on the patio by the manatee fountain. Regular diners praise the friendly and efficient waitstaff—and the cinnamon buns as big as your head. ⊠*100 E. New York Ave.* ☎*386/740–9535* ⚛*Reservations not accepted* ⊟*AE, MC, V.*

$$–$$$ ▥ **Holiday Inn DeLand.** An enormous painting by nationally known local artist Fred Messersmith dominates the welcoming lobby at this slightly dated, yet reliable, hotel. Guest rooms are done in a dizzying array of pastels and come with conveniences like refrigerators, microwaves, and tea/coffeemakers; prestige suites have housed the likes of actor Tom Cruise. Tennis and golf privileges at the DeLand Country Club are offered. Pros: free Wi-Fi, pet friendly, refrigerators and microwaves in every room. Cons: slow elevators, spotty service. ⊠*350 International Speedway Blvd. (U.S. 92), 32724* ☎*386/734–7552* ⎙*386/943–9091* ⊕*www.holiday-inn.com/delandfl* ⇆*148 rooms, 12 suites* ⚿*In-room: refrigerator (some), ethernet. In-hotel: restaurant, room service, bar, pool, gym, laundry facilities, laundry service, executive floor, public Wi-Fi, parking (no fee), some pets allowed (fee), no-smoking rooms* ⊟*AE, D, DC, MC, V.*

¢–$$ ▥ **University Inn.** For years this older motel in historical DeLand has been the choice of business travelers and visitors to Stetson University. The inn is adjacent to campus, and has reasonable rates and a courteous staff. It also doesn't hurt that it's clean, well maintained, and has one of the largest pools in the area. Pros: inexpensive, proximity to campus, clean. Cons: only one suite, dated atmosphere. ⊠*644 N. Woodland Blvd., 32720* ☎*386/734–5711 or 800/345–8991* ⎙*386/734–5716* ⊕*www.universityinndeland.com* ⇆*57 rooms, 1 suite* ⚿*In-room: refrigerator, dial-up. In-hotel: pool, gym, no elevator, parking (no fee), some pets allowed (fee), no-smoking rooms* ⊟*AE, D, MC, V* ▥|*CP.*

THE OUTDOORS

BOATING &
FISHING

Pontoon boats, houseboats, bass boats, and fishing-guide service for the St. Johns River are available from **Hontoon Landing Marina** (⊠*2317 River Ridge Rd.* ☎*386/734–2474 or 800/248–2474*). One of the savviest guides to bass fishing in the St. Johns River and Central Florida lakes is Bob Stonewater of **Bob Stonewater's Trophy Bass Guide Service** (☎*800/835–2851*), who offers five- and nine-hour trips for solo or duo anglers.

SKYDIVING

In addition to hosting competitions, DeLand has tandem jumping. You are literally attached to an experienced instructor-diver, which means that even novices are able to take their maiden voyage after one day. **Skydive DeLand** (⊠*1600 Flightline Blvd.* ☎*386/738–3539*), open daily 8 AM–sunset, offers lessons.

DE LEÓN SPRINGS

42 *7 mi northwest of DeLand, 26 mi southwest of Daytona Beac .*

The town (population 1,500) is a small spot on the map just outs
the eastern edge of the Ocala National Forest.

Near the end of the 19th century, **De León Springs State Park** was promoted as a fountain of youth to winter guests. Today visitors are attracted to the year-round 72°F springs for swimming, fishing, canoeing, and kayaking. Nature trails draw hikers and outdoor enthusiasts. Explore an abandoned sugar mill at **Lake Woodruff National Wildlife Refuge**—accessible through DeLeón Springs—which also has 18,000 acres of lakes, creeks, and marshes for scuba diving, canoeing, and hiking. ⊠ *601 Ponce de León Blvd. at Burt Parks Rd., east off U.S. 17* ☎ *386/985–4212* ⊕ *www.floridastateparks.org/deleonsprings* ⊠ *$5 per vehicle, up to 8 people* ⊙ *Daily 8–sunset.*

WHERE TO EAT

$$–$$$ ✕ **Karlings Inn.** A sort of Bavarian Brigadoon set beside a forgotten highway, this restaurant is decorated like a Black Forest inn inside and out. Karl Caeners oversees the preparation of the sauerbraten, red cabbage, and succulent roast duckling, as well as charcoal-grilled steaks, seafood, and fresh veal. The menu has Swiss, German, French, and Italian selections, and house specialties include blue crab cakes with spicy apricot sauce, seafood sausages (a blend of scallops, shrimp, and fish) served with a sauce made with smoked chorizo and toasted garlic, and roasted duck with Montmorency sauce. Locals say the fried lobster-tail appetizers alone are worth the trip. Be sure to leave room for the dessert tray. ⊠ *4640 N. U.S. Hwy. 17* ☎ *386/985–5535* ▤ *MC, V* ⊙ *Closed Mon. No lunch Tues.–Sat. No dinner Sun.*

¢ ✕ **The Old Spanish Sugar Mill Grill and Griddle House.** You may enjoy poking around the old sugar mill, but there's a lot more fun inside: pitchers of homemade batter arrive at your table, where *you* do the pouring and flipping. Top the pancakes off with blueberries, bananas, pecans, or whatever else is available (get creative since it's all-you-can-eat). Side items include sausage, ham, bacon, eggs, and homemade breads. Although breakfast fare is available until 4 PM (the place closes at 5), salads and sandwiches are also on the menu during lunch hours. You have to pay the $5 admission to the park to eat at the restaurant. ⊠ *De León Springs State Recreation Area, Ponce de León Blvd. at Burt Parks Rd., east off U.S. 17* ☎ *386/985–5644* ▤ *MC, V* ⚏ *Reservations not accepted* ⊙ *No dinner.*

FOREST

*ntrance 40 mi west of Daytona Beach, northern entrance 52
of Jacksonville.*

...thtaking 389,000-acre wilderness with lakes, springs, rivers, ...ails, campgrounds, and historic sites has three major recre-...reas (listed here from east to west): **Alexander Springs** (✉*Off ...ia Rte. 445 S*) has a swimming lake and a campground; **Salt Springs** (✉*Off Rte. 40 via Rte. 19 N*) has a natural saltwater spring where Atlantic blue crabs come to spawn each summer; **Juniper Springs** (✉*Off Rte. 40*) includes a stone waterwheel house, a campground, a natural-spring swimming pool, and hiking and canoe trails. About 30 campsites are sprinkled throughout the park and range from bare sites to those with electric hookups, showers, and bathrooms. Note that credit cards aren't accepted. ✉*Visitor center, 17147 E. Hwy. 40, Silver Springs* ☏*352/625–2520* ⊕*www.fs.fed.us/r8/florida* ⌨*Alexander Springs, Salt Springs, Juniper Springs: $4.*

THE OUTDOORS

CANOEING
The 7-mi **Juniper Springs run** is a narrow, twisting, and winding canoe ride, which, although exhilarating, is not for the novice. Canoe rentals and guided tours are available through **Juniper Springs Canoe Rentals** (☏*352/625–2808*) inside the park.

FISHING
Captain Tom's Custom Charters (☏*352/236–0872*) allows you to charter fishing trips ranging from three hours to a full day, and offers sightseeing cruises as well.

HORSEBACK RIDING
The stable closest to Ocala that's open to the public, **Fiddler's Green Ranch** (✉*Demko Rd., Altoona* ☏*352/669–7111 or 800/947–2624*) organizes trail rides into the national forest.

OCALA

 78 mi west of Daytona Beach, 123 mi southwest of Jacksonville.

This is horse country. Here at the forest's western edge are dozens of horse farms with grassy paddocks and white wooden fences. Hills and sweeping fields of bluegrass make the area feel more like Kentucky than Florida, which is entirely appropriate. The peaceful town is considered a center for thoroughbred breeding and training, and Kentucky Derby winners have been raised in the region's training centers. Sometimes the farms are open to the public.

The **Appleton Museum of Art**, a three-building cultural complex, is a marble-and-granite tour de force with a serene esplanade and reflecting pool. The collection lives up to its surroundings, thanks to more than 6,000 pre-Columbian, Asian, and African artifacts and 19th-century objets d'art. ✉*4333 N.E. Silver Springs Blvd.* ☏*352/291–4455* ⊕*www.appletonmuseum.org* ⌨*$6* ۞*Tues.–Sat. 10–5, Sun. noon–5.*

Retired drag racer Don Garlit pays tribute to the cars and the drivers of that sport at **Garlit's Museum of Drag Racing**. Among his extensive collection are a 1963 Pontiac Firebird Jet, the only car to run more than 290 mph in the ¼ mi; a rare 1904 Orient Buckboard, a consumer automobile built predominantly out of wood; and a 1956 Chrysler sedan once owned by President Eisenhower. ⊠*13700 S.W. 16th Ave.* ☎*877/271–3278* ⊕*www.garlits.com* 🏷*$15 adults, $6 children 5–12* ☉*Daily 9–5.*

OFF THE BEATEN PATH

Silver Springs. The 350-acre natural theme park outside Ocala at the western edge of the Ocala National Forest has the world's largest collection of artesian springs. The state's first tourist attraction, it was established in 1890. Today the park presents wild-animal displays, glass-bottom-boat tours in the Silver River, a Jeep safari through 35 acres of wilderness, and walks through natural habitats. Exhibits include the Panther Prowl, which enables visitors to watch and photograph the endangered Florida panther, and the Big Gator Lagoon, a ½-acre swamp featuring alligators. New attractions include the Fort King River Cruise and the Lighthouse Ride, a combination carousel/gondola ride giving guests a bird's-eye view of the park. A great place to cool off, **Silver Springs Wild Waters** (☎*352/236–2121* ⊕*www.wildwaterspark. com*) has a 450,000-gallon wave pool and eight waterslides and high-speed flumes. The water park is open April through September; admission is $23.99. ⊠*Rte. 40, Exit 352 east off I–75 or Exit 268 west off I–95, 5656 E. Silver Springs Blvd., Silver Springs* ☎*352/236–2121* ⊕*www.silversprings.com* 🏷*Silver Springs: $33.99 adults, $24.99 children 3–10; Wild Waters: $23.99 adults, $20.99 children under 48"; combo ticket, $36.99 adults, $27.99 children* ☉*Silver Springs: daily 10–5, Wild Waters: call for operating schedule.*

WHERE TO STAY & EAT

$$–$$$$ ✕**Arthur's.** Don't pass up this elegant restaurant, in an open area at the back of the lobby in the Ocala Silver Springs Hilton. Filet mignon with port sauce and chicken breast stuffed with spinach and sun-dried tomatoes are favorites. The Sunday brunch is a must. ⊠*3600 S.W. 36th Ave.* ☎*352/854–1400* 🖃*AE, D, DC, MC, V* ☉*No lunch Sat.*

$$$ 🏨**Ocala Silver Springs Hilton.** Only in Ocala would you find a hotel with its own paddock and resident horses (in this case, a Clydesdale named Buddy, a thoroughbred named Spicy Soup, and her foal Holy Guacamole). A winding, tree-lined boulevard leads to this nine-story pink tower nestled in a wooded patch of countryside just off Interstate 75 and a bit removed from downtown. The marble-floor lobby has a piano bar and is home to The Comedy Zone. The spacious guest rooms are decorated in stripes and floral prints in autumn shades of forest green, sand, and burnt orange. Pros: spacious rooms, complimentary breakfast, walking distance to restaurants. Cons: spotty service, small gym, some eyesore views. ⊠*3600 S.W. 36th Ave., 34474* ☎*352/854–1400 or 877/602–4023* 🖨*352/854–6073* ⊕*www.hiltonocala.com* ⇆*193 rooms, 8 suites* ⚭*In-room: refrigerator (some), Wi-Fi. In-hotel: restaurant, room service, bar, tennis court, pool, gym, laundry service, executive level, public Wi-Fi, parking (free), no-smoking rooms,* 🖃*AE, D, DC, MC, V.*

$$–$$$ ⚏ **Seven Sisters Inn.** A pair of showplace Queen Anne mansions func-
★   tions as a B&B, especially popular with honeymooners and anniversary
celebrants. Each themed room (some, quite over the top) has period
antiques and its own bath; some rooms have a fireplace, some a canopy
bed. A loft furnished with wicker sleeps four. Rates include a delicious
breakfast, served in Monet's Morning Room, and afternoon tea. Enjoy
a romantic candlelight dinner in the privacy of your room, or join
your fellow inn-mates for an evening of murder-mystery theater ($55
per person, includes dinner and wine). Pros: romantic, gourmet breakfast, friendly staff. Cons: small rooms, no restaurant. ⊠ *820 S.E. Fort
King St., 32671* ☎ *352/867–1170 or 800/250–3496* 🖷 *352/867–5266*
⊕ *www.sevensistersinn.com* ↩ *13 rooms* 🔑 *In-room: VCR (some),
Wi-Fi. In-hotel: bicycles, no elevator, public Wi-Fi, parking (no fee),
no kids under 12, no-smoking rooms* ⊟ *AE, D, MC, V* ⏐⊙⏐*BP.*

SPORTS & THE OUTDOORS

GOLF   Twenty miles south of Ocala, **El Diablo Golf & Country Club** (⊠ *10405 N.
Sherman Dr., Citrus Springs* ☎ *352/465–0986 or 877/353–4225*) has
a public 18-hole course; green fee: $25–$50.

JAI ALAI   One of the speediest of sports, jai alai is played year-round at **Ocala Jai-
Alai** (⊠ *4601 N.W. Hwy. 318, Orange Lake* ☎ *352/591–2345*).

MICANOPY

45   *36 mi north of Ocala.*

Though this was the state's oldest inland town, site of both a Timucuan
Indian settlement and a Spanish mission, there are few traces left from
before white settlement, which began in 1821. Micanopy (pronounced
micka-*no*-pea) does still draw those interested in the past, however. The
main street of this beautiful little town has quite a few antiques shops,
and in fall roughly 200 antiques dealers descend on the town for the
annual Harvest Fall Festival.

A 20,000-acre wildlife preserve with ponds, lakes, trails, and a visitor
★   center with a museum, **Paynes Prairie State Preserve** is a wintering area
for many migratory birds where alligators, wild horses, and a herd of
American bison also roam. There was once a vast lake here, but a century ago it drained so abruptly that thousands of beached fish died in
the mud. The remains of a ferry stranded in the 1880s can still be seen.
Swimming, boating, picnicking, and camping are permitted. ⊠ *Off
U.S. 441, 1 mi north of Micanopy, 100 Savannah Blvd.* ☎ *352/466–
3397* ⊕ *www.floridastateparks.org/paynesprairie* 🖾 *$4 per vehicle, up
to 8 people* ⊙ *Daily 8–sunset.*

OFF THE
BEATEN
PATH

Marjorie Kinnan Rawlings State Historic Site. The presence of Rawlings,
whose works include *The Yearling* and *Cross Creek*, permeates this
National Historic Landmark home where the typewriter rusts on the
ramshackle porch, the closet where she hid her booze during Prohibition yawns open, and clippings from her scrapbook reveal her legal
battles and marital problems. Bring lunch, and picnic in the shade of

one of Rawlings's citrus trees. Then visit her grave a few miles away at peaceful Island Grove. ✉ *18700 S. C.R. 325, Cross Creek* ☎ *352/466–3672* ⊕ *www.floridastateparks.org/marjoriekinnanrawlings* ◻ *$2 per vehicle, up to 8 people; tours $3* ⊘ *Thurs.–Sun. 10–4; tours at 10, 11, and hourly 1–4 Oct.–July.*

WHERE TO STAY

$$ ☐ **Herlong Mansion.** Spanish moss clings to the stately oak trees surrounding this restored mansion built in the 1800s. The imposing Greek Revival–style B&B has Corinthian columns and wide verandas perfect for relaxing in a rocker. Rooms and suites have period furniture, Oriental rugs, lead-glass windows, and claw-foot tubs; some rooms have whirlpools. A multicourse breakfast, which is included in the rate, is an event here. Emphasis is on personal attention without intrusion; guests appreciate the service without feeling rushed. Pros: large private bathrooms, gourmet breakfast, evening wine and cheese reception. Cons: no phones in rooms, no TVs in some rooms, some small and windowless rooms. ✉ *402 N.E. Cholokka Blvd., 32667* ☎ *352/466–3322 or 800/437–5664* ⊕ *www.herlong.com* ⊃ *12 rooms, 2 cottages* ⟨ *In-room: no phone, kitchen (some), DVD (some), VCR (some), no TV (some) Wi-Fi. In-hotel: no elevator, public Wi-Fi, parking (no fee), no kids under 12, no-smoking rooms* ☰ *AE, D, MC, V* ⌼ *BP.*

GAINESVILLE

46 *11 mi north of Micanopy on U.S. 441.*

The University of Florida anchors this sprawling town. Visitors are mostly Gator football fans and parents of university students, so the styles and costs of accommodations are primarily aimed at budget-minded travelers rather than luxury-seeking vacationers. The surrounding area encompasses several state parks and interesting gardens and geological sites.

On the campus of the University of Florida, the **Florida Museum of Natural History** has several interesting replicas, including a Maya palace, a typical Timucuan household, and a full-size model of a Florida cave and mangrove forest. The collections from throughout Florida's history warrant at least half a day. ✉ *University of Florida, S.W. 34th St. at Hull Rd.* ☎ *352/846–2000* ⊕ *www.flmnh.ufl.edu* ◻ *Free* ⊘ *Mon.–Sat. 10–5, Sun. 1–5.*

About 10,000 years ago an underground cavern collapsed and created a geological treat. At **Devil's Millhopper State Geological Site,** see the botanical wonderland of exotic subtropical ferns and trees growing in the 500-foot-wide, 120-foot-deep sinkhole. You pass a dozen small waterfalls as you head down 232 steps to the bottom. ✉ *4732 Millhopper Rd., off U.S. 441* ☎ *352/955–2008* ⊕ *www.floridastateparks.org/ devilsmillhopper* ◻ *$2 per vehicle, up to 8 people* ⊘ *Wed.–Sun. 9–5.*

WHERE TO STAY & EAT

$$$–$$$$ ✕ **Melting Pot.** Eating is a group activity at this fondue spot; sit down-stairs or upstairs in the cozy loft. Dip slivers of fish or steak in sizzling hot oil, or cubes of crusty French bread in pots of melted cheese. Save room for dessert—more fondue, naturally—pieces of fruit you dip into rich melted chocolate. By the time you leave, you might smell like a fry cook, but most diners agree it's worth any olfactory unpleasant-ries. ⊠418 E. University Ave. ☎352/372–5623 ☰AE, D, DC, MC, V ⊘No lunch.

$$$–$$$$ ✕ **Paramount Grill.** You may be rubbing elbows with your neighbor, but the meal is definitely worth the inconvenience. Try one of the five house salads and such entrées as grilled Angus filet served with shiitake-mush-room sherry-wine sauce and white truffle sauce or pan-roasted pork tenderloin with creamy blue-cheese polenta and apple-cider lemon-thyme sauce. If you miss dinner here, try the Sunday brunch. ⊠12 S.W. 1st Ave. ☎352/378–3398 ☰AE, MC, V ⊘No lunch Sat. and Sun.

$$–$$$$ ✕ **Sovereign.** Crystal and candlelight set a tone of restrained elegance
★ in this 1878 carriage house. An iron gate and a narrow walkway lead back to the elegant dining room. Veal specialties are notable, particu-larly the saltimbocca, braised in white wine, flavored with sage, and topped with ham. Beef Wellington and rack of baby lamb are depend-able choices, too. ⊠12 S.E. 2nd Ave. ☎352/378–6307 ⌂Reserva-tions essential ☰AE, D, DC, MC, V ⊘Closed Sun. No lunch.

$–$$$ ✕ **Emiliano's Cafe.** Linen tablecloths and Art Deco-ish artwork create a casual, elegant feel here. Dine indoors or beneath the stars on the side-walk café. Start with the Galician stew (a family recipe) or the black bean soup, and then move on to one of the chef's signature dishes—Spanish saffron rice with shrimp, clams, mussels, fresh fish, chicken, artichoke hearts, peas, asparagus, and pimientos. Emiliano's also offers an extensive tapas menu with more than 40 items to mix and match. ⊠7 S.E. 1st Ave. ☎352/375–7381 ☰AE, D, MC, V.

$–$$ ✕ **Bistro 1245.** Get high-quality meals at bargain-basement prices at this trendy yet surprisingly down-to-earth restaurant. The bistro sir-loin steak and three-herb pesto with chicken are favorite menu items. For a lighter meal, and a lighter price, order off the lunch menu in the evening. ⊠1245 W. University Ave. ☎352/376–0000 ☰AE, D, DC, MC, V.

¢ ✕ **Leonardo's by the Slice.** It's ironic that the kitschy pizza joint with a '50s flair is surrounded by a white picket fence, since most of its patrons and employees are far from conventional. College students, especially the pierced and tatted-up kind, flock to the Gainesville land-mark not only because it's cheap but because it has the best pizza in town. Available in thick or thin varieties, by the pie and, of course, by the slice, Leonardo's pizza comes in a handful of varieties (like veggie, pepperoni, Greek, and spinach tomato). They also offer calzones, sal-ads, and pasta such as baked ziti and spinach lasagna, with no entrée over $6. ⊠1245 W. University Ave. ☎352/375–2007 ⌂Reservations not accepted ☰AE, D, MC, V.

$$$ ▦ **Hilton University of Florida Conference Center Gainesville.** With 25,000 square feet of meeting space, the University of Florida's flagship hotel

2

caters most obviously to business travelers. Its location on the southwest corner of the campus also makes it a good choice for UF visitors. Guest rooms, which look like they came straight off the Rooms To Go show floor (blond-wood armoires, overstuffed couches with geometric-pattern throw pillows), have two phones with voicemail, large work desks, coffeemakers, MP3 players, and complimentary high-speed Internet. Pros: proximity to college, free Internet, spacious rooms. Cons: 4 PM check-in, spotty service, overrated restaurant. ⊠*1714 S.W. 34th St., 32607* ☎*352/371–3600* 🖷*352/371–0306* ⊕*www.ufhilton. com* ⬅*245 rooms, 3 suites* ♿*In room: kitchen (some), ethernet. In hotel: restaurant, room service, bar, pool, gym, laundry service, concierge, public Wi-Fi, parking (no fee), no-smoking rooms.*

$–$$$ 🏨 **The Magnolia Plantation Bed and Breakfast Inn.** You'll be within minutes of historic downtown and the University of Florida, and owners Joe and Cindy Montalto will welcome you like old friends, whether you stay in the main house or in one of the adorable cottages. The inn's unique French Second Empire architecture is one of only a handful of such examples in the southeastern United States. The lush gardens and gazebos offer quiet, shady spots to relax. All rooms have a private bath. A full breakfast is standard fare and is served in the formal dining room or in the privacy of your cottage. Children and pets are welcome with prior approval. Pros: friendly service, breakfast, nightly social hour. Cons: small rooms, seven-day cancellation policy, some uncomfortable beds. ⊠*309 S.E. 7th St., 32601* ☎*352/375–6653 or 800/201–2379* 🖷*352/338–0303* ⊕*www.magnoliabnb.com* ⬅*5 rooms, 6 cottages* ♿*In-room: kitchen (some), DVD (some), VCR (some), no TV (some), dial-up, Wi-Fi. In-hotel: pool, laundry facilities, parking (no fee), some pets allowed (fee), no-smoking rooms* ▤*AE, D, MC, V* ⋈*CP.*

$–$$$ 🏨 **Sweetwater Branch Inn Bed & Breakfast.** You'll find such modern conveniences as data ports, hair dryers, and business services mixed with Southern charm and hospitality, all wrapped up in two grand Victorian homes surrounded by lush tropical gardens. Gleaming hardwood floors and antique furnishings lend a European flair to nicely appointed rooms. The Sweetwater is in historic downtown, adjacent to the University of Florida, and within walking distance of many of the area's better restaurants and entertainment venues. Pros: Southern breakfast, Jacuzzi suites, location. Cons: spotty service, frequent on-site weddings. ⊠*625 E. University Ave., 32601* ☎*352/373–6760 or 800/595–7760* 🖷*352/371–3771* ⊕*www.sweetwaterinn.com* ⬅*12 rooms, 6 suites* ♿*In-room: kitchen (some), refrigerator (some), Wi-Fi. In-hotel: public Wi-Fi, parking (no fee), no-smoking rooms* ▤*AE, MC, V* ⋈*CP.*

NIGHTLIFE

Locals head to **Calico Jack's Oyster Bar** (⊠*3501 S.W. 2nd Ave.* ☎*352/375–2337*) for seafood, beer, and live music. Get your caffeine and live-music fixes at **Common Grounds** (⊠*210 S.W. 2nd Ave.* ☎*352/372–7320*), which spotlights an eclectic mix of bands. Gainesville's oldest bar, **Lillian's Music Store** (⊠*112 S.E. 1st St.* ☎*352/372–1010*), has rock and Top 40 music, bands, and karaoke. **Market Street Pub** (⊠*120 S.W. 1st Ave.* ☎*352/377–2927*) brews its own beer and has live music on weekends and a DJ some weeknights.

AUTO RACING   The **Gainesville Raceway** ($\boxtimes$*11211 N. County Rd. 225* $\textcircled{a}$*352/377–0046, 626/914–4761 for National Hot Rod Association*) is the site of professional and amateur auto and motorcycle races, including Gatornationals in March, as well as a drag-racing school.

NORTHEAST FLORIDA ESSENTIALS

To research prices, get advice from other travelers, and book arrangements, visit www.fodors.com.

TRANSPORTATION

BY AIR

The main airport for the region is Jacksonville International (JAX). It's served by AirTran, American, Comair, Continental and Continental Connection/Express, Delta, Executive, jetBlue, Midway, Northwest, Southwest, United Express, US Airways, and US Airways Express. Continental, Delta, and Vintage Props & Jets serve Daytona Beach International Airport (DAB). Gainesville Regional Airport (GNV) is served by Delta Connection and US Airways Express. Although Orlando isn't part of the area, visitors to northeastern Florida often choose to arrive at Orlando International Airport (MCO) because of the huge number of convenient flights. Driving east from Orlando on the Beeline Expressway brings you to Cocoa Beach in about an hour. Reach Daytona, about a two-hour drive, by taking the Beeline Expressway to Interstate 95 and driving north.

Contacts AirTran ($\textcircled{a}$*800/247–8726*). **American** ($\textcircled{a}$*800/433–7300*). **Continental and Continental Connection/Express** ($\textcircled{a}$*800/523–3273*). **Delta** ($\textcircled{a}$*800/221–1212*). **Delta Connection** ($\textcircled{a}$*800/282–3424*). **jetBlue** ($\textcircled{a}$*800/538–2583*). **Northwest** ($\textcircled{a}$*800/225–2525*). **Southwest** ($\textcircled{a}$*800/435–9792*). **United Express** ($\textcircled{a}$*800/241–6522*). **US Airways and US Airways Express** ($\textcircled{a}$*800/428–4322*). **Vintage Props & Jets** ($\textcircled{a}$*800/852–0275*).

AIRPORTS &   At Jacksonville International, free shuttles run from the terminal to all
TRANSFERS   parking lots (except the garage) around the clock. Taxi service is available from a number of companies, including Gator City Taxi and Yellow Cab, with fares to downtown approximately $28 and $45 to the beaches and Amelia Island. Shuttle service is available from Gator City Shuttle for approximately $32 for one to four people going downtown, $42 for one to four people going to the beaches and Amelia Island. Limousine service is available from Carey Jacksonville for approximately $78 to downtown and $99 to the beaches and Amelia Island (one to four people), and reservations are required. From Daytona Beach International Airport, taxi fare to beach hotels runs about $18 to $25. Taxi companies include Yellow Cab and Checker Cab. DOTS Transit Service has scheduled service connecting the Daytona Beach and Orlando International airports, the Sheraton Palm Coast area, DeLand (including its train station), New Smyrna Beach, Sanford, and Deltona; fares are $27 one-way and $49 round-trip between the Day-

tona and Orlando airports, $32 one-way and $43 round-trip from the Orlando airport to DeLand or Deltona. From the Gainesville Regional Airport, taxi fare to the center of Gainesville is about $17; some hotels provide free airport pickup.

Airport Contacts **Daytona Beach International Airport** (*[DAB]* ☎ *386/248–8069* ⊕ *www.flydaytonafirst.com*). **Gainesville Regional Airport** (*[GNV]* ☎ *352/373–0249* ⊕ *www.gra-gnv.com*). **Jacksonville International Airport** (*[JAX]* ☎ *904/741–4902* ⊕ *www.jaa.aero*). **Orlando International Airport** (*[MCO]* ☎ *407/825–2001* ⊕ *www.orlandoairports.net*).

Transfer Contacts **Carey Jacksonville** (☎ *904/992–2022*). **Checker Cab** (☎ *904/765–9999*). **DOTS Transit Service** (☎ *386/257–5411 or 800/231–1965*). **Gator City Shuttle** (☎ *904/741–6650*). **Gator City Taxi** (☎ *904/741–0008*). **Yellow Cab** (☎ *904/355–8294*).

BY BOAT

Connecting the north and south banks of the St. Johns River, in Jacksonville, the S.S. Marine Taxi runs between several locations, including the Hilton Jacksonville Riverfront and the Jacksonville Landing. During football season, the water taxi also makes trips to ALLTEL Stadium on game days and for special events like the Florida/Georgia game. The one-way trip takes about five minutes. The ferry runs Sunday–Thursday 11 AM–9 PM; Friday and Saturday 11 AM–11 PM (except during rain or other bad weather). Round-trip fare is $5 adults, $4 children; one-way fare is $3 adults, $2 children.

Contacts **S.S. Marine Taxi** (☎ *904/733–7782* ⊕ *www.jaxwatertaxi.com*).

BY BUS

Greyhound Lines serves the region, with full-service terminals in Jacksonville, Daytona Beach, DeLand, Gainesville, Ocala, and St. Augustine. The Jacksonville Transportation Authority (JTA) serves Jacksonville and the beaches with weekday service to Orange Park, Palatka, and Green Cove Springs. Daytona Beach has an excellent bus network, Votran, which serves the beach area, airport, shopping malls, and major arteries, including service to DeLand and New Smyrna Beach and the Express Link to Orlando. Exact fare is required for Votran ($1–$2) and JTA (75¢–$1.50).

Contacts **Greyhound Lines** (☎ *800/231–2222* ⊕ *www.greyhound.com*). **Jacksonville Transportation Authority** (☎ *904/630–3100* ⊕ *www.jtafla.com*). **Votran** (☎ *386/756–7496* ⊕ *www.votran.com*).

BY CAR

East–west traffic travels the northern part of the state on Interstate 10, a cross-country highway stretching from Los Angeles to Jacksonville. Farther south, Interstate 4 connects Florida's west and east coasts. Signs on Interstate 4 designate it an east–west route, but actually the road rambles northeast from Tampa to Orlando, then heads north–northeast to Daytona. Two interstates head north–south on Florida's peninsula: Interstate 95 on the east coast (from Miami to Houlton, Maine) and Interstate 75 on the west. If you want to drive as close to the Atlantic as possible and are not in a hurry, stick with A1A. It runs along the barrier islands, changing its name several times along the way. Where there are no bridges between islands, cars must return to the mainland via causeways; some are low, with drawbridges that open for boat traffic on the inland waterway, and there can be unexpected delays. The Buccaneer Trail, which overlaps part of Route A1A, goes from St. Augustine north to Mayport (where a ferry is part of the state highway system), through marshlands and beaches, to the 300-year-old seaport town of Fernandina Beach, and then finally into Fort Clinch State Park. Route 13, also known as the William Bartram Trail, runs from Jacksonville to East Palatka along the east side of the St. Johns River through tiny hamlets. It's one of the most scenic drives in north Florida—a two-laner lined with huge oaks that hug the riverbanks—very Old Florida. U.S. 17 travels the west side of the river, passing through Green Cove Springs and Palatka. Route 40 runs east–west through the Ocala National Forest, giving a nonstop view of stately pines and bold wildlife; short side roads lead to parks, springs, picnic areas, and campgrounds.

BY TRAIN

Amtrak schedules stops in Jacksonville, Daytona Beach, DeLand, Gainesville, Waldo (near Gainesville), Ocala, and Palatka. The Auto Train carries cars between Orlando and Lorton, Virginia (just south of Washington, D.C.). Schedules vary depending on the season.

Contacts **Amtrak** (☎ *800/872-7245* ⊕ *www.amtrak.com*).

CONTACTS & RESOURCES

EMERGENCIES
All of the following hospitals have 24-hour emergency rooms.

Emergency Services ☎*911.*

Hospitals **Baptist Medical Center** (⊠ *800 Prudential Dr., Jacksonville* ☎ *904/202-2000*). **Baptist Medical Center Beaches** (⊠ *1350 13th Ave. S, Jacksonville Beach* ☎ *904/627-2900*). **Bert Fish Medical Center** (⊠ *401 Palmetto St., New Smyrna Beach* ☎ *386/424-5000*). **Florida Hospital Oceanside** (⊠ *264 S. Atlantic Ave., Ormond Beach* ☎ *386/672-4161*). **Florida Hospital Ormond Memorial** (⊠ *875 Sterthaus Ave., Ormond Beach* ☎ *386/676-6000*). **Halifax Medical Center** (⊠ *303 N. Clyde Morris Blvd., Daytona Beach* ☎ *386/254-4100*). **Munroe Regional Medical Center** (⊠ *1500 S.W. 1st Ave., Ocala* ☎ *352/351-7200*). **Orange Park Medical Center** (⊠ *2001 Kingsley Ave., Orange Park* ☎ *904/276-8500*). **Shands at AGH** (⊠ *801 S.W. 2nd Ave., Gainesville* ☎ *352/372-4321*). **Shands Jacksonville** (⊠ *655 W. 8th St., Jacksonville* ☎ *904/244-0411*). **St. Luke's Hospital** (⊠ *4201 Belfort Rd., Jacksonville* ☎ *904/296-3700*). **St. Vincent's Medical Center** (⊠ *1800 Barrs St., Jacksonville* ☎ *904/308-7300*).

TOURS
In Jacksonville, River Cruises has relaxing lunch and dinner-dancing cruises and private sightseeing charters aboard the *Annabelle Lee* and *Lady St. Johns* paddleboats; schedules vary with the season. The Jacksonville Historical Society arranges tours only for groups of 20 or more. On Amelia Island, Amelia River Cruises and Charters takes guests on a one-hour narrated tour of Fernandina's historic waterfront, salt

marshes, and Cumberland Sound. In St. Augustine, Old Town Trolley Tours conducts fully narrated tours covering more than 100 points of interest. As the nation's oldest continually operated carriage company, the St. Augustine Transfer Company offers historic and ghost tours via horse-drawn carriage, as well as the Spirits of St. Augustine Ghost Walk. In Daytona Beach, A Tiny Cruise Line leaves from the public marina and explores the Intracoastal Waterway. Tour Time, Inc. offers custom group and individual motorcoach tours of Jacksonville, Amelia Island, and St. Augustine, as well as overnight trips to Silver Springs, Kennedy Space Center, Orlando, Okefenokee Swamp, and Savannah. Prior arrangements are required. New Smyrna Beach's Florida Coastal Cruises takes guests on narrated cruises (lunch, sunset, and dinner) of the Intracoastal Waterway.

Contacts **River Cruises** (☎ *904/306–2200* ⊕ *www.jaxrivercruises.com*). **Jacksonville Historical Society** (☎ *904/665–0064* ⊕ *www.jaxhistory.com*). **Amelia River Cruises and Charters** (☎ *904/261–9972* ⊕ *www.jaxhistory.com*). **Old Town Trolley Tours** (☎ *904/829–3800* ⊕ *www.historictours.com/staugustine*). **St. Augustine Transfer Company** (☎ *904/829–2391* ⊕ *www.staugustinetransfer. com*). **A Tiny Cruise Line** (☎ *386/226–2343* ⊕ *www.visitdaytona.com/tinycruise*). **Tour Time, Inc.** (☎ *904/282–8500 or 800/822–4278* ⊕ *www.tourtimeinc. com*). **Florida Coastal Cruises** (☎ *386/428–0201 or 800/881–2628* ⊕ *www. manateecruise.com*).

VISITOR INFORMATION

Most visitor information offices are open weekdays from 8 or 9 to 5. The St. Augustine Visitor Information Center is open daily 8:30 to 5:30.

Contacts **Amelia Island Tourist Development Council** (✉ *961687 Gateway Blvd., Suite G, Amelia Island 32034* ☎ *904/261–6997 or 800/226–3542* ⊕ *www. ameliaisland.org*). **Cocoa Beach Convention and Visitor's Bureau** (✉ *400 Fortenberry Rd., Merritt Island 32952* ☎ *321/454–2022 or 877/321–8474* ⊕ *www. cocoabeach.com*). **Daytona Beach Area Convention and Visitors Bureau** (✉ *126 E. Orange Ave., Daytona Beach 32114* ☎ *800/544–0415* ⊕ *www.daytonabeach. com*). **Gainesville/Alachua County Visitors and Convention Bureau** (✉ *30 E. University Ave., Gainesville 32601* ☎ *352/374–5231 or 866/778–5002* ⊕ *www. visitgainesville.net*). **Jacksonville and The Beaches Convention & Visitors Bureau** (✉ *550 Water St., Suite 1000, Jacksonville 32202* ☎ *904/798–9100 or 800/733–2668* ⊕ *www.jaxcvb.com*). **Ocala/Marion County Chamber of Commerce** (✉ *110 E. Silver Springs Blvd., Ocala 34470* ☎ *352/629–8051* ⊕ *www. ocalacc.com*). **St. Augustine, Ponte Vedra & The Beaches Visitors & Convention Bureau** (✉ *88 Riberia St., Suite 400, St. Augustine 32084* ☎ *904/829–1711 or 800/653–2489* ⊕ *www.visitoldcity.com*).

Walt Disney World® & the Orlando Area

WORD OF MOUTH

"The best times to go to WDW [are] after Spring Break up till mid May. We sometimes go the week before Mother's Day and it is wonderful. Also the weeks before Thanksgiving—and after Thanksgiving up till mid-December."

—Annabel

"Islands of Adventure [at Universal Orlando] is perfect for teens. My teens have pretty much outgrown Disney."

—eltrain

"We loved SeaWorld—the shows were the best part, and the kids loved being able to feed and pet the dolphins."

—klw25

Updated
by Jennie
Hess, Alicia
Mandigo,
and Rowland
Stiteler

NO MOSS EVER GROWS UNDER the Mouse's trademark yellow clogs (unless it's artfully re-created moss). Walt Disney's original decree that his parks be ever changing, along with some healthy competition from Universal Studios and SeaWorld, keeps the Disney Imagineers on their toes as they dream up new entertainment and install higher-tech attractions. Remember, Disney World is a lot bigger than Disneyland. At 40 square mi, it's twice the size of Manhattan, with four major theme parks—the Magic Kingdom, Epcot, Disney–MGM Studios, and Disney's Animal Kingdom—plus water parks, golf courses, and a host of other attractions. So do a little research, poll family members on their theme-park wishes, make a priority list, then try to relax and have a wonderful time.

3

EXPLORING WALT DISNEY WORLD®

There are two main kinds of travelers to Walt Disney World. There's the family that shows up at the Magic Kingdom around 11, trusting the reputation of Disney to guide them along the way. They'll wander through Main Street and its stores, then reach the other side of Cinderella's castle wondering what to ride first. One child will want to go to Space Mountain, while another will start crying the farther the group gets from Dumbo, which now has a 90-minute line. This family might split up so each child can get in at least one preferred ride before lunch, or they might stick together, causing one child or the other to have a meltdown that ruins everyone's mood. Regardless, by the time they've struggled through the lines at rides and lunch counters, the late-afternoon sun will be beating down.

The second type of traveler does some research. They make their dining reservations in advance, and they decide which rides are must-sees for each person in their party. They learn the cardinal rule of Disney World touring—get there early—and they manage to avoid the worst lines. Above all, they remember that they can't do everything, and they relax long enough to enjoy their experience without stressing out about how much they need to do to merit the cost of their tickets.

Sure, the first family will still have fun, but they'll wait in more lines, probably spend more money, and stress out more than the second family. You don't need to map out every minute of your time to have a good vacation. You just need to know a few basic tips, and the planning can be fun, especially if you get everyone involved. Start by flipping through this chapter and browsing ⊕ *www.disneyworld.com*. And don't worry that your best-laid plans will be stolen by throngs of other guidebook readers. ■ TIP→**Regardless of all the books on the market, most Disney World visitors still don't bother making touring plans. That's why there are still far fewer people in the parks at 9 AM than at 2 PM.** Go ahead, see for yourself. And stay steps ahead of the crowds by purchasing tickets before your trip, mapping out a general itinerary, and using the handiest of theme-park tools: an alarm clock.

TIMING

Avoid school holidays—essentially mid-June through mid-August, Christmastime, Spring Break, and holiday weekends like Presidents Day—which are the most crowded times in the parks. If you have school children, it's nice to avoid prime break times, but if you can't, then plan your itinerary a little more tightly. Spring and fall are the best times to visit.

For the length of your visit, the general rule is one day per park, including the water parks.

TIME-SAVING TIPS

If you remember nothing else, keep in mind these essential strategies, tried and tested by generations of Disney World fans. They are the Eight Commandments for touring Walt Disney World.

Make dining reservations before you leave home, especially for character dining experiences. If you don't, you might find yourself eating a hamburger (again) or leaving Walt Disney World for dinner. The on-site restaurants book up *fast*.

Arrive at the parks at least 30 minutes before they open. Plan to be up by at least 7:30 every day. ∎TIP➜Getting to the parks early is the number-one best way to avoid waiting in line. After transit time, it'll take you 10–15 minutes to park and get to the gates. If you know you want to use the lockers or ATMs, or rent strollers, get there 45 minutes in advance.

See the top attractions first thing in the morning. And we mean first thing. As in, before 10 AM. Decide in advance which attractions you don't want to miss, find out where they are, and hot-foot it to them when the park opens. If you miss any in the morning, the other good times to see the most popular attractions are right before closing and during the parades. Otherwise, use Fastpass.

Use Fastpass. It's worth saying twice. The system is free, easy, and it's your ticket to the top attractions with little or no waiting in line.

Build in rest time. This is the greatest way to avoid becoming overly hot, tired, and grumpy. We recommend starting early and then leaving the theme parks around 3 or 4, the hottest and most crowded time of day. After a couple hours' rest at your hotel, you can have an early dinner and head back to the parks to watch one of the nighttime spectaculars or to ride a couple more of the big-deal rides (lines are shorter around closing time).

Create a rough itinerary, but leave room for spontaneity. Decide which parks to see on each day, and know your priorities, but don't try to plot your trip hour by hour. Instead, break up the day into morning, afternoon, and evening sections. If you're staying at a Disney resort, find out which parks are offering the Extra Magic Hours on which days, and plan to take advantage of the program.

GREAT ITINERARIES

Numbers in the text correspond to numbers in the margin and on the Orlando Area map.

4 DAYS

No stay in the area would be complete without a visit to the **Magic Kingdom ❶** ⌐. The next day, take your pick between the more sophisticated **Epcot ❷** and state-of-the-art **Universal Islands of Adventure ❽**. On Day 3, see **Universal Studios ❼** or the smaller and more manageable **Disney–MGM Studios ❸**. On your fourth day go for **Disney's Animal Kingdom ❹** or **SeaWorld Orlando ❿**. Be sure to catch fireworks one night and one of the local dinner-show extravaganzas on another.

6 DAYS

Spend the first four days exploring in this order: **Magic Kingdom ❶** ⌐, **Universal Islands of Adventure ❽**, **Epcot ❷**, and **Disney's Animal Kingdom ❹** or **Universal Studios ❼**. At night make sure you get to some fireworks, sample at least one of the now-ubiquitous themed dining experiences, and visit Pleasure Island, Downtown Disney, or **CityWalk at Universal ❾**. After all that theme park-ing, you'll need a rest. Depending on your interests and the ages of your children, use Day 5 to relax and play at a Disney water park like **Typhoon Lagoon ❻**, or venture into Orlando and Winter Park. Take a leisurely boat tour and visit the **Charles Hosmer Morse Museum of American Art ⓯** or the **Orlando Science Center ⓮** for its great interactive activities before relaxing at your hotel. The sixth day should be for **SeaWorld Orlando ❿** or the more intimate **Discovery Cove ⓫**. On

your last evening take in Cirque du Soleil's "La Nouba" or a dinner show, perhaps SeaWorld's luau, Disney's Hoop-Dee-Doo Revue, or Kissimmee's Arabian Nights show.

8 DAYS

You'll have time to see *all* the theme parks, but pacing is key. To ensure that the go-go Orlando tourism scene doesn't wear you down, intersperse theme-park outings with low-key sightseeing or shopping. Start with the **Magic Kingdom ❶** ⌐, staying late the first night for the fireworks. The second day, tackle **Epcot ❷** and hit Downtown Disney Pleasure Island that evening. Set aside the third day for a visit to **SeaWorld Orlando ❿**, making luau reservations when you enter the park; or make reservations before your trip to visit **Discovery Cove ⓫** to swim with dolphins. On your fourth day it's back to the theme parks—either **Disney–MGM Studios ❸** or **Universal Studios ❼**, or **Blizzard Beach ❺** or **Typhoon Lagoon ❻** for slower-paced fun. On your fifth and sixth days take in **Disney's Animal Kingdom ❹** and **Universal Islands of Adventure ❽**. Have dinner at a restaurant that suits your fancy. If it rains, substitute the indoor adventures of Disney-Quest. On Day 7, a day of (relative) rest, enjoy a boat tour through Winter Park and visit the **Charles Hosmer Morse Museum of American Art ⓯** or the **Orlando Science Center ⓮**. In late afternoon, stroll along downtown's Lake Eola and grab dinner on the porch of the Lake Eola Yacht Club or at Panera Bread. On your eighth day drive out to **Historic Bok Sanctuary,** and explore Downtown Disney in the evening.

3

Eat at off hours. Have a quick, light breakfast at 8, lunch at 11, and dinner at 5 or 6 to avoid the mealtime rush hours. Between 11:30 and 2:30 during high season, you can wait in line up to 30 minutes for a so-called fast-food lunch in the parks.

Save the high-capacity sit-down shows for the afternoon. You usually don't have to wait in line so long for shows, and you'll be relieved at the chance to sit in an air-conditioned theater during the hottest part of the day.

BEST WAYS TO SAVE

Don't buy a theme-park ticket for the day of your arrival or the day of your departure. It's not worth spending $60 for just a couple of hours in the parks. Instead, use those days to visit Downtown Disney, Disney's Boardwalk, or Universal CityWalk, or lounge around your hotel pool.

Buy your tickets as soon as you know you're going. Prices typically go up about once a year, so you might beat a price hike—and save a little money.

Avoid holidays and school vacation times, or go off-season. You can see more in less time, and lodging rates are lower.

If you plan to eat in a full-service restaurant, do it at lunch. Then have a light dinner. Lunchtime prices are almost always lower than dinnertime prices. Also look for "early bird" menus, which offer dinner entrées at reduced prices during late afternoon and early evening hours.

Watch your shopping carefully. Theme-park merchandisers are excellent at displaying the goods so that you (or your children) can't resist them. Most articles for sale are also available at home—for quite a bit less. One way to cope is to give every member of your family a souvenir budget. Another good option is to shop local CVS or Walgreens stores for cheap but cool souvenirs.

Bring essentials with you. Remember to pack your hat, sunscreen, camera, memory card or film, batteries, diapers, and aspirin. These items are all very expensive within the theme parks.

WALT DISNEY WORLD RESORT ESSENTIALS

ADMISSION

Everyone 10 and older pays adult prices; reductions are available for children ages 3 through 9. Children under three get in free. You won't find discounted tickets at the park, so buy ahead if you're looking for a deal. Prices change at least once a year, so buy your tickets as soon as you know you're going.

THE TICKETING SYSTEM

Once you've decided to take the plunge, Disney fortunately makes buying tickets easy and painless. The **Magic Your Way** ticketing system is all about flexibility. You can tailor your ticket to your interests and desired length of stay. The more days you stay, the greater your savings on per-day ticket prices. A one-day ticket costs $67 for anyone age 10 and up, while a five-day ticket costs $206 or $41.20 per day.

Once you decide how many days to stay, you'll want to decide what options to add on. The **Park Hopper** option lets you move from park to park within the day and adds $45 to the price of your ticket, no matter how many days your ticket covers. So it's an expensive option for a one- or two-day ticket, but it can be well worth the cost for a four-day trip, especially if you know what you want to see at each park.

The **Water Parks & More** option allows a certain number of visits to the water parks and other Disney attractions: Typhoon Lagoon, Blizzard Beach, Pleasure Island, DisneyQuest, and Disney's Wide World of Sports complex. You pay $50 to add this option to your ticket, and you get three to six visits, depending on the length of your stay.

The **No Expiration** option can save you money if you know for sure you're coming back to Disney World again. For example, say you're planning a five-day trip one year, plus a weekend trip sometime the next year. You can buy a seven-day ticket, use it five days during your first trip and keep the remaining two-days' worth of theme-park fun for your next trip to Orlando. It will cost you $10 to $90 to add the No Expiration option to your two- to seven-day tickets.

Note that all Disney admission passes are nontransferable. The ID is your fingerprint. Although you slide your pass through the reader like people with single-day tickets, you also have to slip your finger into a special V-shape fingerprint reader before you'll be admitted.

HOTEL & TICKET PACKAGES
Disney's Magic Your Way basic, premium, and platinum packages help families keep expenses in check by bundling hotel and theme-park expenses. For as low as $1,600, a family of four can plan a six-night, seven-day Magic Your Way Vacation that includes complimentary transportation from the airport and extra hours in the parks. Lower-end package rates offer value-resort accommodations; prices go up with moderate or deluxe accommodations. All Disney resort guests get free bus, boat, and monorail transportation across property. Visit ⊕ *www.disneyworld.com* to explore the different package options.

MEAL PLANS
If you book a package, you can add on a meal plan for more savings. The Magic Your Way Dining Plan allows you one table-service meal, one counter-service meal, and one snack per day of your trip at more than 100 theme-park and resort restaurants. You can add the plan to your package for $38.99 per adult, per day, and $10.99 per child age 3–9, per day (tax and gratuities included). When you consider that the average Disney table-service meal for a child runs about $10.99 *without* gratuity, you realize this plan is a steal. Another advantage of the plan is that you can swap two table-service meals for one of Disney's dinner shows or an evening at one of the high-end signature restaurants like California Grill.

MAGIC YOUR WAY PRICE CHART

TICKET OPTIONS

TICKET	10-DAY	7-DAY	6-DAY	5-DAY	4-DAY	3-DAY	2-DAY	1-DAY
BASE TICKET								
Ages 10-up	$210	$204	$202	$199	$195	$181	$125	$63
Ages 3-9	$171	$165	$164	$162	$160	$149	$103	$52

Base Ticket admits guest to one of the four major theme parks per day's use.
Park choices are: Magic Kingdom, Epcot, Disney-MGM Studios, Disney's Animal Kingdom.

ADD: Park Hopper	$40	$40	$40	$40	$40	$40	$40	$40

Park Hopper option entitles guest to visit more than one theme park per day's use. Park choices are any combination of Magic Kingdom, Epcot, Disney-MGM Studios, Disney's Animal Kingdom.

ADD: Water Parks & More	$50 5 visits	$50 5 visits	$50 4 visits	$50 3 visits	$50 3 visits	$50 2 visits	$50 2 visits	$50 2 visits

Water Parks & More option entitles guest to a specified number of visits (between 2 and 5) to a choice of entertainment and recreation venues. Choices are Blizzard Beach, Typhoon Lagoon, DisneyQuest, Pleasure Island, and Wide World of Sports.

ADD: No Expiration	$135	$65	$50	$40	$20	$10	$10	n/a

No expiration means that unused admissions on a ticket may be used any time in the future.
Without this option, tickets expire 14 days after first use.

MINOR PARKS AND ATTRACTIONS

TICKET	AGES 10-UP	AGES 3-9
TYPHOON LAGOON OR BLIZZARD BEACH 1-Day 1-Park	$34	$28
DISNEYQUEST 1-Day	$34	$28
DISNEY'S WIDE WORLD OF SPORTS	$10.05	$7.48
CIRQUE DU SOLEIL'S *LA NOUBA*	$61–$95	$49–$76
PLEASURE ISLAND 1-Night Multi-Club Ticket	$20.95	$20.95

*Admission to *Pleasure Island* clubs is restricted to guests 18 or older unless accompanied by an adult 21 or older. For some clubs all guests must be 21 or older.

*All prices are subject to Florida sales tax

MONEY MATTERS

Despite relatively low airfares and car-rental rates, cash seems to evaporate out of wallets, and credit-card balances seem to increase on exposure to the hot Orlando sun. Theme-park admission is roughly $60 per day per person—not counting all the $2 soft drinks and $20 souvenirs. Hotels range so wildly—from $60 a night to 10 or more times that—that you have to do some hard thinking about just how much you want to spend. Meal prices away from the theme parks are comparable to those in other midsize cities, ranging from $6.50 per person at a fast-food chain to $40 entrées at a fancy restaurant.

SAMPLE COSTS AT WDW

All prices include sales tax.

- 24 oz. bottle of water $2
- 20 oz. bottle of soda $2
- Cup of coffee $2
- Cheeseburger $4.50
- French fries $2
- Ice-cream treat $3–$4
- Souvenir T-shirt $16–$35
- Roll of film (36 shots) $9.49
- 256 MB digital memory card $69.95
- Autograph Book $6.95
- Plush character toys $8–$50

GETTING AROUND

Walt Disney World Resort has its own transportation system, with boats, buses, and monorails to get you wherever you want to go. It's a fairly simple system—if in doubt, ask the nearest Disney staffer the best way to get where you're going. In general, allow 45–60 minutes to get to your destination. Monorails, launches, buses, and trams operate from early in the morning until at least midnight. (Hours are shorter when the park closes earlier.) Even if you've rented a vehicle in Orlando, it's worthwhile to avail yourself of the public transportation provided within the resort. Some connections can be a little convoluted, but are still convenient: for instance, if you want to reach Downtown Disney from MGM Studios, your best bet is to catch a bus to one of the on-property hotels and then take another bus to get downtown.

OPENING & CLOSING TIMES

Operating hours for the Magic Kingdom, Epcot, Disney–MGM Studios, and Disney's Animal Kingdom vary widely throughout the year. In general, the longest days are in summer and over the year-end holidays, when the Magic Kingdom is open until 10 or 11 (later on New Year's Eve), Epcot is open until 9 or 9:30, and Disney–MGM Studios is open until at least 7, sometimes 8:30. There are so many variations, it pays to call ahead or check the parks' Web site calendar. The Magic Kingdom, Epcot's Future World, and Disney–MGM officially open at 9. Disney's Animal Kingdom opens at 9 and closes at 5, though hours expand from 8 AM to 7 or 8 PM during peak times. The World Showcase at Epcot opens at 11. Parking lots open at least an hour earlier. Arrive at the Magic Kingdom turnstiles before the official opening time; breakfast in a restaurant on Main Street, which opens before the rest of the park; and be ready to dash to one of the popular attractions in other areas as soon as officially possible. Arriving in Epcot, Disney–MGM

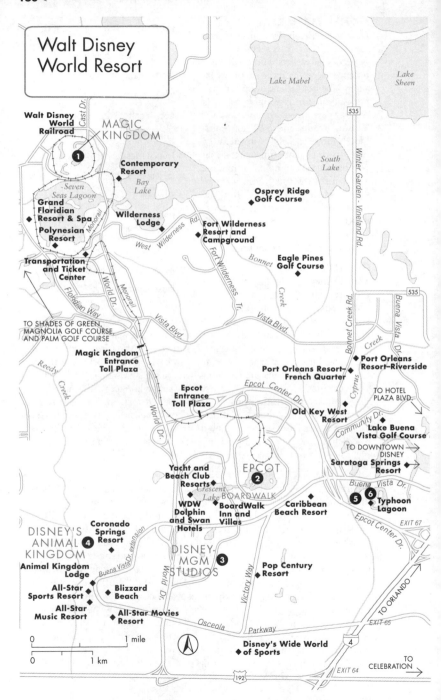

Walt Disney
World Resort

Lake Mabel

Lake Sheen

Walt Disney World Railroad

MAGIC KINGDOM

1

Cast Dr.

535

Contemporary Resort

South Lake

Osprey Ridge Golf Course

Winter Garden - Vineland Rd.

Seven Seas Lagoon

Bay Lake

Grand Floridian Resort & Spa

Wilderness Lodge

Fort Wilderness Resort and Campground

Eagle Pines Golf Course

Polynesian Resort

West Wilderness Rd.

Fort Wilderness Tr.

Bonnet Creek

535

Transportation and Ticket Center

Monorail

Bonnet Creek Rd.

Buena Vista Dr.

TO SHADES OF GREEN, MAGNOLIA GOLF COURSE, AND PALM GOLF COURSE

Floridian Way

World Dr.

Vista Blvd.

Vista Blvd.

Cress

Port Orleans Resort–Riverside

Reedy Creek

Magic Kingdom Entrance Toll Plaza

Port Orleans Resort– French Quarter

Cyprus

TO HOTEL PLAZA BLVD.

Epcot Entrance Toll Plaza

Epcot Center Dr.

Old Key West Resort

Community Dr.

Lake Buena Vista Golf Course

World Dr.

TO DOWNTOWN DISNEY

Yacht and Beach Club Resorts

EPCOT

2

Saratoga Springs Resort

Buena Vista Dr.

Crescent Lake

BOARDWALK

5 6 Typhoon Lagoon

DISNEY'S ANIMAL KINGDOM

Coronado Springs Resort

WDW Dolphin and Swan Hotels

BoardWalk Inn and Villas

Caribbean Beach Resort

Epcot Center Dr.

EXIT 67

4

Buena Vista Dr. extension

DISNEY- MGM STUDIOS

3

TO ORLANDO

Animal Kingdom Lodge

World Dr.

Victory Way

Pop Century Resort

All-Star Sports Resort

Blizzard Beach

All-Star Music Resort

All-Star Movies Resort

EXIT 65

0   1 mile

0   1 km

Osceola Parkway

Disney's Wide World of Sports

192

EXIT 64

TO CELEBRATION

WDW WHAT'S WHERE

❶ The Magic Kingdom. What most people imagine to be Walt Disney World—the Magic Kingdom—actually is a small, but emblematic, part of it. For many of those who have grown up with Cinderella, Snow White, Peter Pan, Dumbo, and Pinocchio, it's a magical place. It's the site of such world-famous attractions as Space Mountain, Pirates of the Caribbean, Splash Mountain, and "it's a small world," as well as new thrills like Stitch's Great Escape and Mickey's Philharmagic. *Take the Magic Kingdom–U.S. 192 exit (Exit 64) off I–4.*

❷ Epcot. Designed to promote enthusiasm for discovery and learning, WDW's Epcot is a sweeping combination of amusement park and world's fair. In Future World, the focus inside 10 landmark pavilions is on the fascinating discoveries of science and technology. Don't miss the funny, often startling, 3-D film and special-effects attraction *Honey, I Shrunk the Audience,* and if you can handle an intense simulation blast-off, try out the Mission: SPACE ride to Mars. In the second major area of Epcot, the World Showcase, you can tour 10 different countries without the jet lag. *Take the Epcot–Downtown Disney exit (Exit 67) off I–4.*

❸ Disney–MGM Studios. This is Disney's re-creation of Hollywood as it might have been in the good old days. Amazing attractions are the

key to "The Studios'" success: there's the Rock 'n' Roller Coaster Starring Aerosmith, the Twilight Zone Tower of Terror, the classic Great Movie Ride, and two stunt shows. Other not-to-be-missed attractions include the closing show, *Fantasmic!,* and the Magic of Disney Animation. *Take the Disney–MGM Studios exit (Exit 64) off I–4.*

❹ Disney's Animal Kingdom. In the center of the park, the huge, sculpted Tree of Life rises 145 feet, towering over all the other trees in the park. Walkways encircle the tree, leading to attractions, including a water ride, a safari ride, and several shows in the Asia, Africa, and Dinoland areas of the park. With a 100-acre savanna and wildlife preserve, the Animal Kingdom is the largest of all the Disney parks. *Take the Disney's Animal Kingdom exit (Exit 65) off I–4.*

❺–❻ The Disney Water Parks. Blizzard Beach and Typhoon Lagoon are two separate water parks that are always jam-packed when the weather's steamy. The best ride—or is it the worst?—is the wild, 55-mph dead-drop to a splashy landing from Blizzard Beach's Summit Plummet, which feels as fast as it sounds. Water babies love Typhoon Lagoon's scaled-down Ketchakiddie Creek and Blizzard Beach's Tyke's Peak.

Studios, or Disney's Animal Kingdom, make dinner reservations before the crowds arrive—in fact, try to reserve tables even before you arrive, utilizing Disney's central reservations number (⇨ *Visitor Information*). Try to take in some of the attractions and pavilions well before the major crowds descend later in the morning.

MAGIC KINGDOM

★ NAME

NAME	Min. Height	Type of Ride	Duration	Suits	Crowds	Strategy
Main Street U.S.A.						
Walt Disney World Railroad	n/a	train	21 min.	All	Heavy	Board with small children for an early start in Toontown or hop on midafternoon.
Adventureland						
Enchanted Tiki Room	n/a	show	12 min.	All	30 min.	Go when you need a refresher in an air-conditioned room.
Jungle Cruise	n/a	boat	10 min.	All	Yes!	Go during the afternoon parade, but not after dark—you miss too much.
Pirates of the Caribbean	n/a	boat	10 min.	All	Less than 30 min.	A good destination, especially in the heat of the afternoon.
The Magic Carpets of Aladdin	n/a	thrill ride	3 min.	All	Fast lines	Visit while waiting for Jungle Cruise Fastpass.
Swiss Family Treehouse	n/a	play area	Up to you.	All	Slow lines	Visit while waiting for Jungle Cruise Fastpass.
Frontierland						
★ Big Thunder Mountain Railroad	40"	thrill ride	4 min.	5 and up	Big crowds	Most exciting at night when you can't anticipate the curves.
Country Bear Jamboree	n/a	show	17 min.	All	Heavy	Visit before 11 AM. Stand to the far left lining up for the front rows.
★ Splash Mountain	40"	thrill ride	11 min.	5 and up	Yes!	Get in line by 9:45 AM or ride during meal or parade times. Bring a change of clothes.
Tom Sawyer Island	n/a	play area	Up to you.	All	ok	Afternoon refresher. It's hard to keep track of toddlers here.
Liberty Square						
Hall of Presidents	n/a	show	30 min.	9 and up	Light	Go in the afternoon for an air-conditioned break.
★ Haunted Mansion	n/a	thrill ride	8 min.	All	Fast lines	Fastpass. Nighttime adds extra fear factor.
Liberty Square Riverboat	n/a	boat	15 min.	All	ok	Good for a break from the crowds.
Fantasyland						
Ariel's Grotto	n/a	play area	Up to you.	Little kids	Yes!	Arrive 20 min. before autograph time.

	Name		Type	Time	Age	Lines	Notes
	Cinderella's Golden Carrousel	n/a	carousel	2 min.	All	Fast lines	Go while waiting for Peter Pan's Fastpass, during afternoon parade, or after dark.
	Dumbo the Flying Elephant	n/a	thrill ride	2 min.	Little kids	Slow lines	Go at Rope Drop. No shade in afternoon.
	Fairytale Garden	n/a	show	25 min.	All	Midday	Share story time with Belle during parade.
	it's a small world	n/a	boat ride	11 min.	All	Fast lines	Tots may beg for a repeat ride; it's worth it.
	Mad Tea Party	n/a	thrill ride	2 min.	All	Slow lines	Go early morning. Skip if wait is 30 min. Spinning ride.
	Mickey's PhilharMagic	n/a	3-D film	12 min.	All	Heavy	Fastpass or arrive early or during a parade.
	Peter Pan's Flight	n/a	ride	2½ min.	All	Steady	Try evening or early morning. Fastpass first.
	Snow White's Scary Adventures	n/a	thrill ride	3 min.	All	Steady	Go very early, during the afternoon parade, or after dark. May scare toddlers.
	The Many Adventures of Winnie the Pooh	n/a	thrill ride	3 min.	All	Heavy	Go early, late in the afternoon, or after dark.
	Tomorrowland						
	Astro-Orbiter	n/a	thrill ride	2 min.	All	Slow lines	Skip unless there's a short line. Better at night. May scare toddlers.
★	Buzz Lightyear's Space Ranger Spin	n/a	thrill ride	5 min.	3 and up	Fast lines	Go early morning and Fastpass. Kids will want more than one ride.
★	Space Mountain	44"	thrill ride	2½ min.	7 and up	Yes!	Fastpass, or go at beginning or end of day or during a parade.
	Stitch's Great Escape	40"	sim. exp.	15 min.	All	Large	Visit early after Space Mountain.
	Timekeeper	n/a	film	11 min.	All	Fast lines	Go when you're waiting for your Buzz Lightyear Fastpass. No seats.
	Tomorrowland Indy Speedway	52" to ride	racetrack	5 min.	Big kids	Steady	Go in the evening or during a parade; skip on a first-time visit.
	Tomorrowland Transit Authority	n/a	tram	10 min.	All	ok	Go with young kids if you need a break.
	Walt Disney's Carousel of Progress	n/a	show	20 min.	All	ok	Skip on a first-time visit unless you're heavily into nostalgia.

★ = FodorsChoice

EPCOT

★ NAME

NAME	Min. Height	Type of Ride	Duration	Suits	Crowds	Strategy
Future World						
Body Wars	40″	sim. ride	5 min.	All	Rarely	Go anytime. Little kids may be scared.
Club Cool	n/a	walk through	Up to you.	All	Fast lines	Visit in midafternoon on a very hot day.
Cranium Command	n/a	show	20 min.	All	Fast lines	Go when everyone else is at Body Wars.
Ellen's Energy Adventure	n/a	ride	30 min.	All	ok	Best seats are to the far left and front of the theater.
Fitness Fairground	n/a	play area	Up to you.	All	ok	Hang loose here with little ones.
★ Honey, I Shrunk the Audience	n/a	show	14 min.	All	Yes!	Go early morning or just before closing. Take off the 3D glasses if little kids get scared.
Innoventions	n/a	walk through	Up to you.	3 and up	at displays	Go before 10 AM or after 2 PM.
Journey into Imagination with Figment	n/a	tour	8 min.		Fast lines	Ride while waiting for Honey, I Shrunk the Audience Fastpass. Toddlers may be scared by darkness and scanner at end of ride.
Living with the Land	n/a	boat	14 min.	Teens	ok	The line moves quickly, so go anytime.
★ Mission: SPACE	44″	thrill ride	4 min.	8 and up	Always	Get there before 10 AM or Fastpass. Don't ride on a full stomach.
Sea Base	n/a	play area	30 min.	All	Yes!	Go in the morning, during lunch, or after 5.
★ Soarin'	40″	sim. ride		5 and up	Heavy	Go early, Fastpass, or use single fliers line. Mild flight ride.

	Height	Type	Duration	Age	Morning	Strategy
Spaceship Earth	n/a	ride	15 min.	All	Morning	Ride while waiting for Mission: SPACE or just before closing.
★ Test Track	40"	thrill ride	5 min.	5 and up	Heavy	The ride can't function on wet tracks, so don't go after a downpour.
The Circle of Life	n/a	film	20 min.	All	Steady	Go early or for your toddler's afternoon nap.
The Seas with Nemo & Friends	n/a	ride, film	8 min.	All	Steady	Get Nemo fans here early in the morning
The Making of Me	n/a	film	14 min.	All	ok	Line up 5–10 min before showtime.
World Showcase						
Age of the Viking Ship	n/a	play area	Up to you.	All	ok	Go anytime.
America Gardens	n/a	show		Varies	Varies	Arrive 30 min to 1 hr ahead of time for holiday and celebrity performances.
El Río del Tiempo	n/a	boat	9 min.	All	Slow lines	Skip this one unless you have small children, who usually enjoy the novelty of a boat ride.
Impressions de France	n/a	film	18 min.	7 and up	late afternoon	Come before noon or after dinner.
Maelstrom	n/a	thrill ride	10 min.	All	Slow lines	Fastpass for after lunch or dinner.
O Canada!	n/a	film	17 min.	All	late afternoon	Go when World Showcase opens or in the evening. No strollers permitted
Reflections of China	n/a	film	19 min.	All	Yes!	Go anytime. No strollers permitted.
The American Adventure Show	n/a	show	30 min.	All	Fast lines	Arrive 10 min before the Voices of Liberty or American Vybe are slated to perform.

★ = Fodor'sChoice

DISNEY–MGM

★ NAME	Min. Height	Type of Ride	Duration	Suits	Crowds	Strategy
Hollywood Blvd.						
Great Movie Ride	n/a	tour	22 min.	5 and up	Medium	Go while waiting for Fastpass on another ride. Lines out the door mean 25-mins. wait.
Sunset Blvd.						
Beauty and the Beast—Live on Stage!	n/a	show	30 min.	All	Yes!	Go 30 min before show time for good seats. Performance days vary, so check ahead.
★ Rock 'n' Roller Coaster Starring Aerosmith	44"	thrill ride	3 min.	7 and up	Huge	Ride early, then Fastpass for another go later.
★ Twilight Zone Tower of Terror	40"	thrill ride	10 min.	7 and up	Yes!	Fastpass. Go early or late evening. Plunging ride.
Animation Courtyard						
Playhouse Disney—Live on Stage!	n/a	show	25 min.	toddlers	Afternoon	Go first thing in the morning, when your child is most alert or to wind down at the end of the day.
★ The Magic of Disney Animation	n/a	tour	30 min.	All	Steady	Go in the morning or late afternoon. Toddlers may get bored.
Voyage of the Little Mermaid	n/a	show	15 min.	All	Yes!	Fastpass Rock 'n' Roller Coaster and ride this first thing. Otherwise, wait until after 5.
Walt Disney: One Man's Dream	n/a	film	20 min.	10 and up	Heavy	Fastpass Who Wants to Be a Millionaire, see this attraction while waiting.
Mickey Avenue						
Disney-MGM Studios Backlot Tour	n/a	tour	35 min.	All	Fast lines	People sitting on the left get wet. Go early; it closes at dusk.
Who Wants to Be a Millionaire—Play It!	n/a	stage show	30 min.	5 and up	Heavy	Line up while waiting on another Fastpass.

Streets of America

Honey, I Shrunk the Kids Movie Set Adventure	n/a	play area	Up to you.	All	Steady	Come after you've done several shows and your kids need to cut loose.
Jim Henson's Muppet*Vision 3-D	n/a	3-D film	20 min.	All	Moderate	Arrive 10 min early or FASTPASS this. And don't worry—there are no bad seats.
Lights, Motors, Action! Extreme Stunt Show	n/a	show	30 min.	All	Heavy	You should be able to get into the theater even if you arrive close to show time. For the best seats line up for the show while others are lining up for the parade.

Echo Lake

Indiana Jones Epic Stunt Spectacular!	n/a	stunt show	30 min.	All	Fast lines	Go at night, when the idols' eyes glow red. Sit up front to feel heat of truck on fire.
Sounds Dangerous Starring Drew Carey	n/a	show	30 min.	6 and up	ok	Arrive 15 min before show. You sit in total darkness.
Star Tours	40"	sim. ride	5 min.	5 and up	Fast lines	Go before closing or early morning. Keep to the left in line, for best seats.

Entertainment

Disney Stars and Motor Cars	n/a	parade	25 min.	All	Heavy	Stake out your curb spot an hr early and hang on to it.
Fantasmic!	n/a	show	25 min.	All	Heavy	Arrive at least 1 hr early and sit toward the rear, near the entrance/exit.

★ = Fodor'sChoice

ANIMAL KINGDOM

NAME	Min. Height	Type of Ride	Duration	Suits	Crowds	Strategy
Discovery Island						
★ Tree of Life—It's Tough to Be a Bug!		3-D film	20 min.	All	ok	Do this after Kilimanjaro Safaris. Good photo opp.
DinoLand U.S.A.						
Boneyard	n/a	play area	Up to you.	Under 7's	Heavy	Play here while waiting for DINOSAUR Fastpass, or come late in the day.
Cretaceous Trail	n/a	walk through	Up to you.	All	ok	Stroll along here as you head toward Chester and Hester's for souvenirs or while you wait for the next Finding Nemo show.
★ DINOSAUR	40"	thrill ride	4 min.	5 and up	Midmorning	Go first thing in the morning or at the end of the day, or use the Fastpass.
Fossil Fun Games	n/a	arcade	Up to you.	6 and up	ok	Bring a pocketful of change
Finding Nemo the MuSEAcal	n/a	show	30 min.	All	Heavy	Arrive 40 min. before showtime. Take little kids here while big kids wait for Expedition Everest.
Primeval Whirl	48"	thrill ride	2½ min.	All	Yes!	Kids may want to ride twice. Take your first spin early, then Fastpass if the wait is more than 20 min. Spinning ride.
TriceraTop Spin	n/a	thrill ride	2 min.	All	Heavy	Ride early while everyone else heads for the safari, or queue up while waiting for your Fastpass appointment for DINOSAUR.
Asia						
★ Expedition EVEREST	44"	thrill ride	2½ min.	7 and up	Yes!	Fastpass. This is the park's biggest thrill ride.
Flights of Wonder	n/a	show	30 min.	All	ok	Arrive 15 min before show time and find a shaded seat beneath one of the awnings—the sun can be brutal.
Kali River Rapids	38"	thrill ride	7 min.	4 and up	Yes!	Use your Fastpass, or go during the parade. You'll get wet.
Maharajah Jungle Trek	n/a	zoo walk	Up to you.	All	ok	Go anytime.
Africa						
★ Kilimanjaro Safaris	n/a	tour	20 min.	All	Morning	Do this first thing in the morning. If you arrive at the park late morning, save this for the end of the day, when it's not so hot.

Attraction	Fastpass	Type	Duration	Audience	Crowds	Strategy
Pangani Forest Exploration Trail	n/a	walk through	Up to you.	All	Midmorning	Go while waiting for your safari Fastpass; try to avoid going at the hottest time of day, when the gorillas like to nap.
Rafiki's Planet Watch	n/a		10 min.	All		Go in late afternoon after you've hit all key attractions.
Wildlife Express Train	n/a	train ride	7 min.	All	Steady	Head straight to Affection Section with little kids to come face-to-face with goats and other critters.
Camp Minnie-Mickey						
★ Festival of the Lion King	n/a	show	30 min.	All	ok	Arrive 15 min before show time. Sit in one of the front rows to increase your kid's chance of being chosen.
★ Mickey's Jammin' Jungle Parade	n/a	parade	15 min.	All	Heavy	Choose your spot along the parade route early, as this is one of Disney's most creative parades, and you should try not to miss it.
Pocahontas and Her Forest Friends	n/a	show	12 min.	All	ok	May not be performed every day in low season; check entertainment guide map and arrive 15 min before show time.

★ = **Fodor's**Choice

PARKING

Every theme park has a parking lot—and all are huge. Always write down exactly where you parked your car and take the note with you. Parking-area trams deliver you to the park entrance. For each lot the cost is $10 for cars (free to WDW resort guests with ID). At Typhoon Lagoon and Blizzard Beach, parking is free.

VISITOR INFORMATION

For general information for Walt Disney World call either the information number or the switchboard. For all accommodations and shows call the central reservations number. There's a single number for all dining reservations. To inquire about resort facilities, call the individual property. For child-care information call KinderCare. One of the easiest ways to get information is via the Web site ⊕*www.disneyworld.com.*

Information **WDW Information** (☎ *407/824–4321, 407/827–5141 TDD*). **WDW Resort Reservations** (☎ *407/934–7639*). **WDW Dining reservations** (☎ *407/939–3463*).

UNIVERSAL ORLANDO

The "umbrella" that is Universal Orlando contains Universal Studios (the original movie theme park), Islands of Adventure (the second theme park), and CityWalk (the dining-shopping-nightclub complex). Although it's bordered by residential neighborhoods and thickly trafficked International Drive, Universal Orlando is surprisingly expansive, intimate, and accessible, with two massive parking complexes, easy walks to all attractions, and a motor launch that cruises to the hotels. Although Universal Orlando emphasizes "two parks, two days, one great adventure," you may find the presentation, creativity, and cutting-edge technology bringing you back for more.

UNIVERSAL STUDIOS

❼ Universal's classic theme park pays tribute to the movie business with well-designed street scenes from Hollywood and New York, and rides devoted to making you feel like you're actually in a movie. Look for The Mummy Returns and Shrek 4-D, as well as *Back to the Future— The Ride* and *Men In Black: Alien Attack. Near the intersection of I–4 and Florida's Tpke. Heading eastbound on I–4, take Exit 75A. Heading west on I–4, take Exit 74B and follow the signs.*

ISLANDS OF ADVENTURE

❽ If you have teenagers or adult thrill seekers in your party, do not miss a day at Islands of Adventure. It has absolutely the best roller coasters in central Florida, and the fantastical designs of its five lands give Disney a run for the money. The screamfest begins at the Incredible Hulk Coaster and continues at the double coaster known as Dueling Dragons. People are still shrieking like babies at the Amazing Adventures of Spider-Man 3-D show. There are plenty of ways to get soaked, too:

Dudley Do-Right's Ripsaw Falls is a flume ride with a serious drop and a splash landing that even gets onlookers wet. Little ones have a land all to themselves: Seuss Landing, where they can enter the world of *One Fish, Two Fish, Red Fish, Blue Fish* and *The Cat in the Hat*. All in all, they've done it all—and they've done it all right. *Near the intersection of I–4 and Florida's Tpke. Heading east on I–4, take Exit 75A; heading west, take Exit 74B.*

UNIVERSAL CITYWALK

3

⑨ With nightspots ranging from a red-hot Latin music club to a cool and smooth jazz lounge, the CityWalk entertainment complex has enough diversity to please any couple or family. Clubgoers should check out "the groove" nightclub or Latin Quarter, and bar hoppers should make it to Jimmy Buffett's Margaritaville. When deciding between here and Disney's Pleasure Island, keep in mind that each is equally entertaining, but CityWalk's $9.49 admission is less than half of Disney's $21 cover.

TIPS FOR MAKING THE MOST OF YOUR VISIT

Universal Express is available to all park guests at all attractions. You check-in at the ride entrance, are assigned a time, and then return later to bypass the line and ride within minutes. Universal Express PLUS is a perk priced from $15 to $25 (depending on the season) that allows you to cut to the front of the line all day long without waiting for a previous Universal Express pass to expire.

If you're staying at a Universal resort, use your room key as your Express ticket to bypass the line at almost all Universal attractions.

In peak seasons, resort hotel guests are admitted to Universal parks an hour before regular park goers.

Call a day or two before your visit to get official park hours, and arrive in the parking lot 45 minutes early. See the biggest attractions first.

Be sure to write down your parking location.

Have a filling snack around 10:30, lunch after 2, and dinner at 8 or later. Or lunch on the early side at a place that takes reservations; then have dinner at 5. Be sure to make your reservations ahead of time or, at the very least, when you enter the park.

UNIVERSAL ORLANDO ESSENTIALS

ADMISSION

Buy your tickets ahead of time for two reasons: one, you avoid the incredibly long and slow lines (even in low season) at the ticket booths at the park entrances; and two, you save a little money if you buy your tickets online at ⊕*www.universalorlando.com*. Plus, there are no shipping costs because you can print your tickets directly from your computer. One such online-only bargain is the EarlyBird Exclusives

UNIVERSAL ORLANDO

★

NAME	Min. Height	Type of Ride	Duration	Suits	Crowds	Strategy
Universal Studios						
A Day in the Park with Barney	n/a	show	20 min.	Toddlers	ok	Arrive 10-15 mins early on crowded days for a good seat.
★ Animal Planet Live!	n/a	show	20 min.	All	Peak times	Come early for a good seat, up front and enter.
Back to the Future . . . The Ride	40″	sim. ride	5 min.	7 and up	Peak times	Go when gates first open, or a half hour later, or go late at night.
Beetlejuice's Graveyard Revue	n/a	show	25 min.	5 and up	Fast lines	Use Universal Express here or go after dark on hot days.
Curious George Goes to Town	n/a	play area	Up to you.	All	Midmorning	Go in late afternoon or early evening.
E.T. Adventure	n/a	thrill ride	5 min.	All	ok	Come early morning.
Earthquake– The Big One	40″	thrill ride	20 min.	5 and up	Heavy	Come early or before closing. This is loud.
Fear Factor Live	n/a	show	25 min.	All	Fast lines	Arrive 30 min. early for good seats. Or use Universal Express. Toddlers may be bored.
Jaws	n/a	thrill ride	7 min.	All	Fast lines	Come after dark for a more terrifying ride.
Jimmy Neutron's Nicktoon Blast	n/a	sim. ride	8 min.	All	Morning	Come at end of day, or Fastpass while you do Shrek ride.
Lucy: A Tribute	n/a	walk through	15 min.	Adults	ok	Save this for a hot afternoon.
Men in Black: Alien Attack	n/a	thrill ride	4½ min.	All	Peak season	Solo riders can take a faster line so split up. Spinning ride.
★ Revenge of the Mummy	48″		3 min.	7 and up	Yes!	Use Universal Express or go first thing in the morning.
Shrek 4-D	n/a	4-D film	12 min.	All	Yes!	Very popular. Use Universal Express.
Terminator 2 3-D	n/a	3-D film	21 min.	7 and up	Yes!	Go first thing in the morning.
Twister . . . Ride It Out	n/a	sim. ride	3 min.	5 and up	Yes!	Go first thing in morning or at closing.

	Height	Type	Duration	Ages	Crowds	Comments
★ Universal Horror Make-Up Show	n/a	show	25 min.	All	Not daunting.	Go in the afternoon or evening. Young children may be frightened; older children eat up the blood-and-guts stories.
Woody Woodpecker's Nuthouse Coaster			1½ min.	4 and up	Midmorning	Go at park closing, when most little ones have gone home.
Universal Islands of Adventure						
Camp Jurassic	n/a	play area	Up to you	Toddlers	ok	Go anytime.
Caro-Seuss-el		carousel	1 min.	All	Fast lines	Universal Express or end day here.
Doctor Doom's Fearfall	52"	thrill ride	1 min.	6 and up	Fast lines	Go later in the day, on empty stomach.
Dudley Do-Right's Ripsaw Falls	44"	thrill ride	8 min.	6 and up	Summer	Go in late afternoon, to cool down, or at day's end. There's no seat where you can stay dry.
★ Dueling Dragons	54"	thrill ride	2¼ min.	6 and up	Yes!	Ride after dark or early morning. Go for the rear car of Fire Dragon
★ Eighth Voyage of Sindbad	n/a	show	25 min.	7 and up	Fast lines	Universal Express or come 15 min. before show time. Don't sit too close up front.
Flying Unicorn	36"	thrill ride	1 min.	Under 7	Fast lines	Use Universal Express if crowded.
Incredible Hulk Coaster	54"	thrill ride	2¼ min.	8 and up	Yes!	Come here first Effects best in the morning. The front row is best
Jurassic Park Discovery Center	n/a	walk through	Up to you	7 and up	ok	Go anytime.
Jurassic Park River Adventure	42"	thrill ride	6 min.	All	Yes!	Universal Express. Toddlers may be scared.
Popeye & Bluto's Bilge-Rat Barges	48"	water-ride	5 min.	All	Yes!	Come early morning or before closing.
Poseidon's Fury	n/a	show	20 min.	6 and up	Heavy	Come at end of day. Stay to the left for best spot. Get in first row each time
Storm Force Accelatron	54"	thrill ride	2 min.	All	ok	Go whenever—except after you've eaten.
★ The Amazing Adventures of Spider-Man	40"	sim. ride	4½ min.	6 and up	Yes!	Use Universal Express or go early or late in day. See bad guys in the WANTED posters.
The Cat in the Hat	n/a	thrill ride		All	Heavy	Universal Express here or go at end of day.

★ = **Fodor'sChoice**

Ticket. For $85 you receive unlimited admission to both theme parks and CityWalk for seven consecutive days—quite a savings. Here are your other ticket options (tax not included).

TICKET	ADULTS	AGES 3–9
1 day, 1 park	$67	$56
1 day, 2 parks	$77	$67
2 days, 2 parks	$114.95	$104.95

You may also want to consider FlexTickets, which let you add visits to SeaWorld, Wet n' Wild, and Busch Gardens Tampa Bay onto visits to Universal. These FlexTickets are good for unlimited admission for 14 consecutive days.

TICKET	ADULTS	AGES 3–9
4-park FlexTicket	$189.95	$155.95
5-park FlexTicket	$234.95	$199.95

People with a disability that limits enjoyment of the park are eligible for a 15% discount off the ticket price. Also, American Automobile Association members get 10% off, sometimes more, at AAA offices. There are discount coupons for most theme parks in tourist flyers distributed around Orlando and if you buy tickets at the **Orlando/ Orange County Convention & Visitors Bureau** (⊠ *8723 International Dr.* ☎ *407/363–5871*), you can save about $5 per adult ticket ($3 on children's prices).

PARKING

Universal's parking garage complex, which serves both theme parks and CityWalk, is the world's largest. Definitely write down your parking space, because everything looks the same inside and after a few go-rounds on the Hulk you might have a hard time remembering whether you parked at King Kong 104 or Jaws 328. Because your vehicle is covered, it's not so sweltering at the end of the day even when it's hot. The cost is $11 for cars and motorcycles, $12 for campers. Valet parking, which puts you just a short walk (and about 15 minutes closer) to the entrance of Universal Studios, is available for $18. Parking in the garage is free after 6 PM.

VISITOR INFORMATION
Universal Information (☎ *407/363–8000 TDD* ⊕ *www.universalorlando.com*). **Universal Resort reservations** (☎ *888/273–1311*).

SEAWORLD & DISCOVERY COVE

Less glitzy than Walt Disney World or Universal, SeaWorld and its sister park, Discovery Cove, are definitely worth a visit for a low-key, relaxing, ocean-theme experience.

SEAWORLD ORLANDO

(10)
Fodor'sChoice
★

It's the animals who are the stars here. Sleek dolphins perform like gymnastic champions, and orcas sail through the air like featherweight Nijinskys. The world's largest zoological park, SeaWorld is devoted to mammals, birds, fish, and reptiles that live in the oceans and their tributaries. Every attraction is designed to explain the marine world and its vulnerability to human use. Yet the presentations are always enjoyable, and almost always memorable. The highlight is Shamu Stadium, where you can see Shamu and his sidekicks propel their trainers high up into the air.

3

ADMISSION

At this writing, regular one-day tickets to SeaWorld cost $64.95 for adults, and $53.95 for children ages 3 to 9, not including tax. For permission to bypass the admission line at the park, purchase and print out your tickets online. Contact **SeaWorld Information** (☎407/351–3600 or 888/800–5447 ⊕www.seaworld.com) with questions.

PARKING

Parking costs $10 per car, $12 for an RV or camper. Preferred parking, which costs $15, allows you to park in the six rows closest to the front gate.

DISCOVERY COVE

(11)
★

An oasis of artificial reefs, white-sand beaches, tropical fish, dolphins, and exotic birds, this limited-admission park is Orlando's most unusual retreat. The major attraction is one-on-one time with a real, live dolphin, which you get to touch, feed, swim with, and even kiss. At $259 per ticket, this is Orlando's most expensive theme park, but the sting of the price is soothed when you realize the price covers meals, towels, a locker, a mask, a snorkel, a wetsuit or swim vest, and admission to sister parks SeaWorld Orlando or Busch Gardens. *Near the intersection of I–4 and the Beeline Expressway; take I–4 to Exit 71 or 72 and follow signs.*

ADMISSION

If you're committed to visiting Discovery Cove, make reservations well in advance—attendance is limited to about 1,000 people a day. All-inclusive tickets (with Dolphin Swim) start at $259 in the off-season and go up to $279 in summer. Prices drop by $100 if you choose to forsake the dolphin. Either fee includes unlimited access to all beach and snorkeling areas and the free-flight aviary; all meals and snacks; use of a mask, snorkel, swim vest, towel, locker, and other amenities; parking; and a pass for seven days of unlimited, come-and-go-as-you-please admission to SeaWorld Orlando or Busch Gardens in Tampa. For reservations and additional information, call **Discovery Cove** (☎877/434–7268 ⊕www.discoverycove.com).

SEAWORLD

★ NAME	Min. Height	Type of Ride	Duration	Suits	Crowds	Strategy
Aviary	n/a	aviary	Up to you.	All	ok	Be sure your camera has memory.
Beaches	n/a	pool	Up to you.	All	ok	Go to Discovery Cove for privacy.
Blue Horizon	n/a	show	30 min.	All	Heavy	Arrive 20 min early.
Clydesdale Hamlet	n/a	zoo	15 min.	All	ok	Go anytime.
Coral Reef	n/a	pool	Up to you.	All	ok	See barracudas and sharks here.
Dolphin Lagoon	n/a	pool	60 min.	6 and up	ok	Beware you'll be cajoled to buy photos.
Dolphin Nursery	n/a	touch pool	Up to you.	All	ok	Go during Shamu show so the kids can be up front.
Journey to Atlantis	42"	thrill ride	6 min.	7 and up	Large	Make a beeline here first thing or go about an hr before closing; this is best at night.
★ Key West at SeaWorld	n/a	touch pool	Up to you.	All	ok	If too crowded, wander until crowds disperse. Feed the dolphins
★ Kraken	54	thrill ride	6 min.	8 and up	Yes!	Get to the park when it opens and head straight to Kraken; otherwise, hit close to closing.
Manatees: The Last Generation?	n/a	touch pool	Up to you.	All	ok	Go during a Shamu show and not right after a dolphin show.
Odyssea	n/a	show	30 min.	All	Fast lines	Arrive fifteen minutes before curtain for a choice of seats. Entertaining pre-show.
Pacific Point Preserve	n/a	sea lions	Up to you.	All	ok	Go anytime.
Penguin Encounter	n/a	touch pool	Up to you.	All	Yes!	Go during dolphin and sea lion shows, and before you've gotten soaked at Journey to Atlantis, or you'll freeze.
Ray Lagoon	n/a	pool	n/a	All	ok	Swim with barbless stingray.
★ Sea Lion & Otter Stadium	n/a	show	40 min.	All	ok	Sit toward the center for the best view, and don't miss the beginning.
★ SeaWorld Theater– Pets Ahoy	n/a	show	20–25 min.	All	Busy	Gauge the crowds and get there early if necessary.
★ Shamu Stadium	n/a	show	30 min.	All	Busy	Go 45 min early for early-afternoon show. Don't miss Close-up encounters.

		play area	Up to you.	Toddlers	Busy	
Shamu's Happy Harbor	n/a	play area	Up to you.			Don't go first thing in morning or you'll never drag your child away; go midafternoon or toward dusk. Bring a towel to dry them off.
Shark Encounter	n/a	aquarium	20 min.	All	Sometimes	Go during the sea lion show.
Sky Tower	n/a	great view	Up to you.	All	ok	Look for a line and go if there's none.
Stingray Lagoon	n/a	aquarium	Up to you.	All	Moderate	Walk by if it's crowded, return before dusk.
Tropical Reef	n/a	aquarium	Up to you.	All	ok	Go at the end of the day—because it's near the entrance, most people stop here on their way in.
Tropical River	n/a	aquarium	Up to you.	All		
Turtle Point	n/a	zoo		All	ok	Go anytime.
Wild Arctic	42"	sim. ride		All	Peak season	Go during a Shamu show. You can skip the ride if you just want to see the mammals.

★ = **Fodor's**Choice

AWAY FROM THE PARKS

Once you've exhausted the theme parks, or have been exhausted by them, turn your attention to a wealth of other area offerings. Although you'll find plenty of other recreational activities of interest to kids, there are also museums and parks and gardens galore, highlighting the cultural and natural heritage of this part of the South.

KISSIMMEE

⓬ *10 mi east of Walt Disney World Resort; take I-4 Exit 64A.*

Although Kissimmee is primarily known as the gateway to Walt Disney World, its non-WDW attractions just might tickle your fancy.

☼ Long before Walt Disney World, there was campy **Gatorland,** which has endured since 1949 without much change, despite major competition. Through the monstrous aqua gator-jaw doorway—a definite photo op—lie thrills and chills in the form of thousands of alligators and crocodiles swimming and basking in the Florida sun. There's a Gator Wrestling Cracker-style show, and although there's no doubt who's going to win the match, it's still fun to see the handlers take on those tough guys with the beady eyes. In the educational Up Close Encounters Snake Show, high drama is provided by the 30–40 rattlesnakes that fill the pit around the speaker. ⊠*14501 S. Orange Blossom Trail, between Orlando and Kissimmee* ☎*407/855–5496 or 800/393–5297* ⊕*www.gatorland.com* ☞*$19.25 adults, $12.95 children 3–12; $3 discount coupons online* ☉*Daily 9–5.*

☼ Friendly farmhands keep things moving on the two-hour guided tour
Fodor'sChoice of **Green Meadows Farm**—a 40-acre property with almost 300 animals.
★ There's no waiting in line because tours are always starting. Everyone can milk the mama cow, and chickens and geese are turned loose in their yard to run and squawk while city slickers try to catch them. Children take a quick pony ride, and everyone gets jostled about on the old-fashioned hayride. Youngsters come away saying, "I milked a cow, caught a chicken, petted a pig, and fed a goat." Take U.S. 192 for 3 mi east of Interstate 4 to South Poinciana Boulevard; turn right and drive 5 mi. ⊠*1368 S. Poinciana Blvd.* ☎*407/846–0770* ⊕*www.greenmeadowsfarm.com* ☞*$19; discount coupons online* ☉*Daily 9:30–5:30; last tour begins at 4.*

OFF THE BEATEN PATH
Fodor'sChoice
★

Historic Bok Sanctuary. If after several days at the theme parks you find that you're in need of a back-to-nature fix, head south along U.S. 27 to the small town of **Lake Wales.** Along the way you see what's left of Central Florida's citrus groves (many of them remain). But the main reason to take this drive is to get to the Historic Bok Sanctuary. Shady paths meander through pine forests in this peaceful world of silvery moats, mockingbirds and swans, blooming thickets, and hidden sundials. You'll be able to boast that you stood on the highest measured point on Florida's peninsula, a colossal 298 feet above sea level. The majestic, 200-foot Bok Tower is constructed of coquina—from sea-

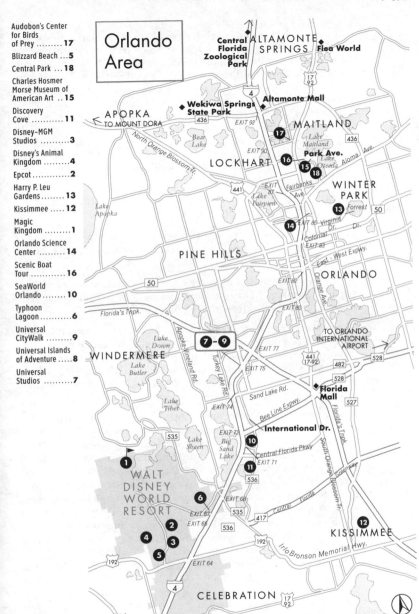

Audobon's Center
for Birds
of Prey **17**

Blizzard Beach ... **5**

Central Park ... **18**

Charles Hosmer
Morse Museum of
American Art .. **15**

Discovery
Cove **11**

Disney-MGM
Studios **3**

Disney's Animal
Kingdom **4**

Epcot **2**

Harry P. Leu
Gardens **13**

Kissimmee **12**

Magic
Kingdom **1**

Orlando Science
Center **14**

Scenic Boat
Tour **16**

SeaWorld
Orlando **10**

Typhoon
Lagoon **6**

Universal
CityWalk **9**

Universal Islands
of Adventure **8**

Universal
Studios **7**

Orlando Area

Central Florida Zoological Park

ALTAMONTE SPRINGS

Flea World

APOPKA

TO MOUNT DORA

Wekiwa Springs State Park

Altamonte Mall

MAITLAND

LOCKHART

Park Ave.

WINTER PARK

PINE HILLS

ORLANDO

TO ORLANDO INTERNATIONAL AIRPORT

WINDERMERE

Florida Mall

International Dr.

WALT DISNEY WORLD RESORT

KISSIMMEE

CELEBRATION

Historic Bok Sanctuary

Cypress Gardens

0   5 miles

0   5 km

KEY

► *Start of itinerary*

shells—and pink, white, and gray marble, and it houses a carillon with 57 bronze bells that ring out each day at 1 and 3 PM. The landscape was designed in 1928 by Frederick Law Olmsted Jr., son of the planner of New York's Central Park. The grounds include the 20-room, Mediterranean-style **Pinewood Estate,** built in 1930. Take I–4 to Exit 55, and head south on U.S. 27 for about 23 mi. Proceed past Eagle Ridge Mall, then turn left after two traffic lights onto Mountain Lake Cut Off Road and follow signs. ✉ *1151 Tower Blvd., Lake Wales* ☎ *863/676–1408* ⊕ *www.boktower.org* ✆ *$10 adults, $3 children 5–12, 50% off admission Sat. 8–9; Pinewood Estate general tour $6 adults, $5 children 5–12; holiday tour prices higher* ⊙ *Daily 8–6; check Web site or call for Pinewood Estate tour schedule, which varies seasonally; holiday tours late Nov.–early Jan.*

DOWNTOWN ORLANDO & ENVIRONS

15 mi northeast of Walt Disney World Resort; take I–4 Exit 83B if you're heading westbound, Exit 83A if eastbound, or Exit 85 for Loch Haven Park sights.

Downtown Orlando is a dynamic community that's constantly growing and changing. Numerous parks, many of which surround lakes, provide pleasant relief from the tall office buildings.

⑬ The former estate of citrus entrepreneur Harry P. Leu, **Harry P. Leu Gardens** provides a quiet respite. On the grounds' 50 acres is a collection of historical blooms, many varieties of which were established before 1900. ✉ *1920 N. Forest Ave., Downtown Orlando* ☎ *407/246–2620* ⊕ *www.leugardens.org* ✆ *$5; $1 children in kindergarten–12th grade* ⊙ *Garden daily 9–5, guided house tours daily 10–3:30.*

With all the high-tech glitz and imagined worlds of the theme parks, which are closer to where most stay, is it worth visiting the

⑭ **Orlando Science Center,** a reality-based science museum in Orlando
☾ proper? That depends. If you're into hands-on educational exhibits
★ about the human body, mechanics, electricity, math, nature, the solar system, and optics, you'll really like the science center. It's in a gorgeous building with, besides the exhibits, a wonderful atrium that's home to live gators and turtles. There's a great DinoDigs room for the dinosaur-crazed, and the Body Zone area is improved with BodyZone3D, a small digital theater show featuring a journey through the circulatory system from the perspective of a red blood cell. The Dr. Phillips CineDome, a movie theater with a giant eight-story screen, offers large-format IWERKS films (Ub Iwerks was an associate of Walt Disney's in the early days), as well as planetarium programs. On Friday and Saturday night, you can peer through Florida's largest publicly accessible refractor telescope to view the planets and many of their moons, plus other galaxies and nebulas. ✉ *777 E. Princeton St.* ☎ *407/514–2000 or 888/672–4386* ⊕ *www.osc.org* ✆ *$14.95 adults, $13.95 students and seniors with ID, $9.95 children 3–11; after 6 Fri. and Sat. $9.95 adults, $8.95 students and seniors, $4.95 children; parking $4; tickets include all exhibits, films, and planetarium shows;*

additional admission charged for special exhibitions ⊙ *Sun.–Thurs.
10–6, Fri. and Sat. 10–11.*

WINTER PARK & MAITLAND

*20 mi northeast of WDW; take I–4 Exit 87 to Winter Park and head
east 3 mi on Fairbanks Ave., or take I–4 Exit 90A, then Maitland Blvd.
east, and turn right (south) on Maitland Ave.*

Spend a pleasant day in upscale Winter Park shopping at chic boutiques, eating at a cozy café, visiting museums, and taking in the scenery along Park Avenue, with its hidden alleyways that lead to peaceful
nooks and crannies. Away from the avenue, moss-covered trees form a
canopy over brick streets, and old estates surround canal-linked lakes.
Just north is the Audubon Center for Birds of Prey in Maitland.

Many works of Louis Comfort Tiffany, including immense stained-
glass windows, lamps, watercolors, and desk sets, are at the

⑮ Fodor'sChoice ★ **Charles Hosmer Morse Museum of American Art.** The 1,082-square-foot Tiffany Chapel was built for the 1893 World's Fair. ⊠ *445 N. Park Ave.*
☎ *407/645–5311* ⤶ *$3; children under 12 free* ⊙ *Tues.–Sat. 9:30–4,
Sun. 1–4; Sept.–May, Fri. until 8.*

⑯ ★ From the dock at the end of Morse Avenue, depart for the **Scenic Boat
Tour,** a Winter Park tradition that's been in continuous operation for
more than 60 years. The one-hour pontoon boat tour, narrated by your
captain, leaves hourly and cruises along 12 mi of Winter Park's opulent
lakeside estates, through narrow canals, and across three lakes. ⊠ *312
E. Morse Blvd.* ☎ *407/644–4056* ⊕ *www.scenicboattours.com* ⤶ *$10;
$5 children 2–11* ⊙ *Daily 10–4.*

⑰ More than 20 bird species, including hawks, eagles, owls, falcons, and
vultures, make their home at **Audubon's Center for Birds of Prey.** This
small wildlife rehabilitation center takes in more than 700 injured wild
birds of prey each year. Fewer than half the birds are able to return
to the wild; permanently injured birds live at the center on outdoor
perches or in the center's aviaries. From Maitland Avenue, turn right on
U.S. 17–92, right on Lake Avenue, and right on Audubon Way. ⊠ *1101
Audubon Way* ☎ *407/644–0190* ⊕ *www.audubonofflorida.org* ⤶ *$5*
⊙ *Tues.–Sun. 10–4.*

**OFF THE
BEATEN
PATH**

Fodor'sChoice
★

Wekiwa Springs State Park. Where the tannin-stained Wekiva River meets
the crystal-clear Wekiwa headspring, you'll find this 6,400-acre park
good for camping, hiking, picnicking, swimming, canoeing, fishing, and
watching for alligators, egrets, and deer. Although it can be crowded on
weekends, on weekdays it's Walden Pond, Florida style. Take Interstate
4 Exit 94 and turn left on Route 434 and right on Wekiwa Springs
Road. ⊠ *1800 Wekiva Circle, Apopka* ☎ *407/884–2008* ⤶ *$5 per
vehicle* ⊙ *Daily 8–sunset.*

CELEBRATION

10 mi southeast of WDW; take I–4 to Exit 64A and follow the Celebration signs.

This Disney-created community reminds some locals of something out of the *The Stepford Wives.* But Celebration, which draws on vernacular architecture from all over the United States and was based on ideas from some of America's top architects and planners, can be a great retreat from the theme parks and from the garish reality of the U.S. 192 tourist strip 1 mi to the east. The town is so perfect it could be a movie set, and it's a delightful place to spend a morning or afternoon. Sidewalks are built for strolling, restaurants have outdoor seating with lake views, and inviting shops beckon. After a walk around the lake, take your youngsters over to the huge interactive fountain, and have fun getting wet. Starting after Thanksgiving and continuing on through the new year, honest-to-goodness snow sprinkles softly over Main Street each evening, to the delight of children of all ages.

WHERE TO EAT

Food in the parks ranges from fast to fabulous. Hamburgers, chicken fingers, and fries dominate at most of the counter-service places, but fresh sandwiches, salads, and fruit are always available, too. Of course, the full-service restaurants offer the best selection, from the Hollywood Brown Derby's signature Cobb salad to steak at Le Cellier. Priority-seating reservations are generally essential for restaurant meals, especially at dinner. Without reservations, you may find yourself having a burger (again) for dinner, or having to leave Walt Disney World, which some people prefer to do anyway.

Although some of Orlando's top restaurants—Victoria and Albert's, the California Grill, Bice, and Emeril's, for example—are in Walt Disney World or Universal, many others are outside the parks. Sand Lake Road, International Drive, and Celebration all have excellent restaurants, such as Seasons 52 and Bonefish Grill, which are perfect for a refreshing and romantic dinner in the real world.

DRESS

Because tourism is king around Orlando, casual dress is the rule. Men need jackets only in the priciest establishments.

MEALTIMES

When you're touring the theme parks, you can save a lot of time by eating in the off-hours. Lines at the counter-service places can get very long between noon and 2, and waiting in line for food can get more frustrating than waiting in line for a ride. Try eating lunch at 11 and dinner at 5, or lunch at 2:30 and dinner at 9.

RESERVATIONS

All WDW restaurants and most restaurants elsewhere in greater Orlando take "priority seating" reservations. A priority-seating reservation is like a FASTPASS to a meal. You don't get your table right away, but you should get the next one that becomes available. Say you make your reservation for 7 PM. Once you arrive, the hostess will give you a round plastic buzzer that looks sort of like a hockey puck. Then you can walk around, get a drink at the bar, or just wait nearby until the buzzer vibrates and flashes red. That means your table is ready and you can go back to the hostess stand to be seated. You will most likely be seated within 15 minutes of your arrival.

WINE & ALCOHOL

The Magic Kingdom's no-liquor policy, a Walt Disney tradition that seems almost quaint in this day and age, does not extend to the rest of Walt Disney World, and in fact, most restaurants and watering holes, particularly those in the on-site hotels, mix elaborate fantasy drinks based on fruit juices or flavored with liqueurs.

For restaurant reservations within Walt Disney World, call ☎407/939–3463 or 407/560–7277. And, although you can't make reservations online at ⊕*www.disneyworld.com*, you can certainly get plenty of information, like the hours, price range, and specialties of all Disney eateries. For Universal Orlando reservations, call ☎407/224–9255.

In reviews, reservations are mentioned only when they're essential or not accepted. Unless otherwise noted, the restaurants listed are open daily for lunch and dinner.

PRICES

WHAT IT COSTS				
¢	$	$$	$$$	$$$$
AT DINNER	under $8	$8–$15	$15–$20	$20–$30	over $30

Prices are per person for a main course at dinner.

WDW CHARACTER MEALS

At these breakfasts, brunches, and dinners staged in hotel and theme-park restaurants all over Walt Disney World, kids can snuggle up to all the best-loved Disney characters. Sometimes the food is served buffet style; sometimes it's served to you banquet style. The cast of characters, times, and prices changes frequently (although locations of performances remain fairly constant), so be sure to call ahead.

Reservations are always available and often required; some meals can fill up more than 60 days in advance. However, you can also book by phone on the same day you plan to dine, and it never hurts to double-check the character lineup before you leave for the meal. If you have your heart set on a specific meal, make your reservations when you book your trip—up to six months in advance. Smoking is not permitted.

BREAKFAST

Main Street, U.S.A.'s **Crystal Palace Buffet** (☎407/939–3463 ✉$18.99 *adults, $10.99 children ages 3–9*) has breakfast with Winnie the Pooh, Eeyore, Piglet, and friends daily from 8 AM to 10:30 AM. Disney–MGM Studios's **Hollywood & Vine** (☎407/939–3463 ✉$22.99 *adults, $12.99 children ages 3–9*) hosts *Playhouse Disney* stars Jo Jo and Goliath from "Jo Jo's Circus" and June and Leo from "The Little Einsteins."

At Disney's Beach Club, characters are on hand at the **Cape May Café** (☎407/939–3463 ✉$18.99 *adults, $10.99 children ages 3–9*) from 7:30 to 11 daily. At the Contemporary Resort, **Chef Mickey's** (☎407/939–3463 ✉$18.99 *adults, $10.99 children ages 3–9*) has a no-holds-barred buffet from 7 to 11:15 daily. The Polynesian Resort's **'Ohana** (☎407/939–3463 ✉$18.99 *adults, $10.99 children ages 3–9*) serves breakfast with Mickey and his friends daily from 7:30 to 11.

At the Swan, the weekend Good Morning Character Breakfast at the **Garden Grove Café** (☎407/934–3000 ✉$16.95 *adults, $8.50 children ages 3–9*) features a couple of dogs—Goofy and Pluto—from 8 to 11.

At the Wyndham Palace Resort & Spa you can drop in Sunday from 8 to 11 for a character meal at the **Watercress Restaurant** (☎407/827–2727 ✉$24 *adults, $13 children ages 3–9*).

BY RESERVATION ONLY

The Princess Storybook Breakfasts with Snow White, Sleeping Beauty, and at least three other princesses are held at Epcot Center in the Norway exhibit at **Restaurant Akershus** (☎407/939–3463 ✉$22.99 *adults, $12.99 children ages 3–9*) in the Norway Pavilion from 8:30 to 10:30 daily. Donald Duck and his friends are at Donald's Breakfastosaurus 8:10 to 10 daily at the **Restaurantosaurus** (☎407/939–3463 ✉$18.99 *adults, $10.99 children ages 3–9*), in Disney's Animal Kingdom. Mary Poppins presides at **1900 Park Fare Restaurant** (☎407/824–2383 ✉$18.99 *adults, $10.99 children ages 3–9*) in the Grand Floridian from 7:30 to 11:30 daily. Cinderella herself hosts Magic Kingdom breakfasts from 8:05 to 10 daily at

Fodor'sChoice **Cinderella's Royal Table** (☎407/939–3463 ✉$31.99 *adults, $21.99 chil-*
★   *dren ages 3–9*). This breakfast is extremely popular, so book six months in advance to be assured seating.

LUNCH

At Cinderella Castle, **Cinderella's Royal Table** (☎407/939–3463 ✉$33.99 *adults, $22.99 children ages 3–9*) is a popular lunchtime option. Your picture is taken as you arrive, then presented to you—in a Cinderella frame, of course. Winnie the Pooh, Tigger, and Eeyore come to the **Crystal Palace Buffet** (☎407/939–3463 ✉$20.99 *adults, $11.99 children ages 3–9*) on Main Street U.S.A. from 11:10 to 2:30. Mickey, Pluto, and Chip 'n' Dale are on hand from noon to 3:50 at the **Garden Grill** (☎407/939–3463 ✉$20.99 *adults, $11.99 children ages 3–9*) in the Land pavilion at Epcot.

The Princess Storybook Lunches with Snow White, Sleeping Beauty, and at least three other princesses are held at Epcot at the Norway Pavilion in **Restaurant Akershus** (☎407/939–3463 ✉$24.99 *adults, $13.99 children ages 3–9*) from 11:40 AM to 2:50 PM.

Jo Jo, Goliath, June, and Leo from *Playhouse Disney* make a comeback at Disney–MGM Studios's **Hollywood & Vine** (☎407/939–3463 ✉$24.99 *adults, $13.99 children ages 3–9*).

AFTERNOON SNACKS

For the *Wonderland* **Tea Party** (☎407/939–3463 ✉$28.17) at the Grand Floridian Resort, Alice and other characters preside over afternoon tea on weekdays from 1:30 to 2:30. With the cast's help, children can bake their own cupcakes and then eat them at the tea party. Open only to children ages 3 to 10; all participants must be potty-trained.

DINNER

All character dinners require reservations. Minnie Mouse and friends (which in this case does not include Mickey) get patriotic during their evening appearance at the Liberty Square **Liberty Tree Tavern** (☎407/939–3463 ✉$27.99 *adults, $12.99 children ages 3–9*). A "revolutionary" feast of smoked pork, turkey, carved beef, and all the trimmings is served nightly from 4 PM to 8:40 PM. Farmer Mickey appears at the Land Pavilion at Epcot's **Garden Grill** (☎407/939–3463 ✉$27.99 *adults, $12.99 children ages 3–9*) from 4 to 8 daily. Winnie the Pooh and friends appear at a nightly buffet from 4 to 8:45 at the **Crystal Palace Buffet** (☎407/939–3463 ✉$27.99 *adults, $12.99 children ages 3–9*) on Main Street, U.S.A.

Every night at 8 (7 in winter), near Fort Wilderness's Meadow Trading Post, there's a **Character Campfire** (☎407/824–2727) with a free singalong. There are usually around five characters there, with Chip 'n' Dale frequent attendees.

Cinderella's Gala Feast is held at the Grand Floridian's **1900 Park Fare** (☎407/939–3463 ✉$28.99 *adults, $13.99 children ages 3–9*), for a buffet served from 4:30 to 8:20 daily. The Contemporary Resort hosts a wildly popular dinner starring the head honcho himself at **Chef Mickey's** (☎407/939–3463 ✉$27.99 *adults, $12.99 children ages 3–9*), from 5 to 9:15 daily. At the Walt Disney World Swan, you can dine with *Lion King* characters Monday and Friday from 5:30 to 10 at **Gulliver's Grill** (☎407/934–1609). Known as the Garden Grove Café during the day, Gulliver's Grill hosts Goofy and Pluto the other five nights of the week. Dinner is $24.99 adults, $10.95 children ages 3 to 11.

The Princess Storybook Dinner with Snow White, Sleeping Beauty, and at least three other princesses are held at Epcot Center at the Norway Pavilion in **Restaurant Akershus** (☎407/939–3463 ✉$28.99 *adults, $13.99 children ages 3–9*) from 4:20 to 8:40.

MAGIC KINGDOM

$$$–$$$$ ✕**Cinderella's Royal Table.** Cinderella and other Disney princesses appear
★ at breakfast time at this eatery in the castle's old mead hall; you should
book reservations up to 180 days in advance to be sure to see them.
Breakfast and lunch are pre-plated meals. Breakfast, which includes
scrambled eggs, sausages, bacon, danishes, potatoes, and beverages is
$32 for adults, $22 for children. Lunch, which includes entrées like
prime rib with mashed potatoes and roasted chicken breast on bread
pudding with spinach, garlic, and red-onion marmalade, is $34 for
adults, $23 for children. The prix-fixe dinner is $40 for adults, $25
for children. When you arrive at the Cinderella Castle, a photographer
snaps a shot of your group in the lobby. A package of photographs
will be delivered to your table during your meal. ✉*Cinderella Castle*
☎*407/939–3463* ⟁*Reservations essential* ▤*AE, MC, V.*

$$–$$$ ✕**Crystal Palace.** Named for the big glass atrium surrounding the res-
taurant, the Crystal Palace is a great escape in summer, when the air-
conditioning is turned to near meat-locker level. The buffet-style meal
includes prime rib, peel-and-eat shrimp, soups, pastas, fresh-baked
breads, and ice-cream sundaes, all part of a one-price package (din-
ner price is $28 for adults). There's also a kids-only buffet with what
many youngsters consider the basic food groups: macaroni and cheese,
pizza, and chocolate chip cookies for $13 per child. The Crystal Palace
is huge but charming with numerous nooks and crannies, comfortable
banquettes, cozy cast-iron tables, and abundant sunlight. It's also one
of the few places in the Magic Kingdom that serves breakfast. Winnie
the Pooh and his pals from the Hundred Acre Wood visit at breakfast,
lunch, and dinner. ✉*At Hub end of Main St. facing Cinderella Castle*
☎*407/939–3463* ▤*AE, MC, V.*

EPCOT

Epcot's World Showcase offers some of the finest dining in Orlando.
Every pavilion has at least one and often two or even three eateries.
Where there's a choice, it's between a relatively expensive full-service
restaurant and a more affordable, ethnic fast-food spot, plus carts and
shops selling snacks ranging from French pastries to Japanese ices—
whatever's appropriate to the pavilion.

Lunch and dinner priority-seating reservations are essential at the full-
service restaurants; you can make them up to 60 days in advance by
calling ☎407/939–3463 or going in person to Guest Relations at the
park (only on the day of the meal) or to the restaurants themselves
when they open for lunch, usually at noon.

CANADIAN

$$–$$$ ✕**Le Cellier.** With the best Canadian wine cellar in the state, this charm-
ing eatery with stone arches and dark-wood paneling has a good selec-
tion of Canadian beer as well. Aged beef is king, although many steaks
appear only on the dinner menu. If you're a carnivore, go for the herb-
crusted prime rib. Even though the menu changes periodically (gone are
the buffalo steaks, alas), they've always got the maple-ginger–glazed

Canadian salmon and free-range chicken with a mustard marinade. For a light meal, try the Prince Edward Island mussels. Dessert salutes to the land up north include a crème brûlée made with maple sugar and the Canadian Club chocolate cake. ⊠ *Canada* ⊟ *AE, MC, V.*

ENGLISH

$$–$$$ ✕ **Rose & Crown.** If you're an Anglophile and you love a good, thick beer, this is the place to soak up both the suds and the British street culture. "Wenches" serve up traditional English fare—fish-and-chips, meat pies, Yorkshire pudding, and the ever-popular bangers and mash, English sausage over mashed potatoes. A good and somewhat eclectic choice is the English pie sampler, with both chicken-and-leek and pork-and-cottage pies (pork with carrots topped with mashed potatoes and cheddar cheese), plus a side of green beans. For vegetarians, there's even an offering of curried veggies and tofu on the menu. For dessert, try the sticky toffee pudding with butter rum sauce. If you are not driving soon after the meal, try the Imperial Ale sampler—five 6-ounce glasses for $9.35. The terrace has a splendid view of IllumiNations. ⊠ *United Kingdom* ⊟ *AE, MC, V.*

FRENCH

$$$$ ✕ **Bistro de Paris.** The great secret in the France pavilion—and, indeed, in
★ all of Epcot—is the Bistro de Paris, upstairs from Les Chefs de France. The sophisticated menu reflects the cutting edge of French cooking; representative dishes include roasted rack of venison with black-pepper sauce, pan-seared lobster served in its own bisque, and seared scallops with black truffle potato puree. Escargot, as an appetizer, is a relative bargain at $10. Save room for the Grand Marnier–flambéed crepes. Come late, ask for a window seat, and plan to linger to watch the nightly Epcot light show. Moderately priced French wines are available by the glass. ⊠ *France* ⊟ *AE, MC, V.*

$$–$$$$ ✕ **Les Chefs de France.** What some consider the best restaurant at Dis-
Fodor'sChoice ney was created by three of France's most famous chefs: Paul Bocuse,
★ Gaston Lenôtre, and Roger Vergé. Classic escargots, a good starter, are prepared in a casserole with garlic butter; you might follow up with duck à l'orange or grilled beef tenderloin with a black pepper sauce. Save room for crepes *au chocolat.* Best guilty pleasure: a sinful version of macaroni and cheese made with cream and Gruyère cheese, a bargain at $17. The nearby Boulangerie Pâtisserie, run by the same team, offers tarts, croissants, éclairs, napoleons, and more to go. ⊠ *France* ⊟ *AE, MC, V.*

GERMAN

$$ ✕ **Biergarten.** Oktoberfest runs 365 days a year here. The cheerful, sometimes raucous, crowds are what you would expect in a place with an oompah band. Waitresses in Bavarian garb serve *breseln,* hot German pretzels, which are made fresh daily on the premises. The menu and level of frivolity are the same at lunch and dinner. For a single price ($21 for adults, $10.99 for kids ages 3–11 at lunch and $24 for adults and $12 for children at dinner), mountains of sauerbraten, bratwurst, chicken schnitzel, apple strudel, and Black Forest cake await you at the all-you-can-eat buffet. And if you aren't feeling too Teutonic,

there's also rotisserie chicken and roast pork. Patrons pound pitchers of all kinds of beer and wine on the long communal tables—even when the yodelers, singers, and dancers aren't egging them on. ⊠ *Germany* ☰ *AE, MC, V.*

ITALIAN

$$$–$$$$ ✕ **L'Originale Alfredo di Roma Ristorante.** Waiters skip around singing
☺ ★   arias, a show in itself. Their voices and the restaurant's namesake dish, made with mountains of imported Italian butter, account for its popularity. The classic dish—fettuccine with cream, butter, and loads of freshly grated Parmesan cheese—was invented by Alfredo de Lelio, whose descendants had a hand in creating this restaurant. Besides the excellent pastas, try the chef's tip of the hat to Florida—roasted grouper with a lemon, butter, and white wine sauce—or the tender, slow-roasted chicken served with polenta. The minestrone is excellent, and if you can't pass up the fettuccine Alfredo, it's available as an appetizer for $7.95 per person, or $19.95 for a platter that serves 3 to 4 people. Dessert offerings include a good tiramisu and an even better cannoli. ⊠ *Italy* ☰ *AE, MC, V.*

JAPANESE

$$–$$$$ ✕ **Mitsukoshi.** Three restaurants and a lounge are enclosed in this complex, which overlooks tranquil gardens. **Yakitori House,** a gussied-up fast-food stand in a small pavilion, is modeled after a teahouse in Kyoto's Katsura Summer Palace. At the **Tempura Kiku,** diners watch the chefs prepare sushi, sashimi, and tempura (batter-dipped deep-fried shrimp, scallops, and vegetables). In the five **Teppanyaki** dining rooms, chefs frenetically chop vegetables, meat, and fish and stir-fry them at the grills set into the communal tables. Specialties include lobster served with either shrimp and scallops or sirloin. The **Matsu No Ma Lounge,** more serene than the restaurants, has a great view of the World Showcase Lagoon. It also offers one of Epcot's great bargains: a 12-piece sushi platter for $21.75. Grown-ups might also go for the sake martini. ⊠ *Japan* ☰ *AE, MC, V.*

MEXICAN

$$–$$$ ✕ **San Angel Inn.** In the dark, grottolike main dining room, a deep purple, dimly lighted mural of a night scene in Central Mexico seems to envelop the diners. San Angel is a popular respite for the weary, especially when the humidity outside makes Central Florida feel like equatorial Africa. At dinner, guitar and marimba music fills the air. Start with the *queso fundido* (melted cheese and chorizo sausage served with soft tortillas) and then try the authentic *filete motuleno* (grilled beef tenderloin over black beans and melted cheese, ranchero sauce, and poblano pepper strips) or the *puntas de filete* (tender beef tips sautéed with onions and chilis and accompanied by rice and refried beans). For dessert, the flan is served with a piña colada sauce and topped with a fresh strawberry. ⊠ *Mexico* ☰ *AE, MC, V.*

MOROCCAN

$$–$$$$ ✗**Marrakesh.** Chef Abrache Lahcen of Morocco presents the best cooking of his homeland in this ornate eatery, which looks like something from the set of *Casablanca*. Your appetizer might be *harira*, a soup with tomatoes, lentils, and lamb that is traditionally served during Ramadan. From there, move on to the chicken, lamb, or vegetable couscous, Morocco's national dish. A good way to try a bit of everything is the Marrakesh Feast ($35 per person), which includes chicken bastilla and beef *brewat* (minced beef in a layered pastry dusted with cinnamon and powdered sugar), plus vegetable couscous and assorted Moroccan pastries; or better still, upgrade to the Royal Feast ($38 per person), which includes everything in the Marrakesh Feast, plus crepes for dessert. Traditional belly dancers perform periodically throughout the day in a show that is completely G-rated. ⊠*Morocco* ▤*AE, MC, V.*

SCANDINAVIAN

$$$
Fodor'sChoice
★

✗**Restaurant Akershus.** The Norwegian buffet at this restaurant is as extensive as you'll find on this side of the Atlantic. Appetizers usually include herring, prepared several ways, and cold seafood, including gravlax (cured salmon served with mustard sauce) or *fiskepudding* (a seafood mousse with herb dressing). For your main course, you might try some hot sausages, venison stew, or grilled Atlantic salmon. The à la carte desserts include raspberry tarts, bread pudding, and chocolate mousse with strawberry sauce. Akershus hosts a princess breakfast with Belle, Jasmine, Sleeping Beauty, and Snow White but *not* Cinderella. Call 407/939–3463 for reservations. ⊠*Norway* ▤*AE, MC, V.*

SEAFOOD

$$–$$$$ ✗**Coral Reef Restaurant.** One of this restaurant's walls is made entirely of glass and looks directly into the 6-million-gallon Living Seas aquarium, where you can get tantalizingly close to sharks, stingrays, groupers, tarpons, sea turtles and even the occasional scuba diver. And with a three-tiered seating area, everyone has a good view. Edible attractions include pan-seared tilapia served with a crab cake; ahi tuna lightly grilled; and Dublin-style mussels and clams steamed in a Harp beer broth. Crab fritters with spicy marinara sauce make a great appetizer. You might finish off with Kahlua tiramisu in raspberry sauce. ⊠*The Living Seas* ▤*AE, MC, V.*

DISNEY–MGM STUDIOS

AMERICAN

$–$$ ✗**'50s Prime Time Café.** Who says you can't go home again? If you grew up in middle America in the 1950s, just step inside. While *I Love Lucy* and *The Donna Reed Show* play on a television screen, you can feast on meat loaf, pot roast, or fried chicken, all served on a Formica tabletop. At $13, the meat loaf is one of the best inexpensive dinners in any local theme park. Follow it up with chocolate cake or a thick milk shake—available in chocolate, strawberry, vanilla, even peanut butter and jelly. The place offers some fancier dishes, such as pan-seared salmon, that are good but out of character with the diner theme. If you're not feeling totally wholesome, go for Dad's Electric Lemonade (rum, vodka, blue curaçao, sweet-and-sour mix, and Sprite), worth every bit of the $9.50 price tag. Just like Mother, the menu admonishes, "Don't put your elbows on the table!" ⊠*Echo Lake, Disney–MGM Studios* ☎*407/939–3463* ⊟*AE, MC, V.*

AMERICAN-CASUAL

$-$$$ ✕**Hollywood & Vine.** This restaurant is designed for those who like lots of food and lots of choices. You can have everything from frittatas to fried rice at the same meal. Even though the buffet ($24 for adults, $12 for children ages 3–11) is all-you-can-eat at a relatively low price, it does offer some upscale entrées like oven-roasted prime rib, sage-rubbed rotisserie turkey, or grilled sirloin in a red wine demi-glace. There are plenty of kids' favorites, such as mac and cheese, hot dogs, and fried chicken. Minnie, Goofy, Pluto, and Chip 'n' Dale put in appearances at breakfast and lunch character meals. There's a Hollywood theme to the place; characters and servers are just hoping to be discovered by some passing Hollywood agent. Priority seating reservations are a must. ⊠*Echo Lake, Disney–MGM Studios* ☎*407/939–3463* ⊟*AE, MC, V.*

ECLECTIC

$$-$$$ ✕**Hollywood Brown Derby.** At this reproduction of the famous 1940s Hollywood restaurant, the walls are lined with movie-star caricatures, just like in Tinseltown, and the staff wears black bow ties. The house specialty is the Cobb salad, which by legend was invented by Brown Derby founder Robert Cobb; the salad consists of lettuce enlivened by loads of tomato, bacon, turkey, blue cheese, chopped egg, and avocado, all tossed table-side. And the butter comes in molds shaped like Mickey Mouse heads. Other menu choices include grilled salmon on creamy polenta and Gorgonzola with sun-dried tomatoes and baby arugula; and pan-roasted pork tenderloin with white-cheddar grits. For dessert, try the Brown Derby grapefruit cake, with layers of cream cheese icing. If you request the *Fantasmic!* dinner package, make a reservation for no later than two hours before the start of the show. ⊠*Hollywood Blvd., Disney–MGM Studios* ☎*407/939–3463* ⊟*AE, MC, V.*

ELSEWHERE IN WALT DISNEY WORLD RESORT

AFRICAN

$$$-$$$$ ✕**Jiko.** The menu here is more African-inspired than purely African, but
Fodor'sChoice does include authentic entrées like jumbo scallops with golden brown
★ mealie pap (a porridge made from ground grain) and steamed golden bass with spicy chaka-laka (a mixture of baked beans, carrots, tomato, onions, and spices—a longtime menu favorite). The menu changes periodically but typically includes such entrées as roasted chicken with mashed potatoes, and pomegranate-glaze quails stuffed with saffron basmati rice. After dinner, try a non-African treat: baklava—the honey-soaked dessert is the best on the menu. Also worth trying is a globe-trotting treat: three flavors of ice cream—vanilla, chocolate, and arugula—with meringue dots. ⊠*Disney's Animal Kingdom Lodge* ☎*407/939–3463* ⚖*Reservations essential* ⊟*AE, D, MC, V.*

CONTEMPORARY

$$$$
Fodor'sChoice
★

✕ **Victoria and Albert's.** At this Disney fantasy, you are served by "Victoria" and "Albert," who recite the menu in tandem. There's also a sommelier to explain the wine pairings. Everyone, of course, is dressed in period Victorian costumes. This is one of the plushest fine-dining experiences in Florida: a regal meal in a lavish, Victorian-style room. The seven-course, prix-fixe menu ($100; wine is an additional $55) changes daily. Appetizer choices might include Iranian caviar, veal sweetbreads, or artichokes in a mushroom sauce; entrées may be Kobe beef with celery-root puree or veal tenderloin with cauliflower-and-potato puree. The restaurant also features a vegetarian menu with exotics such as rutabaga Napoleon with melted leeks and ramps. For most of the year, there are two seatings, at 5:45 and 9. In July and August, however, there's generally just one seating—at 6:30. The chef's table dinner event is $165 to $235 (with wine pairing) per person. Make your reservations 90 days in advance. ⊠ *Grand Floridian* ☎ *407/939–3463* ⌂ *Reservations essential.* Jacket required ▭ *AE, MC, V* ⊘ *No lunch.*

$$$–$$$$

✕ **Citricos.** Although the name implies that you might be eating lots of local citrus-flavor specialties, you won't find them here, aside from drinks like a "Citropolitan" martini, infused with lemon-and-lime liqueur, and an orange-chocolate mousse for dessert. Standout entrées include sautéed salmon fillet with roasted fennel, Yukon gold potatoes, and black-olive butter; and roasted free-range chicken with vegetable quinoa and tomato-cilantro sauce. The wine list, one of Disney's most extensive, includes vintages from around the world. ⊠ *Grand Floridian* ☎ *407/939–3463* ▭ *AE, MC, V.*

$$$–$$$$
☺
Fodor'sChoice
★

✕ **Wolfgang Puck.** There are lots of choices here, from wood-oven pizza at the informal Puck Express to five-course meals in the upstairs formal dining room, where there's also a sushi bar and an informal café. At Express try the barbecue chicken pizza or spinach and mushroom pizza. The dining room always offers inspired pastas with sauces sublimely laced with chunks of lobster, salmon, or chicken. Another good choice is the slow-braised short ribs ($28). Special five-course prix-fixe dinners ($110 with wine, $75 without) require 24-hour notice. ⊠ *Downtown Disney West Side* ☎ *407/938–9653* ▭ *AE, MC, V.*

$$–$$$$
★

✕ **California Grill.** The view of the surrounding Disney parks from this rooftop restaurant is as stunning as the food, especially at night, when you can watch the nightly Magic Kingdom fireworks from the patio. Start with the brick-oven flatbread with grilled duck sausage or the *unagi* (eel) sushi. For a main course, try the oak-fired beef fillet with three-cheese potato gratin and tamarind barbecue sauce, or the seared scallops with risotto, baby carrots, and crustacean butter sauce. Good dessert choices include the orange crepes with Grand Marnier custard, raspberries, and blackberry coulis and the butterscotch, orange, and vanilla crème brûlée. ⊠ *Contemporary Resort* ☎ *407/939–3463* ▭ *AE, MC, V.*

$$$
Fodor'sChoice
★

✕ **Artist Point.** If you're not a guest at the Wilderness Lodge, a meal here is worth it just to see the giant totem poles and huge rock fireplace in the lobby. The specialty is cedar-plank salmon and mashed potatoes with roasted fennel and truffle butter (worth its $29 price tag). Another good option: grilled buffalo sirloin with sweet potato–hazelnut gratin and sweet-onion jam. For dessert, try the wild berry cobbler or the flourless chocolate–whiskey cake with pecans and raspberry sorbet. There's a good northwestern U.S. wine list, and wine pairings for the meal cost $18 to $23 per person. A fixed price dinner, which offers a good cross section of the restaurant's cuisine, is available for $46 per person. ⊠ *Wilderness Lodge* ☎*407/939–3463* ⌕*Reservations essential* ▤*AE, MC, V.*

SEAFOOD

$–$$$$ ✕**Fulton's Crab House.** Set in a faux riverboat docked in a lagoon between Pleasure Island and the Marketplace, this fish house offers fine, if expensive, dining. The signature seafood is flown in daily. Dungeness crab from the Pacific coast, Alaskan king crab, Florida stone crab: it's all fresh. Start with the crab and lobster bisque, then try one of the many combination entrées like the gulf shrimp and crab cake platter. If you have no budget constraints, go for the Lobster Narragansett (a 2-pound lobster tail, oven roasted with scallops, shrimp and red skin potatoes, for $49). The sublime cappuccino ice-cream cake is $13, but one order is easily enough for two. ⊠*Downtown Disney Market Pl.* ☎*407/934–2628* ▤*AE, MC, V.*

STEAK

$$–$$$$ ✕**Yachtsman Steakhouse.** Aged beef, the attraction at this steak house in the ultrapolished Yacht and Beach Club, can be seen mellowing in the glassed-in butcher shop near the entryway. The slow-roasted prime rib is superb, as is a combo featuring an 8-ounce filet mignon and a 6-ounce lobster tail. (At $55, it's one of the most expensive surf-and-turf meals in Orlando.) The oak-fired ribeye is quite tender but at $42 it's not soft on your wallet. For dessert, try the chocolate layer cake with wine-marinated cherries. ⊠*Yacht and Beach Club* ☎*407/939–3463* ▤*AE, MC, V* ☉*No lunch.*

UNIVERSAL ORLANDO

Take I–4 Exit 74B if you're heading westbound, 75A if eastbound.

AMERICAN/CASUAL

$$$–$$$$ ✕**Emeril's.** The popular eatery is a culinary shrine to Emeril Lagasse,
★   the famous Food Network chef who occasionally appears here. The menu changes frequently, but you can always count on New Orleans treats like andouille sausage, shrimp, and red beans appearing in some form or fashion. Entrées may include andouille-crusted redfish with crispy shoestring potatoes; milk-fed veal with shrimp, artichoke hearts, and a mustard hollandaise sauce; and grilled beef fillet with bacon mashed potatoes and buttermilk-breaded onion rings. The wood-baked pizza, topped with exotic mushrooms, is stellar. Save room for Emeril's ice-cream parfait—banana-daiquiri ice cream topped with hot fudge, caramel sauce, walnuts, and a double-chocolate-fudge cookie. ⊠*6000 Universal Blvd., at Universal Orlando's CityWalk* ☎*407/224–2424* ⌕*Reservations essential* ▤*AE, D, MC, V.*

$-$$$ ✕ **NBA City.** The NBA memorabilia and video games are great, but the food is actually the real draw here. Best choices include appetizers of sweet and spicy smoked wings and pecan chicken tenders with orange marmalade sauce. For an entrée, try grilled lemon chicken served with garlic risotto and roasted poblano peppers and artichokes. The brick-oven pizzas include an unusual BLT variety. Finish with Vermont maple syrup pecan tart with fresh cream. The big-screen TVs, which naturally broadcast nonstop basketball action, probably won't surprise you, but the relatively quiet bar upstairs, with elegant blond-wood furniture, probably will. ⊠ *6000 Universal Blvd., at Universal Orlando's City-Walk* ☎ *407/363–5919* ☐ *AE, D, MC, V.*

PAN-ASIAN

$$$-$$$$ ✕ **Tchoup Chop.** With its cathedral ceiling, the inside of this restaurant
★ looks almost churchlike, and the food at Emeril Lagasse's Pacific-influenced restaurant is certainly righteous. Following the theme of the Royal Pacific Resort, the decorators included a tiki bar with lots of bamboo, a couple of indoor waterfalls, and a long pool with porcelain lily pads running the length of the dining room. The menu combines Lagasse's own New Orleans–style cuisine with an Asian theme. Entrées include grilled pork chops with ginger-roasted sweet potatoes, and a Hawaiian-style dinner plate with Kiawe smoked ribs, pork and noodle sauté, and teriyaki grilled chicken. One of the mainstay dishes is fish steamed in a banana leaf and covered with a sake–soy sauce—something to give you that South Pacific feeling. For dessert try the bittersweet chocolate layer cake with banana sauce or the pecan pie with vanilla-bean ice cream. ⊠ *6300 Hollywood Way, Universal Orlando* ☎ *407/503–2467* ⋈ *Reservations essential* ☐ *AE, D, DC, MC, V.*

INTERNATIONAL DRIVE, ORLANDO

Take I–4 Exit 72 or 74A.

AMERICAN/CASUAL

$$-$$$ ✕ **B-Line Diner.** As you might expect from its location in the Peabody
☺ Hotel, this slick, 1950s-style diner with red-vinyl counter seats is not exactly cheap, but the salads, sandwiches, and griddle foods are tops. The greatest combo ever—a thick, juicy burger served with fries and a wonderful milk shake—is done beautifully. You can also get southern favorites like crispy fried red snapper or hickory-smoked chicken, both with sides like white beans or collard greens. Desserts range from hazelnut-orange cake to coconut cream pie to banana splits. It's open 24 hours ⊠ *Peabody Orlando, 9801 International Dr.* ☎ *407/352–4000* ☐ *AE, D, DC, MC, V.*

CARIBBEAN

$$-$$$ ✕ **Bahama Breeze.** Even though the lineage is corporate, the menu here is creative and tasty. The casual fun and the Caribbean cooking draw a crowd, so be prepared for a wait. Meanwhile, you can sip piña coladas and other West Indian delights on a big wooden porch. The food is worth the wait. Start with fried coconut-covered prawns, and move on to the seafood paella or the West Indian–style baby back ribs with a

sweet and smokey guava barbecue glaze. Homemade key lime pie is the perfect finish. ⊠ *8849 International Dr.* ☏ *407/248–2499* ⊠ *8735 Vineland Ave., I–4 Exit 68* ☏ *407/938–9010* ⚬ *Reservations not accepted* ▤ *AE, D, DC, MC.*

ECLECTIC

$$$$
★

✕ **Norman's.** Chef-entrepreneur Norman Van Aken brings impressive credentials to the restaurant that bears his name, as one might expect from the headline eatery in the first and only Ritz-Carlton in Orlando. Van Aken's culinary roots go back to the Florida Keys, where he's credited with creating "Floribbean" cuisine, a blend that is part Key West, part Havana, part Kingston, Jamaica. In the '90s, Van Aken became a star in Miami with his Coral Gables restaurant. The Orlando operation is a formal restaurant with marble floors, starched tablecloths, waiters in black-tie, and a creative, if expensive, prix-fixe menu. The offerings change frequently, but typical dishes include mango-glazed barbecue duck stuffed into a green chili-studded pancake; beef ribs with creamed corn, grilled chayote, and fried onion rings; and Mongolian-style veal chops with grilled Chinese eggplant and Thai fried rice. For dessert, try the "New World banana split," with macadamia nut–brittle ice cream and rum-flambéed banana. The least expensive dinner option is a three-course, prix-fixe meal for $65 per person. ⊠ *Ritz-Carlton Grande Lakes, 4000 Central Florida Pkwy.* ☏ *407/393–4333* ▤ *AE, D, DC, MC, V* ⊗ *No lunch.*

SAND LAKE ROAD

Get away from the theme parks for a meal at one of the excellent restaurants on this boulevard, a mere five minutes or so northeast of Universal Orlando, at Exit 74A.

$$–$$$
Fodor's Choice
★

✕ **Seasons 52.** Parts of the menu change every week of the year at this innovative restaurant, which began with the concept of serving different foods at different times, depending on what's in season. Meals here tend to be light, healthy, and very flavorful. You might have an oak-grilled venison chop with mashed sweet potatoes, mesquite-roasted pork tenderloin with polenta, or salmon cooked on a cedar plank and accompanied by grilled vegetables. An impressive wine list complements the long and colorful menu. Another health-conscious concept adopted at Seasons 52 is the "mini indulgence" dessert: classics like chocolate cake, butterscotch pudding, and rocky road ice cream served in portions designed not to bust your daily calorie budget. Although the cuisine is haute, the prices are modest—not bad for a snazzy, urbane, dark-wood-walled bistro and wine bar. It has live music nightly. ⊠ *7700 Sand Lake Rd., Sand Lake Area* ☏ *407/354–5212* ⊠ *463 E. Altamonte Dr., Altamonte Springs* ☏ *407/767–1252* ▤ *AE, D, DC, MC, V.*

SEAFOOD

$$–$$$ ✕**Bonefish Grill.** After perfecting its culinary act in the Tampa Bay area,
★ this Florida-based seafood chain has moved into the Orlando mar-
ket with a casually elegant eatery that offers seafood from around the
world. Anglers (waiters) serve standout dishes like grilled sea bass in a
mango sauce, Atlantic tilefish piccata, and pistachio-crusted rainbow
trout. Meat-lovers may prefer the boneless pork chops topped with
fontina cheese. For the record, there's no bonefish on the menu. It's
an inedible gamefish, caught for sport in the Florida Keys. ✉*7830
Sand Lake Rd., I–4 Exit 74A, Sand Lake Road Area* ☎*407/355–7707*
◻*AE, D, DC, MC, V* ☉*No lunch.*

DOWNTOWN ORLANDO

*Take I–4 Exit 83B if you're heading westbound, Exit 83A if eastbound,
unless otherwise noted.*

ECLECTIC

$$$–$$$$ ✕**Manuel's on the 28th.** Restaurants with great views don't always have
much more than that to offer, but this lofty spot on the 28th floor
is also a culinary landmark. The menu changes regularly, but there's
always a representative sampling of fish, beef, pork, and duck. Dinner
offerings may include sea scallops covered in macadamia nuts, Black
Angus filet mignon, and even wild boar loin marinated in coconut
milk. For an appetizer, try the smoked confit of duck with boursin (a
creamy white cheese). For dessert, try the baked apples wrapped in
pastry, beggar's-purse style, and topped with caramel sauce. ✉*Bank
of America Bldg., 390 N. Orange Ave., Suite 2800* ☎*407/246–6580*
◻*AE, D, DC, MC, V* ☉*Closed Sun. and Mon. No lunch.*

CUBAN

$–$$$ ✕**Numero Uno.** To the followers of this long-popular Latin restaurant,
the name is no mere hyperbole. Downtowners have been filling the
place at lunch for years. It bills itself as "the home of paella," so just
take their word for it and order some. If you have a good appetite
and you either called ahead to order or can spare the 75-minute wait,
try the *boliche* (a tender pork roast stuffed with chorizo sausage) and
a side order of plantains. Otherwise, go for traditional Cuban fare
like shredded flank steak or *arroz con pollo* (rice with chicken). Finish
with the *tres leches* (three-milk) cake, made with regular, evaporated,
and sweetened-condensed milk. Take I–4 Exit 81A or 81B. ✉*2499
S. Orange Ave., South-Central Orlando* ☎*407/841–3840* ◻*AE, D,
DC, MC, V.*

FRENCH

$$–$$$$ ✕**Le Coq au Vin.** Chef-owner Louis Perrotte is something of a culinary
★ god in Orlando, but he doesn't let it go to his head. He operates a mod-
est little kitchen in a small house in south Orlando. Perrotte's homey
eatery is usually filled with locals who appreciate the lovely traditional
French fare: bronzed grouper with toasted pecans; Long Island duck
with green peppercorns; and braised chicken with red wine, mush-
rooms, and bacon. The menu changes seasonally to insure the freshest

ingredients for house specialties. But the house namesake dish is always available and always excellent. For dessert, try the Grand Marnier soufflé. ⊠*4800 S. Orange Ave., South-Central Orlando* ☎*407/851–6980* ▤*AE, DC, MC, V* ⊗*Closed Mon.*

STEAK

$$–$$$$ ✕**Del Frisco.** Locals like this quiet, uncomplicated steak house, which delivers carefully prepared, corn-fed beef and attentive service. When your steak arrives, the waiter asks you to cut into it and check that it was cooked as you ordered. The menu is simple: T-bones, porterhouses, filet mignon, and such seafood as Maine lobster, Alaskan crab, and a good lobster bisque. There's also an excellent veal osso buco. Bread is baked daily at the restaurant, and the bread pudding, with a Jack Daniels sauce, is worth a try. There's a piano bar next to the dining room. ⊠*729 Lee Rd., North-Central Orlando* ☎*407/645–4443* ▤*AE, D, DC, MC, V* ⊗*Closed Sun. No lunch.*

$$–$$$$ ✕**Linda's La Cantina.** Beef is serious business here. As the menu says, management "cannot be responsible for steaks cooked medium-well and well done." Despite that stuffy-sounding caveat, this down-home steak house has been a favorite among locals since the Eisenhower administration. The menu is short and to the point, including about a dozen steaks and just enough ancillary items to fill a single page. The beef is relatively inexpensive here, with an 18-ounce sirloin going for $21 and a 2-pound T-bone—more beef than most can handle—for $30. With every entrée you get a heaping order of spaghetti (which isn't particularly noteworthy) or a baked potato. The chicken, veal, or eggplant Parmesan topped with marinara sauce is good for nonsteak lovers. ⊠*4721 E. Colonial Dr., near Orlando Executive Airport, Central Orlando* ☎*407/894–4491* ▤*AE, D, MC, V.*

VIETNAMESE

$–$$ ✕**Little Saigon.** This local favorite is one of the best of Orlando's ethnic
★   restaurants. Even though there are more than 100 menu items, you can still create your own dish. Sample the summer rolls (spring-roll filling in a soft wrapper) with peanut sauce, or excellent Vietnamese crepes (stuffed with shredded pork and noodles). Move on to the grilled pork and egg, served atop rice noodles, or the traditional soup filled with noodles, rice, vegetables, and your choice of either chicken or seafood; ask to have extra meat in the soup if you're hungry, and be sure they bring you the mint and bean sprouts to sprinkle in. ⊠*1106 E. Colonial Dr., South-Central Orlando* ☎*407/423–8539* ▤*MC, V.*

WINTER PARK

$$–$$$ ✕**Chef Justin's Park Plaza Gardens.** Sitting at the sidewalk café and bar is like sitting on the main street of the quintessential American small town. But the locals know the real gem is hidden inside—an atrium with live ficus trees, a brick floor, and brick walls that give the place a Vieux Carré feel. Chef Justin Plank's menu combines the best of French and Italian cuisine with an American twist. Much of the dinner menu is composed of traditional Continental fare, like rack of lamb or tenderloin topped with Boursin cheese. One Florida touch is baked grouper

with Tuscan white bean stew. Lunch offerings are lighter, with selections like glazed salmon and a good blue-cheese burger. ⊠ *319 Park Ave. S, Winter Park* ☎ *407/645–2475* ▤ *AE, D, DC, MC, V.*

WHERE TO STAY

Your basic options come down to properties that are (1) owned and operated by Disney on WDW grounds, (2) not owned or operated by Disney but on Disney property, and (3) not on WDW property. There are advantages to each. If you're coming to Orlando for only a few days and are interested solely in the Magic Kingdom, Epcot, and the other Disney attractions, the resorts on Disney property—whether or not they're owned by Disney—are the most convenient. But if you plan to spend time sightseeing in and around Orlando, it makes sense to look into the hotels on International Drive or in Kissimmee, most of which are only 10 minutes from Disney World. Orlando hotels tend to be a little pricier than elsewhere in Florida, but there is little or no charge for children under 18 who share a room with an adult.

PRICES

When it comes to price, the Pop Century and All-Star resorts, at $82 a night, can compete with any off-site budget property. The lodgings we list are the top selections of their type in each category. Rates are lowest from early January to mid-February, from late-April to mid-June, and from mid-August to the third week in December. Always call several places—availability and special deals can often drive room rates at a $$$$ hotel down into the $$ range—and don't forget to ask if you're eligible for a discount. Many hotels offer special rates for members of, for example, the American Automobile Association (AAA) or the American Association of Retired Persons (AARP). Don't overlook the savings to be gained from preparing your own breakfast and maybe a few other meals as well, which you can do if you choose a room or suite with a kitchenette or kitchen. In listings, we always name the facilities that are available, but we don't specify whether they cost extra.

WHAT IT COSTS					
	¢	$	$$	$$$	$$$$
FOR TWO PEOPLE	under $80	$80–$140	$140–$220	$220–$280	over $280

Price categories reflect the range between the least and most expensive standard double rooms in nonholiday high season, based on the European Plan (with no meals) unless otherwise noted. City and state taxes (10%–12%) are extra.

IN WDW: DISNEY-OWNED PROPERTIES

All on-site accommodations that are owned by Disney may be booked through the **Walt Disney World Central Reservations Office** (✉ *Box 10100, Suite 300, Lake Buena Vista 32830* ☎ *407/934–7639* ⊕ *www.disney-world.com*). People with disabilities can call **WDW Special Request Res-**

ervations (☏407/939–7807) to get information or book rooms at any of the on-site Disney properties.

Disney-owned accommodations are noted on the Walt Disney World Resort map.

MAGIC KINGDOM RESORT AREA
Take I–4 Exit 62, 64B, or 65.

The ritzy hotels near the Magic Kingdom all lie on the monorail route and are only minutes away from the park. Fort Wilderness Resort and Campground, with RV and tent sites, is a bit farther southeast of the Magic Kingdom, and access to the parks is by bus.

$$$$
Fodor's Choice
★
Grand Floridian Resort & Spa. On the shores of the Seven Seas Lagoon, this red, gable-roof Victorian is all delicate gingerbread, rambling verandas, and brick chimneys. It's Disney's flagship resort: add a dinner or two at Victoria and Albert's or Cítricos and you may spend more in a weekend here than on your mortgage payment—but you'll have great memories. Although you won't look out of place walking through the lobby in flip-flops, afternoon high tea and a pianist playing nightly in the lobby are among the high-scale touches. The Mouseketeer Clubhouse on the ground floor offers children's programs until midnight daily. Pros: on the monorail; Victoria and Albert's, one of the state's best restaurants. Cons: some say it's not ritzy enough to match the room rates; conference center and convention clientele lend stuffiness. ☏407/824–3000 ⬐900 rooms, 90 suites ⚭In-room: safe, ethernet, Wi-Fi. In-hotel: 5 restaurants, room service, tennis courts, pools, gym, spa, beachfront, concierge, children's programs (ages 4–12), laundry facilities, laundry service, executive floor, no-smoking rooms ▤AE, D, DC, MC, V.

$$$$
Polynesian Resort. If it weren't for the kids in Mickey Mouse caps, you'd think you were in Fiji. In the three-story atrium lobby, orchids bloom alongside coconut palms and banana trees, and water cascades from volcanic-rock fountains. At the evening luau, Polynesian dancers perform before a feast with Hawaiian-style roast pork. Rooms sleep five, since they all have two queen-size beds and a daybed. Most rooms also have a balcony or patio. Lagoon-view rooms—which overlook Magic Kingdom fireworks—are peaceful but costly. Pros: on the monorail; great aloha-spirit atmosphere. Cons: pricey; not good for those bothered by lots of loud children. ☏407/824–2000 ⬐853 rooms, 5 suites ⚭In-room: safe, ethernet. In-hotel: 4 restaurants, room service, bar, pools, gym, beachfront, children's programs (ages 4–12), laundry facilities, laundry service, concierge, executive floor, public Wi-Fi, no-smoking rooms ▤AE, D, DC, MC, V.

$$$–$$$$
Contemporary Resort. You're paying for location, and perhaps tradition, when you stay here. This 15-story, flat-topped pyramid, the first hotel to open here more than 30 years ago, has been completely renovated several times. The 2006 upgrade brought work-station desks, flat-panel TVs, and marble bathroom vanities. The monorail runs through the lobby, so it takes just minutes to get to the Magic Kingdom and Epcot. Upper floors of the main tower (where rooms are

Perks for Disney Resort Guests

Location! Location! Location! You'll get the full WDW experience: every Disney resort has incredible fanciful theming, and you can take Disney transportation everywhere.

Extra Magic Hour. You get special early and late-night admission to certain parks on specified days—call ahead for information about each park's "magic hours" days to plan your early- and late-visit strategies.

Magical Express. If you're coming directly from the airport, you get a free transfer to your Disney resort via the Magical Express coaches. And, of course, you can get a free transfer back to the airport, with your baggage checked in at even check in your baggage.

Package Delivery. Anything you purchase, whether at one of the parks, one of the hotels, or even in Downtown Disney, can be delivered directly to your room at any Disney hotel free of charge. It's a big plus not to have to carry your packages around all day.

Priority Reservations. Hotel guests get priority reservations at Disney restaurants by calling 407/939–3463. Hotel guests also get the choicest tee times at Disney golf courses. Reserve them up to 30 days in advance by calling 407/939–4654.

Charging Privileges. You can charge most meals and purchases throughout Disney to your hotel room.

Free Parking. Parking is free for hotel guests, and that extends beyond hotel parking lots. Show your parking pass when you go to any of the Disney parks and you won't be charged for parking.

more expensive) offer great views of all the activities in and around the Magic Kingdom, including the nightly fireworks. Pros: easy access to Magic Kingdom; Chef Mickey's, the epicenter of the character-meal world; launching point for romantic sunset Bay Lake cruises. Cons: a mix of vacationers and conventioneers (there's an on-site convention center); sometimes too frenzied for the former and too staid for the latter. ☎407/824–1000 ◿1,013 rooms, 25 suites ♨In-room: safe, refrigerator, ethernet. In-hotel: 3 restaurants, room service, tennis courts, pools, gym, beachfront, concierge, children's programs (ages 4–12), laundry facilities, laundry service, executive floor, public Wi-Fi, no-smoking rooms ⊟AE, D, DC, MC, V.

$$–$$$$
Fodor's Choice
★

🏨 **Wilderness Lodge.** The architects outdid themselves with this seven-story hotel modeled after the majestic turn-of-the-20th-century lodges of the American Northwest. The five-story lobby, supported by towering tree trunks, has an 82-foot-high, three-sided fireplace made of rocks from the Grand Canyon and lit by enormous tepee-shaped chandeliers. Two 55-foot-tall hand-carved totem poles complete the illusion. Rooms have leather chairs, patchwork quilts, cowboy art, and a balcony or a patio. The hotel's showstopper is its Fire Rock Geyser, a faux Old Faithful, near the large pool, which begins as an artificially heated hot spring in the lobby. This hotel is a good option if you're a couple without kids looking for more serenity than is found at Disney's other hotels. Pros: high-wow-factor architecture; boarding point for romantic Bay Lake sunset cruises. Cons: ferry toots its horn at every docking; no direct shuttle to Magic Kingdom. ☎407/824–3200 ⬅728 *rooms, 31 suites* ⬥*In-room: safe, ethernet. In-hotel: 3 restaurants, room service, pool, beachfront, bicycles, children's programs (ages 4–12), laundry facilities, laundry service, concierge, executive floor, public Wi-Fi, no-smoking rooms* ⊟*AE, D, DC, MC, V.*

¢–$ ⬥★ **Fort Wilderness Resort Campground.** Bringing a tent or RV is one of the cheapest ways to stay on WDW property, especially considering that sites accommodate up to 10. Tent sites with water and electricity are real bargains. RV sites cost more but are equipped with electric, water, and sewage hookups as well as outdoor charcoal grills and picnic tables. Even with just a good tent and cozy sleeping bag you'll be relatively

comfortable, since the campground has 15 strategically located comfort stations where you can take a hot shower, as well as laundry facilities, restaurants, a general store—everything you need. There are many activities to keep you occupied, such as tennis and horseback riding. Pros: Disney's most economical lodging; pets allowed ($5 nightly fee). Cons: amount of walking within the camp (to reach the store, restaurants, etc.) can be a little much; shuttle rides to Disney parks too long for some. ☎407/824–2900 ⬅788 *campsites, 695 with full hookups, 90 partial hookups* ⬥*Pools, flush toilets, full hookups, dump station, drinking water, guest laundry, showers, picnic tables, food service, electricity, public telephone* ⊟*AE, D, DC, MC, V.*

EPCOT RESORT AREA
Take I–4 Exit 64B, 65, or 67.

From the Epcot resorts you can walk or take a boat to the International Gateway entrance to Epcot, or you can take the shuttle from your hotel or drive to the Future World (front) entrance.

$$$$ ★ 🏨 **BoardWalk Inn and Villas.** Disney's smallest deluxe hotel is a beautiful re-creation of Victorian-era Atlantic City inn. Architectural master Robert A. M. Stern designed it to mimic 19th-century New England building styles. Rooms have floral-print bedspreads and blue-and-white painted furniture. Those overlooking Crescent Lake cost the most and are the noisiest. A 200-foot waterslide in the form of a classic wooden roller coaster cascades into the pool area. The property opens directly onto Disney's BoardWalk entertainment complex, where you can ride surrey bikes, watch a game at the ESPN Sports Club, or dine in some of Disney's better restaurants. The hotel is also a 15-minute walk from

Disney–MGM Studios. Pros: quick access to nighttime fun; rooms are larger than average (390 square feet). Con: shuttle to Magic Kingdom and other parks is slow. ☎407/939–5100 inn, 407/939–6200 villas ⊅370 rooms, 19 suites, 526 villas ♿In-room: safe, ethernet. In-hotel: 4 restaurants, room service, tennis court, pool, gym, concierge, children's programs (ages 4–12), laundry facilities, laundry service, public Wi-Fi, no-smoking rooms ⊟AE, D, DC, MC, V.

$$$$ ⚟**Yacht and Beach Club Resorts.** These Seven Seas Lagoon inns seem
★ straight out of a Cape Cod summer. The five-story Yacht Club has hardwood floors, a lobby full of gleaming brass and polished leather, an oyster-gray clapboard facade, and evergreen landscaping; there's even a lighthouse on its pier. Rooms have floral-print bedspreads and a small ship's wheel on the headboard. At the Beach Club, a croquet lawn and cabana-dotted white-sand beach set the scene. Stormalong Bay, a 3-acre water park with slides and whirlpools, is part of this club. Both lodgings have "quiet pools," which are secluded and largely kid-free, albeit nondescript. Pros: location, location, location—it's easy to walk to Epcot and the BoardWalk, and Disney-MGM is a fun, 20-minute ferry ride away. Cons: distances within the hotel—like, from your room to the front desk—can seem vast; high-noise factor. ☎407/934–8000 Beach Club, 407/934–7000 Yacht Club ⊅1,213 rooms, 112 suites ♿In-room: safe, ethernet, Wi-Fi. In-hotel: 4 restaurants, room service, tennis courts, pools, gym, beachfront, bicycles, children's programs (ages 4–12), laundry service, concierge, public Wi-Fi, no-smoking rooms ⊟AE, D, DC, MC, V.

$$ ⚟**Caribbean Beach Resort.** Six palm-studded "villages," all awash in
★ dizzying pastels and labeld with Caribbean names like Barbados and Trinidad, share 45-acre Barefoot Bay and its white-sand beach. Bridges connect to a 1-acre path-crossed play and picnic area called Parrot Cay. You can rent boats to explore the lake, or rent bikes to ride along the 1½-mi lakefront promenade. The Old Port Royale complex, decorated with cannons, statues, and tropical birds, has a food court, lounge, and pool area with falls and a big slide. Rooms, which have painted–wood furniture, are fresh and done in soft pastels like turquoise and peach. Pros: restaurants sell Jamaica's Red Stripe beer; plenty of on-site outdoor activities; convenient to Epcot, Disney-MGM, and Downtown Disney. Cons: You don't truly feel swept away to a tropical island; only crystalline and swimmable waters are in the pools; walks from your room to the beach or a restaurant can be up to 15 minutes. ☎407/934–3400 ⊅2,112 rooms ♿In-room: safe, ethernet. In-hotel: restaurant, room service, pools, beachfront, bicycles, no elevator, laundry facilities, laundry service, public Wi-Fi, no-smoking rooms ⊟AE, D, DC, MC, V.

$$ ⚟**Coronado Springs Resort.** Because of its 84,000-square-foot exhibit
★ hall, this is Disney's most popular convention hotel. But since the meeting space is in its own wing, the moderately priced resort is also popular with families who appreciate its casual Southwestern architecture, its lively, Mexican-style food court, and its elaborate swimming pool, which has a Mayan pyramid with a big slide. There's a full-service health club and spa, and if you like jogging, walking, or biking

you're in the right place—a pleasant path circles the lake. You can rent bikes, kayaks, canoes, and paddleboats. Pros: great pool with a play area–arcade for kids and a bar for adults; lots of outdoor activities. Cons: some accommodations are a half-mile from the restaurants; standard rooms are on the small side (300 square feet); kids may find the subdued atmosphere boring. ☎407/939–1000 ↜1,967 rooms ♿In-room: safe, ethernet. In-hotel: 2 restaurants, room service, bar, pools, gym, spa, bicycles, laundry service, public Wi-Fi, no-smoking rooms ▤AE, D, DC, MC, V.

DISNEY'S ANIMAL KINGDOM AREA
Take I–4 Exit 64B or 65.

\$\$–\$\$\$\$ **★** 🏨**Animal Kingdom Lodge.** Giraffes, zebras, and other wildlife roam three 11-acre savannas separated by wings of this grand hotel. In the atrium lobby, a massive faux-thatched roof hovers almost 100 feet above hardwood floors with inlaid carvings. Cultural ambassadors give talks about their African homelands, the animals, and the artwork on display; evenings see storytelling sessions around the fire circle on the Arusha Rock terrace. All the romantic rooms (with drapes descending from the ceiling to lend a tentlike feel) have a bit of African art, including carved headboards, pen-and-ink drawings, or original prints. Most rooms also have balconies overlooking the wildlife reserve. Pros: extraordinary wildlife and cultural experiences; Jiko and Boma restaurants serve authentic African cuisine. Cons: shuttle to parks other than Animal Kingdom can take more than an hour; guided savannah tours available only to guests on the concierge level. ☎407/934–7639 ↜1,293 rooms ♿In-room: safe, ethernet. In-hotel: 3 restaurants, bar, pools, gym, spa, children's programs (ages 4–12), laundry facilities, laundry service, public Wi-Fi, no-smoking rooms ▤AE, D, DC, MC, V.

\$ 🏨**All-Star Sports, All-Star Music, and All-Star Movies Resorts.** If you want to immerse yourself in a kids-are-king atmosphere, these megaresorts, in which virtually every guest room seems to house an entire family, are the place to be. The All-Star resorts are as economically priced as any hotel in Orlando, so people without kids stay here, too. (They just ask for rooms away from the pools and other common areas.) In the Sports resort, Goofy is the pitcher in the baseball-diamond pool; in the Music resort you'll walk by giant bongos; and in the Movies resort, huge characters like *Toy Story*'s Buzz Lightyear frame each building. Each room has two double beds, a closet rod, an armoire, and a desk. The food courts sell standard fare, and you can even have pizza delivered to your room. Oddly enough, the resorts do not have the kid's clubs found at other Disney resorts where you can drop off the youngsters when you need a break. ☎407/939–5000 Sports, 407/939–6000 Music, 407/939–7000 Movies ↜1,920 rooms at each ♿In-room: safe, ethernet. In-hotel: room service, bars, pools, laundry facilities, laundry service, public Internet, public Wi-Fi, no-smoking rooms ▤AE, D, DC, MC, V.

\$ 🏨**Pop Century Resort.** Giant jukeboxes and yo-yos, an oversize Big Wheel and Rubik's Cube, and other pop-culture memorabilia are scattered about the grounds. Items from mood rings to eight-track tapes are incorporated into the architecture; wall-mounted shadow boxes display toys, fashions, and fads from each decade since the 1950s. Brightly colored rooms are functional for families, with two double beds or one king. A big food court and a cafeteria serve reasonably priced fare. Pros: great room rates; the trip down memory lane; proximity to Wide World of Sports and Disney-MGM. Cons: big crowds at the front desk; big crowds (and noise) in the food court; small rooms (260 square feet). ☎407/934–7639 ⇱2,880 rooms ♿In-room: safe, ethernet. In-hotel: room service, bar, pools, gym, laundry service, public Wi-Fi, no-smoking rooms ▤AE, D, DC, MC, V.

DOWNTOWN DISNEY RESORT AREA
Take I–4 Exit 67 or 68.

The Downtown Disney resort area, east of Epcot, has two midprice resorts with an Old South theme, plus the upscale Old Key West Resort. From here shuttles are available to all of the parks.

$$$–$$$$ **Old Key West Resort.** A red-and-white lighthouse helps you find your way through this marina-style resort. Freestanding villas resemble turn-of-the-20th-century Key West houses, with white clapboard siding and private balconies that overlook the waterways winding through the grounds. The one-, two-, or three-bedroom houses have whirlpools in the master bedrooms, full-size kitchens (which could save you a fortune on food if you shop at an off-site grocery store), washers and dryers, and patios. The 2,265-square-foot three-bedroom grand villas accommodate up to 12 adults—so bring some friends. The resort is part of the Disney Vacation Club network, but rooms are rented to anyone when they're available. Pros: quiet and romantic; abundance of accommodations with whirlpool baths. Con: distances between rooms and restaurants, recreation facilities, bus stops, etc. ☎407/827–7700 ⇱761 units ♿In-room: safe, ethernet, Wi-Fi. In-hotel: restaurant, tennis courts, pools, gym, spa, bicycles, laundry facilities, laundry service, no-smoking rooms ▤AE, D, DC, MC, V.

$$$–$$$$ **Saratoga Springs Resort.** This large Disney Vacation Club has hundreds of units on 16 acres. Three- and four-story buildings, decorated inside and out to look like the 19th-century resorts of upstate New York, overlook a giant pool with artificial hot springs and faux boulders. Standard rooms, with 355 square feet, have microwaves and refrigerators; suites have full kitchens. Three-bedroom family suites—as big as most homes, with 2,113 square feet—occupy two levels and have dining rooms, living rooms, and four bathrooms. Rich woods, early American–style furniture, and overstuffed couches lend a homey, country-chic look. You can walk to Downtown Disney in 10 minutes or take the ferry, which docks near Fulton's Crab House. Pros: in-room massage; abundance of rooms with whirlpool baths. Con: It's a fair hike from some accommodations to the restaurant and other facilities. ☎407/934–7639 ⇱828 units ♿In-room: safe, ethernet. In-hotel: restaurant, tennis courts, pools, gym, spa, bicycles, public Wi-Fi, no-smoking rooms ▤AE, D, DC, MC, V.

$$ 🏨 **Port Orleans Resort–French Quarter.** Ornate Big Easy–style row houses with vine-covered balconies cluster around squares planted with magnolias. Lamp-lighted sidewalks are named for French Quarter thoroughfares. Because this place is relatively quiet, it appeals more to couples than families with kids. The food court serves Crescent City specialties such as jambalaya and beig-

WORD OF MOUTH

"Pop Century is a wonderful exciting place for families. They have three heated pools, bedtime stories on the phone from Disney characters, a wake-up call from Mickey, etc."

–Geckolips

nets. Scat Cat's Lounge is a serene little bar. Doubloon Lagoon, one of Disney's most exotic pools, includes a clever "sea serpent" slide that swallows and then spits you into the water. Pros: authentic, fun New Orleans atmosphere; lots of water recreation options, including boat rentals. Cons: standard rooms overlook a parking lot (water view rooms cost more); shuttle service is slow; food court is the only on-site dining option. ☎407/934–5000 ⇥1,008 rooms ☐In-room: safe, ethernet. In-hotel: pool, bicycles, laundry facilities, laundry service, public Wi-Fi, no-smoking rooms ☐AE, D, DC, MC, V.

$$ 🏨 **Port Orleans Resort–Riverside.** Buildings look like plantation-style mansions and rustic bayou dwellings. Rooms accommodate up to four in two double beds and have wooden armoires, quilted bedspreads, and gleaming brass faucets; a few rooms have king-size beds. The registration area looks like a steamboat interior, and the 3½-acre, old-fashioned swimming-hole complex called Ol' Man Island has a pool with slides, rope swings, and a nearby play area. Recreation options here include fishing trips on the Sassagoula River, paddleboat and canoe rentals, and evening carriage rides. Pros: carriage rides; river cruises; lots of recreation options for kids. Con: shuttle can be slow. ☎407/934–6000 ⇥2,048 rooms ☐In-room: safe, ethernet. In-hotel: restaurant, pools, gym, bicycles, laundry facilities, laundry service, no-smoking rooms ☐AE, D, DC, MC, V.

OTHER ON-SITE HOTELS

Epcot Resort–area hotels are also noted on the Walt Disney World Resort map.

EPCOT RESORT AREA
Take I–4 Exit 67.

$$$$ 🏨 **Walt Disney World Dolphin.** World-renowned architect Michael Graves
★ designed the neighboring Dolphin and Swan hotels. Outside, a pair of 56-foot-tall sea creatures bookend this 25-story glass pyramid. The fabric-draped lobby resembles a giant sultan's tent. All rooms have either two queen beds or one king, and bright, beach-inspired spreads and drapes. The pillow-top mattresses, down comforters, and multitude of overstuffed pillows make the beds here some of the kingdom's most comfortable. Extensive children's programs include Camp Dolphin summer camp and the five-hour Dolphin Dinner Club. Pros:

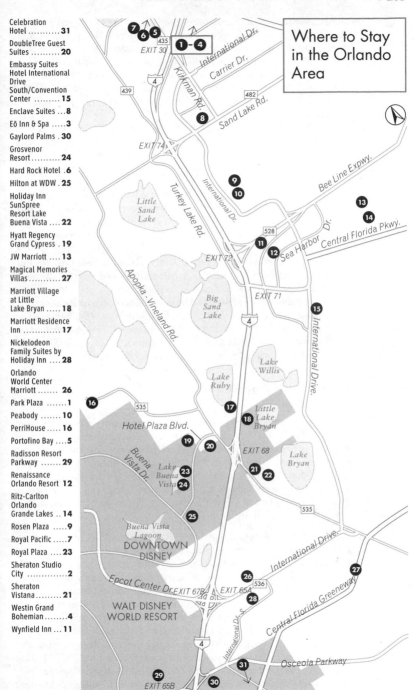

Celebration
Hotel **31**

DoubleTree Guest
Suites **20**

Embassy Suites
Hotel International
Drive
South/Convention
Center **15**

Enclave Suites ... **8**

Eō Inn & Spa **3**

Gaylord Palms .. **30**

Grosvenor
Resort **24**

Hard Rock Hotel . **6**

Hilton at WDW . **25**

Holiday Inn
SunSpree
Resort Lake
Buena Vista **22**

Hyatt Regency
Grand Cypress . **19**

JW Marriott **13**

Magical Memories
Villas **27**

Marriott Village
at Little
Lake Bryan **18**

Marriott Residence
Inn **17**

Nickelodeon
Family Suites by
Holiday Inn **28**

Orlando
World Center
Marriott **26**

Park Plaza **1**

Peabody **10**

PerriHouse **16**

Portofino Bay **5**

Radisson Resort
Parkway **29**

Renaissance
Orlando Resort **12**

Ritz-Carlton
Orlando
Grande Lakes .. **14**

Rosen Plaza **9**

Royal Pacific **7**

Royal Plaza **23**

Sheraton Studio
City **2**

Sheraton
Vistana **21**

Westin Grand
Bohemian **4**

Wynfield Inn ... **11**

Where to Stay in the Orlando Area

3

charge privileges and access to all facilities at the Swan; easy walk to BoardWalk; good on-site restaurants. Con: rooms only dip below $250 in off-season. ⊠*1500 Epcot Resorts Blvd., Lake Buena Vista 32830-2653* ☏*407/934–4000 or 800/227–1500* ⊕*www.swandolphin.com* ⟳*1,509 rooms, 136 suites* ⟲*In-room: safe, ethernet. In-hotel: 9 restaurants, room service, tennis courts, pools, gym, spa, beachfront, children's programs (ages 4–12), executive floor, concierge, public Wi-Fi, no-smoking rooms* ⊟*AE, D, DC, MC, V.*

$$$$ ▦**Walt Disney World Swan.** Facing the Dolphin across Crescent Lake, the Swan is another example of the postmodern "Learning from Las Vegas" school of entertainment architecture characteristic of Michael Graves. Two 46-foot swans grace the rooftop of this coral-and-aquamarine hotel, and the massive main lobby is decorated with a playful mix of tropical imagery. Guest rooms are quirkily decorated with floral and geometric patterns, pineapples painted on furniture, and exotic bird-shape lamps. Every room has two queen beds or one king, two phone lines (one data port), and a coffeemaker; some have balconies. The Grotto, a 3-acre water playground complete with waterslides, waterfalls, and all the trimming, is nearby, as is Disney's BoardWalk and the Fantasia Gardens miniature golf complex. Pros: charge privileges and access to all facilities at the Dolphin; easy walk to BoardWalk; good on-site restaurants. Con: rooms only dip below $250 in off-season. ⊠*1200 Epcot Resorts Blvd., Lake Buena Vista 32830* ☏*407/934–3000 or 800/248–7926* ⊕*www.swandolphin.com* ⟳*756 rooms, 55 suites* ⟲*In-room: safe, ethernet. In-hotel: 6 restaurants, room service, tennis courts, pools, gym, spa, beachfront, children's programs (ages 4–12), executive floor, concierge, public Wi-Fi, no-smoking rooms* ⊟*AE, D, DC, MC, V.*

DOWNTOWN DISNEY RESORT AREA
Take I–4 Exit 68.

A number of non-Disney-owned resorts are clustered on Disney property not far from Downtown Disney, and several more sprawling, high-quality resorts are just outside the park's northernmost entrance. Several of these hotels market themselves as "official" Disney hotels, meaning that they have special agreements with Disney that allow them to offer their guests such perks as early park admission. The hotels on Hotel Plaza Boulevard are within walking distance of Downtown Disney Marketplace, though most offer shuttle service anyway.

$$–$$$$ ▦**Hilton at WDW Resort.** An ingenious waterfall tumbles off the covered entrance and into a stone fountain surrounded by palm trees. Although not huge, rooms are upbeat, cozy, and contemporary, and many on the upper floors have great views of Downtown Disney, which is just a short walk away. The hotel offers two good eateries: Andiamo Italian Bistro, specializing in pasta and grilled seafood, and a Benihana Steakhouse and Sushi Bar. Guests can enter Disney parks an hour before they officially open. Pros: close to Downtown Disney; free shuttle bus; kids' program. Cons: pricier than similar lodgings farther from Disney; inconvenient to Universal and downtown Orlando. ⊠*1751 Hotel Plaza Blvd., Lake Buena Vista 32830* ☏*407/827–4000, 800/782–4414 reservations* ⊕*www.hilton.com* ⟳*814 rooms, 27 suites* ⟲*In-room:*

safe, ethernet. In-hotel: 7 restaurants, room service, pools, gym, children's programs (ages 3–12), laundry facilities, laundry service, public Wi-Fi, no-smoking rooms ☰*AE, DC, MC.*

$–$$$ 🏨**DoubleTree Guest Suites in the WDW Resort.** The lavender-and-pink exterior looks strange, but the interior is another story. Comfortable one- and two-bedroom suites are decorated in tasteful hues, with blue carpeting and orange drapes and bedspreads. Each bedroom has either a king bed or two doubles. Units come with three TVs, including one in the bathroom, and a wet bar, microwave, refrigerator, and coffeemaker. The small lobby has a charming feature—a small aviary with birds from South America and Africa. There's a special "registration desk" for kids, where they can get coloring books and balloons. Pros: within walking distance of Downtown Disney; free shuttle to all Disney attractions. Con: inconvenient to Universal and downtown Orlando. ⊠*2305 Hotel Plaza Blvd., Lake Buena Vista 32830* ☎*407/934–1000 or 800/222–8733* ⊕*www.doubletreeguestsuites.com* ⤶*229 units* ⛁*In-room: safe, refrigerator, ethernet. In-hotel: restaurant, room service, bars, tennis courts, pool, gym, laundry facilities, laundry service, public Wi-Fi, no-smoking rooms* ☰*AE, DC, MC, V.*

$–$$$ 🏨**Royal Plaza.** Spruced-up guest rooms have plasma-screen TVs, pillow-top mattresses, and granite bathroom counters. Some ground-level rooms have semiprivate patios that overlook the swimming pool. The restaurant, the Giraffe Café, is informal but pleasant and specializes in gourmet pizzas with toppings like Boursin cheese and lump crabmeat. You can rent microwaves and refrigerators for your room. Pros: within walking distance of Downtown Disney; free shuttle to all Disney attractions. Con: inconvenient to Universal and downtown Orlando. ⊠*1905 Hotel Plaza Blvd., Lake Buena Vista 32830* ☎*407/828–2828* ⊕*www.royalplaza.com* ⤶*394 rooms, 5 suites* ⛁*In-room: safe, refrigerator, VCR, ethernet. In-hotel: 2 restaurants, room service, tennis courts, pools, laundry service, public Wi-Fi, no-smoking rooms* ☰*AE, DC, MC, V.*

$–$$ 🏨**Grosvenor Resort.** This tan high-rise (the name is pronounced *Grove-*
★ *ner,* just like the one in London) across from Downtown Disney is nondescript on the outside but quite pleasant on the inside. Blond-wood furniture and rose carpeting make the rooms homey, and those in the tower have a great view of Downtown Disney. Public areas are decorated in an easygoing Caribbean style. One of the restaurants, Baskervilles, hosts a Disney character breakfast three days a week and a Saturday murder-mystery dinner show. Pros: within walking distance of Downtown Disney; free shuttle to all Disney attractions. Con: inconvenient to Universal and downtown Orlando. ⊠*1850 Hotel Plaza Blvd., Downtown Disney, Lake Buena Vista 32830* ☎*407/828–4444 or 800/624–4109* ⊕*www.grosvenorresort.com* ⤶*626 rooms, 5 suites* ⛁*In-room: safe, refrigerator, VCR, ethernet. In-hotel: 3 restaurants, room service, tennis courts, pools, laundry service, no-smoking rooms* ☰*AE, DC, MC, V.*

UNIVERSAL ORLANDO
Take I–4 Exit 74B if you're heading westbound, 75A if eastbound.

$$$–$$$$ 🏨**Hard Rock Hotel.** Inside the California mission–style building you'll find such rock memorabilia as the slip Madonna wore in her "Like a

Prayer" video. Rooms have black-and-white photos of pop icons and serious sound systems with CD players. Stay in a suite, and you'll get a big-screen TV and a wet bar. Kid-friendly suites have a small extra room for children. Your hotel key card lets you bypass lines at the Universal. The Kitchen, one of the hotel's restaurants, occasionally hosts visiting musicians cooking their favorite meals at the Chef's Table. Pros: short walk to Universal and CityWalk; preferential treatment at Universal rides. Cons: rooms and meals are pricey; loud rock music in public areas may annoy some people. ⊠*5800 Universal Blvd., Universal Studios, 32819* ☎*407/503–7625 or 800/232–7827* ⊕*www.universalorlando.com* ↪*621 rooms, 29 suites* ⚬*In-room: safe, refrigerator, VCR, ethernet. In-hotel: 3 restaurants, room service, bars, pools, gym, children's programs (ages 4–14), laundry service, public Wi-Fi, no-smoking rooms, some pets allowed (fee)* ⊟*AE, D, DC, MC, V.*

$$–$$$$ ⌗**Portofino Bay Hotel.** The charm and romance of Portofino, Italy, are conjured up at this lovely luxury resort. The illusion is so faultless, right down to the cobblestone streets, that you might find it hard to believe that the different-colored row houses lining the "bay" are a facade. Large, plush rooms here are done in cream and white, with down comforters and high-quality wood furnishings. There are two Italian restaurants, Mama Della's and Delfino Riviera, and gelato machines surround the massive pool. The Feast of St. Gennaro (the patron saint of Naples) is held here in September as are monthly Italian wine tastings. Pros: incredible, Italian villa atmosphere; large spa; short walk or ferry ride to Universal Studios and Islands of Adventure; preferential treatment at Universal rides. Cons: rooms and meals are noticeably expensive; in-room high-speed Internet access costs $10 a day. ⊠*5601 Universal Blvd., Universal Studios, 32819* ☎*407/503–1000 or 800/232–7827* ⊕*www.universalorlando.com* ↪*699 rooms, 51 suites* ⚬*In-room: safe, VCR, ethernet. In-hotel: 3 restaurants, room service, bar, pools, gym, spa, children's programs (ages 4–14), laundry service, public Wi-Fi, some pets allowed (fee)* ⊟*AE, D, DC, MC, V.*

$$–$$$ ⌗**Royal Pacific Resort.** The entrance—a footbridge across a tropical
Fodor'sChoice   stream—sets the tone for the South Pacific theme of this hotel, which is
★   on 53 acres planted with tropical shrubs and trees, most of them palms. The focal point is a 12,000-square-foot, lagoon-style pool, which has a small beach and an interactive water play area. Indonesian carvings decorate the walls everywhere, even in the rooms, and Emeril Lagasse's restaurant, Tchoup Chop, draws crowds. The hotel hosts Polynesian-style luaus every Saturday. Pros: Emeril's restaurant; preferential treatment at Universal rides. Cons: rooms can feel cramped; $10-a-day fee for Internet access unwarranted given rates. ⊠*6300 Hollywood Way, Univeral Orlando, 32819* ☎*407/503–3000 or 800/232–7827* ⊕*www.universalorlando.com* ↪*1,000 rooms, 113 suites* ⚬*In-room: safe, VCR, ethernet. In-hotel: 3 restaurants, room service, bars, pool, gym, children's programs (ages 4–14), laundry facilities, laundry service, executive floor, public Wi-Fi, no-smoking rooms, some pets allowed (fee), minibar* ⊟*AE, DC, MC, V.*

DOWNTOWN DISNEY/LAKE BUENA VISTA AREA
Take I–4 Exit 68.

Many people choose to stay in one of the resorts a bit farther east of Downtown Disney because, though equally grand, they tend to be less expensive than those right on Hotel Plaza Boulevard. Perennially popular with families are the all-suites properties, many with in-room kitchens, just east of Lake Buena Vista Drive. The 1,100-room Marriott Village at Lake Buena Vista, across Interstate 4 from Downtown Disney, is popular for its gated, secure cluster of three hotels, a multi-restaurant complex, a video-rental store, a 24-hour convenience store, and a Hertz rental-car station.

$$$$
★ **Hyatt Regency Grand Cypress Resort.** On 1,500 acres just outside Disney's north entrance, this spectacular resort has a private lake, three golf courses, and miles of trails for bicycling, jogging, and horseback riding. The 800,000-gallon pool has a 45-foot slide and is fed by 12 waterfalls. Tropical birds and plants and Chinese sculptures fill the 18-story atrium. All rooms have tasteful rattan furniture and a private balcony overlooking either the Lake Buena Vista Area or the pool. Villas have fireplaces and whirlpool baths. Accommodations are divided between the hotel and the **Villas of Grand Cypress** (⊠*1 N. Jacaranda Dr., Lake Buena Vista 32836* ☎*407/239–1234 or 800/835–7377*), with 200 villas. Pros: great Sunday brunch at La Coquina; huge pool; lots of recreation options, including nearby equestrian center. Cons: pricey; inconvenient to Universal Orlando and downtown Orlando. ⊠*1 Grand Cypress Blvd., Lake Buena Vista Area, Orlando 32836* ☎*407/239–1234 or 800/233–1234* ⊕*www.hyattgrandcypress.com* ↘*750 rooms* ⚒*In-room: safe, ethernet. In-hotel: 5 restaurants, room service, 18-hole golf courses, 9-hole golf course, tennis courts, pools, gym, spa, bicycles, children's programs (ages 5–12), laundry service, public Wi-Fi, no-smoking rooms* ☰*AE, D, DC, MC, V.*

$$$–$$$$
Orlando World Center Marriott. At 2,000 rooms, this is one of Orlando's largest hotels, and it's very popular with conventions. All rooms have patios or balconies, and the lineup of amenities and facilities seems endless—there's even on-site photo processing. You can rent the upscale Royal Palms, Imperial Palms, and Sabal Palms villas by the day or by the week. Golf at the 6,800-yard championship Hawk's Landing golf course becomes a bargain for guests—a golf package including one round costs about $20 more than the standard rate for a deluxe room, depending on the season. Pros: great steakhouses; golf course; lots of amenities. Con: not much to see or do within walking distance. ⊠*8701 World Center Dr., I–4 Exit 65, Orlando 32821* ☎*407/239–4200 or 800/228–9290* ⊕*www.marriottworldcenter.com* ↘*2,000 rooms, 98 suites, 259 villas* ⚒*In-room: ethernet. In-hotel: 7 restaurants, room service, 18-hole golf course, pool, gym, children's programs (ages 4–12), laundry facilities, laundry service, public Wi-Fi, no-smoking rooms* ☰*AE, D, DC, MC, V.*

$$–$$$$
☺ ★ **Nickelodeon Family Suites by Holiday Inn.** The Nickelodeon theme extends everywhere, from the suites, where separate kids' rooms have bunk beds and SpongeBob wall murals, to the two giant pools built up

like water parks. Kids will look forward to wake-up calls from Nickelodeon stars, character breakfasts, and live entertainment. You can choose between one-, two-, and three-bedroom suites, with or without full kitchens. Pros: extremely kid-friendly; free Disney shuttle; golf course. Cons: not within walking distance of Disney or Downtown Disney; may be too frenetic for folks without kids. ⊠*14500 Continental Gateway, I–4 Exit 67, Orlando 32821* ☎*407/387–5437 or 866/462–6425* ⊕*www.nickhotels.com* ⇨*800 suites* ⌂*In-room: safe, kitchen (some), refrigerator, ethernet. In-hotel: 3 restaurants, room service, pools, 9-hole golf course, gym, children's programs (ages 4–12), laundry facilities, laundry service, public Wi-Fi, no-smoking rooms* ▤*AE, D, DC, MC, V.*

$$–$$$ 🖈**Sheraton Vistana Resort.** Consider this peaceful resort, just across I–4 from Downtown Disney, if you're traveling with a large family or group of friends. The spacious, tasteful, one- and two-bedroom villas and town houses have living rooms, full kitchens, and washers and dryers. Tennis players take note: the clay and all-weather courts are free to guests; private or semiprivate lessons are available for a fee. With seven outdoor heated pools, five kiddie pools, and eight outdoor hot tubs, you can spend the whole day just soaking up the sun. Pros: kitchens let you save money on food; lots of on-site recreation options: Cons: not within walking distance of Downtown Disney (across I–4); shuttles to Disney ($9 round-trip) and Universal and I-Drive ($11 round-trip) are slow. ⊠*8800 Vistana Center Dr., Orlando 32821* ☎*407/239–3100 or 800/325–3535* ⊕*www.starwoodvo.com* ⇨*1,700 units* ⌂*In-room: safe, kitchen, refrigerator, ethernet. In-hotel: 2 restaurants, tennis courts, pools, gym, concierge, children's programs (ages 4–12), public Wi-Fi, no-smoking rooms* ▤*AE, D, DC, MC, V.*

$–$$ 🖈**Marriott Residence Inn.** Billing itself as a Caribbean-style oasis, with lush palms and a waterfall near the swimming pool, this all-suites hotel's most compelling features are more pragmatic: every room has a full kitchen with a stove and dishwasher, and there's an on-site convenience store. (A supermarket is a few blocks down Palm Parkway.) Suites include a separate living room–kitchen and bedrooms. Two-bedroom suites have two baths. The recreation area has both a kids' pool and a putting green. Pros: sequestered, resortlike atmosphere; convenient to Disney and I-Drive; free Disney shuttle. Cons: not within walking distance of much. ⊠*11450 Marbella Palm Ct., Orlando 32836* ☎*407/465–0075* ⊕*www.marriott.com* ⇨*210 suites* ⌂*In-room: safe, kitchen, refrigerator, ethernet. In-hotel: pool, gym, laundry facilities, laundry service, no-smoking rooms* ▤*AE, D, DC, MC, V.*

$–$$ 🖈**PerriHouse Bed & Breakfast Inn.** An eight-room B&B inside a serene
★ bird sanctuary is a unique lodging experience in fast-lane Orlando. The PerriHouse offers you a chance to split your time between sightseeing and spending quiet moments bird-watching: the 16-acre sanctuary has observation paths, a pond, a feeding station, and a small birdhouse museum. It's attractive to bobwhites, downy woodpeckers, red-tail hawks, and the occasional bald eagle. The inn is a romantic getaway, with four-poster and canopy beds and some fireplaces. The staff can book some interesting adventures—anything from bass fish-

ing trips to sessions at an Orlando skydiving simulator. You're free to use the kitchen. Pros: intimate and private; great bird-watching. Cons: not an easy walk to much of interest; need a rental car. ✉*10417 Vista Oak Ct., Lake Buena Vista 32836* ☎*407/876–4830 or 800/780–4830* ⊕*www.perrihouse.com* ⋑*8 rooms* ⌂*In-room: safe, ethernet. In-hotel: pool* ▭*AE, D, DC, MC, V* ⫞*CP.*

¢–$$ 🖭**Marriott Village at Little Lake Bryan.** The private, gated Marriott Village has three hotels. The **Courtyard** welcomes both families and business travelers with 3,000 square feet of meeting space and large standard rooms decorated with yellow and green floral patterns and blond-wood furniture. Each room has a coffeemaker and Web TV, and the indoor-outdoor pool has a swim-up bar. At **SpringHill Suites,** accommodations have kitchenettes, separate sleeping and dining areas, and Sony Playstations. The **Fairfield Inn** is the least expensive of the three, but rooms are as bright and pleasant, if not quite as amenity laden. Continental breakfast is included in the rates, and there are several chain restaurants in the complex. Best of all, there's an on-site Disney planning center where you can buy park tickets. Pros: lots of informal dining options; lower room rates than hotels on the other side of I–4. Cons: Disney shuttle costs $5 per person round trip (hotels across I–4 have free shuttles). ✉*8623 Vineland Ave., Orlando 32821* ☎*407/938–9001 or 877/682–8552* ⊕*www.marriottvillage.com* ⋑*700 rooms, 400 suites* ⌂*In-room: safe, refrigerator, ethernet. In-hotel: 8 restaurants, room service, bars, pools, gym, children's programs (ages 4–12), laundry facilities, laundry service, public Wi-Fi, no-smoking rooms* ▭*AE, D, DC, MC, V* ⫞*CP.*

$ 🖭**Holiday Inn SunSpree Resort Lake Buena Vista.** This family-oriented hotel has a children's registration desk. Off the lobby you'll find the CyberArcade; a small theater where clowns perform weekends at 7 PM; and a buffet restaurant where kids accompanied by adults eat free at their own little picnic tables. Families love the Kidsuites: playhouse-style rooms within a larger room. Pros: extremely kid-friendly; great deal for families. Cons: too noisy at times for adults; street is a tad busy for pedestrians, especially at night. ✉*13351 Rte. 535, Orlando 32821* ☎*407/239–4500 or 800/366–6299* ⊕*www.kidsuites. com* ⋑*507 rooms* ⌂*In-room: safe, refrigerator, ethernet. In-hotel: restaurant, bar, pool, gym, children's programs (ages 4–12), laundry facilities, laundry service, public Wi-Fi, no-smoking rooms* ▭*AE, D, DC, MC, V.*

KISSIMMEE

Take I–4 Exit 64A, unless otherwise noted.

If you're looking for anything remotely quaint, charming, or sophisticated, move on. With a few exceptions (namely, the flashy Gaylord Palms Resort), the U.S. 192 strip—aka the Irlo Bronson Memorial Highway—is a neon-and-plastic strip crammed with bargain-basement motels, cheap restaurants, fast-food spots, nickel-and-dime attractions, overpriced gas stations, and minimarts where a small bottle of aspirin costs $8. In past years, when Disney was in its infancy, this was the best place to find affordable rooms. But now that budget hotels have cropped up all along International Drive, you can often find better rooms closer to the theme parks by passing the Kissimmee motel strip and heading a few exits north.

One Kissimmee caveat: beware of the word "maingate" in many hotel names. It's a good 6 mi from Kissimmee's "maingate" hotel area to the Walt Disney World entrance. The "maingate west" area, however, is about 2 mi from the park.

$$$$
Fodor'sChoice
★
Gaylord Palms Resort. Built in the style of a grand turn-of-the-20th-century Florida mansion, this resort is meant to awe. Inside its enormous atrium, covered by a 4-acre glass roof, are re-creations of such Florida icons as the Everglades, Key West, and old St. Augustine. Restaurants include Sunset Sam's Fish Camp, on a 60-foot fishing boat docked on the hotel's indoor ocean, and the Old Hickory Steak House in an old warehouse overlooking the alligator-ridden Everglades. Rooms carry on the Florida themes with colorful, tropical decorations. With extensive children's programs, two pool areas, and a huge Canyon Ranch spa, the hotel connives to make you never want to leave. The newest room amenity is Gaylord iConnect, complete with a 15-inch flat-screen monitor, that connects you to the Internet plus a hotel network for booking dinner and activity reservations. Pros: you could have a great vacation without ever leaving the grounds; free shuttle to Disney. Cons: Rooms and meals are pricey; not much within walking distance. ⊠*6000 Osceola Pkwy., I–4 Exit 65, Kissimmee 34746* ☎*407/586–0000* ⊕*www.gaylordpalms.com* ⇨*1,406 rooms, 86 suites* ⌂*In-room: safe, ethernet. In-hotel: 5 restaurants, bars, pools, gym, spa, children's programs (ages 4–12), laundry service, public Wi-Fi, no-smoking rooms* ☐*AE, D, DC, MC, V.*

$$–$$$
★
Celebration Hotel. Like everything in the Disney-created town of Celebration, this 115-room hotel borrows from the best of the 19th and 21st centuries. The lobby resembles those of Victorian grand dames, with hardwood floors and decorative millwork throughout. Rooms may look as if they date from the early 1900s, but each has a 25-inch TV, two phone lines, high-speed Internet access, and a six-channel stereo system. Even though it's less than 1 mi south of the U.S. 192 tourist strip in Kissimmee, the hotel's surroundings are serene. The entire hotel is no-smoking. Pros: a mere block from good restaurants; rental bikes and golf carts make touring a breeze. Con: need a rental car (or lots of cab money) to get around off site. ⊠*700 Bloom St., Celebration 34747* ☎*407/566–6000 or 888/499–3800* ⊕*www.celebrationhotel.com* ⇨*115 rooms* ⌂*In-room: ethernet. In-hotel: 2 restaurants, pool, gym, laundry service, public Wi-Fi, no-smoking rooms* ☐*AE, D, DC, MC, V.*

$–$$$
★
Radisson Resort Parkway. This bright, spacious Radisson has an attractive location amid 1½ acres of foliage, good facilities, and competitive prices. The focal point is the giant pool, with wide, gentle waterfalls; a 40-foot slide; and whirlpools. The lively sports bar off the lobby has a massive TV. On-site refueling options include Starbucks, Krispy Kreme, and Pizza Hut. Generously proportioned rooms are decorated

with blond-wood furniture and white down comforters. A free shuttle makes 10-minute trips to Disney. Pros: kids 10 and under eat free at hotel restaurants; kids suites have bunk beds; free Disney shuttle. Con: not an easy walk to area shops or restaurants. ☒*2900 Parkway Blvd., Kissimmee 34746* ☎*407/396–7000 or 800/634–4774* ⊕*www.radissonparkway.com* ⤴*712 rooms, 8 suites* ⌖*In-room: ethernet. In-hotel: 2 restaurants, bar, tennis courts, pools, gym, laundry facilities, laundry service, public Wi-Fi, no-smoking rooms* ☐*AE, D, DC, MC, V.*

$–$$ ☂**Magical Memories Villas.** Despite the name, this resort is not affiliated with Disney, but you'll probably feel the magic anyway when you get your bill. Two-bedroom villas with full kitchens start at $94 a night. Three- and four-bedroom villas are also available. Although the furnishings are standard, the villas are spacious and bright, with large windows and pastel pink walls. All the suites include a washer and dryer, and a set of linens. Pros: sequestered and homey; free long-distance calls with mid-priced and premium rooms. Cons: not an easy walk to area shops or restaurants; extra charge for daily housekeeping (which is required). ☒*5075 U.S. 192 W, Kissimmee 34746* ☎*407/390–8200 or 800/736–0402* ⊕*www.magicalmemories.com* ⤴*140 villas* ⌖*In-room: kitchen, refrigerator, VCR, ethernet. In-hotel: tennis court, pool, gym, laundry facilities, no-smoking rooms, some pets allowed (fee)* ☐*D, MC, V.*

ORLANDO

INTERNATIONAL DRIVE
Take I–4 Exit 28 or 29.

If you plan to visit other attractions besides Walt Disney World, the sprawl of newish hotels, restaurants, and shopping malls known as International Drive—"I–Drive" to locals—makes a convenient base. Parallel to Interstate 4, it's just a few minutes south of downtown Orlando. It's also near SeaWorld and Universal Orlando as well as several popular dinner theaters.

$$$$ ☂**Peabody Orlando.** Every day at 11 AM the celebrated Peabody ducks
★   exit a private elevator and waddle across the lobby to the marble fountain where they pass the day, basking in their fame. At 5 they repeat the ritual in reverse. Built by the owners of the landmark Peabody Hotel in Memphis, this 27-story structure resembles a trio of high-rise office towers, but don't be put off by the austerity. The interior impresses with gilt and marble halls. Some of the oversize upper-floor rooms have views of Disney. A lobby concierge can answer your questions about attractions and cultural events. You can leave your cares behind at the spa or health club. A round-trip shuttle to Disney or Universal is $10 per person. Pros: adjacent to convention center (business travelers take note); good spa; short walk to shops and restaurants. Cons: pricey; adjacent to convention center (leisure travelers take note); on a congested section of I-Drive. ☒*9801 International Dr., I-Drive Area, Orlando 32819* ☎*407/352–4000 or 800/732–2639* ⊕*www.peabodyorlando.com* ⤴*891 rooms* ⌖*In-room: safe, ethernet. In-hotel: 3 res-*

taurants, room service, tennis courts, pool, gym, spa, concierge, public Wi-Fi, no-smoking rooms ▤*AE, D, DC, MC, V.*

$$$–$$$$
Fodor'sChoice
★
🏨**Ritz-Carlton Orlando Grande Lakes.** Orlando's first and only Ritz is a particularly extravagant link in the luxury chain. Service is exemplary, from the fully attended porte-cochere entrance to the 18-hole golf course and 40-room spa. Rooms and suites have large balconies, elegant wood furnishings, down comforters, and decadent marble baths (with separate showers and tubs). A lovely, Roman-style pool area has fountains and a hot tub. Make reservations for dinner at Norman's when you reserve your room. An enclosed hallway connects the Ritz to the nearby JW Marriott Hotel, where you'll find more restaurants and a kid-friendly water park. Pros: truly luxurious; impeccable service; great spa; golf course; shares amenities with Marriott. Cons: pricey; need a rental car to reach Disney and area shops and restaurants. ✉*4012 Central Florida Pkwy., I-Drive Area, Orlando 32837* ☎*407/206–2400 or 800/576–5760* ⊕*www.grandelakes.com* ⬍*520 rooms, 64 suites* ⚷*In-room: ethernet. In-hotel: 4 restaurants, room service, bars, 18-hole golf course, pool, gym, spa, concierge, children's programs (ages 4–12), laundry service, executive floor, public Wi-Fi, no-smoking rooms* ▤*AE, D, DC, MC, V.*

$$–$$$$
★
🏨**JW Marriott Orlando Grande Lakes.** With more than 70,000 square feet of meeting space, this hotel caters to a convention clientele. But because it's part of a lush resort that includes a European-style spa and a Greg Norman–designed golf course, it also appeals to those looking to relax. Rooms are large (420 square feet), and most have balconies that overlook the huge pool complex. Wander down a long connector hallway to the adjoining Ritz-Carlton, where you can use your room charge card in the restaurants and shops. Pros: pool is great for kids and adults; shares amenities with the Ritz. Cons: things are spread out on the grounds; you need a rental car to reach Disney and other area offerings. ✉*4040 Central Florida Pkwy., I-Drive Area, Orlando 32837* ☎*407/206–2300 or 800/576–5750* ⊕*www.grandelakes.com* ⬍*1,000 rooms, 57 suites* ⚷*In-room: ethernet. In-hotel: 4 restaurants, room service, bars, 18-hole golf course, pool, gym, spa, concierge, laundry service, executive floor, public Wi-Fi, no-smoking rooms* ▤*AE, D, DC, MC, V.*

$$–$$$
🏨**Renaissance Orlando Resort at SeaWorld.** The 10-story atrium is full of waterfalls, goldfish ponds, and palm trees; as you shoot skyward in sleek glass elevators, look for the exotic birds—on loan from SeaWorld across the street—twittering in the large, hand-carved, gilded Venetian aviary. Rooms have more floor space than the average Central Florida hotel, plus nice touches like high-speed Internet connections. Atlantis, the formal Mediterranean restaurant, is something of an undiscovered gem. Pros: good on-site restaurants; across from SeaWorld; shuttles to Disney ($7 round trip) and Universal ($14 round trip). Cons: need a rental car to reach area shops and restaurants; $8 daily parking fee; shuttles aren't free; often full of conventioneers. ✉*6677 Sea Harbor Dr., I-Drive Area, Orlando 32821* ☎*407/351–5555 or 800/468–3571* ⊕*www.renaissancehotels.com* ⬍*778 rooms* ⚷*In-room: ethernet. In-hotel: 4 restaurants, room service, tennis courts, pool, gym, spa,*

laundry service, concierge, public Wi-Fi, no-smoking rooms ≡*AE, D, DC, MC, V.*

$-$$ **Embassy Suites Hotel International Drive South/Convention Center.** This all-suites hotel has an expansive Mediterranean-style lobby with marble floors, pillars, hanging lamps, and old-fashioned ceiling fans. The atrium is all about fountains and palm trees. Elsewhere, tile walks and brick arches lend still more flavor. The hotel has a number of good amenities, such as a health club with a fine steam room. Pros: free breakfast and nightly beverages; easy walk to convention center and Pointe*Orlando; free shuttle to Disney and Universal. Con: on congested stretch of I-Drive. ⊠*8978 International Dr., I-Drive Area, Orlando 32819* ☎*407/352–1400 or 800/433–7275* ⊕*www.embassysuitesorlando.com* ⇆*244 suites* ⌂*In-room: safe, ethernet. In-hotel: restaurant, pool, gym, public Wi-Fi, no-smoking rooms* ≡*AE, D, DC, MC, V* ⍥⏐*BP.*

$-$$ **Enclave Suites at Orlando.** With three 10-story buildings surrounding a private lake, an office, restaurant, and recreation area, this all-suites lodging is less a hotel than a condominium complex. Here, what you would spend for a normal room in a fancy hotel gets you an apartment with a living room, a full kitchen, two bedrooms, and small terraces with lake views. KidsQuarter suites, which can sleep six, have small children's rooms with bunk beds and whimsical murals of Shamu. There's free transportation to Universal, SeaWorld, and Wet 'n Wild. Pros: good deals on spacious suites; within walking distance of I-Drive eateries and attractions; free breakfast; free shuttle to Universal, SeaWorld, and Wet 'n Wild. Cons: area traffic can be a hassle. ⊠*6165 Carrier Dr., I-Drive Area, Orlando 32819* ☎*407/351–1155 or 800/457–0077* ⊕*www.enclavesuites.com* ⇆*321 suites* ⌂*In-room: safe, kitchen, refrigerator, ethernet. In-hotel: restaurant, tennis court, pools, gym, laundry facilities, laundry service, public Wi-Fi, no-smoking rooms* ≡*AE, D, DC, MC, V* ⍥⏐*BP.*

$ **Rosen Plaza Hotel.** Harris Rosen, Orlando's largest independent hotel owner, loves to offer bargains, and you can definitely find one here. Although it's essentially a convention hotel, leisure travelers like the prime location and long list of amenities. Rooms have two queen-size beds and are larger than those at many hotels. Two upscale restaurants, Jack's Place and Café Matisse, offer great steaks and a great buffet, respectively. Rossini's serves great pizza, and you can also grab quick eats at the reasonably priced 24-hour deli. With the BAGS service, you can get your airline boarding pass and check your suitcases in the hotel lobby, so you can go straight to the gate at Orlando International. There's a free shuttle to Universal Orlando and SeaWorld; a round-trip shuttle to Disney costs $15 per person. Pros: within walking distanct of I-Drive eateries and attractions; free shuttle to Universal and Sea-World; BAGS check-in service. Cons: convention center traffic can be bad; shuttle to Disney isn't free. ⊠*9700 International Dr., I-Drive Area, Orlando 32819* ☎*407/996–9700 or 800/627–8258* ⊕*www. rosenplaza.com* ⇆*810 rooms* ⌂*In-room: safe, ethernet. In-hotel: 2 restaurants, room service, bar, pool, laundry facilities, laundry service, public Wi-Fi, no-smoking rooms* ≡*AE, D, DC, MC, V.*

$ ⛺**Sheraton Studio City.** Atop this Sheraton is a giant silver globe suitable for Times Square on New Year's Eve. But the interior has a Hollywood theme, with movie posters and black-and-white art deco touches throughout the public spaces and rooms, most of which have two queen beds. The 21st floor has 15 extra-large rooms with floor-to-ceiling windows. Pros: convenient to Universal; free shuttle to theme parks and outlet malls; great night views from upper floors. Con: on an unattractive stretch of I-Drive. ⊠*5905 International Dr., I-Drive Area, Orlando 32819* ☎*407/351–2100 or 800/327–1366* ⊕*www. sheratonstudiocity.com* ⋚*302 rooms* ☐*In-room: safe, ethernet. In-hotel: restaurant, room service, bar, pool, concierge, laundry service, public Wi-Fi, no-smoking rooms* ☐*AE, D, DC, MC, V.*

¢–$ ⛺**Wynfield Inn Convention Center.** If you want a room with more than just the bare essentials but don't have the budget for luxury, this three-story motel is a find. Quarters are comfy if not spectacular; all have two double beds. Children 17 and under stay free in their parents' room (with a maximum of four people per room). The hotel is ¼ mi from SeaWorld. Pros: very economical; short walk to I-Drive; pets allowed ($50 deposit). Con: traffic can be heavy, especially during conventions. ⊠*6263 Westwood Blvd., I-Drive Area, Orlando 32821* ☎*407/345–8000 or 800/346–1551* ⊕*www.wynfieldinn.com* ⋚*144 rooms* ☐*In-room: safe, ethernet. In-hotel: restaurant, bar, pools, laundry facilities, laundry service, no-smoking rooms* ☐*AE, DC, MC, V.*

DOWNTOWN ORLANDO

Downtown Orlando, north of Walt Disney World and slightly north of the International Drive area, is a thriving business district with a tourist fringe in the form of Church Street Station. To get there take Exit 83 off Interstate 4 if you're heading west, Exit 82C if eastbound.

$$–$$$$ ⛺**Westin Grand Bohemian.** This European-style property is downtown Orlando's only luxury hotel. Opposite city hall, the Grand Bohemian showcases more than 100 pieces of art—including an Imperial Grand Bösendorfer piano, one of only two in the world, which sits in a posh ground-floor lounge. Rooms have dark-wood furnishings with brushed-silver accents. Tall headboards are upholstered in iridescent fabrics. Pros: art gallery; quiet, adult-friendly atmosphere; great restaurant; short walk to Lake Eola and Church Street. Con: kids may find it boring. ⊠*325 S. Orange Ave., Downtown, Orlando 32801* ☎*407/313–9000 or 866/663–0024* ⊕*www.grandbohemianhotel.com* ⋚*250 rooms, 36 suites* ☐*In-room: ethernet. In-hotel: restaurant, room service, bar, pool, gym, concierge, executive floor, public Wi-Fi, parking (fee), no-smoking rooms* ☐*AE, D, DC, MC, V.*

$–$$ ⛺**Eō Inn & Urban Spa.** The entrance is at the rear of the building, behind
★   Panera Bread, the bakery–restaurant that occupies the ground floor. Consequently, this three-story boutique hotel in a 1923 building is an undiscovered charmer. The spa does a brisk business on its own, but as a hotel guest you can always get in for a Swedish massage or a beauty treatement. Rooms have black-and-white photographs, thick down comforters, and high-speed Internet connections. Best of all, Lake Eola,

with its 1-mi walking path, is across the street—treat yourself to a king suite overlooking the water. Pros: good spa; very short walk to Lake Eola; short walk to Thornton Park and Church Street. Cons: you have to battle I–4 traffic; Disney is 30 minutes away. ⊠*227 N. Eola Dr., off E. Robinson St., Thornton Park, Orlando 32801* ☎*407/481–8485 or 888/481–8488* ⊕*www.eoinn.com* ✒*17 rooms* ☖*In-room: safe, ethernet. In-hotel: spa, laundry service, public Wi-Fi, no-smoking rooms* ⊟*AE, D, DC, MC, V.*

WINTER PARK

Travel farther afield and find more comforts and facilities for the money, and maybe even some genuine Florida charm—of the warm, cozy, one-of-a-kind country inn variety.

$–$$$ **Park Plaza Hotel.** Small and intimate, this 1922 establishment feels almost like a private home. Best accommodations are front garden suites with a living room that opens onto a long balcony usually abloom with impatiens and bougainvillea. Balconies are so covered with shrubs and ferns that they are somewhat private, inspiring more than a few romantic interludes. A half-dozen sidewalk cafés and many more upscale boutiques and shops surround the hotel. Also, the Charles Hosmer Morse Museum of Art is within two blocks. Park Plaza Gardens, the restaurant downstairs, offers quiet atrium dining and excellent food. Pros: romantic; great balconies overlooking Park Avenue; short walk to shops and restaurants. Cons: no small children allowed; small rooms; Disney is 60 minutes away. ⊠*307 Park Ave. S, Winter Park 32789* ☎*407/647–1072 or 800/228–7220* ⊕*www.parkplazahotel.com* ✒*27 rooms* ☖*In-room: ethernet. In-hotel: restaurant, room service, laundry service, public Wi-Fi, no kids under 5, no-smoking rooms* ⊟*AE, DC, MC, V.*

NIGHTLIFE

BARS, LOUNGES & NIGHTCLUBS

WALT DISNEY WORLD RESORT

When you enter the fiefdom known as Walt Disney World, you're likely to see as many watering holes as cartoon characters. Nightlife awaits at several Disney shopping and entertainment complexes—everywhere you look, rockers, bluesmen, and DJs are tuning up and turning on their amps after dinner's done. Plus, two long-running dinner shows provide an evening of song, dance, and dining, all for a single price. Get information on WDW nightlife from the Walt Disney World information hotline (☎407/824–4321 or 407/824–4500) or check online at ⊕*www.disneyworld.com.* Disney nightspots accept American Express, MasterCard, and Visa, and you can charge your bill to your room if you're staying at a Disney-owned property.

Disney's BoardWalk (☎*407/939–3492 entertainment hotline*), across Crescent Lake from the Yacht and Beach Club Resorts, recalls an Atlantic City–style, turn-of-the-last-century amusement complex by the shore, complete with restaurants, clubs, souvenir sellers, surreys, saltwater taffy vendors, and shops. When the lights go on after sunset, take a nostalgic, romantic stroll. In true Disney fashion, the sports motif at the **ESPN Club** (☎407/939–1177) is carried into every nook and many of the crannies. The vibe is rugged and boisterous at **Jellyrolls** (☎407/560–8770), which has comedians at dueling grand pianos and a sing-along piano bar. Wander the promenade and you'll also come across **Atlantic Dance** (☎407/939–2444) for Top 40 dance tunes, and **Big River Grille & Brewing Works** (☎407/560–0253). Cover charges vary depending on the day of the week. For information on all BoardWalk events, call the entertainment hotline.

Many Disney clubs are at **Pleasure Island,** a 6-acre after-dark entertainment complex connected to the rest of Downtown Disney by footbridges. Despite its location on Disney property, the entertainment has real grit and life, even against the backdrop of the facility's gimmicky underlying concept: every night is New Year's Eve, complete with a nightly countdown to midnight and fireworks. In addition to seven clubs and an Irish pub, you'll find a few restaurants and shops. A pay-one-price admission gets you into all the clubs and shows. Children accompanied by an adult are admitted to all clubs except BET Sound-Stage and Mannequins.

Adventurer's Club re-creates a private club of the 1930s. Much of the entertainment is found in looking at exotic accent pieces that clutter the walls; the rest is in watching actors lead sing-alongs and share tall tales from their adventures. **BET SoundStage Club** is backed by Black Entertainment Television and pays tribute to all genres of African-American music through videos and live performances. The blend has attracted legions of locals who proclaim this the funkiest nightspot in central Florida (and perhaps also the loudest). The comedians at the

Fodor'sChoice **Comedy Warehouse** perform improv games, sing improvised songs, and
★ create off-the-cuff sketches based largely on suggestions from the audience. At **8TRAX,** groove to the recorded music of Donna Summer or the Village People while the disco balls spin. You'll either love or tolerate **Mannequins'** high-tech style, complete with Top 40 hits; a revolving dance floor; elaborate lighting; suggestive, over-the-top Disney dancers; and such special effects as bubbles and snow. **Motion** plays dance music from Zoot Suit Riot to the latest techno junk. The two-story warehouse look is stark, with the emphasis put on the dance floor and the club's twirling lights and thumping sound system. A traditional Irish pub with music, a menu of treats, and a bit o' Blarney just opened at the site of the old Pleasure Island Jazz Company. The **Rock & Roll Beach Club** throbs with live rock music from the '60s to the '90s. ⊠ *Off Buena Vista Dr., Downtown Disney* ☎407/934–7781 or 407/824–4500 🍴*Pay-one-price admission to clubs $20.95 plus tax, shops and restaurants open to all 10:30–7* ⊙ *Clubs daily 7* PM–2 AM; *shops and restaurants daily 10:30* AM–2 AM.

Downtown Disney West Side is a pleasingly hip outdoor complex of shopping, dining, and entertainment. A 24-screen AMC cinema shows first-run movies. For something a little different, drop by for a beer and a *baba-lu* at Gloria Estefan's **Bongos Cuban Café** (☎️*407/828–0999*).

Cirque du Soleil (☎️*407/939–7600*) starts at 100 mph and accelerates from there. It's 90 minutes of extraordinary acrobatics, avant-garde stagings, costumes, choreography, and a grand finale that'll make you double-check Newton's laws of motion. Shows featuring 72 performers are scheduled twice daily, five days a week (call for current performance schedule). Adjacent to the **House of Blues** (☎️*407/934–2583*) restaurant,
which itself showcases cool blues starting at 11, HOB's up-close-and-personal concert venue presents local and nationally known artists playing everything from reggae to rock to R&B.

DisneyQuest is a five-story video–virtual-reality mini-theme park, and there's a **Wolfgang Puck Cafe,** a **Virgin Megastore,** plus an avenue of eclectic shops. ⊠ *Off Buena Vista Dr., Downtown Disney* ☎️*407/824–4321 or 407/824–2222.*

UNIVERSAL ORLANDO

Universal's CityWalk meets the Downtown Disney challenge with its open and airy gathering place, which includes clubs ranging from quiet jazz retreats to over-the-top discotheques. **Bob Marley—A Tribute to Freedom** is a loud reggae club–restaurant with more than a touch of Jamaica. **City Jazz/Bonkerz** has taken on a split personality, with cool jazz and high-energy funk sharing the venue several days a week with a Bonkerz Comedy Club routine. The **groove** has wild lighting, visual effects, disco chrome, and funk music that will have you shakin' your groove thang all night long. The world's largest **Hard Rock Cafe** adjoins the chain's first dedicated live concert venue, **Hard Rock Live.** **The Latin Quarter** is crowded and pulsing and feels like a 21st-century version of Ricky Ricardo's Tropicana, with food and entertainment from 21 Latin American countries. The 20-screen **Loew's Universal Cineplex** (☎️*407/354–5998 tickets, 407/354–3374 box office*) can offer an escape from the crowds.

Jimmy Buffett's Margaritaville has proven itself popular with Parrotheads and margarita drinkers. An exact duplicate of New Orleans's **Pat O'Brien's** blows into Orlando with its signature drink, the hurricane, as well as dueling pianos and a "flaming fountain" patio. Clubs charge individual covers; you can buy a Party Pass (a one price–all clubs admission) for $9.95; or a Party Pass-and-a-Movie for $13. Making these deals even better is the fact that after 6 PM the $8 parking fee drops to nothing. ☎️*407/363–8000 Universal main line, 888/331–9108, 407/224–2692 CityWalk guest services* ⊕*www.citywalkorlando.com.*

ORLANDO

For several years, downtown Orlando clubs had a monopoly on nighttime entertainment—which came to a close when Disney and Universal muscled their way in. Nightspots still attract office workers after hours, but the once-popular Church Street Station entertainment complex has closed. Down Orange Avenue, cool clubs are now sitting beside grungy tattoo and piercing parlors that are making the downtown area look tired, though a revitalization project is currently underway. There are some gems in the surrounding neighborhoods and clubs that are worth a visit—if you're willing to seek them out.

Devoid of stand-up comedians, lively **Sak Comedy Lab** (✉ *380 W. Amelia Ave., Downtown Orlando* ☎ *407/648–0001*) is where you'll find Orlando's premier comedy troupe. Duel of Fools is the regular cast; the Sak Comedy Lab Rats are apprentices with potential, and the Generation S show spotlights Lab Rats with promise. Wayne Brady, star of *Whose Line Is It Anyway?*, got his start here. The troupe plays to sold-out audiences Tuesday through Saturday.

Perhaps the favorite live-music venue of locals, **Social** (✉ *54 N. Orange Ave.* ☎ *407/246–1419* ⊕ *orlandosocial.com*) is a great place to see touring and local musicians. Choose from over 35 bottled beers and a dozen ales and lagers on tap while listening to anything from alternative rock to rockabilly to undiluted jazz. Matchbox Twenty and Seven Mary Three both got their starts here.

Socialite Paris Hilton lent her name to **Club Paris** (✉ *122 W. Church St.* ☎ *407/832–7409*), and then didn't show up to the club's opening party. Three million dollars helped refurbish part of the defunct Church Street Station, and now a South Beach–style courtyard sets the tone for entry. The floor is monitored by "fashion police" who award the trendiest patrons a free bar tab for the evening. There's plenty of room to dance (20,000 square feet) to New York–style DJ noise, as well as varied music on themed nights: Latin, Ladies, Fashion, and '80s. If you're considered worthy or are willing to pay an added admission, you can go upstairs to the VIP club.

Conceptually a world away from Club Paris and its five-for-one drink specials is the **Bösendorfer Lounge** (✉ *325 S. Orange Ave.* ☎ *407/313–9000*) at the Westin Grand Bohemian. This is a place that celebrates the finer things in life by featuring an extensive private art collection, fine wines, and live jazz. In fact, the piano used for performances is a rare Imperial Grand Bösendorfer piano, reportedly one of only two in the world. This a very sophisticated bar that is frequented by local movers and shakers.

SPORTS & THE OUTDOORS

Orlando is the place to visit if you want to be outside. You'll find just about every outdoor sport here—unless it involves a ski lift—that you'll find anywhere else in the country. Although professional sports are limited to the Orlando Magic and the Bay Hill Invitational, Orlando is of course the site for the Walt Disney World Marathon, one of the most popular marathons in the world. It is also home to numerous triathlon events, bike races, and extreme sports such as the NBC Sports Dew Action Sports Tour.

Fodor's Choice
★

Disney's Wide World of Sports (☎407/828–3267) has tournament-type events in more than 30 individual and team sports; serves as the spring-training home of the Atlanta Braves; and offers participatory sports for guests, including basketball, football, baseball, and soccer, as part of its Multi Sport Experience.

> WORD OF MOUTH
>
> "Be ready for a bumpy landing! Our daughter was screeching with laughter, but I was afraid our basket would tip over."–Rong Qian

AUTO RACING

★ **The Richard Petty Driving Experience** allows you to ride in or even drive a NASCAR-style stock car on a real racetrack. Depending on what you're willing to spend—prices range from $99 to $2,999—you can do everything from riding shotgun for three laps on the 1-mi track to taking driving lessons, culminating in your very own solo behind the wheel. The Richard Petty organization has a second Central Florida location at the Daytona International Speedway, but it involves riding in the car with an experienced race-car driver rather than driving a car yourself. ⊠ *Walt Disney World Speedway* ☎ *800/237–3889* ⊕ *www.1800bepetty.com.*

BASKETBALL

Fodor's Choice
★

The **Orlando Magic** has driven the city to new heights of hoop fanaticism, though tickets aren't unattainable. Nosebleed seats run as low as $10; front-and-center viewing goes for up to $150. ⊠ *TD Waterhouse Centre, 600 W. Amelia St., Orlando* ✛ *2 blocks west of I–4 Exit 41* ☎ *407/839–3900 Ticketmaster* ⊕ *www.nba.com/magic.*

GOLF

Golf is extremely popular in central Florida. Be sure to reserve tee times well in advance.

Golfpac (⊠ *483 Montgomery Pl., Altamonte Springs 32714* ☎ *407/ 260–2288 or 800/327–0878* ⊕ *www.golfpactravel.com*) packages golf vacations and prearranges tee times at more than 78 courses around Orlando.

WALT DISNEY WORLD RESORT

Walt Disney World Golf (☎ *407/939–7529*) has five championship 18-hole courses—all on the PGA Tour route. Prices range from $20 for a youngster 17 or under to play 9 holes at Oak Trail walking course, to an adult nonhotel guest paying $165 to play 18 holes at one of Disney's newer courses in peak season. Disney guests get a price break, with rates ranging from $79 for a Disney hotel guest playing Monday through Thursday at the Lake Buena Vista course to $155 for a day visitor playing the Osprey Ridge course. All have a twilight discount rate, $30–$80 for the 18-hole courses, which goes into effect at 2 PM from October 31 to January 14 and at 3 PM from April 1 to October 26. The 9-hole, par-36 Oak Trail course is best for those on a budget, with a year-round rate of $20 for golfers 17 and under and $38 golfers 18 and older, with an additional twilight discount between May 14 and

3

September 27. Rates at all courses except Oak Trail include an electric golf cart. No electric carts are allowed at Oak Trail, and a pull cart for your bag is $6. If you've got the stamina and desire to play the same course twice in the same day, you can do so for half price the second time around, but you can't reserve that option in advance, and this "Re-Play Option," as Disney calls it, is subject to availability. Note that golf rates change frequently, so double-check them when you reserve.

AROUND ORLANDO

Green fees at most non-Disney courses fluctuate with the season. A twilight discount applies after 2 in busy seasons and after 3 during the rest of the year; the discount is usually half off the normal rate.

You can only play at **Arnold Palmer's Bay Hill Club** (✉ *9000 Bay Hill Rd.* ☎ *407/876–2429 or 888/422–9445*) if you're invited by a member or stay at the club's on-property hotel, but room rates that include a round of golf run as low as $219 per person in summer. The course at the **Celebration Golf Club** (✉ *701 Golf Park Dr., Celebration* ☎ *407/566–4653*) was designed by Robert Trent Jones Jr. and Sr. and is 1 mi off the U.S. 192 strip; green fee: $55/$150.

★ **Champions Gate Golf Club** (✉ *1400 Masters Blvd., Champions Gate* ☎ *407/787–4653 or 888/558–9301*), near Walt Disney World, has the feel of the best British Isles courses; green fee: $65/$187. The **Falcon's Fire Golf Club** (✉ *3200 Seralago Blvd., Kissimmee* ☎ *407/239–5445*) course was designed by Rees Jones, green fee: $79/$145. **Hawk's Landing Golf Course** (✉ *Marriott's Orlando World Center, 8701 World Center Dr.* ☎ *407/238–8660*) includes 16 water holes, lots of sand, and exotic landscaping; green fee: $89/$129.

SHOPPING

From fairy-tale kingdoms to Old West–style trading posts to outlet malls, Walt Disney World and Orlando have a plethora of shopping opportunities that won't leave you disappointed. The colors are bright and energetic, the textures soft and cuddly, and the designs fresh and thoughtful. Before you board any roller coaster or giggle at any show, you'll catch yourself window-shopping and delighting in the thought of making a purchase. And when it comes time to do some serious shopping, you may have a hard time deciding what to buy with all the options available. Of course, your best bet is to wait a couple of days before you buy anything; survey the scene a little before spending all the money in your budget. Better yet, save shopping for the last day of your trip.

SHOPPING AREAS, MALLS & DEPARTMENT STORES

WALT DISNEY WORLD RESORT

Shopping is an integral part of the Disney experience, going far beyond the surfeit of Disney trinkets found in every park. The area known as Downtown Disney contains three shopping-entertainment areas with plenty of just about everything. If you're staying at a Disney property,

Best Disney Souvenirs

According to Fodors.com forums users ...

"My friend who is almost 25 still wears her Indiana Jones hat she bought on a senior-year spring break trip to Disney."–jayne1973

"My girls bought inexpensive fans (about $5) in the Epcot China pavilion gift shop. Then the fans were personalized right there (free) with the girls' names written in Chinese."–ajcolorado

"I bought a silver Tinkerbell necklace that I love. They also have these memo holders that are miniatures of the princess dresses. I have Snow White, Cinderella, and Sleeping Beauty, and of course, each is holding the picture of my kids with that princess. So cute!"–missypie

"My best Disney souvenir? Pictures of my kids doing stuff like freaking out on Splash Mountain, etc. These will be around a lot longer than any souvenir. But to officially answer your question it would be the Minnie dress I bought my two-year-old. She did not take it off forever!!"–momof5

"When we went for our honeymoon, we bought the Mickey and Minnie bride-and-groom stuffed toys. Every time I look at them, I think of our honeymoon. And they look so cute in the tux and dress, too!"–travel_addict

"We just returned and we got a Tinkerbell cookie jar and the Cinderella waffle iron."–jetprincess

a nice perk awaits: if you buy anything from a store inside any Disney park, you can ask the salesperson to have it delivered to your room so you don't have to lug it around all day long. The service is free, and your purchase will be waiting for you on your bed when you return to your room.

Fodor's Choice
★

Downtown Disney Marketplace, a pleasant complex of shops, includes the **World of Disney** (☎407/828–1451), the Disney superstore to end all Disney superstores, and the **LEGO Imagination Center** (☎407/828–0065), with an impressive backdrop of elaborate Lego sculptures and an excellent outdoor play area for kids. Among the standouts over at **Downtown Disney West Side** are **Guitar Gallery** (☎407/827–0118), which sells videos, music books, accessories, and guitars, guitars, and more guitars; and the enormous **Virgin Megastore** (☎407/828–0222), with a music, video, and book selection as large as its prices. Don't miss **Hoypolloi,** with its gallery full of museum-quality art and jewelry.

UNIVERSAL ORLANDO

Universal's CityWalk (☎407/363–8000) brings themed shopping experiences along with its cornucopia of restaurants, clubs, bars, and cafés. Retailers include **Endangered Species** (☎407/224–2310), with products representing endangered animals, ecosystems, and cultures worldwide; **Cigarz** (☎407/370–2999), for hand-rolled cigars; and **Universal Studios Store** (☎407/224–2207), for a slew of official merchandise.

TOP 5 SHOPPING DESTINATIONS

Downtown Disney. Why spend valuable touring time shopping in the theme parks when you come here (for no entry fee) on your first or last day? The perfect place for one-stop souvenir shopping, Downtown Disney has dozens of stores, including World of Disney, easily the largest and best store on Disney property.

Epcot World Showcase. Trinkets from all over the world, some hand-crafted and incredibly unique, are sold at the pavilions representing individual countries here. Check out the Japanese bonsai trees and Moroccan fez hats.

Main Street, U.S.A., Magic Kingdom. The Main Street buildings are so adorable with their forced per-spective architecture, pastel colors, and elaborately decorated facades that you want to go inside them and start examining the wares immediately. Don't waste precious touring time shopping in the morning, but definitely come back to check them out in the afternoon or evening.

Mall at Millenia. Visiting this mall is like going to New York for the afternoon. One look at the store names—Gucci, Dior, Chanel, Jimmy Choo, Cartier, Tiffany—and you'll think you've died and gone to the intersection of 5th and 57th.

Park Avenue, Winter Park. If you have the chance to visit the quaint village of Winter Park north of Orlando, carve out an hour or two to stroll up and down this thoroughfare.

ORLANDO

The necessities, such as a 24-hour grocery and pharmacy, post office, bank, and cleaners, are all at **Crossroads of Lake Buena Vista** (⊠ *Rte. 535 and I–4, Lake Buena Vista*), across from Downtown Disney Marketplace. **Florida Mall** (⊠ *8001 S. Orange Blossom Trail*), 4½ mi east of Interstate 4 and International Drive, is the largest mall in central Florida, with 260 specialty shops, Saks and Nordstrom, and one of the better food courts around. **Mall at Millenia** (⊠ *4200 Conroy Rd.* ☎ *407/363–3555* ⊙ *Mon.–Sat. 10–9:30, Sun. 11–7*) has high-end designers like Gucci, Dior, Burberry, Chanel, Jimmy Choo, Hugo Boss, Cartier, and Tiffany, plus Anthropologie, Neiman Marcus, Bloomingdale's, Bang & Olufsen, and Orlando's only Apple store. It's easy to reach: take Exit 78 off Interstate 4.

FACTORY OUTLETS

★ **Prime Outlets Orlando.** Two malls and four annexes make Prime Outlets Orlando the area's largest collection of outlet stores. One of the best places to find deals is Off 5th, the Saks Fifth Avenue Outlet. ⊠ *5401 W. Oak Ridge Rd., at northern tip of International Dr.* ☎ *407/352–9600* ⊕ *www.primeoutlets.com* ⊙ *Mon.–Sat. 10–9, Sun. 10–6*.

Lake Buena Vista Factory Stores. Although there's scant curb appeal, this is a nice gathering of standard outlet stores. The center is roughly 2 mi south of I–4 and includes Reebok, Nine West, Disney's Character Corner, Sony/JVC, Tommy Hilfiger, Ralph Lauren, OshKosh, Fossil, and the area's only Old Navy Outlet. If you can, check the Web site before traveling as some stores post online coupons. Take Exit 68 at

I–4. ✉ *15591 State Rd. 535, 1 mi north of Hwy. 192* ☎ *407/238–9301*
⊕ *www.lbvfs.com* ☾ *Mon.–Sat. 10–9, Sun. 10–6.*

THE ORLANDO AREA ESSENTIALS

*To research prices, get advice from other travelers, and book travel
arrangements, visit www.fodors.com.*

TRANSPORTATION

BY AIR

CARRIERS

More than 20 scheduled airlines and more than 30 charter firms operate into and out of Orlando International Airport, providing direct
service to more than 100 cities in the United States and overseas.

Major Airlines **AirTran** (☎ *800/247–8726* ⊕ *www.airtran.com*). **Alaska Airlines** (☎ *800/252–7522* ⊕ *www.alaskaair.com*). **American** (☎ *800/433–7300*
⊕ *www.aa.com*). **Continental** (☎ *800/523–3273* ⊕ *www.continental.com*).
Delta (☎ *800/221–1212* ⊕ *www.delta.com*). **Northwest/KLM** (☎ *800/225–2525*
⊕ *www.nwa.com*). **United Airlines** (☎ *800/241–6522* ⊕ *www.united.com*). **US
Airways/America West Airlines** (☎ *800/428–4322* ⊕ *www.usairways.com*).

Smaller Airlines **ATA** (☎ *800/225–2995* ⊕ *www.ata.com*). **Frontier** (☎ *800/432–
1359* ⊕ *www.frontierairlines.com*). **JetBlue** (☎ *800/538–2583* ⊕ *www.jetblue.
com*). **Midwest Express** (☎ *800/452–2022* ⊕ *www.midwestairlines.com*). **Southwest** (☎ *800/435–9792* ⊕ *www.iflyswa.com*). **Spirit** (☎ *800/772–7117* ⊕ *www.
spiritair.com*).

AIRPORTS & TRANSFERS

The Orlando airport (MCO on your baggage tag) is ultramodern, huge,
and growing all the time. However, it's relatively easy to navigate. Just
follow the excellent signs. Monorails shuttle you from gate areas to the
core area, where you'll find baggage claim. The complex is south of
Orlando and northeast of Walt Disney World.

Find out in advance whether your hotel offers a free airport shuttle. If
not, you have a few options. Cab fare from the airport to the Disney
World area runs $50–$60. If there are four or more people in your
party, taking a taxi may cost less than paying by the head for an airport shuttle.

A shuttle service, the Mears Transportation Group, meets you at the
gate, helps with the luggage, and whisks you away in either an 11-
passenger van, a town car, or a limo. Vans run to Walt Disney World,
International Drive, and along U.S. 192 in Kissimmee every 30 minutes; prices range from $19 one-way for ($15 for children 4–11) to $31
round-trip ($23 children 4–11). Limo rates run $60–$70 for a town car
that accommodates three or four to $155 for a stretch limo that seats
eight. Town & Country Transportation charges $150 one-way for a
limo seating up to seven or eight people depending on luggage needs.

If you're staying at a Disney hotel (excluding the Walt Disney World Swan, Dolphin, and Downtown Disney Resort area hotels), make arrangements to use Disney's free Magical Express service, which includes shuttle transportation to and from the airport, luggage delivery, and baggage check-in at the hotel. You can't book the service once you've arrived at the airport, so be sure to reserve ahead.

Airport Contacts Orlando International Airport (*(MCO)* ☎*407/825–2001*).

Transport Contacts Magical Express service (☎*866/599–0951*). **Mears Transportation Group** (☎*407/423–5566* ⊕ *www.mearstransportation.com*). **Star Taxi** (☎*407/857–9999*). **Town & Country Transportation** (☎*407/828–3035*). **Yellow Cab Co.** (☎*407/422–2222*).

BY CAR

The Beeline Expressway (State Road 528) is the best way to get from Orlando International Airport to area attractions; however, it's a toll road, so expect to pay about $1.25 in tolls to get from the airport to Interstate 4. Depending on the location of your hotel, follow the expressway west to International Drive, and either exit at SeaWorld for the International Drive area or stay on the Beeline to Interstate 4, and head either west for Walt Disney World and U.S. 192–Kissimmee or east for Universal Studios and downtown Orlando. Call your hotel for the best route. Interstate 4 is the main artery in central Florida, linking the Gulf Coast in Tampa to the Atlantic coast in Daytona Beach. Although Interstate 4 is an east–west highway, it actually follows a north–south track through the Orlando area, so traveling north on Interstate 4 through Orlando would actually be heading east toward Daytona, and traveling south would actually be traveling west toward Tampa. So **think north when Interstate 4 signs say east, and think south when the signs say west.** In 2002 the Florida Department of Transportation changed the exit numbers of several major interstates, including Interstate 4, which intersects Orlando and Walt Disney World. The WDW exits are 64B, 65, 67, and 68, but locals and older maps may still cite the old exits, 25, 24D, 26D, and 27, respectively. The new highway signs display both the old and new exit numbers. Two other main roads you're likely to use are International Drive, also known as I–Drive, and U.S. 192, sometimes called the Space Coast Parkway or Irlo Bronson Memorial Highway. Get onto International Drive from Interstate 4 Exits 72 (formerly Exit 28), 74A (formerly Exit 29), and 75B (formerly Exit 30B). U.S. 192 cuts across Interstate 4 at Exits 64A (formerly 25A) and 64B (formerly 25B).

BY TAXI

Taxi fares start at $3.50 for the first mile and add $2 for each mile thereafter. Sample fares: to WDW's Magic Kingdom, about $25 from International Drive, $14 to $18 from U.S. 192. To Universal Studios, $10 to $14 from International Drive, $27 to $34 from U.S. 192. To Church Street or downtown, $22 to $28 from International Drive, $32 to $44 from U.S. 192. *For information on getting to or from the airport by taxi, see Airport Transfers.*

Contacts A-1 Taxi (☎*407/328–4555*). **Checker Cab Company** (☎*407/699–9999*). **Star Taxi** (☎*407/857–9999*).

CONTACTS & RESOURCES

EMERGENCIES

In an emergency, always call **911**. Disney employees are known for their extreme helpfulness, so don't hesitate to call on anyone with a Disney name tag. All the major theme parks have first-aid centers.

Ambulance or Police **Emergencies** (☎ *911*).

Doctors & Dentists **Dental Emergency Service** (☎ *407/331–2526*).

Hospitals & Clinics **Centra Care** (✉ *12500 S. Apopka Vineland Rd., Lake Buena Vista* ☎ *407/934–2273*). **Florida Hospital Celebration Health** (✉ *400 Celebration Pl., Celebration* ☎ *407/303–4000*). **Orlando Regional Medical Center/ Sand Lake Hospital** (✉ *9400 Turkey Lake Rd., International Drive Area, Orlando* ☎ *407/351–8500*).

VISITOR INFORMATION

Contacts **Kissimmee/St. Cloud Convention and Visitors Bureau** (✉ *1925 Irlo Bronson Memorial Hwy., Kissimmee 34744* ☎ *407/847–5000 or 800/327–9159*). **Orlando/Orange County Convention & Visitors Bureau** (✉ *8723 International Dr., Orlando 32819* ☎ *407/363–5871*). **Winter Park Chamber of Commerce** (✉ *Box 280, Winter Park 32790* ☎ *407/644–8281*).

Palm Beach & the Treasure Coast

WORD OF MOUTH

"The Mizner park shopping area has many outdoor restaurants with nice menus that accommodate families; service is brisker than the finer indoor restaurants but parents can get a nicer meal."

—mitchdesj

"The Vero Beach area has tons of mama turtles laying eggs, from May till August. My relatives used to live just north in Floridana Beach and the whole distance is part of the Archie Carr turtle nesting area. If you walk the beach after 11 PM on a hot summer night (loaded down with DEET 'cause the bugs are pretty awful at night) you will definitely see some turtles laying eggs. My grown daughters still talk about the experience."

—joan

Updated
by Mary
Thurwachter

THIS GOLDEN STRETCH OF ATLANTIC coast resists categorization for good reason. The territory from Palm Beach south to Boca Raton defines old-world glamour and new-age sophistication. North of Palm Beach you'll uncover the comparatively undeveloped Treasure Coast—liberally sprinkled with coastal gems—where towns and wide-open spaces along the road await your discovery. Altogether, there's a delightful disparity, from Palm Beach, pulsing fast with plenty of old-money wealth, to low-key Hutchinson Island and Manalapan. Seductive as the beach scene interspersed with

TOP 5
■ The eye-popping Flagler Museum in Whitehall.
■ Lion Country Safari, the country's first drive-through zoo.
■ The serene Morikami Museum and Japanese Gardens in Delray Beach.
■ The beautiful McKee Botanical Gardens in Vero Beach.
■ Worth Avenue, worth its weight in gold.

4

eclectic dining options can be, you should also take advantage of flourishing commitments to historic preservation and the arts as town after town yields intriguing museums, galleries, theaters, and gardens.

Long reigning as the epicenter of where the crème de la crème go to shake off winter's chill, Palm Beach continues to be a seasonal hotbed of platinum-grade consumption. Yes, other Florida favorites such as Jupiter Island actually rank higher on the per-capita-wealth meters of financial intelligence sources such as *Worth* magazine. But there's no competing with the historic social supremacy of Palm Beach, long a winter address for heirs of icons named Rockefeller, Vanderbilt, Colgate, Post, Kellogg, and Kennedy. Yet even newer power brokers, with names like Kravis, Peltz, and Trump, are made to understand that strict laws govern everything from building to landscaping, and not so much as a pool awning gets added without a town council nod. If Palm Beach were to fly a flag, it's been observed, there might be three interlocking Cs, standing not only for Cartier, Chanel, and Christian Dior but also for clean, civil, and capricious. Only three bridges allow access to the island, and huge tour buses are a no-no. Yet when a freighter ran aground near a Palm Beach socialite's pool, she was quick to lament not having "enough Bloody Mary mix for all these sailors."

To learn who's who in Palm Beach, it helps to pick up a copy of the *Palm Beach Daily News*—locals call it the Shiny Sheet because its high-quality paper avoids smudging society hands or Pratesi linens—for, as it is said, to be mentioned in the Shiny Sheet is to be Palm Beach. All this fabled ambience started with Henry Morrison Flagler, Florida's premier developer, and cofounder, along with John D. Rockefeller, of Standard Oil. No sooner did Flagler bring the railroad to Florida in the 1890s than he erected the famed Royal Poinciana and Breakers hotels. Rail access sent real-estate prices soaring, and ever since, princely sums have been forked over for personal stationery engraved with the 33480 zip code of Palm Beach. To service Palm Beach with servants and other workers, Flagler also developed an off-island community a mile or so west. West Palm Beach now bustles with its own affluent identity, even if there's still no competing with one of the world's toniest island resorts.

With Palm Beach proper representing only 1% of Palm Beach County's land, remaining territory is given over to West Palm and other classic Florida coastal towns, along with—to the west—citrus farms, the Arthur R. Marshall–Loxahatchee National Wildlife Refuge, and Lake Okeechobee, a bass-fishing hot spot and Florida's largest lake. Well worth exploring is the Treasure Coast territory, covering northernmost Palm Beach County, plus Martin, St. Lucie, and Indian River counties. Despite a growing number of malls and beachfront condominiums, much of the Treasure Coast's shoreline remains blissfully undeveloped. Along the coast, the broad tidal lagoon called the Indian River separates barrier islands from the mainland. Inland there's cattle ranching in tracts of pine and palmetto scrub, along with sugar and citrus production. Shrimp farming uses techniques for acclimatizing shrimp from saltwater—land near seawater is costly—to fresh water, all the better to serve demand from restaurants popping up all over the region.

EXPLORING PALM BEACH & THE TREASURE COAST

Palm Beach, with Gatsby-era architecture, stone-and-stucco estates, extravagant landscaping, and highbrow shops, can reign as the focal point for your sojourn any time of year. From Palm Beach, head off in any of three directions: south via the Gold Coast toward Boca Raton along an especially scenic route known as A1A, back to the mainland and north to the barrier-island treasures of the Treasure Coast, or west for more rustic inland activities such as bass fishing and biking on the dikes around Lake Okeechobee.

ABOUT THE RESTAURANTS

Numerous elegant establishments offer upscale continental and contemporary fare, but the area also teems with casual waterfront spots serving affordable burgers and fresh seafood feasts. Grouper, fried or blackened, is especially popular here, along with the ubiquitous shrimp. An hour's drive west of the coast, around Lake Okeechobee, dine on catfish, panfried to perfection and so fresh it seems barely out of the water. Early-bird menus, a Florida hallmark, typically entice the budget-minded with several dinner entrées at reduced prices offered during certain hours, usually before 5 or 6.

ABOUT THE HOTELS

Palm Beach has a number of smaller hotels in addition to the famous Breakers. Lower-priced hotels and motels can be found in West Palm Beach and Lake Worth. To the south, the coastal town of Manalapan has the Ritz-Carlton, Palm Beach; and the posh Boca Raton Resort & Club is near the beach in Boca Raton. To the north in suburban Palm Beach Gardens is the PGA National Resort & Spa. To the west, small towns near Lake Okeechobee offer country-inn accommodations.

WHAT IT COSTS			
	¢	$	$$
RESTAURANTS	under $10	$10–$15	$15–$20
HOTELS	under $80	$80–$100	$100–$140	$

Restaurant prices are per person for a main course at a
standard double room, excluding 6% sales tax (more in
tourist tax.

TIMING

The weather is optimum from November throug   , out the trade-
off is that roadways and facilities are more crowded and prices higher.
In summer, to spend much time outside, it helps to have a tolerance for
heat, humidity, and afternoon downpours. No matter when you visit,
bring insect repellent for outdoor activities.

PALM BEACH

78 mi north of Miami.

Setting the tone in this town of unparalleled Florida opulence is the
ornate architectural work of Addison Mizner, who began designing
homes and public buildings here in the 1920s and whose Moorish-
Gothic style has influenced virtually all community landmarks. Thanks
to Mizner and his lasting influence, Palm Beach remains a playground
of the rich, famous, and discerning.

EXPLORING PALM BEACH

For a taste of what it's like to jockey for position in this status-con-
scious town, stake out a parking place on Worth Avenue or parallel
residential streets, and squeeze in among the Mercedeses, Rolls-Royces,
and Bentleys. Between admiring your excellent parking skills and feeling "car-struck" at the surrounding fine specimens of automobile, be
sure to note the PARKING BY PERMIT ONLY and TWO HOUR parking signs, as
a $25 parking ticket might take the shine off your spot. ■ TIP→The best
course for a half-day visit is to valet-park at the parking deck next to Saks
Fifth Avenue. Away from downtown, along County Road and Ocean
Boulevard (the shore road, also designated as Route A1A), are Palm
Beach's other defining landmarks: Mediterranean-style residences,
some built of coral rock, that are nothing short of palatial, topped
by barrel-tile roofs and often fronted by 10-foot ficus and seagrape
hedges. The low wall that separates the dune-top shore road from the
sea hides shoreline that varies in many places from expansive to eroded.
Here and there, where the strand deepens, homes are built directly on
the beach.

A GOOD TOUR

Start at the **Henry Morrison Flagler Museum ❶**, a 55-room, 60,000-
square-foot villa Flagler built for his third wife, to get your first look
at the eye-popping opulence of the Gilded Age, which defined Palm

Gold Coast &
Treasure Coast

ATLANTIC

OCEAN

4

35 **Sebastian**
TO CAPE
CANAVERAL
A1A
512
510
Winter Beach
Wabasso Beach
Indian River
Shores
60
34 **Vero Beach**
A1A
1
95
A1A
713
Florida's Turnpike
68
33 **Fort Pierce**
70
707
Indian River
709
1
St. Lucie
32 **Hutchinson Island (Jensen Beach)**
609
Florida's Turnpike
Stuart
31
Sewalls Point
TO OKEECHOBEE
95
76
A1A
1
710
76
30 **Jupiter Island & Hobe Sound**
98
441
Indiantown
708
*Lake
Okeechobee*
Port
Mayaca
Tequesta
1
707
706
29 **Jupiter**
710
A1A
Pahokee
Juno
Beach
*Singer
Island*
**Palm Beach
Gardens**
28
95
A1A
**Palm Beach
Shores**
27
Riviera Beach
Belle Glade
98
West Palm Beach
10 – 20
see detail map
Palm Beach
1 – 9
see detail map
TO CLEWISTON
880
80
98
441
Loxahatchee
827
441
21 **Lake Worth**
Lantana
22
Manalapan
23 **Boynton Beach**
0   10 miles
24 **Gulf Stream**
0   15 km
25 **Delray Beach**
Florida's Turnpike
Highland Beach
KEY
▶ *Start of itinerary*
26 **Boca Raton**

TO OKEECHOBEE

GREAT ITINERARIES

Numbers in the text correspond to numbers in the margin and on the Gold Coast and Treasure Coast and the Palm Beach and West Palm Beach maps.

3 DAYS

When time is tight, make ☷ **Palm Beach ❶–❾** ► your base. On the first day, start downtown on **Worth Avenue ❺** to window-shop and gallery-browse. After a *très* chic bistro lunch, head for that other must-see on even the shortest itinerary, the **Henry Morrison Flagler Museum ❶**. Your second day is for the beach. Consider either Lantana Public Beach or Oceanfront Park in **Boynton Beach ㉓**. Budget your last day for exploring other attractions, such as the Morikami Museum and Japanese Gardens in nearby **Delray Beach ㉕**, or Lion Country Safari in ☷ **West Palm Beach ❿–⓴**, yielding tastes of Africa.

5 DAYS

Stay in ☷ **Palm Beach ❶–❾** ► for two nights. The first day visit the **Henry Morrison Flagler Museum ❶** and the luxury hotel known as the **Breakers ❷**, another Flagler legacy. Then head to **Worth Avenue ❺** for lunch and afternoon shopping, even if it's only the window variety. On the second day, drive over to ☷ **West Palm Beach ❿–⓴** and the **Norton Museum of Art ❿**, with many 19th- and 20th-century paintings and sculptures. On Day 3, choose between an overnight visit to ☷ **Lake Okeechobee,** the world's bass-fishing capital, or Palm Beach for another night and a drive of a half hour or so to explore the Arthur R. Marshall–Loxahatchee National Wildlife Refuge. Or head for the

National Croquet Center ⓰. Go to ☷ **Boca Raton ㉖** on the fourth day, and check into a hotel near the beach before spending the afternoon wandering through Mizner Park's shops. On your fifth day, meander through Mizner Park's Boca Raton Museum of Art in the morning and get some sun at South Beach Park after lunch.

7 DAYS

Stay two nights in ☷ **Palm Beach ❶–❾** ►, spending your first day enjoying the sights mentioned in the five-day itinerary. On Day 2, rent a bicycle and follow the bike path along Lake Worth, which provides glimpses at backyards of many Palm Beach mansions. Drive north on Day 3, going first to the mainland and then across Jerry Thomas Bridge to Singer Island and John D. MacArthur Beach State Park. Spend the third night farther north, on ☷ **Hutchinson Island ㉜**, and relax the next morning on the beach at your hotel. On your way back south, explore **Stuart ㉛** and its historic downtown, and pause at the Arthur R. Marshall–Loxahatchee National Wildlife Refuge before ending up in ☷ **Boca Raton ㉖**, for three nights at a hotel near the beach. Split Day 5 between shopping at Mizner Park and sunning at South Beach Park. Day 6 is for cultural attractions: the Boca Raton Museum of Art followed by the Atlantic Avenue galleries and the Morikami in **Delray Beach ㉕**. On your last day, check out Boca's other two beaches, Spanish River and Red Reef parks.

❻ El Solano. No Palm Beach mansion better represents the town's luminous legacy than the Spanish-style home built by Addison Mizner as his residence in 1925. Mizner later sold El Solano to Harold Vanderbilt, and the property was long a favorite among socialites for parties and photo shoots. Vanderbilt, like many of the socially attuned, would open his home to social peers to accommodate worthy causes. Beatle John Lennon and his wife, Yoko Ono, bought it less than a year before Lennon's death. It's still privately owned and not open to the public. ✉ *721 S. County Rd.*

❶ Henry Morrison Flagler Museum. The opulence of Florida's Gilded Age lives on at Whitehall, the palatial 55-room "marble palace" Henry Flagler commissioned in 1901 for his third wife, Mary Lily Kenan. Architects John Carrère and Thomas Hastings were instructed to create the finest home imaginable, and they outdid themselves. Whitehall rivals the grandeur of European palaces and has an entrance hall with baroque ceiling similar to Louis XIV's Versailles. To create the museum, Flagler's granddaughter, Jean Flagler Matthews, in 1960 purchased the property, which had been operating as the Whitehall Hotel since 1929. You'll see original furnishings, a hidden staircase Flagler used to sneak from his bedroom to the billiards room, an art collection, a 1,200-pipe organ, and Florida East Coast Railway exhibits, along with Flagler's personal railcar, the *Rambler,* showcased in an 8,000-square-foot Beaux Arts–style pavilion behind the mansion. Tours take about an hour and are offered at frequent intervals. The café, open after Thanksgiving through mid-April, offers snacks and afternoon tea. ✉ *1 Whitehall Way* ☎ *561/655–2833* ⊕ *www.flagler.org* 🎫 *$15* ⊙ *Tues.–Sat. 10–5, Sun. noon–5.*

Fodor'sChoice ★

❼ Mar-a-Lago. Breakfast-food heiress Marjorie Merriweather Post commissioned a Hollywood set designer to create Ocean Boulevard's famed Mar-a-Lago, a 118-room, 110,000-square-foot Mediterranean Revival palace. Its 75-foot Italianate tower is visible from most areas of Palm Beach and from across the Intracoastal Waterway in West Palm Beach. Owner Donald Trump has turned it into a private membership club. He and wife Melania held their wedding reception in the ballroom here after marrying at Bethesda-by-the-Sea Episcopal Church in 2005. ✉ *1100 S. Ocean Blvd.*

❽ Phipps Ocean Park. In addition to the shoreline, tennis courts, picnic tables, and grills, this park has a Palm Beach County landmark in the **Little Red Schoolhouse.** Dating from 1886, it served as the first schoolhouse in what was then Dade County. No alcoholic beverages are permitted in the park. ✉ *2185 S. Ocean Blvd.* ☎ *561/832–0731* 🎫 *Free* ⊙ *Daily dawn–dusk.*

❹ Society of the Four Arts. Despite widespread misconceptions of members-only exclusivity, this privately endowed institution—founded in 1936 to encourage appreciation of art, music, drama, and literature—is funded for public enjoyment. A gallery building—designed by Addison Mizner, of course—artfully melds an exhibition hall, library, and the Philip Hulitar Sculpture Garden, which underwent a major renovation in 2006. Open from about Thanksgiving to Easter, the museum's programs are extensive, and there's ample free parking. The museum often presents free movie screenings in the auditorium on weekends. ⊠2 *Four Arts Plaza* ☎*561/655–7226* ⊕*www.fourarts.org* ☑*$5* ⊙*Galleries Dec.–mid-Apr., Mon.–Sat. 10–5, Sun. 2–5. Library, children's library, and gardens Nov.–May, weekdays 10–5, Sat. 9–1.*

❺ **Worth Avenue.** Called the Avenue by Palm Beachers, this ¼-mi-long
★ street is synonymous with exclusive shopping. Nostalgia lovers recall an era when faces or names served as charge cards, purchases were delivered home before customers returned from lunch, and bills were sent directly to private accountants. Times have changed, but a stroll amid the Moorish architecture of its shops offers a tantalizing taste of the island's ongoing commitment to elegant consumerism. Explore the labyrinth of eight pedestrian vias, on both sides of Worth Avenue, that wind past boutiques, tiny plazas, bubbling fountains, and the bougainvillea-festooned wrought-iron balconies of second-floor apartments. ⊠*Between Cocoanut Row and S. Ocean Blvd.*

WHERE TO STAY & EAT

$$$$ ✕**Leopard Supper Club and Lounge.** In the Chesterfield hotel, this enclave feels like an exclusive club. Choose a cozy banquette set off by black-and-red lacquer trim or a table near the open kitchen. Start with sweet-corn-and-crab chowder with Peruvian purple potato or a jumbo crab cake, moving on to an arugula or spinach salad followed by a prime strip steak or a glazed rack of lamb. As the night progresses, the Leopard turns into a popular nightclub for Palm Beach's old guard. ⊠*363 Cocoanut Row* ☎*561/659–5800* ☰*AE, D, DC, MC, V.*

$$$–$$$$ ✕**Bice Ristorante.** The bougainvillea-laden trellises set the scene at the main entrance on Peruvian Way, and weather permitting, many patrons prefer to dine on the outdoor patio on the narrow pedestrian walkway. A favorite of Palm Beach society, both the restaurant and the bar become packed and noisy during high season. The aroma of basil, chives, and oregano fills the air as waiters bring out home-baked focaccia to accompany delectable dishes such as seafood risotto, veal chops, and such specialties as duck breast sautéed in mushroom sauce with venison truffle ravioli. ⊠*313½ Worth Ave.* ☎*561/835–1600* ⚐*Reservations essential* ☰*AE, DC, MC, V.*

$$$–$$$$ ✕**Café Boulud.** Celebrated chef Daniel Boulud opened his outpost of
Fodor'sChoice   New York's Café Boulud in the Brazilian Court hotel. The warm and
★   welcoming French-American venue is casual yet elegant, with a palette of honey, gold, and citron, and natural light spilling through arched glass doors opening to a lush courtyard. Lunch and dinner entrées on Boulud's signature four-muse menu include classic French, seasonal, vegetarian, and a rotating selection of international dishes. The lounge, with its backlighted amber glass bar, is the perfect perch to take in the jet-set crowd that comes for a hint of the south of France in South Florida. ⊠*Brazilian Court, 301 Australian Ave.* ☎*561/655–6060* ⚐*Reservations essential* ☰*AE, DC, MC, V.*

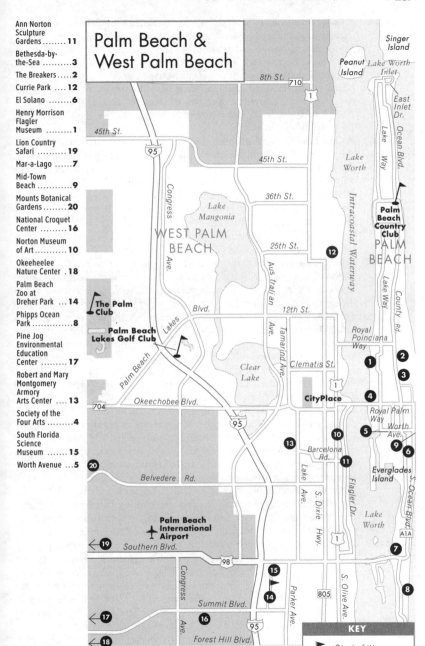

Ann Norton
Sculpture
Gardens 11

Bethesda-by-
the-Sea 3

The Breakers 2

Currie Park 12

El Solano 6

Henry Morrison
Flagler
Museum 1

Lion Country
Safari 19

Mar-a-Lago 7

Mid-Town
Beach 9

Mounts Botanical
Gardens 20

National Croquet
Center 16

Norton Museum
of Art 10

Okeeheelee
Nature Center . 18

Palm Beach
Zoo at
Dreher Park ... 14

Phipps Ocean
Park 8

Pine Jog
Environmental
Education
Center 17

Robert and Mary
Montgomery
Armory
Arts Center 13

Society of the
Four Arts 4

South Florida
Science
Museum 15

Worth Avenue ... 5

$$$–$$$$ ✕**Café L'Europe.** Even after 25 years, the favorite lunch stop of society's movers and shakers remains a regular stop on fine diners' itineraries. Management pays close attention to service and consistency of excellence here. Best sellers include rack of lamb, Dover sole, and Wiener schnitzel, along with creations such as crispy sweetbreads with poached pear and mustard sauce. Depending on your mood, the champagne-caviar bar can provide appetizers or dessert. ⊠*331 S. County Rd.* ☎*561/655–4020* ⌖*Reservations essential* Jacket required ⊟*AE, DC, MC, V* ☉*No lunch.*

$$$–$$$$
Fodor'sChoice
★   ✕**Chez Jean-Pierre.** With walls adorned with Dalí- and Picasso-like art, this is where the Palm Beach old guard likes to let down its guard, all the while partaking of sumptuous French cuisine and an impressive wine list. Forget calorie or cholesterol concerns and indulge in scrambled eggs with caviar or homemade duck foie gras, along with desserts like hazelnut soufflé or profiteroles au chocolat. Waiters are friendly and very attentive. Jackets are not required, although many men wear them. ⊠*132 N. County Rd.* ☎*561/833–1171* ⌖*Reservations essential* ⊟*AE, DC, MC, V* ☉*Closed Sun. No lunch.*

$$–$$$$ ✕**Renato's.** Here at perhaps the most romantic restaurant in Palm Beach, guests can dine in the beautiful courtyard under the stars and twinkling lights on the bougainvillea or in the intimate, low-lighted dining room flickering with candles and enhanced with fresh flowers, quiet classical music, and attentive service. Be sure to try the spit pea soup with small cubes of ham (a meal in itself) and sauteed swordfish with white wine, lemon butter, and capers, all served on pretty, flowered porcelain plates atop crisp white linen tablecloths. Although pricey, dinner here is worth every penny. Jackets are encouraged. ⊠*87 Via Mizner.* ☎*561/655–9752* ⌖*Reservations essential for dinner. Open for lunch 11:30–3 Mon.–Sat.* ⊟*AE, D, MC, V* ☉*Closed Sun.*

$$–$$$$ ✕**Testa's Palm Beach.** Attracting a loyal clientele since 1921 and still owned by the Testa family, the restaurant offers breakfast, lunch, and dinner. Lunches range from burgers to crab salad, and dinner specialties include snapper Florentine and jumbo lump crab cakes. You can dine inside in an intimate pine-paneled room with cozy bar, out back in a gazebo-style room for large groups, or outside at tables with pink tablecloths next to planters of pink hibiscus, with a view of the Breakers in the distance. Friendly waiters greet many customers by name. Don't miss the signature strawberry pie made with fresh Florida berries. ⊠*221 Royal Poinciana Way* ☎*561/832–0992* ⊟*AE, MC, V.*

$$–$$$ ✕**Amici.** The town's premier celebrity-magnet bistro is a crowd pleaser: when it moved across the street and down the block from its original location, a consistent Palm Beach crowd followed. The northern Italian menu highlights house specialties such as rigatoni with spicy tomato sauce and roasted eggplant, potato gnocchi, grilled veal chops, risottos, and pizzas from a wood-burning oven. There are nightly pasta and fresh-fish specials as well. To avoid the crowds, stop by for a late lunch or early dinner. ⊠*375 S. County Rd.* ☎*561/832–0201* ⌖*Reservations essential* ⊟*AE, DC, MC, V* ☉*No lunch Sun.*

$$–$$$ ✕**Echo.** Palm Beach's window on Asia has a sleek sushi bar and floor-to-ceiling glass doors separating the interior from the popular terrace

4

dining area. Chinese, Japanese, Thai, and Vietnamese selections are neatly categorized: Wind (small plates starting your journey), Water (beverages, sushi), Fire (from grill, wok, fry pan), Earth (land and sea), and Flavor (desserts, sweets). Pick from dim sum to sashimi, pad thai to Peking duck, steamed sea bass to lobster lo mein. ⊠ *230-A Sunrise Ave.* ☎ *561/802–4222* ⊟ *AE, D, MC, V* ⊘ *Closed Mon. No lunch.*

$$-$$$ ✕ **Ta-boó.** This peach stucco 60-year-old landmark with green shutters
★ attracts Worth Avenue shoppers looking for a two-hour lunch and a dinner crowd ranging from tuxed and sequined theatergoers to polo-shirted vacationers. Entrées include Black Angus dry-aged beef or roast duck, along with main-course salads, pizzas, and burgers, plus coconut lust, a signature dessert. Drop in late night during the winter season when the nightly music is playing and you'll probably spot a celebrity or two. There's a late-night menu Friday and Saturday. ⊠ *221 Worth Ave.* ☎ *561/835–3500* ⊟ *AE, DC, MC, V.*

¢–$ ✕ **Hamburger Heaven.** A favorite with locals since 1945, the quintessential diner with horseshoe-shaped counter as well as booths and tables is loud and casual and has some of the best burgers on the island. Vegetarian meals, fresh salads, sandwiches, homemade pastries, and daily soup and hot-plate specials featuring comfort foods like meat loaf and chicken potpie are also available. During the week, it's a popular lunch stop for working locals.The staff are friendly and efficient. ⊠ *314 S. County Rd.* ☎ *561/655–5277* ⊟ *MC, V* ⊘ *Closed Sun.*

¢ ✕ **Pizza Al Fresco.** The secret-garden setting is the secret to the success of this popular European pizzeria (beer and wine only), where you can dine under a canopy of century-old banyans in a charming courtyard. Specialties are 12-inch hand-tossed brick-oven pizzas; calzones, salads, and sandwiches round out the selection. Slices are available with such interesting toppings as prosciutto, arugula, and caviar; there's even a dessert pizza topped with Nutella. Look for the grave markers of Addison Mizner's beloved pet monkey, Johnnie Brown, and Rose Sachs's dog Laddie (she and husband Morton bought Mizner's villa and lived there 47 years) next to the patio. Delivery is available, by limo, of course. ⊠ *14 Via Mizner, at Worth Ave.* ☎ *561/832–0032* ⊟ *AE, MC, V.*

$$$$ 🏨 **Brazilian Court.** A short stroll from Worth Avenue shopping, the
★ yellow stucco Spanish-style facade and red-tile roof, and lobby with pecky-cypress ceilings and stone floors, underscore this boutique hotel's Roaring '20s origins. All of the studio and one- and two-bedroom suites have rich limestone baths and showers, Sub-Zero wine refrigerators, and personal butler service. Bay windows look out into the impeccably maintained gardens and enchanting flower-filled courtyards. Amenities include video-conference capabilities in a state-of-the-art business center, a Frederic Fekkai hair salon and spa, and Café Boulud, a New York outpost from famed restaurateur Daniel Boulud; hotel guests reportedly have a better shot than outsiders at procuring a table. Don't feel like dressing up for a table? There's 24-hour in-room dining by Café Boulud. ⊠ *301 Australian Ave., 33480* ☎ *561/655–7740* 📠 *561/655–0801* ⊕ *www.thebraziliancourt.com* ⇆ *80 rooms* 🚪 *In-room: refrigerator, VCR (some), dial-up. In-hotel: restaurant, room*

service, bar, pool, gym, spa, bicycles, laundry facilities, concierge, some pets allowed (fee), no-smoking rooms ⊟*AE, D, DC, MC, V.*

$$$$

Fodor'sChoice

★

The Breakers. Dating from 1896 and on the National Register of Historic Places, this opulent Italian Renaissance–style resort, owned by Henry Flagler's heirs, sprawls over 140 oceanfront acres. Cupids frolic at the main Florentine fountain, and majestic frescoes grace hallways leading to restaurants. More than an opulent hotel, the Breakers is a modern resort packed with amenities, from a 20,000-square-foot luxury spa and beach club to golf and tennis clubhouses that support the 10 tennis courts and two 18-hole golf courses. Jackets and ties are no longer required after 7 PM. ⊠ ⊠*1 S. County Rd., 33480* ☏*561/655–6611 or 888/273–2537* 🖷*561/659–8403* ⊕*www. thebreakers.com* ↩*569 rooms, 57 suites* ♿*In-room: dial-up. In-hotel: 5 restaurants, room service, bars, golf courses, tennis courts, pools, gym, spa, beachfront, children's programs (ages 3–12), concierge* ⊟*AE, D, DC, MC, V.*

$$$$

The Chesterfield. Two blocks north of Worth Avenue, the distinctive white stucco, European-style hotel with red-and-white-striped awnings offers inviting rooms ranging from small to spacious. All have plush upholstered chairs, antique desks, paintings, and marble baths. Settle on a leather couch near the cozy library's fireplace and peruse an international newspaper or classic book. A quiet courtyard surrounds a large pool where you can relax, and the Leopard Lounge draws a convivial crowd. ⊠*363 Cocoanut Row, 33480* ☏*561/659–5800 or 800/243–7871* 🖷*561/659–6707* ⊕*www.chesterfieldpb.com* ↩*44 rooms, 11 suites* ♿*In-room: refrigerator (some), VCR (some). In-hotel: restaurant, room service, bar, pool, concierge, Internet* ⊟*AE, D, DC, MC, V.*

$$$$

The Colony. What distinguishes this legendary pale-yellow British colonial–style hotel is that it's only one short block from Worth Avenue and one block from a beautiful beach on the Atlantic Ocean. An attentive staff, youthful yet experienced, is buzzing with competence and a desire to please. Guest rooms are decorated in Caribbean-Colonial, with sunny yellow walls and dark mahogany desks, and pineapple-carved poster beds grace some rooms. Roomy suites and luxurious two-bedroom villas (rentable by the week or month) have laundry facilities and full kitchens. Reserve early for the dinner cabaret shows, which have featured entertainers such as Faith Prince and Andrea Marcovicci. ⊠*155 Hammon Ave., 33480* ☏*561/655–5430 or 800/521–5525* 🖷*561/659–8104* ⊕*www.thecolonypalmbeach.com* ↩*68 rooms, 14 suites* ♿*In-hotel: restaurant, bar, pools, spa, bicycles, concierge* ⊟*AE, DC, MC, V.*

$$$$

★

Four Seasons Resort Palm Beach. Relaxed elegance is the watchword at this four-story resort on 6 acres with a delightful beach at the south end of town, approximately 5 mi outside the heart of Palm Beach. Fanlight windows, marble, chintz, and palms are serene and inviting. Rooms are spacious, with separate seating areas and private balconies; many have ocean views. On weekends, piano music accompanies cocktails in the Living Room lounge. Jazz groups perform on some weekends in season. The restaurants are worth sampling, and all three have

children's menus. ⊠2800 S. Ocean Blvd., 3348
or 800/432–2335 🖷561/547–1557 ⊕www.four
rooms, 10 suites ⚘In-room: safe, dial-up. In-l
room service, bars, tennis courts, pool, gym, spa,
children's programs (ages 3–12), laundry service,
ing rooms ⊟AE, D, DC, MC, V.

NIGHTLIFE & THE ARTS

THE ARTS

Society of the Four Arts (⊠2 Four Arts Plaza 🖷561/655–7226) has concerts, lectures, and films December through March. Movie tickets can be purchased at time of showing; other tickets may be obtained a week in advance.

NIGHTLIFE

Palm Beach is teeming with restaurants that turn into late-night hot spots, plus hotel lobby bars perfect for tête-à-têtes. Popular for lunch and dinner, **Cucina Dell 'Arte** (⊠257 Royal Poinciana Way 🖷561/655–0770) later becomes the in place for the younger and trendy set. The old guard gathers at the **Leopard Lounge** (⊠363 Cocoanut Row 🖷561/659–5800) in the Chesterfield hotel for piano music during cocktail hour and later to dance until the wee hours. Thursday night happy hours spiked by Flirtinis and live jazz draw a local crowd to the lobby lounge and outdoor patios of the **Brazilian Court** (⊠301 Australian Ave. 🖷561/655–7740).

SPORTS & THE OUTDOORS

BIKING

Bicycling is a great way to get a closer look at Palm Beach. Only 14 mi long, ½ mi wide, flat as the top of a billiard table, and just as green, it's a perfect biking place. The palm-fringed **Lake Trail** (⊠Parallel to Lake Way) skirts the backyards of many palatial mansions and the edge of Lake Worth. The trail starts at the Society of the Four Arts, heading north 8 mi to the end and back—just follow the signs. A block from the bike trail, the **Palm Beach Bicycle Trail Shop** (⊠223 Sunrise Ave. 🖷561/659–4583) rents by the hour or day. It's open daily.

DOG RACING

Since 1932 the hounds have raced year-round at the 4,300-seat **Palm Beach Kennel Club.** Across the bridge in West Palm Beach, the track also offers simulcasts of jai alai and horse racing, and wagering on live and televised sports. There's also a 30-table card room with high-stakes wagers, and fine dining in the Paddock Restaurant. ⊠1111 N. Congress Ave. 🖷561/683–2222 ⊠50¢, terrace level $1, parking free ⊙Racing Mon.–Sat. at 12:40, Fri. and Sat. at 12:40 and 7:30, Sun. at 1. Simulcasts daily at 11:30 and 7:30.

GOLF

Breakers Hotel Golf Club (⊠*1 S. County Rd.* ☎*561/659–8407*) has the historic Ocean Course and the Todd Anderson Golf Academy and is open to members and hotel guests only. A $195 green fee includes range balls, cart, and bag storage at Breakers West or at the redesigned Ocean Course. The **Town of Palm Beach Golf Club** (⊠*2345 S. Ocean Blvd.* ☎*561/547–0598*) has 18 holes, including four on the Atlantic and three on the inland waterway; green fee: $28.

SHOPPING

★ One of the world's premier showcases for high-quality shopping, **Worth Avenue** runs ¼ mi east–west across Palm Beach, from the beach to Lake Worth. The street has more than 250 shops (more than 40 of them sell jewelry), and many upscale stores (Gucci, Hermès, Pucci, Saks Fifth Avenue, Louis Vuitton, Emanuel Ungaro, Chanel, Dior, Cartier, Tiffany, and Tourneau) are represented, their merchandise appealing to the discerning tastes of the Palm Beach clientele. The six blocks of **South County Road** north of Worth Avenue have interesting (and somewhat less expensive) stores. For specialty items (out-of-town newspapers, health foods, and books), try the shops along the north side of **Royal Poinciana Way**. Most stores are closed on Sunday, and many go on hiatus in summer.

Calypso (⊠*247-B Worth Ave.* ☎*561/832–5006*), tucked into Via Encantada, is where owner Christiane Celle—known for handcrafted fragrances—has curated a lively collection of resort wear for the whole family. The thrift store **Church Mouse** (⊠*374 S. County Rd.* ☎*561/659–2154*) is where many high-end resale boutique owners grab their merchandise. **Déjà Vu** (⊠*Via Testa, 219 Royal Poinciana Way* ☎*561/833–6624*) could be the resale house of Chanel, as it has so many gently used, top-quality pieces. There's no digging through piles here; clothes are in impeccable condition and are well organized. **Giorgio's** (⊠*230 Worth Ave.* ☎*561/655–2446*) is over-the-top indulgence, with 50 colors of silk and cashmere sweaters and 22 colors of ostrich and alligator adorning everything from bags to bicycles. Jewelry is very important in Palm Beach, and for more than 100 years **Greenleaf & Crosby** (⊠*236 Worth Ave.* ☎*561/655–5850*) has had a diverse selection that includes investment pieces. **Hollywould** (⊠*36 Via Mizner* ☎*561/366–9016*) stocks the Palm Beach It-Girl uniform of bright jersey dresses, shoes from slides to stilettos, and coordinating handbags. Collector and trader Edmund Lo packs the goods in this tiny shop. **Spring Flowers** (⊠*337 Worth Ave.* ☎*561/832–0131*) has beautiful children's clothing, pajamas, and special-occasion outfits, from tiny to size 12. Little ones start with a newborn gown set by Kissy Kissy or Petite Bateau and grow into fashions by Cacharel and Lili Gaufrette. Holding court for more than 60 years, **Van Cleef & Arpels** (⊠*249 Worth Ave.* ☎*561/655–6767*) is where legendary members of Palm Beach society shop for tiaras and formal jewels.

WEST PALM BEACH

Across the Intracoastal Waterway from Palm Beach.

Long considered Palm Beach's less-privileged stepsister, sprawling West Palm has evolved into an economically vibrant destination of its own, ranking as the cultural, entertainment, and business center of the entire county and territory to the north. High-rise buildings like the mammoth Palm Beach County Judicial Center and Courthouse and the State Administrative Building underscore the breadth of the city's governmental and corporate activity. The glittering Kravis Center for the Performing Arts is Palm Beach County's principal entertainment venue. One of the newest additions to the city is the enormous and extravagant Palm Beach County Convention Center, which cost more than $80 million to build; the 350,000-square-foot campus sits on almost 20 acres across from the Kravis Center and CityPlace.

MOLLY'S TROLLEYS

The relentless Florida sun can be merciless when you're loaded down with Macy's shopping bags and you still have all those other stores to visit. Molly's Trolleys to the rescue! Share space with local lawyers and shoppers on the free and frequent trolley service that makes continuous loops down Clematis Street, the city's century-old main street, and through CityPlace, a shopping-restaurant-theater district. Hop on and off at any of the seven stops—four on Clematis, one next to the Intracoastal Waterway, and two in CityPlace. The trolleys run Sunday–Wednesday 11 AM–9 PM and Thursday–Saturday 11 AM–11 PM. Call ☎561/838-9511.

DOWNTOWN

The heart of revived West Palm Beach is a small, attractive, easy-to-walk downtown area, spurred on by active historic preservation. Along five blocks of beautifully landscaped Clematis Street, which ends at the Intracoastal Waterway, are boutiques and outdoor cafés, plus the 400-seat Cuillo Center for the Arts, which features pre-Broadway shows and concerts; and Palm Beach Dramaworks, an intimate theater, which often shows new plays. An exuberant nightlife has taken hold of the area. In fact, downtown rocks every Thursday from 5:30 PM on with Clematis by Night, a celebration of music, dance, art, and food at Centennial Square. Even on downtown's fringes there are sights of cultural interest.

A GOOD TOUR

From a geographical perspective, the best place to start is at the north end of the city on Flagler Drive, with a walk around **Currie Park** ⑫ ▶, which has two fishing piers on the Intracoastal Waterway and public tennis courts. Flagler hugs the waterway south for 6 mi, with the mansions of Palm Beach clearly visible across the water to the east. The road, lined with stately royal palms, is one of the most scenic drives, and jogging/bike routes, in Florida. You'll see the million-dollar yachts at the Palm Beach Yacht Club and Palm Harbor Marina, Meyers Amphitheater, and Palm Beach Atlantic University. Look for great blue herons, white ibises, and pelicans and the occasional manatees, who live on the waterway in the winter. Pick up maps and information about attractions at the Palm Beach Chamber of Commerce on Flager at Fourth Street. To see the outstanding art collection at the **Norton Museum of Art** ⑩, turn right from Flagler to Diana Place and you'll see the museum one block straight ahead. From here, it's just a few blocks south on Flagler to the peaceful **Ann Norton Sculpture Gardens** ⑪ on the corner of Flagler and Barcelona Road. Finally, you can drive west across Barcelona Road to the **Robert and Mary Montgomery Armory Arts Center** ⑬ to check out the current exhibit.

TIMING

Late morning is ideal for starting this tour, and you can stop for lunch on Clematis Street. In the afternoon you'll need about three hours at the arts-oriented sights. Weekdays are best.

WHAT TO SEE

⑪ **Ann Norton Sculpture Gardens.** This monument to the late American sculptor Ann Weaver Norton, second wife of Norton Museum founder Ralph H. Norton, includes a complex of art galleries in the main house and studio, plus 2½ acres of gardens, where you'll find 300 varieties of palm trees, seven granite figures, and six brick megaliths. The plantings were designed to attract native birdlife. ⊠253 Barcelona Rd. ☎561/832–5328 ⊡$5 ☉ Wed.–Sun. 11–4; call ahead, as schedule is not always observed; or by appointment.

⑩ **Norton Museum of Art.** Constructed in 1941 by steel magnate Ralph H.
Fodor'sChoice Norton, the museum has an extensive collection of 19th- and 20th-century American and European paintings—including works by Picasso,
★ Monet, Matisse, Pollock, and O'Keeffe—and Chinese, contemporary, and photographic art. There's a sublime outdoor covered loggia, Chinese bronze and jade sculptures, and a library. Galleries, including the Great Hall, also showcase traveling exhibits. ∎TIP→**One of the city's best-kept secrets is this museum's café, with its artfully presented dishes that taste as good as they look.** ⊠1451 S. Olive Ave. ☎561/832–5196 ⊕www.norton.org ⊡$8 ☉Mon.–Sat. 10–5, Sun. 1–5.

⑫ **Currie Park.** Frequent weekend festivals, including an annual celebration of seafood, take place at the scenic city park next to the Intracoastal Waterway. Sit on one of the piers and watch the yachts and fishing boats pass by. Put on your jogging shoes—the park is at the north end of a 6.3-mi biking/jogging/skating path. ⊠N. Flagler Dr. at 23rd St.

⑬ **Robert and Mary Montgomery Armory Arts Center.** Built by the WPA in 1939, the facility is now a visual-arts center hosting rotating exhibitions and art classes throughout the year. ⊠1703 Lake Ave. ☎561/832–1776 ⊡Free ☉ Weekdays 9–5:30, Sat. 9–2.

AWAY FROM DOWNTOWN

West Palm Beach's outskirts, flat stretches lined with fast-food outlets and car dealerships, may not inspire, but are worth driving through to reach attractions scattered around the city's southern and western reaches. Several sites are especially rewarding for children and other animal and nature lovers.

A GOOD TOUR

Head south from downtown and turn right on Southern Boulevard, left onto Parker Avenue, and right onto Summit Boulevard to reach the **Palm Beach Zoo at Dreher Park** ⓮ ☞. In the same area (turn right onto Dreher Trail) and also appealing to kids, the **South Florida Science Museum** ⓯, with its Aldrin Planetarium and McGinty Aquarium, is full of hands-on exhibits. If a quick game of croquet intrigues you, head to the **National Croquet Center** ⓰, less than 2 mi from the museum, by turning onto Summit Boulevard from Dreher Trail north and proceeding to Florida Mango Road, where you will again turn right. Backtrack to Summit Boulevard and go west to the 150-acre **Pine Jog Environmental Education Center** ⓱. For more natural adventure, head farther west on Summit until you reach Forest Hill Boulevard, where you turn right to reach the **Okeeheelee Nature Center** ⓲ and its miles of wooded trails. Now retrace your route to Summit Boulevard, drive east until you reach Military Trail, and take a left. Drive north to Southern Boulevard and turn west to reach **Lion Country Safari** ⓳, a 500-acre cageless zoo. For the last stop on this tour, backtrack to Military Trail and travel north to the **Mounts Botanical Gardens** ⓴.

TIMING

Tailor your time based on specific interests, because you could easily spend most of a day at any of these attractions. Prepare yourself for heavy rush-hour traffic, and remember that sightseeing in the morning (not *too* early, to avoid rush hour) will be less congested.

WHAT TO SEE

⓳ **Lion Country Safari.** Drive your own vehicle (with windows closed) on 8 mi of paved roads through a 500-acre cageless zoo with a thousand free-roaming animals. Lions, elephants, white rhinos, giraffes, zebras, antelopes, chimpanzees, and ostriches are among the wild things in residence. Lions are fenced away from roads, but there's a good chance you'll have a giraffe or two nudging at your window. Exhibits include the Kalahari, designed after a South African bush plateau and containing water buffalo and Nilgai (the largest type of Asian antelope), and the Gir Forest, modeled after a game forest in India and showcasing a pride of lions. A walk-through park area has bird feeding and a petting zoo, or take a pontoon boat tour. There's also paddleboating, miniature golf, a children's play area with rides and sports fields, a picnic pavilion, a restaurant, and a snack shop. No convertibles or pets are allowed. ⊠ *2003 Lion Country Safari Rd., at Southern Blvd. W, Loxahatchee* ☎ *561/793–1084* ⊕ *www.lioncountrysafari.com* ☜ *$21.99; $3.50 parking fee* ☉ *Daily 9:30–5:30; last vehicle in by 4:30.*

⑳ **Mounts Botanical Gardens.** Take advantage of balmy weather by walk-
★ ing among the tropical and subtropical plants here. Join a free tour
or explore the 14 acres of exotic trees, rain-forest area, and butterfly
and water gardens on your own. Many plants were significantly damaged during the 2004 and 2005 hurricanes, and new plantings will
take years to reach maturity. There are lots of free brochures about
tropical trees, flowers, and fruits in the main building. If you're feeling
inspired, be sure to check out the gift shop's wide range of gardening
books. ✉ *531 N. Military Trail* ☎ *561/233–1749* ⊕ *www.mounts.org*
✉ *Gardens free; tours $5 suggested donation* ⊙ *Mon.–Sat. 8:30–4:30,*
Sun. noon–4; tours Sun. at 2.

⑯ **National Croquet Center.** The world's largest croquet complex, the 10-
★ acre center is also the headquarters for the U.S. Croquet Association.
Vast expanses of manicured lawn are the stage for fierce competitions—
in no way resembling the casual backyard games where kids play with
wide wire wickets. There's also a clubhouse with a pro shop and Café
Croquet, with verandas for dining and viewing, and a museum hall.
You have to be a member, or a guest of a member, to reserve a lawn
every day but Saturday, when lessons are free and lawns are open to all.
✉ *700 Florida Mango Rd., at Summit Blvd.* ☎ *561/478–2300* ⊕ *www.*
croquetnational.com ✉ *Free admission. Free lessons Sat. Full day of*
play $20 June–Sept., $35 Oct.–May ⊙ *Court times June–Sept., Tues.–*
Sat. 9–5; Oct.–May, daily 9–5.

⑱ **Okeeheelee Nature Center.** Explore 5 mi of trails through 90 acres of
western Palm Beach County's native pine flatwoods and wetlands. A
visitor center–gift shop has hands-on exhibits and offers guided walks
by the center's volunteers. ✉ *7715 Forest Hill Blvd.* ☎ *561/233–1400*
✉ *Free* ⊙ *Visitor center Tues.–Fri. and Sun. 1–4:35, Sat. 8:15–4:35;*
trails daily dawn–dusk.

⑭ **Palm Beach Zoo at Dreher Park.** This wild kingdom is a 23-acre complex
☾ with 400-plus animals representing more than 125 species, from Florida panthers to the giant Aldabra tortoise, and the first outdoor exhibit
of Goeldi's monkeys in the nation. The Tropics of America exhibit has
6 acres of rain forest plus Maya ruins, an Amazon river village, and
an aviary. This was a one-tiger zoo until late 2006, when a pair of
Malayan tiger brothers were added to the mix. The zoo's latest acquisitions are among only 47 Malayan tigers in captivity. Also notable are a
nature trail, the otter exhibit, a children's petting zoo, and a restaurant
overlooking the river. ✉ *1301 Summit Blvd.* ☎ *561/533–0887* ⊕ *www.*
palmbeachzoo.com ✉ *$12.95* ⊙ *Daily 9–5.*

⑰ **Pine Jog Environmental Education Center.** The draw here is 150 acres of
☾ mostly undisturbed Florida pine flatwoods with one self-guided ½-
mi trail. Formal landscaping around five one-story buildings includes
native plants; dioramas and displays illustrate ecosystems. School
groups use the trails during the week; special events include camping and campfires. Call for an event schedule. ✉ *6301 Summit Blvd.*
☎ *561/686–6600* ⊕ *www.pinejog.org* ✉ *Free* ⊙ *Weekdays 9–5.*

⑮ **South Florida Science Museum.** Here at the museum, which includes the
☾ Aldrin Planetarium and McGinty Aquarium, there are hands-on exhibits
with touch tanks, and laser shows with music by the likes of Dave Matthews. Galaxy Golf is a 9-hole science challenge. Weather permitting,
you can observe the heavens Friday night through the most powerful
telescope in South Florida. ⊠*4801 Dreher Trail N* ☎*561/832–1988*
⊕*www.sfsm.org* ⚏*$9, planetarium $4 extra, laser show $5 extra,
galaxy golf $2 extra* ☉ *Weekdays 10–5, Sat. 10–6, Sun. noon–6.*

WHERE TO STAY & EAT

$–$$$ ✕ **Bellagio.** In the center of CityPlace in the 1926 former church, this
European-style bistro offers Italian specialties with a wide variety of
Italian wines. Service is exceptionally friendly and efficient. Sit at the
outdoor tables next to the main plaza's dancing fountains. ⊠*600 S.
Rosemary Ave., CityPlace Plaza* ☎*561/659–6160* ⊟*AE, MC, V.*

$–$$$ ✕ **Columbia.** Columbia's CityPlace location, across from the Conven-
tion Center and next to the Kravis Center, makes it a popular meeting
spot. Unlike the flagship restaurant in Ybor City, there are no flamenco
dancers here, but the 1905 Salad, a house specialty made at your table,
is entertainment enough. The menu reflects Spanish and Cuban cooking, as does the decor—Spanish tile and murals. Try the Red Snapper Alicante, baked with sweet Spanish onions, or the paella. ⊠*651
Okeechobee Blvd.* ☎*561/820–9373* ⊟*AE, D, MC, V* ☉ *Open daily
for lunch and dinner.*

¢–$ ✕ **Flanigan's.** It's not unusual to see Rolls-Royces parked next to pickup
trucks at this rustic restaurant two blocks from the south bridge to
Palm Beach. Big burgers, grilled or fried grouper sandwiches, steamed
shrimp, and conch chowder are the main attractions in the two dining rooms. Pecky-cypress walls (de rigueur in Palm Beach mansions)
are decorated with pictures of customers and the fish that didn't get
away. Arrive early on weekend afternoons to watch the Miami Heat
and Miami Dolphins on small and big-screen TVs. ⊠*330 Southern*
☎*561/659–3129* ⊟*AE, MC, V.*

¢–$ ✕ **Havana.** Decorated with tile floors and vintage posters of its name-
sake city, this two-level restaurant serves such authentic specialties as
Cuban sandwiches and chicken slowly cooked in Spanish sauce. Lunch
and dinner dishes are enhanced by the requisite black beans and rice.
Open until 1 AM Friday and Saturday, it attracts a late-night crowd. The
popular 24/7 walk-up window serves strong Cuban coffee, sugary fried
churros, and fruit juices, including mamey, mango, papaya, guava, and
guanabana. ⊠*6801 S. Dixie Hwy.* ☎*561/547–9799* ⊟*AE, MC, V*
☉ *Open daily.*

¢–$ ✕ **Howley's Restaurant.** Since 1950, this diner's eat-in counter and
"Cooked in sight, it must be right" motto has made a congenial setting
for meeting and making friends. Forgo the counter for the 1950s-style
tables or sit out on the patio. The café attracts a loyal clientele for
breakfast, lunch, and dinner with such specialties as turkey and dressing, burgers, and chicken salad. There's also a bar. ⊠*4700 S. Dixie
Hwy.* ☎*561/833–5691* ⊟*AE, MC, V.*

¢ ✕**Middle East Bakery.** This hole-in-the-wall Middle Eastern bakery, deli, and market fills at lunchtime with regulars who are on a first-name basis with the gang behind the counter. From the nondescript parking lot the place doesn't look like much, but inside, delicious hot and cold Mediterranean treats await. Choose from traditional gyro sandwiches and lamb salads with sides of grape leaves, tabbouleh, and couscous. ✉ *327 5th St., at Olive Ave.* ☎ *561/659–7322* ⊟ *AE, MC, V* ⊘ *Closed Sun.*

$$–$$$$ ⊡**Hibiscus House Downtown.** Business execs repair to this elegant respite from the corporate world between meetings at the Convention Center, which is within walking distance. The nine guest rooms and suites are in two two-story frame houses, both built in 1917. Rooms are decorated with antiques, including desks and high four-poster beds. Breakfast is served on the veranda overlooking the brick street. An elaborate Sunday brunch includes dishes such as paella, eggs Benedict, and beef Wellington, and an outdoor bar serves cocktails, including Sunday-morning mimosas. The city trolley stops in front of the inn, which is just four blocks from the Intracoastal Waterway. The only downside is that the area has been in the news for break-ins and burglaries, especially on the fringes. ✉ *213 S. Rosemary Ave., 33401* ☎ *561/833–8171* 🖷 *561/833–8114* ⊕ *www.hibiscushousedowntown.com* ⏎ *9 rooms* ⊟ *AE, D, MC, V* ⦿ *BP.*

$$$ ⊡**Hotel Biba.** In the El Cid historic district, this 1940s motel has gotten a fun, stylish revamp from Barbara Hulanicki, designer of the 1960s Biba fashion line. Each room has a vibrant mélange of colors, along with handcrafted mirrors, mosaic bathroom floors, and custom mahogany furnishings. Luxury touches include Egyptian-cotton sheets, down pillows and duvets, and lavender-scented closets. The hotel is one block from the Intracoastal Waterway and about a mile from Clematis Street nightlife, and the lobby bar attracts a hip happy-hour crowd. ✉ *320 Belvedere Rd., 33405* ☎ *561/832–0094* 🖷 *561/833–7848* ⊕ *www. hotelbiba.com* ⏎ *43 rooms* ⚴ *In-hotel: bar, pool, no elevator, no-smoking rooms* ⊟ *AE, DC, MC, V.*

$$–$$$ ⊡**Grandview Gardens Bed & Breakfast.** This cheery yellow 1923 Span-
★ ish Mediterranean inn is the new kid on the B&B block in West Palm Beach. It is very conveniently located—next to Howard Park, across from the Armory Art Center, a short walk from the Convention Center, CityPlace, and the Kravis Center, and a 10-minute drive from the airport—and warmly decorated with terra-cotta floors, a coral stone fireplace, and terraces overlooking a swimming pool and gardens. Each spacious room has its own Mediterranean flair as well as a private entrance and French doors opening to private terraces overlooking the pool. The owners are multilingual. ✉ *1608 Lake Ave., 33401* ☎ *561/833–9023* ⊕ *www.grandview-gardens.net* ⏎ *5 rooms and a Bermuda-style guest cottage* ⚴ *In-room: dial-up. In-hotel: pool, no elevator, airport shuttle* ⊟ *AE, DC, MC, V* ⦿ *BP.*

$–$$$ ⊡**Hibiscus House.** The hosts work diligently to promote not only their delightful Cape Cod–style B&B, the sister inn to the Hibiscus House Downtown, but also their neighborhood, Old Northwood; thanks to their efforts, it's listed on the National Register of Historic Places.

LAKE OKEECHOBEE

40 mi west of West Palm Beach.

Rimming the western edges of Palm Beach and Martin counties, the second-largest freshwater lake completely within the United States is girdled by 120 mi of road yet remains shielded from sight for almost its entire circumference. Lake Okeechobee—the Seminole's Big Water and the gateway of the great Everglades watershed—measures 730 square mi, roughly 33 mi north–south, and 30 mi east–west, with an average natural depth of only 10 feet (flood control brings the figure up to 12 feet and deeper). Six major lock systems and 32 separate water-control structures manage the water. Encircling the lake is a 34-foot-high grassy levee—locals call it "the wall"—and the Lake Okeechobee Scenic Trail, a segment of the Florida National Scenic Trail, an easy, flat ride for bikers. ■TIP→**There's no shade, so wear a hat, sunscreen, and bug repellent. Be sure to bring lots of bottled water, too, because restaurants and stores are few and far between.** You are likely to see alligators in the tall grass along the shore, as well as birds, including herons, ibises, and bald eagles, which have made a comeback in the area. The 110-mi trail encircles the lake atop the 34-foot Herbert Hoover Dike. On the lake, you'll spot happy anglers from all over, themselves hooked on some of the best bass fishing in North America. There are 40 species of fish in "Lake O," including largemouth bass, bluegill, Okeechobee catfish, and speckled perch. You can fish from the shore or hire a guide for a half-day or all-day boat trip.

Small towns dot the lakeshore in this predominantly agricultural area. To the southeast is Belle Glade—motto: "her soil is her fortune"—playing a role as the eastern hub of the 700,000-acre Everglades Agricultural Area, the crescent of farmlands south and east of the lake. Southwest lies Clewiston, billing itself as "the sweetest town in America" thanks to the presence of "Big Sugar," more formally known as the United States Sugar Corporation. At the lake's north end, around Okeechobee, citrus production has outgrown cattle ranching as the principal economic engine, and still-important dairying diminishes as the state acquires more acreage in efforts to reduce water pollution. Set back from the lake, Indiantown is the western hub of Martin County, noteworthy for citrus production, cattle ranching, and timbering. The town reached its apex in 1927, when the Seaboard Airline Railroad briefly established its southern headquarters and a model town here.

Detailing city history, the **Clewiston Museum** tells stories not only of Big Sugar and the Herbert Hoover Dike construction but also of a ramie crop grown here to make rayon, of Royal Air Force pilots training at the Clewiston airfield, and of a World War II prisoner-of-war camp. ⊠*112 S. Commercio St., Clewiston* ☎*863/983–2870* ✉*Free* ☉ *Weekdays 9–4.*

In the **Municipal Complex** are the public library and the **Lawrence E. Will Museum,** both with materials on town history. On the front lawn is a Ferenc Verga sculpture of a family fleeing a wall of water rising from the lake during the catastrophic hurricane of 1928. More than

2,000 people perished, and 15,000 families were left homeless by torrential flooding. ⊠*530 Main St., Belle Glade* ☎*561/996–3453* ⌷*Free* ⊙*Mon.–Wed. 10–8, Thurs.–Sat. 10–5.*

WHERE TO STAY & EAT

¢–$$ ✕**Colonial Dining Room.** The Clewiston Inn's restaurant has ladder-back chairs, chandeliers, fanlight windows, and an attitude that's anything but fancy. The regional and continental dishes—chicken, pork, steak, and the ubiquitous catfish—are mighty tasty. ⊠*108 Royal Palm Ave., at U.S. 27, Clewiston* ☎*863/983–8151* ☰*MC, V* ⊙*No dinner Sun.*

¢–$ ✕**Lightsey's.** The pick of the lake, this lodgelike restaurant at the Okee-Tantie Recreation Area started closer to town as a fish company with four tables in a corner. Now folks gladly trek out here for lunch and dinner daily. Get most items fried, steamed, broiled, or grilled. The freshest are the catfish, cooter (freshwater turtle), frogs' legs, and gator. ⊠*10430 Rte. 78 W, Okeechobee* ☎*863/763–4276* ☰*D, MC, V.*

$–$$$ ⬚**Clewiston Inn.** A classic antebellum-style country hotel in the heart of town, this inn was built in 1938. The cypress-paneled lobby, wood-burning fireplace, Colonial Dining Room, and Everglades lounge with a wraparound Everglades mural are standouts. Rooms, with reproduction furniture, are an excellent value, and rates include a full breakfast cooked to order. There's a pool across the street in the park. ⊠*108 Royal Palm Ave., at U.S. 27, Clewiston 33440* ☎*863/983–8151 or 800/749–4466* ⊟*863/983–4602* ⊕*www.clewistoninn.com* ⇥*48 rooms, 5 suites* ⚴*In-hotel: restaurant, bar, tennis courts, no elevator* ☰*AE, D, DC, MC, V* ⎮⊙⎮*BP.*

¢–$$$ ⬚**Pier II Resort.** This two-story motel on the rim canal has a five-story observation tower for peeking over the lake's levee. Large, motel-plain rooms are nicely maintained. Out back are a 650-foot fishing pier and the Oyster Bar, one of the lake area's best hangouts for shooting pool or watching TV, attracting a mix of locals and out-of-towners. The suites were refurbished after Hurricane Wilma in 2005. ⊠*2200 S.E. U.S. 441, Okeechobee 34974* ☎*863/763–8003 or 800/874–3744* ⊟*863/763–2245* ⊕*www.pier2resort.com* ⇥*83 rooms, 6 suites* ⚴*In-room: kitchen (some), refrigerator. In-hotel: bar, pool* ☰*AE, D, DC, MC, V* ⎮⊙⎮*CP.*

$–$$ ⬚**Seminole Inn.** Once the Seaboard Airline Railroad's southern headquarters, this two-story, Mediterranean Revival inn, with cypress ceilings and pine hardwood floors, was restored by Holman Wall. It's now run by the late Indiantown patriarch's daughter, Jonnie Wall Williams, a fifth-generation native. Carpeted rooms are done in country ruffles and prints, with comfy beds. Rocking chairs await on the porch, and there's Indiantown memorabilia in the lobby, a sitting area on the second floor, and good local art throughout. ⊠*15885 S.W. Warfield Blvd., Indiantown 34956* ☎*772/597–3777* ⊟*772/597–2883* ⊕*www.seminoleinn.com* ⇥*22 rooms* ⚴*In-hotel: 2 restaurants, pool, no elevator.* ☰*AE, D, MC, V* ⎮⊙⎮*CP.*

¢   ⬚**Okeechobee Inn.** Rooms in this simple, two-story, L-shaped motel, 2 mi west of Belle Glade, are done in green floral prints. Large windows let in plenty of light, and balconies overlook the pool. Fishing and boat ramps are a mile away. ⊠*265 N. U.S. 27, South Bay 33493* ☎*561/996–6517* ⇥*115 rooms* ⚴*In-hotel: pool, no elevator* ☰*AE, D, DC, MC, V.*

SPORTS & THE OUTDOORS

FISHING

Since the **Okee-Tantie Recreation Area** (⊠*10430 Rte. 78 W, Okeechobee* ☎*863/763–2622*) has direct lake access, it's a popular fishing outpost, with two public boat ramps, fish-cleaning stations, a marina, picnic areas and a restaurant, a playground, restrooms, showers, and a **bait shop** (☎*863/763–9645*) that stocks groceries. In addition to operating the bridge to Torry Island (among Florida's last remaining swing bridges—it's cranked open and closed by hand, swinging at right angles to the road), brothers Charles and Gordon Corbin run **Slim's Fish Camp** (⊠*215 Marina Dr., Belle Glade* ☎*561/996–3844*). The camp, and most of Torry Island, were severely damaged by Hurricane Wilma in 2005, but it's finally up and running again. Torry Island is home to a complete tackle shop, guides, camping facilities, and bass boats. You can also procure the name of a taxidermist to mount your trophy.

GOLF

Belle Glade Municipal Country Club (⊠*Torry Island Rd. [W. Lake Rd.], Belle Glade* ☎*561/996–6605*) has an 18-hole golf course and restaurant open to the public; green fee: $15/$36.

SOUTH TO BOCA RATON

Strung together by Route A1A, the towns between Palm Beach and Boca Raton are notable for their variety, from high-rise condominiums to small-town public beaches. In one town you'll find a cluster of art galleries and fancy dining, and the very next town will yield mostly hamburger joints and mom-and-pop stores.

LAKE WORTH

㉑ *2 mi south of West Palm Beach.*

For years, tourists looked here mainly for inexpensive lodging and easy access to Palm Beach, since a bridge leads from the mainland to a barrier island with Lake Worth's beach. Now Lake Worth has several blocks of restaurants and art galleries, making this a worthy destination on its own.

Also known as Casino Park, **Lake Worth Municipal Park** has a beach, Olympic-size swimming pool, a fishing pier (as of this writing, still partially closed after hurricane damage), picnic areas, shuffleboard, restaurants, and shops. ⊠*Rte. A1A at end of Lake Worth Bridge* ☎*561/533–7367* *Pool $3, parking 25¢ for 15 mins* ☉*Daily 9–5.*

WHERE TO STAY & EAT

$–$$ ✕**Bizaare Avenue Café.** Decorated with a mix of artwork and antiques, this cozy tapas bar–wine bar–bistro fits right into downtown Lake Worth's groovy, eclectic scene. Daily specials are available on both the lunch and dinner menus, where crepes, pizzas, pastas, and salads are the staples. ⊠*921 Lake Ave.* ☎*561/588–4488* ☰*AE, D, DC, MC, V* ⊘*Closed Sun.*

¢–$ ✕**John G's.** Count on a line here until the midafternoon closing. The menu is as big as the crowd: grand fruit platters, sandwich-board superstars, grilled burgers, seafood, eggs every which way, and the house specialty, French toast. Breakfast is served until 11, lunch until 3. ⊠*10 S. Ocean Blvd. (Lake Worth Casino)* ☎*561/585–9860* ⚏*Reservations not accepted* ☰*No credit cards* ⊘*No dinner.*

¢ ✕**Benny's on the Beach.** Perched on the Lake Worth Pier (and nearly wiped out in hurricanes France and Jeanne), Benny's has diner-style food that's cheap and nothing fancy, but the spectacular view of the sun glistening on the water and the waves crashing directly below is what dining here is all about. ⊠*10 Ocean Ave.* ☎*561/582–9001* ☰*No credit cards* ⊘*No dinner.*

$$$–$$$$ 🏠**Sabal Palm House.** Built in 1936, this historic two-story frame
★ enclave is a short walk from the Intracoastal Waterway and a golf course. Three rooms and a suite are in the main house, and three others are across a brick courtyard in the carriage house. Each room is inspired by a different artist—including Renoir, Dalí, Norman Rockwell, and Chagall—and all have oak floors, antique furnishings, and private balconies. There's an inviting parlor where afternoon tea and weekend wine and appetizers are served. A full breakfast is offered indoors or in the courtyard, under the palms. ⊠*109 N. Golfview Rd., 33460* ☎*561/582–1090 or 888/722–2572* 🖷*561/582–0933* ⊕*www. sabalpalmhouse.com* ⇨*6 rooms, 1 suite* ♿*In-hotel: no kids under 14* ☰*AE, MC, V* ⦿*BP.*

$$–$$$ 🏠**Mango Inn.** It's only a 15-minute walk to the beach from this white
★ frame B&B built as a private house in 1915. The two ground-floor rooms have French doors opening onto a patio. A poolside cottage has two bedrooms and two bathrooms. Have your complimentary breakfast of homemade raspberry buttermilk pancakes on the veranda overlooking the heated pool, or in the courtyard next to the fountain. ⊠*128 N. Lakeside Dr., 33460* ☎*561/533–6900 or 888/626–4619* 🖷*561/493–3748* ⊕*www.mangoinn.com* ⇨*7 rooms, 1 cottage* ♿*In-room: kitchen, refrigerator (some), VCR, dial-up. In-hotel: pool, no elevator, no kids, no-smoking rooms* ☰*AE, D, MC, V* ⦿*BP.*

NIGHTLIFE & THE ARTS

NIGHTLIFE

Some nights you'll encounter free concerts by local and regional artists, and other nights the headliners are nationally known professionals. But every night, Tuesday through Saturday, there's traditional blues at the **Bamboo Room** (⊠*25 S. J St.* ☎*561/585–2583*).

THE ARTS

Lake Worth Playhouse (⊠*713 Lake Ave.* ☎*561/586–6410*) presents drama and popular musicals on its main stage, including works by Andrew Lloyd Webber and Tim Rice. The regular season runs from September through June, with two adjacent venues each showing six shows. Tickets are reasonably priced from $18 to $28.

SPORTS & THE OUTDOORS

The **Gulfstream Polo Club,** the oldest such club along the Palm Beaches, began in the 1920s and plays medium-goal polo (for teams with handicaps of 8–16 goals). Seven polo fields and stabling for more than 60 horses make up this facility on the western edge of Lake Worth. ✉ *4550 Polo Rd.* ☎ *561/965–2057* 🍽 *Free* ✹ *Games Dec.–Apr.*

The **Museum of Polo & Hall of Fame** is a good place to start if you're looking for an introduction to polo. See polo memorabilia, art, and a film on the history of the sport. ✉ *9011 Lake Worth Rd.* ☎ *561/969–3210* 🍽 *Free, but donations encouraged* ✹ *10–4 weekdays all year and 10–2 Sat. Jan.–Apr.*

LANTANA

㉒ *2 mi south of Lake Worth.*

Lantana—just a bit farther south from Palm Beach than Lake Worth—has inexpensive lodging and a bridge connecting the town to its own beach on a barrier island. Tucked between Lantana and Boynton Beach is **Manalapan,** a tiny but posh residential community crowned by a luxury Ritz-Carlton beach resort.

Ideal for sprawling, beachcombing, or power-walking, **Lantana Public Beach** is also worthy for its proximity to one of the most popular food concessions in town, the **Dune Deck Cafe.** Here the choices are standard, but the food is particularly fresh and the portions are hearty. Try an omelet with a side of potato fries and melon wedges, Greek salad, homemade yogurt with seasonal fruit topped with honey, or a side of banana nut bread. There are daily breakfast and lunch specials; dining is outdoors under yellow canopies perched over the beach. ✉ *100 N. Ocean Ave.* ☎ *No phone* 🅿 *Parking 25¢ for 15 mins* ✹ *Daily 9–4:45.*

WHERE TO STAY & EAT

$$–$$$ ✕ **Station House Restaurant.** The best Maine lobster in South Florida might well reside at this delicious dive, where all the seafood is cooked to perfection. Sticky seats and tablecloths are an accepted part of the scene, so wear jeans and a T-shirt. Although it's casual and family friendly, reservations are recommended, since it's a local favorite. Station Grill, across the street, is less seafood oriented, but every bite as good. ✉ *233 Lantana Rd.* ☎ *561/547–9487* ⊟ *AE, D, DC, MC, V.*

$$–$$$ ✕ **Suite 225.** On a quaint street with other shops and eateries is this
★ stylish restaurant, an inviting older house that's been renovated into a sleek sushi bar. Glass doors and windows open up to outdoor dining areas, and a bar nestles under large banyan trees. Start with a sample platter from the extensive list of eclectic "suite rolls," which includes nearly 40 choices. Among the good nonseafood bets are grilled sake skirt steak with ginger barbecue sauce and pork chops with Asian-pear chutney. ✉ *225 E. Ocean Ave.* ☎ *561/582–2255* ⊟ *AE, D, MC, V* ✹ *No lunch Sun. and Mon.*

$–$$$ ✕**Old Key Lime House.** Overlooking the Intracoastal Waterway, the 1889 Lyman House has grown in spurts over the years and is now a patchwork of shedlike spaces, housing an informal Old Florida seafood house with prime key lime pie—the house specialty. Although there's air-conditioning, dining is open-air most evenings. The panoramic water views are the main appeal here for adults—kids love to feed the fish and rock in the glider seats on the dock. ✉*300 E. Ocean Ave.* ☎*561/533–5220* ▭*AE, MC, V.*

$$$$ ⚓**Ritz-Carlton, Palm Beach.** Despite its name, this bisque-color, triple-tower landmark is actually in Manalapan, halfway between Palm ★ Beach and Delray Beach. A huge double-sided marble fireplace dominates the elegant lobby and foreshadows the luxury of the guest rooms, which have rich upholstered furnishings and marble tubs. Most rooms have ocean views, and all have balconies. A $15 million room renovation and a $45 million expansion in 2006 added a 3,000-square-foot oceanfront terrace, a new seawall, a second pool, two restaurants, a beauty bar for big and little kids, a grand spa, and a program for teens. Coconut palms shade the pools and courtyard—all of which are served by attendants who can fulfill whims from iced drinks to cool face towels. ✉*100 S. Ocean Blvd., Manalapan 33462* ☎*561/533–6000 or 800/241–3333* ⚓*561/588–4555* ⊕*www.ritz-carlton.com* ⚓*310 rooms* ♿*In-room: dial-up. In-hotel: 4 restaurants, room service, bars, tennis courts, pools, spa, beachfront, water sports, bicycles, children's and teens' programs, laundry service, concierge, no-smoking rooms* ▭*AE, D, DC, MC, V.*

$$$–$$$$ ⚓**Palm Beach Oceanfront Inn.** Families seeking closer-to-earth prices gravitate to this casual two-story resort on the beach. Don't count on anything fancy, but large, adequately furnished rooms and suites face tropical gardens. Beach frontage is the draw here. A wide wooden sundeck surrounds the free-form pool, and both look to the ocean. The informal restaurant and outdoor bar also overlook the water. ✉*3550 S. Ocean Blvd., 33480* ☎*561/582–5631 or 800/457–5631* ⚓*561/588–4563* ⊕*www.palmbeachoceanfrontinn.com* ⚓*50 rooms, 8 suites* ♿*In-room: kitchen (some), refrigerator, VCR (some), dial-up. In-hotel: restaurant, room service, bar, pool, beachfront* ▭*AE, D, MC, V.*

THE ARTS

Florida Stage (✉*262 South Ocean Blvd., Manalapan* ☎*561/585–3433*), in the Plaza Del Mar shopping center across from the Ritz, is a 258-seat theater that presents five new or developing plays from October through June. Tickets range from $42 for previews to $75 for opening-night receptions.

SPORTS & THE OUTDOORS

B-Love Fleet (✉*314 E. Ocean Ave.* ☎*561/588–7612*) offers three deep-sea fishing excursions daily: 8–noon, 1–5, and 7–11. No reservations are needed; just show up 30 minutes before the boat is scheduled to leave. The cost is $35 per person and includes fishing license, bait, and tackle.

BOYNTON BEACH

㉓ *3 mi south of Lantana.*

In 1884, when fewer than 50 settlers lived in the area, Nathan Boynton, a Civil War veteran from Michigan, paid $25 for 500 acres with a mile-long stretch of beachfront thrown in. How things have changed, with today's population at about 118,000 and property values still on an upswing. Far enough from Palm Beach to remain low-key, Boynton Beach has two parts, the mainland and the barrier island—the town of Ocean Ridge—connected by two bridges.

An inviting beach, boardwalk, concessions, grills, a jogging trail, and playground await at **Boynton Beach Oceanfront Park.** Weekend evening concerts are held throughout the year. Parking costs more if you're not a Boynton resident. ⊠*6415 Ocean Blvd. (Rte. A1A)* ☎*No phone* ⊟*Parking $10 per day in winter, $5 per day rest of yr* ☉*Daily 9 AM–midnight.*

Boynton Beach's history is highlighted through interactive exhibits that make the **Schoolhouse Children's Museum** a kid and parent pleaser. In this 1913 schoolhouse, children can milk a mock cow or pick and wash plastic vegetables at the Pepper Patch Farm. Kids can buy tickets and dress up for a "time travel" train ride that immerses them in Boynton's history. A great outdoor playground castle is adjacent to the museum. ⊠*129 E. Ocean Ave.* ☎*561/742–6780* ⊟*$5* ☉*Tues.–Sat. 10–5.*

OFF THE BEATEN PATH

Arthur R. Marshall–Loxahatchee National Wildlife Refuge. The most robust part of the Everglades, this 221-square-mi refuge is one of three huge water-retention areas accounting for much of the Everglades outside the national park. These areas are managed less to protect natural resources, however, than to prevent flooding to the south. Start from the visitor center, where there is a marsh trail to a 20-foot-high observation tower overlooking a pond. The boardwalk takes you through a dense cypress swamp. There's also a 5½-mi canoe trail, best for experienced canoeists since it's overgrown. Wildlife viewing is good year-round, and you can fish for bass and panfish. ⊠*10119 Lee Rd., off U.S. 441 between Boynton Beach Blvd. (Rte. 804) and Atlantic Ave. (Rte. 806), west of Boynton Beach* ☎*561/734–8303* ⊟*$5 per vehicle, pedestrians $1* ☉*Daily 5 AM–6 PM; visitor center, weekdays 9–4, weekends 9–4:30.*

WHERE TO STAY & EAT

$$–$$$ ✕**Nirvana.** Highly stylized dining attracts experimental foodies hungry for Indian food touched with Caribbean, American, and French flavors. Given its strip-mall location, the attentive service is an unexpected treat, as is the intimate interior: sheer fabrics drape from the ceiling, warm woods trim the perimeter, and terra-cotta-color floors and walls contrast with the crisp white tablecloths. ⊠*1701 N. Congress Ave.* ☎*561/752–1932* ⊟*AE, MC, V* ☉*No lunch.*

¢–$$ ✕**Banana Boat.** A mainstay for local boaters, who cruise up and down the intracoastal and dock here, Banana Boat has fish-and-chips, burgers, ribs, and raw seafood. On weekends, casual crowds clad in tank tops, flip-flops, and bikinis dance to live island music while downing frozen drinks. ⊠739 E. Ocean Ave. ☎561/732–9400 ☰AE, MC, V.

$$–$$$$ 🍴Holiday Inn Express. Conveniently perched right off Interstate 95, this four-story hotel has large rooms with purple-and-green fabrics, blond-wood furniture, and small sitting areas. A large sundeck surrounds the heated pool. Complimentary breakfast is served, and free beverages are on tap at the end of the day. The hotel completed a $1 million renovation in 2006, which included a new lobby and breakfast room, a fitness center, a convenience store, and new furniture in guest rooms. ⊠480 W. Boynton Beach Blvd., 33435 ☎561/734–9100 ☎561/738–7193 ⊕www.hiexpress.com ⇆105 rooms, 6 suites ♿In-room: dial-up. In-hotel: pool, laundry facilities ☰AE, DC, MC, V ⛔BP.

$$$ 🍴Emerald Shores Resort. This green-and-white two-story motel has one- and two-bedroom apartments with full kitchens for rent by the week. A large sundeck surrounds the heated pool. The property is well situated—just across Route A1A from the beach—tucked into a quiet residential area with a mix of single and multifamily properties in Ocean Ridge, the barrier island of Boynton Beach. The minimum stay is seven nights. ⊠6600 N. Ocean Blvd., 33435 ☎561/738–2063 or 800/433–0786 ⇆16 rooms, 2 suites ♿In-room: kitchen. In-hotel: pool, no elevator, laundry facilities ☰AE, D, MC, V.

SPORTS & THE OUTDOORS

FISHING

Fish the canal at the **Arthur R. Marshall–Loxahatchee National Wildlife Refuge** (☎561/734–8303). There's a boat ramp, and the waters are decently productive, but bring your own equipment. On the other side of town, catch fish swimming between the Atlantic and intracoastal at the **Boynton Beach Inlet Pier** (☎No phone).

GOLF

Links at Boynton Beach (⊠8020 Jog Rd. ☎561/742–6500) has 18-hole and 9-hole executive courses; green fee: Champion course $13/$41, Family course $39/$49.

GULF STREAM

㉔ *2 mi south of Boynton Beach.*

Quiet money, and quite a lot of it, resides in this small beachfront community, whose architecture reflects Mizner's influence. As you pass the bougainvillea-topped walls of the Gulf Stream Club, don't be surprised if a private security officer stops traffic for a golfer to cross.

DELRAY BEACH

㉕ *2 mi south of Gulf Stream.*

A onetime artists' retreat with a small settlement of Japanese farmers, Delray has grown into a sophisticated beach town. Atlantic Avenue, the once dilapidated main drag, has evolved into a more-than-a-mile-long stretch of palm-dotted sidewalks, lined with stores, art galleries, and dining establishments. Running east–west and ending at the beach, it's a pleasant place for a stroll, day or night. Another active pedestrian way begins at the eastern edge of Atlantic Avenue and runs along the big, broad swimming beach that extends north to George Bush Boulevard and south to Casuarina Road.

Just off Atlantic Avenue, the **Old School Square Cultural Arts Center** has several museums in restored school buildings dating from 1913 and 1926. The **Cornell Museum of Art & History** offers ever-changing art exhibits. During its season, the **Crest Theatre** showcases performances by local and touring troupes in the restored 1925 Delray High School building. ⊠ *51 N. Swinton Ave.* ☎ *561/243–7922* ⊕ *www.oldschool. org* ⊡ *$6* ⊗ *Tues.–Sat. 10:30–4:30, Sun. 1–4:30.*

A restored bungalow-style home that dates from about 1915, **Cason Cottage** serves as the Delray Beach Historical Society's offices. It's filled with Victorian-era relics, including a pipe organ donated by descendants of a Delray Beach pioneer family. Periodic displays celebrate the town's architectural evolution. The cottage is a block north of the cultural center. ⊠ *5 N.E. 1st St.* ☎ *561/243–0223* ⊡ *Free* ⊗ *Call for an appointment for tours.*

The chief landmark along Atlantic Avenue since 1926 is the Mediterranean Revival–style **Colony Hotel,** which is a member of the National Trust for Historic Preservation. Walk through the lobby to the parking lot of the hotel where original stable "garages" still stand—relics of the days when hotel guests would arrive via horse and carriage. ⊠ *525 E. Atlantic Ave.* ☎ *561/276–4123.*

The **Museum of Lifestyle & Fashion History** hosts rotating exhibits, such as the history of the lunchbox, or fashion in architecture, and holds trolley rides through downtown Delray on the fourth Saturday of the month. ⊠ *322 N.E. 2nd Ave.* ☎ *561/243–2662* ⊕ *www.mlfhmuseum. org* ⊡ *$5* ⊗ *Tues.–Sat. 10–5, Sun. 1–5.*

Traditional and digital photography are on display at the **Palm Beach Photographic Centre,** in the Pineapple Grove section of town. There's a small museum, gallery, darkroom, and retail shop. ⊠ *55 N.E. 2nd Ave.* ☎ *561/276–9797* ⊕ *www.workshop.org* ⊡ *$3* ⊗ *Mon.–Sat. 9–5:30.*

Fodor'sChoice
★ Out in the boonies west of Delray Beach seems an odd place to encounter the inscrutable East, but there awaits **Morikami Museum and Japanese Gardens,** a cultural and recreational facility heralding the Yamato Colony of Japanese farmers. The on-site Cornell Café serves light Asian fare. If you don't get your fill of orchids, the American Orchid Society's 20,000-square-foot headquarters is across the street. ⊠ *4000 Morikami Park Rd.* ☎ *561/495–0233* ⊕ *www.morikami.org* ⊡ *$10* ⊗ *Tues.–Sun. 10–5.*

★ Enjoy many types of water-sport rentals—sailing, kayaking, windsurfing, Boogie boarding, surfing, snorkeling—or scuba diving at a sunken Spanish galleon less than ½ mi offshore at **Seagate Beach.** ⊠ *½ mi south of Atlantic Ave. at Rte. A1A.*

A scenic walking path follows the main stretch of the public **Delray Beach Municipal Beach.** ⊠ *Atlantic Ave. at Rte. A1A.*

WHERE TO STAY & EAT

$$-$$$$ ✕ **32 East.** Although restaurants come and go on a trendy street like
  ★   Atlantic Avenue, 32 East is a consistent staple, if not the best restaurant on any given night in Delray Beach. A daily menu of wood-oven pizzas, salads, soups, seafood, meat, and desserts is all based on what is fresh and plentiful. Dark-wood accents and dim lighting make this large restaurant seem cozy. There's a packed bar in front and an open kitchen in back. ⊠ *32 E. Atlantic Ave.* ☎ *561/276–7868* ▤ *AE, D, MC, V* ☉ *No lunch.*

$$-$$$ ✕ **Kyoto.** An energetic crew, from the sushi chefs to the waitstaff, keeps this bustling restaurant running into the wee hours all week long. Sushi and sake are the main draw here, and the less traditional dishes still have Japanese influences. Indoor dining is in a stylish, contemporary setting with sleek black accents and multicolor lighting. You can dine among a bar crowd and watch your sushi being assembled, or take a table in the front courtyard and watch the crowds meander along happening Pineapple Grove. ⊠ *25 N.E. 2nd Ave.* ☎ *561/330–2404* ▤ *AE, DC, MC, V* ☉ *No lunch weekends.*

¢–$$$ ✕ **Pineapple Grille.** A magnet for regulars, this informal tropical enclave serves dependable Caribbean fare. An extensive menu includes macadamia nut–crusted crab cakes and mango goat-cheese chicken, along with imaginative pizzas. There's also a good and affordable wine list and live music on weekends. ⊠ *800 Palm Trail, in Palm Trail Plaza* ☎ *561/265–1368* ▤ *AE, MC, V* ☉ *No lunch Sat., no dinner Sun.*

¢–$$ ✕ **Blue Anchor.** Yes, this pub was actually shipped from England, where it stood for 150 years as the Blue Anchor Pub in London's historic Chancery Lane. There it was a watering hole for famed Englishmen, including Winston Churchill. The Delray Beach incarnation has stuck to authentic British pub fare. Chow down on a ploughman's lunch (a chunk of Stilton cheese, a hunk of bread, and pickled onions), shepherd's pie, fish-and-chips, and bangers and mash (sausages with mashed potatoes). Don't be surprised to find a rugby game on TV. English beers and ales are on tap and by the bottle. It's a late-night place open until at least 2. ⊠ *804 E. Atlantic Ave.* ☎ *561/272–7272* ▤ *AE, MC, V.*

¢–$$ ✕ **Boston's on the Beach.** Restaurants overlooking a beach often rely on location alone to keep tables filled. That's the case at Boston's, where you'll find beer flowing and the ocean breeze blowing. Decent bar fare includes New England clam chowder, several lobster dishes, and fresh fish. The walls are laden with paraphernalia from the Boston Bruins, New England Patriots, and Boston Red Sox, including a shrine to Ted Williams. Kick back on an outdoor deck upstairs. Be warned: Boston's can get loud and rowdy (or lively, depending on your taste) on weekend nights, when rock bands play. ⊠ *40 S. Ocean Blvd. (Rte. A1A)* ☎ *561/278–3364* ▤ *AE, MC, V.*

¢ ✕ **Old School Bakery.** Formerly in a much larger shop where they actually
  ★   baked all the goodies, this purveyor of many restaurants' breads has moved its baking facilities off-site and concentrates on simple sandwich making at its best. Particularly worthy is the cherry chicken salad sand-

wich with Brie on multigrain. Apart from sandwiches and soups served for lunch every day, order from a diverse baked-goods menu with artisan breads, pastries, several kinds of cookies, and even biscotti. The bakery is primarily take-out, but there are a few small tables in an adjacent open-air courtyard. ⊠814 E. Atlantic Ave. ☎561/243–8059 ⊟AE, MC, V ⊘No dinner.

$$$$ ★ ✕▦ **Sundy House.** Just about everything in this bright, bungalow-style inn is executed to perfection. Guest rooms are luxuriously decorated and offer hotel-style amenities, the cottage has its own Jacuzzi and fireplace, and the apartments offer a full kitchen and laundry. Situated a few blocks south of Atlantic Avenue, the only downside is a hearty walk to the beach (although a complimentary beach shuttle lessens the inconvenience). Even if you do not stay here, come see the grounds, where rooms are hidden behind extraordinary tropical gardens. Dine at the exceptional restaurant De la Tierra under an expansive indoor canopy, or on the outside patios under trees and among koi ponds. This is a popular weekend wedding spot. ⊠106 Swinton Ave., 33483 ☎561/272–5678 or 877/434–9601 ⊕www.sundyhouse.com ⊃11 rooms ♿In-hotel: no elevator ⊟AE, DC, MC, V.

$$$–$$$$ ▦ **Colony Hotel & Cabana Club.** In the heart of downtown Delray, this lovely and charming building underwent an exterior renovation that luckily did not do away with the stables in the back, which date back to 1926 when the hotel was built. Today it's listed on Delray's local Register of Historic Places and maintains an air of the 1920s with its Mediterranean Revival architecture. The Cabana Club is a separate property on the ocean about a mile away, with a private beach, club, and heated saltwater pool. A convivial bar and live music on weekend nights make the lobby area a great place to wind down. Fine shops selling leather goods, body products, and stationery fill the lower-level storefronts. ⊠525 E. Atlantic Ave., 33483 ☎561/276–4123 or 800/552–2363 ⊠561/276–0123 ⊕www.thecolonyhotel.com ⊃70 rooms ♿In-room: dial-up. In-hotel: bar, pool, beachfront ⊟AE, DC, MC, V ⏐⊙⏐CP.

$$$–$$$$ ▦ **Delray Beach Marriott.** A bright pink five-story hotel, this is by far the largest property in Delray, with a stellar location at Atlantic Avenue's east end, across the road from the beach and within walking distance of restaurants, shops, and galleries. Rooms and suites are spacious, and many have stunning ocean views. In 2006, the hotel added a spa. The giant, free-form pool is surrounded by a comfortable deck. ⊠10 N. Ocean Blvd., 33483 ☎561/274–3200 ⊠561/274–3202 ⊕www. delraybeachmarriott.com ⊃268 rooms, 88 suites ♿In-room: safe, dial-up. In-hotel: 3 restaurants, room service, bars, pool, gym, spa, beachfront, laundry facilities ⊟AE, DC, MC, V.

NIGHTLIFE & THE ARTS

THE ARTS

The **Crest Theater** (⊠51 N. Swinton Ave. ☎561/243–7922), in the Old School Square Cultural Arts Center, presents productions in dance, music, and theater.

NIGHTLIFE

Bistro 52 (✉ *110 E. Atlantic Ave.* ☎ *561/274–7077*) is packed with local society and celebrity. The drinks flow as does the chatter, but there's no dancing, only posing. **Dada** (✉ *52 N. Swinton Ave.* ☎ *561/330–3232*) presents live music in the living room of a historic house, and movies play on the wall. It's a place where those who don't drink will also feel comfortable. **Elwood's** (✉ *301 E. Atlantic Ave.* ☎ *561/272–7427*) is a fun drinking establishment in a former service station. Harley Davidsons line up on the weekend as locals stop by for the jamming live music and occasional Elvis sighting. **Delux** (✉ *16 E. Atlantic Ave.* ☎ *561/279–4792*) is where the young South Beach wannabe crowd goes to dance all night long.

SPORTS & THE OUTDOORS

BIKING

There's a bicycle path in Barwick Park and a special oceanfront lane along Route A1A. **Richwagen's Bike & Sport** (✉ *32 S.E. 2nd Ave.* ☎ *561/276–4234*) rents bikes by the hour or day and provides lock, basket, helmet, and maps.

TENNIS

Each winter the **Delray Beach Tennis Center** (✉ *201 W. Atlantic Ave.* ☎ *561/243–7360*) hosts professional tournaments such as the Chris Evert Tennis Classic and trains top-ranked players—even Andy Roddick. It offers individual lessons and clinics, and you can practice or learn on 14 clay courts and 5 hard courts year-round. It's open 8 AM–9 PM weekdays, 8 AM–6 PM weekends.

WATERSKIING

At **Lake Ida Park** (✉ *2929 Lake Ida Rd.* ☎ *561/964–4420*), you can water-ski whether you're a beginner or a veteran. The park has a boat ramp, a slalom course, and a trick ski course.

SHOPPING

Street-scaped **Atlantic Avenue** is a showcase for art galleries, shops, and restaurants. This charming area, from Swinton Avenue east to the ocean, has maintained much of its small-town integrity. **Snappy Turtle** (✉ *1038 Atlantic Ave.* ☎ *561/276–8088*) is a multiroom extravaganza where Mackenzie Childs and Lily Pulitzer mingle with other fun fashions for the home and family. A store in the historic Colony Hotel, **Escentials Apothecaries** (✉ *533 Atlantic Ave.* ☎ *561/276–7070*) is packed with all things good-smelling for your bath, body, and home. **Murder on the Beach** (✉ *273 N.E. 2nd Ave.* ☎ *561/279–7790*) specializes in new, used, and antiquarian mystery books, with an impressive selection from local authors. You can also purchase mystery games and puzzles.

BOCA RATON

㉖ *6 mi south of Delray Beach.*

Less than an hour south of Palm Beach and anchoring the county's south end, upscale Boca Raton has much in common with its fabled cousin. Both reflect the unmistakable architectural influence of Addison Mizner, their principal developer in the mid-1920s. The meaning of the name Boca Raton (pronounced boca rah-*tone*) often arouses curiosity, with many folks mistakenly assuming it means "rat's mouth." Historians say the probable origin is Boca Ratones, an ancient Spanish geographical term for an inlet filled with jagged rocks or coral. Miami's Biscayne Bay had such an inlet, and in 1823, a mapmaker copying Miami terrain confused the more northern inlet, thus mistakenly labeling this area Boca Ratones. No matter what, you'll know you've arrived in the heart of downtown when you spot the town hall's gold dome on the main street, Federal Highway.

In a spectacular building in the Mizner Park shopping center *(see Shopping)*, the **Boca Raton Museum of Art** has an interactive children's gallery and changing exhibition galleries showcasing internationally known artists. Upstairs galleries house a permanent collection including works by Picasso, Degas, Matisse, Klee, and Modigliani, as well as notable pre-Columbian art. ✉ *501 Plaza Real* ☎ *561/392–2500* ⊕ *www.bocamuseum.org* 🖅 *$17* ⊙ *Tues., Thurs., and Fri. 10–5, Wed. 10–9, weekends noon–5.*

A big draw for kids, **Gumbo Limbo Nature Center** has four huge saltwater tanks brimming with sea life—from coral to stingrays—and a boardwalk through dense forest with a 40-foot tower you can climb to overlook the tree canopy. In spring and early summer, staffers lead nocturnal turtle walks: you can watch nesting females come ashore and lay eggs. ✉ *1801 N. Ocean Blvd.* ☎ *561/338–1473* ⊕ *www.gumbo-limbo.org* 🖅 *Free; turtle tours $5; tickets must be obtained in advance* ⊙ *Mon.–Sat. 9–4, Sun. noon–4; turtle tours May–Aug., Mon.–Thurs. 9 PM–midnight.*

Built in 1925 as the headquarters of the Mizner Development Corporation, **2 East El Camino Real** is an example of Mizner's characteristic Spanish Revival architectural style, with its wrought-iron grilles and handmade tiles. As for Mizner's grandiose vision of El Camino Real, the architect-promoter once prepared brochures promising a sweeping wide boulevard with Venetian canals and arching bridges. Camino Real is attractive, heading east to the Boca Raton Resort & Club, but don't count on feeling like you're in Venice.

Within a shimmering golden dome, **Town Hall Museum** has a vital repository of archival material and special exhibits on the area's development. Tours and the gift shop are hosted by the Boca Raton Historical Society. One of IBM's first PCs is on display here. ✉ *71 N. Federal Hwy.* ☎ *561/395–6766* ⊕ *www.bocahistory.org* 🖅 *Free, tours $7* ⊙ *Tues.–Fri. 10–4; tour dates and times vary.*

A residential area behind the Boca Raton Art School on Palmetto Park Road, **Old Floresta** was developed by Addison Mizner starting in 1925 and landscaped with varieties of palms and cycads. It includes houses that are mainly in a Mediterranean style, many with upper balconies supported by exposed wood columns. Home tours are held twice a year.

Hands-on interactive exhibits enliven the **Children's Science Explorium,** at Sugar Sands Park. Children can create their own laser-light shows, explore a 3-D kiosk that illustrates wave motion, and try assorted electrifying experiments. There are also wind tunnels, microscopes, and microwave- and radiation-experiment stations. ⊠ *300 S. Military Trail* ☎ *561/347–3913* 🎟 *Free* ⊙ *Weekdays 9–6, weekends 10–5.*

WHERE TO STAY & EAT

$$$–$$$$ ✕ **Mark's at the Park.** Exotic cars pour into valet parking at this Mark Militello property, where a whimsical interpretation of retro and Art-Deco design and a seasonal menu compete for your attention. The eclectic food includes starters of scallops with foie gras–infused mashed potatoes and spicy steamed mussels; main courses range from crab-crusted mahimahi to roast duck with sweet potatoes. Desserts are deliciously old-fashioned. You'll need to make reservations for weekend nights. ⊠ *344 Plaza Real, Mizner Park* ☎ *561/395–0770* 🍴 *AE, D, MC, V.*

$$–$$$$ ✕ **Tiramisu.** The food is an extravaganza of taste treats; veal chops, tuna, and anything with mushrooms draw raves, but count on hearty fare rather than a light touch. Start with the portobello mushroom with garlic or the Corsican baby sardines in olive oil. For a main course, try ricotta ravioli; scaloppine of veal stuffed with crabmeat, lobster, and Gorgonzola; or Tuscan fish stew. ⊠ *855 S. Federal Hwy.* ☎ *561/338–9692* 🍴 *AE, DC, MC, V* ⊙ *Closed Sun.*

$$–$$$ ✕ **Uncle Tai's.** The draw at Boca's most upscale Chinese restaurant is some of the best Szechuan food on Florida's east coast. Specialties include sliced duck with snow peas and water chestnuts in a tangy plum sauce, and orange beef delight—flank steak stir-fried until crispy and then sautéed with pepper sauce, garlic, and orange peel. They'll go easy on the heat on request. Service is quietly efficient. ⊠ *5250 Town Center Circle* ☎ *561/368–8806* 🍴 *AE, MC, V* ⊙ *No lunch Sun.*

$–$$ ✕ **La Tre.** An adventuresome menu distinguishes this simple Vietnamese
★ eatery. Try the crispy eggplant and the happy pancake, a Vietnamese crepe stuffed with pork, shrimp, and vegetables. Tamarind squid is another winner. The restaurant's decor seems to date from the 1980s, with black lacquer furniture and an odd purple hue cast from fluorescent lighting. Don't anticipate a romantic dinner experience, but rather a very good Vietnamese dining experience. ⊠ *249 E. Palmetto Park Rd.* ☎ *561/392–4568* 🍴 *AE, DC, MC, V* ⊙ *No lunch Sat.–Tues.*

¢–$ ✕ **Draft House.** Sports aficionados love this place. It's decorated with sports equipment, memorabilia, and photos of famed coaches, players, and moments in sports, plus a dozen televisions for can't-miss events. Apart from inexpensive draft beer, regulars favor homemade chili wings, fried chicken tenders, and juicy burgers. For the more ravenous, there are char-grilled New York strips or racks of baby back ribs. There are additional locations in east Boca Raton and West Palm Beach. ⊠ *22191 Powerline Rd.* ☎ *561/394–6699* 🍴 *AE, MC, V.*

$$$$ 🏨 **Boca Raton Resort & Club.** Addison Mizner built the Mediterranean-
★ style Cloister Inn here in 1926, and additions over time have created this sparkling, sprawling resort with a beach accessible by shuttle. There are recreational activities here and many lodging options: tra-

ditional Cloister rooms are small but warmly decorated; accommodations in the 27-story Tower are more spacious; Beach Club rooms are light, airy, and contemporary; golf villas are large and attractive. In addition to a redesigned golf course, there's a two-story golf clubhouse, and the deluxe Tennis & Fitness Center. ⊠ *501 E. Camino Real, 33432* ☎*561/447–3000 or 800/327–0101* ⊟*561/447–3183* ⊕*www.bocaresort.com* ⇆*840 rooms, 63 suites, 60 golf villas* ⌂*In-room: safe, kitchen (some). In-hotel: 11 restaurants, room service, bars, golf course, tennis courts, pools, gym, beachfront, water sports, children's programs (ages 2–17), laundry service, concierge* ⊟*AE, DC, MC, V.*

$$$–$$$$ 🏨**Radisson Bridge Resort of Boca Raton.** This pink mid-rise resort sits directly on the Intracoastal Waterway yet has views of the ocean that can't be beat, especially from the top-floor restaurant, which is open only for Sunday brunch (very popular with locals) and private parties. The ground-floor restaurant, Water Color, offers great views of passing boats. The beach is a five-minute walk away, as are restaurants, galleries, and boutiques. Comfortable accommodations, the kind of attentive service found at smaller resorts, and an amazing location are the draws. Rooms are decorated in typical Boca-style light woods and rattan and a watercolor palette—nothing spectacular, yet quite presentable. ⊠ *999 East Camino Real, 33432* ☎*561/368–9500 or 800/333–3333* ⊟*561/362–0492* ⊕*www.radisson.com* ⇆*110 rooms, 11 suites* ⌂*In-room: refrigerator (suites), dial-up. In-hotel: 2 restaurants, room service, bars, pool, gym, beachfront, laundry facilities* ⊟*AE, DC, MC, V.*

$$ 🏨**Ocean Breeze Inn.** If golf is your game, this is an excellent choice. Inn guests can play the outstanding course at the adjoining Ocean Breeze Golf & Country Club, otherwise available only to club members. Rooms are in a three-story building, and most have a patio or balcony. Although the inn is nearly 30 years old, refurbished rooms are comfortable and contemporary. ⊠ *5800 N.W. 2nd Ave., 33487* ☎*561/994–0400 or 800/344–6995* ⊟*561/998–8279* ⊕*www.oceanbreezegolf.com* ⇆*46 rooms* ⌂*In-hotel: restaurant, golf course, tennis courts, pool, laundry facilities* ⊟*AE, DC, MC, V.*

NIGHTLIFE & THE ARTS

THE ARTS
Caldwell Theatre Company (⊠*7873 N. Federal Hwy.* ☎*561/241–7432*) stages four productions each season from November through May in addition to hosting the Play Reading Series for developing playwrights.

NIGHTLIFE
Drop by **Gatsby's Boca** (⊠*5970 S.W. 18th St., Shoppes at Village Point* ☎*561/393–3900*) any night of the week to mingle with a lively crowd. Shoot pool at one of 18 tables or watch sporting events on several giant screens. **Pranzo** (⊠*402 Plaza Real* ☎*561/750–7442*) has a happening weekend bar scene.

SPORTS & THE OUTDOORS

BEACHES

Red Reef Park (✉ *1400 N. Rte. A1A*) has a beach and playground plus picnic tables and grills. Popular **South Beach Park** (✉ *400 N. Rte. A1A*) has a concession stand. In addition to its beach, **Spanish River Park** (✉ *3001 N. Rte. A1A*) has picnic tables, grills, and a large playground.

BOATING

For the thrill of blasting across the water at up to 80 mph, **Palm Breeze Charters** (✉ *107 E. Palmetto Park Rd., Suite 330* ☎ *561/368–3566*) offers weekly cruises and boat charters. Rates are quoted individually depending on boat and charter.

GOLF

Two championship courses and golf programs are at **Boca Raton Resort & Club** (✉ *501 E. Camino Real* ☎ *561/447–3078*), green fee: $100/$195, includes cart. The Dave Pelz Golf School is at the Country Club course.

POLO

Royal Palm Polo Sports Club (✉ *18000 Jog Rd., at Old Clint Moore Rd.* ☎ *561/994–1876*), founded in 1959 by Oklahoma oilman John T. Oxley and now home to the $100,000 International Gold Cup Tournament, has seven polo fields within two stadiums. Games take place January through May, Sunday at 1 and 3. Admission is $10 to $15 for seats, $15 per car.

SCUBA & SNORKELING

Force E (✉ *2181 N. Federal Hwy.* ☎ *561/368–0555*) has information on dive trips and also rents scuba and snorkeling equipment. It has PADI affiliation, provides instruction at all levels, and offers charters.

SHOPPING

Locals know that Boca strip malls contain great shops. While stopping for essentials at Publix, be sure to check out that unassuming consignment, shoe, or fashion boutique next door and you may discover one of Boca's better finds.

★ **Mizner Park** (✉ *Federal Hwy., 1 block north of Palmetto Park Rd.*) is a distinctive 30-acre shopping center with apartments and town houses among its gardenlike retail and restaurant spaces. Some three dozen stores, including national and local retailers, mingle with fine restaurants, sidewalk cafés, galleries, a movie theater, museum, and amphitheater. **Town Center Mall** (✉ *6000 W. Glades Rd.* ☎ *561/368–6000*) is an upscale shopping mall. Major retailers include Nordstrom, Bloomingdale's, Macy's, Lord & Taylor, Saks Fifth Avenue, and Neiman Marcus. The mall's specialty may be women's fashion, but there are more than 200 stores and restaurants.

THE TREASURE COAST

From south to north, the Treasure Coast encompasses the top of Palm Beach County plus Martin, St. Lucie, and Indian River counties. Although dotted with seaside communities, this coastal section is one of Florida's quietest. Beyond the Palm Beach County border, most towns are small, with plenty of undeveloped land in between. Vero Beach, the region's most sophisticated beach area, was hit hard by the hurricanes of 2004 and 2005. Recovery includes new condo-hotels, and refurbishing of fine-dining establishments and upscale shops. Beaches along here are also sought out by nesting sea turtles; join locally organized watches to view the turtles laying their eggs in the sand between late April and August. It's illegal to touch or disturb turtles or their nests.

4

PALM BEACH SHORES

㉗ *7 mi north of Palm Beach.*

Rimmed by mom-and-pop motels, this residential town is at the southern tip of Singer Island, across Lake Worth Inlet from Palm Beach. To travel between the two, however, you must cross over to the mainland before returning to the beach. This unpretentious community has affordable beachfront lodging and is near several nature parks.

In the Intracoastal Waterway between Palm Beach Shores and Riviera Beach, 79-acre **Peanut Island** was opened in 1999 as a recreational park. There's a 20-foot-wide walking path surrounding the island, a 19-slip boat dock, a 170-foot T-shape fishing pier, six picnic pavilions, a visitor center, and 20 overnight campsites. The small **Palm Beach Maritime Museum** (☎ 561/832–7428) is open daily except Friday and showcases the "Kennedy Bunker," a bomb shelter prepared for President John F. Kennedy (call for tour hours). To get to the island, you can use your own boat or take a water taxi (call for schedules and pickup locations). ☎ 561/540–5147 ⊕ *www.pbmm.org* ⊠ *Free, tours $10* ☉ *Daily dawn–dusk for noncampers.*

WHERE TO STAY & EAT

$-$$$ ✕ **Sailfish Marina Restaurant.** Once known as the Galley, this waterfront restaurant looking out to Peanut Island remains a great place to chill out after a hot day of mansion gawking or beach bumming. Sit inside or outdoors to order tropical drinks and mainstays like conch chowder, grouper, or meat loaf. More upscale entrées—this, after all, is still Palm Beach County—include lobster tail or baby sea scallops sautéed in garlic and lemon butter. Breakfast is a winner here, too. ⊠ *98 Lake Dr.* ☎ *561/842–8449* ▤ *AE, MC, V.*

$$-$$$$ ▥ **Sailfish Marina and Sportfishing Resort.** This one-story motel has a marina with 94 deepwater slips and accommodations that include motel-style rooms, small and large efficiencies, and even a three-bedroom house. All rooms open to landscaped grounds, although none are directly on the water. Units 9–11 have ocean views across the blacktop drive. Rooms have peaked ceilings, carpeting, king-size or twin beds, and stall showers; all have ceiling fans. From the seawall, you'll see

Florida's Sea Turtles: The Nesting Season

From May to October it's turtle-nesting season all along the Florida coast. Female loggerhead, Kemp's ridley, and other species living in the Atlantic Ocean or Gulf of Mexico swim up to 2,000 mi to the Florida shore. By night, they drag their 100- to 400-pound bodies onto the beach to the dune line. Then each digs a hole with her flippers, drops in 100 or so eggs, covers them up, and returns to sea.

The babies hatch about 60 days later, typically at night, sometimes taking days to surface. Once they burst out of the sand, the hatchlings must get to sea rapidly or risk becoming dehydrated from the sun or being caught by crabs, birds, or other predators.

Instinctively baby turtles head toward bright light, probably because for millions of years starlight or moonlight reflected on the waves was the brightest light around, serving to guide hatchlings to water. But now light from beach development can lead the babies in the wrong direction, and many hatchlings are crushed by vehicles after running to the street rather than the water. To help, many coastal towns enforce light restrictions during nesting months, and more than one Florida homeowner has been surprised by a police officer at the door requesting that lights be dimmed on behalf of baby sea turtles.

At night, volunteers walk the beaches, searching for signs of turtle nests. Upon finding telltale scratches in the sand, they cordon off the sites, so beachgoers will leave the spots undisturbed. Volunteers also keep watch over nests when babies are about to hatch and assist if the hatchlings get disoriented.

It's a hazardous world for baby turtles. They can die after eating tar balls or plastic debris, or they can be gobbled by sharks or circling birds. Only about 1 in 1,000 survives to adulthood. After reaching the water, the babies make their way to warm currents. East-coast hatchlings drift into the Gulf Stream, spending years floating around the Atlantic.

Males never, ever return to land, but when females attain maturity, in 15–20 years, they return to shore to lay eggs. Remarkably, even after migrating hundreds and even thousands of miles out at sea, most return to the very beach where they were born to deposit their eggs. Sea turtles nest at least twice a season—sometimes as many as 10 times—and then skip a year or two. Each time they nest, they come back to the same stretch of beach. In fact, the more they nest, the more accurate they get, until eventually they return time and again to within a few feet of where they last laid their eggs. These incredible navigation skills remain for the most part a mystery despite intense scientific study. To learn more, check out the Sea Turtle Survival League's and Caribbean Conservation Corporation's Web site at ⊕ www.cccturtle.org.

—Pam Acheson

fish through the clear inlet water. ✉*98 Lake Dr., Singer Island 33404* ☎*561/844–1724 or 800/446–4577* 🖷*561/848–9684* ⊕*www.sailfishmarina.com* 🛏*30 units* 🖕*In-hotel: 2 restaurants, bar, pool, no elevator* ⊟*AE, MC, V.*

SPORTS & THE OUTDOORS

BIKING

To rent bikes by the hour, half day, or full day, head for the **Sailfish Marina and Resort** (✉*98 Lake Dr.* ☎*561/844–1724*). Ask for a free map of the bike trails.

FISHING

The **Sailfish Marina and Resort** (✉*98 Lake Dr.* ☎*561/844–1724*) has a large sportfishing fleet, with 28-foot to 60-foot boats and seasoned captains. Book a full- or half-day of deep-sea fishing for up to six people.

4

PALM BEACH GARDENS

28 *5 mi north of West Palm Beach.*

About 15 minutes northwest of Palm Beach is this relaxed, upscale residential community known for its high-profile golf complex, the PGA National Resort & Spa. Although not on the beach, the town is less than a 15-minute drive from the ocean.

WHERE TO STAY & EAT

$$–$$$$ ✕**Arezzo.** The aroma of fresh garlic will draw you into this Tuscan grill at the PGA National Resort & Spa. Families are attracted by affordable prices (as well as the food), so romantics might be tempted to pass on by, but that would be a mistake. Dishes include chicken, veal, fish, steaks, a dozen pastas, and almost as many pizzas. Thanks to the unusually relaxed attitude of the resort itself, you'll be equally comfortable in khakis or in jacket and tie. ✉*400 Ave. of the Champions* ☎*561/627–2000* ⊟*AE, MC, V* ☼*Closed Mon. No lunch.*

$$$ ✕**Café Chardonnay.** At the end of a strip mall, Café Chardonnay is surprisingly elegant inside. Soft indirect lighting, warm woods, and cozy
★ banquettes set the scene for a quiet lunch or romantic dinner. Established by the Eucalitto husband-and-wife team, the restaurant consistently receives praise for its innovative menu and outstanding wine list. Starters include wild mushroom strudel and truffle-stuffed diver sea scallops; entrées might include Gorgonzola-crusted filet mignon or pan-seared veal scaloppine with rock shrimp. ✉*4533 PGA Blvd.* ☎*561/627–2662* ⊟*AE, MC, V* ☼*No lunch weekends.*

$–$$$ ✕**The Riverhouse.** Patrons keep returning to this waterfront restaurant for large portions of straightforward American fare, the large salad bar, and fresh, slice-it-yourself bread, as well as the competent service. Choices include seafood (with a daily catch), steaks, chops, and seafood-steak combo platters. Booths and freestanding tables are surrounded by light-color wood, high ceilings, and nautical art. Expect a wait on Saturday night in season if you don't make reservations. ✉*2373 PGA Blvd.* ☎*561/694–1188* ⊟*AE, D, DC, MC, V* 🍴*Reservations essential* ☼*No lunch.*

¢–$$ ✕**No Anchovies.** Sharing is half the fun here for either lunch or dinner, so don't be shy about it at this casual and generous neighborhood trattoria. Sandwiches come on Italian loaf, semolina, whole wheat, or a spinach tortilla wrap with fillings such as oven-roasted turkey breast with sun-dried tomatoes or chicken salad. Entrées include pastas, chicken, and shrimp. Consider making your own pizza, perhaps with fresh goat cheese from the Turtle Creek dairy. ⊠*2650 PGA Blvd.* ☎*561/622–7855* ▭*AE, MC, V.*

NIGHTLIFE

For DJ'd Top 40, try the **Club Safari** (⊠*Palm Beach Gardens Marriott, 4000 RCA Blvd.* ☎*561/622–7024*), except on Thursday, when the focus is on oldies, which now means '50s–'80s.

SPORTS & THE OUTDOORS

AUTO RACING

If you yearn for drag racing action, the **Moroso Motorsports Park** (⊠*17047 Beeline Hwy.* ☎*561/622–1400*) awaits with weekly ¼-mi drag racing; monthly 2¼-mi, 10-turn road racing; and monthly AMA motorcycle road racing. These events and swap meets take place all year long. Spectator admission is $12 on Saturday, $15 on Sunday, and there's a $20 two-day pass.

GOLF

PGA National Resort & Spa (⊠*1000 Avenue of the Champions* ☎*561/627–1800*) has a reputedly tough 90 holes, which are available to hotel guests and members. Among them are the Champion Course, designed by Tom Fazio and Jack Nicklaus, green fee: $109/$280; the General Course, designed by Arnold Palmer, green fee: $109/$180; the Haig Course, the first course opened at the resort, green fee: $109/$160; the Estate Course, with a practice range and putting green, green fee: $109/$160; and the Tom Fazio–designed Squire Course, green fee: $109/$180. Lessons are available at the Golf Digest Academy.

SHOPPING

The **Gardens Mall** (⊠*3101 PGA Blvd.* ☎*561/775–7750*) offers an above-par shopping-mall experience—a calm, spacious, airy, and well-lighted environment. Anchors Bloomingdale's, Macy's, Nordstrom, Saks Fifth Avenue, and Sears Roebuck support more than 160 specialty retailers, including Swarovski, Louis Vuitton, Tiffany, Burberry, Godiva, Tommy Bahama, J. Jill, and Gymboree. **Downtown at the Gardens** (⊠*11701 Lake Victoria Gardens Ave.* ☎*561/340–1600*) offers open-air shopping with a movie theater, Whole Foods Market, restaurants, and shops like Urban Outfitters, Smith & Hawken, and Sur La Table.

EN ROUTE

John D. MacArthur Beach State Park. Almost 2 mi of beach, good fishing and shelling, and one of the finest examples of subtropical coastal habitat remaining in southeast Florida are among the treasures here. To learn about what you see, take an interpretive walk to a mangrove estuary along the upper reaches of Lake Worth. Or visit the **William T. Kirby Nature Center** (☎*561/624–6952*), open daily from 9 to 5, which has exhibits on the coastal environment. ✉*10900 Rte. A1A, North Palm Beach* 📞*561/624–6950* ⊕*www.macarthurbeach.org* 💲*$4 per vehicle, up to 4 people* 🕐*Daily 8–sundown.*

Loggerhead Park Marine Life Center of Juno Beach. Established by Eleanor N. Fletcher, the "turtle lady of Juno Beach," the center focuses on sea turtle history, including loggerheads and leatherbacks, with displays of coastal natural history, sharks, whales, and shells. You can adopt a turtle for a donation, and although you can't take it home with you, the center will watch over your pet. ✉*14200 U.S. Hwy. 1, Juno Beach* 📞*561/627–8280* ⊕*www.marinelife.org* 💲*Free* 🕐*Mon.–Sat. 10–4, Sun. noon–3.*

4

JUPITER

㉙ *12 mi north of Palm Beach Shores.*

Jupiter is one of the few little towns in the region not fronted by an island. Beaches here are part of the mainland, and Route A1A runs for almost 4 mi along the beachfront dunes and beautiful estates.

A beach is just one of the draws of **Carlin Park,** which has picnic pavilions, hiking trails, a baseball diamond, a playground, six tennis courts, and fishing sites. The Park Galley, serving snacks and burgers, is open daily 9–5. ✉*400 Rte. A1A* 📞*No phone* 🕐*Daily dawn–dusk.*

Take a look at how life once was at the **Dubois Home,** a modest pioneer outpost dating from 1898. Sitting atop an ancient Jeaga Indian mound 20 feet high and looking onto Jupiter Inlet, it has Cape Cod as well as Cracker (Old Florida) design. Even if you arrive when the house is closed, surrounding **Dubois Park** is worth the visit for its lovely beaches and swimming lagoons. ✉*Dubois Rd.* 📞*561/747–6639* ⊕*www.lrhs. org* 💲*$2; park is free* 🕐*Tues. and Wed. 1–4; park daily dawn–dusk.*

Permanent exhibits at the **Loxahatchee River Historical Museum** review not only modern-day development along the Loxahatchee River but also shipwrecks, railroads, and steamboat-era, Seminole, and pioneer history. ✉*805 N. U.S. 1, Burt Reynolds Park* 📞*561/747–6639* ⊕*www. lrhs.org* 💲*$5* 🕐*Tues.–Fri. 10–5, weekends noon–5.*

★ Designed by Civil War hero General George Meade, the redbrick Coast Guard **Jupiter Inlet Lighthouse** has operated here since 1860. Tours of the 105-foot-tall landmark unfold every half hour, and there's a small museum. The lighthouse has undergone significant change, courtesy of an $858,000 federal grant, transforming it from bright red to natural brick, the way it looked from 1860 to 1918. Children must be at least 4 feet tall to go to the top of the lighthouse. ✉*500 Capt. Armour's Way (U.S. 1 and Beach Rd.)* 📞*561/747–8380* ⊕*www.jupiterlighthouse.org* 💲*Tour $7* 🕐*Tues.–Sun. 10–5; last tour at 3:15.*

Maltz Jupiter Theatre. This renovated 550-seat theater is open all year with comedy and dramatic performances, but the major shows, such as *Anna in the Tropics,* run from September to April. Shows have both evening and matinee performances, and tickets range from

$15 to $50. ⊠*1001 E. Indiantown Rd.* ☎*561/743–0714* ⊕*www. jupitertheatre.org.*

WHERE TO STAY & EAT

$–$$$ ✕**Sinclairs Ocean Grill.** This popular spot in the Jupiter Beach Resort has French doors looking out to the pool, and a menu with a daily selection of fresh fish, such as cashew-encrusted grouper, Cajun-spice tuna, and mahimahi with pistachio sauce. There are also thick, juicy steaks—filet mignon is the house specialty—or chicken and veal dishes. Sunday brunch is a big draw. ⊠*5 N. Rte. A1A* ☎*561/745–7120* ⊟*AE, MC, V.*

$–$$ ✕**Food Shack.** This barlike shack filled with locals is a bit tricky to find, but worth the search. Fried-food standards typical of such a casual place are not found at the Food Shack; instead there are fried tuna rolls with basil and fried grouper cheeks with a fruity side slaw. A variety of beers are fun to pair with the creatively prepared seafood dishes that include wahoo, mahimahi, dolphin, and snapper. ⊠*103 South U.S. 1* ☎*561/741–3626* ⊟*DC, MC, V* ⊙*Closed Sun.*

¢–$ ✕**Lighthouse Restaurant.** Low prices match the plain look in this coffee shop–style building. The same people-pleasing formula has been employed since 1936: round-the-clock service (except 10 PM Sunday–6 AM Monday) and a menu that changes daily to take advantage of in-season market buys. Order chicken breast stuffed with sausage and vegetables, burgundy beef stew, crab cakes, and great pastries. ⊠*1510 U.S. 1* ☎*561/746–4811* ⊟*D, DC, MC, V.*

$$–$$$$ ⌂**Jupiter Beach Resort.** Although unpretentious, this time-share resort had a multimillion-dollar makeover before 2004's hurricane season and then another refurbishing after, and it shows. Caribbean-style rooms with mahogany sleigh beds and armoires are within a nine-story tower. Most rooms have balconies, and those on higher floors have great ocean views. Plentiful activities and a casual approach draw families here, and the resort offers turtle watches in season, May through October. Snorkeling equipment and bicycles are available for rent. ⊠*5 N. Rte. A1A, 33477* ☎*561/746–2511 or 800/228–8810* ⊠*561/747–3304* ⊕*www. jupiterbeachresort.com* ⌐*88 rooms, 65 suites* ♻*In-room: dial-up. In-hotel: 3 restaurants, bars, tennis court, pool, gym, beachfront, diving, laundry facilities* ⊟*AE, D, MC, V.*

SPORTS & THE OUTDOORS

BASEBALL

Both the **St. Louis Cardinals and Florida Marlins** (⊠*4751 Main St.* ☎*561/775–1818*) train at the $28 million Roger Dean Stadium, which seats 7,000 and has 12 practice fields.

CANOEING

Canoe Outfitters of Florida (⊠*9060 W. Indiantown Rd.* ☎*561/746–7053*) runs two- to three-hour trips (Thurs.–Mon.) and six-hour trips (weekends) along 8 mi of the Loxahatchee River, Florida's only government-designated Wild and Scenic River, where you can see animals in the wild, from otters to eagles. Canoe or kayak rental for two to three hours is $25, six hours $40, with drop-off and pickup.

GOLF

Abacoa Golf Club (⊠*105 Barbados Dr.* ☎*561/622–0036*), with 18 holes, is a recommended alternative to nearby private courses; green fee: $40/$130, including cart. The **Golf Club of Jupiter** (⊠*1800 Central Blvd.* ☎*561/747–6262*) has 18 holes of varying difficulty; green fee: $40/$59, including cart. **Jupiter Dunes Golf Club** (⊠*401 Rte. A1A* ☎*561/746–6654*) has an 18-hole golf course named Little Monster and a putting green near the Jupiter River estuary; green fee: $22/$34.

JUPITER ISLAND & HOBE SOUND

30 *5 mi north of Jupiter.*

Northeast across the Jupiter Inlet from Jupiter is the southern tip of Jupiter Island, including a planned community of the same name. Here expansive and expensive estates often retreat from the road behind screens of vegetation, and at the north end of the island, turtles come to nest in a wildlife refuge. To the west, on the mainland, is the little community of Hobe Sound.

In **Blowing Rocks Preserve,** within the 73-acre Nature Conservancy holding, are plant communities native to beachfront dune, coastal strand (the landward side of the dunes), mangrove, and hammock (tropical hardwood forests). The best time to visit is when high tides and strong offshore winds coincide, causing the sea to blow spectacularly through holes in the eroded outcropping. Park in the lot; police ticket cars parked along the road. ⊠*574 South Beach Rd. (Rte. 707), Jupiter Island* ☎*561/744–6668* ☜*$2* ⊙*Daily 9–4:30.*

Two tracts make up **Hobe Sound National Wildlife Refuge:** 232 acres of sand-pine and scrub-oak forest in Hobe Sound and 735 acres of coastal sand dune and mangrove swamp on Jupiter Island. Trails are open to the public in both places. Turtles nest and shells wash ashore on the 3½-mi-long beach, which has been severely eroded by 2004 and 2005 hurricanes' high tides and strong winds. ⊠*13640 S.E. Federal Hwy., Hobe Sound* ☎*772/546–6141* ☜*$5 per vehicle* ⊙*Daily dawn–dusk.*

Although on the Hobe Sound National Wildlife Refuge, **Hobe Sound Nature Center** is an independent organization. Its museum, which has baby alligators and crocodiles, and a scary-looking tarantula, is a child's delight. Interpretive exhibits focus on the environment, and a ½-mi trail winds through a forest of sand pine and scrub oak—one of Florida's most unusual and endangered plant communities. As of this writing, a new visitor center was nearing completion after the former structure was destroyed by Hurricanes Frances and Jeanne in 2004. ⊠*13640 S.E. Federal Hwy., Hobe Sound* ☎*772/546–2067* ☜*Donation suggested* ⊙*Trail daily dawn–dusk; nature center weekdays 9–3, call to verify hrs.*

Once you've gotten to **Jonathan Dickinson State Park,** follow signs to **Hobe Mountain.** An ancient dune topped with a tower, it yields a panoramic view across the park's 10,285 acres of varied terrain, as well as the Intracoastal Waterway. The Loxahatchee River, part of the federal government's Wild and Scenic Rivers program, cuts through the park and harbors manatees in winter and alligators year-round. Two-hour boat tours of the river leave daily at 9, 11, 1, and 3. Among amenities are a dozen cabins for rent, tent sites, bicycle and hiking trails, a campground, and a snack bar. ⊠*16450 S.E. Federal Hwy., Hobe Sound* ☎*772/546–2771* ⊠*$4 per vehicle for up to 4 people, boat tours $14.50* ☉*Daily 8–dusk.*

SPORTS & THE OUTDOORS

Jonathan Dickinson's River Tours (⊠*Jonathan Dickinson State Park* ☎*561/746–1466*) offers boat tours of the river and canoe, kayak, and motor-vessel rentals for use around the park from 9 to 5 daily. The fee is $10 for the first two hours and $4 for each additional hour.

STUART

③ *7 mi north of Hobe Sound.*

This compact little town on a peninsula that juts out into the St. Lucie River has a remarkable amount of river shoreline for its size as well as a charming historic district. The ocean is about 5 mi east.

★ Strict architectural and zoning standards guide civic-renewal projects in **historic downtown Stuart,** which has antiques shops, restaurants, and more than 50 specialty shops within a two-block area. A self-guided walking-tour pamphlet is available at assorted locations downtown to clue you in on this once small fishing village's early days.

On the National Register of Historic Places, the **Lyric Theatre** (⊠*59 S.W. Flagler Ave.* ☎*772/286–7827*) has been revived for performing and community events; a gazebo has free music performances.

The old courthouse has become the **Court House Cultural Center** (⊠*80 E. Ocean Blvd.* ☎*772/288–2542*) and presents folk art and other art exhibits.

The George W. Parks General Store is now the **Stuart Heritage Museum** (⊠*161 S.W. Flagler Ave.* ☎*772/220–4600*).

For information on the historic downtown, contact the **Stuart Main Street** (⊠*201 S.W. Flagler Ave., 34994* ☎*772/286–2848*).

★ Linking the watery past with a permanent record of maritime and yachting events contributing to Treasure Coast lore, the **Maritime & Yachting Museum** is near a marina with many old ships as well as historic exhibits to explore. Ship modelers are usually on hand, too; call for an events and activities schedule. Among those leading Saturday tours is a retired ship captain who has many interesting stories to share. ⊠*3250 S. Kanner Hwy.* ☎*772/692–1234* ⊠*Free* ☉*Mon.–Sat. 11–4, Sun. 1–4.*

WHERE TO STAY & EAT

$$–$$$ ✕**Courtine's.** A husband-and-wife team oversees this quiet and hospitable restaurant under the new Roosevelt Bridge. The Swiss chef's food represents French Continental and American influences, from his seafood and poultry dishes to the grilled house special of filet mignon stuffed with Roquefort, fresh spinach, and a port wine–balsamic reduction. The formal dining room has subtle touches of elegance, such as soft lighting and fresh flowers on each table. A full bar and extensive wine list are available. A more casual and light menu is also available at the bar. ⊠ *514 N. Dixie Hwy. (SR707)* ☎ *772/692–3662* ☰ *AE, MC, V* ⊗ *Closed Sun. and Mon. No lunch.*

¢–$$ ✕ **The Ashley.** Despite the hanging plants and artwork, this restaurant still has elements of the old bank that was robbed three times early in the 20th century by the Ashley Gang (hence the name). Situated at the end of the main historic street in downtown Stuart, The Ashley is easy to spot because of its redbrick facade. Spacious tables, comfortable seats, and good service make this restaurant a consistently pleasant place to eat. The continental menu has lots of salads, fresh fish, and pastas, and all are served in large portions. Crowds head to the lounge for a popular happy hour. Brunch is the only meal served on Sunday. ⊠ *61 S.W. Osceola St.* ☎ *772/221–1769* ☰ *AE, MC, V.*

$$$ ⛾ **Pirates Cove Resort and Marina.** On the banks of the St. Lucie River and the Intracoastal Waterway in the heart of Sailfish Alley, this cozy enclave is the perfect place to recoup after a day at sea. This midsize resort is relaxing and casual but packed with recreational activities for the day. The Pirates Loft Lounge gets lively at night, but the restaurant can be rather dull during the day. The tropically furnished rooms are large, with balconies to enjoy the waterfront views. The few suites include microwaves and refrigerators. A continental breakfast is included. ⊠ *4307 S.E. Bayview St., Port Salerno 34997* ☎ *772/287–2500 or 800/332–1414* ⧉ *772/220–2704* ⊕ *www.piratescoveresort. net* ⇆ *48 rooms, 2 mini suites* ⟨ *In-room: dial-up, refrigerators. In-hotel: restaurant, room service, bar* ☰ *AE, D, DC, MC, V.*

SPORTS & THE OUTDOORS

Deep-sea charters are available at the **Sailfish Marina** (⊠ *3565 S.E. St. Lucie Blvd.* ☎ *772/221–9456*).

SHOPPING

More than 60 restaurants and shops with antiques, art, and fashions have opened along **Osceola Street** in the restored downtown area. Operating for more than two decades, the **B&A Flea Market,** the oldest and largest such enterprise on the Treasure Coast, has a street-bazaar feel with shoppers happily scouting for the practical and unusual. ⊠ *2885 S.E. Federal Hwy.* ☎ *772/288–4915* ⧈ *Free* ⊗ *Weekends 8–3.*

HUTCHINSON ISLAND (JENSEN BEACH)

32 *5 mi northeast of Stuart.*

Area residents have taken pains to curb the runaway development that has created the commercial crowding found to the north and south, although some high-rises have popped up along the shore. The small town of Jensen Beach, occupying the core of the island, stretches across both sides of the Indian River. Citrus farmers and anglers still play a big community role, anchoring the area's down-to-earth feel. Between late April and August more than 600 turtles come here to nest along the town's Atlantic beach.

★ The **Florida Oceanographic Coastal Center** consists of a coastal hardwood hammock-and-mangrove forest. Expansion has yielded a visitor center, a science center with interpretive exhibits on coastal science and environmental issues, and a ½-mi interpretive boardwalk. Guided nature walks through trails and stingray feedings are offered at various times during the day. Eco-boat tours are 1½ hours long and include a 20-minute stop at a bird sanctuary. Dolphins, manatees, and turtles are often seen on the boat tour, for which reservations are required. ⊠ *890 N.E. Ocean Blvd.* ☎ *772/225–0505* ⊕ *www.floridaoceanographic.org* ⊠ *$8; $22 boat tour* ☉ *Mon.–Sat. 10–5, Sun. noon–4; guided nature walks Mon.–Sat. 11 and 3, Sun. at 2; boat tours Tues. and Thurs.–Sat. at 11 and Thurs. at 4.*

The pastel-pink **Elliott Museum** was erected in 1961 in honor of Sterling Elliott, inventor of an early automated addressing machine and a four-wheel cycle. The museum, with its antique cars, dolls, toys, and vintage baseball cards, is a nice stop for anyone fond of nostalgic goods. There are also antique fixtures from an early general store, blacksmith shop, and apothecary shop. ⊠ *825 N.E. Ocean Blvd.* ☎ *772/225–1961* ⊠ *$6* ☉ *Mon.–Sat. 10–4, Sun. 1–4.*

Built in 1875, **Gilbert's House of Refuge Museum** on Hutchinson Island is the only remaining building of nine such structures built by the U.S. Life Saving Service (a predecessor of the Coast Guard) to aid stranded sailors. Exhibits include antique lifesaving equipment, maps, artifacts from nearby wrecks, and boatbuilding tools. ⊠ *301 S.E. MacArthur Blvd.* ☎ *772/225–1875* ⊠ *$4* ☉ *Mon.–Sat. 10–4, Sun. 1–4.*

WHERE TO STAY & EAT

$$$ ✕ **11 Maple Street.** With a mere 16 tables, this spot is as good as it
★ gets on the Treasure Coast, with a menu that changes nightly. Soft recorded jazz and friendly staff satisfy, as does food served in ample portions. Although the cuisine is progressive, the place is filled with antiques and many vintage collectibles. Appetizers run from panfried conch and crispy calamari to spinach salad, and entrées include pan-seared rainbow trout, wood-grilled venison with onion-potato hash, and beef tenderloin with white-truffle-and-chive butter. Desserts such as a white-chocolate custard with blackberry sauce are seductive, too. ⊠ *3224 Maple Ave.* ☎ *772/334–7714* ⌖ *Reservations essential* ▭ *MC, V* ☉ *Closed Mon. and Tues. No lunch.*

$$–$$$ ✕ **Baha Grill.** Replacing the former Scalawags restaurant, but in a slightly different locale (the main dining room is now on the first floor), this spot serves breakfast, lunch, and dinner daily, though from a more limited menu than before. The food is basically the same—assorted soups, salads, and entrées consistent with most Marriott hotels. Standouts include a prime-rib buffet on Friday night and the all-you-can-eat Wednesday-evening seafood extravaganza with jumbo shrimp, Alaskan crab legs, clams on the half shell, marinated salmon, and

fresh catch. The decor is also standard for a Marriott dining room—a tasteful assemblage of wood accents, floral patterns, and subtle hues. ✉ *Marriott Beach Resort, 555 N.E. Ocean Blvd.* ☎ *772/225–6818* ▭ *AE, D, DC, MC, V.*

¢–$$ ✕ **Conchy Joe's.** This rustic Florida stilt house full of antique fish mounts, gator hides, and snake skins dates from the 1920s, although Conchy Joe's, like a hermit crab sliding into a new shell, moved up from West Palm Beach in 1983. It's a popular tourist spot, but its waterfront location, supercasual attitude, and seafood continue to attract locals, too. Staples are grouper marsala, broiled sea scallops, and fried cracked conch. There's live music Friday, heady rum drinks on Saturday, and a happy hour daily 3 to 6 and during NFL games. ✉ *3945 N.E. Indian River Dr.* ☎ *772/334–1130* ▭ *AE, D, MC, V.*

$$$$ 🏨 **Hutchinson Island Marriott Beach Resort & Marina.** With golf, tennis, a 77-slip marina, and a full water-sports program, plus many restaurants and bars, this 200-acre self-contained resort is excellent for families. Reception, some restaurants, and many rooms are in a trio of yellow four-story buildings that form an open courtyard with a large pool. Additional rooms and apartments with kitchens are spread over the property, some overlooking the Intracoastal Waterway and marina, others looking onto the ocean or tropical gardens. ✉ *555 N.E. Ocean Blvd., Hutchinson Island 34996* ☎ *772/225–3700 or 800/775–5936* 🖶 *772/225–0003* ⊕ *www.marriotthotels.com* 🛏 *213 rooms, 70 suites, 70 condominiums* ⅋ *In-room: kitchen (some). In-hotel: 3 restaurants, room service, bars, tennis courts, pools, gym, spa, beachfront, children's programs (2–12), laundry facilities, some pets allowed* ▭ *AE, D, DC, MC, V.*

SPORTS & THE OUTDOORS

BASEBALL

The **New York Mets** (✉ *525 N.W. Peacock Blvd., Port St. Lucie* ☎ *772/871–2115*) train at Tradition Field. It's also the home of the St. Lucie Mets Minor League Team.

BEACHES

Bathtub Reef Park (✉ *MacArthur Blvd. off Rte. A1A*), at the north end of the Indian River Plantation, is ideal for children because the waters are shallow for about 300 feet offshore and usually calm. At low tide bathers can walk to the reef. Facilities include restrooms and showers.

GOLF

Hutchinson Island Marriott Golf Club (✉ *555 N.E. Ocean Blvd.* ☎ *772/225–6819*) has 18 holes for private-club members and hotel guests; green fee: $28/$77. The PGA-operated **PGA Golf Club at the PGA Villages** (✉ *1916 Perfect Dr., Port St. Lucie* ☎ *772/467–1300 or 800/800–4653*) is a public facility with the PGA Learning Center and three courses designed by Pete Dye and Tom Fazio; green fee for North Course, South Course, and Dye Course: $25/$89, including cart.

FORT PIERCE

㉝ *11 mi north of Stuart.*

About an hour north of Palm Beach, this community has a distinctive rural feel, focusing on ranching and citrus farming. There are several worthwhile stops, including those easily seen while following Route 707. As a result of being directly hit by two hurricanes in 2004 and Hurricane Wilma in 2005, the landscape from Fort Pierce to Vero Beach has been greatly altered. Although there are pockets of destruction, pockets of beauty have sprung up, too. It will take years before the trees and plantings are lush and full again, perhaps hundreds of years for the glorious banyan and live oaks to reach their former statuesque size.

☾ Once a reservoir, the 550-acre **Savannas Recreation Area** has been returned to its natural state. Today the semi-wilderness area has campsites, boat ramps, and trails. ⊠ *1400 E. Midway Rd.* ☎ *772/464–7855* ⧉ *$1 per vehicle. RV hookups $20.* ☾ *Daily 8–6.*

A self-guided tour of the 3½-acre **Heathcote Botanical Gardens** takes in a palm walk, a Japanese garden, and subtropical foliage. There is also a pioneer house, orchid house, and gift shop with whimsical and botanical knickknacks. Guided tours are available Tuesday through Saturday by appointment. ⊠ *210 Savannah Rd.* ☎ *772/464–4672* ⊕ *www.heathcotebotanicalgardens.org* ⧉ *$6* ☾ *Tues.–Sat. 9–5; Nov.–Apr., also Sun. 1–5.*

As the home of the Treasure Coast Art Association, the **A. E. "Bean" Backus Gallery** displays works of one of Florida's foremost landscape artists. The gallery mounts changing exhibits and offers exceptional buys on work by local artists. ⊠ *500 N. Indian River Dr.* ☎ *772/465–0630* ⊕ *www.backusgallery.com* ⧉ *Free* ☾ *Tues.–Sat. 10–4, Sun. noon–4; summer hrs by appointment.*

Accessible only by footbridge, the **Ft. Pierce State Park** has 4 mi of trails around Jack Island. The 1½-mi Marsh Rabbit Trail across the island traverses a mangrove swamp to a 30-foot-tall observation tower overlooking the Indian River. ⊠ *Rte. A1A* ☎ *772/468–3985* ⧉ *$3* ☾ *Daily 8–5:30.*

★ Commemorating more than 3,000 navy frogmen who trained along Treasure Coast shoreline during World War II, the **Navy SEAL Museum** has weapons and equipment on view and exhibits depicting the history of the UDTs (Underwater Demolition Teams). Patrol boats and vehicles are displayed outdoors. ⊠ *3300 N. Rte. A1A* ☎ *772/595–5845* ⧉ *$6* ☾ *Mon.–Sat. 10–4, Sun. 1–4.*

Highlights of the **St. Lucie County Historical Museum** include early-20th-century memorabilia, photos, vintage farm tools, a restored 1919 American La France fire engine, replicas of a general store and the old Fort Pierce railroad station, and the restored 1905 Gardner House. ⊠ *414 Seaway Dr.* ☎ *772/462–1795* ⧉ *$3.50* ☾ *Tues.–Sat. 10–4, Sun. noon–4.*

$$–$$$ ✕**Ocean Grill.** Opened by Waldo Sexton as a hamburger shack in 1938, the Ocean Grill combines its ocean view with Tiffany-style lamps, wrought-iron chandeliers, and paintings of pirates and Seminoles. Count on at least three kinds of seafood any day on the menu, along with pork chops, tasty soups, and salads. The house drink, the Leaping Limey—a curious blend of vodka, blue curaçao, and lemon—commemorates the 1894 wreck of the *Breconshire*, which occurred just offshore and from which 34 British sailors escaped. ⊠*Sexton Plaza, 1050 Ocean Dr.* ☎*772/231–5409* ▤*AE, D, DC, MC, V* ◷*Closed 2 wks after Labor Day. No lunch weekends.*

$$$–$$$$ ⊞**Disney's Vero Beach Resort.** On 71 pristine oceanfront acres, this sprawling family-oriented retreat, operating both as a time-share and a hotel, is Vero's top resort. The main four-story building, three freestanding villas, and six beach cottages, all painted in pastels with gabled roofing in an approximation of turn-of-the-19th-century Old Florida style, are nestled among tropical greenery. Units, some with kitchens and many with balconies, have bright interiors with rattan furniture and tile floors. Shutters, one of two restaurants, has American food. Disney-wary adults need not worry; you have to go out of your way to track down a Disney character. ⊠*9250 Island Grove Terr., 32963* ☎*772/234–2000 or 800/359–8000* ⊟*772/234–2030* ⊕*www.dvc.disney.go.com* ⇄*161 rooms, 14 suites, 6 cottages* ⌂*In-room: safe, kitchen (some), refrigerator (some), VCR. In-hotel: 3 restaurants, room service, bar, tennis courts, pool, gym, beachfront, bicycles, children's programs (ages 4–12), laundry facilities, no-smoking rooms* ▤*AE, MC, V.*

$$–$$$$ ⊞**Driftwood Inn.** Listed on the National Register of Historic Places, this unique 1935 inn was built entirely from ocean-washed timbers and decorated with such artifacts as cathedral and ship bells, Spanish tile, and a cannon from a 16th-century Spanish galleon. The time-share hotel complex includes nine buildings on the beach with both modern and historic rooms. The inn attracts guests from around the world, who sit in wooden rockers facing the beach. ⊠*3150 Ocean Dr., 32963* ☎*772/231–0550* ⊟*772/234–1981* ⊕*www.thedriftwood. com* ⇄*86 rooms, 12 1- and 2-bedroom suites, 2 cottages* ⌂*In-room: kitchen (some), refrigerator. In-hotel: restaurant, bar, pools, beachfront* ▤*AE, DC, MC, V.*

THE ARTS

The **Civic Arts Center** (⊠*Riverside Park*), a cluster of cultural facilities, includes the **Riverside Theatre** (⊠*3250 Riverside Park Dr.* ☎*772/231–6990*), which stages six productions each season in its 633-seat performance hall; and the **Agnes Wahlstrom Youth Playhouse** (⊠*3280 Riverside Park Dr.* ☎*772/234–8052*), mounting children's productions.

Ⓒ **Riverside Children's Theatre** (⊠*3280 Riverside Park Dr.* ☎*772/234–8052*) offers a series of professional touring and local productions, as well as acting workshops, at the Agnes Wahlstrom Youth Playhouse. **Vero Museum of Art** (⊠*3001 Riverside Park Dr.* ☎*772/231–0707* ◷*Mon.–Sat. 10–4, Sun. 1–4:30*) is part of the Riverside Park's 26-acre campus dedicated to the arts. The museum is where a full schedule of exhibitions, art movies, lectures, workshops, and classes are hosted. The museum's five galleries and sculpture garden make it the largest art facility in the Treasure Coast.

SPORTS & THE OUTDOORS

BASEBALL

The **Los Angeles Dodgers** (⊠*4101 26th St.* ☎*772/569–4900*) train at Holman Stadium in Vero Beach's Dodgertown.

BEACHES

Humiston Park is one of the beach-access parks along the east edge of town that have boardwalks and steps bridging the dunes. There are picnic tables and a children's play area. ⊠*Ocean Dr. below Beachland Blvd.* ☎*772/231–5790* ☲*Free* ☉*Lifeguards 9* AM–*5* PM. There are many services at **Treasure Shores Park** (⊠*A1A, 3 mi north of County Rd. 510 at the Wabasso Bridge* ☎*772/581–4997*). **Wabasso Beach Park** (⊠*County Rd. 510, east of A1A intersection, north of Disney Resort* ☎*772/581–4998*) is a good option for a day in the sun.

GOLF

Sandridge Golf Club (⊠*5300 73rd St.* ☎*772/770–5000*) has two public 18-hole courses designed by Ron Garl; green fee: Dunes Course or Lakes Course $16/$42, including cart.

SHOPPING

Along **Ocean Drive** near Beachland Boulevard, a shopping area includes art galleries, antiques shops, and upscale clothing stores. The eight-block area of Oceanside has an interesting mix of boutiques, specialty shops, and eateries. Just west of Interstate 95, **Outlets at Vero Beach** (⊠*1824 94th Dr.* ☎*772/770–6171* ☉*Stores open Mon.–Sat. 9–8, Sun. 11–6*) is a discount shopping destination with 85 brand-name stores, including Ann Taylor, Ralph Lauren Polo, Mikasa, Bombay, and Jones New York.

SEBASTIAN

 14 mi north of Vero Beach.

One of few sparsely populated areas on Florida's east coast, this fishing village has as remote a feeling as you're likely to find between Jacksonville and Miami Beach. That adds to the appeal of the recreation area around Sebastian Inlet, where you can walk for miles along quiet beaches and catch some of Florida's best waves for surfing.

You'll really come upon hidden loot when entering **Mel Fisher's Treasure Museum.** See some of what was recovered in 1985 from the Spanish treasure ship *Atocha* and its sister ships of the 1715 fleet. The museum certainly piques one's curiosity about what is still buried at sea: treasures continue to be discovered each year. A similar museum in Key West is also operated by the late Mel Fisher's family. ⊠*1322 U.S. Hwy. 1* ☎*772/589–9875* ⊕*www.melfisher.com* ☲*$6.50* ☉*Mon.–Sat. 10–5, Sun. noon–5.*

Founded in 1903 by President Theodore Roosevelt as the nation's first national wildlife refuge, **Pelican Island National Wildlife Refuge** is in the Indian River Lagoon between Sebastian and Wabasso. The island is accessible only by boat. Public facilities—a boardwalk and observation tower, built for the refuge's centennial—enable visitors to see birds, endangered species, and habitats.

Because of the highly productive fishing waters of Sebastian Inlet, at the north end of Orchid Island, the 578-acre **Sebastian Inlet State Recreation Area** is one of the Florida park system's biggest draws. Both sides of the high bridge spanning the inlet—views are spectacular—attract plenty of anglers as well as those eager to enjoy the fine sandy shores, known for having some of the best waves in the state. A concession stand on the inlet's north side sells short-order food, rents various craft, and has a small apparel and surf shop. There's a boat ramp, and not far away is a dune area that's part of the **Archie Carr National Wildlife Refuge,** a haven for sea turtles and other protected Florida wildlife. ⊠9700 S. Rte. A1A, Melbourne Beach ☎321/984–4852 ⊕www.floridastate-parks.org ☜$3 for single occupancy, $5 for more than 1 in vehicle ☉Daily; bait and tackle shop 7:30–6, concession stand 8–5.

A National Historical Landmark, the **McLarty Treasure Museum** underscores the credo "Wherever gold glitters or silver beckons, man will move mountains." It has displays of coins, weapons, and tools salvaged from a fleet of Spanish treasure ships that sank in the 1715 storm, leaving some 1,500 survivors struggling to shore between Sebastian and Fort Pierce. The museum's last video showing begins at 3:15. ⊠13180 N. Rte. A1A ☎772/589–2147 ☜$1 ☉Daily 10–4:30.

WHERE TO STAY & EAT

$$–$$$ ✕**Hurricane Harbor Seafood Company.** Built in 1927 as a garage and used during Prohibition as a smugglers' den, this restaurant draws a year-round crowd for lunch and dinner. Waterfront window seats are especially coveted on stormy nights, when waves break outside in the Indian River Lagoon. Count on seafood, steaks, and grills, along with lighter fare. There's live music most nights. Peek into the Antique Dining Room, with a huge breakfront, used for special occasions. ⊠1540 Indian River Dr. ☎772/589–1773 ☐AE, D, MC, V ☉Closed Mon.

$–$$$ ✕**Capt. Hiram's Restaurant.** This family-friendly outpost on the Indian River Lagoon is easygoing, fanciful, and fun. Don't miss Capt. Hiram's Sandbar, where kids can play while parents enjoy drinks at stools and booths set in the sand and on wooden decks overlooking the water. Order the fresh catch, crab cakes, stuffed shrimp, raw-bar items, or a juicy steak. There's a weekday happy hour and nightly entertainment in season. ⊠1606 N. Indian River Dr. ☎772/589–4345 ☐AE, D, MC, V.

$$$ ⛳**Capt. Hiram's Resort.** A Key West–style inn with a lobby embellished with a classic surfboard collection brings the Florida Keys to Sebastian's Riverfront, about 17 mi north of Vero at Marker 66 on the intracoastal. All rooms have a private balcony and most have oak furnishings. Minisuites include microwave, refrigerator, and wet bar; deluxe suites also include dishwasher and stove. A heated pool has a

tropical sundeck, shaded by tables with umbrellas. A continental breakfast is included. ✉ *1580 U.S. 1, 32958* ☎ *772/388–8588* 📠 *772/589–4346* 🌐 *www.hirams.com* *56 rooms* *In-room: kitchen (some), dial-up. In-hotel: 2 restaurants, bar, pool* 💳 *AE, D, MC, V* *CP.*

SPORTS & THE OUTDOORS

CANOEING & KAYAKING

The boating stand at **Sebastian Inlet State Recreation Area** (✉ *9700 S. Rte. A1A, Melbourne Beach* ☎ *321/724–5424*) rents canoes, kayaks, and powerboats daily.

FISHING

The region's best inlet fishing is at **Sebastian Inlet State Recreation Area** (✉ *9700 S. Rte. A1A, Melbourne Beach*), where the catch includes bluefish, flounder, jack, redfish, sea trout, snapper, snook, and Spanish mackerel. For bottom fishing, try **Incentive Charter Fishing** (✉ *Dock at Capt. Hiram's Restaurant* ☎ *321/676–1948*). For sport fishing, try **The Big Easy Fishing Charters** (✉ *Dock at Capt. Hiram's Restaurant* ☎ *772/664–4068*). Another good sportfishing choice is **Skipper Sportfishing Charters** (✉ *Dock at Capt. Hiram's Restaurant* ☎ *772/589–8505*).

PALM BEACH & THE TREASURE COAST ESSENTIALS

To research prices, get advice from other travelers, and book travel arrangements, visit www.fodors.com.

TRANSPORTATION

BY AIR

CARRIERS

Palm Beach International Airport (PBIA) is served by Air Canada, AirTran, American, Bahamasair, CanJet, Comair, Continental, Delta, jetBlue, Laker Air, Northwest, Song, Southwest Airlines, Spirit Airlines, United, and US Airways/US Airways Express.

Contacts **Air Canada** (☎ *800/247–2262*). **AirTran** (☎ *800/247–8726*). **American** (☎ *800/433–7300*). **Bahamasair** (☎ *800/222–4262*). **CanJet** (☎ *800/809–7777*). **Comair** (☎ *800/354–9822*). **Continental** (☎ *800/525–0280*). **Delta** (☎ *800/221–1212*). **JetBlue** (☎ *800/538–2583*). **Northwest** (☎ *800/225–2525*). **Song** (☎ *800/359–7664*). **Southwest Airlines** (☎ *800/435–9792*). **Spirit Airlines** (☎ *800/772–7117*). **United** (☎ *800/241–6522*). **US Airways/US Airways Express** (☎ *800/428–4322*).

AIRPORTS & TRANSFERS

PalmTran Routes 44 and 40 run from the airport to Tri-Rail's nearby Palm Beach airport station daily. Palm Beach Transportation provides taxi and limousine service from PBIA. Reserve at least a day in advance for a limo. The lowest fares are $2 per mile, with the meter starting at

$1.25. Depending on your destination, a flat rate (from PBIA only) may save money. Wheelchair-accessible vehicles are available.

Contacts Palm Beach International Airport (PBIA) (✉ *Congress Ave. and Belvedere Rd., West Palm Beach* ☎ *561/471–7420*). **Palm Beach Transportation** (☎ *561/689–4222*). **Tri-Rail Commuter Bus Service** (☎ *800/874–7245*).

BY BUS

Greyhound Lines buses arrive at the station in West Palm Beach. Palm-Tran buses, running between Worth Avenue and Royal Palm Way in Palm Beach and major areas of West Palm Beach, require exact change. Fares are $1.25, or 60¢ for students, senior citizens, and people with disabilities (with reduced-fare ID). Service operates seven days a week. Call for schedules, routes, and rates for multiple-ride punch cards.

Contacts Greyhound Lines (☎ *800/229–9424* ✉ *205 S. Tamarind Ave., West Palm Beach* ☎ *561/833–8536*). **PalmTran** (☎ *561/841–4200*).

BY CAR

Interstate 95 runs north–south, linking West Palm Beach with Fort Lauderdale and Miami to the south and with Daytona, Jacksonville, and the rest of the Atlantic coast to the north. To access Palm Beach, exit east at Southern Boulevard, Belvedere Road, or Okeechobee Boulevard. Florida's Turnpike runs from Miami north through West Palm Beach before angling northwest to reach Orlando. U.S. 1 threads north–south along the coast, connecting most coastal communities, whereas the more scenic Route A1A ventures out onto the barrier islands. Interstate 95 runs parallel to U.S. 1 but a few miles inland. A nonstop four-lane route, Okeechobee Boulevard carries traffic from west of downtown West Palm Beach, near the Amtrak station in the airport district, directly to the Flagler Memorial Bridge and into Palm Beach. The best way to access Lake Okeechobee from West Palm is to drive west on Southern Boulevard from Interstate 95 past the cutoff road to Lion Country Safari. From there, the boulevard is designated U.S. 98/441.

CAR RENTAL

Contacts Alamo (☎ *800/462–5266*). **Avis** (☎ *800/331–1212*). **Budget** (☎ *800/527–7000*). **Hertz** (☎ *800/654–3131*). **National** (☎ *800/227–7368*).

BY TAXI

Palm Beach Transportation has a single number serving several cab companies. Meters start at $2, and the charge is $2.25 per mile. Some cabs may charge more.

Contacts Palm Beach Transportation (☎ *561/689–4222*).

BY TRAIN

Amtrak connects West Palm Beach with cities along Florida's east coast and the northeast daily. Since Hurricane Katrina hit Florida and the Gulf Coast in 2005, the Sunset Limited no longer connects West Palm Beach to New Orleans. Included in Amtrak's service is transport from West Palm Beach to Okeechobee; the station is unmanned. Tri-Rail, the commuter rail system, has 13 stops altogether between West Palm

Beach and Miami, where tickets can be purchased. The one-way fare is $5.50.

Contacts Amtrak (☎ 800/872–7245 ✉ 201 S. Tamarind Ave., West Palm Beach ☎ 561/832–6169 ✉ 801 N. Parrott Ave., Okeechobee). **Tri-Rail** (☎ 800/874–7245).

CONTACTS & RESOURCES

EMERGENCIES
Ambulance or Police Emergencies (☎ 911).

Late-Night Pharmacies CVS (✉ 3187 S. Congress Ave., Palm Springs ☎ 561/965–3367). **Walgreens** (✉ 1634 S. Federal Hwy., Boynton Beach ☎ 561/737–1160 ✉ 1208 Royal Palm Beach Blvd., Royal Palm Beach ☎ 561/798–9048 ✉ 1800 W. Indiantown Rd., Jupiter ☎ 561/744–6822 ✉ 2501 Broadway, Riviera Beach ☎ 561/848–6464).

MEDIA

NEWSPAPERS & MAGAZINES
To keep abreast of local issues and find what's new in entertainment options, pick up copies of the *Sun-Sentinel, Palm Beach Post, Palm Beach Daily News, The Press Journal, South Florida Business Journal,* and *New Times,* or *Boca Magazine, Palm Beach Illustrated,* and *Palm Beach Society* magazines.

RADIO
WLRN 91.3 FM is a public radio station. Tune into WLVE 93.9 FM for jazz; WZTA 94.9 for rock; WFLC 97.3 and WRMF 97.9 for adult contemporary; WLDI 95.5 and WHYI 100.7 for top 40; WMXJ 102.7 for oldies; WPBZ 103.1 for alternative; WMGE 103.5 for disco; and WKGR 98.7 and WBGG 105.9 for classic rock.

TOURS
Jonathan Dickinson's River Tours runs two-hour guided riverboat cruises daily at 9, 11, 1, and 3. The cost is $12. Loxahatchee Everglades Tours operates airboat tours year-round from west of Boca Raton through the marshes between the built-up coast and Lake Okeechobee. The *Manatee Queen,* a 49-passenger catamaran, offers day and evening cruises November through May on the Intracoastal Waterway and into the park's cypress swamps for $19.99. *Pilgrim Belle* operates two-hour sightseeing cruises along the Intracoastal Waterway. Water Taxi Scenic Cruises has several different daily sightseeing tours in a 16-person launch. All include a close-up look at the mansions of the rich and famous. The southern tour passes Peanut, Singer, and Munyan islands, and Palm Beach mansions. A second tour runs solely along the shore of Jupiter Island. A third tour passes the Craig Norman estate and goes into Lake Worth and Sawgrass Creek.

The Boca Raton Historical Society offers tours of the Boca Raton Resort & Club and trolley tours of city sites during season. Main Street Fort Pierce gives walking tours of the town's historic section, past buildings erected by early settlers, the second Wednesday of each month. The Indian River County Historical Society conducts walking tours of downtown Vero by reservation. Old Northwood Historic District Tours leads two-hour walking tours that include visits to historic home interiors. During season they typically start Sunday at 2, and a $5 donation is suggested. Tours for groups of six or more can be scheduled almost any day.

Contacts **Audubon Society of the Everglades** (✆ Box 16914, West Palm Beach 33416 ☎ 561/588–6908). **Boca Raton Historical Society** (✉ 71 N. Federal Hwy., Boca Raton ☎ 561/395–6766). **Capt. Doug's** (✉ Sebastian Marina, Sebastian ☎ 772/589–2329). **Indian River County Historical Society** (✉ 2336 14th Ave., Vero Beach ☎ 772/778–3435). **Jonathan Dickinson's River Tours** (✉ Jonathan Dickinson State Park, 16450 S.E. Federal Hwy., Hobe Sound ☎ 561/746–1466). **Loxahatchee Everglades Tours** (✉ 15490 Loxahatchee Rd. ☎ 561/482–8026). **Main Street Fort Pierce** (✉ 122 A. E. Backus Ave., Fort Pierce ☎ 772/466–3880). **Manatee Queen** (✉ Jonathan Dickinson State Park, 1065 N. Hwy. A1A, Hobe Sound ☎ 561/744–2191). **Old Northwood Historic District Tours** (✉ 501 30th St., West Palm Beach ☎ 561/863–5633). **River Rose Riverboat** (✉ 801 E. Atlantic Ave., Delray Beach ☎ 561/243–0686). **Water Taxi Scenic Cruises** (✉ Panama Hatties Restaurant, 11511 Ellison Wilson Rd., North Palm Beach ☎ 561/775–2628).

VISITOR INFORMATION

Tourist Information **Belle Glade Chamber of Commerce** (✉ 540 S. Main St., Belle Glade 33430 ☎ 561/996–2745). **Chamber of Commerce of the Palm Beaches** (✉ 401 N. Flagler Dr., West Palm Beach 33401 ☎ 561/833–3711). **Clewiston Chamber of Commerce** (✉ 109 Central Hwy, Clewiston 33440 ☎ 863/983–7979). **Delray Beach Chamber of Commerce** (✉ 64-A S.E. 5th Ave., Delray Beach 33483 ☎ 561/278–0424). **Glades County Chamber of Commerce** (✉ 998 U.S. 27 SE, Moore Haven 33471 ☎ 863/946–0440). **Indian River Chamber of Commerce** (✉ 1216 21st St., Vero Beach 32960 ☎ 772/567–3491). **Indiantown and Western Martin County Chamber of Commerce** (✆ Box 602, Indiantown 34956 ☎ 772/597–2184). **Okeechobee County Chamber of Commerce** (✉ 55 S. Parrott Ave., Okeechobee 34974 ☎ 863/763–6464). **Pahokee Chamber of Commerce** (✉ 115 E. Main St., Pahokee 33476 ☎ 561/924–5579). **Palm Beach County Convention & Visitors Bureau** (✉ 1555 Palm Beach Lakes Blvd., Suite 800, West Palm Beach 33401 ☎ 561/233–3000). **St. Lucie County Tourist Development Council** (✉ 2300 Virginia Ave., Fort Pierc e34982 ☎ 800/344–8443). **Stuart/Martin County Chamber of Commerce** (✉ 1650 S. Kanner Hwy., Stuart 34994 ☎ 772/287–1088). **Town of Palm Beach Chamber of Commerce** (✉ 400 Royal Palm Way, Palm Beach 33480 ☎ 561/655–3282). **U.S. Army Corps of Engineers (Okeechobee area information)** (✉ South Florida Operations Office, 525 Ridgelawn Rd., Clewiston 33440-5399 ☎ 863/983–8101).

Fort Lauderdale & Broward County

WORD OF MOUTH

"The Fort Lauderdale [Water] Taxi was a great way to see the city and get around. The drivers always have a few stories to tell and point out lots of things along the way too and make the trip entertaining. Certainly listening to the driver dishing the dirt on all the rich owners of homes on Millionaire's Row on the Intracoastal Waterway was funny."

–Dave

"At nighttime in Fort Lauderdale, try the Riverwalk area on the New River. Lots of restaurants and bars, right on the river (of course). If you want something upscale, go east on Las Olas Blvd. $$$! But really nice!"

–birdergirl

Updated by
Lynne Helm

COLLEGIATES OF THE 1960S RETURNING to Fort Lauderdale for vacations today would be hard pressed to recognize the onetime "Sun and Suds Spring Break Capital of the Universe." Back then, Fort Lauderdale's beachfront was lined with T-shirt shops, and downtown consisted of a lone office tower, dilapidated buildings, and motley other structures waiting to be razed. Today, the beach has upscale shops and restaurants, and downtown growth of recent years has exploded with luxury resort hotels equipped with enough high-octane amenities to light up skies all the way to western Broward's Alligator Alley. At risk of losing small-town 45-rpm magic in iPod times—when hotel parking fees alone threaten to eclipse room rates of old—Greater Fort Lauderdale somehow seems to be melding disparate eras into nouveau nirvana, seasoned with a little Gold Coast sand.

Credit the 1960 film *Where the Boys Are* for catapulting sleepy Lauderdale environs onto that era's *Haute List* for spring-fling campus escape. The movie depicted college students—upward of 20,000—swarming into town for the spring-break phenomenon. By 1985 the 20,000 had mushroomed to 350,000. Hotel owners bemoaned students cramming into standard-size hotel rooms by the dozen, with civility hitting new lows. Drug trafficking and petty theft proliferated, along with downscale bars staging wet T-shirt and banana-eating contests. Fed up, city leaders adopted policies and restrictions designed to encourage spring breakers to go elsewhere. They did, and the complaints of lost business are few—given a new era attracting a far more sophisticated, affluent crowd.

A major beneficiary is Las Olas Boulevard, a shopping street once moribund after 5 PM, which has reinvented itself as a hot venue, with a mix of trendy shops and eateries. Ever more restaurants have sprung up, and both visitors and locals often make an evening of strolling the boulevard. Farther west, along New River, is evidence of Fort Lauderdale's cultural renaissance: the Arts and Entertainment District and its crown jewel, the Broward Center for the Performing Arts. Still farther west, in the community of Sunrise, is the BankAtlantic Center (formerly the Office Depot Center, and before that the National Car Rental Center), serving as Broward's top sports, concert, and lecture circuit venue, and as home arena for the National Hockey League's Florida Panthers. Upscale shopping of an open-air-outlet nature arrived with the Colonnade Outlets at Sawgrass in Sunrise, featuring a slew of design stars, from Kate Spade and David Yurman to Valentino. Even so, a wave-capped shoreline with wide ribbons of golden sand for beach-

5

TOP 5

Don't miss the beaches along Lauderdale-by-the-Sea and Hollywood's Broadwalk.

Fort Lauderdale's Riverwalk before performances or dinner.

If you're feeling lucky, try Hollywood's Seminole Hard Rock Casino or Isle of Capri Pompano Park.

See the Everglades via airboat.

Head out to sea on a deep-sea fishing adventure, or stick around town with a riverboat cruise.

combing and sunbathing is the major draw for Fort Lauderdale and Broward County.

Tying all this together is a transportation system that, though less congested than elsewhere in South Florida, is rapidly becoming overwhelmed by traffic overload. Interstate 595 connects the city and suburbs and provides a direct route to the Fort Lauderdale–Hollywood International Airport and Port Everglades, but be sure to avoid morning and evening rush hours, when lanes slow to a crawl. For a more scenic way to really see this canal-laced city, simply hop on a water taxi, now known as a water bus. None of this was envisioned by Napoleon Bonaparte Broward, Florida's governor from 1905 to 1909, for whom the county was named. His drainage schemes opened much of the marshy Everglades region for farming, ranching, and settling (in retrospect, an environmental disaster). It was for Major William Lauderdale, who built a fort at the river's mouth in 1838 during the Seminole Indian wars, that the city was named.

Incorporated in 1911 with just 175 residents, Fort Lauderdale grew rapidly during the Florida boom of the 1920s. Today its population is 150,000, and the suburbs keep growing—1.6 million live in the county's 31 municipalities and unincorporated areas. Once oriented toward retirees, Broward now attracts younger families, many living in such newer communities as Weston, southwest of Fort Lauderdale. A revitalized downtown and a skyline (marked by ever more highrises) now includes multiuse complexes mixing retail and loft housing, and the city's young professionals are buying and revamping aging beachside condominiums.

Gaming has further rouged the area's complexion. Although South Florida's Indian tribes have long offered bingo, poker, and machines resembling slots—Hollywood's Seminole Hard Rock Hotel & Casino, where beleagured Anna Nicole Smith spent her final hours in 2007, ranks as the most glittering example—big change came at the behest of Broward voters (despite foot-dragging by conservative state legislators). In 2005, Broward's electorate gave a thumbs-up to becoming Florida's first county to offer Las Vegas–style gambling with true slot machines at four wagering facilities: Gulfstream Park Racing & Casino, the Mardi Gras Racetrack & Gaming Center, Dania Jai Alai Casino, and Isle of Capri Pompano Park Harness Track. As of this writing, slots were whirring at Gulfstream and Pompano Park.

Defying forecasts, the newly exfoliated face of Greater Fort Lauderdale—pockmarked with plywood-covered windows and blue "heck of a job" FEMA roofs after no fewer than seven hurricanes touched or boldly swept through the area in 2004 and 2005—is fresh and wrinkle free after a blissfully hurricane-free 2006. Monikers like Charlie, Frances, Ivan, Jeanne, Katrina, Rita, and the most devastating, Wilma, won't make it onto favorite-names lists here for quite a while, but I survived Hurricane ___ T-shirts are still in stock at some beach shops.

EXPLORING FORT LAUDERDALE & BROWARD COUNTY

The Fort Lauderdale metro area is laid out in a basic grid system, and only myriad canals and waterways interrupt the mostly straight-line path of streets and roads. Nomenclature is important here. Streets, roads, courts, and drives run east–west. Avenues, terraces, and ways run north–south. Boulevards can (and do) run any which way. For visitors, Las Olas Boulevard is one of the most important east–west thoroughfares from the beach to downtown, whereas Route A1A—referred to as Atlantic Boulevard, Ocean Boulevard, and Fort Lauderdale Beach along some stretches—runs along the north–south oceanfront. These names can confuse visitors, since there are separate streets called Atlantic and Ocean in Hollywood and Pompano Beach. Boulevards, composed of either pavement or water, give Fort Lauderdale its distinct "Venice of America" character. Honeycombed with more than 260 mi of navigable waterways, the city is home port for about 44,000 privately owned boats. An easy, pleasant way to tour the canals is via Fort Lauderdale's water-taxi system, made up of motor launches carrying up to 70 passengers, providing transportation and quick, narrated tours. Larger, multiple-deck touring vessels and motorboat rentals for self-guided tours are other options. The Intracoastal Waterway, paralleling Route A1A, is the nautical equivalent of an interstate highway. It runs north–south between downtown Fort Lauderdale and the beach and provides easy access to neighboring beach communities. Keep in mind that Broward and adjacent Miami-Dade and Palm Beach counties regularly rank in Florida's top five for pedestrian deaths.

ABOUT THE RESTAURANTS

Greater Fort Lauderdale offers some of the finest, most varied dining of any U.S. city its size. From among nearly 4,000 wining and dining establishments in Broward, choose from basic Americana or cuisines of Asia, Europe, or Central and South America and enjoy more than just food in an atmosphere with a subtropical twist.

ABOUT THE HOTELS

Although not as posh as Palm Beach or as Deco-trendy as Miami Beach, Fort Lauderdale has a growing roster of more than respectable lodging choices, from beachfront luxury suites to intimate bed-and-breakfasts to chain hotels along the Intracoastal Waterway. If you want to be *on* the beach, be sure to ask specifically when booking your room, since many hotels advertise "waterfront" accommodations that are actually on inland waterways.

WHAT IT COSTS	¢	$	$$	$$$	$$$$
RESTAURANTS	under $10	$10–$15	$15–$20	$20–$30	over $30
HOTELS	under $80	$80–$100	$100–$140	$140–$220	over $220

Restaurant prices are per person for a main course at dinner. Hotel prices are for a standard double room, excluding 6% sales tax (more in some counties) and 1%–4% tourist tax.

GREAT ITINERARIES

Since many Broward County attractions are close, it's realistic to pack a lot into a day—if you have wheels. Catch the history, museums, and shops and bistros in Fort Lauderdale's downtown and along Las Olas Boulevard. Then if you feel like hitting the beach, head east to the intersection of Las Olas and A1A and you're there. Neighboring communities like Lauderdale-by-the-Sea and Pompano Beach (to the north) or Dania Beach and Hollywood (to the south) have attractions of their own, and you may not even be aware when you've crossed municipal lines. As a result, you'll be able to cover most of the high points in 3 days, and with 7 to 10 days, you can experience virtually all of Broward's mainstream charms.

Numbers in the text correspond to numbers in the margin and on the Broward County and Fort Lauderdale maps.

3 DAYS

With a bigger concentration of hotels, restaurants, and attractions than its suburbs, ☷ **Fort Lauderdale ❶–❸ ▶** makes a logical base of operations for any visit. On your first day, see the downtown, especially Las Olas Boulevard between Southeast 3rd and Southeast 15th avenues. After lunch at a sidewalk café, head for the nearby Arts and Science District and the downtown **Riverwalk ❻**; enjoy it at a leisurely pace in half a day or less. On your second day, spend some time at the **Fort Lauderdale Beachfront ⓫**, shopping or having a cooling libation at an oceanfront lounge if heat drives you off the sand. Tour the waterways on the third day, either on a rented boat

from one of the marinas along Route A1A, or via a sightseeing vessel or water taxi. Reachable by water taxi are attractions such as Gallery at Beach Place, Broward Center for the Performing Arts, Galleria Mall, Las Olas Boulevard shops, Las Olas Riverfront, and the **Museum of Art ❸** and **Museum of Discovery and Science/Blockbuster IMAX Theater ❼**; restaurants such as 15th Street Fisheries, Grill Room at Riverside Hotel, Shula's on the Beach, and dozens of others; and hotels such as the Hyatt Regency Pier Sixty-Six, and Radisson Bahia Mar.

5 DAYS

With additional time, see more of the beach and the arts district and still work in some outdoor sports—and you'll be able to rearrange your plans depending on weather. On the first day, visit the Arts and Science District and the downtown **Riverwalk ❻ ▶**. Set aside the next day for an offshore adventure, perhaps a deep-sea fishing charter, a reef-diving trip, or some parasailing along the beach. Landlubbers might go for hiking at Markham Park or at Tradewinds Park (home of **Butterfly World ⓮**). On Day 3, shop, dine, and relax along the **Fort Lauderdale Beachfront ⓫**, and at the end of the day, sneak a peek at the Hillsboro Light, at **Lighthouse Point ⓴**. Day 4 can be spent at the **Hugh Taylor Birch State Recreation Area ⓬**. Enjoy your fifth day in ☷**Hollywood ⓴**.

TIMING

Tourists visit all year long, arriving in winter or summer, depending on budget, interests, hobbies, and the climate where they live. The winter season, roughly Thanksgiving through March, attracts the biggest crowds and regular "snowbirds"—seasonal residents showing up when snow starts up north. Concert, art, and entertainment seasons are at their height then, packing restaurants and roadways. In summer, waits at even the top restaurants are likely to be shorter, although some venues curtail hours. Summer can be rainy—although weather patterns have been less predictable in recent years—with showers arriving about midafternoon and typically soon gone. Heat and humidity do not quickly subside, and summer moves into fall at a slow, sticky pace. Recent years, notably 2004–2005, have brought hurricanes to Greater Fort Lauderdale in August and September, and hurricane activity offshore has extended beyond the traditional end of hurricane season in November. For golfers, almost any time is great for play, though waits for tee times are longer on weekends year-round. Remember that sun can burn all year long, even in cloudy weather and especially at midday. If you jump in the water to cool off when the sun is strongest, rays reflecting off the water can substantially increase your chance of burning. Plan beach time for early morning and late afternoon, with sightseeing, shopping, or a siesta in between.

> **CAUTION**
>
> Avoid unguarded waters, and be aware that Florida has yet to implement uniform color codes. In Fort Lauderdale, double red flags mean water is closed to the public, often because of lightning or sharks; a lone red flag means strong currents; purple signals dangerous marine life such as men-of-war; green means calm conditions. In Hollywood, orange signals rip currents with easterly onshore winds; blue means dangerous marine life such as jellyfish; red means hazardous; green means good conditions

FORT LAUDERDALE

Like many southeast Florida neighbors, Fort Lauderdale has been revitalizing for several years. In a state where gaudy tourist zones often stand aloof from workaday downtowns, Fort Lauderdale exhibits consistency at both ends of the 2-mi Las Olas corridor. The sparkling look results from efforts to upgrade both beachfront and downtown. Matching the downtown's innovative arts district, cafés, and boutiques is an equally inventive beach area, with hotels, cafés, and shops facing an undeveloped shoreline, and new resort-style hotels replacing faded icons of yesteryear. Despite wariness of pretentious overdevelopment, city leaders have allowed a striking number of glittering high-rises. Some nostalgia buffs fret over the diminishing vision of sailboats bobbing in waters near downtown, now that a boxy high-rise has erased one of the area's oldest marinas. Sharp demographic changes are also altering the faces of Greater Fort Lauderdale communities, increasingly cosmopolitan with more minorities, including Hispanics and people of Caribbean descent, as well as gays and lesbians. In Fort Lauderdale, especially, a younger populace is growing, whereas longtime residents are dying off or heading north, to a point where one former city commissioner likens the change to that of the city's historic New River—moving with the tide and sometimes appearing at a standstill. "The river of our population is at still point, old and new in equipoise, one pushing against the other."

DOWNTOWN

The jewel of downtown along New River is the Arts and Entertainment District, with Broadway shows, ballet, and much more at the riverfront Broward Center for the Performing Arts. Clustered within a five-minute walk are the Museum of Discovery and Science, the expanding Fort Lauderdale Historical Museum, and the Museum of Art (MOA/FL), home to blockbuster touring exhibits like Princess Diana's wedding dress and "Tutankhamun and the Golden Age of the Pharaohs." (Ancient Egyptians surely rest easy knowing that the county has added wireless broadband network or Wi-Fi hot spots downtown, providing free Internet access to anyone using suitably equipped laptops, etc.) Restaurants, sidewalk cafés, bars, and blues, folk, jazz, reggae, and rock clubs flourish. Las Olas Riverfront, a multistory entertainment, dining, and retail complex along several waterfront blocks once owned by pioneers William and Mary Brickell, has been a retail disappointment to developers, and is evolving with more luxury housing. Tying this district together is the Riverwalk, extending 2 mi along the New River's north and south banks. Tropical gardens with benches and interpretive displays fringe the walk on the north, boat landings on the south. Along Riverwalk's north side near the New River tunnel is the pioneer Stranahan House, and Las Olas shopping and dining begins a block east. Tropical landscaping and trees separate traffic lanes in some blocks, setting off fine shops, restaurants, and popular nightspots. From here, depending on traffic, it's 10 to 15 minutes by car or about a half hour by water bus/taxi back to the beach.

A GOOD TOUR

Start on Southeast 6th Avenue at Las Olas Boulevard, where you'll find **Stranahan House ❶** ▶, holding strong against an onslaught of controversial development. Between Southeast 6th and 15th avenues, Las Olas has Spanish colonial buildings with fashion boutiques, jewelry shops, and art galleries. Driving east, you'll cross into the Isles, among Fort Lauderdale's most prestigious neighborhoods, where homes line waterways with seawalls embellished by yachts. Return west on Las Olas to Andrews Avenue, turn right, park in one of the municipal garages, and walk around downtown. First stop is the **Museum of Art ❸**. Walk one block north to the **Broward County Main Library ❹** to see works from Broward County's Public Art and Design Program. Go west on Southeast 2nd Street to Southwest 2nd Avenue, turn left, and stop at the **Old Fort Lauderdale Village & Museum ❺**, surveying the city's beginnings. Just to the south is the palm-lined **Riverwalk ❻**, a good place for strolling.

Head north toward the Arts and Science District's outdoor Esplanade, whose exhibits include a hands-on display of the science and history of navigation, the **Museum of Discovery and Science/Blockbuster IMAX Theater ❼**; adjacent to the museum is the Broward Center for the Performing Arts. Finally, to glimpse one of the city's oldest neighborhoods, go west along Las Olas Boulevard to Southwest 7th Avenue and the entrance to **Sailboat Bend ❽**. Return to the start of the tour by traveling east along Las Olas Boulevard.

TIMING   Depending on how long you like to linger in museums and how many hours you want to spend in the shops on Las Olas Boulevard, you can devote anywhere from half a day to an entire day to this tour.

WHAT TO SEE

❾ **African-American Research Library and Cultural Center.** A two-story, $14 million gem, a few miles west of downtown, this resource provides locals and researchers from around the world with more than 75,000 books, documents, and artifacts centering on experiences of people of African descent. The family of the late Emmy Award winner Esther Rolle—Florida Evans on television's *Good Times*—has donated much of her memorabilia, from beaded gowns to letters, photos, and awards for display. Rolle, of Bahamian descent, died in 1998, and grew up with 17 siblings in Pompano Beach. There's a gift shop and a small café, and parking is free. ✉ *2650 Sistrunk Blvd.* ☎ *954/625–2800* ⊕ *www. broward.org/library/aarlcc.htm* ⊠ *Free* ☽ *Mon.–Thurs. 10–9, Fri. and Sat. 10–6, Sun. 1–5.*

❹ **Broward County Main Library.** One of more than 30 libraries in the Broward County system, this eight-story building of Florida limestone with a terraced glass facade that stood up remarkably well to Hurricane Wilma was designed by Marcel Breuer to complement the environment. Works are displayed here from Broward's Public Art and Design Program, including paintings, sculpture, photographs, and weavings by nationally renowned and Florida artists. A technology center has personal computers for public use and assistant/adaptive devices for patrons with disabilities. A 300-seat theater hosts productions from theater to poetry readings. ✉ *100 S. Andrews Ave.* ☎ *954/357–7444, 954/357–7457 for self-guided Art in Public Places walking tour brochure* ⊕ *www.broward.org/library* ⊠ *Free* ☽ *Mon.–Thurs. 9–9, Fri. and Sat. 9–5, Sun. noon–5:30.*

NEED A
BREAK?   Don't miss **Charcuterie Too** (✉ *100 S. Andrews Ave.* ☎ *954/463–9578*), a cozy cafeteria on Broward County Main Library's second floor. Breakfast treats include muffins, scones, and coffee cakes, and a lunch menu with quiche, soups, salads, and entrées. Open weekdays from 8 to 2:30, it caters to library bookworms and downtown worker bees.

❷ **Fort Lauderdale Antique Car Museum.** Retired floral company owner Arthur O. Stone set up a foundation to preserve these eye-poppers. Nostalgia includes nearly two dozen Packards from 1900 to the 1940s, along with a gallery saluting Franklin Delano Roosevelt. Within a quick commute of both Port Everglades and the airport, this museum has everything from spark plugs and gearshift knobs to Texaco Oil signage. ⊠*1527 S.W. 1st Ave.* ☎*954/779–7300* ⊕*www.antiquecar-museum.org* ☜*$8* ⊙*Weekdays 10–4.*

❸ **Museum of Art.** In an Edward Larrabee Barnes–designed building
★ that's considered an architectural masterpiece, this newly renovated
museum, which started in a storefront and now makes a habit of hosting world-class touring exhibits, has an impressive permanent collection of 20th-century European and American art, including works by
Picasso, Calder, Dalí, Mapplethorpe, Warhol, and Stella, as well as
works by celebrated Ashcan School artist William Glackens. ⊠*1 E.
Las Olas Blvd.* ☎*954/763–6464* ⊕*www.moafl.org* ☜*$7 and up,
depending on exhibit* ⊙*Daily 11–7, Thurs. open until 9; closed Tues.
mid-Dec.–Jan.*

Museum of Discovery and Science/Blockbuster IMAX Theater. Open 365
days barring weather-related events, the aim here is to show children—*and* adults—the wonders of science in an entertaining fashion.
The courtyard's 52-foot-tall Great Gravity Clock lets arrivals know a
cool experience awaits. Inside, exhibits include Kidscience, encourag-
ing youngsters to explore the world; and Gizmo City, a look at how
gadgets work. Florida Ecoscapes has a living coral reef as well as live
bees, bats, frogs, turtles, and alligators. An IMAX theater, part of the
complex, shows films (some 3-D) on a five-story-high screen. ⊠*401
S.W. 2nd St.* ☎*954/467–6637 museum, 954/463–4629 IMAX* ⊕*www.
mods.org* ☜*Museum $14, includes one IMAX show* ⊙*Mon.–Sat. 10–
5, Sun. noon–6.*

❺ **Old Fort Lauderdale Village & Museum.** Surveying city history from the
Seminole era to more recent times, the museum has expanded into sev-
eral adjacent historic buildings, including the King-Cromartie House,
the Historical Society's Hoch Heritage Center, and the New River Inn.
The research facility archives original manuscripts, maps, and more
than 250,000 photos. Walking tours of the historic district depart the
New River Inn at noon on Saturday, with the $10 fee including admis-
sion and tours of the inn and King-Cromartie House. ⊠*231 S.W. 2nd
Ave.* ☎*954/463–4431* ⊕*www.oldfortlauderdale.org* ☜*$7* ⊙*Tues.–
Sat. 10–5, weekends noon–5.*

Riverwalk. Fantastic views and entertainment prevail on this lovely,
paved promenade on the New River's north bank. On the first Sunday of every month a jazz brunch attracts visitors. The walk has been
extended 2 mi on both sides of the beautiful urban stream, connecting
the facilities of the Arts and Science District.

❽ **Sailboat Bend.** Between Las Olas and the river lies a neighborhood with
much of the character of Key West's Old Town and Miami's Coconut
Grove, except there are no shops or services here. Across the river lies
another tree-lined neighborhood called Tarpon River, alluding to the
river looping off New River from the southeast quadrant and running
to the southwest section, returning to New River near Sailboat Bend.

❶ **Stranahan House.** The oldest residence in the city, increasingly dwarfed
☛ by high-rise development, was once home for businessman Frank Stra-

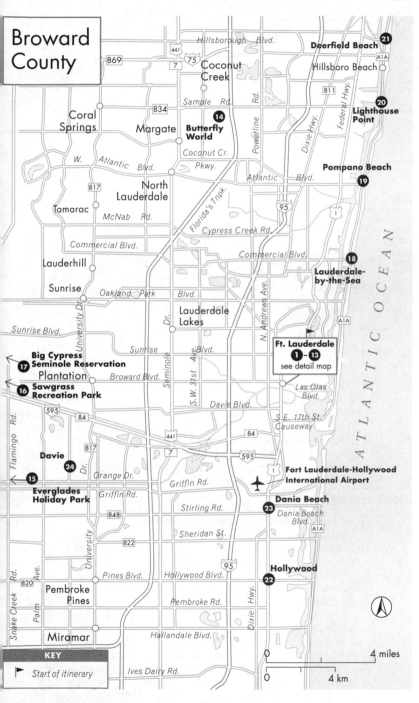

African-American Research Library and Cultural Center **9**

Bonnet House **13**

Broward County Main Library **4**

Fort Lauderdale Antique Car Museum **2**

Fort Lauderdale Beachfront **11**

Hugh Taylor Birch State Recreation Area **12**

International Swimming Hall of Fame Museum and Aquatic Complex **10**

Museum of Art ...**3**

Museum of Discovery and Science/ Blockbuster IMAX Theater **7**

Old Fort Lauderdale Village & Museum **5**

Riverwalk **6**

Sailboat Bend ...**8**

Stranahan House **1**

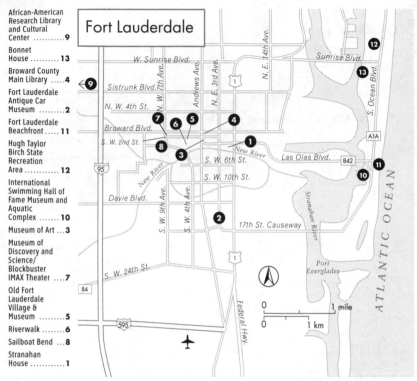

nahan, who arrived in 1892. With his wife, Ivy, the city's first school-teacher, he befriended Seminole Indians, traded with them, and taught them "new ways." In 1901 he built a store and later made it his home. Now it's a museum, with many original furnishings, and tours on the hour. ⊠ *335 S.E. 6th Ave., at Las Olas Blvd.* ☎ *954/524–4736* ⊕ *www.stranahanhouse.org* ⊠ *$10* ⊙ *Wed.–Sat. 10–3, Sun. 1–3.*

ALONG THE BEACH

Fort Lauderdale's increasingly stylish beachfront offers easy access not only to a wide band of beige sand but also to restaurants and shops. For 2 mi heading north, beginning at the Bahia Mar yacht basin along Route A1A, you'll have clear ocean views, typically across rows of colorful beach umbrellas, to ships passing in and out of nearby Port Everglades. If you're on the beach, gaze back on an exceptionally grace-ful promenade. Broad walkways line both sides of the beach roadway, and traffic has been trimmed to two gently curving northbound lanes, where in-line skaters skim past slow-moving cars. On the beach side, a low masonry wall doubles as an extended bench, separating sand from the promenade. At night the wall is accented with pretty ribbons of fiber-optic color, often on the blink despite an ongoing search for a permanent fix. The beach is most crowded between Las Olas and

Sunrise boulevards. North of the redesigned beachfront is another 2 mi of open and natural coastal landscape. Much of the way parallels Hugh Taylor Birch State Recreation Area, a preserved patch of primeval Florida, largely recovered from hurricane-force winds toppling trees and denuding landscape in 2005.

A GOOD TOUR

Go east on Southeast 17th Street across the newly improved (higher and wider) bridge over the Intracoastal Waterway and bear left onto Seabreeze Boulevard (Route A1A). You'll pass through a neighborhood of older homes set in lush vegetation before emerging at the south end of Fort Lauderdale's beachfront strip. On your left is the Radisson Bahia Mar Beach Resort, where novelist John McDonald's fictional hero, Travis McGee, is honored with a plaque at marina slip F-18. It's here that McGee docked his also-fictional houseboat, the *Busted Flush*. Three blocks north, visit the **International Swimming Hall of Fame Museum and Aquatic Complex ❿** ▶. As you approach Las Olas Boulevard, you'll see the lyrical styling that has given a distinctly European flavor to the **Fort Lauderdale Beachfront ⓫**. Plan to break for lunch and perhaps some shopping at Beach Place, the entertainment, retail, and dining complex just north of Las Olas. Turn left off Route A1A at Sunrise Boulevard, then right into **Hugh Taylor Birch State Recreation Area ⓬**, where outdoor activities can be enjoyed amid vivid flora and fauna. Cross Sunrise Boulevard and visit the **Bonnet House ⓭** to marvel at both the whimsical home and surrounding subtropical acreage.

NEED A BREAK?

Catch an orange-bottomed, yellow-topped **Sun Trolley**—running every 15 minutes, either free or for less than $1, depending on routes—and catch a break. Sun Trolley's *Convention Connection,* at 50¢ per person, runs round-trip from Cordova Road's Harbor Shops near Port Everglades to past the Convention Center, over the 17th Street Causeway, and north along A1A to Beach Place. Wave at trolley drivers—yes, they will stop—for pickups anywhere along the route. (☎954/761–3543 ⊕*www.suntrolley.com*)

TIMING

The beach is all about recreation and leisure. To enjoy it as it's meant to be, allow at least a day to loll about. For shade there's a stand of resilient trees at the southern portion near the Yankee Clipper hotel.

WHAT TO SEE

⓭ **Bonnet House.** A 35-acre oasis in the heart of the beach area, this subtropical estate survived a big hit from Hurricane Wilma, and stands as a tribute to the history of Old South Florida. The charming home was the winter residence of the late Frederic and Evelyn Bartlett, artists whose personal touches and small surprises are evident throughout. Whether you're interested in architecture, artwork, or the natural environment, this is a special place. Be on the lookout for playful monkeys swinging from trees, a source of amusement at even some of the most solemn weddings on the grounds. Hours can vary, so call first. ⊠*900 N. Birch Rd.* ☎*954/563–5393* ⊕*www.bonnethouse.org* ✍*$15 for house tours, $9 for grounds only* ⊙ *Wed.–Fri. 10–3, weekends noon–4.*

⓫ Fort Lauderdale Beachfront. A wave theme unifies the setting—from the low, white, wave-shaped wall between the beach and beachfront promenade to the widened and bricked inner promenade in front of shops, restaurants, and hotels. Alone among Florida's major beachfront communities, Fort Lauderdale's beach remains gloriously open and uncluttered. More than ever, the boulevard is worth promenading.

⓬ Hugh Taylor Birch State Recreation Area. Amid the tropical greenery of this 180-acre park, stroll along a nature trail, visit the Birch House Museum, picnic, play volleyball, or paddle a rented canoe. Since parking is limited on A1A, park here and take a walkway underpass to the beach (between 9 and 5). ⊠ *3109 E. Sunrise Blvd.* ☎ *954/564–4521* ⊕ *www.abfla.com/parks* ⊡ *$4 per vehicle with up to 8 people, $1 per pedestrian* ⊘ *Daily 8–sunset; ranger-guided nature walks Fri. at 10:30.*

❿ International Swimming Hall of Fame Museum and Aquatic Complex. This monument to underwater accomplishments took a swipe from Hurricane Wilma, but lived to tell the tale. It has two 10-lane, 50-meter pools that are open daily to the public, when not hosting international competitions. The exhibition building has photos, medals, and other souvenirs from major swimming events worldwide, as well as a theater that shows vintage films such as Esther Williams in *Million Dollar Mermaid.* ⊠ *1 Hall of Fame Dr., 1 block south of Las Olas at A1A* ☎ *954/462–6536 museum, 954/828–4580 pool* ⊕ *www.ishof.org* ⊡ *Museum $5, $10 per family; pool $5* ⊘ *Museum and pro shop mid-Jan.–late Dec., weekdays 9–7, weekends 9–5; pool mid-Jan.–late Dec., weekdays 8–4, weekends 9–5.*

WHERE TO EAT

AMERICAN

$$$–$$$$ ✕ **Shula's on the Beach.** For anyone getting positively misty-eyed at mere
Fodor'sChoice mention of Don Shula's Miami Dolphin 17–0 Perfect Season of '72, the
★ good news for steak—and sports—fans is that the staff here also turns out culinary winners. Certified Angus beef is cut thick and grilled over a superhot fire for quick charring. Try Steak Mary Anne, named for Shula's wife, consisting of two sliced fillets in a savory sauce. Seafood is excellent, too, as is the apple cobbler à la mode. Patio tables provide views of sand and ocean, and inside seating provides access to sports memorabilia and large-screen TVs. Complimentary valet parking is a nice alternative to pricey beach-area parking. ⊠ *Sheraton Yankee Trader, 321 N. Fort Lauderdale Beach Blvd.* ☎ *954/355–4000* ⊟ *AE, D, DC, MC, V.*

$$–$$$ ✕ **Casablanca Cafe.** You'll get a fabulous ocean view and a good meal to
Fodor'sChoice boot at this historic two-story Moroccan-style villa, built in the 1920s
★ by local architect Francis Abreu. The menu is an American potpourri with both tropical and Asian influence (try the mussels in Thai curry sauce) along with North African specialties like lamb shank and couscous. There's a bar downstairs, and a deck for outside dining. Service

Cruising for a Taxi

Shout "Taxi! Taxi" in Fort Lauderdale, and look for your ship to come in.

Actually, you'll be catching a water bus or water taxi, depending on your point of view, since the original fleet of water taxis has been replaced by water buses carrying up to 70 passengers. Either way, they're floating "cabs" that you can "hail" along the Intracoastal Waterway and New River.

For sightseeing, the water-taxi-cum-bus can pick you up at any of several docking spots along the intracoastal or New River, and you can stop off at attractions like the Performing Arts Center, the Museum of Discovery & Science, Stranahan House, or the Gallery at Beach Place. For lunch, sail away to restaurants on Las Olas Boulevard or Las Olas Riverfront. As the sun disappears, water taxis are a superb way to head out for dinner or bar-hop, letting your pilot play the sober role of designated driver.

The water-transport venture was started by Bob Bekoff, a longtime Broward resident and outspoken tourism promoter, who decided to combine the need for transportation with one of the area's most captivating features: miles of waterways that make Fort Lauderdale the Venice of America.

Some seasons ago, Water Taxi and Broward County Mass Transit partnered to create Water Bus, with larger ecofriendly electric ferries, phasing out the original motley fleet. Since then, Bekoff and county power brokers have parted company, with the water bus fleet now operating on a private basis. You can still ride all you want with a day pass from 10:30 AM to 12:30 AM for $11. Family all-day passes for two adults and up to four youths are $35, and after 7 PM passes are $8. Annual passes are $150. A dozen or so scheduled stops include the Bahia Mar, the Gallery at Beach Place, Galleria Mall, Seville Street, Pier 66, the Convention Center, and the historic Downtowner Saloon. The South Beach shuttle, a socko day-trip to the Art Deco District of Miami Beach ($19 Tuesday only), leaves Fort Lauderdale at 8:45 AM and Hollywood at 10 AM, returning to Hollywood at 5:45 PM and to Fort Lauderdale at 7 PM. For family reunions and such, group tours like the Sunset Cruise, Great River Safari, and Mansions and Marinas are on tap. To get around town by Water Bus, call 954/467–6677 about 20 minutes ahead of when you want to be picked up, or check out the schedule at ⊕ *www. watertaxi.com.* —Lynne Helm

is friendly and attentive. ⊠*A1A and Alhambra St.* ☎*954/764–3500* ▤*AE, D, MC, V.*

$$–$$$ ✕**Tropical Acres.** The Studiale family's sprawling icon restaurant has served up sizzling steaks from a fireplace grill since 1949—a millennium by South Florida standards. Juicy prime rib is big here, and you'll find some of the best early-bird specials around. Choose from more than 40 entrées, including sautéed frogs' legs, rack of lamb, and boneless New York strip for two, or ask the friendly waitstaff for recommendations. A wine list of some 60 labels ranges from $17 to $65, with more than a dozen poured by the glass. ⊠*2500 Griffin Rd.* ☎*954/989–2500* ▤*AE, DC, MC, V.*

¢–$ ✕**Alligator Alley.** As a native Florida taproom and music hall big on nightly rockabilly to funk rock, Alley chefs ladle up memorable signature gumbo, and alligator ribs once featured on the Food Network. Wash down your beer with gator bites or Buffalo fingers. Vegetarians can stroke out on cheese fries or go with a garden salad. ✉*1321 E. Commercial Blvd.* ☎*954/771–2220* ⊕*www.alligatoralleyflorida.com* ▭*AE, D, MC, V.*

¢–$ ✕**Elbo Room.** You can't go wrong wallowing in the past, lifting a drink, and exercising your elbow at the Elbo, a noisy, suds-drenched hot spot since 1938. This watering hole phased out food (except for light nibbles) a long time ago, but they kept their hokey sense of humor: upstairs a sign proclaims "We Don't Serve Women Here … You Have to Bring Your Own." ✉*241 S. Fort Lauderdale Beach Blvd.* ☎*954/463–4615* ▭*AE, D, MC, V.*

> **A LITTLE ELBO ROOM**
>
> Nothing says nostalgia in Fort Lauderdale like a cold one at the Elbo Room, anchoring Las Olas and A1A. It's so revered as the last bar standing from a washed-out era that an impassioned coterie calling themselves "Sons of the Beach" wants the old joint anointed as an official historic city landmark.

¢–$ ✕**Floridian.** This Las Olas landmark with photos of Monroe, Nixon, and local notables past and present dishes up some of the best breakfasts around, with oversize omelets that come with biscuits, toast, or English muffins, plus a choice of grits or tomatoes. With sausage or bacon on the side, the feast will make you forget about eating again soon. Count on savory sandwiches and hot platters for lunch, a tempting three-cheese meat-loaf plate for dinner, and friendly efficient service all day. It's open 24 hours—even during hurricanes, as long as the power holds out. Feeling flush? Try the Fat Cat Breakfast (New York strip steak, hash browns or grits, toast, and a worthy champagne) or the Not-So-Fat-Cat, with the same grub and a lesser-quality vintage. ✉*1410 E. Las Olas Blvd.* ☎*954/463–4041* ▭*No credit cards.*

¢–$ ✕**Lester's Diner.** Home to big cups of strong coffee and a demanding skip-your-dinner dessert display, Lester's has stood as a 24-hour haven for the hungry along State Road 84 since 1967. Truckers head in here on their way to Port Everglades, as do workers from the area's thriving marine industry, suits from downtown toting briefcases, and tourists packing beach bags. Patronage gets even more eclectic in the wee hours. A stick-to-the-ribs menu includes breakfast anytime, homemade soups, sandwiches (try the Monte Cristo), salads, and dinners of generous portions. If your cholesterol count can take the hit, try the country-fried steak for less than $10 or the chicken-liver omelet (under $6). Smokers like the patio dining, under a red awning on the east side, but don't count on a view beyond what's in the parking lot. Two other Lester's—in western Broward's Margate and Sunrise—close at midnight on weeknights. ✉*250 State Rd. 84* ☎*954/525–5641* ✉*4701 Coconut Creek Pkwy., Margate* ☎*954/979–4722* ✉*1399 N.W. 136th Ave., Sunrise* ☎*954/838–7473* ▭*D, MC, V.*

¢–$ ✕**Southport Raw Bar.** You can't go wrong at this unpretentious spot where the motto, seen on bumper stickers for miles around, proclaims EAT FISH, LIVE LONGER, EAT OYSTERS, LOVE LONGER, EAT CLAMS, LAST LONGER. Raw or steamed clams, raw oysters, and combos, along with peel-and-eat shrimp, are market priced. Hoagies, subs, and burgers are the ticket for less than $10. Side orders range from Bimini bread to key lime pie, with conch fritters, beer-battered onion rings, and corn on the cob in between. Order wine by the bottle or glass and beer by the pitcher, bottle, or can. Eat outside overlooking a canal, or inside at booths, tables, or the bars, in front and back. Limited parking is free, and a grocery store parking lot is across the street. ✉*1536 Cordova Rd.* ☎*954/525–2526* ▤*MC, V.*

¢–$ ✕**Tom Jenkins.** Big portions of drippingly delicious barbecue are dispensed at this handy spot for eat-in or takeout, south of the New River Tunnel and north of the 17th Street Causeway. If you think you don't have time to stop, roll down your window and inhale on the way by, and you're likely to change your mind. Furnishings include an old Singer sewing machine and a wringer washer, and diners partake at picnic-style tables. Side dishes with dinners for less than $10 include baked beans, collards, and mighty tasty macaroni and cheese. For lunch, Tom's pork, beef, and catfish sandwiches are a surefire shortcut to satisfaction. Leave room for sweet-potato pie or apple cobbler. ✉*1236 S. Federal Hwy.* ☎*954/522–5046* ▤*MC, V* ☉*Closed Sun. and Mon.*

¢ ✕**Ernie's Barbecue.** Walls once plastered with philosophical quotes from a former owner have been scrubbed clean at Ernie's, where the menu proclaims CONCH IS KING, BARBECUE IS A WAY OF LIFE, AND THE BAR IS OPEN LATE. Fortunately for patrons, barbecue platters of pork or beef and conch chowder are as lip-smacking as ever. Bimini bread, thick-sliced for sandwiches, is also sold by the loaf to go, along with racks of ribs and conch chowder by the quart. Seafood, salads, and burgers also pass muster here, and there's a children's menu. Eat downstairs, or, if you don't mind the buzz of Federal Highway traffic, take the stairs to second-floor open-air patio tables near a couple of pool tables. ✉*1843 S. Federal Hwy.* ☎*954/523–8636* ▤*AE, D, MC, V.*

¢ ✕**Georgia Pig.** When heading out to the area's western reaches, this postage-stamp-size outpost can add down-home zing to your day. Breakfast, including sausage gravy and biscuits, is served from 6 to 11 AM. But the big attraction is barbecue beef, pork, or chicken, on platters or in sandwiches. Alternatives include a spicy Brunswick stew and fried jumbo shrimp. There's apple, peach, cherry, and pecan pie, and a small-fry menu. Order takeout (25¢ extra) or eat at the counter, at wooden tables, or at a half dozen or so booths. ✉*1285 S.W. 40th Ave. (State Rd. 7–U.S. 441, just south of Davie Blvd.)* ☎*954/587–4420* ▤*No credit cards.*

¢ ✕**Skyline Chili.** Cincinnati's famed brand has made a name for itself among locals fond of debating the merits of coneys or three-, four-, or five-way chili, each making for a meal well under $10. A chili sandwich is made just like the Skyliner coneys but without the wiener. Eat inside or at a couple of glider-style tables out front. ⊠*2590 N. Federal Hwy.* ☎*954/566–1541* ⊟*D, MC, V.*

¢   ✕**Stork's Café.** In trendy Wilton Manors (a municipality in remarkable renaissance), Stork's Café stands out as a gay-friendly, straight-friendly, just plain friendly place to plot sightseeing strategy (or catch up on news from local papers). Sit indoors or outside under red umbrellaed tables. Custom Barbie Cakes (real dolls, edible ball gowns) are hot here. Divine baked goods range from croissants, tortes, cakes, and pies to Monster Cookies ($1.60 each), including gingersnap and snickerdoodle. The Pilgrim (turkey) or Hello Kitty (tuna) sandwiches go with salads or soups like Vegan Split Pea. Offshoot Stork's Las Olas is becoming the tail wagging the dog, with a similar menu, friendly staff, a great view of the Himmarshee Canal, and even gondola service promoted by owner Jim Stork. ⊠*2505 N.E. 15th Ave., Wilton Manors* ☎*954/567–3220* ⊠*1109 E. Las Olas Blvd., Fort Lauderdale* ☎*954/522–4670* ⊟*AE, D, MC, V.*

ASIAN

$$$ ✕**Mai-Kai.** You'll think you've tripped off to the South Seas rather than South Florida upon arrival at this torchlighted landmark, anchoring Federal Highway since this particular stretch was a two-laner. Yes, it's touristy, yet somehow magnetic. Specialties include Peking duck, exotic tropical drinks, and a pulsating Polynesian dance review with a flaming finale. Valet parking is available. ⊠*3599 N. Federal Hwy.* ☎*954/563–3272* ⊟*AE, D, MC, V.*

$–$$ ✕**Siam Cuisine.** Some locals claim this eatery, tucked away in a small storefront in Wilton Manors, serves the best Thai in the Fort Lauderdale area, and they may be right. The family-run kitchen turns out appealing, flavorful delights from $10 to around $25 for a whole fish, usually red snapper. Curry dishes with chicken or shrimp are favorites, along with steamed dumplings and roast duck. ⊠*2010 Wilton Dr.* ☎*954/564–3411* ⊟*AE, MC, V.*

CONTEMPORARY

★ $$$–$$$$ ✕**By Word of Mouth.** Unassuming but outstanding, this restaurant never advertises, hence its name. But word has sufficed for nearly a quarter century because locals consistently put this dining spot along the railroad tracks just off Oakland Park Boulevard at the top of "reader's choice" polls. There's no menu. Patrons are shown the day's specials to make their choice. Count on a solid lineup of fish, fowl, beef, pasta, and vegetarian entrées. A salad is served with each dinner entrée, and there's a retail bakery for takeout. ⊠*3200 N.E. 12th Ave.* ☎*954/564–3663* ⊟*AE, D, MC, V.*

$$–$$$$
FodorsChoice
★   ✕**Mark's Las Olas.** Mark Militello, a star among chefs in South Florida and beyond, commands this offshoot of north Miami's long-gone Mark's Place. Militello's loyal following remains enchanted with his Florida-style preparation, blending flavors from Caribbean, Mediterranean, and southwestern traditions. Entrées change daily, but patrons can count on signatures like crab-crusted black grouper. Appearing on occasion is Italian baby chicken grilled under a brick. And some patrons rave about the wild mushroom polenta with roasted shallots and por-

cini oil. Dishes are occasionally paired off with combos of callaloo (West Indian spinach), chayote, ginger, jícama, and plantain. Be aware that substitutions are frowned upon, although servers are warmly hospitable. The wine list is mostly California, with many offered by the glass. ⊠ *1032 E. Las Olas Blvd.* ☎*954/463–1000* ⚑*Reservations essential* ⊟*AE, D, DC, MC, V* ☉*No lunch weekends.*

$–$$$ ✗**Creolina's.** Since it moved to Himmarshee Village from a more modest storefront birthplace not far away, it's still not uncommon to see chef-owner Mark Sulzinski cooking up Cajun-creole delights for city power brokers, including the longtime mayor. Try Gumbo Ya Ya, crawfish rémoulade, or alligator piquant (tender strips crisp-fried) for starters. Also consider the catfish with pecans or plain old red beans and rice. Warm bread pudding with bourbon sauce is a worthy finale. Prices are up with the fancier digs, but remain a good deal. ⊠ *209 S.W. 2nd St.* ☎*954/524–2003* ⊟*AE, D, DC, MC, V.*

CONTINENTAL

$$$–$$$$ ✗**Grill Room on Las Olas.** After soaking in the area's trendiest spots, you may be ready for tried-and-true fare at the historic Riverside Hotel. Grill Room decor reflects the grand style of a colonial British officers' club, and the menu has grilled steaks, or chateaubriand and rack of lamb, both for two. Many dishes are prepared tableside, including a grand Caesar salad. Choose from an extensive wine list. The adjacent Golden Lyon Bar has the feeling of a pub somewhere in India. ⊠ *Riverside Hotel, 620 E. Las Olas Blvd.* ☎*954/467–2555* ⊟*AE, MC, V.*

FRENCH

$$–$$$ ✗**Le Café de Paris.** Serving the classics for lunch and dinner under ownership of Swiss-born (and jeans-clad) Louis Flematti (former owner of the now-closed French Quarter), Le Café seats upward of 150 but keeps everything cozy with comfort foods like crusty bread, onion soup, and crepes, as well as duck, lamb, and beef dishes. There's also a mouthwatering pastry wagon. ⊠ *715 Las Olas Blvd.* ☎*954/467–2900* ⊟*AE, D, DC, MC, V* ☉*Closed Sun. No lunch Sat.*

GERMAN

$–$$$ ✗**Old Heidelberg Restaurant & Deli.** Likened to a Bavarian mirage plucked from the Alps and plopped along State Road 84 near airport and seaport, the Old Heidelberg's beer stein–cowbell–cuckoo clock decor accents the veal loaf, sauerkraut, and other specialties, from apple strudel to Black Forest cake. Owners Heidi Bruggermann and Dieter Doerrenberg hit South Florida to thaw out in 1984. After opening a wholesale sausage factory, they bought a onetime seafood eatery in 1991 for transformation into a German-style haven for breaded pork cutlets, fried burgers, panfried flounder, and stuffed roast pork with bread dumplings. For better or wurst in takeout, the Old Heidelberg Deli next door (open Tuesday through Saturday 9–6) stocks kielbasa, liver dumplings, Bitburger beer, breads, and nearly a dozen mustards. ⊠ *900 State Rd. 84* ☎*954/463–6747 or 954/463–3880* ⊟*AE, D, MC, V* ☉*Closed Mon. No lunch Sat.*

IRISH

¢–$ ✕**Biddy Early's.** This dark, somewhat Gothic lunch and dinner watering hole stands out on a somewhat forlorn stretch of Andrews Avenue, beckoning with assorted East Clare sandwiches, West Clare burgers (if you haven't guessed, the owner hails from Ireland's County Clare), and Irish fare, including beef Guinness stew ($7.50) and bangers and mash ($9.95). Bread-and-butter pudding, quite comforting, is $3.50, and there's more comfort in a Monday through Friday happy hour, from 4 to 7. ✉*3419 N. Andrews Ave., Oakland Park* ☎*954/567–1990* ⊟*AE, D, MC, V.*

¢–$ ✕**Maguire's Hill 16.** With the requisite lineup of libations and sandwiches, this comfortable and long-popular Irish pub has a very tasty potato soup, shepherd's pie, bangers and mash, corned beef and cabbage, and Irish stew. ✉*535 N. Andrews Ave.* ☎*954/764–4453* ⊟*AE, D, DC, MC, V.*

ITALIAN

$$–$$$$ ✕**Primavera.** Tucked inside an ordinary shopping plaza is this extraordinary find. Apart from fresh pasta with rich sauces and risotto entrées, choose from creative fish, poultry, veal, and beef dinners. Among chef-owner Giacomo Dresseno's favorites is a double-cut veal chop. If you're in town for a while, check out the chef's lunch ($45) or dinner ($50) cooking classes. Ticket holders appreciate the pretheater menu. ✉*830 E. Oakland Park Blvd.* ☎*954/564–6363* ⊕*www.trueitalian. com* ⊟*AE, D, DC, MC, V* ☉*Closed Mon. No lunch.*

$–$$$$ ✕**Casa D'Angelo.** Owner-chef Angelo Elia has re-created his former Café D'Angelo into a gem of a Tuscan-style white-tablecloth restaurant, tucked in the Sunrise Square shopping center. Casa D'Angelo's oak oven turns out marvelous seafood and beef dishes. The pappardelle with porcini mushrooms takes pasta to pleasant heights. Another favorite is the calamari-and-scungilli salad with garlic and lemon. Be sure to ask about the oven-roasted fish of the day. ✉*1201 N. Federal Hwy.* ☎*954/564–1234* ⊟*AE, D, DC, MC, V* ☉*No lunch.*

¢–$$$ ✕**Louie, Louie Bistro.** Some of the best pasta dishes on Las Olas are served at this friendly, tavern-style establishment. Try thin-crust pizzas, sandwiches, or complete dinners. Fresh-fish specials are offered daily. Grouper, when available, is excellent. Wash it all down with any of eight on-tap beers, or select from the wine list. ✉*1404 E. Las Olas Blvd.* ☎*954/524–5200* ⊟*AE, MC, V.*

MEDITERRANEAN

$$$–$$$$ ✕**Trina.** You might well fill up on eyefuls of Fort Lauderdale beach during breakfast or lunch at this spot on the ground level of the Atlantic hotel, but come dinnertime your focus will shift to the crackling activity in the open kitchen and among the well-heeled crowd. The warm wood tones and minimalist fixtures mirror the Atlantic's restrained elegance, but there's a touch of New York fanfare on the menu, in part because Don Pintabona, former executive chef of Tribeca Grill, is running the kitchen. Seafood dominates, with some interesting results: scallops and sweetbreads mingle in one entrée, whereas Florida favorites like snapper and sole get Mediterranean touches. One successful leitmotif

is flatbread: a tasty herbed variation with pancetta at breakfast, or with such toppings as rock shrimp or spicy Moroccan lamb at dinner. Another good bet is a Trina Trio, which might include an appetizer of tuna carpaccio, salmon tartare, and snapper ceviche, or a crème brûlée sampler including coffee, chocolate and, most worthy, coconut. Reservations are recommended. ⊠ *601 N. Fort Lauderdale Beach Blvd.* ☎ *954/567–8020* ☐ *AE, D, DC, MC, V.*

MEXICAN

$$–$$$$ ✕ **Eduardo de San Angel.** Authentic chilies, spices, and herbs enhance classic seafood, meat, and poultry dishes here. Specialties are beef tenderloin tips sautéed with portobello mushrooms and onions in a chipotle chili sauce, and terrific peppercorn-crusted Keys yellowtail. ⊠ *2822 E. Commercial Blvd.* ☎ *954/772–4731* ☐ *AE, D, DC, MC, V* ☽ *Closed Sun.*

¢–$ ✕ **Cafe del Rio.** This Tex-Mex eatery next to an Outback Steakhouse kicks things off with tortilla chips and fresh, zingy salsa. Appetizers, soups, salads, combo plates, and fajitas make it easy for two to dine heartily for around $20. Enchiladas have chunk meat, and tamales are stuffed with ground beef. Complimentary serve-yourself soft ice cream provides a cordial finale. Huge, high-ceiling dining rooms are less than cozy, and those in the know often head outside to the landscaped patio, where tables are on gliders under canopies. ⊠ *1821 S.E. 10th Ave.* ☎ *954/463–5490* ☐ *AE, MC, V.*

¢ ✕ **Tortilleria Mexicana.** With a machine about the size of an old home-style Mixmaster cranking out 1,000 pounds of cornmeal tortillas daily (double that on weekends) as you watch, the tiny hole-in-the-wall Tortilleria Mexicana, near Oakland Park City Hall, has authentic fare that attracts Broward's growing Mexican population and plenty of gringos to boot. Try such staples as tacos, tamales, chicken with rice and beans, enchiladas, quesadillas, and flautas with chicken, salad, and hot pepper slices. Owner Eliseo Martinez opened a second tortilla haven, in Pompano Beach, this one with a bakery and butcher shop. ⊠ *4115 N. Dixie Hwy., Oakland Park* ☎ *954/563–2503* ⊠ *1614 E. Sample Rd., Pompano Beach* ☎ *954/943–0057* ☐ *MC, V.*

SEAFOOD

★ $$$–$$$$ ✕ **Blue Moon Fish Company.** Most tables have stellar views of the Intracoastal Waterway, but Blue Moon's true magic comes from the kitchen, where chefs Baron Skorish and Bryce Statham create moon-and-stars-worthy seafood dishes. Start with the raw bar, a sushi sampler, or pan-seared fresh-shucked oysters. Salads include a hydroponic bibb with hearts of palm, and entrée favorites include shiitake mushroom–crusted halibut or peppercorn-crusted big-eye tuna with sticky rice. Carnivores might opt for prosciutto-stuffed veal tenderloin. To wrap up an evening, indulge in the Tartelette of Bananas Foster Blue Moon. Book early, even in the off-season, for the popular Sunday champagne brunches ($29.95). ⊠ *4405 W. Tradewinds Ave.* ☎ *954/267–9888* ☐ *AE, D, DC, MC, V.*

$$–$$$$ ✕ **15th Street Fisheries.** A prime Intracoastal Waterway view is a big part of allure at this two-story seafood landmark alternately drawing praise and pans from patrons, some complaining about lackluster service during financial seminars—also known as plate lickers—booked upstairs. Now back under original ownership, it's time to give the old 15th another try for cold seafood salad and a spicy conch chowder. Homemade breads, a specialty, come with a cheese-and-chive spread. Grilled mahimahi and alligator are among the more than 50 entrées. Key lime pie has an Oreo crust. Valet parking costs $2 at dinner, but it's free at lunch. ⊠ *1900 S.E. 15th St.* ☎ *954/763–2777* ⊟ *AE, D, DC, MC, V.*

$$–$$$$ ✕ **Rustic Inn Crabhouse.** The late Wayne McDonald started with a cozy one-room roadhouse in 1955, when this stretch was a remote service road just west of the little airport. Now run by Wayne's family, the still-rustic place brags that it is still crackin' after 50 years. The ample menu luring entertainer Arthur Godfrey, and more recently Johnny Depp and Dan Marino, stars a garlic crab dinner, with patrons banging crabs open with mallets on tables covered with newspapers, and peel-and-eat shrimp, served either with garlic and butter or spiced and steamed. Lunch includes a fine fish sandwich with fries and a soda for less than $5. Finish off with pie or cheesecake. ⊠ *4331 Ravenswood Rd.* ☎ *954/584–1637* ⊟ *AE, D, DC, MC, V.*

SOUTHWESTERN

$$–$$$ ✕ **Canyon Southwest Cafe.** Adventurous southwestern fusion fare helps you escape the ordinary at this small, stylish enclave (next to the Gateway movie theater at Sunrise Boulevard and Federal Highway) run for the past dozen years by owner and executive chef Chris Wilber. Take, for example, the ostrich skewers, smoked salmon tostada, or coriander-crusted tuna with sticky rice. Chipotle, wasabi, jalapeño, mango, and red chilies accent fresh seafood and wild game. Start off with Canyon's famous prickly-pear margaritas or choose from a well-rounded wine list or beer selection. ⊠ *1818 E. Sunrise Blvd.* ☎ *954/765–1950* ⊟ *AE, MC, V* ⊗ *No lunch.*

WHERE TO STAY

DOWNTOWN & BEACH CAUSEWAYS

$$$–$$$$ 🔝 **Hyatt Regency Pier Sixty-Six.** Unfortunately, the trademark of this
Fodor's Choice high-rise resort on the Intracoastal Waterway—the rooftop Pier Top
★ Lounge—has closed, and is now a banquet-meeting space for private soirees. Still, the 17-story tower dominates a lovely 22-acre spread that includes Spa 66, a full-service European-style spa. Each room has a balcony with views of the 142-slip marina, pool, ocean, or intracoastal. Some guests prefer the ground-level lanai rooms. Lush landscaping and convenience to the beach, shopping, and restaurants add to overall allure. Hail the water bus at the resort's dock for access to downtown or the beach. ⊠ *2301 S.E. 17th St. Causeway, 33316* ☎ *954/525–6666 or 800/327–3796* 🖷 *954/728–3551* ⊕ *www.pier66.com* ↪ *380 rooms, 8 suites* ♿ *In-hotel: 6 restaurants, bars, tennis courts, pools, gym, spa, water sports* ⊟ *AE, D, DC, MC, V.*

$$$–$$$$ 🔝 **Riverside Hotel.** On Las Olas Boulevard, just steps from boutiques, restaurants, and art galleries, Fort Lauderdale's oldest hotel was built in 1936, and within the past decade added luster with a $25 million

renovation and expansion. Penthouse suites in the newer 12-story executive tower have balconies with sweeping views of Las Olas, New River, and downtown's skyline. Historic photos grace hallways, and rooms are outfitted with antique oak furnishings and framed French prints. Enjoy afternoon tea in the newly spruced-up lobby, and dine at Indigo, where American favorites include steaks and seafood; the elegant Grill Room; or the new Brio Mediterranean Wine Bar & Restaurant. The hotel's new Wine Room for private dining has a 1,500-bottle cellar. ⊠ *620 E. Las Olas Blvd., 33301* ☎ *954/467–0671 or 800/325–3280* 🖷 *954/462–2148* ⊕ *www.riversidehotel.com* 📞 *206 rooms, 11 suites* 🖒 *In-hotel: 3 restaurants, bars, pool, no-smoking rooms* 🖃 *AE, DC, MC, V.*

$$$–$$$$ 🖫 **Schubert Resort.** This restored 1950s Art-Deco property is an all-male, clothing-optional, luxury boutique resort tucked into tropical landscaping within the Victoria Park neighborhood. Suites are oversize and have marble-and-granite baths; most have either a king-size bed or two double-size beds. Continental breakfast is served overlooking the pool and Jacuzzi. The property feels secluded yet is a short walk from shopping and restaurants. ⊠ *855 N.E. 20th Ave., 33304* ☎ *954/763–7434 or 866/338–7666* 🖷 *954/763–4132* ⊕ *www. schubertresort.com* 📞 *30 rooms* 🖒 *In-room: kitchen (some). In-hotel: pool* 🖃 *AE, DC, MC, V* 🍴 *CP.*

ALONG THE BEACH

★ $$$$ 🖫 **The Atlantic.** Functional but elegant is the principle behind this luxury condo hotel, a Starwood newcomer steps from Las Olas Boulevard and the Atlantic beyond. In lieu of having you hunch over the front desk, staffers check you in one-on-one while you sip an icy libation in the lobby, a marriage of marble and wood, beiges and browns. This British-colonial scheme is picked up in the spacious, unfussy rooms, which have simple, dark-wood furniture, ample marble kitchen areas, and creamy fabrics and plush carpeting that smartly frame rather than compete with the main event—balcony views of the city or ocean (go for the latter). Little in-room touches include Bose Wave CD/radio systems and a host of Internet connection options; among on-premises amenities are a European-style spa offering treatments and massages within the spa or in-room, and the tony Trina lounge and restaurant, or Spuma, for light fare with a pool view. ⊠ *601 N. Fort Lauderdale Beach Blvd., 33304* ☎ *954/567–8020* 🖷 *954/567–8040* ⊕ *www.luxurycollection. com/atlantic* 📞 *61 rooms, 58 suites, 5 penthouses* 🖒 *In-room: kitchen, refrigerator (some), dial-up, Wi-Fi. In-hotel: 2 restaurants, bar, pool, gym, spa, concierge, laundry service, parking (fee), no-smoking rooms* 🖃 *AE, D, DC, MC, V.*

★ $$–$$$$ 🖫 **Best Western Pelican Beach.** On the beach and under new ownership, 🌣 this already lovely property has been transformed into an entirely new nonsmoking resort with a restaurant and lounge, an old-fashioned ice-cream parlor, and Fort Lauderdale's only Lazy River pool, allowing guests to float around a moatlike "river." For small fry, there's also a Funky Fish program. Of 156 rooms and one-bedroom suites in the new building, 117 are oceanfront. With the new building all aglow, the original Sun Tower is getting a makeover. ⊠ *2000 N. Atlantic Blvd.,*

33305 ☎954/568–9431 or 800/525–6232 📠954/565–2622 ⊕*www. pelicanbeach.com* ➪*180 rooms* &*In-hotel: restaurant, bar, pools* ⊟*AE, DC, MC, V.*

★ $$–$$$ ⊡**Lago Mar Resort & Club.** The sprawling Lago Mar has been owned by the Banks family since the early 1950s and, after renovations, its sparkle remains. Most accommodations are suites, ideal for families. Suite highlights include a king-size bed, pull-out sofa, and full kitchen. Trellises and bougainvillea plantings edge the swimming lagoon, and you have direct access to a large private beach in an exclusive neighborhood. ✉*1700 S. Ocean La., 33316* ☎*954/523–6511 or 800/524– 6627* 📠*954/524–6627* ⊕*www.lagomar.com* ➪*52 rooms, 160 suites* &*In-hotel: 3 restaurants, tennis court, pools* ⊟*AE, DC, MC, V.*

$$–$$$ ⊡**The Pillars Hotel at New River Sound.** Described as Fort Lauderdale's "small secret" by locals in the know, this property is one block in from the beach on the intracoastal. Its design recalls the colorful architecture of 18th-century British-colonial Caribbean plantations. Most rooms have views of the waterway or pool, with French doors opening to individual patios or balconies. Rooms have rattan-and-mahogany headboards, antique reproduction desks and nightstands, and lush draperies. Suites include wet bars with refrigerators and microwaves. ✉*111 N. Birch Rd., 33304* ☎*954/467–9639* 📠*954/763–2845* ⊕*www.pillarshotel.com* ➪*19 rooms, 4 suites* &*In-room: refrigerator (some), VCR, ethernet. In-hotel: room service, pool, no elevator, concierge, no kids under 12, no-smoking rooms* ⊟*AE, D, DC, MC, V.*

$–$$$ ⊡**The Worthington.** This gay-friendly hotel exclusively for men has a 24/7 hot tub for up to 12, great landscaping with rare palms and fountains, and tastefully decorated rooms. It's close to the beach, and continental breakfast is served poolside with fresh-ground Starbucks coffee. ✉*543 N. Birch Rd., 33306* ☎*954/563–6819 or 800/445–7036* 📠*954/563–6819* ➪*12 rooms, 5 junior suites* &*In-hotel: pool, no elevator* ⊟*AE, D, DC, MC, V* ⊠*CP.*

¢–$$ ⊡**The Alcazar Resort.** For decades known as the family-owned, family-oriented Sea Chateau, this property has been acquired by owners of the Worthington (next door), who transformed the two-story enclave about a block from the beach into a gay-friendly place. A 24-hour clothing-optional heated swimming pool and shaded courtyard are within the now-fenced property, and corner efficiencies with kitchenettes are now called junior suites. Each room received a makeover, with carpeting removed to expose trendy terrazzo. Most beds are king-size, although some rooms have pairs of queen-size beds. ✉*555 N. Birch Rd., 33304* ☎*954/567–2525* 📠*954/563–6819* ➪*15 rooms, 5 suites* &*In-room: kitchen (some), refrigerator. In-hotel: pool, no elevator* ⊟*AE, D, DC, MC, V.*

CAMPING

GREATER FORT LAUDERDALE

⚠**Kozy Kampers RV Park.** This quiet and friendly park with a restaurant next door serves as a central point for exploring Greater Fort Lauderdale or relaxing with horseshoes and shuffleboard. Leashed dogs up to 35 pounds are allowed, as are big rigs and slide-outs. There are 13 pull-through sites. Stay the night (around $40), or pay a weekly ($250) or monthly ($725) rate in winter; rates are lower in summer. Reservations are a near necessity in winter. ⚲ *Laundry facilities, full hookups, dump station, public telephone* ⤳*104 sites* ✉*3631 W. Commercial Blvd.* ☎*954/731–8570* 🖷*954/731–3140* ⊕*www.kozykampers.com* ▭*MC, V* ☾ *Year-round.*

🏕**Paradise Island RV Resort.** You'll find this long-established park, formerly known as Buglewood, well situated for heading east to the beach or west to attractions. Relax in a large heated pool surrounded by umbrellaed tables or chaise longues. Or, head for the resource room with modem hookup, big-screen TV, and a library. Planned group activities including cookouts and ice-cream socials unfold November through April. There's fax service at the front office, and daily trash pickup at no extra cost. Rates for two November through April range from $42 daily to $228 weekly and $772 monthly, with lower rates available in summer. Reservations are advised, especially in winter. ⚲*Full hookups, electricity* ⤳*232 paved, level sites* ✉*2121 N.W. 29th Ct.* ☎*800/487–7395* 🖷*954/485–5701* ⊕*www.paradiserv.com* ▭*AE, D, MC, V* ☾ *Year-round.*

🏕**Twin Lakes Travel Park.** Unwind here in the clubhouse or in the adjacent heated pool overlooking the lake. The park offers free daily trash removal. Rates for two people range from $50 daily to $265 weekly to $835 monthly. Reservations are advised, especially in winter. ⚲*Full hookups, electricity* ⤳*379 paved, level sites* ✉*3055 Burris Rd.* ☎*954/587–0101* 🖷*954/587–9512* ▭*AE, D, MC, V* ☾ *Year-round.*

🏕**Yacht Haven Park and Marina.** Along the New River, this park is pet-friendly for animals up to 30 pounds, but call to make sure yours is acceptable. Scheduled activities in the recreation hall during the winter season include cookouts and ice-cream socials. A heated pool and spa and fishing are available on the property. Depending on location, daily rates for two range from $45 to $65 in winter, $29 to $50 in summer, with $15 for each extra person, plus tax. Weekly and monthly rates are also available. Reservations are recommended. ⚲*Laundry facilities, dump station, showers* ⤳*250 paved RV sites, some waterfront* ✉*2323 State Rd. 84* ☎*954/583–2322 or 800/581–2322* ⊕*www. yachthavenpark.com* ▭*AE, D, MC, V* ☾ *Year-round.*

NIGHTLIFE & THE ARTS

For the most complete weekly listing of events, read the "Showtime!" entertainment section and events calendar in the Friday *South Florida Sun-Sentinel.* "Weekend," in the Friday Broward edition of *The Herald,* also lists area happenings. The weekly *City Link* is principally an entertainment and dining paper with an "underground" look. *New Times* is a free alternative weekly circulating a Broward–Palm Beach County edition. *East Sider* is another free weekly entertainment guide. A 24-hour **Arts & Entertainment Hotline** (☎*800/249–2787*) has updates

An African-American Gem

West of downtown Fort Lauderdale's Arts & Sciences District, in the heart of the African-American community along Sistrunk Boulevard, lies a gem once discounted as a grand idea unlikely to get off the ground.

Yet in late 2002, Fort Lauderdale's African-American Research Library and Cultural Center soared into reality as a sparkling two-story, $14 million repository of history and heritage of African, African-American, and Caribbean cultures, with historic books, papers, and art, much of it pertaining to the African Diaspora. There's a 300-seat auditorium, a story-time area, and 5,000 square feet of gallery space for exhibits. African symbols appear as part of the decor.

For Samuel F. Morrison, now-retired Broward County Library director, the center is the culmination of his dream, a vision to create a worthy showcase reflecting African-American heritage. Broward County anted up $5 million for the 60,000-square-foot center, and Morrison raised the rest.

Of the nation's three major African-American public research facilities, Fort Lauderdale's is the only one that includes a Caribbean focus. Among the Fort Lauderdale center's offerings is the Alex Haley Collection, including eight unfinished manuscripts. Other components range from Fisk University research of slave narratives to books on Jamaica and the Caribbean.

You'll also find the Kitty Oliver Oral Histories Collection on Broward and Okeechobee and the Niara Sudarkasa Collection of papers, artwork, and other materials of the former president of Lincoln University.

And there's the collection of Dorothy Porter Wesley—in some eyes the greatest of the black bibliophiles. Her collection includes about 500 inscribed and autographed books—some date to 1836—with personal narratives, histories, fiction, and reference works. Wesley's daughter, Constance Porter Uzelac, refers to "Mama's stuff," noting that "it's not just books and manuscripts ... what's interesting is the associations she had with the authors and the people." Wesley was known for going to the homes of the recently deceased to make sure nothing of value was thrown away. Her daughter recalls, "She'd get to the house before the body was cold," heading straight to attics and basements to retrieve bits and scraps of history.

Passionate about his dream, Morrison also remains adamant about the library's widespread appeal, noting that "these pieces provide glimpses [into] the hearts and minds of people who have made a difference in the lives of not only people of color and African culture, but people of many colors and cultures."

—Lynne Helm

on attractions and events. Get tickets at individual box offices and through **Ticketmaster** (☎954/523–3309); there's a service charge.

THE ARTS
Broward Center for the Performing Arts (✉201 S.W. 5th Ave. ☎954/462–0222) is the waterfront centerpiece of Fort Lauderdale's arts district. More than 500 events unfold annually at the 2,700-seat architectural masterpiece, including Broadway-style musicals, plays, dance,

symphony, opera, rock, film, lectures, comedy, and children's theater. **Cinema Paradiso** (⊠*503 S.E. 6th St.* ☎*954/525–3456* ⊕*www.cinemaparadiso.org*) operates as an art-house movie theater from a former church (south of New River). The space doubles as headquarters for FLIFF, the Fort Lauderdale International Film Festival. Screenings stretch from extreme sports to anime.

★ **Chef Jean-Pierre Cooking School** (⊠*1436 N. Federal Hwy.* ☎*954/563–2700* ⊕*www.chefjp.com* ☕*$50 per class, $285 per series* ◷*10 AM–7 PM*) carries on from the fondly remembered Left Bank by New River Tunnel, with Chef Jean-Pierre Brehier now presiding at his school and cookware shop. Teaching basics from boiling water onward to more than 7,000 avid learners since 1997, the enthusiastic Gallic transplant has appeared on PBS, NBC's *Today,* and CNN's *Larry King Live.* Chef J-P's fun cooking facility also sells nifty gadgets, pots, pastas, oils, and other irresistibles. **Laffing Matterz.** Across from the Museum of Art in an old five-and-dime that still has its circa 1936 McCrory logo carved on the facade, all-American guffaws at this live musical comedy review target politics, sports, and celebrity machinations. Entrance, $45 to $49.50 for reserved tiered circular seating surrounding the stage, covers show, house salad, and entrées like beef tenderloin and teriyaki salmon. Appetizers, desserts, and libations such as the Laffing Martini ($8.95) are extra. Laffing Matterz thinks nothing of spoofing itself along with patrons, promising that although it's fine to dress casual, you might get stares if you show up in bathing suits. Geared toward grown-ups, there's no kid's menu. ⊠*219 S. Andrews Ave.* ☎*954/763–5236* ▭*AE, D, MC, V.*

NIGHTLIFE

BARS & LOUNGES

Hurricane Bar & Grill (⊠*The Gallery at Beach Pl.* ☎*954/522–0050*) has stepped into space once occupied by both the defunct Crazy Louie's and Cafe Iguana. **Howl at the Moon Saloon/Sloppy Joe's** (⊠*The Gallery at Beach Place, 17 S. Fort Lauderdale Beach Blvd.* ☎*954/522–5054*) has dueling piano players and sing-alongs Wednesday through Sunday. Sloppy Joe's, a take-off on the iconic Key West bar, is open nightly. **Maguire's Hill 16** (⊠*535 N. Andrews Ave.* ☎*954/764–4453*) highlights excellent bands in classic Irish-pub surroundings. **O'Hara's Jazz Café** (⊠*722 E. Las Olas Blvd.* ☎*954/524–1764*) has live jazz, blues, R&B, and funk nightly. Its big crowd spills onto this prettiest of downtown streets. **Coyote Ugly** (⊠*220 S.W. 2nd St.* ☎*954/764–8459*) continues a tradition of being one of the hottest spots in Broward. **Tarpon Bend** (⊠*200 S.W. 2nd St.* ☎*954/523–3233*) specialties—food, fishing gear, and bands covering current hits—draw a casual, beer-drinking crowd. **Tavern 213** (⊠*213 S.W. 2nd St.* ☎*954/463–6213*) is a small, no-frills club where cover bands do classic rock nightly. **Voodoo Lounge** (⊠*111 S.W. 2nd Ave.* ☎*954/522–0733*) plays the latest in club music inside the nightclub and hip-hop on the elegant outside deck. There's a new VIP room, and the scene here doesn't start until almost midnight.

SPORTS & THE OUTDOORS

BASEBALL
From mid-February to the end of March the **Baltimore Orioles** (⊠*Fort Lauderdale Stadium, 1301 N.W. 55th St.* ☎*954/776–1921*) are in spring training, although squabbles over team-sought stadium upgrades could put a damper on plans for expanded, cushier seating.

BIKING
Among the most popular routes are Route A1A and Bayview Drive, especially in early morning before traffic builds, and a 7-mi bike path that parallels State Road 84 and the New River and leads to Markham Park, which has mountain-bike trails. ■TIP→Alligator alert: Do not dangle your legs from seawalls.

FISHING
If you're interested in a saltwater charter, check out the **Radisson Bahia Mar Beach Resort** (⊠*801 Seabreeze Blvd.* ☎*954/627–6357 or 954/764– 2233*). Both sportfishing and drift-fishing bookings can be arranged.

GOLF
Ten miles from Fort Lauderdale in Dade County are two newly revamped 18-hole courses reflecting $100,000 of landscaping per hole, and a new driving range at **Turnberry Isle Resort & Club** (⊠*19999 W. Country Club Dr., Aventura* ☎*305/933–6929 or 800/327–7028* ⊕*www.turnberryisle.com*); green fee: $95/$150.

SCUBA DIVING & SNORKELING
Lauderdale Diver (⊠*1334 S.E. 17th St. Causeway* ☎*954/467–2822 or 800/654–2073*), which is PADI-affiliated, arranges dive charters throughout the county. Dive trips typically last four hours. Nonpackage reef trips are open to divers for $45; scuba gear is extra. **Pro Dive** (⊠*515 Seabreeze Blvd.* ☎*954/761–3413 or 800/776–3483*), a PADI five-star facility, is the area's oldest diving operation and offers packages with several hotels, including the Radisson Bahia Mar Beach Resort, from which its 60-foot boat departs. Snorkelers can go out for $29 on a two-hour snorkeling trip, which includes equipment. Scuba divers pay $45 using their own gear or $84 with full scuba rentals included.

TENNIS
With 21 courts, 18 of them lighted clay courts, the **Jimmy Evert Tennis Center at Holiday Park** is Fort Lauderdale's largest public tennis facility. Chris Evert learned the sport here under the watchful eye of her father, Jimmy, who retired after 37 years as the center's tennis pro. ⊠*701 N.E. 12th Ave.* ☎*954/828–5378* ⊞*$5 per person per hr* ☉ *Weekdays 8 AM–9 PM, weekends 8–6.*

SHOPPING

MALLS
Just north of Las Olas Boulevard on Route A1A is **The Gallery at Beach Place** (⊠*17 S. Fort Lauderdale Beach Blvd. [A1A]*). Browse shops, have lunch or dinner at restaurants ranging from casual Caribbean

to elegant American, or carouse at assorted nightspots—all open late. Lower-level eateries tend toward the more upscale, whereas upper-level prices are lower (go figure), with superior ocean views. ■TIP→Beach **Place has covered parking, but you can pinch pennies by using a nearby municipal lot.** Just west of the Intracoastal Waterway, the split-level **Galleria Mall** (⊠*2414 E. Sunrise Blvd.*) entices with Neiman Marcus, Dillard's, Macy's, and Saks Fifth Avenue, plus 150 specialty shops for anything from cookware to sportswear and fine jewelry. Chow down at Capital Grille, Blue Martini, Red Star Tavern, Mama Sbarro's, and Seasons 52, or head for the food court, a decided cut above at this upscale mall open 10 to 9 Monday through Saturday, and noon to 5:30 Sunday. The **Swap Shop** (⊠*3291 W. Sunrise Blvd.*) is the South's largest flea market, with 2,000 vendors open daily. While exploring this indoor–outdoor entertainment and shopping complex, hop on the carousel or stick around for Swap Shop drive-in movies.

SHOPPING DISTRICTS

When you're downtown, check out **Las Olas Riverfront** (⊠*1 block west of Andrews Ave. along New River*), a shopping, dining, and entertainment complex. **Vogue Italia** (⊠*Las Olas Riverfront, 300 S.W. 1st Ave.* ☎*954/527–4568*) is packed with trendy fashions by D&G, Ferré, Versus, Moschino, and Iceberg, among others, at wholesale prices. If only for a stroll and some window-shopping, don't miss **Las Olas Boulevard** (⊠*1 block off New River east of Andrews Ave.*). The city's best boutiques plus top restaurants and art galleries line a beautifully landscaped street. **American Soul** (⊠*810 E. Las Olas Blvd.* ☎*954/462–4224*) carries menswear from suits to socks, along with leather goods and gifts. **Casa Chameleon** (⊠*619 E. Las Olas Blvd.* ☎*954/763–2543*) has antiques, linens, and beautiful things to top your table. The sweet smell of waffle cones lures pedestrians to **Kilwin's of Las Olas** (⊠*809 E. Las Olas Blvd.* ☎*954/523–8338*), an old-fashioned confectionery that also sells hand-paddled fudge and scoops of homemade ice cream. **Lauderdale Lifestyle–A Lilly Pulitzer Signature Store** (⊠*819 E. Las Olas Blvd.* ☎*954/524–5459*) specializes in the South Florida dress requisite—clothing and accessories in Lilly Pulitzer's signature tropical colors and prints. **Seldom Seen** (⊠*817 E. Las Olas Blvd.* ☎*954/764–5590*) is a gallery of contemporary and folk art, including furniture, jewelry, ceramics, sculpture, and blown glass. **Zola Keller** (⊠*818 E. Las Olas Blvd.* ☎*954/462–3222*) sells special-occasion dresses—cocktail dresses, evening gowns, vow-renewal apparel, and, yes, Miss Florida and Mrs. America pageant dresses.

SIDE TRIPS

THE WESTERN SUBURBS & BEYOND

West of Fort Lauderdale is ever-growing suburbia, with most of Broward's golf courses, attractions, and malls. As you head west, the terrain takes on more characteristics of the Everglades, and you'll occasionally see alligators sunning on canal banks. Cute as they appear, please refrain from feeding them. Keep Fido out of sight, too, as gators find small dogs especially tasty. Iguanas, often discarded as pets (and com-

CLOSE UP

Swap till You Drop

Just when you thought it was safe to head for the beach, the siren's song of dirt-cheap bargain-hunting draws you to a sprawling, sun-baked patch of land where you can park free, get in free, browse free, and load up with eclectic acquisitions or plain swell stuff for darned-near free.

From Barbie dolls to slightly used miter saws, here's a place where you can feel free to squeeze nickels until the buffalos moan. Fort Lauderdale's Swap Shop—among Florida's largest tourist draws long before the arrival of roller-coaster economics—is a 180,000-square-foot shopping-entertainment complex on 88 acres that makes it possible to find a Carly Simon *Hotcakes* album for a dime, apparel items for 10¢ each (make that a dozen for a dollar), or 30 sticks of hand-dipped mango incense for a couple of bucks. Psychic readings are negotiable, and it's $15 for 15 minutes at the Chinese Backrub Booth, near a stall where you can get tailoring done while you wait. A small midway with a merry-go-round near the pedestrian walkway over Sunrise Boulevard houses a giant video arcade and eateries. You can hang around past dusk to catch flicks from *Texas Chainsaw Massacre* to *Rocky Balboa* at the Swap Shop Drive-In, now grown to 15 screens.

Established in 1963 by Betty and Preston Henn, the Fort Lauderdale Swap Shop stems from what originally was known as the Thunderbird, one of America's then-ubiquitous drive-ins. By 1966, Henn started farming out his land as a weekend flea market. As drive-ins went bust, the Thunderbird held on, propped up by Swap Shop revenues. By 1979, Henn had put up a building as an open-air food court surrounded by vendors. In 1988 he walled it in, adding air-conditioning and a stage where local bands jammed at no charge. Next came the long-running Hanneford Family Circus, later phased out in favor of a high-end auto display. In 1990 singer Ronnie Milsap kicked off a free-concert tradition. And the rest, as they say, is drive-in-movie-aficionado history.

Henn, a handsome devil now well into the un-sunny side of 70, made news in 2005 when he got into a scuffle with a tenant, after which Broward Sheriff's Office deputies took a notion to taser-gun the Swap Shop king. Henn bounced back with an ad campaign proclaiming "Crazy ... Loco ... Insane ... Our Swap Shop prices are so low that they're tasering me." The Swap Shop pulls in more than 12 million visitors a year.

Tri-Rail runs Swap Shop shuttles on Saturday from points in Broward, Palm Beach, and Dade counties, and some hotels arrange transportation. Fort Lauderdale Swap Shop grounds are between Interstate 95 and Florida's Turnpike at 3291 E. Sunrise Blvd., 954/791–7927. —Lynne Helm

paratively harmless except for spreading salmonella when handled), are proliferating here as sunbathers. Waterbirds, fish, and other creatures populate canals and lakes throughout the western areas. No matter how dedicated developers are to building over this area, the Everglades keeps asserting itself.

As many as 80 butterfly species from South and Central America, the Philippines, Malaysia, Taiwan, and other Asian nations are typically found within **Butterfly World,** a 3-acre site inside Tradewinds Park. A screened aviary called North American Butterflies is reserved for native species. The Tropical Rain Forest Aviary is a 30-foot-high construction, with observation decks, waterfalls, ponds, and tunnels where thousands of colorful butterflies flutter. Kids bug out on the bug zoo. ✉3600 W. Sample Rd., Coconut Creek ☎954/977–4400 ⊕www.butterflyworld.com ✆$19.95 ⊙Mon.–Sat. 9–5, Sun. 11–5.

The 30-acre Everglades **Holiday Park** provides brag-worthy glimpses of the Everglades. Take an airboat tour, look at an 18th-century-style Native American village, or catch the alligator-wrestling (not to be reenacted at home). A souvenir shop, a deli, a convenience store, and a campground with RV hookups ($24.40 per night) and tent sites ($22 nightly) are all here. ✉21940 Griffin Rd. ☎954/434–8111 ⊕www.evergladesholidaypark.com ✆Free, airboat tour $21 ⊙Daily 9–5.

16 For an ever-so-thrilling Everglades experience, take an airboat ride at **Sawgrass Recreation Park.** You'll see all sorts of plants and wildlife, from birds and alligators to turtles, snakes, and fish. Besides the ride, your entrance fee covers admission to an Everglades nature exhibit, a native Seminole village, and exhibits about alligators, other reptiles, and birds of prey. A souvenir shop, food service, and an RV park with hookups are also at the park. ✉U.S. 27 north of I–595 ☎954/389–0202 ⊕www.evergladestours.com ✆$19.50 ⊙Weekdays 7–6, weekends 6–6; airboat rides daily 9–5.

A stretch from Fort Lauderdale's beaches, but worth the hour-plus drive, is the **Big Cypress Seminole Reservation** and its two very different attractions. At the **Billie Swamp Safari,** experience the majesty of the Everglades firsthand. Daily tours of the wetlands and hammocks, where wildlife abounds, yield sightings of deer, water buffalo, bison, wild hogs, hawks, eagles, alligators, and occasionally the rare Florida panther. Animal and reptile shows are entertaining. Ecoheritage tours are conducted aboard motorized swamp buggies, and airboat rides are available, too. On the property is Swamp Water Café, serving gator nuggets, frogs' legs, catfish, and Indian fry bread with honey, along with burgers and more. ✉19 mi north of I–75 Exit 49 ☎863/983–6101 or 800/949–6101 ⊕www.seminoletribe.com ✆Seminole Village reservation, free; combined ecotour, reptile or critter show, and airboat ride, $43 ⊙Daily 8–5.

Not far from the Billie Swamp Safari is the **Ah-Tha-Thi-Ki Museum,** whose name means "a place to learn, a place to remember." It is just that. The museum documents and honors the culture and tradition of the Seminole Tribe of Florida through artifacts, exhibits, and reenactments of rituals and ceremonies. The site includes a living-history Seminole village, nature trails, and a boardwalk through a cypress swamp. ✉17 mi north of I–75 Exit 49 ☎863/902–1113 ⊕www.seminoletribe.com ✆$6 ⊙Tues.–Sun. 9–5.

$$–$$$$ ☑**Coral Springs Marriott Hotel, Golf Club and Convention Center.** Adjacent to the Tournament Players Club golf course in Heron Bay, this resort's perch near the Sawgrass Expressway also makes it convenient to area attractions. Spacious, updated rooms are furnished with oak and cherrywood. There's an outdoor terrace and a game room. ⊠*11775 Heron Bay Blvd., Coral Springs 33076* ☎*954/753–5598* 🖷*954/753–2888* ⊕*www.marriott.com* ⇆*224 rooms, 7 suites* ⚲*In-room: Wi-Fi. In-hotel: restaurant, bar, golf course, pool, gym* ⊟*AE, D, MC, V.*

$$–$$$$ ⊡**Hyatt Regency Bonaventure Conference Center Hotel & Spa.** Formerly a
Fodor's Choice Wyndham, the new name asserts itself as a more upscale venue target-
★   ing conventioneers as well as visitors who value golf or the Everglades over beach proximity. Factor in the allure of a huge Elizabeth Arden's Red Door Lifestyle Spa (48,000 square feet with 30 treatment rooms) with a Pilates studio, Zen Garden, and more, and you'll understand why leisure guests also flock here. Shop & Drop packages with free transport to nearby Sawgrass Mills extends the appeal to an even wider audience. Spacious guest rooms (and public areas) have a light British-colonial-amid-an-oasis look, with plentiful modern amenities, including clock radios with iPod docks. Banyan Restaurant serves American and continental fare, and the Bamboo Spa Café dishes up tasty, nutritional fare. Golf and tennis facilities adjacent to the hotel are independent of the resort. ⊠*250 Racquet Club Rd., Westin 33326* ☎*954/616–1234* 🖷*954/384–6157* ⊕*www.bonaventure.hyatt.com* ⇆*400 rooms, 96 suites* ⚲*In-hotel: 3 restaurants, bars, golf courses, tennis courts, pools, gym, spa* ⊟*AE, D, DC, MC, V.*

SPORTS & THE OUTDOORS

FISHING

The marina at **Everglades Holiday Park** (⊠*21940 Griffin Rd.* ☎*954/434–8111*) caters to freshwater fishing. For $98, you get a five-hour rental of a 14-foot johnboat (with a 9.9-horsepower Yamaha outboard) that carries up to four. A rod and reel rent for $10 a day with a refundable $20 deposit; bait is extra. For two, a fishing guide for a half day (four hours) is $225; for a full day (eight hours), $300. A third person adds $45 for a half day, $90 for a full day. Buy a mandatory freshwater fishing license here; a seven-day nonresident license is $17. At **Sawgrass Recreation Park** (⊠*U.S. 27 and I–75* ☎*954/389–0202* ⊕*www.evergladestours.com*) you can rent boats, get fishing licenses, and buy live bait.

GOLF

Bonaventure Country Club (⊠*200 Bonaventure Blvd.* ☎*954/389–2100*) has 36 holes; green fee: west course, $29/$49; east course, $34/$56. **Colony West Country Club** (⊠*6800 N.W. 88th Ave. [Pine Island Rd.], Tamarac* ☎*954/726–8430*) offers play on 36 holes; green fee: $15.50/$95. **Heron Bay Golf Club** (⊠*11801 Heron Bay Blvd., Coral Springs* ☎*954/796–2000 or 800/511–6616*) has a public 18-hole course; green fee: $41/$150. Just west of Florida's Turnpike, the **Inverrary Country Club** (⊠*3840 Inverrary Blvd., Lauderhill* ☎*954/733–7550*) has two 18-hole championship courses and an 18-hole executive course; green fee: $69/$100. **Jacaranda Golf Club** (⊠*9200 W. Broward Blvd., Plantation* ☎*954/472–5836*) has 36 holes to play. Green fee: $29/$99.

Ice Hockey & Concerts. BankAtlantic Center (formerly the Office Depot Center and before that the National Car Rental Center) is home of Sinatra Theatre, with 3,000 to 4,000 seats, depending on what show is booked, and the National Hockey League's **Florida Panthers** (✉ *2555 N.W. 137th Way [Panther Pkwy.], Sunrise* ☎ *954/835–8326*).

SHOPPING

Surveys reveal that shopping is vacationers' number-one activity. With 26 million visitors annually, **Sawgrass Mills** (✉ *12801 W. Sunrise Blvd., at Flamingo Rd., Sunrise*), 10 mi west of downtown Fort Lauderdale, proves the point, ranking as Florida's second-biggest tourist attraction, after Disney. The ever-growing complex has a basic alligator shape, and walking it all amounts to about a 2-mi jaunt, making comfy shoes a near necessity. Count on 11,000 self-parking spaces (note your location, or you'll be working those comfy shoes), valet parking, and two information centers. More than 400 shops—many manufacturer's outlets, retail outlets, and name-brand discounters—include Abercrombie & Fitch Outlet, assorted Gaps, Chico's Outlet, Polo Ralph Lauren Factory Store, Super Target, and Ron Jon Surf Shop. Restaurants such as Cajun Grill, Cheeburger Cheeburger, the Cheesecake Factory, Rainforest Cafe, and others are joined by the inevitable Starbucks and entertainment venues Regal 23 Cinemas, GameWorks, and Wannado City, a $40 million indoor recreation enterprise that bills itself as the nation's first interactive empowerment environment for ages 4 to 11. While parents shop, kids can role-play as firefighters, reporters, doctors, chefs, archaeologists, even King Tut, the boy-king from Egypt, among hundreds of occupations. And for the upscale shopping promenade pièce de résistance head to the Mediterranean-inspired, open-air **Colonnade Outlets at Sawgrass,** catering to the well-heeled—and those who want to look that way—with a David Yurman jewelry outlet, along with Valentino, Burberry, Kate Spade, Feraud/Rosch, Fitelle, Nurielle, and Vilebrequin outlets, for tantalizing openers. There's also a Coach Factory, MaxMara Outlet, Salvatore Ferragamo Company Store, and to top it off, a Grand Lux Cafe, serving lunch, dinner, and afternoon tea, with a Paul (à la Paris) bakery. An expanded Neiman Marcus Last Call Clearance and the Off 5th Saks Fifth Avenue Outlet have relocated from Sawgrass Mills proper to the Colonnade.

NORTH ON SCENIC A1A

North of Fort Lauderdale's Birch Recreation Area, Route A1A edges away from the beach through a stretch known as the Galt Ocean Mile, and a succession of oceanside communities lines up against the sea. Traffic can line up, too, as it passes through a changing pattern of beach-blocking high-rises and modest family vacation towns and back again. Here and there a scenic lighthouse or park dots the landscape, and other attractions and recreational activities are found inland.

LAUDERDALE-BY-THE-SEA

⑱ *5 mi north of Fort Lauderdale.*

Just north of Fort Lauderdale's northern boundary, this low-rise family resort town traditionally digs in its heels at the mention of high-rises. The result is choice shoreline access that's rapidly disappearing in similar communities, and Lauderdale-by-the-Sea (L-B-T-S) takes delight in enhancing the beachgoing experience, adding such amenities as showers and bike racks. Dedicated to pioneers Marie White and her late husband, Stanley, who settled in when roads were of dirt with little traffic, a beach access portal at the intersection of El Mar Drive and Pal Avenue is one of five (including Hibiscus, Datura, Washingtonia, and Pine avenues). Enjoy driving along lawn-divided El Mar Drive, lined with garden-style motels. Getting along without a car in L-B-T-S is doable—it's only 3 mi long, with eateries and shops near hotels and the beach. Where Commercial Boulevard meets the ocean, **Anglin's Fishing Pier** (shored up by new owners after repeated storm damage) stretches 875 feet into the Atlantic. Even when closed for fishing, you can sit on nearby canopied benches to soak up pier atmosphere or grab a bite at restaurants clustered around the seafront plaza.

WHERE TO STAY & EAT

$-$$$$ ✕**Sea Watch.** For more than 25 years this nautical-themed restaurant with a prime beach location has catered to the crowds for lunch and dinner. Among the appetizers are oysters Rockefeller, gulf shrimp, clams casino, and Bahamian conch fritters. Daily entrées might include oat-crusted sautéed yellowtail snapper with roasted red bell-pepper sauce and basil, or charbroiled swordfish or dolphin fillet marinated with soy sauce, garlic, black pepper, and lemon juice. Try the crème brûlée or the strawberries Romanoff. ✉*6002 N. Ocean Blvd. (Rte. A1A), Fort Lauderdale* ☎*954/781–2200* 🖃*AE, MC, V.*

$-$$$ ✕**Aruba Beach Café.** A big beachside barn of a place—very casual, always crowded, always fun—Aruba serves big portions of Caribbean conch chowder and a Key West soup loaded with shrimp, calamari, and oysters, plus fresh tropical salads, sandwiches, and seafood. For less than $10, Aruba serves a mighty juicy burger with custom toppings. A band performs day and night, so head for the back corner with eye-popping views of the beach if you want conversation while you eat and drink. ✉*1 E. Commercial Blvd.* ☎*954/776–0001* 🖃*AE, D, DC, MC, V.*

Fodor'sChoice
★

$$-$$$$ 🎬**Best Florida Resort.** Although the name might seem a bit cocky, this fenced two-story oasis a block or so from the beach seduces with subtropical palm-fringed landscaping, creative decor, and other whimsical touches, including a supply-room sign warning of a make-believe attack alligator. Rooms showcase fresh takes on classic rattan and bamboo. Hospitable owners Bozena and Tomasz Jurczak, fluent in several languages, provide no-smoking, pet-free respite without spring-break revelry. Besides wireless Internet access, there's a barbecue grill for guest use, and one apartment unit has a private patio. ✉*4628 N. Ocean Dr.* ☎*954/772–2500* ⊕*www.wakacjefloryda.com* ⤴*12 units, including 1 and 2-bedroom units* ₾ 🖃*AE, D,MC, V.*

$$–$$$$ ⬚**Tropic Seas Resort Motel.** It's only a block off A1A, yet this two-story property has a multimillion-dollar location—directly on the beach and two blocks from municipal tennis courts. Built in the 1950s, units are plain but clean and comfortable, with tropical rattan furniture and ceiling fans. Muffins and coffee are served daily. ⊠*4616 El Mar Dr., 33308* ☎*954/772–2555 or 800/952–9581* 🖷*954/771–5711* ⊕*www. tropicseasresort.com* ☞*3 rooms, 6 efficiencies, 7 apartments* ⬧*In-hotel: pool, beachfront, no elevator* ⊟*AE, D, DC, MC, V.*

$–$$$$ ⬚**Sea Lord Hotel & Suites.** You won't need to wonder "are we there yet" since Sea Lord is spelled out loud and clear in huge letters on this attractive oceanside building, along a stretch of private beach. Enjoy a complimentary continental breakfast by the pool overlooking the ocean. Efficiencies and one- and two-bedroom units all have coffee-makers and refrigerators, and some have full kitchens. The staff prides itself on creating a warm, hospitable environment. Depending on the time of year, market conditions, and area events, there can be four-night or longer minimum stays for some rooms. ⊠*4140 El Mar Dr., 33308* ☎*954/776–1505 or 800/344–4451* 🖷*954/776–1505* ⊕*www. sealord.com* ☞*48 rooms* ⬧*In-room: kitchen (some). In-hotel: pool, beachfront, laundry facilities* ⊟*AE, D, MC, V* ⎮⚆⎮*CP.*

$$–$$$ ⬚**A Little Inn by the Sea.** Subtropical charm flourishes at this two-story inn, which caters to an international clientele—French and English are spoken here. Rooms have bamboo-and-rattan furniture and nice views from private balconies, many facing the beach. ⊠*4546 El Mar Dr., 33308* ☎*954/772–2450 or 800/492–0311* 🖷*954/938–9354* ⊕*www. alittleinn.com* ☞*10 rooms, 7 suites, 12 efficiencies* ⬧*In-hotel: pool, beachfront, bicycles, no elevator* ⊟*AE, D, DC, MC, V* ⎮⚆⎮*BP.*

¢–$$ ⬚**Blue Seas Courtyard.** Innkeeper Cristie Furth, with her husband, Marc, runs this small one- and two-story motel in a quiet resort area across from the beach. Lattice fencing, fountains, and gardens of cactus and impatiens provide privacy around the brick patio and pool. Guest quarters have a Mexican hacienda look, with hand-painted and stenciled furnishings and terra-cotta tiles. ⊠*4525 El Mar Dr., 33308* ☎*954/772–3336* 🖷*954/772–6337* ⊕*www.blueseascourtyard.com* ☞*12 rooms* ⬧*In-room: kitchen. In-hotel: pool, no elevator, laundry facilities* ⊟*MC, V.*

¢–$$ ⬚**Great Escape Hotel.** For comfortable accommodations amid palms and other tropical plants in a poolside courtyard, this could be your great—and economical—escape. Among the units are four hotel rooms, five efficiencies, and two one-bedroom apartments. ⊠*4620 N. Ocean Dr., 33308* ☎*954/772–1002* 🖷*954/772–6488* ⊕*www.greatescape-hotel.com* ☞*11 units* ⬧*In-hotel: pool, no elevator, laundry facilities* ⊟*AE, MC, V.*

★ ¢–$$ ⬚**High Noon Beach Resort.** Flanked by the Nautilus Resort to the north and the Sea Foam Resort to the south, High Noon—family owned and run—plays the central role for this resort trio on the beach, where you'll find a comfortable place to relax morning, high noon, or night. Accommodations, either poolside or oceanfront, range from rooms to efficiency apartments with kitchens, to apartments with separate bedrooms and one or two baths. Wicker furnishings and a color scheme of sea foam, sage, and beiges prevail at High Noon; Sea Foam rooms have terra-cotta tile, and High Noon and Nautilus rooms have beige tile. ⊠*4424 El Mar Dr., 33308* ☎*954/776–1121 or 800/382–1265* 🖷*954/776–1124* ⇆*40 rooms* ⚉*In-room: kitchen (some), refrigerator (some). In-hotel: pool, beachfront, no elevators* ☰*AE, D, DC, MC, V.*

¢–$$　⛬ **Villa Orleans.** With a touch of New Orleans architecture, this beach-area property rests behind an inviting pool and well-groomed grounds. Rooms are spacious. ⊠*4513 N. Ocean Dr., 33308* ☎*888/301–2363* 🖷🖷*954/491–2363* ⊕*www.villaorleans.com* ⇆*12 rooms* ⚉*In-room: ethernet. In-hotel: pool, no elevator, laundry facilities* ☰*AE, MC, V.*

¢–$　⛬ **Rainbow by the Sea Resort.** This family-oriented, owner-managed property has all no-smoking rooms. A rusty-brown carpeted sundeck equipped with loungers faces the ocean on top of the main building. Both pools are pictures in landscaping. ⊠*4553 El Mar Dr., 33308* ☎*954/772–0514* 🖷*954/772–6569* ⇆*30 rooms* ⚉*In-hotel: pools, no elevator, laundry facilities, no-smoking rooms* ☰*AE, MC, V.*

THE OUTDOORS

★ **Anglin's Fishing Pier** (☎*954/491–9403*), a longtime favorite for 24-hour fishing, has new ownership and a fresh, newly renovated appearance after sustaining repeated storm damage that has closed the pier at intervals. Its tiny restaurant—with a friendly staff and seats inside and outdoors—has survived the damage and renovation.

POMPANO BEACH

⑲　*3 mi north of Lauderdale-by-the-Sea.*

As Route A1A enters this town directly north of Lauderdale-by-the-Sea, the high-rise scene resumes. Sportfishing is big in Pompano Beach, as its name implies, but there's more to beachside attractions than the popular Fisherman's Wharf. Behind a low coral-rock wall, Alsdorf Park extends north and south of the wharf along the road and beach.

WHERE TO STAY & EAT

★ $$$–$$$$　✕ **Cafe Maxx.** New-wave epicurean dining had its South Florida start here in the early 1980s, and Cafe Maxx remains new. The menu changes nightly, showcasing tropical appeal with grilled rabbit tenderloin and citrus gnocci or jumbo stone-crab claws with honey-lime mustard sauce and black-bean and banana-pepper chili with Florida avocado. Appetizers include caviar pie and crispy sweetbreads. Desserts such as Hawaiian vintage chocolate soufflé cake stay the tropical course. Select from 300 wines by the bottle, and many by the glass. ⊠*2601 E. Atlantic Blvd.* ☎*954/782–0606* ☰*AE, D, DC, MC, V* ⊘*No lunch.*

$$–$$$　⛬ **Beachcomber Resort & Villas.** This property's beach location is central to most Broward County attractions and a mile from the Pompano Pier. Ocean views are everywhere, from the oversize guest-room balconies to dining rooms. Although there are also villas and penthouse suites atop the eight-story structure, standard rooms are spacious. The multilingual staff is attentive to guest requests. ⊠*1200 S. Ocean*

Blvd., 33062 ☎*954/941–7830 or 800/231–2423* 🖶*954/942–7680* ⊕*www.beachcomberresort.com* ⇱*143 rooms, 9 villas, 4 suites* ⚓*In-room: ethernet. In-hotel: restaurant, bar, pools, beachfront* ▤*AE, D, DC, MC, V.*

$$–$$$ 🏨**Fairfield Fairways of Palm-Aire Resort & Spa.** In its heyday (and hey, that's many a day ago), stars like Elizabeth Taylor checked in here to let loose and relax. Now a time share, this resort has studios and one-, two-, and four-bedroom apartments that are individually owned but share similar decor. Some units have whirlpool tubs and washers and dryers; kitchens range from partial to full. Housekeeping is provided weekly, and more frequently for a charge. The spa and fitness complex has a sauna, a steam room, cardiovascular machines, weight equipment, fitness classes, and body treatments. Five championship golf courses at the Palm-Aire Country Club are just a chip shot away. The Tiki Hut serves lunch and drinks. ⊠*2601 Palm-Aire Dr. N, 33069* ☎*954/972–3300* 🖶*954/968–2711* ⊕*www.efairfield.com* ⇱*298 units* ⚓*In-hotel: tennis courts, pools, gym, spa* ▤*AE, D, DC, MC, V.*

SPORTS & THE OUTDOORS

FISHING

Pompano Pier (☎954/773–1346) extends more than 1,000 feet into the Atlantic and is getting a $12 million upgrade to add style and stability. A two-story Pompano Beach Pier & Promenade will have upscale seafood and steak restaurants, tiki bar, and more, with completion planned for the city's 2008 centennial celebration. Admission is $3 to fish, $1 to sightsee; rod-and-reel rental is $5.25, plus $5 deposit and a driver's license. Anglers brag about catching barracuda, jack, and snapper here in the same sitting, along with bluefish, cobia, and, yes, pompano. For drift-fishing try *Fish City Pride* (⊠*Fish City Marina, 2621 N. Riverside Dr.* ☎*954/781–1211*). Morning, afternoon, and evening trips cost $35 and include fishing gear and bait. Arrange for a saltwater charter boat through the **Hillsboro Inlet Marina** (⊠*2629 N. Riverside Dr.* ☎*954/943–8222*). The 10-boat fleet offers half-day charters for $500, including gear for up to six people.

GOLF

Crystal Lake South Course (⊠*3800 Crystal Lake Dr.* ☎*954/943–2902*) has 36 holes; green fee: $21/$69. **Palm-Aire Country Club** (⊠*3701 Oaks Clubhouse Dr.* ☎*954/978–1737, 954/975–6244 tee line*) has five golf courses, including an executive course with four extra practice holes; green fee: $25/$45.

HORSE RACING

Isle of Capri Pompano Park Harness Track, Florida's only harness track, has world-class trotters and pacers during its October through August meet. It now pulls the punters with Vegas-style slot machines. The Top o' the Park restaurant overlooks the finish line. The track also has a poker room and afternoon and evening simulcast betting. ⊠*1800 S.W. 3rd St.* ☎*954/972–2000* 🎫*Grandstand and clubhouse free* ⊙*Racing Mon., Wed., Fri., and Sat. at 7:30 PM.*

ICE-SKATING

Skate at the **Glacier Ice and Snow Arena** during morning, afternoon, or evening sessions. ✉ *4601 N. Federal Hwy.* ☎ *954/943–1437* ✆ *Sessions $7, skate rental $3 ($3 for hockey skates)* ☉ *Mon.–Thur. 9:40 AM–4:00 PM, Fri. 9:40 PM–10 PM, 7:30–10 PM, Sat. 8–10 PM, Sun. 11:15–3:45 PM.*

SHOPPING

Bargain hunters head to the **Festival Flea Market Mall** (✉ *2900 W. Sample Rd.* ☎ *954/979–4555* ⊕ *www.festivalfleamarket.com*), where more than 800 stores, booths, and kiosks sell new brand-name merchandise at discounts. For diversion, there's also an arcade, beauty salon, farmers' market, and food court. On acreage formerly occupied by Pompano Square Mall, **Citi Centre** (✉ *2001 N. Federal Hwy., at Copans Rd.*) is an indoor/outdoor retail hub with Loew's, Macy's, JCPenney, and Sears, along with smaller enterprises, boutiques, fine dining, and casual outdoor cafés.

LIGHTHOUSE POINT

㉑ *2 mi north of Pompano Beach.*

The big attraction here is the view across Hillsboro Inlet to **Hillsboro Light,** oft called the brightest lighthouse in the southeast. Mariners have used this landmark for decades. When at sea you can see the light almost halfway to the Bahamas. Although the lighthouse is on private property inaccessible to the public, it's well worth a peek, even from afar.

WHERE TO EAT

★ $$$ ✕ **Cap's Place.** On an island once a bootlegger's haunt, Lighthouse Point's ramshackle seafood spot reached by launch has served the famous as well as the infamous, including the likes of Winston Churchill, FDR, JFK, and Al Capone. Cap was Captain Theodore Knight, born in 1871, who, with partner-in-crime Al Hasis, floated a derelict barge to the area in the 1920s. Broward's oldest restaurant, built on the barge, is run by Hasis descendants. Sesame Crusted Dolphin ($27.95) is served with soy ginger sauce, flaky rolls are baked fresh several times a night, and tangy lime pie ($5.95) is a great finale. Cap's is no cheapie; even a plate of linguine and clams will cost you $20. ✉ *Cap's Dock, 2765 N.E. 28th Ct.* ☎ *954/941–0418* ▱ *AE, D, MC, V* ☉ *No lunch, closed Mon. May–Dec.*

▮ EN
ROUTE
To the north, Route A1A traverses the so-called Hillsboro Mile (actually more than 2 mi), a millionaire's row of some of Broward's most beautiful and expensive homes. The road runs along a narrow strip of land between the Intracoastal Waterway and the ocean, with bougainvillea and oleander edging the way and yachts docked along both banks. Traffic often moves at a snail's pace, especially in winter, as vacationers (and sometimes even envious locals) gawk.

DEERFIELD BEACH

㉑ *3½ mi north of Lighthouse Point.*

The name **Quiet Waters Park** belies what's in store for kids here. Splash Adventure is a high-tech water-play system with slides and tunnels, among other activities. There's also cable waterskiing and boat rental on the park's lake. ⊠*401 S. Powerline Rd.* ☎*954/360–1315* 🕿*Park $1 weekends, free weekdays; Splash Adventure $3* ⊘*Apr.–Sept., daily 8–7; Oct.–Mar., 8–5:30; Splash Adventure May–Labor Day, daily 9:30–5:30; Labor Day–Apr., weekends 9:30–5:30.*

Deerfield Island Park, reached only by boat, is a group of coastal hammock islands. Officially designated an Urban Wilderness Area along the Intracoastal Waterway, it contains a mangrove swamp that provides a critical habitat for gopher tortoises, gray foxes, raccoons, and armadillos. As of this writing, Deerfield Island Park remained closed because of damage stemming from Hurricane Wilma. When open, boat shuttles run on the hour Wednesday 10–noon and Sunday 10–3; space is limited, so call for reservations. Call also for special events. ⊠*1720 Deerfield Island Park* ☎*954/360–1320* 🕿*Free.*

WHERE TO STAY & EAT

★ **$$–$$$$** ✕**Brooks.** Long known as one of Broward's more elegant dining spots, thanks to French perfectionist Bernard Perron, who turned over operations to son-in-law John Howe, updated continental meals are served in a series of rooms filled with replicas of Old Masters, cut glass, antiques, and floral wallpaper. Fresh ingredients go into distinctly Floridian dishes, including sea bass and mustard-crusted lamb chops. Put your order in early for the chocolate soufflé. ⊠*500 S. Federal Hwy.* ☎*954/427–9302* ▭*AE, D, MC, V.*

★ **¢–$$$** ✕**Whale's Rib.** For a casual, almost funky nautical experience near the beach, look no farther. If you want to blend in, order a fish special with whale fries—thinly sliced potatoes that look like hot potato chips. Lesser appetites can choose from salads and fish sandwiches, or raw-bar favorites like Ipswich clams. ⊠*2031 N.E. 2nd St.* ☎*954/421–8880* ▭*AE, MC, V.*

$$$–$$$$ 🏨**Ocean Club of Deerfield Beach.** This motel-turned-condominium, renting only by the week, is just south of the Palm Beach County line, across the narrow shore road from the beach. Large units—efficiencies and one- and three-bedroom, three-bath apartments—all have full-size kitchens and big balconies overlooking the sea. Units vary, some with new tile and newer rattan furnishings. The property recently added a fifth floor with two penthouse apartments. ⊠*2080 E. Hillsboro Blvd., 33441* ☎*954/421–7112* 🖷*954/421–8693* ⊕*www.oceanfrontrental-sondeerfieldbeach.com* ⬂*34 units* ⚲*In-room: kitchen. In-hotel: pool, laundry facilities* ▭*AE, D, DC, MC, V.*

$$–$$$$ 🏨**Royal Flamingo Villas.** A small community of houselike villas built in the 1970s reaches from the Intracoastal Waterway to the ocean on 7.5 acres of manicured grounds. Roomy one- and two-bedroom villas are decorated in Florida pastels, rattan, and wicker, all keeping with the tropical theme. If you don't need lavish public facilities, this is your upscale choice at a reasonable price. ⊠*1225 Hillsboro Mile (Rte. A1A), Hillsboro Beach 33062* ☎*954/427–0660 or 800/241–2477* 📠*954/427–6110* ⊕*www.royalflamingovillas.com* 🛏*40 villas* &*In-hotel: pool, beachfront, no elevator, laundry facilities* ▤*D, MC, V.*

¢–$$　🏨**Carriage House Resort Motel.** This tidy motel is one block from the ocean. The white, two-story, colonial-style property with black shutters is actually two buildings connected by a second-story sundeck. Steady improvements have been made to the facility, and kitchenettes are equipped with good-quality utensils. Rooms are quiet and have walk-in closets and safes. ⊠*250 S. Ocean Blvd., 33441* ☎*954/427–7670* 📠*954/428–4790* ⊕*www.carriagehouseresort.com* 🛏*6 rooms, 14 efficiencies, 10 1-bedroom apartments* &*In-room: ethernet. In-hotel: pool, no elevator, laundry facilities* ▤*AE, D, DC, MC, V.*

SPORTS & THE OUTDOORS

FISHING

The **Cove Marina** (⊠*Hillsboro Blvd. and the Intracoastal Waterway* ☎*954/427–9747*) has a deep-sea charter fleet. In winter there are excellent runs of sailfish, kingfish, dolphin, and tuna. A half-day charter costs about $500 for six people. Enter the marina through the Cove Shopping Center, where The Cove Restaurant and Marina (954/421–9272) does a spirited happy hour with a complimentary buffet.

GOLF

Off Hillsboro Boulevard west of Interstate 95, **Deer Creek Golf Club** (⊠*2801 Country Club Blvd.* ☎*954/421–5550*) has 18 holes. Green fee: $55/$145; there are six fee structures depending on the season.

SCUBA DIVING

One of the area's most popular dive operators, **Dixie Divers** (⊠*Cove Marina, Hillsboro Blvd. and the Intracoastal Waterway* ☎*954/420–0009*) has morning and afternoon dives aboard the 48-foot *Lady-Go-Diver*, plus evening dives on weekends. Snorkelers and certified divers can explore the marine life of nearby reefs and shipwrecks. The cost is $45; ride-alongs are welcome for $35.

SOUTH BROWARD

From Hollywood's Broadwalk, a 27-foot-wide thoroughfare paralleling 2 mi of palm-fringed beach, to the western reaches of Old West–flavored Davie, this region has a personality all its own. South Broward's roots are in early Florida settlements. Thus far it has avoided some of the glitz and glamour of neighbors to the north and south, and folks here like it that way. Still, there's plenty to see and do—excellent restaurants in every price range, world-class pari-mutuels, now gussied up with gaming on the side, and a new focus on the arts.

HOLLYWOOD

㉒ *7 mi south of Fort Lauderdale.*

Hollywood has had a face-lift, with more nips and tucks to come as Young Circle, plagued in recent times by derelicts, becomes Broward's first Arts Park. Things have not exactly gone smoothly for the revamp, given an unrealistic timetable and a developer's inclination to walk from the project. On Hollywood's western outskirts, the flamboyant Seminole Hard Rock Hotel & Casino has arguably etched the previously downtrodden section of State Road 7/U.S. 441 corridor on the map of trendy excitement for good, drawing local weekenders, architecture buffs, and gamblers. But Hollywood's redevelopment effort doesn't end there: new shops, restaurants, and art galleries open at a persistent clip, and the city has spiffed up its Broadwalk—a wide pedestrian walkway along the beach—where Rollerbladers are as commonplace as visitors from the north. Trendy sidewalk cafés have opened, vying for space with mom-and-pop T-shirt shops. Downtown, along Harrison Street and Hollywood Boulevard, jazz clubs and still more fashionable restaurants draw young professionals to the scene. Design studios and art galleries are also abundant along these two streets. In 1921 Joseph W. Young, a California real-estate entrepreneur, began developing the community of Hollywood from the woodsy flatlands. It quickly became a major tourist magnet, with casino gambling and whatever else made Florida hot. Reminders of Young-era glory days remain in places like Young Circle (the junction of U.S. 1 and Hollywood Boulevard) and the stately old homes on east Hollywood streets.

The **Art and Culture Center of Hollywood** is a visual and performing-arts facility with an art reference library, outdoor sculpture garden, and arts school. It's just east of Young Circle, melding urban open space with a fountain, a 2,000-plus seat amphitheater, and an indoor theater. Nearby, on trendy Harrison Street and Hollywood Boulevard, are chic lunch places, bluesy entertainment spots, and shops. ✉*1650 Harrison St.* ☎*954/921–3274* ☜*$5* ☉*Tues., Wed., Fri., and Sat. 10–5, Thurs. 10–8, Sun. 1–4.*

☾ With the Intracoastal Waterway nearby to its west and the beach and FodorśChoice ocean immediately east, the newly spiffed-up 2¹⁄₅-mi paved promenade ★ known as the **Broadwalk** has lured pedestrians and cyclists since 1924. Thanks to a $14 million makeover, this stretch has taken on new luster for the buff, the nubile, the laid-back, and the retired. Kids also thrive here: there are play areas, rental bicycles-for-two, trikes, and other wheeled, pedal-powered gizmos. Expect to hear French spoken along this scenic stretch that now has an 18-inch decorative wall separating sand and the promenade, since Hollywood Beach has been a favorite getaway for Québecois ever since Joseph Young hired French-Canadians to work here in the 1920s. Conversations in Spanish and Portuguese are also frequently overheard on this path.

Hollywood North Beach Park is at the Broadwalk's north end. No highrises overpower the scene, and there's nothing hip or chic about the park. It's just a laid-back, old-fashioned place for enjoying the sun, sand, and sea. ⊠ *Rte. A1A and Sheridan St.* ☎*954/926–2444* ⊑*Free; parking $5 until 2, $3 thereafter* ⊙*Daily 8–6.*

ↁ Comprising 1,500 acres at the Intracoastal Waterway, **West Lake Park** is one of Florida's largest urban nature facilities. Rent a canoe, kayak, or boat with an electric motor (no fossil fuels are allowed in the park) or take the 40-minute environmental boat tour. Extensive boardwalks traverse mangroves, sheltering endangered and threatened species. A 65-foot observation tower showcases the entire park. More than $1 million in exhibits are on display at the **Anne Kolb Nature Center,** named after the late county commissioner and leading environmental advocate. The center's exhibit hall has 27 interactive displays, an ecology room, and a tri-level aquarium. ⊠*1200 Sheridan St.* ☎*954/926–2410* ⊑*Weekends $1, weekdays and holidays free; exhibit hall $1* ⊙*Daily 9–5.*

ↁ At the edge of Hollywood lies **Seminole Native Village,** a reservation where you can pet a cougar, hold a baby alligator, and take in wildlife demonstrations. The Seminole also sell their art and crafts here. Across the street, **Hollywood Seminole Gaming** (⊠*4150 N. State Rd. 7* ☎*954/961–3220*) is open 24/7 and, although downscale in atmosphere compared to the newer, glitzy Seminole Hard Rock, has bingo, poker, and more than 1,000 gaming machines. ⊠*3551 N. State Rd. 7* ☎*954/961–4519* ⊑*Self-guided tour $5, guided tour including alligator wrestling and snake demonstrations $10* ⊙*Daily 9–5.*

WHERE TO STAY & EAT

$$$$ ✕**Nikki Marina Hollywood Restaurant & Bar.** As part of the growing global village of Nikki Beach outposts, stretching from St. Tropez to Sardinia, Marrakech to Miami Beach, Hollywood's own is situated at Diplomat Landing across from the Westin Diplomat Resort. This is a good spot to sample sushi, sip mojitos, and gawk at mega yachts. At lunch, go for the Nikki Marina Salad ($10) with Stilton cheese, pears, grapefruit, toasted cashews, and greens. A dinner menu stretches from Cowboy Steak ($42) to Paella ($40), with lobster, shrimp, clams, and mussels amid the saffron rice. High rollers can order Nikki's Delight of the Sea Platter ($200), loaded with Alaskan crab legs, Maine lobster, shrimp, oysters, and more. Sunday Brunch ($38) includes a raw bar. Arrive by vehicle or boat, and prepare to be upstaged by something a little bigger or snazzier than whatever you're steering. ⊠*3660 S. Ocean Dr.* ☎*954/602–8750.*

$$–$$$$ ✕**Giorgio's Grill.** Good food and service are hallmarks of this 400-seat restaurant overlooking the Intracoastal Waterway. Seafood is a specialty, but you'll also find pasta and meat dishes. A great water view and friendly staff add to the experience. A surprisingly extensive wine list is reasonably priced. ⊠*606 N. Ocean Dr.* ☎*954/929–7030* ⊟*AE, D, DC, MC, V.*

$$–$$$ ✕**Las Brisas.** Next to the beach, this cozy bistro offers seating inside or out, and the food is Argentine with Italian flair. A small pot, filled with *chimichurri*—a paste made of oregano, parsley, olive oil, salt, garlic, and crushed pepper—for spreading on steaks, sits on each table. Grilled fish is a favorite, as are pork chops, chicken, and pasta entrées. Des-

serts include a flan like *mamacita* used to make, and a *dulce con leche* (sweet milk pudding). ✉ *600 N. Surf Rd.* ☎ *954/923–1500* 🖃 *AE, D, DC, MC, V* ⊘ *No lunch.*

$–$$ ✕ **Sushi Blues Café and Blue Monk Lounge.** Raw fish, burgers, and soul food complement the American roots music and vintage lamps at this hip (read: far from stodgy) Hollywood institution, open daily from 11:30 AM until the wee hours. It's operated by husband-and-wife team Kenny Millions and Junko Maslak. Japanese chefs prepare conventional and macrobiotic-influenced dishes, from sushi and rolls (California, tuna, and the Yozo roll, with snapper, flying-fish roe, asparagus, and Japanese mayonnaise) to steamed vegetables with tofu and steamed snapper with miso sauce. Poached pears steamed in cabernet sauce and cappuccino custard are popular desserts. The Sushi Blues Band performs on many evenings. ✉ *2009 Harrison St.* ☎ *954/929–9560* 🖃 *AE, MC, V.*

¢–$$ ✕ **Le Tub.** Formerly a Sunoco gas station, this place is now a quirky waterside saloon with an enduring affection for claw-foot bathtubs. Hand-painted tubs, sinks, and toilets are everywhere—under ficus, sea grape, and palm trees. If a potty doesn't appeal, there's a secluded swing facing the water north of the main dining area. Despite molasses-slow service and an abundance of flies at sundown, this eatery is favored by locals for affordable fare, and management seemed genuinely appalled when hordes of trend-seeking city slickers started jamming bar stools and tables after *GQ* magazine and Oprah declared its thick, juicy Angus burgers the best around. ✉ *1100 N. Ocean Dr.* ☎ *954/921–9425* 🖃 *No credit cards.*

$$–$$$$ 🏨 **Seminole Hard Rock Hotel & Casino.** Springing up from the flatlands of western Hollywood as if a virtual mirage, the Seminole Hard Rock Hotel & Casino—where tragedy-plagued Anna Nicole Smith spent her final hours in 2007—has become a magnet for Vegas-style excitement, entertainment, and dining with a subtropical appeal. The 4½-acre pool complex inspires a wow-reaction, where a rock mountain doubles as a backdrop to a 182-foot-long waterslide. A Lazy River circulating pool, waterfalls, hot tubs, and a shallow play area are capped by a nearly 22,000-square-foot spa. Partially embracing this landscaping is a starkly white 12-story tower. Amenities include Tivoli stereos and ultra-luxe beds dressed in Egyptian cottons and European duvets. Dining options include the memorabilia-packed Hard Rock Cafe Hollywood, the Council Oak, with steak and seafood, and the 24-hour Blue Plate, which borders the casino action. The facility is designed in a somewhat dizzying fashion so that eateries, lounges, and elegant outlying lobby area form a peripheral map of sorts for the casino floor, where poker pulsates at 40 tables, to spectator delight, along with a couple of thousand electronic gaming machines. A ballroom theater just off the casino hosts stage extravaganzas; and "Hard Rock Live!," a 5,600-seat live performance venue, hosts performers like Prince, touring bands, theater, championship boxing, and rodeo. Seminole Paradise, a retail, restaurant, and live-entertainment district, will relieve you of any casino-floor winnings. A billboard along Interstate 95 blares news of hefty daily payouts at this playground with seemingly acres of free parking, now expanded to accommodate more big wheels. ✉ *1*

Seminole Way, 33314 ☎954/364–4171 or 800/937–0010 ⊕www.
hardrock.com ⇨500 rooms, including 100 suites &In-room: dial-
up. In-hotel: 3 restaurants, bars, golf course, tennis courts, pools, gym,
spa, minibar ⊟AE, DC, MC, V.

★ $$–$$$$ ▦**The Westin Diplomat Resort & Spa.** Opened in 2002 on the site of the
original 1950s hotel of the same name, the Diplomat is a grand 39-
story, dual-tower property. The hotel has a lobby-atrium area with
ceilings soaring to 60 feet. A signature of the resort is its 120-foot
bridged pool, extending from lobby to oceanfront. To offset ero-
sion, a beach replenishment project is in the works, though the effort
seems a never-ending, if not a forever-losing, battle. A Mediterranean-
inspired spa offers fitness facilities and more than 20 luxury treat-
ments. The Diplomat's country club, across the intracoastal, has 60
guest rooms, golf, tennis, and spa. You'll have use of facilities at both
properties; shuttle service is provided. ⊠1995 E. Hallandale Beach
Blvd., 33309 ☎954/457–2000 or 800/327–1212 ⊕www.starwood-
hotels.com ⇨900 rooms, 100 suites &In-room: dial-up. In-hotel: 3
restaurants, bars, golf course, tennis courts, pools, gym, spa, minibar
⊟AE, DC, MC, V.

★ $–$$$ ▦**Manta Ray Inn.** Canadians Donna and Dwayne Boucher run this
immaculate, affordable two-story inn on a beach, perfect for a low-
key getaway. Dating from the 1940s, the inn offers casual, comfortable beachfront accommodations with amenities such as cable TV
with VCR, and wireless Internet access. Kitchens are equipped with
pots, pans, and many appliances. One-bedroom apartments have marble shower stalls, and two-bedroom units also have tubs. ⊠1715 S.
Surf Rd., 33019 ☎954/921–9666 or 800/255–0595 ⊟954/929–8220
⊕www.mantarayinn.com ⇨12 units &In-room: VCR, Wi-Fi. In-
hotel: beachfront, no elevator ⊟AE, D, MC, V.

¢–$$$ ▦**Sea Downs.** Directly facing the Broadwalk, this three-story lodg-
ing is a good choice for efficiency or apartment living (one-bedroom
units can be joined to make two-bedroom apartments). All but two
units have ocean views. Kitchens are fully equipped, and most units
have tub-showers and closets. Housekeeping is provided once a week.
In between, fresh towels are provided daily and sheets upon request,
but you'll need to make your own bed. ⊠2900 N. Surf Rd., 33019
☎954/923–4968 ⊟954/923–8747 ⊕www.seadowns.com ⇨4 effi-
ciencies, 8 1-bedroom apartments &In-room: Wi-Fi. In-hotel: pool,
no elevator, laundry facilities ⊟No credit cards.

¢–$ ▦**Driftwood on the Ocean.** Facing the beach at the secluded south end of
Surf Road is this attractive late-1950s resort motel that clearly shows
its age. The setting is what draws guests, but attention to maintenance
and refurbishing efforts are what make it a value. Accommodations
range from a studio to a deluxe two-bedroom, two-bath suite. Most
units have a kitchen; all have balconies or terraces, and wireless Internet
access. ⊠2101 S. Surf Rd., 33019 ☎954/923–9528 or 800/944–3148
⊟954/922–1062 ⊕www.driftwoodontheocean.com ⇨7 rooms, 9 2-
bedroom apartments, 13 1-bedroom apartments, 20 efficiencies &In-
room: kitchen (some), Wi-Fi. In-hotel: pool, beachfront, bicycles, no
elevator, laundry facilities ⊟AE, D, MC, V.

NIGHTLIFE & THE ARTS

THE ARTS

Harrison Street Art and Design District in downtown Hollywood has galleries featuring original artwork (eclectic paintings, sculpture, photography, and mixed media), Costa Rican collectibles, and African artifacts. Friday night the artists' studios, galleries, and shops stay open later while crowds meander along Hollywood Boulevard and Harrison Street. The colorful home furnishings gallery **Alliage** (⊠*2035 Harrison St.* ☎*954/922–7017*) has tables, wall consoles, and sculptures handcrafted from brushed aluminum and sand-blasted glass. **Indaba** (⊠*2029 Harrison St.* ☎*954/920–2029*) celebrates African art with an extensive collection of masks, statues, cloth, and baskets. **Mosaica** (⊠*2020 Hollywood Blvd.* ☎*954/923–7006*) is a design studio with handcrafted, one-of-a-kind mosaic tile tables, mirrors, and art.

NIGHTLIFE

Although downtown Hollywood has a small-town feel, it has an assortment of coffee bars, Internet cafés, sports bars, martini lounges, and dance clubs. The downtown area is known for its live jazz and blues venues. **O'Hara's Hollywood** (⊠*1903 Hollywood Blvd.* ☎*954/925–2555*) highlights top local jazz and blues talent six nights a week. Sushi café and wine bar **Sushi Blues** (⊠*1836 Young Circle* ☎*954/929–9560*) serves up live blues Friday and Saturday nights starting at 9.

SPORTS & THE OUTDOORS

DOG RACING

Mardi Gras Racetrack & Gaming Center, long known as the Hollywood Greyhound Track before the arrival of slot machine action, has live dog racing during its December through May season and simulcasting every day. Relax at the Dog House sports bar and grill. ⊠*831 N. Federal Hwy., Hallandale* ☎*954/924–3200* ☒*Grandstand $1, clubhouse $2, parking free* ☉*Racing nightly at 7:30, and Tues., Thurs., and Sat. at 12:30* PM.

BOATING

Adventure World at the Landing (⊠*3570 South Ocean Dr.* ☎*954/457–9575*) provides Jet Ski, Air Cat, and other boat rentals, and runs fishing trips as well as kayak and canoe expeditions through the mangroves and lagoons of local parks. Electric bikes, all-terrain Segways, and bicycle rentals are also available, and handy package deals allow you to try out combinations of water and land equipment over a five-hour period.

FISHING

Sea Leg's III (⊠*5400 N. Ocean Dr.* ☎*954/923–2109*) runs drift-fishing trips from 8 AM to 12:30 PM and 1:30 to 6 and bottom-fishing trips from 7 PM to midnight. Trips cost $32 to $36, including rod rental.

GOLF

The **Diplomat Country Club & Spa** (⊠*501 Diplomat Pkwy., Hallandale* ☎*954/883–4000*) has 18 holes and a spa. Green fee: $69/$209. The course at **Emerald Hills** (✉*4100 N. Hills Dr.* ☎*954/961–4000*) has 18 holes. Green fee: $55/$175, depending on the season.

HORSE RACING

Gulfstream Racing & Casino is the winter home of some of the nation's top thoroughbreds, trainers, and jockeys, and now the year-round home of slot machine action. In addition to races, there are family days with attractions for kids and scheduled concerts with well-known performers. The season is capped by the $1 million Florida Derby, with Kentucky Derby hopefuls. Racing unfolds January through April. ✉*901 S. Federal Hwy., Hallandale* ☎*954/454–7000 or 800/771–8873* ⌨*Grandstand $3, clubhouse $5* ☉*Racing Wed.–Mon. at 1 and nightly simulcasting.*

DANIA BEACH

㉓ *3 mi north of Hollywood, 4 mi south of Fort Lauderdale.*

This town at the south edge of Fort Lauderdale is probably best known for its antiques dealers, but there are other attractions as well.

The once pine-dotted **John U. Lloyd Beach State Recreation Area** has lost significant shaded ambience, thanks to government-driven efforts to pull out all but indigenous plants, leaving taxpayers to gripe that myopic bureaucrats could have waited for Hurricane Wilma to decide what might stay and what should go. Disappointed shade-seeking park goers are advised that, eventually, sea grape, gumbo limbo, and other native plantings will fill the void. Meanwhile, gate attendance has declined appreciably, hurricane damage has closed the jetty pier for fishing, and erosion has done a number on what remains of the beach. Nature trails and a marina remain open, along with canoeing on Whiskey Creek. Despite setbacks, this is a prime spot to watch cruise ships enter and depart Port Everglades. ✉*6503 N. Ocean Dr.* ☎*954/923–2833* ⌨*$5 per vehicle with up to 8 people* ☉*Daily 8–sunset.*

★ **IGFA Fishing Hall of Fame and Museum** is a shrine to the sport. Near the Fort Lauderdale airport at Interstate 95 and Griffin Road, the center is the creation of the International Game Fishing Association. In addition to checking out the World Fishing Hall of Fame, a marina, and an extensive museum and research library, visit seven galleries with fantasy fishing and other interactive displays. And in the Catch Gallery, cast off via virtual reality and try to reel in a marlin, sailfish, trout, tarpon, or bass. ✉*300 Gulfstream Way, Dania Beach* ☎*954/922–4212* ⊕*www.igfa.org* ⌨*$6* ☉*Daily 10–6.*

WHERE TO EAT

¢–$ ✕**Grampa's Bakery & Restaurant.** A magnet for local politicos, Grampa's provides a cheery, homey fix of comfort foods from the charbroiler, fryer, and grill. You won't go hungry with Grampa's Chili with cheese, lox, eggs, an onion omelet, or biscuits and gravy. Check out the sweets, at the bakery counter up front. ✉*17 S.W. 1st St.* ☎*954/923–2163* ▭*MC, V.*

¢–$ ✕**Jaxson's Ice Cream Parlor.** Across from the Dania United Methodist Church, the half-century-old Jaxson's whips up malts, shakes, and jumbo sundaes, plus sandwiches and salads, amid an antique-license-plate decor. Platters include the New York–style mile-long all-beef hot dog. Ice creams and toppings are prepared daily on the premises. Owner Monroe Udell has trademarked The Kitchen Sink—a small sink full of ice cream, topped by sparklers—reserved for parties of four or more for $10 per person. Less-ambitious appetites lean toward Jaxson's Sampler (Junior or Senior), the Praline Pecan Supreme or the Banana Skyscraper. Chocoholics can ponder the Jug-O-Fudge or Chocolate Suicide. ✉*128 S. Federal Hwy.* ☎*954/923–4445* ▭*AE, D, MC, V.*

¢–$ ✕**Tarks of Dania.** Started in 1966 as a small stand for clams, wings, and beer, Tarks hasn't changed much, with a counter and a few tables for neighbors and drop-ins to eat, drink, and rejuvenate. From Tarks's raw bar come topneck and littleneck clams along with raw oysters. From the fryer are clams (bellies or strips), oysters, scallops, shrimp, wings, and curly fries. For around $10 you can order a gator-tail dinner (gently marinated and deep-fried) or a tasty conch salad. Nightly specials include Alaskan snow crab on Friday. Tarks markets its own bottled "terminator" sauce, and there's a "Frequent Tarks Club" to accumulate points for special offers. ✉*1317 S. Federal Hwy.* ☎*954/925–8275* ▭*AE, D, MC, V.*

SPORTS & THE OUTDOORS

JAI ALAI

Dania Jai-Alai Casino has one of the fastest ball games on the planet, scheduled year-round. Simulcast wagering from other tracks and a poker room are also available, with slot machines on the near horizon. ✉*301 E. Dania Beach Blvd.* ☎*954/920–1511* ▭*$1.50, reserved seats $2–$7* ☉*Games Tues. and Sat. at noon, Sun. at 1, nightly Tues.–Sat. at 7:15.*

MINIATURE GOLF

☉ **Boomers!** has action games for kids of all ages—go-kart and Nas-kart racing, miniature golf, batting cages, bumper boats, Lasertron, and a skycoaster. ✉*1801 N.W. 1st St.* ☎*954/921–1411* ☉*Mon.–Thurs. noon–midnight, Fri. noon–2 AM, Sat. 10 AM–2 AM, Sun. 10 AM–midnight.*

ROLLER COASTER

☉ **Dania Beach Hurricane,** visible from Interstate 95, isn't the world's highest, fastest, or longest roller coaster, but it's near the top in all those categories, and it's the tallest wooden coaster south of Atlanta. This retro-feeling ride creaks like an old staircase while you race along 3,200 feet of track and plummet from a height of 100 feet at speeds up to 55 mph. ✉*1760 N.W. 1st St.* ☎*954/921–7433* ▭*$6.25* ☉*Sun.–Thurs. 10 AM–11:30 PM, Fri. and Sat. 10 AM–1:30 AM.*

SHOPPING

Despite moans over eBay competition encroachment, dozens of dealers along **Dania Antique Row** do a thriving business buying and selling everything from antique furniture to vintage knickknacks. You never know what you'll find here, but Depression-era glassware seems plenti-ful, and shop owners are quite friendly. This two-square-block area is on Federal Highway (U.S. 1), ½ mi south of the Fort Lauderdale airport and ½ mi north of Hollywood. Take the Stirling Road or Griffin Road East exit off Interstate 95.

DAVIE

㉔ *4 mi west of Dania Beach.*

Davie's horse farms and estates are the closest thing to the Old West in South Florida. Folks in Western wear ride their fine steeds through downtown—where they have the same right of way as motorists—and order up takeout at "ride-through" windows. With 70,000 residents, Davie has doubled in size in 15 years, and gated communities are pop-ping up alongside ranches. A weekly rodeo at the Bergeron Rodeo Grounds and Entertainment Center is the town's most famous howdy, pardner activity.

★ ☾ Gators, crocodiles, river otters, and birds of prey can be seen at **Fla-mingo Gardens and Wray Botanical Collection,** as can a 25,000-square-foot walk-through aviary, plant house, and Everglades museum in the pio-neer Wray Home. A half-hour guided tram ride winds through a citrus grove and wetlands area. ⊠ *3750 S. Flamingo Rd.* ☎ *954/473–2955* ⊕ *www.flamingogardens.org* ⊠ *$17, tram ride $3* ☾ *Daily 9:30–5:30; closed Mon. June–Sept.*

☾ At the **Young at Art Children's Museum,** kids can work with paint, graph-ics, sculpture, and crafts according to themes that change three times a year. Then they take their masterpieces home with them. ⊠ *11584 W. State Rd. 84, in the Plaza* ☎ *954/424–0085* ⊕ *www.youngatartmu-seum.org* ⊠ *$8* ☾ *Mon.–Sat. 10–5, Sun. noon–5.*

WHERE TO EAT

$$–$$$$ ✕**Darrel & Oliver's East City Grill.** Weston's East City Grill, born on Fort Lauderdale beach, quickly grew up to relocate westward for smart, sophisticated dining under the tutelage of Darrel Broek and Chef Oliver Saucy. Amid a dressy-casual atmosphere with a lake view, try the lolli-pop lamb chops ($13.75) or the Jurassic shrimp cocktail ($6.50). Entrées include rice-flour-dusted sautéed yellowtail snapper ($28) and twin breast of duck ($26). Among desserts, chocolate truffle cheesecake is a stand-out. Martinis—chocolate, butterscotch, mango, or cappuccino—provide liquid dessert finales. ⊠ *1800 Bell Tower La.* ☎ *954/659–3339* ⊟ *AE, D, DC, MC, V.*

THE ARTS

Bailey Concert Hall (⊠ *Central Campus of Broward Community Col-lege, 3501 S.W. Davie Rd.* ☎ *954/201–6884)* schedules classical-music concerts, dance, drama, and other performing-arts activities, especially from October to April.

NIGHTLIFE

Round Up Country Western Club (⊠ *9020 W. State Road 84* ☎ *954/423–1990*), South Florida's hot country-music venue, is in the heart of Broward's horse country, with a quartet of bars, drink specials, food, dance lessons, large-screen TVs, and theme nights (Wednesday is ladies' night). Open from 6 PM to 4 AM, it's closed Monday and Tuesday. **Chocolate Moose Music Cafe** (⊠ *9118 State Road 84* ☎ *954/474–5040*) is themed and geared to moose, but this coffeehouse also serves beer and wine, and runs open mikes several times weekly.

THE OUTDOORS

BIKING

Bicycle and in-line-skating enthusiasts can ride at the **Brian Piccolo Skate Park and Velodrome** (⊠ *9501 Sheridan St., Cooper City* ☎ *954/437–2626*), south of Davie. Hours are geared to after-school and weekend skating and biking.

RODEO

The **Davie Rodeo** (⊠ *4271 Davie Rd.* ☎ *954/680–3555*) is staged at the Bergeron Rodeo Grounds and Entertainment Center at frequent intervals. Saturday-night bull riding starts at 8. National rodeos come to town some weekends.

FORT LAUDERDALE & BROWARD ESSENTIALS

To research prices, get advice from other travelers, and book travel arrangements, visit www.fodors.com.

TRANSPORTATION

BY AIR

More than 40 scheduled airlines, commuters, and charters serve Fort Lauderdale–Hollywood International Airport.

Contacts **Air Canada** (☎ *888/247–2462*). **Air Jamaica** (☎ *800/523–5585*). **AirTran** (☎ *800/247–8726*). **America West** (☎ *800/235–9292*). **American** (☎ *800/433–7300*). **Continental** (☎ *800/525–0280*). **Delta** (☎ *800/221–1212*). **JetBlue** (☎ *800/538–2583*). **MetroJet** (☎ *888/638–7653*). **Northwest** (☎ *800/225–2525*). **Southwest** (☎ *800/435–9792*). **Spirit** (☎ *800/772–7117*). **TWA** (☎ *800/221–2000*). **United** (☎ *800/241–6522*). **US Airways** (☎ *800/428–4322*).

Fort Lauderdale–Hollywood International Airport, 4 mi south of downtown Fort Lauderdale and just off U.S. 1, serves more than 21 million travelers a year, and provides free Internet access throughout terminals and concourses through its wireless system. All airport coffee shops have converted to Dunkin' Donuts brand, with regular, flavored, and specialty coffees, plus Dunkin' Donuts. Ongoing expansion has added a terminal, parking, and access roads. Broward County Mass Transit operates bus route No. 1 between the airport and its main terminal at Broward Boulevard and Northwest 1st Avenue, in the center of Fort Lauderdale. Service from the airport is every 20 minutes and begins daily at 5:40 AM; the last bus leaves the airport at 11:15 PM. The fare is $1. Airport Express provides limousine service to all parts of Broward County. Fares to most Fort Lauderdale beach hotels are in the $25 range.

Airport Contacts Fort Lauderdale–Hollywood International Airport (☏ 954/359–6100). **Airport Express** (☏ 954/561–8888). **Broward County Mass Transit** (☏ 954/357–8400).

BY BOAT & FERRY

Water Taxi, also known as Water Bus, provides service along the Intracoastal Waterway in Fort Lauderdale between the 17th Street Causeway and Oakland Park Boulevard daily from 10:30 AM until midnight.

Contacts Water Bus, Water Taxi (☏ 954/467–6677).

BY BUS

Greyhound Lines buses stop in Fort Lauderdale. Broward County Mass Transit bus service covers the county on 275 fixed routes and ventures into Dade and Palm Beach counties. The fare is $1, and BUZ pass options include unlimited daily ($2.50), weekly ($9), monthly ($32), and 10 rides for $8 any day, any time, sold at bus stations, libraries, and elsewhere. Route service starts at 5 AM and continues to 11:30 PM, except on Sunday. Call for route information. Fort Lauderdale's Sun Trolley is free on some routes or costs 25¢ to 50¢ per ride, depending on the route (flow of federal grant money, and whims of local transporation czars), and covers both the downtown loop and the beach area. The Courthouse Route generally runs every 10 minutes weekdays from 7:30 until 6. The Las Olas & Beach Route runs on the half hour 5:45 PM–1:45 AM.

Contacts Broward County Mass Transit (*Main Bus Terminal* ✉ *Broward Blvd. at N.W. 1st Ave., Fort Lauderdale* ☏ 954/357–8400). **Greyhound Lines** (✉ *515 N.E. 3rd St., Fort Lauderdale* ☏ 800/231–2222 or 954/764–6551). **TMAX** (☏ 954/761–3543).

Broward County Mass Transit offers seven-day passes that cost $9 and are good for unlimited use on all county buses. Get passes at some hotels, Broward County libraries, and the main bus terminal.

BY CAR

Access to Broward County from north or south is via Florida's Turnpike, Interstate 95, U.S. 1, or U.S. 441. Interstate 75 (Alligator Alley, requiring a toll despite being part of the nation's interstate highway system) connects Broward with Florida's west coast and runs parallel to State Road 84 within the county. Except during rush hour, Broward County is easier than elsewhere in South Florida for driving. East–west Interstate 595 runs from westernmost Broward County and links Interstate 75 with Interstate 95 and U.S. 1, providing handy access to the airport. The scenic but slow Route A1A generally parallels the beach. The Sawgrass Expressway (also known as State Road 869 north of Interstate 595 and Interstate 75 south) is a toll road that links to Sawgrass Mills shopping and the ice-hockey arena, both in Sunrise.

Contacts **Alamo** (☎ *954/525–4713*). **Avis** (☎ *954/359–5250*). **Budget** (☎*954/359–4700*). **Dollar** (☎*954/359–7800*). **Enterprise** (☎*954/760–9888*). **Hertz** (☎*954/764–1199*). **National** (☎*954/359–8303*).

BY TAXI

It's difficult to hail a cab on the street. Sometimes you can pick one up at a major hotel. Otherwise, phone for taxi service. Meters run at a rate of $4.50 for the first mile and $2.40 for each additional mile; waiting time is 40¢ per minute, with rates likely to rise as fuel costs escalate. The major company serving the area is Yellow Cab.

Contacts **Yellow Cab** (☎*954/565–5400*).

BY TRAIN

Amtrak provides daily service to the Fort Lauderdale station as well as other Broward County stops at Hollywood and Deerfield Beach. Tri-Rail operates train service daily 4 AM–11 PM (limited service on weekends) through Broward, Miami-Dade, and Palm Beach counties. There are six Broward stations west of Interstate 95: Hillsboro Boulevard in Deerfield Beach, Pompano Beach, Cypress Creek, Fort Lauderdale, Fort Lauderdale Airport, Sheridan Street in Hollywood, and Hollywood Boulevard.

Contacts **Amtrak** (✉*200 S.W. 21st Terr., Fort Lauderdale* ☎*800/872–7245*). **Tri-Rail** (☎*800/874–7245*).

CONTACTS & RESOURCES

TOURS

Carrie B., a 300-passenger day cruiser, gives 90-minute tours on the New River and Intracoastal Waterway. Cruises depart at 11, 1, and 3 each day and cost $14.95. *Jungle Queen III* and *Jungle Queen IV* are 175-passenger and 527-passenger tour boats taking day and night cruises up New River through the heart of Fort Lauderdale. Sightseeing cruises at 10 and 2 cost $14.95, and the evening dinner cruise costs $34.95. You can also take a daylong trip to Miami's Bayside Marketplace ($17.95) on Biscayne Bay on Wednesday and Saturday, departing at 9:15. Professional Diving Charters operates the 60-foot glass-bottom boat *Pro Diver II*. On Tuesday through Saturday mornings and Sunday afternoon, two-hour sightseeing trips costing $22 take in offshore reefs.

Contacts **Carrie B.** (✉*Riverwalk at S.E. 5th Ave., Fort Lauderdale* ☎*954/768–9920*). **Jungle Queen III** and **Jungle Queen IV** (✉*Radisson Bahia Mar Beach Resort, 801 Seabreeze Blvd., Fort Lauderdale* ☎*954/462–5596*). **Professional Diving Charters** (✉*515 Seabreeze Blvd., Fort Lauderdale* ☎*954/761–3413*).

VISITOR INFORMATION

Contacts **Chamber of Commerce of Greater Fort Lauderdale** (✉*512 N.E. 3rd Ave., Fort Lauderdale 33301* ☎*954/462–6000* ⊕*www.ftlchamber.com*). **Davie/Cooper City Chamber of Commerce** (✉*4185 S.W. 64th Ave., Davie 33314* ☎*954/581–0790* ⊕*www.davie-coopercity.org*). **Greater Deerfield Beach Chamber of Commerce** (✉*1601 E. Hillsboro Blvd., Deerfield Beach 33441* ☎*954/427–1050* ⊕*www.deerfieldchamber.com*). **Greater Fort Lauderdale Con-**

vention & Visitors Bureau (✉ *100 E. Broward Blvd., Suite 200, Fort Lauderdale 33301* ☎ *954/765–4466* ⊕ *www.broward.org*). **Hollywood Chamber of Commerce** (✉ *330 N. Federal Hwy., Hollywood 33020* ☎ *954/923–4000* ⊕ *www.hollywoodchamber.org*). **Lauderdale-by-the-Sea Chamber of Commerce** (✉ *4201 N. Ocean Dr., Lauderdale-by-the-Sea 33308* ☎ *954/776–1000* ⊕ *www.lbts.com*). **Pompano Beach Chamber of Commerce** (✉ *2200 E. Atlantic Blvd., Pompano Beach 33062* ☎ *954/941–2940* ⊕ *www.pompanobeachchamber.com*).

Miami &
Miami Beach

WORD OF MOUTH

"Head to the Little Havana area. Walk around a little and wander into a market in hopes of securing some Cuban or Hispanic soda and a mango."
—ajcolorado

"You must stop by the pool bar at the Delano (a walk through the lobby is a South Beach must) for the very best mojitos in Miami."
—GoTravel

"The club scene in South Beach is ever-changing and getting a little past its 'That's so hot' stage, so don't be too intimidated. You DO want to dress a bit flashily for the better places, certainly, but don't go too over the top."
—rjw_lgb_ca

Updated by
LoAnn Halden
and Suzy
Buckley

THINK OF MIAMI AS A teenager: a young beauty with growing pains, cocky yet confused, quick to embrace the latest fads, exasperating yet lovable. It may help you understand how best to tackle this imperfect paradise.

As cities go, Miami and Miami Beach really are young. Just a little more than 100 years ago, Miami was mosquito-infested swampland, with an Indian trading post on the Miami River. Then hotel builder Henry Flagler brought his railroad to the outpost known as Fort Dallas. Other visionaries—Carl Fisher, Julia Tuttle, William Brickell, and John Sewell, among others—set out to tame the unruly wilderness. Hotels were erected, bridges were built, the port was dredged, electricity arrived. The narrow strip of mangrove coast was transformed into Miami Beach. And the tourists started to come.

TOP 5
Grab an outdoor table on Lincoln Road Mall for noshing and people-watching.
Visit elegant Vizcaya Museum and Gardens. At night, the grounds are as magical as in a fairy tale.
Photography lovers should run, not walk, to the Margulies Collection at the Warehouse near the Design District.
Browse the posh boutiques of the Bal Harbour Shops, which include Tiffany and Co.
Ditch the city bustle and head for Oleta River State Park. It has plenty of cozy niches among the palms.

Greater Miami is many destinations in one. At its best it offers an unparalleled multicultural experience: melodic Latin and Caribbean tongues, international cuisines and cultural events, and an unmistakable joie de vivre—all against a frankly beautiful beach backdrop. In Little Havana the air is tantalizing with the perfume of strong Cuban coffee. In Coconut Grove, Caribbean steel drums ring out during the Miami/Bahamas Goombay Festival. Anytime in colorful Miami Beach restless crowds wait for entry to the hottest new clubs.

Many visitors don't know that Miami and Miami Beach are really separate cities. Miami, on the mainland, is South Florida's commercial hub. Miami Beach, on 17 islands in Biscayne Bay, is sometimes considered America's Riviera, luring refugees from winter with its warm sunshine; sandy beaches; graceful, shady palms; and tireless nightlife. The natives know well that there's more to Greater Miami than the bustle of South Beach and its Art Deco District. In addition to well-known places such as Coconut Grove and Bayside, the less reported spots, like the Museum of Contemporary Art in North Miami; the burgeoning Design District in Miami; and the mangrove swamps of Matheson Hammock Park, in Coral Gables, are great insider destinations.

GREAT ITINERARIES

Numbers in the text correspond to numbers in the margin and on the Miami Beach; Downtown Miami; Miami, Coral Gables, Coconut Grove, and Key Biscayne; and South Dade maps.

3 DAYS

Grab your lotion and head to the ocean, more specifically **Ocean Drive** on **South Beach,** and catch some rays while relaxing on the white sands. Afterward, take a guided or self-guided tour of the **Art Deco District** ❷ to see what all the fuss is about. Keep the evening free to socialize at Ocean Drive cafés. The following day drive through **Little Havana** to witness the heartbeat of Miami's Cuban culture on your way south to Coconut Grove's Vizcaya. Wrap up the evening a few blocks away in downtown **Coconut Grove,** enjoying its partylike mood and many nightspots. On the last day head over to **Coral Gables** to take in the eye-popping display of 1920s Mediterranean Revival architecture in the neighborhoods surrounding the city center and the majestic **Biltmore Hotel** ㉖; then take a dip in the fantastic thematic **Venetian Pool** ㉔. Early evening, set aside a little time to shop at Village of Merrick Park (at the corner of Ponce and Bird), and later that night have a fine meal in Coral Gables.

5 DAYS

Follow the suggested three-day itinerary, and on Day 4 visit the beaches of **Virginia Key** ㉙ and **Key Biscayne** ㉚–㉛. Take a diving trip or fishing excursion, learn to windsurf, or just watch the water. On Day 5, step back to the 1950s with a cruise up **Collins Avenue** to some of the monolithic hotels, such as the **Fontainebleau Hilton** and **Eden Roc**; continue north to the elegant shops of **Bal Harbour**; and return to **South Beach** for an evening of shopping, drinking, and outdoor dining at **Lincoln Road Mall** ❻.

7 DAYS

A week is enough time to experience fully the multicultural, cosmopolitan, tropical mélange that is Greater Miami. On Day 6 see where it all began. Use the Miami Metromover to ride above downtown Miami before touring the streets (if possible, on a tour with historian Dr. Paul George). Visit the **Miami-Dade Cultural Center** ⑫, home of art and history museums. Or go check out the **Miami Design District's** art galleries, which showcase local and international artists amidst decorator showrooms and antiques stores.. The nearby **Wynwood Art District** ⑬ is also worth exploring. In the evening, check out the shops at **Bayside Marketplace.** The final day can be used to visit **South Miami.**

EXPLORING MIAMI & MIAMI BEACH

If you had arrived here 40 years ago with a Fodor's guide in hand, chances are you'd be thumbing through listings looking for alligator wrestlers and you-pick strawberry fields or citrus groves. Well, things have changed. While Disney sidetracked families in Orlando, Miami was developing a grown-up attitude courtesy of the original *Miami Vice,* European fashion photographers, and historic preservationists.

Nowadays the wildest ride is the city itself. Climb aboard and check out the different sides of Greater Miami.

To find your way around Greater Miami, learn how the numbering system works. Miami is laid out on a grid with four quadrants—northeast, northwest, southeast, and southwest—which meet at Miami Avenue and Flagler Street. Miami Avenue separates east from west, and Flagler Street separates north from south. Avenues and courts run north–south; streets, terraces, and ways run east–west. Roads run diagonally, northwest–southeast. But other districts—Miami Beach, Coral Gables, and Hialeah—may or may not follow this system, and along the curve of Biscayne Bay, the symmetrical grid may shift diagonally. It's best to buy a detailed map, stick to the major roads, and ask directions early and often. However, make sure you're in a safe neighborhood or public place when you seek guidance; cabdrivers and cops are good resources.

SOUTH BEACH

The hub of South Beach is the 1-square-mi Art Deco District, fronted on the east by Ocean Drive and on the west by Alton Road. In recent years the story of South Beach has become a big part of the story of Miami. Back in the early 1980s the neighborhood's vintage hotels were badly run down. But a group of visionaries led by the late Barbara Baer Capitman, a spirited New York transplant, saw this group of buildings as architecturally significant and worth protecting from mindless urban renewal. Capitman was well into her sixties when she stepped in front of bulldozers ready to tear down the Senator, an Art Deco hotel. The Senator fell, but thanks to preservationists 40 others were saved. As the movement picked up, investors started restoring the interiors and repainting the exteriors of classic South Beach buildings. The area is now distinguished as the nation's first 20th-century district to be listed on the National Register of Historic Places, with 800 significant buildings making the roll.

Life along Ocean Drive now unfolds 24 hours a day. Beautiful people pose in hotel lounges and sidewalk cafés, tanned cyclists zoom past palm trees, and visitors flock to see the action. On Lincoln Road café crowds spill onto the sidewalks, weekend markets draw all kinds of visitors and their dogs, and thanks to a few late-night lounges the scene is just as alive at night.

You'll notice right away that several things are plentiful in South Beach. Besides the plethora of surgically enhanced bodies and cell phones, there are a lot of cars for a small area, and plenty of attentive meter maids. On-street parking is scarce, tickets are given freely when meters expire, and towing charges are high. Check your meter to see when you must pay to park; times vary by district. No quarters? Try the municipal lot west of the convention center; the 17th Street Garage between Pennsylvania and Meridian; the 16th Street Garage between Collins and Washington; or the 7th Street Garage at Washington and Collins.

Better yet, take advantage of the South Beach Local shuttle—it costs only a quarter and runs until the wee hours of the morning.

Numbers in the text correspond to numbers in the margin.

TWO GOOD WALKS

South Beach is the most pedestrian-friendly part of Miami, so if you've got the time, spend a couple of days exploring it on foot. Work the southern end of the beach one day, savoring the Art Deco architecture along Ocean Drive, the local museums, and the shops of Española Way. The next day, set your sights on the many pleasures of Lincoln Road and its neighboring attractions.

DAY 1

Start this walk early (8 AM) if you want to watch the awakening city without distraction. At this hour you're also likely to see a fashion photo shoot in progress, since photographers like early morning light. If you're really up for a good walk, start your day at the up-and-comingest part of South Beach: SoFi, so called because it's South of Fifth Street. Here South Pointe Park is a good place to watch cruise ships glide by. Walk north on Ocean Drive and two blocks west (Washington Avenue) to the **Sanford L. Ziff Jewish Museum of Florida ❶** ▶. From here return to Ocean Drive and head north, or, if you don't have the legs for it, begin your South Beach walking tour north of Fifth.

A bevy of Art Deco jewels hugs the drive here, and across the street lies palm-fringed Lummus Park. Cross to the west side of Ocean Drive and walk north, taking note of the Park Central Hotel (No. 640), built in 1937 by Deco architect Henry Hohauser. If you're in the vicinity of 10th Street after 10 AM, recross Ocean Drive to the beach side and visit the **Art Deco District Welcome Center ❷**. Rent a tape or hire a guide for an Art Deco District tour.

Look back across Ocean Drive and take a peek at the wonderful flying-saucer architecture of the Clevelander, at No. 1020. On the next block you'll see the late Gianni Versace's Spanish-Mediterranean Casa Casuarina. Graceful fluted columns stand guard at the Leslie (No. 1244) and the 1941 Carlyle (No. 1250); to their north is the much-photographed Cardozo. Walk two blocks west (away from the ocean) on 13th Street to Washington Avenue, and step inside the 1937 Depression moderne Miami Beach Post Office, designed by Howard Cheney, to see the rotunda and the Works Project Administration–era mural. Turn left on Washington and walk 2½ blocks south to the **Wolfsonian–Florida International University ❸**, where design and art used as propaganda from 1885 to 1945 are the focus.

Return north on Washington—without kids in tow—for a stop at the **World Erotic Art Museum ❹**, then continue past 14th Street, and turn left to end the tour on **Española Way ❺**. Return to Ocean Drive in time to pull up a chair at an outdoor café, order an espresso, and settle down for some people-watching, South Beach's most popular pastime. Or grab some late rays at the beach, which has unofficial gay, mixed, and family zones.

6

TIMING

To see only the Art Deco buildings on Ocean Drive, allow one hour. Schedule six hours for the whole tour, including a stop at a café and browsing time in the shops.

DAY 2

Start at **Lincoln Road Mall** ❻ ⌐, three blocks north of Española Way, and part of must-see South Beach. Look beyond the lively parade of pedestrians and you'll find architectural gems.

The next main street north of Lincoln Road is 17th Street, and to the east is the Miami Beach Convention Center, where Muhammad Ali (then known as Cassius Clay) defeated Sonny Liston for the world heavyweight boxing championship in 1964. Walk behind the massive building to the corner of Meridian Avenue and 19th Street to see the chilling **Holocaust Memorial** ❼. Just east is the compact Miami Beach Botanical Garden.

On the east side of the Convention Center, you'll find Park Avenue, site of such architectural jewels as the Adams Tyler Hotel at 2030 Park and the Streamline-style Plymouth at 336 21st Street. Continue east through Collins Park and its enormous baobab trees to the **Bass Museum of Art** ❽. Then make a loop back to Lincoln for a tour-ending shopping spree (you don't want to lug bags all day) or grab a libation at the Delano Hotel or the National Hotel. If you have kids—and energy—make a beeline by cab or rental car for the **Miami Children's Museum** ❾ and **Parrot Jungle Island** ❿, two attractions right across the road from each other on MacArthur Causeway.

TIMING

Allow about four hours to amble down Lincoln Road and visit the museums, gardens, and architectural sights a few blocks to the north. It's worth planning the tour around a meal, given the abundance of Lincoln Road's outdoor dining options. Set aside an entire day to include a side trip to MacArthur Causeway.

WHAT TO SEE

❷ **Art Deco District Welcome Center.** Run by the Miami Design Preservation League, the center provides information about the buildings in the district. A gift shop sells 1930s–1950s Art Deco memorabilia, posters, and books on Miami's history. Several tours—covering Lincoln Road, Española Way, North Beach, and the entire Art Deco District, among others—start here. You can rent audiotapes for a self-guided tour, join one of the regular morning (Wednesday and Friday through Sunday) or Thursday-evening walking tours, or take a bicycle tour. All of the options provide detailed histories of the Art Deco hotels. Don't miss the special boat tours during Art Deco Weekend, in early January. ✉ *1001 Ocean Dr., at Barbara Capitman Way (10th St.), South Beach* ☎ *305/531–3484* ☒ *Tours $20* ☉ *Sun.–Thurs. 10–7, Fri. and Sat. 10–6.*

❽ **Bass Museum of Art.** The Bass, in historic Collins Park, is part of the Miami Beach Cultural Park, which includes the Miami City Bal-

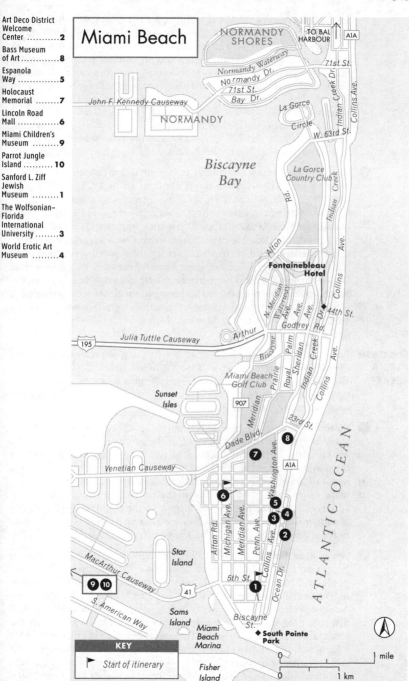

Art Deco District
Welcome
Center **2**

Bass Museum
of Art **8**

Espanola
Way **5**

Holocaust
Memorial **7**

Lincoln Road
Mall **6**

Miami Children's
Museum **9**

Parrot Jungle
Island **10**

Sanford L. Ziff
Jewish
Museum **1**

The Wolfsonian–
Florida
International
University **3**

World Erotic Art
Museum **4**

Miami Beach

NORMANDY
SHORES

TO BAL
HARBOUR

A1A

71st St.

Normandy Waterway

Normandy Dr.

71st St.
Bay Dr.

John F. Kennedy Causeway

NORMANDY

La Gorce
Circle

W. 63rd St.

Collins Ave.

Indian Creek Dr.

*Biscayne
Bay*

La Gorce
Country Club

Indian Creek

Alton Rd.

**Fontainebleau
Hotel**

6

Collins Ave.

N. Meridian Ave.

Waterway Ave.

Palm Ave.

44th St.

Collins Rd.

Godfrey

195

Julia Tuttle Causeway

Arthur

Biscayne

Prairie

Palm

Royal

Sheridan

Indian Creek

Collins

Ave.

Miami Beach
Golf Club

Sunset
Isles

907

Meridian

Dade Blvd.

23rd St.

A T L A N T I C   O C E A N

8

7

A1A

Venetian Causeway

6

Washington Ave.

Alton Rd.

Michigan Ave.

Meridian Ave.

Penn. Ave.

Collins Ave.

5

3

4

2

Star
Island

MacArthur Causeway

9 **10**

S. American Way

41

5th St.

Collins Ave.

Ocean Dr.

1

Sams
Island

Biscayne
St.

Miami
Beach
Marina

◆ **South Pointe
Park**

Fisher
Island

KEY

► *Start of itinerary*

0   1 mile

0   1 km

let's Arquitectonica-designed facility and the Miami Beach Regional Library. The original building, constructed of keystone, has unique Maya-inspired carvings. The expansion designed by Japanese architect Arata Isozaki houses another wing and an outdoor sculpture garden. Special exhibitions join a diverse collection of European art. Works on permanent display include *The Holy Family*, a painting by Peter Paul Rubens; *The Tournament*, one of several 16th-century Flemish tapestries; and works by Albrecht Dürer and Henri de Toulouse-Lautrec. Special exhibits often cost a little extra. ⊠*2121 Park Ave., at 21st St., South Beach* ☎*305/673–7530* ⊕*www.bassmuseum.org* ☞*$8* ☉*Tues.–Sat. 10–5, Thurs. 10–9, Sun. 11–5.*

⑤ Española Way. There's a decidedly Bohemian feel to this street lined with Mediterranean Revival buildings constructed in 1925. Al Capone's gambling syndicate ran its operations upstairs at what is now the Clay Hotel, a youth hostel. At a nightclub here in the 1930s, future bandleader Desi Arnaz strapped on a conga drum and started beating out a rumba rhythm. Visit this quaint avenue on a weekend afternoon, when merchants and craftspeople set up shop to sell everything from handcrafted bongo drums to fresh flowers. Between Washington and Drexel avenues the road has been narrowed to a single lane, and Miami Beach's trademark pink sidewalks have been widened to accommodate sidewalk cafés and shops selling imaginative clothing, jewelry, and art. ⊠*Española Way, between 14th and 15th Sts. from Washington to Jefferson Aves., South Beach.*

NEED A BREAK? Before taking on Española, head for hot dog heaven at **Dogma Grill** (⊠*1500 Washington Ave., at 15th St., South Beach* ☎*305/695–8259* ⊕*www.dogmagrill.com*), where their 20-plus toppings will seriously tempt you. You can also get turkey and veggie dogs, salads, and killer mint lemonade.

⑦ Holocaust Memorial. A bronze sculpture depicts refugees clinging to a giant bronze arm that reaches out of the ground and 42 feet into the air. Enter the surrounding courtyard to see a memorial wall and hear the music that seems to give voice to the 6 million Jews who died at the hands of the Nazis. It's easy to understand why Kenneth Triester's dramatic memorial is in Miami Beach: the city's community of Holocaust survivors was once the second largest in the country. ⊠*1933–1945 Meridian Ave., at Dade Blvd., South Beach* ☎*305/538–1663* ⊕*www. holocaustmmb.org* ☞*Free, donations welcome* ☉*Daily 9–9.*

⑥ Lincoln Road Mall. A playful 1990s redesign spruced up this open-air pedestrian mall, adding a grove of 20 towering date palms, five linear pools, and colorful broken-tile mosaics to the futuristic 1950s vision of Fontainebleau designer Morris Lapidus. Some of the shops are owner-operated boutiques with a delightful variety of clothing, furnishings, garden supplies, and decorative design. Others are the typical chain stores of American malls. Remnants of tired old Lincoln Road—beauty-supply and discount electronics stores on the Collins end of the strip—somehow fit nicely into the mix. The new Lincoln Road is fun, lively, and friendly for people old, young, gay, and straight—and their dogs. Folks skate, scoot, bike, or jog here. The best times to hit the road are during Sunday morning farmers' markets and on weekend evenings, when cafés bustle, art galleries open shows, street performers make the sidewalk their stage, and stores stay open late.

Two of the landmarks worth checking out at the eastern end of Lincoln Road are the massive 1940s keystone building at 420 Lincoln Road, which has a 1945 Leo Birchanky mural in the lobby, and the 1921 mission-style Miami Beach Community Church, at Drexel Avenue. The Lincoln Theatre (No. 541–545), at Pennsylvania Avenue, is a classical four-story Art Deco gem with friezes. The New World Symphony, a national advanced-training orchestra led by Michael Tilson Thomas, rehearses and performs here, and concerts are often broadcast via loudspeakers, to the delight of visitors. Just west, facing Pennsylvania, a fabulous Cadillac dealership sign was discovered underneath the facade of the Lincoln Road Millennium Building, on the south side of the mall. At Euclid Avenue there's a monument to Lapidus, who in his nineties watched the renaissance of his whimsical creation. At Lenox Avenue, a black-and-white Art Deco movie house with a Mediterranean barrel-tile roof is now the Colony Theater (No. 1040), where live theater and experimental films are presented. ⊠ *Lincoln Rd., between Collins Ave. and Alton Rd., South Beach.*

NEED A BREAK?

Lincoln Road is a great place to cool down with an icy treat while touring South Beach.

Try the homemade ice cream and sorbets—including Indian mango, key lime, and litchi—from the **Frieze Ice Cream Factory** (⊠ *1626 Michigan Ave., south of Lincoln Rd., South Beach* ☎ *305/538–2028*). Or try an authentic Italian gelato at the sleek glass-and-stainless-steel **Gelateria Parmalat** (⊠ *670 Lincoln Rd., between Euclid and Pennsylvania Aves., South Beach* ☎ *786/276–9475*). If you visit on a Sunday, stop at one of the many juice vendors, who will whip up made-to-order smoothies from mangos, oranges, and other fresh local fruits.

❾ Miami Children's Museum. This Arquitectonica-designed museum, both imaginative and geometric in appearance, is directly across the MacArthur Causeway from Parrot Jungle Island. Twelve galleries house hundreds of interactive, bilingual exhibits. Children can scan plastic groceries in the supermarket, scramble through a giant sand castle, climb a rock wall, learn about the Everglades, and combine rhythms in the world-music studio. ⊠ *980 MacArthur Causeway, Watson Island, Miami* ☎ *305/373–5437* ⊕ *www.miamichildrensmuseum.org* ⊠ *$10, parking $1 per hr* ☉ *Daily 10–6.*

❿ Parrot Jungle Island. South Florida's original tourist attraction—it opened in 1936 in South Miami—closed in 2002 but reopened in 2003 on an island between Miami and Miami Beach. The park is home to more than 1,100 exotic birds, a few orangutans and snakes, a squadron of flamingos, a rare albino alligator, and a liger (lion and tiger mix), plus amazing orchids and other flowering plants. There's also the Hippo, but in this case, it's a three-story waterslide open Wednesday through Sunday. Kids enjoy the hands-on (make that wings-on) experience of having parrots perch on their shoulders. The Japanese garden that once stood on this site is next door—it's open on weekends and free to enter. ■TIP➜**You can eat at the indoor-outdoor lakeside café, overlooking the Caribbean flamingos, without paying the park's admission fee.** ⊠*1111 Parrot Jungle Trail, off MacArthur Causeway (I–395), Watson Island, Miami* ☎*305/400–7000* ⊕*www.parrotjungle.com* ⊠*$27.95 plus $7 parking* ☉*Daily 10–6.*

❶ **Sanford L. Ziff Jewish Museum of Florida.** Listed on the National Register of Historic Places, this former synagogue, built in 1936, contains Art Deco chandeliers, 80 impressive stained-glass windows, and a permanent exhibit, MOSAIC: Jewish Life in Florida, which depicts more than 235 years of the Florida Jewish experience. The museum also hosts changing exhibits and events and has a museum store. ⊠*301 Washington Ave., at 3rd St., South Beach* ☎*305/672–5044* ⊕*www.jewishmuseum.com* ⊠*$6, free on Sat.* ☉*Tues.–Sun. 10–5.*

❸ **Wolfsonian–Florida International University.** An elegantly renovated 1927 storage facility is now both a research center and home to the 70,000-plus-item collection of modern design and "propaganda arts" amassed by Miami native Mitchell ("Micky") Wolfson Jr., a world traveler and connoisseur. Broad themes of the 19th and 20th centuries—nationalism, political persuasion, industrialization—are addressed in permanent and traveling shows. Included in the museum's eclectic holdings, which represent Art Deco, art moderne, art nouveau, Arts and Crafts, and other aesthetic movements, are 8,000 matchbooks collected by Egypt's King Farouk. ⊠*1001 Washington Ave., at 10th St., South Beach* ☎*305/531–1001* ⊕*www.wolfsonian.org* ⊠*$7, free after 6 on Fri.* ☉*Mon., Tues., Sat., and Sun. noon–6, Thurs. and Fri. noon–9.*

❹ **World Erotic Art Museum (WEAM).** The prudish can skip right on to the next stop, but anyone with an appreciation for the offbeat should check out whimsical, wonderful WEAM. The sexy collection, all owned by millionaire Naomi Wilzig, unfolds with contemporary and historical art of varying quality—there are amazing fertility statues from around the globe dating to 500 BC sharing the space with knickknacks that look like they came from the bawdiest yard sale on earth. An original phallic prop from Stanley Kubrick's *A Clockwork Orange* and an over-the-top Kama Sutra bed are worth the price of admission, but the real standout is "Miss Naomi," who is usually on hand to answer questions and provide behind-the-scenes anecdotes. Kids 17 and under are not admitted. ⊠*1205 Washington Ave., at 12th St., South Beach* ☎*305/532–9336* ⊕*www.weam.com* ⊠*$15* ☉*Daily 11 AM–midnight.*

DOWNTOWN MIAMI

Downtown Miami dazzles from a distance. Rapid-transit trains zoom across a bridge arcing high over the Miami River before disappearing into a cluster of high-rises. Business is the key to downtown Miami's daytime bustle. Traffic congestion from the high-rise offices and expensive parking tend to keep the locals away, unless they're bringing out-of-town guests to touristy Bayside Marketplace. But change is in the air—and a high-rise condo building boom is under way. Although it hasn't yet grown into its artsy new identity, Downtown deserves exploring. Thanks to the free Metromover, which runs inner and outer loops through Downtown and to nearby neighborhoods to the south and north, this is an excellent tour to take by rail. Attractions are conveniently located within about two blocks of the nearest station. If you're coming from north or east of Downtown, leave your car near a Metromover stop and take the Omni Loop downtown. If you're coming from south or west of Downtown, park your car at a Metrorail station and take a leg of the 21-mi elevated commuter system downtown.

Numbers in the text correspond to numbers in the margin and on the Downtown Miami map.

A GOOD TOUR

Make your way to the Metrorail/Metromover Government Center Station, board the southbound Brickell Avenue Loop, and get off at the Financial District stop. From the station, turn left and head up Brickell Avenue, where sleek high-rises, international banks, and a handful of restaurants have replaced the mansions of yesteryear. For retail therapy or a bite, take a left on Southeast 10th Street to check out **Brickell Village ⑪ ⌐**. This burgeoning neighborhood of low-rise condos and shops clustered around South Miami Avenue has some rather popular restaurants, so you might want to save it for an evening visit. Return to Brickell at Southeast 8th Street and cross the street to look at the First Presbyterian Church, a 1949 keystone structure with a distinctive verdigris roof two blocks north.

As you walk across the Miami River via the Brickell Avenue Bridge, check out the parcel of riverfront land on the right, the site of the Miami Circle. A multimillion-dollar development was halted here when archaeologists discovered a circular stone formation and other ancient artifacts. After crossing the bridge, go left to the Hyatt Regency Miami, adjacent to the James L. Knight Convention Center. Walk down Southeast 4th Street to an old yellow-frame house, Flagler Palm Cottage, a 19th-century anachronism in this modern neighborhood. From the adjoining Bijan's on the River you can look out over the Miami River, a hub of Native American commerce hundreds of years ago (and, more recently, drug running).

From here you can reboard the Metromover at Riverwalk Station to ride past the following sights, or you can remain on foot and walk up Southeast 1st Avenue to Southeast 2nd Street. You'll instantly notice the proliferation of Brazilian flags in the storefronts. This lively part of Downtown draws crowds of South American shoppers. Turn right at Southeast 2nd Street and continue for three blocks, passing the towering 55-story Wachovia Financial Center, the second-tallest building in Florida; royal palms grace its 1-acre Palm Court plaza. Proceed until you reach Biscayne Boulevard at the southwest corner of Bayfront Park. Rising up in the corner of the park is the white *Challenger* Memorial, commemorating the space shuttle that exploded in 1986. Continue north on Biscayne on foot, past Plaza Bolivar, a tribute by

Downtown Miami

KEY

☐ M	Metro stops
---	Metromover
►	Start of itinerary

Brickell Village **11**

Miami-Dade
Cultural Center **12**

Wynwood Art District **13**

Cuban immigrants to their adopted country. You'll reach the JFK Torch of Friendship, a plaza adorned with plaques representing all the South and Central American countries except Cuba, and Bayside Marketplace, the popular entertainment, dining, and retail complex. If you reboarded Metromover, get off at the College/Bayside Station to visit Bayside and to continue the next part of the tour on foot. From Bayside, cross Biscayne and walk up Northeast 3rd Street to Northeast 2nd Avenue, where you'll come upon Miami Dade College, home of two worthy art galleries. One block farther west stands the U.S. Courthouse, notable for the epic Depression-era mural inside that depicts Floridian progress.

Turn south on Northeast 1st Avenue and walk one block to Northeast 2nd Street. On the corner stands the 1922 Historic Gesu Church, one of South Florida's oldest. Return to Northeast 2nd Avenue; then turn right. Before you is the architectural clutter that characterizes downtown Miami: a cacophony of gaudy outlet shops, homely storefronts, and the occasional gem of a building. At 174 East Flagler, the landmark Gusman Center for the Performing Arts is a stunning movie palace that now serves as a concert hall. Now head west on Flagler Street, downtown Miami's commercial spine. You'll see the 1936 Streamline moderne building housing Macy's department store. After one more block on Flagler, the Dade County Courthouse comes into view. After crossing 1st Avenue you'll arrive at the **Miami-Dade Cultural Center ⑫**, home of the Miami Art Museum, the Historical Museum of Southern Florida, and the Miami-Dade Public Library. From the adjacent Metrorail/Metromover Government Center Station, you can reboard the Metromover's Downtown Inner Loop and get a bird's-eye view of the downtown area.

TIMING

To walk and ride to the various points of interest, allow three hours. If you want to spend additional time eating and shopping at Bayside, allow at least five hours. To include museum visits, allow seven hours.

WHAT TO SEE

⑪ **Brickell Village.** You can spend a delightful evening outdoors in Brickell Village, a neighborhood rarely discovered by visitors. After checking out the shops and condos by day, return at sunset for drinks at the **Big Fish** (✉ 55 S.W. Miami Avenue Rd., at S.E. 5th St. ☎ 305/373–1770), a riverfront restaurant decorated with metal fish scales that's hard to find but worth the effort. From here you can see Downtown's dazzling skyline, the neon art that adorns the span of the Metrorail bridge, and the nonstop activity along the Miami River. You can get homemade gelato or tiramisu at **Perricone's Marketplace and Café** (✉ 15 S.E. 10th St. ☎ 305/374–9449). The venerable blues and rock bar (est. 1912) **Tobacco Road** (✉ 626 S. Miami Ave. ☎ 305/374–1198) is a great stop for live music. And there's no hurry to leave, as they close at 5 AM. Just north at the Miami River is the **Brickell Avenue Bridge.** More of an outdoor art piece than a mere bridge, it's decorated with a bronze sculpture of a Tequesta Indian, a collage of native wildlife, and a series of smaller bronze plaques of area fauna on both sides of the bridge, works of Manuel Carbonell (1995). ⊠*Brickell Ave. between S.E. 5th St. and Biscayne Blvd. Way, Downtown.*

⑫ **Miami-Dade Cultural Center.** Containing three cultural resources, this
★ fortresslike 3-acre complex is a Downtown focal point. The **Miami**
☺ **Art Museum** (☎*305/375–3000* ⊕*www.miamiartmuseum.org*) presents major touring exhibitions of work by international artists, focusing on art since 1945. Open Tuesday–Friday 10–5 (until 9 the third Thursday of the month) and weekends noon–5, the museum charges $5 admission ($6 including the historical museum). At the **Historical Museum of Southern Florida** (☎*305/375–1492* ⊕*www.hmsf.org*) you'll be treated to pure South Floridiana, with exhibits celebrating Miami's multicultural heritage and history, including an old Miami streetcar, cigar labels, and a railroad exhibit, plus a display on prehistoric Miami. Admission is $5 ($6 including the art museum), and hours are Monday to Saturday 10–5, and Sunday noon–5. The **Main Public Library** (☎*305/375–2665*)—open Monday to Wednesday and Friday to Saturday 9–6, Thursday 9–9, plus Sunday 1–5 from August to May—contains nearly 4 million holdings and a Florida Department that includes rare books, documents, and photographs recording Miami history. It also has art exhibits in the auditorium and in the second-floor lobby. ⊠*101 W. Flagler St., between N.W. 1st and 2nd Aves., Downtown.*

⑬ **Wynwood Art District.** Just north of downtown Miami, the up-and-coming Wynwood Art District is peppered with galleries, art studios, and private collections that are open to the public. Visit during Wynwood's monthly gallery walk to maximize viewing of the smaller venues. Make sure a visit includes a stop at the

★ **Margulies Collection at the Warehouse** (⊠*591 N.W. 27th St., between N.W. 5th and 6th Aves., Downtown* ☎*305/576–1051* ⊕*www.margulieswarehouse.com*). Martin Margulies's collection of vintage and contemporary photography, videos, and installation art in a 45,000-square-foot space makes for eye-popping viewing. It's free to enter and open from October to April, Wednesday to Saturday, 11 to 4. Fans of edgy art will appreciate the **Rubell Family Collection** (⊠*95 N.W. 29th St., between N. Miami Ave. and N.W. 1st Ave., Downtown* ☎*305/573–6090* ⊕*www.rubellfamilycollection.com*). Mera and Don Rubell have accumulated work by artists from the 1970s to the present, including Jeff Koons, Cindy Sherman, Damien Hirst, Keith Haring, and Ansel M. Keifer. Admission is $5, and the gallery is open Wednesday to Sunday 10 to 6. ⊠*N.W. 10th St. to N.W. 37th St. between Biscayne Blvd. and N.W. 6th Ave., Wynwood Art District* ⊕*www.wynwoodartdistrict. com* ☉*times vary, approx. 10–5; gallery walks 2nd Sat. 7–10.*

LITTLE HAVANA

First settled en masse by Cubans in the early 1960s, after that country's Communist revolution, Little Havana is a predominantly working-class area and the core of Miami's Hispanic community. Spanish is the language that predominates, but don't be surprised if the cadence is less Cuban and more Salvadoran or Nicaraguan. The main commercial zone is bounded by Northwest 1st Street, Southwest 9th Street, Ronald Reagan Avenue (Southwest 12th Avenue), and Teddy Roosevelt Boulevard (Southwest 17th Avenue). Calle Ocho (Southwest 8th Street) is the axis of the neighborhood.

Some of the restaurants host traditional flamenco performances and Sevillaña *tablaos* (dances performed on a wood-plank stage, using castanets), and some clubs feature recently arrived Cuban acts. Intimate neighborhood theaters host top-notch productions ranging from Spanish classics to contemporary satire. Throughout the year a variety of festivals commemorate Miami's Hispanic heritage, and residents from no fewer than five countries celebrate their homeland's independence days in Little Havana. On the last Friday of every month Little Havana takes its culture to the streets for Cultural Fridays, between 6:30 and 11 PM on 8th Street from 14th to 17th avenues. Art expositions, music, and avant-garde street performances bring a young, hip crowd to the neighborhood.

Numbers in the text correspond to numbers in the margin.

A GOOD WALK

An ideal place to discover the area's flavor, both literally and figuratively, is along Calle Ocho (Southwest 8th Street), at the eastern end of Tamiami Trail between Southwest 12th and 27th avenues. You'll need to drive in, but definitely park, since the only way to really experience the neighborhood is on foot; metered spots are readily available, and it's not too hard to find a free spot on a side street. Start at **Cuban Memorial Boulevard** ⑭ ☞ , a section of Southwest 13th Avenue just south of Calle Ocho. Memorials to Cuban patriots line the boulevard, and the plaza here is the scene of frequent political rallies. On Mother's Day older women adorn a statue of the Virgin Mary with floral wreaths and join in song to honor her. Believers claim a miracle occurs here each midafternoon, when a beam of sunlight shoots through the foliage overhead directly onto the Christ child in the Virgin's arms.

On Calle Ocho to the east of the boulevard is El Aguila Vidente (The Seeing Eagle), one of many neighborhood *botánicas* (stores selling spiritual items). The shop welcomes the respectfully curious. A particularly worthwhile stop is next door at the **El Credito Cigar Factory** ⑮. At this family-owned business, one of about a half-dozen cigar factories in the neighborhood, employees deftly hand-roll more than a million stogies each year. On Calle Ocho, between Southwest 13th and 17th avenues, you'll find the Walkway of the Stars. The Latin version of its Hollywood namesake, the strip of sidewalk embedded with stars honors many of the world's top Hispanic celebrities, among them the late salsa queen Celia Cruz, crooner Julio Iglesias, and superstar Gloria Estefan. Stop in at La Casa de los Trucos, a magic store where the owners sometimes demonstrate their skills. Farther west on Calle Ocho is Domino Park, at 15th Avenue. The game tables are always two deep with guayabera-clad men—it wasn't until the last decade that the park's male domino aficionados even allowed women into their domain.

6

TIMING   If a quick multicultural experience is your goal, set aside an hour or two to do this tour on foot. For real ethnic immersion, allow more time; eating is a must, as well as a peek at the area's residential streets lined with distinctive homes. Especially illuminating are Little Havana tours led by Dr. Paul George (101 W. Flagler St. ☎305/375–1621), a history professor at Miami Dade College and historian for the Historical Museum of Southern Florida.

WHAT TO SEE

⑭ **Cuban Memorial Boulevard.** Two blocks in the heart of Little Havana ⚑ are filled with monuments to Cuba's freedom fighters. Among the memorials are the *Eternal Torch of the Brigade 2506,* commemorating those who were killed in the failed Bay of Pigs invasion of 1961; a bust of 19th-century hero Antonio Maceo; and a bas-relief map of Cuba depicting each of its *municipios.* There's also a bronze statue in honor of Tony Izquierdo, who participated in the Bay of Pigs invasion, served in Nicaragua's Somozan forces, and interestingly enough was also on the CIA payroll. ⊠*S.W. 13th Ave., south of S.W. 8th St., Little Havana.*

⑮ **El Credito Cigar Factory.** Through the giant storefront windows you can see cigars being rolled. Many of the workers at this family business dating back three generations learned their trade in prerevolutionary Cuba. Today the tobacco leaf they use comes primarily from the Dominican Republic and Mexico, and the wrappers from Connecticut, making theirs a truly multinational product. A walk-in humidor has more than 40 brands favored by customers such as Arnold Schwarzenegger, Bill Clinton, Robert De Niro, and Bill Cosby. ⊠*1106 S.W. 8th St., near S.W. 11th Ave., Little Havana* ☎*305/858–4162* ⊘ *Weekdays 8–5:30, Sat. 9–4.*

▮ **NEED A BREAK?**   Sorry, there's no Starbucks in Little Havana—the locals probably wouldn't touch the stuff, anyway—but everywhere are walk-up windows peddling the quick energy of thimble-size *café cubano* for as little as 40¢. The locals call it *un cafecito* (literally, "a small coffee"), but be warned that it's high-octane and sure to keep you going through this tour. In the mood for something refreshing? Try **Las Pinareños** (⊠*1334 S.W. 8th St., Little Havana* ☎*305/285–1135*), a *fruteria* (fruit stand), for fresh cold coconut juice served in a whole coconut, mango juice, or other *jugos* (juices). For something a little more substantial, pop into **Exquisito Restaurant** (⊠*1510 S.W. 8th St., Little Havana* ☎*305/643–0227*), next to the Tower Theatre. The unassuming Cuban café serves up delectable yuca with garlic sauce and other traditional dishes.

COCONUT GROVE

Eclectic and intriguing, Miami's Coconut Grove can be considered the tropical equivalent of New York's Greenwich Village. A haven for writers and artists, the neighborhood has never quite outgrown its image as a small village. During the day it's business as usual in Coconut Grove, much as in any other Miami neighborhood. But in the evening, especially on weekends, it seems as if someone flips a switch and the streets come alive. Locals and tourists jam into small boutiques, sidewalk cafés, and stores lodged in two massive retail-entertainment complexes. For blocks in every direction, students, honeymooning couples, families, and prosperous retirees flow in and out of a mix of galleries, restaurants, bars, bookstores, comedy clubs, and theaters. With this weekly influx of traffic, parking can pose a problem. There's a well-lighted city garage at 3315 Rice Street, or look for police to direct you to parking lots where you'll pay $5–$10 for an evening's slot. If you're staying in the Grove, leave the car behind, and your night will get off to an easier start.

Nighttime is the right time to see Coconut Grove, but in the day you can take a casual drive around the neighborhood to see its diverse architecture. Posh estates mingle with rustic cottages, modest frame homes, and stark modern dwellings, often on the same block. If you're into horticulture, you'll be impressed by the Garden of Eden–like foliage that seems to grow everywhere without care. In truth, residents are determined to keep up the Grove's village-in-a-jungle look, so they lavish attention on exotic plantings even as they battle to protect any remaining native vegetation.

Numbers in the text correspond to numbers in the margin.

A GOOD TOUR

From downtown Miami take Brickell Avenue south. Follow the signs to Vizcaya and Coconut Grove, and you'll reach South Miami Avenue. This street turns into South Bayshore Drive a few miles down. Continue south and watch on your left for the entrance to the don't-miss **Vizcaya Museum and Gardens** 16 ☞, an estate with an Italian Renaissance–style villa. Spend some time in the building and on the grounds; then head less than 100 yards farther down the road. On your right is the **Miami Museum of Science and Planetarium** 17, a hands-on museum with animated displays for all ages.

As you leave the museum and head toward the village center of Coconut Grove, South Bayshore switches from four lanes to two and back again. Before you hit the village, you may wish to stop at David T. Kennedy Park, which has 28 waterfront acres of Australian pine, lush lawns, and walking and jogging paths. Return to Main Highway and to the historic village of Coconut Grove. As you reenter the village center, note on your left the Coconut Grove Playhouse. On your right, beyond the benches and shelter, is the entrance to the **Barnacle Historic State Park** 18, a residence built by Commodore Ralph Munroe in 1891. The house and grounds offer a glimpse into Miami's early Anglo years. After getting your fill of history, relax and spend the evening mingling with Coconut Grove's artists and intellectuals. Shop along Grand Avenue and Mary Street, and be sure to check out **CocoWalk** 19 and the **Mayfair in the Grove** 20, two collections of stores and restaurants.

Plan on devoting from six to eight hours to enjoy Vizcaya, other bayfront sights, and the village's shops, restaurants, and nightlife.

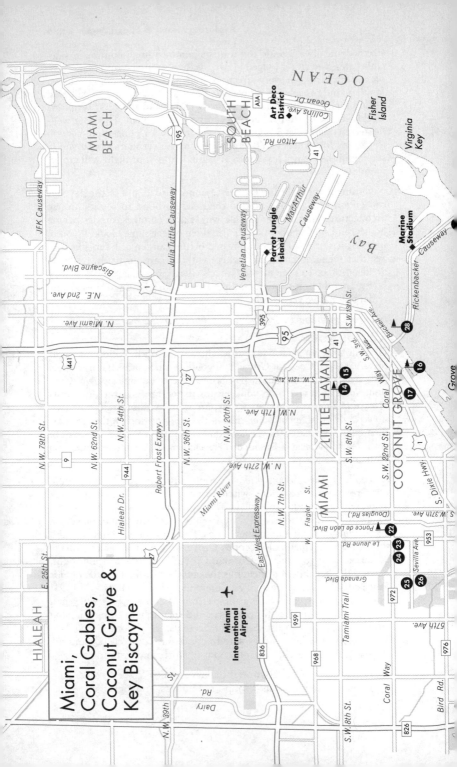

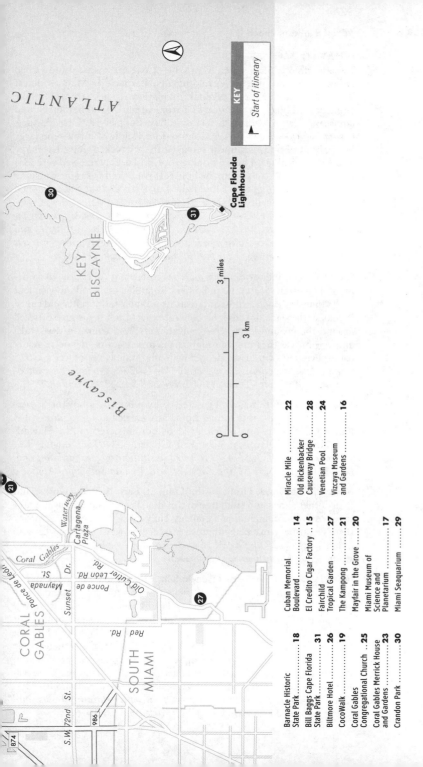

KEY

▲ Start of itinerary

ATLANTIC

Biscayne

Cape Florida
Lighthouse

**KEY
BISCAYNE**

**CORAL
GABLES**

**SOUTH
MIAMI**

Cartagena
Plaza

Coral Gables

Ponce de León

Ponce de León Blvd.

Sunset Dr.

Old Cutler Rd.

Red Rd.

Maynada St.

Waterway

S.W. 72nd St.

874

986

0   3 km

0   3 miles

Barnacle Historic
State Park **18**

Bill Baggs Cape Florida
State Park **31**

Biltmore Hotel **26**

CocoWalk **19**

Coral Gables
Congregational Church .. **25**

Coral Gables Merrick House
and Gardens **23**

Crandon Park **30**

Cuban Memorial
Boulevard **14**

El Credito Cigar Factory .. **15**

Fairchild
Tropical Garden **27**

The Kampong **21**

Mayfair in the Grove **20**

Miami Museum of
Science and
Planetarium **17**

Miami Seaquarium **29**

Miracle Mile **22**

Old Rickenbacker
Causeway Bridge **28**

Venetian Pool **24**

Vizcaya Museum
and Gardens **16**

WHAT TO SEE

⓲ **Barnacle Historic State Park.** A pristine bayfront manse sandwiched between cramped luxury developments, Barnacle is Miami's oldest house still standing on its original foundation. To get here, you'll hike along an old buggy trail through a tropical hardwood hammock and landscaped lawn leading to Biscayne Bay. Built in 1891 by Florida's first snowbird—New Yorker Commodore Ralph Munroe—the large home, built of timber Munroe salvaged from wrecked ships, has many original furnishings, a broad sloping roof, and deeply recessed verandas that channel sea breezes into the house. If your timing is right, you may catch one of the monthly Moonlight Concerts, and the old-fashioned picnic on the Fourth of July is popular. *✉3485 Main Hwy., Coconut Grove ☎305/442–6866 ⊕www.floridastateparks.org/thebarnacle ✎$1, concerts $5 ⊗Fri.–Mon. 9–4; tours at 10, 11:30, 1, and 2:30; group tours for 10 or more Tues.–Thurs. by reservation; concerts Sept.–May on evenings near the full moon 6–9, call for dates.*

⓳ **CocoWalk.** This indoor-outdoor mall has three floors of nearly 40 name-brand (Victoria's Secret, Gap, Banana Republic, etc.) and independent shops that stay open almost as late as its popular restaurants and clubs. Kiosks with beads, incense, herbs, and other small items are scattered around the ground level; street entertainers hold court on weekends; and the movie theaters and nightspots are upstairs. If you're ready for an evening of touristy people-watching, this is the place. *✉3015 Grand Ave., Coconut Grove ☎305/444–0777 ⊕www.galleryatcocowalk.com ⊗Sun.–Thurs. 11–10, Fri. and Sat. 11 AM–midnight.*

The Kampong. With nearly 11 acres of exquisite, flamboyant flowering trees and fruits, this former home and garden of horticulturist Dr. David Fairchild is one of five gardens administered by the Hawaii-based National Tropical Botanical Garden. *✉4013 Douglas Rd., Coconut Grove ☎305/442–7169 ⊕www.ntbg.org/gardens/kampong.php ✎$10 ⊗Tours by appointment, usually 2nd Sat. Sept.–Apr.*

⓴ **Mayfair in the Grove.** Home to the Limited, Bath & Body Works, and many other shops and restaurants, this mall is best known for its entertainment venues, including a comedy club and a lounge. On Saturday there's a farmers' market with fresh produce, flowers, baked goods, and handicrafts. *✉2911 Grand Ave., Coconut Grove ☎305/448–1700 ⊕www.mayfairinthegrove.net ⊗Daily 11–11.*

⓱ **Miami Museum of Science and Planetarium.** This museum is chock-full of hands-on sound, gravity, and electricity displays for children and adults alike. A wildlife center houses native Florida snakes, turtles, tortoises, and birds of prey. Outstanding traveling exhibits appear throughout the year, and virtual reality, life-science demonstrations, and Internet technology are on hand every day. If you're here the first Friday of the month, stick around for a laser-light rock-and-roll show, presented in the planetarium at 9 and 10, or just check out the Weintraub Observatory for free. *✉3280 S. Miami Ave., Coconut Grove ☎305/646–4200 ⊕www.miamisci.org ✎Museum exhibits, planetarium shows, and wildlife center $17, laser show $7 ⊗Museum daily 10–6.*

Vizcaya Museum & Gardens. Of the 10,000 people living in Miami between 1912 and 1916, about 1,000 of them were gainfully employed by Chicago industrialist James Deering to build this Italian Renaissance–style winter residence. Once comprising 180 acres, the grounds now occupy a 30-acre tract that includes a native hammock and more than 10 acres of formal gardens with fountains overlooking Biscayne Bay. The house, open to the public, contains 70 rooms, 34 of which are filled with paintings, sculpture, antique furniture, and other fine and decorative arts. The pieces date from the 15th through the 19th century and represent the Renaissance, baroque, rococo, and neoclassical movements. So unusual and impressive is Vizcaya that visitors have included many major heads of state. Guided tours are available. Moonlight tours, in particular, offer a unique look at the gardens; call for reservations. ⊠ *3251 S. Miami Ave., Coconut Grove* ☎ *305/250–9133* ⊕ *www.vizcayamuseum.org* ⊠ *$12* ⊗ *Daily 9:30–4:30, garden 9:30–5:30.*

CORAL GABLES

You can easily spot Coral Gables from the window of a Miami-bound jetliner—just look for the massive orange tower of the Biltmore Hotel rising from a lush green carpet of trees concealing the city's gracious homes. The canopy is as much a part of this planned city as its distinctive architecture, all attributed to the vision of George E. Merrick nearly 100 years ago.

The story of this city began in 1911, when Merrick inherited 1,600 acres of citrus and avocado groves from his father. Through judicious investment he nearly doubled the tract to 3,000 acres by 1921. Merrick dreamed of building an American Venice here, complete with canals and homes. Working from this vision, he began designing a city based on centuries-old prototypes from Mediterranean countries. Unfortunately for Merrick, the devastating no-name hurricane of 1926, followed by the Great Depression, prevented him from fulfilling many of his plans. He died at 54, an employee of the post office. Today Coral Gables has a population of about 43,000. In its bustling downtown, more than 150 multinational companies maintain headquarters or regional offices, and the University of Miami campus in the southern part of the Gables brings a youthful vibrancy to the area. A southern branch of the city extends down the shore of Biscayne Bay through neighborhoods threaded with canals. The gorgeous Fairchild Tropical Botanic Garden and beachfront Matheson Hammock Park dominate this part of the Gables.

Numbers in the text correspond to numbers in the margin.

A GOOD TOUR

Heading south from downtown Miami on Brickell Avenue, turn right onto Coral Way, a historic roadway characterized by an arch of banyan trees, and continue until you reach the grand entrance onto **Miracle Mile** ㉒ ▶. Actually only a half mile long, this stretch of Coral Way, from Douglas Road (Southwest 37th Avenue) to Le Jeune Road (Southwest 42nd Avenue) is the heart of downtown Coral Gables. Park your car and take time to explore the area on foot.

At some point you'll want to get back on wheels. Head west on Coral Way past the plentiful shops. Cross Le Jeune Road and bear right to continue on Coral Way, catching an eyeful of the ornate 1928 Spanish Renaissance Coral Gables City Hall and the adjacent Merrick Park. Heading west, you will see the Granada Golf Course—the oldest operating course in Florida. Make a slight right onto South Greenway Drive to continue along the golf course, and notice the stands of banyan trees that separate the fairways. At the end of the golf course the road makes a horseshoe bend, but continue west and cross Alhambra Circle to loop around the restored Merrick-designed Alhambra Water Tower. Return to Alhambra and follow it south to the next light, at Coral Way, where you can turn left and ogle beautifully maintained Spanish-style homes from the 1920s. Although there is only a small sign to announce it, at the corner of Coral Way and Toledo Street is the **Coral Gables Merrick House and Gardens** ㉓, Merrick's boyhood home. After a stop there, take a right back onto Coral Way and turn left on Granada. Four blocks ahead is the De Soto Plaza and Fountain, also Merrick designed.

Head to 9 o'clock, three-quarters of the way around the roundabout surrounding the fountain, and turn right onto De Soto Boulevard. Coming into view on your right is the Merrick-designed **Venetian Pool** ㉔, which Esther Williams made famous. After visiting the pool, double back on De Soto, crossing Granada at the fountain roundabout, and continue on DeSoto for a magnificent vista of the Biltmore Hotel, which, you guessed it, was designed by Merrick. Before you reach the hotel, you'll see the **Coral Gables Congregational Church** ㉕ on your right, one of the first churches built in this planned community. At the **Biltmore Hotel** ㉖ (parking to the right), enjoy the grounds and public areas. After you've visited the hotel, turn right on Anastasia Avenue, and proceed to the four-way stop at Granada. Turn right on Granada and follow its winding way south past Bird Road; you'll eventually reach Ponce de León Boulevard. Turn right and follow the boulevard until you reach the entrance to the main campus of the University of Miami. Turn right at the first stoplight (Stanford Drive) to enter the campus, and park in the lot on your right, which is designated for visitors to the Lowe Art Museum, where you can view fine art.

Now take a drive through Merrick's internationally themed Gables neighborhoods, which he called villages. He planned these residential areas, some of which are very small, to contrast with the Mediterranean look of the rest of the city. From Lowe Art Museum, cross Ponce De León and stay right to follow Maynada Street south to Hardee Road. Turn left on Hardee; between Leonardo and Cellini streets is French City Village. Continuing east on Hardee, you'll pass French Country Village between San Vincente and Maggiore streets. When you reach Le Jeune, turn right and drive five blocks south to Maya Avenue to see Dutch South African Village. At the end of the block, turn right on San Vicente and then left on Aurelia to reach Riviera Drive. At Riviera, turn right and enjoy the sprawling, elegant homes on both sides of the street. At the corner of Castania Avenue, you will see the Chinese Village. Turn right at Castania, and in two blocks turn left on Le Jeune and cross Dixie Highway. Then take a left turn onto Ponce De León and veer right onto Blue Road, which wends its way west through Riviera Country Club to Santa Maria Street, where you'll turn right. As you head north through the golf course toward Bird, you'll encounter Southern Colonial Village, also known as Florida Pioneer Village. When you reach Bird, take a right and proceed back to Le Jeune. Turn left on Le Jeune and drive four blocks north to Viscaya Avenue. If you turn left here, you'll see French Normandy Village.

Returning to Le Jeune, you can head north, back to Miracle Mile, or south about 1 mi to the large roundabout that connects to scenic Old Cutler Road. Old Cutler Road curves down through the uplands of southern Florida's coastal ridge toward the 83-acre **Fairchild Tropical Botanic Garden** ㉗. After admiring the tropical flora, you can backtrack ¼ mi north on Old Cutler Road to the entrance of the lovely Matheson Hammock Park and its beach.

TIMING

To see all the sights described here, you'll need two full days. Strolling Miracle Mile should take a bit more than an hour unless you plan to shop (don't forget the side streets); in that case, allow four hours. Save time—perhaps an hour or two—for a refreshing dip at the Venetian Pool, and plan to spend at least an hour getting acquainted with the Biltmore, longer if you'd like to order a drink and linger poolside or enjoy the elaborate Sunday brunch. Allow an hour to visit the Lowe Art Museum and another hour for the drive through the villages. You'll need a minimum of two hours to do Fairchild Tropical Garden justice, and if you want to spend time at the beach, Matheson Hammock Park will require at least another two hours.

WHAT TO SEE

Biltmore Hotel. Bouncing back stunningly from its dark days as an army hospital, this hotel has become the jewel of Coral Gables—a dazzling architectural gem with a colorful past. First opened in 1926, it was a hot spot for the rich and glamorous of the Jazz Age until it was converted to an army–air force regional hospital in 1942. The Veterans Administration continued to operate the hospital after World War II, until 1968. Then the Biltmore lay vacant for nearly 20 years before it underwent extensive renovations and reopened as a luxury hotel in 1987. Its 16-story tower, like the Freedom Tower in downtown Miami, is a replica of Seville's Giralda Tower. The magnificent pool, reportedly the largest hotel pool in the continental United States, is steeped in history—Johnny Weissmuller of Tarzan fame was a lifeguard there, and in the 1930s grand aquatic galas featuring alligator wrestling, synchronized swimming, and bathing beauties drew thousands. More recently it was President Clinton's preferred place to stay and golf. To the west is the Biltmore Country Club, a richly ornamented Beaux Arts–style structure with a superb colonnade and courtyard; it was reincorporated into the hotel in 1989. On Sunday free tours are offered at 1:30, 2:30, and 3:30. ✉ *1200 Anastasia Ave., near De Soto Blvd., Coral Gables* ☎ *305/445–1926* ⊕ *www.biltmorehotel.com.*

㉕ Coral Gables Congregational Church. With George Merrick as a charter member (he donated the land on which it stands), this parish was organized in 1923. Rumor has it Merrick built this small church, the first in the Gables, in honor of his father, a Congregational minister. The original interiors are still in magnificent condition, and a popular jazz series is held here. ✉ *3010 De Soto Blvd., at Anastasia Ave., Coral Gables* ☎ *305/448–7421* ⊕ *www.coralgablescongregational.org* ⊙ *Weekdays 8:30–5, Sun. services at 9:15 and 11.*

㉓ Coral Gables Merrick House and Gardens. In 1976 the city of Coral Gables acquired Merrick's boyhood home. Restored to its 1920s appearance, it contains Merrick family furnishings and artwork. The breezy veranda and coral rock construction are details you'll see repeated on many of the grand homes along Coral Way. ✉ *907 Coral Way, at Toledo St., Coral Gables* ☎ *305/460–5361* ☜ *House $5, grounds free* ⊙ *House tours Wed. and Sun. at 1, 2 and 3; grounds daily 8–sunset.*

OFF THE BEATEN PATH

Everglades Alligator Farm. Here's your chance to see gators, gators, gators—2,000 or so—and other wildlife, of course, such as blue herons, snowy egrets, and perhaps a rare roseate spoonbill. You can also take in alligator wrestling, reptile shows, and other animal exhibits as well as an airboat ride (they're not allowed inside Everglades National Park). This place is a little over 30 mi south of Miami, just south of the former pioneer town of Homestead. ✉ *40351 S.W. 192nd Ave., Florida City* ☎ *305/247–2628* ⊕ *www.everglades.com* ☜ *$13.50, $19 with airboat tour* ⊙ *Daily 9–6.*

Fairchild Tropical Botanic Garden. With 83 acres of lakes, sunken gardens, a 560-foot vine pergola, orchids, bellflowers, coral trees, bougainvillea, rare palms, and flowering trees, Fairchild is the largest tropical botanical garden in the continental United States. The tram tour highlights the best of South Florida's flora; then set off exploring on your own. A 2-acre rain-forest exhibit showcases tropical rain-forest plants from around the world complete with a waterfall and stream. The conservatory, Windows to the Tropics, houses rare tropical plants, including the Titan Arum (*Amorphophallus titanum*), a fast-growing variety that attracted thousands of visitors when it bloomed in 1998. (It was only the sixth documented bloom in this country in the 20th century.) The Keys Coastal Habitat, created in a marsh and mangrove area in 1995 with assistance from the Tropical Audubon Society, provides food and shelter to resident and migratory birds. Check out the Montgomery Botanical Center, a research facility devoted to palms and cycads. Spicing up Fairchild's calendar are plant sales, afternoon teas, and genuinely special events year-round, such as the International Mango Festival the second weekend in July. The excellent bookstore–gift shop carries books on gardening and horticulture, and the Garden Café serves sandwiches and, seasonally, smoothies made from the garden's own crop of tropical fruits. ✉ *10901 Old Cutler Rd., Coral Gables* ☎ *305/667– 1651* ⊕ *www.fairchildgarden.org* ☜ *$20* ⊙ *Daily 9:30–4:30.*

**OFF THE
BEATEN
PATH**

Metrozoo. Don't miss a visit to this top-notch zoo, the only subtropical zoo in the continental United States. Its 290 acres, 14 mi south of Miami, are home to more than 900 animals that roam on islands surrounded by moats. Take the monorail for a cool overview, then walk around to take a closer look at such attractions as the Tiger Temple, where white tigers roam, and the African Plains exhibit, where giraffes, ostriches, and zebras graze in a simulated natural habitat. You can even feed veggies to the giraffes at Samburu Station. The Wings of Asia aviary has about 300 exotic birds representing 70 species flying free within the junglelike enclosure. There's also a petting zoo with a meerkat exhibit and interactive opportunities, such as those at Dr. Wilde's World and the Ecology Theater, where kids can touch Florida animals like alligators and opossums. An educational and entertaining wildlife show is given three times daily. In addition to standard fare, the snack bar offers local favorites such as Cuban sandwiches, *arepas* (corn pancake sandwiches), and Cuban coffee—and cold beer. ⊠ *12400 Coral Reef Dr. (S.W. 152nd St.), Richmond Heights, Miami* ☎ *305/251–0400* ⊕ *www.miamimetrozoo.com* ☏ *$11.50, 45-min tram tour $4* ☉ *Daily 9:30–5:30; last admission at 4.*

Miracle Mile. Even with competition from some impressive malls, this half-mile stretch of retail stores continues to thrive because of its intriguing mixture of unique boutiques, bridal shops, art galleries, charming restaurants, and upscale nightlife venues. ⊠ *Coral Way between S.W. 37th and S.W. 42nd Aves., Coral Gables.*

㉔
Fodor'sChoice
★

Venetian Pool. Sculpted from a rock quarry in 1923 and fed by artesian wells, this 825,000-gallon municipal pool remains quite popular because of its themed architecture—a fantasized version of a waterfront Italian village—created by Denman Fink. The pool has earned a place on the National Register of Historic Places and showcases a nice collection of vintage photos depicting 1920s beauty pageants and swank soirées held long ago. Paul Whiteman played here, Johnny Weissmuller and Esther Williams swam here, and you should, too (but no kids under three). A snack bar, lockers, and showers make this must-see user-friendly as well. ⊠ *2701 De Soto Blvd., at Toledo St., Coral Gables* ☎ *305/460–5356* ⊕ *www.venetianpool.com* ☏ *Apr.–Oct., $9; Nov.–Mar., $6, free parking across De Soto Blvd.* ☉ *June–Aug., weekdays 11–7:30, weekends 10–4:30; Sept. and Oct., Apr. and May, Tues.–Fri. 11–5:30, weekends 10–4:30; Nov.–Mar., Tues.–Fri. 10–4:30, weekends 10–4:30.*

KEY BISCAYNE & VIRGINIA KEY

Once upon a time, these barrier islands were an outpost for fishermen and sailors, pirates and salvagers, soldiers and settlers. The 95-foot Cape Florida Lighthouse stood tall during Seminole Indian battles and hurricanes. Coconut plantations covered two-thirds of Key Biscayne, and there were plans as far back as the 1800s to develop the picturesque island as a resort for the wealthy. Fortunately, the state and county governments set much of the land aside for parks, and both keys are now home to top-ranked beaches and golf, tennis, softball, and picnicking facilities. The long and winding bike paths that run through the islands are favorites for in-line skaters and cyclists. Incorporated in 1991, the village of Key Biscayne is a hospitable community of about 10,500; Virginia Key remains undeveloped at the moment, making these two playground islands especially family-friendly.

Numbers in the text correspond to numbers in the margin.

A GOOD TOUR

Day or night, there are few drives prettier than the one to Key Biscayne and Virginia Key. And if you're in a convertible on a balmy day—well, this kind of drive is what South Florida living is all about. You can also make this tour on in-line skates or bicycle.

From I–95 take the Key Biscayne exit to the Rickenbacker Causeway (a $1.25 toll covers your round-trip). If you plan to skate or bike, just park anywhere along the causeway after the tollbooth and take off. The beaches on either side of the causeway are popular for water sports, with sailboards, sailboats, and Jet Skis available for rental. The causeway bridge rises 75 feet, providing a spectacular if fleeting view of the cruise ships at the Port of Miami, to the north. You can also see the high-rises looming at the tip of South Beach to the northeast, the bright blue Atlantic straight ahead, and sailboat-dotted Biscayne Bay to the south. South of Powell Bridge you'll see anglers fishing off the **Old Rickenbacker Causeway Bridge** 28 ⌐ among the hungry seabirds.

After the causeway turns southeast on Virginia Key, you can spy the gold geodesic dome of the **Miami Seaquarium** 29. Visit the undersea world of South Florida and beyond; then cross the Bear Cut Bridge (popular for fishing) onto lush Key Biscayne. Past the marina on your right, winding Crandon Boulevard takes you to **Crandon Park** 30, home to one of South Florida's best-loved beaches. As you approach the village of Key Biscayne, take note of the iguana-crossing signs warning motorists of the many green reptiles that scamper about the area. As you drive through town, you'll see luxurious beachfront condos and smaller buildings on your left and single-family houses on your right. Peek down some of the side streets—especially those along waterways—and you can spot spectacular bayfront mansions. Crandon turns into Grapetree Drive as you enter **Bill Baggs Cape Florida State Park** 31, a 410-acre park with great beaches, an excellent café, picnic areas, and at its southern tip the brick Cape Florida Lighthouse and light keeper's cottage. After you've taken the sun, or perhaps a bicycle ride, in the park, backtrack on Crandon to the causeway. On your way to the mainland, there's a panoramic view of downtown Miami as you cross the bridge.

TIMING   Set aside the better part of a day for this tour, saving a few afternoon hours for Crandon Park and the Cape Florida Lighthouse.

WHAT TO SEE

③1 Bill Baggs Cape Florida State Park.

Fodor'sChoice ★ Thanks to great beaches, sunsets, and a lighthouse, this park at Key Biscayne's southern tip is worth the drive. It has boardwalks, 18 picnic shelters, and two cafés that serve light lunches. A stroll or ride along walking and bicycle paths provides wonderful views of Miami's dramatic skyline. From the southern end of the park you can see a handful of houses rising over the bay on wooden stilts, the remnants of Stiltsville, built in the

1940s and now dying a natural death. Bill Baggs has bicycle rentals, a playground, fishing piers, and guided tours of the **Cape Florida Lighthouse,** South Florida's oldest structure. The lighthouse was erected in 1845 to replace an earlier one destroyed in an 1836 Seminole attack, in which the keeper's helper was killed. Plantings around the lighthouse and keeper's cottage recall the island's past. The restored cottage and lighthouse offer free tours at 10 AM and 1 PM Thursday–Monday. Be there a half hour beforehand. ⌂*1200 S. Crandon Blvd., Key Biscayne* ☎*305/361–5811 or 305/361–8779* ⊕*www.floridastateparks. org/capeflorida* ☜*$3 per single-occupant vehicle, $5 per vehicle with 2–8 people; $1 per person on bicycle, bus, motorcycle, or foot* ☉*Daily 8–dusk, tours Thurs.–Mon. at 10 and 1; sign up ½ hr beforehand.*

③0 Crandon Park. This laid-back park in northern Key Biscayne is popular with families, and many educated beach enthusiasts rate the 3½-mi beach here among the top 10 beaches in North America. The sand is soft, there are no riptides, there's a great view of the Atlantic, and parking is both inexpensive and plentiful. Because it's a weekend favorite of locals, you'll get a good taste of multicultural Miami flavor: salsa and hip-hop, jerk chicken and barbecue ribs. **Crandon Gardens** at Crandon Park was once the site of a zoo. There are swans, waterfowl, and even hundreds of huge iguanas running loose. Nearby is a restored carousel (open weekends and major holidays), outdoor roller rink, and playground. At the north end of the beach is the free **Marjory Stoneman Douglas Biscayne Nature Center** (☎*305/361–6767*), open daily 9–4. Here you can explore sea-grass beds on a tour with a naturalist; see red, black, and white mangroves; and hike along the beach and hammock in the Bear Cut Preserve. ⌂*4000 Crandon Blvd., Key Biscayne* ☎*305/361– 5421* ⊕*www.miamidade.gov/parks/parks/crandon_beach.asp* ☜*Free, parking $5 per vehicle* ☉*Daily 8–sunset.*

②9 Miami Seaquarium. This classic but aging visitor attraction stages shows with sea lions, dolphins, and Lolita the killer whale. The Crocodile Flats exhibit has 26 Nile crocodiles. Discovery Bay, an endangered mangrove habitat, is home to indigenous Florida fish and rays, alligators, herons, egrets, and ibis. You can visit a shark pool, a tropical reef aquarium, and West Indian manatees. The big draw now is the Swim with Our Dolphins program. A two-hour session offers one-on-one interaction with the dolphins. It's expensive—$189 to touch, kiss, and swim with them—but the price does include park admission, towel, and snacks. Call for reservations. ✉ *4400 Rickenbacker Causeway, Virginia Key, Miami* ☎ *305/361–5705* ⊕ *www.miamiseaquarium.com* ✑ *$32, dolphin swim program $189, parking $7* ◷ *Daily 9:30–6, last admission at 4:30; dolphin swim daily at 8:30, noon, and 3:30.*

28 **Old Rickenbacker Causeway Bridge.** Here you can watch boat traffic pass through the channel, pelicans and other seabirds soar and dive, and dolphins cavort in the bay. Park at the bridge entrance, about a mile from the tollgate, and walk past anglers tending their lines to the gap where the center draw span across the Intracoastal Waterway was removed. On the right, on cool, clear winter evenings, the water sparkles with dots of light from hundreds of shrimp boats. ✉ *Rickenbacker Causeway south of Powell Bridge, east of Coconut Grove, Miami.*

WHERE TO EAT

Restaurants listed here have passed the test of time, but you might double-check by phone before you set out for the evening. At many of the hottest spots, you'll need a reservation to avoid a long wait for a table. And when you get your check, note whether a gratuity is already included; most restaurants add between 15% and 18% (ostensibly for the convenience of, and protection from, the many Latin-American and European tourists who are used to this practice in their homelands), but reduce or supplement it depending on your opinion of the service.

WHAT IT COSTS				
	¢	$	$$	$$$	$$$$
AT DINNER	under $10	$10–$15	$15–$20	$20–$30	over $30

Prices are per person for a main course at dinner.

MID-BEACH & NORTH

CONTINENTAL

$$$–$$$$ ✕ **The Forge.** Legendary for its opulence, this restaurant has been wowing patrons in its present form since 1970. The Forge is a steak house, but a steak house the likes of which you haven't seen before. Antiques, gilt-framed paintings, a chandelier from the Paris Opera House, and Tiffany stained-glass windows from New York's Trinity Church are the fitting background for some of Miami's best steaks. The tried-and-true menu also includes prime rib, lobster thermidor, chocolate soufflé, and Mediterranean side dishes. For its walk-in humidor alone, the over-the-top Forge is worth visiting. ✉ *432 Arthur Godfrey Rd., Mid-Beach, Miami Beach* ☎ *305/538–8533* ⚏ *Reservations essential* ☰ *AE, DC, MC, V* ◷ *No lunch.*

DELICATESSEN

¢–$ ✕**Arnie and Richie's.** Take a deep whiff when you walk in, and you'll know what you're in for: onion rolls, smoked whitefish salad, half-sour pickles, herring in sour-cream sauce, chopped liver, corned beef, pastrami. Deli doesn't get more delicious than in this family-run operation that's casual to the extreme. Most customers are regulars and seat themselves at tables that have baskets of plastic knives and forks; if you request a menu, it's a clear sign you're a newcomer. Service can be brusque, but it sure is quick. ⊠ *525 41st St., Mid-Beach, Miami Beach* ☎*305/531–7691* ▤*AE, MC, V.*

ITALIAN

$$$$ ✕**Timo.** Located 5 mi north of South Beach, Timo (Italian for "thyme")
Fodor'sChoice is worth the trip. The handsome bistro, co-owned by chef Tim Andriola,
★ has dark-wood walls, Chicago brick, and a dominating stone-encased wood-burning stove. Banquettes around the dining room's periphery and a large flower arrangement at its center add to the quietly elegant feel. Andriola has an affinity for robust Mediterranean flavors: sweet-breads with bacon, honey, and aged balsamic; artisanal pizzas; and homemade pastas. Wood-roasted chicken and Parmesan dumplings in a truffled broth are not to be missed. Every bite of every dish attests to the care given. ⊠ *17624 Collins Ave., Sunny Isles* ☎*305/936–1008* ▤*AE, DC, MC, V.*

★ $$–$$$ ✕**Café Prima Pasta.** One of Miami's many signatures is this exemplary Argentine-Italian spot, which rules the emerging North Beach neighborhood. Service can be erratic, but you forget it all on delivery of fresh-made bread with a bowl of spiced olive oil. Tender carpaccio and plentiful antipasti are a delight to share, but the real treat here is the hand-rolled pasta, which can range from crab-stuffed ravioli to simple fettuccine with seafood. If overexposed tiramisu hasn't made an enemy of you yet, try this legendary one to add espresso notes to your unavoidable garlic breath. ⊠ *414 71st St., North Beach, Miami Beach* ☎*305/867–0106* ▤*MC, V.*

SOUTH BEACH

AMERICAN

$$–$$$ ✕**Joe Allen.** Crave a good martini along with a terrific burger? Locals head to this hidden hangout in an exploding neighborhood of condos, town houses, and stores. The eclectic crowd includes kids and grandparents, and the menu has everything from pizzas to calves' liver to steaks. Start with an innovative salad, such as arugula with pear, prosciutto, and a Gorgonzola dressing, or roast-beef salad on greens with Parmesan. Home-style desserts include banana cream pie and ice-cream-and-cookie sandwiches. Comfortable and homey, this is the perfect place to go when you don't feel like going to a restaurant. ⊠*1787 Purdy Ave., South Beach* ☎*305/531–7007* ▤*MC, V.*

6

Where to Eat in the Miami Area

South Beach

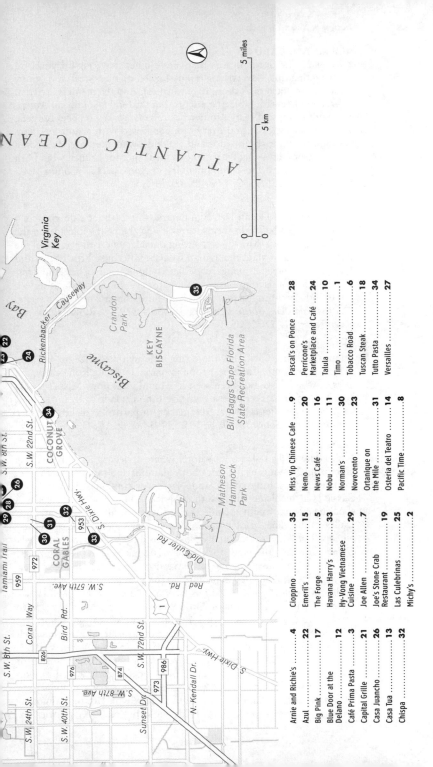

ATLANTIC OCEAN

Virginia
Key

Rickenbacker Causeway

Bay

Crandon
Park

KEY
BISCAYNE

Bill Baggs Cape Florida
State Recreation Area

Biscayne

COCONUT
GROVE

Matheson
Hammock
Park

CORAL
GABLES

S. Dixie Hwy.

Old Cutler Rd.

Red Rd.

S.W. 57th Ave.

Bird Rd.

Coral Way

Tamiami Trail

S.W. 8th St.

S.W. 22nd St.

S.W. 8th St.

S.W. 24th St.

S.W. 40th St.

Sunset Dr.

S.W. 72nd St.

S.W. 87th Ave.

N. Kendall Dr.

S. Dixie Hwy.

5 km

5 miles

Arnie and Richie's 4
Azul 22
Big Pink....................17
Blue Door at the
Delano 12
Café Prima Pasta 3
Capital Grille 21
Casa Juancho 26
Casa Tua 13
Chispa 32

Cioppino 35
Emeril's 15
The Forge 5
Havana Harry's 33
Hy-Vong Vietnamese
Cuisine 29
Joe Allen 7
Joe's Stone Crab
Restaurant 19
Las Culebrinas 25
Michy's 2

Miss Yip Chinese Cafe 9
Nemo 20
News Café 16
Nobu 11
Norman's 30
Novecento 23
Ortanique on
the Mile 31
Osteria del Teatro 14
Pacific Time................8

Pascal's on Ponce 28
Perricone's
Marketplace and Café ..24
Talula 10
Timo 1
Tobacco Road 6
Tuscan Steak..............18
Tutto Pasta................34
Versailles 27

AMERICAN/CASUAL

$–$$

Fodor'sChoice

★

✕**Big Pink.** The decor in this innovative diner may remind you of a roller-skating rink—everything is pink Lucite, stainless steel, and campy (think sports lockers as decorative touches). And the menu is a virtual book, complete with table of contents. But the food is solidly all-American, with dozens of tasty sandwiches, pizzas, turkey or beef burgers, and side dishes, each and every one composed with a gourmet flair. Customers comprise club kids and real kids, who alternate, depending on the time of day—Big Pink makes a great spot for brunch—but both like to color with the complimentary crayons. ✉157 Collins Ave., South Beach ☎305/532–4700 ⊟AE, MC, V.

CAFÉ

$–$$$

✕**News Café.** An Ocean Drive landmark, this 24-hour café attracts a crowd with snacks, light meals, drinks, and the people parade on the sidewalk out front. Most prefer sitting outside, where they can feel the salt breeze and gawk at the human scenery. Offering a little of this and a little of that—bagels, pâtés, chocolate fondue, sandwiches, and a terrific wine list—this joint has something for everyone. Although service can be indifferent to the point of laissez-faire, the café remains a scene. ✉800 Ocean Dr., South Beach ☎305/538–6397 ⚑Reservations not accepted ⊟AE, DC, MC, V.

CHINESE

¢–$

✕**Miss Yip Chinese Cafe.** This interesting little gem specializes in dim sum as well as authentic Cantonese food prepared by Hong Kong chefs, the likes of which have not been seen in Miami until now. Miss Yip also houses a small market offering up to 40 homemade sauces, oils, and spices and ingredients packaged together for particular dishes. ✉1661 Meridian Ave., South Beach ☎305/534–5488 ⊟AE, D, DC, MC, V.

FRENCH

$$$–$$$$

Fodor'sChoice

★

✕**Blue Door at the Delano.** In a hotel where style reigns supreme, this high-profile restaurant provides both glamour and tantalizing cuisine. Acclaimed consulting chef Claude Troisgros combines the flavors of classic French cuisine with South American influences to create a seasonal menu that might include the Big Ravioli, filled with crab-and-scallop mousseline, or osso buco in Thai curry sauce with caramelized pineapple and bananas. Equally pleasing is dining with the crème de la crème of Miami (and New York and Paris) society. Don't recognize the apparent bigwig next to you? Just eavesdrop on his cell phone conversation, and you'll be filled in pronto. ✉1685 Collins Ave., South Beach ☎305/674–6400 ⚑Reservations essential ⊟AE, D, DC, MC, V.

$$$–$$$$

Fodor'sChoice

★

✕**Nemo.** The SoFi (South of Fifth Street) neighborhood may have emerged as a South Beach hot spot, but Nemo's location is not why this casually comfortable restaurant receives raves. It's the menu, which often changes but always delivers, blending Caribbean, Asian, Mediterranean, and Middle Eastern influences and providing an explosion of cultures in each bite. Popular appetizers include garlic-cured salmon rolls with tobiko caviar and wasabi mayo, and crispy prawns with spicy salsa cruda. Main courses might include wok-charred salmon or grilled Indian-spice pork chop. Hedy Goldsmith's funky pastries are exquisitely sinful. Bright colors and copper fixtures highlight the tree-shaded courtyard. ✉ *100 Collins Ave., South Beach* ☎ *305/532–4550* 🖃 *AE, DC, MC, V.*

★ $$$–$$$$ ✗ **Talula.** Husband and wife Frank Randazzo and Andrea Curto have each collected numerous awards and fabulous press. At Talula they are cooking together for the first time while keeping their own styles: she, the cuisine she developed at Wish, joining Asian and tropical influences; he, from the Gaucho Room, grills with a Latin influence. Together they call their style "American creative." Barbecued quail, steamed mussels in a saffron broth, grouper with lime and chili, and a tender and moist barbecued pork tenderloin stand out. The key lime pie alone is worth a visit. ✉ *210 23rd St., South Beach* ☎ *305/672–0778* 🖃 *AE, MC, V.*

ITALIAN

★ $$$–$$$$ ✗ **Casa Tua.** To accommodate the demanding clientele of this exclusive boutique hotel as well as anyone willing to wait two weeks for a reservation, Casa Tua provides a charming restaurant. You can dine inside or alfresco under the trees. Either way, the idea is to make you feel as if you were at home in a Mediterranean beach house. The food is Italian—sophisticated yet simple dishes, such as truffle risotto and whole roasted *branzino* (sea bass) made with impeccable ingredients. The service is seamless and relaxed. And the elegant experience is a peaceful respite from Miami Beach's dizzing energy. ✉ *1700 James Ave., South Beach* ☎ *305/673–1010* ⬧ *Reservations essential* 🖃 *AE, MC, V.*

★ $$–$$$$ ✗ **Osteria del Teatro.** Thanks to word of mouth, this northern Italian restaurant is constantly full. Orchids grace the tables in the intimate gray-on-gray room with a low, laced-canvas ceiling, Deco lamps, and the most refined clink and clatter along Washington Avenue. Regulars know not to order off the printed menu, however. A tremendous variety of daily specials offers the best options here. A representative appetizer is poached asparagus served over polenta triangles with a Gorgonzola sauce. Stuffed pastas, including spinach crepes overflowing with ricotta, can seem heavy but taste light; fish dishes yield a rosemary-marinated tuna or salmon in a pink peppercorn–citrus sauce. ✉ *1443 Washington Ave., South Beach* ☎ *305/538–7850* ⬧ *Reservations essential* 🖃 *AE, DC, MC, V* ⊙ *Closed Sun. No lunch.*

★ $$–$$$$ ✗ **Tuscan Steak.** Dark wood, mirrors, and green upholstery define this chic, masculine place, where big platters of meats and fish are served family-style, assuming yours is a royal family. Tuscan can be as busy as a subway stop, and still the staff is gracious and giving. The chefs take their cues from the Tuscan countryside, where pasta is rich with truffles and main plates are simply but deliciously grilled. Sip red wine with a house specialty: three-mushroom risotto with white truffle oil, gnocchi with Gorgonzola cream, Florentine T-bone with roasted garlic puree, or filet mignon with a Gorgonzola crust in a red wine sauce. Portions are enormous. Bring your friends and share, share, share. ✉ *431 Washington Ave., South Beach* ☎ *305/534–2233* 🖃 *AE, DC, MC, V.*

JAPANESE

$$–$$$ ✕**Nobu.** The wildly popular Peruvian-Japanese restaurant within The Shore Club hotel is a must-stop stop for those with extra cash. Lines can be long for the famous yellowtail jalapeño and miso black cod, but it's worth the wait. Grab a drink at the bar, saunter around the adjoining Sky Bar lounge, and ogle your fellow diners, likely to be along the lines of Anna Kournikova and Jay-Z. ⊠*1901 Collins Ave., South Beach* ☎*305/695–3232* ▭*AE, D, DC, MC, V.*

PAN-ASIAN

$$$–$$$$ ✕**Pacific Time.** Packed nearly every night, chef-proprietor Jonathan Eismann's superb eatery has a high blue ceiling, banquettes, plank floors,
Fodor'sChoice   and an open kitchen. The brilliant American-Asian menu changes
★   daily, but usually includes such entrées as cedar-roasted salmon, rosemary-roasted chicken, and dry-aged Colorado beef grilled with shiitake mushrooms. The cuttlefish appetizer and the Florida pompano entrée are masterpieces. Desserts include a fresh pear-pecan spring roll and the famous chocolate "bomb." ⊠*915 Lincoln Rd., South Beach* ☎*305/534–5979* ⌦*Reservations essential* ▭*AE, DC, MC, V.*

SEAFOOD

$$$–$$$$ ✕**Joe's Stone Crab Restaurant.** This Miami phenomenon stubbornly refuses reservations despite phenomenal crowds. Prepare to wait up to an hour just to sign up for a table and another *three* hours to get one. The centerpiece of the ample à la carte menu is, of course, stone crab, with a piquant mustard sauce. Popular side orders include creamed garlic spinach, french-fried onions, fried green tomatoes, and hash browns. Desserts range from a famous key lime pie to apple pie with crumb-pecan topping. If you can't stand loitering hungrily while self-important patrons try to grease the maître d's palm, come for lunch, or get takeout and picnic on the beach. ⊠*11 Washington Ave., South Beach* ☎*305/673–0365, 305/673–4611 for takeout, 800/780–2722 for overnight shipping* ⌦*Reservations not accepted* ▭*AE, D, DC, MC, V* ☉*Closed May–mid-Oct. No lunch Sun. and Mon.*

SOUTHERN

$$–$$$ ✕**Emeril's.** "It's getting happy in here" is one of Emeril Lagasse's stock phrases, and now he has brought his brand of happy to Miami Beach. You can expect a different gumbo each day and other New Orleans specialties at Lagasse's ninth restaurant, which appears to have the winning formula down, though the seafood naturally shines in these parts (an andouille-crusted redfish and a Louisiana crabmeat salad signal the imported Lagasse touch) and the chef has his own worthy, meringue-happy take on key lime pie. As a bonus, the restaurant delivers without even a hint of South Beach attitude. ⊠*1601 Collins Ave., South Beach* ☎*305/695–4550* ▭*AE, D, DC, MC, V.*

DOWNTOWN MIAMI

AMERICAN/CASUAL

¢-$ ✕ **Tobacco Road.** If you like your food the way you like your blues—gritty, honest, and unassuming—then this octogenarian joint will earn your respect. A musician wailing the blues also cooks jambalaya on-stage, although entertainment varies. And no one's weeping about the food. The Road-burger is a popular choice, as are the chili worthy of a fire hose and appetizers such as nachos and chicken wings. Don't let the rough-edged exterior deter you from finer dining. On Tuesday during the season, Tobacco Road offers a Maine lobster special, and fine single-malt Scotches are stocked behind the bar. ⊠ *626 S. Miami Ave., Downtown* ☎ *305/374–1198* ⊟ *AE, D, DC, MC, V.*

ARGENTINE

¢-$$ ✕ **Novecento.** This Argentine eatery is known for its empanadas (tender chicken or spinach and cheese), simple grilled meats (luscious grilled skirt steak with chimichurri), and flavorful pastas (crab ravioli in a creamy saffron sauce). It's no wonder it has established itself as one of Brickell Avenue's best lunch and dinner hot spots. But come for breakfast and/or lunch on Saturday and Sunday from 11 to 4 for a leisurely Latin spin on the à la carte brunch: indulge in tasty Latin dishes such as huevos rancheros and arepas Colombianas with eggs. ⊠ *1414 Brickell Ave., Downtown Miami* ☎ *305/403–0900* ⊟ *AE, D, DC, MC, V.*

ITALIAN

$-$$$ ✕ **Perricone's Marketplace and Café.** Brickell Avenue south of the Miami River is burgeoning with Italian restaurants, and this lunch place for local bigwigs is the biggest and most popular among them. It's housed partially outdoors and partially indoors in a 120-year-old Vermont barn. Recipes were handed down from grandmother to mother to daughter, and the cooking is simple and good. Buy your wine from the on-premises deli, and enjoy it (for a small corking fee) with homemade minestrone; a generous antipasto; linguine with a sauté of jumbo shrimp, fresh asparagus, and chopped tomatoes; or gnocchi with four cheeses. The homemade tiramisu and fruit tart are top notch. ⊠ *Brickell Village, 15 S.E. 10th St., Downtown* ☎ *305/374–9449* ⊟ *AE, MC, V.*

MEDITERRANEAN

$$-$$$ ✕ **Michy's.** Miami's homegrown star chef Michelle Bernstein now has her own gig. The funky, blue, late 1960s–inspired dining room on the mainland's "Upper East Side" serves exquisite French- and Mediterranean-influenced seafood dishes at over-the-causeway (read: non-tourist-trap) prices. Can't-miss plates include the blue cheese and fig croquetas and the steak frite au poivre. ⊠ *6927 Biscayne Blvd., Upper East Side* ☎ *305/759–2001* ⊟ *AE, D, DC, MC, V.*

SEAFOOD

$$-$$$$ ✕ **Azul.** Azul has sumptuously conquered the devil in the details, from chef Clay Conley's exotically rendered French-Caribbean cuisine to the thoughtful service staff who graciously anticipate your broader dining needs. Does your sleeveless blouse leave you too cold to properly

Fodor's Choice
★

appreciate the poached eggs with lobster-knuckle hollandaise? Ask for one of the house pashminas, available in a variety of fashionable colors. Forgot your reading glasses and can't decipher the hanger steak with foie-gras sauce? Request a pair from the host. Want to see how the other half lives? Descend the interior staircase to Cafe Sambal, the all-day casual restaurant downstairs. ⊠ *Mandarin Oriental Hotel, 500 Brickell Key Dr., Brickell Key* ☎ *305/913–8288* ⚓ *Reservations essential* ⊟ *AE, MC, V* ⊗ *Closed Sun. No lunch weekends.*

STEAK

★ $$$ ✕ **Capital Grille.** Downtown's most elegant restaurant is a palace of protein. That is, the menu is traditional and oriented to beef, and the dining room handsome and filled mostly with men on a power lunch. Porterhouse, steak au poivre, various sirloins, and fillets, many of which hang in a locker in the center of the dining room to age, head the list. All is à la carte, even the baked potato. The cheesecake is tops. Still, service can be so relentlessly formal it's ridiculous—the waiters will walk miles to ensure that women get their menus first. ⊠ *444 Brickell Ave., Downtown* ☎ *305/374–4500* ⊟ *AE, D, DC, MC, V.*

LITTLE HAVANA

CUBAN

$–$$$ ✕ **Versailles.** One of Miami's first Cuban restaurants and still its most ornate budget restaurant, Versailles dishes out heaping platters of traditional Cuban food amid mirrors, candelabras, and white tablecloths. The fun of Versailles is people-watching, though—that and the waitresses who call you *mi amor*. The coffee counter serves the city's strongest cafecito, but if you can't handle it, ask for a *cortadito*, the same strong demitasse coffee but with steamed milk to soften the blow, and unless you like coffee syrup (Cuba equals sugar, after all), ask for it *sin azúcar* and add sugar to taste. ⊠ *3555 S.W. 8th St., between S.W. 35th and S.W. 36th Aves., Little Havana* ☎ *305/444–0240* ⊟ *AE, D, DC, MC, V.*

ITALIAN

¢–$ ✕ **Tutto Pasta.** Some of the city's best Italian for the money comes out of this kitchen. Entrées rarely top $12, but they always please, especially homemade pastas with red sauces. Start with delicious bruschetta, mozzarella with pignoli, prosciutto and sun-dried tomatoes, or a homemade soup. Spaghetti with marinara, the cheapest entrée, might well be the best because the sauce is that good. Pleasant service matches the casual atmosphere. Fettuccine with chicken, mushrooms, and sun-dried tomatoes; homemade ravioli with spinach and ricotta; and a stew of snapper, seafood, and tomato sauce excel, as do housebaked desserts. ⊠ *1751 S.W. 3rd Ave. at S.W. 18th Rd., Little Havana* ☎ *305/857–0709* ⊟ *MC, V.*

SPANISH

$$–$$$$ ✕ **Casa Juancho.** This meeting place for the movers and shakers of the Cuban *exilio* community is also a haven for lovers of fine Spanish regional cuisine. Strolling balladeers serenade surrounded by brown

brick, rough-hewn dark timbers, hanging smoked meats, and colorful Talavera platters. Try the hake prepared in a fish stock with garlic, onions, and Spanish white wine or the *carabineros a la plancha* (jumbo red shrimp with head and shell on, split and grilled). For dessert, *crema Catalana* is a rich pastry custard with a delectable crust of burnt caramel. The house features the largest list of reserved Spanish wines in the States. ⊠ *2436 S.W. 8th St., Little Havana* ☎ *305/642–2452* ⊟ *AE, D, DC, MC, V.*

VIETNAMESE

★ ¢–$$ ✕ **Hy-Vong Vietnamese Cuisine.** Spring springs forth in spring rolls of ground pork, cellophane noodles, and black mushrooms wrapped in homemade rice paper. Folks'll mill about on the sidewalk for hours—come before 7 PM to avoid a wait—to sample the whole fish panfried with *nuoc man,* a garlic-lime fish sauce, not to mention the thinly sliced pork barbecued with sesame seeds, almonds, and peanuts. Beer-savvy proprietor Kathy Manning serves a half-dozen top brews (Double Grimbergen, Moretti, and Spaten, among them) to further inoculate the experience from the ordinary. Well, as ordinary as a Vietnamese restaurant on Calle Ocho can be. ⊠ *3458 S.W. 8th St., Little Havana* ☎ *305/446–3674* ⊟ *AE, D, MC, V* ☉ *Closed Mon. and Tues. No lunch.*

6

COCONUT GROVE & KEY BISCAYNE

ITALIAN

★ $$$–$$$$ ✕ **Cioppino.** Choose your view: the ornate dining room near the exhibition kitchen or the alfresco area with views of landscaped gardens or breeze-brushed beaches. Then select your food, which may be even more difficult, given the many rich, luscious Italian options—items range from creamy mozzarella with green beans to tantalizing risotto with lobster, white wine, and zucchini. Aria is fortunate to have a master sommelier, whose palate is impeccable and whose wine list is impossible to resist. ⊠ *Ritz-Carlton, Key Biscayne, 455 Grand Bay Dr., Key Biscayne* ☎ *305/365–4286* ⋨ *Reservations essential* ⊟ *AE, D, DC, MC, V.*

CORAL GABLES

CARIBBEAN

$$–$$$$ ✕ **Ortanique on the Mile.** First, the place is gorgeous. Soft ochre walls and columns are hand-painted with cascading ortaniques, a Jamaican hybrid orange, creating a warm, welcoming, and soothing atmosphere. Next, the food is vibrant in taste and color, as delicious as it is beautiful. Though there is no denying that the strong, full flavors are imbued with island breezes, chef/partner Cindy Hutson's personal cuisine goes beyond Caribbean refinements. The menu centers on fish, since Hutson has a special way with it, and the Caribbean bouillabaisse is not to be missed. ⊠ *278 Miracle Mile, Coral Gables* ☎ *305/446–7710* ⊟ *AE, DC, MC, V.*

CUBAN

$-$$

Fodor'sChoice

★

✕**Havana Harry's.** When Cuban families want a home-cooked meal but don't want to cook it themselves, they come to this spacious, airy restaurant. In fact, you're likely to see whole families here, from babes in arms to grandmothers. The fare is traditional Cuban: the long thin steaks known as *bistec palomilla*, roast chicken with citrus marinade, and fried pork chunks; contemporary flourishes—mango sauce and guava-painted pork roast—are kept to a minimum. Most dishes come with white rice, black beans, and a choice of ripe or green plantains. The sweet ripe ones offer a good contrast to the savory dishes. This is an excellent value. ⊠*4612 Le Jeune Rd., Coral Gables* ☎*305/661–2622* ▤*AE, MC, V.*

SEAFOOD

$$$$

Fodor'sChoice

★

✕**Norman's.** Chef Norman Van Aken has created an international buzz by perfecting the art of new-world cuisine—an imaginative combination rooted in Latin, North American, Caribbean, and Asian influences. Bold tastes are delivered in every dish, from a simple black-and-white-bean soup with sour cream, chorizo, and tortillas to a rum-and-pepper-painted grouper on a mango–habañero chili sauce. The emphasis here is on service, and the ultragracious staff never seems harried, even when all seats are filled (usually every minute between opening and closing). ⊠*21 Almeria Ave., Coral Gables* ☎*305/446–6767* ▤*AE, DC, MC, V* ☉*Closed Sun. and Mon. No lunch.*

FRENCH

$$-$$$

Fodor'sChoice

★

✕**Pascal's on Ponce.** Though not a native son, chef-proprietor Pascal Oudin has been cooking around Miami since the 1980s, when he opened Dominique's in the Alexander Hotel. His streamlined French cuisine disdains trends and discounts flash. Instead, you're supplied with substantive delicacies such as sautéed sea bass wrapped in a crispy potato crust with braised leeks, veal rib eye au jus, and tenderloin of beef sautéed with snails and wild mushrooms. Service is proper, textures are perfect, and wines are ideally complementary. The only dilemma is deciding between Oudin's tarte tatin (apple tart), Miami's only perfect soufflé, and a cheese course for dessert. ⊠*2611 Ponce de León Blvd., Coral Gables* ☎*305/444–2024* ▤*AE, D, DC, MC, V* ☉*Closed Sun. No lunch Sat.*

LATIN

$$-$$$$

Fodor'sChoice

★

✕**Chispa.** Meaning "spark" in Spanish, Chispa indeed sparkles. Chef Robbin Haas has taken command of the open kitchen, basing the menu on a melting pot of Latin flavors that reflects Miami's population. *Cazuelitas* let you have smaller portions as appetizers—from mussels with chipotle chili to Spanish *cava* (sparkling wine) fondue. Ceviches are assertively marinated, croquettes melt in your mouth, and skeptics can have flatbreads with various toppings (read: pizzas). Share plates and platters of grilled shrimp or suckling pig before guava cheesecake or churros with chocolate sauce. Exotic drinks are served at the 40-foot bar, and leather banquettes, Bahama shutters, and colorful Cuban tiles complete the hacienda feel. ⊠*225 Altara Ave., Coral Gables* ☎*305/648–2600* ▤*AE, MC, V.*

SPANISH

¢–$$ ✕**Las Culebrinas.** At this Spanish *tapacería* (house of little plates), live each meal as if it were your last, though you may wait as long as some inmates do for an appeal. Tapas here are not small; some are entrée size: the succulent mix of garbanzos, ham, sausage, red peppers, and oil, or the Frisbee-size Spanish tortilla (omelet). Indulge in a tender fillet of crocodile, fresh fish, grilled pork, or the kicker, goat in Coca-Cola sauce. For dessert there's *crema Catalana,* caramelized at your table with a blowtorch. This is a good time to remind your kids not to touch. ⊠*4700 W. Flagler St., at N.W. 47th Ave., Coral Gables* ☎*305/445–2337* ▤*AE, MC, V.*

WHERE TO STAY

In high season, which is January to May, expect to pay at least $150 per night. In summer, however, prices can be as much as 50 percent lower than the dizzying winter rates. You can also find great values between Easter and Memorial Day, which is actually a delightful time in Miami, and in September and October, the height of hurricane season.

Two important considerations that greatly affect price are balcony and view. Whether a property has a pool generally does not affect cost. If you're willing to have a room without an ocean view, you can sometimes get a price much lower than the standard rate. Many hotels are aggressive with specials and change their rates like stock prices—hour to hour—so it's worth calling around.

WHAT IT COSTS					
	¢	$	$$	$$$	$$$$
FOR TWO PEOPLE	under $150	$150–$200	$200–$300	$300–$400	over $400

Prices are for two people in a standard double room in high season, excluding 12.5% city and resort taxes.

SOUTH BEACH

Now that it's a scene of international celeb partying, synonymous with glamour and style, it's hard to imagine that South Beach was a derelict district 15 years ago. These days the hotels themselves are attractions to see, both outside and in, on a visit to Miami. The inventory of playful 1930s Art Deco buildings is unmatched anywhere in the world. What's different today from even 10 years ago is their total renovation into glistening, historic, architectural gems. Feel free to visit the hotels to explore their lobbies, restaurants, lounges, and bars, where you'll find much of the city's nightlife taking place.

$$$$ ▦**Delano Hotel.** "I am the movie director of the clients of this hotel.
Fodor'sChoice They are the actors, not the spectators—never!" Never was "never" so
★ visionary. When you stay at the Delano today, 20 years after designer Philippe Starck uttered these words to *Vanity Fair* about his brainchild

6

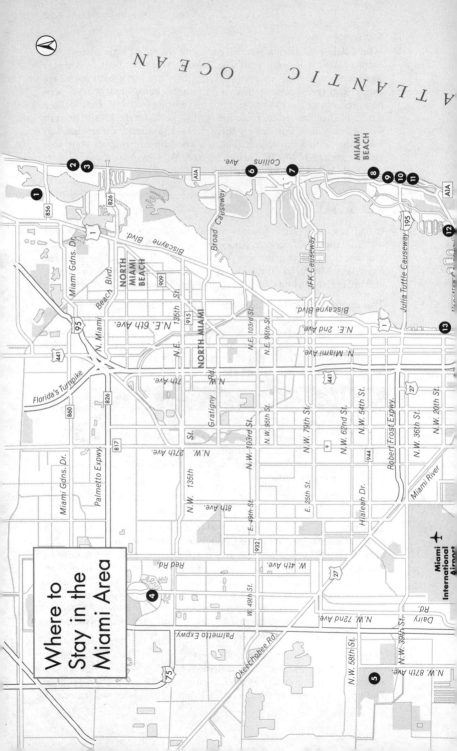

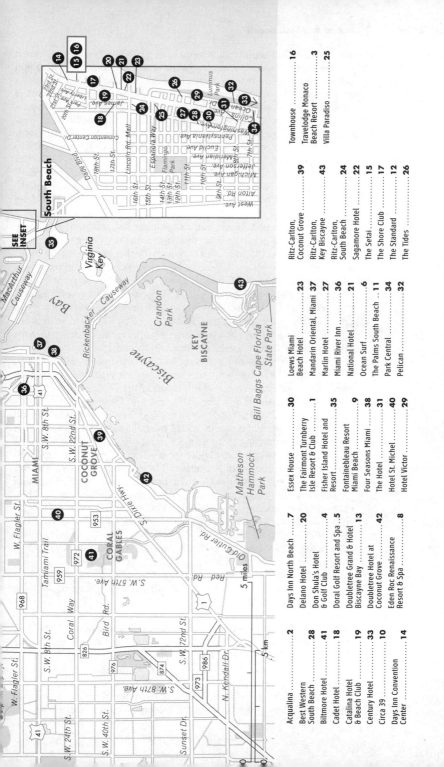

South Beach

SEE INSET

Virginia Key

MacArthur Causeway

Biscayne Bay

Rickenbacker Causeway

Crandon Park

KEY BISCAYNE

Bill Baggs Cape Florida State Park

Matheson Hammock Park

MIAMI

COCONUT GROVE

CORAL GABLES

Acqualina 2
Best Western
South Beach 28
Biltmore Hotel 41
Cadet Hotel 18
Catalina Hotel
& Beach Club 19
Century Hotel 33
Circa 39 10
Days Inn Convention
Center 14

Days Inn North Beach 7
Delano Hotel 20
Don Shula's Hotel
& Golf Club 4
Doral Golf Resort and Spa . . 5
Doubletree Grand & Hotel
Biscayne Bay 13
Doubletree Hotel at
Coconut Grove 42
Eden Roc Renaissance
Resort & Spa 8

Essex House 30
The Fairmont Turnberry
Isle Resort & Club 1
Fisher Island Hotel and
Resort 35
Fontainebleau Resort
Miami Beach 9
Four Seasons Miami 38
The Hotel 31
Hotel St. Michel 40
Hotel Victor 29

Loews Miami
Beach Hotel 23
Mandarin Oriental, Miami . . 37
Marlin Hotel 27
Miami River Inn 36
National Hotel 21
Ocean Surf 6
The Palms South Beach . . 11
Park Central 34
Pelican 32

Ritz-Carlton,
Coconut Grove 39
Ritz-Carlton,
Key Biscayne 43
Ritz-Carlton,
South Beach 24
Sagamore Hotel 22
The Setai 15
The Shore Club 17
The Standard 12
The Tides 26

Townhouse 16
Travelodge Monaco
Beach Resort 3
Villa Paradiso 25

hotel, you're still within the spectacle of glamour. The Delano was a pioneer that defined what Miami hotels were to become. And here you can still live the fantasy: catwalk through massive, white, billowing drapes, and try to act casual while celebs, models, and moguls gather beneath cabanas and pose by the pool. A rooftop bathhouse and solarium, and the fabulous Blue Door restaurant complete the picture. Pros: electrifying design, lounging amidst the beautiful and famous. Cons: crowded, scene-y, small rooms, expensive. ⊠*1685 Collins Ave., South Beach 33139* ☎*305/672–2000 or 800/555–5001* 🖷*305/532–0099* ⊕*www.delano-hotel.com* 🛏*184 rooms, 24 suites* ⚷*In-room: safe, refrigerator, Wi-Fi. In-hotel: 2 restaurants, room service, bars, pool, gym, spa, beachfront, laundry service, concierge, public Wi-Fi, parking (fee), no-smoking rooms* ▤*AE, D, DC, MC, V.*

$$$$

Fodor'sChoice

★

🏨 **Fisher Island Hotel & Resort.** Want to explore Fisher Island? Assuming you don't have a private yacht, there are three ways to gain access to the ferry from just off South Beach: you can either become a club member (initiation fee alone: $25,000), be one of the 750 equity members who have vacation places here (starting price: $8 million), or book a night at the club hotel (basic villa: $750 a night). Once you've made it, you'll be welcomed at reception with champagne. Considering you get a private house, a golf cart, and a fenced-in backyard with a hot tub, villas are a value for a memorable honeymoon or other lifetime event, if not a casual weekend. Families should stay in one of three former guest cottages of the former Italianate mansion of William K. Vanderbilt (in 1925 he swapped Carl Fisher *his* yacht for the island), which forms the centerpiece of this resort. An 18-hole golf course, the surprisingly affordable Spa Internazionale, and 18 lighted tennis courts (hard, grass, and clay), kids' programs, and 1 mi of very private (and very quiet) white sand beach imported from the Bahamas means there's plenty of sweet nothing to do here. Oh, and there are eight restaurants and a fun sunset tiki bar to choose from—Porto Cervo is the best Italian restaurant nobody knows about. The Garwood Lounge features nightly piano and seats just 16. Remarkably, this true exclusivity and seclusion is minutes from South Beach. Pros: great private beaches, exclusive surroundings, varied dining choices. Cons: expensive, ferry rides take time. ⊠*1 Fisher Island Dr., Fisher Island, Miami 33109* ☎*305/535–6000 or 800/537–3708* 🖷*305/535–6003* ⊕*www.fisher-island.com* 🛏*55 suites, 6 villas, 3 cottages* ⚷*In-room; safe, refrigerator. In-hotel: 8 restaurants, golf course, tennis courts, pools, gym, spa, beachfront, water sports, children's programs (ages 4–12), laundry service, concierge, public Internet, parking (no fee), some pets allowed, no-smoking rooms* ▤*AE, D, DC, MC, V.*

★ **$$$$**

🏨 **Hotel Victor.** Parisian designer Jacques Garcia turned this long-abandoned Art Deco building into Ocean Drive's hippest hotel. The signature jellyfish tank in the lobby is mesmerizing, and the tentacle theme continues in the lighting and decorations throughout the hotel. Most rooms are fairly small and overlook the second-floor pool and the ocean; ask for a room in one of the newly constructed wings, which have little balconies and better views. Instead of walls, drapes and sliding mirrors allow you to control the space in your room. Deep tubs in the middle of the rooms create intimacy. The spa here, also designed by Garcia, is a knockout, the artsiest one around. The Victor hosts the city's hottest Thursday night party, a boon, since you're invited, but it stays noisy till 2 AM. Pros: great design, views of Ocean Drive from the pool deck, high hip factor, good service. Cons: distant and somewhat unfriendly staff, small pool. ⊠ *Ocean Dr., South Beach 33139* ☎ *305/932–6200 or 800/327–7028* 🖷 *305/933–6560* ⊕ *www.hotel-victorsouthbeach.com* 🛏 *91 rooms.* ⚿ *In-room: safe, kitchen (some), refrigerator, DVD (some), Wi-Fi. In-hotel: 2 restaurants, room service, bar, pool, gym, spa, laundry service, public Wi-Fi, parking (fee), some pets allowed, no-smoking rooms* ▭ *AE, D, DC, MC, V.*

★ $$$$ 🏨 **Loews Miami Beach Hotel.** Marvelous for families, businesspeople, and groups, the Loews combines top-tier amenities, a massive new spa, a great pool, and direct beachfront setting in its pair of enormous 12- and 18-story towers. When it was built in 1998, Loews managed not only to snag 99 feet of beach, but also to take over the vacant St. Moritz next door and restore it to its original 1939 Art Deco beauty. The entire complex combines boutique charm with updated opulence. How big is it? The Loews has 85,000 square feet of meeting space and an enormous ocean-view grand ballroom. Emeril Lagasse opened a restaurant here, and a three-story spa opened in 2007 with 15 treatment rooms and a state-of-the-art fitness center. In the grand lobby you'll find a dozen black-suited staffers behind the counter, and a half dozen other bellboys and valets. Rooms are great: contemporary and very comfortable, with flat-screens and high-end amenities. If you like big hotels with all the services, this is your choice in South Beach. Pros: top-notch amenities include a beautiful oceanfront pool and immense spa. Cons: intimacy is lost in the size of the place, and parking costs $30. ⊠ *1601 Collins Ave., South Beach 33139* ☎ *305/604–1601 or 800/235–6397* 🖷 *305/604–3999* ⊕ *www.loewshotels.com/miamibeach* 🛏 *733 rooms, 57 suites* ⚿ *In-room: dial-up. In-hotel: 3 restaurants, room service, bars, pool, gym, spa, beachfront, laundry service, concierge, public Internet, public Wi-Fi, parking (fee), some pets allowed, no-smoking rooms* ▭ *AE, D, DC, MC, V.*

★ $$$$ 🏨 **Ritz-Carlton South Beach.** A sumptuous affair, the Ritz-Carlton is the only truly luxurious property on the beach that *feels* like it's on the beach because its long pool deck leads you right out to the water. There are all the usual high-level draws the Ritz is known for, that is, attentive service, a kids club, a club level with five food presentations a day, and high-end restaurants. The spa has exclusive brands of scrubs and creams, and dynamite staff, including a "tanning butler" named Malcolm, who, from 11 AM to 3 PM Thursday to Sunday, will make sure you're not burning, and will apply lotions in the hard-to-reach places. He manages to make this gimmick such a real treat you may end up buying a "tanning butler" T-shirt. Synchronized swimmers perform Saturdays. The diLido Beach club restaurant, believe it or not, is one of the very few places in Miami where you can get a beachside meal. Overall, this landmarked 1954 art-moderne hotel, designed by Melvin Grossman and Morris Lapidus, has never been hotter. Pros: luxury rooms, beachside restaurant, fine spa. Cons: too big to be intimate

6

and the lobby feels corporate. ⊠*1 Lincoln Rd., South Beach 33139* ☎*786/276–4000 or 800/241–3333* 🖷*786/276–4100* ⊕*www.ritzcarl-ton.com* 🖘*375 rooms* ⚐*In-room: safe, refrigerator, Wi-Fi. In-hotel: 3 restaurants, room service, bars, pools, gym, spa, beachfront, children's programs (ages 5–12), laundry service, concierge, executive floor, pub-lic Wi-Fi, parking (fee), some pets allowed, no-smoking rooms* ⊟*AE, D, DC, MC, V.*

$$$$ 🔝**Setai.** This is, by far, the most expensive hotel in Miami (the cheapest room in high season is $950). What do you get for this price? Perfect, state-of-the-art rooms, a tranquil, luxurious setting, and the quietest hotel on the beachfront in the heart of hip South Beach. What you won't necessarily get is the warm, relaxed, casual vibe you might want from a beach vacation. The hotel seems as famous now for its aloof service as for the irresistible comfort and Asian furnishings of its rooms. The 40-story luxury residence tower and the eight-story courtyard hotel offer rooms from 550 to 900 square feet, and it's hard not to consider these the best rooms in the city. Teak-latticed cabanas tucked within a lush landscape of gardens and fountains, and three consecutive pools make for blissful perambulations. Beach facilities are excellent. Most striking of all is its inner reflecting pool in the courtyard, the most serene setting for drinks, and one of Miami's highlights. Pros: perfection in rooms; private beach amenities; a quiet, celebrity site. Cons: spotty service; somewhat cold aura; doesn't feel like South Beach. ⊠*101 20th St., South Beach 33139* ☎*305/520–6000 or 888/625–7500* 🖷*305/520–6111* ⊕*www.setai.com* 🖘*110 rooms* ⚐*In room: safe, refrigerator, Wi-Fi. In-hotel: restaurant, room service, bars, pools, gym, spa, beach-front, laundry service, concierge, public Wi-Fi, parking (fee), some pets allowed, no-smoking rooms* ⊟*AE, D, DC, MC, V.*

$$$$ 🔝**Shore Club.** Exuding the glamour of Old Hollywood, this SoBe pied-à-terre is a hot spot for today's Tinseltown A-listers and visitors hoping to spy them. The sprawling, six-building property has room for private cabanas and a beach house on the sand and a series of gardens sepa-rated by courtyards and reflecting pools. Rooms are fairly large and serenely beautiful, with dashes of color among the blond-wood fur-niture and stainless-steel accents. Part of the upscale Nobu chain, the restaurant serves Japanese-Peruvian cuisine and draws healthy crowds. Other healthy crowds can be found at the rooftop Spa at the Shore Club. In terms of lounging, people-watching, and poolside glitz, this is the best of South Beach. Pros: great outdoor lounge, good restau-rants and bars, nightlife in your backyard. Cons: bustling scene makes it less private for guests. ⊠*1901 Collins Ave., South Beach 33139* ☎*305/695–3100 or 877/640–9500* 🖷*305/695–3299* ⊕*www.shore-club.com* 🖘*322 rooms* ⚐*In-room: safe, refrigerator, Wi-Fi. In-hotel: 2 restaurants, room service, bars, pools, gym, spa, beachfront, laundry service, concierge, public Wi-Fi, parking (fee), some pets allowed, no-smoking rooms* ⊟*AE, D, DC, MC, V.*

$$$$
Fodor'sChoice
★

🔝**The Tides.** The Tides is the best boutique hotel in Miami, offering exceptional, personalized service in large, luxurious, and stylish rooms with perfect ocean views. Under new owners, it was wholly reinvented in 2007: the lobby, terrace, and all 45 suites were completely redone, replacing a strict all-white minimalism with a soothing palette that suggests South Beach has arrived at the next phase of sophistication. Pretty public spaces include a dining terrace at the gorgeous contemporary restaurant, 1220. The pool is among the biggest on Ocean Drive, though to see the sea you'll have to peer through a couple of sets of portholes. Pros: superior service, great beach location, and ocean views from all suites plus the terrace restaurant. Cons: no views from pool deck. ✉ *1220 Ocean Dr., South Beach 33139* ☎ *305/604–5070 or 866/438–4337* 📠 *305/604–5180* 🌐 *www.thetideshotel.com* *45 suites* *In-room: safe, dial-up. In-hotel: restaurant, pool, gym, beachfront, concierge, laundry service, parking (fee), no-smoking rooms* 💳 *AE, D, DC, MC, V.*

★ $$–$$$$ **The Hotel.** Despite its minimalist name, this boutique hotel has gotten maximum applause thanks to fashion designer Todd Oldham, who brought the colors of the sand and the sea indoors. Individually painted tiles, pale ash desks, and mosaic-pattern rugs delight the eyes. Bejeweled bathrooms, decidedly petite, are the most colorful in Miami, and they even have separate temperature controls. Add soft lighting and two-person bathtubs, and you have all the makings of a romantic retreat. The excellent restaurant Wish serves creative cuisine indoors or out. Best of all is the intimate rooftop pool with spectacular, unobstructed views of the sea. Have breakfast here. Also on the rooftop is a bar set around the 1939 landmark spire with the hotel's original name: Tiffany. Pros: great service and beautiful pool deck with free cabana usage, good for couples. Cons: a block from the beach, "designer" rooms have no views. ✉ *801 Collins Ave., South Beach 33139* ☎ *305/531–2222 or 877/843–4683* 📠 *305/531–3222* 🌐 *www.thehotelofsouthbeach.com* *48 rooms, 4 suites* *In-room: safe, Wi-Fi. In-hotel: restaurant, room service, bar, pool, laundry service, concierge, public Internet, public Wi-Fi, parking (fee), no-smoking rooms* 💳 *AE, D, DC, MC, V.*

$–$$$$ Fodor'sChoice ★ **The National Hotel.** Elegant and aloof, the timeless National Hotel is a dramatic and popular backdrop for the film crews that often work here. In the middle of the coolest block of hotels anywhere in the world, the National's gorgeous 1939 tower stands out and yet the hotel relaxes at its own pace, indifferent to what's going on next door at the Delano or the Sagamore or the Ritz. The most spectacular feature is the palm-lined "infinity" pool—Miami Beach's longest, at 205 feet, and most beautiful. Add to that a private beach and hammocks swinging in the tropical garden, and you have an oasis you'll never want to leave. If you can splurge, go for a room in the poolside cabana wing. Rooms in the historic main tower are a bit disappointing and far from the pool. Step into the 1930s-style Martini Room bar and you'll be looking for Bogie. Pros: beautiful tropical garden, stunning pool, perfect location. Cons: tower rooms not nearly as nice as cabanas, neighbors can be noisy weekend nights. ✉ *1677 Collins Ave., South Beach 33139* ☎ *305/532–2311 or 800/327–8370* 📠 *305/534–1426* 🌐 *www.nationalhotel.com* *143 rooms, 9 suites* *In-room: safe, DVD, VCR (some), ethernet, Wi-Fi. In-hotel: 2 restaurants, room service, bars, pools, gym, beach-*

6

front, laundry service, concierge, public Internet, public W-Fi, parking (fee), some pets allowed, no-smoking rooms ☰AE, DC, MC, V.

$–$$$$
Fodor'sChoice
★

☷**Sagamore.** This super-sleek all-white hotel in the middle of the action looks and feels more like a Chelsea art gallery, filled with brilliant contemporary art. Its restaurant, Social Miami, is one of the hottest reservations in town. With all the mind-bending hipness, you might expect some major flaw, like small rooms, but in fact they're all suites here, and some of the largest on the strip, starting at 525 square feet. All have full kitchens with big fridges, mini ovens, microwaves, and dishwashers. You can also expect huge flat-screen TVs and whirlpool baths. Hallways have artists' quotes lining the halls, and public restrooms have video installations. The poolside duplex bungalows make posh party pads on weekend nights, when the Sagamore is *the* place to be in all of Miami (no surprise there). Staying here saves you the long wait and the begging to get in. Don't worry—it's still safe for kids here, and they'll love the glass, flourescent-lighted swing in the lobby. A VIP kids card entitles them to unlimited free ice cream, hot dogs, and soda (what the heck, it's vacation). Pros: sensational pool, Friday and Saturday night parties, great location, quiet on weekdays, good rate specials. Cons: basic rooms are not as stylish as public areas, noisy on weekends. ✉*1671 Collins Ave., South Beach 33139* ☎*305/535–8088* ☷*305/535–8185* ⊕*www.sagamorehotel.com* ☞*93 suites* ♿*In-room: safe, kitchen, refrigerator, Wi-Fi. In-hotel: restaurant, room service, bars, pool, spa, beachfront, laundry service, concierge, parking (fee), no-smoking rooms* ☰AE, D, DC, MC, V.

★ **$$–$$$**

☷**Essex House.** You'll get your own South Beach people-watching perch on the outdoor patio at this wonderfully restored Art Deco gem. A favorite with Europeans, especially the British, Essex House has average-size rooms with midcentury-style red furniture and marble tubs. The suites, reached by crossing a lovely tropical courtyard, are well worth the price: each has a wet bar, king-size bed, pull-out sofa, 100-square-foot bathroom, refrigerator, and hot tub. The lobby mural was created in 1938 by artist Earl Le Pan, and touched up by him 50 years later. Pros: a social, heated pool; great Art Deco patio; good service. Cons: small pool. ✉*1001 Collins Ave., South Beach 33139* ☎*305/534–2700 or 800/553–7739* ☷*305/532–3827* ⊕*www.essex-hotel.com* ☞*61 rooms, 19 suites* ♿*In-room: Wi-Fi. In-hotel: bar, pool, laundry service, parking (fee)* ☰AE, D, DC, MC, V.

$$–$$$
Fodor'sChoice
★

☷**Townhouse.** Sandwiched between the Setai and the Shore Club—two of the hottest hotels on the planet—the Townhouse looks like a big adult playhouse and fits the bill as the most lighthearted hotel on South Beach. A red plastic beach ball welcomes you to spotless rooms bleached white. The rooftop terrace has red waterbeds and a signature water tower. It's no wonder you find loud parties here on weekend nights. The hotel was designed by India Madhavi; thank him for the bright, inviting lobby with two, big, red (of course) bikes, kickstands down, for rent. Off to one side, a delightful sunroom is a great place to read the paper over a generous continental breakfast. Just outside, a porch deck has swings and comfortable chairs. A hip sushi restaurant, Bond St. Lounge, is downstairs. With its clean white backdrops and discounts for crew members, there's always a good chance a TV production or magazine shoot is happening. Pros: a great budget buy for the style hungry. Cons: no pool, rooms not designed for long stays. ✉*150 20th St., east of Collins Ave., South Beach 33139* ☎*305/534–3800 or 877/534–3800* 🖷*305/534–3811* ⊕*www.townhousehotel. com* ⮑*69 rooms, 3 suites* ⌂*In-room: safe, ethernet, Wi-Fi. In-hotel: restaurant, room service, bar, bicycles, laundry facilities, laundry service, public Wi-Fi, parking (fee), no-smoking rooms* ▭*AE, D, DC, MC, V* ��*CP.*

$$ 🛏 **Marlin Hotel.** Music-industry luminaries who come to record at the on-site South Beach Studios often stay at this mini boutique property, which has attracted the likes of Mick Jagger, U2, and Aerosmith. Every room is different, but hardwood floors, stainless-steel fixtures, and muted earth tones in all create a commonality. Studio suites, with rattan sitting areas, are a fairly good deal for their size. Larger suites feel more like villas. You can sunbathe on the rooftop deck. Pros: intimate 11-suite property. Cons: spotty service, no pool. ✉*1200 Collins Ave., South Beach 33139* ☎*305/604–5063 or 800/688–7678* 🖷*305/672–2881* ⊕*www.marlinhotel.com* ⮑*12 suites* ⌂*In-room: safe, kitchen, Wi-Fi. In-hotel: restaurant, room service, bar, laundry service, public Wi-Fi, parking (fee), no-smoking rooms* ▭*AE, D, DC, MC, V.*

★ $–$$ 🛏 **Catalina Hotel & Beach Club.** Need an inexpensive base where you can party in Miami? The Catalina will pick you up from the airport with its free shuttle, give you free drinks every night from 7 to 8, and get you in the mood with its red shag carpets and funky red-and-white lounges, one of which has two-story glass windows and monumental sheer drapes. When it's time to move on, head across the street to South Beach's hottest bars. If you don't wake up with too bad of a hangover, hop on the hotel's complimentary bikes to explore South Beach. Otherwise, stake out a beach chair for a little sun-rejuvenation time. In short, this is the best budget party hotel in the city. Rooms are all white and sparsely furnished, with Tempur-pedic mattresses and Italian Mascioni sheets. No. 400 is special—it hovers above Collins Avenue and is washed in light. Perhaps the staff is *too* laid-back. Service can be spotty and you sometimes feel like the bartenders are running the place. Pros: free drinks, free bikes, free airport shuttle, good people-watching. Cons: $15 wireless fee, service not a high priority, loud. ✉*1732 Collins Ave., Miami Beach 33139* ☎*305/674–1160* 🖷*305/674–7522* ⊕*www. catalinahotel.com* ⮑*138 rooms.* ⌂*In-room: safe, refrigerator, Wi-Fi. In-hotel: restaurant, bars, pool, bicycles, laundry service, public Wi-Fi, airport shuttle, parking (fee), some pets allowed, no-smoking rooms* ▭*AE, D, DC, MC, V.*

$–$$ 🛏 **Century Hotel.** Designed in 1939 by Art Deco master Henry Hohauser, the Century now garners an *InStyle* guest list. Like the Marriott across the street, it's a little south of the action, but that can be a good thing: the Century is a favorite of celebrities trying to keep a low profile. Next door, the renowned Italian restaurant Joia casts a heavy shadow of cool aided by a steady influx of A-listers and local glitterati. The rooms have a certain spartan warmth and definitely feel stylish, if a little remote—but that's probably the point. Pros: free continental breakfast, great Art

6

Deco exterior. Cons: not in the heart of South Beach, no pool. ✉*140 Ocean Dr., South Beach 33139* ☎*305/674–8855 or 888/982–3688* 🖷*305/538–5733* ⊕*www.centurysouthbeach.com* ⬦*26 rooms* ♿*In-room: safe, dial-up. In-hotel: restaurant, bar, parking (fee), no-smoking rooms* ⊟*AE, DC, MC, V* ⦿*CP.*

$–$$ 🏨**Park Central.** Park Central operates as three side-by-side, much-photographed, Art Deco hotels on Ocean Drive: the Imperial, which has oceanfront and standard rooms; the Heathcote, which has 12 suites; and the seven-story, 1937, flagship building, also called Park Central, which has rooms in many categories. The crowning "blue jewel" of the three, it has wraparound corner windows, a sculpture garden, and a compact pool, the setting of much parading about in swimsuits. Black-and-white photos of old beach scenes decorate rooms in all three buildings. You'll also find mahogany furnishings from the Philippines and ceiling fans. There's a roof deck for sunning, where people also gather to watch movies shown here Thursday and Sunday nights all year, with free popcorn and soda. Pros: spacious rooftop sundeck, comfy beds, perfect location for first trip to Miami. Cons: small bathrooms, most rooms have limited views. ✉*640 Ocean Dr., South Beach 33139* ☎*305/538–1611 or 800/727–5236* 🖷*305/534–7520* ⊕*www.theparkcentral.com* ⬦*115 rooms, 12 suites* ♿*In-room: refrigerator, dial-up. In-hotel: 2 restaurants, room service, bars, pool, gym, laundry service, concierge, public Internet, public Wi-Fi, parking (fee), no-smoking rooms* ⊟*AE, D, DC, MC, V.*

$–$$ 🏨**Pelican.** The Diesel clothing company opened this contemporary boutique hotel in 1994, an experiment that has paid off in spades. Every room is individually decorated in Diesel's signature hip, youthful, zany style. For example, the "Me Tarzan, You Vain" room has a jungle theme, with African wood sculptures and a stick lamp; "Up, Up in the Sky" has a space theme, with a model rocket and off-kilter furniture; and the "Best Whorehouse" has a tall, plush, upholstered headboard, chairs with heart-shape backs, and red lamp shades. Sadly, however, most rooms have tiny sleeping chambers in contrast to their triple-size bathrooms with outrageous industrial piping. A relatively inexpensive restaurant on the first-floor patio makes a great Ocean Drive people-watching perch. Pros: unique, over-the-top design; central Ocean Drive location. Cons: tiny rooms. ✉*826 Ocean Dr., South Beach 33139* ☎*305/673–3373 or 800/773–5422* 🖷*305/673–3255* ⊕*www.pelicanhotel.com* ⬦*25 rooms, 5 suites* ♿*In-room: safe, refrigerator, Wi-Fi. In-hotel: restaurant, room service, bar, beachfront, laundry service, parking (fee), no-smoking rooms* ⊟*AE, D, DC, MC, V.*

$ 🏨**The Standard.** An extension of André Balazs's trendy, budget hotel chain, the Standard is a Hollywood newcomer that set up shop a few minutes from South Beach on an island just over the Venetian Causeway. The message: we'll do what we please, and the cool kids will follow. The scene is trendy 30- and 40-year-olds interested in the hotel's many "do-it-yourself" spa activities, including mud bathing, scrubbing with sea salts, soaking in hot or arctic-cold waters, and yoga. An 8-foot, 103-degree cascade into a Roman hot tub is typical of the handful of adult pleasures spread around the pool deck. An informal restaurant overlooks the bay's Mediterranean-style mansions and the cigarette boats that float past. If you choose, you can go kayaking around the island. On the hotel facade you'll see the monumental signage of a bygone occupant, the Lido Spa Hotel, and the much smaller sign of its current occupant, hung, with a wink, upside down. The rooms are small and simple, though they have thoughtful touches like a picnic basket and embroidered fabric covers for the small flat-screen TVs. First-floor rooms have outdoor soaking tubs but very limited privacy, so few take that plunge. Pros: interesting island location, free bike and kayak rentals, swank pool scene, great spa, inexpensive. Cons: removed from South Beach nightlife, small rooms with no views, outdoor tubs are gimmicks, mediocre service. ⊠ *40 Island Ave., Belle Isle, Miami Beach 33139* ☎*305/673–1777* 📠*305/673–8181* ⊕*www.standardhotel.com* ⤳*104 rooms, 1 suite* ♿*In-room: safe, refrigerator, DVD, ethernet. In-hotel: restaurant, room service, bars, pool, gym, spa, water sports, bicycles, laundry service, concierge, Wi-Fi, parking (fee), some pets allowed, no children under 14, no-smoking rooms* ⊟*AE, D, DC, MC, V.*

★ ¢–$ 🏨**Cadet Hotel.** You can trace the fact that this is one of the sweetest, quietest hotels in South Beach to the ways of its independent female owner. (There are very few privately owned hotels here anymore.) The placid patio-garden is the perfect spot to enjoy a full breakfast, included in your rate. Little touches, like candles in the lobby, fresh flowers all around, 600-thread-count sheets, and small pouches that contain fresh lavender or sea shells, depending on the season, show the care and sophistication that are of utmost importance here. The boutique hotel is two blocks from Lincoln Road and the beach, across the street from Casa Tua, and yet you feel like a local resident when you stay here. Clark Gable stayed in Room 225 when he came to Miami for Army Air Corps training in the 1940s; he'd been enrolled at West Point, and thus the hotel's name. Right now the rates are an incredibly good value, but they're likely to double if the property becomes a Relais & Chateaux–managed property, as is under consideration. A 50-person French restaurant is expected to open in late 2007. Pros: well run with friendly service, a lovely garden, and great value. Cons: no pool. ⊠*1701 James Ave., South Beach 33139* ☎*305/672–6688 or 800/432–2338* 📠*305/532–1676* ⊕*www.cadethotel.com* ⤳*33 rooms, 3 suites* ♿*In-room: safe, Wi-Fi. In-hotel: restaurant, room service, bar, pool, laundry service, public Wi-Fi, no-smoking rooms* ⊟*AE, D, DC, MC, V* ⧆*CP.*

★ ¢–$ 🏨**Villa Paradiso.** One of South Beach's best deals, Paradiso has huge floor-through, apartmentlike rooms with kitchens, and a charming tropical courtyard with benches for hanging out at all hours. There's even another smaller courtyard on the other side of the rooms. Peeking out from a sea of tropical foliage, the hotel seems at first to be a rather unassuming piece of Deco architecture. But for all its simplicity, value shines bright. Rooms have polished hardwood floors, French doors, and quirky wrought-iron furniture. They are well suited for extended visits—discounts begin at 10% off for a week's stay. Pros: great hangout spot in courtyard, huge rooms with kitchens, good value, great location. Cons: no wireless Internet, no pool, no restaurant. ⊠*1415 Collins Ave., South Beach 33139* ☎*305/532–0616* ⊟*305/673–5874* ⊕*www.villaparadisohotel.com* ✍*17 studios* ⌂*In-room: kitchen, refrigerator, dial-up. In-hotel: some pets allowed, no-smoking rooms* ⊟*AE, D, DC, MC, V.*

¢ ⊞ **Best Western South Beach.** If you want a cheap stay in the heart of South Beach, and don't care much about service or a fancy room, the Best Western has five, walled-in, Art Deco hotels for your choosing. The Kenmore houses the main lobby, a curvaceous room with block glass and tables for a continental breakfast. Three others, the Taft, Bel-Aire, and the Davis, provide more guest rooms, and the Coral House next door houses a restaurant. The whole complex projects a no-nonsense vibe; for instance, gated entrances to the various hotels are chained off. A big pool in the courtyard is surrounded by plastic lounge chairs. Self-service is the best kind you'll get here. Pros: cheap, central location. Cons: small rooms, no frills, spotty service. ⊠*1050 Washington Ave., South Beach 33139* ☎*305/674–1930 or 888/343–1930* ⊟*305/534–6591* ⊕*www.bestwestern.com* ✍*139 rooms* ⌂*In-room: safe, refrigerator (some). In-hotel: restaurant, bar, pool, public Internet, public Wi-Fi, no-smoking rooms* ⊟*AE, MC, V* ⌾*CP.*

¢ ⊞ **Days Inn Convention Center.** Wedged, improbably, in the space that should by sheer size and might belong to the Setai, which towers above and around it, this cheesy little Days Inn has managed to hold on to its claim to prime beachfront (*someone's* not selling). Unfortunately, it doesn't seem to be taking full advantage of its privileged location. The big pool, which should have amazing ocean views right next to the boardwalk, is fenced in so no views are possible. To reach the sand you have to walk back out through the lobby and down 30 steps. The lobby itself is like a bad parody of Miami Beach, with a big sunset mural, a bridge over a fountain, and a dozen old-fashioned lampposts. But if you're in the right frame of mind, meaning you're willing to put up with mediocre rooms and service, you can get beachfront accommodations for a little more than $100 room. Spend a little extra for one of the 30 oceanfront rooms with balconies. Pros: cheap beachfront rooms in a prime location. Cons: cheesy, older hotel with spotty service. ⊠*100 21st St., South Beach 33139* ☎*305/538–6631 or 800/451–3345* ⊟*305/674–0954* ⊕*www.daysinnsouthbeach.com* ✍*172 rooms* ⌂*In-room: safe, refrigerator (some), ethernet, Wi-Fi. In-hotel: bar, pool, beachfront, laundry facilities, laundry service, concierge, public Internet, public Wi-Fi, parking (fee), no-smoking rooms* ⊟*AE, D, DC, MC, V.*

MID-BEACH AND BAL HARBOUR

Where does South Beach end and Mid-Beach begin? With the massive amount of money being spent on former 1950s pleasure palaces like the Fontainebleau and Eden Roc, it could be that Mid-Beach will soon just be considered part of South Beach. North of 24th Street, Collins Avenue curves its way to 44th Street, where it takes a sharp left turn after running into the Fontainebleau Resort. The area between these two points—24th Street and 96th Street—is Mid-Beach. This stretch is undergoing a renaissance, as formerly rundown hotels are renovated and new hotels and condos are being built.

At 96th Street, the town of Bal Harbour takes over Collins Avenue from Miami Beach. The town runs a mere 10 blocks to the north before the bridge to Sunny Isles. Bal Harbour is famous for its outdoor upscale shops. If you take your shopping seriously, you'll probably want to stay in this area.

$$$-$$$$ **Eden Roc Renaissance Resort & Spa.** Like its next door neighbor, the Fontainebleau, this grand 1950s hotel designed by Morris Lapidus is undergoing a head-to-toe renovation, as well as the construction of a new wing and huge pool complex, both expected to open in 2008. When they do, the Eden Roc will be one of the biggest hotels in the city. The original hotel, which has the free-flowing lines of Deco at its best, is slated to reopen after a thorough restoration in late 2007. (Until then no rooms are open.) The public areas are landmarks and will retain their grand elegance, including monumental columns. The room renovations should renew the allure and perhaps return the swagger of a stay at the Eden Roc to the heights it had reached after opening in the 1950s. For a glimpse of the old glamour, visit Harry's Grille, which has murals of former guests, a veritable roll call of '50s and '60s stars. Pros: all new rooms and facilities. Cons: not on South Beach. ⊠*4525 Collins Ave., Mid-Beach, Miami Beach 33140* ☎*305/531–0000 or 800/327–8337* ⚏*305/674–5555* ⊕*www.edenrocresort.com* ⌕*365 rooms* ⚫*In-room: safe, kitchen (some), refrigerator, ethernet. In-hotel: 2 restaurants, room service, bars, pools, gym, spa, beachfront, parking (fee), no-smoking rooms* ⊟*AE, D, DC, MC, V.*

$$-$$$$ **Fontainebleau Resort and Towers.** Look out, South Beach. When Hilton reopens the Fontainebleau in 2008 as Miami's biggest hotel—twice the size of the Loews, with more than 1,500 rooms—it will be the fruit of the most ambitious and expensive hotel renovation project in the history of Greater Miami. The impact could be even more astonishing to the travel industry here than its original opening in 1954. Planned are 11 restaurants, a huge nightclub, sumptuous pools with cabana islands, a state-of-the-art fitness center and spa, and more than 60,000 square feet of meeting and ballroom space—all of it built from scratch. A 36-story all-suites tower was completed in 2005 and remains open continuously during construction. Suites in the lavish tower offer a peek at the luxury to come in the rest of the resort, with full kitchens including dishwashers and outstanding views looking south over Miami Beach. A second all-suites tower is set to open in late 2007. You may have been wondering if any part of the original hotel is left, and it is. Two Morris Lapidus–designed and landmarked exteriors and lobbies are being restored to their original state. All original rooms, however, were completely gutted, down to the beams, to create new, contemporary rooms. Pros: historic design mixed with all-new facilities, fabulous pools. Cons: away from the South Beach pedestrian scene, too big to be intimate. ⊠*4441 Collins Ave., Mid-Beach, Miami Beach 33140* ☎*305/538–2000 or 800/548–8886* ⚏*305/673–5351* ⊕*www.*

6

fontainebleau.com ☞*1,504 rooms* ⌂*In-room: safe, kitchen (some), refrigerator, DVD (some), Wi-Fi. In-hotel: 11 restaurants, bars, pools, gym, spa, water sports, laundry service, public Internet, public Wi-Fi, parking (fee), no-smoking rooms* ☰*AE, D, DC, MC, V.*

★ **$–$$$** ⛱ **The Palms South Beach.** Stay here if you're seeking an elegant, relaxed property away from the noise but still near South Beach. Like its sister property, the National Hotel, to the south, The Palms has an exceptional beach, an easy pace, and beautiful gardens with a gazebo, fountains, soaring palm trees, and inviting hammocks. There are more large palms inside, in the Great Room lounge just off the lobby, and designer Patrick Kennedy used subtle, natural hues of ivory, green, and blue for the homey, well-lighted rooms. Pros: tropical garden, relaxed and quiet. Cons: no balconies, away from South Beach, city-view rooms feel detached. ✉*3025 Collins Ave., Mid-Beach, Miami Beach 33140* ☎*305/534–0505 or 800/550–0505* 🖷*305/534–0515* ⊕*www.thepalmshotel.com* ☞*220 rooms, 22 suites* ⌂*In-room: safe, refrigerator, Wi-Fi. In-hotel: restaurant, room service, bars, pool, beachfront, laundry service, concierge, public WiFi, parking (fee), no-smoking rooms* ☰*AE, D, DC, MC, V.*

¢–$ ⛱ **Days Inn North Beach.** Here you'll find lots of quiet and a wide expanse of white sand just off Collins and across a quiet street from the beach. Although the rooms and baths are small, the hotel itself is adequate and very clean. Paid public parking is the only option until 6 PM, but there's plenty of availability, and the lobby desk has lots of quarters. A good bet for families, this hotel has a game room and a bright breakfast room, where a free continental breakfast is served. Pros: inexpensive, off the beaten track, quiet. Cons: basic rooms, meter parking. ✉*7450 Ocean Terr., North Beach, Miami Beach 33141* ☎*305/866–1631 or 888/825–6800* 🖷*305/868–4617* ⊕*www.daysinn.com* ☞*92 rooms* ⌂*In-room: safe, refrigerator, Wi-Fi. In-hotel: restaurant, bar, pool, laundry facilities, no-smoking rooms* ☰*AE, D, DC, MC, V.*

★ ¢–$ ⛱ **Ocean Surf.** Did a tornado lift this colorful charmer of an Art Deco hotel and drop it 60 blocks north? If so, the prices got left behind as well, with nights as low as $79. It has one of the most soda-pop-cute exteriors anywhere, and it's right by the beach with an outdoor sundeck (but no pool). As long as you don't need a lot of hotel staff attention and you can vacation in a "do-it-yourself" fashion, this hotel is an excellent choice for the price. It's one of a clustered trio of hotels (the Days Inn is one) a block east of Collins Avenue. Buy a parking pass for your car, and cross the quiet street to the nearly private white sands. Rooms are generic hotel style, with doubles or queens; oceanfront rooms add a balcony overlooking the blue Atlantic. Pros: adorable Art Deco hotel, cheap, free continental breakfast. Cons: basic rooms, no Internet, sloppy service. ✉*7436 Ocean Terr., North Beach, Miami Beach 33141* ☎*305/866–1648 or 800/555–0411* 🖷*305/866–1649* ☞*49 rooms* ⌂*In-room: safe, refrigerator. In-hotel: beachfront, parking (fee), no-smoking rooms* ☰*AE, MC, V* ⊚*CP.*

¢ ⛱ **Circa 39.** This stylish, budget, boutique hotel pays attention to every
Fodor'sChoice detail and gets them all right. In its lobby, inspired by Miami's legend-
★ ary Delano hotel, tall candles burn all night. The pool has cabanas and

umbrella-shaded chaises that invite all-day lounging. Beyond the pool, a bar invites you to linger all night, and possibly play the on-site *Sex and the City, The Sopranos,* or *Desperate Housewives* trivia games. A garden courtyard connecting two wings of the hotel is another great place to lounge. Rooms have wood floors and a cool, crisp look with white furnishings dotted with pale blue pillows. A full-service concierge is called the "Agent of Desires," and the staff wears T-shirts that say "Let Us Spoil You." Done. Note that preservation laws mandate keeping the name plaque "Copley Plaza" outside—that's how you'll know you've found it. The name Circa 39? It was built in 1939 and is on 39th Street. Pros: affordable, chic, and intimate. Cons: wrong side of Collins Avenue (no beach), north of South Beach. ✉ *3900 Collins Ave., Mid-Beach, Miami Beach 33140* ☎ *305/538–4900 or 877/8CIRCA39* 🖷 *305/538–4998* ⊕ *www.circa39.com* �'82 rooms 🔑 *In-room: safe, kitchen, refrigerator, ethernet, Wi-Fi. In-hotel: restaurants, bar, pool, gym, concierge, public Wi-Fi, parking (fee), some pets allowed, no-smoking rooms* ▭ *AE, D, DC, MC, V.*

SUNNY ISLES, AVENTURA & MIAMI LAKES

6

Twenty minutes north of South Beach lies the newly fashionable stretch of beach hotels and condos in the formerly anonymous town of Sunny Isles. Because it's accessible to South Beach, but miles away in spirit, Sunny Isles is an appealing, calm, predominantly upscale choice for families looking for a beautiful beach.

There is no nightlife to speak of in Sunny Isles, and yet the half-dozen mega-luxurious skyscraper hotels that have sprung up here since 2005 have created a niche resort town from the demolished ashes of much older, affordable hotels. It's funny in this context to see the last remnant of the old, two-story, humble beach motels, the Monaco, wedged in between two monster luxury high-rises. That hotel's days are numbered, but things are just starting for the next generation.

$$$$
Fodor'sChoice
★

🏨 **Acqualina.** When it opened in 2006, this hotel raised the bar for luxury in Miami. You'll pay for it, too: Acqualina promises a lavish Mediterranean lifestyle with lawns and pool set below terraces that evoke Vizcaya, and Ferraris and Lamborghinis lining the driveway. There is much to love about the amenities here, including a private beach club, the colossal ESPA spa, gorgeous pools, and the trendiest of restaurants, including one of only a handful in Miami to offer unobstructed beach views. And, upon arrival, you're escorted to your room for a personal, in-room check-in. Rooms are sinfully comfortable, with every conceivable frill. Even standard rooms facing away from the ocean seem grand; they have huge flat-screens that rise out of the foot of the bed, making recumbent TV watching seem like a theater experience. If you're planning to pop the big question on your vacation, a Proposal Concierge will help set the scene. Pros: in-room check-in, luxury amenities, huge spa. Cons: in-room lighting is complicated to use. ✉ *17875 Collins Ave., Sunny Isles 33160* ☎ *305/918–8000* 🖷 *305/918–8100* ⊕ *www. acqualinaresort.com* �'54 rooms, 43 suites 🔑 *In-room: safe, refrigera-*

tor, Wi-Fi. In-hotel: 3 restaurants, room service, bars, pools, gym, spa, beachfront, water sports, children's programs (ages 5–12), laundry service, concierge, public Internet, public Wi-Fi, parking (fee), no-smoking rooms ⊟*AE, D, DC, MC, V.*

★ $$$$ 🗇**Fairmont Turnberry Isle Resort & Club.** Covering a tapestry of islands and waterways on 300 superbly landscaped acres by the bay, the Fairmont Turnberry Isle is a state-of-the-art golf, tennis, and spa resort for people who want to completely get away. It was designed by Addison Mizner on the Intracoastal Waterway in the 1920s and has been completely renovated multiple times since then, most recently to the tune of $100 million in 2007. Oversize rooms are decorated in light woods and earth tones and have large curving terraces and hot tubs. The marina has moorings for 117 boats, there are two Robert Trent Jones golf courses, and a free shuttle takes you to the Aventura Mall. Perks for all ages include a private Ocean Club at Collins Avenue and 17th Street, a quick shuttle ride away. Pros: lots of activity. Cons: no beach nightlife. ✉*19999 W. Country Club Dr., Aventura 33180* 🕾*305/932–6200 or 800/327–7028* 🖷*305/933–6560* ⊕*www.turnberryisle.com* ➴*392 rooms, 41 suites* ♿*In-room: safe, kitchen (some), refrigerator, DVD (some), Wi-Fi. In-hotel: 4 restaurants, bars, golf courses, tennis courts, pools, gym, spa, water sports, bicycles, laundry service, executive floor, public Internet, public Wi-Fi, parking (fee), some pets allowed, no-smoking rooms* ⊟*AE, D, DC, MC, V.*

¢–$$ 🗇**Don Shula's Hotel & Golf Club.** In leafy Miami Lakes, about 14 mi northwest of downtown Miami, the hotel is part of the Main Street shopping, dining, and entertainment complex. The golf club, with par-72 championship and par-3 executive courses, is less than a mile away. Both wings have rooms with sports prints, and a shuttle runs between them and all around the 500-acre property. If you're not teeing off, you can work out or play tennis in the hotel's 40,000-square-foot athletic club. Need to fortify yourself with some protein? Don Shula's Steak House serves hefty cuts of prime beef in an atmosphere that can best be described as "football elegant." Pros: good golf, fun sports atmosphere, unpretentious vibe. Cons: suburban location, far from beaches. ✉*6842 Main St., Miami Lakes 33014* 🕾*305/821–1150 or 800/247–4852* 🖷*305/820–8071* ⊕*www.donshulahotel.com* ➴*188 rooms, 17 suites in hotel, 84 rooms in club* ♿*In-room: safe, refrigerator, Wi-Fi. In-hotel: 2 restaurants, bars, golf courses, tennis courts, pools, gym, spa, laundry service, public Internet, public Wi-Fi, parking (no fee), no-smoking rooms* ⊟*AE, DC, MC, V.*

¢ 🗇**Travelodge Monaco Beach Resort.** Book a room here today, before
Fodor'sChoice the Monaco is demolished to make way for another high-rise luxury
★ hotel. Peek inside the courtyard and you'll see older men and women playing shuffleboard. Some have been coming here for 50 years, and it seems almost out of charity that the Monaco stays open for them today. In high season rooms are only $100. Want a kitchen? Ten dollars more. Naturally the furnishings are simple, but they're clean and the oceanfront wing literally extends out onto the sand. So there's no wireless Internet here—who needs it? Read a book under one of the tiki huts on the beach. You don't need to reserve them, and you don't

pay extra. This is easily the best value of any hotel in Miami. Pros: steps to great beach, wholly unpretentious, bottom-dollar cost. Cons: older rooms, not service oriented. ✉ *17501 Collins Ave., Sunny Isles 33160* ☎*305/932–2100 or 800/227–9006* 📠*305/931–5519* ⊕*www. monacomiamibeachresort.com* 🛏*110 rooms* 🔑*In-room: safe, kitchen (some), refrigerator (some). In-hotel: restaurant, bar, pool, beachfront, parking (fee)* ☰*AE, D, DC, MC, V.*

DOWNTOWN MIAMI

$$$$ 🛏**Four Seasons Hotel Miami.** Stepping off busy Brickell Avenue into
Fodor'sChoice this hotel, you see a soothing water wall trickling down from above.
★ Inside, a cavernous lobby is barely big enough to hold the enormous sculptures—part of the hotel's collection of local and Latin American artists. A 2-acre pool terrace on the seventh floor overlooks downtown Miami while making you forget you're in downtown Miami. Three heated pools include a foot-high wading pool with 24 palm tree "islands." Service is tops for Miami. Pros: sensational service, amazing pool deck. Cons: no balconies. ✉ *1435 Brickell Ave., Downtown 33131* ☎*305/358–3535 or 800/819–5053* 📠*305/358–7758* ⊕*www. fourseasons.com/miami* 🛏*182 rooms, 39 suites* 🔑*In-room: safe. In-hotel: restaurant, bars, pools, gym, spa, children's programs (ages 4– 12), public Internet* ☰*AE, D, DC, MC.*

$$$$ 🛏**Mandarin Oriental, Miami.** If you can afford to stay here, do. The loca-
Fodor'sChoice tion, at the tip of Brickell Key in Biscayne Bay, is superb. Rooms fac-
★ ing west overlook the downtown skyline; to the east are Miami Beach and the blue Atlantic. There's also beauty in the details: sliding screens that close off the baths, dark wood, crisp linens, and room numbers hand-painted on rice paper at check-in. The Azul restaurant, with an eye-catching waterfall and private dining area at the end of a catwalk, serves a mix of Asian, Latin, Caribbean, and French cuisine. The hotel has a 20,000-square-foot private beach and an on-site spa. Pros: only beach (man-made) in downtown, intimate feeling, top luxury hotel. Cons: small pool, few beach cabanas. ✉ *500 Brickell Key Dr., Brickell Key 33131* ☎*305/913–8288 or 866/888–6780* 📠*305/913–8300* ⊕*www.mandarinoriental.com* 🛏*327 rooms, 31 suites* 🔑*In-room: safe, dial-up. In-hotel: 2 restaurants, bars, pool, spa, laundry service, concierge, parking (fee)* ☰*AE, D, DC, MC, V.*

$$–$$$ 🛏**Doubletree Grand Hotel Biscayne Bay.** Like the Biscayne Bay Marriott, this elegant waterfront option is at the north end of downtown off a scenic marina, and near many of Miami's headline attractions: the Port of Miami, Bayside, the Arena, and the Carnival Center. Rooms are spacious, and most have a view of Biscayne Bay and the port. Some suites have full kitchens. You can rent Jet Skis or take deep-sea fishing trips from the marina. Pros: great bay views, deli and market on-site. Cons: need a cab to get around. ✉ *1717 N. Bayshore Dr., Downtown 33132* ☎*305/372–0313 or 800/222–8733* 📠*305/539–9228* ⊕*www. doubletree.com* 🛏*152 suites* 🔑*In-room: safe, kitchens (some), Wi-Fi. In-hotel: restaurant, bar, pool* ☰*AE, D, DC, MC, V.*

6

¢
Fodor's Choice
★
⊞**Miami River Inn.** Billed as Miami's only bed-and-breakfast, this inn dispenses the attentive, personalized hospitality often lost in Miami Beach's gleaming Deco towers. The inn's five restored 1904 clapboard buildings are the only group of Miami houses left from that period. A glass of wine at check-in sets the tone. Rooms (some with tub but no shower) are filled with antiques, and many have hardwood floors. All have TVs and phones. The most popular rooms overlook the river from the second and third floors. The heart of the city is a 10-minute stroll across the 1st Street Bridge. The inn is eco-friendly and sponsors a community garden down the street. Pros: free continental breakfast, unusual but central location, quaint and inexpensive. Cons: no pool. ⊠*118 S.W. South River Dr., Little Havana, 33130* ☎*305/325–0045 or 800/468–3589* ☐*305/325–9227* ⊕*www.miamiriverinn.com* ⇶*40 rooms, 2 with shared bath* ⚐*In-hotel: pool, laundry facilities, parking (no fee), some pets allowed, no-smoking rooms* ☰*AE, D, DC, MC, V* ⦿*CP.*

WEST MIAMI-DADE

$$$–$$$$
⊞**Doral Golf Resort & Spa.** With its five championship golf courses, including the Blue Monster—home of the annual PGA Ford Championship—this 650-acre resort is definitely golf central in Greater Miami. But there's more: the Arthur Ashe Tennis Center with 11 courts, the lavish spa with its own luxury suites, two fitness centers, on-site shops and boutiques, a kids' camp, a water park with a 125-foot slide, and five restaurants. Pros: kids' water park, great golf, garden walkways. Cons: suburban location far from Miami Beach and downtown Miami, unexciting rooms. ⊠*4400 N.W. 87th Ave., Doral, Miami 33178* ☎*305/592–2000 or 800/713–6725* ☐*305/591–4682* ⊕*www.doralresort.com* ⇶*696 rooms, 48 suites* ⚐*In-room: safe, refrigerator, Wi-Fi. In-hotel: 5 restaurants, room service, bars, golf courses, tennis courts, pool, spa, children's programs (ages 5–12), laundry service, concierge, public Internet, public Wi-Fi, parking (no fee), some pets allowed, no-smoking rooms.* ☰*AE, D, DC, MC, V.*

COCONUT GROVE

Coconut Grove is blessed with a number of excellent luxury properties. All are within walking distance of its principal entertainment center, Coco Walk, as well as its marinas. Although this area certainly can't replace the draw of Miami Beach, or the business convenience of downtown, about 20 minutes away, it's an exciting bohemian-chic neighborhood with a gorgeous waterfront.

$$$–$$$$
⊞**Ritz-Carlton, Coconut Grove.** Although it's the least exciting of the Ritz-Carlton's three properties in the Miami area, it provides the best service experience in Coconut Grove. Overlooking Biscayne Bay, rooms are appointed with marble baths, a choice of down or nonallergenic foam pillows, and private balconies. And there's a butler to solve every dilemma—technology butlers to resolve computer problems, travel butlers to meet your flight and guide you to the hotel, dog butlers to

watch after your version of Tinkerbell, and shopping and style guides to make sure you don't drop while you shop. A 5,000-square-foot spa is on hand to soothe away stress, and the open-air Bizcaya is among Coconut Grove's loveliest dining spots. Pros: best service in Coconut Grove, high-quality spa. Cons: least exciting of the three Miami Ritz-Carltons. ⊠*3300 S.W. 27th Ave., Coconut Grove 33133* ☎*305/644–4680 or 800/241–3333* 🖷*305/644–4681* ⊕*www.ritzcarlton.com* ↩*88 rooms, 27 suites* ⌂*In-room: safe, refrigerator, ethernet, Wi-Fi. In-hotel: 2 restaurants, room service, bar, pool, gym, spa, children's programs (ages 5–12), laundry service, concierge, executive floor, public Internet, public Wi-Fi, parking (fee), some pets allowed, no-smoking rooms* ▤*AE, D, DC, MC, V.*

¢–$ 🏨**Doubletree Hotel at Coconut Grove.** Along Coconut Grove's hotel row, which faces some of the best waterfront in the country, the Doubletree is a short walk from popular Grove shops and restaurants and a quick drive from Miami's beaches and business districts. Most rooms have terraces open to breezes from the bay, plus work desks, coffeemakers, movies, and complimentary Internet access. Pros: cookies at check-in, nice marina views. Cons: drab, older exterior. ⊠*2649 S. Bayshore Dr., Coconut Grove 33133* ☎*305/858–2500 or 800/222–8733* 🖷*305/858–9117* ⊕*www.coconutgrove.doubletree.com* ↩*173 rooms, 19 suites* ⌂*In-room: safe, Wi-Fi. In-hotel: restaurant, room service, bars, pool, parking (fee), no-smoking rooms* ▤*AE, D, DC, MC, V.*

KEY BISCAYNE

Key Biscayne is the southernmost barrier island in the country yet it's only 5 mi from downtown Miami.

$$$$ 🏨**The Ritz-Carlton, Key Biscayne.** There is probably no other place in
Fodor'sChoice   Miami where slowness is lifted to a fine art. On Key Biscayne, there are
★   no pressures, there's no nightlife, and the dining choices are essentially limited to the hotel. In this kind of setting, you'll appreciate the Ritz brand of pampering. Need something to do? The "tequilier" at the seaside Cantina Beach will educate you on the finer points of his native region's drink. Hitting the spa? In one of 21 treatment rooms, try the 42 Movement Minerale Massage. An 11-court tennis "garden" with tennis butler, a private beach, and beachside water sports are other options. In-room luxuries like robes, slippers, fine linens and toiletries, and scales are of course expected. The club level offers five food presentations a day, and the Ritz Kids club has full- and half-day, and Saturday night, programs. Borrow bikes here to explore Billy Baggs park and its lighthouse. Pros: top tennis facility, private beach, good family retreat. Cons: beach is gray sand, you have to drive to Miami for nightlife. ⊠*455 Grand Bay Dr., Key Biscayne 33149* ☎*305/365–4500 or 800/241–3333* 🖷*305/365–4505* ⊕*www.ritzcarlton.com/resorts/key_biscayne* ↩*365 rooms, 37 suites* ⌂*In-room: safe, DVD (some), VCR (some), ethernet, Wi-Fi. In-hotel: 2 restaurants, room service, bars, tennis courts, pools, gym, spa, beachfront, water sports, bicycles, laundry service, concierge, executive floor, public Internet,*

public Wi-Fi, parking (fee), some pets allowed, no-smoking rooms ▤*AE, D, DC, MC, V.*

CORAL GABLES

Coral Gables is a beautiful town, set around its beacon, the national landmark Biltmore Hotel. It also has a couple of big business hotels and one smaller boutique property. The University of Miami is nearby.

$$$–$$$$
Fodor'sChoice
★

🏨 Biltmore Hotel. Built in 1926, this landmark hotel has had several incarnations over the years—including a stint as a hospital during World War II—and has changed hands more than a few times. Through it all, this grandest of grande dames remains an opulent reminder of yesteryear, with its palatial lobby and grounds, enormous pool, and distinctive 315-foot tower, which rises above the canopy of trees shading Coral Gables. Fully updated, the Biltmore has on-site golf and tennis, a spa and fitness center, extensive meeting facilities, and the celebrated Palme d'Or restaurant. Pros: historic property, possibly best pool in Miami, great tennis and golf. Cons: far from Miami Beach. ⊠*1200 Anastasia Ave., Coral Gables 33134* ☎*305/445–1926 or 800/727–1926* ▤*305/913–3159* ⊕*www.biltmorehotel.com* ⊅*241 rooms, 39 suites* ♿*In-hotel: 4 restaurants, bars, golf course, tennis courts, pool, gym, spa, public Internet* ▤*AE, D, DC, MC, V.*

★ **$–$$**

🏨 Hotel St. Michel. There is no other hotel quite like the St. Michel, where each room is individually decorated with antiques imported from England, Scotland, and France by the owner. Built in 1926, this historic and intimate inn has glass chandeliers suspended from vaulted ceilings in the public areas. Dinner at the superb Restaurant St. Michel is a must, but there is also a more casual bar and dining area behind the lobby, better suited for quiet breakfasts or late-night aperitifs. The St. Michel is nearly always fully booked, so reserve early. Pros: personal service, good free continental breakfast, European sensibility. Cons: slightly less than luxurious. ⊠*162 Alcazar Ave., Coral Gables 33134* ☎*305/444–1666 or 800/848–4683* ▤*305/529–0074* ⊕*www.hotelstmichel.com* ⊅*29 rooms* ♿*In-room: Wi-Fi. In-hotel: restaurant, room service, bar, laundry service, parking (fee), no-smoking rooms* ▤*AE, D, DC, MC, V* ❘⊚❘*CP.*

NIGHTLIFE

Updated
by Carolyn
Keating

Miami's pulse pounds with nonstop nightlife that reflects the area's potent cultural mix. On sultry, humid nights with the huge full moon rising out of the ocean and fragrant night-blooming jasmine intoxicating the senses, who can resist Cuban salsa, Jamaican reggae, and Dominican merengue, with some disco and hip-hop thrown in for good measure? When this place throws a party, hips shake, fingers snap, bodies touch. It's no wonder many clubs are still rocking at 5 AM.

How to get past the velvet ropes at the hottest South Beach nightspots? First, if you're staying at a hotel, use the concierge. Decide which clubs you want to check out (consult *Ocean Drive* magazine celebrity pages if you want to be among the glitterati), and the concierge will e-mail, fax, or call your names in to the clubs so you'll be on the guest list when you arrive. This means much easier access and usually no cover charge (which can be upward of $20) if you arrive before midnight. Guest list or no guest list, follow these pointers: make sure there are more women than men in your group. Dress up—casual chic is the dress code. For men this means no sneakers, no shorts, no sleeveless vests, and no shirts unbuttoned past the top button. For women, provocative and seductive is fine; overly revealing is not. Black is always right. At the door: don't name-drop—no one takes it seriously. Don't be pushy while trying to get the doorman's attention. Wait until you make eye contact, then be cool and easygoing. If you decide to tip him (which most bouncers don't expect), be discreet and pleasant, not big-bucks obnoxious—a $10 or $20 bill quietly passed will be appreciated, however. With the right dress and the right attitude, you'll be on the dance floor rubbing shoulders with South Beach's finest clubbers in no time.

FIND OUT WHAT'S GOING ON

The *Miami Herald* ⊕*www.herald.com* is a good source for information on what to do in town. The "Weekend" section, included in the Friday edition, has an annotated guide to everything from plays and galleries to concerts and nightclubs. The "Ticket" column of this section details the week's entertainment highlights. You can pick up the free weekly tabloid *Miami New Times* ⊕*www.miaminewtimes.com*, the city's largest free alternative newspaper, published each Thursday. It lists nightclubs, concerts, and special events; reviews plays and movies; and provides in-depth coverage of the local music scene. "Night & Day" is a rundown of the week's cultural highlights. *Ocean Drive*, Miami Beach's model-strewn, upscale fashion and lifestyle magazine, squeezes club, bar, restaurant, and events listings in with fashion spreads, reviews, and personality profiles. Paparazzi photos of local party people and celebrities give you a taste of Greater Miami nightlife before you even put on your black going-out ensemble.

The Spanish-language *El Nuevo Herald,* published by the *Miami Herald,* has extensive information on Spanish-language arts and entertainment, including dining reviews, concert previews, and nightclub highlights. *Spanish-language radio,* primarily on the AM dial, is also a good source of information about arts events. Tune in to WXDJ (95.7 FM), Amor (107.5 FM), or Radio Mambi (710 AM).

Much news of upcoming events is disseminated through flyers tucked onto windshields or left for pickup at restaurants, clubs, and stores. They're technically illegal to distribute, but they're mighty useful. And if you're a beachgoer, chances are that as you lie in the sun you'll be approached by kids handing out cards announcing the DJs and acts appearing in the clubs that night.

BARS & LOUNGES

One of Greater Miami's most popular pursuits is bar hopping. Bars range from intimate enclaves to showy see-and-be-seen lounges to loud, raucous frat parties. There's a decidedly New York flair to some of the newer lounges, which are increasingly catering to the Manhattan party crowd who escape to South Beach for long weekends. If you're looking for a relatively unfrenetic evening, your best bet is one of the chic hotel bars on Collins Avenue.

SOUTH BEACH

B.E.D. Innocently standing for "beverages, entertainment, and dining," B.E.D. also offers king pillow–strewn beds in place of tables. ✉929 *Washington Ave., South Beach* ☎305/532–9070.

Club Deuce. Although it's completely unglam, this pool hall attracts a colorful crowd of clubbers, locals, celebs—and just about anyone else. Locals consider it the best spot for a cheap drink. ✉222 14th St., at *Collins Ave., South Beach* ☎305/531–6200.

Laundry Bar. Do your laundry while listening to house music or quaffing a drink at the bar (you can leave your dry cleaning, too). It's mostly gay (with a ladies' night), but definitely straight-friendly. ✉721 N. Lincoln *La., 1 block north of Lincoln Rd., South Beach* ☎305/531–7700.

Lost Weekend. Players at this pool hall are serious about their pastime, so it's hard to get a table on weekends. The full bar, which has 150 kinds of beers, draws an eclectic crowd, from yuppies to drag queens to slumming celebs like Lenny Kravitz and the guys in Hootie and the Blowfish. ✉218 Española Way, at Collins Ave., South Beach ☎305/672–1707.

Rex at the Marlin. It's the Austin Powers look here—fuchsia and orange pillows and cushions and mirrors everywhere. DJs spin a different type of music every night for the 25-to-40 crowd. ✉1200 Collins Ave., *South Beach* ☎305/604–3595.

Mynt Ultra Lounge. The name of this upscale lounge is meant to be taken literally—not only are the walls bathed in soft green shades, but an aromatherapy system pumps out different fresh scents, including mint. Celebs like Enrique Iglesias, Angie Everhart, and Queen Latifah have cooled down here. ✉1921 Collins Ave., South Beach ☎786/276–6132.

★ **The National.** Don't miss a drink at the hotel's nifty wooden bar, one of many elements original to the 1939 building, which give it such a sense of its era that you'd expect to see Ginger Rogers and Fred Astaire hoofing it along the polished lobby floor. The adjoining Martini Room has a great collection of cigar and old airline stickers and vintage Bacardi ads on the walls. There's live jazz most nights. Don't forget to take a peek at the long, sexy pool. ✉1677 Collins Ave., South Beach ☎305/532–2311.

Fodor'sChoice **Pearl.** An airy space lab of white and orange bathed in lavender light, ★ this restaurant-cum-nightclub overlooks the ocean and is next door to Nikki Beach Club. The food's not bad either. ✉1 Ocean Dr., South *Beach* ☎305/538–1111.

Fodor'sChoice ★ **Rose Bar at the Delano.** The airy lobby lounge at South Beach's trendiest hotel manages to look dramatic but not cold, with long gauzy curtains and huge white pillars separating conversation nooks (this is where Ricky Martin shot the video for "La Vida Loca"). A pool table brings the austerity down to earth. There's also a poolside bar with intimate waterside cabanas. ✉ *1685 Collins Ave., South Beach* ☎ *305/672-2000.*

Fodor'sChoice ★ **SkyBar at the Shore Club.** Splendor-in-the-garden is the theme at this haute spot by the sea, where multiple lounging areas are joined together. Daybeds, glowing Moroccan lanterns, and maximum atmosphere make a visit to this chic outdoor lounge worthwhile. Groove to dance music in the Red Room, or enjoy an aperitif and Japanese bar bites at Nobu Lounge. The Red Room, Nobu Restaurant and Lounge, Italian restaurant Ago, and SkyBar all connect around the Shore Club's pool area. ✉ *1901 Collins Ave., South Beach* ☎ *305/695-3100.*

Snatch. An upscale rock-and-roll bar with a sophisticated edge, this VIP mecca is where you can hear your favorite hard rock and hip-hop tunes from the '80s and '90s, swing on a stripper pole, and/or ride a mechanical bull. ✉ *1439 Washington Ave., Miami Beach* ☎ *305/604-8889.*

Tantra. With its grass-floor lobby and aphrodisiacal dinner menu, this place takes sensory enhancement a step further when it transforms into a nightclub on Friday and Saturday and hosts its popular Goddess Party on Monday nights. ✉ *1445 Pennsylvania Ave., South Beach* ☎ *305/672-4765.*

DOWNTOWN MIAMI & DESIGN DISTRICT

Gordon Biersch. This financial district brew house is classier than most, with glass-enclosed copper pots cranking out tasty ales and lagers, an inspired menu, live music on Fridays, and a steady happy-hour crowd. ✉ *1201 Brickell Ave., Downtown* ☎ *786/425-1130.*

Fodor'sChoice ★ **Tobacco Road.** Opened in 1912, this classic holds Miami's oldest liquor license: No. 0001! Upstairs, in a space that was occupied by a speakeasy during Prohibition, local and national blues bands perform nightly. There are excellent bar food, a dinner menu, and a selection of single-malt Scotches, bourbons, and cigars. This is the hangout of grizzled journalists, bohemians en route to or from nowhere, and club kids seeking a way station before the real parties begin. ✉ *626 S. Miami Ave., Downtown* ☎ *305/374-1198.*

COCONUT GROVE

Monty's in the Grove. The outdoor bar here has Caribbean flair, thanks especially to live calypso and island music. It's very kid-friendly on weekends, when Mom and Dad can kick back and enjoy a beer and the raw bar while the youngsters dance to live music. Evenings bring a DJ and reggae music. ✉ *2550 S. Bayshore Dr., at Aviation Ave., Coconut Grove* ☎ *305/858-1431.*

CORAL GABLES

Bar at Ponce and Giralda. One of the oldest bars in South Florida, the old Hofbrau has been reincarnated and now serves no-nonsense, live homegrown rock-and-roll and a nontouristy vibe. ✉ *172 Giralda Ave., at Ponce de León Blvd., Coral Gables* ☎ *305/442–2730.*

Globe. The centerpiece of Coral Gables' emphasis on nightlife draws crowds of twentysomethings who spill into the street for live jazz Wednesday through Saturday and a bistro-style menu nightly. Outdoor tables and an art-heavy, upscale interior are comfortable, if you can find space to squeeze in. ✉ *377 Alhambra Circle, at Le Jeune Rd., Coral Gables* ☎ *305/445–3555.*

John Martin's Restaurant and Irish Pub. The cozy upscale Irish pub hosts an Irish cabaret on Saturday nights, with live contemporary and traditional music—sometimes by an Irish band—storytelling, and dancers. ✉ *253 Miracle Mile, at Ponce de León Blvd., Coral Gables* ☎ *305/445–3777.*

CABARET, COMEDY & SUPPER CLUBS

If you're in the mood for scantily clad showgirls and feathered headdresses, you can still find the kind of song-and-dance extravaganzas that were produced by every major Miami Beach hotel in the 1950s. Modern-day offerings include flamenco shows, salsa dancing, and comedy clubs.

Casa Panza. The visionary Madrileñan owners of this Little Havana restaurant have energized the neighborhood with a twice-weekly tribute to *La Virgen del Rocío* (the patron saint of a province in Andalusia), in which the room is darkened and diners are handed lighted candles and sheet music. Everyone readily joins in the singing, making for a truly enjoyable evening. There is flamenco dancing on Tuesday, Thursday, Friday, and Saturday. ✉ *1620 S.W. 8th St., Little Havana, Miami* ☎ *305/643–5343* 🎫 *Free.*

Improv Comedy Club. This long-standing comedy club hosts nationally touring comics nightly. Comedy club faithfuls will recognize Margaret Cho and George Wallace, and everyone knows Damon Wayans and Chris Rock, both of whom have taken the stage here. Urban Comedy Showcase is held Tuesday and Wednesday, with an open mike part of the evening on Wednesday. A full menu is available. ✉ *Streets of Mayfair, 3390 Mary St., at Grand Ave., Coconut Grove, Miami* ☎ *305/441–8200.*

Lombardi's. You can shake it salsa-style or merengue until midnight to the music of three different bands on Friday, Saturday, and Sunday nights at this downtown restaurant and bar. ✉ *Bayside Marketplace, 401 Biscayne Blvd., Downtown, Miami* ☎ *305/381–9580.*

DANCE CLUBS

SOUTH BEACH

Fodor'sChoice ★ **Cameo.** Sophisticated and fun, this newly renovated disco-era-inspired club combines sleek with a state-of-the-art light and sound systems to dazzle the senses. It's housed in the historic Cameo Theater, which is, unfortunately, carpeted. ⊠*1445 Washington Ave., South Beach* ☎*305/532–2667.*

Nikki Beach Club. With its swell on-the-beach location, the full-service Nikki Beach Club has become a favorite pretty-people and celeb hangout. Tepees and hammocks on the sand, dance floors both under the stars and inside, and beach parties make this a true South Beach experience. ⊠*1 Ocean Dr., South Beach* ☎*305/538–1111.*

Opium Garden. Enter the Asian temple and behold a lush waterfall, lots of candles, dragons, and tapestries. Casually chic twenty- and thirtysomethings go for the exotic intrigue of the popular nightspot and dance to house music and hip-hop. The particularly stylish set should set their sights on the club's upstairs VIP lounge, Privé—a more intimate dance club and lounge experience. ⊠*136 Collins Ave., South Beach* ☎*305/531–5535.*

DOWNTOWN

Space. Want 24-hour partying? Here's the place. Created from four downtown warehouses, Space has three dance rooms, an outdoor patio, a New York industrial look, and a 24-hour liquor license. It's open on weekends only, and you'll need to look good to be allowed past the velvet ropes. ⊠*34 N.E. 11th St., Downtown* ☎*305/375–0001.*

COCONUT GROVE

★ **Oxygen Lounge.** Latin and dance sounds dominate at this sleek, belowground lounge. Water cascades down a wall, and blue neon light casts a glow over the crowd of mainly young professionals out for a good time and a little dancing. ⊠*2911 Grand Ave., Coconut Grove* ☎*305/476–0202.*

GAY NIGHTLIFE

Aside from a few bars and lounges on the mainland, Greater Miami's gay action centers on the dance clubs in South Beach. That tiny strip of sand rivals New York and San Francisco as a hub of gay nightlife—if not in the number of clubs then in the intensity of the partying. The neighborhood's large gay population and the generally tolerant attitudes of the hip straights who live and visit here encourage gay-friendliness at most South Beach venues that are not specifically gay. In addition, many mixed clubs, like Cameo, have one or two gay nights. To find out what's going on, log on to *The Express* (⊕*www.express-gaynews.com*) or OutInMiami.com (⊕*www.outinmiami.com*).

Fodor's Choice ★ **Cameo.** Steamy club windows on Monday nights are caused by the fantastically popular Back Door Bamby night, with go-go girls and boys. Keep in mind the carpeted dance floor—your lug soles will resist movement. ⊠*1445 Washington Ave., South Beach, Miami Beach* ☎*305/532–2667.*

Twist. This longtime hot spot and local favorite with two levels, an outdoor patio, and a game room is crowded from 8 PM on, especially on Monday, Thursday (two-for-one), and Friday nights. ⊠*1057 Washington Ave., South Beach, Miami Beach* ☎*305/538–9478.*

LIVE MUSIC

★ **Jazid.** Thanks to a sleek interior design job in aqua tones, Jazid is an intimate, candlelighted standout on the strip. The music is jazz, with blues and R&B. Bands play downstairs in the cozy barroom and upstairs on an even tinier stage. Call ahead to reserve a table. ✉*1342 Washington Ave., South Beach, Miami Beach* ☎*305/673–9372.*

Fodor'sChoice   **Tobacco Road.** Live blues, R&B, and jazz are on tap along with the food
★   and drink at this Miami institution. ✉*626 S. Miami Ave., Downtown* ☎*305/374–1198.*

BEACHES, SPORTS & THE OUTDOORS

Sun, sand, and crystal-clear water mixed with an almost nonexistent winter and a cosmopolitan clientele make Miami and Miami Beach ideal for year-round sunbathing and outdoor activities. Whether the priority is showing off a toned body, jumping on a Jet Ski, or relaxing in a tranquil natural environment, there's a beach tailor-made to please. But tanning and water sports are only part of this sun-drenched picture. Greater Miami has championship golf courses and tennis courts, miles of bike trails along placid canals and through subtropical forests, and skater-friendly concrete paths amidst the urban jungle. For those who like their sports of the spectator variety, the city offers up a bonanza of pro teams for every season. The Miami Dolphins remain the only NFL team to have ever played a perfect season, the scrappy Florida Marlins took the World Series title in 2003, and the Miami Heat are the 2006 NBA champions. There's even a crazy ball-flinging game called jai alai that's billed as the fastest sport on earth.

In addition to contacting the venues below directly, get tickets to major events from **Ticketmaster** (☎*305/358–5885*).

AUTO RACING

★ For NASCAR Nextel Cup events, head south to the **Homestead–Miami Speedway,** which hosts the Ford 400 Nextel Cup Series season finale. The highlight of the speedway schedule, it's held the third Sunday in November in conjunction with the NASCAR Craftsman Truck Series season finale and other races. The speedway, built in 1995 and improved with steeper banking in 2003, is also home to the Toyota Indy 300 IRL season opener each February and other Indy-car racing. ✉*1 Speedway Blvd., Exit 6 of Florida's Tpke. (Rte. 821) at S.W. 137th Ave., Homestead* ☎*866/409–7223* ⊕*www.homesteadmiamispeedway.com* ⊙ *Weekdays 9–5* ☒*Prices vary according to event.*

BASEBALL

☼ The **Florida Marlins** did what few thought possible: they came out of nowhere to beat the New York Yankees and win the 2003 World Series. Now the only thing lacking is a baseball-only stadium with a retractable roof to use on rainy days; they currently play home games at Dolphin Stadium, April through early October. ⊠*Dolphin Stadium, 2267 N.W. 199th St., 16 mi northwest of Downtown, between I–95 and Florida's Tpke., Miami* ☎*305/626–7400 or 877/627–5467* ⊕*www. marlins.mlb.com* ⊠*$9–$80, parking $10.*

BASKETBALL

The **Miami Heat,** the 2006 NBA champs, play at the 19,449-seat, waterfront AmericanAirlines Arena. The state-of-the-art venue has indoor fireworks, restaurants, a wide patio overlooking Biscayne Bay, and a silver sun-shape special-effects scoreboard with rays holding widescreen TVs. During Heat games, when the 1,100 underground parking spaces are reserved for season-ticket holders, you can park across the street at Miami's Bayside Marketplace ($20), at metered spaces along Biscayne Boulevard, or in lots on side streets, where prices range from $20 to $35, depending on the distance from the arena (a limited number of spaces for people with disabilities are available on-site for non-season-ticket holders). Better yet, take the Metromover to the Park West or Freedom Tower station. Home games are held November through April. ⊠*AmericanAirlines Arena, 601 Biscayne Blvd., Downtown* ☎*786/777–4328, 800/462–2849 ticket hotline* ⊕*www. nba.com/heat* ⊠*$10–$265.*

6

BEACHES

Almost every side street in Miami Beach dead-ends at the ocean. Sandy shores also stretch along the southern side of the Rickenbacker Causeway to Key Biscayne, where you'll find more popular beaches. Greater Miami is best known for its ocean beaches, but there's freshwater swimming here, too, in pools and lakes. Below are the highlights for the get-wet set.

MID-BEACH & NORTH

Let's cut to the chase. There are plenty of beaches in Miami, but only one lets you return home without a single trace of a tan line. Park in the North Lot of **Haulover Beach Park** to hit the clothing-optional stretch of sand. It's unofficial, but the gay crowd gathers to the left. The sections of beach requiring swimwear are popular, too, given the park's ample parking and relaxed atmosphere. Tunnels leading from the beach to the lots are less than pristine, but the park is nice for those who want to get to the water without a long march across hot sand. There are lifeguards on duty, barbecue grills, tennis, and volleyball, plus showers for rinsing off after a day in the sun and surf. Or check out the kite rentals, charter fishing excursions, and a par-3, 9-hole golf course. ⊠*10800 Collins Ave., north of Bal Harbour, North Miami-Dade, Miami Beach* ☎*305/947–3525* ⊠*$5 per vehicle* ☉*Daily sunrise–sunset.*

★ ℃ Across the Intracoastal Waterway from Haulover is **Oleta River State Park,** 1,033 acres of subtropical beauty along Biscayne Bay. Swim in the calm bay waters and bicycle, canoe, and bask among egrets, manatees, bald eagles, and fiddler crabs. Highlights include picnic pavilions, five on the Intracoastal and four adjacent to a man-made swimming beach; a playground for tots; a mangrove island accessible only by boat; mountain-bike trails; and primitive but air-conditioned cabins ($45 per night, reservations required) for those who wish to tackle the trails at night. In early 2007, the Historic Blue Marlin Fish House and Outdoor Experience, a casual café and self-guided interpretative center, opened on park land just west of the entrance. ⊠ *3400 N.E. 163rd St., North Miami Beach* ☎ *305/919–1846* ⊕ *www.floridastateparks. org/oletariver/* ⊠ *$1 per person on foot or bike; $5 per vehicle up to 8 people, $1 each additional* ☉ *Daily 8–sunset.*

Parlez-vous français? If you do, you'll feel quite comfortable at **Surfside Beach.** This stretch of beach is filled with the many French Canadians who spend the winter here. ⊠ *Collins Ave. between 88th and 96th Sts., Surfside.*

SOUTH BEACH

Fodor'sChoice
★ The stretch of beach along **Ocean Drive**—primarily the 10-block stretch from 5th to 15th streets—is one of the most talked-about beachfronts in America. The beach is wide, white, and bathed by warm aquamarine waves. Separating the sand from the traffic of Ocean Drive is palm-fringed Lummus Park, with its volleyball nets and chickee huts for shade. The beach also plays host to some of the funkiest lifeguard stands you'll ever see, pop stars shooting music videos, and visitors from all over the world. The beach at 12th Street is popular with gays. Because much of South Beach has an adult flavor—women are often casually topless—many families prefer the beach's quieter southern reaches, especially 3rd Street Beach. Unless you're parking south of 3rd Street, metered spaces near the waterfront are rarely empty. Instead, opt for a public garage and walk; you'll have lots of fun people-watching, too. ⊠ *Ocean Dr., between 1st and 22nd Sts., South Beach, Miami Beach* ☎ *305/673–7714.*

KEY BISCAYNE & VIRGINIA KEY

Fodor'sChoice
★ Beyond Key Biscayne's commercial district, at the southern tip of the island, is **Bill Baggs Cape Florida State Park,** a natural oasis with an excellent swimming beach frequently ranked among the top 10 in North America by the University of Maryland's esteemed sandman, Dr. Beach. Sea grass–studded dunes, blue-green waters, and plenty of native plants and trees add to the tranquil setting. The 410-acre park has a restored lighthouse, 18 picnic shelters, and a casual seafood restaurant, which also serves beer and wine. A stroll or bike ride along paths and boardwalks provides wonderful views of the bay and Miami's skyline. You can rent bikes, beach chairs, and umbrellas, and there are fishing platforms and a playground. ⊠ *1200 S. Crandon Blvd., Key Biscayne* ☎ *305/361–5811 or 305/361–8779* ⊠ *$1 per person on foot, bike, motorbike, or bus; $5 per vehicle up to 8 people* ☉ *Daily 8–sunset, lighthouse tours Thurs.–Mon. 10 and 1.*

★
☾ The 3½-mi-long beach at **Crandon Park** has a great view of the Atlantic, and parking is inexpensive and plentiful at several different entry points. On busy days be prepared for a long hike from your car to the

beach. There are bathrooms, outdoor showers, plenty of picnic tables, and concession stands. The entire park is family-friendly and the sand is equally soft no matter where you place your towel, but the South Beach entrance has boredom-busting access to marine-theme play sculptures, a dolphin-shaped spray fountain, an old-fashioned outdoor roller rink, and a restored carousel (it's open weekends and major holidays 10–5, until 6 in summer, and you get three rides for $1). Then there's **Crandon Gardens**, a former zoo site that's home to free-roaming swans, iguanas, and at least one American crocodile. Enter at North Beach for the weekend kayak rental concession, bike path, and the $4 million **Marjory Stoneman Douglas Biscayne Nature Center** (☎305/361–6767 ☉ *daily 9–4*), home of interactive aquatic exhibits and walking trails through Bear Cut Preserve. Eco-tours can be arranged through the center as well. ⊠*4000 Crandon Blvd., Key Biscayne* ☎*305/361–5421* ☎*$5 per vehicle* ☉*Daily 8–sunset.*

BICYCLING

Perfect weather and flat terrain make Miami-Dade County a popular place for cyclists. Add a free color-coded map that points out streets best suited for bicycles, rated from best to worst, and it's even better. Also available are printouts listing parks with multiuse paths and information about local bike clubs. The map is available from the **Miami-Dade County Bicycle Coordinator** (⊠*Metropolitan Planning Organization, 111 N.W. 1st St., Suite 910, Miami 33128* ☎*305/375–1647*), whose purpose is to share with you the glories of bicycling in South Florida. There's some especially good cycling to be had in South Miami-Dade. On Key Biscayne, **Mangrove Cycles** (⊠*260 Crandon Blvd., #6, Key Biscayne* ☎*305/361–5555*) rents bikes for $10 for two hours or $15 per day and will offer helpful suggestions for the island's 12 mi of paved bike trails. On Miami Beach the proximity of the **Miami Beach Bicycle Center** (⊠*601 5th St., South Beach, Miami Beach* ☎*305/674–0150*) to Ocean Drive and the ocean itself makes it worth the $24 per day (or $8 per hour).

BOATING & SAILING

Boating, whether on sailboats, powerboats, or luxury yachts, Wave Runners or windsurfers, is a passion in greater Miami. The Intracoastal Waterway, wide and sheltered Biscayne Bay, and the Atlantic Ocean provide ample opportunities for fun aboard all types of watercraft.

The best windsurfing spots are on the north side of the Rickenbacker Causeway at Virginia Key Beach or to the south at, go figure, Windsurfer Beach. Kitesurfing adds another level to the water-sports craze. The shallow waters off the parking lot in Matheson Hammock Park are like catnip for local kiteboarders. They also blast off from 87th Street in Miami Beach at North Shore Open Space Park.

MARINAS

Haulover Marine Center (⊠*15000 Collins Ave., north of Bal Harbour, North Miami-Dade, Miami Beach* ☏*305/945–3934*), which has a bait-and-tackle shop and a 24-hour marine gas station, is low on glamour but high on service.

Near the Art Deco District, **Miami Beach Marina** (⊠*MacArthur Causeway, 300 Alton Rd., South Beach, Miami Beach* ☏*305/673–6000* ⊕*www.miamibeachmarina.com*) has plenty to entice sailors and land-lubbers alike: restaurants, charters, boat rentals, a complete marine-hardware store, a dive shop, excursion vendors, a large grocery store, a fuel dock, concierge services, and 400 slips accommodating vessels of up to 250 feet. There's also a U.S. Customs clearing station and a charter service, Florida Yacht Charters. Picnic tables along the docks make this marina especially visitor-friendly.

One of the busiest marinas in Coconut Grove is **Bayshore Landing Marina** (⊠*2550 S. Bayshore Dr., Coconut Grove, Miami* ☏*305/854–7997*), home to a lively seafood restaurant that's good for viewing the nautical eye candy.

RENTALS & CHARTERS

You can rent 19- to 54-foot powerboats through **Club Nautico** (⊠*Miami Beach Marina, 300 Alton Road, #112, South Beach, Miami Beach* ☏*305/673–2502* ⊕*www.clubnauticousa.com* ⊠*Crandon Park Marina, 5400 Crandon Blvd., Key Biscayne* ☏*305/361–9217*), a national powerboat rental company. Half- to full-day rentals range from $200 to $699. You may want to consider buying a club membership; it'll cost a bundle at first, but you'll save about 50% on all your future rentals. The family-owned **Florida Yacht Charters** (⊠*MacArthur Causeway, 390 Alton Rd., Suite 3, South Beach, Miami Beach* ☏*305/532–8600 or 800/537–0050*), at the full-service Miami Beach Marina, will give you the requisite checkout cruise and paperwork. Then you can take off for the Keys or the Bahamas on a catamaran, sailboat, or motor yacht. Charts, lessons, and captains are available if needed.

Playtime Watersports (⊠*Collins Ave., Mid-Beach, Miami Beach* ☏*786/234–0184* ⊠*Eden Roc, 4525 Collins Ave.* ⊠*Miami Beach Resort and Spa, 4833 Collins Ave.* ⊠*Alexander Hotel, 5225 Collins Ave.*) sells and rents high-end water-sports equipment, including Wave Runners and wind-driven devices, from concessions at several Collins Avenue hotels and the Ritz-Carlton on Key Biscayne. In addition to renting equipment, the friendly folks at **Sailboards Miami** (⊠*Site E1 Rickenbacker Causeway, mi past toll plaza, Key Biscayne* ☏*305/361–7245* ⊕*www.sailboardsmiami.com*) say they teach more windsurfers each year than anyone in the United States and promise to teach you to windsurf within two hours—for $69. Rentals average $25–$30 for one hour and $100 for four hours.

FOOTBALL

Fodor'sChoice
★ Consistently ranked as one of the top teams in the NFL, the **Miami Dolphins** have one of the largest average attendance figures in the league. Fans may be secretly hoping to see a repeat of 1972's perfect season, when the team, led by legendary coach Don Shula, compiled a 17–0 record (a record that still stands). September through January, on home game days the Metro Miami-Dade Transit Agency runs buses to the stadium. ✉*Dolphin Stadium, 2267 N.W. 199th St., 16 mi northwest of Downtown, between I–95 and Florida's Tpke., Miami* ☎*305/620–2578* ⊕*www.miamidolphins.com.*

GOLF

Greater Miami has more than 30 private and public courses. Costs at most courses are higher on weekends and in season, but you can save by playing on weekdays and after 1 or 3 PM, depending on the course—call ahead to find out when afternoon–twilight rates go into effect. To get a **"Golfer's Guide for South Florida,"** which includes information on most courses in Miami and surrounding areas, call 800/864–6101. The 18-hole, par-71 championship **Biltmore Golf Course** (✉*1210 Anastasia Ave., Coral Gables* ☎*305/460–5364*), known for its scenic layout, has been restored to its original Donald Ross design, circa 1925. Green fees range from $65 to $70 in season, and an optional cart is $26. The gorgeous hotel makes a great backdrop.

Overlooking the bay, the **Crandon Golf Course** (✉*6700 Crandon Blvd., Key Biscayne* ☎*305/361–9129*) is a top-rated 18-hole, par-72 public course in a beautiful tropical setting. Expect to pay $150–$167 for a round in winter, $61 in summer, cart included. Twilight rates from $31 to $39 apply after 3. **Don Shula's Hotel & Golf Club** (✉*7601 Miami Lakes Dr., 154th St. Exit off Rte. 826, Miami Lakes* ☎*305/820–8106* ⊕*www.donshulahotel.com*), in northern Miami, has one of the longest championship courses in the area (7,055 yards, par-72), a lighted par-3 course, and a golf school. Green fees are $80–$170, depending on the season. You'll pay in the lower range on weekdays, more on weekends, and $45 after 3 PM. Golf carts are included. The lighted par-3 course is $12 weekdays, $16 weekends. The club hosts more than 75 tournaments a year.

Among its five courses and many annual tournaments, the **Doral Golf Resort and Spa** (✉*4400 N.W. 87th Ave., 36th St. Exit off Rte. 826, Doral, Miami* ☎*305/592–2000 or 800/713–6725* ⊕*www.doralresort. com*), just west of Miami proper, is best known for the par-72 Blue Monster course and the PGA's annual Ford Championship. (The week of festivities planned around this tournament, which offers $5 million in prize money, brings hordes of pro-golf aficionados in late February and early March.) Fees range from $95 to $295. Carts are not required. For a casual family outing or for beginners, the 9-hole, par-3 **Haulover Golf Course** (✉*Haulover Beach Park, 10800 Collins Ave.North Miami-Dade, Miami Beach* ☎*305/940–6719*) is right on the Intracoastal Waterway at the north end of Miami Beach. The longest hole on this walking course is 120 yards; green fees are only $7, plus $5 for parking. Hit the links in the heart of South Beach at the lovely 18-hole, par-72 **Miami Beach Golf Club.** (⊠*2301 Alton Rd.South Beach, Miami Beach* ☎*305/532–3350* ⊕*www.miamibeachgolfclub.com*). The 2002 redesign from Arthur Hills took the course to the next level. Green fees are $95 in summer, $200 in winter, including mandatory cart.

IN-LINE SKATING

Miami Beach's ocean vistas, wide sidewalks, and flat terrain make it a perfect locale for in-line skating. And don't the locals know it. Very popular is the **Lincoln Road Mall** from Washington Avenue to Alton Road; many of the restaurants along this pedestrian mall have outdoor seating where you can eat without shedding your skates. For a great view of the Art Deco District and action on South Beach, skate along the sidewalk on the east side of **Ocean Drive** from 5th to 14th streets. In South Miami an often-traversed concrete path winds **under the elevated Metrorail** from Vizcaya Station (across U.S. 1 from the Miami Museum of Science) to Red Road at U.S. 1 (across from the Shops at Sunset Place). You don't have to bring your own; a number of in-line skate shops offer rentals that include protective gear. **Fritz's Skate and Bike Shop** (⊠*730 Lincoln Rd., South Beach, Miami Beach* ☎*305/532–1954*) charges $10 an hour or $24 for 24 hours.

POOL

★ The 820,000-gallon **Venetian Pool,** fed by artesian wells, is so special
♨ that it's on the National Register of Historic Places. The picturesque pool design and lush landscaping place it head and shoulders above typical public pools, and a snack bar, lockers, showers, and free parking make an afternoon here pleasant and convenient. Children must be at least 38ʺ tall or three years old. ⊠*2701 De Soto Blvd., Coral Gables* ☎*305/460–5306* ⊕*www.venetianpool.com* ☞*$7–$10, free parking across De Soto Blvd.* ⏱*June–July, weekdays 11–7:30, weekends 10–4:30; Aug.–Oct. and Apr.–May, Tues.–Fri. 11–5:30, weekends 10–4:30; Nov.–Mar., Tues.–Sun. 10–4:30.*

SCUBA DIVING & SNORKELING

Diving and snorkeling on the off-shore coral wrecks and reefs on a calm day can be comparable to the Caribbean. Chances are excellent you'll come face-to-face with a flood of tropical fish. One option is to find Fowey, Triumph, Long, and Emerald reefs in 10- to 15-foot dives that are perfect for snorkelers and beginning divers. On the edge of the continental shelf a little more than 3 mi out, these reefs are just ¼ mi away from depths greater than 100 feet. Another option is to paddle around the tangled prop roots of the mangrove trees that line the coast, peering at the fish, crabs, and other creatures hiding there.

It's a bit of a drive, but the best diving and definitely the best snorkeling to be had in Miami-Dade is on the incredible living coral reefs

✆ in **Biscayne National Park** (✉9710 S.W. 328th St., Exit 6 of Florida's Tpke., Homestead ☎305/230–1100 ⊕www.nps.gov/bisc/), in the rural southeast corner of the county. With 95 percent of its 173,000 acres underwater, this is the national park system's largest marine park. The huge park includes the northernmost islands of the Florida Keys and the beginning of the world's third-longest coral reef. Guided snorkeling and scuba trips, offered from the concession near the visitor center, cost $35 for a three-hour snorkel trip (daily 1:30–4:30), including equipment, and $54 for a 4½-hour, two-tank dive trip (weekends 8:30–1). Scuba equipment is available for rent.

Perhaps the area's most unusual diving options are its **artificial reefs** (✉1920 Meridian Ave., South Beach, Miami Beach ☎305/672–1270). Since 1981, Miami-Dade County's Department of Environmental Resources Management has sunk tons of limestone boulders and a water tower, army tanks, and almost 200 boats of all descriptions to create a "wreckreational" habitat where divers can swim with yellow tang, barracudas, nurse sharks, snapper, eels, and grouper. Most dive shops sell a book listing the locations of these wrecks. Information on wreck diving can be obtained from the Miami Beach Chamber of Commerce.

Divers Paradise of Key Biscayne (✉5400 Crandon Blvd., Key Biscayne ☎305/361–3483 ⊕www.keydivers.com) has a complete dive shop and diving-charter service next to the Crandon Park Marina, including equipment rental and scuba instruction with PADI and NAUI affiliation. Dive trips are offered Tuesday through Friday at 1, weekends 8:30 and 1:30. **South Beach Dive and Surf Center** (✉850 Washington Ave., South Beach, Miami Beach ☎305/531–6110), an all-purpose dive shop with PADI affiliation, runs night and wreck dives right in the center of it all. Its boats depart from marinas in Miami Beach and Key Largo, in the Florida Keys.

SHOPPING

Miami teems with sophisticated shopping malls and the bustling avenues of commercial neighborhoods. But this is also a city of tiny boutiques tucked away on side streets—such as South Miami's Red, Bird, and Sunset roads intersection—and outdoor markets touting unusual and delicious wares. Stroll through Spanish-speaking neighborhoods where shops sell clothing, cigars, and other goods from all over Latin America. At an open-air flea-market stall, score an antique glass shaped like a palm tree and fill it with some fresh Jamaican ginger beer from the table next door. Or stop by your hotel gift shop and snap up an alligator magnet for your refrigerator, an ashtray made of seashells, or a bag of gumballs shaped like Florida oranges. Who can resist?

6

MALLS

People fly to Miami from all over the world just to shop, and the malls are high on their list of spending spots. Stop off at one or two of these climate-controlled temples to consumerism, many of which double as mega–entertainment centers, and you'll understand what makes Miami such a vibrant shopping destination.

Fodor'sChoice **Bal Harbour Shops.** Local and international shoppers flock to this swank
★ collection of 100 high-end shops, boutiques, and department stores, which include such names as Christian Dior, Gucci, Hermès, Salvatore Ferragamo, Tiffany, and Valentino. Many European designers open their first North American signature store at this outdoor, pedestrian-friendly mall, and many American designers open their first boutique outside of New York here. Restaurants and cafés, in tropical garden settings, overflow with style-conscious diners. People-watching at outdoor café Carpaccio is the best in town. ✉ *9700 Collins Ave., Bal Harbour* ☎ *305/866–0311* ⊕ *www.balharbourshops.com.*

CocoWalk. It's got three floors containing nearly 40 chain and specialty shops (Koko & Palenki, Victoria's Secret, and Edward Beiner, among others), blending the bustle of a mall with the breathability of an open-air venue. Kiosks with cigars, beads, incense, herbs, and other small items are scattered around the ground level, and restaurants and nightlife (Hooters, Fat Tuesday, and a 16-screen AMC theater, to name a few) are upstairs. Hanging out and people-watching is somewhat of a pastime here. The stores stay open almost as late as the popular restaurants and clubs. ✉ *3015 Grand Ave., Coconut Grove, Miami* ☎ *305/444–0777.*

Mayfair in the Grove. This open-air complex of promenades, balconies, and sidewalk cafés bustles both day and night, thanks to its Coconut Grove setting and its popular tenants: an improv comedy club, martini lounge, and a few all-night dance clubs. Banana Republic, Palm Produce, Bath + Body Works, and a dozen other shops and restaurants are also here. ✉ *2911 Grand Ave., Coconut Grove, Miami* ☎ *305/448–1700* ⊕ *www.mayfairinthegrove.net.*

Fodor'sChoice **Village of Merrick Park.** At this Mediterranean-style shopping and din-
★ ing venue Neiman Marcus and Nordstrom anchor 115 specialty shops. Designers such as Etro, Tiffany, Burberry, Carolina Herrera, and Bottega Veneta fulfill most high-fashion needs, and luxury-linen purveyor Ann Gish and Brazilian contemporary-furniture designer Artefacto provide a taste of the haute-decor shopping options. International food venues and a day spa, Elemis, offer further indulgences. ✉ *358 San Lorenzo Ave., Coral Gables* ☎ *305/529–0200* ⊕ *www.villageofmerrickparkl.com.*

SHOPPING DISTRICTS

If you're over the climate-controlled slickness of shopping malls and can't face one more food-court "meal," you've got choices in Miami. Head out into the sunshine and shop the city streets, where you'll find big-name retailers and local boutiques alike. Take a break at a sidewalk café to power up on some Cuban coffee or fresh-squeezed OJ and enjoy the tropical breezes.

MIAMI DESIGN DISTRICT

★ Miami is synonymous with good design, and this visitor-friendly shopping district is an unprecedented melding of public space and the exclusive world of design. Covering a few city blocks around N.E. 2nd Avenue and N.E. 40th Street, the Design District contains more than 200 showrooms and galleries, including Kartell, Ann Sacks, Poliform, and Luminaire. Unlike most showrooms, which are typically the beat of decorators alone, the Miami Design District's showrooms are open to the public and occupy windowed, street-level spaces. Bring your quarters, as all of the parking is on the street and metered. Visitor-friendly touches include art galleries and cafés, and the neighborhood even has its own high school (of art and design, of course) and hosts street parties and gallery walks. Although in many cases you'll need a decorator to secure your purchases, browsers are encouraged to consider for themselves the array of rather exclusive furnishings, decorative objects, antiques, and art. ⊠*N.E. 36th St. to N.E. 42nd St. between N.E. 2nd Ave. and N. Miami Ave., Design District, Miami* ⊕*www.miamidesigndistrict.net.*

MIRACLE MILE–DOWNTOWN CORAL GABLES

Lined with trees and busy with strolling shoppers, Miracle Mile is the centerpiece of the downtown Coral Gables shopping district, which is home to men's and women's boutiques, jewelry and home furnishing stores, and a host of exclusive couturiers and bridal shops. More than 30 first-rate restaurants offer everything from French to Indian cuisine, and art galleries and the Actors' Playhouse give the area a cultural flair. ⊠*Douglas Rd. to LeJeune Rd. and Aragon Ave. to Andalusia Ave., Coral Gables* ☎*305/569–0311* ⊕*www.shopcoralgables.com.*

SOUTH BEACH–COLLINS AVENUE

★ Give your plastic a workout in shopping the many high-profile tenants on this densely packed two-block stretch of Collins Avenue between 5th and 10th streets. Think Club Monaco, MAC, Kenneth Cole, Barney's Co-Op, and A/X Armani Exchange. Sprinkled amid the upscale vendors are hair salons, spas, cafés, and such familiar stores as the Gap, Urban Outfitters, and Banana Republic. Be sure to head over one street east and west to catch the shopping on Ocean Drive and Washington Avenue. ⊠*Collins Ave. between 6th and 8th Sts., South Beach, Miami Beach* ☎*305/672–1270.*

SOUTH BEACH–LINCOLN ROAD MALL

Fodor's Choice ★ This eight-block-long pedestrian mall is home to more than 150 shops, 20-plus art galleries and nightclubs, about 50 restaurants and cafés, and the renovated Colony Theatre. Tiffany & Co. was one of the first of the exclusive boutiques here in the 1940s, when Lincoln Road was known as the 5th Avenue of the South. Although the Tiffany's outpost is long gone, today an 18-screen movie theater anchors the west end of the street, which is where most of the worthwhile shops are; the far east end is mostly discount and electronic shops. Sure, there's a Pottery

Barn, a Gap, and a Williams-Sonoma, but the emphasis is on emporiums with unique personalities, like En Avance, Chroma, Base, and Jonathan Adler. Do as the locals do, and meander along "the Road" day or night, stopping for a refreshment at one of the top-flight bistros or open-air eateries. ⊠*Lincoln Rd. between Alton Rd. and Washington Ave., South Beach, Miami Beach* ☎*305/672–1270.*

SPECIALTY STORES

Beyond the shopping malls and the big-name retailers, Greater Miami has all manner of merchandise to tempt even the casual browser. For consumers on a mission to find certain items—Art Deco antiques or cigars, for instance—the city streets burst with a rewarding collection of specialty shops.

ANTIQUES

Alhambra Antiques (⊠*2850 Salzedo St., Coral Gables* ☎*305/446–1688*) houses a collection of high-quality decorative pieces acquired on annual jaunts to Europe.

★ **Architectural Antiques** (⊠*2520 S.W. 28th La., Coconut Grove, Miami* ☎*305/285–1330*) carries large and eclectic items—railroad crossing signs, statues, English roadsters—along with antique furniture, lighting, paintings, and silverware, all in a cluttered setting that makes shopping an adventure.

Artisan Antiques Art Deco (⊠*110 N.E. 40th St., Design District, Miami* ☎*305/573–5619*) purveys china, crystal, mirrors, and armoires from the French Art Deco period, but an assortment of 1930s radiator covers, which can double as funky sideboards, are what's really neat here.

★ **Senzatempo** (⊠*1680 Michigan Ave., Ste. 1015, South Beach, Miami Beach* ☎*305/534–5588* ⊕*www.senzatempo.com*) was once a popular showroom yet now operates as a warehouse, but buyers can stop into their Lincoln Road area offices to place orders for great vintage home accessories by European and American designers of the 1930s through the 1970s, including electric fans, klieg lights, and chrome furniture.

Valerio Antiques (⊠*250 Valencia Ave., Coral Gables* ☎*305/448–6779*) carries fine French Art Deco furniture, bronze sculptures, shagreen boxes, and original art glass by Gallé and Loetz, among others.

BEAUTY

Fodor'sChoice **Brownes & Co.** (⊠*841 Lincoln Rd., South Beach, Miami Beach*
★ ☎*305/532–8703* ⊕*www.brownesbeauty.com*) provides luxurious products to those who appreciate them the most. Cosmetics include Molton Brown, Body & Soul, Le Clerc, and others. It also sells herbal remedies and upscale hair and body products from Bumble and Bumble. Try to resist something from the immense collection of scented European soaps in all sizes and colors. A popular in-house salon, **Some Like It Hot** (☎*305/538–7544*), offers some of the best waxing in town. **The Fragrance Shop** (⊠*612 Lincoln Rd., South Beach, Miami Beach* ☎*305/535–0037*) carries more than 800 perfume oils, including those that mimic famous brands, in a setting that resembles an 18th-century apothecary. The staff will customize a unique blend for

you or sell you a handblown perfume bottle made by one of many international artisans.

BOOKS

Barnes & Noble (✉ *152 Miracle Mile, Coral Gables* ☎ *305/446–4152*), like others in the superstore chain, encourages customers to pick a book off the shelf and lounge on a couch. A well-stocked magazine and international news rack and an espresso bar–café make it even easier to while away a rainy afternoon here or at the Kendall, North Miami Beach, or South Miami locations.

Fodor's Choice
★
Books & Books, Inc. (✉ *265 Aragon Ave., Coral Gables* ☎ *305/442–4408* ✉ *933 Lincoln Rd., South Beach, Miami Beach* ☎ *305/532–3222* ✉ *9700 Collins Ave., Bal Harbour Shops, Bal Harbour* ☎ *305/864–4241*), Greater Miami's only independent English-language bookshops, specialize in contemporary and classical literature as well as in books on the arts, architecture, Florida, and Cuba. At any of its three locations, you can lounge at a café or browse the photography gallery. All stores host regular poetry and other readings. **La Moderna Poesia** (✉ *5739 N.W. 7th St., Little Havana, Miami* ☎ *305/262–1975*), with more than 100,000 titles, is the region's largest and most complete source for *los libros en español*.

CIGARS

Bill's Pipe & Tobacco (✉ *2309 Ponce de León Blvd., Coral Gables* ☎ *305/444–1764*) has everything for the smoker, including a wide selection of pipes and pipe tobacco, cigars, accessories, and gifts. **Tropical Cigars** (✉ *741 Lincoln Rd., South Beach, Miami Beach* ☎ *305/673–3194*) is a cigar, coffee, and cocktail bar where you can get boxes of cigars with personalized labels. Name a dozen after yourself or your new kid. **El Credito Cigars** (✉ *1106 S.W. 8th St., Little Havana, Miami* ☎ *305/858–4162*), in the heart of Little Havana, employs rows of workers at wooden benches. They rip, cut, and wrap giant tobacco leaves, and press the cigars in vises. Dedicated smokers find their way here to pick up a $90 bundle or to peruse the *gigantes, supremos,* panatelas, and Churchills available in natural or *maduro* wrappers. **Macabi Cigars** (✉ *3473 S.W. 8th St., Little Havana, Miami* ☎ *305/446–2606*) carries cigars, cigars, and more cigars, including premium and house brands. Humidors and other accessories are also available.

CLOTHING FOR MEN & WOMEN

★ **Base** (✉ *939 Lincoln Rd., South Beach, Miami Beach* ☎ *305/531–4982*) is a constantly evolving shop with a cutting-edge magazine section, an international CD station with DJ, and groovy home accessories. Stop here for men's and women's eclectic clothing, shoes, and accessories that mix Japanese design with Caribbean-inspired materials. The often-present house label designer may help select your wardrobe's newest addition. **Chroma** (✉ *920 Lincoln Rd., South Beach, Miami Beach* ☎ *305/695–8808*) is where fashionistas go for Barbara Bui, Catherine Malandrino, and Mint, as well as up-and-coming designers. **Genius Jones** (✉ *1661 Michigan Ave., South Beach, Miami Beach* ☎ *305/534–7622*) is a modern design store for kids and parents. It's the best—and one of few—places to buy unique children's gifts on South Beach. Pick up furniture, strollers, clothing, home accessories, and playthings, including classic wooden toys, vintage rock T-shirts by Claude and Trunk, and toys designed by Takashi Murakami and Keith Haring. **Intermix** (✉ *634 Collins Ave., South Beach, Miami Beach* ☎*305/531–5950)* is a modern New York boutique with the variety of a department store. You'll find fancy dresses, stylish shoes, slinky accessories, and trendy looks by sassy and somewhat pricey designers like Chloé, Stella McCartney, Marc Jacobs, Moschino, and Diane von Furstenberg.

Kristine Michael (✉*7271 S.W. 57th Ave., South Miami* ☎*305/665–7717)* is a local fashion institution with suburban moms and University of Miami students. The store's hip and up-to-the-minute selection of pieces from Theory, Alice & Olivia, Kors, and C & C California stands out from the national retailers across the street at the Shops at Sunset Place.

★ **MIA Jewels** (✉*1439 Alton Rd., Miami Beach* ☎*305/532–6064)* is an Alton Road jewelry and accessories boutique known for its colorful, gem- and bead-laden, gold and silver earrings, necklaces, bracelets, and brooches by lines such as Cousin Claudine, Amrita, and Alexis Bittar. This is a shoo-in store for everyone: you'll find things for trend lovers (gold-studded chunky Lucite bangles), classicists (long, colorful, wraparound beaded necklaces), and ice lovers (long Swarovski crystal cabin necklaces) alike.

★ **Silvia Tcherassi** (✉*358 San Lorenzo Ave., Coral Gables* ☎*305/461–0009)*, the Colombian designer's signature boutique, in the Village of Merrick Park, features feminine and frilly dresses and separates accented with chiffon, tulle, and sequins.

SHOES

Giroux (✉*638 Collins Ave., South Beach, Miami Beach* ☎*305/672–3015)* carries some men's and women's shoes by American, Spanish, and house-label designers. But the highlight of the selection is the Italian shoe company of brothers Goffredo Fantini and Enrico Fantini, who design independent men's lines and collaborate on their women's shoe collection, Materia Prima. **Koko & Palenki** (✉*CocoWalk, 3015 Grand Ave., Coconut Grove, Miami* ☎*305/444–1772)* is where Grovers go for a well-edited selection of trendy shoes by Calvin Klein, Casadei, Charles David, Stuart Weitzman, Via Spiga, and others. Handbags, belts, and men's shoes add to the selection. Koko & Palenki also has stores in the Aventura and Dadeland malls.

SWIMWEAR

Absolutely Suitable (✉*1560 Collins Ave., South Beach, Miami Beach* ☎*305/604–5281)* carries women's and men's swimwear and accessories for lounging poolside. The salespeople will put you in a suit that fits just right and dress you from sunhat to flip-flop. **Everything but Water** (✉*Aventura Mall, 19501 Biscayne Blvd., Aventura* ☎*305/932–7207)* lives up to its name, selling everything for the water (except the water itself). The complete line of women's and junior's swimwear includes one- and two-piece suits and tankinis (tank tops with bikini or high-top bottoms). **South Beach Surf & Dive Shop** (✉*850 Washington Ave., South Beach, Miami Beach* ☎*305/531–6110* ⊕*www.southbeachdivers.com)*

is a one-stop shop for beach gear—from clothing and swimwear for guys and gals to wake-, surf-, and skateboards. The shop also offers multilingual surfing, scuba, snorkeling, and dive lessons and trips.

VINTAGE CLOTHING

★ **Consign of the Times** (⊠*1635 Jefferson Ave., South Beach, Miami Beach* ☎*305/535–0811*) sells vintage and consignment items by top designers at pre-owned prices, including Chanel suits, Fendi bags, and Celine and Prada treasures.

★ **Fly Boutique** (⊠*650 Lincoln Rd., South Beach, Miami Beach* ☎*305/604–8508*) is where South Beach hipsters flock for the latest arrival of used clothing. At this resale boutique '80s glam designer pieces fly out at a premium price, but vintage camisoles and Levi's corduroys are still a resale deal. Be sure to look up—the eclectic lanterns are also for sale.

Fodor'sChoice
★ **Miami Twice** (⊠*6562 S.W. 40th St., South Miami* ☎*305/666–0127*) has fabulous vintage clothes and accessories from the last three decades. After all, everyone needs a leisure suit or platform shoes. Check out the vintage home collectibles and furniture, too. **Sasparilla Vintage** (⊠*1630 Pennsylvania Ave., South Beach, Miami Beach* ☎*305/532–6611*), just off Lincoln Road, teems with a well-chosen selection of gotta-have-it vintage. Resale accessories in excellent condition from Gucci, Dolce, Dries, and Pucci are neatly organized among colorful party outfits like a vintage Missoni rainbow-color dress.

JEWELRY

Beverlee Kagan (⊠*5831 Sunset Dr., South Miami* ☎*305/663–1937*) deals in vintage and antique jewelry, including Art Deco–era bangles, bracelets, and cuff links. **Jose Roca Designs** (⊠*297 Miracle Mile, Coral Gables* ☎*305/441–9696*) designs fine jewelry from precious metals and stones. If you have a particular piece that you would like to create, this is the place to have it meticulously executed. **Me & Ro** (⊠*Shore Club hotel, 1901 Collins Ave., South Beach, Miami Beach* ☎*305/672–3566* ⊕*www.meandrojewelry.com*) is a trendy New York–based jewelry shop run by Michele Quan and Robin Renzi, with a celebrity clientele that reads like a who's who. Designs are crafted from silver, gold, and semiprecious stones.

MUSIC

Do-Re-Mi Music Center (⊠*1829 S.W. 8th St., Little Havana, Miami* ☎*305/541–3374*) satisfies shoppers who want to go home with suitcases full of salsa, merengue, or other Latin dance music. **Sam Ash Music** (⊠*5360 N.W. 167th St., West Miami-Dade, Miami* ☎*305/628–3510* ⊠*Dolphin Mall, 11421 N.W. 12th St., West Miami-Dade, Miami* ☎*786/331–9688*) stocks music supplies from guitar strings and drumsticks to amps and keyboards and has DJ-demo, drum-percussion, and keyboard rooms that let you sample the merchandise before buying. The 48,000-square-foot store also offers instrument repairs and international sales.

ODDS & ENDS

Condom USA (✉*3066 Grand Ave., Coconut Grove, Miami* ☎*305/445–7729*) sells condoms by the gross, sexually oriented games, and other titillating objects. If you're easily offended, stay away, but if you're easily aroused, stay the night (or at least until closing—2 AM on Friday and Saturday, midnight the rest of the week). **La Casa de los Trucos (The House of Costumes)** (✉*1343 S.W. 8th St., Little Havana, Miami* ☎*305/858–5029*) is a popular magic store that first opened in Cuba in the 1930s; the exiled owners reopened it here in the 1970s. When they're in, the owners perform for you.

ONLY IN MIAMI

ABC Costume Shop (✉*3704 N.E. 2nd Ave., Design District, Miami* ☎*305/573–5657* ⊕*www.abccostumeshop.com*) is a major costume source for TV, movie, and theatrical performances. Open to the public, it rents and sells outfits from Venetian kings and queens to Tarzan and Jane. Hundreds of costumes and accessories, such as wigs, masks, gloves, tights, and makeup, are available to buy off the rack, and thousands are available to rent.

★ **Dog Bar** (✉*723 N. Lincoln La., South Beach, Miami Beach* ☎*305/532–5654*), just north of Lincoln Road's main drag, caters to enthusiastic animal owners who simply must have that perfect leopard-skin pet bed, gourmet treats, and organic food.

La Casa de las Guayaberas (✉*5840 S.W. 8th St., Little Havana, Miami* ☎*305/266–9683*) sells custom-made guayaberas, the natty four-pocket dress shirts favored by Latin men. Hundreds are also available off the rack. **Miami Orchids** (✉*2662 S. Dixie Hwy., Coconut Grove, Miami* ☎*305/665–3278*) will satisfy your yen for mysteriously beautiful varieties of orchids, bromeliads, and bonsai.

SPORTING GOODS

Bikes to Go (✉*6600 S.W. 80th St., Miami* ☎*305/666–7702*) sells wheels and products that protect you from the hazards of biking but does not rent equipment.

★ **South Beach Scooters** (✉*215 6th St., South Beach, Miami Beach* ☎*305/532–6700* ⊕*www.electricrentals.com*) is a one-stop shop for scooters and Segways, the dynamic human transporter. Renting a Segway or scooter at this storefront between Washington and Collins avenues includes hands-on training and instruction on the rules of the road. Tours are also available. **Miami Golf Discount Superstore** (✉*111 N.E. 1st St., 2nd fl., Downtown* ☎*800/718–8006* ⊕*www.miamigolfdiscount. com*) has 10,000 square feet of golf equipment, including clubs, balls, shoes, and clothing. A practice net lets you test your swing.

OUTDOOR MARKETS

Pass the mangos! Greater Miami's farmers' markets and flea markets take advantage of the region's balmy weather and tropical delights to lure shoppers to open-air stalls filled with produce and collectibles.

★ **Coconut Grove Farmers Market.** The most organic of Miami's outdoor markets specializes in a mouthwatering array of local produce as well as such ready-to-eat goodies as cashew butter, homemade salad dressings, and fruit pies. If you are looking for a downright granola crowd and experience, pack your Birkenstocks, because this is it. ⊠*Grand Ave. and Margaret St., Coconut Grove, Miami* ☎*305/238–7747.*

Coral Gables Farmers Market. Some 25 local produce growers and plant vendors sell herbs, fruits, fresh-squeezed juices, chutneys, cakes, and muffins at this market between Coral Gables' City Hall and Merrick Park. Artists also join in. Regular events include gardening workshops, children's activities, and cooking demonstrations offered by Coral Gables' master chefs. ⊠*405 Biltmore Way, Coral Gables* ☎*305/460–5311.*

Española Way Market. This market has been a city favorite since its debut in the heart of South Beach in 1995. Along a two-block stretch of balconied Mediterranean-style storefronts, the road closes to traffic, and vendors set up tables on the wide sidewalks as street musicians beat out Latin rhythms. You might find silver jewelry, antique lanterns, orchids, leather jackets, cheap watches, imports from India and Guatemala, or antique Venetian painted beads. Scattered among the merchandise, food vendors sell tasty but inexpensive Latin snacks and drinks. Park along a side street. ⊠*Española Way between Drexel and Washington Aves., South Beach, Miami Beach* ☎*305/531–0038.*

Lincoln Road Farmers Market. With all the familiar trappings of a farmers' market, this is quickly becoming a must-see event before or after visiting the Antique and Collectibles Market. It brings local produce and bakery vendors to the Lincoln Road Mall and often features plant workshops, art sales, and children's activities. This is a good place to pick up live orchids, too. ⊠*Lincoln Rd. between Meridian and Euclid Aves., South Beach, Miami Beach* ☎*305/673–4166.*

★ **Lincoln Road Antique and Collectibles Market.** Interested in picking up samples of Miami's ever-present modern and moderne furniture and accessories? This outdoor show offers eclectic goods that should satisfy post-impressionists, Deco-holics, Edwardians, Bauhausers, Goths, and '50s junkies. ⊠*Lincoln and Alton Rds., South Beach, Miami Beach* ☎*305/673–4991.*

SIDE TRIP TO SOUTH DADE

In 1992 Hurricane Andrew forever changed the face of these scattered suburbs southwest of Miami-Dade County's urban core, with many residents moving out and millions of dollars of aid pouring in, evident today in the charmingly rebuilt Deering Estate, Metrozoo, and Fruit and Spice Park. The Redland, the southernmost area also known as America's winter vegetable basket, offers a welcome change from urbane Miami. A complete exploration of all the attractions would probably take two days. Keep an eye open for hand-painted signs announcing orchid farms, fruit stands, you-pick farms, and horseback riding.

❸❽ Coral Castle of Florida. The castle was born when 26-year-old Edward Leedskalnin, a Latvian immigrant, was left at the altar by his 16-year-old fiancée. She went on with her life, and he went off the deep end and began carving a castle out of coral rock. It's hard to believe that Eddie, only 5 feet tall and 100 pounds, could maneuver tons of coral rock single-handedly. Built between 1920 and 1940, the 3-acre castle is one of South Florida's original tourist attractions. There's a 9-ton gate a child could open, an accurate working sundial, and a telescope of coral rock aimed at the North Star. ☒28655 S. Dixie Hwy. ☎305/248–6345 ⊕www.coralcastle.com ☜$9.75 ⊙Daily 7 AM–9 PM.

③② Deering Estate at Cutler. In 1913 Charles Deering, brother of James Deering, who built Vizcaya in Coconut Grove, bought this property for a winter residence. Nine years later he built the Mediterranean Revival house that stands here today. Far more austere than its ornate cousin Vizcaya, Charles's stone house, with a magnificent view of Biscayne Bay, has wrought-iron gates, copper doors, and a unique stone ceiling. Next door, the fully restored Richmond Cottage, the first inn to be built between Coconut Grove and Key West (1900), is a fine example of South Florida frame vernacular architecture. Take a naturalist-guided tour to learn more about the area's archaeology: scientists discovered human remains here and carbon-dated them to 10,000 years ago; they may belong to Paleo-Indians. A fossil pit contains the bones of dog-size horses, tapirs, jaguars, peccaries, sloths, and bison. Coastal tropical hardwood hammocks, rare orchids and trees, and wildlife, such as gray foxes, bobcats, limpkins, peregrine falcons, and cormorants, populate the property. A huge environmental education and visitor center, with wide viewing porches, presents programs for children and adults. Nature tours and canoe trips to nearby Chicken Key are available. Admission includes parking and three guided tours. ☒16701 S.W. 72nd Ave. ☎305/235–1668 ⊕www.deeringestate.org ☜$7 ⊙Daily 10–5; last admission at 4.

③④ Gold Coast Railroad Museum. Historic railroad cars on display here include a 1949 *Silver Crescent* dome car and the *Ferdinand Magellan,* the only Pullman car constructed specifically for U.S. presidents. It was used by Franklin Delano Roosevelt, Harry Truman, Dwight Eisenhower, and Ronald Reagan. Every weekend the museum offers $2.25 train rides; on the second Sunday of each month you can ride the presidential Pullman for $5.50 ($11 for the engine car). ☒12450 S.W. 152nd St. ☎305/253–0063 ⊕www.goldcoast-railroad.org ☜$5 ⊙Weekdays 10–4, weekends 11–4.

③⑤ Metrozoo. One of the few zoos in the United States in a subtropical environment, the 290-acre Metrozoo is state of the art. Inside the cageless zoo, some 800 animals roam on islands surrounded by moats. Take the monorail to see major attractions, including the Tiger Temple, where white tigers roam, and the African Plains exhibit, where giraffes, ostriches, and zebras graze in a simulated habitat. There are also koalas and Komodo dragons. The free-flight aviary, demolished by Hurricane Andrew, reopened in 2003 with 300 birds, waterfalls, and lush tropical foliage. The children's petting zoo has a meerkat exhibit, and Dr. Wilde's World is an interactive facility with changing exhibits. Kids can touch Florida animals such as alligators and possum at the Ecology Theater. ☒12400 S.W. 152nd St. ☎305/251–0400 ⊕www.miami-

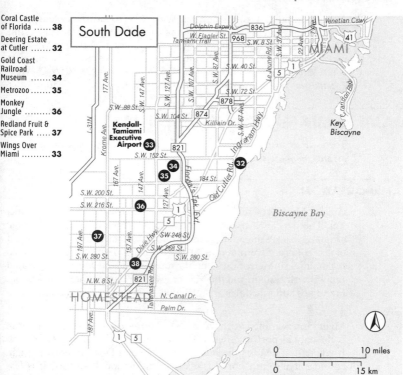

Coral Castle
of Florida **38**

Deering Estate
at Cutler **32**

Gold Coast
Railroad
Museum **34**

Metrozoo **35**

Monkey
Jungle **36**

Redland Fruit &
Spice Park **37**

Wings Over
Miami **33**

South Dade

metrozoo.com ⊠*$11.50, 45-min tram tour $2.50* ☉*Daily 9:30–5:30; last admission at 4.*

36 **Monkey Jungle.** Still a kitschy attraction for adults, more than 300 monkeys representing 25 species—including orangutans from Borneo and Sumatra and golden lion tamarins from Brazil—roam free here. Exhibits include Lemurs of Madagascar, Parrots of the Amazon, and the Cameroon Jungle. Perhaps the most fun is feeding monkeys who scurry across the fences overhead, hauling up peanuts you place in a metal cup. ⊠*14805 S.W. 216th St.* ☎*305/235–1611* ⊕*www.monkeyjungle. com* ⊠*$19.95* ☉*Daily 9:30–5; last admission at 4.*

37 **Redland Fruit & Spice Park.** The 35 acres here have been a Dade County treasure since 1944, when it was opened as a showcase of tropical fruits and vegetables. Plants are grouped by country of origin and include more than 500 varieties of exotic fruits, herbs, spices, nuts, and poisonous plants from around the world. A sampling reveals 90 types of bananas, 40 varieties of grapes, and dozens of citrus fruits. The park store offers many varieties of tropical-fruit products, jellies, seeds, aromatic teas, and reference books. ⊠*24801 S.W. 187th Ave.* ☎*305/247–5727* ⊕*www.co.miami-dade.fl.us* ⊠*$5* ☉*Daily 10–5, tours at 11, 1:30, and 3.*

③③ Aviation enthusiasts touch down at **Wings Over Miami** to see planes from World War II and the Korean War and earlier vintage biplanes in a still-evolving museum filling the space that once housed Weeks Air Museum, which moved to the Sun 'n' Fun complex in Lakeland. The museum is inside Tamiami Airport. ⊠*14710 S.W. 128th St.* ☎*305/233–5197* ⊕*www.wingsovermiami.com* ✑*$10* ☉*Thurs.–Sun. 10–5:30.*

MIAMI & MIAMI BEACH ESSENTIALS

To research prices, get advice from other travelers, and book travel arrangements, visit www.fodors.com.

TRANSPORTATION

Greater Miami resembles Los Angeles in its urban sprawl and traffic. You'll need a car to visit many attractions and points of interest. Some are accessible via the public transportation system, run by a department of the county government—the Metro-Dade Transit Agency, which maintains 650 Metrobuses on 70 routes; the 21-mi Metrorail elevated rapid-transit system; and the Metromover, an elevated light-rail system. Free maps and schedules are available.

BY AIR

Miami International Airport (MIA), 7 mi west of downtown Miami, is the only airport in Greater Miami that provides scheduled service. If you're destined for the north side of Miami-Dade County, though, consider flying into Fort Lauderdale International Airport. It is less crowded and more user-friendly, and you may also find greatly reduced fares on airlines that don't serve MIA. Approximately 32 million visitors pass through MIA annually, just less than half of them international travelers. Altogether, more than 80 airlines serve nearly 150 cities with nonstop or one-stop service from here.

Getting around MIA is easy if you envision a horseshoe or U-shaped terminal. Eight concourses extend out from the terminal; Concourse A is on the right or north side, E is in the center, and H is on the left or south side (a map of the airport is available on the MIA Web site, ⊕*www.miami-airport.com*). If you're headed from one concourse to another, **take the Moving Walkway** on the skywalk (third) level; it links all eight concourses and the parking garages. Skycaps are available for hire throughout the airport, but on busy days be prepared to wait. Within Customs, portage is free only from baggage claim to the inspection line. A better bet: **grab a luggage cart**—they're free within Customs and $3 elsewhere.

A Tourist Information Center, open 5 AM–9 PM, is on Level 2, Concourse E; free brochures here tell you everything you'd want to know about the airport. Long-term parking is $4 per hour for the first and second hour, $2 for the third hour, and a maximum of $15 per 24-hour period. Short-term parking is $2.50 per half hour, with a maximum of $30 per day.

International flights arrive at Concourses A, B, D, E, and F, as well as at the International Satellite Terminal ¼ mi west of the main terminal. International passengers can be met outside U.S. Customs exits on the lower level of Concourse E or on the third level of Concourse B.

Airport Contacts Miami International Airport (☎ *305/876–7000* ⊕ *www.miami-airport.com*). **Fort Lauderdale–Hollywood International Airport** (☎ *954/359–1200* ⊕ *www.fll.net*). **Miami International Airport Hotel** (✉ *Concourse E, upper level* ☎ *305/871–4100* ⊕ *www.miahotel.com*).

GROUND TRANSPORTATION

Taxi, shuttle, and limousine service are available outside baggage claim areas on Level 1. **Look for a uniformed county dispatcher** to hail a cab for you. On the mainland (i.e., west of Biscayne Bay) cabs cost $2.50 when the meter starts and $.40 for each 1/6 of a mile thereafter (plus a $2 surcharge for trips originating at MIA or the Port of Miami); the fare from the airport to downtown Miami averages $22, and from the Port it's a flat fare of $24.

Flat-rate fares are set for five zones along the barrier island generally referred to as Miami Beach. The long, thin stretch of beachfront actually encompasses not only Miami Beach proper but Indian Creek Village, Surfside, Bay Harbor Islands, Bal Harbour, Sunny Isles, Golden Beach, and adjacent unincorporated areas. The fare zones comprise five east–west bands bound on the east by the Atlantic Ocean and on the west by the mainland. Flat-rate fares run $32 (South Beach)–$52 (North Dade, Sunny Isles) per trip, not passenger; they include tolls and the airport surcharge, but no gratuity.

For taxi service to destinations in the immediate vicinity of the airport, **ask the dispatcher to call an ARTS (Airport Region Taxi Service) cab** for you. These blue cars offer a short-haul flat fare in two zones. An inner-zone ride costs $10; the outer-zone fare is $14. The area of service runs north to 36th Street, west to the Palmetto Expressway (77th Avenue), south to Northwest 7th Street, and east to Douglas Road (37th Avenue). Maps are posted in cab windows on both sides.

Limo service is available through prior arrangement only, but SuperShuttle vans transport passengers on demand between MIA and local hotels, the Port of Miami, the Greyhound terminal, and even individual residences on a 24-hour basis. Shuttles are available throughout the lower level of the terminal outside baggage claim areas. Service extends from Palm Beach to Monroe County (including the Lower Keys). It's best to **make reservations 24 hours in advance for the return,** although the firm will try to arrange pickups within Miami-Dade County on as little as four hours' notice. Per-person rates average $9–$25; additional members of a party pay a lower rate for many destinations, and children under three ride free with their parents. There's a pet transport fee of $5 for a pet less than 20 pounds, $8 for 20–50 pounds, or $10 for more than 50 pounds in kennels.

Greyhound offers two departures daily (1 PM and 9:50 PM) connecting the airport with a number of its local terminals, including its Bayside (downtown) terminal (1012 N.W. 1st Ave.). If those times don't work out, more routes are available from Greyhound's main hub (4111 N.W. 27th St.), a short taxi ride from the airport.

Contacts **Greyhound** (☎ *305/871–1810* ⊕ *www.greyhound.com*). Miami-Dade Transit, **Metrobus** (☎ *305/770–3131* ⊕ *www.miamidade.gov/transit*). **SuperShuttle** (☎ *305/871–2000 from MIA, 954/764–1700 from Fort Lauderdale, 800/258–3826 elsewhere* ⊕ *www.supershuttle.com*). **Tri-County Airport Express** (☎ *954/561–8888 or 800/244–8252* ⊕ *www.floridalimo.com*.) is a car service that leaves from Fort Lauderdale International Airport. **TriRail** (☎ *800/874–7245* ⊕ *www.tri-rail.com*).

BY BIKE

Great weather and flat terrain make Miami great for cycling, but as a general method of transportation it shouldn't be your first choice, given traffic and limited bike paths. You can opt for Miami-Dade Transit's "Bike and Ride" program, which lets cyclists take single-seat two-wheelers on Metrorail, Metrobus, or Metromover at any time. A bike permit is required for Metrorail only. Applications are filled on the spot at the downtown Government Center Metrorail station (101 N.W. 1st St.), weekdays 8 AM to 4 PM. To apply by mail, call 305/884–7567. You can also store your bicycle in lockers at most Metrorail stations; leases are available for 3, 6, or 12 months.

BY BUS, TO MIAMI

Most motor coaches that stop in the Miami area are chartered tour buses. Regularly scheduled, interstate Greyhound buses stop at four terminals in Greater Miami. The Cutler Ridge location connects to several destinations in the Keys, including Key West.

Bus Information **Greyhound** (☎ *800/231–2222* ⊕ *www.greyhound.com*).

Bus Terminal Information **Cutler Ridge** (✉ *10801 Caribbean Blvd.* ☎ *305/296–9072*). **Miami Downtown** (✉ *1012 N.W. 1st Ave.* ☎ *305/374–6160*). **Miami North** (✉ *16000 N.W. 7th Ave.* ☎ *305/688–7277*). **Miami West–Airport** (✉ *4111 N.W. 27th St.* ☎ *305/871–1810*).

BY BUS, AROUND MIAMI

Metrobus stops are marked with blue-and-green signs with a bus logo and route information. If you want to get around by bus or rapid transit, **call Miami-Dade Transit for exact bus routes.** It's staffed with people who can give you specific information and route schedules. If you call from your hometown, they can also mail you a map of Miami-Dade showing all the bus routes and their numbers.

The frequency of service varies widely from route to route, depending on the demand, so call in advance to **obtain specific bus schedules.** Buses on the most popular routes run every 10 to 15 minutes. The fare is $1.50 (exact change only). Transfers cost 50¢. Some express routes carry surcharges of $1.85.

Contacts Miami-Dade Transit, **Metrobus** (☎ *305/770–3131* ⊕ *www.miamidade. gov/transit*).

BY CAR

I–95 is the major expressway connecting South Florida with points north; State Road 836 is the major east–west expressway and connects to Florida's Turnpike, State Road 826, and I–95. Seven causeways link Miami and Miami Beach, I–195 and I–395 offering the most convenient routes; the Rickenbacker Causeway extends to Key Biscayne from I–95 and U.S. 1. **Remember U.S. 1 (aka Biscayne Boulevard)**—you'll hear it often in directions. It starts in Key West, hugs South Florida's coastline, and heads north straight through to Maine.

Greater Miami traffic is among the nation's worst, so definitely **avoid driving during the rush hours of 7–9 am and 5–7 pm. The hour just after and right before the peak times also can be slow going.**

Road construction is constant; **pay attention to the brightly lighted, roadside Smart Signs that warn drivers of work zones and street closings.** During rainy weather be especially cautious of flooding in South Beach and Key Biscayne. The Web site www.dot.state.fl.us lists roadwork updates for Florida's interstates.

Courtesy may not be the first priority of Miami drivers, who are allergic to turn signals and may suddenly change lanes or stop to drop off passengers where they shouldn't. **Watch out for short-tempered drivers** who may shout, gesticulate, honk, or even approach the car of an offending driver.

Even when your driving is beyond censure, you should **be especially careful in rental cars.** Despite the absence of identifying marks and the stepped-up presence of TOP (Tourist Oriented Police) patrols, cars piled with luggage or driven by hesitant drivers are prime targets for thieves. Keep car doors locked, and ask questions only at tollbooths, gas stations, and other evidently safe locations. Don't stop if your car is bumped from behind, you see a disabled vehicle, or even if you get a flat tire. Drive to the nearest gas station or well-lighted locale and telephone the police from there. It's a good idea to **bring or rent a cellular phone,** as well.

CAR RENTAL

The following agencies have booths near the baggage-claim area on MIA's lower level: Avis, Budget, Dollar, Hertz, National, and Royal. Avis and Budget also have offices at the Port of Miami. If money is no object, check out Excellence Luxury Car Rental. As the name implies, rent some wheels (a Ferrari, perhaps?) to cruise SoBe. If you can't find the excellent car you want, rent a Dodge Viper, BMW, Hummer, Jaguar, Porsche, or Rolls-Royce from Exotic Toys. Airport pickup is provided.

Contacts **Alamo** (☎ *800/468–2583*). **Avis** (☎ *800/331–1212*). **Budget** (☎ *800/527–0700*). **Dollar** (☎ *800/800-4000*). **Excellence Luxury Car Rental** (☎ *305/526–0000*). **Exotic Toys Car Rental** (☎ *305/888-8448*). **Hertz** (☎ *800/654-3131*). **National** (☎ *800/227–7368*). **Royal** (☎ *800/314–8616*).

PARKING

Many parking garages fill up at peak times. This is particularly true in Miami Beach and Coconut Grove, where streetside parking is impossible and spaces in municipal lots cost a fortune. Thankfully, these neighborhoods are the most pedestrian-friendly in Greater Miami. On Miami Beach valet parking is offered at most dining and entertainment venues (although it can cost as much as $20 on a busy weekend night). "Cabbing" it in South Beach is easy and inexpensive, but if you have to drive, call the **City of Miami Beach's Parking Hotline** (☎ *305/673–PARK*) for garages convenient to where you're going. **Don't be tempted to park in a tow-away zone,** as the fees are high and you'll be surprised at how quickly the tow trucks arrive. If your car is towed, contact the municipality for details on how to retrieve your vehicle.

RULES OF THE ROAD

Drive to the right and pass on the left. Keep change handy, since tolls are frequent and can range from 75¢ to as much as $1.50. Right turns are permitted at red lights (after a complete stop), unless otherwise indicated. At four-way stop signs it's first-come, first-go; when in doubt, yield to the right. Speed limits are 55 mph on state highways, 30 mph within city limits and residential areas, and 55–70 mph on interstates and Florida's Turnpike. Be alert for signs announcing exceptions and school zones (15 mph).

All front-seat passengers are required to wear seat belts, and children under 5 must be fastened securely in child safety seats or boosters; children under 12 are required to ride in the rear seat. Florida's Alcohol–Controlled Substance DUI Law is one of the toughest in the United States. A blood alcohol level of .08 or higher can have serious repercussions even for the first-time offender. Cell phone use while driving is discouraged, although it's currently still legal.

BY SCOOTER

You'll notice that scooters are a popular mode of transportation in Miami Beach and rentals are offered at a few locations. It's a good idea to reserve ahead around peak holiday times. You'll need a credit card and valid driver's license. Expect to pay a security deposit.

Scooters are available from about $15/hour or $50 a day. Ask about hotel pickup service.

Information **American Road Collection** (⊠ *1416 18th St., Miami Beach* ☎ *305/673-8113*). **Beach Scooter Rentals** (⊠ *1341 Washington Ave., Miami Beach* ☎ *305/538-7878* ⊠ *1435 Collins Ave., Miami Beach* ☎ *305/538-0977* ⊕ *www.beachscooter.com*). **South Beach Scooters** (⊠ *215 6th St., Miami Beach* ☎ *305/538-0202* ⊠ *2935 Collins Ave., Miami Beach* ☎ *305/534-7433* ⊕ *www. southbeachscooters.com*).

BY TAXI

Except in South Beach, it's difficult to hail a cab on the street; in most cases you'll need to call a cab company or have a hotel doorman hail one for you. Fares run $4.50 for the first mile and $2.40 every mile thereafter; flat-rate fares are also available from the airport to a variety of zones. Fares are set by the board of county commissioners, so if you have a question or complaint, call the **Metro-Dade Passenger Transportation Regulatory Service** (☎305/375–2460), informally known as the Hack Bureau. There's no additional charge for up to five passengers or for luggage. Many cabs now accept credit cards; inquire when you call or before you get in the car.

Recent taxi-regulating legislation, hospitality training, and increased competition should rein in most surly drivers. But Greater Miami still has cabbies who are rude and in some cases even dishonest, taking advantage of visitors who don't know the area, so **try to be familiar with your route and destination.**

Taxi Companies **Central Taxicab Service** (☎305/532–5555). **Diamond Cab Company** (☎305/545–5555). **Flamingo Taxi** (☎305/759–8100). **Metro Taxi** (☎305/888–8888). **Society Cab Company** (☎305/757–5523). **Super Yellow Cab Company** (☎305/888–7777). **Tropical Taxicab Company** (☎305/945–1025). **Yellow Cab Company** (☎305/633–0503).

BY TRAIN, TO MIAMI

Amtrak provides service from 500 destinations to the Greater Miami area, including two trains daily from New York City. The trains make several stops along the way; north–south service stops in the major Florida cities of Jacksonville, Orlando, Tampa, West Palm Beach, and Fort Lauderdale. For extended trips, or if you want to visit other areas in Florida, come via Auto Train from Lorton, Virginia, just outside of Washington, D.C., to Sanford, Florida, just outside of Orlando. From there it's less than a four-hour drive to Miami. Note: you must be traveling with an automobile to purchase a ticket on the Auto Train.

The Auto Train runs daily with one departure at 4 PM (however, car boarding ends one hour earlier). Fares vary depending on class of service and time of year, but expect to pay between $269 and $346 for a basic sleeper seat and car passage each way.

Train Information **Amtrak** (✉8303 N.W. 37th Ave., Miami ☎800/872-7245 ⊕www.amtrak.com).

BY TRAIN, AROUND MIAMI

Elevated Metrorail trains run from downtown Miami north to Hialeah and south along U.S. 1 to Dadeland. The system operates daily 5 AM–midnight. Trains run every 6 minutes during peak hours, every 15 minutes during weekday mid-hours, and every 30 minutes after 8 PM and on weekends. The fare is $1.50; 50¢ transfers to Metromover or Metrobus must be purchased at the station where you originally board the system. Parking at Metrorail stations costs $4.

Metromover resembles an airport shuttle and runs on two loops around downtown Miami, linking major hotels, office buildings, and shopping areas. The system spans 4½ mi, including the 1½-mi Omni Loop, with six stations to the north, and the 1-mi Brickell Loop, with six stations to the south. Service runs daily, every 90 seconds during rush hour and every three minutes off-peak, 5 AM–midnight along all loops. There is no fee to ride; transfers to Metrorail are $1.50.

Tri-Rail, South Florida's commuter train system, offers daily service connecting Miami-Dade with Broward and Palm Beach counties via Metrorail (transfer at the TriRail–Metrorail Station at the Hialeah station, at 79th Street and East 11th Avenue). They also offer shuttle service to and from MIA from their airport station at 3797 N.W. 21st Street. Tri-Rail stops at 18 stations along a 71-mi route. Fares are established by zones, with prices ranging from $3.50 to $9.25 for a round-trip ticket.

Information **Metrorail** and **Metromover** (☎ *305/770–3131* ⊕ *www.miamidade. gov/transit*). **TriRail** (☎ *800/874–7245* ⊕ *www.tri-rail.com*).

CONTACTS & RESOURCES

E-MAIL SERVICE

Save the cost of phone calls and avoid the delays of postal service by using e-mail. If you're sans laptop and modem, get a free e-mail account from any of the larger service providers or try www.hotmail. com. You can log on free at the local library, or try Kafka's Kafe in South Beach. A used bookstore, newsstand, and cybercafé, it's very Europeanlike. High-speed access for 10 minutes is $1, for one hour $6; discounted rates available before noon and after 8 PM. If you're in one of the larger hotels, you can use their business center to send and receive e-mail.

E-mail Service **Kafka's Cybernet Kafe** (✉ *1464 Washington Ave., Miami Beach* ☎ *305/673–9669*).

EMERGENCIES

Doctors & Dentists **Miami-Dade County Medical Association** (☎ *305/324–8717*) is open weekdays 9–5 for medical referrals. **East Coast District Dental Society** (☎ *305/667–3647 or 800/344–5860* ⊕ *www.sfdda.org*) is open weekdays 9–4:30 for dental referrals. After hours, stay on the line and a recording will direct you to a dentist. **Dental Referral Service** (☎ *800/577–7322*) is open 24 hours for dental referrals. **Visitors Medical Hotline** (☎ *305/674–2273*) is available weekdays 8:30–6:30 for medical referrals provided by Mt. Sinai Medical Center.

Emergency Services Dial 911 for police, ambulance, or fire rescue. You can dial free from pay phones. For 24-hour **Poison Control,** call 800/222-1222.

Hospitals **Baptist Hospital of Miami** (✉ *8900 N. Kendall Dr., Miami* ☎ *786/596–1960, 786/596–6556 emergency, 786/596–6557 physician referral* ⊕ *www. baptisthealth.net*). **Jackson Memorial Medical Center** (✉ *1611 N.W. 12th Ave., near Dolphin Expressway, Miami* ☎ *305/585–1111, 305/585–6901 emergency, 305/547–5757 physician referral* ⊕ *www.jhsmiami.org*). **Mercy Hospital** (✉ *3663 S. Miami Ave., Coconut Grove* ☎ *305/854–4400, 305/285–2171 emergency, 305/285–2929 physician referral* ⊕ *www.mercymiami.org*). **Miami Children's Hospital** (✉ *3100 S.W. 62nd Ave., Miami* ☎ *305/666–6511* ⊕ *www.mch.com*). **Mt. Sinai Medical Center** (✉ *4300 Alton Rd., I-195 off Julia Tuttle Causeway, Miami Beach* ☎ *305/674–2121, 305/674–2200 emergency, 305/674–2273 physician referral* ⊕ *www.msmc.com*). **Jackson North Medical Center** (✉ *160 N.W. 170th St., North Miami Beach* ☎ *305/651–1100, 888/836–3848 physician referral* ⊕ *www.jhsmiami.org*).

Hotlines **Abuse Registry** (☎800/962–2873, 800/453–5145 *TTY*). **Drug Helpline** (☎800/662–4357). **Mental Health/Suicide Intervention** (☎305/358–4357). **Missing Children Information Clearing House** (☎888/356–4774). **Rape Treatment Center Hotline** (☎305/585–7273).

MEDIA

NEWSPAPERS & MAGAZINES

Greater Miami's major newspaper is the *Miami Herald*. Your best bet for weekend happenings is the free alternative weekly *New Times*. For Spanish-language news, turn to *El Nuevo Herald*. Regional editions of the *Wall Street Journal* and the *New York Times* can be found just about everywhere—including vending machines—and many of Europe and Latin America's major dailies and fashion glossies are available at newsstands.

TOURS

Coconut Grove Rickshaw centers its operations at CocoWalk. Two-person rickshaws scurry along Main Highway in Coconut Grove's Village Center from 7 PM to midnight. Take a 10-minute ride through Coconut Grove or a 20-minute lovers' moonlight ride to Biscayne Bay; prices start at $5 per person, and you can pick them up curbside.

BOAT TOURS

Duck Tours Miami (✉1665 *Washington Ave., Miami Beach* ☎877/382–5849 *or* 786/276–8300 ⊕*www.ducktoursmiami.com*) uses amphibious vehicles to offer daily 90-minute tours of Miami that combine land and sea views. Comedy and music are part of the mix. Tickets are $32 per person, $18 for children 4–12. *Island Queen, Island Lady,* **and** *Pink Lady* (✉401 *Biscayne Blvd., Miami* ☎305/379–5119) are 150-passenger double-decker tour boats docked at Bayside Marketplace. They offer daily 90-minute narrated tours of the Port of Miami and Millionaires' Row, at a cost of $19 per person, $10 for those under 12. For something a little more private and luxe, **RA Charters** (☎305/854–7341 *or* 305/989–3959 ⊕*www.racharters.com*) sails out of the Dinner Key Marina in Coconut Grove. Full- and half-day charters include snorkeling and even sailing lessons, with extended trips to the Florida Keys and Bahamas. For a romantic night, have Captain Masoud pack some gourmet fare and sail sunset to moonlight while you enjoy Biscayne Bay's spectacular skyline view of Miami. Call for prices and details.

WALKING TOURS

The **Art Deco District Tour** (✉1001 *Ocean Dr., South Beach, Miami Beach* ☎305/531–3484 ⊕*www.mdpl.org*) operated by the Miami Design Preservation League is a 90-minute guided walking tour that departs from the league's welcome center at the Oceanfront Auditorium. It costs $20 (tax-deductible) and starts at 10:30 AM Wednesday and Friday–Sunday and 6:30 PM Thursday. Private group tours can be arranged with advance notice. You can go at your own pace with the league's self-guided $15 audio tour, which takes roughly an hour and a half.

6

Professor Paul George (✉ *1345 S.W. 14th St., Miami* ☎*305/858–6021*), a history professor at Miami Dade College and historian for the Historical Museum of Southern Florida, leads a variety of walking, bike, and boat tours, as well as tours via Metrorail and Metromover. Pick from tours covering downtown, the Miami River, or neighborhoods such as Little Havana and Coconut Grove. George starts Saturdays at 10 and Sundays at 11 at various locations, depending on the tour; the tours generally last 2–2½ hours. Call for each weekend's schedule and for additional tours by appointment. Tours start at $15 per person, and prices vary by tour and group size.

VISITOR INFORMATION

Florida Gold Coast Chamber of Commerce serves the beach communities of Bal Harbour, Bay Harbor Islands, Golden Beach, North Bay Village, Sunny Isles Beach, and Surfside.

Contacts **Coconut Grove Chamber of Commerce** (✉*2820 McFarlane Rd., Coconut Grove, Miami 33133* ☎*305/444–7270* 🖶*305/444–2498* ⊕*www.coconutgrove. com*). **Coral Gables Chamber of Commerce** (✉*224 Catalonia Ave., Coral Gables 33134* ☎*305/446–1657* 🖶*305/446–9900* ⊕*www.gableschamber.org*). **Florida Tourism Industry Marketing Corporation (Visit Florida)** (☎*888/7FLA–USA automated* ⊕*www.visitflorida.com*). **Greater Miami Convention & Visitors Bureau** (✉*701 Brickell Ave., Suite 2700, Miami 33131* ☎*305/539–3000 or 800/933–8448 in U.S.* ⊕*www.gmcvb.com*). **Key Biscayne Chamber of Commerce & Visitors Center** (✉*88 W. McIntyre St., Suite 100, Key Biscayne 33149* ☎*305/361–5207* 🖶*305/361–9411* ⊕*www.keybiscaynechamber.org*). **Miami Beach Chamber of Commerce & Visitors Center** (✉*1920 Meridian Ave., Miami Beach 33139* ☎*305/674–1300 or 800/666–4519* 🖶*305/538–4336* ⊕*www.miamibeachchamber.com*). **Sunny Isles Beach Resort Association Visitor Information Center** (✉*18070 Collins Ave., Sunny Isles Beach 33160* ☎*305/947–5826* ⊕*www.sunnyislesfla.com*). **Surfside Tourist Board** (✉*9301 Collins Ave., Surfside, 33154* ☎*305/864–0722 or 800/327–4557*).

The Florida Keys

WORD OF MOUTH

"The beach at Bahia Honda is the best in the Keys. In fact, it is one of the nicest beaches I have ever visited. The water is very shallow there and you can walk for a long way in knee-deep water that is so clean and clear that you would think it was a swimming pool."

–CarolSchwartz

"The 'real Keys' are typified by small places like Tavernier, Islamorada, Marathon, and Big Pine. I'm not saying that these places are any better than Key West for a vacation, but if you could pick only one place in all the Keys that most typified all the Keys, it would not be Key West."

–Larry1

Update by
Diane Bair
and Pamela
Wright

BEING A CONCH IS A condition of the heart, and foreclosure on the soul. Many throughout the Florida Keys wear that label proudly, yet there is anything but a shared lifestyle here. To the south, Key West has a Mardi Gras mood with Fantasy Festivals, Hemingway look-alike contests, and the occasional threat to secede from the Union. It's an island whose melting-pot character allows crusty natives to mingle (more or less peacefully) with eccentrics and escape artists who lovingly call this 4-mi sandbar "Paradise." Although life elsewhere in the island chain isn't quite as offbeat, it's nearly as diverse. Flowering jungles, shimmering seas, and mangrove-lined islands are also,

TOP 5
■ Snorkel around Christ of the Deep off John Pennekamp Coral Reef State Park.
■ Camp on a sugar-white beach at Bahia Honda State Park.
■ Kayak amidst a tangle of black, red, and white mangroves in the backcountry passages of Florida Bay.
■ Marvel at the sunset celebration (and maybe a green flash) at Mallory Square.
■ Revel in the unabashedly trashy side of Key West's Duval Street.

conversely, overburdened. A river of tourist traffic gushes along U.S. 1 (also called the Overseas Highway), the 110-mi artery linking the inhabited islands. Residents of Monroe County live by diverting the river's flow of dollars to their own pockets. In the process, the fragile beauty of the Keys—or at least the 45 that are inhabited and linked to the mainland by 43 bridges—is paying an environmental price. At the top, nearest the mainland, is Key Largo, becoming more congested as it evolves into a bedroom community and weekend hideaway for residents of Miami and Fort Lauderdale. At the bottom, 106 mi southwest, is Key West, where hundreds of passengers from multiple cruise ships swarm the narrow streets. Offshore is the Florida Keys National Marine Sanctuary, established by Congress in 1990, a wondrous but fragile environment of sea-grass meadows, mangrove islands, and living coral reefs.

The expansion of U.S. 1 to the mainland to four lanes will open the floodgates to increased traffic, population, and tourism. Observers wonder if the four-laning of the rest of U.S. 1 throughout the Keys can be far away. For now, however, take pleasure as you drive down U.S. 1 along the islands. Gaze over the silvery blue-and-green Atlantic and its still-living reef, with Florida Bay, the Gulf of Mexico, and the backcountry on your right (the Keys extend east–west from the mainland). At a few points the ocean and gulf are as much as 10 mi apart. In most places, however, they are from 1 to 4 mi apart, and on the narrowest landfill islands, they are separated only by the road. Try to get off the highway. Once you do, rent a boat, anchor, and then fish, swim, or marvel at the sun, sea, and sky. In the Atlantic, dive spectacular coral reefs or pursue grouper, blue marlin, and other deepwater game fish. Along Florida Bay's coastline, kayak and canoe to secluded islands and bays or seek out the bonefish, snapper, snook, and tarpon that lurk in the grass flats and in the shallow, winding channels of the backcountry.

More than 600 kinds of fish populate the reefs and islands. Diminutive Key deer and pale raccoons, related to but distinct from their mainland cousins, inhabit the Lower Keys. And throughout the islands you'll find such exotic West Indian plants as Jamaican dogwood, pigeon plum, poisonwood, satin leaf, and silver-and-thatch palms, as well as tropical birds, including the great white heron, mangrove cuckoo, roseate spoonbill, and white-crowned pigeon. Mangroves, with their gracefully bowed prop roots, appear to march out to sea. Day by day they busily add more keys to the archipelago. With virtually no distracting air pollution or obstructive high-rises, sunsets are a pure, unadulterated spectacle that each evening attracts thousands to waterfront parks, piers, restaurants, bars, and resorts throughout the Keys. Weather is another attraction: winter is typically 10°F warmer than on the mainland; summer is usually 10°F cooler. The Keys also get substantially less rain, around 30 inches annually, compared with an average 55 to 60 inches in Miami and the Everglades. Most rain falls in quick downpours on summer afternoons, except in June, September, and October, when tropical storms can dump rain for two to four days. Winter cold fronts occasionally stall over the Keys, dragging overnight temperatures down to the high 40s.

The Keys were only sparsely populated until the early 20th century. In 1905, however, railroad magnate Henry Flagler began building the extension of his Florida railroad south from Homestead to Key West. His goal was to establish a Miami–Key West rail link to his steamships that sailed between Key West and Havana, just 90 mi across the Straits of Florida. The railroad arrived at Key West in 1912 and remained a lifeline of commerce until the Labor Day hurricane of 1935 washed out much of its roadbed. The Overseas Highway, built over the railroad's old roadbeds and bridges, was completed in 1938.

EXPLORING THE FLORIDA KEYS

Getting lost in the Keys is almost impossible once you understand the unique address system. Many addresses are simply given as a mile marker (MM) number. The markers are small, green, rectangular signs along the side of the Overseas Highway (U.S. 1). They begin with MM 126, a mile south of Florida City, and end with MM 0, in Key West. Keys residents use the abbreviation BS for the bay side of U.S. 1 and OS for the ocean side. From Marathon to Key West, residents may refer to the bay side as the gulf side. The Keys are divided into four areas: the Upper Keys, from Key Largo to the Long Key Channel (MM 106–65) and Ocean Reef and North Key Largo, off Card Sound Road and Route 905, respectively; the Middle Keys, from Conch (pronounced *konk*) Key through Marathon to the south side of the Seven Mile Bridge, including Pigeon Key (MM 65–40); the Lower Keys, from Little Duck Key south through Big Coppitt Key (MM 40–9); and Key West, from Stock Island through Key West (MM 9–0).

ABOUT THE RESTAURANTS

Seafood rules on the Keys—no surprise there—and your biggest decision of the day might well be "grilled, fried, or blackened?" But just when you think you can't bear the thought of another plate of grouper or mahimahi, you stumble upon a little Japanese restaurant with tasty sushi, or a place that serves barbecued ribs and chicken right off the smoker. The Keys are full of smallish, chef-owned restaurants with good, not-fancy food (bonus points for ice-cold beer and sunset views). Things get more exotic once you reach Key West, where you can pretty much find anything you want (except maybe a bargain). Pricier restaurants serve tantalizing fusion cuisine that reflects the Keys' proximity to Cuba and other Caribbean islands. Florida citrus, seafood, and tropical fruits figure prominently—and those fruits definitely show up on the beverage side of the menu! Florida lobster should be local and fresh from August to March and stone crabs from mid-October to mid-May. Also keep an eye out for authentic key lime pie. The real McCoy has yellow custard in a graham-cracker crust and tastes tart as hell. (If it's green, just say "no.") And don't you dare leave the islands without sampling conch, be it in a fritter or seviche-style. Restaurants may close for a two- to four-week vacation during the slow season—between mid-September and mid-November.

ABOUT THE HOTELS

Resorts and water sports marry throughout the Keys, giving couples and families, novices and veterans, chances to snorkel and dive. Some properties charge a required $15 (or more) daily resort fee for equipment rental, which can cover spa use and other services. Key West's lodging portfolio includes historic cottages, restored Conch houses, and large resorts. A few rooms cost as little as $65 a night, but most range from $100 to $300. Some guesthouses and inns do not welcome children under 16, and some do not permit smoking.

	¢	$	$$	$$$	$$$$
WHAT IT COSTS					
RESTAURANTS	under $10	$10–$15	$15–$20	$20–$30	over $30
HOTELS	under $80	$80–$100	$100–$140	$140–$220	over $220

Restaurant prices are per person for a main course at dinner. Hotel prices are for a standard double room, excluding 6% sales tax (more in some counties) and 1%–4% tourist tax.

TIMING

High season in the Keys is mid-December through March, and traffic on the Overseas Highway is inevitably heavy. From November to the middle of December, crowds are thinner, the weather is superlative, and hotels and shops drastically reduce their prices. Summer, which is hot and humid, is becoming a second high season, especially among families and Europeans. Key West's annual Fantasy Fest is the last week in October; if you plan to attend this wildy popular event (emphasis on wild), reserve at least six months in advance. Rooms are also scarce the first few weekends of lobster season, which starts in early August and runs through March. There's also a two-day sport season in late July.

THE UPPER KEYS

Diving and snorkeling rule here, thanks to the tropical-coral-reef tract that runs a few miles off the seaward coast. Divers benefit from accessible islands and dive sites and an established tourism infrastructure. Yet anglers, kayakers, and nature lovers won't be shortchanged. Within 1½ mi of the bay coast lie the islands of Everglades National Park; here naturalists lead ecotours to see one of the world's few saltwater forests, endangered manatees, dolphins, roseate spoonbills, and tropical-bird rookeries. Although the number of birds has dwindled since John James Audubon captured their beauty on a visit to the Keys, bird-watchers will find plenty to see. At sunset flocks take to the skies, and in spring and autumn migrating birds add their numbers. Tarpon and bonefish teem in the shallow waters surrounding the islands, providing food for birds and a challenge to light-tackle anglers. These same crystal-clear waters attract windsurfers, sailors, and powerboaters. Wherever you go, you'll find a pleasant mix of locals, visitors, snowbirds (in season), and South Floridian weekenders.

Don't bring dressy duds. With few exceptions, dining in the Upper Keys tends toward the casual in food, service, and dress—though for the sake of your fellow diners, perhaps you could leave the string bikini in your room. Speaking of which, accommodations are as varied as they are plentiful. The majority are in small waterfront resorts, with efficiency and one- or two-bedroom units. They offer dockage and often provide or will arrange boating, diving, and fishing excursions. Depending on which way the wind blows and how close the property is to the highway, noise from U.S. 1 can be bothersome. In high season, expect to pay $85 to $165 for an efficiency unit (in low season, $65 to $145). Campground and RV park rates with electricity and water run $25 to $55. Some properties require two- or three-day minimum stays during holidays and high-season weekends. Conversely, discounts are given for midweek, weekly, and monthly stays, and rates can drop 20% to 40% April through June and October through mid-December. Keep in mind that salty winds and soil play havoc with anything man-made, and constant maintenance is a must; inspect your accommodations before checking in.

KEY LARGO

❶ *56 mi south of Miami International Airport.*

The first Key reachable by car, 30-mi-long Key Largo—named Cayo Largo ("long key") by the Spanish—is also the largest island in the chain. Comprising three areas—North Key Largo, Key Largo, and Tavernier—it runs northeast–southwest between Lake Surprise and Tavernier Creek, at MM 95. Most businesses are on the four-lane divided highway (U.S. 1) that runs down the middle, and the cars whiz past—

something to remember when you're booking that room. Most properties sit right on the highway, so you'll want to be as far back (toward the water) as you can afford to be. The feel is more "suburbia" than Key West here. Keep that in mind, and you won't be disappointed. Still, you're at the gateway to the Keys, and an evening of seafood and sunset on the water will get you in that Key-easy state of mind. What's there to do on Key Largo, besides make like Bogie and Bacall and gaze into the sunset? Frankly, not much, if you're not into diving or snorkeling. If you aren't, but maybe you want to be, this is the place to learn. Dive companies galore will be more than happy to show you the ropes and get you down there. Even neophyte snorkelers can catch a glimpse of Christ of the Deep, an underwater statue that's a few miles out to sea. You might luck out and catch an underwater wedding. Nobody comes to Key Largo without visiting John Pennkamp Coral Reef State Park, one of the jewels of Florida's state park system.

American crocodiles, Key Largo wood rats, Key Largo cotton mice, Schaus swallowtail butterflies, and 100 other rare critters and plants call 2,400-acre **Dagny Johnson Key Largo Hammocks Botanical State Park** their home. It's also a user-friendly place to explore the largest remaining stand of the vast West Indian tropical hardwood hammock and mangrove wetland that once covered most of the Keys' upland areas. Interpretive signs describe many of the tropical tree species along a 1¼-mi paved road (2½ mi round-trip) that invites walking, rollerblading, and biking. Rangers give guided tours and encourage you to taste the fruits of native plants. Pets are welcome if on a leash no longer than 6 feet. You'll also find restrooms, information kiosks, and picnic tables. ✉ *1 mi north of U.S. 1 on Rte. 905, OS, North Key Largo* ☎ *305/451–1202* 💲 *$1.50* ☉ *Daily 8–sundown. Tours Thurs. and Sun. at 10.*

Taking the Overseas Highway from the mainland lands you closer to Key Largo proper, abounding with shopping centers, chain restaurants, and, of course, dive shops.

Best diving and snorkeling sites in the Sunshine State? **John Pennekamp Coral Reef State Park** is on everyone's list of faves. This underwater gem encompasses 78 square mi of coral reefs, sea-grass beds, and mangrove swamps. Its reefs contain 40 of the 52 species of coral in the Atlantic Reef System and more than 650 varieties of fish. Its visitor center–aquarium has a large floor-to-ceiling tank surrounded by smaller ones, plus a video room and exhibits. A concessionaire rents canoes and powerboats and offers snorkel, dive, and glass-bottom-boat trips to the reef. The park also has short nature trails, two man-made beaches, picnic shelters, a snack bar, and a campground. No pets are allowed for visitors who are camping or going on a boat trip. You also can arrange a 30-minute boat trip to see Christ of the Deep, the 9-foot-tall, 2-ton underwater statue of Jesus at Key Largo National Marine Sanctuary. ✉ *MM 102.5, OS, Box 487, 33037* ☎ *305/451–1202* ⊕ *www.floridastateparks.org/pennekamp/default.cfm* 💲 *$3.50. or $6 per vehicle for 2 people plus 50¢ each additional person; $1.50 per pedestrian or bicyclist; $29–$50 for dive and snorkel tours; $22 for glass-bottom-boat tours.* ☉ *Daily 8–sunset.*

GREAT ITINERARIES

Numbers in the text correspond to numbers in the margin and on the Florida Keys and Key West maps.

3 DAYS

Don't push your luck. You can fly and then dive; but if you dive, you can't fly for 24 hours, so spend your first morning diving or snorkeling at John Pennekamp Coral Reef State Park in 🔅 **Key Largo ❶** ▶. If you aren't certified, take a resort course, and you'll be exploring the reefs by afternoon. Dinner or cocktails at a bayside restaurant or bar will give you your first look at a fabulous Keys sunset. On Day 2 get an early start to savor the breathtaking views on the two-hour drive to Key West. Along the way make stops at the natural-history museum that's part of the Museums and Nature Center of Crane Point Hammock, in **Marathon ❷**, and Bahia Honda State Park, on **Bahia Honda Key ❽**; stretch your legs on a forest trail or snorkel on an offshore reef. Once in 🔅 **Key West ⓫–㉜**, watch the sunset before dining at one of the island's first-class restaurants. Spend the next morning strolling Duval Street, visiting any of the myriad museums, or taking a walking or trolley tour of Old Town before driving back to the mainland.

4 DAYS

Spend the first day as you would above, overnighting in 🔅 **Key Largo ❶** ▶. Start Day 2 by renting a kayak and exploring the mangroves and small islands of Florida Bay, or take an ecotour of the islands in Everglades National Park. In the afternoon, stop by the Florida Keys Wild Bird Rehabilitation Center before driving down to 🔅 **Islamorada ❸**. Pause to read the inscription on the Hurricane Monument, and before day's end, make plans for the next day's fishing. After a late lunch on Day 3—perhaps at one of the many restaurants that will prepare your catch for you—set off for 🔅 **Key West ⓫–㉜**. Enjoy the sunset celebration at Mallory Square, and spend the last day as you would above.

7 DAYS

Spend your first three days as you would in the four-day itinerary, but stay the third night in 🔅 **Islamorada ❸**. In the morning catch a boat, or rent a kayak to paddle to Lignumvitae Key Botanical State Park before making the one-hour drive to 🔅 **Marathon ❼**. Visit the natural-history museum that's part of the Museums and Nature Center of Crane Point Hammock and walk or take a train across the Old Seven Mile Bridge to Pigeon Key. The next stop is just 10 mi away at Bahia Honda State Park, on 🔅 **Bahia Honda Key ❽**. Take a walk on a wilderness trail, go snorkeling on an offshore reef, wriggle your toes in the beach's soft sand, and spend the night in a waterfront cabin, letting the waves lull you to sleep. Your sixth day starts with either a half day of fabulous snorkeling or diving at Looe Key Reef or a visit to the National Key Deer Refuge, on **Big Pine Key ❾**. Then continue on to 🔅 **Key West ⓫–㉜**, and get in a little sightseeing before watching the sunset.

7

❷ Have a nose-to-beak encounter with ospreys, hawks, herons, and other birds on the mend at the **Florida Keys Wild Bird Center,** which is at **Tavernier,** the southernmost part of Key Largo. They live in large, screened enclosures lining a winding boardwalk on some of the best waterfront real estate in the Keys. The center is especially popular among photographers, who arrive at 3:30 PM, when hundreds of wild waterbirds fly in and feed within arm's distance. Rehabilitated birds are set free, whereas others become permanent residents. A short nature trail runs into the mangrove forest (bring bug spray May through October), and a video explains the center's mission. (Warning: This place can be stinky. Must be that fishy pelican breath.) ⊠*MM 93.6, BS, Tavernier* ☎*305/852–4486* ⊕*www.fkwbc.org* ⊠*Free* ☉*Daily sunrise–sunset.*

☉ **Jacobs Aquatic Center.** Take the plunge at one of three swimming pools: an eight-lane, 25-meter lap pool with a diving well; a 3- to 4-foot-deep ramp-accessible pool; and an interactive play pool with a waterslide, pirate ship, waterfall, and beachfront entry. ⊠*320 Laguna Ave., MM 99.6, OS* ☎*305/453–7946* ⊕*www.jacobsaquaticcenter.org* ⊠*$7, discounted multiday passes available* ☉*Weekdays 11–6, weekends 10–7.*

WHERE TO STAY & EAT

★ $$–$$$$ ✕**Sundowners.** The name don't lie. If it's a clear night and you can get a reservation, you'll be treated to a sherbet-hued sunset over Florida Bay. If you're here in mild weather—anytime other than the dog days of summer or the rare winter cold snap—the best seats are on the patio. The view and food are excellent, and you won't have to get gussied up to eat in style. Try the key lime seafood, a happy combo of sautéed shrimp, lobster, and lump crab swimming in a garlic-and-vegetable lime sauce spiked with Tabasco. Wednesday and Saturday are prime-rib nights, and Friday features an all-you-can-eat fish fry. ⊠*MM 104, BS* ☎*305/451–4502* ⊕*sundownerskeylargo.com* ⊟*AE, D, MC, V.*

$$–$$$ ✕**Snapper's.** "You hook 'em, we cook 'em" is the motto here. Alas, it doesn't extend to "cleanin' 'em." The DIY dinner will set you back $13.95 per person. Otherwise, they'll catch and cook you a yellowtail snapper, roasted on a cedar plank with a basil-cream sauce, a grilled tuna steak slathered with Asian barbecue sauce alongside a mound of chipotle mashed potatoes, or a little something from the raw bar. The aromatic steamed mussels are worth the hours of garlic breath, and the ceviche of yellowtail (merrily spicy) wins raves, too. All this is served up in a lively, mangrove-ringed waterfront setting with live music, killer rum drinks, and seating alongside the fishing dock. Not for the weak of heart is the Nutty Lobster entrée, in which they cover a spiny lobster with mixed nuts and throw it into the deep fryer. ⊠*139 Seaside Ave.* ☎*305/852–5956* ⊟*AE, D, MC, V.*

★ $–$$$ ✕**The Fish House.** The pan-sautéed black grouper will make you moan with pleasure, but it's just one of many headliners in this nautical, Keys-y eatery. On the fin side, the choices include mahimahi, swordfish, tuna, and yellowtail snapper that can be broiled, blackened, baked, fried, or jerked Jamaican-style. Prefer shellfish or crustaceans? There are nearly as many choices on the shrimp, lobster, and, during the

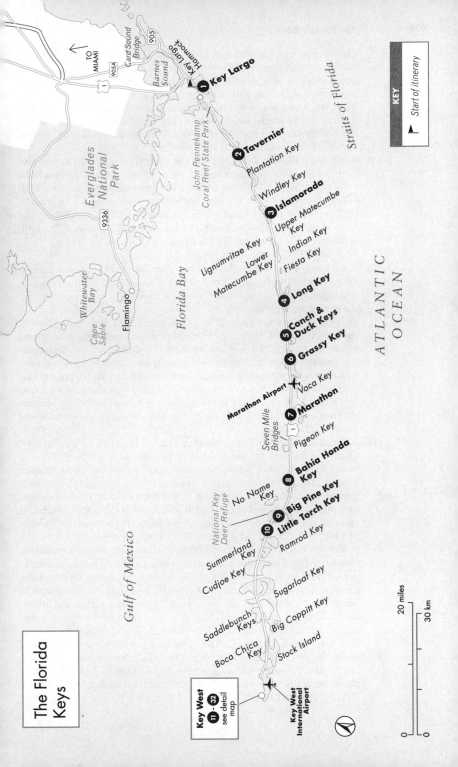

The Florida Keys

KEY

▲ Start of itinerary

TO MIAMI

Card Sound Bridge

905A
905

Key Largo Hammock

▲ **① Key Largo**

Barnes Sound

John Pennekamp Coral Reef State Park

② Tavernier

Plantation Key

Windley Key

③ Islamorada

Upper Matecumbe Key

Lignumvitae Key

Indian Key

Lower Matecumbe Key

Fiesta Key

④ Long Key

⑤ Conch & Duck Keys

⑥ Grassy Key

Vaca Key

Marathon Airport

⑦ Marathon

Pigeon Key

Seven Mile Bridges

⑧ Bahia Honda Key

No Name Key

⑨ Big Pine Key

National Key Deer Refuge

⑩ Little Torch Key

Summerland Key

Ramrod Key

Cudjoe Key

Sugarloaf Key

Saddlebunch Keys

Big Coppitt Key

Boca Chica Key

Stock Island

Key West ⑪–㉜
see detail map

Key West International Airport

Everglades National Park

9336

Whitewater Bay

Cape Sable

Flamingo

Florida Bay

ATLANTIC OCEAN

Straits of Florida

Gulf of Mexico

20 miles
30 km

October through May season, stone-crab side of the menu. For a sweet ending, try the homemade key lime pie. To ease the long lines, they've added outdoor seating and opened Encore next door; it has many of the same dishes, but with slightly higher prices, a more formal dining room, and a piano-bar dining area, where Sunday karaoke performances can be loud—unless you're singing, of course. ⊠ *MM 102.4, OS* ☎*305/451–4665 or 305/451–0650* ⊕*www.fishhouse.com* ⊟*AE, D, MC, V* ⊙*Closed early Sept.–early Oct.*

$–$$$ ✕**Mrs. Mac's Kitchen.** Townies pack the counters and booths at this tiny eatery, where decor runs to license plates stuck on the walls and folks talk fishing. Got a hankering for tuna casserole or Caribbean-style crab cakes? You'll find it here, along with the reliably good TJ Dolphin, a mahimahi fillet with a spicy tomato salsa served with black beans and rice. There's also an assortment of burgers and barbecue. The chili wins raves. Open for breakfast, lunch, and dinner. ⊠*MM 99.4, BS* ☎*305/451–3722* ⊟*AE, D, MC, V* ⊙*Closed Sun.*

$–$$$ ✕**Rib Daddy's Steak & Seafood.** When Bob Marshall's smoker experiments resulted in finger-licking ribs that almost fell off the bone, he whispered to his wife, "Who's your rib daddy?" The phrase became the restaurant's name, servers' T-shirts pose the question, and Bob's shirt reads, I'M YOUR RIB DADDY. You'll swoonfully agree after tasting the mesquite-smoked prime rib, beef ribs, and pork baby back and spare ribs flavored with Bob's own rubs and sauces. The Flintstone-size smoked turkey drumsticks are slightly less messy but just as tasty. Must-try sides include grilled corn on the cob and sweet-potato casserole. Key lime pie comes standard or with a chocolate cookie crust and a drizzle of chocolate. All this, and free Texas Hold 'Em tourneys on Tuesdays. ⊠*MM 102.5, BS* ☎*305/451–0900* ⊿*Reservations not accepted* ⊟*MC, V.*

¢–$$ ✕**Chad's Deli & Bakery.** It's a deli! It's a bakery! It's a pasta place! By day, Chad's serves monster sandwiches in pita wraps or on freshly baked bread. By night (after 5 PM), there are also pizza (try the garlic chicken white pizza), pasta dishes (everyone loves the chicken parm), even veggie goulash … and beer and wine to wash it all down. Of course, you may bypass all this and make a meal out of one of Chad's white-chocolate macadamia nut or chocolate-chip cookies, approximately the size of your head. ⊠*MM 92.3, BS* ☎*305/853–5566* ⊟*MC, V.*

¢–$ ✕**Alabama Jack's.** Cholesterol count be damned—the conch fritters here taste like heaven on a plate. Regulars at this weathered restaurant floating on two roadside barges in an old fishing community include Keys characters, Sunday cyclists, local retirees, and boaters, who come to admire tropical birds in the nearby mangroves, the occasional crocodile in the canal, or the bands that play on weekend afternoons. Some locals say that Jack's doesn't have the biker-bar feel it used to, but the food's still good, and cheap. The menu also has fish sandwiches, burgers, fries, salads, and lots of beer. The crab cakes, made from local blue crabs, earn some hallelujahs, too. Jack's closes by 7 or 7:30, when the mosquitoes start biting. ⊠*58000 Card Sound Rd., Card Sound* ☎*305/248–8741* ⊟*MC, V.*

¢–$ ✕**Harriette's Restaurant.** Mmmm—home cookin'. If you're looking for comfort food (the buttermilk biscuits are melt-in-your-mouth), try this refreshing throwback. Little has changed over the years in this vivid yellow-and-turquoise-hued roadside eatery. Owner Harriette Mattson personally welcomes the visitors and regulars who come for breakfast: steak and eggs with hash browns or grits and toast and jelly, or old-fashioned hotcakes with butter and syrup and sausage or bacon. ⊠*MM 95.7, BS* ☎*305/852–8689* ▭*No credit cards* ✆*No dinner.*

$$$$ ⊡**Jules' Undersea Lodge.** You can truly sleep with the fishies at this underwater inn. But don't plan a dip if you're claustrophobic—each of the two bedrooms is a very cozy 8 by 10 feet, though the entire chamber (a former research lab) has 640 square feet. You'll spend your visit at 5 fathoms (30 feet) below the surface with three 42-inch round windows for viewing sea life. The only way to gain access to the lodge is by diving, and guests must either be certified divers or take the hotel's three-hour introductory course (an additional $80). Two guest rooms share a kitchen and bathroom. Rates include breakfast and a full or light dinner (delivered by a mer-chef), unlimited dives, and use of diving gear. Because of the length of stay underwater, once you're back on terra firma, you can't fly for 24 hours. The office is open only from 8 AM to 4 PM. ⊠*MM 103.2, OS, 51 Shoreland Dr., 33037* ☎*305/451–2353* 🖷*305/451–4789* ⊕*www.jul.com* ⬌*2 rooms* ♿*In-room: kitchen, VCR. In-hotel: pool, diving, no elevator, no kids under 10, no-smoking rooms* ▭*AE, D, MC, V* ⫿*MAP.*

$$$$ ⊡**Key Largo Grande Resort & Beach Club.** Nestled within a hardwood hammock near the southern border of Everglades National Park, this sprawling hotel is undergoing some changes under new ownership. Formerly the Sheraton Beach Key Largo, the property got a $12 million makeover, and the management aims to improve the level of service and the caliber of the resort's restaurants. Spacious guest rooms each have a private balcony. Most rooms overlook the water or woods, but some face the parking lot. Lighted nature trails and boardwalks wind through the woods to a small beach. Two small pools are separated by a coral rock wall and waterfall. Both restaurants, one of which is very casual, overlook the water. The beach is small, but the vistas are tremendous. Pros: nice nature trail on bay side, pool has waterfalls. Cons: pools are between the parking lot and the highway, $10 daily charge for parking. ⊠*MM 97, BS, 97000 Overseas Hwy., 33037* ☎*305/852–5553 or 866/597–5397* 🖷*305/852–8669* ⊕*www.keylargogrande.com* ⬌*190 rooms, 10 suites* ♿*In-room: safe, Internet, refrigerators (some). In-hotel: 2 restaurants, room service, bars, tennis courts, pools, gym, beachfront, water sports, bicycles, some pets allowed (fee), no-smoking rooms* ▭*AE, D, DC, MC, V.*

★ $$$$ ⊡**Kona Kai Resort.** Bougainvilleas, coconut palms, and guava trees decorate a 2-acre hideaway that's one of the prettiest places to stay in the Keys. Each of the intimate cottages has tropical furnishings, a CD player, and fruit-scented toiletries. Spacious studios and one- and two-bedroom suites—with full kitchens and original art—are light filled. Outside, kick back in a lounge chair or hammock, soak in the Jacuzzi, or try a paddleboat or kayak (complimentary here). The resort also

7

has an art gallery and an orchid house with more than 250 blooms. Maid service is every third day to prolong your privacy; however, fresh linens and towels are available at any time. The resort closes during September. Pros: lush landscaping, complimentary use of kayaks and paddleboat. Cons: costly smallish rooms, lack of privacy in some rooms, no continental breakfast. ⊠ *MM 97.8, BS, 97802 Overseas Hwy., 33037* ☎ *305/852–7200 or 800/365–7829* ⊕ *www.konakairesort.com* ⇌ *8 suites, 5 rooms* ⚘ *In-room: no phone, kitchen (some), refrigerator, DVD. In-hotel: tennis court, pool, beachfront, no elevator, concierge, public Internet, no kids under 16, no-smoking rooms* ⊟ *AE, D, MC, V.*

$$$$ 🏨 **Marriott's Key Largo Bay Beach Resort.** Park the car and toss the keys
Ⓒ in the bottom of your bag; there's no need to go anywhere from here (except maybe John Pennekamp Coral Reef State Park, just a half mile north). This 17-acre bayside resort has diversion aplenty, including a white-sand beach and outdoor activities ranging from personal watercraft and parasailing to tennis and volleyball courts and a day spa. Given all that, the pool still rules, so an occasional stroll to the tiki bar could well be your most vigorous activity of the day. The resort's lemon-yellow, grille-balconied stories slice between highway and bay and exude an air of warm, indolent days. This isn't the poshest Marriott you've ever encountered, but it's fresh looking and suitably tropical in style. Some of the choicest rooms and suites offer sunset views. Pros: trips to the reef, lots to do, lively atmosphere. Cons: rooms facing the Overseas Highway get traffic noise. ⊠ *MM 103.8, BS, 103800 Overseas Hwy., 33037* ☎ *305/453–0000 or 866/849–3753* 🖷 *305/453–0093* ⊕ *www.marriottkeylargo.com* ⇌ *132 rooms, 20 2-bedroom suites, 1 penthouse suite* ⚘ *In-room: safe, kitchen (some), Wi-Fi. In-hotel: restaurant, room service, bars, tennis court, pool, gym, spa, beachfront, diving, water sports, bicycles, children's programs (ages 5–13), laundry facilities, laundry service, no-smoking rooms* ⊟ *AE, D, DC, MC, V.*

$$$–$$$$ 🏨 **Azul Del Mar.** Palms bathe the grounds in shade and the dock points the way to many beautiful sunsets at this adults-only boutique hotel. Advertising director Karol Marsden and her husband, Dominic, a commercial travel photographer, transformed a run-down waterfront mom-and-pop place into Azul Del Mar in 2004. As you'd expect from innkeepers with a background in the image business, the property offers great visuals, from the marble floors, dark-wood furniture, and Provençal yellow leather sofas to the ice-blue bath tiles, Tom Seghi paintings, and dark granite countertops. Behind the pretty facade is real warmth, as the well-traveled proprietors envision Azul Del Mar as a great place for grownups to stay and play. They're avid sailors, so water toys are plentiful. If you mix business with pleasure, take your laptop to the beach; the resort is a Wi-Fi hot spot. Pros: great garden, barbecue grills, kayaks. Cons: smallish beach. ⊠ *MM 104.3, BS, 104300 Overseas Hwy., Key Largo 33037* ☎ *305/451–0337 or 888/253–2985* 🖷 *305/451–0339* ⊕ *www.azulkeylargo.com* ⇌ *5 suites* ⚘ *In-room: no phone, kitchen, refrigerator, VCR, Wi-Fi. In-hotel: beachfront, water sports, bicycles, no elevator, Wi-Fi, no kids under age 16, no-smoking rooms* ⊟ *AE, MC, V.*

$$$–$$$$ 🖼 **Coconut Palm Inn.** Like home, only better, this low-key waterfront lodge is set in a quiet residential neighborhood of towering gumbo-limbo and buttonwood trees. Built in the 1930s, this little inn draws repeat guests with its friendly, relaxed vibe. A 400-foot sandy beach is dotted with the requisite hammocks and swaying palm trees. Screened porches are a welcome touch, letting Caribbean breezes in and keeping mosquitoes out. Rooms, which are decorated in West Indies–plantation style, vary from one-room efficiencies to one- and two-bedroom suites. No two rooms are alike, although seafoam green paint is used liberally. Pros: beach, tranquil location. Cons: Not much going on here. ✉ *MM 92, BS, 198 Harborview Dr., Tavernier 33070* 🕾 *305/852–3017* 🖷 *305/852–3880* ⊕ *www.coconutpalminn.com* 🛏 *8 suites, 12 rooms* 🕭 *In-room: kitchen (some), refrigerator, VCR (some). In-hotel: pool, beachfront, no elevator. laundry facilities, no-smoking rooms* 🖃 *AE, MC, V.*

$$$ 🖼 **Dove Creek Lodge.** Old-school fishermen would be scandalized by the luxury of this stylish fishing camp, with its sherbet-hued paint and plantation-style furniture, heated pool, and Jacuzzi. Then they'd get a load of the giant, flat-panel TV in the lobby, the comfy leather couch, and the nice tall stack of fishing magazines, and never want to leave. That is until they smell fish grilling at Snappers, the restaurant next door. One of the owners of the lodge is also owner of Snappers, and it seems like a match made in heaven. You can head out from the marina at Snappers with a fishing guide, chase billfish offshore or bonefish on the flats, and come back to eat and brag about the one that got away—until the sun sets and the band plays. Sweet. The rooms are surprisingly plush, and range in size from simple lodge rooms to luxury suites that sleep six. Given the proximity of the restaurant, it's a lively scene—liveliest if you stay in Room 201 or 202, where you'll hear the music until 10 PM. Pros: no minimum-stay requirements, lodge will arrange transportation from the airport (no car needed), live music next door every night. Cons: Formica countertops in a luxury suite, a too-new feel for some, loud music. ✉ *147 Seaside Ave., 33037* 🕾 *305/852–6200 or 800/401–0057* ⊕ *www.dovecreeklodge.com* 🛏 *14 rooms* 🕭 *In-room: safe, kitchen (some), refrigerator, ethernet. In hotel: pool, public Wi-Fi, airport shuttle, parking (no fee), no-smoking rooms.* 🖃 *AE, D, MC, V.*

$–$$$ 🖼 **Coconut Bay Resort & Bay Harbor Lodge.** Some 200 feet of waterfront is the main attraction here, framed with Easter egg–hued cottages and efficiencies. Most of the rooms, all simply furnished, have been renovated with new tile floors and appliances. Large gumbo-limbo trees shade the 2½-acre grounds, except at the beach, where coconut palms whisper in the breeze. Nice features abound, like well-placed lounge chairs for gazing out over the water, and kayaks and paddleboats (for when you want to get closer). Everybody shows up on the sundeck or the 30-foot dock to watch the sun slip into Davy Jones's Locker for the night. Restaurants are within walking distance. Ask for Unit 25 and you'll have extra space and a water view. Pros: lush foliage masks traffic noise from the Overseas Highway. Cons: guests all seem to know one another. ✉ *MM 97.7, BS, 97770 Overseas Hwy., 33037* 🕾 *305/852–*

1625 or 800/385–0986 ⊕www.thefloridakeys.com/coconutbay ⊲*21 units, 9 rooms, 5 efficiencies, 7 1-bedroom cottages* ⌂*In-room: kitchen (some), refrigerator. In-hotel: pool, beachfront, no elevator, some pets allowed (fee)* ⊟*AE, D, MC, V.*

★ $–$$$ ▣**Largo Lodge.** Drive under the dense canopy of foliage at the entrance of Largo Lodge, and you'll feel like you've gone through a time warp. Vintage 1950s duplex guest cottages are tucked amidst 3 acres of palms, sea grapes, and orchids. Vacationing baby-boomer couples seem right at home here, in one-bedroom guest cottages (no kids allowed) that probably resemble the places they vacationed when they were kids. Accommodations—surprisingly spacious but very basic—feature small kitchens with a dining area, rattan furniture, and screened porches. A lavish swath of bay frontage is perfect for sitting and contemplating. For swimming, you'll need to go to Pennekamp state park, about a mile away. Pros: lush, a good bargain for the Keys, 100-foot dock for watching the sunset. Cons: no Internet access, no pool, traffic noise when you're outdoors. ⊠*MM 101.7, BS, 101740 Overseas Hwy., 33037* ☎*305/451–0424 or 800/468–4378* ⊕*www.largolodge.com* ⊲*6 cottages* ⌂*In-room: no phone, kitchen. In-hotel: beachfront, no elevator, no kids under 16* ⊟*MC, V.*

¢–$$ ▣**The Pelican Motel.** If you're into nostalgia, consider this 1950s throwback, reminiscent of the days when vacationers packed the kids into the station wagon and came to the Keys to stay in no-frills seaside motels. Head toward the water, and you might see an old-timer or a little kid fishing off the dock. New owners are spiffing things up, and adding a beach, but basically, it is what it is: a clean and friendly motel, not fancy but comfortable. Picnic tables, palm trees, hammocks, Adirondack chairs, and animal statuary surround the colony of duplex bungalows and efficiency units, painted white with pastel trim. Guests include seniors, baby-boomer bikers, and families, who don't mind skipping a bit of space and a few frills in favor of homey digs and a low price tag. Some bring their boats; cozy up to a boat owner and maybe you'll get asked along on a fishing trip. Pros: hammocks strung between palms, well-maintained boat docks, inexpensive. Cons: slight trailer-park feel (there are two trailers on-site), some small rooms, some things that need fixing (cracked pottery, etc.). ⊠*MM 99.3, BS, 33037* ☎*305/451–3576* ⎙*305/451–4407* ⊕*www.hungrypelican.com* ⊲*13 rooms, 4 efficiencies, 2 trailers, 4 suites* ⌂*In-room: no phone, kitchen (some), refrigerator, VCR. In-hotel: beachfront, water sports, bicycles, no elevator, no-smoking rooms* ⊟*AE, D, DC, MC, V* ⎊*CP.*

$ ▣**Popp's Motel.** A high wall with stylized metal white herons marks the entrance to this 50-year-old family-run motel. The third and fourth generation of Popps are currently at the helm here, where basic-but-clean bedroom units and efficiencies have kitchens, dark-wood paneling, and terrazzo floors. A weeklong stay is required during busy periods; a three-night minimum is standard. Room 9 is closest to the beach. Family-friendly as it seems, no kids under age 13 are welcome. Pros: nice beach area, budget prices. Cons: rooms could use some updating, minimum-stay requirement eliminates the "just passing through" guest. ⊠*MM 95.5, BS, 95500 Overseas Hwy., 33037* ☎*305/852–5201*

☎305/852–5200 🌐*www.popps.com* 🛏*10 units* ♿*In-room: kitchen. In-hotel: beachfront, water sports, no elevator* 🚫*AE, MC, V.*

¢–$ 🏨**Seafarer Resort & Dive Center.** It's budget-basic but not without niceties, thanks to recently upgraded interiors that gave this resort new air conditioners, tiled floors, appliances, and linens. Outdoors, there's a pond and hammocks. Most rooms boast water views. Rooms 3 and 4 are spacious and best for families. Unit 6, a one-bedroom cottage called the "beach house," has a large picture window with an awesome view of the bay. Some units have private patios. Guests gather at the beachfront picnic table for alfresco dining and on the dock and lounge chairs for sunset watching. The dive shop offers scuba certification and uses state-of-the-art equipment. ⊠*MM 97.6, BS, 97684 Overseas Hwy., 33037* ☎*305/852–5349* ☎*305/852–0474* 🌐*www.seafarerresort.com* 🛏*15 units, 7 rooms, 2 studios, 3 1-bedroom cottages, 1 2-bedroom cottage, 2 apartments* ♿*In-room: no phone, kitchen (some), refrigerator. In-hotel: beachfront, diving, water sports, bicycles, no elevator, public Internet, no-smoking rooms* 🚫*MC, V.*

🏕**Kings Kampground.** Florida Bay breezes keep things cool, and the neighboring waterway gives boat toters access to John Pennekamp Coral Reef State Park. The campground has a marina for storing boats 23 feet or less ($10 per day). The park can accommodate RVs up to 40 feet long, and if you don't want to bring your own, you can rent one ($110–$125). This property also has a cottage ($120–$150), motel-style units ($45–$65), and tent sites ($30–$40). ♿*Partial hookups (electric and water), dump station, drinking water, picnic tables, electricity, public telephone, swimming (ocean)* 🛏*60 hookups for RVs and tents* ⊠*MM 103.5, BS* ☎*305/451–0010* 🌐*www.kingskamp.com* 🚫*MC, V.*

★ ☾ 🏕**John Pennekamp Coral Reef State Park.** Divers, snorkelers, and campers won't find a better location in the Upper Keys. Pennekamp's campsites are carved out of hardwood hammock, providing shade and privacy away from the heavy day-use areas. Nearby, water laps the shore, providing a soothing lullaby. Groups have numerous facilities and plenty of space to play. There's a campground host, campfire programs, and vending machines for late-night snack attacks. Day-use activities and facilities include boating, fishing, hiking, boat-slip rentals, a dock, boat tours, a nature center, a marina, scuba diving and snorkeling, and volleyball. ♿*Flush toilets, partial hookups (electric and water), dump station, drinking water, showers, fire pits, picnic tables, electricity, public telephone, general store, ranger station, swimming (ocean)* 🛏*47 partial hookups for RVs and tents* ⊠*MM 102.5, OS* ☎*305/451–1202 park, 800/326–3521 reservations* 🌐*www.reserveamerica.com* 🚫*AE, D, MC, V.*

NIGHTLIFE

The semiweekly *Keynoter* (Wednesday and Saturday), weekly *Reporter* (Thursday), and Friday through Sunday editions of the *Miami Herald* are the best sources of information on entertainment and nightlife.

Mingle with locals over cocktails and sunsets at **Breezers Tiki Bar** (⊠*MM 103.8, BS* ☎*305/453–0000*), in Marriott's Key Largo Bay

Beach Resort. Walls plastered with Bogart memorabilia remind customers that the classic 1948 Bogart-Bacall flick *Key Largo* was shot in the **Caribbean Club** (⊠*MM 104, BS* ☎*305/451–4466*). An archetype of a laid-back Keys bar, it draws a beards-and–baseball caps crowd, happy to shoot the breeze while shooting pool. Postcard-perfect sunsets and live entertainment draw revelers on Friday and Saturday and at 5 on Sunday evening, and *American Idol* wannabes show up for karaoke on Wednesday night. **Coconuts** (⊠*MM 100, OS, 528 Caribbean Dr.* ☎*305/453–9794*), next to Marina Del Mar Resort, has entertainment Monday and Wednesday through Sunday year-round, except Monday during football season. The crowd is primarily thirty- and fortysomething, sprinkled with a few more-seasoned townies.

THE OUTDOORS

BIKING
Tavernier Bicycle & Hobbies (⊠*MM 91.9, BS, 91958 Overseas Hwy., Tavernier* ☎*305/852–2859*) rents single-speed adult bikes. Cruisers go for $15 a day, $75 a week. Helmets and locks are free with rental. Closed on Sunday.

FISHING
Sailors Choice (⊠*MM 99.7, OS* ☎*305/451–1802 or 305/451–0041*) runs a party boat twice daily ($35 for half-day trips plus $3 fuel surcharge) plus a night trip ($40 plus $3 surcharge) on Friday and Saturday. The ultramodern 65-foot, 49-passenger boat with air-conditioned cabin leaves from the Holiday Inn docks. Rods, bait, and license are included.

SCUBA & SNORKELING
Much of what makes the Upper Keys a singular dive destination is variety. Places like Molasses Reef, which rises as high as 3 feet below the surface and descends to 55 feet, have something for snorkelers, novice divers, and experienced divers. The latest addition to the Keys diving wrecks is the *Spiegel Grove*, a 510-foot vessel that was sunk 6 mi off Key Largo in June 2002. It lies on its starboard side in 130 feet of water, but reaches up as high as 45 feet below the surface. Expect to pay about $75 for a two-tank, two-site dive trip with tanks and weights, or $35 to $40 for a two-site snorkel outing and for nonswimming accompanying guests. Get big discounts with multiple trips.

Ocean Divers (⊠*MM 105.5, BS, 522 Caribbean Dr.* ⊠*MM 100, OS* ☎*305/451–0037, 877/451–0037, 305/451–1113, or 800/451–1113* ⊕*www.oceandivers.com*) operates two shops in Key Largo. Both are PADI five-star CDC facilities and offer day and night dives, fully stocked stores, instruction, and dive-lodging packages. The cost is $80 for a two-tank reef dive with tank and weight rental ($85 for wrecks), $122 if you need everything; $136 includes a wet suit, suggested in winter. Snorkel trips cost $45 with snorkel, mask, and fins. **Amy Slate's Amoray Dive Resort** (⊠*MM 104.2, BS* ☎*305/451–3595 or 800/426–6729* ⊕*www.amoray.com*) makes diving easy. Get out of bed, walk out of your room and into a full-service dive shop (NAUI, PADI, TDI, and BSAC certified), then onto a 45-foot catamaran. The rate for one two-dive trip is $75.

Ask about multidive discounts, accommodations packages, and underwater weddings. **Coral Reef Park Co.** (⊠ *John Pennekamp Coral Reef State Park, MM 102.5, OS* ☎*305/451–6322* ⊕*www.pennekamppark.com*) gives scuba and snorkeling tours of the park aboard sailing and motorized boats. **Conch Republic Divers** (⊠*MM90.8, BS* ☎*305/852–1655 or 800/274–3483* ⊕*www.conchrepublicdivers.com*) gives instruction as well as scuba and snorkeling tours of the Pennekamp, Molasses, and other reefs. Two-location dives are $80 with tank and weights. Other options are available. **Divers City, USA** (⊠*MM 90.5, OS* ☎*305/852–0430 or 800/649–4659* ⊕*www.diverscityusa.com*) is eco- and diver-friendly. They repair scuba gear and also have the best prices for "Bubble Watchers"—passengers accompanying a diver ($25). Two-tank, two-location dives are $75; three-location dives will set you back a Benjamin. **Quiescence Diving Service, Inc.** (⊠*MM 103.5, BS* ☎*305/451–2440* ⊕*www.quiescence.com*) sets itself apart in two ways: it limits groups to six to ensure personal attention and offers day, night, and twilight (in summer) dives an hour before sundown, the time when sea creatures are most active. Two-tank, two-dive trips are $75.

WATER SPORTS

Kayaking is the fastest-growing water sport in the Keys, thanks in part to the many new outfitters offering tours, but also because of advances in equipment—such as foot pedals, rudders, and sails—that make sea kayaking easier. You can paddle for a few hours or the whole day, paddle on your own, or take a guided tour. Some outfitters also offer overnight trips. The 110-mi Florida Keys Overseas Paddling Trail, part of a statewide system, runs from Key Largo to Key West. You can paddle the entire trip, which takes approximately seven days, or just cover a section. Contact outfitters for information on campgrounds and participating hotels along the route, or visit www.dep.state.fl.us/gwt/paddling. The state parks along the trail have vowed to create some primitive campsites for paddlers, but that hasn't happened yet. For now, trail-trippers either stealth camp (you didn't hear it from us!) or reserve in advance and stay and pay. **Coral Reef Park Co.** (⊠*John Pennekamp Coral Reef State Park, MM 102.5, OS* ☎*305/451–1202*) frequently renews its fleet of canoes and kayaks for gliding around the mangrove trails or the sea. Rent a canoe, a single or double sea kayak, or even camping equipment from **Florida Bay Outfitters** (⊠*MM 104, BS* ☎*305/451–3018*). They help with trip planning and match the equipment to the skill level, and are the go-to folks for setting up self-guided trips on the Florida Keys Overseas Paddling Trail. They also run myriad guided tours and sell camping and outdoor accessories, kayaks, and canoes.

SHOPPING

Key Largo isn't all about tiki bars and dive trips. Pick up an old Hemingway novel or the latest tome from a local poet at **Cover to Cover Books** (⊠*Tavernier Towne Shopping Center, MM 91.2, BS, 91272 Overseas Hwy.* ☎*305/853–2464*). The children's department is especially strong. Beyond books, the shop offers a gourmet coffee bar, open-mike nights, book signings, lectures, kid's story hours, and assorted literary events. Original works by major international artists—including American pho-

MIND YOUR P'S & CRACKERS

If you spend enough time in Florida, sooner or later you'll start hearing about Crackers. Depending on whom you ask, and in which part of the state, you might get a very different answer. Some folks are proud to identify themselves as Crackers; others consider it a racial epithet and a violation under the Florida Hate Crimes Act.

In the early 1500s the Spanish came to the Americas, bringing caballeros and horses. These early cowboys got the nickname "crackers" for the cracking sound they made with their whips. This was also the name given to the small Spanish horses, which were agile and ideal for working with cattle. Florida Cracker horses are still an active breed in Florida and essential to the cattle industry.

Another theory is that the term is derived from the practice of "corn-cracking," a way to grind dried corn kernels into grits and cornmeal.

Often the term is used disparagingly about people who can't afford much to eat, especially those who live in the Panhandle near the Georgia border. Call somebody a Cracker in these parts, and you might be adding hefty insult to injury.

Many Floridians will agree that "Cracker" refers to people who can claim native Floridian heritage. Crackers were frontiersmen and pioneers, mostly living off the land, hunting, raising their own meat, and building their own houses. Original Cracker houses were akin to log cabins but styled more like two cabins separated by a long hallway. These shotgun houses were built this way to make it possible to fire a gun through the front door and not hit any other wall in the house. Nowadays, a Cracker house is usually a clapboard home with a wraparound porch common in the northern and western part of the state.

tographer Clyde Butcher, sea captain–turned-painter Dirk Verdoorn, and French sculptor Polles—are shown at the **Gallery at Kona Kai** (⊠*MM 97.8, BS, 97802 Overseas Hwy.* ☎*305/852–7200*), in the Kona Kai Resort. Go into olfactory overload—you'll find yourself sniffing every single bar of soap and scented candle—at **Key Lime Products** (⊠*MM 95.2, BS, 95200 Overseas Hwy.* ☎*305/853–0378 or 800/870–1780* ⊕*key-limeproducts.com*). Take home some key lime juice and bake a pie; the (super-easy) directions are right on the bottle. You can find lots of shops in the Keys that sell cheesy souvenirs—snow globes, gators, and shell-encrusted anything. **Shellworld** (⊠*MM 97.5, center median* ☎*305/852–8245*) is the great big granddaddy. The sprawling Keys-style building is stuffed with home furnishings, CDs of local music, shells, cards, resort clothing, jewelry, and, yes, delightfully tacky souvenirs. There's a super-sale the weekend after Thanksgiving.

ISLAMORADA

❸ *MM 90.5–70.*

True story: Early settlers named this key after their schooner, the *Island Home,* but to make the name more romantic, they translated it into

Spanish—*isla morada*. The Floridian spin on the foreign tongue is pronounced *eye*-la-mor-*ah*-da. The chamber of commerce prefers to say it
means "the purple isles." Early maps show Islamorada as only Upper
Matecumbe Key, but the incorporated "Village of Islands" comprises
the islands between Tavernier Creek at MM 90 and Fiesta Key at MM
70, including Plantation Key, Windley Key, Upper Matecumbe Key,
Lower Matecumbe Key, Craig Key, and Fiesta Key. In addition, two
islands—Indian Key, in the Atlantic Ocean, and Lignumvitae Key, in
Florida Bay—belong to the group. Islamorada is one of the world's
most renowned sportfishing areas. For nearly 100 years, seasoned
anglers have fished these clear, warm waters teeming with game fish
as well as lobster, shrimp, and crabs. The rich, famous, and powerful
who have come to wet a line include Lou Gehrig, Ted Williams, Zane
Grey, and presidents Hoover, Truman, Carter, and George H.W. Bush.
More than 150 backcountry guides and 400 offshore captains operate
out of this 20-mi stretch. Activities include fishing tournaments and
historic reenactments. During September and October, Heritage Days
highlights include free lectures on Islamorada history, a golf tournament, and the Indian Key Festival.

Between 1885 and 1915, settlers earned good livings growing pineapples at **Plantation Key,** using black Bahamian workers to plant and
harvest their crops. The plantations are gone, replaced by a dense concentration of homes, businesses, and a public park. ⊠ *MM 90.5–86.*
Windley Key is the highest point in the Keys, though at 16 feet above
sea level it's not likely to give anyone altitude sickness. Originally two
islets, the area was first inhabited by Native Americans, who left mid-
dens and other remains, and then by settlers, who farmed and fished in
the mid-1800s and called the islets the Umbrella Keys. Henry Flagler
bought the land from homesteaders in 1908 for his Florida East Coast
Railway, filled in the inlet between the two islands, and changed the
name. His workers quarried rock for the rail bed and bridge approaches
in the Keys—the same rock used in many historic South Florida structures, including Miami's Vizcaya and the Hurricane Monument on
Upper Matecumbe. Although the Quarry Station stop was destroyed
by the 1935 hurricane, quarrying continued until the 1960s. Today a
few resorts occupy the island. ⊠ *MM 86–84.*

Islamorada Founder's Park. Formerly part of a commercial resort, this
public park boasts a nice little palm-shaded beach, marina, dog park,
skate park, boat rentals, an Olympic-size pool, and restrooms and
showers. If you're staying in Islamorada hotels, enter the park free
and pay the village rate of $3 for use of the pool. Guests of other Keys
hotels pay $4 to enter the park and $7 to use the pool, possibly worth
it if your lodgings place is pool-less or the kids want a change of scenery. A spiffy new amphitheater will host concerts, plays, and shows.
For event information, call the Islamorada Chamber of Commerce at
305/664-4503. ⊠ *MM 87, BS* ☎ *305/853–1685.*

The fossilized coral reef at **Windley Key Fossil Reef Geological State Park,**
laid down about 125,000 years ago, shows that the Florida Keys were
at some time underwater. Excavation of Windley Key's limestone bed

by the Florida East Coast Railway exposed the petrified reef. The park contains the **Alison Fahrer Environmental Education Center,** with historic, biological, and geological displays about the area. There also are guided and self-guided tours along trails that lead to the railway's old quarrying equipment and cutting pits, where you can take rubbings of beautifully fossilized brain coral and sea ferns from the quarry walls. There's an annual festival in February. ⊠*MM 85.5, BS* ☎*305/664–2540* ⊕*www.dep.state.fl.us/parks* 🎫*Education center free, quarry trails $1.50, ranger-guided tours $2.50* ☉*Education center Thurs.–Mon. 8–5; tours at 10 and 2.*

℃ The lush, tropical, 17-acre **Theater of the Sea** is the second-oldest marine mammal center in the world, a throwback that doesn't attempt to compete with more modern, higher-priced parks such as the Miami Seaquarium. Still, it's among the better tourist stops between the latter attraction and Key West. Entertaining educational shows provide insight into conservation issues, natural history, and mammal anatomy, physiology, and husbandry. Interactive programs include dolphin, sea lion, and sting ray encounters ($50–$165 including general admission), a marine tour, and a boat ride; reservations are recommended. Shows run continuously. Ride a glass-bottom boat and take a four-hour Dolphin Adventure Snorkel Cruise or guided tours to view marine life, raptors, and reptiles. Visit dolphins and sea lions. Try lunch at the grill, shop, and sunbathe at a lagoon-side beach. ⊠*MM 84.5, OS, 84721 Overseas Hwy., 33036* ☎*305/664–2431* ⊕*www.theaterofthesea.com* 🎫*$23.95* ☉*Daily 9:30–4.*

Early homesteaders were so successful at growing pineapples in the rocky soil of **Upper Matecumbe Key** that at one time the island had the largest U.S. pineapple crop. However, Cuban pineapples and the hurricane of 1935 killed the industry. Today, life centers on fishing and tourism, and the island is lively with homes, charter-fishing boats, bait shops, restaurants, stores, nightclubs, marinas, nurseries, and offices. It's one of the earliest of the Upper Keys to be permanently settled. ⊠*MM 84–79.*

Tucked away behind the Islamorada library is **Islamorada County Park,** with a small beach on a creek. The water isn't very deep, but it is crystal clear. Currents are swift, making swimming unsuitable for young children, but kids can enjoy the playground. There are also picnic tables, grassy areas, and restrooms. ⊠*MM 81.5, BS.*

▌OFF THE BEATEN PATH   **Indian Key Historic State Park.** Murder, mystery, and misfortune surround 10½-acre Indian Key, on the ocean side of the Matecumbe islands. Before it became one of the first European settlements outside of Key West, it was inhabited by Native Americans for several thousand years. The islet served as a county seat and base for 19th-century shipwreck salvagers until an Indian attack wiped out the settlement in 1840. Dr. Henry Perrine, a noted botanist, was killed in the raid. Today his plants overgrow the town's ruins. In October the Indian Key Festival celebrates the key's heritage. Take a ranger-guided tour, Thursday through Monday at 9 and 1 ($1), or roam among the marked trails and sites.

Because of hurricane damage, the Indian Key public dock is closed, but you can get there by rental kayak or canoe. Locals kayak out from **Indian Key Fill** (⊠ *MM 78.5, BS*). Rentals are available from Florida Keys Kayak and Sail. ⊠ *MM 78.5, OS* ☏ *305/664–4878.*

Lignumvitae Key Botanical State Park. On the National Register of Historic Places, this 280-acre bayside island is the site of a virgin hardwood forest and home and gardens that chemical magnate William Matheson built as a private retreat in 1919. Access is by boat—your own, a rental, or a ferry operated by Robbie's Marina, with twice-daily ferry service (10 AM and 2 PM) Thursday through Monday. Robbie's also rents kayaks. (Paddling here from Indian Key Fill, at MM 78.5, is a popular pastime.) On the key, take a guided ranger walk, offered Thursday through Monday at 10 and 2. Wear long sleeves and pants, and bring mosquito repellent. On the first weekend in December is the Lignumvitae Christmas Celebration. ⊠ *MM 78.5, BS* ☏ *305/664–9814 ferry service, 305/664–2540 Windley Key State Park* ⓥ *Free; tour $1.50; ferry $20* ⊙ *Tours Thurs.–Mon. at 10 and 2; last ticket sold 30 mins before tour.*

ↂ Tarpon, large prehistoric-looking denizens of the not-so-deep, congregate around the docks at **Robbie's Marina** on Lower Matecumbe Key, where children—and lots of adults—buy a $2 bucket of bait fish to feed them. Count your fingers when you're finished. ⊠ *MM 77.5, BS* ☏ *305/664–9814 or 877/664–8498* ⊕ *www.robbies.com* ⊠ *Dock access $1* ⊙ *Daily 8–5.*

On Lower Matecumbe Key, **Anne's Beach** is a popular village park whose beach is best enjoyed at low tide. The nicest feature here is a ½-mi elevated wooden boardwalk that meanders through a natural wetland hammock. Covered picnic areas along the boardwalk provide a place to linger and enjoy the view. Restrooms are at the north end. Weekends are packed with Miami day-trippers. ⊠ *MM 73.5, OS* ☏ *305/853–1685.*

WHERE TO STAY & EAT

★ $$–$$$$ ✕ **Marker 88.** With a seemingly endless supply a few yards away in Florida Bay, it's no wonder marine cuisine rules at Chef Sal Barrios's eatery, which over the last 30 years has become a "must" for visitors. Large picture windows offer great sunset views, but the bay views are lovely anytime. Irresistible entrées include grilled yellowfin tuna served with wasabi and ginger and yellowtail snapper in a delicate meunière sauce. Landlubbers find veal piccata, chicken française, and a few other options, and there's also a long list of sandwiches ($8–$12). The extensive wine list is an oenophile's delight. Reservations are recommended. ⊠ *MM 88, BS* ☏ *305/852–9315* ⊕ *www.marker88.info* ⊟ *AE, MC, V.*

$$–$$$$ ✕ **Pierre's.** One of the Keys' most elegant dining addresses, Pierre's
FodorsChoice draws foodies from Miami and beyond, and more than a few guys
★ with George Hamilton tans dining with their younger, blonder … daughters? Put on your best "tropical chic" duds and decide to be as fabulous as the food. A two-story sister to the Morada Bay restaurant,

7

Pierre's marries British colonial decadence with South Florida trendiness. It oozes style, with dark wood, rattan, French doors, Indian and Asian architectural artifacts, and a wicker chair–strewn veranda that overlooks the bay. The food, drawn from those same Asian, Indian, and Floridian influences, is complex: layered, colorful, and beautifully presented. Diners gush about the sauces and "fabulous" desserts. The changing menu might include sea bass over baby bok choy or potato-crusted grouper. Among the appetizer choices, few can resist the lobster cake. Weather permitting, dine outside. The sophisticated downstairs bar provides a perfect vantage point for sunset watching. Reservations are recommended. ⊠*MM 81.5, BS* ☎*305/664–3225* ▤*AE, MC, V* ⊘*Closed Mon.*

$–$$$$ ✕**Island Grill.** If you sat any closer to the water at this oceanfront restaurant, you'd need a towel. There's indoor and outdoor seating. If you're seated outdoors, know that boats pull up within a few feet of your table discharging diners—and exhaust—so opt for a table a little farther away; you'll still get the sea view, but without the fumes. Pop music is piped as waiters take orders from an eclectic menu with such dishes as Reuben mahimahi, guava barbecue shrimp with pineapple salsa, and tuna nachos. Southern-inspired fare includes low-country shrimp or shrimp and andouille sausage, both with grits or, as some locals call them, "gree-its." There's a bar indoors and another outdoors, with live entertainment Wednesday through Sunday. ⊠*MM 85.5, OS* ☎*305/664–8400* ▤*AE, MC, V.*

$$–$$$ ✕**Uncle's Restaurant.** Former fishing guide Joe LePree adds flair to seafood recipes by offering options such as française, Milanese, parmigiana, or LePree (with artichokes, mushrooms, and garden-grown spices) in addition to the usual grilled, broiled, or blackened options. You also can feast on mussels or littleneck clams in red or white sauce. Specials sometimes combine game (bison, caribou, or elk) with seafood. Portions are huge, so share dishes or take home a doggie bag. Weather permitting, sit outdoors in the garden; poor acoustics make dining indoors unusually noisy. ⊠*MM 81, OS* ☎*305/664–4402* ▤*AE, D, DC, MC, V* ⊘*Closed Sun.*

★   ✕**Morada Bay.** Readers give this wildly popular, bayfront restaurant
$–$$$ high marks for a funky Keys vibe, sunsets viewed from Adirondack chairs, and tiki torches that bathe the evening in romance. "It's great bistro food—original and tasty," as one recent guest put it. Entrées feature alluring combinations like potato-crusted dolphin with scallop mousse and asparagus risotto, and carmelized jumbo sea scallops with braised leeks and wild mushrooms. Seafood takes center stage, but you can always get chicken (infused with lemon, here) or a steak. The decor showcases renowned photographer Clyde Butcher's black-and-white Everglades photography. Popularity has made the kitchen's performance inconsistent in the preparation of an inventive menu, which includes tapas, mostly from the sea. Dine indoors (noisy) or outdoors overlooking a beach dotted with kids playing in the sand—as everywhere, they've eaten faster than their parents. There's frequently live entertainment, especially on weekends, and a monthly full-moon party. ⊠*MM 81, BS* ☎*305/664–0604* ▤*AE, MC, V.*

¢–$$$ ✗**Kaiyo.** Chef-owner Dawn Sieber, formerly of Cheeca Lodge, designed
    🕙   Kaiyo with as much artistry as she applies to the food. The setting
includes a colorful abstract mosaic, polished wood floors and bars,
earth tones, and upholstered banquettes. The menu, a fusion of East
and West—Sieber calls it Flor-Asian—has sushi and sashimi, classic
rolls, and her signature rolls that combine local ingredients with tra-
ditional Japanese tastes. Key lime lobster roll is a blend of Florida
lobster with hearts of palm and essence of key lime ($13.75). Kaiyo
roll includes local stone crab, wahoo, edamame, jerk-spiced sunflower
seeds, and stone-ground mustard mayonnaise ($13.50). Wash it down
with an ice-cold Voss—naturally, hip water is served here—or one
of Kaiyo's beloved sake mojitos. ⊠*MM 82, OS* ☎*305/664–5556*
⊕*www.kaiyokeys.com* ⊟*AE, MC, V* ⊙*Closed Sun.*

$$$$ 🏨**Casa Morada.** Three female hoteliers brought their cumulative 50
Fodor'sChoice   years of New York and Miami Beach experience to the Keys. Using
    ★   their transformative magic, they've turned this waterfront resort into
an all-suites showcase befitting the French Riviera, with a Caribbean
accent, of course. Lush landscaping, a pool surrounded by a sandy
"beach," artwork, blooming orchids, CD players, and outdoor lounges
at the water's edge are just the start. Complimentary yoga classes, a
Zen garden, and a rock waterfall lend a wholesome spa vibe. Clean,
cool tile-and-terrazzo floors invite you to kick off your shoes and step
out to your private patio overlooking the gardens and bay. Break-
fast and lunch are served on the waterside terrace. Pros: cool design
touches everywhere, hammock set at end of dock, complimentary use
of bikes and kayaks. Cons: trailer park across the street, not much of
a beach. ⊠*MM 82, BS, 136 Madeira Rd., 33036* ☎*305/664–0044
or 888/881–3030* 🖷*305/664–0674* ⊕*www.casamorada.com* ⌖*16
suites* ⌂*In-room: safe, DVD. In-hotel: restaurant, room service, bar,
pool, bicycles, no elevator, concierge, laundry service, public Wi-Fi, no
kids under 16, no-smoking rooms* ⊟*AE, MC, V* ⊙|*CP.*

$$$$ 🏨**Cheeca Lodge & Spa.** Stretching across 27 oceanfront acres, this clas-
sic resort has luxury beachfront bungalows, suites, and rooms, as well
as fish-filled lagoons. Accommodations include West Indies–style furni-
ture (think mahogany and marble) and 42-inch plasma TVs. Beckoning
are the beach and water sports, as well as massages, facials, and body
treatments at the spa. Rooms have views of ocean, garden, or golf
course. A $39-plus-tax per-day resort fee covers tennis, golf, fishing
tackle, and kayaks. The Cheeca is the local leader in green activism,
with everything from recycling programs to ecotours. Camp Cheeca
for kids, $40 per child per day (ages 5–12, Tuesday–Saturday 9 AM–1
PM), $40 per night (6–10 PM), is fun and educational. High season tends
to draw lots of spring-breaking families, so Cheeca is not the place to
be if you're single or not fond of small fry. Pros: pillow-top mattresses
and other luxurious touches, beautifully landscaped grounds, wildlife.
Cons: slow service, especially in restaurants, kids' lagoon could be
cleaner, minimum-stay requirement may apply in season. ⊠*MM 82,
OS, Box 527, 33036* ☎*305/664–4651 or 800/327–2888* 🖷*305/664–
2893* ⊕*www.cheeca.com* ⌖*139 rooms, 64 suites* ⌂*In-room: safe,
refrigerator (some), DVD, Wi-Fi. In-hotel: 2 restaurants, room ser-*

vice, bar, golf course, tennis courts, pools, gym, spa, beachfront, diving, water sports, bicycles, concierge, children's programs (ages 5–12), laundry service, Wi-Fi, no-smoking rooms ⊟*AE, D, DC, MC, V.*

$$$$ 🏨 **The Islander Resort.** The vintage sign is straight out of a *Happy Days* rerun, but don't let first impressions fool you. This circa-1951 property made an ugly-duckling-to-swan transformation in 2004. Inside the suites and villas, the look is Beachhouse Modern, with white cottage-style furnishings and contrasting lapis fabrics. Sunny yellow, white-trimmed bedrooms look like pages from a Pottery Barn catalog. Private screened porches lead to 1,300 feet of coral-shell beach, curved palm trees bending in the breeze, and ocean views that seem to go on forever. Families snap up suites in the oceanfront Beach House; couples looking for a more tranquil escape head to rooms set back from the pool and beach area. The pools—one saltwater, one freshwater—win raves from guests, as do the spacious rooms and full kitchens. A 200-foot dock, lighted at night, adds to the resort-y feel. Tip: Book directly with the resort for the best deals. Pros: clean, full kitchens, beach, spacious rooms. Cons: somewhat overpriced, beach is more shell-y than sandy. ⊠*MM 81.2, OS, 33026* ☎*305/664–2031 or 800/753–6002* 🖷*305/664–5503* ⊕*www.islanderfloridakeys.com* ⬚*114* ⚭*In-room: safe, kitchen, Wi-Fi. In-hotel: restaurant, bar, pools, gym, beachfront, water sports, bicycles, no elevator, laundry facilities, laundry service* ⊟*AE, D, DC, MC, V* ⦿*CP.*

★ $$$$ 🏨 **The Moorings.** Pinch yourself: your tropical fantasy retreat with hammocks swaying between tall palm trees, and a sugar-white beach lapped by aqua-green waves is right here. West Indies–style cottages with colorful Bahama shutters, verandas, and wicker furniture are enveloped by a canopy of coconut palms on a residential street off the highway. This is a high-end slice of Old Florida, so don't expect tiki bars on the beach (or even room service.) The one-, two-, and three-bedroom cottages are outfitted with batik fabrics, pristine kitchens, plush towels, and cushy bedcovers. Four original cottages date back to the 1930s; the other houses were built in the early '90s. A palm-lined walkway leads to the beach, where Adirondack chairs, hammocks, and a swimming dock await. The spa offers massages and beauty treatments. There's a two-night minimum-stay requirement for one-bedroom cottages, a one-week minimum on other lodgings, and a $15-per-day resort fee (includes the use of the fitness room, kayaks, and windsurfing equipment). Often compared to Cheeca Lodge, The Moorings feels like a private island, whereas Cheeca feels like a resort. Pros: romantic, good restaurants on property, beautiful beach. Cons: no room service, extra fee for housekeeping. ⊠*MM 81.6, OS, 123 Beach Rd., 33036* ☎*305/664–4708* 🖷*305/664–4242* ⊕*www.themooringsvillage.com* ⬚*5 cottages, 13 houses* ⚭*In-room: kitchen, Wi-Fi. In-hotel: tennis court, pool, spa, beachfront, water sports, no elevator, laundry facilities* ⊟*AE, MC, V.*

$$$ 🏨 **White Gate Court.** Pack your puppy: this seven-unit, circa-1940s inn is a dog lover's paradise, with plenty of open space for pooches to play. Susanne Orias de Cargnelli restored the property in 1995. All the units, which sleep either two or five, are well equipped, and the backyard has a barbecue and an umbrella-shaded table under palm trees. Rates include use of bicycles, paddleboat, and snorkeling gear. Pros: pet-friendly, homey feel, mature trees. Cons: preference to guests with longer stays, no pool, access to the water is slippery. ⊠ *MM 76, BS, 76010 Overseas Hwy., 33036* ☎ *305/664–4136 or 800/645–4283* ⊕ *www.whitegatecourt.com* ⟱ *7 units* ⚒ *In-room: kitchen, dial-up. In-hotel: beachfront, water sports, bicycles, no elevator, laundry facilities, some pets allowed (fee)* ⊟ *MC, V.*

★ **$$–$$$** 🏠 **Drop Anchor Resort & Marina.** It's easy to find your cottage here, even after a night on the town. Did you look great in lavender? or perhaps the Lily Pulitzer lime-and-pink cottage? Cute, colorful, and immaculate, this place has the charming feel of your college chum's beach house, and the owners keep making it better. (Planned improvements include the addition of plantation-style porches and Bahama shutters.) Inside you'll find soothing West Indies–type furnishings and kitschy-cool, 1950s-era tile in the bathrooms. Welcoming as the rooms may be, you didn't come to the Keys to sit indoors: there's a luscious expanse of white sand awaiting your piggies, and you can catch ocean breezes from either your balcony, a Crayola-color Adirondack chair, or a picnic table perched in the sand. Pros: colorful, attention to detail, laid-back charm. Cons: close to the highway (noise is a factor). ⊠ *84959 Overseas Hwy., MM 85, OS* ✉ *Box 222, 33036* ☎ *305/664–4863 or 888/664–4863* 📠 *305/664–4801* ⊕ *www.dropanchorresort.com* ⟱ *18 rooms* ⚒ *In-room: kitchen (some), refrigerator. In-hotel: pool, no elevator, laundry facilities* ⊟ *AE, D, DC, MC, V.*

¢–**$$$** 🏠 **Ragged Edge Resort.** Call it the anti–Casa Morada. This small colony of duplexes, tucked away in a residential area at the ocean's edge, is big on value but short on style. With almost no advertising, Ragged Edge draws returning guests who would rather fish off the dock and hoist a brew with proprietor Mike than loll in Egyptian cotton sheets. Even those who turn their noses up at cheap plastic deck furniture and pine paneling would admit that Ragged Edge has a million-dollar setting, with ocean views all around. There's no beach to speak of, but you can ride a bike (complimentary) across the street to Islamorada Founder's Park, where you'll find a nice little beach and water toys for rent. If a bit of partying puts you off, look elsewhere. Plain-Jane though they are, rooms are very clean and fairly spacious. Ground-floor units have screened porches; upper units have large decks, more windows, and beam ceilings. Pros: oceanfront location on the cheap, quiet neighborhood, clean. Cons: rooms and furnishings need updating, style is '60s rec room, no room phones or Internet. ⊠ *MM 86.5, OS, 243 Treasure Harbor Rd., 33036* ☎ *305/852–5389 or 800/436–2023* ⊕ *www. ragged-edge.com* ⟱ *10 units* ⚒ *In-room: no phone, kitchen (some), refrigerator (some), no TV (some). In-hotel: pool, bicycles, no elevator* ⊟ *MC, V.*

NIGHTLIFE

Hog Heaven (⊠ *MM 85.3, OS* ☎ *305/664–9669*) is a lively sports bar with three satellite dishes that give way on weekends to a DJ or live bands if there's no sports event worth watching. Behind a larger-than-life mermaid is this Keys-easy, over-the-water cabana bar, the **Lorelei**

(⊠*MM 82, BS* ☎*305/664–4656*). This is the kind of place you fanta-size about during those long, cold winters up north. It's all about good drinks, tasty bar grub, and sherbet-hued sunsets set to music. Live bands (nightly) play reggae and light rock. **Zane Grey Long Key Lounge** (⊠*MM 81.5, BS* ☎*305/664–4244*), above the World Wide Sports-man, was created to honor Zane Grey, one of South Florida's greatest legends in fishing and writing and one of the most famous members of the Long Key Fishing Club. The lounge displays the author's photo-graphs, books, and memorabilia and has live blues, jazz, and Motown Thursday–Saturday and a wide veranda that invites sunset watching.

SPORTS & THE OUTDOORS

BOATING

Bump & Jump (⊠*MM 81.2, OS* ☎*305/664–9404 or 877/453–9463*) is a one-stop shop for windsurfing, sailboat, and powerboat rentals, sales, and lessons. This company understands what you need to make your vacation a blast. They deliver to your hotel, house, or beach. They also rent bicycles. Their motto: "We rent nice clean recent equipment, just like what we would like to use while on vacation." Wildlife in the Keys is most active at sunrise and sunset. See it all, from the comfort of your own boat (captain's cap optional) with **Houseboat Vacations of the Florida Keys** (⊠*MM 85.9, BS, 85944 Overseas Hwy.* ☎*305/664–4009* ⊕*www.thefloridakeys.com/houseboats*), which rents a fleet of 42- to 44-foot boats that accommodate six to eight people and come outfit-ted with safety equipment and necessities—except food. (You provision yourself at a nearby grocery store.) The three-day minimum starts at $1,112; one week costs $1,854. Kayaks, canoes, and 17- to 27-foot skiffs suitable for the ocean are also available. **Robbie's Boat Rentals & Charters** (⊠*MM 77.5, BS, 77520 Overseas Hwy.* ☎*305/664–9814 or 877/664–8498* ⊕*www.robbies.com*) does it all. They'll deliver your boat to your hotel, and give you a crash course in how not to crash it. The rental fleet includes an 18-foot Wagner with a 60-horsepower outboard for $135 for four hours and $185 for the day, an 18-foot skiff (same rates), and a 23-foot deck boat, yours for $185 for the half day and $235 for eight hours. They also rent fishing and snorkeling gear (there's good snorkeling nearby) and sell bait, drinks, snacks, and gas. Rather go out with a guide who knows local waters and where the fish lurk? Robbie's offers offshore sportfishing trips, patch reef trips, and party-boat fishing. Backcountry flats trips are a specialty. When you're in the Keys, do as the locals do: get out on the water, preferably for a few days. Captains Pam and Pete Anderson of **Treasure Harbor Marine** (⊠*MM 86.5, OS, 200 Treasure Harbor Dr.* ☎*305/852–2458 or 800/352–2628* ⊕*www.treasureharbor.com*) provide everything you'll need for a vacation at sea: linens, safety gear, and, best of all, advice on where to find the best anchorages, snorkeling spots, marinas, and lobstering sites, tailored to your interests. Rent a crewed sailboat or a bareboat; vessels range from a 19-foot Cape Dory to a 51-foot Mor-gan Out Island. Rates start at $110 a day, $450 a week ($95 and $400 respectively for the Cape Dory). Hire a captain for $150 a day. Marina facilities are basic—water, electric, ice machine, laundry, picnic tables, and shower-restrooms—and dockage is only $1.50 a foot. A ship's store sells snacks, beverages, and sundries.

FISHING

Long before fly-fishing became a trendy sport, Sandy Moret was fishing the Keys for bonefish, tarpon, and redfish. Now he operates **Florida Keys Outfitters** (✉ *MM 81.2, at the Green Turtle* ☎ *305/664-5423* ⊕ *www.floridakeysoutfitters.com*), with a store and the Florida Keys Fly Fishing School, which attracts anglers from around the world. Two-day weekend fly-fishing classes, which include classroom instruction, equipment, arrival cocktails, and daily breakfast and lunch, cost $985. Add another $1,070 for two days of fishing. Guided fishing trips cost $395 for a half day, $535 for a full day. Fishing and accommodations packages (at Cheeca Lodge) are available. The 65-foot party boat *Miss Islamorada* (✉ *Bud n' Mary's Marina, MM 79.8, OS* ☎ *305/664-2461*) has full-day trips ($60 includes everything). Bring your lunch or buy one from the dockside deli.

★ Captain Ken Knudsen of the *Hubba Hubba* (✉ *MM 79.8, OS* ☎ *305/664-9281*) quietly poles his flatboat through the shallow water, barely making a ripple. Then he points and his clients cast. Five seconds later there's a zing, and the excitement of bringing in a snook, redfish, trout, or tarpon begins. Knudsen has fished Keys waters since he was 12. That's more than 40 years. Now a licensed backcountry guide, he's ranked among the top 10 guides in Florida by national fishing magazines. He offers four-hour sunset trips for tarpon ($375) and two-hour sunset trips for bonefish ($200), as well as half- ($325) and full-day ($450) outings. Prices are for one or two anglers, and tackle and bait are included. Like other top fly-fishing and light-tackle guides, Captain Geoff Colmes of **Fishabout Charters** (✉ *105 Palm La.* ☎ *305/853-0741 or 800/741-5955* ⊕ *www.floridakeysflyfish.com*) helps his clients land double-figure fish in the waters around the Keys ($300–$425). But unlike the others, he also heads across Florida Bay to fish the coastal Everglades on three- and four-day trips (from $3,900 for two anglers) off his 65-foot mother ship, the *Fishabout*. It has four staterooms, private baths, living room, kitchen, satellite TV, phone, and separate crew quarters. It's especially ideal when cold, windy weather shuts out fishing around the Keys. Rates include captain, crew, guide fees, lodging, all meals, tackle, and use of canoes for getting deep into shallow Everglades inlets.

SCUBA & SNORKELING

Florida Keys Dive Center (✉ *MM 90.5, OS* ☎ *305/852-4599 or 800/433-8946* ⊕ *www.floridakeysdivectr.com*) organizes dives from John Pennekamp Coral Reef State Park to Alligator Light. The center has two Coast Guard–approved dive boats, offers scuba training, and is one of the few Keys dive centers to offer Nitrox (mixed gas) diving. With a resort, pool, restaurant, entertainment, store, lessons, and twice-daily dive and snorkel trips, **Holiday Isle Dive Shop** (✉ *MM 84, OS, 84001 Overseas Hwy.* ☎ *305/664-3483 or 800/327-7070* ⊕ *www.*

diveholidayisle.com) is a one-stop dive shop. Rates start at $60 for a two-tank dive.

TENNIS

Not all Keys recreation is on the water. Play tennis year-round at the **Islamorada Tennis Club** (⊠*MM 76.8, BS* ☎*305/664–5340* ⊕*www.islamoradatennisclub.com*). It's a well-run facility with four clay and two hard courts (all lighted), same-day racket stringing, ball machines, private lessons, a full-service pro shop, night games, and partner pairing. Rates are from $16 a day.

WATER SPORTS

Florida Keys Kayak (⊠*MM 77.5, BS, 77522 Overseas Hwy., in Robbie's Marina* ☎*305/664–4878*) rents kayaks within a 20- to 30-minute paddle of Indian and Lignumvitae keys, two favorite destinations for paddlers. They also offer guided two- and three-hour tours ($39 and $49 per person). Kayak rental rates are $20 per hour for a single, and $27.50 for a double. Half-day rates (and you'll need plenty of time to explore those mangrove canopies) are $40 for a single kayak and $55 for a double.

SHOPPING

At the **Banyan Tree** (⊠*MM 81.2, OS, 81197 Overseas Hwy.* ☎*305/664–3433*), a sharp-eyed husband-and-wife team successfully combines antiques and contemporary gifts for the home and garden with plants and pots in a stylishly sophisticated indoor–outdoor setting. At **Down to Earth** (⊠*MM 82.2, OS, 82205 Overseas Hwy.* ☎*305/664–9828*), indulge your passion for *objets* that are at once practical and fanciful, such as salad tongs carved from polished coconut shells or Indonesian furniture. Prices are reasonable, too. The go-to destination for a one-of-a-kind gift is **Gallery Morada** (⊠*MM 81.6, OS, 81611 Old Hwy.* ☎*305/664–3650*), where blown glass and glassware are beautifully displayed, as well as home furnishings, original paintings and lithographs, sculptures, and hand-painted scarves and earrings by top South Florida artists. Among the best buys in town are the used best sellers and hardbacks that sell for less than $5 after locals trade them in for store credit at **Hooked on Books** (⊠*MM 82.6, OS, 82681 Overseas Hwy.* ☎*305/517–2602*). There are also new titles, audio books, cards, and CDs. **Island Silver & Spice** (⊠*MM 82, OS* ☎*305/664–2714*) has everything you need to re-create that Keys-y cool vibe at home. Shop for women's and men's resort wear, tropical-style furnishings, rugs and home decor, cards, toys and games, and bath goods. They also stock a large jewelry selection with high-end Swiss watches and marine-theme pieces. Former U.S. presidents, celebrities, and record holders beam alongside their catches in black-and-white photos on the walls at **World Wide Sportsman** (⊠*MM 81.5, BS* ☎*305/664–4615*), a two-level attraction and retail center that sells upscale fishing equipment, art, resort clothing, and gifts. Think of it as a mini–L. L. Bean, except it isn't open 24/7 (doors close at 9 PM). There's a certain entertainment value in watching city-slicker guys dress up like Ernest Hemingway. Also on-site: a marina and the Zane Grey Long Key Lounge.

ART GALLERIES

The **Rain Barrel** (⊠*MM 86.7, BS* ☎*305/852–3084*) is a natural and unhurried shopping showplace. Set in a tropical garden of shady trees, native shrubs, and orchids, the 1977 crafts village has shops with works by local and national artists and eight resident artists in studios, including John Hawver, noted for Florida landscapes and seascapes. The **Garden Café** (☎*305/852–6499*) is a beautiful outdoor respite, and serves a primarily vegetarian menu of sandwiches and salads until 5 PM. The **Redbone Gallery** (⊠*MM 81.5, OS, 200 Industrial Dr.* ☎*305/664–2002*), the largest sporting-art gallery in Florida, stocks hand-stitched clothing and giftware, in addition to work by wood and bronze sculptors such as Kendall Van Sant; watercolorists Chet Reneson, Jeanne Dobie, and Kathleen Denis; and painters C. D. Clarke and Tim Borski.

LONG KEY

❹ *MM 70–65.5.*

Long Key isn't a tourist hot spot, which is what makes it attractive to travelers looking to avoid the masses and enjoy some cultural and ecological history in the process. Offering both is **Long Key State Park.** On the ocean side, the Golden Orb Trail leads onto a boardwalk through a mangrove swamp alongside a lagoon, where waterfowl congregate. The park has a campground, picnic area, restrooms and showers, a canoe trail through a tidal lagoon, and a broad expanse of shallow grass flats. Bring a mask and snorkel to observe the marine life in this rich nursery area. The water is very shallow, though. Repairs and replantings after four hurricanes have left the park with improved facilities, but with very little shade. Replanting efforts continue, as do hurricanes. Across the road, near a marker partially obscured by foliage, is the **Layton Nature Trail** (⊠*MM 67.7, BS*), which takes 20–30 minutes to walk and leads through tropical hardwood forest to a rocky Florida Bay shoreline overlooking shallow grass flats. A marker relates the history of the Long Key Viaduct, the first major bridge on the rail line, and the exclusive Long Key Fishing Camp, which Henry Flagler established nearby in 1906 and which attracted sportsman Zane Grey, the noted Western novelist and conservationist, who served as its first president. The camp was washed away in the 1935 hurricane and never rebuilt. For Grey's efforts, the creek running near the recreation area was named for him. Good news: the park is adding kayaks to its rental fleet, so visitors can explore the shoreline leading to Long Key Point. ⊠*MM 67.5, OS, Box 776, 33001* ☎*305/664–4815* ⊕*www. dep.state.fl.us/parks* ☜*$3.50 per person/$6 for 2, and 50¢ for each additional person in the group; canoe rental $5 per hr, $10 per day; Layton Nature Trail free* ☽*Daily 8–sunset.*

WHERE TO STAY & EAT

$–$$$ ✕**Little Italy.** It's your basic little Italian joint that looks like it's been around forever. The menu offers no real surprises—except maybe conch parmigiana—but that's the whole point. Lunch favorites include caesar salad, chicken marsala, stone crabs, and stuffed snapper for

$4.95 to $8.95. The dinner menu offers plenty of variety—including chicken, seafood, veal, and steak—but few can resist the pull of the pasta (maybe it's the garlicky aroma that permeates the place). The light-bites menu has smaller portions for kids and calorie watchers. Reward those light bites with a slice of decadent chocolate pecan pie. Little Italy is open for breakfast, too. ⊠*MM 68.5, BS* ☎*305/664–4472* ⊟*AE, MC, V.*

$–$$$ ⚏ **Lime Tree Bay Resort.** Easy on the eye and wallet, this popular 2½-acre Florida Bay stop is far from the hubbub of the larger islands. You can get a good workout on the water or simply break a sweat turning the pages of a good book while lolling on the beach or in a hammock in the pleasantly landscaped garden. Colorful bedding and coordinating valances, tropical art, and walls painted in complementary faux finishes create a sophisticated, upscale look. Five mini and family suites have become the best places to stay, followed by the cottages out back (no bay views) and four deluxe rooms upstairs that have cathedral ceilings and skylights. The best bet for two couples traveling together is the upstairs Tree House. Most units have a balcony or porch. Pros: great views, friendly staff, close to Long Key State Park. Cons: only one nearby restaurant (Little Italy). ⊠*MM 68.5, BS* ⬡*Box 839, Layton 33001* ☎*305/664–4740 or 800/723–4519* ⬛*305/664–0750* ⊕*www. limetreebayresort.com* ⬎*34 rooms* ⬙*In-room: kitchen (some), refrigerator, dial-up. In-hotel: tennis court, pool, beachfront, water sports, bicycles, no elevator, no-smoking rooms* ⊟*AE, D, DC, MC, V.*

⚠ **Long Key State Park.** Trees and shrubs border all of these oceanfront tent and RV sites. Maximum length for RVs is 32 feet. By day there are biking, hiking 10 mi of trail, boating, and fishing for bonefish, permit (bigger than bonefish), and tarpon in the near-shore flats. By night there are seasonal campfire programs. All sites have water and electricity, and campground hostesses are available to help out. Reserve up to 11 months in advance by phone or online—campsites on the Keys go quickly in winter. A two-night minimum stay is required on holidays and weekends. Arrive early; gates close at sunset. Sites cost $26. ⬙*Flush toilets, partial hookups (electric and water), dump station, drinking water, showers, picnic tables, electricity, public telephone, ranger station, swimming (ocean), some pets allowed* ⬎*60 partial hookups, 50 RV sites, 10 tent sites* ⊠*MM 67.5, OS, Box 776, 33001* ☎*305/664–4815 or 800/326–3521 (campsite reservations)* ⊕*www. reserveamerica.com* ⊟*AE, D, MC, V.*

▌
EN
ROUTE
As you cross Long Key Channel, look beside you at the old **Long Key Viaduct.** The second-longest bridge on the former rail line, this 2-mi-long structure has 222 reinforced-concrete arches. The old bridge is popular with anglers, who fish off the sides day and night.

THE MIDDLE KEYS

If you get bridge fever—the heebie-jeebies when driving over water—you may need a pair of blinders (or a tranquilizer) before tackling the Middle Keys. Stretching from Conch Key to the far side of the

Seven Mile Bridge, this zone contains U.S. 1's most impressive stretch, MM 65–40, and the Keys' two longest bridges—Long Key Viaduct and Seven Mile Bridge, both historic landmarks. Activity centers on the town of Marathon, the Keys' third-largest metropolitan area. Fishing and diving are the main attractions. The deepwater fishing is superb in both bay and ocean, at places like Marathon West Hump, whose depth ranges from 500 to more than 1,000 feet. Anglers successfully fish from a half-dozen bridges, including Long Key Bridge, the Old Seven Mile Bridge, and both ends of Toms Harbor. There are also many beaches and natural areas to enjoy in the Middle Keys.

CONCH & DUCK KEYS

⑤ *MM 63–61.*

This stretch of islands is rustic. Fishing dominates the economy, and many residents are descendants of immigrants from the mainland South. Across a causeway from the tiny fishing and retirement village of Conch Key is Duck Key, an upscale community and resort.

WHERE TO STAY

$$$$ 🏨**Hawk's Cay Resort.** A kids' club, kids' night out, and pirate ship with ★ water cannons make this sprawling resort a family favorite. Opened in ☾ 1959, it's a rambling Caribbean-style retreat, with two-bedroom villas and spacious rooms with wicker and earthy colors. Recreational facilities are extensive, as are supervised programs for kids and teens. The Dolphin Connection provides three educational experiences with dolphins, including the in-the-water Dolphin Discovery program, which lets you get up-close and personal with the intelligent mammals. The room rate does not include a $10 to $20 daily resort fee. Pros: huge rooms, discounted off-season packages. Cons: no real beach, a bit cut off from rest of keys, on-site restaurants aren't very good. ⊠*MM 61, OS, Duck Key* ☎*305/743–7000 or 888/443–6393* 🖷*305/743–5215* ⊕*www.hawkscay.com* ⇗*177 rooms, 16 suites, 295 2-bedroom villas* ⚘*In-room: kitchen (some), refrigerator, ethernet. In-hotel: 4 restaurants, room service, bars, tennis courts, pools, gym, spa, diving, water sports, children's programs (ages 5–12), laundry facilities, laundry service, concierge, public Wi-Fi, airport shuttle, no-smoking rooms* ⊟*AE, D, DC, MC, V.*

GRASSY KEY

⑥ *MM 60–57.*

Local lore has it that this sleepy little key was named not for its vegetation—mostly native trees and shrubs—but for an early settler with the name Grassy. It's primarily inhabited by a few families who operate small fishing camps and motels.

The original *Flipper* movie popularized the notion of dolphins interacting with humans. The film's creator, Milton Santini, also created this facility, the **Dolphin Research Center,** now home to a colony of dolphins

CLOSE UP

Close Encounters of the Flipper Kind

Here in the Florida Keys, where Milton Santini created the original 1963 *Flipper* movie, close encounters of the Flipper kind are an everyday occurrence at a handful of facilities that allow you to commune with trained dolphins. There are in-water and water-side programs. The former are the most sought-after and require advance reservations. All of the programs emphasize education and consist of three parts: first, you learn about dolphin physiology and behavior from a marine biologist or researcher; then you go water side for an orientation on dos and don'ts (for example, don't talk with your hands—you might, literally, send the wrong signal); finally, you interact with the dolphins—into the water you go.

For the in-water programs, the dolphins swim around you and cuddle up next to you. If you lie on your back with your feet out, they use their snouts to push you around; or grab onto a dorsal fin and hang on for an exciting ride. The in-water encounter lasts about 10 to 25 minutes, depending on the program. On water-side-interaction programs, participants feed, shake hands, kiss, and do tricks with the dolphins from a submerged platform. The programs vary from facility to facility and the entire program, from registration to departure, takes about two hours. The best time to go is when it's warm, from March through December. You spend a lot of time near or in and out of the water, and you can get cold on a chilly day.

Dolphin Connection at Hawk's Cay Resort. Marine biologists at the Dolphin Connection promote conservation through programs at this stylish mid-Keys resort. The resort offers three programs, including Dockside

Dolphins, a 30-minute encounter from the dry training docks ($50 resort guests, $60 nonguests); Dolphin Discovery, an in-water, nonswim program that lasts about 45 minutes and lets you kiss, touch, and feed the dolphins ($135, $150); and Trainer for a Day, a three-hour session with the animal training team ($275, $285). ⌧ MM 61, OS, 61 Hawks Cay Blvd., Duck Key ☎ 888/814–9154 ⊕ www.dolphinconnection.com.

Dolphin Cove. The educational part of the Dolphin Encounter program takes place on a 30-minute boat ride on adjoining Florida Bay. Then it's back to the facilities lagoon for a get-acquainted session from a platform. Finally, you slip into the water for the program's highlight: swimming and playing with your new dolphin pals. ⌧ MM 101.9, BS, 101900 Overseas Hwy., Key Largo ☎ 305/451–4060 ⊕ www.dolphinscove.com ⌨ $125–$300.

Dolphins Plus, Inc. Programs here emphasize education and therapy. Natural Swim begins with a one-hour briefing; then you enter the water to become totally immersed in the dolphins' world. ⌧ MM 99, 31 Corrine Pl., Key Largo ☎ 305/451–1993 or 866/860–7946 ⊕ www.dolphinsplus. com ⌨ $125.

Dolphin Research Center. This not-for-profit organization has a colony of bottlenose dolphins and California sea lions. Dolphin Encounter is a swim-interaction program, and in Dolphin Splash you stand on a submerged platform rather than swim. ⌧ MM 59, Marathon Shores ☎ 305/289–1121 or 305/289–0002 ⊕ www.dolphins.org ⌨ Dolphin Encounter $180, Dolphin Splash $130.

and sea lions. The not-for-profit organization has tours, narrated programs every 30 minutes, and several programs that allow interaction with dolphins in the water (Dolphin Encounter) or from a submerged platform (Dolphin Splash). You can even paint a T-shirt with a dolphin—you pick the paint, the dolphin "designs" your shirt ($55, plus T-shirt). The center recently added special-needs programs designed for people with an amputation and those with mental and emotional conditions such as autism. Some programs have age or height restrictions, and some require 30-day advance reservations. ⊠ *MM 59, BS* 🏠 *Box 522875, Marathon Shores 33052* 🕾 *305/289–1121 general information, 305/289–0002 interactive program information* ⊕ *www. dolphins.org* 🖃 *Tours $19.50, Dolphin Splash $130, Dolphin Encounter $180, Trainer for a Day $650* ⊙ *Daily 9–4:30; walking tours daily at 10, 11, 12:30, 2, 3:30, 4:30.*

OFF THE BEATEN PATH

Curry Hammock State Park. Looking for a slice of the Keys that's far removed from tiki bars and Jet-Skis? On the ocean and bay sides of U.S. 1, this littoral park covers 260 acres of upland hammock, wetlands, and mangroves. On the bay side, there's a trail through thick hardwoods to a rocky shoreline. The ocean side is more developed, with a sandy beach, a clean bathhouse, picnic tables, a playground, grills, and a 28-site campground (open November–May). A 1.5-mi walking path winds through a hardwood hammock. Locals consider the trails that meander under canopies of arching mangroves one of the best areas for kayaking in the Keys. Manatees frequent the area, and it's a great spot for bird-watching. Herons, egrets, ibis, plovers, and sanderlings are commonly seen. Raptors are often seen in the park, too, especially during migration periods. ⊠ *MM 57, OS, Crawl Key* 🕾 *305/289–2690. For campground reservations, call 800/326–3521* ⊕ *www.reserveamerica.com* 🖃 *$3.50 for single visitor, $6 for 2, plus 50¢ per passenger* ⊙ *Daily 8–sunset.*

WHERE TO STAY & EAT

$$–$$$$ ✕**Hideaway Café.** The name captures the location—it's tucked between Grassy Key and Marathon, easily missed if you're barnstorming through the middle islands. When you find it (just look on the ocean side before crossing to Marathon), you'll find a favorite of locals who appreciate a great menu, scenic ocean view, and quiet evening away from the crowds. For starters, dig into escargots à la Edison (sautéed with vegetables, garlic, pepper, cognac, and cream). Then feast on several specialties, such as a rarely-found-in-the-Keys charbroiled veal chop, cooked to order; a belly-busting whole roasted duck; or the seafood special, which combines the catch of the day with scallops and shrimp in a savory scampi sauce. ⊠ *MM 58, OS, Grassy Key* 🕾 *305/289–1554* ⊕ *www.hideawaycafe.com* 🖃 *AE, D, DC, MC, V.*

$$–$$$ 🛌 **Gulf View Waterfront Resort.** You may be greeted with "Hey, baby! I love you!" at the easygoing Gulf View, but it's not a randy proprietor who's being so forward, it's Coco, a white cockatiel. With a flock of 15 birds on property, this homey duplex is part resort, part aviary. Owner-occupied, the Gulf View took a big hit from Hurricane Wilma and has been remodeled in bright but simple fashion with wicker furniture, tropical pastels, white tiles, and ceiling fans. The only jarring design note is the the green-painted concrete ledge that supports the elevated swimming pool. Guests—mostly couples during the winter and families during spring break and holidays—appreciate the close proximity to the Dolphin Research Center, practically next door (the resort offers discount passes). Canoes, paddleboats, and kayaks are also available for guests for free. Pros: friendly owners, parklike area leads to dock and bay, restaurant and Dolphin Research Center nearby. Cons: ground-level units are somewhat musty and dark, some traffic noise. ⊠*MM 58.5, BS, 58743 Overseas Hwy., 33050* ☎*305/289–1414* 🖷*305/743–8629* ⊕*www.gulfviewwaterfrontresort.com* ⇆*2 rooms, 6 suites, 3 efficiencies* ⚒*In-room: kitchen (some), refrigerator, Wi-Fi. In-hotel: pool, no elevator, laundry facilities, parking, some pets allowed (fee), no-smoking rooms* ▤*AE, D, MC, V.*

¢–$$$ 🏨**Bonefish Resort.** Set on a skinny lot bedecked with palms, banana leaves, and hibiscus plantings, this motel-style hideaway is the best choice in a 'hood of small, back-to-basics properties. It's not fancy, but it's clean, cheap, and a good base for paddling a kayak, wading for bonefish, and watching the waves roll in from a lounge chair. Rooms, efficiencies, and suites are decorated with floral linens, wicker, tile floors, and tropical motifs painted by a local artist on entrance doors and some interior walls. A narrow gravel courtyard lined with umbrellaed tables leads to a small beach and a waterfront pool. The communal deck, with hammocks and chaises, invites relaxation, and kayaks and paddleboats encourage exploration. Check-in is at next-door sister property Yellowtail Inn, which has cottages and efficiencies starting at $119 in winter. Pros: good price point for oceanside digs. Cons: decks off rooms are small and dark, guests have to pay to rent boats and bicycles. ⊠*MM 58, OS, 58070 Overseas Hwy., 33050* ☎*305/743–7107 or 800/274–9949* 🖷*305/743–9014* ⊕*www.bonefishresort.com* ⇆*2 rooms, 5 suites, 6 efficiencies* ⚒*In-room: kitchen (some), refrigerator, VCR. In-hotel: beachfront, bicycles, no elevator, laundry facilities, some pets allowed (fee)* ▤*D, MC, V.*

MARATHON

❼ *MM 53–47.5.*

This municipality began as a commercial fishing village in the early 1800s, then served as a base for pirates, salvagers (aka "wreckers"), spongers, and, later, farmers who eked out a living, traveling by boat between islands. According to local lore, Marathon was renamed when a worker commented that it was a marathon task to rebuild the railway across the 6-mi island after a 1906 hurricane. The railroad brought businesses and a hotel, and today Marathon is a bustling town by Keys standards. Basically, that means it has a Publix Supermarket, a Kmart, and a Home Depot along its commercial strip. It shouldn't be your first choice of places to stay in the Keys (it leaves something to be desired in the charm department), but there are a surprising number of good places to eat, so you'll definitely want to stop for a bite, even if you're just passing through en route to Key West. Fishing, diving, and boating are the main attractions.

Tucked away from the highway behind a stand of trees, Crane Point—part of a 63-acre tract that includes the last-known undisturbed thatch-palm hammock—is delightfully undeveloped greenery. It's the site of the **Museums and Nature Center of Crane Point Hammock,** which includes the **Museum of Natural History of the Florida Keys,** with a few dioramas, a shell exhibit, and displays on Keys geology, wildlife, and cultural history. Also here is the **Children's Activity Center,** with a replica of a 17th-century galleon and pirate dress-up room where children can play swashbuckler. Outside, on the 1-mi indigenous loop trail, visit the remnants of a Bahamian village, site of the restored **George Adderly House,** the oldest surviving example of Bahamian tabby (a concrete-type material created from sand and seashells) construction outside of Key West. A newly constructed Cracker house demonstrates the vernacular housing of the early 1900s. A boardwalk crosses wetlands, a river, and mangroves before ending at Adderly Village. From November to Easter, docent-led tours, included in the price, are available; bring good walking shoes and bug repellent during warm weather. Events include a Bahamian Heritage Festival in January, an Earth Day event, a Native American Cultural Festival, family stargazing nights, and more. ⊠ *MM 50.5, BS, 5550 Overseas Hwy., Box 536, 33050* ☎ *305/743–9100* ⊕ *www.cranepoint.org* ⊠ *$7.50* ☉ *Mon.–Sat. 9–5, Sun. noon–5; call to arrange trail tours.*

NEED A
BREAK?

If you don't get a buzz from breathing in the robust aroma at **Leigh Ann's (More Than Just A) Coffee House** (⊠ *7537 Overseas Hwy.* ☎ *305/743–2001*), order an espresso shot, Cuban or Italian, for a satisfying jolt. Pastries are baked fresh daily, but the biscuits with sausage gravy and the Italian frittata cooked with no fat are among the big movers. Business is so good, Leigh Ann's is now open for dinner. (Try the risotto, followed by the ultimate seven-layer brownie.) Soups, salads, and sandwiches, as well as beer and wine, make up the rest of the menu, served until 9 PM in season. They accept major credit cards and are closed on Sunday.

Pleasant, shaded picnic kiosks overlook a grassy stretch and the Atlantic Ocean at **Sombrero Beach.** Separate areas allow swimmers, jet boaters, and windsurfers to share the beach. Facilities include a grassy park with barbecue grills, picnic kiosks, showers, and restrooms, plus a baseball diamond, a large playground, and a volleyball court. Sunday afternoons draw lots of local families toting picnic baskets and burgers for the grill. The park is accessible for travelers with disabilities and allows leashed pets. Turn left at the traffic light in Marathon and follow signs to the end. ⊠ *MM 50, OS, Sombrero Rd.* ☎ *305/743–0033* ⊠ *Free* ☉ *Daily 8–sunset.*

OFF THE
BEATEN
PATH

Pigeon Key. There's much to like about this 5-acre island under the Old Seven Mile Bridge. It's reached by walking or riding a shuttle across a 2¼-mi section of the old bridge. Once there, tour the island on your own with a brochure or join a guided tour (hourly until 2 PM). The tour explores the buildings that formed the early-20th-century work camp for the Overseas Railroad, which linked the mainland to Key West. Later, their uses changed as the island became a fish camp, then a park, and then government administration headquarters. Today, the focus is on Florida Keys culture, environmental education, and marine research. Exhibits in a museum and a video recall the history of the railroad, the Keys, and railroad baron Henry M. Flagler. Pick up the shuttle at the gift shop on Knight's Key (MM 47, OS). ⊠ *MM 45, OS, Box 500130, Pigeon Key 33050* ☎ *305/289–0025 general information, 305/743–5999 tickets* ⊇ *$8.50* ☉ *Daily 10–5, tours hourly 10–2.*

WHERE TO STAY & EAT

$$-$$$$
Fodor'sChoice
★
✕ **Barracuda Grill.** It's not much to look at, but when it comes to the kitchen, the Barracuda Grill delivers. The sophisticated, eclectic menu capitalizes on local seafood (take a test drive with the Mangrove snapper and mango) but is equally represented by tender, aged Angus beef, rack of lamb, and braised pork shank. Innovation is in everything but not at the expense of good, solid cooking. Local favorites include Francesca's voodoo stew, with scallops, shrimp, and vegetables in a spicy tomato-saffron stock, and sashimi of yellowfin tuna with wasabi and tamari. For dessert, slices of oh-so-rich key lime cheesecake fly out of the kitchen. The well-thought-out wine list is heavily Californian. ⊠ *MM 49.5, BS, 4290 Overseas Hwy.* ☎ *305/743–3314* ⊘ *Reservations not accepted* ☐ *AE, MC, V* ☉ *Closed Sun. No lunch.*

$$-$$$
✕ **Keys Fisheries Market and Marina.** From the parking lot the commercial warehouse with fishing boats docked alongside barely hints at the restaurant inside. Order at the window outside, pick up your food in the market, then dine at waterfront picnic tables, some under a plastic canopy. Fresh seafood and a token hamburger are the only things on the menu. A lobster Reuben ($13.95) served on thick slices of toasted bread is the signature dish. There's also a 16-flavor ice-cream bar and a beer-wine bar. ⊠ *MM 49, BS, end of 35th St.* ☎ *305/743–4353 or 866/743–4353* ⊕ *www.keysfisheries.com* ☐ *MC, V.*

¢–$$$
✕ **Key Colony Inn.** The inviting aroma of an Italian kitchen pervades this popular family-owned restaurant. The menu has well-prepared chicken, steak, pasta, and veal dishes, and the service is friendly and attentive. For lunch there are fish and steak entrées served with fries, salad, and bread. At dinner you can't miss with traditional continental dishes like veal Oscar and New York strip, or such specialties as seafood Italiano, a light dish of scallops and shrimp sautéed in garlic butter, served over a bed of linguine with a hint of marinara sauce. The Inn is known locally for its broad menu, and as Marathon's best value. ⊠ *MM 54, OS, 700 W. Ocean Dr., Key Colony Beach* ☎ *305/743–0100* ☐ *AE, MC, V.*

★ ¢–$$
✕ **7 Mile Grill.** With its whirling ceiling fans, this 50-plus-year-old open-air restaurant easily could serve as a movie set for a 1950s-era film noir based in the tropics. The crowd is a mix of visitors who can't resist a place that looks like this and fisher-folk from the marina next door. At the Marathon end of the Seven Mile Bridge, this restaurant's menu won't wow you, but you can count on friendly servers delivering casual food at breakfast, lunch, and dinner. Standards on the mostly seafood menu include creamy shrimp bisque, stuffed crabs, beer-steamed

shrimp, and mahimahi—grilled, blackened, or fried. Don't pass up the authentic key lime pie, which won the local paper's "Best in the Keys" award three years in a row. ⊠*MM 47, BS* ☎*305/743–4481* ▤*MC, V* ⊘*Closed Wed.; closed Thurs. mid-Apr.–mid-Nov. and at owner's discretion Aug. and Sept.*

¢–$ ✕**Fish Tales Market and Eatery.** Fans of the Island City Fishmarket won't be too disappointed about its sale once they learn that the new owners are George, Jackie, Johnny, and Gary Eigner of the former Grassy Key DB Seafood Grille (which has closed). They serve some of the DB's favorite dishes, such as oysters on a roll and snapper on grilled rye with slaw and melted cheese. You also can slurp lobster bisque or red conch chowder. Plan to dine early, as it's open only until 6:30 Monday through Thursday and 8:30 Friday and Saturday. ⊠*MM 53, OS, 11711 Overseas Hwy.* ☎*305/743–9196 or 888/662–4822* ⊕*www. floridalobster.com* ▤*AE, MC, V* ⊘*Closed Sun.*

¢–$ ✕**The Stuffed Pig.** With only eight tables and a counter, this breakfast-and-lunch place is always hopping. The kitchen whips up daily specials like meat loaf–and–mashed and pulled pork (with hand-cut fries) for lunch, but a quick glance around the room reveals that the all-day breakfast is the main draw. You can get the usual breakfast plates, but why not spring for something different, say the lobster omelet, gator tail, or "grits and grunts" (that's fish, to the rest of us). Greet Porky and Petunia Pig on your way out to the shady backyard patio, the best place to eat on a nice day. ⊠*MM 49, BS, 3520 Overseas Hwy.* ☎*305/743–4059* ▤*D, DC, MC, V.*

$$$$ ☷**Tranquility Bay.** It's Pottery Barn–meets–Ralph Lauren at this recently opened luxury beach house resort. The 87 two- and three-bedroom town houses have little lawns, white picket fences, and open-floor-plan interiors decorated in trendy seaside cottage style. The picture-perfect theme continues with the palm-fringed pool to a sandy beach, edged with a ribbon of blue bay (and echoed in the blue-and-white stripes of the poolside umbrellas). Guests look like models on a photo shoot: attractive young families enjoying the zero-edge pool, the large beach, the gourmet kitchens, the oversize decks, and the outdoor casual dining. ▮**TIP**→ **Check their Web site for sharply discounted rates, even in high season.** Pros: set back from the road, lovely crescent beach. Cons: could be anywhere in Florida, a bit sterile and too-new. ⊠*MM 48.5, BS, 2600 Overseas Hwy., 33050* ☎*305/289–0888 or 866/643–5397* ☷*305/289–0667* ⊕*www.tranquilitybay.com* ⇝*87 rooms* ⚘*In-room: kitchen, refrigerator, DVD, Wi-Fi. In-hotel: tennis court, pool, gym, beachfront, water sports, children's programs, concierge, no-smoking rooms* ▤*AE, D, MC, V.*

$$$ ☷**Crystal Bay Resort & Marina.** This resort is what it is: a retro motel with rooms, efficiencies, and suites, a kitschy minigolf course, shuffleboard, and a self-serve BYO tiki bar. Room 20 offers the best digs, with a bay view that goes on forever. We're told the Wright Brothers stayed in Unit 29—and who's to argue? The fish stories come fast and furious here. Folks bring their boats down and stay two or three weeks at a time; one guy seemingly came and never left. If all this sounds eccentrically charming to you, you'll have a grand old time here; if it just

7

sounds weird, stay away. Pros: all rooms have refrigerators and microwave ovens, friendly staff, very casual. Cons: some rooms are musty smelling and need updating, $20 charge for extra guests, including kids. ⊠*MM 49, BS, 4900 Overseas Hwy., 33050* ☎*305/289–8089 or 888/289–8089* ⊕*www.crystalbayresort.com* ⇆*29 rooms* ⬙*In-room: kitchen, refrigerator. In-hotel: tennis courts, beachfront, water sports, no elevator, laundry facilities* ▤*AE, MC, V.*

SPORTS & THE OUTDOORS

BIKING

Tooling around on two wheels is a good way to see Marathon. There are paved paths along Aviation Boulevard on the bay side of Marathon Airport, the four-lane section of the Overseas Highway through Marathon, Sadowski Causeway to Key Colony Beach, Sombrero Beach Road to the beach, and the roads on Boot Key (across a bridge on 20th Street, OS). There's easy cycling on a 1-mi off-road path that connects to the 2 mi of the Old Seven Mile Bridge that leads to Pigeon Key.

"Have bikes, will deliver" could be the motto of **Bike Marathon Bike Rentals** (☎*305/743–3204*), which gets beach cruisers to your hotel door for $45 per week, including a helmet. It's open Monday through Saturday 9 to 4 and Sunday 9 to 2. **Overseas Outfitters** (⊠*MM 48, BS* ☎*305/289–1670*) rents aluminum cruisers and hybrid bikes for $10 per day, $50 per week. They also rent tandem bikes and kids' bikes, and offer a retail shop with sports clothes, gear, skateboards, and the like. Open weekdays 9 to 6, Saturday 9 to 5, and Sunday 10 to 3.

BOATING

Captain Pip's (⊠*MM 47.5, OS* ☎*305/743–4403 or 800/707–1692* ⊕*www.captainpips.com*) rents 19- to 24-foot outboards, $145 to $330 per day, as well as tackle and snorkeling gear. You also can charter a small boat with a guide, $620 to $685 per half day and $875 to $925 for a full day's excursion. **Fish 'n' Fun** (⊠*MM 53.5, OS* ☎*305/743–2275 or 800/471–3440* ⊕*www.fishnfunrentals.com*), next to the Boat House Marina, lets you get out on the water on 18- to 25-foot powerboats starting at $115 for a half day, $160 to $250 for a full day. You also can pick up bait, tackle, licenses, and snorkel gear. For those who want a live-aboard vacation, **Florida Keys Bareboat Charters** (☎*305/743–0090* ⊕*www.floridakeysbareboatchartercompany.com*) rents 27-foot Catalina and Balboa sailboats for $200 a day, $950 a week, with a two-day minimum. The fee includes home-port dockage.

FISHING

Morning and afternoon, fish for mahimahi, grouper, and other tasty catch aboard the 75-foot *Marathon Lady* (⊠*MM 53, OS, at 117th St.* ☎*305/743–5580* ⊕*www.marathonlady.com*) that departs on half-day ($40, plus $5 for equipment) excursions from the Vaca Cut Bridge, north of Marathon. Join them for night fishing ($40, plus $5) from 6:30 to midnight from Memorial Day to Labor Day; it's especially beautiful on a full-moon night. Captain Jim Purcell, a deep-sea specialist for ESPN's *The American Outdoorsman,* provides one of the best values in fishing in the Keys. His

★ **Sea Dog Charters** (⌧*MM 47.5, BS* ☎*305/743–8255* ⊕*www. seadogcharters.net*), next to the 7 Mile Grill, has half- and full-day offshore, reef and wreck, tarpon, and backcountry fishing trips as well as combination fishing and snorkeling trips on the 32-foot *Bad Dog* for up to six people. The cost is $59.99 per person for a half day, regardless of whether your group fills the boat, and includes bait, light tackle, licensing, ice, and coolers. If you prefer an all-day private charter on a 37-foot boat, he offers those, too, for $850 for up to six people. A fuel surcharge may apply.

GOLF **Key Colony Golf & Tennis** (⌧*MM 53.5, OS, 8th St., Key Colony Beach* ☎*305/289–1533*), a 9-hole par-3 course near Marathon, charges $9 for the course ($7 for each additional 9 holes), $2 per person for club rental, and $1 for a pull cart. There are no tee times and there's no rush. Play from 7:30 to dusk. A little golf shop meets basic golf needs. Two lighted tennis courts are open from 7:30 to 10. Hourly rates are $4 for singles, $6 for doubles.

SCUBA & SNORKELING

Hall's Diving Center and Career Institute (⌧*MM 48.5, BS, 1994 Overseas Hwy., 33050* ☎*305/743–5929 or 800/331–4255* ⊕*www.hallsdiving. com*) has been diving and training divers for more than 40 years. Along with conventional twice-a-day snorkel and two-tank dive trips ($45–$55) to the reefs at Sombrero Lighthouse and wrecks, including *Thunderbolt,* the company also offers wet submarine dives, diver propulsion vehicles, rebreathers, and digital and video photography.

EN ROUTE

The **Seven Mile Bridge** is one of the most-photographed images in the Keys. Actually measuring 6.79 mi long, it connects the Middle and Lower Keys and is believed to be the world's longest segmental bridge. It has 39 expansion joints separating its concrete sections. Each April, runners gather in Marathon for the annual Seven Mile Bridge Run. The expanse running parallel to it is what remains of the **Old Seven Mile Bridge,** an engineering marvel in its day that's now on the National Register of Historic Places. It rested on a record 546 concrete piers. No cars are allowed on the old bridge today, but a 2-1/5-mi segment is open for biking, walking, and rollerblading, with a terminus at historic Pigeon Key.

THE LOWER KEYS

In truth, the Lower Keys include Key West, but since it's covered in its own section and is as different from the rest of the Lower Keys as peanut butter is from jelly, this section covers just the limestone keys between MM 37 and MM 9. From Bahia Honda Key south, islands are clustered, smaller, and more numerous, a result of ancient tidal waters' flowing between the Florida Straits and the gulf. Here you're likely to see more birds and mangroves than other tourists, and more refuges, beaches, and campgrounds than museums, restaurants, and hotels. The islands are made up of two types of limestone, both denser than the highly permeable Key Largo limestone of the Upper Keys. As a result, fresh water forms pools rather than percolating, creating watering holes that support Key deer, alligators, fish, snakes, Lower Keys rabbits, raccoons, migratory ducks, Key cotton and silver rice rats, pines, saw palmettos, silver palms, grasses, and ferns. (Many of these animals and plants can be seen in the National Key Deer Refuge on Big Pine Key.) Nature was generous with her beauty in the Lower Keys, which have both Looe Key Reef, arguably the Keys' most beautiful coral reef tract, and Bahia Honda State Park, considered one of the best beaches in the world for its fine sand dunes, clear warm waters, and panoramic vista of bridges, hammocks, and azure sky and sea.

BAHIA HONDA KEY

8 *MM 38–36.*

Most first-time visitors to the Keys are dismayed by the lack of beaches. But then, they discover Bahia Honda, and all is forgiven! Sun-soaked, 524-acre **Bahia Honda State Park** sprawls across both sides of the highway, giving it 2½ mi of fabulous white sandy coastline—three beaches in all—on both the Atlantic Ocean and the Gulf of Mexico. It's regularly declared the best beach in Florida, and you'll be hard pressed to argue: the sand is baby-powder soft, and the aqua water is warm, clear, and shallow, with mild currents. It's great for swimming, even with small fry. The snorkeling isn't bad, either; there's underwater life to see (soft coral, queen conchs, random little fish) just a few hundred feet offshore. Although swimming, kayaking, fishing, and boating are the main reasons to come, you shouldn't miss a walk along the Silver Palm Trail, with rare West Indian plants and several species found nowhere else in the Keys. Seasonal ranger-led nature programs might include illustrated talks on the history of the Overseas Railroad. There are 3½ mi of flat park roads for biking, rental cabins, a campground, a snack bar, gift shop, 19-slip marina, and a concessionaire for snorkeling. Get a panoramic view of the island from what's left of the railroad—the Bahia Honda Bridge. ✉*MM 37, OS, 36850 Overseas Hwy., 33043* ☎*305/872–2353* ⊕*www.floridastateparks.com* ✇*$3.50 for 1 person, $6 per vehicle for 2 people, plus 50¢ per additional person; $1.50 per pedestrian or bicyclist* ⊙*Daily 8–sunset.*

WHERE TO STAY

¢–$$ 🏕**Bahia Honda State Park.** Elsewhere, you'd have to pay big bucks for the outrageously wonderful water views available at the state park's duplex cabins, set directly on Florida Bay. Each cabin-on-stilts is completely furnished, with air-conditioning (although there's no television, radio, or phone); has two bedrooms, full kitchen, and bath; and sleeps six ($136.30, including tax). The park also has popular campsites ($31.49 per night), suitable for motor homes and tents. Some campsites are directly on the beach—talk about a room with a view! Cabins and campsites usually book up early, so reserve up to 11 months before your planned visit. Pros: great bayfront views in cabins, beachfront camping, affordable. Cons: must book in advance (although you can sometimes luck into a walk-in campsite during the week in season), can be buggy. ⊠*MM 37, OS, 36850 Overseas Hwy., 33043* ☎*305/872–2353 or 800/326–3521* ⊕*www.reserveamerica.com* ⫷*80 campsites, 48 RV sites, 32 tent sites; 3 duplex cabins* ⴄ*In-room: no phone, kitchen, no TV. In-hotel: beachfront, water sports, bicycles, no elevator* ⊟*AE, D, MC, V.*

THE OUTDOORS

Bahia Honda Dive Shop (⊠*MM 37, OS* ☎*305/872–3210* ⊕*www. bahiahondapark.com*), the concessionaire at Bahia Honda State Park, manages a 19-slip marina; rents wet suits, snorkel equipment, and corrective masks; and operates twice-a-day offshore-reef snorkel trips ($28.95 plus $6 for equipment) off-season and thrice a day in-season that run almost three hours (with 90 minutes on the reef). Park visitors looking for other fun can rent kayaks ($10 per hour single, $18 double) and beach chairs.

BIG PINE KEY

❾ *MM 32–30.*

In the Florida Keys, more than 20 animals and plants are endangered or threatened. Among them is the Key deer, which stands about 30 inches at the shoulders and is a subspecies of the Virginia white-tailed deer. The 8,542-acre **National Key Deer Refuge** was established in 1957 to protect the dwindling population. These deer once ranged throughout the Lower and Middle Keys, but hunting, habitat destruction, and a growing human population caused their numbers to decline to 27 by 1957. Under the refuge's aegis the deer have made a comeback, increasing their numbers to around 800. The best place to see Key deer in the refuge is at the end of Key Deer Boulevard (Route 940), off U.S. 1, and on No Name Key, a sparsely populated island just east of Big Pine Key. Deer may turn up along the road at any time of day, so drive slowly. Feeding them is against the law and puts them in danger. The refuge also has 22 listed endangered and threatened species of plants and animals, including five that are found nowhere else. The **Blue Hole**, a quarry left over from railroad days, is the largest body of fresh water in the Keys. From the observation platform and nearby walking trail, you might see alligators, birds, turtles, Key deer, and other wildlife. There are two well-marked trails: the Jack Watson Nature Trail (2/3 mi), named after an environmentalist and the refuge's first warden; and the Fred Mannillo Nature Trail, one of the most wheelchair-accessible places to see an unspoiled pine rockland forest. The visitor center has exhibits on Keys biology and ecology. The refuge also provides information on the Key West National Wildlife Refuge and the Great White Heron National Wildlife Refuge. Both, accessible only by water, are popular with kayak outfitters. ⊠*Visitor Center–Headquarters, Big Pine Shopping Center, 28950 Watson Blvd., MM 30.5, BS* ☎*305/872–2239 or 305/872–0774* ⊕*www.fws.gov/nationalkeydeer* ⛁*Free* ☉*Daily sunrise–sunset; headquarters weekdays 8–5.*

WHERE TO STAY & EAT

¢–$$ ✗**No Name Pub.** This no-frills, clapboard, Keys-style honky-tonk has been around since 1936, delighting locals and bold vacationers who come for cold beer, excellent pizza, and … interesting companionship. The decor, such as it is, amounts to the autographed dollar bills that cover every inch of the place. The owners have conceded to the times by introducing a full menu, adding "city food" like a half-pound fried grouper sandwich, spaghetti and meatballs, seafood baskets ($11.50), and chicken wings. The lighting is poor, the furnishings are rough, and the jukebox doesn't play hip-hop. It's hard to find this former brothel–bait shop but worth the search if you want a singular Keys experience. ⊠*MM 30, BS, N. Watson Blvd.* ⊕ *turn north at Big Pine Key traffic light, right at the fork, left at the 4-way stop, and go over a humpback bridge; pub is on left, before the No Name Bridge* ☎*305/872–9115* ⊕*www.nonamepub.com* ⊟*D, MC, V.*

¢ ✗**Good Food Conspiracy.** Like good wine, this small natural-foods eatery and market surrenders its pleasures a little at a time. Step inside to the aroma of brewing coffee, and then pick up the scent of fresh strawberries or carrots blending into a smoothie, followed by an earthy hummus redolence. Order raw or cooked vegetarian and vegan dishes, organic soups, salads, sandwiches, and desserts, along with organic and vegan coffees, smoothies, juices, and teas. Bountiful sandwiches like the popular organic turkey on whole-wheat pita or chapati are served with vegetables, sprouts, and mixed greens. If you can't sit down for a bite, stock up on healthful snacks-to-go, like dried fruits, raw nuts, and carob-covered almonds. Dine early: the shop closes at 7, and at 5 on Sunday. You also can call in your order in advance. ⊠*MM 30.2, OS* ☎*305/872–3945.*

$$$–$$$$ 🏨**Deer Run Bed & Breakfast.** Key deer wander the grounds of this beachfront B&B, set on a quiet, dead-end street lined with buttonwoods and mangroves. The "natural beauty" angle is already covered here; now, new innkeepers Jen and Harry are working to elevate the level of lodgings. Two large oceanfront rooms are decorated in soothing earth tones and furnished with mahogany rattan and pecan-wood furnishings. The beach-level unit is decorated in key lime and flamingo pink, with wicker furnishings, and the garden-view room is an eclectic mix that includes Victorian farmhouse doors serving as the headboard of the queen-size bed. Guests share a living room and a veranda. The animal-friendly atmosphere extends to the kitchen, with a mostly organic breakfast menu suitable for vegans. Fresh baked goods and a hot item (perhaps flax pancakes with organic fruit or veggie scramble with soy sausage) come out of the kitchen with Fair Trade coffee and tea. Guest rooms are stocked with organic cotton towels and cruelty-free toiletries. The Key deer, we think, would approve, as do we. Pros: quiet location, emphasis on fresh, healthful ingredients on breakfast menu, enthusiastic new owners. Cons: the exterior of the house is cluttered and lacks eye appeal, price is high for a B&B with shared common areas. ⊠*MM 33, OS, 1997 Long Beach Dr., 33043* ☎*305/872–2015* ⊕*www.deerrunfloridabb.com* ➥*4 rooms* ⌂*In-room: refrigerator,*

Wi-Fi. In-hotel: beachfront, water sports, bicycles, no elevator, no kids under 18, no-smoking rooms ⊟*D, MC, V.*

★ ¢–$$ ⊡**Big Pine Key Fishing Lodge.** There's a genial, sporty vibe at this lively family-owned lodge-campground-marina. It's a happy mix of tent campers (who have the choicest waterfront real estate on the property), RVers who look pretty permanent (the lawn gnomes are a clue), and motel-dwellers who like to mingle at the roof-pool and maybe play a little poker later. Rooms have tile floors, wicker furniture, doors that allow sea breezes to blow through, queen-size beds, a second-bedroom loft, and vaulted ceilings. A skywalk joins them with a pool and deck. Camping sites range from rustic to full hookups. Everything is clean—even the campers' bathhouse—and service is good-natured but efficient. They'll book you a room, sell you bait, hook you up with a fishing charter—and even let you try on a T-shirt to show you how it fits, if you ask nicely. Separate game and recreation rooms have TVs, organized family-oriented activities, and other amusements, and there's dockage along a 735-foot canal. Advance reservations require a three-day minimum. Discounts are available for weeklong or longer stays. Pros: local fishing crowd, nice roof-deck pool, great price point. Cons: the RV park is really close to motel units, Key deer will eat your food (unless you take precautions) if you're camping. ⊠*MM 33, OS, Box 430513, 33043* ☏*305/872–2351* 📠*305/872–3868* ⤳*16 rooms; 158 campsites, 101 with full hookups, 57 without hookups* ⟐*In-room: kitchen (some), refrigerator (some). In-hotel: pool, dial-up, no elevator* ⊟*MC, V.*

THE OUTDOORS

BIKING

A good 10 mi of paved and unpaved roads run from MM 30.3, BS, along Wilder Road, across the bridge to No Name Key, and along Key Deer Boulevard into the National Key Deer Refuge, where you might see some Key deer. Stay off the trails that lead into wetlands, where fat tires can do damage to the environment.

Marty Baird, owner of **Big Pine Bicycle Center** (⊠*MM 30.9, BS* ☏*305/872–0130*), is an avid rider and enjoys sharing his knowledge of great places to ride. He's also skilled at selecting the right bike for customers to rent or purchase, and he knows his repairs, too. His old-fashioned single-speed, fat-tire cruisers for adults rent for $7 per half day, $9 for a full day (overnight), and $38 a week, second week $20 more. Helmets, baskets, and locks are included. Although the shop is closed on Sunday, join Marty there most Sunday mornings at 8 in winter for a free off-road fun ride.

FISHING

Fish with pros year-round in air-conditioned comfort with **Strike Zone Charters** (⊠*MM 29.6, BS, 29675 Overseas Hwy.* ☏*305/872–9863 or 800/654–9560*). Deep-sea charter rates are $550 for a half day, $695 for a full day. It also offers flats fishing in the Gulf of Mexico.

SCUBA & SNORKELING

Strike Zone Charters (✉ *MM 29.6, BS, 29675 Overseas Hwy.* ☎ *305/872–9863 or 800/654–9560*) leads dive excursions to the wreck of the 210-foot *Adolphus Busch* ($50), and scuba ($40) and snorkel ($30) trips to Looe Key Reef. Strike Zone also offers a five-hour island excursion that combines snorkeling, fishing, history, and an island cookout for $49 per person. A large, new dive shop is on-site.

WATER SPORTS

Big Pine Kayak Adventures (✉ *Old Wooden Bridge Fishing Camp, MM 30, BS, turn right at traffic light, continue on Wilder Rd. toward No Name Key* ☎ *305/872–7474* ⊕ *www.keyskayaktours.com*) has a complete rental fleet and makes it very convenient to rent kayaks. Along with bringing kayaks to your lodging or put-in point anywhere between Seven Mile Bridge and Stock Island, the group, headed by Captain Bill Keogh, author of *The Florida Keys Paddling Guide,* will rent you a kayak and then ferry you—called taxi-yaking—to remote islands with explicit instructions on how to paddle back on your own. Rentals are by the half day or full day. Group kayak tours ($50, three hours) explore the mangrove forests of Great White Heron and Key Deer National Wildlife Refuges, and custom tours ($125 and up, four hours) transport you to exquisite backcountry areas teeming with wildlife. Kayak fishing charters are also popular excursions.

LITTLE TORCH KEY

 MM 29–10.

With a few exceptions, Little Torch Key and its neighbor islands, Cudjoe Key and Geiger Key, are more jumping-off points for divers headed for Looe Key Reef, a few miles offshore, than destinations themselves. They also serve as a refuge for those who want to make forays into Key West but not stay there.

NEED A BREAK? The aroma of rich, roasting coffee beans at **Baby's Coffee** (✉ *MM 15, OS, Saddlebunch Keys* ☎ *305/744–9866 or 800/523–2326*) arrests you at the door of "the Southernmost Coffee Roaster." Buy it by the pound or by the cup along with fresh-baked goods.

The undeveloped backcountry is at your door, making this an ideal location for fishing and kayaking. Nearby **Ramrod Key,** which also caters to divers bound for Looe Key, derives its name from a ship that wrecked on nearby reefs in the early 1800s.

WHERE TO STAY & EAT

$$$$ ✕ **Little Palm Island Resort & Spa Restaurant.** It's a setting worthy of St. Barth's, with food that's presented as art-on-a-plate. Keep that in mind as you reach for the bill, which can be equally swoon-worthy. The waterfront dining room at the exclusive Little Palm Island resort is one of the most romantic spots, and indeed luxurious dining experiences, in the Keys. The menu is a melding of French and Latin flavors, with exotic little touches. Think yellowtail-snapper ceviche with passionfruit-and-coconut gelée as a starter, followed by Serrano ham–wrapped diver scallops with crispy cilantro polenta and a flourish of squid-ink aioli—all enhanced with candlelight, live music, and seating indoors or outdoors on the beachfront terrace. The tropical Sunday brunch buffet and the full-moon jazz dinners are very popular. The dining room is open to nonguests on a reservations-only basis. ⊠*MM 28.5, OS, 28500 Overseas Hwy.* ☎*305/872–2551* ⚓*Reservations essential* ⊟*AE, D, DC, MC, V.*

$$–$$$ ✕**Square Grouper.** Although this restaurant's food draws raves, its name earns snickers—a grouper is a fine eating fish, but a square grouper is the moniker for bales of marijuana dropped into the ocean off the coast during the drug-running 1970s. Inside an unassuming strip mall, the room is surprisingly suave, with white-clothed tables and West Indies–style sofas separating a wood-topped stainless-steel bar from the dining rooms. (Slightly jarring: they sell thong underwear that say, "Got grouper?") Owners Lynn and Doug Bell give the dishes whimsical and artistic presentations, making them look as good as they taste. Seared sesame-encrusted tuna looks like a fish and is lightly crunchy outside, like butter inside. The square grouper sandwich is a steaming pan-sautéed grouper fillet with key lime tartar sauce topped with onion rings, lettuce, and tomato on ciabatta. ⊠*MM 22.5, OS, Cudjoe Key* ☎*305/745–8880* ⊟*AE, MC, V* ☉*Closed Sun. and Mon. and several weeks in summer.*

¢–$ ✕**Geiger Key Marina Smokehouse.** There's a hint of the old Keys at this oceanfront marina restaurant where locals usually outnumber tourists even in high season. They come for the daily dinner specials of meat loaf on Monday, corned beef and cabbage Tuesday, and so on. Weekends are the most popular; the place is packed Saturday for steak-on-the-grill night, and Sunday for the "Famous Chicken & Ribs BBQ" ($10.95) accompanied by live music. Along with lunch and dinner, this spot serves breakfast, catering to local fishermen and RVers who park their "land cruisers" within shouting distance of their boats for early fishing getaways. ⊠*MM 10, Geiger Key* ☎*305/296–3553 or 305/294–1230* ⊕*www.geigerkeymarina.com* ⊟*MC, V.*

$$$$
Fodor's Choice
★
🏨**Little Palm Island Resort & Spa.** *Haute tropicale* best describes this luxury retreat, and "second mortgage" might explain how some can afford to stay here. But to those who can, it's worth the price. This property is on a 5-acre palm-fringed island 3 mi offshore. The 28 oceanfront one-bedroom, thatch-roof bungalow suites have slate-tile baths, mosquito netting–draped king beds, and British colonial–style furnishings. Other comforts include an indoor and outdoor shower, private veranda, separate living room, and robes and slippers. Two Island Grand Suites are twice the size of the others and offer his-and-her bathrooms, an outdoor hot tub, and uncompromising ocean views. Cellular phones are verboten in public areas. ⊠*MM 28.5, OS, 28500 Overseas Hwy., 33042* ☎*305/872–2524 or 800/343–8567* ☎*305/872–4843* ⊕*www. littlepalmisland.com* ⇨*30 suites* ☺*In-room: no phone, safe, refrigerator, no TV, dial-up. In-hotel: restaurant, room service, bars, pool, gym, spa, beachfront, diving, water sports, no elevator, concierge, airport shuttle, parking (no fee), no kids under 16, no-smoking rooms* ⊟*AE, D, DC, MC, V* ⎢⎢*MAP.*

7

★ $$–$$$　　🔲 **Parmer's Resort.** Don't let the off-the-beaten-track, behind-the-Jeho-vah's-Witness-Hall-location put you off. Almost every unit here has a view of Pine Channel, with the lovely curl of Big Pine Key in the foreground. So what if the decor feels a little grandma's-house and you have to pay extra for housekeeping services. Waterfront cottages, with decks or balconies, are spread out on 5 landscaped acres, with a heated swimming pool in the middle. There are water activities galore, and they'll book you a kayak tour or a fishing trip, or tell you which local restaurants will deliver to your room, if you prefer to stay put. Value-minded couples (mostly European) flock here, sharing the landscape with 70-some tropical birds. Pros: bright, clean, good value. Cons: a bit out of the way, maid service costs extra; little shade or landscaping around the pool. ⊠ *MM 29, BS, 565 Barry Ave., 33042* ☎*305/872-2157* 🖷*305/872-2014* ⊕*www.parmersresort.com* ☞*18 rooms, 12 efficiencies, 15 apartments* ⚴*In-room: no phone, kitchen (some). In-hotel: pool, bicycles, no elevator, laundry facilities, public Internet, no-smoking rooms* ⊟*AE, D, MC, V* �ⓄⅠ*CP.*

¢–$　　🔲 **Ed & Ellen's Lodgings.** Homey, in a quiet residential neighborhood, these well-maintained 800-square-foot duplexes scream, "Bring the family, the big family." Units (of which there are three) sleep up to seven, with double beds in two bedrooms and three daybeds in the living room. There's a breakfast bar and good appliances in the fully outfitted kitchen, one bathroom, and a small canal-front balcony, where a plastic table and four chairs barely fit. You can tie up a boat at the wooden dock along the canal lined with mangroves and other homes, but bring bug spray. Wildlife abounds, including Key deer, raccoons, squirrels, and iguanas. Rental includes a free pass to Bahia Honda State Park. Pros: cozy, low-cost lodgings. Cons: off the beaten track. ⊠*1547 Narcissus Ave., MM 30, BS, 33043* ☎*305/872-0703 or 888/333-5536* ⊕*www.ed-ellens-lodgings.com* ☞*3 duplexes* ⚴*In-room: no phone, kitchen, VCR. In-hotel: bicycles, no elevator, no-smoking rooms* ⊟*MC, V.*

SPORTS & THE OUTDOORS

SCUBA & SNORKELING

In 1744 the HMS *Looe*, a British warship, ran aground and sank on one of the most beautiful and diverse coral reefs in the Keys. Today, **Looe Key Reef** (⊠*MM 27.5, OS, 216 Ann St., Key West 33040* ☎*305/292-0311*) owes its name to the ill-fated ship. The 5.3-square-nautical-mi reef, part of the **Florida Keys National Marine Sanctuary**, has stands of elkhorn coral on its eastern margin, purple sea fans, and abundant sponges and sea urchins. On its seaward side, it drops almost vertically 50 to 90 feet. Snorkelers and divers will find the sanctuary a quiet place to observe reef life, except in July, when the annual Underwater Music Festival pays homage to Looe Key's beauty and promotes reef awareness with six hours of music broadcast via underwater speakers. Dive shops and private charters transport hundreds of divers and snorkelers (more than 600 last year) to hear the spectacle, which includes Caribbean, classical, jazz, and New Age, plus Elvis imitators and, of course, Jimmy Buffett. ("Fins" seems apropos here.) Rather than the customary morning and afternoon two-tank, two-location trips offered by most dive shops, **Looe Key Reef Resort & Dive Center** (⊠*MM 27.5, OS, Box 509, Ramrod Key* ☎*305/872–2215 Ext. 2 or 800/942–5397* ⊕*www.diveflakeys.com*), the closest dive shop to Looe Key Reef, runs a single three-tank, three-location dive from 10 to 3 ($80 for divers, $40 for snorkelers). The maximum depth is 30 feet, so snorkelers and divers go on the same boat. On Saturday and Wednesday, they run a 3/3 dive on wrecks (for qualified divers) and reefs in the area ($80). It's part of the full-service Looe Key Reef Resort, which, not surprisingly, caters to divers. The dive boat, a 45-foot Corinthian catamaran, is docked outside the hotel, whose guests get a 10% discount on trips. Bring lunch or buy food and sodas on board.

EN ROUTE The huge object that looks like a white whale floating over Cudjoe Key (MM 23–21) is not a figment of your imagination. It's Fat Albert, a radar balloon that monitors local air and water traffic.

KEY WEST

MM 4–0.

Situated 150 mi from Miami and 90 mi from Havana, this tropical island city has always maintained a strong sense of detachment, even after it was connected to the rest of the United States—by the railroad in 1912 and by the Overseas Highway in 1938. The U.S. government acquired Key West from Spain in 1821 along with the rest of Florida. The Spanish had named the island Cayo Hueso (Bone Key) after the Native American skeletons they found on its shores. In 1823 Uncle Sam sent Commodore David S. Porter to chase pirates away. For three decades, the primary industry in Key West was wrecking—rescuing people and salvaging cargo from ships that foundered on the nearby reefs. According to some reports, when pickings were lean, the wreckers hung out lights to lure ships aground. Their business declined after 1849, when the federal government began building lighthouses.

In 1845 the army started construction of Fort Taylor, which kept Key West on the Union team during the Civil War. After the war, an influx of Cuban dissidents unhappy with Spain's rule brought the cigar industry here. Fishing, shrimping, and sponge-gathering became important industries, and a pineapple-canning factory opened. Major military installations were established during the Spanish-American War and World War I. Through much of the 19th century and into the second decade of the 20th, Key West was Florida's wealthiest city in per-capita terms. But in 1929 the local economy began to unravel. Modern ships no longer needed to provision in Key West, cigar making moved to Tampa, Hawaii dominated the pineapple industry, and the sponges succumbed to a blight. Then the Depression hit, and the military moved out. By 1934 half the population was on relief. The city defaulted on its bond payments, and the Federal Emergency Relief Administration took over the city and county governments. By promoting Key West as a tourist destination, federal officials attracted 40,000 visitors during the 1934–35 winter season, but when the 1935 Labor Day hurricane struck the Middle Keys, it wiped out the railroad—and some slow-moving tourists.

An important naval center during World War II and the Korean War, the island remains a strategic listening post on the doorstep of Fidel Castro's Cuba. It was during the 1960s that the fringes of society began moving here and the mid-'70s that gay guesthouses opened in rapid succession. In April 1982 the U.S. Border Patrol threw a roadblock across the Overseas Highway just south of Florida City to catch drug runners and illegal aliens. Traffic backed up for miles as Border Patrol agents searched vehicles and demanded that the occupants prove U.S. citizenship. City officials in Key West, outraged at being treated like foreigners by the federal government, staged a protest and formed their own "nation," the so-called Conch Republic. They hoisted a flag and distributed mock border passes, visas, and Conch currency. The embarrassed Border Patrol dismantled its roadblock, and now an annual festival recalls the city's victory.

Key West reflects a diverse population: native "Conchs" (white Key Westers, many of whom trace their ancestry to the Bahamas), fresh-water Conchs (longtime residents who migrated from somewhere else years ago), black Bahamians (descendants of those who worked the railroads and burned charcoal), Hispanics (primarily Cuban immigrants), recent refugees from the urban sprawl of mainland Florida, navy and air force personnel, and an assortment of vagabonds, drifters, and dropouts in search of refuge. The island was once Florida's gay vacation hot spot, and it remains decidedly gay-friendly, although gays are a declining demographic here. Some of the most renowned gay guesthouses no longer cater exclusively to a gay clientele.

Although the rest of the Keys are highly outdoor oriented, Key West has more of a city feel. Few open spaces remain, as promoters continue to churn out restaurants, galleries, shops, and museums to interpret the city's intriguing past. As a tourist destination, Key West has a lot to sell—an average temperature of 79°F, 19th-century architecture, and a laid-back lifestyle. There's also a growing calendar of festivals and artistic and cultural events—including the Conch Republic Celebration in April and a Halloween Fantasy Fest. Few cities of its size—a mere 2 mi by 4 mi—offer the joie de vivre of this one. Yet, as elsewhere, when preservation has successfully revived once-tired towns, next have come those unmindful of style and eager for a buck. Duval Street can look like a mini Las Vegas strip (with ubiquitous T-shirt shops and tour shills instead of casinos). Mass marketers directing the town's tourism have attracted cruise ships, which dwarf the town's skyline, and Duval Street floods with day-trippers who gawk at the earringed hippies with dogs in their bike baskets, gay couples walking down the street holding hands, and the oddball lot of locals, some of whom bark louder than the dogs.

)LD TOWN

The heart of Key West, this historic area runs from White Street west to the waterfront. Beginning in 1822, wharves, warehouses, chandleries, ship-repair facilities, and eventually in 1891 the U.S. Custom House sprang up around the deep harbor to accommodate the navy's large ships and other sailing vessels. Wealthy wreckers, merchants, and sea captains built lavish houses near the bustling waterfront. A remarkable number of these fine Victorian and pre-Victorian structures have been restored to their original grandeur and now serve as homes, guesthouses, and museums. These, along with the dwellings of famous writers, artists, and politicians who've come to Key West over the past 175 years, are among the area's approximately 3,000 historic structures. Old Town also has the city's finest restaurants and hotels, lively street life, and popular nightspots.

A GOOD TOUR

To cover many sights, take the Old Town Trolley, which lets you get off and reboard a later trolley, or the Conch Tour Train. Old Town is also very manageable on foot, bicycle, or moped, but be warned that this tour is expansive; you'll want either to pick and choose from it or break it into two or more days. Start on Whitehead Street at the **Ernest Hemingway Home & Museum** ⑪ ▶, and then cross the street and climb to the top of the **Lighthouse Museum** ⑫ for a spectacular view. Return to Whitehead Street and follow it north to Angela Street; then turn right. At Margaret Street, the **City Cemetery** ㉕ has above-ground vaults and unusual headstone inscriptions. Head north on Margaret to Southard Street, turn left, then right onto Simonton Street. Halfway up the block, Free School Lane is occupied by **Nancy Forrester's Secret Garden** ⑭. After touring it, return west on Southard to Duval Street, turn right, and look at the lovely tiles and woodwork in the **San Carlos Institute** ⑮. Return again to Southard Street, turn right, and follow it through Truman Annex to **Fort Zachary Taylor State Park** ⑬; after viewing the fort, take a dip, and a moment at the beach.

Walk west into Truman Annex to see the **Harry S Truman Little White House Museum** ⑱, President Truman's vacation residence. Return east on Caroline and turn left on Whitehead to visit the **Audubon House and Gardens** ⑯, honoring the artist-naturalist. Follow Whitehead north to Greene Street and turn left to see the salvaged sea treasures of the **Mel Fisher Maritime Heritage Society Museum** ⑰. At Whitehead's north end are the **Key West Aquarium** ⑳ and the **Key West Museum of Art and History** ⑲, the former historic U.S. Custom House. By late afternoon you should be ready to cool off with a dip or catch a few rays at the beach. (Heed signs about the water's condition.) From the aquarium, head east two blocks to the end of Simonton Street, where you'll find the appropriately named **Simonton Street Beach** ㉑. On the Atlantic side of Old Town is **South Beach** ㉖, named for its location at the southern end of Duval Street. If you've brought your pet, stroll a few blocks east to **Dog Beach** ㉗, at the corner of Vernon and Waddell streets. A little farther east is **Higgs Beach–Astro Park** ㉘, on Atlantic Boulevard between White and Reynolds streets. As the sun starts to sink, return to the north end of Old Town and follow the crowds to Mallory Square, behind the aquarium, to watch Key West's nightly sunset spectacle. (Those lucky enough may see a green flash—the brilliant splash of green or blue that sometimes appears as the sun sinks into the ocean on a clear night.) For dinner, head east on Caroline Street to **Historic Seaport at Key West Bight** ㉔ (formerly known simply as Key West Bight), a renovated area where there are numerous restaurants and bars.

If you're not entirely a do-it-yourselfer, **Key West Promotions** (✉422 *Fleming St.* ☎*305/744–9804* ⊕*www.keywestwalkingtours.com*) offers a variety of guided walking tours, including a pub crawl.

TIMING

Allow two full days to see all the Old Town museums and homes, especially with a little shopping thrown in. For a narrated trip on the tour train or trolley, budget 1½ hours to ride the loop without getting off, an entire day if you plan to get off and on at some of the sights and restaurants.

WHAT TO SEE

⓰ **Audubon House and Gardens.** If you've ever seen an engraving by ornithologist John James Audubon, you'll understand why his name is synonymous with birds. See his works in this three-story house, which was built in the 1840s for Captain John Geiger but now commemorates Audubon's 1832 stop in Key West while he was traveling through Florida to study birds. Several rooms of period antiques and a children's room are also of interest. Admission includes an audiotape (in English, French, German, or Spanish) for a self-guided tour of the house and tropical gardens, complemented by an informational booklet and signs that identify the rare indigenous plants and trees. ✉*205 Whitehead St.* ☎*305/294–2116 or 877/294–2470* ⊕*www.audubonhouse.com* ☞*$10* ☉*Daily 9:30–5, last tour starts at 4.*

㉕ **City Cemetery.** You can learn almost as much about a town's history through its cemetery as through its historic houses. Key West's celebrated 20-acre burial place may leave you wanting more, with headstone epitaphs such as "I told you I was sick" and, for a wayward husband, "Now I know where he's sleeping at night." Among the interesting plots are a memorial to the sailors killed in the sinking of the battleship USS *Maine*, carved angels and lambs marking graves of children, and grand aboveground crypts. There are separate plots for Catholics, Jews, and martyrs of Cuba. You're free to walk around the cemetery on your own, but the best way to see it is on a 60-minute tour given by the staff and volunteers of the Historic Florida Keys Foundation. Tours leave from the main gate, and reservations are required. ✉*Margaret and Angela Sts.* ☎*305/292–6718* ☞*$10* ☉*Daily sunrise–6 PM, tours Tues. and Thurs. at 9:30; call for additional times.*

㉗ **Dog Beach.** Next to Louie's Backyard, this small beach—the only one in Key West where dogs are allowed—has a shore that's a mix of sand and rocks. ✉*Vernon and Waddell Sts.* ☎*No phone* ☞*Free* ☉*Daily sunrise–sunset.*

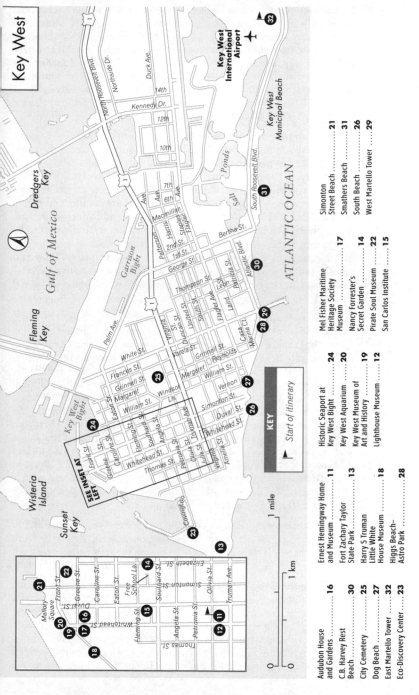

Key West

★ ㉓ **Eco-Discovery Center.** Walk through a model of Key Largo's Aquarius, the world's only underwater ocean laboratory, to discover what lurks beneath the sea. Opened in January 2007, this 6,400-square-foot underwater attraction encourages visitors to venture through a variety of Florida Key habitats, from pinelands, beach dunes, and mangroves to the deep sea. Touch-screen computer displays and live underwater cameras show off North America's only contigious barrier coral reef. ✉ *35 East Quay Rd., at end of Southard St. in Truman Annex* ☎ *305/809–4750* ⊕ *www.nmsfocean.org* 🎫 *Free* ⊘ *Tues.–Sat. 9–4.*

★ ⑪ **Ernest Hemingway Home & Museum.** Guided tours of Ernest Hemingway's home are full of anecdotes about the author's life in the community and his household quarrels with wife Pauline. While living here between 1931 and 1942, Hemingway wrote about 70% of his life's work, including *For Whom the Bell Tolls*. Few of the family's belongings remain, but photographs help illustrate his life, and scores of descendants of Hemingway's cats—many named for actors, artists, and authors—have free rein of the property. Literary buffs should be aware that there are no curated exhibits from which to gain insight into Hemingway's writing career. Tours begin every 10 minutes and take 25 to 30 minutes; then you're free to explore on your own. ✉ *907 Whitehead St.* ☎ *305/294–1136* ⊕ *www.hemingwayhome.com* 🎫 *$10* ⊘ *Daily 9–5.*

⑬ **Fort Zachary Taylor State Park.** Construction of the fort began in 1845, and in 1861, even though Florida seceded from the Union during the Civil War, Yankee forces used the fort as a base to block Confederate shipping (more than 1,500 Confederate vessels were detained in Key West's harbor). The fort, finally completed in 1866, was also used in the Spanish-American War. Take a 30-minute guided tour of this National Historic Landmark at noon and 2. On the first weekend in March, a celebration called Civil War Days includes costumed reenactments and demonstrations. The park's beach is the best in Key West. There's an adjoining picnic area with barbecue grills and shade trees, a snack bar, and rental equipment, including snorkeling gear and kayaks. ✉ *End of Southard St., through Truman Annex* ☎ *305/292–6713* ⊕ *www. floridastateparks.org/forttaylor* 🎫 *$3.50 for 1 person, $6 per vehicle for 2 people, plus 50¢ per additional person; $1.50 per pedestrian or bicyclist* ⊘ *Daily 8–sunset, tours noon and 2.*

▌ **NEED A BREAK?** Check out the pretty palm garden next to the Key West Library at 700 Fleming Street, just off Duval. This leafy, outdoor reading area, with shaded benches, is the perfect place to escape the frenzy and crowds of downtown Key West. There's free Internet access in the library, too.

⑱ **Harry S Truman Little White House Museum.** In a letter to his wife during one of his visits, President Harry S. Truman wrote, "Dear Bess, you should see the house. The place is all redecorated, new furniture and everything." If he visited today, he'd write something similar. There's a photographic review of visiting dignitaries and permanent audiovisual and artifact exhibits on the Florida Keys as a presidential retreat; Ulysses S. Grant, John F. Kennedy, and Jimmy Carter are among the chief executives who passed through here. Tours lasting 45 minutes begin every 15 minutes until 4:15. On the grounds of **Truman Annex,** a 103-acre former military parade grounds and barracks, the home served as a winter White House for presidents Truman, Eisenhower, and Kennedy. ⊠*111 Front St.* ☎*305/294–9911* ⊕*www.trumanlittle-whitehouse.com* ✍*$11* ⊘*Daily 9–5, grounds 8–sunset; last tour at 4:30.*

㉘ Higgs Beach–Astro Park. This Monroe County park is a popular sunbathing spot. But bather beware: the Natural Resources Defense Council lists this as one of the Florida beaches most often closed because of sewage runoff. A nearby grove of Australian pines provides shade, and the West Martello Tower provides shelter should a storm suddenly sweep in. Across the street, **Astro Park** is a popular children's playground. The beach also has a marker commemorating the gravesite of 295 enslaved Africans who died after being rescued from three South America–bound slave ships in 1860. ⊠*Atlantic Blvd. between White and Reynolds Sts.* ☎*No phone* ✍*Free* ⊘*Daily 6 AM–11 PM.*

㉔ Historic Seaport at Key West Bight. What used to be a funky—in some places even seedy—part of town is now an 8½-acre historic restoration project of 100 businesses, including waterfront restaurants, open-air people- and dog-friendly bars, museums, clothing stores, bait shops, docks, a marina, a wedding chapel, the Waterfront Market, the Key West Rowing Club, and dive shops. It's all linked by the 2-mi waterfront **Harborwalk,** which runs between Front and Grinnell streets, passing big ships, schooners, sunset cruises, fishing charters, and glass-bottom boats. Additional construction continues on outlying projects.

㉒ Key West Aquarium. Feed a nurse shark and explore the fascinating underwater realm of the Keys without getting wet at this kid-friendly aquarium. Hundreds of tropical fish and sea creatures live here. A touch tank enables you to handle starfish, sea cucumbers, horseshoe and hermit crabs, even horse and queen conchs—living totems of the Conch Republic. Built in 1934 by the Works Progress Administration as the world's first open-air aquarium, most of the building has been enclosed for all-weather viewing. Guided tours include shark petting and feedings. ⊠*1 Whitehead St.* ☎*305/296–2051 or 800/868–7482* ⊕*www.keywestaquarium.com* ✍*$10 including tour* ⊘*Daily 10–6; tours at 11, 1, 3, and 4:30.*

⑲ Key West Museum of Art and History. When Key West was designated a U.S. port of entry in the early 1820s, a customhouse was established. Salvaged cargoes from ships wrecked on the reefs could legally enter here, thus setting the stage for Key West to become the richest city in Florida. After a $9 million restoration, the imposing redbrick-and-terra-cotta Richardsonian Romanesque–style U.S. Custom House reopened as a museum and art gallery featuring major rotating exhibits. Smaller galleries have long-term and changing exhibits about the history of Key West, including a fine collection of folk artist Mario Sanchez's wood paintings. ⊠*281 Front St.* ☎*305/295–6616* ⊕*www. kwahs.com* ✍*$10* ⊘*Daily 9–5.*

7

Hemingway Was Here

In a town where Pulitzer Prize–winning writers are almost as common as coconuts, Ernest Hemingway stands out. Bars and restaurants around the island claim that he ate or drank there, and though he may not have been at all of them, his larger-than-life image continues to grow.

Hemingway came to Key West in 1928 at the urging of writer John dos Passos and rented a house with wife number two, Pauline Pfeiffer. They spent winters in the Keys and summers in Europe and Wyoming, occasionally taking African safaris. Along the way they had two sons, Patrick and Gregory. In 1931 Pauline's wealthy uncle Gus gave the couple the house at 907 Whitehead Street. Now known as the Ernest Hemingway Home & Museum, it's Key West's number one tourist attraction. Renovations included the addition of a pool and a tropical garden with peacocks.

In 1935, when the visitor bureau included the house in a tourist brochure, Hemingway promptly built the high brick wall that surrounds it today. He wrote of the visitor bureau's offense in a 1935 essay for *Esquire,* saying, "The house at present occupied by your correspondent is listed as number eighteen in a compilation of the forty-eight things for a tourist to see in Key West. So there will be no difficulty in a tourist finding it or any other of the sights of the city, a map has been prepared by the local F.E.R.A. authorities to be presented to each arriving visitor ... This is all very flattering to the easily bloated ego of your correspondent but very hard on production."

During his time in Key West, Hemingway penned some of his most important works, including *A Farewell to Arms, To Have and Have Not, Green Hills of Africa,* and *Death in the Afternoon.* His rigorous schedule consisted of writing almost every morning in his second-story studio above the pool, then promptly descending the stairs at midday. By afternoon and evening he was ready for drinking, fishing, swimming, boxing, and hanging around with the boys.

One close friend was Joe Russell, a craggy fisherman and owner of the rugged bar Sloppy Joe's, originally at 428 Greene Street but now at 201 Duval Street. Russell was the only one in town who would cash Hemingway's $1,000 royalty check. Russell and Charles Thompson introduced Hemingway to deep-sea fishing, which became fodder for his writing. Another of Hemingway's loves was boxing. He set up a ring in his yard and paid local fighters to box with him, and he refereed matches at Blue Heaven, then a saloon but now a restaurant, at 729 Thomas Street.

Hemingway honed his macho image dressed in cutoffs and old shirts and took on the name Papa. In turn, he gave his friends new names and used them as characters in his stories. Joe Russell became Freddy, captain of the *Queen Conch* charter boat in *To Have and Have Not.*

Hemingway stayed in Key West for 11 years before leaving Pauline for wife number three. Pauline and the boys stayed on in the house, which sold in 1951 for $80,000, 10 times its original cost.

—Jim & Cynthia Tunstall

⑫ **Lighthouse Museum.** For the best view in town and a history lesson at the same time, climb the 88 steps to the top of this 92-foot lighthouse. It was built in 1847. About 15 years later, a Fresnel lens was installed at a cost of $1 million. The keeper lived in the adjacent 1887 clapboard house, which now exhibits vintage photographs, ship models, nautical charts, and lighthouse artifacts from all along the Key reefs. ✉*938 Whitehead St.* ☎*305/295–6616* ⊕*www.kwahs.com* ☟*$10* ☉*Daily 9:30–4:30; last admission at 4:15.*

⑰ **Mel Fisher Maritime Heritage Society Museum.** In 1622 two Spanish galleons laden with riches from South America foundered in a hurricane 40 mi west of the Keys. In 1985 diver Mel Fisher recovered the treasures from the lost ships, the *Nuestra Señora de Atocha* and the *Santa Margarita.* Fisher's incredible adventure tracking these fabled hoards and battling the state of Florida for rights is as amazing as the loot you'll see, touch, and learn about in this museum. Artifacts include a gold bar weighing 6.3 troy pounds and a 77.76-carat natural emerald crystal worth almost $250,000. Exhibits on the second floor rotate and might cover slave ships, including the excavated 17th-century *Henrietta Marie,* or the evolution of Florida maritime history. ✉*200 Greene St.* ☎*305/294–2633* ⊕*www.melfisher.org* ☟*$11* ☉*Daily 9:30–5.*

⑭ **Nancy Forrester's Secret Garden.** It's hard to believe that this green escape exists in the middle of Old Town Key West. Despite damage by hurricanes and pressures from developers, Nancy Forrester has maintained her naturalized garden for more than 35 years. Growing in harmony are rare palms and cycads, ferns, bromeliads, bright gingers and heliconias, gumbo-limbos strewn with orchids and vines, and a colorful crew of birds, reptiles, cats, and a few surprises. An art gallery has botanical prints and environmental art. One-hour private tours cost $15 per person, four-person minimum. ✉*1 Free School La.* ☎*305/294–0015* ⊕*www.nfsgarden.com* ☟*$6* ☉*Daily 10–5.*

㉒ **Pirate Soul Museum.** Sniff, peek, and enter if you dare! The $10 million attraction, on the waterfront across from Fort Zachary Taylor State Park, combines an animatronic Blackbeard, hands-on displays, and a collection of nearly 500 pirate artifacts, including the only authentic pirate chest in America. Don't miss the Disney-produced, three-dimensional sound program that takes you belowdecks into a completely dark mock prison cell. *Eerie.* ✉*524 Front St.* ☎*305/292–1113* ⊕*www. piratesoul.com* ☟*$13.95* ☉*Daily 10–7.*

⑮ **San Carlos Institute.** South Florida's Cuban connection began long before Fidel Castro was born. The institute was founded in 1871 by Cuban immigrants. Now it contains a research library and museum rich with the history of Key West and 19th- and 20th-century Cuban exiles. Cuban patriot Jose Martí delivered speeches from the balcony of the auditorium, and opera star Enrico Caruso sang in the Opera House, which reportedly has exceptional acoustics. It's frequently used for concerts, lectures, films, and exhibits. ✉*516 Duval St.* ☎*305/294–3887* ☟*Free* ☉*Tues.–Fri. 1:30–7, weekends 11–5.*

㉑ **Simonton Street Beach.** This small beach facing the gulf is a great place to watch boat traffic in the harbor. Parking, however, is difficult. There are restrooms and a boat ramp. ✉*North end of Simonton St.* ☎*No phone* 🔳*Free* ☉*Daily 7 AM–11 PM.*

㉖ **South Beach.** On the Atlantic, this stretch of sand, also known as City Beach, is popular with travelers staying at nearby motels, but the Natural Resources Defense Council lists it as one of Florida's most-often-closed beaches because of sewage runoff. Enjoy the water, but from afar perhaps. It has limited parking. ✉*Foot of Duval St.* ☎*No phone* 🔳*Free* ☉*Daily 7 AM–11 PM.*

NEW TOWN

The Overseas Highway splits as it enters Key West, the two forks rejoining to encircle New Town, the area east of White Street to Cow Key Channel. The southern fork runs along the shore as South Roosevelt Boulevard (Route A1A), past municipal beaches, salt ponds, and Key West International Airport. Along the north shore, North Roosevelt Boulevard (U.S. 1) passes the Key West Welcome Center, shopping centers, chain hotels, and fast-food eateries. Part of New Town was created with dredged fill. The island would have continued growing this way had the Army Corps of Engineers not determined in the early 1970s that it was detrimental to the nearby reef.

A GOOD TOUR

Attractions are few in New Town. The best way to take in the sights is by car or moped. Take South Roosevelt Boulevard from the island's entrance to the historical museum exhibits at **East Martello Tower** ㉜ ▶, near the airport. Continue past the Riggs Wildlife Refuge salt ponds and stop at **Smathers Beach** ㉛ for a dip, or continue west onto Atlantic Boulevard to **C.B. Harvey Rest Beach** ㉚. A little farther along, at the end of White Street, is the **West Martello Tower** ㉙, with its lovely tropical gardens.

TIMING

Allow one to two hours to include brief stops at each attraction. If your interests lie in art, gardens, or Civil War history, you'll need three or four hours. Throw in time at the beach and make it a half-day affair.

WHAT TO SEE

㉚ **C. B. Harvey Rest Beach.** This beach and park were named after Cornelius Bradford Harvey, former Key West mayor and commissioner. It has half a dozen picnic areas, dunes, and a wheelchair and bike path. ✉*Atlantic Blvd., east side of White St. Pier* ☎*No phone* 🔳*Free* ☉*Daily 7 AM–11 PM.*

★ ㉜ **East Martello Tower.** This Civil War citadel was *semper paratus,* or "always ready" as the U.S. Coast Guard motto says, but like most of Florida during the war it never saw a lick of action. Today it serves as a museum, with historical exhibits about the 19th and 20th centuries. Among the latter are relics of the USS *Maine,* a Cuban refugee raft, and books by famous writers—including seven Pulitzer Prize winners—who have lived in Key West. The tower, operated by the Key West Art and Historical Society, also has a collection of Stanley Papio's "junk art" sculptures and Cuban folk artist Mario Sanchez's chiseled and painted wooden carvings of historic Key West street scenes. ⊠ *3501 S. Roosevelt Blvd.* ☏ *305/296–3913* ⊕ *www.kwahs.com* 💲 *$6* ⊙ *Daily 9:30–4:30; last admission at 4:15.*

③① **Smathers Beach.** This beach has nearly 2 mi of sand, plus restrooms, picnic areas, and volleyball courts, all of which make it popular with the spring-break crowd. Trucks along the road rent rafts, windsurfers, and other beach "toys." ⊠ *S. Roosevelt Blvd.* ☏ *No phone* 💲 *Free* ⊙ *Daily 7 AM–11 PM.*

②⑨ **West Martello Tower.** Within the ruins of this Civil War–era fort is the Key West Garden Club, which maintains lovely gardens of native and tropical plants. It also holds art, orchid, and flower shows in March and November and leads private garden tours in March. ⊠ *Atlantic Blvd. and White St.* ☏ *305/294–3210* ⊕ *www.keywestgardenclub.com* 💲 *Donation welcome* ⊙ *Tues.–Sat. 9:30–3:15.*

WHERE TO EAT

AMERICAN

$$–$$$$ ✕ **Michael's Restaurant.** White tablecloths, subdued lighting, oil paintings, and light music give Michael's the feel of a favorite restaurant in an urban neighborhood. Garden seating reminds that you are in a favorite restaurant in the Keys. Chef-owner Michael Wilson flies in prime rib, cowboy steaks, and rib eyes from Allen Brothers in Chicago, which has supplied top-ranked steakhouses for more than 100 years. Also on the menu is a melt-in-your-mouth Provimi veal chop (stuffed with mozzarella and prosciutto, topped with mushrooms); grouper Oscar, a locally caught fillet stuffed with jumbo lump crab; and a variety of fondue dishes (try the pesto pot, spiked with hot pepper and basil.) The Hemingway (rum, lime, and mint) and the Third Degree (raspberry vodka and white crème de cacao) top the martini menu. ⊠ *532 Margaret St.* ☏ *305/295–1300* ⊕ *www.michaelskeywest.com* ▤ *AE, DC, MC, V* ⊙ *No lunch.*

¢–$$ ✕ **The Deli Restaurant.** Decent affordable food is the appeal of this fourth-generation family-run restaurant. Decor is a maritime theme gone awry, with strewn fish netting, plastic sea horses, and bad artwork. But the food is a hit, especially the no-frills, hearty breakfasts (try fish and grits) and lunchtime sandwiches, chili, and chowders. Roast pork and roast beef dinners, papa's fish cakes, and baked chicken with stuffing and cranberries are among the comfort foods. Most dinner dishes cost $8.95 to $12.95 and include a choice of two vegetables and a biscuit or corn muffin. You can order breakfast, lunch, and dinner all day. ⊠ *531 Truman Ave.* ☏ *305/294–1464* ▤ *D, MC, V* ⊙ *Closes at 4 PM.*

¢–$$ ✕ **PT's Late Night Bar and Grill.** Locals like the dimly lighted hominess (booths, TVs, pool tables), low prices (most entrées are around $13), and late hours (open until 4 AM, food service until 1 AM). Start with the ultra-spicy "911" chicken wings, then calm your firing appetite with comfort food like turkey potpie, onion-smothered pork chops, and Yankee pot roast. Fajitas are a specialty, with a choice of steak, chicken, shrimp, vegetables, or a combo. ⊠ *920 Caroline St.* ☎ *305/296–4245* ⊕ *www.ptslatenight.com* ⊟ *AE, D, MC, V.*

¢ ✕ **Lobo's Mixed Grill.** If White Castle has attained national cult status with its burgers, then the equivalent among Key West denizens might very well be Lobo's belly buster. The 7-ounce, char-grilled chunk of ground chuck is thick and juicy and served with lettuce, tomato, and pickle on a toasted bun. The choice of 30 wraps (rib eye, oyster, grouper, and others) is equally popular. The menu includes salads and quesadillas, as well as a fried-shrimp-and-oyster combo. Beer and wine are also served. It's an outdoor eatery that closes at 6, so eat early. Lobo's offers free delivery within Old Town. ⊠ *5 Key Lime Sq., between Southard and Angela Sts.* ☎ *305/296–5303* ⊕ *www.loboskeywest.com* ⊟ *No credit cards* ☉ *Closed Sun. Apr.–early Dec.*

ECLECTIC

$$$–$$$$
Fodor'sChoice
★
✕ **Café Marquesa.** It's showtime in the show kitchen as Chef Susan Ferry, who trained with Norman Van Aken at his Coral Gables restaurant, works her magic in this relaxed elegant 50-seat eatery that adjoins the intimate Marquesa Hotel. Susan presents 10 or so entrées each night, and although every dish is a sure bet, frequent guests call attention to the peppercorn-dusted seared yellowfin tuna, the ginger coconut almond–crusted hogfish, and the pan-roasted duck breast. End your meal on a sweet note with Key Lime Napoleon with tropical fruits and berries. There's also a fine selection of wines and a choice of microbrewery beers. Dinner is served until 11. ⊠ *600 Fleming St.* ☎ *305/292–1244* ⊕ *www.marquesa.com* ⊟ *AE, DC, MC, V* ☉ *No lunch.*

$$$–$$$$
✕ **Louie's Backyard.** Feast your eyes on a steal-your-breath-away view and beautifully presented dishes prepared by executive chef Doug Shook. Once you get over sticker shock (appetizers cost around $14 to $16; entrées hover around the $35 mark), settle in and enjoy dishes like oven-roasted salmon on a crisp potato cake, grilled tuna with Somen noodles, or grilled chili-rubbed pork chop with smoked applesauce. Louie's key lime pie has a gingersnap crust and is served with a raspberry coulis. Come for lunch if you're on a budget; the menu is less expensive (but still expect to pay about $17 for your dish) and the view is just as fantastic. For night owls, the Afterdeck Bar serves cocktails on the water until the wee hours. ⊠ *700 Waddell Ave.* ☎ *305/294–1061* ⊕ *www.louiesbackyard.com* ⚲ *Reservations essential* ⊟ *AE, DC, MC, V.*

$$–$$$$
Fodor'sChoice
★
✕ **Alice's Key West Restaurant.** A rather plain-Jane storefront gives way to a warm and cozy dining room, where chef-owner Alice Weingarten works whimsical creations that are very far from plain. Color, zing, and spice are Weingarten's main ingredients. Take the tuna tartare tower: it's spiced with a garlic-chili paste, topped with tomato-ginger jam, and served between crisp wonton wafers. The Brazilian churrasco pan-seared skirt steak is served with garlicky chimichurri sauce and green chili and manchego cheese mashed potatoes. Or, try the Asian-spiced wild boar baby back ribs or the marinated ostrich. It's open for break-

fast and lunch, too; end your Duval Crawl here for a breakfast of eggs, fries, and toast for as little as $4. ⊠*1114 Duval St.* ☎*305/292–5733* ⊕*www.aliceskeywest.com* ⊟*AE, D, MC, V* ⊘*No lunch.*

$$–$$$$ ✕**915 Duval.** Twinkling lights draped along the lower- and upper-level outdoor porches of a 100-year-old Victorian mansion set an elegant— though unstuffy—stage at this very cool tapas-style eatery. If you like to sample and sip, you'll appreciate the variety of smaller plate selections and wines by the glass. Amply portioned tapas include adventurous combos, like the bacon-wrapped dates stuffed with sweet garlic and soy citrus, clams and chorizo, Thai beef salad rolls, and the signature Tuna Dome, with fresh crab, lemon-miso dressing, and an ahi tuna sashimi wrapping. There are larger plates, too, if you're craving a hunk of something, like grilled double pork chops or steak frites au poivre. Dine outdoors and people-watch along upper Duval, or sit inside at a table or the sleek bar while listening to light jazz. ⊠*915 Duval St.* ☎*305/296–0669* ⊕*www.915duval.com* ⊟*AE, MC, V* ⊘*No lunch.*

$–$$$$ ✕**Rick's Blue Heaven.** The outdoor dining area here is often referred to as "the quintessential Keys experience," and it's hard to argue. There's much to like about this historic restaurant where Hemingway refereed boxing matches and customers watched cockfights. Although the cockfights are no more, the free-roaming chickens and cats add that "what-a-hoot" factor. Nightly specials include seared and spice-rubbed grouper or sautéed yellowtail snapper in citrus beurre-blanc sauce. Desserts and breads are baked on-site. ∎**TIP→Dinner can be crowded and service spotty; your best bet is to come for breakfast or lunch.** ⊠*305 Petronia St.* ☎*305/296–8666* ⌫*Reservations not accepted* ⊟*D, MC, V.*

★ ¢–$ ✕**The Cafe, A Mostly Vegetarian Place.** You don't have to be a vegetarian to love this New Age–ish café, serving fresh soups, salads, sandwiches, grilled pizza, and more. Local favorites include homemade veggie burgers (order them with a side of sweet potato fries), as well as portobello mushroom salad, Szechuan vegetable stir-fry, and the Gorgonzola pizza. There are fewer than a dozen tables and an eat-at bar with backless stools that fill the dining space, but there are a couch and chairs for waiting. Sit down and relax—the food is worth the wait. ⊠*509 Southard St.* ☎*305/296–5515* ⊟*MC, V* ⊘*Closed Sun.*

CARIBBEAN

$$$–$$$$ ✕**Mangoes.** The outdoor dining patio with potted plants, soft lights, and oversize umbrellas is the place to see and be seen on lively Duval Street. The chef plays it safe with conventional dishes, like mustard-rubbed rack of lamb, filet mignon, pan-seared veal chop and rosemary-lemon roasted chicken, but all are well prepared and rarely disappoint. Adventurous diners may find more satisfaction in the salads and starters selection. Try the fabulous tempura-fried ahi tuna, lightly crisped and fried rare; the conch spring rolls with Asian spiced vegetables; the wild mushroom martini; or shrimp sambuca. Then sit back and watch the Key weird world go by. ⊠*700 Duval St.* ☎*305/292–4606* ⊕*www. mangoeskeywest.com* ⊟*AE, MC, V.*

7

CUBAN

¢–$ ✕**El Siboney.** Dining at this sprawling three-room, family-style restaurant is like going to Mom's for Sunday dinner—that is, if your mother is Cuban. It's noisy and the food is traditional (and inexpensive) cubanano. There's a well-seasoned black-bean soup; local fish grilled, stuffed, and breaded; and a memorable paella Valencia for two ($40.75). Dishes come with plantains, bread, and two sides. ✉*900 Catherine St.* ☎*305/296–4184* ▤*No credit cards.*

FRENCH

★ $$$–$$$$ ✕**Café Solé.** Welcome to the self-described "home of the hog snapper." No, it's not the owners' pet, but a deliciously roasted local fish seasoned with shrimp and red peppers. This little piece of France is concealed behind a high wall and a gate in a residential neighborhood. Inside, Chef John Correa shows culinary wizardry that extends well beyond the hog. Marrying his French training with local foods and produce, he creates delicious takes on classics like half rack of lamb rubbed with *herbes de Provence* and some of the best bouillabaisse that you'll find outside of Marseilles. From the land, there is filet mignon casa nova with a wild-mushroom demi-glace with foie gras. His salads are lightly kissed with balsamic vinegar. ✉*1029 Southard St.* ☎*305/294–0230* ⊕*www.cafesole.com* ▤*D, MC, V.*

IRISH

¢–$$$ ✕**Finnegan's Wake Irish Pub and Eatery.** From friendly, accented waitresses to pictures of Beckett, Shaw, Yeats, and Wilde to creaky wood floors, this restaurant exudes Irish country warmth. The certified Angus beef is a bit pricey ($29.95 for an 18-ounce rib eye), but most other dishes are bargains. Traditional fare includes bangers and mash, Irish stew, Dublin chicken potpie with chunks of chicken and vegetables in a creamy broth, and colcannon—rich mashed potatoes with scallions, sauerkraut, and melted aged white cheddar cheese. Bread pudding soaked in whiskey and topped with whipped cream is a true treat. There's live music on weekends, happy hour daily from 4 to 7 PM and midnight to 2 AM, and a boast of the "world's largest selection on tap." ✉*320 Grinnell St.* ☎*305/293–0222* ⊕*www.keywestirish. com* ▤*AE, D, MC, V.*

ITALIAN

★ $$–$$$$ ✕**Salute Ristorante Sul Mare.** This funky indoor and open-air restaurant is on Higgs Beach, giving it one of the island's best lunch views (and a bit of sand and salt spray on a windy day). The dinner menu includes homemade pastas, like the cappellini puttanesca with calamari, capers, olives, and tomatoes, or linguine with Key West pink shrimp, tomatoes, garlic, and basil. Start with a salad of mixed greens, feta, artichoke hearts, olives, and roasted red pepper or the Tuscan bean soup with grilled bread. At lunch there are bruschetta, panini, and calamari marinara, as well as a fresh-fish sandwich and daily specials, like bacon-wrapped grilled shrimp Caesar salad. ✉*1000 Atlantic Blvd., Higgs Beach* ☎*305/292–1117* ▤*AE, MC, V* ☾*No lunch Sun.*

★ $–$$ ✕**Mangia Mangia.** Elliot and Naomi Baron, ex-Chicago restaurateurs, serve large portions of homemade pastas that can be matched with one of the homemade sauces. Tables are arranged in a twinkly brick garden with specimen palms and in a nicely dressed-up old-house dining room. Everything that comes out of the open kitchen is outstanding, including the *bollito misto di mare* (fresh seafood sautéed with garlic, shallots, and white wine) or the memorable capellini "schmappellini," wafer-thin pasta with asparagus, tomatoes, pine nuts, and Parmesan. The wine list—with more than 350 offerings it's the largest in Monroe County—has a good under-$20 selection. ⊠*900 Southard St.* ☎*305/294–2469* ⊕*www.mangia-mangia.com* ⊟*AE, MC, V* ⊘*No lunch.*

JAPANESE

$–$$$ ✕**Ambrosia.** Ask any savvy Key West local where to get the best sushi on the island and you'll undoubtedly be pointed to this tiny wood-and-tatami paneled dining room tucked in a quiet neighborhood. Grab a seat at the sushi bar and watch owner and head sushi chef Masa prepare an impressive array of super-fresh sashimi delicacies. You can't go wrong with the Ambrosia Special, a seven-piece sampling, including five kinds of sashimi. There's an assortment of lightly fried tempura and teriyaki dishes and a killer bento box. Enjoy it all with a cup of sake or a cold glass of Sapporo beer. ⊠*1100 Packer St.* ☎*305/293–0304* ⊟*AE, MC, V* ⊘*No lunch Apr.–Nov. Closed Sun.*

STEAK/SEAFOOD

★ $$$–$$$$ ✕**Pisces.** Don't be dismayed when you see the sign for Pisces on the Café des Artistes building: Chef Andrew Berman and staff are still there. They've changed the name, updated the menu, and gone contemporary with a granite bar and sparkling mirrors. Some old favorites remain on the menu, such as Lobster Tango Mango, flambéed in cognac and served with a saffron-basil butter sauce and sliced mangoes. Other dishes include tuna served rare with wild mushrooms, and champagne-braised black grouper. Menu names sounded better when they were in French, but the taste lost nothing in the translation. ⊠*1007 Simonton St.* ☎*305/294–7100* ⊕*www.pisceskeywest.com* ⊟*AE, MC, V* ⊘*No lunch.*

★ $–$$$ ✕**Seven Fish.** A local hot spot, this off-the-beaten-track, tiny dining room is good for an eclectic mix of dishes like tropical shrimp salsa, wild-mushroom quesadilla, seafood marinara, and sometimes even an old-fashioned meat loaf with real mashed potatoes. Those in the know arrive early to snag one of the 12 or so tables clustered in the bare-bones dining room. ⊠*632 Olivia St.* ☎*305/296–2777* ⊕*www.7fish. com* ⊟*AE, MC, V* ⊘*Closed Tues. No lunch.*

¢–$$ ✕**Turtle Kraals.** Turtle races are held Monday and Friday evenings at 6 in this restaurant and saloon named for the kraals, or corrals, where turtles were kept until they went to the cannery. This practice ended in the 1970s, when the U.S. Endangered Species Act prohibited the slaughter of green and other sea turtles for their meat. Today, much smaller box turtles provide the live entertainment and the menu offers an assortment of marine cuisine that includes seared jerk tuna, seafood enchiladas, and mango crab cakes. ⊠*231 Margaret St.* ☎*305/294–2640* ⊕*www.turtlekraals.com* ⊟*MC, V.*

7

WHERE TO STAY

Historic cottages, restored turn-of-the-last-century Conch houses, and large resorts are among the offerings in Key West, with the majority charging $100 to $300 a night. In high season, December through March, you'll be hard pressed to find a decent room for less than $200, and most places raise prices considerably during October's Fantasy Fest week and other popular events. Many guesthouses and inns do not welcome children under 16, and some do not permit smoking indoors but provide ashtrays outside. Most tariffs include an expanded continental breakfast and, often, afternoon wine or snack.

GUESTHOUSES

★ $$$$ ⛅**Ambrosia House.** If you desire personal attention, a casual mood with a dollop of style, and bang for your buck, stay at these twin inns with pool-view rooms, suites, town houses, and cottages spread out on nearly 2 acres. Ambrosia is more intimate. Ambrosia Too is a delightful art-filled hideaway. Rooms have original work by Keys artists, wicker or wood furniture, and spacious bathrooms. Each has a private entrance and deck, patio, or porch. Poolside continental breakfast is included, and children are welcome. Pros: suites are spacious and nicely furnished, poolside breakfast offers hot items, friendly staff. Cons: on-street parking can be tough to come by. ⊠ *615, 618, 622 Fleming St., 33040* ☎ *305/296–9838 or 800/535–9838* 🖷 *305/296–2425* ⊕ *www. ambrosiakeywest.com* 🛏 *22 rooms, 3 town houses, 1 cottage, 6 suites* ⟠ *In-room: kitchen (some), refrigerator. In-hotel: 3 pools, bicycles, no elevator, concierge, public Wi-Fi, parking (no fee), some pets allowed (fee), no-smoking rooms* ⊟ *AE, D, MC, V* ⦿ *CP.*

$$$$ ⛅**The Gardens Hotel.** Built in 1875, this gloriously shaded property
Fodor's Choice   covers one-third of a city block in Old Town. Peggy Mills, who bought
★   it as a private estate in 1931, coiffed it with orchids, ponytail palms, and black bamboo. She added walks, fountains, and *tinajones* (earthen pots) brought from Cuba. After her death in 1971, the property was turned into a romantic inn that offers several classes of rooms, from standards to garden and courtyard views to a two-bedroom carriage house suite. Decorated with Bahamian plantation-style furnishings, the quiet and elegant rooms are a luxurious tropical retreat; most have private verandas. Rates include continental breakfast. Pros: luxurious bathrooms with Aveda toiletries, secluded garden seating, free phone calls. Cons: hard to get reservations. ⊠ *526 Angela St., 33040* ☎ *305/294–2661 or 800/526–2664* 🖷 *305/292–1007* ⊕ *www.garden- shotel.com* 🛏 *17 rooms* ⟠ *In-room: refrigerator. In-hotel: bar, pool, spa, no elevator, concierge, parking (no fee), no kids under 16, no- smoking rooms* ⊟ *AE, MC, V* ⦿ *CP.*

$$$$ ⛅**Island City House Hotel.** A garden oasis with brick walkways, tropical plants, a palm canopy, and a real sense of conviviality set this guesthouse, of three unique buildings, apart from the pack. The vintage-1880s Island City House has wraparound verandas, antiques, and pine floors. Arch House, a former carriage house, has a dramatic entry that opens into a lush courtyard. Although all suites front on busy Eaton Street, only Nos. 5 and 6 face it. A reconstructed cigar factory

has become the poolside Cigar House, with spacious rooms, porches, decks, and plantation-style teak and wicker furnishings. The private tropical garden wraps around a spacious pool area. Children are welcome—a rarity in Old Town guesthouses. Pros: private gardens, knowledgeable staff. Cons: Wi-Fi is hit-or-miss in some rooms, no front desk staff at night, Arch House rooms are small. ☒ *411 William St., 33040* ☎*305/294–5702 or 800/634–8230* 🖳*305/294–1289* ⊕*www.island-cityhouse.com* ⮑*24 suites* 🖒*In-room: kitchen (some), VCR (some), Wi-Fi (some). In-hotel: pool, bicycles, no elevator, laundry facilities, concierge, no-smoking rooms* ▤*AE, D, DC, MC, V* ⦿ICP.

$$$$ 🏨**Key Lime Inn.** This 1854 Grand Bahama–style house on the National Register of Historic Places, with adjacent cottages and cabanas, succeeds by offering amiable service, good location, and simple rooms with natural-wood and white furniture. The cluster of pastel-painted cottages, surrounded by white picket fences, has a residential feel, a bit like a beach colony without the beach, or the backlot of a movie set. The least-expensive Cabana rooms, some with patios, surround the pool. The Garden Cottages have one room; some include a porch or balcony. Some rooms in the historic Maloney House have a porch or patio. Pros: free parking, deluxe rooms have private porch or patio. Cons: standard rooms are pricey yet basic, pool faces a busy street, mulch-covered paths and grounds. ☒ *725 Truman Ave., 33040* ☎*305/294–5229 or 800/549–4430* 🖳*305/294–9623* ⊕*www.key-limeinn.com* ⮑*30 rooms, 7 cottages* 🖒*In-room: safe, refrigerator (some), VCR (some), dial-up. In-hotel: pool, no elevator, public Wi-Fi, parking (no fee), no-smoking rooms* ▤*AE, D, MC, V* ⦿ICP.

$$$–$$$$ 🏨**Azul Key West.** The ultramodern—nearly minimalistic—redo of this classic Queen Anne mansion provides a visual vacation from the sensory overload of Key West's other abundant Victorian guesthouses. The adults-only boutique hotel, 3½ blocks from Duval, combines original dark trimwork and shiny floors with sleek furnishings, including a curved frosted glass and chrome check-in desk, leather loungers, and a state-of-the-art sound system. Spacious, serene rooms, some with private verandas, have leather headboards, flat-screen TVs, and remote-controlled fans and lights. Pros: seaglass scattered on beds is a nice touch; deluxe linens and toiletries in marble-floored baths. Cons: on a busy street. ☒ *907 Truman Ave., 33040* ☎*305/296–5152 or 888/253–2985* 🖳*305/296–3524* ⊕*www.azulhotels.us.* ⮑*10 rooms, 1 suite* 🖒*In-room: Wi-Fi. In-hotel: pool, bicycles, no elevator, public Wi-Fi, no kids under 21, no-smoking rooms* ▤*AE, D, MC, V* ⦿ICP.

$$$–$$$$ 🏨**Heron House Court.** Formerly called Fleur de Key Guesthouse, this stately inn (circa 1900) changed its name and now welcomes all guests rather than a strictly gay clientele. Its Conch-style architecture harks back to the property's origins as a boardinghouse and cigar makers' cottages. Standard rooms in the main house are small, so opt for a superior room, which is slightly more expensive but much larger. Airy, bright rooms have tiled floors and a complementary mix of antiques and reproductions, and are tastefully decorated in whites and tropical colors. The guest rooms are nicer than the public areas, which include a pool and weathered deck. Pros: complimentary weekend wine and

social hours, fluffy bathrobes. Cons: property faces Eaton Street and can be noisy, owner's suite is dated and smells musty. ⊠*412 Frances St., 33040* ☎*305/296–4719 or 888/265–2395* ⊕*www.heronhousecourt.com* ⤢*2 suites, 14 rooms* ⏃*In-room: refrigerator. In-hotel: pool, no elevator, concierge, public WI-Fi, no kids under 21, no-smoking rooms* ▤*AE, D, MC, V* ⑩*CP.*

★ $$$–$$$$ 🔲**Mermaid & the Alligator.** An enchanting combination of personality and style, and flora and fauna makes this 1904 Victorian house a welcoming retreat. The property is bathed in palms, banyans, birds of paradise, and poincianas, with cages of colorful, live parrots and swarms of butterflies adding tropical punch. Rooms are Caribbean colonial–inspired, with wooden floors, furniture, and trim as well as French doors that complement the key lime, cantaloupe, and other rich colors. Some downstairs rooms open onto the deck, pool, and gardens designed by one of the resident owners, a landscape designer. Upstairs room balconies overlook the gardens. A full breakfast is served poolside. Pros: inviting hot tub and massage pavillion, large-screen TV in public sitting area, island getaway feel. Cons: dark public areas, you may find resident dog at your feet, cheesy plastic lawn chairs. ⊠*729 Truman Ave., 33040* ☎*305/294–1894 or 800/773–1894* 🖶*305/295–9925* ⊕*www.kwmermaid.com* ⤢*6 rooms* ⏃*In-room: no phone, no TV. In-hotel: pool, no elevator, public Wi-Fi, no kids under 16, no-smoking rooms* ▤*AE, MC, V* ⑩*BP.*

★ $–$$$$ 🔲**Popular House/Key West Bed & Breakfast.** Local art—large, splashy canvases, a mural in the style of Gauguin—hangs on the walls, bright, handmade textiles (owner Jody Carlson is a talented weaver) drape chairs, couches and beds, and tropical gardens and music set the mood here. You'll find both inexpensive rooms with shared bath (there is one with a private bath) and luxury rooms, reasoning that budget travelers deserve the same good style (and lavish continental breakfast) as the rich. Less-expensive rooms burst with colors; the hand-painted dressers add a whimsical flourish. Balconies added to second-floor rooms overlook the gardens, making these quarters the best in the house after the spacious (and most expensive) third-floor rooms, decorated with a paler palette and original furniture. Pros: feels like an art gallery; tiled outdoor shower, Jacuzzi and dry sauna area is a welcome hangout. Cons: some rooms and gathering areas are small. ⊠*415 William St., 33040* ☎*305/296–7274 or 800/438–6155* 🖶*305/293–0306* ⊕*www.keywestbandb.com* ⤢*8 rooms, 4 with bath* ⏃*In-room: no phone, no TV. In-hotel: pool, bicycles, no elevator, public Internet, no kids under 18, no-smoking rooms* ▤*AE, D, DC, MC, V* ⑩*CP.*

$$$ 🔲**Courtney's Place.** If you like kids, cats, and dogs, you'll feel right at home in this collection of gardens and cottages ranging from Bahamian and cigar-maker cottages to Caribbean and shotgun houses. The interior is equally varied in coloring and furnishings, but all the rooms have at least a refrigerator, microwave, and coffeepot, if not a full kitchen. The family-owned property is tucked into a residential neighborhood, though within easy walking distance of Duval Street. Note: all rooms are not created equal here; the tiny Room 5 is tucked into an attic space. Pros: near Duval Street, decent bargain option. Cons: small parking lot,

dated bed linens. ✉*720 Whitemarsh La., 33040* ☎*305/294–3480 or 800/869–4639* 🖷*305/294–7019* ⊕*www.courtneysplacekeywest.com* ⇨*6 rooms, 3 suites, 8 cottages* ⌂*In-room: kitchen (some), refrigerator, Wi-Fi. In-hotel: pool, bicycles, no elevator, concierge, laundry facilities, parking (no fee), some pets allowed (fee), no-smoking rooms* ⊟*AE, MC, V* ⦿*CP.*

★ $$$ 🏠**Eden House.** From the vintage metal rockers on the streetside porch to the old neon hotel sign in the lobby, this 1920s rambling Key West mainstay hotel is high on character, low on gloss. Forget fancy; here, you'll get a taste of authentic old Key West, without sacrificing convenience, comfort, or budget. Rooms come in all shapes and sizes, from bare-bones, shared-bath basic to large apartments with full kitchens and private decks or porches. The spacious outdoor area has towering palms, waterfalls, decks, porches, and swaying hammocks. Grab a book and plop in a hammock in the outdoor library, tucked into a sun-dappled corner with a gurgling waterfall and potted bonsai. Pros: lots of shady and sunny spots to linger; hot tub is actually hot; daily happy hour celebrations around the pool. Cons: cutesy signage is overdone. ✉*1015 Fleming St., 33040* ☎*305/296–6868 or 800/533–5397* 🖷*305/294–1221* ⊕*www.edenhouse.com* ⇨*35 rooms, 8 suites.* ⌂*In-room: kitchen (some), refrigerator (some). In-hotel: restaurant, pool, bicycles, no elevator, public Internet, parking (no fee), no-smoking rooms* ⊟*AE, MC, V.*

$$$ 🏠**La Pensione.** Hospitality and period furnishings give this 1891 home, once owned by a cigar executive, a wonderful imagination of Key West life in the late 19th century. All rooms have private baths and king-size or double beds. All but one have sitting areas—the exception being a handicapped-accessible room. None have televisions, but not to worry, there's plenty of entertainment (and distraction) from Duval Street, a few yards away. Rates include daily continental breakfast in the dining room or on the veranda. Pros: historic hand-planed pine-paneled walls, off-street parking, some rooms have wraparound porches. Cons: street rooms are noisy, baths and bedding need updating. ✉*809 Truman Ave., 33040* ☎*305/292–9923 or 800/893–1193* 🖷*305/296–6509* ⊕*www.lapensione.com* ⇨*9 rooms* ⌂*In-room: no TV. In-hotel: pool, no elevator, parking, no kids under 18* ⊟*AE, D, MC, V* ⦿*CP.*

★ $$$ 🏠**Merlin Guesthouse.** Key West guesthouses don't usually welcome families, but this laid-back jumble of rooms, suites, and cottages is an exception, and if you can live with a few flaws, you'll grab a bargain. Rooms in the 1930s Simonton House are most suitable for couples. They have four-poster beds and porches. Suites have wooden floors, French doors, rugs, four-poster beds, sundecks or porches, and sofa beds; the one- and two-bedroom suites, with kitchens, are popular with families. Bright, roomy cottages have similar furnishings. Get a room in the back, if you like to sleep. The leafy courtyard and pool area are fun (noisy) hangouts. Pros: just off Duval Street, back rooms have hammocks and small sitting areas. Cons: neighbor noise, common areas need TLC, cold hot tub. ✉*811 Simonton St., 33040* ☎*305/296–3336 or 800/642–4753* 🖷*305/296–3524* ⊕*www.merlinguesthouse.com* ⇨*10 rooms, 6 suites, 4 cottages* ⌂*In-room: no phone, safe, kitchen*

7

(some), refrigerator (some). In-hotel: pool, no elevator, public Internet, no-smoking rooms ☐*AE, D, MC, V* ⦿|*CP.*

$$–$$$ ⌂**Angelina Guest House.** The high rollers and ladies of the night were chased away long ago, but this charming guesthouse can still tickle your imagination with its jaded past as a gambling hall and bordello. Two blocks off Duval Street, in the heart of Old Town Key West, it's a home away from home that offers simple, clean, attractively priced accommodations. Rooms range from those sharing a hallway bath, community refrigerator, and microwave, to spacious rooms with king beds and sleeper sofas. Built in the 1920s, this rambling, yellow-and-white wooden building has second-floor porches, gabled roofs, and a white picket fence. The current owners prettied the rooms with flower-print curtains and linens and added homemade cinnamon rolls, which receive rave reviews in the guest book, to the inclusive breakfast bar. A lagoon-style pool, fountain, and old bricks accent a lovely garden that begs you to sip a tropical concoction and forget what's left behind. Pros: good value, clean, friendly staff. Cons: thin walls, shared balcony porch, basic. ✉*302 Angela St., 33040* ☎*305/294–4480 or 888/303–4480* ⊕*www.angelinaguesthouse.com* ⇋*13 rooms* ♤*In-room: no phone, refrigerator (some), no TV. In-hotel: pool, bicycles, no elevator, no kids under 18, no-smoking rooms* ☐*D, MC, V* ⦿|*CP.*

¢–$$ ⌂**Speakeasy Inn.** During Prohibition, Raul Vasquez smuggled liquor from Cuba and taxi drivers stopped here to fill suitcases with the boot-leg. Today, the booze is legal and the Speakeasy survives as an attractively priced, no-frills inn within walking distance of the beach. Studios, suites, and two-bedroom units have bright white walls offset by bursts of color in rugs, pillows, and seat cushions; queen-size beds and tables made from salvaged pine; Saltillo tiles in the bathrooms; oak floors; and some claw-foot bathtubs. Room 1 fronts Duval Street with a deck that's good for people-watching. Note: the smaller rooms and suites can seem as cramped as a Midtown Manhattan studio. Pros: good location, budget bed, high-quality cigars at the attached cigar store. Cons: no pool, no complimentary breakfast, no maid service. ✉*1117 Duval St., 33040* ☎*305/296–2680 or 800/217–4884* 🖷*305/296–2680* ⊕*www.speakeasyinn.com* ⇋*4 suites, 4 studios, 2 2-bedroom units* ♤*In-room: kitchen (some), refrigerator. In-hotel: bicycles, no elevator, public Internet, no-smoking rooms* ☐*AE, D, MC, V.*

HOTELS

$$$$ ⌂**Best Western Key Ambassador Resort Inn.** You know what to expect from this chain hotel: standard, well-maintained rooms, predictable service, and competitive prices. This one also happens to be on a prime 7-acre piece of property with ocean views. Accommodations are cheerful, if uninspired, with Caribbean-style light-color furniture and linens in coordinated tropical colors. Rooms have screened-in balconies, too. The palm-shaded pool looks over the Atlantic, and a covered picnic area with a large barbecue grill encourages socializing. Pros: big pool area, Tiki Bar. Cons: overhead plane noise, a trek to Duval Street. ✉*3755 S. Roosevelt Blvd., New Town, 33040* ☎*305/296–3500 or 800/432–4315* 🖷*305/296–9961* ⊕*www.keyambassador.com* ⇋*100 rooms* ♤*In-room: refrigerator, dial-up, Wi-Fi. In-hotel: restaurant, bar,* *pool, laundry facilities, public Wi-Fi, airport shuttle, parking (no fee), no-smoking rooms* ⊟*AE, D, DC, MC, V* ⊚|*CP.*

$$$$ 🏨 **Casa Marina Resort.** At any moment, you expect the landed gentry to walk across the oceanfront lawn, just as they did in the 1920s, when this 13-acre resort was built. Set on a private beach, it has the same rich lobby with a beamed ceiling, polished pine floor, and art. Guest rooms are stylishly decorated. Armoires and wicker chairs with thick cushions add warmth. Fluffy bathrobes and luxurious designer toiletries make it feel like home. Two-bedroom loft suites with balconies face the ocean. The main building's ground-floor lanai rooms open onto the lawn, and the pools have a nice view of the Atlantic. ⊠*1500 Reynolds St., 33040* ☎*305/296–3535 or 866/397–6342* 🖷*305/296–9960* ⊕*www. casamarinaresort.com* ⇋*239 rooms, 72 suites* ⌂*In-room: safe, dial-up, Wi-Fi. In-hotel: 2 restaurants, room service, bars, tennis courts, pools, gym, spa, beachfront, diving, water sports, bicycles, children's programs (ages 4–12), laundry service, concierge, public Internet, public Wi-Fi, airport shuttle, no-smoking rooms* ⊟*AE, D, DC, MC, V.*

$$$$
Fodor'sChoice ★
🏨 **Marquesa Hotel.** In a town that prides itself on its laid-back luxe, this complex of four restored 1884 houses stands out. Guests—typically shoeless in Marquesa robes—relax among richly landscaped pools and peaceful gardens (you're asked to turn off your cell phones in common areas) against a backdrop of steps rising to the villalike suites. Elegant rooms surround a courtyard and have antique and reproduction furnishings, creamy-white and aqua fabrics, and marble baths. The lobby resembles a Victorian parlor, with antiques, Audubon prints, flowers, and photos of early Key West. The clientele is well traveled and affluent 40- to 70-year-olds, mostly straight, but the hotel is very gay-friendly. Pros: elegant outdoor setting, romantic, deluxe baths. Cons: street-facing rooms can be noisy. ⊠*600 Fleming St., 33040* ☎*305/292–1919 or 800/869–4631* 🖷*305/294–2121* ⊕*www.marquesa.com* ⇋*27 rooms* ⌂*In-room: safe, dial-up. In-hotel: restaurant, room service, pools, spa, bicycles, no elevator, laundry service, concierge, public Wi-Fi* ⊟*AE, DC, MC, V.*

★ $$$$ 🏨 **Ocean Key Resort.** A pool and lively open-air bar make their homes on the Sunset Pier here, which provides the perfect view come sundown. Toast the day's end from private balconies that extend from spacious, brightly colored rooms that are both stylish and homey. High ceilings, hand-painted furnishings, a sleigh bed, a plaid couch, and a wooden chest for a coffee table create a personally designed look. This is a full-service resort with excellent amenities, including a great on-site spa. Pros: well-trained staff, lively pool scene, best spa on the island. Cons: layout is confusing. ⊠*Zero Duval St., 33040* ☎*305/296–7701 or 800/328–9815* 🖷*305/292–7685* ⊕*www.oceankey.com* ⇋*75 rooms, 25 suites* ⌂*In-room: kitchen (some), refrigerator, dial-up. In-hotel: 2 restaurants, room service, bars, pool, spa, diving, water sports, bicycles, laundry service, concierge, public Wi-Fi, parking (fee), some pets allowed, no-smoking rooms* ⊟*AE, D, DC, MC, V.*

$$$$ 🏨 **Pier House Resort & Caribbean Spa.** Great service, great location. The staff go out of their way to pamper you, and the location—on a quiet stretch of beach at the foot of Duval—is ideal as a buffer from, and gateway to, the action. It's a sprawling complex of weathered gray buildings, including an original Conch house. The courtyard is dotted with tall coconut palms and hibiscus blossoms, and rooms are cozy and colorful, with a water, pool, or garden view. Most rooms are smaller than those at newer hotels, except in the more expensive Caribbean Spa section, which has hardwood floors, two-poster plantation beds, and CD players. The best lodgings are in the Harbor Front, each with a private balcony. Sunset on the Havana Docks is a special event. Rooms nearest the public areas can be noisy. Pros: nice beach, good location, restaurant has water views. Cons: strong convention clientele, buildings feel cookie-cutter, poolside rooms are small and basic. ⊠*1 Duval St., 33040* ☎*305/296–4600 or 800/723–2791* 🖶*305/296–7569* ⊕*www. pierhouse.com* 🗪*126 rooms, 16 suites* ⚲*In-room: refrigerator, VCR (some), dial-up, Wi-Fi. In-hotel: 3 restaurants, room service, bars, pool, gym, spa, beachfront, bicycles, laundry service, concierge, Wi-Fi, no-smoking rooms* ⊟*AE, D, DC, MC, V.*

★ **$$$$**   ⛱ **Sunset Key.** This private island retreat offers the best of two worlds: secluded, luxurious cottage living, minutes away from the downtown Key West action. Board a 10-minute launch to the one-, two-, and three-bedroom cottages on 27-acre Sunset Key, 100 yards offshore, where you'll find sandy beaches, swaying palms, flowering gardens, and a delicious sense of privacy. The comforts are first-class and appeal to adults and children. Baked goods, juice, and a newspaper are delivered each morning, grocery shopping service is provided (fee), a private chef is available (fee), and you can use all the facilities at the Westin Key West Resort (where you check in and board the boat shuttle). Shuttle between the island and Key West around the clock at no extra charge, or remain at Sunset Key to dine, play, and relax at the very civilized beach, complete with attendants and cabanas. Pros: peace and luxury, roomy verandas, free 24-hour water shuttle. Cons: luxury doesn't come cheap. ⊠*245 Front St., 33040* ☎*305/292–5300 or 888/477–7786* 🖶*305/292–5395* ⊕*www.sunsetkeyisland.com* 🗪*37 cottages* ⚲*In-room: safe, kitchen, DVD, VCR, dial-up. In-hotel: restaurant, room service, tennis courts, pool, beachfront, laundry facilities, laundry service, concierge, public Internet, no-smoking rooms* ⊟*AE, D, DC, MC, V* ⑩*CP.*

★ **$$$–$$$$**   ⛱ **Southernmost Hotel & Resorts.** Sparkling clean and energetic, this hotel offers resort-style living at modest motel prices. Its location on the quiet, south end of Duval means you don't have to deal with the hustle and bustle of downtown unless you want to (it's within a 20-minute walk). Rooms are cookie-cutter but light and airy with cottage-style furnishings and the required tropical Keys colors. Grab a cold drink from the Tiki Hut bar and join the crowd around the pool, or venture across the street to the beach. Looking for something more upscale and intimate? They own two additional properties, La Mer boutique hotel and Dewey House in the same location. Pros: pool and Tiki Hut attract a lively crowd, access to additional pools on adjacent properties, free parking. Cons: public beach is small. ⊠*1319 Duval St., 33040* ☎*305/296–6577 or 800/354–4455* 🖶*305/294–8272* ⊕*www. southernmostresorts.com* 🗪*127 rooms* ⚲*In-room: safe, refrigerator,* *dial-up, Wi-Fi (some). In-hotel: Bar, pool, beachfront, laundry facilities, public Wi-Fi, parking (no fee), no-smoking rooms* ⊟*AE, D, DC, MC, V* ⃝|*CP.*

NIGHTLIFE & THE ARTS

THE ARTS

Catch the classics and the latest art, independent, and foreign films shown daily by the **Key West Film Society** (⊠*416 Eaton St.* ☎*305/295–9493*) in the two-screen Tropic Cinema theater. In a wickedly indulgent style that is so Key West, **Cinema Shores** (⊠*510 South St.* ☎*305/296–2491*), at Atlantic Shores Resort, an adult alternative resort, shows classic, foreign, and new films ($5) on a large outdoor screen on Thursday evenings. Viewers enjoy free popcorn and chocolate bars and cocktail service as they stretch out on lounge chairs on the lawn. Sebrina Alfonso directs the **Key West Symphony** (⊠*Tennessee Williams Fine Arts Center, 5901 College Rd.* ☎*305/292–1774*) during the winter season. With more than 20 years' experience, the **Red Barn Theatre** (⊠*319 Duval St., rear* ☎*305/296–9911 or 866/870–9911*), a small professional theater, performs dramas, comedies, and musicals, including works by new playwrights. The **Tennessee Williams Fine Arts Center** (⊠*Florida Keys Community College, 5901 College Rd.* ☎*305/296–1520*), on Stock Island, presents chamber music, dance, jazz concerts, and dramatic and musical plays with major stars, as well as other performing arts events. The community-run **Waterfront Playhouse** (⊠*Mallory Sq.* ☎*305/294–5015*) is a mid-1850s wrecker's warehouse that was converted into a 180-seat regional theater presenting comedy and drama from December to June. It's Florida's longest continuously running theater company.

NIGHTLIFE

BARS & LOUNGES

No matter your mood, **Durty Harry's** (⊠*208 Duval St.* ☎*305/296–4890*) can fit the bill. The mega-size entertainment complex has live music in a variety of indoor-outdoor bars, plus the tiny Red Garter strip club. Belly up to the bar for a cold mug of the signature Hog's Breath Lager at the infamous **Hog's Breath Saloon** (⊠*7400 Front St.* ☎*305/296–4222*), a must-stop on the Key West bar crawl. Live entertainment plays daily 10 AM–2 AM. Pick your entertainment at the **Bourbon Street Complex** (⊠*722–801 Duval St.* ☎*305/296–1992*), a gay-oriented club with five bars and two restaurants. There are two nightly drag shows in the 801 Bourbon Bar and 10 video screens along with male dancers grooving to the latest music spun by DJs at the Bourbon Street Pub. **Capt. Tony's Saloon** (⊠*428 Greene St.* ☎*305/294–1838*) was the original Sloppy Joe's in the mid-1930s, when Hemingway was a regular. Later, a young Jimmy Buffett sang here and made this Key's watering hole famous in his song "Last Mango in Paris." Bands play nightly. Pause for a libation at the open-air **Green Parrot Bar** (⊠*601 Whitehead St., at Southard St.* ☎*305/294–6133*). Built in 1890, the bar is said to be Key West's oldest, a sometimes-rowdy saloon where locals outnumber out-of-towners, especially on weekends when bands play. **LaTeDa Hotel and Bar** (⊠*1125*

Duval St. ☎*305/296–6706 or 877/528–3520*) hosts a riotously funny cabaret show nightly in the Crystal Room Cabaret Lounge. There's also live entertainment nightly, including the popular local singer Lenore Troia, in the Terrace Garden Bar and smooth piano jazz and pricey martinis in the ultracool lounge bar. A youngish, touristy crowd, sprinkled with aging Parrot Heads, frequents **Margaritaville Café** (✉ *500 Duval St.* ☎*305/292–1435*), owned by former Key West resident and recording star Jimmy Buffett, who has been known to perform here. The drink of choice is, of course, a margarita. There's live music nightly, as well as lunch and dinner. Nightlife at the **Pier House** (✉ *1 Duval St.* ☎*305/296–4600 or 800/723–2791*) begins with a steel-drum band (weekends) to celebrate the sunset on the beach, then moves indoors to the piano bar for live jazz (Thursday to Sunday). The **Schooner Wharf Bar** (✉ *202 William St.* ☎*305/292–3302*), an open-air waterfront bar and grill in the historic seaport district, retains its funky Key West charm. There's live island music all day. There's more history and good times at **Sloppy Joe's** (✉ *201 Duval St.* ☎*305/294–5717*), the successor to a famous 1937 speakeasy named for its founder, Captain Joe Russell. Decorated with Hemingway memorabilia and marine flags, the bar is popular with travelers and is full and noisy all the time. The **Top Lounge** (✉ *430 Duval St.* ☎*305/296–2991*) is on the 7th floor of the La Concha Crowne Plaza and is one of the best places in town to view the sunset and enjoy live entertainment Wednesday to Saturday. In the best traditions of a 1950s cocktail lounge, **Virgilio's** (✉ *524 Duval St.* ☎*305/296–8118*) serves chilled martinis to the soothing tempo of live jazz and blues nightly. It's part of the La Trattoria restaurant complex.

SPORTS & THE OUTDOORS

BIKING

Key West is a cycling town, but ride carefully: narrow and one-way streets along with car traffic result in several bike accidents a year. Some hotels rent or lend bikes to guests; others will refer you to a nearby shop and reserve a bike for you. ■**TIP→** Lock up; bikes—and porch chairs!—are favorite targets for local thieves.

Keys Moped & Scooter (✉ *523 Truman Ave.* ☎*305/294–0399*) rents beach cruisers with large baskets as well as scooters. Rates for scooters start at $30 for one to four hours. Look for the huge American flag on the roof. **Moped Hospital** (✉ *601 Truman Ave.* ☎*305/296–3344 or 866/296–1625*) supplies balloon-tire bikes ($12 per day) with yellow safety baskets for adults and kids, as well as mopeds ($40) and double-seater scooters for adults ($65). **Paradise Scooter Rentals** (✉ *112 Fitzpatrick St., next to the cruise-ship docks, and 430 Duval St.* ☎*305/923–6063*) rents bikes for about $13 a day and scooters from $54 (single) to $75 (double) a day.

FISHING

Key West Fishing Pro Guides (☎866/259–4205) has several guides and trips, including flats fishing ($400–$600), backcountry fishing ($400–$600), wreck/reef fishing ($500–$800), and offshore fishing ($500–$800). **Key West Bait and Tackle** (✉241 Margaret St. ☎305/292–1961) carries live bait, frozen rigged and unrigged bait, and fishing and rigging equipment. It also has the Live Bait Lounge; unwind and sip ice-cold beer while telling tall post-trip tales.

GOLF

Key West Resort Golf Course (✉6450 E. College Rd. ☎305/294–5232) is an 18-hole, par 70 course on the bay side of Stock Island. Nonresident fees are $150 for 18 holes (cart included) in season, $85 off-season.

SCUBA & SNORKELING

Adventure Charters & Tours (✉6810 Front St., 33040 ☎305/296–0362 or 888/817–0841) has sail-and-snorkel coral reef adventure tours ($35) aboard the 42-foot trimaran sailboat *Fantasea*, with a maximum of 16 people. There are two daily departures. They also offer full-day backcountry kayaking excursions ($129). **Captain's Corner** (✉Corner of Greene and Elizabeth ☎305/296–8865), a PADI five-star shop, has dive classes in several languages and twice-daily snorkel and dive trips ($30–$35) to reefs and wrecks aboard the 60-foot dive boat *Sea Eagle*. Safely dive the coral reefs without getting a scuba certification with **Snuba of Key West** (✉Garrison Bight Marina, Palm Ave. between Eaton St. and N. Roosevelt Blvd. ☎305/292–4616). Ride out to the reef on a catamaran, listen to a 20-minute orientation, then follow your guide underwater for a one-hour tour of the coral reefs. You wear a regulator with a breathing hose that is attached to a floating air tank on the surface of the water. No prior diving or snorkeling experience is necessary, but you must know how to swim. The $95 cost includes beverages.

SHOPPING

You'll find colorful local art, all things key lime, a handful of boutiques carrying designer labels, and the raunchiest T-shirts, thongs, and costumes in the civilized world. Browsing shops—with frequent pub stops along the way—makes for an entertaining stroll down Duval. Cocktails certainly help the appreciation of some goods (such as the doubled-over naked man who blows bubbles out his backside or the swashbuckling pirate fantasy-wear at the Fairvilla Megastore).

BahamaVillage is an enclave of spruced-up shops, restaurants, and vendors leading the way in the restoration of the historic district where black Bahamians settled in the 19th century. The village lies roughly between Whitehead and Fort streets and Angela and Catherine streets. Hemingway frequented the bars, restaurants, and boxing rings in the village.

ARTS & CRAFTS

Cuba, Cuba! (⊠*814 Duval St.* ☎*305/295–9442*) stocks paintings, sculptures, and photos by Cuban artists. The **Gallery on Greene** (⊠*606 Greene St.* ☎*305/294–1669*) showcases politically incorrect art by Jeff MacNelly and three-dimensional paintings by local artist Mario Sanchez, among others, in the largest gallery exhibition space in Key West. The oldest private art gallery in Key West, **Gingerbread Square Gallery** (⊠*1207 Duval St.* ☎*305/296–8900*), represents local and internationally acclaimed artists, including Sal Salinero and John Kiraly, in media ranging from graphics to art glass. Historian, photographer, and painter Sharon Wells opened **KW Light Gallery** (⊠*534 Fleming St.* ☎*305/294–0566*), a contemporary photographic art gallery, showcasing her own fine art photography and paintings as well as the works of other national artists. **Lucky Street Gallery** (⊠*1130 Duval St.* ☎*305/294–3973*) sells high-end contemporary paintings, watercolors, and a few pieces of jewelry by internationally recognized Key West–based artists. Changing exhibits, artist receptions, and special events make this Duval gallery a lively venue. **Pelican Poop** (⊠*314 Simonton St.* ☎*305/296–3887*) sells Caribbean art around a lush tropical courtyard garden with a fountain and pool. The owners buy direct from Caribbean artisans every year, so prices are very attractive. (Hemingway wrote *A Farewell to Arms* while living in the complex's apartment.) Potters Charles Pearson and Timothy Roeder *are* **Whitehead St. Pottery** (⊠*322 Julia St.* ☎*305/294–5067*), where they display their porcelain stoneware and raku-fired vessels. The setting, around two koi ponds with a burbling fountain, is as sublime as the art. **Glass Reunion** (⊠*825 Duval St.* ☎*305/294–1720*) showcases a collection of wild and impressive fine art glass. It's worth a stop in just to see the imaginative and over-the-top glass chandeliers, jewelry, dishes, and platters.

BOOKS

The **Key West Island Bookstore** (⊠*513 Fleming St.* ☎*305/294–2904*) is the literary bookstore of the large Key West writers' community. It carries new, used, and rare titles and specializes in Hemingway, Tennessee Williams, and South Florida mystery writers.

CLOTHES & FABRICS

Take home a shopping bag full of scarlet hibiscus, fuchsia heliconias, blue parrot fish, and even pink flamingos from the **Seam Shoppe** (⊠*1114 Truman Ave.* ☎*305/296–9830*), which specializes in the city's widest selection of tropical fabrics for indoor and outdoor upholstery, as well as quilts and fashions. Since 1964, **Key West Hand Print Fashions** (⊠*201 Simonton St.* ☎*305/294–9535 or 800/866–0333*) has been noted for its vibrant tropical prints, yard goods, and resort wear for men and women. It's in the Curry Warehouse, a brick building erected in 1878 to store tobacco. Get beach ready with the plush, colorful towels and robes at **Towels of Key West** (⊠*806 Duval St.* ☎*305/292–1120 or 800/927–0316*). There are more than 45 towel designs alone, some standard tourist design, some whimsical. All are hand-sewn on the island. Don't leave town without a browse through the legendary **Fairvilla Megastore** (⊠*520 Duval St.* ☎*305/292–0448*), where you'll find an astonishing array of fantasy wear, costumes (check out the pirate section), and "interesting" souvenirs.

FOOD & DRINK

The **Blond Giraffe** (✉ *802 Duval St.* ☎ *305/293–7874* ✉ *614 Front St.* ☎ *305/296–2020* ✉ *1209 Truman Ave.* ☎ *305/295–6776* ✉ *107 Simonton St.* ☎ *305/296–9174*) turned an old family recipe for key lime pie into a commercial success story. Its two stores often have a line for the pie, with delicate pastry, sweet-tart custard filling, and thick meringue topping. The key lime rum cake is the best-selling product for shipping home. For a snack on the run, try the pie on a stick. You'll be pleasantly surprised with the tropical fruit and vegetable wines sold at the **Key West Winery** (✉ *103 Simonton St.* ☎ *305/292–2254 or 866/880–1717*). Display crates hold bottles of wines made from blueberries, blackberries, pineapples, cherries, carrots, citrus, mangoes, watermelons, tomatoes, and, of course, key limes. Stop in for a free tasting. **Fausto's Food Palace** (✉ *522 Fleming St.* ☎ *305/296–5663* ✉ *1105 White St.* ☎ *305/294–5221*) may be under a roof, but it's a market in the traditional town-square sense. Since 1926, Fausto's has been the spot to catch up on the week's gossip and to chill out in summer—it has groceries, organic foods, marvelous wines, a sushi chef on duty from 8 to 6, and box lunches to go. If you like it hot, you'll love **Peppers of Key West** (✉ *602 Greene St.* ☎ *305/295–9333 or 800/597–2823*). The shop has hundreds of sauces, salsas, and sweets guaranteed to light your fire on the way in and out. You'll spend your first five minutes at the family-owned **Waterfront Market** (✉ *201 William St.* ☎ *305/296–0778*) wondering how to franchise one of these great markets in your hometown. The upscale market sells items from around the world, including health food, organic produce, fresh salads, gourmet coffees, imported cheeses, baked goods, and more. Don't miss the fish market, arguably the best in town; there's also a juice bar, sushi, and vegan dishes.

GIFTS & SOUVENIRS

Like a parody of Duval Street T-shirt shops, the hole-in-the-wall **Art Attack** (✉ *606 Duval St.* ☎ *305/294–7131*) throws in every icon and trinket anyone nostalgic for the days of peace and love might fancy: beads, necklaces, harmony bells, and psychedelic T-shirts. Best sellers are photographic postcards of Key West by Tony Gregory. It's open until 11 nightly. **Fast Buck Freddie's** (✉ *500 Duval St.* ☎ *305/294–2007*) sells a classy, hip selection of crystal, furniture, tropical clothing, and every flamingo item imaginable. It also carries such imaginative items as a noise-activated rat in a trap and a raccoon tail in a bag. **Half Buck Freddie's** (✉ *306 William St.* ☎ *305/294–2007*) is the discount-outlet store for Fast Buck's. It's closed Tuesday and Wednesday. In a town with a gazillion T-shirt shops,

★ **Last Flight Out** (✉ *503 Greene St.* ☎ *305/294–8008*) stands out for its selection of classic namesake Ts, specialty clothing, and gifts that appeal to aviation types and others who reach for the stars. For that unique souvenir of your trip to Key West head to **Montage** (✉ *512 Duval St.* ☎ *877/396–4278*), where you'll discover hundreds of hand-

7

crafted signs of popular Key West guesthouses, inns, hotels, restaurants, bars, and streets. If you can't find what you're looking for, they'll make it for you.

HEALTH & BEAUTY

Key West Aloe (✉ *540 Greene St., at Simonton St.* ☎ *305/294–5592 or 800/445–2563*) was founded in a garage in 1971; today it produces some 300 perfume, sunscreen, and skin-care products for men and women.

THE FLORIDA KEYS ESSENTIALS

To research prices, get advice from other travelers, and book travel arrangements, visit www.fodors.com.

TRANSPORTATION

BY AIR

CARRIERS Service between Key West International Airport and Miami, Fort Lauderdale/Hollywood, Fort Myers, West Palm, Atlanta, Naples, Orlando, St. Petersburg, and Tampa is provided by American Eagle, Comair/Delta Connection, Gulfstream/Continental Connection, and US Airways/US Airways Express. However, flights to Key West are among the most frequently canceled—as many as one out of three at some airports, including Tampa—because of fuel costs and low passenger counts.

Contacts American Eagle (☎ *800/433–7300* ⊕ *www.aa.com*). **Comair/Delta Connection** (☎ *800/354–9822* ⊕ *www.comair.com*). **Gulfstream/Continental Connection** (☎ *800/523–3273* ⊕ *www.gulfstreamair.com*). **US Airways/US Airways Express** (☎ *800/428–4322* ⊕ *www.usairways.com*).

AIRPORTS & Airporter operates scheduled van and bus pickup service from all
TRANSFERS Miami International Airport (MIA) baggage areas to wherever you want to go in Key Largo ($40) and Islamorada ($45). A group discount is given for three or more passengers. There are three departures daily; reservations are required. Keys Shuttle runs scheduled service six times a day in 15-passenger vans (9 passengers maximum) between Miami Airport and Key West with stops throughout the Keys for $70 to $90 per person. The SuperShuttle charges about $150 per passenger for trips to the Upper Keys. To go farther into the Keys, you must book an entire van (up to 11 passengers), which costs about $250 to Marathon, $350 to Key West. SuperShuttle requests 24-hour notice for transportation back to the airport.

Airport Contacts Key West International Airport (✉ *S. Roosevelt Blvd., Key West* ☎ *305/296–7223* ⊕ *www.keywestinternationalairport.com*). **Miami International Airport** (☎ *305/876–7000* ⊕ *www.miami-airport.com*). **Airporter** (☎ *305/852–3413 or 800/830–3413*). **Keys Shuttle** (☎ *305/289–9997 or 888/765–9997* ⊕ *www.floridakeysshuttle.com*). **SuperShuttle** (☎ *305/871–2000* ⊕ *www.supershuttle.com*).

BY BOAT & FERRY

Boaters can travel to and along the Keys either along the Intracoastal Waterway (5-foot draft limitation) through Card, Barnes, and Blackwater sounds and into Florida Bay or along the deeper Atlantic Ocean route through Hawk Channel, a buoyed passage. Refer to NOAA Nautical Charts Numbers 11451, 11445, and 11441. The Keys are full of marinas that welcome transient visitors, but they don't have enough slips for everyone. Make reservations in advance and ask about channel and dockage depth—many marinas are quite shallow.

For nonemergency information contact Coast Guard Group Key West; VHF-FM Channel 16. Safety and weather information is broadcast at 7 AM and 5 PM Eastern Standard Time on VHF-FM Channels 16 and 22A. There are stations in Islamorada and Marathon.

Key West Express operates air-conditioned ferries between the Key West Terminal (Caroline and Grinnell Streets) and Marco Island and Fort Myers Beach, on the mainland's southwest coast. The trip takes 3½ hours each way. Ferries depart in the morning at 9 and return in the afternoon between 5:30 and 6. Tickets start at $73 one-way, $128 round-trip. The round-trip includes continental breakfast. A current, legal photo ID is required for each passenger. All bags are subject to search. Advance reservations are recommended.

Chambers of commerce, marinas, and dive shops offer free Teall's Guides, land and nautical charts that pinpoint popular fishing and diving areas throughout the Keys.

Contacts Coast Guard Group for the Florida Keys (⊠ *Key West* ☎ *305/292–8856 or 800/368–5647* ⊠ *Islamorada* ☎ *305/664–8077 information, 305/664–4404 emergencies* ⊠ *Marathon* ☎ *305/743–6778 information, 305/743–6388 emergencies*). **Key West Express Ferry** (☎ *888/539–2628 or 239/394–9700* ⊕ *www.keywestferry.com*). **Teall's Guides** (⌂ *Box 522409, Marathon Shores 33052* ☎ *305/872–3123*).

BY BUS

Greyhound Lines runs a special Keys shuttle three or four times a day (depending on the day of the week) between Miami International Airport (departing from Concourse E, lower level) and stops throughout the Keys. Fares run from around $15 for Key Largo (Howard Johnson, MM 102) to around $35 for Key West (3535 S. Roosevelt, Key West Airport).

City of Key West Department of Transportation has six color-coded bus routes traversing the island from 6:30 AM to 11:30 PM. Stops have signs with the international symbol for bus. Schedules are available on buses and at hotels, visitor centers, and shops. The fare is $1 (exact change) or $3 for an all-day pass that you purchase on board.

American Coach Lines (formerly the Dade–Monroe Express) provides daily bus service from MM 50 in Marathon to the Florida City Wal-Mart Supercenter on the Mainland. The bus stops at major shopping centers as well as on-demand anywhere along the route during daily round-trips on the hour from 6 AM to 9:55 PM. The cost is $1.85 each way, exact change needed. The Lower Keys Shuttle bus runs from Marathon to Key West ($2 one way), with scheduled and on-demand stops along the way.

Contacts **City of Key West Department of Transportation** (☎ *305/292–8160*). **American Coach Lines** (☎ *305/770–3131*). **Greyhound Lines** (☎ *800/410–5397 or 800/231–2222*). **Lower Keys Shuttle** (☎ *305/292–8160* ⊕ *www.monroecounty-fl.gov*).

BY CAR

From MIA follow signs to Coral Gables and Key West, which put you on Lejeune Road, then Route 836 west. Take the Homestead Extension of Florida's Turnpike south (toll road), which ends at Florida City and connects to U.S. 1. Tolls from the airport run approximately $2.25. The alternative from Florida City is Card Sound Road (Route 905A), which has a bridge toll of $1. Continue to the only stop sign and turn right on Route 905, which rejoins U.S. 1 31 mi south of Florida City.

In Key West's Old Town, parking is scarce and costly. Some lodgings provide parking or discounts at municipal lots. If you're really lucky, you'll snag a free spot on one of the side streets—just be sure it's not marked for residential parking only. It's better to take a taxi, rent a bicycle or moped, walk, or take a shuttle to get around. Elsewhere in the Keys, a car is crucial. Gas costs more than on the mainland, so fill your tank in Miami and top it off in Florida City. Most of the Overseas Highway is narrow and crowded (especially weekends and in high season). Expect delays behind RVs, trucks, cars towing boats, and rubbernecking tourists. The best Keys road map, published by the Homestead–Florida City Chamber of Commerce, can be obtained for $5.50 from the Tropical Everglades Visitor Center.

Contacts **Tropical Everglades Visitor Center** (✉ *160 U.S. 1, Florida City 33034* ☎ *305/245–9180 or 800/388–9669* ⊕ *www.tropicaleverglades.com*).

CAR RENTAL Unless you plan to veg out and wander within a very small radius, a car for at least part of your stay is a necessity. Two- and four-passenger open-air electric cars that travel about 25 mph are an environmentally friendly way to get around the island. Rent them from Key West Cruisers for $89 to $129 a half day for the two- or four-seater, or $139 to $189 a day.

Avis, Budget, and Enterprise serve Marathon Airport. Key West's airport has booths for Alamo, Avis, Budget, Dollar, and Hertz. Enterprise Rent-A-Car has offices in Key Largo, Marathon, and Key West. Thrifty Car Rental has an office in Tavernier.

Avoid flying into Key West and driving back to Miami; there are substantial drop-off charges for leaving a Key West car there.

Contacts **Alamo** (☎ *305/294–6675 or 800/327–9633* ⊕ *www.alamo.com*). **Avis** (✉ *Key West Airport* ☎ *305/294–4846* ✉ *Marathon Airport* ☎ *305/743–5428 or 800/331–1212* ⊕ *www.avis.com*). **Budget** (✉ *Key West Airport* ☎ *305/294–8868* ✉ *Marathon Airport* ☎ *305/743–3998 or 800/527–0700* ⊕ *www.budget.com*). **Dollar** (☎ *305/296–9921 or 800/800–4000* ⊕ *www.dollar.com*). **Enterprise**

Rent-A-Car (☎800/325–8007 ⊕ www.enterprise.com). **Hertz** (☎305/294–1039 or 800/654–3131 ⊕ www.hertz.com). **Key West Cruisers** (✉500 Truman Ave., at Duval St. ☎305/294–4724 or 888/800–8802). **Thrifty Car Rental** (✉MM 91.8, OS, Tavernier ☎305/852–6088 or 800/847–4389 ⊕ www.thrifty.com).

BY TAXI

Serving the Keys from Ocean Reef to Key West, Luxury Limousine has luxury sedans and limos that seat up to eight passengers, as well as vans and buses. It'll pick up from any airport in South Florida. In the Upper Keys (MM 94–74), Village Taxi has been operating since 1982 and charges a $5 pickup charge plus $2 per mi for vans that hold six. It also makes airport runs. Florida Keys Taxi Dispatch (also called Five Sixes Taxi) operates around the clock in Key West. The fare for two or more from the Key West airport to Old Town or New Town is $7.50 per person. Otherwise meters register $2.75 to start, 55¢ for each $^1/_5$ mi, and 55¢ for every 50 seconds of waiting time. Their pink taxis all have bike racks.

Contacts Florida Keys Taxi Dispatch (also called Five Sixes Taxi) (☎305/296–6666 or 305/296–1800 ⊕ www.keywesttaxi.com). **Luxury Limousine** (☎305/367–2329 or 800/664–0124). **Village Taxi** (☎305/664–8181).

CONTACTS & RESOURCES

EMERGENCIES

Keys Hotline provides information and emergency assistance in six languages. Florida Marine Patrol maintains a 24-hour telephone service to handle reports of boating emergencies and natural-resource violations. Coast Guard Group Key West responds to local marine emergencies and reports of navigation hazards. The Keys have no 24-hour pharmacies. Hospital pharmacists will help with emergencies after regular retail business hours. Fishermen's Hospital, Lower Florida Keys Health System, and Mariners Hospital have 24-hour emergency rooms.

Contacts Emergencies (☎911). **Coast Guard Group Key West** (☎305/292–8727). **Fishermen's Hospital** (✉MM 48.7, OS, Marathon ☎305/743–5533 ⊕www.fishermenshospital.com). **Florida Marine Patrol/Fish and Wildlife Conservation Commission** (✉MM 48, BS, 2796 Overseas Hwy., Suite 100, State Regional Service Center, Marathon33050 ☎305/289–2320, 800/342–5392 after 5 PM ⊕www.myfwc.com). **Lower Florida Keys Health System** (✉MM 5, BS, 5900 College Rd., Stock Island ☎305/294–5531). **Mariners Hospital** (✉MM 91.5, BS, Tavernier ☎305/434–3000 ⊕www.baptisthealth.net).

MEDIA

NEWSPAPERS & MAGAZINES — The best of the publications covering Key West are the weekly *Solares Hill* and the daily *Key West Citizen*. For the Upper and Middle Keys, turn to the semiweekly *Keynoter*. The *Free Press, Reporter,* and *Upper Keys Independent* cover the same area once a week. The *Miami Herald* publishes a Keys edition with good daily listings of local events. The weekly *Celebrate* and the monthly *Southern Exposure* are good sources of entertainment and information for gay and lesbian travelers.

TELEVISION &   WLRN (National Public Radio) is 91.3, 92.1, and 93.5, depending on
RADIO   where you are in the Keys. Try WKLG 102.1 bilingual (English and
Spanish) for adult contemporary; WCTH 100.3 for country; WFKZ
103.1 for classic rock; WKEZ 96.9 for easy listening; WFFG AM 1300
Keys for talk radio, sports, and news; and WKYZ 101.3 for country.

LODGING

The Key West Innkeepers Association is an umbrella organization for
dozens of local properties. Vacation Rentals Key West lists historic cottages, homes, and condominiums for rent. Although it prefers to handle
reservations for all types of accommodations in advance, the Key West
Welcome Center gets a lot of walk-in business because of its location on
U.S. 1 at the entrance to Key West. Property Management of Key West,
Inc. has lease and rental service for condominiums, town houses, and
private homes. Rent Key West Vacations specializes in renting vacation
homes and condos for a week or longer. Vacation Key West lists all
kinds of properties throughout Key West.

Contacts **Key West Innkeepers Association** (⊠ *Key West 33040* ☎ *800/492–*
1911 ⊕ *www.keywestinns.com).* **Vacation Rentals Key West** (⊠ *1511 Truman Ave.,*
Key West 33040 ☎ *305/292–7997 or 800/621–9405* 🖷 *305/294–7501* ⊕ *www.*
keywestvacations.com). **Key West Welcome Center** (⊠ *24746 Overseas Hwy.,*
Summerland Key 33042 ☎ *305/296–4444 or 800/284–4482* ⊕ *www.keywest-*
welcomecenter.com). **Rent Key West Vacations** (⊠ *1107 Truman Ave., Key West*
33040 ☎ *305/294–0990 or 800/833–7368* ⊕ *www.rentkeywest.com).* **Vacation**
Key West (⊠ *100 Grinnell St., Key West 33040* ☎ *305/295–9500 or 800/595–5397*
⊕ *www.vacationkw.com).*

TOURS

Island Aeroplane Tours flies up to two passengers in a 1941 Waco, an
open-cockpit biplane. Tours range from a 15-minute overview of Key
West ($120 for two) to a 55-minute look at the offshore reefs ($325 for
two). Seaplanes of Key West has half- and full-day trips to the Dry Tor-
tugas; explore Fort Jefferson, built in 1846, and snorkel on the beautiful protected reef. Soft drinks and snorkel equipment are included in
the $199 half-day, $345 full-day per-person fee, plus a $5 park fee.

Key West's Ghosts & Legends offers nightly tours at 7 and 9 ($18),
including a visit to the Old City Morgue, haunted Victorian mansions,
and the Key West Cemetery to hear fascinating and sometimes bone-
chilling stories of real-life events and people. Lloyd's Original Tropical
Bike Tour, led by a 30-year Key West veteran, explores the natural,
noncommercial side of Key West at a leisurely pace, stopping on back-
streets and in backyards of private homes to sample native fruits and
view indigenous plants and trees; at City Cemetery; and at the Medi-
cine Garden, a private meditation garden. The behind-the-scenes tours
run two hours and cost $35, including bike rental. Captain Sterling's
Everglades Eco-Tours operates Everglades and Florida Bay ecology
tours ($49 per person), sunset cruises ($59 per person), the four-hour
out-island excursion to a remote island in Florida Bay ($299 for up to
six people), and the Flamingo Express, a five-hour boat tour from Key

Largo to Flamingo, in mainland Everglades National Park ($399 for up to six people.)

Key Largo Princess offers two-hour glass-bottom-boat trips ($25) and sunset cruises on a luxury 70-foot motor yacht with a 280-square-foot glass viewing area, departing from the Holiday Inn docks three times a day. M/V *Discovery*'s glass-bottom boats have submerged viewing rooms for 360-degree marine watching ($35). Strike Zone Charters has glass-bottom-boat excursions into the backcountry and Atlantic Ocean. The five-hour Island Excursion ($49) emphasizes nature and Keys history. Besides close encounters with birds, sea life, and vegetation, there's a fish cookout on an island. Snorkel and fishing equipment, food, and drinks are included. This is one of the few nature outings in the Keys with wheelchair access.

Victoria Impallomeni, noted wilderness guide and authority on the ecology of Florida Bay, invites nature lovers—and especially children—aboard the *Imp II,* a 25-foot Aquasport, for four-hour ($500) and seven-hour ($700) ecotours that frequently include encounters with wild dolphins. While island-hopping, you visit underwater gardens, natural shoreline, and mangrove habitats. Play Like a Dolphin lets you get pulled through the water on a dolphin board. Tours also include Dancing Water Spirits retreats, a self-transformational retreat with healing therapies. All equipment is supplied. Tours leave from Murray's Marina.

The Conch Tour Train is a 90-minute narrated tour of Key West, traveling 14 mi through Old Town and around the island. Board at Mallory Square and Flagler Station (901 Caroline St.) every half hour (9–4:30 from Mallory Square, later at other stops). The cost is $25. Old Town Trolley operates trackless trolley-style buses, departing from the Mallory Square and Roosevelt Boulevard depots every 30 minutes (9–4:30 from Mallory Square, later at other stops), for 90-minute narrated tours of Key West. The smaller trolleys go places the train won't fit. You may disembark at any of 10 stops and reboard a later trolley. The cost is $25, but you can save a little by booking online. Key West Business Guild's 75-minute Gay and Lesbian Historic Trolley Tours highlight the contributions gay and lesbian writers, artists, politicians, designers, and celebrities have made to Key West's past. Tours, which cost $25, depart Saturday at 11 AM from 512 South Street. Look for the rainbow flags on the trolley.

Adventure Charters & Tours loads kayaks onto the 42-foot catamaran *Island Fantasea* in Key West and heads out to the Great White Heron National Wildlife Refuge for guided kayak nature tours with a maximum of 14 passengers. Full-day trips ($129) depart at 9:30 and include snorkeling, fishing, a grilled lunch, and drinks. They also offer 2½-hour trips ($35) at 10 and 2 that paddle out from Key West. Lazy Dog Island Outfitters runs full-day guided sea-kayak natural-history tours around the mangrove islands just east of Key West. The $60 charge covers transportation, bottled water, a snack, and supplies, including snorkeling gear.

7

Captain Bill Keogh (naturalist, educator, photographer, and author of *The Florida Keys Paddling Guide*) operates Big Pine Kayak Adventures, which takes visitors into remote areas of two national wildlife refuges in the Lower Keys to explore mangrove hammocks, islands, creeks, and sponge and grass flats on kayak nature tours, shallow-water skiff eco-tours, backcountry catamaran sailing cruises, and shallow-water fishing expeditions. Prices start at $50 per person for a three-hour tour.

The folks at Florida Bay Outfitters know Upper Keys and Everglades waters well. Take a full-moon paddle, or a one- to seven-day canoe or kayak tour to the Everglades, Lignumvitae, or Indian Key. Trips run $50 to $795. In addition to publishing several good guides on Key West, the Historic Florida Keys Foundation conducts tours of the City Cemetery Tuesday and Thursday at 9:30. As the former state historian in Key West and the current owner of a historic-preservation consulting firm, Sharon Wells of Island City Strolls knows plenty about Key West. She's authored many works, including the annually revised "Walking and Biking Guide to Historic Key West," which has 14 self-guided tours of the historic district. It's available at guesthouses, hotels, and Key West bookstores. If that whets your appetite, sign on for one of her walking or biking tours, including the Famous Writers and Artists of Key West and the Off-the-Beaten-Track Old Town tour, which cost $25, with a four-person minimum. "Pelican Path" is a free walking guide to Key West published by the Old Island Restoration Foundation. The guide discusses the history and architecture of 43 structures along 25 blocks of 12 Old Town streets. Pick up a copy at the Chamber of Commerce.

Contacts **Adventure Charters & Tours** (✉ *6810 Front St., Stock Island 33040* ☎ *305/296–0362 or 888/817–0841* ⊕ *www.keywestadventures.com*). **Big Pine Kayak Adventures** (✉ *Box 431311, Big Pine Key 33043* ☎ *305/872–7474* ⊕ *www. keyskayaktours.com*). **Conch Tour Train** (☎ *305/294–5161 or 800/868–7482* ⊕ *www.conchtrain.com*). **Everglades Eco-Tours** (✉ *Dolphin's Cove, MM 102, BS, Key Largo 33037* ☎ *305/853–5161 or 888/224–6044* ⊕ *www.captainsterling.com*). **Florida Bay Outfitters** (✉ *MM 104, BS, 104050 Overseas Hwy., Key Largo 33037* ☎ *305/451–3018* ⊕ *www.kayakfloridakeys.com*). **Historic Florida Keys Foundation** (✉ *510 Greene St., Old City Hall, Key West 33040* ☎ *305/292–6718*). **Island Aeroplane Tours** (✉ *Key West Airport, 3469 S. Roosevelt Blvd.* ☎ *305/294–8687* ⊕ *www.keywestairtours.com*). **Island City Strolls** (✉ *Box 56, Key West 33041* ☎ *305/294–8380* ⊕ *www.seekeywest.com*). **Key Largo Princess** (✉ *MM 100, OS, 99701 Overseas Hwy., Key Largo 33037* ☎ *305/451–4655 or 877/648–8129* ⊕ *www.keylargoprincess.com*). **Key West Business Guild (gay)** (✉ *513 Truman Ave.* ✉ *Box 1208, Key West 33041* ☎ *305/294–4603 or 800/535–7797* ⊕ *www. gaykeywestfl.com*). **Lazy Dog Island Outfitters** (✉ *5114 Overseas Highways, Key West 33040* ☎ *305/295–9898* ⊕ *www.mosquitocoast.net*). **Lloyd's Original Tropical Bike Tour** (✉ *Truman Ave. and Simonton St., Key West* ☎ *305/304–4700* ⊕ *www.lloydstropicalbiketour.com*). **Murray's Marina** (✉ *5710 U.S. Highway 1, MM 5, Key West 33040* ☎ *305/296–0364* ⊕ *www.murraymarine.com*). **M/V** *Discovery* (✉ *Land's End Marina, 251 Margaret St., Key West 33040* ☎ *305/293–0099 or 800/262–0099* ⊕ *www.discoveryunderseatours.com*). **Old Town Trolley** (✉ *6631 Maloney Ave., Key West* ☎ *305/296–6688* ⊕ *www.oldtowntrolley.com*). **Seaplanes**

of Key West (✉ *Key West Airport, 3471 S. Roosevelt Blvd.* ☎ *305/294–0709 or 800/950–2359* ⊕ *www.seaplanesofkeywest.com*). **Strike Zone Charters** (✉ *MM 29.6, BS, 29675 Overseas Hwy., Big Pine Key 33043* ☎ *305/872–9863 or 800/654–9560*). **Victoria Impallomeni** (✉ *5710 U.S. 1, Key West 33040* ☎ *305/304–7562 or 888/822–7366* ⊕ *www.captainvictoria.com*).

VISITOR INFORMATION

Contacts **Big Pine and the Lower Keys Chamber of Commerce** (✉ *MM 31, OS, 31020 Overseas Hwy.* 🖆 *Box 430511, Big Pine Key 33043* ☎ *305/872–2411 or 800/872–3722* 🖨 *305/872–0752* ⊕ *www.lowerkeyschamber.com*). **Florida Keys & Key West Visitors Bureau** (✉ *402 Wall St., Box 1146, Key West 33041* ☎ *800/352–5397* ⊕ *www.fla-keys.com*). **Florida Keys Council of the Arts** (✉ *1100 Simonton St., Key West 33040* ☎ *305/295–4369* 🖨 *305/295–4372* ⊕ *www.keysarts. org*). **Gay and Lesbian Community Center of Key West** (✉ *513 Truman Ave., Key West 33040* ☎ *305/292–3223* 🖨 *305/292–3237* ⊕ *www.glcckeywest.org*). **Greater Key West Chamber of Commerce (mainstream)** (✉ *402 Wall St., Key West 33040* ☎ *305/294–2587 or 800/527–8539* ⊕ *www.keywestchamber.org* 🖨 *305/294–7806*). **Greater Marathon Chamber of Commerce & Visitor Center** (✉ *MM 53.5, BS, 12222 Overseas Hwy., Marathon 33050* ☎ *305/743–5417 or 800/262–7284* 🖨 *305/289–0183* ⊕ *www.floridakeysmarathon.com*). **Islamorada Chamber of Commerce** (✉ *MM 83.2, BS, Box 915, Islamorada 33036* ☎ *305/664–4503 or 800/322–5397* 🖨 *305/664–4289* ⊕ *www.islamoradachamber.com*). **Key Largo Chamber of Commerce** (✉ *MM 106, BS, 106000 Overseas Hwy., Key Largo 33037* ☎ *305/451–14747 or 800/822–1088* 🖨 *305/451–4726* ⊕ *www.keylargochamber. org*). **Key West Business Guild (gay)** (✉ *513 Truman Ave.* 🖆 *Box 1208, Key West 33041* ☎ *305/294–4603 or 800/535–7797* ⊕ *www.gaykeywestfl.com*).

The Everglades

WORD OF MOUTH

"Check the tides, and plan a bike trip down Snake Bite Trail. You want to arrive at the end of the trail at low tide, because the trail ends at Florida Bay, and the birds will be all over feeding. When we went last time, we didn't go at low tide, but it was still wonderful, with lots of wildlife."

–birder

Updated by
Chelle Koster
Walton

MIAMI IS THE ONLY CITY in the country that has two national parks and a national preserve in its backyard. Everglades National Park, created in 1947, was meant to preserve the slow-moving River of Grass—a freshwater river 50 mi wide but only 6 inches deep, flowing from Lake Okeechobee through marshy grassland into Florida Bay. Along the Tamiami Trail (U.S. 41), marshes of saw grass extend as far as the eye can see, interspersed only with hammocks or tree islands of bald cypress and mahogany, while overhead, southern bald eagles make circles in the sky. An assembly of plants and flowers, including ferns, orchids, and bromeliads, shares the brackish waters with river otters, turtles, alligators, and occasionally that gentle giant, the

TOP 5
Everglades National Park: Spend a day or two driving, biking, hiking, or boating in deep, raw wilderness.
Biscayne National Park underwater adventure: Scuba dive, snorkel, or take a glass-bottom boat.
Big Cypress National Preserve: Walk the boardwalk over alligators and drive Loop Road for a backwoods experience.
Miccosukee Indian Village: Take an airboat ride to a Native American camp.
Ride a swamp buggy: Several tour operators offer forays.

Florida manatee. Not so gentle, though, is the saw grass. Deceptively graceful, these tall, willowy sedges have small, sharp teeth on the edges of their leaves.

Biscayne National Park, established as a national monument in 1968 and 12 years later expanded and designated a national park, is the nation's largest marine park and the largest national park within the continental United States with living coral reefs. A small portion of the park's almost 274 square mi consists of mainland coast and outlying islands, but 95% is under water, much of it in Biscayne Bay. Of particular interest are the mangroves and their tangled masses of stiltlike roots that thicken the shorelines. These "walking trees," as locals call them, have striking curved prop roots, which arch down from the trunk, while aerial roots drop from branches. The trees draw fresh water from saltwater and create a coastal nursery capable of sustaining myriad types of marine life. Congress established Big Cypress National Preserve in 1974 after buying up one of the least-developed watershed areas in South Florida to protect Everglades National Park. The preserve, on the northern edge of Everglades National Park, entails extensive tracts of prairie, marsh, pinelands, forested swamps, and sloughs. Although preservation and recreation are the preserve's mainstay, hunting and off-road vehicle use are allowed. Ten Thousand Islands National Wildlife Refuge, accessible only by boat, spreads to the south of Everglades National Park on its gulf side; and Florida Panther National Wildlife Refuge, accessible by two new trails, and Fakahatchee Strand Preserve State Park both lie to the northwest.

Hurricanes Katrina and Wilma took their toll on the Everglades in 2005, knocking down trees, flooding, and flattening the landscape.

8

Although nature heals quickly, towns take a little longer, particularly Flamingo, which took the brunt of the storm before it moved northward. The lodge, restaurant, and some marina tours and facilities were still closed as of this writing.

More long-term in effect, Miami's backyard is threatened by suburban sprawl, agriculture, and business development. What results is competition among environmental, agricultural, and developmental interests. The biggest issue is water. Starting in the 1930s, a giant flood-control system began diverting water to canals running to the gulf and the ocean. The unfortunate side effect of flood control has been devastation of the wilderness. Park visitors decry diminished bird counts, the black bear population has been nearly eliminated, and the Florida panther once neared extinction. Meanwhile, the loss of fresh water has made Florida Bay saltier, devastating breeding grounds and creating dead zones where pea-green algae have replaced sea grasses and sponges.

The nearly $8 billion, 10-year comprehensive plan worked out between government agencies and a host of conservation groups and industries to restore, protect, and preserve the ecosystem is under way. More than 200 projects tear down levees, fill canals, construct new water-storage areas on land formerly preserved for agriculture or new development, channel water to estuaries and Everglades National Park, and provide flood protection and a reliable water supply. The expectation is that new policies and projects implemented over the next decade will go a long way toward reviving the natural system.

EXPLORING THE EVERGLADES

Most sports and activities in both national parks are based on water, on the study of nature, or both. So even when you're on land, be prepared to get a bit damp on the region's marshy trails. Although relatively compact compared with the national parks of the West, these parks still require time to see. The narrow, two-lane roads through the Everglades make for slow travel, whereas sightseeing by boat, a necessity at Biscayne, takes time. The southern tip of the Florida peninsula is largely taken up by Everglades National Park, and land access to it is primarily by two roads. The main park road traverses the southern Everglades from the gateway towns of Homestead and Florida City to the outpost of Flamingo, on Florida Bay. In the northern Everglades, take the Tamiami Trail (U.S. 41) east from the Greater Miami area to the western park entrance in Everglades City at Route 29 near Naples.

ABOUT THE RESTAURANTS

With a few exceptions, dining centers on low-key mom-and-pop places that serve hearty home-style food, and small eateries that specialize in local fare: alligator, fish, stone crab, frogs' legs, and fresh Florida lobster from the Keys. Native American restaurants add another dimension, serving local favorites as well as catfish, Indian fry bread (a flour-and-water flat bread), pumpkin bread, Indian burgers (ground beef browned, rolled in fry-bread dough), and tacos (fry bread with chili, lettuce, tomato, and shredded cheddar cheese on top). Because of its large Hispanic farm-worker population, Homestead restaurants specializing in authentic and inexpensive Mexi and fresh produce. Diners looking for something more tren the Keys or Miami. Restaurants in Everglades City, especi along the river, have the freshest seafood, particularly stone cra ...ese places can be casual to the point of rustic, and often close for a month or two in the fall. The nearest fine restaurants to Everglades City are in Marco Island and Naples, each about a half hour away. Although both Everglades and Biscayne national parks and Big Cypress National Preserve are wilderness areas, there are restaurants within a short drive. Most are between Miami and Shark Valley along the Tamiami Trail (U.S. 41), in the Homestead–Florida City area, in Everglades City, and in the Florida Keys along the Overseas Highway (U.S. 1). There are also fast-food establishments on the Tamiami Trail east of Krome Avenue and along U.S. 1 in Homestead–Florida City, and west of Everglades City in Naples.

ABOUT THE HOTELS

If you're spending several days exploring the East Coast Everglades, stay either in one of the park's campgrounds—11 mi away in Homestead–Florida City, where there are reasonably priced motels and RV parks—or in the Florida Keys or the Greater Miami–Fort Lauderdale area. Lodgings and campgrounds are also available on the Gulf Coast in Everglades City, Naples, and Marco Island. Florida City's selection is mostly of the chain variety and geared toward business travelers, with Internet service and continental breakfast. Accommodations near the parks range from inexpensive to moderate and offer off-season rates in summer, when rampant mosquito populations essentially preclude going outdoors for any length of time. If you crave luxury and lots of extras, head for Miami or Naples—where you'll pay more.

8

WHAT IT COSTS					
	¢	$	$$	$$$	$$$$
RESTAURANTS	under $10	$10–$15	$15–$20	$20–$30	over $30
HOTELS	under $80	$80–$100	$100–$140	$140–$220	over $220

Restaurant prices are per person for a main course at dinner. Hotel prices are for a standard double room, excluding 6% sales tax (more in some counties) and 1%–4% tourist tax.

TIMING

Winter is the best time to visit Biscayne National Park, Everglades National Park, and Big Cypress National Preserve. Temperatures and mosquito activity are low to moderate, low water levels concentrate the resident wildlife around sloughs that retain water all year, and migratory birds swell the avian population. Winter is also the busiest time in the park. Make reservations and expect crowds at Flamingo, the main visitor center (known officially as the Ernest F. Coe Visitor Center), and Royal Palm Visitor Center. In late spring the weather turns hot and rainy, and tours and facilities are less crowded. Migratory birds depart, and you must look harder to see wildlife. Even if you're not staying in

Everglades National Park, try to stick around until dusk, when dozens of bird species feed around the ponds and trails. While shining a flashlight over the water in marshy areas after dark, look for two yellowish-red reflections above the surface—telltale signs of alligators.

■ TIP→ **In the dry winter season, be careful with campfires and matches; this is when the wildfire-prone saw-grass prairies and pinelands are most vulnerable.** Summer brings intense sun and billowing clouds unleashing torrents of rain almost every afternoon. Start your outdoor activities early to avoid the rain and the sun's strongest rays, and use sunscreen. Water levels rise and wildlife disperses as the day goes on, and mosquitoes hatch, swarm, and descend on you in voracious clouds, making outdoor activity virtually unbearable, unless you swath yourself in netting. Mosquito repellent is a necessity any time of year.

BISCAYNE NATIONAL PARK

Occupying 173,000 acres along the southern portion of Biscayne Bay, south of Miami and north of the Florida Keys, this national park is 95% under water, and its altitude ranges from 4 feet above sea level to 60 feet below. Contained within it are four distinct zones, which from shore to sea are mangrove forest along the coast, Biscayne Bay, the undeveloped upper Florida Keys, and coral reefs. Mangroves line the mainland shore much as they do elsewhere along South Florida's protected bay waters. Biscayne Bay functions as a lobster sanctuary and a nursery for fish, sponges, and crabs. Manatees and sea turtles frequent its warm, shallow waters. Unfortunately, the bay is under assault from forces set on a course of destruction. To the east, about 8 mi off the coast, lie 44 tiny keys, stretching 18 nautical miles north–south and accessible only by boat. There's no commercial transportation between the mainland and the islands, and only a handful can be visited: Elliott, Boca Chita, Adams, and Sands keys. The rest are either wildlife refuges or too small, have rocky shores or waters too shallow for boats. It's best to explore the Keys between December and April, when the mosquito population is relatively quiescent. Bring repellent just in case. Diving is best in summer, when calmer winds and smaller seas result in clearer waters. Another 3 mi east of the Keys, in the ocean, lies the park's main attraction—the northernmost section of Florida's living tropical coral reefs. Some are the size of a student's desk, others as large as a football field. You can take a glass-bottom-boat ride to see this underwater wonderland, but you really have to snorkel or scuba dive to appreciate it fully. A diverse population of colorful fish—angelfish, gobies, grunts, parrot fish, pork fish, wrasses, and many more—flits through the reefs. Shipwrecks from the 18th century are evidence of the area's international maritime heritage, and a Shipwreck Trail is being developed that will string together five of the major sites. A Native American midden (shell mound) dating from AD 1000, and Boca Chita Key, listed on the National Register of Historic Places for its 10 historic structures, illustrate the park's rich cultural heritage. More than 170 species of birds have been seen around the park. Although all the Keys are excellent for birding, Jones Lagoon, south of Adams Key, between Old Rhodes Key and Totten Key, is one of the best. It's approachable only by nonmotorized craft.

CONVOY POINT

❶ *9 mi east of Florida City, 30 mi south of downtown Miami.*

★ The **Dante Fascell Visitor Center** has a wide veranda with views across mangroves and Biscayne Bay. Inside the museum, artistic vignettes and on-request videos explore the park's four ecosystems. Among the facilities are the park's canoe and tour concessionaire, restrooms with showers, a ranger information area, a gift shop, and vending machines. Ranger programs take place daily, along with monthly family festivals and bimonthly narrated paddling trips. Outside are picnic tables and grills. A short trail and boardwalk lead to a jetty and launch ramp. This is the only area of the park accessible without a boat. ✉*9700 S.W. 328th St., Homestead* ☎*305/230–7275* ⊕*www.nps.gov/bisc* 🚗*Free* ⊙*Daily 9–5.*

THE OUTDOORS

CANOEING

Biscayne National Underwater Park, Inc. (✉*Convoy Point Visitor Center, Box 1270, 9710 S.W. 328th St., Homestead* ☎*305/230–1100*), the park's official concessionaire, has canoes and kayaks for rent on a first-come, first-served basis. Canoe prices are $12 an hour, kayaks $16 an hour. December through April, rangers lead guided paddling trips the second and fourth Saturday of the month. Rentals are available weekdays 8:30–5, weekends 8–5.

DIVING & SNORKELING

★ **Biscayne National Underwater Park, Inc.** (✉*Convoy Point Visitor Center, Box 1270, 9710 S.W. 328th St., Homestead* ☎*305/230–1100*) rents equipment and conducts snorkel and dive trips aboard the 45-foot *Boca Chita.* Three-hour snorkel trips ($37.50) leave daily at 1:15 and include use of mask, fins, snorkel, and buoyancy vest; and instruction. About half the time is spent on the reef and wrecks. Two-tank scuba trips to shallow reef or wall dives depart weekends at 8:30 AM, costing $56.50, tanks and weights included. Additional trips, including night dives, may be offered according to demand. Complete gear rental ($42 extra, including two tanks) is available. Even with a reservation (recommended), you should arrive one hour before departure to sign up for gear.

8

BOCA CHITA KEY

② *10 mi northeast of Convoy Point.*

★ This island was once owned by the late Mark C. Honeywell, former president of Minneapolis's Honeywell Company. A ½-mi hiking trail curves around the south side of the island. Climb the 65-foot-high ornamental lighthouse (by ranger tour only) for a panoramic view of Miami and surrounding waters. There's no fresh water, access is by private boat only, and no pets are allowed.

WHERE TO STAY

⚠ **Boca Chita Campground.** This small, flat island has a grassy, waterside campground shaded by palm trees that whisper in the breeze. The views are awesome, and a nature trail circles the island. Check with the park concessionaire for drop-off and pickup service ($38.45 roundtrip). Reservations are required. There's no running fresh water. Campers must carry out all trash. ⚐ *Flush toilets, picnic tables* ⤳*39 sites* ✉*9700 S.W. 328th St., Homestead 33033* ☎*305/230–7275, 305/230–1100 transportation* ⊕*www.nps.gov/bisc* ▭*No credit cards.*

ELLIOTT KEY

③ *9 mi east of Convoy Point.*

This key, accessible only by boat (on your own or from the concessionaire for $38.45 round-trip), has a boardwalk made from recycled plastic and two nature trails with tropical plant life. Take an informal, ranger-led nature walk or hike the 7-mi trail on your own along socalled Spite Highway, a 225-foot-wide swath of green that developers mowed down in hopes of linking this key to the mainland. Luckily the federal government stepped in, and now it's a hiking trail through tropical hardwood hammock. Facilities include restrooms, picnic tables, fresh drinking water, showers (cold), grills, and a campground. Pets are allowed on the island but not on trails. A 30-foot-wide sandy beach about a mile north of the harbor on the west (bay) side of the key is the only one in the national park. Boaters like to anchor off it to swim. For day use only, it has picnic areas and a short trail that follows the shore and cuts through the hammock.

WHERE TO STAY

⚠ **Elliott Key Campground.** The grassy, beachfront tent sites are populated with plenty of native hardwood trees, and there's no light pollution here, so the night sky is brilliant with stars. Spend the day swimming, snorkeling, hiking trails, and fishing. Parties of up to 25 people and six tents can share the group campsite for $25 a night, and leashed pets are welcome. Regular ferry service and boat rental are nonexistent, but the park concessionaire's snorkel boat provides drop-off and pickup service to campers ($28.45 round-trip). Reservations are required. If you bring a boat, dock in the marina overnight for an additional $5. Bring plenty of insect repellent and try to pick a breezy spot to plant your tent. Keep in mind you must carry out all garbage, and bring some drinking water: the pumps are known to go out on occasion. ⚐ *Flush toilets, drinking* *water, showers (cold), picnic tables, swimming (bay)* ⇆*40 sites* ⊠*9700 S.W. 328th St., Homestead 33033* ☎*305/230–7275, 305/230–1100 transportation, 305/230–1144 Ext. 3074 for group campsite* ⊕*www. nps.gov/bisc* ⊟*No credit cards.*

ADAMS KEY

❹ *9 mi southeast of Convoy Point.*

This small key, a stone's throw from the western tip of Elliott Key, is open for day use and has picnic areas, restrooms, dockage, and a short trail that runs along the shore and through a hardwood hammock. Access is by private boat.

OK, KILL JAWS MUSIC

One thing you won't see at Shark Valley is sharks. The name comes from the Shark River, also called the River of Grass, which flows through the area. Several species of shark swim up this river from the coast (about 45 mi south of Shark Valley) to give birth. The young sharks aren't able to tolerate salt water and need to experience the waters of the slough before they can swim out to sea.

EVERGLADES NATIONAL PARK

11 mi southwest of Homestead, 45 mi southwest of Miami International Airport.

The best way to experience the real Everglades is to get your feet wet either by taking a walk in the muck, affectionately called a "slough slog," or by paddling a canoe into the maze of mangrove islands to stay in a backcountry campsite. Most day-trippers don't want to do that, however. Luckily, there are several ways to see the wonders of the park with relatively dry feet. Take a boat tour in Everglades City or Flamingo, ride the tram or bike the loop road at Shark Valley, or walk the boardwalks that extend out from the main park road. And there's more to see than natural beauty. Miccosukee Indians operate a number of attractions and restaurants meriting a stop. Admission to Everglades National Park's two pay gates (main entrance and Shark Valley) is valid at both entrances for seven days. Coverage in the following section begins in the southeastern Everglades, followed by the northern Everglades, starting in the east and ending in Everglades City.

THE MAIN PARK ROAD

The main park road (Route 9336) travels from the main visitor center to Flamingo, across a section of the park's eight distinct ecosystems: hardwood hammock, freshwater prairie, pinelands, freshwater slough, cypress, coastal prairie, mangrove, and marine-estuarine. Highlights of the trip include a dwarf cypress forest, the ecotone (transition zone) between saw grass and mangrove forest, and a wealth of wading birds at Mrazek and Coot Bay ponds. Boardwalks, looped trails, several short spurs, and observation platforms allow you to stay dry.

8

⑤ Numerous interactive exhibits and films make the **Ernest F. Coe Visitor**
☺ **Center** a worthy and important stop during your tour of the region.
Fodor'sChoice Stand in a simulated blind and peer through a spyglass to watch birds
★ in the wild; although it's actually a film, the quality is so good you'll
think you're outside. Move on to a bank of telephones to hear differ-
ing viewpoints on the Great Water Debate. Another exhibit re-creates
sights and sounds of the Everglades. A 15-minute film on the park, a
movie on hurricanes, and a 35-minute wildlife film for children are
rotated in the theater. Computer monitors present a schedule of daily
ranger-led activities parkwide as well as information on canoe rentals
and boat tours. In the Everglades Discovery Shop, browse through neat
nature, science, and kids' stuff and pick up extra insect repellent. Park
admission fees permit entry for a seven-day period, including at the
Shark Valley access. The Coe Visitor Center, however, has free admission, as it's outside the park gates. ⊠*11 mi southwest of Homestead
on Rte. 9336* ☎*305/242–7700* ⊕*www.nps.gov/ever* ⊠*Park $10 per
vehicle, $5 per pedestrian, bicycle, or motorcycle* ⊙*Daily 8–5; hrs
sometimes shortened in off-season.*

⑥ A must for anyone who wants to experience the real Everglades, the
★ **Royal Palm Visitor Center** permits access to the Anhinga Trail boardwalk, where in winter spying alligators congregating in watering holes
is almost guaranteed. Or follow the neighboring Gumbo Limbo Trail
through a hardwood hammock. Do both strolls, as they're short (½
mi) and expose you to two Everglades ecosystems. Rangers conduct
twice-daily Anhinga Ambles in season (mid-December through mid-
April) starting at 10:30 and 3:30 on Monday, Wednesday, Friday, and
Saturday. Ask also about slough slogs and bike tours. The visitor center
has interpretive displays, a bookstore, and vending machines. ⊠*4 mi
west of Ernest F. Coe Visitor Center on Rte. 9336* ☎*305/242–7700*
⊙*Daily 8–4.*

HOMESTEAD

⑦ *30 mi southwest of Miami.*

In recent years, the Homestead area has redefined itself as a destination for tropical agro- and ecotourism. The emphasis is on "tropical,"
because as you cross Quail Roost Trail along north Krome Avenue
(Route 997), you actually cross latitudes into the tropical zone. Seated
at the juncture between Miami and the Keys as well as Everglades
National Park and Biscayne National Park, it has the added dimension of shopping centers, residential development, hotel chains, and
the Miami-Dade Homestead Motorsports Complex—when car races
are scheduled there, hotels increase rates and have minimum stays.
The historic downtown area has become a preservation-driven Main
Street. Krome Avenue, where it cuts through the city's heart, is lined
with restaurants, an arts complex, antiques shops, and low-budget, but
sometimes undesirable, accommodations. West of north–south Krome
Avenue, miles of fields grow fresh fruits and vegetables. Some are harvested commercially, and others have U-PICK signs, inviting you to harvest

your own. Stands selling farm-fresh produce and nurseries that grow and sell orchids and tropical plants abound. In addition to its agricultural legacy, the town has an eclectic flavor, attributable to its population mix: descendants of pioneer Crackers, Hispanic growers and farm workers, professionals escaping Miami's hustle and bustle, and latter-day northern retirees.

> **WITNESS PROTECTION PROGRAM**
>
> Fifteen federally protected threatened and endangered creatures survive within the protection of Everglades National Park, including manatees, crocodiles, snail kites, and sea turtles.

With a saltwater atoll pool that's flushed by tidal action, **Homestead Bayfront Park,** adjacent to Biscayne National Park, is popular among local families as well as anglers and boaters. Facilities include a sandy beach with lifeguards, a playground, ramps for people with disabilities (including a ramp that leads into the swimming area), and a picnic pavilion with grills, showers, and restrooms. ✉*9698 S.W. 328th St.* ☎*305/230–3034* 💲*$4 per passenger vehicle, $10 per vehicle with boat, $12 per RV* ☉*Daily sunrise–sunset.*

Because it officially qualifies for tropical status, **Fruit & Spice Park,** in Homestead's Redland historic agricultural district, is the only public garden of its type in the United States. More than 500 varieties of herbs, spices, citrus, and nuts typically grow in the 35-acre park, but it is most famous for its exotic fruits, such as pomelo, carambola, sugar apple, and monstera. There are 70 varieties of bananas alone, plus 70 varieties of avocado, and 140 of mangos. Tours and tastings are available three times daily. ✉*24801 S.W. 187th Ave.* ☎*305/247–5727* ⊕*www.fruitandspicepark.org* 💲*$5* ☉*Daily 9–5; guided tours at 11, 1:30, and 3.*

Enjoy Homestead's fruity bounty in liquid form at **Schnebly Redland's Winery.** Opened to the public in 2005, it began producing fruit wines as a way to avoid wasting thousands of pounds of fruit from the family groves each year, fruit not quite perfect enough for shipping. Three bucks buys you a taste of six varieties of surprisingly tasty fruit wines, from the oaky Islamorada brand made from carambola to the slightly sweet and acidic passion fruit. You get to keep your souvenir wineglass and can bring it back anytime for free refills. ✉*30205 S.W. 217th Ave.* ☎*305/242–1224 or 888/717–WINE* ⊕*www.schneblywinery.com* 💲*$3* ☉*Weekdays 10–5, Sat. 10–6, Sun. noon–5.*

☺ Driven by unrequited love, 100-pound immigrant Ed Leedskalnin built **Coral Castle** in the early 1900s out of massive slabs of coral rock, a feat likened to the building of the pyramids. Visitors can learn how he peopled his fantasy world with his imaginary wife and three children, studied astronomy, and built his simple home and elaborate courtyard with no engineering education and tools he mostly fashioned himself. Highlights of the National Register of Historic Places site include the Polaris telescope built to spot the North Star, a working sundial, a

8

5,000-pound heart-shaped table featured in Ripley's *Believe It or Not*, a banquet table in the shape of Florida, and a playground Ed named "Grotto of the Three Bears." ⊠*28655 S. Dixie Hwy.* ☎*305/248–6345* ⊕*www.coralcastle.com* ▨*$9.75* ⊗*Mon.–Thurs. 9–6, Fri.–Sun. 9–9.*

This groundbreaking project centers on a 3½-acre complex, **ArtSouth,** which includes the historic First Baptist Church, 45 artist studios, galleries, workshops, sculpture garden, and stage. Watch artists at work, take classes, and enjoy concert performances. Check Second Saturdays opening exhibits, which include live entertainment, hands-on art demonstrations, self-guided tours, and refreshments served from 3 to 8 PM. ⊠*240 N. Krome Ave.* ☎*305/247–9406* ⊕*www.artsouthhomestead. org* ▨*Free* ⊗*Tues.–Fri. 10–6, weekends noon–6.*

WHERE TO STAY & EAT

$–$$$ ✕**Tiffany's Cottage Dining.** If a bright, pleasant setting and well-made sandwiches and salads make you feel you've escaped the rushing world for a brief time, then join the local working population and women-who-lunch at Tiffany's, a country Victorian–style restaurant complete with gingerbread on the outside and ruffles and lace inside. The lunch menu describes Buffalo chicken wraps, seafood- and egg-salad sandwiches on fresh-baked croissants, and the most popular dish, the daily quiche. Dinner favorites include lobster ravioli, chicken cordon bleu, steak, and fresh fish of the day. Among the homemade desserts, choose from a very tall carrot cake and a harvest pie that has layers of fruits, walnuts, and a caramel topping. There is a Saturday breakfast and a Sunday brunch buffet. ⊠*22 N.E. 15th St.* ☎*305/246–0022* ⚞*Reservations essential* ▤*AE, D, MC, V* ⊗*No dinner Sun.–Tues.*

$$ ✕**Hiatari Sushi Bar.** Visit this downtown Japanese-Thai restaurant, in a simple storefront café setting, for a change of taste from Homestead's seafood and Mexican staples. Off the Japanese side of the menu, choose from a dazzling selection of rolls and sushi, including the home-town Homestead Roll, with fried snapper, avocado, and cream cheese. Entrées include pan-seared tuna, teriyakis, and tempura shrimp. Thai takes over with entrées in the curry, noodle, vegetarian, and fried-rice departments. Ask for tatami Japanese-style seating in private booths or American-style tables, and stay for karaoke. ⊠*109 N. Krome Ave.* ☎*305/248–7426* ▤*MC, V* ⊗*Closed Sun.*

★ ¢–$ ✕**El Toro Taco.** This simple, family-run favorite gets high marks for its generous portions, homemade tortilla chips (sometimes a little greasy), and friendly service. Selections include tasty fajitas, enchiladas, and burritos, and other traditional Mexican dishes such as *mole de pollo,* which combines unsweetened chocolate and Mexican spices with chicken. Order spicing from mild to tongue-challenging. And if you're tired of the same old morning fare, consider stopping here for breakfast, available 8–11 AM. ⊠*1 S. Krome Ave.* ☎*305/245–8182* ▤*AE, D, MC, V* ⚟*BYOB* ⊗*Closed Mon.*

¢–$ ✕**Sam's Country Kitchen.** For good old Southern-style home cooking, Sam's is the choice of the local population. Burgers, sandwiches, and dinners—including chicken livers, hamburger steaks, and fried clams—come with fresh-baked corn bread and a daily selection of sides such as okra with tomatoes, turnip greens, pickled beets, or onion rings. Don't miss out on the changing selection of homemade soups and desserts. All this goodness comes cheaply, but at the expense of an anything-but-glamorous dining area and often slow service. ⊠ *1320 N. Krome Ave.* ☎ *305/246–2990* ⊟ *MC, V* ☉ *Closed Sun.*

¢ ✕**NicaMex.** Among the local Latin population, this is a favorite and the lowest priced. It helps if you speak Spanish, but there's usually one staffer who speaks English, and the menu is bilingual. Although they term it *comidas rapidas* (fast food), the cuisine is not Americanized. You can get authentic huevos rancheros or *chilaquiles* (corn tortillas cooked in red-pepper sauce) for breakfast, and specialties such as *chicharron en salsa verde* (fried pork skin in hot green-tomato sauce) and shrimp in garlic all day. Seafood and beef soups are best sellers and have generous amounts of vegetables and seafood or meat. Choose a domestic or imported beer, pop a coin into the Wurlitzer jukebox, select a Latin tune, and escape to a foreign land. ⊠ *32 N.W. 1st St., across from the Krome Ave. bandstand* ☎ *305/246–8300* ⊟ *AE, D, MC, V.*

★ \$–\$\$ 🏨**Redland Hotel.** Of downtown Homestead's smattering of mom-and-pop motels, this is the most desirable and has the most character. When it opened in 1904, the inn was the town's first hotel. It later became the first mercantile store, the first post office, the first library, and the first boardinghouse. Today, each room has a different layout and furnishings, and some have access to a shared balcony. The style is Victorian, with lots of pastels and reproduction antique furniture. The pub is popular with locals, and there are good restaurants and antiques shops nearby. A coffee shop–Internet café with free Wi-Fi connections was added in 2006. Pros: historic character, convenient to downtown, well maintained. Cons: traffic noise, small rooms, ugly street location. ⊠ *5 S. Flagler Ave., 33030* ☎ *305/246–1904 or 800/595–1904* ⊕ *www. redlandhotel.com* ⌨ *13 rooms* ⌂ *In-room: VCR, ethernet, dial-up. In-hotel: room service, bar, public Wi-Fi, no-smoking rooms,* ⊟ *AE, D, DC, MC, V.*

★ \$ 🏨**Grove Inn Country Guesthouse.** Away from downtown but close to Homestead's agricultural attractions, Grove Inn derives much of its personality from co-owner Paul, a former show man. The garden is lush with organic, tropical fruit trees and native plants (instead of a guest book there's a live autograph tree in the courtyard, where people sign the leaves) and the rooms are decorated fussily with antique furnishings and table settings. The owners go out of their way to pamper you, starting with a country breakfast using local produce, served family-style in a dining room done in deep Victorian florals. They offer behind-the-scenes tours of orchid nurseries and farms not otherwise open to the public. A vending machine dispenses complimentary cold drinks. Pros: fresh fruit, privacy, delicious breakfast, rural location. Cons: far from downtown and national parks, no restaurants nearby, not suited to families. ⊠ *22540 S.W. Krome Ave., 6 mi north of downtown, 33170* ☎ *305/247–6572 or 877/247–6572* ⊕ *www.groveinn. com* ⌨ *13 rooms, 1 2-bedroom suite, 1 cottage* ⌂ *In-room: kitchen (some), refrigerator, dial-up. In-hotel: pool, laundry facilities, some pets allowed, no-smoking rooms* ⊟ *AE, D, MC, V* ⚏ *BP.*

8

SPORTS & THE OUTDOORS

AUTO RACING

The **Miami-Dade Homestead Motorsports Complex** (⊠ *1 Speedway Blvd., 33035* ☎ *305/230–7223* ⊕ *www.homesteadmiamispeedway.com*) is a state-of-the-art facility with 65,000 grandstand seats and two tracks: a 2.21-mi continuous road course and a 1.5-mi oval. There's a schedule of year-round manufacturer and race-team testing, club racing, and other national events.

BOATING

Boaters give high ratings to the facilities at **Homestead Bayfront Park.** The 174-slip marina has a ramp, dock, bait-and-tackle shop, fuel station, ice, dry storage, and boat hoist, which can handle vessels up to 50 feet long if they have lifting rings. The park also has a tidal swimming area. ⊠ *9698 S.W. 328th St.* ☎ *305/230–3033* ⊠ *$4 per passenger vehicle, $10 per vehicle with boat, $10 per RV, $10 hoist* ⊙ *Daily sunrise–sunset.*

SHOPPING

In addition to Homestead Boulevard (U.S. 1) and Campbell Drive (Southwest 312th Street and Northeast 8th Street), **Krome Avenue** is popular for shopping. In the heart of old Homestead, it has a brick sidewalk, art galleries, and antiques stores. The **Antique Mall** contains six dealer shops plus a coffee shop.

FLORIDA CITY

8 *2 mi southwest of Homestead.*

The Florida Turnpike ends in this southernmost town on the peninsula, spilling thousands onto U.S. 1 and eventually west to Everglades National Park, east to Biscayne National Park, or south to the Florida Keys. As the last outpost before 18 mi of mangroves and water, this stretch of U.S. 1 is lined with fast-food eateries, service stations, hotels, bars, dive shops, and restaurants. Hotel rates increase significantly during NASCAR races at the nearby Miami-Dade Homestead Motorsports Complex. Like Homestead, Florida City is rooted in agriculture, with hundreds of acres of farmland west of Krome Avenue and a huge farmers' market that processes produce shipped nationwide.

WHERE TO STAY & EAT

$$–$$$ ✕**Mutineer Restaurant.** Families and older couples prefer the quirky yet well-dressed setting of this roadside steak-and-seafood restaurant with an indoor-outdoor fish-and-duck pond. It was built to look like a ship in 1980, back when Florida City was barely on the map. Etched glass divides the bi-level dining rooms, with velvet upholstered chairs, an aquarium, and nautical antiques. The big menu has 15 seafood entrées, including stuffed grouper (a favorite), Florida lobster tails, and snapper Oscar, plus another half dozen daily seafood specials, as well as poultry, ribs, and steaks. There's a $9.95 hot buffet and salad bar Monday through Saturday 11 AM to 3 PM, a $21.95 Sunday seafood buffet from 11 AM to 9 PM, and live music and dancing Friday and Saturday

evenings. ✉ *11 S.E. 1st Ave. (U.S. 1), at Palm Dr.* ☎*305/245–3377* ⊕*www.mutineer.biz* ▤*AE, D, DC, MC, V.*

$–$$$ ✕**Capri Restaurant.** Locals have been coming here for affordable Italian food in a wide selection since 1958. Outside it's a rock-walled building with a big parking lot that fills up nightly. The interior has dark-wood paneling with redbrick accents and heavy wooden furniture. The tasty fare ranges from pizza with a light, crunchy crust and ample toppings to spaghetti 16 different ways, and broiled steaks and seafood-pasta classics. This is traditional Italian-American cuisine with no surprises and little flourish. Bargain hunters have two choices: the daily early-bird entrées, 4:30 to 6:30 for $12 to $14, which include soup or salad and potato or spaghetti, and the Tuesday family night (after 4 PM), which has all-you-can-eat pasta with salad or soup for $7.95. Top-shelf scotches and cognacs supplement the small wine list. ✉*935 N. Krome Ave.* ☎*305/247–1544* ⊕*www.the-capri.com* ▤*AE, D, MC, V* ⊘*Closed Sun.*

¢–$$ ✕**Gusto's Grill & Bar.** This fun and friendly place is mostly about drinking and watching sports on TV, yet it's also good for catching a reasonably priced meal, especially during happy hour (4 to 7 PM), when there's a free buffet and a dozen raw oysters costs only $4. Sit indoors or out (televisions are situated throughout) to order your honey garlic wings, shrimp corn chowder, pasta, burgers, pizza, steak, cashew salmon, and crab cakes. Shoot pool and sip a Razzeberri Mojito while you wait. ✉*326 S.E. 1st Ave.* ☎*786/243–9800* ▤*AE, D, MC, V.*

★ $ ✕**Farmers' Market Restaurant.** Although it's in the farmers' market and serves fresh vegetables, seafood figures prominently on the menu of home-cooked specialties. A family of fishermen runs the place, so fish and shellfish are only hours from the sea. Catering to the fishing and farming crowd, it opens at 5:30 AM, serving pancakes, jumbo eggs, and fluffy omelets with home fries or grits in a pleasant dining room with checkered tablecloths on the edge of town. The lunch and dinner menus have fried shrimp, seafood pasta, country-fried steak, roast turkey, and fried conch, as well as burgers, salads, and sandwiches. ✉*300 N. Krome Ave.* ☎*305/242–0008* ▤*MC, V.*

★ ¢ ✕**Rosita's Restaurante.** With its population of immigrant farm workers, this area can boast the real thing in Mexican, a flavor you just don't get in the Tex-Mex chains. Order à la carte specialties or dinners and combos with beans and rice, and salad. Forty-three breakfast, lunch, and dinner entrées are served all day and range from Mexican eggs, enchiladas, and taco salad to stewed beef, shrimp rancheros style, and fried pork chop. The food is on the spicy side, and if you like more fire, each table comes prepared with fresh-tasting salsa, jalapeños, and bottled habanero sauce. Clean (with lingering faint whiffs of bleach to prove it) and pleasant, with an open kitchen, take-out counter, and Formica tables, it's a favorite with locals and budget-minded guests at the hostel across the street. ✉*199 W. Palm Dr.* ☎*305/245–8652* ▤*AE, MC, V.*

$–$$$$ ▥**Best Western Gateway to the Keys.** If you want easy access to Everglades and Biscayne national parks as well as the Florida Keys, you'll be well placed at this pretty, modern, two-story motel two blocks off the Florida Turnpike. Standard rooms, done in tropical colors, have two queen-size beds or one king-size bed. Rooms around the lushly landscaped pool cost the most. There's high-speed Internet access available in the rooms, plus wireless access in the lobby. Pros: convenient to national parks and Keys, business services, pretty pool area. Cons: traffic noise, generic rooms, fills up fast during high season. ⊠ *411 S. Krome Ave., 33034* ☎ *305/246–5100* 📠 *305/242–0056* 🌐 *www.bestwestern.com* 💭 *114 rooms* 🔑 *In-room: refrigerator, ethernet, dial-up. In-hotel: pool, laundry facilities, Wi-Fi, no-smoking rooms* ☰ *AE, D, DC, MC, V* ⭕ *CP.*

$–$$$ 🖭 **Fairway Inn.** Two stories high with a waterfall pool, this motel has some of the area's lowest chain rates, and it's next to the chamber of commerce. Rooms, with either one king-size bed or two doubles, have tiled bathroom and closet areas. Pros: affordability, convenient to restaurants, parks, and raceway, free wireless connections in room. Cons: no character, plain rooms, small rooms. ⊠ *100 S.E. 1st Ave., 33034* ☎ *305/248–4202 or 888/340–4734* 🌐 *www.fairwayinnfl.com* 📠 *305/245–8578* 💭 *160 rooms* 🔑 *In-room: dial-up, Wi-Fi. In-hotel: pool, laundry facilities, no-smoking rooms* ☰ *AE, D, MC, V* ⭕ *CP.*

¢–$$$ 🖭 **Travelodge.** This bargain motor lodge is close to the Florida Turnpike, Everglades and Biscayne national parks, the Florida Keys, and the Miami-Dade Homestead Motorsports Complex. Clean and colorful rooms are smallish, but they have more amenities than usually found in this price range, including complimentary breakfast and newspaper, coffeemaker, hair dryer, iron with ironing board, high-speed Internet access, and voice mail. Fast-food and chain eateries, gas stations, and a visitor's bureau are within walking distance. Pros: in-room refrigerator, convenience to U.S. 1, complimentary deluxe breakfast. Cons: lack of character, small rooms, busy location. ⊠ *409 S.E. 1st Ave., 33034* ☎ *305/248–9777 or 800/758–0618* 📠 *305/248–9750* 🌐 *www.tlflcity. com* 💭 *88 rooms* 🔑 *In-room: safe, refrigerator, ethernet, dial-up. In-hotel: pool, laundry facilities* ☰ *AE, D, DC, MC, V* ⭕ *CP.*

$$ 🖭 **Comfort Inn.** Rooms are large, have contemporary tropical furnishings, and are on one of two floors (there's no elevator). They're outfitted with irons, hair dryers, and coffeemakers. Continental breakfast and newspapers are free. In-room Internet connections are high speed. It's in an asphalt complex of hotels, gas stations, and restaurants just off U.S. 1. Pros: free continental breakfast, close to restaurants and services, in-room conveniences. Cons: no elevator, noisy location, nondescript rooms. ⊠ *333 S.E. 1st Ave., 33034* ☎ *305/248–4009 or 888/352–2489* 📠 *305/248–7935* 🌐 *www.ciflcity.com* 💭 *124 rooms* 🔑 *In-room: safe, refrigerator, ethernet, dial-up. In-hotel: pool, no elevator, laundry facilities, no-smoking rooms* ☰ *AE, D, DC, MC, V* ⭕ *CP.*

★ $$ 🖭 **Hampton Inn.** Racing fans can hear the engines roar from this two-story motel next to an outlet mall and within 15 minutes of the raceway and Everglades and Biscayne national parks. If you're looking for an upgrade from the other chains, this one offers more amenities and comfort, such as 37-inch plasma TVs. Carpeted rooms are bright and clean and have upholstered chairs, a coffeemaker, and an iron and ironing board. Included are a continental breakfast and local calls. Pros: extra room amenities, business clientele perks, convenient location. Cons: busy location, chain anonymity, no sense of place. ⊠ *124 E. Palm Dr., 33034* ☎*305/247–8833 or 800/426–7866* 🖷*305/247–6456* ⊕*www.hamptoninnfloridacity.com* ⇥*123 rooms* ⚲*In-room: refrigerator (some), dial-up, Wi-Fi. In-hotel: pool, laundry service, no-smoking rooms* ⊟*AE, D, DC, MC, V* ⦿*CP.*

¢–$ 🏠**Econo Lodge.** Close to the Florida Turnpike and with access to the Keys, this is a good pullover spot for an overnight. The rooms are uncramped, with attractive bedspreads, and have coffeemakers and data ports. The pool sits in the middle of the parking lot. Pros: convenient location, business services, microwaves and refrigerators for rent. Cons: urban-ugly location, noisy, lack of character. ⊠*553 N.E. 1st Ave., 33034* ☎*305/248–9300 or 800/553–2666* 🖷*305/245–2753* ⊕*www.econolodge.com* ⇥*42 rooms* ⚲*In-room: refrigerator (some), dial-up. In-hotel: pool, laundry facilities, public Internet, no-smoking rooms* ⊟*AE, D, DC, MC, V* ⦿*CP.*

¢ 🏠**Everglades Hostel.** Stay in clean and spacious private or dorm-style rooms (generally six to a room; $2 charge for linen); relax in indoor and outdoor quiet areas; watch videos or TV on a big screen; and take airboat, hiking, biking, and sightseeing tours. This HI-AYH facility is in a minimally restored Art Deco building on a lush, private acre between Everglades and Biscayne national parks, 20 mi north of Key Largo. At mealtime, enjoy a free all-you-can-make pancake breakfast in the communal kitchen, pitch in for a communal dinner (according to demand, $3 each), or walk to a nearby restaurant. Pets are welcome. You can make free domestic long-distance calls from the phone in the lobby. Pros: affordability, Everglades tours, free services. Cons: communal living, no elevator, old structure. ⊠*20 S.W. 2nd Ave., 33034* ☎*305/248–1122 or 800/372–3874* 🖷*305/245–7622* ⊕*www.evergladeshostel.com* ⇥*46 beds in dorm-style rooms with shared bath, 2 private rooms with shared bath* ⚲*In-room: no a/c (some), no phone, no TV. In-hotel: bicycles, no elevator, laundry facilities, public Internet, public Wi-Fi, some pets allowed, no-smoking rooms* ⊟*MC, V.*

SHOPPING

Prime Outlets at Florida City (⊠*250 E. Palm Dr.* ☎*888/545–1798* ⊕*www.primeoutlets.com*) has nearly 50 discount stores plus a small food court.

★ **Robert Is Here** (⊠*19200 Palm Dr. [S.W. 344th St.]* ☎*305/246–1592* ⊕*www.robertishere.com*), a remarkable fruit stand, sells vegetables, fresh-fruit milk shakes (the key lime shake is fabulous), 10 flavors of honey, more than 100 flavors of jams and jellies, fresh juices, salad dressings, and some 30 kinds of tropical fruits, including (in season) carambola, lychee, egg fruit, monstera, sapodilla, dragonfruit, genipa, sugar apple, and tamarind. The stand started in 1960, when seven-year-old Robert sat at this spot selling his father's bumper crop of cucumbers. Now Robert ships around the world, and everything is first quality. Seconds are given to needy area families. An odd assortment of animals out back—from goats to emus—adds to the entertainment

8

value. The stand opens at 8 and never closes earlier than 7. It does shut down, however, during September and October.

FLAMINGO

❾ *38 mi southwest of Ernest F. Coe Visitor Center.*

Here at the far end of the main road lies a marina (from which sightseeing tours and fishing charters into Everglades National Park depart), a visitor center, and a campground on Florida Bay. The marina also rents kayaks and motorboats. Before Hurricanes Katrina and Wilma washed them away in 2005, a lodge, cabins, and restaurants provided Everglades National Park's only accommodations. At press time, no information was available about the rebuilding of Flamingo Lodge. Nearby is Eco Pond, one of the most popular wildlife observation areas, but still closed at press time because of hurricane damage. Recovery efforts continue, so check ⊕*www.nps.gov/ever* for a facilities update before you visit.

The **Flamingo Visitor Center** provides an interactive display and has natural-history exhibits in the small Florida Bay Flamingo Museum. Check the schedule for ranger-led activities, such as naturalist discussions, evening programs in the campground amphitheater, and hikes along area trails. Some of the park's best birding is at nearby Eco Pond. Eco Pond was still deemed unsafe as of this writing, so be sure to call ahead for accessibility information. ☎*239/695–2945* ⊘*Hrs vary.*

WHERE TO STAY

For an intense stay in the "real" Florida, consider one of the 45 backcountry campsites deep in the park, many inland, with some on the beach. You'll have to carry your food, water, and supplies in; take care to carry out all your trash. You'll also need a site-specific permit, available on a first-come, first-served basis from the Flamingo or Gulf Coast Visitor Center. These sites cost $10 or more, depending on group size.

⚠**Everglades National Park.** About 12 mi southwest of Florida City, the park has two developed campsites available through a reservation system from mid-November through mid-April; the rest of the year they're first-come, first-served. Six miles west of the park's main entrance, **Long Pine Key** has no-permit hiking, though you will need separate permits for freshwater and saltwater fishing. ♿*Flush toilets, dump station, drinking water, picnic tables, public telephone* ⬳*108 drive-up sites* ☎*800/365–2267 campsite reservations, 305/242–7700, 239/695–2945 park information* ⊕*reservations.nps.gov* ▤*D, MC, V.*

> ### KIDS IN THE GLADES
>
> Although kids of all ages can enjoy the park, they will get the most out of the experience at age seven and up. Consider how much you as a parent will enjoy keeping tabs on tiny ones around so much water and so many teeth. Also consider that some young children are frightened by sheer wilderness.

★ Thirty-eight miles southwest of the park's main entrance, ⚠️**Flamingo** has hiking and nature trails. Of its 234 drive-in sites, 55 have a view of the bay; 9 of its 40 walk-in sites are on the water. At press time, only a portion of the sites were accessible because of 2005's hurricane damage. ♿*Flush toilets, dump station, drinking water, showers (cold), general store* ⚑234 *drive-up sites, 40 walk-in sites, 20 on the water* ☎800/365–2267 *campsite reservations, 305/242–7700, 239/695–2945 park information* ⊕*reservations.nps.gov* ▭*D, MC, V.*

> ### ALL BARK, NO BITE?
>
> Only four out of the Everglades' 27 species of snakes are venomous: cottonmouths, diamondback rattlesnakes, dusky pigmy rattlesnakes, and coral snakes. Wear sturdy boots when hiking in wooded or grassy areas to avoid bites.

THE OUTDOORS

BIKING

Flamingo Lodge, Marina & Outpost Resort (☎239/695–3101) usually rents (check ahead; rentals were closed by hurricane damage) old but sturdy bikes for $14 a day, $8 per half day. Snake Bight Trail and the park's main road are good places to ride to see wildlife.

BOATING

★ (Note: At press time, rentals and ramp facilities were limited at Flamingo; check status before you go.) The marina at **Flamingo Lodge, Marina & Outpost Resort** (☎239/695–3101) rents 17-foot power skiffs for $155 per day, $65 per half day. Several private boats are also available for charter. Currently, only the backcountry ramp is open because the hoist across the plug dam separating Florida Bay from the Buttonwood Canal is closed. A small store sells food, camping supplies, bait and tackle, propane, and fuel. A concessionaire rents rods, reels, binoculars, and coolers by the half and full day.

CANOEING & KAYAKING

Everglades has well-marked canoe trails in the Flamingo area, plus the southern end of the 99-mi Wilderness Trail from Everglades City to Flamingo.

★ **Flamingo Lodge, Marina & Outpost Resort** (☎239/695–3101) rents canoes in two sizes: small (up to two paddlers) and family size (up to four). Small canoes rent for $8 per hour; family-size run $10. Daily and overnight rates also available. Saltwater crocodiles like to hang out around the marina on Buttonwood Canal, so you're practically guaranteed a sighting.

FISHING

★ **Flamingo Lodge, Marina & Outpost Resort** (☎239/695–3101) helps arrange two-person charter fishing trips. The cost is $400 a day for one or two people, $300 for a half day. Per-person costs lower with three or four people.

8

TAMIAMI TRAIL

141 mi from Miami to Fort Myers.

In 1915, when officials decided to build an east–west highway linking Miami to Fort Myers and continuing north to Tampa, it made sense to call it the Tamiami Trail. In 1928 the road became a reality, cutting through the Everglades and altering the natural flow of water and the lives of the Miccosukee Indians, who eked out a living fishing, hunting, farming, and frogging here.

Today the highway's traffic streams through Everglades National Park, Big Cypress National Preserve, and Fakahatchee Strand Preserve State Park. The landscape is surprisingly varied, changing from hardwood hammocks to pinelands, then abruptly to tall cypress trees dripping with Spanish moss and back to saw-grass marsh. Those who slow down to take in the scenery are rewarded with glimpses of alligators sunning themselves along the banks of roadside canals and in the shallow waters, and hundreds of waterbirds, especially in the dry winter season. The man-made landscape has chickee huts, Native American villages, and airboats parked at roadside enterprises.

Businesses along the trail give their addresses either based on their distance from Krome Avenue, Florida Turnpike, and Miami on the east coast or Naples on the west coast. Between Miami and Naples, the road goes by several names, including Tamiami Trail, U.S. 41, Ninth Street in Naples, and, at the Miami end, Southwest 8th Street.

⑩ A perennial favorite with tour-bus operators, **Everglades Safari Park** has an arena that seats up to 300 people to watch an educational alligator show and wrestling demonstration. Before and after the show, get a closer look at the alligators on Gator Island, walk through a small wildlife museum, or climb aboard an airboat for a 30-minute ride through the River of Grass (included in admission). There's also a restaurant, a gift shop, and an observation platform that looks out over the Glades. Small, private airboat tours are available for an extra charge and last 20 minutes to 2½ hours. ✉*26700 Tamiami Trail, 15 mi west of Florida Tpke.* ☎*305/226–6923 or 305/223–3804* ⊕*www.evsafaripark. com* ☜*$20* ⊗*Daily 9–5.*

☾ **⑪** After visiting **Everglades Gator Park** you can tell your friends you came face-to-face with—and even touched—an alligator, albeit a baby one. You can also squirm in a "reptilium" of venomous and nonpoisonous native snakes or learn about Native Americans of the Everglades through a reproduction of a Miccosukee village. The park also has wildlife shows with native and exotic animals, 45-minute airboat tours, and RV campsites, as well as a gift shop and restaurant. The last airboat ride departs 45 minutes before sunset. ✉*24050 Tamiami Trail, 12 mi west of Florida Tpke.* ☎*305/559–2255 or 800/559–2205* ⊕*www. gatorpark.com* ☜*Tours, wildlife show, and park $20* ⊗*Daily 9–6.*

★ ☾ **⑫** It takes a bit of nerve to walk the paved 15-mi loop in **Shark Valley** because in the winter months alligators lie on and alongside the road, basking in the sun—most, however, do move quickly out of the way.

You can also ride a bicycle or take a tram tour (reservations recommended in winter). Stop at the halfway point to climb the concrete observation tower's ramp, which spirals skyward 50 feet. From there the River of Grass spreads as far as the eye can see. Observe waterbirds as well as alligators and, if you're lucky, river otters crossing the road, and follow a short trail into the habitat. Just behind the bike-rental area a short boardwalk trail meanders through the saw grass and another one passes through a tropical hardwood hammock. A small visitor center has rotating exhibits, a bookstore, and park rangers ready to answer questions. The park had plans to install an underwater live camera in the canal behind the center by 2007 so visitors can watch the alligators and otters. Shark Valley is the national park's north entrance; however, no roads here lead directly to other parts of the park. ⊠ *23½ mi west of Florida Tpke.* ☎ *305/221–8455, 305/221–8776 tram tours* ⊠ *Park $10 per vehicle, $4 per pedestrian, bicyclist, or motorcyclist* ☉ *Visitor center daily 9–5; gate daily 6:30–6.*

★ ☺ **⑬** The cultural center at **Miccosukee Indian Village** showcases the Miccosukees' foods, crafts, skills, and lifestyle. It also presents cultural alligator shows, which explain how the animals and Native Americans have historically interacted, and crafts demonstrations. Narrated 30-minute airboat rides take you into the heart of the wilderness to which these Native Americans escaped after the Seminole Wars and Indian Removal Act of the mid-1800s. In modern times, the Miccosukee clans have relocated to this village along Tamiami Trail, but most still maintain their hammock farming and hunting camps. The village's museum shows a film and displays chickee structures and artifacts that explain this ancient culture. Guided tours are available throughout the day. The Everglades Music & Craft Festival falls on a July weekend, and the weeklong Indian Arts Festival is in late December. There's a restaurant and gift shop on-site. ⊠ *Just west of Shark Valley entrance, 25 mi west of Florida Tpke.* ☎ *305/223–8380* ⊕ *www.miccosukeetribe.com* ⊠ *Village $10, rides $10* ☉ *Daily 9–5.*

⑭ Clyde Butcher does for the River of Grass and Big Cypress Swamp
Fodor'sChoice what Ansel Adams did for the West; check out his stunning photo-
★ graphs at his **Big Cypress Gallery.** Working with large-format black-and-white film, Butcher captures every blade of grass, wisp of cloud, and flicker of light. If you're lucky, Butcher will be on hand to sign your prints. He's always there on Thanksgiving and Labor Day weekends. Special exhibits, lectures, tours, photo expeditions, and slide presentations are given throughout the year. ⊠ *52388 Tamiami Trail, 45 mi west of Florida Tpke., Ochopee* ☎ *239/695–2428 or 888/999–9113* ⊕ *www.clydebutcher.com* ⊠ *Free* ☉ *Daily 10–5; closed Tues. and Wed. in summer.*

⑮ Slow down—the **Oasis Visitor Center** is a welcome respite along the Tamiami Trail. If you blow by here as you speed between Miami and Naples, you'll miss out on an opportunity to learn about the surrounding preserve. The biggest attraction is the huge gators you can view from the boardwalk in front. Inside the center are a small exhibit area, an information center, a bookshop, and a theater that shows a dated

8

but informative 15-minute film on the preserve and Big Cypress Swamp. The center also has myriad seasonal ranger-led and self-guided activities, such as campfire and wildlife talks, slough slogs, and canoe excursions. The 8-mi Turner River Canoe Trail begins nearby and crosses through Everglades National Park before end-

> ### GRRRREAT MATES!
>
> To bring back Florida panther numbers, threatened by inbreeding as well as human impact, Florida Panther National Wildlife Refuge has introduced a compatible subspecies from Texas.

ing in Chokoloskee Bay, near Everglades City. Rangers lead four-hour canoe trips on most Saturdays and Sundays in season beginning at 9:30 AM. Two-hour ranger swamp walks take place most Sundays beginning at 1:30 PM and Mondays at 10 AM. Reservations are required (☎239/695–1201) for ranger programs up to 14 days in advance. Hikers on their own can join the Florida National Scenic Trail, which begins in the preserve and is divided in three segments 6.5 to 28 mi each. Two 5-mi trails, Concho Billy and Fire Prairie, can be accessed a few miles east off Turner River Road. Turner River Road and Birdon Road form a 17-mi gravel loop drive that's excellent for birding. Bear Island has about 32 mi of scenic, flat, looped trails that are ideal for bicycling. Most trails are hard-packed lime rock, but a few miles are gravel. Cyclists share the road with off-road vehicles, which are most plentiful during General Gun Hunting season, from mid-November through December. To see the best variety of wildlife from your car, follow 26-mi Loop Road, south of U.S. 41 and west of Shark Valley, where alligators, raccoons, and soft-shell turtles crawl around right beside the gravel road and swallowtail kites and brown-shouldered hawks swoop. Stop at H.P. Williams Roadside Park, west of the Oasis, and walk along the boardwalk to spy gators, turtles, and garfish in the clear river waters. ⊠ *24 mi east of Everglades City, 50 mi west of Miami, 20 mi west of Shark Valley* ☎*239/695–1201* ⊕*www.nps.gov/bicy* ⊠*Free* ⊙*Daily 9–4:30.*

⓰ The tiny **Ochopee Post Office** is the smallest in North America. Buy a picture postcard of the little one-room shack and mail it to a friend, thereby helping to keep this picturesque spot in business. ⊠*4 mi east of Rte. 29, Ochopee* ☎*800/275–8777* ⊙ *Weekdays 10–noon and 1–4:30, Sat. 10–11:30.*

☉ A classic Florida roadside attraction, **Wooten's Airboat Tours** offers a typical Everglades array of alligators, snakes, panthers, and other creatures, including a Siberian tiger, in addition to airboat and swamp-buggy tours. See wildlife and an old fishing camp complete with a moonshine still on the swamp-buggy tour. Visit the animal exhibits separately or as part of a tour combo. ⊠*Tamiami Trail, 1½ mi east of Rte. 29, Ochopee* ☎*239/695–2781 or 800/282–2781* ⊕*www.wootenseverglades.com* ⊠*$21 for half-hour tour, $8 for animal exhibits* ⊙*Daily 8:30–4:30.*

Since it opened in 1989, **Florida Panther National Wildlife Refuge** has remained off-limits to human access to protect the endangered cougar subspecies. In 2005, driven by public input, the refuge opened two short loop trails in a region lightly traveled by panthers so visitors could get a taste of the wet prairies, tropical hammocks, and pine uplands where panthers range and wild orchids thrive. The trails, less than 2 mi total, range from muddy in spots in winter to thigh-high under water in summer, and may be closed when particularly flooded. If you look closely, you may see signs of deer, black bear, and even panthers, but sightings are rare. ⊠*Off Rte. 29, ½ mi north of I–75 Exit 80* ☐*3860 Tollgate Blvd., Naples* ☎*800/344–9453* ⊕*floridapanther. fws.gov* ☒*Free* ☉*Daily dawn–dusk; trails may be closed July–Nov. because of rain.*

★ ⓱ The ½-mi boardwalk at **Fakahatchee Strand Preserve State Park** gives you an opportunity to see rare plants, bald cypress, and North America's largest stand of native royal palms and largest concentration and variety of epiphytic orchids, including 31 varieties of threatened and endangered species that bloom most extravagantly in the hot months. You can drive through the 12-mi-long (one-way) W. J. Janes Memorial Scenic Drive and hike the spur trails that lead off it. Ranger-led swamp walks and canoe trips are given November through April. ⊠*Boardwalk on north side of Tamiami Trail 7 mi west of Rte. 29 W.J. Janes Scenic Dr. ¾ mi north of Tamiami Trail on Rte. 29; ranger station on W.J. Janes Scenic Dr., Box 548, Copeland* ☎*239/695–4593* ⊕*www. floridastateparks.org/fakahatcheestrand* ☒*Free* ☉*Daily 8–sunset.*

★ ⓲ Nature trails, biking, camping, and canoeing into Everglades territory make **Collier-Seminole State Park** an easy introduction to this often forbidding land. Of historical interest, a Seminole War blockhouse has been re-created to hold the interpretative center, and one of the "walking dredges"—invented to carve the Tamiami Trail out of the muck—adorns the grounds. ⊠*20200 E. Tamiami Trail, Naples* ☎*239/394–3397* ⊕*www.floridastateparks.org/collier-seminole* ☒*$4 per car* ☉*Daily 8–sunset.*

8

WHERE TO STAY & EAT

$–$$ ✕**Joanie's Blue Crab Café.** It could be a movie set: it has that swamp café look down to an art without even trying. Slumped roadside in the middle of nothing but Everglades, this red-painted, corrugated tin-sided shanty offers welcome paddle fan–cooled respite to hungry and thirsty travelers looking for something in the way of genuine 'Glades grub—hearty she-crab soup, gator tail, soft-shell crab, frogs' legs, and Seminole fry bread. Come on in, help yourself to a drink out of the cooler, or order a strawberry shake. The restaurant usually closes at 5 PM except certain nights during the winter-spring season when bands

> **CROCS OR GATORS?**
>
> You can tell you're looking at a crocodile, not an alligator, if you can see its lower teeth protruding when its jaws are shut. Gators are much darker in color—a grayish black—compared with the lighter tan color of crocodiles. Alligators' snouts are also much broader than their long, thin crocodilian counterparts.

play. ✉ *39395 Tamiami Trail, 50 mi west of Florida Tpke., Ochopee* ☎ *239/695–2682* 🖃 *AE, D, MC, V.*

¢–$$ ✕**Coopertown Restaurant.** Make this pit stop for local color and cuisine fished straight from the swamp. For more than a half century this small, casual eatery inside an airboat concession storefront has attracted the famous and the humbly hungry. House specialties are frogs' legs and alligator tail prepared cornmeal-breaded and deep-fried, served simply on paper ware with a lemon wedge and Tabasco. Also choose from more conventional selections, such as catfish, shrimp, or sandwiches. ✉ *22700 S.W. 8th St., 11 mi west of Florida Tpke., Miami* ✆ *Box 940176* ☎ *305/226–6048* ⊕ *www.coopertownairboats.com* 🖃 *AE, MC, V.*

$ ✕**Empeek Aaweeke.** Whether you're staying at the Miccosukee Resort or just spending the day at the slot machines, the all-day buffet will bolster you with salads, cold cuts, chicken, fish, steak, and desserts. There's a Friday night seafood buffet. The restaurant's bright Art Deco furnishings and tribal art murals are in keeping with the rest of the resort. Kids under age 6 eat free; ages 6 to 12 eat half price. ✉ *500 S.W. 177th Ave., 6 mi west of Florida Tpke., Miami* ☎ *305/925–2555 or 877/242–6464* ⊕ *www.miccosukee.com* 🖃 *AE, D, MC, V.*

★ ¢–$ ✕**Miccosukee Restaurant.** For a taste of local culture at a reasonable price, this restaurant at the Miccosukee Indian Village overlooking the River of Grass provides the best variety of food along Tamiami Trail in Everglades territory. A mural depicting Native American women cooking and men engaged in a powwow is the only nod toward atmosphere in this roadside cafeteria setting. Favorites are catfish and frogs' legs breaded and deep-fried, Indian fry bread, pumpkin bread, and Indian burgers and tacos, but you'll also find more common fare, such as burgers, fish, and Hispanic dishes. Try the Miccosukee Platter ($22.95) for a sampling of local favorites, including gator bites. Breakfast and lunch are served daily. ✉ *25 mi west of Florida Tpke.* ☎ *305/223–8380 Ext. 2374* 🖃 *AE, D, MC, V.*

★ ¢–$ ✕**Pit Bar-B-Q.** At the edge of Miami, this old-fashioned roadside eatery
🕄 is a holdout from the Everglades' backwoods heritage and a popular, affordable option for families. Order at the counter, pick up your food, and eat at one of the picnic tables indoors on the screened porch or outdoors. Specialties include barbecued chicken and ribs with a tangy sauce, french fries, coleslaw, and a fried biscuit, plus burgers and fish sandwiches. The whopping double-decker beef or pork sandwich with slaw requires at least five napkins. Locals flock here, bringing the kids on weekends for pony rides. ✉ *16400 Tamiami Trail, 5 mi west of Florida Tpke., Miami* ☎ *305/226–2272* 🖃 *AE, D, MC, V.*

$$ 🖭**Miccosukee Resort & Convention Center.** Big-name entertainers, major sporting events, and gaming draw crowds to this nine-story resort at the crossroads of Tamiami Trail and Krome Avenue. Like an oasis on the horizon, it's the only facility for miles, and it's situated to attract the attention of travelers going to the Everglades, driving across the state, or looking for casino action. The casino occupies the lobby, making for a cigarette-smoky welcome as visitors enter to check in. Most units have a view of Everglades saw grass and wildlife. In addition

to an enormous indoor play area for children and a game arcade for teens and 'tweens, there are tours to Everglades National Park and the Miccosukee Indian Village, shuttles to area malls, and a golf course about 9 mi away. Pros: casino, most modern resort in these parts, golf. Cons: cigarette smell in lobby, parking lot fills with gamblers, doesn't feel compatible with the Everglades. ⊠*500 S.W. 177th Ave., 6 mi west of Florida Tpke., Miami 33194* ☎*305/925–2555 or 877/242–6464* ⊕*www.miccosukee.com* ⇥*256 rooms, 46 suites* ⌂*In-room: safe, dial-up. In-hotel: 2 restaurants, bar, golf course, pool, gym, spa, children's programs (ages 0–12), laundry service, airport shuttle, public Internet, no-smoking rooms* ▭*AE, D, DC, MC, V.*

⚠ **Everglades Gator Park.** At an airboat tour facility in the heart of the Everglades, this RV park is especially popular with snowbirds, as it's close to the Port of Miami and Miami airport and offers short-term RV storage. Campers are surrounded by the sounds of alligators, birds, and frogs by night, departing and arriving airboats by day. There's a restaurant inside the park. ⌂*Restaurant, flush toilets, full hookups, drinking water, electricity, public telephone, general store* ⇥*10 full hookups, 20 partial hookups* ⊠*24050 S.W. 8th St., Miami* ✉*Box 787, Miami33194* ☎*305/559–2255 or 800/559–2205* 🖷*305/559–2844* ⊕*www.gatorpark.com* ▭*AE, D, DC, MC, V.*

THE OUTDOORS

★ **Shark Valley Tram Tours** (⊠*Shark Valley* ☎*305/221–8455*) rents one-speed, well-used bikes daily 8:30–4 (last rental at 3; bikes must be returned by 4) for $6 per hour.

SHOPPING

The shopping alone should lure you to the **Miccosukee Indian Village** (⊠*25 mi west of Florida Tpke., just west of Shark Valley entrance* ☎*305/223–8380*). Wares include Native American crafts such as beadwork, moccasins, dolls, pottery, baskets, and patchwork fabric and clothes.

EVERGLADES CITY

🔟 *35 mi southeast of Naples, 83 mi west of Miami.*

Aside from a chain gas station or two, this is perfect Old Florida. No high-rises (other than an observation tower) mar the landscape at this western gateway to Everglades National Park, just off the Tamiami Trail. It was developed in the late 19th century by Barron Collier, a wealthy advertising man. Collier built it as a company town to house workers for his numerous projects, including construction of the Tamiami Trail. It grew and prospered until the Depression and World War II. Today it draws people to the park for canoeing, fishing, and bird-watching excursions. Airboat tours, though popular with visitors, are banned within the preserve and park because of the environmental damage they cause to the mangroves. The annual Seafood Festival, held the first weekend of February, draws 60,000 to 75,000 visitors to eat seafood, hear nonstop music, and buy crafts. At other times, dining choices are limited to a handful of basic eateries. The town is small, fishing oriented, and unhurried, making it excellent for boating and bicycling. Pedal along the waterfront on a 2-mi ride along the strand out to Chokoloskee Island.

The best place to find information about Everglades National Park's watery western side is at the **Gulf Coast Visitor Center.** During the winter season, it's filled with canoeists checking in for trips to the Ten Thousand Islands and 99-mi Wilderness Waterway Trail, visitors viewing interpretive exhibits about local flora and fauna while they wait for the departure of a naturalist-led boat trip, rangers answering questions, and backcountry campers purchasing permits. In season (Christmas through Easter), rangers lead bike tours and canoe trips. There are no direct roads from here to other sections of the park. ⊠*Rte. 29* ☎*239/695–3311* ☞*Park free* ☉*Mid-Nov.–mid-Apr., daily 8–4:30; mid-Apr.–mid-Nov., daily 9–4:30.*

You can climb 108 steps to the top of the **Observation Tower** (across the road from the visitor center entrance), which was built in 1984 and recently reopened to visitors behind the chamber of commerce office. The office does not have regular hours, so call ahead to see when you can visit. ⊠*905 Copeland Ave.* ☎*239/695–3172* ☞*$2* ☉*Call for hrs.*

Through artifacts and photographs at the **Museum of the Everglades,** meet the Native Americans, pioneers, businesspeople, and fishermen who played a role in the development of southwest Florida. Exhibits and a film chronicle the tremendous feat of building Tamiami Trail through the mosquito- and gator-infested Everglades wetlands. The only unaltered structure original to the town of Everglades, where it opened in 1927 as the town's laundry, the building is on the National Register of Historic Places. In addition to the permanent displays, there are occasional rotating exhibits and works by local artists. ⊠*105 W. Broadway* ☎*239/695–0008* ⊕*www.colliermuseum.com* ☞*Free* ☉*Tues.–Sat. 10–4.*

OFF THE BEATEN PATH

Smallwood Store. Ted Smallwood pioneered this last American frontier in 1906 and built a 3,000-square-foot pine trading post raised on pilings on Chokoloskee Bay. Smallwood's granddaughter Lynn McMillin reopened it in 1989, after it had been closed for several years, and installed a small gift shop and a museum chock-full of goods from the store, including historic photographs and original store ledgers; Native American clothing, furs, and hides; and area memorabilia. An annual festival in March celebrates the century-long relationship the store has had with local Native Americans. ⊠*360 Mamie St., Chokoloskee Island* ☎*239/695–2989* ☞*$3* ☉*Dec.–Apr., daily 10–5; May–Nov., daily 11–5.*

WHERE TO STAY & EAT

★ $$–$$$ ✕**Rod and Gun Club.** The striking, polished pecky cypress woodwork in this historic building dates from the 1920s, when wealthy hunters, anglers, and yachting parties from around the world came for the winter season. The main dining room holds the overflow from the popular enormous screened porch that overlooks the river. Like life in general here, servers move slowly and upkeep is minimal. Fresh seafood domi-nates a menu that includes stone crab claws in season, a turf-and-surf combo of steak and grouper, a swamp-and-turf combo of frogs' legs and steak, seafood and pasta pairings, and yummy key lime pie. If you lack the nerve to go native for your entrée, you can sample frogs' legs or gator nuggets as an appetizer. Arrive by boat or land. ⊠*200 Riverside Dr.* ☎*239/695–2101* ▤*No credit cards.*

$–$$　✕**Oyster House Restaurant.** One of the town's oldest and most old-fash-
☺　ioned fish houses, it serves all the local staples—shrimp, gator tail, frogs' legs, oysters, stone crab, and grouper. Shrimp scampi and grou-per smothered in tomatoes are among the few exceptions to fried prep-aration. But deep-frying is an art in these parts, so if you're going to indulge, do it here. Try to dine at sunset. ⊠*Hwy. 29 S.* ☎*239/695–2073* ⊕*www.oysterhouserestaurant.com* ▤*AE, D, MC, V.*

¢–$$　✕**Everglades Seafood Depot.** Come for affordable, scenic breakfast, lunch, or dinner to this storied 1928 Spanish-style stucco structure on Lake Placid. It began its life as the original Everglades depot, was part of the University of Miami, appeared in the film *Winds across the Everglades,* and has housed several restaurants. Today's menu has a wide selection of well-prepared seafood—from shrimp and grouper to frogs' legs and alligator—and combinations thereof. For big appetites, there are generously portioned entrées of steak and fish specials and combination platters that include warm, fresh-baked biscuits. Weekly specials include a taco bar one day and all-you-can-eat specials others. Ask for a table on the back porch overlooking the lake or a window seat. ⊠*102 Collier Ave.* ☎*239/695–0075* ▤*AE, D, MC, V.*

¢–$　✕**Havana Café.** Cuban specialties are a tasty change from the shanty seafood houses of Everglades City: brightly painted walls and floral tablecloths make this little eatery and its 10 indoor tables and 4 porch tables a cheerful spot. Service is order-at-the-counter for breakfast and lunch (until 3 PM). Start the day with the sweet punch of café con leché and a pressed egg sandwich. For lunch, you'll find the ubiquitous Cuban sandwich, burgers, and shrimp, grouper, steak, and pork plates with rice and beans and yucca. ⊠*Chokoloskee Mall* ☎*239/695–2214* ▤*No credit cards.*

¢–$　✕**Triad Seafood.** Along the Barron River, seafood houses, fishing boats, and crab traps populate one shoreline; mangroves the other. Some of the seafood houses, selling fresh off the boat, added picnic tables and eventually grew into restaurants. Triad is one, with a deck overhang-ing the river and holding about nine outdoor tables where you can enjoy the view and fresh seafood during stone crab season, October 15 to May 15. Nothing fancy, but you won't find a better grouper sandwich anywhere. Roughly from 11 AM to 4 PM the house also serves fried shrimp, conch, crab cake, and soft-shell blue crab baskets, plus Reubens, hamburgers, Philly cheesesteak sandwiches, and, on Fri-day, smoked ribs. ⊠*401 School Dr.* ☎*239/695–2662* ▤*AE, MC, V* ⊗*Closed May 16–Oct. 15.*

$$　▥**Everglades Spa & Lodge.** Formerly a bank dating from 1923, this inn focuses on offering spa and tour services. On the second floor are spa-cious, individually decorated rooms, suites, and efficiencies, all homey,

8

no-frills, and comfortable with private baths. A licensed massage thera-pist operates the first-floor, five-room day spa, offering such services as massages and facials, colon hydrotherapy, and clay baths. State-certi-fied ecotourism guides lead outings to local attractions, packaged with spa services. Continental breakfast is delivered to your door. Bicycle use is complimentary. Pros: holistic spa, affordability, close to restaurants. Cons: not on the water, dated, cluttered lobby area. ⊠*201 W. Broad-way, Box 570, 34139* ☎*239/695–3151* 🖷*239/695–3335* ⊕*www.evergladeslodge.com* ➦*7 rooms* ⚒*In-room: no phone, kitchen (some), refrigerator. In-hotel: spa, bicycles, public Internet, no-smoking rooms* ⊟*AE, D, DC, MC, V* ⦿*CP.*

¢–$$ 🛏 **Ivey House.** A remodeled 1928 boardinghouse originally for workers
Fodor's Choice   building the Tamiami Trail, the Ivey House today fits many budgets.
★   One part is a friendly bed-and-breakfast bargain with shared baths and a cottage. The newer inn, connected to the B&B by a ramp, has rooms with private baths—some of Everglades City's plushest accom-modations. Most inn rooms surround the screen-enclosed pool and courtyard. Display cases of local flora and fauna decorate the inn, as do photographs of the Everglades and Ten Thousand Islands. The layout is designed to promote camaraderie, but there are secluded patios with chairs and tables for private moments. Rates include a hot breakfast buffet. The Ivey House is run by the owners of NACT-Everglades Rent-als & Eco Adventures, so stay here before or after the ecotours and save 20% on canoe and kayak rentals and tours. Pros: canoe and kayak rentals and tours, pleasant atmosphere, affordability. Cons: not on the water, small rooms, sparse amenities, breakfast for guests only. ⊠*107 Camellia St., 34139* ☎*239/695–3299* 🖷*239/695–4155* ⊕*www.ivey-house.com* ➦*31 rooms, 18 with bath; 1 2-bedroom cottage* ⚒*In-room: refrigerator (some), dial-up. In-hotel: restaurant, room service, pool, laundry facilities, no-smoking rooms* ⊟*MC, V* ⊗*Closed June–Sept.* ⦿*BP.*

$ 🛏 **Glades Haven Cozy Cabins.** Bob Miller wanted to build a Holiday Inn next to his Oyster House Restaurant on marina-channel shores. When that didn't go through, he sent for cabin kits and set up mobile home–size units around a pool on his property. Guests who rent these cabins get free boat docking. A full cabin, done up in wood, tin roof, and polished floor, has a full kitchen and separate bedroom with screened porch. Duplex cabins—one of the best deals in town—come with a small fridge and microwave, with or without a screened porch. Pros: convenient to ENP boating, good food options, marina. Cons: crowded trailer park feel, no phones. ⊠*801 Copeland Ave., 34139* ☎*239/695–2746 or 888/956–6251* ⊕*www.gladeshaven.com* ➦*24 cabins, 5 3-bedroom houses* ⚒*In-room: no phone, kitchen (some). In-hotel: 2 restaurants, pool, laundry facilities* ⊟*AE, D, MC, V.*

★   ⚠ **Outdoor Resorts.** This clean, amenity-rich RV resort, set at the water's edge on secluded Chokoloskee Island, has sunny sites with concrete pads. Tropical vegetation adds shade and color. All sites have a water view. The property has boat rentals, tennis and shuffleboard, a marina, and a bait shop. A TV hookup and use of a recreation hall and health club are included in the rates and help while the hours away on rainy days. A motel accommodates those who come without an RV. ♿ *Pools, flush toilets, full hookups, drinking water, guest laundry, showers, electricity, general store* ⚓*283 sites, 8 efficiencies with kitchens* ✉*Rte. 29, 6 mi south of Tamiami Trail* ✉*Box 39, Chokoloskee Island, 34138* ☎*239/695–3788* 🖨*239/695–3338* ⊕*www.outdoor-resorts.com* ▤*MC, V.*

THE OUTDOORS

BOATING

Glades Haven Marina (✉*801 S. Copeland Ave.* ☎*239/695–2628* ⊕*www.gladeshaven.com*) can put you on the water to explore the Ten Thousand Islands in 16-foot Carolina skiffs and 24-foot pontoon boats. Rates start at $150 a day, with half-day options. It also rents kayaks, canoes, and fishing tackle, and has a 24-hour boat ramp and dockage for vessels up to 24 feet long.

CANOEING & KAYAKING

Everglades National Park Boat Tours (✉*Gulf Coast Visitor Center* ☎*239/695–4731 or 866/628–7275*) rents 17-foot canoes for day and overnight use. Rates are $25.44 per day, including tax. Car-shuttle service is available, for an additional fee for canoeists paddling the Wilderness Trail in season, and travelers with disabilities can be accommodated. Reservations are strongly suggested from December through April.

Fodor'sChoice **NACT-Everglades Rentals & Eco Adventures** (✉*Ivey House, 107 Camel-*
★ *lia St.* ☎*239/695–3299* ⊕*www.evergladesadventures.com*) is an established source for canoes, sea kayaks, and guided Everglades trips (November through April). Canoes cost from $35 the first day, $27 for each day thereafter, and kayaks are from $45 for the first day. Half-day rentals from 1 to 5 PM are available. Shuttles deliver you to major launching areas in the region, such as the Turner River ($30 for two people and one vessel) and Collier-Seminole State Park ($60).

BIG CYPRESS NATIONAL PRESERVE

Through the 1950s and early 1960s, the world's largest cypress-logging industry prospered in the Big Cypress Swamp. The industry died out in the 1960s, and the government began buying parcels. Today, 729,000 acres, or nearly half of the swamp, have become this national preserve. The word "big" in its name refers not to the size of the trees but to the swamp, which juts down into the north side of Everglades National Park like a piece in a jigsaw puzzle. Its size and strategic location make it an important link in the region's hydrological system, in which rainwater first flows through the preserve, then south into the park, and eventually into Florida Bay. Its variegated pattern of wet prairies, ponds, marshes, sloughs, and strands provides a wildlife sanctuary, and thanks to a policy of balanced land use—"use without abuse"—the watery wilderness is devoted to research and recreation as well as preservation. The preserve allows—in limited areas—hunting, off-road vehicle (airboat, swamp buggy, four-wheel-drive vehicles) use by permit, and cattle grazing. Compared with Everglades National Park, the preserve is less developed and has fewer visitors. That makes it ideal for naturalists, birders, and hikers who prefer to see more wildlife than humans. Several scenic drives link off Tamiami Trail; some require four-wheel-drive vehicles, especially in wet summer months. A few lead to camping areas. Roadside picnic areas are off the Tamiami Trail. There are three types of trails—walking (including part of the extensive Florida National Scenic Trail), canoeing, and bicycling. All three trail types are easily accessed from the Tamiami Trail near the preserve's visitor center, and one boardwalk trail departs from the center. Canoe and bike equipment can be rented from outfitters in Everglades City, 24 mi west, and Naples, 40 mi west.

CAMPING

⚠ **Big Cypress National Preserve.** There are four no-fee primitive campgrounds within Big Cypress National Preserve along the Tamiami Trail and Loop Road. One of them, Burns Lake, is open September through January 6 and camping is free. Others may close seasonally for repairs or because of flooding, so check ahead. A fifth site, Monument Lake Campground (open September through mid-April), has restrooms, a cold shower, an amphitheater, and activities and seasonal programs (mid-December through March). Campers can use the dump station on Dona Drive in Ochopee. ♿ *Flush toilets, dump station, running water (nonpotable), showers (cold)* ⟐ *40 sites at Burns Lake; 10 tent, 26 RV or tent sites at Monument Lake* ⊠ *Tamiami Trail (Hwy. 41), between Miami and Naples* ⏚ *HCR 61, Box 110, Ochopee 34141* ☎ *239/695–1201* ⊕ *www.nps.gov/bicy* ▭ *No credit cards.*

THE EVERGLADES ESSENTIALS

To research prices, get advice from other travelers, and book travel arrangements, visit www.fodors.com.

TRANSPORTATION

BY AIR

Miami International Airport (MIA) is 34 mi from Homestead and 83 mi from Flamingo in Everglades National Park. *For airline carriers to MIA, refer to the Miami chapter.* Airporter runs shuttle buses three times daily that stop at the Hampton Inn in Florida City on their way between MIA and the Florida Keys. Shuttle service, which takes about an hour, runs 6:10 AM to 5:20 PM from Florida City, 7:30 AM to 6 PM from the airport. Reserve at least 24 hours in advance. Pickups can be arranged for all baggage-claim areas. The cost is $30 one-way. SuperShuttle operates 11-passenger air-conditioned vans to Homestead. Service from MIA is available around the clock; booths are outside most luggage areas on the lower level. For the return to MIA, reserve 24 hours in advance. The one-way cost is $41 per person. Southwest Florida International Airport (RSW) in Fort Myers, about an hour away from Everglades City, is the closest major airport to the Everglades western access. For carrier information see *the Southwest Florida chapter.* On-demand taxi transportation from the airport to Everglades City runs about $100.

Contacts **Miami International Airport (MIA)** (☎ *305/876–7000* ⊕ *www.miami-airport.com*). **Southwest Florida International Airport (RSW)** (☎ *239/768–1000* ⊕ *www.flylcpa.com*). **Airporter** (☎ *800/830–3413*). **SuperShuttle** (☎ *305/871–2000* ⊕ *www.supershuttle.com*).

BY BOAT

If you're entering the United States by pleasure boat, you must phone U.S. Customs either from a marine phone or upon first arriving ashore. Bring aboard the proper *NOAA Nautical Charts* before you cast off to explore park waters. The charts are available at many marine stores in South Florida, from the Florida National Parks and Monuments Association's online bookstore (⊕ *www.nps.gov/ever/fnpma.htm*), and at Flamingo Marina in the Everglades. The annual *Waterway Guide* (Southern Edition) is widely used by boaters. Bookstores all over South Florida sell it, or you can order it from the publisher for $40 plus shipping and handling.

Contacts **U.S. Customs** (☎ *800/432–1216*). *Waterway Guide* (⊠ *326 1st St., Suite 400, Annapolis, MD 21403* ☎ *800/233–3359* ⊕ *www.waterwayguide.com*).

BY BUS

Metrobus travels daily through the Miami–Homestead–Florida City area on weekdays. Regular fare is $1.50. The Dade-Monroe Express provides daily bus service from the Florida City Wal-Mart Supercenter to Mile Marker 50 in Marathon. The bus makes several stops in Florida City and the Keys, during daily round-trips on the hour from 6 AM to 10 PM. The cost is $1.85 each way.

Contacts **Dade-Monroe Express** (☎ *305/770–3131* ⊕ *www.miamidade.gov/transit*). **Metrobus** (☎ *305/770–3131* ⊕ *www.miamidade.gov/transit*).

BY CAR

From Miami the main highways to the area are U.S. 1, the Homestead Extension of Florida Turnpike, and Krome Avenue (Route 997). To reach Biscayne National Park from Homestead, take U.S. 1 or Krome Avenue to Route 9336 (Palm Drive) and turn east. Follow Palm Drive for about 8 mi until it becomes Southwest 344th Street and follow signs to the park headquarters. To reach Everglades National Park's Ernest F. Coe Visitor Center and Flamingo, head west on Palm Drive in Florida City and follow signs. From Florida City the Ernest F. Coe Visitor Center is 11 mi; Flamingo is 49 mi. The north entrance of Everglades National Park at Shark Valley is reached by taking the Tamiami Trail about 20 mi west of Krome Avenue. To reach the west entrance of Everglades National Park at the Gulf Coast Visitor Center in Everglades City, take Route 29 south from the Tamiami Trail.

CAR RENTAL Agencies in the Homestead area include Budget and Enterprise Rent-a-Car.

Contacts **Budget** (⊠ *29949 S. Dixie Hwy., Homestead* ☎ *305/248–4524 or 800/527–0700*). **Enterprise Rent-a-Car** (⊠ *29130 S. Dixie Hwy., Homestead* ☎ *305/246–2056 or 800/736–8222*).

CONTACTS & RESOURCES

EMERGENCIES

In national parks, rangers answer police, fire, and medical emergencies. The Florida Fish and Wildlife Conservation Commission, a division of the Florida Department of Natural Resources, maintains a 24-hour telephone service for reporting boating emergencies and natural-resource violations. The Miami Beach Coast Guard Base responds to local marine emergencies and reports of navigation hazards. The base broadcasts on VHF-FM Channel 16. The National Weather Service supplies local forecasts.

Contacts **Emergencies** (☎ *911*). **Hospital emergency line** (☎ *305/596–6556*). **Homestead Hospital** (✉ *160 N.W. 13th St., Homestead* ☎ *305/248–3232, 305/596–6557 physician referral*). **Florida Fish and Wildlife Conservation Commission** (☎ *305/956–2500*). **Miami Beach Coast Guard Base** (✉ *100 MacArthur Causeway, Miami Beach* ☎ *305/535–4300 or 305/535–4314*). **National Parks** (☎ *305/247–7272*). **National Weather Service** (☎ *305/229–4522*).

MEDIA

NEWSPAPERS & MAGAZINES The *South Dade News Leader* is published twice weekly and covers south Miami, Homestead, Florida City, and the Redland areas. *Everglades Echo* comes out on Wednesday in Everglades City.

TELEVISION & RADIO WLRN is National Public Radio at FM 91.3. Two FM stations broadcast information on Everglades flora, fauna, and attractions along Interstate 75: tune in to FM 98.7 or 107.9. Out of Miami, WLVE 93.9 plays jazz; WZTA 94.9, rock.

TOURS

Many Everglades-area tours operate only in season, roughly November through April. The National Park Service has free programs, typically focusing on native wildlife, plants, and park history. At Biscayne National Park, for example, rangers give informal tours of Elliott and Boca Chita keys, which you can arrange in advance, depending on ranger availability. Contact the respective visitor center for details. Wings Ten Thousand Islands Aero-Tours operates scenic, low-level flight tours of the Ten Thousand Islands National Wildlife Refuge, Big Cypress National Preserve, Everglades National Park, and the Gulf of Mexico in an Alaskan floatplane. On the 20- to 90-minute flights, see saw-grass prairies, Native American shell mounds, alligators, and wading birds. Prices start at $30 per person with a group of three or four. For an all- or multiday outing, opt for flights across the gulf to the Florida Keys or Dry Tortugas. Wooten's Everglades Airboat Tours runs airboat and swamp-buggy tours ($21) through the Everglades. (Swamp buggies are giant tractorlike vehicles with oversize rubber wheels.) Tours last approximately 30 minutes. Combination tours, including a visit to the animal sanctuary, cost $40. Southwest of Florida City near the entrance to Everglades National Park, Everglades Alligator Farm runs a 4-mi, 30-minute tour of the River of Grass with departures 20 minutes after the hour. The tour ($19) includes free hourly alligator, snake, and wildlife shows, or take in the shows only ($13.50).

From the Shark Valley area, Buffalo Tiger's Florida Everglades Airboat Ride is operated by a former chairman of the Miccosukee tribe. Miccosukee Indian guides narrate the 40-minute trip from the perspective of the Native Americans, who have lived there since the 1800s. Trips run on the north side of Tamiami Trail, where there's more water and wildlife, and include a stop at an old Native American camp. Tours cost $25 each for two people and operate 10 to 5 daily. Reservations are not required. Coopertown Airboat Ride operates the oldest airboat rides in the Everglades (since 1945). The 35- to 40-minute tour ($19) takes you 9 mi to hammocks and alligator holes. Everglades Gator Park offers 45-minute narrated airboat tours ($18, including park tour and wildlife show). Everglades Safari Park runs 40-minute airboat rides for $20 and small, private airboat tours for an extra charge; they last 20 minutes to 2½ hours. The price includes a show and gator tour. The Miccosukee Indian Village 30-minute narrated airboat ride stops at a 100-year-old family camp in the Everglades to hear tales and allow passengers to walk around and explore ($10).

Tours at Biscayne National Park are run by people-friendly Biscayne National Underwater Park, Inc. Daily trips (at 10, with a second trip at 1 during high season, depending on demand) explore the park's living coral reefs 10 mi offshore on *Reef Rover IV*, a 53-foot glass-bottom boat that can carry 48 passengers. On days when the weather is unsuitable for reef viewing, an alternative three-hour, ranger-led interpretive tour visits Boca Chita Key. (Rangers also conduct the Boca Chita tour on certain Sundays in season.) Reservations are recommended. The cost is $26.95, and you should arrive at least one hour before departure.

Flamingo Marina Boat Tours is the official concession operating sightseeing excursions through Everglades National Park. The two-hour backcountry *Pelican* cruise ($18) is the most popular. The boat winds under a heavy canopy of mangroves, revealing abundant wildlife— from alligators, crocodiles, and turtles to herons, hawks, and egrets.

Starting at the Shark Valley visitor center, Shark Valley Tram Tours follows a 15-mi loop road, especially good for viewing gators, into the interior, stopping at a 50-foot observation tower. Two-hour narrated tours cost $14 and depart hourly 9 to 4 December through April; the rest of the year tours run every two hours from 9:30 to 3. Reservations are recommended December through April. On the west side, Everglades National Park Boat Tours operates 1½-hour trips ($26.50) through the Ten Thousand Islands National Wildlife Refuge and mangrove wilderness, where passengers often see dolphins, manatees, bald eagles, and roseate spoonbills. In the height of season, three tour boats run four times daily. Boats can accommodate large parties and wheelchairs (not electric) and have drink concessions. Everglades Rentals & Eco Adventures leads one-day to seven-night Everglades paddling tours November through April. Highlights include bird and gator sightings, mangrove forests, no-man's-land beaches, relics of the hideouts of infamous and just-plain-reclusive characters, and spectacular sunsets. Included in the cost of overnight tours ($500 to $1,375) are canoe or kayak rental, all necessary equipment, a guide, meals, and lodging for the first night at the Ivey House. There's a four-person minimum.

Contacts **Biscayne National Underwater Park, Inc.** (✉ *Convoy Point, east end of North Canal Dr., 9710 S.W. 328th St.* ✆ *Box 1270, Homestead 33090* ☎ *305/230–1100* ⊕ *www.nps.gov/bisc*). **Buffalo Tiger's Florida Everglades Airboat Ride** (✉ *30 mi west of Florida Tpke. on Tamiami Trail* ☎ *305/382–0719*). **Coopertown Airboat Ride** (✉ *11 mi west of Florida Tpke. on Tamiami Trail* ☎ *305/226–6048* ⊕ *www.coopertownairboats.com*). **Everglades Alligator Farm** (✉ *40351 S.W. 192nd Ave.* ☎ *305/247–2628* ⊕ *www.everglades.com*). **Everglades Gator Park** (✉ *12 mi west of Florida Tpke. on Tamiami Trail* ☎ *305/559–2255 or 800/559–2205* ⊕ *www.gatorpark.com*). **Everglades National Park Boat Tours** (✉ *Gulf Coast Visitor Center, Everglades City* ☎ *239/695–2591 or 866/628–7275* ⊕ *www.nps.gov/ever*). **Everglades Rentals & Eco Adventures** (✉ *Ivey House, 107 Camellia St.* ✆ *Box 5038, Everglades City 34139* ☎ *239/695–3299* ⊕ *www. evergladesadventures.com*). **Everglades Safari Park** (✉ *26700 Tamiami Trail, 15 mi west of Florida Tpke.* ☎ *305/226–6923 or 305/223–3804* ⊕ *www.evsafaripark. com*). **Flamingo Lodge, Marina & Outpost Resort Boat Tours** (✉ *1 Flamingo Lodge Hwy., Flamingo* ☎ *239/695–3101* ⊕ *www.flamingolodge.com*). **Miccosukee Indian Village** (✉ *25 mi west of Florida Tpke. on Tamiami Trail* ☎ *305/223–8380* ⊕ *www.miccosukeetours.com*). **Shark Valley Tram Tours** (✆ *Box 1739, Tamiami Station, Miami 33144* ☎ *305/221–8455* ⊕ *www.nps.gov/ever/visit/tours.htm*). **Wings Ten Thousand Islands Aero-Tours** (✉ *Everglades Airport, 650 Everglades City Airpark Rd.* ✆ *Box 482, Everglades City 34139* ☎ *239/695–3296* ☽ *Nov.–May*). **Wooten's Everglades Airboat Tours** (✉ *Wooten's Alligator Farm, 1½ mi east of Rte. 29 on Tamiami Trail* ☎ *239/695–2781 or 800/282–2781* ⊕ *www.wootensairboats.com*).

VISITOR INFORMATION

Contacts **Big Cypress National Preserve** (✆ *HCR 61, Box 11, Ochopee 34141* ☎ *239/695–1201* ⊕ *www.nps.gov/bicy*). **Biscayne National Park** (*Dante Fascell Visitor Center,* ✉ *9700 S.W. 328th St., Homestead 33033–5634* ☎ *305/230–7275* ⊕ *www.nps.gov/bisc*). **Everglades Area Chamber of Commerce** (✉ *Rte. 29 and Tamiami Trail* ✆ *Box 130, Everglades City 34139* ☎ *239/695–3172* ⊕ *www. florida-everglades.com/chamber*). **Everglades National Park** (*Ernest F. Coe Visitor Center* ✉ *40001 Rte. 9336, Homestead 33034* ☎ *305/242–7700* ⊕ *www.nps. gov/ever*). **Flamingo Visitor Center** (✉ *1 Flamingo Lodge Hwy., Flamingo 33034* ☎ *239/695–2945*). **Gulf Coast Visitor Center** (✉ *Rte. 29, Everglades City 34139* ☎ *239/695–3311* ⊕ *www.nps.gov/ever*). **Tropical Everglades Visitor Center** (✉ *160 U.S. 1, Florida City 33034* ☎ *305/245–9180 or 800/388–9669* ⊕ *www. tropicaleverglades.com*).

The Lower Gulf Coast

WORD OF MOUTH

"Within [Naples] there are only a couple of beach-front hotels, as the beach is lined with all private homes at the southern end, and condominiums as you go farther north, but that doesn't mean that the beach is private or belongs to any of those people. In fact it means that if you go to the more southern end, particularly south of the pier, you have the beach much more to yourself."

–Patrick

"Spent a day on Sanibel Island, enjoyed the beach and wonderful shelling … We shopped at Miromar, which was nice, but not much different from our nearby outlets, just a more tropical feel!"

–luugis

Updated by
Chelle Koster
Walton

WITH ITS SUBTROPICAL CLIMATE AND beckoning family-friendly beaches, the Lower Gulf Coast, also referred to as the state's southwestern region, is a favorite vacation spot of Florida residents as well as visitors. There's lots to do in addition to the sun and surf scene throughout its several distinct travel destinations. Small and historic downtown Fort Myers, recently dubbed the River District, rises inland along the Caloosahatchee River, and the rest of the town sprawls in all directions. It got its nickname, the City of Palms, from the hundreds of towering royal palms that inventor Thomas Edison planted between 1900 and 1917 along McGregor Boulevard, a historic residential street and site

TOP 5

Edison & Ford Winter Estates, Fort Myers: Two geniuses left Fort Myers their enduring legacy.

Island-Hopping: Hop aboard and explore islands accessible only by boat.

J.N. "Ding" Darling National Wildlife Refuge, Sanibel Island: More than 6,000 acres preserve wetland habitat for many creatures.

Naples Shop & Dine: Hit 5th Avenue South with a credit card and an open mind.

Fishing: Fish the entire coast, especially Maco Island.

of his winter estate. Edison's idea caught on, and more than 2,000 royal palms now line 15 mi of McGregor Boulevard. Museums and educational attractions are the draw here, as downtown diligently tries to shape itself as an entertainment destination and makes slow but sure headway. Across the river, Cape Coral has evolved from a mostly residential community to a resort destination for water-sports enthusiasts. North of Fort Myers, Punta Gorda is the center of a fishing-frenzied vacationland that remains a well-kept secret. Off the coast west of Fort Myers are more than 100 coastal islands in all shapes and sizes—among them Sanibel and Captiva, two thoughtfully developed resort islands. Connected to the mainland by a 3-mi causeway, Sanibel is known for its superb shelling, fine fishing, beachfront resorts, and wildlife refuge. Here and on Captiva, to which it is connected by a short bridge, multimillion-dollar homes line both waterfronts, but the gulf beaches are readily accessible. Just southwest of Fort Myers is Estero Island, home of busy Fort Myers Beach, and farther south, Lovers Key State Park and the growing area of Estero and Bonita Springs.

Farther down the coast lies Naples, once a small fishing village and now a thriving and sophisticated town, a smaller, more understated version of Palm Beach with fine restaurants, chichi shopping areas, and—locals will tell you—more golf holes per capita than anywhere else in the world. There's a lovely small art museum in the 1,473-seat Naples Philharmonic Center, which is the west-coast home of the Miami City Ballet. The beaches are soft and white, and access is relatively easy. East of Naples stretch the Big Cypress National Preserve and Everglades National Park, and a half hour south basks Marco Island, which people visit mostly for beaches and fishing. See a maze of pristine miniature mangrove islands when you take a boat tour departing from the island's marinas into Ten Thousand Islands National

Wildlife Refuge. Although high-rises line much of Marco's waterfront, natural areas have been preserved, including the tiny fishing village of Goodland, an outpost of Old Florida that tries valiantly to stave off new development.

XPLORING THE LOWER GULF COAST

In this region vacationers tend to spend most of their time outdoors—swimming, sunning, shelling, fishing, boating, and playing tennis or golf. Fort Myers is the only major inland destination; it has several interesting museums and parks. The barrier islands vary from tiny and undeveloped to sprawling and chockablock with hotels and restaurants.

Be aware that the destination's growing popularity, especially during winter, means traffic congestion at peak times of day. Avoid driving when the locals are getting to and from work and visitors are getting to and from the beach.

ABOUT THE RESTAURANTS

In this part of Florida fresh seafood reigns supreme. Succulent native stone crab claws, a particularly tasty treat, in season from mid-October through mid-May, are usually served with drawn butter or tangy mustard sauce. Supplies should remain plentiful, since these crabs are not killed to harvest their claws and their limbs regenerate in time for the next season. In Naples's excellent restaurants, mingle with locals, winter visitors, and other travelers and catch up on the latest culinary trends.

ABOUT THE HOTELS

Lodging in Fort Myers, the islands, and Naples can be pricey, but there are affordable properties even during the busy winter season. If these destinations are too rich for your budget, consider visiting in the off-season, when rates drop drastically. Beachfront properties tend to be more expensive; to spend less, look for properties away from the water. Punta Gorda and Charlotte Harbor have more in the budget range. In high season—Christmas through Easter—always reserve ahead for the top properties. Fall is the slowest season: rates are low and availability is high, but this is also the prime time for hurricanes. Hurricanes, in fact, took out some of the coastline's accommodations inventory in 2004 and 2005, but resorts are slowly coming back or being replaced. The reopening of Captiva Island's South Seas Island Resort, severely damaged by Hurricane Charley, was a significant stride in the island's recovery. In Charlotte County, hard hit in 2004, several new chain hotels have opened, or soon will, to replace 200 lost rooms. Intercontinental Hotels has broken ground on the first new hotel construction in Downtown Fort Myers in 20 years. As of this writing, Hotel Indigo Fort Myers was slated to open in late 2007. Across the river in Cape Coral, The Resort at MarinaVillage was hoping to break ground by 2008. Naples awaits the fall 2007 opening of the Naples Bay Resort, an 85-unit luxury hotel, rental cottage, and marina complex. Between

Naples and Everglades City, new owners renovated Port of the Islands Resort and reopened it in January 2007.

WHAT IT COSTS					
	¢	$	$$	$$$	$$$$
RESTAURANTS	under $10	$10–$15	$15–$20	$20–$30	over $30
HOTELS	under $80	$80–$100	$100–$140	$140–$220	over $220

Restaurant prices are per person for a main course at dinner. Hotel prices are for a standard double room, excluding 6% sales tax (more in some counties) and 1%–4% tourist tax.

TIMING

In winter this is one of the warmest areas of the United States, although occasionally temperatures drop below freezing in December or January. From February through April you may find it next to impossible to find a hotel room. Numbers drop off-season, but visitors from within driving range and convention clientele still keep things busy. Temperatures and humidity soar, but discounted room rates make summer attractive, and there's plenty of water for keeping cool.

FORT MYERS AREA

In Fort Myers, old Southern mansions and their modern-day counterparts peek out from behind stately palms. Views over the broad Caloosahatchee River, which borders the city's small but businesslike cluster of office buildings downtown, soften the look of the area. These days, it's showing the effects of age and urban sprawl, but renowned planner Andres Duany, father of "new urbanism," has been engaged to help revive what has been termed the River District. North of Fort Myers are small fishing communities and new retirement towns, including Boca Grande on Gasparilla Island; Englewood Beach on Manasota Key; Port Charlotte, north of the Peace River; and Punta Gorda, at the convergence of the Peace River and Charlotte Harbor.

FORT MYERS

▶ ❶ *90 mi southeast of Sarasota, 140 mi west of Palm Beach.*

The inviting city core lies inland along the banks of the Caloosahatchee River, a half hour from the nearest beach. The town is best known as the winter home of inventors Thomas A. Edison and Henry Ford.

Majestic palms, some planted by Thomas Edison, line **McGregor Boulevard**, one of the city's most scenic streets. It runs from downtown to Summerlin Road, which takes you to the barrier islands.

Fodor'sChoice   **Edison & Ford Winter Estates,** Fort Myers's premier attraction, pays homage to two of America's most ingenious inventors: Thomas A. Edison, who gave the world the stock ticker, the incandescent lamp, and the phonograph, among other inventions; and his friend and neighbor,

GREAT ITINERARIES

Numbers in the text correspond to numbers in the margin and on the Lower Gulf Coast map.

2 DAYS

⊞ **Fort Myers ❶** ► is a good base for a short visit. It's not directly on the beach, but its central location makes day trips easy. On the morning of your first day, visit Edison & Ford Winter Estates, in downtown Fort Myers, and then take McGregor Boulevard and Summerlin Road to ⊞ **Sanibel Island ❽**. There, stop by the Bailey-Matthews Shell Museum and the J.N. "Ding" Darling National Wildlife Refuge before heading to Bowman's Beach for shelling, swimming, and its famous sunset. The next day drive down Interstate 75 to ⊞ **Naples ⓬–㉑**. If you have a heart for art, stop by the **Naples Museum of Art ⓭** before hitting Old Naples for some shopping and relaxing on the nearby beach. Check out the subtropical plants and exotic animals at **Naples Zoo ⓯**.

4 DAYS

Stay near the water on ⊞ **Sanibel Island ❽** ►. Spend your first day shelling and swimming, taking a break from the beach for a stop at the Bailey-Matthews Shell Museum. On Day 2, head into **Fort Myers ❶** to Edison & Ford Winter Estates and, if you have kids, the hands-on Imaginarium nearby. Spend your third day back on Sanibel, dividing your time between the beach and the J.N. "Ding" Darling National Wildlife Refuge; go kayaking or try bird-watching in the early morning or evening. On Day 4, drive south to ⊞ **Naples ⓬–㉑** and the sights mentioned in the two-day itinerary, or for even more wildlife, head to the Corkscrew Swamp Sanctuary, a nature preserve east of **Bonita Springs ⓫**.

10 DAYS

An extended stay enables you to move your base and explore several areas in more depth. With two days in the area around **Fort Myers ❶** ►, add Babcock Wilderness Adventures and the Calusa Nature Center and Planetarium to the sights on the four-day itinerary. An extra day on ⊞ **Sanibel Island ❽** allows you to visit by boat an isolated island such as **Cabbage Key ❻** or the little town of Boca Grande, on **Gasparilla Island ❹**. For the second half of your trip, relocate to ⊞ **Naples ⓬–㉑**, stopping en route at Lovers Key State Park for some sensational shelling along its 2½ mi of white-sand beach. Once in Naples, divide your time between the beach and the galleries and shops. **Naples Zoo ⓯** and the Corkscrew Swamp Sanctuary are good bets for kids; to try your hand at paddling, rent a canoe or kayak at the **Naples Nature Center ⓰**. Or get your dose of culture at the impressive **Naples Museum of Art ⓭**. As a diversion, head to **Marco Island ㉒** for a day of fishing or a wildlife-viewing boat trip in the Everglades.

9

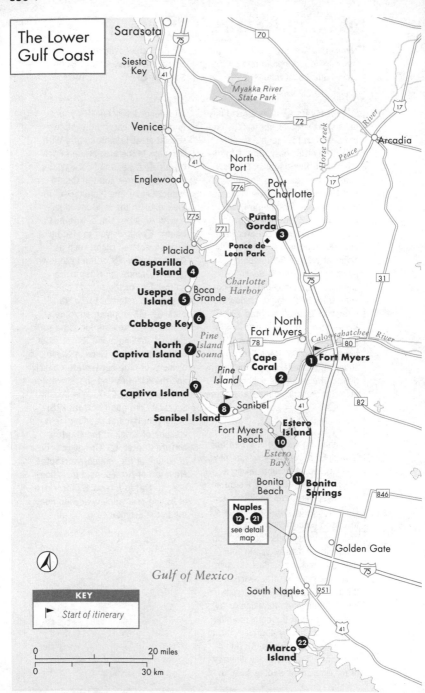

The Lower Gulf Coast

Sarasota

Siesta Key

Myakka River State Park

Venice

North Port

Englewood

Port Charlotte

Arcadia

Punta Gorda ③

Ponce de Leon Park

Placida

Gasparilla Island ④

Charlotte Harbor

Useppa Island ⑤   Boca Grande

Cabbage Key ⑥

Pine Island Sound

North Captiva Island ⑦

North Fort Myers

Caloosahatchee River

Cape Coral ②

Fort Myers ①

Captiva Island ⑨

Pine Island

Sanibel ▶

Sanibel Island ⑧

Fort Myers Beach

Estero Island ⑩

Estero Bay

Bonita Beach

Bonita Springs ⑪

Naples
⑫ - ㉑
see detail map

Golden Gate

Gulf of Mexico

South Naples

Marco Island ㉒

KEY
▶ Start of itinerary

0 ———— 20 miles
0 ———— 30 km

automaker Henry Ford. Donated to the city by Edison's widow, his 12-acre estate, reopened in 2006 after a $9 million historic renovation, is a remarkable place with three homes, a laboratory, botanical gardens, and a museum. The laboratory is just as Edison left it when he died in 1931. Edison traveled south from New Jersey and devoted much of his time here to inventing things (there are 1,093 patents to his name), experimenting with rubber for friend and frequent visitor Harvey Firestone, and planting some 600 species of plants collected around the world. Next door to Edison's two identical homes is Ford's "Mangoes," the more modest seasonal home of Edison's fellow inventor. It's said that the V-8 engine in essence was designed on the back porch. The recent renovation opened for the first time the property's oldest building, the Caretaker's House, circa 1860. Research garden renovation is ongoing. Tours are guided or audio self-guided. One admission covers both homes; laboratory-museum-only tickets are also available. ✉ *2350 McGregor Blvd.* ☎ *239/334–3614* ⊕ *www.efwefla.org* ✐ *$20* ⏱ *Tours daily 9–4.*

In a restored railroad depot, the **Southwest Florida Museum of History** showcases the area's history dating to 800 BC. Displays include prehistoric Calusa artifacts, a reconstructed *chickee* hut, canoes, clothing and photos from Seminole settlements, historical vignettes, changing exhibits, and a replicated Florida Cracker house. A favorite attraction is the *Esperanza*, a private railcar from the 1930s. ✉ *2300 Peck St.* ☎ *239/332–5955* ⊕ *www.cityftmyers.com/museum* ✐ *$9.50* ⏱ *Tues.–Sat. 10–5,.*

☾ ★ Kids can't wait to get their hands on the wonderful interactive exhibits at the **Imaginarium Hands-On Museum,** a lively museum-aquarium combo that explores the environment, physics, anatomy, weather, and other science and lifestyle topics. Check out the marine life in the aquariums, the touch pool, the living-reef tank, and the outdoor lagoon; visit tarantulas, a kinkajou, snakes, a juvenile alligator, and other live critters in the Animal Lab; dig for dinosaur bones; slap a hockey puck; watch a 3-D movie in the theater or a hands-on show; then prepare to get blown away in the Hurricane Experience. ✉ *2000 Cranford Ave.* ☎ *239/337–3332* ⊕ *www.cityftmyers.com/imaginarium* ✐ *$8* ⏱ *Mon.–Sat. 10–5, Sun. noon–5.*

☾ For a look at exhibits on wildlife, fossils, and Florida's native animals and habitats, head to the **Calusa Nature Center and Planetarium.** Boardwalks lead through subtropical wetlands, a birds-of-prey aviary, a butterfly house, and a re-created Seminole Indian village. There are snake, alligator, and other live-animal demonstrations several times daily. The 90-seat planetarium has astronomy shows daily and special laser shows. ✉ *3450 Ortiz Ave.* ☎ *239/275–3435* ⊕ *www.calusanature.com* ✐ *Nature center and planetarium $8* ⏱ *Mon.–Sat. 9–5, Sun. 11–5; call for astronomy and laser show schedule.*

☾ ★ At **Manatee Park** you may glimpse Florida's most famous marine mammal. When gulf waters are cold—usually from November to March—the gentle sea cows congregate in these waters, which are warmed by the outflow of a nearby power plant. Pause at any of the three observation decks and watch for bubbles. Hydrophones allow you to eavesdrop on their songs. Periodically one of the mammoth creatures—mature adults weigh hundreds of pounds—will surface. The park rents kayaks in winter and on summer weekends, and kayaking clinics and free guided walks are available. ⊠ *1½ mi east of I–75 Exit 141 at 10901 Rte. 80* ☎ *239/694–3537* ⊕ *www.leeparks.org* ⊠ *Parking $1 per hr to maximum of $5 per day* ⊙ *Daily 8–sunset. Gates lock automatically and promptly at closing time. Visitor center daily 9–4.*

WHERE TO STAY & EAT

$$$–$$$$ ✕ **Biddle's Restaurant & Piano Bar.** Refined, intimate surroundings and a karaoke piano bar set the mood for seafood, pasta, and chops infused with flavor and accompanied with creative sides and sauces. Seafood pasta comes with brandy-tomato cream sauce, chicken breast stuffed with prosciutto, New Zealand grilled lamb chops with pan-seared polenta, and seafood Wellington topped with lobster cream sauce. The glamorous chocolate piano dessert brings the meal to a fitting end. Stay for late-night dancing on weekends. ⊠ *20351 Summerlin Rd.* ☎ *239/433–4449* ⊟ *AE, MC, V.*

★ $$$–$$$$ ✕ **The Veranda.** Restaurants come and go quickly as downtown reinvents itself, but this one has endured since 1979. A favorite of business and government bigwigs, it serves imaginative Continental fare with a trace of a Southern accent. Notable are tournedos with smoky sour-mash whiskey sauce, rack of lamb with rosemary merlot sauce, herb-crusted honey grilled salmon, and a grilled seafood sampler, all served with homemade honey-drizzled bread and muffins with pepper jelly. The restaurant is a combination of two turn-of-the-20th-century homes, with a two-sided central brick fireplace, and sconces and antique oil paintings on its pale-yellow walls. Ask for an outdoor courtyard table when weather permits. ⊠ *2122 2nd St.* ☎ *239/332–2065* ⊕ *www.verandarestaurant.com* ⊟ *AE, MC, V* ⊙ *Closed Sun. No lunch Sat.*

★ $$–$$$ ✕ **Bistro 41.** Shoppers and business folk meet here for some of the town's most dependable and inventive cuisine. Amid brightly painted, textured walls, the menu roams from meat loaf and rotisserie chicken to pasta dishes and snapper roasted in a banana leaf. To experience the kitchen at its imaginative best, check the night's specials, which often include daringly done seafood (crabmeat-crusted tripletail fish with caramelized plantains and passion-fruit beurre blanc, for instance) and usually cost more than regular menu items. When weather permits, ask for a table on the patio. ⊠ *13499 S. Cleveland Ave.* ☎ *239/466–4141* ⊕ *www.bistro41.com* ⊟ *AE, D, MC, V* ⊙ *No lunch Sun.*

★ $$–$$$ ✕ **Mille Saporé.** If you're looking for finally crafted, flavorful (its name means "a thousand flavors") Mediterranean interpretations in a range from gourmet pizza to fine seafood and grilled meats, this intimate, candlelit corner belies its strip-mall location. Fans—shoppers and local business folk—rave about its seafood pizza, Brie calzone, red snapper with sour oranges, vegetable pasta, and nightly specials.

$–$$$ ✕ **French Roast Café.** Irish omelet, Belgian waffles, steak au poivre, Vietnamese sea bass, American burgers: French Roast clearly travels farther abroad than its name implies. And it does it with utmost taste and flavor, as its faithful local clientele will attest. The best deals are the lunchtime Vietnamese and early-bird (4:30 to 5:30) meals. At dinner, leave room for crepes à la Grand Marnier tableside or something from the bakery, and a cup of fresh-roasted coffee (hence the second part of its name). The interior poses a soothing surprise in a busy part of town with a water feature, fireplace, and classic columns. ⊠*12995 S. Cleveland. Ave. #118* ☎*239/936–2233* ▤*AE, D, MC, V* ☾*Closed Mon. in summer.*

$–$$ ✕**Shrimp Shack.** Seafood lovers flock to these two locations with their ☾ vivacious staff, bustle, and tropical color. There's a wait for lunch in winter season and a brisk take-out business at both addresses. Southern-style deep frying prevails—whole-belly clams, grouper, shrimp, onion rings, hush puppies, and pork loin planks—though you can get some selections broiled or blackened. The Pirate's Pleasure ($16) combines broiled grouper, shrimp, and scallops on a bed of crabmeat stuffing. This is your place if you like your seafood simple. The Colonial location has outdoor seating. ⊠*13361 Metro Pkwy.* ☎*239/561–6817* ⊠*Royal Palm Sq., 1400 Colonial Blvd. #57* ☎*239/277–5100* ▤*AE, D, DC, MC, V.*

¢–$ ✕**Chile Ranchero.** The local gringo population converges regularly on this authentic little corner of Mexicana along busy Tamiami Trail. You can't beat the prices or the portions. The staff speak Spanish and so does the menu, with English subtitles. Dishes appeal to American and Latin palates, with a range from pita sandwiches and steak ranchero to liver tacos and excellent nachos de ceviche. ⊠*11751 S. Cleveland Ave. #18* ☎*239/275–0505* ▤*AE, D, MC, V.*

¢–$ ✕**Mel's Diner.** A mostly older crowd swarms here for inexpensive comfort food prepared and served with nostalgia. Burgers are properly juicy, and the mile-high pies are impossibly huge (enough to feed up to four on one $4.99 slice). Stick with the diner-style specialties. Daily blue-plate specials—pot roast, chicken potpie, country-fried steak, for example—come with real mashed potatoes. Or try the Windy City chili, ribs, or an omelet. This place has become so popular it has spawned a chain on Florida's west coast. ⊠*4820 S. Cleveland Ave.* ☎*239/275–7850* ⊕*www.melsdiners.com* ▤*AE, DC, MC, V.*

★ ¢ ✕**Philly Junction.** From the bread (Amorosa rolls) to the beer (Yuengling), it comes from Philadelphia. Not only are the Philly cheesesteaks delicious and authentic, but the burgers and other sandwiches are excellent—and the prices are among the lowest around. Stay for an old-fashioned sundae, or join the Philly natives for pork roll and scrapple at breakfast. The café occupies two rooms sided with natural wood board-and-bead paneling in a strip mall. Signs at every table humorously reveal "25 Ways To Tell You're From Philly." ⊠*4600 Summerlin Rd.* ☎*239/936–6622* ▤*MC, V* ☾*No dinner Sun.*

$$$$ 🏨**Sanibel Harbour Resort & Spa.** Families and business folk who want ☾ luxury without Sanibel Island price tags flock to this high-rise resort FodorśChoice complex. It is not on Sanibel proper but instead towers over the bay at ★ the last mainland exit before the causeway. Choose from three lodging options—a concierge club–style inn, the hotel, and condos—all with sweeping views of island-studded San Carlos Bay. There's also tennis,

the best resort spa in the Fort Myers area, restaurants (one of which is a buffet-dining yacht), the gorgeous circular windowed Charley's Bar, and a large free-form pool, among other facilities and activities. Rent a kayak, take a wildlife-viewing cruise, or go fishing. The beach is small and bayside, but transportation to Sanibel's beaches is free. Pros: luxury accommodations, full amenities, great views. Cons: daily amenities fee added to rate, unspectacular beach, high rates. ⊠*17260 Harbour Pointe Dr., Fort Myers 33908* ☎*239/466–4000 or 800/767–7777* 🖷*239/466–6050* ⊕*www.sanibel-resort.com* 📞*281 rooms, 66 suites, 53 condominiums* ⚙*In-room: safe, ethernet. In-hotel: 5 restaurants, room service, bars, tennis courts, pools, gym, spa, beachfront, children's programs (ages 5–12), executive floor, public Wi-Fi, no-smoking rooms* ▭*AE, D, DC, MC, V.*

$$$–$$$$　🏨**Hilton Garden Inn.** This compact, prettily landscaped low-rise is near Fort Myers's cultural and commercial areas, and business clientele favors it for its convenience. Rooms, done in florals and light-color wood, are spacious, with marble vanities in the bath, and have high-speed Internet access and free HBO. A huge aquarium in the lobby adds a nice Florida feel for vacationers. Pros: near performing arts center, enjoyable restaurant, large and convenient rooms. Cons: chain feel, small pool, at busy intersection. ⊠*12600 University Dr., 33907* ☎*239/790–3500* 🖷*239/790–3501* ⊕*www.hilton.com* 📞*109 rooms, 17 suites* ⚙*In-room: refrigerator, ethernet, dial-up. In-hotel: restaurant, bar, pool, laundry facilities, laundry service, Wi-Fi* ▭*AE, DC, MC, V.*

$$　🏨**Ambassador Riverfront Hotel.** Towering 24 stories over the city harbor downtown, this hotel, formerly a Ramada Inn, caters equally to business and pleasure travelers with an elegant marble atrium lobby, mezzanine restaurant, two swimming pools, and easy access to downtown's street parties and clubs. Shuttles take you to the Edison & Ford Winter Estates, the mall, and the airport. The best rooms have views of the harbor; all are done up tropical-style, with bright bedspreads and white walls and furnishings. Pros: river views, convenient to downtown's restaurants and attractions, roomy accommodations. Cons: unstable (it changes hands often). ⊠*2500 Edwards Dr., 33901* ☎*239/337–0300 or 800/833–1620* 🖷*239/337–1530* ⊕*www.ambassadorfl.com* 📞*216 rooms, 195 suites* ⚙*In-room: refrigerator (some), dial-up, Wi-Fi. In-hotel: restaurant, room service, bar, tennis court, pools, gym, airport shuttle, some pets allowed (fee), public Wi-Fi* ▭*AE, D, DC, MC, V.*

NIGHTLIFE & THE ARTS

THE ARTS

The **Barbara B. Mann Performing Arts Hall** (⊠*Edison Community College, 13350 Edison Pkwy., off College Pkwy.* ☎*239/481–4849* ⊕*www.bbmannpah.com*) presents Broadway plays, concerts, musicals, and comedians.

★　The **Broadway Palm Dinner Theater** (⊠*1380 Colonial Blvd.* ☎*239/278–4422* ⊕*www.broadwaypalm.com*) serves buffet dinners along with some of Broadway's best comedies and musicals. There's also a 90-seat black-box theater that plays smaller-scale comedies and musicals. In the restored circa-1920 Arcade Theatre downtown,

★ **Florida Repertory Theatre** (✉ *12267 1st St.* ☎ *239/332–4488 or 877/787–8053* ⊕ *www.floridarep.org*) stages professional entertainment, from Neil Simon shows to musical revues.

NIGHTLIFE

Lively every night in season (Thursday through Sunday the rest of the year), **Bahama Breeze** (✉ *14701 Tamiami Trail* ☎ *239/454–9234*) sways tropical with calypso, soca, and other island sounds.

★ **Dwyer's Pub** (✉ *13851 S. Cleveland Ave.* ☎ *239/425–0782*) hops and jigs on Wednesday and weekends with live Irish bands. **Laugh In Comedy Café** (✉ *College Plaza, 8595 College Pkwy.* ☎ *239/479–5233*), south of downtown, has comedians Thursday, Friday, and Saturday. **Stevie Tomato's Sports Page** (✉ *11431 S. Cleveland Ave.* ☎ *239/939–7211*) has big-screen TVs and good munchies. ■ TIP➜Tickets are half-price for the Thursday 8 PM show at Laugh In Comedy Café.

SPORTS & THE OUTDOORS

BASEBALL

The **Boston Red Sox** (✉ *2201 Edison Ave.* ☎ *239/334–4700* ⊕ *www.red-sox.com*) train in Fort Myers every spring. The **Minnesota Twins** (✉ *Lee County Sports Complex, 14100 Six Mile Cypress Pkwy.* ☎ *239/768–4210*) play exhibition games in town during March and early April. From April through August, the Miracle, a Twins single-A affiliate, play home games at the Complex.

BIKING

The longest bike path in Fort Myers is along Summerlin Road. It passes commercial areas, and close to Sanibel through dwindling wide-open spaces. Linear Park, which runs parallel to Metro Parkway, offers more natural, less-congested views. A trailhead park is in the planning stages for parking and bike trails access. For a good selection of rentals, try the **Bike Route** (✉ *8595 College Parkway Suite B-1* ☎ *239/481–3376* ⊕ *thebikeroute.com*).

FISHING

Anglers head for the gulf, its bays, and estuaries for saltwater fishing—snapper, sheepshead, mackerel, and other species. The Caloosahatchee River, Orange River, canals, and small lakes offer freshwater alternatives.

GOLF

★ The driving range and 18-hole course at the **Eastwood Golf Club** (✉ *4600 Bruce Herd La.* ☎ *239/275–4848*) are affordable, especially if you don't mind playing at unfavorable times (midday in summer, for example). Many golfers enjoy the lack of development around the course, which poses challenges with its water hazards and doglegs. Fees include cart and tax; fees without cart included are available at certain times. Green fee: $45/$45. The **Fort Myers Country Club** (✉ *3591 McGregor Blvd.* ☎ *239/936–2457*), with 18 holes, challenges golfers with its small greens. It's the town's oldest course. Lessons are available. Green fee: $45/$45. Head to the **Shell Point Golf Club** (⊠*16401 On Par Blvd.* ☎*239/433–9790*) for an 18-hole course and a driving range. Green fee: $90/$90 (including cart).

ICE SKATING

☼ Recreational ice-skating (including figure skating) and ice-hockey programs plus skate rentals are offered at downtown's **Fort Myers Skatium** (⊠*2250 Broadway Ave.* ☎*239/461–3145* ⊕*www.fmskatium.com*).

SAILING

★ **Southwest Florida Yachts** (⊠*3444 Marinatown La. NW* ☎*239/656–1339 or 800/262–7939* ⊕*www.swfyachts.com*) charters sailboats and offers lessons.

SHOPPING

★ **Bell Tower Shops** (⊠*Cleveland Ave. and Daniels Pkwy.* ☎*239/489–1221* ⊕*www.thebelltowershops.com*), an open-air shopping center, has about 40 stylish boutiques and specialty shops, a Saks Fifth Avenue, and 20 movie screens. **Edison Mall** (⊠*Colonial Blvd. at Cleveland Ave.*) is the largest air-conditioned indoor mall in Fort Myers, with several major department stores and more than 150 specialty shops. Along its boardwalks, **Sanibel Tanger Factory Outlets** (⊠*McGregor Blvd. and Summerlin Rd.* ☎*888/471–3939* ⊕*www.tangeroutlet.com*) has outlets for Dexter, Van Heusen, Maidenform, Coach, Liz Claiborne, and Samsonite, among others. Just east of Fort Myers, more than 900 vendors sell new and used goods at **Fleamasters Fleamarket** (⊠*1 mi west of I–75 Exit 138 on Rte. 82* ⊕*www.fleamall.com*), Friday through Sunday between 8 and 4.

CAPE CORAL & NORTH FORT MYERS

❷ *Cape Coral is 13 mi from downtown Fort Myers via North Fort Myers, just across the river (1 mi) from south Fort Myers.*

Four bridges cross from Fort Myers to Cape Coral and its eastern neighbor, North Fort Myers. Families especially find fun in these residential communities and their rural backyards, including undiscovered Pine Island.

☼
Fodor'sChoice
★
Sun Splash Family Waterpark is the place to cool off when summer swelters. It has a dozen wet and dry attractions, including four thrill waterslides; the Lilypad Walk, where you step from one floating "lily pad" to another; an arcade; a family pool and Tot Spot; and a river tube ride. ⊠*400 Santa Barbara Blvd.* ☎*239/574–0557* ⊕*www.sunsplashwaterpark.com* ☜*$15* ☼*Mid-Mar.–Sept., call for hrs.*

OFF THE BEATEN PATH

ECHO Global Farm & Nursery. Educational Concerns for Hunger Organization is a small Christian ministry group striving to end world hunger via creative farming. A fascinating 90-minute tour of its working farm takes you through five simulated tropic-zone gardens and has you tasting leaves and berries, walking through rain-forest habitat, visiting farm animals, stopping at a simulated Haitian school, witnessing urban gardens grown inside tires on rooftops, and learning all about ECHO's mission. The edible landscape nursery and gift shop sell fruit trees and the same seeds ECHO distributes to impoverished tropical farmers in 180 countries. ⊠ *17391 Durrance Rd., North Fort Myers* ☎ *239/543–3246* ⊕ *www.echonet.org* 🖼 *$8* 🕙 *Tours Jan.–Mar., Tues.–Fri. at 10 and 2, Sat. at 10; Apr.–Dec., Tues., Fri., and Sat. at 10; or by appointment. Nursery open Mon.–Sat. 9–noon.*

WHERE TO STAY & EAT

Cape Coral determinedly moves from its pigeon hole as a residential community to attract tourism with its downtown reconfiguration and the happy appearance of destination restaurants at the Cape Harbour residential marina development. In September 2008, The Resort at MarinaVillage, a separate 184-unit property, is scheduled to open and drastically change the face of Cape Coral tourism.

★ $$–$$$ ✕**Rumrunners.** Cape Coral's best casual cuisine is surprisingly affordable, considering the luxury condo development that rises around it and the size of the yachts that pull up to the docks. Caribbean in spirit, with lots of indoor and outdoor views of a mangrove-fringed waterway, it serves bistro specialties such as seafood potpie, pork marinated with rum and orange juice, bronzed salmon, and a warm chocolate bread pudding that is addictive. ⊠ *5848 Cape Harbour Dr. at the Marina at Cape Harbour, off Chiquita Blvd. at Cape Coral Pkwy.* ☎ *239/542–0200* ⌖ *Reservations suggested.*

★ ¢–$ ✕**Bert's Bar & Grill.** Looking to hang out with the locals on Pine Island? You get that, cheap eats, live entertainment, a pool table, and a water view to boot at Bert's. Speaking of boots, you're likely to see much of the clientele wearing white rubber fishing boots, known here as Pine Island Reeboks. Order pizza, a burger, fried oysters, or grouper Reuben from the no-nonsense menu. ⊠ *4271 Pine Island Rd., Matlacha* ☎ *239/282–3232* ⊕ *www.bertsbar.com* ☰ *MC, V.*

¢–$ ✕**Siam Hut.** Lunch and dinner menus at this Cape Coral fixture let you design your own stir-fry, noodle, or fried-rice dish. Dinner specialties include fried crispy frogs' legs with garlic and black pepper, a sizzling shrimp platter, fried whole fish with curry sauce, salads, and pad thai (rice noodles, shrimp, chicken, egg, ground peanuts, and vegetables). Get your food fiery hot or extra mild. Two traditional Thai tables allow you to sit on floor pillows (conveniently with backs) or you can opt for a more conventional table or booth. ⊠ *4521 Del Prado Blvd.* ☎ *239/945–4247* ☰ *MC, V* 🕙 *Closed Sun. No lunch Sat.*

$$–$$$$ 🛏 **Tarpon Lodge Sportsman Inn.** If you're looking for no-frills escape and fishing, this aptly named lodge, built in 1926 on a sweep of green lawn with magnificent views out to sea, may do the trick. Rooms are small and simple, and the sunny restaurant dishes up creative surprises. It's in the fishing village of Pineland, on the edge of Pine Island Sound, settled in the 16th century by Calusa Indians and stocked with charming Cracker fishing shacks in the 1920s. Pros: waterfront view, historic, great restaurant. Cons: old digs, far from other restaurants, far from beach. ⊠ *13771 Waterfront Dr., Pineland 33945* ☎ *239/283–3999* 🖨 *239/283–7658* ⊕ *www.tarponlodge.com* ⇌ *21 rooms, 2 cottages*

9

In-room: no phones. In-hotel: restaurant, bar, pool, public Wi-Fi, no elevator, ⊟AE, MC, V ⏿CP.

$$–$$$ 🏨 **Casa Loma Motel.** Stay at this pretty little motel, 15 minutes from Fort Myers at the end of the Croton Canal, to be close to Cape Coral's attractions and escape the sticker shock of the beaches. All units are efficiencies with a porch or balcony, some overlooking the canal. Pros: affordable, kitchen facilities, canal access. Cons: far from beaches, on a busy street, must drive to restaurants. ⊠*3608 Del Prado Blvd., 33904* ☎*239/549–6000 or 877/227–2566* ⊞*239/549–4877* ⊕*www.casalomamotel.com* ⇌*48 efficiencies, 1 suite* *In-room: kitchen, dial-up. In-hotel: pool, laundry facilities, no-smoking rooms, no elevator* ⊟*AE, D, MC, V.*

SPORTS & THE OUTDOORS

GOLF

Coral Oaks Golf Course (⊠*1800 N.W. 28th Ave.* ☎*239/573–3100*) has an 18-hole layout and a practice range. Arthur Hill designed the championship par-72 course, which has lots of lakes, ponds, wildlife, and mammoth live oaks. Green fee: $25/$55 (including cart).

TENNIS

Cape Coral Yacht and Racquet Club (⊠*5819 Driftwood Pkwy.* ☎*239/574–0808*) has five lighted hard courts. Guest fees apply.

SHOPPING

A survivor from Florida's roadside-attraction era, the vast ☾ **Shell Factory & Nature Park** (⊠*2787 N. Tamiami Trail, North Fort Myers* ☎*239/995–2141 or 800/282–5805* ⊕*www.shellfactory.com*) is the place to buy seashells, coral, sponges, and fossils. Bazaarlike shops also sell everything from Florida-style Christmas decorations to jewelry and teddy bears. But this is as much entertainment complex as store, so you'll find bumper boats, miniature golf, and a musical lighted fountain show (admission $5 each attraction). The nature park (admission $6, open daily 10–9) contains a petting zoo with camels, llamas, and goats; a walk-through aviary; an EcoLab with reptiles and small animals; a prairie dog habitat; and a gator slough.

PUNTA GORDA

❸ *23 mi north of Cape Coral and Fort Myers.*

In this small, old town on the mouth of the Peace River, where it empties into Charlotte Harbor, street art, water views, and murals enliven the compact downtown historic district. Art and creative dining are the area's long suits. Although there's plenty of waterfront in the area, between this town and sprawling adjacent Port Charlotte there's only a single beach—and it's man-made and on the river rather than on the gulf. This is a place to come for fishing, canoeing, walking in the woods, and, most of all, escaping the crowds.

The **Ponce de León Historical Park and Peace River Wildlife Center** is named for the famous conquistador who, according to local lore, took a fatal arrow here. A humble shrine and historic marker pay homage, but the park's best features are the fishing, wildlife, and view at the mouth of the Peace River. The wildlife rehabilitation facility that shares the point of land conducts tours. ⊠ *3400 W. Marion Ave.* ☎ *941/637–3830* ☜ *Donations accepted* ☉ *Wildlife center daily 11–4, park daily sunrise–sunset.*

Hands-on and glass-encased permanent and changing exhibits explore the region's pirate lore, Native Americans, fishing heritage, and other facets of the past at **Charlotte Harbor Historical Center.** It resides in a waterfront facility next to a fishing-pier park and hosts special kids' programs. ⊠ *22959 Bayshore Rd., Charlotte Harbor* ☎ *941/629–7278* ☜ *Donations accepted* ☉ *Weekdays 10–5, Sat. 10–3.*

OFF THE BEATEN PATH

★

Babcock Wilderness Adventures. To see what Florida looked like centuries ago, visit Babcock Crescent B Ranch, southeast of Punta Gorda and northeast of Fort Myers. During the 90-minute swamp-buggy excursion you ride in a converted school bus through several ecosystems, including the unusual and fascinating Telegraph Cypress Swamp. Along the way an informative and amusing guide describes the area's social and natural history while you keep an eye peeled for alligators, wild pigs, all sorts of birds, and other denizens of the wild. The tour also takes in the ranch's bison herd, resident cattle, and Florida panthers in captivity. Reservations are needed for tours. ⊠ *8000 Rte. 31* ☎ *941/637–4611 or 800/500–5583* ⊕ *www.babcockwilderness.com* ☜ *Bus tour $17.95* ☉ *Tours daily 9–3 Nov.–May; mornings only June–Oct. (call for hours)* ☜ *Reservations essential.*

WHERE TO STAY & EAT

★ **$$–$$$** ✕ **Amimoto Japanese Restaurant.** Most popular for lunch, Amimoto offers a nice selection of *obentos,* Japanese box lunches, which might include pork loin or shrimp dumplings. The extensive sushi and appetizer menus give you many grazing options. Entrées involve grilled or breaded chicken, pork, beef, and seafood, with wasabi or teriyaki sauce. Sit at the sushi bar or a table in the small dining room decorated simply with Japanese art prints and artifacts. ⊠ *Towles Plaza, 2705 S. Tamiami Trail* ☎ *941/505–1515* ⊟ *AE, D, DC, MC, V* ☉ *No lunch weekends.*

$–$$ ✕ **River City Grill.** Sparking a dining renaissance on West Marion Avenue, this eatery remodeled a vintage brick building with artistic yet homey panache. Imaginative dishes such as salmon in phyllo, and mango and balsamic-glazed butterfish share the menu with grilled prime cuts of beef, pasta, and seafood. The abundant seating spills out onto the sidewalk. ⊠ *131 W. Marion Ave.* ☎ *941/639–9080* ⊕ *www.rivercitygrill. org* ⊟ *AE, D, MC, V.*

$$$ ⊞ **Fishermen's Village Villas.** Go for a shopping spree or hire a fishing charter without leaving the premises when you stay at this complex of affordable, nicely decorated two-bedroom time-share units. Sleeping up to eight in two bedrooms, a loft, and on a pull-out couch, they're above Punta Gorda's lively shopping center, on the site of an old crab-packing plant. The comfortable units are warmly decorated spaces with modern appliances. Pros: near shopping and restaurants, full marina, like-

9

home comfort. Cons: noise and traffic from shopping center, far from beaches. ✉ *1200 W. Retta Esplanade, No. 58, 33950* ☎ *941/639–8721 or 800/639–0020* 🖷 *941/637–1054* ⊕ *www.fishville.com* ⏎ *47 suites* ⚫ *In-room: kitchen. In-hotel: 7 restaurants, bars, tennis court, pool, spa* ⊟ *AE, DC, MC.*

¢–$$ 🏠 **Budget Inn.** Five minutes from downtown's shop-and-dine scene and close to the chain restaurants along the highway, it is both convenient and pleasant, with a garden feel. Rooms in the two-story building, each outfitted with a full-size refrigerator, look newly painted and furnished. Pros: convenient location, free local calls, clean rooms. Cons: on heavily traveled highway, stark outside appearance, low on personality. ✉ *1520 Tamiami Trail, Punta Gorda 33950* ☎ *941/639–8000* ⏎ *45 rooms* ⚫ *In-room: kitchens (some), refrigerator, Wi-Fi (some). In-hotel: pool, laundry facilities, public Wi-Fi* ⊟ *AE, D, MC, V.*

$ 🏠 **Banana Bay on Charlotte Harbor.** Here's a neighborhood that one day will be coveted for its harbor views, but in the meantime, lodging is humble and affordable. Painted banana-tree murals and potted staghorn ferns add character to this motel, near minigolf and the fishing pier. Rooms and efficiencies underwent post-hurricane renovation in 2004 and are comfortable and clean. Pros: lovely river view, quiet setting, small beach and miniature golf next door. Cons: no nearby shopping, old facility, limited amenities. ✉ *23285 Bayshore Rd., Port Charlotte 33980* ☎ *941/743–4441* 🖷 *941/743–4172* ⊕ *www.bananabaymotel.com* ⏎ *3 rooms, 13 efficiencies* ⚫ *In-room: kitchen (some), refrigerator, dial-up, ethernet (some). In-hotel: some pets allowed, Internet* ⊟ *AE, D, DC, MC, V.*

SPORTS & THE OUTDOORS

BIKING

For information on bike trails, which range from bike lanes through local neighborhoods to recreational trails such as the Cape Haze Pioneer Trail and the rails-to-trails Boca Grande Trail, visit www.ccmpo.com/maps1.htm.

FISHING

For half- and full-day fishing trips in the bay or the gulf, call **King Fisher Fleet** (✉ *Fishermen's Village* ☎ *941/639–0969* ⊕ *www.kingfisherfleet.com*). Prices start at $140 per person for a full day in the gulf. For back-bay fishing, up to three can fish for $250 a half day.

GOLF

There are 18 holes to play at the **Deep Creek Golf Club** (✉ *1260 San Cristobal Ave., Port Charlotte* ☎ *941/625–6911*), green fee: $50 (including cart).

THE COASTAL ISLANDS

A maze of islands in various stages of habitation fronts the mainland from Charlotte County to Fort Myers, separated by the Intracoastal Waterway. Some are accessible via a causeway; to reach others, you need a boat. If you cut through bay waters, you have a good chance of being escorted by bottlenose dolphins. Mostly birds and other wild creatures inhabit some islands, which are given over to state parks. Traveler-pampering hotels on Sanibel, Captiva, and Fort Myers Beach give way to rustic cottages, old inns, and cabins on quiet Cabbage Key and Pine Island, which have no beaches because they lie between the barrier islands and mainland. Still more are devoted to resorts. When exploring island beaches, keep one eye on the sand: shelling is a major pursuit in these parts.

> ### KING FISHERS
>
> Pine Island Sound and Boca Grande Pass spawned the sport of tarpon-fishing in the late 1880s. A wealthy Chicago streetcar mogul built the Izaak Walton Club on Useppa Island in 1911 for the famed and wealthy who descended to capture the "Silver King."

GASPARILLA ISLAND (BOCA GRANDE)

④ *43 mi northwest of Fort Myers, 23 mi southwest of Punta Gorda.*

Before roads to the lower Gulf Coast were even talked about, wealthy Northerners came by train to spend the winter at the **Gasparilla Inn,** built in 1912 in Boca Grande on Gasparilla Island, named, legend has it, for a Spanish pirate who set up headquarters in these waters. Although condominiums and modern sprawl creep up on the rest of Gasparilla, much of the town of Boca Grande looks like another era. The mood is set by the Old Florida homes and tree-framed roadways. The island's calm is disrupted in the spring when anglers descend with a vengeance on Boca Grande Pass, considered among the best tarpon-fishing spots in the world. North of it stretches a long island, home to Don Pedro Island State Park and Palm Island Resort, both accessible only by boat, then the off-the-beaten-path island of Manasota Key and its fishing resort community of Englewood Beach.

The island's beaches are its greatest prize and lie within **Gasparilla Island State Park and Boca Grande Lighthouse Museum** at the south end. The long, narrow beach ends at Boca Grande Pass, famous for its deep waters and tarpon fishing. The pretty, two-story, circa-1890 lighthouse once marked the pass for mariners. In recent years, it has been restored as a museum that explores the island's fishing and railroad heritage in rooms once occupied by the lighthouse keeper. ⊠*Boca Grande* ☎*941/964–0060* ⊕*www.barrierislandparkssociety.org/museum.html* 🎫*$2 per vehicle; $1 suggested donation to lighthouse* ☉*Park daily 8–sunset; lighthouse Nov.–May, daily 10–4; June–Oct., Wed.–Sun. 10–4; closed Aug.*

WHERE TO STAY & EAT

★ $$$$ ✕**Boca Bistro.** Part of the island's new Boca Grande Resort complex, the bistro brings to Boca a new level of creative dining with an elevated waterside view. Red lacquered walls threaded with gold and copper leaf frame a bank of windows on the second-story restaurant. Nightly specials complement a menu including blue-cheese tomato soup, warm duckling spinach salad, and bouillabaisse with lobster tails. ⊠*5800*

9

Gasparilla Rd., Boca Grande ☎*941/964–8020* ▭*AE, D, MC, V* ⊘*Closed Mon. and Tues. Easter–Thanksgiving.*

★ **$$$$**   🏠**Gasparilla Inn.** Social-register members such as the Vanderbilts and DuPonts still winter at the gracious pale-yellow wooden hotel built by shipping industrialists in the early 1900s. Lodge rooms are not lavishly decorated by today's standards. The cottage rooms are more modern and less spartan, but some are without TVs. The inn takes up much of the town of Boca Grande with its rich-blooded amenities—sprawling lawns, golf course, and beach club. In summer (mid-Apr.–mid-June), rates are for Modified American Plan or European Plan; October through mid-December no meals are served. Two of its restaurants are off the main campus. Gentlemen are required to wear jacket and tie in the hotel after 6 PM. Pros: historic property, newly painted and upgraded. Cons: forced meal plan is limiting, expensive, hotel rooms are sparse. ⊠*500 Palm Ave., Boca Grande 33921* ☎*941/964–2201 or 800/996–1913* ⊕*www.gasparillainn.com* 🖷*941/283–1384* ⇌*140 rooms* ⚭*In-room: no TV (some). In-hotel: 3 restaurants, golf course, tennis courts, pools, gym, beachfront* ▭*No credit cards* ⦿*FAP.*

SPORTS & THE OUTDOORS

BIKING

Boca Grande's erstwhile railroad bed has been paved for a 7-mi bike path that golf cart drivers also share. **Island Bike 'N Beach** (⊠*333 Park Ave., Boca Grande* ☎*941/964–0711*) rents bikes as well as golf carts.

CANOEING & KAYAKING

🐾 **Grande Tours** (⊠*12575 Placida Rd., Placida* ☎*941/697–8825* ⊕*www. grandetours.com*) leads kayaking ecotours along the creeks and open waters around Charlotte Harbor. Cost is $50 for 2½ hours. Also available are kayaking lessons, kayak fishing excursions, kids kayak camp, and rentals.

USEPPA ISLAND

5 *2 mi south of Boca Grande Pass.*

Unless you're spending the night, the only way to visit this historic island, at Mile Marker 63 on the Intracoastal Waterway and occupied by an exclusive club, is on a tour with the *Lady Chadwick* cruise through Captiva Cruises on Captiva Island. Go for lunch and a tour of the fascinating little Useppa Museum, which tells about the island's ancient Calusa mounds and its role in training fighters for the Cuban Bay of Pigs confrontation.

WHERE TO STAY

★ **$$$–$$$$**   🏠**Collier Inn & Cottages.** Should you decide to spend some time away from civilization, you can lodge at the inn here, built in 1908 as the Izaak Walton Club, a fishing getaway for the rich and tarpon-seeking. Rooms and suites in the inn and a couple of other historic buildings reflect the island's sporting past, but in the finest taste. The Useppa Island Club also has some two-bedroom cottages on a rental program.

The club can make transportation arrangements from Pine Island or Boca Grande. Continental breakfast is complimentary for guests without kitchens. ⌂ *Box 640, Useppa Island 33922* ☎*239/283–1061* ⎙*239/283–0290* ⊕*www.useppa.com* ⇩*4 rooms, 9 suites, 2 2-bedroom cottages, 2 3-bedroom cottages* ⌂*In-room: kitchen (some), refrigerator, dial-up, Wi-Fi. In-hotel: 2 restaurants, bars, tennis courts, pool, gym, beachfront, bicycles, laundry facilities, Wi-Fi* ▤*AE, MC, V* ⎮⊙⎮*CP.*

CABBAGE KEY

6 *5 mi south of Boca Grande.*

You'll have to take a boat—from Bokeelia, on Pine Island, or from Captiva Island—to get to this island, which sits at Mile Marker 60 on the Intracoastal Waterway.

WHERE TO STAY

$ 🏨 **Cabbage Key Inn.** Atop an ancient Calusa Indian shell mound and accessible only by boat is the friendly, somewhat quirky inn built by novelist and playwright Mary Roberts Rinehart in 1938. It's surrounded by 100 acres of tropical vegetation, through which a natural trail runs. In addition to the inn rooms, there are guest cottages scattered throughout the property, some of which have kitchens and can accommodate up to eight guests. Rooms range from bare-bones to more modern and family friendly. There's a full-service marina and a restaurant whose dining room is papered with thousands of dollar bills. One of the many perks of staying here is close access to the remote and pristine beach of Cayo Casto, a short boat trip from Cabbage Key. ⌂ *Box 200, Pineland 33945* ☎*239/283–2278* ⎙*239/283–1384* ⊕*www.cabbagekey.com* ⇩*6 rooms, 7 cottages* ⌂*In-room: no phone, kitchen (some), no TV. In-hotel: restaurant, bar* ▤*MC, V.*

9

NORTH CAPTIVA ISLAND

7 *3 mi south of Cabbage Key.*

No bridges lead to this 750-acre island, and most visitors arrive by prearranged water taxi from Pine Island. They come for the isolation and complete absence of "civilization." Some of the private houses can be rented through **North Captiva Island Club Resort** (☎*239/395–1001 or 800/576–7343* ⊕*www.northcaptiva.com*). The complex has two pools and a sauna, which you're free to use, plus bike, kayak, and golf cart (the main mode of motorized transportation on the island) rentals and two restaurants and a pool bar that serve food. The island also holds another public restaurant outside the resort. It's a good idea to bring your own groceries; there's only one small store, and it's quite pricey. Walk to secluded beaches at the south end, where Hurricane Charley split the island in two in 2004.

SANIBEL & CAPTIVA ISLANDS

8 *23 mi southwest of downtown Fort Myers.*

Sanibel Island, accessible from the mainland via the Sanibel Causeway (toll $6 round-trip), is famous as one of the world's best shelling grounds, a function of the unusual east–west orientation of the island's south end. Just as the tide is going out and after storms, the pickings can be superb, and shell seekers with the telltale "Sanibel stoop" patrol every beach carrying bags of conchs, whelks, cockles, and other bivalves and gastropods. (Remember, it's unlawful to pick up live shells.) Away from the beach, flowery vegetation decorates small shopping complexes, pleasant resorts and condo complexes, mom-and-pop motels, and casual restaurants. But much of the narrow road down the spine of the island is bordered by nature reserves that have made Sanibel as well known among bird-watchers as it is among seashell collectors.

9 **Captiva Island,** connected to the northern end of Sanibel by a bridge, is quirky and engaging. At the end of a twisty road lined with million-dollar mansions lies a delightful village of shops and eateries.

At Sanibel's southern tip, the frequently photographed **Sanibel Lighthouse,** built in 1884, before the island was settled, guards **Lighthouse Beach.** Although the lighthouse is not open to the public, the area around it has been a wildlife refuge since 1950. A fishing pier, nature trail, and restrooms are available. ✉*Periwinkle Way, Sanibel* ☎*239/472–6477* 🚗*Parking $2 per hr.*

★ The charming **Sanibel Historical Village and Museum** shows off buildings from the island's past—a 1927 post office, a garage housing a Model T Ford, the Old Bailey general store, a teahouse, a 1925 winter vacation cottage, and the 1913 Rutland House Museum, with old documents and photographs and a Calusa Indian exhibit. The newest addition is a 19th-century one-room schoolhouse, which was moved in 2004 from its original location on Periwinkle Way, where it served as a theater for more than 20 years. ✉*950 Dunlop Rd., Sanibel* ☎*239/472–4648* 🚗*$5* ☉*Nov.–May, Wed.–Sat. 10–4; June–mid-Aug., Wed.–Sat. 10–1; closed mid-Aug.–Oct.*

☾ The beach in **Gulfside Park** is quiet, safe from strong currents, and good for solitude and shells. There are restrooms and picnic tables and long stretches to stroll. ✉*Algiers La. off Casa Ybel Rd., Sanibel* ☎*239/472–6477* 🚗*Parking $2 per hr.*

Tarpon Bay Beach is centrally located and safer for swimming than beaches at the passes, where waters move swiftly. It is, however, one of the more populated beaches, lined with low-rise condos and resorts. You can walk for miles in either direction. Sometimes in season there's a mobile concession stand. ✉*Tarpon Bay Rd. off Sanibel–Captiva Rd., Sanibel* ☎*239/472–6477* 🚗*Parking $2 per hr.*

☾ To help you identify your Sanibel Island beach finds, stop at the **Bai-**
Fodor'sChoice **ley-Matthews Shell Museum,** where a shell-finder display identifies speci-
★ mens from local waters in sizes ranging from tiny to huge. Thirty-five

vignettes and exhibits explore shells in the environment, art, and history, including a life-size display of native Calusa and how they used shells for tools and food. Handle shell specimens and play games in the colorful kids' lab. A 6-foot globe at the center of the museum rotunda highlights shells from around the world. ✉ *3075 Sanibel–Captiva Rd., Sanibel* ☎ *239/395–2233 or 888/679–6450* ⊕ *www.shellmuseum.org* ✉ *$7* ⊙ *Daily 10–5.*

↻ More than half of Sanibel is occupied by the subtly beautiful **J.N.**
Fodor's Choice **"Ding" Darling National Wildlife Refuge,** 6,300 acres of wetlands and
★ lush, jungly mangrove forests named after a conservation-minded Pulitzer Prize–winning political cartoonist, who fathered the federal Duck Stamp program. The masses of roseate spoonbills and ibis and the winter flock of white pelicans here make for a good show even if you're not a die-hard bird-watcher. Birders have counted some 230 species, including herons, ospreys, and the timid mangrove cuckoo. Raccoons, otters, alligators, and a lone American crocodile also can be spotted. The 4½-mi Wildlife Drive is the main way to explore the preserve; drive, walk, or bicycle along it, or ride a specially designed open-air tram with a naturalist on board. There are also a couple of short walking trails, including one to a Calusa shell mound. Or explore from the water via canoe or kayak (guided tours are available). The best time for bird-watching is in the early morning about an hour before or after low tide, and the observation tower along the road offers prime viewing. Interactive exhibits in the center, at the entrance to the refuge, demonstrate the refuge's various ecosystems and explain its status as a rest stop along a major bird migration route. Because Wildlife Drive is closed to vehicular traffic on Friday, try to time your visit for another day. ✉ *1 Wildlife Dr., off Sanibel–Captiva Rd. at MM 2, Sanibel* ☎ *239/472–1100, 239/472–8900 tram* ⊕ *www. fws.gov/dingdarling* ✉ *$5 per car, $1 for pedestrians and bicyclists, tram $12, Education Center free* ⊙ *Education Center Jan.–Apr., daily 9–5; May–Dec., daily 9–4; Wildlife Drive Sat.–Thurs. 7:30–8.*

↻ For a good look at snowy egrets, great blue herons, alligators, and other inhabitants of Florida's wetlands, follow the 4½ mi of walking trails at the 1,800-acre wetlands managed by the **Sanibel–Captiva Conservation Foundation.** See island research projects and nature displays, visit a butterfly house, and touch sea creatures. Guided walks are available on and off property; the beach walk is especially enjoyable and easily educational. ✉ *3333 Sanibel–Captiva Rd., Sanibel* ☎ *239/472–2329* ⊕ *www.sccf.org* ✉ *$3* ⊙ *May–Nov., weekdays 8:30–3; Dec.–Apr., weekdays 8:30–3, Sat. 10–3.*

★ Long, wide **Bowman's Beach,** on Sanibel's northwest end, is the island's most secluded strand. Walk the length of it and leave humanity behind, finding some of the greatest concentrations of shells along the way. The sunsets at the north end are spectacular—try to spot the green flash said to occur just as the sun sinks below the horizon. Here's where, you may have heard, nudists once sunbathed—but current laws prohibit it, and local officials police against it. ✉ *Bowman Beach Rd., Sanibel*

🕾 *239/432–2006* 🅿 *Parking $2 per hr.* ■ TIP→ Red tide, a common natural beach occurrence that kills fish, also has negative effects on the human respiratory system. It causes scratchy throats, runny eyes and noses, and coughing. Although the effects are not long term, it's a good idea to avoid the beach when red tide is in the vicinity (look for posted signs).

Turner Beach is the sunset-watching spot on the southern tip of Captiva. Strong currents through the pass make swimming tricky, and parking is limited. Surfers head here when winds whip up the waves. ⊠ *Captiva Dr., Captiva* 🅿 *Parking $2 per hr.*

Captiva Beach, widened in 2005, is acclaimed as one of the nation's most romantic beaches for its fabulous sunsets—the best view on Sanibel and Captiva. The parking lot is small, so arrive early. Facilities are limited to portable restrooms, but stores and restaurants are nearby. ⊠ *Captiva Dr., Captiva* 🅿 *Parking $2 per hr.*

WHERE TO STAY & EAT

$$$ ✕ **Bubble Room.** This lively, kitschy favorite is fun for families and nostalgic types with fat wallets. Servers wear scout uniforms and funny headgear. Electric trains circle overhead, glossies of 1940s Hollywood stars line the walls, and tabletops showcase old-time toys. After grazing your basket of cheesy bubble bread and sweet, yeasty sticky buns, go for aged prime rib or the grouper steamed in a paper bag. It's more about the atmosphere than the food here, but the homemade triple-layer cakes, delivered in hefty wedges, are stand-out. The red velvet is a classic favorite. Be prepared to wait for a table. ⊠ *15001 Captiva Dr., Captiva* 🕾 *239/472–5558* ⊕ *www.bubbleroomrestaurant.com* ⚲ *Reservations not accepted* ▭ *AE, D, DC, MC, V.*

★ $$$ ✕ **Traders Store & Cafe.** In the midst of a warehouse-size import store, this bistro, accented with artifacts from Africa and other exotic places, is a favorite of locals. The marvelous sesame-seared tuna lunch salad with Asian slaw and wasabi vinaigrette exemplifies the creative fare. For dinner, go for the barbecued baby back ribs, macadamia-crusted grouper, or any of the day's finely crafted specials. A local crooner entertains two nights a week. ⊠ *1551 Periwinkle Way, Sanibel* 🕾 *239/472–7242* ▭ *AE, D, MC, V.*

$–$$$ ✕ **Green Flash.** Good food and second-story, sweeping views of quiet waters and a mangrove island keep boaters and others coming back to this casual indoor-outdoor restaurant. Seafood dominates, but there's a bit of everything on the menu, from shrimp in beer batter and grilled swordfish to pork tenderloin Wellington. For lunch, try the Green Flash sandwich (smoked turkey and prosciutto or vegetables, both with cheese on grilled focaccia). On cool, sunny days, grab a table out back dockside. ⊠ *15183 Captiva Dr., Captiva* 🕾 *239/472–3337* ▭ *AE, D, DC, MC, V.*

$$ ✕ **McT's Shrimphouse and Tavern.** In this informal Sanibel landmark, the menu predictably spotlights fresh seafood. The baked oysters make great starters. If you're a seafood fiend, go for the Sanibel steamer or all-you-can-eat shrimp and crab. Besides more than 15 shrimp entrées, ribs, prime rib, and Cajun-style chicken are available. Few can resist the Sanibel mud pie, an enormous ice-cream concoction heavy on the

Oreos. Stop in for a before- or after-dinner drink in the bar with the upside-down tree forest. ⊠*1523 Periwinkle Way, Sanibel* ☎*239/472–3161* ⬢*Reservations not accepted* ▤*AE, D, MC, V.*

$ ✕**Lazy Flamingo.** At two Sanibel locations, this is the friendly neigh-
☺ borhood hangout enjoyed by locals and visitors alike. The original in Santiva (between Sanibel and Captiva) is small, with counter service only; the other is larger (but there's still often a wait) and provides table service. Both have a funky nautical look à la Key West and a popu-lar following for their "Dead Parrot Wings" (Buffalo wings coated with tongue-scorching hot sauce), grouper sandwiches, burgers, and steamer pots. ⊠*6520C Pine Ave., Sanibel* ☎*239/472–5353* ⊠*1036 Periwinkle Way, Sanibel* ☎*239/472–6939* ⬢*www.lazyflamingo.com* ⬢*Reservations not accepted* ▤*AE, D, MC, V.*

¢ ✕**Amy's Over Easy Café.** Locals head to this bright, chicken-decorated eatery for breakfast and lunch. Kick-start the day with the egg Reu-ben sandwich, veggie Benedict, or a custom omelet made with whole eggs, whites only, or egg substitute. The lunch menu includes salads, vegetarian wraps, burgers, a mahimahi sandwich, and blackberry cob-bler. If there's a wait for breakfast, spend it browsing and sipping free coffee at the café's gift shop. Early dinner is served Tuesday–Saturday. ⊠*630-1 Tarpon Bay Rd., Sanibel* ☎*239/472–2625* ⬢*Reservations not accepted* ▤*D, MC, V* ⊘*No dinner Sun. and Mon.*

$ ✕**Redfish Bluefish.** Despite the whimsical name and brightly painted, gar-bage-art decor, there's nothing frivolous about the food. There's not a green egg to be found on the dinner menu in this intimate spot, which lists three courses of well-designed dishes shrunk to taster size and con-centrated with multilevel flavor, such as the yellowfin ahi tuna nachos, scallop knee-high in lobster bisque, and the braised short ribs with Maytag blue cheese. ⊠*Behind Tower Gallery, 751 Tarpon Bay Rd., Sanibel* ☎*239/472–1956* ⬢*www.redfishbluefishcaptiva.com* ▤*AE, D, MC, V* ⊘*Closed Mon. No lunch.*

$$$$ ⌂**Casa Ybel Resort.** At this time-share resort, palms, ponds, a foot-
☺ bridge, and gazebos set the mood on 23 acres of gulf-facing grounds. Inside the two-floor stilt buildings, the one- and two-bedroom apart-ments are roomy and contemporary, with full kitchens, wicker furni-ture, tasteful patterns, and big screened-in porches that look out to the beach. The respected Thistle Lodge restaurant is in a re-created historic home with a beach view. In season (mid-March through April), the minimum stay is seven days. Pros: on the beach, good restaurants, lots of recreational opportunities. Cons: spa treatments in-room only or beachside, minimum stay requirement. ⊠*2255 W. Gulf Dr., Sanibel 33957* ☎*239/472–3145 or 800/276–4753* ⊠*239/472–2109* ⬢*www. casaybelresort.com* ⬢*40 1-bedroom units, 74 2-bedroom units* ⬢*In-room: safe, kitchen, VCR, ethernet, dial-up. In-hotel: 2 restaurants, bars, tennis courts, pool, beachfront, children's programs (ages 4–11)* ▤*AE, D, DC, MC, V.*

$$$$ ⌂**Sanibel's Seaside Inn.** Tucked among the subtropical greenery, right on the beach, this quiet inn is a pleasant alternative to the area's larger resorts. Cottage suites are done up in charming island cottage style with rattan, and have full kitchens and flat-screen TVs. Rooms come

with a handy wet-bar area stocked with dishware, a coffeemaker, toaster, microwave, and small fridge. Continental breakfast and bike use are complimentary, and DVDs are on hand to borrow. You may use amenities at Sundial Beach Resort and the Dunes Golf Club. ⊠*541 E. Gulf Dr., Sanibel 33957* ☎*239/472–1400 or 888/295–4560* 🖨*239/481–4947* ⊕*www.seasideinn.com* 📠*22 rooms, 10 cottage suites* ⚒*In-room: kitchen (some), refrigerator, VCR, Wi-Fi. In-hotel: pool, beachfront, bicycles, laundry facilities, no-smoking rooms* ⊟*AE, D, DC, MC, V* ⧉*CP.*

$$$$
☺
Fodor's Choice
★

⌂ **South Seas Island Resort.** This massive 330-acre resort closed for about a year and a half after extensive hurricane damage in August 2004. It partially reopened in March 2006 under new ownership with all-new, upgraded guest accommodations, 19 swimming pools, reinvented private restaurants and shops, and a remodeled 9-hole golf course with lush water features. The resort is now operating full swing and at its best ever. As in the past, stylish, low-rise hotel rooms, villas, and houses are all over the property but are concentrated at either end, near the marina and, to the south, near the entry gate and the small shopping complex. Dunes fringe a pristine 2½-mi beach, and mangroves edge the single main road. Entry gates and water on three sides give the resort a delicious seclusion, but trolleys take you around property and into Captiva village. A new Golden Door Spa is expected to open in 2008. Pros: full-service amenities, security, isolation, exclusivity, car-free transportation. Cons: high rates, isolation (a pro for some, con for others), spread out. ⊠*5400 Plantation Rd., Box 194, Captiva 33924* ☎*239/472–5111 or 800/965–7772* 🖨*239/481–4947* ⊕*www.south-seas.com* 📠*138 rooms, 482 suites* ⚒*In-room: kitchen. In-hotel: 2 restaurants, room service, bars, golf course, tennis courts, pools, gym, spa, beachfront, water sports, bicycles, children's programs (ages 3–18)* ⊟*AE, D, DC, MC, V.*

★ **$$$$**
☺

⌂ **Sundial Beach & Golf Resort.** Sanibel's largest resort encompasses 400 privately owned, individually decorated one- and two-bedroom condos, about 260 of which are in its rental program. It caters to groups in fall, families in winter. The latter hang around the main pool with its seashell slide, the shell-strewn beach, and the Eco-Center, where they can pet live shells and sign up for family activities and kids camp. Pros: full-service amenities, great beach. Cons: conference crowds, crowded pool area. ⊠*1451 Middle Gulf Dr., Sanibel 33957* ☎*239/472–4151 or 866/565–5093* 🖨*239/472–8892* ⊕*www.sundialresort.com* 📠*1300 1-bedroom units, 130 2-bedroom units* ⚒*In-room: safe, kitchen, VCR, dial-up. In-hotel: 2 restaurants, bars, tennis courts, pools, gym, beach-front, water sports, bicycles, children's programs (ages 4–12), public Wi-Fi, no-smoking rooms* ⊟*AE, D, DC, MC, V.*

$$$–$$$$

⌂ **Shalimar.** Well-maintained grounds and an inviting beach are the appeal of this small property. Units occupy tin-roof two-story cottages and a two-story motel set back from the beach amid palm trees and other subtropical greenery. The small pool is in the courtyard, and there are barbecue grills. Pros: on the beach, intimate, free Wi-Fi, variety of accommodations. Cons: no restaurants or shopping on property or nearby. ⊠*2823 W. Gulf Dr., Sanibel 33957* ☎*239/472–1353 or*

800/472–1353 🖨*239/472–6430* ⊕*www.shalimar.com* ⬦*20 efficiencies, 11 1-bedroom units, 2 2-bedroom units* ⚭*In-room: kitchen, VCR, dial-up, Wi-Fi. In-hotel: pool, beachfront, bicycles, laundry facilities, public Internet, public Wi-Fi.* ⊟*AE, D, MC, V.*

$$$–$$$$ 🖥 **'Tween Waters Inn.** Besides its great beach-to-bay location, this inn has historic value. In the 1930s, Pulitzer Prize–winning cartoonist and conservationist "Ding" Darling, namesake of Sanibel's refuge, stayed in its historic cottages, which are the most charming of the property's accommodations. Water-sports enthusiasts especially like all the available rentals and charters out of the marina. The pool bar and Crow's Nest lounge, both of which serve food, are popular with locals and visitors alike. Pros: great views, lots of water-sports options, free Wi-Fi. Cons: beach is across the road from accommodations, rooms are bland. ⊠*Captiva Dr., Captiva 33924* ☎*239/472–5161 or 800/223–5865* 🖨*239/481–0249* ⊕*www.tween-waters.com* ⬦*48 rooms, 24 efficiencies, 40 suites, 4 2-bedroom suites, 2 3-bedroom suites, 19 cottages* ⚭*In-room: kitchen (some), Wi-Fi. In-hotel: restaurant, bar, tennis courts, pool, gym, spa, beachfront, bicycles, laundry facilities, public Internet, public Wi-Fi, no-smoking rooms* ⊟*AE, D, DC, MC, V* ⊙|*CP.*

$$$–$$$$ 🖥 **Waterside Inn.** Palm trees and white sand set the scene at this quiet beachside vacation spot made up of white one- and two-story buildings. Rooms and efficiencies are modestly furnished, with bright cobalt-blue-and-white interiors, and have balconies or patios and at least a partial view of the gulf. Single-story cottages are named and painted for apricot, kiwi, raspberry, and other fruit. Pros: beachfront, intimate, small pets allowed. Cons: no restaurants on-site or within walking distance, no high-speed Internet access. ⊠*3033 W. Gulf Dr., Sanibel 33957* ☎*239/472–1345 or 800/741–6166* 🖨*239/472–2148* ⊕*www.watersideinn.net* ⬦*4 rooms, 10 efficiencies, 13 cottages* ⚭*In-room: kitchen (some), refrigerator, dial-up. In-hotel: pool, beachfront, bicycles, laundry facilities, some pets allowed* ⊟*AE, D, MC, V.*

SPORTS & THE OUTDOORS

BIKING

Everyone bikes around flatter-than-a-pancake Sanibel and Captiva—on bikeways that edge the main highway in places, on the road through the wildlife refuge, and along side streets. Free maps are available at bicycle liveries. On Sanibel, rent by the hour or the day at **Billy's Bikes** (⊠*1470 Periwinkle Way, Sanibel* ☎*239/472–5248* ⊕*www.billysrentals.com*), which also rents motorized scooters and conducts Segway tours. On Captiva, bikes are available at **Jim's Rentals** (⊠*11534 Andy Rosse La., Captiva* ☎*239/472–1296* ⊕*www.yolo-jims.com*).

BOATING

The Boat House (⊠*Sanibel Marina, 634 N. Yachtsman Dr., Sanibel* ☎*239/472–2531*) rents 21-foot powerboats starting at $132.50 for a half day. **Sweet Water Boat Rental** (*'Tween Waters Marina,* ⊠*15951 Captiva Dr., Captiva* ☎*239/472–6336*) can set you up with a 19-foot center-console powerboat starting at $160 for a half day.

CANOEING & KAYAKING

One of the best ways to scout out the wildlife refuge is by paddle. Rent a canoe or kayak from the refuge's official concessionaire,

★ **Tarpon Bay Explorers** (✉ *900 Tarpon Bay Rd., Sanibel* ☎*239/472–8900* ⊕*www.tarponbayexplorers.com*). Guided tours are also available.

FISHING

Local anglers head out to catch mackerel, pompano, grouper, reds, snook, snapper, tarpon, and shark. To find a charter captain on Sanibel, ask around at its main public marina, **Sanibel Marina** (✉*634 N. Yachtsman Dr., Sanibel* ☎*239/472–2723*). On Captiva, the place to look for guides is **'Tween Waters Marina** (✉*15951 Captiva Dr., Captiva* ☎*239/472–5161*).

GOLF

Rent clubs and take lessons as well as test your skills against the water hazards on the 18-hole course at the **Dunes Golf & Tennis Club** (✉*949 Sandcastle Rd., Sanibel* ☎*239/472–2535*), green fee: $110.

TENNIS

At the **Dunes Golf & Tennis Club** (✉*949 Sandcastle Rd., Sanibel* ☎*239/472–3522*), there are seven clay courts and two pros who give lessons.

SHOPPING

Sanibel is known for its art galleries, shell shops, and one-of-a-kind boutiques; the several small open-air shopping complexes are inviting, with their tropical flowers and shady ficus trees. The largest cluster of complexes is **Periwinkle Place** (✉*2075 Periwinkle Way, Sanibel* ⊕*www.periwinkleplace.com*), with nearly 30 shops. At **She Sells Sea Shells** (✉*1157 Periwinkle Way, Sanibel* ☎*239/395–2266*), everything imaginable is made from shells, from decorative mirrors and lamps to Christmas ornaments. The owner wrote the book on shellcraft, and you can buy it there.

Fodor'sChoice   Expect the unexpected in wildlife art at **Jungle Drums** (✉*11532 Andy*
★   *Rosse La., Captiva* ☎*239/395–2266* ⊕*www.jungledrumsgallery.com*), where fish, sea turtles, and other wildlife are depicted with utmost creativity and touches of whimsy.

ESTERO ISLAND (FORT MYERS BEACH)

⑩   *18 mi southwest of Fort Myers.*

Crammed with motels, hotels, and restaurants, this island is one of Fort Myers's more frenetic gulf playgrounds. Dolphins are frequently spotted in Estero Bay, a protected arm of the gulf, and marinas provide a starting point for boating adventures, including sunset cruises, sightseeing cruises, and deep-sea fishing. At the southern tip, a bridge leads to Lovers Key State Park.

↻   At the 17-acre **Lynn Hall Memorial Park,** in the commercial northern part of Estero Island, the shore slopes gradually into the usually tranquil and warm gulf waters, providing safe swimming for children. And since houses, condominiums, and hotels line most of the beach, you're never far from civilization. There are picnic tables, barbecue grills, playground equipment, and a free fishing pier. A bathhouse with restrooms, a pedestrian mall, and a number of restaurants are nearby. Parking is metered; 25¢ buys only eight minutes and meters are closely surveyed. ⊠ *Estero Blvd.* ☎ *239/463–1116* ⊙ *Daily 7 AM–11 PM.*

OFF THE
BEATEN
PATH

Fodor'sChoice
★

Lovers Key State Park. Once a little-known secret, this out-of-the-way park encompassing 1,616 acres on four barrier islands and several uninhabited islets is gaining popularity among beachers and birders. Bike, hike, or walk the park's trails; go shelling on its 2½ mi of white-sand beach; take a boat tour; or rent a canoe, kayak, or bike. Trams run regularly 9 to 5 to deliver you and your gear to South Beach. The ride is short but often dusty. North Beach is a five-minute walk from the concession area and parking lot. Watch for osprey, bald eagles, herons, ibis, pelicans, and roseate spoonbills, or sign up for an excursion to learn fishing or cast-netting. Weddings often take place at the gazebo on the beach. There are also restrooms, picnic tables, a snack bar, and showers. On the bayside, playgrounds and another picnic area cater to families. ⊠ *8700 Estero Blvd.* ☎ *239/463–4588* ⊕ *www.floridastateparks.org/loverskey* ⊴ *$4 2–8 people in 1 vehicle, $2 for 1 person in 1 vehicle, $1 for pedestrians and bicyclists* ⊙ *Daily 8–sunset.*

WHERE TO STAY & EAT

$–$$$ ╳ **Warfields.** The newest sensation in Fort Myers Beach, this spot in a refined, off-the-beach location does steaks with a Latin flair that has locals raving. The lively bar scene and dance floor add to its popularity, and the flavorful, exotically prepared meats—oregano sirloin, coffee rib eye with *soubise* (creamy onion-mango sauce), and filet mignon stuffed with roasted shallots and cheese—set it apart from the area's sudden steak-house proliferation. Intriguing appetizers, entrées, salads, and seafood dishes round out the menu. Mood lighting warms the interior, and Italian leather couches warm the bar. ⊠ *19220 San Carlos Blvd.* ☎ *239/463–3510* ⊕ *www.warfieldssteakhouse.com* ⊟ *AE, D, MC, V* ⊙ *No lunch Sun. in off-season.*

$$ ╳ **Matanzas Inn.** Watch boats coming and going whether you sit inside or out at this rustic Old Florida–style restaurant right on the docks alongside the Intracoastal Waterway. When the weather cooperates, tables outdoors, under umbrellas, provide the best ambience. Inside, a rustic shack gives way to a more formal dining area in the back; there's a bar upstairs with sweeping views. You can't miss with shrimp from the local fleets—delicately cornmeal-breaded, stuffed, or done Alfredo with scallops. The Matanzas Steamer, a house specialty, heaps on the fish and shellfish. This is true Fort Myers Beach style, meaning service can be a bit gruff—and slow. ⊠ *416 Crescent St.* ☎ *239/463–3838* ⊕ *www.matanzasrestaurant.com* ⊲ *Reservations not accepted* ⊟ *AE, D, MC, V.*

$$ ╳ **Parrot Key Caribbean Grill.** For something more contemporary than Fort Myers Beach's traditional shrimp and seafood houses, head to San Carlos Island on the east side of the high bridge where the shrimp boats

9

dock. Parrot Key sits marina-side near the shrimp docks and exudes merriment with its flair for Floribbean cuisine and island music. The all-day menu takes tropical cues with dishes such as habanero (hot chili) wings, chicken sandwich with kiwi-strawberry-mango barbecue sauce, filet au poivre with a brandy-mango demi-glace, and fried oysters with creole mustard. There's live entertainment weekends from 7 to 10 PM. ⊠*2400 Main St.* ☎*239/463–3257* ⊕*www.myparrotkey.com* ⌘*Reservations not accepted* ⊟*AE, D, MC, V.*

¢–$ ✕**Plaka.** A casual long-timer and a favorite for a quick breakfast, lunch breaks, and sunset dinners, Plaka—Greek for "beach"—has typical Greek fare such as moussaka, pastitsio, gyros, and roast lamb, as well as burgers, hot dogs, sandwiches, fried seafood, and strip steak. It lies along a strip of casual sidewalk restaurants in a pedestrian mall near the beach. There's indoor dining, but grab a seat on the porch or under an umbrella on the patio. ⊠*1001 Estero Blvd.* ☎*239/463–4707* ⌘*Reservations not accepted* ⊟*AE, D, MC, V.*

$$$$ ☗**DiamondHead.** This 12-story, all-suites resort sits on the beach, and many rooms, especially those on higher floors, have stunning views. Units are done in rich fall tones but show a little wear and tear. Each has a living room with queen-size sleeper sofa, a separate bedroom, and a kitchenette. The well-organized children's programs include everything from crafts to scavenger hunts to sand golf. Pros: right on beach, walking distance to Times Square, kitchen facilities. Cons: heavy foot and car traffic, very small fitness center, not the best value on the beach. ⊠*2000 Estero Blvd., 33931* ☎*239/765–7654 or 888/765–5002* 🖷*239/765–1694* ⊕*www.diamondheadfl.com* ⌇*124 suites* ⌘*In-room: kitchen, dial-up, ethernet. In-hotel: 2 restaurants, bar, pool, gym, beachfront, children's programs (ages 4–14), laundry facilities, public Wi-Fi* ⊟*AE, D, MC, V.*

★ $$$–$$$$ ☗**Lovers Key Beach Club & Resort.** Views can be stupendous from upper floors in this 14-story waterfront resort just north of Lovers Key State Park. The gulf seems to stretch forever, and dolphins and manatees in the estuary put on quite a show. Most of the plantation-style condominiums have spa bathtubs with a window view. All of the one- and two-bedroom units have full kitchens and handsome decor that continues the lobby theme of bamboo, palms, and pineapples. The lagoon-style waterfall pool sits bayside, where a narrow strip of protected sand constitutes the beach. Pros: excellent views, off the beaten path, spacious accommodations. Cons: not a true beach, far from shopping, limited amenities. ⊠*8771 Estero Blvd., 33931* ☎*239/765–1040 or 877/798–4879* 🖷*239/765–1055* ⊕*www.loverskey.com* ⌇*99 condominiums* ⌘*In-room: kitchen, dial-up. In-hotel: restaurant, pool, gym, beachfront, laundry facilities, public Internet* ⊟*AE, D, DC, MC, V.*

$$–$$$ ☗**Outrigger Beach Resort.** On a wide gulf beach, this casual resort has ☾ rooms and efficiencies with configurations to suit different families and budgets. The standard rooms offer your basic motel setup; efficiencies are roomier and work well for families. All open up to a shared porch or balcony. You'll also find a broad sundeck, tiki cabanas, sailboats, and a beachfront pool with a popular tiki bar. Pros: beautiful beach, cabana and water-sports rentals, family friendly. Cons: can be

noisy, crowded pool area, old-school look and feel. ⊠*6200 Estero Blvd., 33931* ☎*239/463–3131 or 800/657–5659* ⊟*239/463–6577* ⊕*www.outriggerfmb.com* ↝*74 rooms, 68 efficiencies* ⅋*In-room: safe, kitchen (some), refrigerator, dial-up. In-hotel: 2 restaurants, bar, pool, beachfront, bicycles, no-smoking rooms* ⊟*AE, MC, V.*

$–$$$ 📺**Pierview Hotel & Suites.** In the thick of things at Fort Myers Beach's so-called Times Square, this three-story property, formerly a Ramada Inn, has pretty gingerbread trim. Inside, cheery florals and wallpaper borders along the ceiling make the rooms homey, and all have a porch or balcony. The new private owner has plans to tear the old building down and start over, so call ahead to learn the status of the hotel. Pros: near all the action, right on the beach, affordable. Cons: old building, limited amenities, no Internet access. ⊠*1160 Estero Blvd., 33931* ☎*239/463–6158 or 800/544–4592* ⊟*239/765–4240* ↝*56 rooms, 14 suites* ⅋*In-room: safe, kitchen (some), dial-up. In-hotel: bar, pool, beachfront, laundry facilities, some pets allowed (fee), no-smoking rooms* ⊟*AE, D, MC, V.*

SPORTS & THE OUTDOORS

BIKING

Fort Myers Beach has no designated trails, so most cyclists ride along the road. **Fun Rentals** (⊠*1901 Estero Blvd.* ☎*239/463–8844*) advertises bike rental rates anywhere from two hours to a week. Rent bikes in Lovers Key State Park through **Nature Recreation Management** (⊠*8700 Estero Blvd., Fort Myers Beach* ☎*239/314–0110* ⊕*www.naturerecreationmanagement.com*). Fees are $10 for a full day.

CANOEING

Lovers Key State Park offers both kayak rentals and guided kayaking tours of its bird-rich estuary. The concessionaire, **Nature Recreation Management** (⊠*8700 Estero Blvd., Fort Myers Beach* ☎*239/314–0110* ⊕*www.naturerecreationmanagement.com*), charges $35 for its guided tour, which is offered Monday, Wednesday, and Saturday. Rentals begin at $20 for a half day, $30 for a full day.

FISHING

Getaway Deep Sea Fishing (⊠*18400 San Carlos Blvd.* ☎*800/641–3088 or 239/466–3600* ⊕*www.getawaymarina.com*) rents fishing equipment, sells bait, and can arrange half- and full-day charters. Rates start at $42 for a half day and include bait, license, and equipment.

GOLF

The **Fort Myers Beach Golf Course** (⊠*4200 Bay Beach La., off Estero Blvd.* ☎*239/463–2064*) has 18 holes and a practice range in the midst of a condo community but filled with birds. Green fee: $20/$25.

ΝAPLES AREA

As you head south from Fort Myers on U.S. 41, you soon come to Estero and Bonita Springs, followed by the Naples and Marco Island areas, which are sandwiched between Big Cypress Swamp and the

Gulf of Mexico. East of Naples the land is largely undeveloped and mostly wetlands, all the way to Fort Lauderdale. Here, along the northern border of the Florida Everglades, there are stunning nature preserves and parks. Tours and charters out of Everglades City explore the mazelike Ten Thousand Islands National Wildlife Refuge. These waters are full of fish and wildlife. Between Naples and Everglades City, acres of breeze-swept saw grass stretch off to the horizon. Keep your eyes peeled and you may even spot alligators in the waterways alongside the road. Naples itself is a major vacation destination that has sprouted pricey high-rise condominiums and golfing developments, plus a spate of restaurants and shops to match. A similar but not as thorough evolution has occurred on Marco Island, the largest of the Ten Thousand Islands.

ESTERO/BONITA SPRINGS

⑪ *10 mi south of Fort Myers.*

Towns below Fort Myers have started to flow seamlessly into one another since the opening of Florida Gulf Coast University in San Carlos Park and as a result of the growth of Estero and Bonita Springs, agricultural communities until not long ago. Bonita Beach, the closest beach to Interstate 75, has evolved from a fishing community into a strip of upscale homes and beach clubs built to provide access for residents of inland golf developments.

★ Tour one of Florida's quirkier chapters from the past at **Koreshan State Historic Site.** Named for a religious cult that was active at the turn of the 20th century, Koreshan preserves a dozen structures where the group practiced arts, worshipped a male-female divinity, and created its own branch of science called cosmogony. The cult floundered when leader Cyrus Reed Teed died in 1908, and in 1961, the four remaining members deeded the property to the state. Rangers lead tours, and the grounds are lovely for picnicking and camping. Canoeists paddle the Estero River, fringed by a forest of exotic vegetation the Koreshans planted. ✉ *Tamiami Trail, Estero* ☎ *239/992–0311* ⊕ *www.floridastateparks.org/koreshan* 🎫 *$4 per vehicle with up to 8 passengers; $3 for a single driver; $1 per bicyclist, pedestrian, or extra passenger* ☉ *Daily 8* AM*–sunset.*

☙ Opened in 1936 and one of the first attractions of its kind in the state, **Everglades Wonder Gardens** captures the beauty of untamed Florida. The old-fashioned zoological gardens have Florida panthers, black bears, crocodiles and alligators, tame Florida deer, flamingos, and trained otters and birds. There's also a funky natural-history museum. Tours, which include an otter show and alligator feedings, run continuously, the last starting at 4. The swinging bridge over the alligator pit is a real thrill. ✉ *27180 Old U.S. 41* ☎ *239/992–2591* 🎫 *$15* ☉ *Daily 9–5.*

Bonita Springs Public Beach, at the south end of Bonita Beach, has picnic tables, beach concessions, and a restaurant next door. As far as local beaches goes, it's the easiest to access and the most popular south of Fort Myers Beach. ⊠*Hickory Blvd. at Bonita Beach Rd.* ☎*239/461–7400* ⚓*Parking $1 per hr up to $5 per day.*

★ The 342-acre **Barefoot Beach Preserve** is a quiet, out-of-the-way place, accessible via a road around the corner from the buzzing public beach. It has picnic tables, a nature trail and learning center, a butterfly garden, a canoe trail, and refreshment stands. Gopher tortoises often cross the road right in front of your car, so drive slowly. Park rangers lead nature walks and canoe trips. ⊠*Lely Beach Rd.* ☎*239/498–4364* ⚓*$5.*

> **FOR THE BIRDS**
>
> The last leg of the Great Florida Birding Trail, the South Trail lists more than 20 stops in the area covered by this chapter. Visit www.floridabirdingtrail.com/sites_south.htm for a complete listing.

OFF THE
BEATEN
PATH
Fodor'sChoice

★
☺

Corkscrew Swamp Sanctuary. To get a feel for what this part of Florida was like before civil engineers began draining the swamps, drive 13 mi east of Bonita Springs (30 mi northeast of Naples) to these 11,000 acres of pine flatwood and cypress, grass-and-sedge "wet prairie," saw-grass marshland, and lakes and sloughs filled with water lettuce. Managed by the National Audubon Society, the sanctuary protects North America's largest remaining stand of ancient bald cypress, 600-year-old trees as tall as 130 feet, as well as endangered birds, such as wood storks, which often nest here. This is a favorite destination for serious birders and in 2006 was designated the gateway to the new Great Florida Birding South Trail. If you spend a couple of hours to take the 2¼-mi self-guided tour along the boardwalk, you'll spot ferns, orchids, and air plants, as well as wading birds and possibly alligators and river otters. A nature center educates you about this precious, unusual habitat with a dramatic re-creation of the preserve and its creatures in the Swamp Theater. ⊠*16 mi east of I–75 on Rte. 846* ☎*239/348–9151* ⊕*www.audubon.org* ⚓*$10* ☉*Oct. 1–Apr. 10, daily 7–5:30; Apr. 11–Sept. 30, daily 7* AM*–7:30* PM.

9

WHERE TO STAY & EAT

$$ ✕**Toucan Grille.** Come casual and come for your booster shot of Caribbean atmosphere and tastes. Spinning lazily from high ceilings, paddle fans swirl cool air and hot reggae around this sandy-hued place, which is done in rattan, wicker, and bamboo and splashed with bright tropical colors. With its offerings of coconut shrimp, jerk chicken, and chili-rum-glazed salmon, the menu, too, makes an island statement—nothing too brazen, custom-fit to American palates. At happy-hour time, the bar stools fill with local businesspeople. ⊠*4480 Bonita Beach Rd., Bonita Springs* ☎*239/495–9464* ⊕*www.toucangrille.com* ⊟*D, MC, V* ☉*Closed Sun. and Mon. May–Nov.*

¢–$ ✕**Doc's Beach House.** Right next door to the public beach access, Doc's
☺ has fed hungry beachers for decades. Come barefoot and grab a quick libation or meal downstairs, outside on the beach, or in the courtyard. When the thermometer reaches "searing," take refuge on the air-conditioned second floor, with its great view of beach action. Basic fare

on the breakfast and all-day menu includes a popular Angus burger, pizza, and seafood plates. ✉*27908 Hickory Blvd., Bonita Springs* ☎*239/992–6444* ⚓*Reservations not accepted* ⊕*www.docsbeach-house.com* ▤*No credit cards.*

$$$–$$$$
Ↄ
Fodor'sChoice
★

▥**Hyatt Coconut Point Resort & Spa.** This secluded luxury Hyatt, with its marble-and-mahogany lobby and 18 floors, makes a lovely sanctuary for golfers, families, and conferences. Man-made water features include a slide pool, lap pool, lazy-river pool, and fountain-waterfall pool. For nature-made water features, catch a ferry to the hotel's private island beach. Handsomely appointed rooms overlook the water or the golf course. Its spa is known for its rare Watsu (water shiatsu) pool, and an interpretive center showcases natural and prehistoric history. Pros: luxury amenities, top spa, great ceviche bar in one restaurant. Cons: boat shuttle to the beach, expensive restaurants and no others very close by. ✉*5001 Coconut Rd., Bonita Springs 34134* ☎*239/444–1234 or 800/554–9288* 🖨*239/390–4277* ⊕*www.coconutpoint.hyatt.com* ⮑*426 rooms, 30 suites* ⚒*In-room: safe, refrigerator, VCR, ethernet, dial-up, Wi-Fi. In-hotel: 5 restaurants, room service, bars, golf course, tennis courts, pools, gym, spa, beachfront, concierge, children's programs (ages 3–12), executive floor, public Internet, public Wi-Fi, no-smoking rooms* ▤*AE, D, DC, MC, V.*

$$$
▥**Trianon Bonita.** Convenient to Bonita Springs' best shopping and dining at The Promenade shopping center, this branch of a downtown Naples favorite feels European in its peaceful, sophisticated way. It's very similar to its predecessor Naples property, and has a new poolside-lakeside alfresco bar and grill. Rooms are oversize and the lobby has a vaulted, coved ceiling and marble columns. Cocktails and complimentary breakfast are served in the library, where a fireplace and baby grand piano dominate. Pros: shops and restaurants within walking distance, intimate atmosphere, refined amenities. Cons: sometimes less-than-friendly front desk staff, far from beach, slightly stuffy. ✉*3401 Bay Commons Dr., Bonita Springs 34134* ☎*239/948–4400 or 800/859–3939* 🖨*239/948–4401* ⊕*www.trianon.com* ⮑*100 rooms* ⚒*In-room: safe, refrigerator (some), dial-up, Wi-Fi. In-hotel: pool, public Internet, public Wi-Fi, no-smoking rooms* ▤*AE, D, DC, MC, V* ⏣*CP.*

SPORTS & THE OUTDOORS

BIKING
Rent bicycles by the day or by the week at **Bonita Bike & Baby** (✉*No physical address; by cell phone and delivery only* ☎*239/947–6377*).

BOATING
Bonita Beach Resort Motel (✉*26395 Hickory Blvd.* ☎*239/992–2137*) rents pontoon boats for a minimum of two hours or by the half day and day.

CANOEING
The meandering Estero River is pleasant for canoeing as it passes through Koreshan State Historic Site to the bay. **Estero River Outfitters**

($\boxtimes$ *20991 Tamiami Trail S, Estero* $\blacksquare$ *239/992–4050* $\oplus$ *www.esteroriveroutfitters.com*) provides rental canoes, kayaks, and equipment.

DOG RACING

Greyhounds race year-round at the **Naples/Fort Myers Greyhound Track** ($\boxtimes$ *10601 Bonita Beach Rd. SE* $\blacksquare$ *239/992–2411* $\oplus$ *www.naplesfortmyersdogs.com*).

ICE HOCKEY

Fort Myers's minor-league hockey team, the **Florida Everblades** ($\boxtimes$ *Germain Arena, 11000 Everblades Pkwy., Estero* $\blacksquare$ *239/948–7825* $\oplus$ *www. floridaeverblades.com*), battle their opponents from October to April.

ICE SKATING

★ Skaters can head to the **Germain Arena** ($\boxtimes$ *11000 Everblades Pkwy.,*
$\mathfrak{C}$ *Estero* $\blacksquare$ *239/948–7825* $\oplus$ *www.germainarena.com*) for ice, in-line, and figure skating, plus hockey and clinics.

SHOPPING

★ **Miromar Outlets complex** ($\boxtimes$ *Corkscrew Rd. at I–75 Exit 123 in Estero, near Germain Arena* $\blacksquare$ *239/948–3766* $\oplus$ *www.miromar.com/florida. html*) includes Adidas, Nike, Nautica, Off 5th Saks Fifth Avenue, and more than 130 other stores and eateries. **Gulf Coast Town Center** ($\boxtimes$ *Airways Blvd. and Marathon Way* $\oplus$ *www. gulfcoasttowncenter. com*) began rolling out in fall 2006 with a 123,000-square-foot Bass Pro Shops. When completed, it will include Borders, Best Buy, two Marriott hotels, several restaurants, and movie theaters. **Coconut Point Town Center** ($\boxtimes$ *23106 Fashion Dr., Estero* $\blacksquare$ *239/992–4259* $\oplus$ *www. coconutpointretail.com*), a 500-acre planned community, opened its shopping-entertainment district in November 2006. The **Promenade at Bonita Bay** ($\boxtimes$ *South Bay Dr.*) in the Bonita Bay subdivision is Bonita Springs' chic shopping venue, with an upscale collection of shops and restaurants.

9

NAPLES

12–**21** *21 mi south of Bonita Springs.*

Poised between the Gulf of Mexico and the Everglades, Naples belies its wild setting and Indian-post past with the trappings of wealth—neo-Mediterranean-style mansions, neatly manicured golfing developments, revitalized downtown streets lined with galleries and one-of-a-kind shops, and a reputation for lively and eclectic dining. Visitors come for its luxury hotels—including two Ritz-Carltons—its fabulous white-sand beaches, fishing, shopping, theater and arts, and a lofty reputation for golf. Yet with all the highfalutin living, Naples still appeals to family, especially with a new water park at North Collier Regional Park and a Children's Museum slated to open there in 2008.

12 The well-maintained 166-acre **Delnor-Wiggins Pass State Park** has one
Fodor'sChoice of Naples's best beaches, barbecue grills, picnic tables, a boat ramp,
★ an observation tower, restrooms with wheelchair access, bathhouses,

Clam Pass
Beach Park **14**

Collier County
Museum **19**

Delnor–
Wiggins Pass
State Park **12**

Lowdermilk
Park **17**

Naples Botanical
Garden **20**

Naples Museum
of Art **13**

Naples Nature
Center **16**

Naples Zoo at
Caribbean
Gardens **15**

Palm Cottage .. **18**

Sun-N-Fun
Lagoon **21**

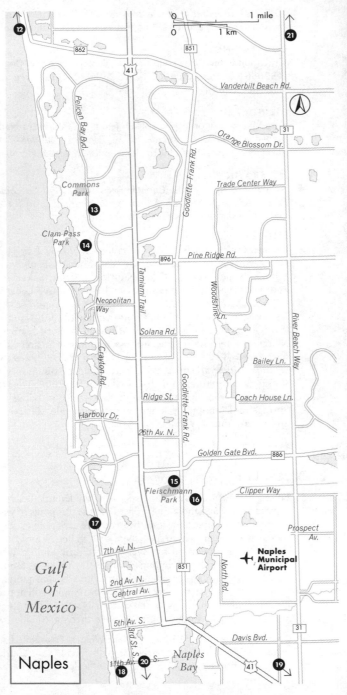

Naples

showers, boat ramps, and lots of parking. Fishing is best in Wiggins Pass, at the north end of the park. Rangers conduct sea-turtle walks in summer, and birding and other tours year-round. ✉ *11100 Gulf Shore Dr. N, at Rte. 846* ☎ *239/597–6196* ⊕ *www.floridastateparks.org/delnor-wiggins* ✍ *$5 per vehicle with up to 8 people, $3 for single driver, $1 for pedestrians and bicyclists* ⊙ *Daily 8–sunset.*

🐾 ㉑ The **Sun-N-Fun Lagoon** brings splashy fun to a county park east of town. Interactive water features such as water pistols and dumping buckets are designed for children age seven and under. The whole family will go for the lazy river and slides. ✉ *15000 Livingston Rd. at North Collier Regional Park* ☎ *239/254–4021* ⊕ *www.colliergov.net* ✍ *$10* ⊙ *Call or visit Web site for hours.*

⓭ The cool, contemporary **Naples Museum of Art**, around the corner from the Waterside Shops in the Naples Philharmonic Center for the Arts, displays provocative, innovative pieces, including American miniatures, antique walking sticks, modern American and Mexican masters, and traveling exhibits. Dazzling installations by glass artist Dale Chihuly include a fiery cascade of a chandelier and an illuminated ceiling layered with many-hued glass bubbles, glass corkscrews, and other shapes that suggest the sea; alone, this warrants a visit. ✉ *5833 Pelican Bay Blvd.* ☎ *239/597–1900 or 800/597–1900* ⊕ *www.thephil.org* ✍ *$8* ⊙ *Tues.–Sat. 10–4, Sun. noon–4 May–Oct.; closed Mon. and Aug.–Labor Day; open an hour later in the winter season.*

Fodor's Choice
★

⓮ Kayak through the mangroves or into the surf at **Clam Pass Beach Park.** Next to the Naples Grande Resort, a ¾-mi boardwalk winds through the mangrove area to the beach. Convenient for north-end Naples residents and hotel guests, it provides tram service down the boardwalk. ✉ *Next to the Naples Grande Resort on Seagate Dr.* ☎ *239/353–0404* ✍ *Parking $6* ⊙ *Daily 8–sunset.*

🐾 ⓯ The lush and entertaining 52-acre **Naples Zoo**, established in 1919 as a botanical garden, today draws visitors curious to see lions, African wild dogs, tigers, lemurs, antelope, and monkeys. Central exhibits include Panther Glade and its new in 2007 Leopard Rock, but it's the shows that distinguish this nationally accredited zoo. The presentations in Planet Predator and Serpents: Fangs & Fiction star the extreme in wild animals. The Primate Expedition Cruise takes you through islands of monkeys and lemurs. Youngsters can amuse themselves in three separate play areas, and there are meet-the-keeper times and alligator feedings. ✉ *1590 Goodlette Rd.* ☎ *239/262–5409* ⊕ *www.napleszoo.com* ✍ *$15.95* ⊙ *Daily 9:30–5:30; gates close at 4:30.*

🐾 ⓰ On 14 acres bordering a tidal lagoon teeming with wildlife, the **Naples Nature Center** includes an aviary, a wildlife rehabilitation clinic, a Discovery Center with a serpentarium, and a 3,000-gallon sea-turtle aquarium. Short trails are dotted with interpretive signs, and there are free (with paid admission) guided walks and boat tours on the mangrove-bordered Gordon River several times daily. Canoes and kayaks are available for rent. ✉ *1450 Merrihue Dr.* ☎ *239/262–0304*

9

⊕*www.conservancy.org* ✉*$7.50* ⊙*Mon.–Sat. 9–4:30; Nov.–Apr. also Sun. noon–4.*

★ ☾ **⑰**   Stretching along Gulf Shore Boulevard, **Lowdermilk Park** is great for families. It has more than 1,000 feet of beach as well as volleyball courts, a playground, restrooms, showers, vending machines, and picnic tables. ✉*Gulf Shore Blvd. at Banyan Blvd.* ☎*239/213–3029* ✉*Parking 25¢ per 15 min* ⊙*Daily 7–sunset.*

⑱   Houses in 19th-century South Florida were often built of a concrete-like material made of sand and seashells. For a fine example of such tabby construction, stop by   **Palm Cottage,** built in 1895 and one of the Lower Gulf Coast's few surviving tabby homes. The historically accurate interior contains simple furnishings typical of the period. Docents give guided tours of the home and, for $15, a historic walking tour of the area. ✉*137 12th Ave. S* ☎*239/261–8164* ⊕*www.napleshistoricalsociety.org* ✉*$6* ⊙*Guided tours Nov.–Apr., Tues.–Sat. 1–4; May–Oct., Wed. and Sat. 1–4.*

★ ☾ **⑲**   To get a feel for local history, stop by the **Collier County Museum,** where a Seminole chickee hut, native plant garden, swamp buggy, reconstructed 19th-century fort, steam logging locomotive, and other historical exhibits capture important developments from prehistoric times to the World War II era. ✉*3301 Tamiami Trail E* ☎*239/774–8476* ⊕*www.colliermuseum.com* ✉*Free* ⊙*Weekdays 9–5, Sat. 9–4.*

★ **⑳**   Developing in phases, the **Naples Botanical Garden** is worth a visit even as it grows. Self-guided tours take in a lovely Date Palm Allée backdropped by an artistic mosaic wall, a fruit and spice garden, a fragrance garden, and the Pollination Pavilion filled with butterflies, bees, geckos, hummingbirds, and lories. ✉*4820 Bayshore Dr.* ☎*239/643–7275* ⊕*www.naplesgarden.org* ✉*$6* ⊙*Nov.–Apr., Wed.–Sat. 10–4, Sun. noon–4; July–Sept., Thurs.–Sat. 9–1; May, June, and Oct., Wed.–Sat. 10–4.*

WHERE TO STAY & EAT

$$$$

Fodor's Choice

★

✗**Artisans in the Dining Room.** The crème de la crème of Naples dining, the Ritz's main restaurant is equally rich in food and decor. Exquisite molding, solid European furnishings, and ever-changing themed exhibits from local galleries set an elegant mood, and the imaginative cuisine reflects what's fresh that day: trio of foie gras with peaches and Sauternes sorbet, bamboo-steamed Dover sole, and lobster risotto, for instance. Dinners are arranged and priced as three-, four-, and seven-course meals. ✉*280 Vanderbilt Beach Rd.* ☎*239/598–3300* ⌂*Reservations essential* ⊟*AE, D, DC, MC, V* ⊙*No lunch.*

$$$

✗**Aura.** The newest sensation at the new Naples Grande Resort breaks all the rules with a chic wall-less lobby setting and a short menu of multidimensional and artistically plated creations. A tuna sashimi appetizer, for instance, comes with a soy-ginger tuna tartare, a shot of pureed cucumber spiked with champagne and grenadine, and the suggestion of a lime vodka and chili-pepper-water martini. Main plates include sugarcane "lacquered" halibut, strip steak with truffle Parmesan fries, and Dijon-panko crusted rack of lamb. Save room for the innovative dessert shooters. Breakfast and lunch menus are equally bold. ✉*475*

Seagate Dr., Naples Grande Resort ☎*239/597–3232* ⊕*www.naples-grande.com* ⊟*AE, D, DC, MC, V.*

\$\$–\$\$\$ ✕**Brio's Tuscan Grille.** With its open Tuscan marketplace atmosphere around an outdoor bar, Brio is the hot new place to see and be seen enjoying drinks and noshes in a range from affordable to fine. Archways with massive billowing curtains separate the patio component from the milling restaurant section at Waterside Shops. Indoors is more traditional, less convivial. Because of its popularity, the service tends to be slow, but the food is dependably tasty, ranging from pizza and flatbreads to entrée salads, pasta, grilled steaks, and specialties such as proscuitto-stuffed chicken breast and rosemary beef tenderloins. ⊠*5505 Tamiami Trail N at Waterside Shops* ☎*239/593–5329* ⊕*www.brioitalian.com* ⊟*AE, D, MC, V.*

\$\$–\$\$\$ ✕**Chops City Grill.** Count on high-quality cuisine that fuses, as its name
Fodor'sChoice reflects, a personality split between chopstick cuisine and fine cuts of
★ meat. Ultrasophisticated yet resort-wear casual, it draws everyone from young business folk to the local retired population. Sushi and Pacific Rim inspirations such as beef satay, sushi, and teriyaki roasted sea bass represent its Asian persuasion; dry-aged T-bone, fillets, and New Zealand lamb rack, its meaty side. They come together in the Asian barbecue pork porterhouse. Dine inside with a view of the kitchen or, at the Bonita Springs branch, alfresco in the courtyard. ⊠*837 5th Ave. S* ☎*239/262–4677* ⊠*Hwy. 41 at Brooks Grand Plaza, Bonita Springs* ☎*239/992–4677* ⌖*Reservations essential* ⊕*www.chopsbonita.com* ⊟*AE, DC, MC, V* ☾*No lunch.*

\$\$–\$\$\$ ✕**Tommy Bahama's Tropical Café.** Here, Naples takes a youthful curve. Island music sounds on the umbrella-shaded courtyard at this, the prototype for the chain. It has that trademark rattan look that identifies the Tommy Bahama label in clothing and furniture stores across the nation. Indoors and out, everybody's munching sandwiches, salads, ribs, and grilled seafood and steaks with a tropical flair (Trinidad tuna pan-seared with a cilantro-lemongrass crust, Wha'Jamaican jerk pork) and sampling Tommy's Bungalow Brew beer. ⊠*1220 3rd St. S* ☎*239/643–6889* ⊕*www.tommybahama.com* ⊟*AE, MC, V.*

★ **\$\$** ✕**Bha! Bha!** Classic and fusion Middle Eastern cooking—some of Naples's finest ethnic food—fill the menu with wonderful, adventurous taste treats. Specialties include dried plum lamb, garlic eggplant chicken, mango-ginger shrimp, and spicy beef in saffron sauce with cucumber yogurt. Ocher walls, stuffed ottomans, and exotic tapestries confirm the "Persian bistro" on the restaurant's sign. The service lags at times, but intrepid palates still declare it worth finding (hidden in a strip mall) and waiting for. ⊠*847 Vanderbilt Rd.* ☎*239/594–5557* ⊕*www.bhabhapersianbistro.com* ⊟*AE, MC, V.*

\$ ✕**Cilantro Tamales.** The salsa and chips alone are worth a visit to this bright and lively little spot, with slabs of clay tile for placemats. The signature dish, smoked Gouda–stuffed tamales, sets an example for freshness, authenticity, and a flair of creativity. Imaginative touches are also added to other Tex-Mex standards, including enchiladas, fajitas, rellenos, and a Mexican rice bowl. ⊠*10823 N. Tamiami*

9

Trail ☎*239/597–5855* ⊕*www.cilantrotamales.com* ☰*MC,* V ⊘ *Closed Mon.*

¢–$ ✕**Aurelio's Is Pizza.** Transplanted from Chicago, the pizza here is steeped in tradition and flavor. The selections are typical, with a few show-offs such as taco, shrimp barbecue, and the low-cholesterol spinach Calabrese. There's also pasta with homemade sauces and chicken Parmesan or Alfredo. Red-and-white tablecloths and old Illinois license plates accent this neighborhood-style strip-mall café. ⊠*590 N. Tamiami Trail* ☎*239/403–8882* ⊕*aureliosofnaples.com* ☰*AE, MC,* V ⊘ *Closed Mon. No lunch.*

¢–$ ✕**Old Naples Pub.** Local blue- and white-collar workers gather with visitors for affordable sandwiches and seafood in the courtyard of this 20-year-old traditional pub, tucked away from shopping traffic at 3rd Street Plaza. It strikes one as an everybody-knows-your-name kind of place, with jars of pickles on the tables and friendly bartenders. Taste some 20 kinds of beer and order fried grouper sandwich, burgers, crispy chicken salad, and nachos, as well as such not-so-traditional pub snacks as grilled ahi tuna and fried gator tail. There's musical entertainment nightly between Thanksgiving and Easter. ⊠*255 13th Ave. S* ☎*239/649–8200* ☰*AE, D, MC, V.*

★ $$$$ 🏨**Bellasera.** It is "off 5th" just enough (less than two blocks) for privacy and convenience. Right off a Tuscany postcard, it feels quite villa with its red-tile roofs and burnt-gold stucco. The privately owned studios and one- to three-bedroom suites, keeping in theme with earthy hues and terra-cotta tiles, huddle three-story high around a beautifully tiled pool, fountain, and courtyard. Private cabanas line the pool on two sides and Zizi restaurant spills out onto the patio on another. The studios have in-room whirlpool tubs with plantation shutters opening onto the master bedroom so you can watch TV from your bubble bath. Pros: near shops and restaurants, spacious rooms, you can watch TV from jetted tubs. Cons: must take shuttle to beach, on a busy highway, average restaurant. ⊠*221 9th St. S, 34102* ☎*239/649–7333 or 888/612–1115* 🖷*239/649–6233* ⊕*www.bellaseranaples.com* ⇗*10 studios, 30 1-bedroom suites, 48 2-bedroom suites, and 12 3-bedroom suites* ♿*In-room: kitchen, Wi-Fi. In-hotel: restaurant, room service, bar, pool, gym, concierge, public Internet, public Wi-Fi* ☰*AE, D, DC, MC, V.*

$$$$ 🏨**Edgewater Beach Hotel.** This compact waterfront seven-story hotel anchors the north end of fashionable Gulf Shore Boulevard. The one- and two-bedroom suites are brightly decorated and have gingerbread-trimmed patios or balconies, many with exquisite gulf views. Have meals by the pool or in the elegant restaurant in the newly renovated lobby. You'll also find the new fitness center and business facilities on the same floor. Guests have certain dining and recreational privileges (including golfing) at the Naples Grande Resort, a sister property. ⊠*1901 Gulf Shore Blvd. N, 34102* ☎*239/403–2000, 800/821–0196, 800/282–3766 in Florida* 🖷*239/403–2100* ⊕*www.edgewaternaples. com* ⇗*97 1-bedroom suites, 28 2-bedroom suites* ♿*In-room: safe, refrigerator, ethernet, dial-up. In-hotel: restaurant, bars, golf course, pool, gym, beachfront, bicycles, public Internet, public Wi-Fi* ☰*AE, DC, MC, V.*

$$$$ ⬚**Inn on Fifth.** To plant yourself in the heart of Naples nightlife and shopping, you can't beat this swank property whose rooms are well soundproofed to shut out the activity when you're ready to seclude yourself in comfort. When you're not, slide open the French doors and tune in to 5th Avenue from the balcony. A spa completes a list of urban amenities that also include a lively Irish pub, a rooftop pool, and an arched, columned marble lobby hung with crystal chandeliers. A theater is next door and the beach is six blocks away. The pub is ultra-friendly, but the front desk staff is known to be less than helpful. Pros: near shopping and restaurants, metro vibe, very comfortable rooms. Cons: a little bustly if you prefer quiet, staff with an attitude, not on the beach. ⊠*699 5th Ave. S, 34102* ☎*239/403–8777 or 888/403–8778* 🖶*239/403–8778* ⊕*www.naplesinn.com* ⬚*76 rooms, 11 suites* ⬚*In-room: safe, dial-up, Wi-Fi. In-hotel: restaurant, bar, pool, gym, spa, concierge, laundry service, public Internet, public Wi-Fi.* ⊟*AE, D, DC, MC, V* ⦿*CP.*

$$$$ ⬚**LaPlaya Beach & Golf Resort.** LaPlaya bespeaks posh and panache
Fodor'sChoice down to the smallest detail—custom-designed duvet covers, marble
★ bathrooms, and a palm-tree-patterned teddy bear on the pillow, for instance. The boutique resort features a Thai-style spa, rock-waterfalls pools, a tony Miami-style beachfront restaurant, and a casual tiki bar that serves food. Of its 189 units, 141 are beachfront with private balconies. Some have jetted soak tubs with a view of the gulf. Pros: right on the beach, high-end amenities, beautiful rooms. Cons: golf course is off-property, no locker rooms in spa. ⊠*9891 Gulf Shore Dr., 34108* ☎*239/597–3123 or 800/237–6883* 🖶*239/567–6278* ⊕*www.laplayaresort.com* ⬚*180 rooms, 9 suites* ⬚*In-room: ethernet, dial-up. In-hotel: restaurant, bars, golf course, pools, gym, spa, bicycles, concierge, public Wi-Fi, no-smoking rooms* ⊟*AE, D, MC, V.*

$$$$ ⬚**Naples Beach Hotel and Golf Club.** Family-owned and -managed for
☺ more than 50 years, this beach resort is a piece of Naples history. On a prime stretch of powdery sand, it stands out for its par-72, 18-hole championship golf course, the first resort course in the state with a pro shop and golf school. The hotel's lobby has skylights, a coral rock fireplace, an aquarium, and a baby grand piano. Rooms, decorated in light colors, are in six high- and mid-rise pink buildings, and packages make an extended stay affordable. Pros: terrific beach, good recreational amenities. Cons: expensive, shows its age in places, have to cross street to reach spa and golf facilities. ⊠*851 Gulf Shore Blvd. N, 34102* ☎*239/261–2222 or 800/237–7600* 🖶*239/261–7380* ⊕*www.naplesbeachhotel.com* ⬚*256 rooms, 42 suites, 20 efficiencies* ⬚*In-room: kitchen (some), dial-up, Wi-Fi. In-hotel: 3 restaurants, bars, golf course, tennis courts, pool, gym, spa, beachfront, children's programs (ages 5–12), laundry service, public Internet, public Wi-Fi, no-smoking rooms* ⊟*AE, D, DC, MC, V.*

$$$$ ⬚**Naples Grande Resort & Club.** A beach, full amenities, and top-shelf
☺ luxury: formerly the Registry Resort, its new branding reflects its golf-
Fodor'sChoice club focus. And if the links aren't your thing, a recently opened Golden
★ Door Spa just might be. Rooms are spacious and comfortable at this high-rise hotel. One of the glories of the property—at least for fami-

9

lies—is the immense free-form family swimming pool, with zero entry (water begins at a depth of zero feet), and a 100-foot waterslide. The hotel sits behind dusky, twisted mangrove forests; to get to the 3 mi of powdery white sand, it's a short walk or tram ride. Indigenous cypress and pines frame the Naples Grande Golf Club, the hotel's 18-hole Rees Jones layout, a short drive away. Pros: great tennis and golf, top-notch restaurant. Cons: not right on the beach, high room rates with resort fee. ⊠*475 Seagate Dr., 34103* ☎*239/597–3232 or 800/247–9810* 🖶*239/566–7919* ⊕*www.naplesgrande.com* 🛏*395 rooms, 79 suites* 🛆*In-room: ethernet, dial-up. In-hotel: 4 restaurants, room service, bars, golf course, tennis courts, pools, gym, spa, beachfront, water sports, bicycles, children's programs (ages 4–12), laundry service, public Wi-Fi* ▤*AE, DC, MC, V.*

★ $$$$ 🏨**Ritz-Carlton Golf Resort.** Ardent golfers with a yen for luxury will find their dream vacation at Naples's most elegant golf resort. Ritz style prevails all the way but in a more contemporary verve than at its sister resort, the Ritz-Carlton, Naples. The lobby is done up in rich upholstery, with floor-to-ceiling windows looking out onto greens and grounds manicured like a French château's. Rooms are regal, with marble bathrooms and color schemes in shades of greens and burgundies; half of them have balconies with links views. The golf academy can help you polish your skills, and you have access to the spa, kids' program, and other amenities of the beachside Ritz-Carlton, which is nearby. Dining at Tuscan-style Lemonia is divine, and the cigar bar next door is inviting, with its billiards and fireplace. Pros: great golfing, fine dining, very elegant. Cons: must take shuttle bus to beach. ⊠*2600 Tiburón Dr., 34109* ☎*239/593–2000 or 800/241–3333* 🖶*239/593–2010* ⊕*www.ritzcarlton.com* 🛏*257 rooms, 38 suites* 🛆*In-room: safe, dial-up, Wi-Fi. In-hotel: 2 restaurants, room service, bars, golf course, tennis courts, pool, concierge, laundry service, executive floor, public Internet, public Wi-Fi, no-smoking rooms* ▤*AE, D, DC, MC, V.*

$$$$ 🏨**Ritz-Carlton, Naples.** This is a classic Ritz-Carlton, awash in marble, FodorśChoice antiques, and 19th-century European oil paintings. In the rooms, the ★ comforts of home prevail—assuming your home is a palace. Outside, steps away, the beach is soft, white, and dense with seashells. Given the graciousness of the staff, you quickly get over the incongruity of traipsing through the regal lobby in flip-flops, clutching a plastic bag of beach finds. It doesn't hurt that the kitchen is a wonder as well, making meals at Artisans in the Dining Room and the oh-so-clubby Grill, and even dessert in the lobby, just a little bit special. Then there's the elegant spa, one of the first and largest under the Ritz-Carlton brand with a complete menu of indulgences. Pros: very luxurious, flawless service, great beach. Cons: valet parking only, short walk to the beach. ⊠*280 Vanderbilt Beach Rd., 34108* ☎*239/598–3300 or 800/241–3333* 🖶*239/598–6691* ⊕*www.ritzcarlton.com* 🛏*450 rooms, 25 suites* 🛆*In-room: safe, Wi-Fi. In-hotel: 7 restaurants, room service, bars, tennis courts, pools, gym, spa, beachfront, concierge, children's programs (ages 5–12), laundry service, executive floor, public Internet, public Wi-Fi, no-smoking rooms* ▤*AE, D, DC, MC, V.*

$$$–$$$$ ⊞**Trianon Old Naples.** Oh so Euro in feel, this boutique hotel is just enough removed from 5th Avenue's traffic to feel private while convenient. Wrought-iron balconies and shade trees set the stage outside; inside, the elegant lobby has high ceilings, a working granite fireplace, plush furnishings, and a library that doubles as a wine-and-beer bar and breakfast room. Rooms are large and lavishly furnished, with heavy draperies. Pros: close to stores and restaurants, elegant setting, spacious rooms. Cons: limited facilities, must drive to beach. ⊠*955 7th Ave. S, 34102* ☎*239/435–9600 or 877/482–5228* ☐*239/261–0025* ⊕*www. trianon.com* ⇆*55 rooms, 3 suites, 1 cottage* ⚲*In-room: safe, dial-up. In-hotel: bar, pool, public Internet* ⊟*AE, D, DC, MC, V* ⦿*CP.*

$$–$$$ ⊞**Holiday Inn.** Although this two-story motel is on a major highway, it's set back from the road and the rooms are quiet because most of them are behind the restaurant and pool. Decorated with dark wood and carpeting and pastel bedspreads, they're also clean and comfortable. Landscaping is well maintained and the location is convenient if you plan to sightsee. New in 2005, handsome Pate's Steak House, a big name to local meat eaters, opened on-site. Pros: free Wi-Fi, nice steak house, fair rates. Cons: 15-minute drive to beach, on busy highway, not conducive to walking to restaurants and shopping. ⊠*1100 9th St. N, 34102* ☎*239/263–3434 or 800/325–1135* ☐*239/261–3809* ⊕*www. hinaples.com* ⇆*137 rooms* ⚲*In-room: dial-up, Wi-Fi. In-hotel: restaurant, bar, pool, public Wi-Fi* ⊟*AE, D, DC, MC, V.*

NIGHTLIFE & THE ARTS

THE ARTS

★ Naples is the cultural capital of this stretch of coast. The **Naples Philharmonic Center for the Arts** (⊠*5833 Pelican Bay Blvd.* ☎*239/597–1900 or 800/597–1900* ⊕*www.thephil.org*) has a 1,473-seat performance center with plays, concerts, and exhibits year-round. It's home to the 85-piece Naples Philharmonic, which presents both classical and pop concerts. The Miami Ballet Company performs here during its winter season. The **Naples Players** (⊠*Sugden Community Theatre, 701 5th Ave. S* ☎*239/263–7990* ⊕*www.naplesplayers.org*), on 5th Avenue, performs musicals and dramas year-round; winter shows often sell out well in advance.

NIGHTLIFE

Downtown's 5th Avenue South is the scene of lively nightclubs and sidewalk cafés. **McCabe's Irish Pub** (⊠*699 5th Ave. S* ☎*239/403–7170*) hosts Irish bands most weekends and some weeknights. Audiences often join in on the lusty lyrics. Hit **Fusion** (⊠*15495 U.S. 41 N* ☎*239/514–3790*) for live music, from hip-hop to '50s tunes, Tuesday through Saturday.

SPORTS & THE OUTDOORS

BIKING

Try **Clint's Bicycle Shoppe of Naples** (⊠*8789 Tamiami Trail N* ☎*239/566–3646*) for rentals by the week or month, starting at $30 a week. For daily rentals, try **Naples Cyclery** (⊠*813 Vanderbilt Beach Rd. at Pavilion Shopping Center* ☎*239/566–0600* ⊕*naplescyclery.com*), where

9

rates range from $5 to $30 for two hours and selections include recumbent bikes, two- and four-passenger surreys, tandems, and more.

BOATING

Naples Watersports at Port-O-Call Marina (✉*550 Port-O-Call Way* ☎*239/774–0479*) rents 21-foot deck boats starting at $175 for a two-hour minimum.

FISHING

The *Lady Brett* (✉*Tin City* ☎*239/263–4949* ⊕*www.tincityboats. com*) makes half-day fishing trips twice daily at $60 each. Take a guided boat and learn to cast and tie flies at **Mangrove Outfitters** (✉*4111 E. Tamiami Trail* ☎*239/793–3370 or 888/319–9848* ⊕*www.mangrove-outfitters.com*).

GOLF

★ **Tiburón Golf Club** (✉*Ritz-Carlton Golf Resort, 2600 Tiburón Dr.* ☎*239/593–2000*) is one of Naples's newest and brightest, with two 18-hole Greg Norman–designed courses, the Black and the Gold, and a golf academy. Challenging and environmentally pristine, the links include narrow fairways, stacked sod wall bunkers, coquina sand, and no roughs. Green fee: $280. At **Lely Flamingo Island Club** (✉*8004 Lely Resort Blvd.* ☎*239/793–2600* ⊕*www.lely-resort.net*), there are three 18-hole courses—The Classics, Flamingo Island, and The Mustang—plus a golf school. Mustang is the easiest and most wide open. Green fee: $154. **Naples Beach Hotel & Golf Club** (✉*851 Gulf Shore Blvd. N* ☎*239/435–2475* ⊕*www.naplesbeachhotel.com*) has 18 holes, a golf school, and a putting green. The region's oldest course, a par 72, it was built in 1929 and last renovated in 1998. Green fee: $140 (cart and balls included). At affordable **Riviera Golf Club** (✉*48 Marseille Dr.* ☎*239/774–1081*), there are 18 holes. Green fee: $55/$47 (includes cart).

TENNIS

Cambier Park Tennis Center (✉*775 8th Ave. S* ☎*239/213–3060*) offers clinics and play on 12 Hydro-Grid lighted clay courts for members and visitors.

SHOPPING

Old Naples encompasses two distinct shopping areas marked by historic buildings and flowery landscaping: 5th Avenue South and 3rd Street South. Both are known for their abundance of fine-art galleries and monthly musical entertainment. Near 5th Avenue South, **Old Marine Market Place at Tin City** (✉*1200 5th Ave. S* ⊕*www.tin-city.com*), in a collection of tin-roof former boat docks along Naples Bay, has more than 30 boutiques, eateries, and souvenir shops, with everything from jewelry to T-shirts and seafood. At the classy **Village on Venetian Bay** (✉*4200 Gulf Shore Blvd.* ⊕*www.venetianvillage.com*), nearly 60 shops and restaurants have been built at water's edge. Only in South Florida can you find something like

★ **Waterside Shops** (⊠*Seagate Dr. and U.S. 41* ⊕*www.watersideshops. net*), four dozen stores plus eateries wrapped around a series of water-falls, waterways, and shaded open-air promenades, all renovated in 2006. Saks Fifth Avenue is one of the anchors. **Gattle's** (⊠*1250 3rd St. S* ☎*239/262–4791 or 800/344–4552*) stocks pricey, beautifully made linens. **Marissa Collections** (⊠*1167 3rd St. S* ☎*239/263–4333*) showcases designer women's wear. At the **Mole Hole** (⊠*1201 3rd St. S* ☎*239/262–5115*), gift items large and small, from glassware to paper-weights to knickknacks, cover every surface. **Kirsten's Boutique** (⊠*Wa-terside Shops, 5495 Tamiami Trail N* ☎*239/598–3233*) is filled with African-inspired clothing, jewelry, and decorative art. Among 5th Ave-nue South's upscale selection,

★ **Regatta** (⊠*750 5th Ave. S* ☎*239/262–3929*) sells personal and home accessories with a sense of humor and style. Naples's ladies-who-lunch often donate their year-old Armani castoffs and fine collectibles to a spate of terrific thrift shops such as **Options** (⊠*968 2nd Ave. N* ☎*239/434–7115*). The most upscale clothes sometimes go to consign-ment shops such as **New to You** (⊠*933 Creech Rd.* ☎*239/262–6869*).

Pawing through wealthy folks' high-end designer castoffs is a favor-ite Naples activity for penny-pinching vacationers and residents alike at **Lynne's Consignment** (⊠*13560 Tamiami Trail N* ☎*239/514–1410*), where you'll find a wide selection of name-brand clothes. **Encore Shop** (⊠*3105 Davis Blvd.* ☎*239/775–0032*) carries designer furniture, paintings, decorative items, and collectibles. For more bargains, hit **Prime Outlets Naples** (⊠*Rte. 951 west of Marco Island* ☎*239/545–7196 or 877/466–8853*), home to more than 40 factory outlets.

MARCO ISLAND

㉒ *20 mi south of Naples.*

High-rises line part of the shore of Marco Island, which is connected to the mainland by two bridges. Yet it retains an isolated feeling much appreciated by those who love this corner of the world. Some natural areas have been preserved, and the down-home fishing village of Good-land is resisting change. Fishing, boating, sunning, swimming, and ten-nis are the primary activities.

☾ ★ In the midst of 110,000-acre Rookery Bay National Estuarine Reserve, **Rookery Bay Environmental Learning Center** interprets the Ever-glades environment and local history with interactive models, aquari-ums, original art, a film, and classes. It's on the edge of the estuary, about five minutes east of Marco's north bridge on Collier Boulevard. A new audio tour option was initiated in 2007 for a nominal fee. In 2008, the center is scheduled to debut a million-dollar, 250-foot pedestrian suspension bridge that will span the reserve's creek from the center's second floor. ⊠*300 Tower Rd.* ☎*239/417–6310* ⊕*www.rookerybay. org* ⊒*$5* ☉*Mon.–Sat. 9–4* ☉*Closed Sat. in summer.*

☾ **Tigertail Beach** is on the southwest side of the island, 2,500 feet along both developed and undeveloped areas. Facilities include playgrounds, volleyball, a butterfly garden, free use of a beach wheelchair, a concession stand, restrooms, and showers. Sailboat and kayak rentals are available, and rangers conduct nature programs. ✉*490 Hernando Ct.* ☎*239/353–0404, 239/591–8596 for ranger programs* 🚗*Parking $5* ☉*Daily 8–sunset.* ■TIP→The Conservancy of Southwest Florida conducts free educational beach walks at Tigertail Beach every weekday from 8:30 to 9:30 AM January–mid-April.

Marco Island was once part of the ancient Calusa kingdom. The Marco Cat, a statue found in 1896 excavations, has become symbolic of the island's prehistoric significance. A replica of the original, which is kept by the Smithsonian Institution, is among displays illuminating ancient past to modern present at the **Marco Island Historical Society Museum.** Both it and its unstaffed branch location interpret local history through vignettes, video, and artifacts. ✉*140 Waterway Dr. at Bald Eagle Dr.* ☎*239/642–7468* 🎫*Free* ☉*Weekdays 9–4* ✉*Shops of Olde Marco, 168 Royal Palm Dr., 2nd fl.* ☎*239/389–6447* 🎫*Free* ☉*Daily 7–7* ⊕*www.themihs.org.*

WHERE TO STAY & EAT

$$$ ✗**Verdi's.** There's a Zen feel to this American bistro with a devoted clientele built on creative American and fusion cuisine. You might start with steamed littleneck clams in garlic butter or shrimp egg roll, then move on to entrées such as grilled swordfish, crispy duck, or the New Zealand rack of lamb. Cuban coffee crème brûlée and deep-dish apple strudel are among the tempting desserts. ✉*Sand Dollar Plaza, 241 N. Collier Blvd.* ⊕*www.verdisbistro.com* ☎*239/394–5533* ▤*D, DC, MC, V* ☉*Closed Sun.*

$$$ ✗**Café de Marco.** This cozy, cottagelike little bistro with cheery yellow walls and elegantly draped windows serves fresh local fish with original preparations, and there are always good daily specials. Try stuffed Florida lobster, sautéed frogs' legs, or the broiled seafood platter. Steaks, chicken, and a vegetarian dish are also available. ✉*244 Palm St.* ☎*239/394–6262* ⊕*www.cafedemarco.com* ▤*AE, MC, V* ☉*Closed Sun. Easter–Christmas. No lunch.*

★ $$$ ✗**Olde Marco Island Inn.** Dating from the turn of the 20th century, this inn lends grace to intimate meals. Continental style heavily influences the menu, which includes scallops Saint Jacques in a creamy mushroom sauce, Florida lobster tails (market price), pork porterhouse, and prime rib. The inn serves dinner only, plus a Sunday brunch in season. The cottagelike veranda room feels pleasantly Florida, but the more formal cranberry room is gorgeous. A piano player entertains Wednesday, Friday, and Saturday nights. ✉*100 Palm St.* ☎*239/394–3131 or 877/475–3466* ▤*AE, D, MC, V* ☉*Closed Sun. after Mother's Day through Jan. 1.*

★ $$$ ✗**Sale e Pepe.** Marco's best dining view comes also with some of its finest cuisine. The name means "salt and pepper," an indication that this palatial restaurant with patio seating overlooking the beach adheres to the basics of home-style Italian cuisine. Pasta, sausage, and sinful pastries are made right here in the kitchen. Simple dishes, such as veal ravioli, risotto, asparagus soup, sautéed salmon with cauliflower sauce, grilled lamb chops, and venison tenderloin explode with home-cooked, long-cooked flavors. For a gourmet adventure, splurge on the chef's tasting menu for $55 ($30 extra with wine pairings). Breakfast, lunch, and dinner are served here, but only the dinner is prepared by the restaurant's award-winning culinary team. ⊠*Marco Beach Ocean Resort, 480 S. Collier Blvd.* ☎*239/393–1600* ⊕*www.sale-e-pepe.com* ⊟*AE, D, DC, MC, V.*

$$–$$$ ✕**Arturo's.** This place is huge, with expansive Romanesque dining
Fodor's Choice rooms and more seating on the patio. Still it fills up year-round with
★ a strong following that appreciates the attitude of fun and serious Italian cuisine done comprehensively and traditionally. Start with the plump mussels marinara, then choose from three pages of classic Italian entrees. The stuffed pork chop, a nightly special, is a winner, as is the New York–style cheesecake. ⊠*844 Bald Eagle Dr.* ☎*239/642–0550* ⚑*Reservations essential* ⊕*www.arturosmarcoisland.com* ⊟*AE, D, DC, MC, V.*

$$–$$$ ✕**Old Marco Lodge Crab House.** Built in 1869, this waterfront restaurant is Marco's oldest landmark, and boaters often cruise in and tie up dock-side to sit on the veranda and dine on local-seafood and pasta entrées. The all-you-can-eat salad bar is a popular lunch option. For dinner, start with a wholesome bowl of vegetable crab soup. The blue crabs in garlic butter are a specialty (market price), but the menu includes all manner of shellfish, pasta, grouper, and steak. Save room for the authentic key lime pie. A game room keeps antsy kids occupied. ⊠*1 Papaya St., Goodland* ☎*239/642–7227* ⊕*www.oldmarcolodge.com* ⊟*AE, D, MC, V* ☉*Closed Sept.; Mon. and Tues. May–Aug.; and Mon. Oct.–mid-Dec.*

¢–$$ ✕**Sunset Grille.** Head to this popular spot, formerly Tide Beachfront Bar & Grill, for the best casual dining with a view of the beach and a menu of sandwiches, burgers, New Jersey–style thin-crust pizza (after 5 PM), wings, and seafood. The lively sports bar scene adds to the fun indoors; a porch accommodates alfresco diners with the most inexpensive dining view in Marco. Just beware if you leave your table: the porch has no screens and the local gulls are thieves. ⊠*Apollo Condominiums, 900 S. Collier Blvd.* ☎*239/393–8433* ⊟*AE, D, MC, V.*

¢–$ ✕**The Crazy Flamingo.** Burgers, seafood, finger foods such as conch fritters and chicken wings, and late-night hours are the draw at this neighborhood bar, where there's counter service only and seating indoors and outdoors on the sidewalk. Try the seafood steamer pot, mussels marinara, or grouper sandwich. ⊠*Marco Island Town Center, 1035 N. Collier Blvd.* ☎*239/642–9600* ⚑*Reservations not accepted* ⊟*No credit cards.*

$$$$ ⛉**Marco Beach Ocean Resort.** One of the island's first condo hotels, this
Fodor's Choice 12-story class act has one- and two-bedroom suites, done in royal blues
★ and golds. All rooms face the gulf and the property's crescent-shaped rooftop pool (on the fifth floor). The bathrooms are full of marble. The Sale e Pepe Tuscan-style restaurant wins raves and awards. Golf and tennis are nearby. Pros: top-rate dining, beach location, full amenities with a boutique feel. Cons: high-priced, a rather squeezed feel, near big, busy resort. ⊠*480 S. Collier Blvd., 34145* ☎*239/393–1400*

9

or 800/260–5089 🖨*239/393–1401* ⊕*www.marcoresort.com* 🛏*87 1-and 16 2-bedroom suites* ⅃*In-room: kitchen, dial-up, ethernet, Wi-Fi (some). In-hotel: restaurant, bars, tennis courts, pool, gym, spa, beach-front, concierge, public Internet* ▤*AE, D, DC, MC, V.*

★ **$$$$** ⊡ **Marco Island Marriott Resort, Golf Club & Spa.** A circular drive and ☾ manicured grounds front this beachfront resort made up of two 11-story towers. In 2007, it completed a massive, three-year renovation that includes a new spa. It's delightfully beachy outside, where Marco's crescent beach reaches its widest, yet the interior is elegant, with many shops and restaurants, a polished marble lobby, and large, plush rooms with good to exceptional water views. The stand-alone spa is massive and ultra-pampering. Kids love the zero-entry rock-waterfalls pool with slides. The hotel's golf course is 10 minutes away by tram. Pros: terrific beach, top-notch amenities, great spa. Cons: huge size, lots of convention business, parking across the street in uncovered lot. ⊠*400 S. Collier Blvd., 34145* ☎*239/394–2511 or 800/438–4373* 🖨*239/642–2672* ⊕*www.marcoislandmarriott.com* 🛏*727 rooms, 54 suites* ⅃*In-room: refrigerator. In-hotel: 5 restaurants, bars, golf course, tennis courts, pools, gym, spa, beachfront, water sports, bicy-cles, concierge, children's programs (ages 5–12), laundry service, Inter-net* ▤*AE, DC, MC, V.*

$$$–$$$$ ⊡ **Hilton Marco Island Beach Resort.** This 11-story beachfront hotel is smaller and more conservative than the Marriott, and it seems less busy and crowded. All rooms are spacious and have private balco-nies with unobstructed gulf views, a sitting area, a dry bar, bathrobes, and a mini-refrigerator. Pros: gorgeous wide beach, complete business services, exclusive feel. Cons: a little stuffy, expensive, business focus. ⊠*560 S. Collier Blvd., 34145* ☎*239/394–5000 or 800/394–5000* 🖨*239/394–8410* ⊕*www.hiltonmarcoisland.com* 🛏*271 rooms, 26 suites* ⅃*In-room: safe, refrigerator, ethernet, dial-up. In-hotel: 2 res-taurants, bar, tennis courts, pool, gym, beachfront, water sports, chil-dren's programs (ages 5–12), public Wi-Fi* ▤*AE, D, DC, MC, V.*

$$–$$$ ⊡ **Boat House Motel.** For a great location at a good price, check into this two-story motel. Modest but appealing with its white facade and turquoise trim, it's at the north end of Marco Island, on a canal close to the gulf. Units are light and bright and furnished with blond woods, rattan, and tropical print fabrics. All have a balcony or walled-in ter-race, and some have great water views. You can fish from the motel's dock. Pros: away from busy beach traffic, affordable, boating docks and access. Cons: no beach, hard to find, tight parking area. ⊠*1180 Edington Pl., 34145* ☎*239/642–2400 or 800/528–6345* 🖨*239/642–2435* ⊕*www.theboathousemotel.com* 🛏*20 rooms, 3 condomini-ums, 1 2-bedroom house* ⅃*In-room: kitchen (some), refrigerator, dial-up, Wi-Fi. In-hotel: pool, public Wi-Fi, some pets allowed, no elevator* ▤*MC, V.*

SPORTS & THE OUTDOORS

BIKING

Rentals are available at **Scootertown Island Bike Shop** (⊠*845 Bald Eagle Dr.* ☎*239/394–8400*) for use on the island's bike path along beachfront condos, resorts, and residential areas. Charges begin at $5 an hour, but you can also rent by the day, week, and month.

FISHING

Sunshine Tours (⊠ *Rose Marco River Marina, 951 Bald Eagle Dr.* ☎ *239/642–5415* ⊕ *www.sunshinetoursmarcoisland.com*) operates deep-sea ($95 per person for half day) and backcountry ($55 per person for three hours) fishing charters.

SAILING

Sail Kahuna (⊠ *Rose Marco River Marina, 951 Bald Eagle Dr.* ☎ *239/642–7704* ⊕ *www.sail-kahuna.com*) can help you sail into the sunset or take you out in search of dolphins and shells for $35 to $45.

THE LOWER GULF COAST ESSENTIALS

To research prices, get advice from other travelers, and book travel arrangements, visit www.fodors.com.

TRANSPORTATION

BY AIR

Southwest Florida International Airport (RSW) is served by Air Canada, AirTran Airways, American, Cape Air, Comair, Condor, Continental, Delta, Frontier, JetBlue, LTU International Airways, Midwest, Northwest, Southwest, Spirit, Sun Country, United, US Airways, USA 3000 Airlines, and WestJet. Delta Connection services Naples Municipal Airport.

Contacts Air Canada (☎ *888/247–2262*). **AirTran Airways** (☎ *800/247–8726*). **American** (☎ *800/433–7300*). **Cape Air** (☎ *800/352–0714*). **Comair** (☎ *800/221–1212*). **Condor** (☎ *800/524–6975*). **Continental** (☎ *800/525–0280*). **Delta** (☎ *800/221–1212*). **Frontier Airlines** (☎ *800/432–1359*). **JetBlue Airways** (☎ *800/538–2583*). **LTU International Airways** (☎ *866/266–5588*). **Midwest Airlines** (☎ *800/452–2022*). **Northwest** (☎ *800/225–2525*). **Southwest Airlines** (☎ *800/435–9792*). **Spirit** (☎ *800/772–7117*). **Sun Country** (☎ *800/359–6786*). **United** (☎ *800/241–6522*). **US Airways** (☎ *800/428–4322*). **USA 3000 Airlines** (☎ *877/872–3000*). **WestJet** (☎ *888/937–8538*).

Southwest Florida International Airport, which debuted an entirely new terminal in 2005 and continues to grow, is about 12 mi southwest of Fort Myers and 25 mi north of Naples. An on-demand taxi for up to three passengers to Fort Myers, Sanibel, or Captiva costs about $20 to $75, and it's about $50 to $90 to Naples. Extra people are charged at $10 each. Other transportation companies include Aaron Airport Transportation, Boca Grande Limo, Charlotte Limousine Service, and Sanibel Island Taxi. The Naples Municipal Airport is a small facility east of downtown principally serving Delta Airlines, private planes, commuter flights, and charters. Once you have arrived, call Naples Taxi.

Airport Contacts Naples Municipal Airport (☎ *239/643–0733* ⊕ *www.flynaples.com*). **Southwest Florida International Airport** (☎ *239/768–1000* ⊕ *www.fly-lcpa.com*). **Aaron Airport Transportation** (☎ *239/768–1898 or 800/998–1898*).

Boca Grande Limo (☎941/964-0455 or 800/771-7433). **Charlotte Limousine Service** (☎941/627-4494 or 800/208-6106). **Naples Airport Shuttle** (☎239/430-4747 or 888/569-2227 ⊕www.naplesairportshuttle.com). **Naples Taxi** (☎239/643-2148). **Sanibel Island Taxi** (☎239/472-4160).

BY BOAT

Key West Shuttle operates a ferry from Marco Island (from Thanksgiving through May) and Fort Myers Beach (year-round) to Key West. The cost for the round-trip (four hours each way) from Marco Island and Fort Myers Beach is $123.

Contact Key West Shuttle (☎239/394-9700 or 888/539-2628 ⊕www.keywestshuttle.com).

BY BUS

Greyhound Lines has service to Fort Myers and Naples. LeeTran serves most of the Fort Myers area. In Naples and Marco Island, Collier Area Transit (CAT) runs regular routes.

Contacts Greyhound Lines (☎800/231-2222 ✉2250 Peck St., Fort Myers ☎239/334-1011 ✉2669 Davis Blvd., Naples ☎239/774-5660 ✉26505 N. Jones Loop Rd., Punta Gorda ☎941/875-2781 ✉900 Kings Hwy., Port Charlotte ☎941/627-5836). **LeeTran** (☎239/275-8726 ⊕www.rideleetran.com). **Collier Area Transit (CAT)** (☎239/596-7777 ⊕www.colliergov.net).

BY CAR

Interstate 75 spans the region from north to south. Once you cross the Georgia border into Florida, it's about six hours to Fort Myers and another half hour to Naples. Alligator Alley, a section of Interstate 75, is a toll road ($2 to enter) that runs from Fort Lauderdale through the Everglades to Naples. The trip takes about three hours. U.S. 41 also runs the length of the region. Also known as the Tamiami Trail, U.S. 41 goes through downtown Fort Myers and Naples and is also called Cleveland Avenue in the former and 9th Street in the latter. McGregor Boulevard (Route 867) and Summerlin Road (Route 869), Fort Myers's main north–south city streets, head toward Sanibel and Captiva islands. San Carlos Boulevard runs southwest from Summerlin Road to Fort Myers Beach, and Pine Island–Bayshore Road (Route 78) leads from North Fort Myers through northern Cape Coral onto Pine Island. In Naples, east–west trunks exiting off Interstate 75 include, from north to south, the Immokalee Road (Route 846) at the north edge of town, Pine Ridge Road (Route 896), and Route 951, which takes you also to Marco Island.

CAR RENTAL

Contacts Alamo (☎800/462-5266). **Avis** (☎800/331-1212). **Budget** (☎800/527-7000). **Hertz** (☎800/654-3131). **National** (☎800/227-7368).

CONTACTS & RESOURCES

EMERGENCIES
Ambulance or Police **Emergencies** (☎ *911*).

VISITOR INFORMATION
The following are open to the public weekdays 9 to 5: Charlotte County Visitor's Bureau, Charlotte County Chamber of Commerce, and Marco Island Area Chamber of Commerce. In season, the Marco Chamber also opens Saturday 10 to 3. The Naples Area Chamber of Commerce also opens Saturday 9 to 5. The Sanibel & Captiva Islands Chamber of Commerce stays open weekdays 9 to 6 and weekends 9 to 5.

Contacts **Charlotte County Visitor's Bureau** (⊠ *18501 Murdock Circle, Suite 502, Port Charlotte 33948* ☎ *941/743–1900* ⊕ *www.pureflorida.com*). **Charlotte County Chamber of Commerce** (⊠ *2702 Tamiami Trail, Port Charlotte 33952* ☎ *941/627–2222* ⊠ *326 W. Marion Ave., Suite 112, Punta Gorda 33950* ☎ *941/639–2222* ⊕ *www.charlottecountychamber.org*). **Lee County Visitor & Convention Bureau** (⊠ *12800 University Dr., Suite 550, Fort Myers 33907* ☎ *239/338–3500 or 800/237–6444* ⊕ *www.fortmyers-sanibel.com*). **Marco Island Area Chamber of Commerce** (⊠ *1102 N. Collier Blvd., Marco Island 34145* ☎ *239/394–7549 or 800/788–6272* ⊕ *www.marcoislandchamber.org*). **Naples, Marco Island, Everglades Convention and Visitors Bureau** (⊠ *3050 N. Horseshoe Dr., #218, Naples 34104* ☎ *239/403–2425* ⊕ *www.paradisecoast. com*). **Sanibel & Captiva Islands Chamber of Commerce** (⊠ *1159 Causeway Rd., Sanibel 33957* ☎ *239/472–1080* ⊕ *www.sanibel-captiva.org*).

9

The Tampa Bay Area

WORD OF MOUTH

"State park beaches are always less crowded than public beaches. In the Clearwater area, Caladesi Island off Dunedin is a nice beach, well maintained, completely noncommercial, and family friendly. There are just a few concessions (food and drink) and the carnival atmosphere that prevails in Clearwater, St. Pete, and Panama City is conspicuously absent."

—kswl

"Depending on when you are here, baseball spring training may be in full swing. St. Pete, Clearwater, Tampa, and Dunedin all have teams. If it's not on the weekend, you may be able to just walk up and get tickets."

—champ21e

Updated
by Jim and
Cynthia
Tunstall

GROWTH HAS CHANGED MOST CORNERS of Florida, and the Tampa Bay area is no exception, but planning and an abundance of preserves have shielded most of it from the overdevelopment that saturates much of the Atlantic Coast. Granted, this is one of the state's largest metro areas, but it is less fast-lane than Miami. Whereas Tampa has Florida's third-busiest airport and a vibrant business community, St. Petersburg, Clearwater, and Sarasota have exceptional beaches, and the entire bay area has superior hotels and resorts that make this an excellent place to spend a week or a lifetime. Native Americans were the sole inhabitants of the region for many years. (Some say *Tampa* means "sticks of fire" in the language of the ancient Calusa Indians.) Spanish explorers Juan Ponce de León, Pánfilo de Narváez, and Hernando de Soto passed through in the mid-1500s, and the U.S. Army and civilian settlers arrived in 1824. The Spanish-American War was very good to Tampa, enabling industrialist Henry Plant to create an economic momentum that was sustained into the third millennium. A military presence remains in Tampa at MacDill Air Force Base, the U.S. Operations Command.

TOP 5
Browsing through the shops of Ybor City.
Going on a docent-led tour of the Salvador Dalí Museum in St. Petersburg.
Feasting on smoked mackerel, German potato salad, and a cold one at Ted Peters in South Pasadena.
Spending the afternoon on the white-sand beach at Siesta Key in Sarasota—then staying for sunset.
Touring the impressive baroque and Renaissance collection at the FSU Ringling Center for the Cultural Arts,

Today the region offers equal elements of old and new Florida. Terrain ranges from the pine-dotted northern reaches to the coast's white-sand beaches and barrier islands. Tampa is a full-fledged city, with a high-rise skyline and highways jammed with traffic. Across the bay lies the peninsula that contains Clearwater and St. Petersburg. The compact St. Petersburg downtown, which has interesting restaurants, shops, and museums, is on the southeast side of the peninsula, facing Tampa. Inland is largely classic American suburbia. The peninsula's western periphery is rimmed by barrier islands with beaches, quiet parks, and little, laid-back beach towns. To the north are communities that celebrate their ethnic heritage—such as Tarpon Springs, settled by Greek sponge divers—and, farther north, land dotted with crystal-clear rivers, springs, and nature preserves. To the south lie resort towns, including Sarasota, which, like the Pinellas County beaches, fill up in winter with snowbirds escaping the cold.

10

EXPLORING THE TAMPA BAY AREA

Whether you feel like walking on white-sand beaches, watching sponge divers, or wandering through upscale shopping districts, there's something to your liking in the diverse Tampa Bay Area. Bright, modern

Tampa is the area's commercial center. Peninsular St. Petersburg lies across the bay. Tarpon Springs, to the northwest, is still Greek in flavor. The Nature Coast, to the north, is quite rural, with extensive preserves. To the south are Bradenton, which has several museums and beaches; Sarasota, a sophisticated resort town; and small, canal-crossed Venice.

ABOUT THE RESTAURANTS
Fresh gulf seafood is plentiful, and raw bars serving oysters, clams, and mussels are everywhere. Tampa's many Cuban and Spanish restaurants serve fresh seafood, perhaps in spicy paella, along with black beans and rice. Tarpon Springs adds hearty helpings of classic Greek specialties. In Sarasota the emphasis is on ritzier dining, but many restaurants offer extra-cheap early-bird menus for seatings before 6 PM.

ABOUT THE HOTELS
Many convention hotels in the Tampa Bay area double as family-friendly resorts—taking advantage of nearby beaches, marinas, spas, tennis courts, and golf links. However, unlike Orlando and some other parts of Florida, the area has been bustling for more than a century, and its accommodations often reflect a sense of its history. You'll find a turn-of-the-20th-century beachfront resort where Zelda and F. Scott Fitzgerald stayed, a massive all-wood building from the 1920s, plenty of Art Deco, and throwbacks to the Spanish-style villas of yore. But one thing they all have in common is a certain Gulf Coast charm.

WHAT IT COSTS					
	¢	$	$$	$$$	$$$$
RESTAURANTS	under $10	$10–$15	$15–$20	$20–$30	over $30
HOTELS	under $80	$80–$100	$100–$140	$140–$220	over $220

Restaurant prices are per person for a main course at dinner. Hotel prices are for a standard double room, excluding 6% sales tax (more in some counties) and 1%–4% tourist tax.

TIMING
Winter and spring are high season, and the level of activity is double what it is in the off-season. In summer there are huge afternoon thunderstorms, and temperatures hover around 90°F during the day. Luckily the mercury drops to the mid-70s at night, and beach towns have a consistent on-shore breeze that starts just before sundown, which enabled civilization to survive here before air-conditioning was invented.

NORTH & WEST AROUND TAMPA BAY

The core of the northern bay comprises the cities of Tampa, St. Petersburg, and Clearwater. A semitropical climate and access to the gulf make Tampa an ideal port for the cruise industry. The waters around Clearwater and St. Petersburg are often filled with pleasure and commercial craft, including dozens of boats with day trips and night trips featuring what purveyors euphemistically call "Las Vegas action":

gambling in international waters. It's fitting that an area with a thriving international port should also be populated by a wealth of nationalities. The center of the Cuban community is the east Tampa enclave of Ybor City, whereas north of Clearwater, in Dunedin, the heritage is Scottish. North of Dunedin, Tarpon Springs has supported a large Greek population for decades and is the largest producer of natural sponges in the world. Inland, to the east and north of Tampa, it's all suburban sprawl, freeways, shopping malls, and—the main draw—Busch Gardens.

TAMPA

84 mi southwest of Orlando.

The west coast's business and commercial hub, Tampa has numerous high-rises and heavy traffic. Amid the bustle is a concentration of restaurants, nightlife, stores, and cultural events.

❶ ★ ☾ Eels, sharks, and stingrays are part of the fun, but the **Florida Aquarium** is much more than a giant fishbowl. This is a dazzling architectural landmark with an 83-foot-high multitier glass dome and 200,000 square feet of air-conditioned exhibit space. It has more than 10,000 aquatic plants, and animals representing species native to Florida and the rest of the world. The major exhibit areas reflect the diversity of Florida's natural habitats—Wetlands, Bays and Beaches, and Coral Reef. Creature-specific exhibits are the No Bone Zone (lovable invertebrates) and Sea Hunt, with predators ranging from sharks to exotic lion fish. The aquarium's most impressive single exhibit is the Coral Reef, in a 500,000-gallon tank ringed with viewing windows, including an awesome 43-foot-wide panoramic opening. Part of the tank is a walkable tunnel, almost giving the illusion of venturing into underwater depths. There you see a thicket of elkhorn coral teeming with tropical fish. A dark cave reveals sea life you would normally see only on night dives. For $75, visitors 6 and up can swim with fish, and for $150 certified divers 15 and up can dive with sharks. If you have two hours, try *Bay Spirit,* Wild Dolphin Ecotour, which takes up to 49 passengers onto Tampa's bay in a 64-foot catamaran for an up-close look at bottlenose dolphins and other wildlife. The outdoor Explore-a-Shore exhibit, which packs appeal for younger kids, is an aquatic playground with a waterslide, water jet sprays, and a climbable replica pirate ship. ⊠ *701 Channelside Dr., Downtown* ☎ *813/273–4000* ⊕ *www.flaquarium.org* ᗌ *Aquarium $17.95, Bay Spirit, Wild Dolphin Ecotour $19.95; parking $5* ☾ *Daily 9:30–5.*

Downtown Tampa's **Riverwalk** connects some developed-area waterside entities such as the Marriott Waterside, the Channelside shopping and entertainment complex, and the Florida Aquarium. **Cotanchobee Fort Brooke Park** includes a wall of bronze plaques telling the story of Tampa's Seminole War fort from the Seminole perspective. The landscaped park is 6 acres and extends along the Garrison cruise-ship channel and along the Hillsborough River downtown. The walkway is being expanded as waterside development continues.

10

Adventure Island **6**

Bayside Tours .. **19**

BayWalk **14**

Busch Gardens ..**5**

Cedar Key
Historical Society
Museum **38**

Children's Museum
of Tampa **9**

Clearwater
Beach **27**

Clearwater Marine
Aquarium **26**

Crystal River
Wildlife Refuge **37**

Dunedin **28**

Egmont Key **23**

Florida Aquarium **1**

Florida Holocaust
Museum **12**

Florida
Int'l Museum ... **15**

Fort De Soto
Park **20**

Friendship
TrailBridge **10**

Great
Explorations ... **18**

Homosassa
Springs Wildlife
State Park **35**

Howard Park
Beach **33**

Konger
Aquarium **29**

Lowry Park Zoo ..**4**

Museum of
Fine Arts **13**

Museum of Science
and Industry **7**

Pass-A-Grille
Beach **21**

St. Nicholas
Cathedral **30**

St. Petersburg
Museum of
History **16**

Salvador Dalí
Museum **17**

Sand Key Park . **25**

Seminole Hard
Rock Hotel &
Casino **8**

Sponge Factory **31**

Suncoast Seabird
Sanctuary **24**

Sunken Gardens **11**

Sunset Beach .. **32**

Tampa Museum
of Art **3**

Treasure Island **22**

Weeki Wachee **34**

Ybor City **2**

Yulee Sugar Mill
State Park **36**

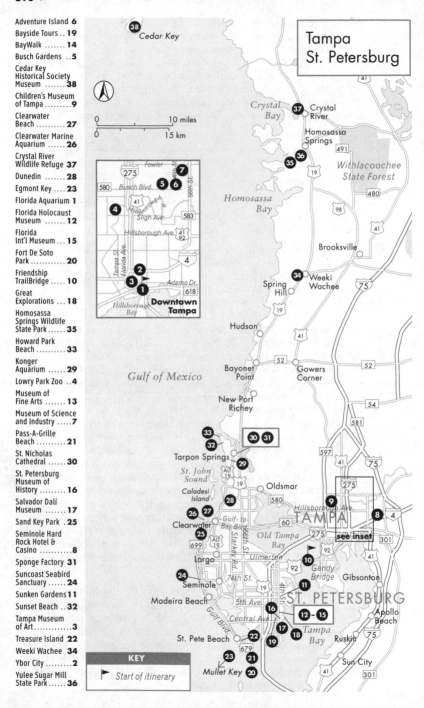

Tampa
St. Petersburg

GREAT ITINERARIES

Numbers in the text correspond to numbers in the margin and on the Tampa/St. Petersburg and Bradenton/Sarasota maps.

3 DAYS

Florida Aquarium ❶ ⚐ and **Busch Gardens ❺**, 8 mi northeast of ☷ **Tampa ❶–❼**, are probably the two most popular attractions in the area. You need a half day for the aquarium and a full day for Busch Gardens. Then it's on to ☷ **Sarasota ❸❾–❺❷**, with the **FSU Ringling Center for the Cultural Arts ❹❸** and **Mote Marine Aquarium ❹❽**.

4 DAYS

Start in ☷ **Tampa ❶–❼** ⚐ with a half day at the **Florida Aquarium ❶**. Then it's just a short drive to **Ybor City ❷**. Rest your feet over lunch before an hour or two of strolling through the shops. **Busch Gardens ❺** takes your whole second day. Start your third day in downtown St. Petersburg at the **Florida International Museum ❶❺**. Catch lunch in the **BayWalk ❶❹** dining and entertainment complex just across the street. A few blocks east is the **Florida Holocaust Museum ❶❷**. On Day 4, choose between the beach or the streets of Sarasota. One of the best spots for a day at the beach is pristine **Fort De Soto Park ❷⓪**, a perfect place to picnic or watch the sun set over the Gulf of Mexico. Spend your last day in **Sarasota ❸❾– ❺❷**, seeing the museums at the **FSU Ringling Center for the Cultural Arts ❹❸** and at **Mote Marine Aquarium ❹❽**.

10 DAYS

With this much time, linger three days in ☷ **St. Petersburg ❶❷–❶❺** ⚐. Catch a meal or two and do some shopping at **BayWalk ❶❹**, which is across the street from the **Florida International Muse ❶❺**, in turn a short walk from the **Florida Holocaust Museum ❶❷** and a five-minute drive from the **Salvador Dalí Museum ❶❼**. You could easily spend a full day in downtown **Tampa ❶–❼**. Start the morning with the spectacular **Florida Aquarium ❶**. Then head to **Ybor City ❷** for a bit of touring, shopping, and lunch. End the day with the **Tampa Museum of Art ❸** and the Channelside dining and entertainment district for dinner. The next three attractions, northeast of Tampa, are 45–60 minutes by car from St. Petersburg. Spend a day at **Busch Gardens ❺**. If you are into waterslides, set aside another day for **Adventure Island ❻**, Busch Gardens' water-park cousin. Spend a day around **Tarpon Springs ❸⓪–❸❶**, the self-described Sponge Capital of the World. Consider Caladesi Island State Park or nearby Honeymoon Island State Park, outside **Dunedin ❷❽**, for a day at the beach.

☷ **Sarasota ❹❹–❺❷** is a convenient base for the second part of your stay. Drive up to **Bradenton ❸❾–❹❷** to take in its sights and beaches for a day. In Sarasota, allow about four hours to cover the museums at the **FSU Ringling Center for the Cultural Arts ❹❸** and **Sarasota Jungle Gardens ❹❺**. In the afternoon you might drive to St. Armands Circle on Lido Key to see shops and **Mote Marine Aquarium ❹❽**. On another day explore the **Marie Selby Botanical Gardens ❹❼** and downtown Sarasota. **Venice ❺❷** makes an enjoyable half- or full-day trip.

10

② Lively **Ybor City,** Tampa's Latin quarter, is one of only four National
Fodor'sChoice Historic Landmark districts in Florida. It has antique-brick streets and
★ wrought-iron balconies. Cubans brought their cigar-making industry
to Ybor (pronounced *ee*-bore) City in 1886, and the smell of cigars—
hand-rolled by Cuban immigrants—still wafts through the heart of this
east Tampa area, along with the strong aroma of roasting coffee. These
days the neighborhood is emerging as Tampa's hot spot, as empty cigar
factories and historic social clubs are transformed into trendy boutiques, art galleries, restaurants, and nightclubs that are a microcosm
of Miami's sizzling South Beach. Take a stroll past the ornately tiled
Columbia restaurant and the stores lining 7th Avenue. Guided walking
tours of the area ($6) enable you to see artisans hand-roll cigars follow-
ing time-honored methods. Step back into the past at **Centennial Park**
(⊠*8th Ave. and 18th St.*), which re-creates a period streetscape and
hosts the Fresh Market every Saturday. Ybor City's destination within a
destination is the dining and entertainment palace **Centro Ybor** (⊠*1600
E. 7th Ave.*). It has shops, trendy bars and restaurants, a 20-screen
movie theater, and GameWorks, an interactive playground developed
by Steven Spielberg. The **Ybor City Museum State Park** provides a look
at the history of the cigar industry. Admission includes a tour of La
Casita, one of the shotgun houses occupied by cigar workers and their
families in the late 1890s. ⊠*1818 E. 9th Ave., between Nuccio Pkwy.
and 22nd St., from 7th to 9th Ave.* ☏*813/247–6323* ⊕*www.ybormu-
seum.org* ☞*$3* ⊙*Daily 9–5; walking tours Sat. 10:30, $6.*

③ The 35,000-square-foot **Tampa Museum of Art** has an impressive permanent collection of Greek and Roman antiquities and 20th- to
21st-century sculpture, along with five galleries that host traveling
exhibits, which range from contemporary to classical. ⊠*600 N.
Ashley Dr., Downtown* ☏*813/274–8130* ⊕*www.tampagov.net/
dept%5FMuseum* ☞*$8* ⊙*Tues.–Sat. 10–5, Sun. 11–5; open until 8
3rd Thurs. of month.*

⑨ The **Children's Museum of Tampa** is a great place for families to spend a
☺ half day exploring 16 pint-size buildings where youngsters can cash a
check, play doctor, buy a house or groceries, pedal a bike or scooter
through "town," explore a firehouse, and more. There are Under the
Sea and By the Seashore exhibits for preschoolers, free crafts and activity nights the first Friday of the month, and reading, art, and stamp programs on weekends. ⊠*7550 N. Blvd., west of I–275 Sligh Ave. Exit,
Central Tampa* ☏*813/935–8441* ⊕*www.flachildrensmuseum.com*
☞*$5* ⊙*Tues.–Thurs. 9:30–2:30, Fri. and Sat. 9:30–5, Sun. noon–5.*

④ *Child* magazine in 2005 rated the 56-acre **Lowry Park Zoo** the number
☺ one kids' zoo in the United States because of park safety and its exotic
creatures, which live in lush, natural habitats. Visit the zoo's newest
exhibit area, Safari Africa, to see Tamani, a young African elephant
(born in October 2005) and four adult elephants. Feed a giraffe, ride a
camel, and experience a "white rhino encounter." Check out the Asian
Domain, with tigers, Persian leopards, and Indian rhinos, and Primate
World, including chimpanzees and orangutans. Spot some fancy flying in the free-flight bird aviary, see red-tailed hawks and other rap-

tors in the Birds of Prey Center, and come face-to-face with alligators, panthers, bears, and red wolves at the Florida Wildlife Center. Gentle goats and kangaroos populate the Wallaroo Station children's zoo, and gentle creatures of another kind headline at the Manatee Aquatic Center. Manatees, turtles, hawks, and herons also are the highlights of the Hillsborough River Odyssey Ecotour ($14, Wed.–Sun.). This zoo is particularly attuned to night events: parties range from food and beer tastings for adults to chaperoned sleepovers for children ages six and up. The zoo also has water-play areas, rides, and restaurants. ⊠ *1101 W. Sligh Ave., Central Tampa* ☎ *813/935–8552* ⊕ *www.low-ryparkzoo.com* ⊠ *$14.95* ☉ *Daily 9:30–5.*

❺ With five roller coasters, **Busch Gardens** is paradise for thrill-ride jockeys. But this state-of-the-art theme park also is a world-class zoo with more than 2,000 animals and a live entertainment venue that provides a full day (or more) of entertainment for the whole family. The 335-acre adventure park's habitats offer views of some of the world's most endangered and exotic animals. You can experience up-close animal encounters on the **Serengeti Plain,** a 65-acre free-roaming habitat that is home to reticulated giraffe, Grevy's zebras, white rhinos, bongo, eland, impala, and more. **Myombe Reserve: The Great Ape Domain** allows you to view lowland gorillas and chimpanzees in a lush, tropical-rain-forest environment. **Edge of Africa** is an intense walking tour of lions, hippos, and hyenas. The Broadway-style theater extravaganza **KaTonga: Tales from the Jungle** is a 35-minute celebration of animal folklore, and the hapless Leslie Nielsen leads a bumbling band of buccaneers on the big screen in *Pirates 4-D.*

SheiKra, North America's first dive coaster, opened in mid-2005. On the wings of an African hawk, riders fly through a three-minute journey 200 feet up, then (gulp!) plunge 90 degrees straight down at 70 mi per hour. The park's coaster lineup also includes steel giants **Kumba** and **Montu,** a double wooden roller coaster called **Gwazi,** and **Cheetah Chase**—a five-story family coaster full of hairpin turns and breathtaking dips. The off-road safari **Rhino Rally** brings you face-to-face with elephants, white rhinos, and Nile crocodiles. (When it's running properly, which isn't always the case, a flash flood adds a river-raft element.) **Land of the Dragons** is a 4-acre playland for children that has rides, special shows, play areas, and a three-story tree house with towers and stairways. For those 21 years or older, the **Hospitality House** in the Bird Gardens offers complimentary Anheuser-Busch products and the **Budweiser Beer School** hosts a 30-minute lesson in the art, science, and tradition of beer brewing. Allow six to eight hours to experience Busch Gardens. ⊠ *3000 E. Busch Blvd., 8 mi northeast of downtown Tampa and 2 mi east of I–275 Exit 50, Central Tampa* ☎ *813/987–5082 or 888/800–5447* ⊕ *www.buschgardens.com* ⊠ *$61.95; parking $9* ☉ *Daily 10–6; later in summer during special events.*

❻ Ride-names like Tampa Typhoon, Gulf Scream, and Key West Rapids hint to the wild watery fun awaiting at **Adventure Island,** a corporate cousin of Busch Gardens that features waterslides and artificial wave pools in a 30-acre package. The park's newest thrill ride, Riptide, is

10

Fodor's Choice
★

an adventure enabling you to race three other riders on a sliding mat through twisting tubes and hairpin turns. Planners of this water park took the younger kids into account, with offerings such as Fabian's Funport, which has a scaled-down wave pool and interactive water gym. Along with a volleyball complex and a surf pool, there are cafés, snack bars, picnic and sunbathing areas, and changing rooms. ⊠ *1001 Malcolm McKinley Dr., less than 1 mi north of Busch Gardens, Central Tampa* ☎ *813/987–5660 or 888/800–5447* ⊕ *www.adventureisland. com* ⊿ *$34.95; parking $5* ⊙ *Mid-Mar.–late Oct., daily 10–5.*

❼ The **Museum of Science and Industry (MOSI)** is a fun and stimulating sci-
Ⅽ entific playground, though at times several exhibits aren't working properly. When it's hitting on all cylinders, you learn about Florida weather, anatomy, flight, and space by seeing *and* by doing. At the Gulf Coast Hurricane Exhibit, experience what a hurricane and its 74-mph winds feel like. The BioWorks Butterfly Garden is a 6,400-square-foot engineered ecosystem project that demonstrates how wet-lands can clean water plus serve as a home for butterflies. The 100-seat Saunders Planetarium—Tampa's only planetarium—has afternoon and evening shows, one of them a trek through the universe. For adven-turous spirits, there's a high-wire bicycle ride 30 feet above the floor. There's also an impressive IMAX theater, where films are projected on a hemispherical 82-foot dome. Kids in Charge, a 40,000-square-foot science center with interactive exhibits aimed at the 12-and-under set, opened in 2005, complete with a flight simulator ($3.50 additional charge). Disasterville, an exhibit about—you guessed it—natural disas-ters, opened in mid-2006, giving visitors a chance to walk through a simulated town hit by natural disasters. ⊠ *4801 E. Fowler Ave., 1 mi north of Busch Gardens, Northeast Tampa* ☎ *813/987–6000 or 800/995–6674* ⊕ *www.mosi.org* ⊿ *$19.95* ⊙ *Daily 9–5.*

❽ If you've brought your body to Tampa but your heart's in Vegas, satisfy that urge to hang around a poker table at 4 AM at the **Seminole Hard Rock Hotel & Casino.** The casino has poker tables and video gaming machines, and Las Vegas–style level-three slot machines opened in mid-2006. The casino lounge serves drinks 24 hours a day. Floyd's restaurant has din-ner and nightlife. ⊠ *5223 N. Orient Rd., off I–4 at N. Orient Rd. Exit* ☎ *813/627–7625 or 866/762–5463* ⊕ *www.seminolehardrock.com* ⊿ *Free* ⊙ *Daily 24 hrs.*

WHERE TO STAY & EAT

★ $$$–$$$$ ✕ **Armani's.** Business and downtown professionals flock to this northern-Italian-style rooftop restaurant for two reasons: good service and great views of the bay, city, and, on clear days, sunsets along the gulf. Crowd pleasers include veal tenderloin with a crabmeat and lobster gratin bonnet that comes with mustard sauce on the side. Another specialty is rack of lamb with Gorgonzola potatoes. For those with a gamier hankering, there's pan-seared boar with apple-parsnip puree. ⊠ *Grand Hyatt Tampa Bay, 2900 Bayport Dr., Airport Area* ☎ *813/207–6800* ⊕ *www.armanisrestaurant.com* ⊟ *AE, D, DC, MC, V* ⊙ *Closed Sun. No lunch.*

$$$–$$$$ ✕**Bern's Steak House.** For those who love meat, this is one of Florida's fin-
Fodor'sChoice est steak houses, an elegant eatery with the air of an exclusive club. Fine
★ mahogany paneling and ornate chandeliers define the legendary Bern's,
where owner David Laxer ages his own beef, grows his own organic
vegetables, roasts his own coffee, and maintains his own saltwater fish
tanks. Cuts of topmost beef are sold by weight and thickness. There's
a 60-ounce, 3-inch porterhouse that's big enough to feed your pride (of
lions). The wine list includes some 6,500 selections (with 1,800 dessert
wines). After dinner, tour the kitchen and wine cellar before having
dessert upstairs in a cozy booth. ⊠*1208 S. Howard Ave., Hyde Park*
☎*813/251–2421 or 800/282–1547* ⊕*www.bernssteakhouse.com*
⚲*Reservations essential* ⊟*AE, D, MC, V* ⊘*No lunch.*

$$–$$$$ ✕**Castaway.** The specialty of this midprice casual restaurant with bay
views is local seafood—grilled, broiled, or blackened—but the menu
also includes grilled steaks, such as New York strip, and several pasta
dishes, making it popular with mainstream diners, including a lot of
locals. The menu changes frequently, but favorites have included Can-
tonese-style shrimp with snow peas, baby corn, and shiitake mushrooms. Dine inside or on the expansive deck, popular for lunch and
at sunset. The jets dipping down over the bay on their final approach
are just far enough away to avoid a noise problem. ⊠*7720 Courtney
Campbell Causeway, east side, 1 mi west of Tampa International Airport, Airport Area* ☎*813/281–0770* ⊕*www.castawayrestaurant.com*
⊟*AE, D, DC, MC, V.*

★ **$$–$$$** ✕**Mise en Place.** Chef Marty Blitz and his wife, Maryann, have delighted
downtown diners for years with an inventive, ever-changing menu that
has made this one of Tampa's most celebrated restaurants. How to
decide between the creole-grilled salmon delivered with collard greens
and smoked-cheddar bacon grits (pronounced gree-its by true South-
erners) and the ostrich tenderloin crusted with pumpkinseed and
accompanied by maple orange-roasted acorn squash? Don't. Come
twice. There's also a rotating tasting menu. ⊠*442 W. Kennedy Blvd.,
entrance off Grand Central Pl., Central Tampa* ☎*813/254–5373*
⊕*www.miseonline.com* ⊟*AE, D, DC, MC, V* ⊘*Closed Sun. and
Mon. No lunch Sat.*

$$–$$$ ✕**Roy's.** Tampa Bay has a taste for trendy national restaurant names, so
it's no surprise that Roy's, the Hawaiian fusion-style restaurant chain
that has swept the United States in the past decade, has an outpost here
that attracts business and leisure travelers. Chef Roy Yamaguchi flies in
fresh ingredients daily from around the Pacific. The menu changes daily,
but typical dishes include roasted macadamia-nut-crusted mahimahi
with lobster-essence sauce, blackened island ahi tuna with spicy soy-
mustard sauce, and tender braised short-rib beef with natural or butter
sauce. Dessert choices include a melting chocolate soufflé and a fresh-
fruit cobbler. ⊠*4342 Boy Scout Blvd., Airport Area* ☎*813/873–7697*
⊕*www.roysrestaurant.com* ⊟*AE, D, DC, MC, V.*

$–$$$ ✕**Bernini.** Named for the 17th-century Italian baroque sculptor Giovanni
Bernini, this trendy restaurant is something of a gallery for copies of his
works. In the former Bank of Ybor City building, it has a classy look
and such fare as cioppino (clams, mussels, scallops, crab, shrimp, and

10

fish swimming in marinara broth), grilled salmon with basil pesto, and veal lasagna. The Caesar pizza (basically topped with Caesar salad) is among the best of the wood-fired pizzas. ⊠*1702 E. 7th Ave., Ybor City* ☎*813/248–0099* ⊕*www.berniniofybor.com* ⊟*AE, D, DC, MC, V* ⊙*No lunch weekends.*

$–$$$ ✕**Columbia.** Make a date for some of the best Latin cuisine in Tampa.
Fodor'sChoice   A fixture since 1905, this magnificent structure with an old-world air,
★   spacious dining rooms, and a sunny courtyard takes up an entire city block and seems to feed the entire city—locals as well as travelers—throughout the week, but especially on weekends. The paella, bursting with seafood, chicken, and pork, arguably is the best in Florida, and the 1905 salad—with ham, olives, cheese, and garlic—is legendary. The menu has Cuban classics such as *boliche criollo* (tender eye of round stuffed with chorizo sausage), *ropa vieja* (shredded beef with onions, peppers, and tomatoes) and *arroz con pollo* (chicken with yellow rice). Don't miss the flamenco dancing show (Monday–Saturday, $6 cover). Buy hand-rolled cigars in the bar. ⊠*2117 E. 7th Ave., Ybor City* ☎*813/248–4961* ⊕*www.columbiarestaurant.com/ybor.asp* ⊟*AE, D, DC, MC, V.*

¢–$$$ ✕**Café Dufrain.** Lassie can tag along if you dine on the patio at dog-friendly Café Dufrain, a riverside eatery popular with an upscale crowd. For a little something different, try the Brazilian *moquecca* (a stew made of fish, shrimp, lobsters, and clams in lemon and coconut milk) or the chili-marinated short ribs with goat-cheese smashed potatoes and grilled asparagus. Seal the deal with the homemade flan topped with vanilla caramel. ⊠*707 Harbour Post Dr., Downtown* ☎*813/275–9701* ⊕*www.cafedufrain.com* ⊟*AE, D, MC, V.*

¢–$$ ✕**Byblos Cafe.** Nothing flashy here—just good grub and a friendly crowd, and if you come Thursday through Saturday evenings, you can watch bellies (other than your own) dance. The mainly Greek and Lebanese cuisine adds to the city's diversity with dishes such as grape leaves stuffed with beef, rice, onions, and tomatoes; herb- and spice-marinated lamb chops; and spicy sausage kabobs. ⊠*2832 S. MacDill Ave., South Tampa* ☎*813/805–7977* ⊟*AE, MC, V.*

¢–$$ ✕**Estela's Mexican Restaurant.** In the tiny business district of Davis Islands, a sidewalk café gives this otherwise nondescript storefront a spark of vibrancy. It's the perfect place to munch on nachos and drink imported Mexican beer on a spring afternoon. The standard Tex-Mex cuisine is nothing special, so go for chicken soup (with avocado and a touch of cilantro) or chili Colorado steak (rib-eye steak with rice, beans, and guacamole salad). Warning: Like all eateries in this neighborhood, Estela's fills up fast with the weekday lunch crowd. ⊠*209 E. Davis Blvd., 1½ mi across bridge from downtown Tampa, Davis Island* ☎*813/251–0558* ⊕*www.estelas.com* ⊟*AE, MC, V.*

¢–$$ ✕**Kojak's House of Ribs.** Family-run since its doors opened in 1978, this casual eatery has been voted a Tampa favorite year after year in local polls. Day and night the three indoor dining rooms and outdoor dining terrace are crowded with hungry patrons digging into tender barbecued ribs. There's chicken on the menu, too, and heaping sides of coleslaw, potato salad, parsley potatoes, and corn on the cob. ⊠*2808 Gandy*

Blvd., South Tampa ☎*813/837–3774* 🌐*www.kojaksbbq.com* ▭*AE, D, MC, V* ⏲*Closed Mon.*

¢–$$ ✕ **Stumps Supper Club.** The menu is as lively as the entertainment at this downtown Tampa restaurant-nightclub combo. The food is a big draw: Southern cooking (Brunswick stew, barbecued pork chops, country-fried steak and, of course, cornbread, cheese grits, black-eyed peas, and collard greens). Decorated in flea-market chic, it pokes fun at Southern food while taking it quite seriously. Friday and Saturday nights after 9 you'll bump into Jimmy James & The Velvet Explosion, a six-piece band that relives Elvis, Abba, Motown, and KC & the Sunshine Band. ✉*615 Channelside Dr., Downtown* ☎*813/226–2261* 🌐*www.stumpssupperclub.com* ▭*AE, D, DC, MC, V* ⏲*No lunch weekdays.*

¢–$ ✕ **Newk's Lighthouse Cafe.** A popular choice with the downtown work crowd, Newk's has the feel of a neighborhood bar, though a sea-and-sky mural gives the illusion of waterfront dining. Staples are burgers and fish-house fare. Grouper sandwiches come five different ways; notable are the crunchy version, with a cornflake-and-almond coating, and the spicy Buffalo-style. The café has indoor and outdoor seating. ✉*514 Channelside Dr., Downtown* ☎*813/307–6395* ▭*AE, D, MC, V* ⏲*Closed Mon.*

¢ ✕ **Mel's Hot Dogs.** Just look for the red wienermobile on the north side of the highway—just east of Busch Gardens—and you'll find a hot-diggity-doggery that's heaven for tube-steak fans. It's a roll-up-your-sleeves place that's very popular with the workday crowd as well as vacationers wanting to step outside the theme park for a bite. You can order a traditional dog, but we recommend something with a little more pizzazz, such as a bacon-cheddar Reuben-style bow-wow on a poppy-seed bun. To avoid lunch crowds, arrive before 11:30 or after 1:30. ✉*Central Tampa, 4136 E. Busch Blvd., Tampa* ☎*813/985–8000* ⏲Closed *Sun.*

$$$$ 🏨 **Tampa Marriott Waterside.** Across from the Tampa Convention Center, this downtown hotel was built for conventioneers but is also convenient to tourist spots such as the Florida Aquarium, the St. Pete Times Forum, and shopping and entertainment districts Channelside, Hyde Park, and Ybor City. At least half the rooms and most of the suites overlook the channel to Tampa Bay; the bay itself is visible from the higher floors of the 27-story hotel. The lobby coffee bar overlooks the water. Il Terrazzo is the hotel's formal, Italian dining room. Pros: great downtown location. Cons: traffic gridlock during rush hour, streets unsafe on foot after dark. ✉*700 S. Florida Ave., Downtown, 33602* ☎*813/221–4900* 📠*813/221–0923* 🌐*http://marriott.com/property/propertypage/TPAMC* ⇨*681 rooms, 36 suites* 👍*In-room: safe, kitchen (some), high-speed Internet. In-hotel: 3 restaurants, room service, bars, pool, gym, spa, laundry facilities, laundry service, concierge, executive floor, public Wi-Fi, parking (fee), no-smoking rooms* ▭*AE, D, DC, MC, V.*

★ $$$–$$$$ 🏨 **Saddlebrook Resort Tampa.** If you can't get enough golf and tennis, then here's your cure. Saddlebrook is one of west Florida's premier resorts of its type, largely because it has so many things in one spot—36 holes of championship golf, the Arnold Palmer Golf Academy, 45 clay, grass, and artificial-surface tennis courts, a Harry Hopman tennis program, a sophisticated spa, and sprawling convention space. Varied accommodations include one- and two-bedroom suites; breakfast and dinner are included in the rates, which are per person, and wireless high-speed Internet access is available throughout the hotel. There's also a 5-acre executive challenge course. Pros: heavily wooded grounds are a nice buffer from urban sprawl; great choice for the fitness-minded. Cons: isolated at 12 mi from the heart of Tampa's action. ⊠ *5700 Saddlebrook Way, Wesley Chapel 33543* ☎ *813/973–1111 or 800/729–8383* 🖷 *813/973–4504* ⊕ *www.saddlebrookresort.com* ↩ *800 rooms, 420 suites* ⌂ *In-room: kitchen (some), high-speed Internet, Wi-Fi. In-hotel: 4 restaurants, room service, bars, golf courses, tennis courts, pools, gym, spa, bicycles, no elevator, children's programs (ages 4–12), laundry service, concierge, Wi-Fi* ☐ *AE, D, DC, MC, V* ☉ *MAP.*

$$$–$$$$ 🔝**Seminole Hard Rock Hotel & Casino.** If gambling's your game, this is the place to stay. Rooms are decorated with sophisticated, clean lines and neutral tones. Beds have cotton duvets, and many of the bathrooms have natural light via a skylight. That said, the casino is open 24 hours, so chances are you won't see much of your lovely room. The Hard Rock is the only show around if you're looking for a gaming base camp. But it definitely isn't the place to be if you're not into wagering or find the moderate casino-hotels in Las Vegas or Reno a bit on the sterile side. ⊠ *5223 Orient Rd., off I–4 at Orient Rd. Exit, 33610* ☎ *813/627–7625 or 800/937–0010* 🖷 *813/627–7655* ⊕ *www. seminolehardrock.com* ↩ *248 rooms, 2 suites* ⌂ *In-room: safe, high-speed Internet. In-hotel: 2 restaurants, room service, bars, pool, gym, spa, parking (no fee)* ☐ *AE, D, DC, MC, V.*

$$$–$$$$ 🔝**Westin Tampa Harbour Island.** Few folks think of the islands when visiting Tampa, but this 12-story hotel on a 177-acre islet in the Bay is just an eight-minute walk and short drive from downtown Tampa. Many units have terrific views of the water or the downtown skyline. Service is attentive. There's a marina, and you may use the extensive health and fitness center and 20 tennis courts at the Harbour Island Athletic Club, next door, for a fee. Pros: close to downtown but doesn't feel like it, trolley from hotel to the convention center or to the electric streetcar (TECO) station (from which you can travel to Channelside, the Florida Aquarium, or Ybor City). Cons: not the best choice if you want the freedom to roam the Bay area. ⊠ *725 S. Harbour Island Blvd., Harbour Island, 33602* ☎ *813/229–5000* 🖷 *813/229–5322* ⊕ *www.westin.com* ↩ *280 rooms, 19 suites* ⌂ *In-room: safe, refrigerator (some), ethernet, Wi-Fi. In-hotel: restaurant, room service, bar, pool, laundry service, airport shuttle, parking (fee), some pets allowed, no-smoking rooms* ☐ *AE, DC, MC, V.*

$$$ 🔝**Equus Meadow Inn.** Horse lovers won't find a better bunkhouse than this lovely, two-unit (cottage and suite) bed-and-breakfast. The Carriage House Cottage has a bedroom and sitting room with a woody Victorian decor and modern trimmings such as satellite television. The Meadowlook Suite has a balcony, a parlor, a claw-foot tub, and inside or outside stairway access, ruling it out for guests with mobility problems. It, too, has satellite TV. Both units have private baths (the suite's

is down a hall) and daily breakfast. For $40 per hour you can rent one of the inn's six steeds for a guided trail ride. Kids under 18 are not permitted. Pros: intimate, nice escape, horses. Cons: feels special only if you love horses. ⊠*6812 George Rd., North Tampa Area, 33634* ☎*813/806–5566* ⊕*www.equusmeadowinn.com* ⇆*2 units* ⚲*In-room: kitchen (one), small refrigerator, microwave (one), no elevator* ▭*MC, V.*

★ $$–$$$ ⌂**Casita de la Verdad.** The home of a cigar worker in the factory district, this inn is one of the most intimate places to stay in the Bay area. In the heart of Ybor City, it has the same kind of clapboard siding and picket fences that were originally part of the home. Inside, you'll find marble floors, a claw-foot tub, and two queen-size beds. There's also a full kitchen, but don't let it stop you from going out for a traditional breakfast—*café cubano* or *café con leche* with a wedge of buttered Cuban bread. Pros: romantic, nostalgic. Cons: sense of isolation. ⊠*1609 E. 6th Ave., Ybor City 33605* ☎*813/654–6087* ⊕*www.yborcityguesthouse.com* ⇆*1 room* ⚲*In-room: kitchen, refrigerator, ethernet* ▭*AE, MC, V.*

★ $$–$$$ ⌂**Don Vicente de Ybor Historic Inn.** Built as a home in 1895 by town founder Don Vicente de Ybor this inn shows that the mainly working-class cigar city had an elegant side, too. From the beige stucco exterior to the white marble staircase in the main lobby, this boutique hotel is an architectural tour de force. Rooms have parquet floors, canopied beds, and private baths; most have wrought-iron balconies. Common areas have crystal chandeliers, Tiffany lamps, and Persian carpets. Pros: elegant, rich in history, within walking distance of Ybor City's salsafied nightlife. Cons: things can get a bit rowdy outside on weekend nights. ⊠*1915 Republica de Cuba, Ybor City 33605* ☎*813/241–4545 or 866/206–4545* ⊟*813/241–6104* ⊕*www.donvicenteinn.com* ⇆*13 rooms, 3 suites* ⚲*In-room: ethernet. In-hotel: restaurant, bar, laundry service, Wi-Fi* ▭*AE, D, DC, MC, V* ⎮◯⎮*BP.*

$$–$$$ ⌂**Hilton Garden Inn Tampa Ybor Historic District.** Architecturally, this property pales when compared with the century-old classic structures around it. But it is convenient: it's across the street from the Centro Ybor complex, 3 mi from downtown Tampa, and 7 mi from Tampa International Airport. The hotel restaurant has a full breakfast buffet and doesn't try to compete with the culinary heavyweights in a six-block radius. Rooms are business traveler–friendly, with high-speed Internet access, dual phone lines, large desks, and ergonomic chairs. Pros: good location if Ybor City is central to your plans. Cons: chain property, aesthetics between the hotel and the neighborhood are not in sync. ⊠*1700 E. 9th Ave., Ybor City 33605* ☎*813/769–9267* ⊟*813/769–3299* ⊕*www.tampayborhistoricdistrict.gardeninn.com* ⇆*84 rooms, 11 suites* ⚲*In-room: refrigerator, ethernet. In-hotel: restaurant, pool, laundry facilities, laundry service, Wi-Fi* ▭*AE, D, DC, MC, V* ⎮◯⎮*EP.*

NIGHTLIFE & THE ARTS

THE ARTS

Occupying 9 acres along the Hillsborough River, the 345,000-square-foot **Tampa Bay Performing Arts Center** (⊠*1010 W.C. MacInnes Pl.,*

10

Downtown ☎*813/229–7827 or 800/955–1045* ⊕*www.tbpac.org*) is the largest such complex south of the Kennedy Center in Washington, D.C. Among the facilities are the new 200-seat Teco Theater, the 2,500-seat Carol Morsani Hall, a 1,047-seat playhouse, a 300-seat cabaret theater, and a 120-seat black box theater. Opera, concerts, drama, and ballet performances are presented here. In a restored 1926 movie palace, the **Tampa Theatre** (✉*711 N. Franklin St., Downtown* ☎*813/274–8982* ⊕*www.tampatheatre.org*) has films, concerts, and special events.

NIGHTLIFE

The biggest concentration of nightclubs, as well as the widest variety, is found along 7th Avenue in Ybor City. It becomes a little like Bourbon Street in New Orleans after the sun goes down. Popular **Adobe Gilas** (✉*1600 E. 8th Ave., Ybor City* ☎*813/241–8588*) has live music Thursday through Sunday nights and a balcony overlooking the crowds on 7th Avenue. There's a large selection of margaritas and more than 30 brands of tequila, and food is served until 2 AM. Considered something of a dive—but a lovable dive—by a loyal local following that ranges from esteemed jurists to nose ring–wearing night owls, the **Hub** (✉*719 N. Franklin St., Downtown* ☎*813/229–1553*) is known for one of Tampa's best martinis and one of its most eclectic jukeboxes. **Improv Comedy Theater & Restaurant** (✉*Centro Ybor, 1600 E. 8th Ave., Ybor City* ☎*813/864–4000* ⊕*www.improvtampa.com*) stars top comedians in performances Wednesday through Sunday. **Metropolis** (✉*3447 W. Kennedy Blvd., Central Tampa* ☎*813/871–2410*), a gay club near the University of Tampa, has DJs and male strippers. Catch comedians Wednesday through Sunday nights at **Side Splitters** (✉*12938 N. Dale Mabry Hwy., Central Tampa* ☎*813/960–1197* ⊕*www.sidesplitterscomedy.com*). **Skippers Smokehouse** (✉*910 Skipper Rd., Northeast Tampa* ☎*813/971–0666* ⊕*www.skipperssmokehouse.com*), a junkyard-style restaurant and oyster bar, has live reggae Wednesday, Grateful Dead night on Thursday, blues Friday through Sunday, and great smoked fish every night. **Stumps Supper Club** (✉*615 Channelside Dr., Downtown* ☎*813/226–2261* ⊕*www.stumpssupperclub.com*) serves Southern food, and has live dance music daily and a DJ on Friday and Saturday. **Blue Martini Lounge** (✉*2323 N. Westshore Blvd., West Tampa* ☎*813/873–2583* ⊕*www.bluemartinilounge.com/tpahome.htm*) at International Plaza has live entertainment nightly except Monday and a menu of killer martinis à la *Sex and the City*.

International Plaza's **Bay Street** (✉*2223 N. West Shore Blvd., Airport Area*) has become one of Tampa's dining and imbibing hot spots.

SPORTS & THE OUTDOORS

BASEBALL

Locals and tourists flock each March to see the **New York Yankees** (✉*Legends Field, 1 Steinbrenner Dr., near corner of Dale Mabry Hwy. and Martin Luther King Jr. Blvd., off I–275 Exit 41B, Central Tampa* ☎*813/879–2244 or 813/875–7753*) play about 17 spring-training games at their 10,382-seat stadium. Call for tickets. From April through September, the stadium belongs to a Yankee farm team, the **Tampa Yankees,** who play 70 games against the likes of the Daytona Cubs and the Sarasota Red Sox.

CANOEING

In northeast Tampa, **Canoe Escape** (⊠ *9335 E. Fowler Ave., ½ mi east of I–75* ☎*813/986–2067*) arranges guided or self-guided trips from two hours' to all-day duration on the upper Hillsborough River, abounding with alligators, ibises, hawks, and other wildlife. They also rent canoes and kayaks.

DOG RACING

Tampa Greyhound Track (⊠ *8300 N. Nebraska Ave.* ☎*813/932–4313* ⊕*www.tampadogs.com*) holds dog races from early June to December.

FISHING

Captain Jim Lemke of **Light Tackle Adventures** (⊠ *8613 Beth Ct., Odessa* ☎*813/917–4989 or 813/920–5460* ⊕*www.lighttackleadventures. com*) is an outfitter who arranges bay, backwater, offshore, and flats-fishing trips for everything from snook to tarpon.

FOOTBALL

Seeing the National Football League's **Tampa Bay Buccaneers** (⊠ *Raymond James Stadium, 4201 N. Dale Mabry Hwy., Central Tampa* ☎*813/879–2827 or 800/282–0683* ⊕*www.buccaneers.com*) play isn't easy without connections, since the entire stadium is booked by season-ticket holders years in advance. The Arena Football League **Tampa Bay Storm** (⊠ *St. Pete Times Forum, 401 Channelside Dr., Downtown* ☎*813/301–6900* ⊕*www.tampabaystorm.com*) plays about 16 games in its January-to-May season. The Storm is a perennial contender in the Arena League and has a hot rivalry with the Orlando Predators.

GOLF

Babe Zaharias Golf Course (⊠ *11412 Forest Hills Dr., Northeast Tampa* ☎*813/631–4374*) is a challenging 18-hole public course with water hazards on 8 holes; green fee: $22/$32. A pro is on hand to give lessons. **Bloomingdale Golfers Club** (⊠ *4113 Great Golfers Pl., Southeast Tampa* ☎*813/685–4105*) has 18 holes, a two-tiered driving range, a 1-acre putting green, and a restaurant; green fee: $55/$85. **The Claw at USF** (⊠ *13801 N. 46th St., North Tampa* ☎*813/632–6893*) is named for its many dog-legged fairways. The 18-hole par-71 course is on a preserve with moss-draped oaks and towering pines, and is free of any on-course housing developments; green fee: $31/$53. **The Club at Eaglebrooke** (⊠ *1300 Eaglebrooke Blvd., Lakeland* ✛*Polk County, 30 mi from Tampa* ☎*863/701–0101*) is an 18-hole course; green fee: $59/$69. Twenty miles north of Tampa, **Lake Jovita Golf & Country Club** (⊠ *12900 Lake Jovita Blvd., Dade City* ☎*352/588–9200 or 877/481–2652*) has a semiprivate 36-hole course; green fee: $89/$119. Golfers rotate from the back 9 holes to the front 9. The **Saddlebrook Resort** (⊠ *5700 Saddlebrook Way, Wesley Chapel* ☎*813/973–1111*) has 36 holes; green fee: $180. There's also a driving range, golf shop, on-site

10

pro, and resort spa. The public, 18-hole course at **Tournament Players Club of Tampa Bay** (⊠ *5300 W. Lutz Lake Fern Rd., Lutz* ☎ *813/949–0090*), 15 mi north of Tampa, was designed by Bobby Weed and Chi Chi Rodriguez; green fee: $119/$155.

HORSE RACING

Tampa Bay Downs (⊠ *Race Track Rd., off Rte. 580, Oldsmar* ☎ *813/855–4401* ⊕ *www.tampadowns.com*) holds thoroughbred races from December to May, plus simulcast TV broadcasts of other thoroughbred races at tracks around the nation.

ICE HOCKEY

The National Hockey League's **Tampa Bay Lightning** (⊠ *St. Pete Times Forum, 401 Channelside Dr., Downtown* ☎ *813/301–6600* ⊕ *www.tampabaylightning.com*) play at the 21,500-seat St. Pete Times Forum (formerly the Ice Palace), a classy, $153 million downtown waterfront arena. It's near the Florida Aquarium and Channelside and close enough to both Ybor City and Hyde Park to venture to either spot to eat before the game. There's a trolley from the forum to Ybor City, and those with a ticket stub can get discounts at several restaurants.

TENNIS & RACQUETBALL

The **City of Tampa Tennis Complex at HCC** (⊠ *3901 W. Tampa Bay Blvd., Central Tampa* ☎ *813/223–8602*), across from Raymond James Stadium and immediately north of Tampa International Airport, has 12 clay courts and 16 hard courts ($5 an hour for clay courts; $2.50 an hour for hard courts). All courts are lighted. The complex also has four racquetball courts.

SHOPPING

For the mildly unusual to the downright bizarre, stop at **Squaresville** (⊠ *508 S. Howard Ave., Near Downtown* ☎ *813/259–9944*), which stocks everything from Cuban clothing to Elvis posters to Betty Page clocks. The **Channelside shopping and entertainment complex** (⊠ *615 Channelside Dr., Downtown*) offers movie theaters, shops, restaurants, and clubs; the official Tampa Bay visitor center is also here. If you want to grab something at Neiman Marcus on your way to the airport, the upscale **International Plaza** (⊠ *2223 N. Westshore Blvd., Airport Area*) mall, which includes Betsey Johnson, J. Crew, L'Occitane, Louis Vuitton, Tiffany & Co., and many other shops, is immediately south of the airport. Bay Street, the mall's dining "district," is one of Tampa's hot spots. **Old Hyde Park Village** (⊠ *Swan Ave. near Bayshore Blvd., Hyde Park*) is a gentrified shopping district like the ones you find in every major American city. Williams-Sonoma and Brooks Brothers are mixed in with bistros and sidewalk cafés. More than 120 shops, department stores, and eateries are in one of the area's biggest market complexes, **Westfield Shopping Town at Brandon** (⊠ *Grand Regency and Rte. 60, Brandon*), an attractively landscaped complex near Interstate 75, about 20 minutes east of downtown by car. If you are shopping for hand-rolled cigars, head for 7th Avenue in **Ybor City**, where a few handrollers practice their craft in small shops.

T. PETERSBURG

21 mi west of Tampa.

St. Petersburg and the Pinellas Coast form the thumb of the hand that juts out of Florida's west coast and grasps Tampa Bay. There are two distinct parts of St. Petersburg: the downtown and cultural area, centered on the bay, and the beach area, a string of barrier islands that faces the gulf and includes St. Pete Beach, Treasure Island, and Madeira Beach. Causeways link beach communities to the mainland peninsula.

⑩ If you can't decide whether to go in-line skating or saltwater fishing, do both at once (depending on your level of athleticism) on Tampa Bay's car-free **Friendship TrailBridge,** formerly the Gandy Bay Bridge (U.S. Highway 92), which connects Tampa and St. Petersburg. The trail runs parallel to the newer Gandy Bridge and can be accessed from either city. The 2½-mi bridge will eventually connect to another 21 mi of trails, and when complete, will make it the world's second-longest over-the-water recreational trail. It has no facilities except for portable potties that have been placed at either end of the two-lane concrete span. The recreational-trail experience is like going to sea on foot. Long wooden decks on each side of the bridge (open 24 hours) are reserved for anglers, and the former traffic lanes of the bridge are open sunrise to sunset to runners, walkers, bicyclists, and in-line skaters. ☎727/549–6099 ⊕*www.friendshiptrail.org.*

⑪ **Sunken Gardens** is one of Florida's most beautiful natural attractions. It's a 100-year-old botanical paradise—check out photos of its colorful past in the gift shop—that has cascading waterfalls, koi ponds, a walk-through butterfly house, and exotic gardens where more than 50,000 tropical plants and flowers thrive amid groves of some of the area's most spectacular palm trees. You can arrange a guided tour (no charge, Monday, Thursday, Friday, and Saturday at 1:30), and there are special events and workshops year-round. The on-site restaurant, open for dinner, and Great Explorations, a hands-on kids' museum (ask for the dual-admission ticket and save a few bucks), make this place a family favorite. ✉*1825 4th St. N* ☎727/551–3100 ⊕*www.sunkengardens. org* ✍*$8* ☉*Mon.–Sat. 10–4:30, Sun. noon–4:30.*

⑱ At **Great Explorations** you'll never hear "Don't touch." The museum is hands-on through and through, with a Robot Lab, Climb Wall, Lie Detector, and other interactive play areas, including the new Fire House. Smart exhibits like the Tennis Ball Launcher, which uses compressed air to propel a ball through a series of tubes, and Sounds Waves, where Styrofoam pellets in a clear tube show differences in sound frequencies, employ low-tech to teach kids (and parents) high-tech principles. ✉*1925 4th St. N* ☎727/821–8992 ⊕*www.greatexplorations.org* ✍*$9* ☉*Mon.–Sat. 10–4:30, Sun. noon–4:30.*

⑮ The **Florida International Museum,** a Smithsonian Institution affiliate, has become a major focal point of the central business district. Dedicated to historical, cultural, and educational exhibitions, the museum dis-

10

plays new treasures each season. Continually changing exhibits have included Diana, Princess of Wales, *Titanic,* and Treasures of the Czars. ✉244 2nd St. N, off I–275 Exit 23A ☎727/341–7900 ⊕*www.floridamuseum.org* ✑*$10; special event tickets higher* ⊙*Tues.–Sat. 10–5, Sun. noon–5.*

⑭ Downtown St. Petersburg got a massive infusion of vibrancy with the opening of **BayWalk,** a shopping, dining, and entertainment mall in a square-block complex incorporating California mission–style design and courtyard areas lined with trendy eateries, bars, shops, and a 20-screen movie theater. It's best for adults to stroll the plaza and restaurants in the afternoon and early evening, since teenagers overtake BayWalk at night. Among the restaurants at 2nd Avenue North and 2nd Street (off I–275 Exit 23A) are Dan Marino's Fine Food & Spirits; dish; Johnny Rockets, of hamburger-chain fame; and Wet Willies, a see-and-be-seen bar. ✉*Bordered by 2nd St. N, 2nd Ave. N, 1st St. N, and 3rd Ave. N.*

⑫ The downtown **Florida Holocaust Museum** is the fourth-largest museum of its kind in the United States. It has the permanent History, Heritage, and Hope exhibit, an original boxcar, and an extensive collection of photographs, art, and artifacts. A popular display includes portraits and biographies of Holocaust survivors. The museum was conceived as a learning center for children, so many of the exhibits avoid overly graphic content; parents are warned before entering a gallery if any of the subject matter is potentially too intense for kids. ✉55 5th St. S ☎727/820–0100 or 800/960–7448 ⊕*www.flholocaustmuseum.org* ✑*$8* ⊙*Daily 10–5.*

⑬ Outstanding examples of European, American, pre-Columbian, and Asian art are at the **Museum of Fine Arts,** a gorgeous Mediterranean Revival structure on the waterfront one block from the Pier. You'll find major works by American artists ranging from Whistler to O'Keeffe to Rauschenberg and Lichtenstein, but the museum is known for its collection of French artists, including Fragonard, Cézanne, Monet, Rodin, Gauguin, and Renoir. There are also photography exhibits that draw from a permanent collection of more than 1,200 works. Docents give narrated gallery tours. Admission prices and museum hours are sometimes increased for special exhibits. ✉255 Beach Dr. NE ☎727/896–2667 ⊕*www.fine-arts.org* ✑*$8* ⊙*Tues.–Sat. 10–5, Sun. 1–5.*

⑯ Learn about the history of the Tampa Bay region, from the Tocobaga Indians to America's first commercial airline, at the **St. Petersburg Museum of History.** Exhibits include those on Native American primitive shell tools, a 400-year-old dugout canoe, an early-European settlement, the railroad era, the growth of tourism, St. Petersburg's Webb's City (long gone but once hailed as the world's largest drugstore), and a full-size replica of the Benoist Airboat flown by pioneer aviator Tony Jannus. Admission to the museum is free Monday 5 to 7. ✉335 2nd Ave. NE ☎727/894–1052 ⊕*www.spmoh.org* ✑*$5* ⊙*Mon. noon–7, Tues.–Sat. 10–5, Sun. noon–5.*

⑰ The Spanish surrealist certainly had a different way of viewing our
Fodor'sChoice world as evidenced by exhibits at the **Salvador Dalí Museum,** which holds
★ the world's most comprehensive collection of his work. Paintings such
as "Eggs on a Plate without a Plate" and "The Hallucinogenic Tore-
ador" are among the 95 oils, more than 100 watercolors and drawings, and 1,300 graphics, sculptures, photographs, and objets d'art
displayed here. Frequent hour-long tours are led by well-informed
docents. How did the collection end up here? A rich industrialist and
friend of Dalí, Ohio magnate A. Reynolds Morse, was looking for
a museum site after his huge Dalí collection began to overflow his
mansion. The people of St. Petersburg vied admirably for the collection, and the museum was established here as a result. ⊠ *1000 3rd St.
S* ☎ *727/823–3767 or 800/442–3254* ⊕ *www.salvadordalimuseum.
org* ☑ *$15* ⊗ *Mon.–Wed. 9:30–5:30, Thurs. 9:30–8, Fri. 9:30–6, Sat.
9:30–6:30, Sun. noon–5:30.*

⑲ **Bayside Tours** is a fun way to see downtown St. Petersburg and the
★ Tampa Bay waterfront on one of man's more recent chariots—a Segway, a cross between a chariot of sorts and a motorized scooter. Each
tour starts with an easy 15- to 20-minute training session. Much of
the trick is simply a matter of leaning—forward to reach warp speed
of about 12 mph, backward to slow down or brake, and sideways to
turn. Tours are 60 to 90 minutes and are offered up to three times
daily. ⊠ *335 NE 2nd Ave.* ☎ *727/896–3640* ⊕ *www.gyroglides.com*
☑ *tours $35–$50* ⊗ *Tues.–Sat. 10:30 and 2, Sun. 12:30 and 2, Mon.
12:30, 2:30, and 4:30.*

⑳ Spread over five small islands, or keys, 1,136-acre **Fort De Soto Park**
lies at the mouth of Tampa Bay. It has 7 mi of beaches, two fishing
piers, a 4-mile hiking-skating trail, picnic and camping grounds, and
a historic fort. The fort for which it's named was built on the southern
end of Mullet Key to protect sea lanes in the gulf during the Spanish-American War. Roam the fort or wander the beaches of any of
the islands within the park. ⊠ *3500 Pinellas Bayway S, Tierra Verde*
☎ *727/582–2267* ☑ *Free* ⊗ *Beaches, daily sunrise–sunset; fishing and
boat ramp, 24 hrs.*

㉑ **Pass-A-Grille Beach,** at the southern end of St. Pete Beach, has parking
meters, a snack bar, restrooms, and showers. ⊠ *Off Gulf Blvd. (Rte.
699), St. Pete Beach.*

㉒ **Treasure Island** (⊠ *11260 Gulf Blvd.*) is a free beach north of Pass-A-
Grille with dressing rooms, metered parking, and a snack bar.

㉓ In the middle of the mouth of Tampa Bay lies a small (350 acres) and
largely unspoiled island, **Egmont Key,** now a state park, national wildlife
refuge, national historic site, and bird sanctuary. On the island are the
ruins of Fort De Soto's sister fortification, **Fort Dade,** built during the
Spanish-American War to protect Tampa Bay. The primary inhabitant
of the 2-mi-long island is the threatened gopher tortoise. Shelling and
nature-viewing are rewarding. The only way to get here, however, is
by boat. **Dolphin Landings Tours** (☎ *727/367–4488* ⊕ *www.dolphinland-*

10

IF YOU LIKE

BEACHES

Every barrier island from Clearwater to Venice has excellent swimming beaches facing out on the Gulf of Mexico. Waters are calmer and warmer here than on the Atlantic Coast, a boon to families but a disappointment to surfers. Don't swim in Tampa Bay, Sarasota Bay, or the inland waterway, all of which have been polluted by boaters, marinas, and industry.

BIKING

The 34-mi-long Pinellas Trail, a paved route that follows the path of a former railroad, makes it possible to bike all the way from Tarpon Springs, at the north end of Pinellas County, to a spot not far north of the Sunshine Skyway Bridge, at the south end of the county. Opened in 2001, Suncoast Trail runs north from Tampa's outskirts—beginning in

north Hillsborough County and ending in north Hernando County—for nearly 42 mi. The paved surface will eventually connect to the Upper Bay Trail and extend another 58 mi.

CANOEING

Several inland rivers offer superb canoeing, and outfits at different points along their shores rent equipment and lead guided tours. Sculling teams from the University of Tampa and colleges nationwide train in downtown's Hillsborough River.

FISHING

Anglers flock to southwest Florida's coastal waters to catch tarpon, kingfish, speckled trout, snapper, grouper, sea trout, snook, sheepshead, and shark. Charter a fishing boat or join a group on a party boat for full- or half-day outings. Avoid fishing in polluted Tampa Bay.

ings.com) does a four-hour shelling trip, a two-hour dolphin-sighting excursion, back-bay fishing or party-boat fishing, and other outings.

WHERE TO STAY & EAT

★ $$$–$$$$ ✕**Redwoods Restaurant.** A sophisticated and intimate spot, Redwoods had a bit of an identity crisis when it arrived several years ago, drifting from Pacific Rim to Latino before finally settling on a less confining menu, which changes regularly. That said, it always includes fresh fish brought in daily. Menu items have included swordfish medallions on a bed of corn and avocado, seared tuna with mango relish, wild Atlantic salmon, and grilled house-smoked pork chops. The terrazzo flooring and crisp white table linens define cleanliness, and the staff and chef make this one of St. Pete's best restaurants. ⊠*247 Central Ave.* ☎*727/896–5118* ⊟*AE, D, MC, V* ⊙*No lunch. Closed Mon.*

★ $$–$$$$ ✕**Marchand's Grill.** Once the Pompeii Room in the Vinoy Hotel, opened in 1925, this wonderful eatery has frescoed ceilings and a spectacular view of Tampa Bay and the nearby boat docks. The food is impressive as well. The imaginative, changing menu lists temptations such as asparagus ravioli, roasted eggplant soup, browned gnocchi with wild mushrooms and pinot grigio broth, and seafood bouillabaisse. The wine list is extensive, including a number of by-the-glass selections. There's live music Tuesday through Saturday nights. ⊠*Renaissance Vinoy Resort, 501 5th Ave. NE* ☎*727/894–1000* ⊟*AE, D, DC, MC, V.*

$–$$$$ ✕**Salt Rock Grill.** Locals flock to this beach hangout, attesting to its good-time atmosphere (a band plays Saturday and Sunday nights during summer) and rock-solid menu. The showstoppers include aged steaks, roasted Caribbean lobster tail, and cioppino (shrimp, king crab, lobster, mussels, fish, and clams with a sourdough crust). In fair weather, dine on the dock; otherwise ask for a table with a view of the water. ✉ *19325 Gulf Blvd.* ☎ *727/593–7626* ⊕ *www.saltrockgrill.com* ⊟ *AE, MC, V.*

¢–$$$$ ✕**Hurricane Seafood Restaurant.** Sunsets and gulf views are two of the magnets that bring tourists as well as locals to this Pass-A-Grille Beach seafood establishment, which has been serving the Tampa Bay area since 1977. One of the most popular entrées is the catch-of-the-day (mahimahi and flounder, among others) prepared however you like, which could include fried, grilled, blackened, or jerk. Grilled grouper with tomato tapenade, basil olive oil, mango coulis, and seasonal lobster selections are other top menu items. Sunset seekers throng to the rooftop sundeck for gorgeous views. ✉ *807 Gulf Way, St. Pete Beach* ☎ *727/360–9558* ⊟ *AE, D, MC, V.*

$$–$$$ ✕**Spoto's Steak Joint.** Simple formula here: aged Angus beef, expertly prepared. The restaurant serves about every cut one can imagine, from a huge porterhouse to a petit filet. And if steak is not your thing, smoked baby-back ribs is another specialty. You'll find chicken, duck, and seafood. Dishes are served with hot bread, fresh vegetables, and soup or salad. ✉ *4871 Park St.* ☎ *727/545–9481* ⊕ *www.spotossteakjoint.com* ✉ *1280 Main St., Dunedin* ☎ *727/734–0008* ⊟ *AE, D, MC, V* ☾ *No lunch.*

$–$$$ ✕**Bonefish Grill.** A great sampling of local seafood is the trademark of this urbane eatery near downtown. Shrimp fettuccine diablo and wood-grilled grouper are local offerings. Mussels sautéed with tomatoes, garlic, basil, and lemon-wine sauce is a must-try appetizer. If you don't care for fish, pork tenderloin portobello piccata is stellar. You won't find the namesake fish on the menu, incidentally; bonefish is popular for sportfishing in the keys, but it's far too bony to eat. ✉ *5901 4th St. N* ☎ *727/521–3434* ⊕ *www.bonefishgrill.com* ⊟ *AE, D, DC, MC, V* ☾ *No lunch.*

¢–$$$ ✕**Crabby Bill's.** Come for fresh, expertly cooked Florida seafood in a friendly family atmosphere. The fried grouper sandwich (it also comes grilled, blackened, and broiled) is highly recommended, but crustaceans are the house specialty. That means your choice of blue, softshell, king, and, from October to May, delicious stone crabs, among others. There's also a good selection of other treats, including flounder, bay scallops, and farm-raised oysters. Diners usually dress in the official uniform of Florida beaches: shorts, T-shirt, and flip-flops. ✉ *5300 Gulf Blvd.* ☎ *727/360–8858* ⊕ *www.crabbybills.com* ⊟ *D, MC, V.*

$–$$ ✕**Saffron's Caribbean Cuisine.** You'll feel like you've cocooned yourself in a 1930s jungle resort at Saffron's, which fittingly is in a vintage west St. Petersburg resort called Jungle Prada (featured in the 1985 film *Cocoon*). Try the curried goat (slow cooked with potatoes and onions)—it's a great way to sample a meat not often served in American restaurants. Another solid choice is jerk chicken marinated and grilled

10

with a topping of jerk sauce, onions, peppers, and spices. Shrimp swimming in tomatoes, peppers, and Jamaican beer Red Stripe is popular among regulars. ⊠ *1700 Park St.* ☎ *727/345–6400* ⊕ *www.saffroncuisine.com* ⊟ *AE, D, DC, MC, V* ⊗ *No lunch Sun.*

¢–$$
FodorśChoice
★

✕ **Ted Peters Famous Smoked Fish.** Picture this: flip-flop–wearing anglers and beach-towel clad bathers lolling on picnic benches, soaking up a beer or three, and devouring flavorful oak-smoked salmon, mullet, and mackerel. Everything comes to the table with heaped helpings of German potato salad or coleslaw. If you're industrious enough to have hooked your own fish, the crew will smoke it for about $1.50 per pound. If not, there's always what many consider to be the best burger in the Tampa Bay region. The popular smoked-fish spread is available to go. There's also indoor seating. Closing time is 7:30 PM. ⊠ *1350 Pasadena Ave. S, South Pasadena* ☎ *727/381–7931* ⚮ *Reservations not accepted* ⊟ *No credit cards* ⊗ *Closed Tues.*

¢–$

✕ **Luck Dill Deli.** This New York–style deli serving breakfast and lunch is usually packed. Favorites include Cuban sandwiches, pastrami sandwiches, Angus burgers, cheese blintzes, and potato knishes. ⊠ *277 Central Ave., St. Petersburg* ☎ *727/895–5859* ⚮ *Reservations not accepted* ⊟ *MC, V* ⊗ *No dinner. Closed Sun.*

¢–$

✕ **TooJay's.** Knishes and roast brisket with potato pancakes are the mainstays at this kosher-style deli with a busy dining room at lunch and dinner. Other selections include salmon cakes, shepherd's pie, and shrimp salad. Don't miss the éclair, a house specialty. The restaurant is nothing fancy, but it's bright and friendly, and management ensures you're waited on promptly. Everything on the menu is available for takeout. ⊠ *141 2nd Ave. N, BayWalk, St. Petersburg* ☎ *727/823–3354* ⊕ *www.toojays.com* ⚮ *Reservations not accepted* ⊟ *AE, D, DC, MC, V.*

$$$$
FodorśChoice
★

⊞ **Don CeSar Beach Resort, a Loews Hotel.** Once a favorite of Scott and Zelda Fitzgerald, Babe Ruth, and Clarence Darrow, this sprawling, sybaritic beachfront "Pink Palace," now part of the Loews hotel chain, has long been a Gulf Coast landmark because of its remarkable architecture. Steeped in turn-of-the-last-century elegance and old-world service, the hotel claims a rich history, complete with a resident ghost—founder Thomas Rowe. The restaurant, Maritana Grille, specializes in Florida seafood and is lined with huge fish tanks. The more casual Beach House Suites by the Don CeSar, less than ½ mi from the main building, has one-bedroom condos and a great little beach bar. Pros: romantic, great beach, great dining options. Cons: pricey. ⊠ *3400 Gulf Blvd., St. Pete Beach 33706* ☎ *727/360–1881 or 800/282–1116* 🖷 *727/363–5034* ⊕ *www.doncesar.com* ⊲ *Resort: 277 rooms, 40 suites; Beach House: 70 condos* ⚮ *In-room: safe (some), ethernet, Wi-Fi. In-hotel: 3 restaurants, room service, bars, pools, gym, spa, beachfront, children's programs (ages 5–12), laundry service, concierge, parking (fee), no-smoking rooms, some pets allowed* ⊟ *AE, D, DC, MC, V.*

$$$–$$$$ Inn at the Bay. In a three-story 1910 Victorian home, this charmer is near downtown and a short distance from the museums and the Pier. Rooms have four-poster beds and antique furniture. The Sailboat Suite has a fireplace and whirlpool bath. A full hot breakfast is served at your leisure. Like most B&Bs, it doesn't have an elevator, but there is a wheelchair ramp, and there are rooms on the lower floor. Pros: quiet, tree-lined neighborhood but still close to downtown. Cons: no elevator ⊠126 4th Ave. NE, 33701 ☎727/822–1700 or 888/873–2122 ⊟727/896–7411 ⊕www.innatthebay.com ⇆7 rooms, 5 suites ♿In-room: ethernet, Wi-Fi. In-hotel: parking (no fee), no kids under 9, no-smoking rooms ⊟AE, D, DC, MC, V ❍BP.

$$$–$$$$ Renaissance Vinoy Resort and Golf Club. Built in 1925, the Vinoy is
Fodor'sChoice   a luxury resort in a quiet, quaint neighborhood not far from down-
★   town St. Petersburg's attractions. The same vintage as the Don CeSar, the resort's $93 million renovation in the early 1990s allowed it to keep its yesteryear glamour and place on the National Register of Historic Places. All the spacious units are comfortable and stylish. The resort overlooks Tampa Bay, and a tiny bayside beach several blocks away is good for strolling (though unswimmable). Transportation is provided to gulf beaches 20 minutes away. Other offerings include access to a Ron Garl–designed golf course with a stunning clubhouse, a big marina, and pool attendants who deliver drinks. The hotel is convenient to downtown museums, the Pier, or BayWalk. Pros: charm, history, proximity to downtown museums. Cons: pricey, not beachfront. ⊠501 5th Ave. NE, 33701 ☎727/894–1000 ⊟727/822–2785 ⊕www.vinoyrenaissanceresort.com ⇆345 rooms, 15 suites ♿In-room: ethernet. In-hotel: 5 restaurants, room service, bars, golf course, tennis courts, pools, gym, spa, laundry facilities, laundry service, concierge, no-smoking rooms ⊟AE, D, DC, MC, V.

$$$–$$$$ TradeWinds Islands Resort.Most rooms have a view of the beach at this
☾   sprawling gulf-front property, which is actually two resorts in one. It is very popular with business, European, and Latin American guests, and it has some of the showmanship of an Orlando hotel, with a huge man-made waterway inside the complex, complete with paddleboats. The resort's own kids character, Beaker the Pelican, makes appearances at kids' programs and can even tuck your child into bed at night for a fee. There are on-site swimming lessons for children and adults. Pros: great beachfront location, close to several outside restaurants. Cons: heavy convention trade. ⊠5500 Gulf Blvd., St. Pete Beach 33706 ☎727/363–2212 ⊟727/363–2222 ⊕www.tradewindsresort. com ⇆434 rooms, 310 suites (Island Grand: 378 rooms, 207 suites; Sandpiper: 56 rooms, 103 suites) ♿In-room: safe, kitchen, refrigerator, ethernet, Wi-Fi. In-hotel: 11 restaurants, bars, tennis courts, pools, gym, spa, beachfront, children's programs (ages 4–15), laundry facilities, laundry service, concierge, parking (fee), no-smoking rooms ⊟AE, D, DC, MC, V.

$$$–$$$$ Mansion House Bed & Breakfast Boutique Inn. A pleasant 15-minute walk from the Pier, Mansion House B&B is actually two 20th-cen-

10

tury next-door-neighbor wood frame mansions in charming Arts and Crafts style. One house is said to have been home to the first mayor of St. Petersburg. The first and second floors of each house have inviting, individually decorated rooms; the most appealing might be the Carriage Room, which has a cathedral ceiling and an old-fashioned, custom-made, built-in four-poster bed. Wi-Fi is accessible throughout the property, including poolside. Pros: within walking distance of pier, restaurants, shops, and art galleries. Cons: not wheelchair accessible. ⊠*105 5th Ave. NE, 33701* ☎*727/821–9391 or 800/274–7520* 🖷*727/821–6906* ⊕*www.mansionbandb.com* ⮌*12 rooms, 1 carriage house* ☼*In-room: ethernet, Wi-Fi. In-hotel: pool, no elevator, Wi-Fi, parking (no fee), some pets allowed (fee), no-smoking rooms* ▤*AE, D, DC, MC, V* ⦿|*BP.*

$$–$$$$ ▦**Island's End Resort.** Sunrise and sunset views are part of the charm of this 1950s-vintage motel, which offers one- and three-bedroom cottages. Outdoors, the grounds are dotted with huge live oaks, sea grapes, teak deck chairs, and a weathered fishing pier that adds to the resort's character. The grounds are nicely landscaped, and it's an easy walk to the beach, restaurants, and shops. Grills are available if you want to barbecue. The small resort makes a great place for families who want to enjoy the beach life. Continental breakfast is served on Tuesday, Thursday, and Saturday. Pros: good value, nice views, nice location. Cons: access via a narrow road with creeping traffic. ⊠*1 Pass-A-Grille Way, St. Pete Beach 33706* ☎*727/360–5023* 🖷*727/367–7890* ⊕*www. islandsend.com* ⮌*6 cottages* ☼*In-room: kitchen, DVD, VCR, Wi-Fi. In-hotel: laundry facilities, some pets allowed* ▤*MC, V* ⦿|*CP.*

NIGHTLIFE & THE ARTS

THE ARTS

American Stage (⊠*211 3rd St. S* ☎*727/823–7529* ⊕*www.americanstage.org*) performs in an intimate 130-seat theater. In April and May, the company takes Shakespeare's plays outdoors.

NIGHTLIFE

Carlie's (⊠*7020 49th St. N* ☎*727/527–5214* ⊕*www.carlieslounge. com*) is hopping practically every night, with plenty of dancing to local bands. At **Cha Cha Coconuts** (⊠*The Pier* ☎*727/822–6655*), crowds catch live contemporary music Friday through Sunday year-round. **Coliseum Ballroom** (⊠*535 4th Ave. N* ☎*727/892–5202*) has ballroom dancing and group lessons on most Wednesday afternoons and Saturday nights. Call ahead. At **Marchand's** (⊠*501 5th Ave. NE* ☎*727/894–1000*), a fine-dining spot inside the posh Vinoy Hotel, sophisticated locals and well-informed out-of-towners gather at the bar for after-dinner cocktails and dancing to top-notch jazz bands. It's the most genteel place in town for a nightcap. The **Rare Olive** (⊠*300 Central Ave., corner of 3rd St.* ☎*727/822–7273* ⊕*www.rareolive.com*) adds a touch of class to an otherwise jeans-and-T-shirt nightlife scene with martinis, banquettes, and an assortment of bands and DJs. It also has Texas Hold 'Em tournaments.

Stormy's at the Hurricane (⊠807 *Gulf Way, Pass-A-Grille Beach* ☎727/360–9558) is a fine place to watch the sunset and then dance to DJ music every Friday and Sunday.

SPORTS & THE OUTDOORS

BASEBALL

Hometown favorites, the **Tampa Bay Devil Rays** (⊠*Tropicana Field, 1 Tropicana Dr., off I–275* ☎727/825–3137 or 888/326–7297 ⊕*http:// tampabay.devilrays.mlb.com*) play in an air-conditioned domed stadium. Spring training is at **Progress Energy Park** (⊠230 *First St. S* ☎727/898–7297).

DOG RACING

Greyhound races are held from early December through mid-June at **Derby Lane** (⊠10490 *Gandy Blvd. N* ☎727/812–3339 ⊕*www.derbylane.com*).

GOLF

Mangrove Bay Golf Course (⊠875 *62nd Ave. NE* ☎727/893–7800) has 18 holes and a driving range; green fee: $27/$43.

SHOPPING

One of the state's more notable bookstores is **Haslam's** (⊠2025 *Central Ave.* ☎727/822–8616), a family-owned emporium that's been doing business just west of downtown St. Petersburg for more than 70 years. The store carries some 300,000 volumes, from cutting-edge best sellers to ancient tomes. If you value a good book or simply like to browse, you could easily spend an afternoon here. Designer boutiques, movie theaters, and trendy restaurants can be found at the downtown shopping plaza **Florida Craftsmen Galleries** (⊠501 *Central Ave.* ☎727/822–4294), which gives 125 homegrown craftsmen a chance to exhibit glassware, jewelry, furniture, and more. **John's Pass Village and Boardwalk** (⊠12901 *Gulf Blvd., Madeira Beach*) is a collection of shops and restaurants in an old-style fishing village, where you can pass the time watching pelicans cavorting and dive-bombing for food. A five-story structure on the bayfront, the **Pier** (⊠800 *2nd Ave. NE*), near the Museum of Fine Arts, looks like an inverted pyramid. Inside are numerous shops and eating spots. More than 150 art dealers sell their wares at **Art & Antiques** (⊠*Beach Street between 1st and 2nd Aves.*).

10

CLEARWATER

12 mi north of St. Petersburg.

Residential areas are a buffer between the commercial areas that center on U.S. 19 and the beach, which is moderately quiet during winter, but buzzing with life during spring break and summer. There's a semi-quaint downtown area on the mainland, just east of the beach.

24 When pelicans become entangled in fishing lines, locals sometimes carry them to the nonprofit **Suncoast Seabird Sanctuary,** founded by Ralph Heath and dedicated to the rescue, repair, recuperation, and release of sick and injured birds. At times there are between 500 and 600 land

and sea birds in residence, including pelicans, egrets, herons, gulls, terns, sandhill cranes, hawks, owls, and cormorants. ⊠ *18328 Gulf Blvd., Indian Shores* ☎ *727/391–6211* ⊕ *www.seabirdsanctuary.org* ⊠ *Donation welcome* ☉ *Daily 9–sunset; tours Wed. and Sun. at 2.*

㉕ South of Clearwater Beach, on Sand Key at Clearwater Pass, **Sand Key Park** (⊠ *1060 Gulf Blvd.* ☎ *727/588–4852*) has a lovely beach, plenty of green space, a playground, and a picnic area.

㉖ The **Clearwater Marine Aquarium** is a laid-back attraction offering an opportunity to participate in the work of saving and caring for endangered marine species. Many of the sea turtles, dolphins, and other animals living at the aquarium were brought there to be rehabilitated from an injury or saved from danger. The aquarium conducts tours of the bays and islands around Clearwater, including a daily ecocruise on a pontoon boat (you might just see a dolphin or two), and kayak tours of Clearwater Harbor and St. Joseph Sound. ⊠ *249 Windward Passage* ☎ *727/441–1790* ⊕ *www.cmaquarium.org* ⊠ *$9* ☉ *Weekdays 9–5, Sat. 9–4, Sun. 11–4.*

㉗ Connected to downtown Clearwater by Memorial Causeway, **Clearwater Beach** (⊠ *Western end of State Rd. 60, 2 mi west of downtown Clearwater*) is on a narrow island between Clearwater Harbor and the gulf. It has a widespread reputation for beach volleyball. There are lifeguards here as well as a marina, concessions, showers, and restrooms. Around Pier 60 there's a big, modern playground. This is the site of a nightly sunset celebration complete with musicians and artisans. It's one of the area's nicest and busiest beaches, but it's also one of the costliest in terms of parking fees.

Fodors Choice
★

OFF THE BEATEN PATH

Pinewood Cultural Park. Three out-of-the-way but worthwhile attractions grace this space. **Florida Botanical Gardens** (⊠ *12175 125th St. N, Largo* ☎ *727/582–2200* ⊕ *www.flbg.org* ⊠ *Free* ☉ *Daily 7–7*) welcomes you to 150 acres of native and exotic ornamental plants. Demonstrations teach environmentally friendly gardening techniques. The University of Florida Pinellas County Extension maintains the gardens. More than 27 historic local structures are gathered at **Heritage Village** (⊠ *11909 125th St. N, Largo* ☎ *727/582–2123* ⊠ *Donations accepted* ☉ *Tues.–Sat. 10–4, Sun. 1–4*), including a log cabin and Victorian-era home, tracing local history back to the 1850s. **Gulf Coast Museum of Art** (⊠ *12211 Walsingham Rd., Largo* ☎ *727/518–6833* ⊠ *$8* ☉ *Tues.–Sat. 10–4, Sun. noon–4*) completes the complex with permanent showings of Florida artists and visiting exhibits.

WHERE TO STAY & EAT

$–$$$ ✕ **PJ's Oyster Bar & Seafood Restaurant.** Follow the crowds to this back-alley, everyman's selection where rolls of paper towels spin overhead on wire hangers and beer flows freely. Seafood selections range from fried catfish and grouper to more elegant choices such as blackened yellowfin tuna. The all-day menu balances seafood with sandwiches and pastas. ⊠ *500 1st St., Indian Rocks Beach* ☎ *727/596–5898* ⊕ *www. pjsoysterbar.com* ⊟ *AE, MC, V.*

$$ ✕**Frenchy's Rockaway Grill.** Quebec native Mike "Frenchy" Preston runs four eateries in the area, including this fabulous place. The headliner here is a killer grouper sandwich that's moist and not battered into submission. (It's also real grouper, something that's not a given these days in Florida, because of fishing restrictions.) Mike also gets a big thumbs-up for his she-crab soup. ⊠*7 Rockaway St.* ☎*727/446–4844* ⊕*www.frenchysonline.com* ▤*AE, D, MC, V.*

$$$–$$$$ ⊡**Safety Harbor Resort & Spa.** The focus here is the 50,000-square-foot Aveda-concept spa, with all the latest in therapies and treatments. The pleasant hamlet of Safety Harbor is also a point of interest, with charming shops along the nearby main street. The resort was built over hot springs on Tampa Bay in 1926, but little of the original architecture remains. The springs still function, however, feeding into pools, the spa, and water coolers. The property has on-site golf and tennis instruction, and golf courses are 5 mi away. Pros: charm, good choice for spa lovers. Cons: far from local attractions, staff can be chilly. ⊠*105 N. Bayshore Dr., Safety Harbor 34695* ☎*727/726–1161 or 888/237–8772* ☎*727/724–8772* ⊕*www.safetyharborspa.com* ➳*189 rooms, 4 suites* ♿*In-room: ethernet, Wi-Fi. In-hotel: restaurant, tennis courts, pools, gym, spa, laundry facilities, laundry service, some pets allowed, no-smoking rooms* ▤*AE, D, DC, MC, V.*

$$$–$$$$ ⊡**Sheraton Sand Key Resort.** This is a supreme spot for sun, sand, and surf. On 10 well-manicured acres, the nine-story, T-shaped resort has many rooms with excellent gulf views, and others that look out over an adjacent park. All rooms have balconies or patios. Considered one of the top corporate-meeting and convention hotels in the Clearwater area, the resort has amenities—such as a beautiful private beach—that make it ideal for leisure travelers, too. Pros: private beach, great views. Cons: Clearwater Beach crowds just off-property. ⊠*1160 Gulf Blvd., Clearwater Beach 33767* ☎*727/595–1611* ☎*727/596–8488* ⊕*www. sheratonsandkey.com* ➳*375 rooms, 15 suites* ♿*In-room: ethernet. In-hotel: 4 restaurants, room service, bars, tennis courts, pool, gym, beachfront, water sports, children's programs (ages 3–15), Wi-Fi, some pets allowed, no-smoking rooms* ▤*AE, D, DC, MC, V.*

$–$$$$ ⊡**Belleview Biltmore Resort & Spa.** Built by railroad magnate Henry Plant, this huge 1896 Victorian resort looks like a *Great Gatsby* movie set. It is one of the world's largest wooden structures and is on the National Register of Historic Places. Units range from cozy little rooms to spacious suites that lie off long, creaky corridors. The 21 acres overlook a narrow part of Clearwater Bay. The spa matches the Victorian opulence of the rest of the hotel, with the convenience of modern facilities. The hotel staff conducts daily historical tours. Pros: nostalgic, off the beaten tourist path. Cons: in addition to being creaky it's also a bit musty. ⊠*25 Belleview Blvd., 33756* ☎*727/373–3000 or 800/237–8947* ☎*727/441–4173* ⊕*www.belleviewbiltmore.com* ➳*246 rooms, 38 suites* ♿*In-room: ethernet, Wi-Fi. In-hotel: 3 restaurants, bars, golf course, tennis courts, pools, gym, spa, bicycles, Wi-Fi, some pets allowed, no-smoking rooms* ▤*AE, D, DC, MC, V.*

$$–$$$ ⊡**Wingate Inn–Clearwater/St. Petersburg.** The Wingate is a pleasant business-class hotel that's clearly a good choice if you're going to be visit-

10

ing attractions throughout Pinellas County. Pros: friendly staff, clean rooms, free breakfast. Cons: location—between St. Pete and Clearwater—can be a problem if you're spending most of your time in one city. ⊠*5000 Lake Blvd., Clearwater 33767* ☎*727/299–9800* ⊟*727/299– 0088* ⊕*www.wingateinnclearwater.com* ⇆*84 rooms* ⚐*In room: high-speed and wireless Internet, work area, microwave, mini fridge. In-hotel: pool, gym, laundry facilities, no-smoking rooms* ⊟*AE, D, DC, MC, V.*

THE ARTS

Ruth Eckerd Hall (⊠*1111 N. McMullen Booth Rd.* ☎*727/791–7400* ⊕*www.rutheckerdhall.com*) hosts many national performers of ballet, opera, and pop, classical, or jazz music.

SPORTS & THE OUTDOORS

BASEBALL

The **Philadelphia Phillies** (⊠*Brighthouse Networks Field, 601 N. Old Coachman Rd.* ☎*727/441–8638, 727/442–8496 tickets*) get ready for the season with spring training here (February–March). The stadium also hosts the Phillies' farm team.

BIKING

Lou's Bicycle Center (⊠*8990 Seminole Blvd., Largo* ☎*727/398–2453*) rents bikes, does quick repairs, and sells new bikes. There's an access point to the Pinellas Trail a couple of blocks west of Lou's on 86th Avenue Southwest.

The **Pinellas Trail** is a 35-mi paved route that spans Pinellas County. Once a railway, the trail runs adjacent to major thoroughfares, no more than 10 feet from the roadway, so you can access it from almost any point. You get the flavor of neighborhoods and an amalgam of suburbs along the way. The trail, also popular with in-line skaters, has spawned trailside businesses such as repair shops and health-food cafés. There are also many lovely rural areas to bike through and plenty of places to rent bikes. Be wary of traffic in downtown Clearwater and on the congested areas of the Pinellas Trail, which still needs more bridges for crossing over busy streets. To start riding from the route's south end, park at Trailhead Park (37th Street South at 8th Avenue South) in St. Petersburg. To ride south from the north end, park your car in downtown Tarpon Springs (East Tarpon Avenue at North Stafford Avenue). The 2½-mi car-free **Friendship Trail** is part of the Pinellas Trail system. It's accessible from either Tampa or St. Petersburg, immediately adjacent to the Gandy Bridge. ☎*727/464–8201* ⊕*www.pinellascounty. org/trailgd/default.htm.*

GOLF

Clearwater Executive Golf Course (⊠*1875 Airport Dr.* ☎*727/447–5272*) has 18 holes and a driving range; green fee: $20/$29.

MINIATURE GOLF

The live alligators advertised on the roadside sign for **Congo River Golf & Exploration Co.** (⊠*20060 U.S. 19 N* ☎*727/797–4222*) are not in the water traps, just in a small, fenced-off lagoon adjacent to the course. The reptiles do, however, add a Florida touch to this highly landscaped course tucked into a small parcel of land adjacent to Clearwater's busiest north–south thoroughfare. Admission is $7. Closed mid-October–April, weekends only April, May, October.

TENNIS

Shipwatch Yacht & Tennis Club (⊠*11800 Shipwatch Dr., Largo* ☎*727/596–6862*) has 11 clay courts, 3 of which are lighted for night play, and 2 hard courts.

DUNEDIN

28 *3 mi north of Clearwater.*

If the sound of bagpipes and the sight of men in kilts appeals to you, head to this town, named by two Scots in the 1880s. In March the Highland Games and in November the Celtic Festival pay tribute to the town's heritage. Dunedin also has a nicely restored historic downtown area—only about five blocks long—that has become a one-stop shopping area for antiques hunters and is also lined with gift shops and good, nonchain eateries.

WHERE TO EAT

$$–$$$ ✕**Black Pearl.** Dinner is an elegant experience with a cut-above menu. Choices include lump crab meat with slaw and lemon horseradish sauce and herb-rubbed cedar plank salmon. Come here with friends for a leisurely, upscale meal. ⊠*315 Main St.* ☎*727/734–3463* ⊕*www.theblackpearlofdunedin.com* ▤*AE, MC, V.*

$–$$$ ✕**Bon Appetit.** Known for its creative fare, this restaurant has views of the Intracoastal Waterway and the gulf. Expect a menu that changes as frequently as twice a month and offers salads and light entrées as well as such selections as broiled rack of lamb in herbed walnut crust and sautéed veal sweetbreads with mushrooms in brown butter. This is an excellent place to catch a sunset. ⊠*148 Marina Plaza* ☎*727/733–2151* ▤*AE, D, DC, MC, V.*

★ $–$$ ✕**Casa Tina.** The focus here is on Mexican dishes, including several vegetarian entrées. Try the enchiladas (with vegetables or chicken) or chiles rellenos, roasted cheese-stuffed peppers. Cactus salad won't prick your tongue, but the tantalizing flavor created by tender pieces of cactus, cilantro, tomatoes, onions, lime, and *queso fresco* (a mild white cheese) might prick your taste buds. The place is often crowded, and service can be slow, but it's worth it. ⊠*369 Main St.* ☎*727/734–9226* ⊕*www.casatinas.com* ▤*AE, D, DC, MC, V* ☉*Closed Mon.*

OFF THE BEATEN PATH

Caladesi Island State Park. Quiet, secluded, and still wild, this 3½-mile-long barrier island is one of the best shelling beaches (scallops, nautilus, baby's ear, and various other varieties) on the Gulf Coast, second only to Sanibel. The park also has plenty of sights for birders—from common sandpipers to majestic blue herons to rare black skimmers—and miles of trails through scrub oaks, saw palmettos, and cacti (with tenants such as armadillos, rabbits, raccoons, and rattlesnakes). The

10

landscape also features mangroves and dunes, and the gradual slope of the sea bottom makes this a good swim for novice swimmers and kids. You have to get to Caladesi Island by private boat (there's a 108-slip marina) or through its sister park, Honeymoon Island State Recreation Area, where you take the 15-minute ferry ride across to Caladesi. The park has the only section of beach north of Venice where it's okay to bring your pets—on a leash. ✉*Dunedin Causeway to Honeymoon Island, then board ferry* ☎*727/734–5263 ferry information, 727/469–5942 or 469–5918 parks information* ✉*Honeymoon $6 per car, ferry $8* ⊘*Daily 8–sunset; ferry hourly 10–4:30 in fair weather.*

SPORTS & THE OUTDOORS

BASEBALL
The **Toronto Blue Jays** (✉*Knology Park, 373 Douglas Ave., north of State Rd. 580* ☎*727/733–9302*) play about 18 spring training games here in March.

GOLF
Dunedin Country Club (✉*1050 Palm Blvd.* ☎*727/733–7836*), a semi-private course, has 18 holes, a driving range, and a pro shop; green fee: $59/$65.

TARPON SPRINGS

10 mi north of Dunedin.

Tucked into a little harbor at the mouth of the Anclote River, this growing town was settled by Greek immigrants at the end of the 19th century. They came to practice their generations-old craft of sponge diving. Although bacterial and market forces seriously hurt the industry in the 1940s, sponging has had a modest return, mostly as a focal point for tourism. The docks along Dodecanese Boulevard, the main waterfront street, are filled with sweet old buildings with shops and eateries. Tarpon Springs' other key street is Tarpon Avenue, about a mile south of Dodecanese. This old central business district has become a hub for antiques hunters. The influence of Greek culture is omnipresent; the community's biggest celebration is the annual Greek Orthodox Epiphany Celebration in January, in which teenage boys dive for a golden cross in Spring Bayou, a few blocks from Tarpon Avenue, during a ceremony followed by a street festival in the town's central business district.

30 Don't miss **St. Nicholas Greek Orthodox Cathedral,** which is a replica of St. Sophia's in Istanbul and an excellent example of New Byzantine architecture. ✉*36 N. Pinellas Ave.* ☎*727/937–3540* ✉*Donation suggested* ⊘*Daily 9–4.*

31 **The Sponge Factory** is a shop, museum, and cultural center that reveals more than you ever imagined about how a lowly sea creature, the sponge, created the industry that built this village. See a film about these much-sought-after creatures from the phylum *porifera* and how they helped the town prosper in the early 1900s. You'll come away converted to (and loaded up with) natural sponges and loo-fahs. ⊠*510 Dodecanese Blvd., off Rte. 19* ☎*727/938–5366* ⊡*Free* ⊙*Daily 10–6.*

㉙ The **Konger Tarpon Springs Aquarium** is a privately owned attraction not nearly as extensive as the big aquariums in Tampa or Clearwater, but it's got some good exhibits, including a 120,000-gallon shark tank with a living coral reef inside. Divers feed the sharks in a show performed twice daily. There's also a baby-shark-and-stingray feeding tank, where you can feed the animals yourself—without going in the water, of course. The freshwater tank has three 7-foot-long alligators. ⊠*850 Dodecanese Blvd.* ☎*727/938–5378* ⊡*$5.25* ⊙*Mon.–Sat. 10–5, Sun. noon–5.*

㉜ **Sunset Beach** (⊠*Gulf Rd.*) is a small public beach with restrooms, picnic tables, grills, and a boat ramp.

㉝ **Howard Park Beach** (⊠*Sunset Dr.*) comes in two parts: a shady mainland picnic area and a white-sand beach island. The causeway is a popular hangout for windsurfers. The park has restrooms, picnic tables, and grills.

WHERE TO STAY & EAT

¢–$$ ✕**Costas.** In the heart of the Greek community, Costas is a favorite among locals and visitors alike hungry for authentic fare. Around since 1977, its specialties include dolmades, lamb shank, fried or grilled grouper fillets, and charbroiled lamb chops. It's a great laid-back place to stop after wandering around this Greek village. ⊠*521 Athens St.* ☎*727/942–3011* ⊟*AE, D, MC, V.*

¢–$ ✕**Bridie Gannon's Pub & Eatery.** In a town known for its Greek food, you might think it's a mistake to go to an Irish pub, but once you taste the classic Irish dishes, you'll know you've made a good choice. The menu includes bangers and mash, corned beef and cabbage, and shepherd's pie. There's Guinness on tap, a late-night menu, and live music on weekend nights. ⊠*200 E. Tarpon Ave.* ☎*727/942–3011* ⊟*AE, D, MC, V.*

★ $$$–$$$$ ▦**Westin Innisbrook Golf Resort.** A massive pool complex with a 15-foot waterslide and a sand beach are part of the allure of this sprawling, 1,100-acre resort. But 72 holes of golf, including the Copperhead course (home of October's Chrysler Championship), are the real magnets. The resort's grounds are beautifully maintained, and guest suites are in 24 two- and three-story lodges tucked among the trees between golf courses. The rooms were all remodeled in 2004, and some of the roomy junior, one-bedroom, and two-bedroom suites have balconies or patios. Innisbrook has enough restaurants and lounges to make it self-contained, though today the area around it offers a little competition. Pros: great for serious golfers, varied dining options. Cons: removed from other attractions. ⊠*36750 U.S. 19 N, Palm Harbor 34684* ☎*727/942–2000 or 800/456–2000* ⊟*727/942–5576* ⊕*www. innisbrookgolfresort.com* ⊷*600 suites* ⚐*In-room: kitchen (some), ethernet. In-hotel: 4 restaurants, bars, golf courses, tennis courts,*

10

CLOSE UP

Bobbing for Sponges

ANIMALS THAT SWIM or slither their way through Florida's semitropical waters have a vaunted place in state folklore. Several have been chosen as team mascots—the Miami Dolphins, Florida Marlins, and the University of Florida Gators, to name a few—a sign of the influence these animals have had on the state. But no aquatic creature has had a greater effect on the Tampa Bay area than the sponge.

Unlike the reputedly intelligent dolphin, the sponge is no genius. It's hard to be smart when you consist of only one cell. The sponge that divers retrieve from the seabed, or perhaps the one you reach for in the shower, is actually a colony of millions of the one-cell organisms bound together in an organic matrix that makes up a soft, flexible lump.

As you learn if you check out Tarpon Springs' aging and modest Spongeorama, sponge diving predates the birth of Christ, and the first Greek sponge seekers actually worshipped the god Poseidon. For the past millennium or so, most spongers have been devoutly Greek Orthodox, and today many sponge boats carry a small shrine to St. Nicholas, the patron saint of mariners. The divers' deep devotion to their religion—and to Greek culture—resulted in the development of Tampa Bay's own little Greek village.

Sponge gathering actually began in the Florida Keys circa 1850, but it gained momentum around Tampa Bay after 1905, when George Cocoris brought to Florida the first mechanical diving apparatus, complete with a brass-helmeted diving suit and pump system, that enabled divers to stay in 75 to 100 feet of water for two hours at a time. Cocoris and those who worked with him soon discovered a particularly marketable type of sponge: the Rock Island wool sponge, so named because it resembles fine wool and is found in abundance around Rock Island, off Florida's west coast. When word of Cocoris's success got back to Greece, more sponge-diving families headed west, and within a decade or so, several thousand of his fellow Greeks had settled around Tarpon Springs to share in its prosperity.

By the 1930s, Tarpon Springs was the largest U.S. sponging port, but in the late '40s and early '50s a sponge blight and the growing popularity of synthetic sponges nearly wiped out the local industry. Still, the hardy Greeks held on. They discovered that tourists were drawn more by the town's Hellenic culture than by the sponges sold in the dockside markets. In the ensuing 40 years Tarpon Springs' waterfront area has been turned into a delightful tourist district filled with Greek restaurants, Greek pastry shops, and Greek art galleries. And should you choose to see divers pull sponges from the seabed, you can book passage on one of the glass-bottom boats that leave hourly from the town docks.

And so the town owes its success to the humble sponge. But even though you'll find bronze statues of sponge divers, with the exception of Spongeorama there is no tribute to the monocellular creature itself. Perhaps a future Florida sports team will choose the "Fightin' Sponges" as its mascot.

—Rowland Stiteler

pools, gym, bicycles, laundry facilities, laundry service, concierge, Wi-Fi, no-smoking rooms ⊟*AE, D, DC, MC, V.*

THE NATURE COAST

The coastal area north of Tampa is sometimes called the Nature Coast, and aptly so. Flora and fauna have been well preserved in this area, and West Indian manatees are show stoppers. These gentle vegetarian water mammals, distantly related to elephants, remain an endangered species, though their numbers have grown to about 3,500 or more today. Many manatees have massive scars on their backs from run-ins with boat propellers. Extensive nature preserves and parks have been created to protect them and other wildlife indigenous to the area, and these are among the best spots to view manatees in the wild. Although they are far from mythical beauties, it is believed that manatees inspired ancient mariners' tales of mermaids. U.S. 19 is the prime route through this rural region, and traffic flows freely once you've left the congestion of St. Petersburg, Clearwater, and Port Richey. If you're planning a day trip from the bay area, pack a picnic lunch before leaving, since most of the sights are outdoors.

WEEKI WACHEE

㉞ *27 mi north of Tarpon Springs.*

At **Weeki Wachee Springs,** the spring flows at the remarkable rate of 170 million gallons a day with a constant temperature of 74°F. The spring has long been famous for its live "mermaids," clearly not the work of Mother Nature, as they wear bright costumes and put on an Esther Williams–like underwater choreography show that's been virtually unchanged in the more than 50 years the park has been open. The attraction has lost much of its luster as modern theme parks have lured tourists away from this area. But it still has snorkel tours and canoe trips on the river, and a wilderness boat ride gives an up-close look at raccoons, otters, egrets, and other semitropical Florida wetlands wildlife. In summer, Buccaneer Bay water park opens for swimming, beaching, and riding its thrilling slides and flumes. There's a tiki bar on the grounds, and during high season there's live music on Friday and Saturday. ⊠*6131 Commercial Way, at U.S. 19 and Rte. 50* ☎*352/596–2062* ⊕*www.weekiwachee.com* ⊠*$21.95 mid-Mar.–Sept., $13.95 Oct.–mid-Mar.; parking $3* ⊗*Hrs vary; call ahead.*

SPORTS & THE OUTDOORS

The 48 holes at **World Woods Golf Club** (⊠*17590 Ponce de León Blvd., Brooksville* ☎*352/796–5500* ⊕*www.worldwoods.com*) are some of the best in Florida (green fee: $40/$140). The club also has a 22-acre practice area with a circular driving range and a 2-acre putting course.

10

HOMOSASSA SPRINGS

③⑤   *20 mi north of Weeki Wachee.*

At the **Homosassa Springs Wildlife State Park,** see many manatees and species of fish through a floating glass observatory known as the Fish Bowl—except in this case the fish are outside the bowl and the people are inside it. The park's wildlife-walk trails lead you to excellent manatee, alligator, and other animal programs. Among the species are bobcats, a western cougar, white-tailed deer, a black bear, pelicans, herons, snowy egrets, river otters, whooping cranes, and even a hippopotamus named Lucifer, a keepsake from the park's days as an exotic-animal attraction. Boat cruises on Pepper Creek lead you to the Homosassa wildlife park (which takes its name from a Creek Indian word meaning "place where wild peppers grow"). ⊠*4150 S. Suncoast Blvd. (U.S. 19)* ☎*352/628–2311 or 352/628–5343* ⊕*www.citrusdirectory.com/hsswp/main.html* ⊠*$9* ⊙*Daily 9–5:30; boats run every ½ hr 9:15–3:15.*

③⑥   At the **Yulee Sugar Mill Ruins Historic State Park** are the remains of a circa-1851 sugar mill and other remnants of a 5,100-acre sugar plantation owned by Florida's first U.S. senator, David Levy Yulee. It makes for pleasant picnicking, although it is somewhat lacking visually. ⊠*3 mi off Hwy. 19/98 on State Rd. 490/Yulee Dr., Old Homosassa* ☎*352/795–3817* ⊕*www.floridastateparks.org* ⊠*Free* ⊙*Daily 8 AM–sunset.*

WHERE TO STAY & EAT

¢–$ ✕**Dan's Clam Stand.** Three reasons to go: the fried grouper burger, the clam "chow-da," and anything else seafood. (Make that four: the beef burgers are killer, too.) This is a small, divelike place about 2 mi east of Homosassa Springs State Wildlife Park and U.S. 19, but it's very popular among locals—just check out the packed parking lot at lunch and dinner. New England seafood is a house specialty, including whole-belly clams and "lob-sta," but the grouper and mahimahi are home-grown, and Dan's won't bust your budget. ⊠*7364 Grover Cleveland Blvd.* ☎*352/628–9588* ⊠*2315 N. Sunshine Path/off Highway 44, Crystal River* ☎*352/795–9081* ▤*Debit only* ⊙*Closed Sun.*

¢–$$$ ▥**Homosassa Riverside Resort.** Five villas with multiple guest rooms fill this big (by Homosassa standards) complex. There's a marina with boat and scuba-equipment rentals, a restaurant and bar that overlook the river, and an island where monkeys cavort in the trees. Resort grounds cover 9 acres of semitropical forest along the riverfront. Pros: right on the river, basic but clean. Cons: out of the way. ⊠*5297 Cherokee Way, 34448* ☎*352/628–2474 or 800/442–2040* ▤*352/628–5208* ⊕*www.riversideresorts.com* ↻*43 suites* ⌂*In-room: kitchen (some), refrigerator (some). In-hotel: restaurant, bar, laundry facilities, no-smoking rooms* ▤*D, MC, V.*

¢–$$ ▥**MacRae's.** Fishing aficionados pick this fixture in the Homosassa lodge scene. Simple rooms occupy one-story structures built to look like log cabins. Efficiencies contain full kitchens. The focus is the riverside marina, complete with boat rentals, bait shop, and fishing charters. Pros: great location for anglers. Cons: out of the way, feels more rustic than its 15 years. ✉ *5300 Cherokee Way, 34487* ☎ *352/628–2602* 🛏 *12 rooms, 10 efficiencies* ♿ *In-room: no phone, kitchen (some). In-hotel: bar, no elevator, laundry facilities* ▭ *AE, D, MC, V.*

¢–$ 🏨 **Bella Oasis Hotel & Spa.** Adjacent to the Homosassa Springs Wildlife State Park, this simple motor inn has king-size beds in most rooms. Many rooms were renovated in early 2006. There's a full-service spa next door with water therapy treatments, among other services. The on-site restaurant is popular for its variety of chicken wings, and that's about it. Pros: good base to hit and run a few attractions. Cons: very basic motel, pay-for-it television. ✉ *4076 Hwy. 19, 34446* ☎ *352/628–4311* 🖷 *352/628–0650* ⊕ *www.bellaoasis.com* 🛏 *104 rooms* ♿ *In-room: refrigerator (some). In-hotel: restaurant, bar, pool, spa, some pets allowed (fee), no-smoking rooms* ▭ *AE, D, MC, V* ⑩ *CP.*

CRYSTAL RIVER

③⑦ *7 mi north of Homosassa Springs.*

The **Crystal River National Wildlife Refuge** is a U.S. Fish and Wildlife Service sanctuary for the endangered manatee. The main spring, around which manatees congregate in winter (generally from November to March), feeds crystal-clear water into the river at 72°F year-round. This is one of the best sure-bet places to see manatees in winter, since more than 350 typically congregate at this 40-acre refuge, which includes Kings Spring, which forms the headwaters of the Crystal River. The small visitor center has displays about the manatee and other refuge inhabitants. In warmer months, when most manatees scatter (about 80 stay here year-round), the main spring is fun for a swim or scuba diving. Though accessible only by boat, the refuge provides neither tours nor boat rentals. For these, contact marinas in the town of Crystal River, such as the **American Pro Diving Center** (✉ *821 S.E. Hwy. 19* ☎ *352/563–0041 or 800/291–3483* ⊕ *www.americanprodiving.com*) or the **Crystal Lodge Dive Center** (✉ *Behind Best Western, 614 N.W. U.S. 19 N* ☎ *352/795–6798* ⊕ *www.manatee-central.com*). ✉ *1502 S. Kings Bay Dr.* ☎ *352/563–2088* 🎟 *Free* ⊙ *Mid-Nov.–mid-Mar., daily 8–4; mid-Mar.–mid-Nov., weekdays 8–4.*

WHERE TO STAY & EAT

$–$$ ✕ **Crystal River Wine & Cheese Co.** Excellent salads and good wine at affordable prices make this a very popular eatery, but the service can be a tad tardy, and the limited seating coupled with lingering diners make it difficult to park your keister during prime time, especially weekends. ✉ *734 S.E. U.S. 19* ☎ *352/795–0008* ▭ *AE, D, MC, V.*

$$ 🏨 **Plantation Inn & Golf Resort.** On the shore of Kings Bay, this two-story plantation-style resort is on 232 acres near several nature preserves and rivers. Although the resort's exterior looks like that of a huge Southern mansion, the rooms are more comfortable than palatial, with blond-wood furniture and wall-to-wall carpeting. Some rooms have patios. Condos and villas have views of the golf course. Pros: good location for golfers and boaters. Cons: stuffy old-Southern-club feel. ✉ *9301 W. Fort Island Trail, 34429* ☎ *352/795–4211 or 800/632–6262* 🖷 *352/795–1368* ⊕ *www.plantationinn.com* 🛏 *126 rooms, 2 suites,*

10

5 condos, 12 villas ₺*In-room: kitchen (some), refrigerator (some), dial-up. In-hotel: 2 restaurants, bars, golf course, tennis courts, pool, diving, public Internet, public Wi-Fi, no-smoking rooms* ☰*AE, D, DC, MC, V.*

$ 🖫 **Best Western Crystal River Resort.** Divers favor this cinder-block road-side motel close to Kings Bay and its manatee population. Dive boats depart for scuba and snorkeling excursions from the marina. The property was renovated in 2004, and the rooms are nestled under large oak trees that make the place feel like the Old South. Pros: great Kings Bay location. Cons: pretty standard chain motel. ⊠*614 N.W. U.S. 19, 34428* ☎*352/795–3171 or 800/435–4409* 🖷*352/795–3179* ⊕*www. seawake.com* ⮑*114 rooms, 18 efficiencies* ₺*In-room: kitchen (some), Wi-Fi. In-hotel: restaurant, bar, pool, diving, water sports, laundry facilities, public Wi-Fi, airport shuttle, no-smoking rooms* ☰*AE, D, DC, MC, V.*

SPORTS & THE OUTDOORS
GOLF
The **Plantation Inn & Golf Resort** (⊠*9301 W. Fort Island Trail* ☎*352/795–7211 or 800/632–6262)*, open to the public, has 27 holes, a driving range, and a putting green; green fee: $21/$55.

CEDAR KEY

57 mi northwest of Crystal River; from U.S. 19, follow Rte. 24 southwest to the end.

In the area known as the Big Bend, Florida's long, curving coastline north of Tampa, you won't find many beaches. You will find an idyllic collection of small cays and a little island village tucked in among the marshes and scenic streams feeding the Gulf of Mexico. Once the base of a prolific pencil factory, remote Cedar Key is today a commercial clamming center. Change is in the air, however. Though the town used to be a well-kept secret with sparse tourism, it's becoming increasingly popular as a getaway and a retirement paradise where prices have all but driven the locals out. It has a spring arts festival and fall seafood festival that take over the streets of the rustic downtown area. There are at least a dozen commercial galleries, a sign that Cedar Key is attracting those who carry platinum credit cards. It's also long been a favorite of the college crowd, because it's only an hour from the main campus of the University of Florida in Gainesville. The upside of this popularity is that creative bars and restaurants abound; several are on a Cannery Row–style pier a block from downtown.

38 The **Cedar Key Historical Society Museum**, in an 1871 home, displays photographs dating to 1850, Native American artifacts, and exhibits about the area's development. ⊠*Rte. 24 and 2nd St.* ☎*352/543–5549* 🗊*$1* ☾*Sun.–Fri. 1–4, Sat. 11–5.*

WHERE TO STAY & EAT

$–$$$ ✕ **Tony's.** Come for belly-busting fried grouper sandwiches and, on mild days, a patio dining area reminiscent of eating in a favorite aunt's back-yard. Tony's is an island staple popular with tourists as well as locals thanks to steamed local clams, a softshell crab platter, and sweet sea scallops. You won't find fancy French sauces, but you will find some excellently prepared Florida seafood that in many cases is caught only a few hundred yards away. ⊠ *597 2nd St.* ☎ *352/543–0022* ▭ *AE, D, MC, V.*

$–$$ ✕ **Island Room.** Like virtually every other downtown restaurant, this place in a waterfront condo complex has a good gulf view and focuses on seafood. Excellent upscale cuisine includes such treats as grouper *piccata* (cooked in white wine and lemon juice), linguine *alle vongole* (with fresh herbs, garlic, and local clams sautéed in oil), and a very worthy crab bisque. Sunday mornings, you can order brunch. ⊠ *Cedar Cove Beach and Yacht Club, 10 E. 2nd St.* ☎ *352/543–6520* ⊕ *www. islandroom.com* ▭ *AE, D, MC, V* ◔ *No lunch Mon.–Sat.*

$–$$$ ⯐ **Island Place.** Gulf views are the big attraction at this waterfront condo-style hotel, and all the guest rooms have them from their private balconies. Suites, which have either one bedroom and one bath or two bedrooms and two baths, are set up for those who might want to linger in this lovely town awhile and enjoy the historic Old Florida flavor. There is a dining room and a washer, dryer, and dishwasher in every room—making your family vacation much easier. Pros: great views. Cons: no frills. ⊠ *550 1st St., 32625* ☎ *352/543–5307 or 800/780–6522* ⊕ *www.islandplace-ck.com* ⊷ *30 suites* ⚓ *In-room: kitchen, refrigerator. In-hotel: pool, no elevator, laundry facilities, no-smoking rooms* ▭ *AE, D, MC, V.*

$–$$ ⯐ **Island Hotel.** Having enjoyed its heyday during the Confederacy, this property built in 1859 is now on the National Register of Historic Places and has been carefully restored to reflect what it was like a century ago. Rooms have antique furnishings and claw-foot bathtubs. The restaurant and bar is under new (and very friendly) ownership, and the cooked-to-order breakfast includes a hot specialty item and toasted coconut bread. Local seafood dominates the lunch and dinner menus. Pros: two blocks from the gulf, pleasant staff. Cons: no gulf views. ⊠ *373 2nd St., 32625* ☎ *352/543–5111 or 800/432–4640* ◳ *352/543–6949* ⊕ *www.islandhotel-cedarkey.com* ⊷ *10 rooms* ⚓ *In-room: no phone, no TV. In-hotel: restaurant, bar, no elevator. no-smoking rooms* ▭ *MC, V* ⧄ *BP.*

¢–$$ ⯐ **Faraway Inn.** Cheery stucco cottages, efficiencies, and motel rooms accommodate at this typical Old Cedar Key establishment on the gulf. It's made for escaping and fishing—and the office provides movies for you to watch on in-room VCRs. Bikes, canoes, and kayaks are available on the property. Bring your pets; the Faraway declares itself as totally pet-friendly. ⊠ *3rd and G Sts., 32625* ☎ *352/543–5330 or 888/543–5330* ⊕ *www.farawayinn.com* ⊷ *5 rooms, 2 efficiencies, 5 cottages* ⚓ *In-room: kitchen (some), refrigerator, VCR. In-hotel: beachfront, bicycles, some pets allowed (fee), no-smoking rooms* ▭ *MC, V.*

10

SOUTH OF TAMPA BAY

Bradenton and Sarasota anchor the southern end of Tampa Bay. A string of barrier islands borders the two cities with fine beaches. Sarasota County has 35 mi of gulf beaches, as well as two state parks, 22 municipal parks, and more than 30 golf courses, many open to the public. Sarasota has a thriving cultural scene, thanks mostly to circus magnate John Ringling, who chose this area for the winter home of his circus and his family. Bradenton, to the north, maintains a lower profile, and Venice, a few miles south on the Gulf Coast, claims beaches known for their prehistoric sharks' teeth.

BRADENTON

49 mi south of Tampa.

This city on the Manatee River has some 20 mi of beaches and is well situated for access to fishing, both fresh- and saltwater. It also has its share of golf courses and historic sites dating to the mid-1800s.

③ The **Manatee Village Historical Park** is the real thing. You can see an 1860 courthouse, 1887 church, 1903 general store and museum, and 1912 settler's home. The Old Manatee Cemetery, which dates to 1850, has graves of early Manatee County settlers. An appointment is necessary for a cemetery tour. ☒*1404 Manatee Ave. E/State Rd. 64* ☎*941/749–7165* ☞*Free* ☉*Weekdays 9–4:30, Sun. 1:30–4:30; closed Sun. July and Aug.*

④ Florida history showcased at the **South Florida Museum and Parker Manatee Aquarium** includes state-of-the-art Native American cultural displays, prehistoric artifacts and casts, and a collection of vignettes depicting eras past in South Florida. Snooty, the oldest manatee in captivity, lives here. There are manatee presentations at feeding time in the 60,000-gallon tank. A planetarium opened in mid-2005, and includes a digital multipurpose theater. ☒*201 10th St. W* ☎*941/746–4132* ⊕*www.southfloridamuseum.org* ☞*$15.95* ☉*Jan.–Apr. and July, Mon.–Sat. 10–5, Sun. noon–5; May, June, and Aug.–Dec., Tues.–Sat. 10–5, Sun. noon–5.*

④ Hernando de Soto, one of North America's first Spanish explorers, ★ set foot in Florida in 1539 near what is now Bradenton; that feat is commemorated at the **De Soto National Memorial.** In high season (late December–early April), park employees dressed in 16th-century costumes demonstrate period weapons and show how European explorers prepared and preserved food for their journeys over the untamed land. A film, exhibits, and a short nature trail into the mangroves and along the shoreline round out the offerings. ☒*75th St. NW* ☎*941/792–0458* ☞*Free* ☉*Visitor center daily 9–5, grounds daily dawn–dusk.*

④ **Anna Maria Island,** Bradenton's 7-mi barrier island to the west, has a number of worthwhile beaches. Manatee Avenue connects the mainland to the island via the **Palma Sola Causeway,** adjacent to which is a long, sandy beach fronting Palma Sola Bay. There are boat ramps, a

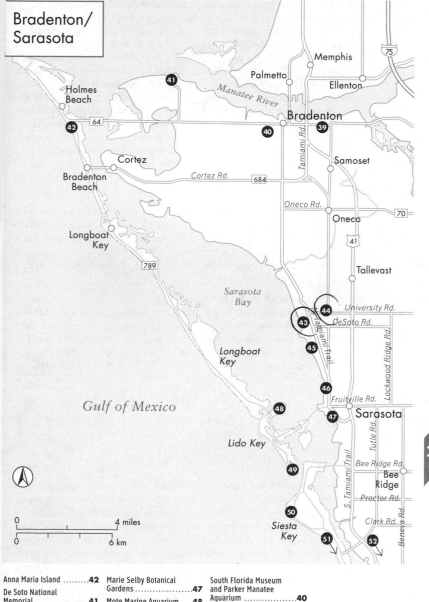

Bradenton/ Sarasota

Memphis

Palmetto

Ellenton

Holmes Beach

41

Manatee River

75

42 64

Bradenton

40 **39**

Cortez

Samoset

Bradenton Beach

Cortez Rd. 684

Oneco Rd.

Oneco

Longboat Key

70

789

41

Sarasota Bay

Tallevast

44 *University Rd.*

43 *DeSoto Rd.*

45

Longboat Key

46

Fruitville Rd.

48

47 Sarasota

Gulf of Mexico

Lido Key

Tuttle Rd.

10

49

South Lido Park

Bee Ridge Rd.

Bee Ridge

Proctor Rd.

50

Siesta Key

Clark Rd.

51 **52**

0   4 miles
0   6 km

S. Tamiami Trail

Beneva Rd.

Anna Maria Island **42**

De Soto National
Memorial **41**

FSU Ringling Center for the
Cultural Arts **43**

G.WIZ (the Hands-on Science
Museum) **46**

Manatee Village
Historical Park **39**

Marie Selby Botanical
Gardens **47**

Mote Marine Aquarium **48**

Sarasota Classic
Car Museum **44**

Sarasota Jungle Gardens ..**45**

Siesta Beach **50**

South Florida Museum
and Parker Manatee
Aquarium **40**

South Lido Park **49**

Turtle Beach **51**

Venice **52**

dock, and picnic tables. **Anna Maria Bayfront Park** (⊠ *N. Bay Blvd., adjacent to a municipal pier*) is a secluded beach fronting the Intracoastal Waterway and the Gulf of Mexico. Facilities include picnic grounds, a playground, restrooms, showers, and lifeguards. In the middle of the island, **Manatee County Beach** (⊠ *Gulf Dr. at 44th St., Holmes Beach*) is popular with beachgoers of all ages. It has picnic facilities, a snack bar, showers, restrooms, and lifeguards. **Cortez Beach** (⊠ *Gulf Blvd., Bradenton Beach*) is popular with those who like their beaches without facilities—nothing but sand, water, and trees. Singles and families flock to **Coquina Beach,** at the southern end of the island. There are lifeguards here, as well as a picnic area, boat ramp, playground, refreshments stand, restrooms, and showers. Just across the inlet on the northern tip of Longboat Key, **Greer Island Beach** is accessible by boat or via North Shore Boulevard. The secluded peninsula has a wide beach and excellent shelling, but no facilities.

OFF THE BEATEN PATH

Gamble Plantation Historic State Park. Built in the 1840s, this, the only pre–Civil War plantation house in South Florida, displays period furnishings. The Confederate secretary of state took refuge here when the Confederacy fell to Union forces. ⊠ *3708 Patten Ave., Ellenton* ☎ *941/723–4536* 🖾 *Free, tours $5* ☉ *Thurs.–Mon. 8–4:30; tours at 9:30, 10:30, and hourly 1–4.*

WHERE TO STAY & EAT

★ $-$$$$ ✕**Lee's Crab Trap and Crab Trap II.** Rustic furnishings, ultrafresh seafood, gator tail, and wild pig are among the trademarks of this casual two-house chain. Crab cakes and three-crab soup are excellent choices. The extensive menu also sways to the exotic with ostrich, octopus, kangaroo, and African rock lobster. ⊠ *5611 U.S. 19 N at Terra Ceia Bridge, Palmetto* ☎ *941/722–6255* ⊠ *4815 17th St. E, Ellenton* ☎ *941/729–7777* 🖎 *Reservations not accepted* ☐ *D, MC, V.*

$$-$$$ ✕**Sandbar Seafood & Spirits.** The outside deck sits right on the beach— the view is spectacular and a great place from which to watch the sunset. Sandbar has a formal indoor menu and a more casual outdoor menu. Options range from hamburgers to sesame-crusted tuna to stuffed snapper. ⊠ *100 Spring Ave., Anna Maria Island* ☎ *941/778–0444* ☐ *AE, D, DC, MC, V.*

$-$$$ ✕**Mangrove Grill & Bar.** Elegant dark-wood tables, sophisticated tropical accents, and overall cleanliness attract a good crowd here each night. Mangrove is a waterfront restaurant right on the Manatee River, where popular entrées include paella, ahi tuna steak crusted with black and white sesame seeds and splashed with a soy-ginger reduction, pork tenderloin grilled with a Pacific Rim garlic rub accompanied with apple compote, or the chef's selected fresh fish of the day. ⊠ *102 Riviera Dunes Way, Palmetto* ☎ *941/723–2556* ☐ *AE, D, DC, MC, V* ☉ *No lunch Mon.*

¢-$$ ✕**Gulf Drive Café.** Especially popular for breakfast (served all day), this unassuming landmark squats on the beach and serves cheap sit-down eats: mostly sandwiches, but also a sampling of entrées after 4 PM. ⊠ *900 N. Gulf Dr. N, Bradenton Beach* ☎ *941/778–1919* ☐ *D, MC, V.*

★ $$$–$$$$ 🏨**BridgeWalk, a landmark resort.**An all-in-one beach resort on Bradenton Beach's historic street, the BridgeWalk sits across the road from the beach. It has studio suites, one-bedroom suites (it calls them "apartos"), and two-bedroom town homes with Jacuzzi baths, granite countertops, and terra-cotta tile floors; the town homes have electric fireplaces. The suites range in size from 750 to 1,650 square feet. The handsome tin-roof multicolor resort is within walking distance of a pier that's popular for fishing and strolling, as well as restaurants and shops, including some on-property. Minimum stays may be required during high season (February through April). Pros: great location, variety of lodgings. Cons: can be pricey. ✉*100 Bridge St., Bradenton Beach 34217* ☎*941/779–2545 or 866/779–2545* 🖷*941/779–0828* ⊕*www. silverresorts.com* ⇴*28 apartments* ⌂*In-room: kitchen (some), dial-up. In-hotel: restaurant, bar, pool, spa, laundry facilities, no-smoking rooms* ▭*AE, D, DC, MC, V.*

$$$–$$$$ 🏨**Silver Surf Gulf Beach Resort.** It's hard to beat the location of this terra-cotta-color two-story hotel. Its private beach is right out front, there is a heated pool, many restaurants are nearby, and the staff can arrange scooter, jet ski, and kayak rentals for you. Rooms are comfortable, and renovations were done in 2005. A free trolley takes you to and from each tip of Anna Maria Island. ✉*1301 Gulf Dr. N, Anna Maria Island, Bradenton Beach 34217* ☎*941/778–6626 or 800/441–7873* 🖷*941/778–4308* ⊕*www.silverresorts.com* ⇴*4 rooms, 46 suites* ⌂*In-room: kitchen (some), refrigerator (some), dial-up. In-hotel: pool, beachfront, bicycles, laundry facilities* ▭*AE, D, DC, MC, V.*

$–$$$ 🏨**Holiday Inn Bradenton Riverfront.** Near the Manatee River, this Spanish Mediterranean–style motor inn is easily accessible from Interstate 75 and U.S. 41. Every room has its own balcony, many overlooking the river. Pros: nice views from top floor. Cons: still feels like a Holiday Inn. ✉*100 Riverfront Dr. W, Manatee Ave. to 3rd St. W, 34205* ☎*941/747–3727* 🖷*941/746–4289* ⇴*96 rooms, 57 suites* ⌂*In-room: refrigerator (some), ethernet, Wi-Fi. In-hotel: 2 restaurants, room service, bar, pool, gym, laundry service, public Wi-Fi* ▭*AE, D, DC, MC, V.*

SPORTS & THE OUTDOORS

BASEBALL

The **Pittsburgh Pirates** (✉*McKechnie Field, 17th Ave. W and 9th St.* ☎*941/748–4610*) have spring training here in March.

BIKING

Ringling Bicycles (✉*3606 Manatee Ave. W* ☎*941/749–1442*) rents bicycles for all needs and speeds for adults and kids starting at $10 a day, $40 a week.

GOLF

The excellent county-owned 18-hole **Buffalo Creek Golf Course** (✉*8100 Erie Rd., Palmetto* ☎*941/776–2611*), designed by Ron Garl, resembles a Scottish links course; green fee: $26/$49. Arnold Palmer was among the designers of **The Legacy Golf Course at Lakewood Ranch** (✉*8255 Legacy Blvd.* ☎*941/907–7920*), a public 18-hole course; green fee:

10

$55/$99. **Manatee County Golf Course** (⌧*6415 53rd Ave. W* ☎*941/792–6773*) has a driving range and 18 holes of golf; green fee: $24/$48. **Peridia Golf & Country Club** (⌧*4950 Peridia Blvd.* ☎*941/753–9097*), an executive course, has 18 holes and a driving range; green fee: $35/$55. **Waterlefe Golf & River Club** (⌧*1022 Fish Hook Cove* ☎*941/744–9771*) has a public 18-hole course; green fee: $45/$100.

SHOPPING

Find discount factory-outlet bargains at **Ellenton Prime Outlets** (⌧*5461 Factory Shops Blvd., off I–75 Exit 224* ☎*888/260–7608*), with more than 135 name-brand and other stores. **EarthBox Research Center** (⌧*1023 Ellenton-Gillette Rd.* ☎*941/723–2911 or 800/821–8838*) is closer to being a retail store that's a gardeners' paradise. EarthBox is a unique fruit and vegetable growing system—a garden in a box as the name implies—invented by farmer Blake Whisenant, who still gives demonstrations Saturdays at 10 AM. The center is open Monday through Friday 9–4 and Saturday 9–2.

SARASOTA

16 mi south of Bradenton.

A sophisticated resort town, Sarasota is traditionally the home of some ultra-affluent residents, dating back to John Ringling of circus fame. Cultural events are scheduled year-round, and there is a higher concentration of upscale shops, restaurants, and hotels than in much of the Tampa Bay area. Across the water from Sarasota lie the barrier islands of **Siesta Key, Longboat Key,** and **Lido Key,** with myriad beaches, shops, hotels, condominiums, and houses.

Decades ago, circus tycoon John Ringling found this area an ideal spot for his clowns and performers to recuperate from their months of travel while preparing for their next journey. Today, this spot is home to three spectacular attractions in one at the

㊽ FSU Ringling Center for the Cultural Arts. Along Sarasota Bay, Ringling ☾ built himself a grand home called *Cà d'Zan* ("House of John," in **Fodor's**Choice Venetian dialect), patterned after the Palace of the Doges in Venice, ★ Italy. This exquisite mansion of 32 rooms, 15 bathrooms, and a 61-foot Belvedere Tower was completed in 1925, restored in 2002, and is a must-visit today. Its 8,000-square-foot terrace overlooks the dock where Ringling's wife, Mable, moored her gondola. The **John and Mable Ringling Museum of Art** is the State Art Museum of Florida and houses 500 years of art, including a world-renowned collection of Rubens paintings and tapestries. The **Ringling Circus Museum** displays circus memorabilia from its ancient roots to modern day. The Tibbals Learning Center, which opened in early 2006, focuses on the American circus and the collection of Howard Tibbals, master model-builder, who spent 40 years building the world's largest miniature circus. This impressive to-scale replica of the circa 1920s and '30s Ringling Bros. and Barnum & Bailey Circus is authentic from the number of pancakes the circus cooks are flipping, to the exact likenesses and costumes of the performers (painstakingly re-created from photography and written accounts), to the correct names of the animals marked on the miniature mess buckets. Tibbals's passion to re-create every exact detail continues in his on-site workshop, where kids can ask him questions and watch him carving animals and intricate wagons. ⊠ *U.S. 41, ½ mi west of Sarasota-Bradenton Airport* ☎ *941/359–5700* ⊕ *www.ringling.org or www.fsu.edu/~ringling* ⚏ *$15* ⊘ *Daily 10–5:30.*

44 On display at the **Sarasota Classic Car Museum** are 100 restored antique, classic, and muscle cars—including Rolls-Royces, Pierce Arrows, and Auburns. The collection includes rare cars and vehicles that belonged to famous people, such as John Lennon and John Ringling. ⊠ *5500 N. Tamiami Trail* ☎ *941/355–6228* ⊕ *www.sarasotacarmuseum.org* ⚏ *$8.50* ⊘ *Daily 9–6.*

45 It takes about three hours to stroll through the 10-acre spread of tropical plants and animals at the **Sarasota Jungle Gardens.** The lush gardens, created in 1936, are filled with native species and exotic plants from around the world, such as the rare Australian nut tree and the Peruvian apple cactus. Also on-site are flocks of flamingos, reptiles, birds of prey, a butterfly garden, and a variety of animal shows and entertainment. ⊠ *3701 Bayshore Rd.* ☎ *941/355–5305* ⊕ *www.sarasotajunglegardens.com* ⚏ *$12* ⊘ *Daily 9–5.*

46 Kids and parents alike love state-of-the-art **G.WIZ** *(the Hands-on Science Museum).* Exhibits teach visitors about sight, sound, motion, magnetism, electricity, and more. Included are the ExploraZone, a butterfly garden, and the ecozone with snakes, a kids' lab, a technology gallery, and other exhibits. ⊠ *1001 Blvd. of the Arts* ☎ *941/309–4949* ⊕ *www.gwiz.org* ⚏ *$9* ⊘ *Weekdays 10–5, Sat. 10–6, Sun. noon–6.*

47 **Marie Selby Botanical Gardens** and her home are a don't-miss attraction for plant and flower lovers. You can stroll through the Tropical Display House with orchids and colorful bromeliads, and wander the garden pathway past plantings of bamboo, under ancient banyans, and through the mangrove along Little Sarasota Bay with spectacular views of downtown. There are rotating exhibits of botanical art and photography in a 1924 restored mansion. Enjoy lunch at the Selby Café in the historic Selby House. Shop at the Banyan Treasures Store for unique gifts as well as the Rainforest Store, specializing in orchids and tropical plants. ⊠ *811 S. Palm Ave.* ☎ *941/366–5731* ⊕ *www.selby. org* ⚏ *$12* ⊘ *Daily 10–5.*

48 The 135,000-gallon shark tank at **Mote Marine Aquarium** lets you view its inhabitants from above and below the water's surface. Additional tanks show off eels, rays, and other marine creatures native to the area. There's also a touch tank where you can get friendly with horseshoe crabs, conchs, and more. Hugh and Buffett are the resident manatees that have lived at the aquarium since 1995, and there's also a permanent sea turtle exhibit. Many visitors take the 105-minute boat trip onto Sarasota Bay, conducted by **Sarasota Bay Explorers** (☎ *941/388–4200* ⊕ *www.sarasotabayexplorers.com*). The crew brings marine life on board in a net, explains what it is, and throws it back to swim

10

away. You are almost guaranteed to see bottlenose dolphins. Reservations are required for the excursion. ✉*1600 Ken Thompson Pkwy., City Island, Sarasota* ☎*941/388–4441* ⊕*www.mote.org* ✇*Aquarium $15, boat excursion $26, combined ticket $35* ☉*Aquarium daily 10–5; boat tours daily 11, 1:30, and 4.*

49 **South Lido Park,** at the southern tip of the island, has one of the best beaches in the region, but also no lifeguards. The sugar-sand beach offers little for shell collectors, but try your luck at fishing, take a dip in the gulf, roam the 100-acre park, or picnic as the sun sets through the Australian pines into the water. Facilities include nature trails, a canoe trail and kayak launch and trail, volleyball court, playground, horseshoe pits, restrooms, and picnic grounds. ✉*2201 Ben Franklin Dr., Lido Key, Sarasota.*

50 **Siesta Beach** and its 40-acre park have nature trails, a concession stand,
Fodor'sChoice   fields for soccer and softball, picnic facilities, a playground, restrooms,
★   a fitness trail, and tennis and volleyball courts. In 1987 this beach was recognized internationally as having the whitest and finest sand in the world, a powdery, quartz-based compound that squeaks under your feet. ✉*948 Beach Rd., Siesta Key, Sarasota.*

51 Only 14 acres, **Turtle Beach** is a beach-park that's popular with families and is more secluded than most gulf beaches. It doesn't have the soft, white sand of Siesta Beach, but it does have boat ramps, a canoe and kayak launch, fishing from both the bay and gulf, horseshoe pits, picnic and play facilities, a recreation building, restrooms, and a volleyball court. ✉*8918 Midnight Pass Rd., Siesta Key, Sarasota.*

**OFF THE
BEATEN
PATH**   **Myakka River State Park.** With 28,900 acres, this outstanding wildlife preserve is absolutely lovely and is great for bird-watching and gator-sighting. Tram tours explore hammocks, airboat tours whiz over the lake, and there are hiking trails and bike rentals. A 100-foot-long can-
Fodor'sChoice   opy walkway gives you a bird's-eye view from 25 feet above ground. If
★   you care to stay awhile, the park rents cabins that have kitchens, fireplaces, and air-conditioning. There's also a campground. Reservations are essential for cabins and camping. ✉*Rte. 72, 9 mi southeast of Sarasota* ☎*941/365–0100 tours, 941/361–6511 camping, 800/326–3521 cabin reservations* ⊕*www.myakkariver.org* ✇*$5 per vehicle up to 8 people; tours $10; cabins $60 per night* ☉*Daily 8 AM–dusk; boat tours daily at 10, 11:30, 1, and 2:30.*

WHERE TO STAY & EAT

$$$$ ✕**Beach Bistro.** Standards here include a melt-in-your-mouth, herb-rubbed rack of lamb; a lobster, shrimp, fish, and calamari bouillabaisse; and roast duck with a peppercorn-and-cognac demi-glace. There also are five or six nightly specials such as veal scaloppine, New York strip, and nut-and-coconut-crusted grouper. Smaller appetites can save some pesos with a "beginnings" menu that features duck, steak, and a lonely lamb chop ($11–$24). ✉*6600 Gulf Dr., Anna Maria Island* ☎*941/778–6444* ⊕*www.beachbistro.com* ▤*AE, D, DC, MC, V.*

$$$–$$$$ ✕**Café L'Europe.** Located in an upscale neighborhood, this sidewalk and indoor eatery has a courteous staff, and a menu that's respectable if not

spectacular. When available, you can't miss with the veal osso buco sprouting asparagus and Alaskan king crab. There's also a nice choice of wines by the glass. ⊠ *431 St. Armands Circle* ☎ *941/388–4415* ⊕ *www.cafeleurope.com* ⊟ *AE, DC, D, MC, V.*

$$$–$$$$ ✗ **Ophelia's on the Bay.** The menu changes nightly at this intimate water-front spot. Favorites include grouper with coconut-and-cashew crust with papaya jam and habanero mashed potatoes; mushroom and asiago ravioli; and maple roasted duckling with pecan rice. ⊠ *9105 Midnight Pass Rd., Siesta Key* ☎ *941/349–2212* ⊕ *www.opheliasonthebay.net* ⊟ *AE, D, DC, MC, V* ⊗ *No lunch.*

$$–$$$$ ✗ **Euphemia Haye.** Named for its original owner, this refueling stop is
Fodor'sChoice a pleasant find with good food, a friendly staff, and intimate lighting.
★ Treats include Grecian lamb shank braised in a red wine garlic sauce, crispy barbecue duckling in a sweet and spicy sauce, and a very tasty pistachio-crusted red snapper. The upstairs Haye Loft, once the home of the original owner's grandson, has been converted into a lounge and dessert room. ⊠ *5540 Gulf of Mexico Dr., Longboat Key* ☎ *941/383–3633* ⊕ *www.euphemiahaye.com* ⊟ *AE, D, MC, V.*

$$–$$$$ ✗ **Michael's on East.** Dine in trendy elegance at this downtown Sarasota favorite. The fare ranges from Maine lobster bow-tie pasta to rack of lamb to grilled duck breast to pan-seared Chilean sea bass. Desserts, such as the house specialty chocolate lava, are standouts here. A light menu is served in the intimate bar, where there's often piano music or jazz in the evening. The lunch menu includes sandwiches such as fire-roasted chicken. ⊠ *1212 East Ave. S* ☎ *941/366–0007* ⊕ *www.michaelsoneast.com* ⊗ *Closed Sun. No lunch Sat.* ⊟ *AE, D, DC, MC, V.*

$$–$$$ ✗ **Bijou Café.** Wood, brass, and sumptuous carpeting surround diners
Fodor'sChoice in this 1920 gas station–turned-restaurant. Specialties on the regularly
★ changing menu could include superb crab cakes with rémoulade, a wonderfully spicy shrimp dish inspired by Mozambique, crispy roast duckling with orange-cognac sauce or port-wine cherry sauce, pepper steak, and crème brûlée for dessert. An extensive international wine list includes vintages ranging from an Australian cabernet-shiraz blend to a South African merlot and, of course, numerous selections from France and California. Opera season—typically February and March—is the only time Sunday dinner is served. ⊠ *1287 1st St.* ☎ *941/366–8111* ⊕ *www.bijoucafe.net* ⊟ *AE, D, DC, MC, V* ⊗ *Closed Sun. Apr.–Jan. No lunch weekends.*

$$–$$$ ✗ **Columbia.** On trendy St. Armands Circle, this eatery isn't quite as good as the original landmark in Ybor City, which celebrated its 100th birthday in 2005, yet it is still worth a visit. The menu reflects Spanish and Cuban cooking, and includes three versions of Spanish paella and a superb black-bean soup. A house specialty is pompano papillote (pompano with shrimp, crabmeat, and artichoke in a white wine sauce, baked in parchment), and the 1905 salad is deserving of its cult status. ⊠ *411 St. Armands Circle, Lido Key* ☎ *941/388–3987* ⊕ *www.colum-biarestaurant.com* ⊟ *AE, D, DC, MC, V.*

$$–$$$ ✗ **Patrick's.** A longtime favorite among locals, this upscale restaurant with a sports bar attracts crowds that belly up to the bar after work and

10

end up staying for steak sandwiches, juicy cheeseburgers, pizza, pasta, and char-grilled steaks. Local *Sarasota Magazine* continually ranks the burgers here as the best in the area. ✉*1400 Main St.* ☎*941/952–1170* ⊕*www.patricksrestaurant.net* ♨*Reservations not accepted* ⊟*AE, D, DC, MC, V.*

$–$$ ✕**Café Baci.** For 14 straight years its northern Italian cuisine has earned Café Baci the best restaurant award from *Sarasota Magazine.* Menu highlights include osso buco; snapper à la Baci, cooked with tomatoes, black olives, rosemary, and white wine; and veal shank. The interior is not as enticing as the entrées, but resembles an English garden, with splashes of green and white and slightly outdated floral accents. ✉*4001 S. Tamiami Trail* ☎*941/921–4848* ⊕*www.cafebaci. net* ⊟*AE, D, DC, MC, V.*

¢–$ ✕**The Broken Egg.** A local institution in the heart of Siesta Village, the Broken Egg serves breakfast and lunch. Some favorites are crab cakes Benedict, chicken ranch wrap, and banana-nut-bread French toast. The café is decorated with art by local artists, and the large patio is surrounded by lush greens. ✉*210 Avenida Madera, Siesta Village* ☎*941/346–2750* ⊕*www.thebrokenegg.com* ⊟*AE, D, DC, MC, V* ⊘*No dinner.*

¢–$ ✕**The Old Salty Dog.** A view of New Pass between Longboat and Lido keys and affordable eats make this a popular stop, especially for visitors to Mote Marine Aquarium. It's open-air but comfortable even in summer, thanks to a pleasant breeze. Quarter-pound hot dogs, fish-and-chips, wings, and burgers set the menu's tone. Locals hang out at the beer bar, shaped from the hull of an old boat. ✉*1601 Ken Thompson Pkwy., City Island* ☎*941/388–4311* ⊕*www.theoldsaltydog.com* ✉*5023 Ocean Blvd., Sarasota* ☎*941/349–0158* ♨*Reservations not accepted* ⊟*MC, V.*

¢–$ ✕**TooJay's.** A sister deli to its St. Pete's location, TooJay's is bright and cheerful and has warm wood tones. The menu has Reubens, matzo-ball soup, cheese blintzes, corned beef or pastrami sandwiches, old-fashioned pot roast, and roast chicken. ✉*Westfield Shoppingtown-Southgate, 3501 S. Tamiami Trail* ☎*941/362–3692* ⊕*www.toojays.com* ♨*Reservations not accepted* ⊟*AE, D, DC, MC, V.*

¢–$ ✕**Yoder's.** Pies—key lime, Dutch apple, egg custard, strawberry rhubarb, and others—are among the main events at this Amish family restaurant in the heart of Sarasota's Amish community, but don't miss enjoying at least one meal here. Entrées, served family style—feeding two to three people—typically include meat loaf, liver and onions, turkey and dressing, a wonderful goulash, and other hearty dishes, and breakfasts include big stacks of pancakes. The desserts might be the best part of the meal, particularly the pies. The place gets crowded around noon and early evening. ✉*3434 Bahia Vista* ☎*941/955–7771* ⊕*www.yodersrestaurant.com* ♨*Reservations not accepted* ⊟*MC, V* ⊘*Closed Sun.*

$$$$ ▦**Hyatt Sarasota on Sarasota Bay.** The Hyatt is contemporary in design and is in the heart of the city, across from the Van Wezel Performing Arts Hall. All the spacious rooms overlook Sarasota Bay or the marina and the lagoon-style pool and hot tub, which have waterfalls flowing

into them. Your concierge will arrange fishing, golfing, and babysitting if you desire. ✉ *1000 Blvd. of the Arts, 34236* ☎ *941/953–1234 or 800/233–1234* 🖨 *941/952–1987* 🌐 *www.sarasota.hyatt.com* ⤴ *294 rooms, 12 suites* ♿ *In-room: dial-up, Wi-Fi. In-hotel: 2 restaurants, room service, bars, pool, gym, bicycles, laundry facilities, laundry service, concierge, Wi-Fi, airport shuttle, some pets allowed, no-smoking rooms* ▤ *AE, D, DC, MC, V.*

$$$$ 🏨 **Longboat Key Club and Resort.** This beautifully landscaped 410-acre property is one of *the* places to golf in the state and one of the top tennis resorts in the country. Water is the test on both golf courses, which have excellent pro shops, lessons, and clinics. Tennis courts are Har-Tru–surfaced. Hobie Cats, kayaks, Sunfish, deep-sea charters, and ecology trips are also available. All rooms have balconies overlooking a golf course, beach, or private lagoon where manatees and bottle-nose dolphins are occasionally seen. Golf and dining facilities are for resort guests and club members only. ✉ *301 Gulf of Mexico Dr., Longboat Key 34228* ☎ *941/383–8821, 800/237–8821, or 888/237–5545* 🖨 *941/383–0359* 🌐 *www.longboatkeyclub.com* ⤴ *14 rooms, 142 suites* ♿ *In-room: kitchen (some), refrigerator, ethernet. In-hotel: 5 restaurants, room service, bars, golf course, tennis courts, pool, gym, beachfront, bicycles, children's programs (ages 5–12), laundry facilities, concierge, Wi-Fi, no-smoking rooms* ▤ *AE, DC, MC, V.*

★ $$$$ 🏨 **Ritz-Carlton, Sarasota.** Developers like to say that this hotel is circus magnate John Ringling's realized dream, and it certainly has a style Ringling would have coveted. Fine artwork and fresh-cut flowers decorate marble-floored hallways. Rooms have marble bathrooms, and private balconies with views of Sarasota Bay, the marina, or the downtown skyline. In late 2005, the Ritz opened a private 18-hole Tom Fazio–designed golf course 12 mi northeast of the property on the Braden River. A European-style spa and guest-and-members-only beach facility on Lido Key, about 4 mi away, make this city resort full service. Vernona restaurant serves regional organic cuisine, and overlooks yachts in the marina. Pros: Ritz-glitz. Cons: separation of some amenities, such as the golf course and beach facility. ✉ *1111 Ritz-Carlton Dr., 34236* ☎ *941/309–2000 or 800/241–3333* 🖨 *941/309–2100* 🌐 *www.ritzcarlton.com/resorts/sarasota* ⤴ *266 rooms, 30 suites* ♿ *In-room: safe, Wi-Fi . In-hotel: 2 restaurants, room service, bars, golf course, tennis courts, pool, gym, spa, children's programs (ages 5–12), laundry service, concierge, executive floor, Wi-Fi, some pets allowed, no-smoking rooms* ▤ *AE, D, DC, MC, V.*

★ $$$–$$$$ 🏨 **Colony Beach & Tennis Resort.** If tennis is your game, this is the place to stay—it's one of Florida's best racquet clubs, and tennis greats such as Björn Borg have made the Colony their home court. Ten of its courts are clay hydrosurfaced (the other 11 are hard), and the pros are all USPTA-certified. They run clinics and camps at all levels, and with the guaranteed match-making program, you can play with a pro when no one else is available. There are even rackets and lessons for children, plus excellent free kids' programs. The Colony dining room has a local reputation for excellence and fine wine. Suites sleep up to eight. Among the suites are a two-story penthouse as well as three private

10

beach houses that open onto sand and sea. The exterior of the lodging buildings could stand to be updated. Pros: *the* place for tennis fans, just 3 mi from St. Armands Circle, the Rodeo Drive of Florida's West Coast. Cons: pricey, not a good choice for nonplayers. ⊠*1620 Gulf of Mexico Dr., Longboat Key 34228* ☎*941/383–6464 or 800/426–5669* ⊟*941/383–7549* ⊕*www.colonybeachresort.com* ☞*235 suites* ♿*In-room: safe, kitchen, ethernet. In-hotel: 2 restaurants, bars, tennis courts, pool, gym, spa, beachfront, water sports, bicycles, children's programs (ages 3–17), laundry facilities, laundry service, concierge, public Wi-Fi, no-smoking rooms* ⊟*AE, D, DC, MC, V.*

★ **$$$–$$$$** 🏨**The Cypress, a Bed & Breakfast Inn.** The only B&B in downtown Sarasota, the inn has a delightful assortment of themed rooms. The Martha Rose Suite has French accessories with a balcony overlooking the gulf, a sitting area, and a separate powder room. French doors in the Mango Suite open onto a garden, and the furnishings include a couch, armchair, and Victorian writing desk. Aptly named Kathryn's Garden Room has a floral feel with wicker furnishings, a sitting area, and views of live oaks and mango trees. The Victorian-style Elizabeth Brittany Suite has an oak high-back bed and tropical sitting room. And the Essie Leigh Key West Room has a front-porch view of the bay, a pewter-and-brass bed, and private entrance. All have private baths. Rates include full breakfast and afternoon hors d'oeuvres and refreshments. Guests under 21 aren't permitted. Pros: friendly staff, convenient to downtown, a five-minute drive from the beaches at Lido Key. Cons: no in-room phones. ⊠*621 Gulfstream Ave. S, 34236* ☎⊟*941/955–4683* ⊕*www.cypressbb.com* ☞*5 rooms* ♿*In-room: no phone, Wi-Fi. In-hotel: concierge, public Wi-Fi, parking (no fee), no kids under 21, no-smoking rooms* ⊟*AE, D, MC, V* ⦿*BP.*

$$$–$$$$ 🏨**Turtle Beach Resort.** Reminiscent of a quieter, friendlier time, many of the cottages here date to the 1940s, a romantic plus for yesteryear lovers, especially given that they are well maintained. In all, there are two studios, two one-bedroom units, and six two-bedroom cottages with full kitchens. Some units have courtyards. The grounds are private, shielded by high wooden fences and palms, bougainvilleas, and other tropical foliage. The inn sits on Sarasota Bay and is named for the sea turtle nesting sites that lie across the street. If you really want to escape, use one of the resort's canoes or kayaks to paddle a short distance south to a beach dotted with sand dunes and sea oats. Pros: nice location Cons: inconvenient to the area's cultural attractions. ⊠*4099 Midnight Pass Rd., Siesta Key 34242* ☎*941/349–4554* ⊟*941/312–9034* ⊕*www.turtlebeachresort.com* ☞*20 cottages and rooms* ♿*In-room: kitchen, refrigerator, DVD (some), VCR, Wi-Fi. In-hotel: pools, no elevator, laundry facilities, parking (no fee), no-smoking rooms* ⊟*D, MC, V.*

$$–$$$$ 🏨**A Beachfront Sea Castle Accommodations.** The 10 buildings that make up this property are two-story in the Old Florida style, and all rooms lead out to the beach at Siesta Key. Rooms are bright and decorated in tasteful pastel colors, and have balconies with lounge chairs. During high season (mid-December–April), the owners mainly rent out weekly. Pros: beachfront. Cons: 1950s Florida rustic isn't for everyone. ⊠*1001–1019 Seaside Dr., Siesta Key 34242* 📠*941/349–8858 or 800/720–6885* ⊕*www.sea-castle.com* ⚲*40 rooms, 10 apartments* ⚷*In-room: kitchen (some), refrigerator, VCR (some), dial-up (some). In-hotel: pool, beachfront, no elevator, laundry facilities, parking (no fee), no-smoking rooms* ▤*D, MC, V (varies by building).*

$$–$$$$ 🏨**Lido Beach Resort.** Superb gulf views can be found at this classy beachfront resort. The South Tower was completed in May 2002, and the majority of rooms there have beach and gulf views. There are two free-form pools and three Jacuzzis, all right on the beach. The resort is equipped with Wi-Fi hot spots. Pros: gulf views, beachfront. Cons: bland furnishings. ⊠*700 Ben Franklin Dr., Lido Beach 34236* 📠*941/388–2161 or 800/441–2113* 🖨*941/388–3175* ⊕*www.lido-beachresort.com* ⚲*158 rooms, 64 suites* ⚷*In-room: kitchen (some), refrigerator, dial-up. In-hotel: 2 restaurants, bars, pools, beachfront, children's programs (ages 8–13), laundry facilities, laundry service, concierge, public Wi-Fi, no-smoking rooms* ▤*AE, D, DC, MC, V.*

$–$$$ 🏨**Best Western Midtown.** Here's a three-story motel that's comfortable, and very affordable during its off-season, from mid-April through early February. Set back from U.S. 41 and somewhat removed from traffic noise, it's within walking distance of a shopping center and several restaurants—including the popular Michael's on East—and is central to area attractions and downtown. Rooms have sitting areas. Pros: central location. Cons: bland chain feel. ⊠*1425 S. Tamiami Trail, 34239* 📠*941/955–9841 or 800/937–8376* 🖨*941/954–8948* ⊕*www. bwmidtown.com* ⚲*100 rooms* ⚷*In-room: refrigerator (some), ethernet. In-hotel: pool, laundry facilities, no-smoking rooms* ▤*AE, D, DC, MC, V* ⏀*CP.*

¢–$$$ 🏨**Gulf Beach Resort.** Lido Key's first motel has been named a historic property by the county. The resort is beachfront and is composed of condominium units that are rented out as motel rooms; since each unit is individually owned, renovations at the property are continuous. Rooms are bright and each has a different decor—many return visitors have their favorite rooms and book several years in advance. Pros: just 2 mi from St. Armands Circle, well maintained. Cons: pretty basic motel. ⊠*930 Ben Franklin Dr., Lido Key34236* 📠*941/388–2127 or 800/232–2489* 🖨*941/388–1312* ⊕*www.gulfbeachsarasota.com* ⚲*8 rooms, 41 suites* ⚷*In-room: dial-up. In-hotel: pool, beachfront, no elevator, laundry facilities, no-smoking rooms* ▤*AE, D, DC, MC, V.*

$$ 🏨**Sarasota Cay Club Resort & Marina.** Near the airport and just a 10-minute drive from downtown and a 25-minute drive from the beaches, this hotel has its own marina, and the back of the building looks out at Sarasota Bay. Rooms are standard and clean, and the restaurant often has a popular Friday night seafood buffet. ⊠*7150 N. Tamiami Trail, 34243* 📠*941/355–2781 or 888/818–2781* 🖨*941/355–1605* ⊕*www. cayclubs.com/resorts/sarasota* ⚲*178 rooms, 4 suites* ⚷*In-room: kitchen (some), refrigerator (some), dial-up (some). In-hotel: restaurant, room service, bars, pool, gym, laundry facilities, laundry service, Wi-Fi, airport shuttle, parking (no fee), some pets allowed (fee), no-smoking rooms* ▤*AE, D, DC, MC, V.*

10

NIGHTLIFE & THE ARTS

THE ARTS

Sarasota has free cultural events most Friday nights. The first Friday of each month, historic Palm Avenue downtown has **Art Walks** from 6 to 9. Members of the Palm Avenue Arts Alliance open their galleries to the public and entertain with dancing and singing. The third Friday of each month, from 6 to 10, **Towles Court Artists Colony** (✉ *1938 Adams La., Downtown* ⊕ *www.towlescourt.com*) hosts an evening for folks to wander in and out of its galleries, ask the artists about their work, and enjoy wine and cheese. The fourth Friday night (October to May, 6–9 PM) brings **Smooth Jazz on St. Armands Circle.** Musicians perform in the center of the circle; bring a blanket, relax, and enjoy refreshments from on-site kiosks.

Among the many theaters in Sarasota, the $5 million **Asolo Repertory Theatre** (✉ *5555 N. Tamiami Trail* ☎ *941/351–8000 or 800/361–8388* ⊕ *www.asolo.org*) mounts rotating-repertory productions November through mid-June. The small **Florida Studio Theatre** (✉ *1241 N. Palm Ave.* ☎ *941/366–9000*) presents contemporary dramas, comedies, and musicals, and has acting classes for both adults and children. Performers at the **Florida West Coast Symphony Center** (✉ *709 N. Tamiami Trail* ☎ *941/953–4252* ⊕ *www.fwcs.org*) include the Florida West Coast Symphony, Florida String Quartet, Florida Brass Quintet, Florida Wind Quintet, and New Artists Piano Quartet. **Golden Apple Dinner Theatre** (✉ *25 N. Pineapple Ave.* ☎ *941/366–5454*) serves a standard buffet along with musicals. A long-established community theater, **The Players Theatre** (✉ *838 N. Tamiami Trail /U.S. 41 and 9th St.* ☎ *941/365–2494*), launched such actors as Montgomery Clift and Paul Reubens. The troupe performs comedies, special events, live concerts, and musicals. The **Sarasota Concert Band** (✉ *1345 Main St.* ☎ *941/364–2263*), which celebrated its 50th anniversary in 2005, has 50 players, many of them full-time musicians; performance venues change with each event. **Theatre Works** (✉ *1247 1st St.* ☎ *941/952–9170*) presents professional non-Equity productions at the Palm Tree Playhouse. The **Van Wezel Performing Arts Hall** (✉ *777 N. Tamiami Trail* ☎ *941/953–3368 or 800/826–9303* ⊕ *www.vanwezel.org*) is easy to find—just look for the purple shell rising along the bay front. It hosts some 200 performances each year, including Broadway plays, ballet, jazz, rock concerts, symphonies, and children's shows.

The **Sarasota Film Society** (✉ *Burns Court Cinema, 506 Burns La.* ☎ *941/364–8662, 941/955–3456 theater* ⊕ *www.filmsociety.org*) shows foreign and art films daily. Call the theater for film titles and show times, and see the society's Web site for detailed descriptions of films.

Celebrating its 46th season in 2005, the **Sarasota Opera** (✉ *The Edwards Theater, 61 N. Pineapple Ave.* ☎ *941/366–8450 or 888/673–7212*) performs from February through March in a historic 1,033-seat downtown theater. Internationally known artists sing the principal roles, supported by a professional chorus of 24 young apprentices.

NIGHTLIFE

The **Gator Club** (✉ *1490 Main St.* ☎ *941/366–5969*), in a classy, historic building downtown, has live music and dancing 365 days a year. Much like Centro Ybor in Tampa, **The Quay** (✉ *U.S. 41 and Fruitville Rd.* ☎ *941/957–0120*) is a great spot for bar hopping or a casual stroll. Cover charges vary.

SPORTS & THE OUTDOORS

BASEBALL

The **Cincinnati Reds** (✉ *Ed Smith Stadium, 2700 12th St.* ☎ *941/954–4101*) have spring training here in March.

BIKING

CB's Saltwater Outfitters (✉ *1249 Stickney Point Rd., Siesta Key* ☎ *941/349–4400* ⊕ *www.cbsoutfitters.com*) rents boats, fishing gear, and bikes hourly or by the day.

DOG RACING

The greyhounds run from late November through mid-April at the **Sarasota Kennel Club** (✉ *5400 Bradenton Rd.* ☎ *941/355–7744* ⊕ *www.sarasotakennelclub.com*).

FISHING

Flying Fish Fleet (✉ *U.S. 41, on the bay front at Marina Jack* ☎ *941/366–3373* ⊕ *www.flyingfishfleet.com*) has several boats that can be chartered for deep-sea fishing and has daily group trips on its "party" fishing boat.

GOLF

Bobby Jones Golf Course (✉ *1000 Circus Blvd.* ☎ *941/955–8097*) has 45 holes and a driving range; green fee: $39/$44. **Bobcat Trail Golf Club** (✉ *1350 Bobcat Trail, North Port* ☎ *941/429–0500*) is a semiprivate 18-hole course 35 mi from Sarasota; green fee: $35/$75. Semiprivate **Forest Lakes Golf Club** (✉ *2401 Beneva Rd.* ☎ *941/922–1312*) has a practice range and 18 holes, green fee: $27/$50. Fifteen miles from Sarasota, **Heron Creek Golf & Country Club** (✉ *5303 Heron Creek Blvd., North Port* ☎ *941/423–6955* or *800/877–1433*) has a semiprivate 27-hole course; green fee: $30/$90. There are 27 holes at the Ron Garl–designed **University Park Country Club** (✉ *7671 Park Blvd., University Park* ☎ *941/359–9999*); green fee: $70/$125. This club is private, but does allow nonmembers limited play after 11 AM.

KAYAKING

Siesta Sports Rentals (✉ *6551 Midnight Pass Rd., Siesta Key* ☎ *941/346–1797* ⊕ *www.siestasportsrentals.com*) rents kayaks, bikes, beach chairs, scooters, and beach wheelchairs and strollers. Guided kayaking trips are also available.

SHOPPING

St. Armands Circle (✉ *John Ringling Blvd. [Rte. 789] at Ave. of the Presidents*) is a cluster of oh-so-exclusive shops and restaurants just east of Lido Beach. The **Ringling Art Museum Store** (✉ *5401 Bay Shore*

Rd. ☏941/359–5700 ⊕*www.ringling.org/museum_store.asp*) is a fun place to pick up clown noses, circus poster-books, T-shirts, and more.

Downtown Sarasota has many unique boutiques and eateries. **Sarasota News & Books** (✉*1341 Main St., Downtown* ☏941/365–6332) is an independent bookstore that carries a good selection of books and periodicals, hosts author-signing events, and has a café with outdoor tables. **Lotus** (✉*1451 Main St., Downtown* ☏941/906–7080 ⊕*www.lotussarasota.com*) is a home-decor and clothing boutique, specializing in shoes, accessories, Bliss cosmetics, and cotton bedding. They also display and sell works by local artists. **Rousseau's** (✉*1385 Main St., Downtown* ☏941/365–1072) has fun and unusual women's clothing and jewelry in a SoHo-style boutique. **Whole Foods** (✉*1451 1st St. at Lemon Ave., Downtown* ☏941/955–8500) carries organic produce, has a specialty wine-and-cheese market, and has a deli with prepared meals that make great picnic lunches for the beach.

VENICE

❺❷ *18 mi south of Sarasota.*

This small town is crisscrossed with canals like the city for which it was named. Venice beaches are good for shell collecting, but they're best known for their wealth of sharks' teeth and fossils, washed up from the ancient shark burial grounds just offshore.

Nokomis Beach (✉*901 Casey Key Rd., Nokomis*) is one of two notable beaches in the area, on the island just north of Venice Beach, across the pass near North Jetty Park. It has restrooms, a concession stand, picnic equipment, play areas, two boat ramps, a volleyball court, and fishing.

North Jetty Park (✉*Albee Rd., Casey Key*), at the south end of Casey Key, is a favorite for family outings and fishermen. Facilities include restrooms, a concession stand, play and picnic equipment, horseshoes, and a volleyball court.

Caspersen Beach (✉*Beach Dr., South Venice*) is the county's largest park and is known for its fossil finds. It has a nature trail, fishing, picnicking, restrooms, and lots of beach, but few amenities.

Manasota Beach (✉*Manasota Beach Rd., Manasota Key*) has a boat ramp, picnic area, and restrooms. Reach it by foot from Caspersen Beach. By road, it's a lot less direct.

At **Blind Pass Beach** (✉*Manasota Beach Rd., Manasota Key*), fish, swim, and hike the nature trail. There are restrooms and showers.

Englewood Beach (✉*Off Rte. 776, near the Charlotte–Sarasota county line*) is popular with teenagers, although beachgoers of all ages frequent it. There are barbecue grills, picnic facilities, boat ramps, a fishing pier, a playground, and showers. There's a charge for parking.

WHERE TO STAY & EAT

$$-$$$$
Fodor's Choice
★

✕**Crow's Nest Marina Restaurant & Tavern.** Open since 1976, this waterfront restaurant on the south jetty is a lively local favorite, always teeming with patrons. The upstairs main dining room, where business-casual dress is enforced, is more formal than the downstairs dark-wood tavern. The menu includes pan-seared grouper Key Largo, which is topped with lobster, shrimp, scallops, and mushrooms, and roasted Bahamian lobster tail. ⊠*1968 Tarpon Center Dr.* ☎*941/484–9551* ⊕*www.crowsnest-venice.com* ⊟*AE, D, DC, MC, V.*

$-$$$

✕**Sharky's on the Pier.** Gaze out on the beach and sparkling waters while dining on grilled seafood at this very casual eatery. You choose whether the catches of the day are broiled, blackened, grilled, or fried. Specialties include macadamia grouper and sea pasta. There's an outdoor veranda in addition to the tables indoors, and entertainment five nights a week. ⊠*1600 S. Harbor Dr.* ☎*941/488–1456* ⊕*www.sharkyson-thepier.com* ⊟*AE, D, MC, V* ⊗*Closed Mon. July–Sept.*

$$$-$$$$

▥**Inn at the Beach.** Across from the beach, this little one- and two-story resort is popular with families. Some of the one- and two-bedroom suites, which have spacious living rooms, have views of the gulf. Others look out on tropical gardens. A continental breakfast is served in the lobby each morning. ⊠*725 W. Venice Ave., 34285* ☎*941/484–8471* or *800/255–8471* 🖷*941/484–0593* ⊕*www.innatthebeach.com* ⬉*37 rooms, 12 suites* ⚐*In-room: safe, kitchen (some), refrigerator, dial-up, Wi-Fi . In-hotel: pool, no elevator, laundry facilities, parking (no fee), no-smoking rooms* ⊟*AE, D, DC, MC, V* ⓄⅠCP.

THE ARTS

Venice Little Theatre (⊠*140 W. Tampa Ave.* ☎*941/488–1115* ⊕*www. venicestage.com*) is a community theater showing comedies, musicals, dramas, and contemporary works on two stages during its October through May season.

SPORTS & THE OUTDOORS

BIKING

Bicycles International (⊠*1744 S. Tamiami Trail* ☎*941/497–1590*) rents some of its varied stock weekly and daily.

FISHING

At **Florida Deep Sea Fishing Charters** (⊠*1968 Tarpon Center Dr., Crow's Nest Marina, Venice* ☎*941/473–4603* ⊕*www.charter-boatfishing. com*), Captain Dave Pinkham offers half-day and full-day deep-sea-fishing trips for tarpon, shark, amberjack, and other fighting fish.

GOLF

Bird Bay Executive Golf Course (⊠*602 Bird Bay Dr. W* ☎*941/485–9333*) is a public course that has 18 holes; green fee: $15/$19.

WATER SPORTS

Don and Mike's Boat and Jet Ski Rental (⊠*482 Blackburn Point Rd.* ☎*941/966–4000*) rents water skis, jet skis, ski boats, tech boats, and pontoon boats, and has instruction for all activities.

10

SHOPPING

If you like flea markets, check out the **Dome** (⊠ *Rte. 775, west of U.S. 41*), where dozens of sheltered stalls sell new and recycled wares. It's open October through August, Friday through Sunday 9 to 4.

THE TAMPA BAY AREA ESSENTIALS

To research prices, get advice from other travelers, and book travel arrangements, visit www.fodors.com.

TRANSPORTATION

BY AIR

Many carriers serve Tampa International Airport. Sarasota's airport is served by major carriers (⇨ *Smart Travel Tips).* Scheduled service to St. Petersburg–Clearwater International is limited, and from many areas of the country, you have to supply your own plane. American TransAir connects to U.S. cities, and Air Transat flies from Toronto.

Contacts **Air Transat** (☎ *877/872–6728* ⊕ *www.airtransat.com).* **American TransAir** (☎ *800/435–9282* ⊕ *www.ata.com).* **Cayman Airways** (☎ *800/422–9626* ⊕ *www.caymanairways.com).* **Condor Airlines** (☎ *800/524–6975* ⊕ *www.condor.com).* **Discover Air** (☎ *866/359–3247* ⊕ *www.discoverair.com).* **Southeast** (☎ *800/383–7807* ⊕ *www.flyseal.com).* **Gulfstream International** (☎ *800/525–0280* ⊕ *www.gulfstreamair.com).*

Central Florida Limousine provides Tampa International Airport service to and from Hillsborough (Tampa, Plant City) and Polk (east of Tampa-Lakeland) counties, and Super Shuttle serves Pinellas County (St. Pete Beach, St. Petersburg, Clearwater). Expect taxi fares to be about $12 to $25 for most of Hillsborough County and about twice that for Pinellas County. Transportation to and from Sarasota–Bradenton Airport is provided by West Coast Executive Sedan. The average cab fare between the airport and downtown is $12 to $25.

Airport Contacts **Tampa International Airport** (⊠ *5503 Spruce St., 6 mi from downtown Tampa* ☎ *813/870–8700* ⊕ *www.tampaairport.com).* **St. Petersburg–Clearwater International Airport** (⊠ *14700 Terminal Blvd., off Rte. 686, 9 mi from downtown St. Petersburg* ☎ *727/453–7800* ⊕ *www.fly2pie.com).* **Sarasota–Bradenton International Airport** (⊠ *600 Airport Circle, off U.S. 41, just north of Sarasota* ☎ *941/359–2777* ⊕ *www.srq-airport.com).*

Transfer Contacts **Super Shuttle** (☎ *727/572–1111 or 800/282–6817* ⊕ *www.supershuttle.com).* **West Coast Executive Sedan** (☎ *941/359–8600).*

BY BUS

Service to and throughout the state is provided by Greyhound Lines. Around Tampa, the Hillsborough Area Regional Transit (HART) serves the county, and the TECO Line Streetcars replicate the city's first electric streetcars, transporting cruise-ship passengers to Ybor City. Around St. Petersburg, Pinellas Suncoast Transit Authority serves Pinellas County. The Looper trolley operates to downtown area attractions. In Sarasota the public transit company is Sarasota County Area Transit (SCAT). Fares for local bus service range from 50¢ to $2.50 (for an all-day pass), and exact change is required.

Contacts Greyhound Lines (☎ *800/231–2222* ⊕ *www.greyhound.com*). **Greyhound Sarasota** (✉ *575 N. Washington Blvd., Sarasota* ☎ *941/955–5735*). **Greyhound Clearwater** (✉ *2811 Gulf-to-Bay Blvd., Clearwater* ☎ *727/796–7315*). **Greyhound St. Petersburg** (✉ *180 9th St. N, St. Petersburg* ☎ *727/898–1436*). **Greyhound Tampa** (✉ *610 E. Polk St., Tampa* ☎ *813/229–2174*). **Hillsborough Area Regional Transit** (*(HART)* ☎ *813/254–4278* ⊕ *www.hartline.org*). **Pinellas Suncoast Transit Authority** (*(PSTA)* ☎ *727/540–1900* ⊕ *www.psta.net*). **Sarasota County Area Transit** (*(SCAT)* ☎ *941/316–1234*). **TECO Line Street Cars** (☎ *813/254–4278*).

BY CAR

Interstate 75 spans the region from north to south. Once you cross the Florida border from Georgia, it should take about 4½ hours to reach Tampa and another hour to reach Sarasota. Interstate exits are numbered according to mileage from their southern terminus, rather than sequentially. Coming from Orlando, you're likely to drive west into Tampa on Interstate 4. Along with Interstate 75, U.S. 41 (which runs concurrently with the Tamiami Trail for much of the way) stretches the length of the region. U.S. 41 links the business districts of many communities, so it's best to avoid it and all bridges during rush hours (7–9 AM and 4–6 PM). U.S. 19 is St. Petersburg's major north–south artery; traffic can be heavy, and there are many lights, so use a different route when possible. Interstate 275 heads west from Tampa across Tampa Bay to St. Petersburg, swings south, and crosses the bay again on its way to Terra Ceia, near Bradenton. Along this last leg—the Sunshine Skyway and its stunning suspension bridge—you'll get a bird's-eye view of bustling Tampa Bay. The Gandy Bridge (Highway 92) also yields a spectacular view of Tampa Bay, and Route 679 takes you along two of St. Petersburg's most pristine islands, Cabbage and Mullet keys. Route 64 connects Interstate 75 to Bradenton and Anna Maria Island. Route 789 runs over several slender barrier islands, past miles of blue-green gulf waters, beaches, and waterfront homes. The road does not connect all the islands, however; it runs from the village of Anna Maria off the Bradenton coast south to Lido Key, then begins again on Siesta Key and again on Casey Key south of Osprey, and runs south to Nokomis Beach.

10

BY TRAIN

Amtrak trains run from the Northeast, Midwest, and much of the South to the Tampa station.

Contacts Amtrak (✉ *Tampa Union Station, 601 N. Nebraska Ave., Tampa* ☎ *800/872–7245 or 813/221–7600* ⊕ *www.amtrak.com*).

CONTACTS & RESOURCES

EMERGENCIES

There are 24-hour emergency rooms at Bayfront Medical Center, Manatee Memorial Hospital, Sarasota Memorial Hospital, and University Community Hospital.

Contacts **Emergencies** (☎ *911*). **Bayfront Medical Center** (✉ *701 6th St. S, St. Petersburg* ☎ *727/893-6100*). **Manatee Memorial Hospital** (✉ *206 2nd St. E, Bradenton* ☎ *941/745-7559*). **Sarasota Memorial Hospital** (✉ *1700 S. Tamiami Trail, Sarasota* ☎ *941/917-9000*). **University Community Hospital** (✉ *3100 E. Fletcher Ave., Tampa* ☎ *813/971-6000*).

MEDIA

Daily newspapers in the area are the *Bradenton Herald, Sarasota Herald–Tribune, St. Petersburg Times,* and *Tampa Tribune.* The *Cedar Key Beacon, Longboat Observer,* and *Tampa Bay Business Journal* are weekly newspapers. *Tampa Bay Life* is a monthly magazine.

TOURS

West Florida Helicopters gives bay-area tours. There's a daily hovercraft tour from St. Petersburg, operated by Hover USA. The *American Victory* Mariners Memorial & Museum Ship offers weekend day trips aboard the restored World War II–era merchant marine vessel with historical reenactments of life aboard during its wartime service. Gourmet meals and a stunning view of the Tampa skyline are available aboard StarShip Cruises, with lunch and dinner cruises aboard its namesake *StarShip,* which seats up to 350 people in the dining room.

On Captain Memo's Pirate Cruise, crew members dressed as pirates take you on sightseeing and sunset cruises in a replica of a 19th-century sailing ship. Dolphin Landings Charter Boat Center has daily, four-hour cruises to unspoiled Egmont Key at the mouth of Tampa Bay. Aboard the glass-bottom boats of St. Nicholas Boat Line, you take a sightseeing cruise of Tarpon Springs' historic sponge docks and see a diver at work. The *Starlite Princess,* an old-fashioned paddle wheeler, and *Starlite Majesty,* a sleek yacht-style vessel, make sightseeing and dinner cruises.

Contacts *American Victory* **Mariners Memorial & Museum Ship** (✉ *705 Channelside Dr., Berth 271, behind Florida Aquarium, Tampa* ☎ *813/228-8766* ⊕ *www.americanvictory.org*). **Captain Memo's Pirate Cruise** (✉ *Clearwater Beach Marina, Clearwater Beach* ☎ *727/446-2587*). **Dolphin Landings Charter Boat Center** (✉ *4737 Gulf Blvd., St. Pete Beach* ☎ *727/360-7411*). **St. Nicholas Boat Line** (✉ *693 Dodecanese Blvd., Tarpon Springs* ☎ *727/942-6425*). **Starlite Princess and Starlite Majesty** (✉ *Clearwater Beach Marina, at the end of Rte. 60, Clearwater Beach* ✉ *Corey Causeway, 3400 S. Pasadena, South Pasadena* ☎ *727/462-2628* ⊕ *www.starlitecruises.com*). **StarShip Cruises** (✉ *603 Channelside Dr., Tampa* ☎ *813/223-7999 or 877/744-7999*). **West Florida Helicopters** (✉ *Albert Whitted Airport, 107 8th Ave. SE, St. Petersburg* ☎ *727/823-5200*).

VISITOR INFORMATION

Contacts **Bradenton Area Convention & Visitors Bureau Tourist Information Center** (✉ *1 Haven Blvd., Palmetto 34221* ✉ *Kiosk in Prime Outlets Ellenton, 5461 Factory Shops Blvd., Ellenton 34222* ☎ *941/729-9177* ⊕ *www.floridasgulfislands. com*). **Cedar Key Chamber of Commerce** (✉ *525 2nd St., Box 610, Cedar Key 32625* ☎☎ *352/543-5600* ⊕ *www.cedarkey.org*). **Clearwater Regional Chamber of Commerce** (✉ *1130 Cleveland St., Clearwater 33755* ☎ *727/461-0011* ⊕ *www.clearwaterflorida.org*). **Greater Dunedin Chamber of Commerce** (✉ *301 Main St., Dunedin 34698* ☎ *727/733-3197* ⊕ *www.dunedin-fl.com*). **Greater Tampa Chamber of Commerce** (✉ *615 Channelside Dr., Box 420, Tampa 33601* ☎ *813/228-7777, 813/223-1111 Ext. 44 for Visitors Information Department* ⊕ *www.tampachamber.com*). **Sarasota Convention and Visitors Bureau** (✉ *655 N. Tamiami Trail, Sarasota 34236* ☎ *941/957-1877 or 800/522-9799* ⊕ *www. sarasotafl.org*). **St. Petersburg Area Chamber of Commerce** (✉ *13850 58th St. N, Suite 2200, St. Petersburg 33760* ☎ *727/821-4069* ⊕ *www.stpete.com*). **St. Petersburg/Clearwater Area Convention & Visitors Bureau** (✉ *14450 46th St. N, Suite 108, St. Petersburg 33762* ☎ *727/464-7200 or 877/352-3224* ⊕ *www. floridasbeach.com*). **Tampa Bay Beaches Chamber of Commerce** (✉ *6990 Gulf Blvd., St. Pete Beach 33706* ☎ *727/360-6957 or 800/944-1847* ⊕ *www. tampabaybeaches.com*). **Tampa Bay Convention and Visitors Bureau** (✉ *400 N. Tampa St., Suite 2800, Tampa 33602* ☎ *800/368-2672 or 813/223-1111* ⊕ *www. visittampabay.com*). **Tarpon Springs Chamber of Commerce** (✉ *11 E. Orange St., Tarpon Springs 34689* ☎ *727/937-6109* ⊕ *www.tarponsprings.com*). **Ybor City Chamber Visitor Bureau** (✉ *1600 E. 8th Ave., Suite B104, 33605* ☎ *813/248-3712* ⊕ *www.ybor.org*).

10

Florida Essentials

PLANNING TOOLS, EXPERT INSIGHT, GREAT CONTACTS

There are planners and there are those who, excuse the pun, fly by the seat of their pants. We happily place ourselves among the planners. Our writers and editors try to anticipate all the issues you may face before and during any journey, and then they do their research. This section is the product of their efforts. Use it to get excited about your trip to, Florida to inform your travel planning, or to guide you on the road should the seat of your pants start to feel threadbare.

GETTING STARTED

We're really proud of our Web site: Fodors.com is a great place to begin any journey. Scan "Travel Wire" for suggested itineraries, travel deals, restaurant and hotel openings, and other up-to-the-minute info. Check out "Booking" to research prices and book plane tickets, hotel rooms, rental cars, and vacation packages. Head to "Talk" for on-the-ground pointers from travelers who frequent our message boards. You can also link to loads of other travel-related resources.

■ RESOURCES

ONLINE TRAVEL TOOLS
The state of Florida is very visitor-oriented and has a terrific Web site—⊕ *www.visitflorida.com*—with superb links to help you find out all you want to know. It's a wonderful place to learn about everything from fancy resorts to camping trips to car routes to beach towns.

All About Florida Visit Florida (⊕www.visitflorida.com).

Safety Transportation Security Administration (TSA; ⊕www.tsa.gov).

Time Zones Timeanddate.com (⊕www.timeanddate.com/worldclock) can help you figure out the correct time anywhere in the world.

Weather Accuweather.com (⊕www.accuweather.com) is an independent weather-forecasting service with especially good coverage of hurricanes. **Weather.com** (⊕www.weather.com) is the Web site for the Weather Channel.

Other Resources CIA World Factbook (⊕www.odci.gov/cia/publications/factbook/index.html) has profiles of every country in the world. It's a good source if you need some quick facts and figures. A Gulf Coast Journal, hosted by Jack Perkins, formerly of NBC and A&E Biography, airs monthly on WEDU stations in the Venice–Sarasota–Tampa region. In each episode, Perkins discovers and visits little-known gems in the Gulf Coast region. These Emmy Award–winning episodes can be purchased through the Web site ⊕www.wedu.org, and the Journal's archives on the site have Web links to sites that Perkins has covered.

VISITOR INFORMATION
For general information about Florida's attractions, contact the office below; welcome centers are on Interstate 10, Interstate 75, Interstate 95, and U.S. 231 (near Graceville), and in the lobby of the New Capitol in Tallahassee. *For regional tourist bureaus and chambers of commerce see individual chapters.*

Contacts Visit Florida (✉661 E. Jefferson St., Suite 300, Tallahassee# 32301 ☏Box 1100, Tallahassee # 32302 ☎850/488–5607 ☐850/224–9589 ⊕www.visitflorida.com).

■ THINGS TO CONSIDER

GOVERNMENT ADVISORIES
If you travel frequently, look into the TSA's Registered Traveler program (⊕www.tsa.gov). The program, which is still being tested in several U.S. airports, is designed to cut down on gridlock at security checkpoints by allowing prescreened travelers to pass quickly through kiosks that scan an iris and/or a fingerprint. How sci-fi is that?

If you are visiting Florida during the June through November hurricane season and a hurricane is imminent, be sure to follow directions from local authorites.

GEAR

The northern part of the state is much cooler in winter than the southern part, and you'll want to take a heavy sweater if you plan on traveling north in winter months. Even in summer, ocean breezes can be cool, so always take a sweater or jacket just in case.

The Miami area and the Naples–Fort Myers area are warm year-round and often extremely humid in summer months. Be prepared for sudden storms all over Florida in summer, but keep in mind that plastic raincoats are uncomfortable in the high humidity. Often the storms are quick and the sun comes back in no time.

Dress is casual throughout the state, with sundresses, jeans, or walking shorts appropriate during the day; bring comfortable walking shoes or sneakers for theme parks. A few restaurants request that men wear jackets and ties, but most do not. Be prepared for air-conditioning working in overdrive.

You can generally swim year-round in peninsular Florida from about New Smyrna Beach south on the Atlantic coast and from Tarpon Springs south on the Gulf Coast. Be sure to take a sun hat and sunscreen, because the sun can be fierce, even in winter and even if it's chilly or overcast. Don't leave valuables on your beach blanket while you walk the beach or go for a dip.

SHIPPING LUGGAGE AHEAD

Imagine globe-trotting with only a carry-on in tow. Shipping your luggage in advance via an air-freight service is a great way to cut down on backaches, hassles, and stress—especially if your packing list includes strollers, car seats, etc. There are some things to be aware of, though. First, research carry-on restrictions; if you absolutely need something that's isn't practical to ship and isn't allowed in carry-ons, this strategy isn't for you. Second, plan to send your bags several days in advance to U.S. destinations and as much as two

weeks in advance to some international destinations. Third, plan to spend some money: it will cost at least $100 to send a small piece of luggage, a golf bag, or a pair of skis to a domestic destination, much more to places overseas. Some people use Federal Express to ship their bags, but this can cost even more than air-freight services. All these services insure your bag (for most, the limit is $1,000, but you should verify that amount); you can, however, purchase additional insurance for about $1 per $100 of value.

Contacts Luggage Concierge (☎ 800/288–9818 ⊕ www.luggageconcierge.com). **Luggage Express** (☎ 866/744–7224 ⊕ www.usxpluggageexpress.com). **Luggage Free** (☎ 800/361–6871 ⊕ www.luggagefree.com). **Sports Express** (☎ 800/357–4174 ⊕ www.sportsexpress.com) specializes in shipping golf clubs and other sports equipment. **Virtual Bellhop** (☎ 877/235–5467 ⊕ www.virtualbellhop.com).

TRIP INSURANCE

What kind of coverage do you honestly need? Do you even need trip insurance at all? Take a deep breath and read on.

We believe that comprehensive trip insurance is especially valuable if you're booking a very expensive or complicated trip (particularly to an isolated region) or if you're booking far in advance. Who knows what could happen six months down the road? But whether or not you get insurance has more to do with how comfortable you are assuming all that risk yourself.

Comprehensive travel policies typically cover trip-cancellation and interruption, letting you cancel or cut your trip short because of a personal emergency, illness, or, in some cases, acts of terrorism in your destination. Such policies also cover evacuation and medical care. Some also cover you for trip delays because of bad weather or mechanical problems as well as for lost or delayed baggage. Another type of coverage to look for is financial

Trip Insurance Resources

INSURANCE COMPARISON SITES		
Insure My Trip.com	800/487–4722	www.insuremytrip.com
Square Mouth.com	800/240–0369	www.quotetravelinsurance.com
COMPREHENSIVE TRAVEL INSURERS		
Access America	866/807–3982	www.accessamerica.com
CSA Travel Protection	800/873–9855	www.csatravelprotection.com
HTH Worldwide	610/254–8700 or 888/243–2358	www.hthworldwide.com
Travelex Insurance	888/457–4602	www.travelex-insurance.com
Travel Guard International	715/345–0505 or 800/826–4919	www.travelguard.com
Travel Insured International	800/243–3174	www.travelinsured.com
MEDICAL-ONLY INSURERS		
International Medical Group	800/628–4664	www.imglobal.com
International SOS	215/942–8000 or 713/521–7611	www.internationalsos.com
Wallach & Company	800/237–6615 or 504/687–3166	www.wallach.com

default—that is, when your trip is disrupted because a tour operator, airline, or cruise line goes out of business. Generally you must buy this when you book your trip or shortly thereafter, and it's available to you only if your operator isn't on a list of excluded companies.

If you're going abroad, consider buying medical-only coverage at the very least. Neither Medicare nor some private insurers cover medical expenses anywhere outside of the United States besides Mexico and Canada (including time aboard a cruise ship, even if it leaves from a U.S. port). Medical-only policies typically reimburse you for medical care (excluding that related to preexisting conditions) and hospitalization abroad, and provide for evacuation. You still have to pay the bills and await reimbursement from the insurer, though.

Expect comprehensive travel insurance policies to cost about 4% to 7% of the total price of your trip (it's more like

12% if you're over age 70). A medical-only policy may or may not be cheaper than a comprehensive policy. Always read the fine print of your policy to make sure that you are covered for the risks that are of most concern to you. Compare several policies to make sure you're getting the best price and range of coverage available.

■TIP→ OK. You know you can save a bundle on trips to warm-weather destinations by traveling in rainy season. But there's also a chance that a severe storm will disrupt your plans. The solution? Look for hotels and resorts that offer storm/hurricane guarantees. Although they rarely allow refunds, most guarantees do let you rebook later if a storm strikes.

BOOKING YOUR TRIP

Unless your cousin is a travel agent, you're probably among the millions of people who make most of their travel arrangements online. But have you ever wondered just what the differences are between an online travel agent (a Web site through which you make reservations instead of going directly to the airline, hotel, or car-rental company), a discounter (a firm that does a high volume of business with a hotel chain or airline and accordingly gets good prices), a wholesaler (one that makes cheap reservations in bulk and then re-sells them to people like you), and an aggregator (one that compares all the offerings so you don't have to)? Is it truly better to book directly on an airline or hotel Web site? And when does a real live travel agent come in handy?

ONLINE

You really have to shop around. A travel wholesaler such as Hotels.com or Hotel-Club.net can be a source of good rates, as can discounters such as Hotwire or Priceline, particularly if you can bid for your hotel room or airfare. Indeed, such sites sometimes have deals that are unavailable elsewhere. They do, however, tend to work only with hotel chains (which makes them just plain useless for getting hotel reservations outside of major cities) or big airlines (so that often leaves out upstarts like jetBlue and some foreign carriers like Air India). Also, with discounters and wholesalers you must generally prepay, and everything is nonrefundable. And before you fork over the dough, be sure to check the terms and conditions, so you know what a given company will do for you if there's a problem and what you'll have to deal with on your own.

■TIP➜To be absolutely sure everything was processed correctly, confirm reservations made through online travel agents, discounters, and wholesalers directly with your hotel before leaving home.

Booking engines like Expedia, Travelocity, and Orbitz are actually travel agents, albeit high-volume, online ones. And airline travel packagers like American Airlines Vacations and Virgin Vacations—well, they're travel agents, too. But they may still not work with all the world's hotels.

An aggregator site will search many sites and pull the best prices for airfares, hotels, and rental cars from them. Most aggregators compare the major travel-booking sites such as Expedia, Travelocity, and Orbitz; some also look at airline Web sites, though rarely the sites of smaller budget airlines. Some aggregators also compare other travel products, including complex packages—a good thing, as you can sometimes get the best overall deal by booking an air-and-hotel package.

WITH A TRAVEL AGENT

If you use an agent—brick-and-mortar or virtual—you'll pay a fee for the service. And know that the service you get from some online agents isn't comprehensive. For example Expedia and Travelocity don't search for prices on budget airlines like jetBlue, Southwest, or small foreign carriers. That said, some agents (online or not) *do* have access to fares that are difficult to find otherwise, and the savings can more than make up for any surcharge.

A knowledgeable brick-and-mortar travel agent can be a godsend if you're booking a cruise, a package trip that's not available to you directly, an air pass, or a complicated itinerary including several overseas flights. What's more, travel agents that specialize in a destination may have exclusive access to certain deals and insider information on things such as charter flights. Agents who specialize in types of travelers (senior citizens, gays and lesbians, naturists) or types of trips (cruises, luxury travel, safaris) can also be invaluable.

A top-notch agent planning your trip to Russia will make sure you get the correct visa application and complete it on time; the one booking your cruise may get you a cabin upgrade or arrange to have a bottle of champagne chilling in your cabin when you embark. And complain about the surcharges all you like, but when things don't work out the way you'd hoped, it's nice to have an agent to put things right.

▪TIP➔Remember that Expedia, Travelocity, and Orbitz are travel agents, not just booking engines. To resolve any problems with a reservation made through these companies, contact them first.

Agent Resources **American Society of Travel Agents** (☎703/739-2782 ⊕www.travelsense.org).

Florida Travel Agents **Florida State Travel Center** (✉2000 S. Tamiami Trail, Sarasota 34239 ☎800/430-2435 or 941/955-2525 ⊕www.floridatravelusa.com). **The British in Florida** (☎877/878-6731 ⊕sunnybrits.com/british/travel/index.htm).

▪ ACCOMMODATIONS

Florida has every conceivable type of lodging—from tree houses to penthouses, mansions for hire to hostels. Even with occupancy rates inching above 70%, there are almost always rooms available, except maybe at Christmas and other holidays.

Children are welcome generally everywhere in Florida. Pets are another matter, so inquire ahead of time if you're bringing an animal with you.

In the busy seasons—over Christmas and from late January through Easter in the southern half of the state, during the summer along the Panhandle and around Jacksonville, and all over Florida during holiday weekends in summer—always reserve ahead for the top properties. Fall is the slowest season: rates are low and availability is high, but this is also the

prime time for hurricanes. St. Augustine stays busy all summer because of its historic flavor. Key West is jam-packed for Fantasy Fest at Halloween. If you're not booking through a travel agent, call the visitors bureau or the chamber of commerce in the area you'll be visiting to check whether a special event is scheduled for the period of your trip.

CATEGORY	COST
¢	under $80
$	$80–$100
$$	$100–$140
$$$	$140–$220
$$$$	over $220

All prices are for a standard double room in high season, based on the European Plan (EP) and excluding tax and service charges, which vary throughout the state: Sarasota charges a 7% sales tax and 3% tourist tax, totaling 10%; in Miami the sales and tourist taxes combined are 13%.

Most hotels and other lodgings require you to give your credit-card details before they will confirm your reservation. If you don't feel comfortable e-mailing this information, ask if you can fax it (some places even prefer faxes). However you book, get confirmation in writing and have a copy of it handy when you check in.

Be sure you understand the hotel's cancellation policy. Some places allow you to cancel without any kind of penalty—even if you prepaid to secure a discounted rate—if you cancel at least 24 hours in advance. Others require you to cancel a week in advance or penalize you the cost of one night. Small inns and bed-and-breakfasts are most likely to require you to cancel far in advance. Most hotels allow children under a certain age to stay in their parents' room at no extra charge, but others charge for them as extra adults; find out the cutoff age for discounts.

Online Booking Resources

AGGREGATORS		
Kayak	www.kayak.com	also looks at cruises and vacation packages.
Mobissimo	www.mobissimo.com	
Qixo	www.qixo.com	also compares cruises, vacation packages, and even travel insurance.
Sidestep	www.sidestep.com	also compares vacation packages and lists travel deals.
Travelgrove	www.travelgrove.com	also compares cruises and packages.
BOOKING ENGINES		
Cheap Tickets	www.cheaptickets.com	a discounter.
Expedia	www.expedia.com	a large online agency that charges a booking fee for airline tickets.
Hotwire	www.hotwire.com	a discounter.
lastminute.com	www.lastminute.com	specializes in last-minute travel the main site is for the U.K., but it has a link to a U.S. site.
Luxury Link	www.luxurylink.com	has auctions (surprisingly good deals) as well as offers on the high-end side of travel.
Onetravel.com	www.onetravel.com	a discounter for hotels, car rentals, airfares, and packages.
Orbitz	www.orbitz.com	charges a booking fee for airline tickets, but gives a clear breakdown of fees and taxes before you book.
Priceline.com	www.priceline.com	a discounter that also allows bidding.
Travel.com	www.travel.com	allows you to compare its rates with those of other booking engines.
Travelocity	www.travelocity.com	charges a booking fee for airline tickets, but promises good problem resolution.
ONLINE ACCOMMODATIONS		
Hotelbook.com	www.hotelbook.com	focuses on independent hotels worldwide.
Hotel Club	www.hotelclub.net	good for major cities worldwide.
Hotels.com	www.hotels.com	a big Expedia-owned wholesaler that offers rooms in hotels all over the world.
Quikbook	www.quikbook.com	offers "pay when you stay" reservations that let you settle your bill at check out, not when you book.
OTHER RESOURCES		
Bidding For Travel	www.biddingfortravel. com	a good place to figure out what you can get and for how much before you start bidding on, say, Priceline.

■TIP➔Assume that hotels operate on the European Plan (**EP**, no meals) unless we specify that they use the Breakfast Plan (**BP**, with full breakfast), Continental Plan (**CP**, continental breakfast), Full American Plan (**FAP**, all meals), Modified American Plan (**MAP**, breakfast and dinner), or are all-inclusive (**AI**, all meals and most activities).

APARTMENT & HOUSE RENTALS

Contacts (⌂ Box 1133, Captiva 33924 ☎800/547–0127 ⊕www.captiva-island.com). **Florida Keys Rental Store/Marr Properties** (⌂ Box 600, ✉99980 Overseas Hwy., Key Largo # 33037 ☎800/585–0584 or 305/451–3879 ⊕www.floridakeysrentalstore.com). **Florida Sunbreak** (✉90 Alton Rd., Suite 16, Miami Beach # 33139 ☎800/786–2732 or 305/532–1516 ⊕www.floridasunbreak.com). **Freewheeler Vacations** (✉85992 Overseas Hwy., MM 86, Islamorada # 33036 ☎866/664–2075 or 305/664–2075 ⊕www.freewheeler-realty.com). **Interhome** (☎954/791–8282 or 800/882–6864 ⊕www.interhome.us). **Resort-Quest International** (✉35000 Emerald Coast Pkwy., Destin # 32541 ☎877/588–5800 ⊕www.resortquest.com). **Sa nd Key Realty** (✉2701 Gulf Blvd., Indian Rocks Beach # 33785 ☎866/353–8911 or 727/595–5441 ⊕www.sandkey.com). **Suncoast Realty** (✉224 Franklin Blvd., St. George Island # 32328 ☎800/341–2021 ⊕www.uncommon-florida.com). **Vacation Home Rentals Worldwide** (☎201/767–9393 or 800/633–3284 ⊕www.vhrww.com). **Villas International** (☎415/499–9490 or 800/221–2260 ⊕www.villasintl.com). **Wyndham Vacation Resorts** (✉5259 Coconut Creek Pkwy., Margate # 33063 ☎800/251–8736 ⊕www.fairfieldresorts.com).

BED & BREAKFASTS

Small inns and guesthouses are increasingly numerous in Florida, but they vary tremendously, ranging from economical places that are plain but serve a good home-style breakfast to elegantly furnished Victorian houses with four-course breakfasts and rates to match. Many offer a homelike setting. In fact, many are in private homes with owners who treat

10 WAYS TO SAVE

1. Join "frequent guest" programs. You may get preferential treatment in room choice and/or upgrades.

2. Call direct. You can sometimes get a better price if you call a hotel's local toll-free number (if available) rather than a central reservations number.

3. Check online. Check hotel Web sites, as not all chains are represented on all travel sites.

4. Look for specials. Always inquire about packages and corporate rates.

5. Look for price guarantees. For overseas trips, look for guaranteed rates. With your rate locked in you won't pay more, even if the price goes up in the local currency.

6. Look for weekend deals at business hotels. High-end chains catering to business travelers are often busy only on weekdays; to fill rooms they often drop rates dramatically on weekends.

7. Ask about taxes. Check if taxes are included in quoted rates. In some places taxes can add 20% or more to your bill.

8. Read the fine print. Watch for add-ons, including resort fees, energy surcharges, and "convenience" fees for such things as local phone service you won't use or a newspaper in a language you can't read.

9. Know when to go. If high season is December through April and you're trying to book, say, in late April, you might save money by changing your dates by a week or two. Ask when rates go down, though: if your dates straddle peak and nonpeak seasons, a property may still charge peak-season rates for the entire stay.

10. Weigh your options (we can't say this enough). Weigh transportation times and costs against the savings of staying in a hotel that's cheaper because it's out of the way.

you almost like family; others are more businesslike. It's a good idea to make specific inquiries of B&Bs you're interested in. The association listed below offers descriptions and suggestions for B&Bs throughout Florida. *Superior Small Lodging, a Guide to Fine Small Hotels,* is available through the Daytona Beach Convention and Visitors Bureau.

Reservation Services Bed & Breakfast. com (☎512/322–2710 or 800/462–2632 ⊕www.bedandbreakfast.com) also sends out an online newsletter. **Bed & Breakfast Inns Online** (☎800/215–7365 ⊕www.bbonline. com). **BnB Finder.com** (☎212/432–7693 or 888/547–8226 ⊕www.bnbfinder.com). **Florida Bed and Breakfast Inns** (✍Box 6187, Palm Harbor # 34684 ☎800/524–1880 or 281/499–1374 ⊕www.florida-inns.com). Superior Small Lodging, a Guide to Fine Small Hotels (✉126 E. Orange Ave., Daytona Beach # 32114 ☎800/854–1234 or 386/255–0415).

HOME EXCHANGES

With a direct home exchange you stay in someone else's home while they stay in yours. Some outfits also deal with vacation homes, so you're not actually staying in someone's full-time residence, just their vacant weekend place.

Exchange Clubs Home Exchange.com (☎800/877–8723 ⊕www.homeexchange. com); $59.95 for a 1-year online listing. **HomeLink International** (☎800/638–3841 ⊕www.homelink.org or www.homelink-usa. com); $80 yearly for Web-only membership; $130 includes Web access and two catalogs. **Intervac USA Home Exchange** (☎800/756–4663 ⊕www.intervacus.com ✍info@intervacusa.com); $78.88 for Web-only membership; $126 includes Web access and a catalog.

HOTELS

Wherever you look in Florida, it seems, you'll find lots of plain, inexpensive motels and luxurious resorts, independents alongside national chains, and an ever-growing number of modern properties as well as quite a few timeless classics. In fact, since Florida has been a

favored travel destination for some time, vintage hotels are everywhere: there are grand edifices like the Breakers in Palm Beach, the Boca Raton Resort & Club in Boca Raton, the Biltmore in Coral Gables, and the Casa Marina in Key West; and smaller, historic places, like the Governors Inn in Tallahassee and the New World Inn in Pensacola.

All hotels listed have private bath unless otherwise noted.

▌AIRLINE TICKETS

Most domestic airline tickets are electronic; international tickets may be either electronic or paper. With an e-ticket the only thing you receive is an e-mailed receipt citing your itinerary and reservation and ticket numbers. The greatest advantage of an e-ticket is that if you lose your receipt, you can simply print out another copy or ask the airline to do it for you at check-in. You usually pay a surcharge (up to $50) to get a paper ticket, if you can get one at all. The sole advantage of a paper ticket is that it may be easier to endorse over to another airline if your flight is canceled and the airline with which you booked can't accommodate you on another flight.

▌RENTAL CARS

When you reserve a car, ask about cancellation penalties, taxes, drop-off charges (if you're planning to pick up the car in one city and leave it in another), and surcharges (for being under or over a certain age, for additional drivers, or for driving across state or country borders or beyond a specific distance from your point of rental). All these things can add substantially to your costs. Request car seats and extras such as GPS when you book.

Rates are sometimes—but not always—better if you book in advance or reserve through a rental agency's Web site. There are other reasons to book ahead, though: for popular destinations, during busy times of the year, or to ensure that you get certain types of cars (vans, SUVs, exotic sports cars).

■TIP➔Make sure that a confirmed reservation guarantees you a car. Agencies sometimes overbook, particularly for busy weekends and holiday periods.

Car rental is highly recommended for travelers in Florida since public transportation is limited and restrictive. In-season rates in Miami begin at $36 a day and $170 a week for an economy car with air-conditioning, an automatic transmission, and unlimited mileage. Rates in Orlando begin at $35 a day and $149 a week. Rates in Fort Lauderdale begin at $36 a day and $159 a week. Rates in Tampa begin at $34 a day and $149 a week. This does not include tax on car rentals, which varies from county to county. Bear in mind that rates fluctuate tremendously—both above and below these quoted figures—depending on demand and the season.

In the past, major rental agencies were at the airport, whereas cheaper firms weren't. Now, however, all over Florida, even the majors might be off airport property. Speedy check-in and frequent shuttle buses make off-airport rentals almost as convenient as on-site service. However, it's wise to allow a little extra time for bus travel between the rental agency and the airport.

CAR-RENTAL INSURANCE

Everyone who rents a car wonders whether the insurance that the rental companies offer is worth the expense. No one—including us—has a simple answer. It all depends on how much regular insurance you have, how comfortable you are with risk, and whether or not money is an issue.

If you own a car and carry comprehensive car insurance for both collision and liability, your personal auto insurance will probably cover a rental, but read your policy's fine print to be sure. If you don't have auto insurance, then you should probably buy the collision- or loss-damage waiver (CDW or LDW) from the rental company. This eliminates your liability for damage to the car. Some credit cards offer CDW coverage, but it's usually supplemental to your own insurance and rarely covers SUVs, minivans, luxury models, and the like. If your coverage is secondary, you may still be liable for loss-of-use costs from the car-rental company (again, read the fine print). But no credit-card insurance is valid unless you use that card for *all* transactions, from reserving to paying the final bill.

■TIP➔Diners Club offers primary CDW coverage on all rentals reserved and paid for with the card. This means that Diners Club's company—not your own car insurance—pays in case of an accident. It *doesn't* mean that your car-insurance company won't raise your rates once it discovers you had an accident.

You may also be offered supplemental liability coverage; the car-rental company is required to carry a minimal level of liability coverage insuring all renters, but it's rarely enough to cover claims in a really serious accident if you're at fault. Your own auto-insurance policy will protect you if you own a car; if you don't, you have to decide whether you are willing to take the risk.

10 WAYS TO SAVE

1. Nonrefundable is best. If saving money is more important than flexibility, then nonrefundable tickets work. Just remember that you'll pay dearly (as much as $100) if you change your plans.

2. Comparison shop. Web sites and travel agents can have different arrangements with the airlines and offer different prices for exactly the same flights.

3. Beware those prices. Many airline Web sites—and most ads—show prices *without* taxes and surcharges. Don't buy until you know the full price.

4. Stay loyal. Stick with one or two frequent-flier programs. You'll get free trips faster and you'll accumulate more quickly the perks that make trips easier. On some airlines these include a special reservations number, early boarding, and upgrades.

5. Watch those ticketing fees. Surcharges are usually added when you buy your ticket anywhere but on an airline Web site (that includes by phone, and paper tickets regardless of how you book).

6. Check early and often. Start looking for cheap fares up to a year in advance, and keep looking until you see something you can live with.

7. Don't work alone. Some Web sites have tracking features that will e-mail you immediately when good deals are posted.

8. Fly mid-week. Look for departures on Tuesday, Wednesday, and Thursday, typically the cheapest days to travel.

9. Be flexible. Check on prices for departures at different times and to and from alternative airports.

10. Weigh your options. What you get can be as important as what you save. A cheaper flight might have a long layover, or it might land at a secondary airport, where your ground transportation costs might be higher.

U.S. rental companies sell CDWs and LDWs for about $15 to $25 a day; supplemental liability is usually more than $10 a day. The car-rental company may offer you all sorts of other policies, but they're rarely worth the cost. Personal accident insurance, which is basic hospitalization coverage, is an especially egregious rip-off if you already have health insurance.

■ TIP➔You can decline the insurance from the rental company and purchase it through a third-party provider such as Travel Guard (www.travelguard.com)—$9 per day for $35,000 of coverage. That's sometimes just under half the price of the CDW offered by some car-rental companies.

In Florida you must be 21 to rent a car, and rates may be higher if you're under 25.

■ VACATION PACKAGES

Packages *are not* guided excursions. Packages combine airfare, accommodations, and perhaps a rental car or other extras (theater tickets, guided excursions, boat trips, reserved entry to popular museums, transit passes), but they let you do your own thing. During busy periods packages may be your only option, as flights and rooms may be sold out otherwise. Packages will definitely save you time. They can also save you money, particularly in peak seasons, but—and this is a really big "but"—you should price each part of the package separately to be sure. And be aware that prices advertised on Web sites and in newspapers rarely include service charges or taxes, which can up your costs by hundreds of dollars.

■ TIP➔Some packages and cruises are sold only through travel agents. Don't always assume that you can get the best deal by booking everything yourself.

Each year consumers are stranded or lose their money when packagers—even large ones with excellent reputations—

Car Rental Resources

AUTOMOBILE ASSOCIATIONS

American Automobile Association	315/797–5000	www.aaa.com;
		most contact with the organization is through state and regional members.
National Automobile Club	650/294–7000	www.thenac.com; membership open to CA residents only.

LOCAL AGENCIES

Continental Florida Auto Rental	800/327–3791 or 954/764–1008 in Fort Lauderdale
Sunshine Rent-A-Car	305/294–8136, in Fort Lauderdale
Tropical Rent-A-Car	954/467–8100, in Key West
U-Save Auto Rental/Specialty Van Rental	888/440–8744, in Clearwater, Fort Lauderdale, Miami, Orlando, Palm Harbor, Sanford, and Tampa–St. Petersburg

MAJOR AGENCIES

Alamo	800/462–5266	www.alamo.com
Avis	800/230–4898	www.avis.com
Budget	800/527–0700	www.budget.com
Hertz	800/654–3131	www.hertz.com
National Car Rental	800/227–7368	www.nationalcar.com

go out of business. How can you protect yourself? First, always pay with a credit card; if you have a problem, your credit-card company may help you resolve it. Second, buy trip insurance that covers default. Third, choose a company that belongs to the United States Tour Operators Association, whose members must set aside funds to cover defaults. Finally, choose a company that also participates in the Tour Operator Program of the American Society of Travel Agents (ASTA), which will act as mediator in any disputes. You can also check on the tour operator's reputation among travelers by posting an inquiry on one of the Fodors.com forums.

Organizations American Society of Travel Agents ([ASTA] ☎703/739–2782 or 800/965–2782 ⊕www.astanet.com). **United States Tour Operators Association** ([USTOA] ☎212/599–6599 ⊕www.ustoa.com). ∎TIP➔**Local tourism boards can provide information about lesser-known and small-niche operators that sell packages to only a few destinations.**

∎ GUIDED TOURS

Guided tours are a good option when you don't want to do it all yourself. You travel along with a group (sometimes large, sometimes small), stay in prebooked hotels, eat with your fellow travelers (the cost of meals sometimes included in the price of your tour, sometimes not), and follow a schedule. But not all guided tours are an if-it's-Tuesday-this-must-be-Belgium experience. A knowledgeable guide can take you places that you might never discover on your own, and you may be pushed to see more than you would have otherwise. Tours aren't for everyone, but they can be just the thing for trips to places where making travel arrangements is difficult or time-consuming (particularly when you don't speak the language). Whenever you book a guided tour, find out what's included and what

10 WAYS TO SAVE

1. Beware of cheap rates. Those great rates aren't so great when you add in taxes, surcharges, and insurance. Such extras can double or triple the initial quote.

2. Rent weekly. Weekly rates are usually better than daily ones. Even if you only want to rent for five or six days, ask for the weekly rate; it may very well be cheaper than the daily rate for that period of time.

3. Don't forget the locals. Price local companies as well as the majors.

4. Airport rentals can cost more. Airports often add surcharges, which you can sometimes avoid by renting from an agency whose office is just off airport property.

5. Wholesalers can help. Investigate wholesalers, which don't own fleets but rent in bulk from firms that do, and which frequently offer better rates (note that you must usually pay for such rentals before leaving home).

6. Look for rate guarantees. With your rate locked in, you won't pay more, even if the price goes up in the local currency.

7. Fill up farther away. Avoid hefty refueling fees by filling the tank at a station well away from where you plan to turn in the car.

8. Pump it yourself. Don't buy the tank of gas that's in the car when you rent it unless you plan to do a lot of driving.

9. Get all your discounts. Find out whether a credit card you carry or organization or frequent-renter program to which you belong has a discount program. And confirm that such discounts really are a deal. You can often do better with special weekend or weekly rates offered by a rental agency.

10. Check out package rates. Adding a car rental onto your air/hotel vacation package may be cheaper than renting a car separately on your own.

isn't. A "land-only" tour includes all your travel (by bus, in most cases) in the destination, but not necessarily your flights to and from or even within it. Also, in most cases prices in tour brochures don't include fees and taxes. And remember that you'll be expected to tip your guide (in cash) at the end of the tour.

Royal Palm Tours arranges a variety of special-interest tours ranging from literary to history, Harley motorcycles, eco-tours, and more. Gatortrax Adventure Tours specializes in guided motor-coach group tours to the Everglades, St. Augustine, Kennedy Space Center, Key West, Orlando, and the Keys. Groups cannot be mixed, and to make the best of your budget, it is recommended that you have at least 20 people in your group. Flamingo Tours of Florida specializes in group tours through the city of Miami, Key West, Orlando, and the Everglades. Rates start at $45 per person.

Recommended Companies Flamingo Tours of Florida (✉ 7915 N.W. Fifth Ct., Miami # 33150 ☎ 305/751–8600 ⊕ www.usaflamingotours.com). **Gatortrax Adventure Tours** (✉ 71 N.E. 97th St., Miami # 33138 ☎ 305/756–1000 ⊕ www.gatortrax.com). **Royal Palm Tours** (✉ Box 60079, Fort Myers# 33906 ☎ 239/368–0760 ⊕ www.royalpalmtours.com).

SPECIAL-INTEREST TOURS

FISHING

Contacts Canaveral National Seashore (✉ 308 Julia St., Titusville # 32796 ☎ 321/267–1110 ⊕ www.nbbd.com/godo/cns) maintains a list of guides on their Web site who have approved permits to operate along the Canaveral National Seashore. **Fishing-Florida.com** (⊕ www.fishing-florida.com) maintains a list of charter companies that specialize in freshwater and saltwater trips in southwest Florida. **Florida Bass Adventures** (✉ Kissimmee, FL ☎ 352/603–5467 ⊕ www.orlandobassguide.com) operated by Steve Boyd arranges fishing trips: $225 for hours; $325 for eight hours.

TRANSPORTATION

Travel Times from Miami

To	By Air	By Car or Bus	By Train
Key West	1 hour	3½ hours	N/A
Tampa	2 hours	4½ hours	5½ hours
Palm Beach	NA	1½ hours	N/A
Cape Canaveral	1 hour	3½ hours	N/A
Tallahassee	2 hours	7 hours	N/A
St. Augustine	no nonstop flights available	5 hours	N/A
Orlando	1 hour	3½ hours	5½ hours
Fort Myers	1 hour	2½ hours	N/A
Everglades	NA	1½ hours	N/A

■TIP➔Ask the local tourist board about hotel and local transportation packages that include tickets to major museum exhibits or other special events.

■ BY AIR

Flying times to Florida vary based on the city you're flying to, but typical times are 3 hours from New York, 4 hours from Chicago, 2¾ hours from Dallas, 4½ to 5½ hours from Los Angeles, and 8 to 8½ hours from London.

Airlines & Airports Airline and Airport Links.com (⊕www.airlineandairportlinks.com) has links to many of the world's airlines and airports.

Airline Security Issues Transportation Security Administration (⊕www.tsa.gov) has answers for almost every question that might come up.

Air Travel Resources in Florida Better Business Bureau (☎703/276–0100 ⊕www.bbb.org). **Florida Attorney General** (☎850/414–3300 ⊕http://myfloridalegal.com/consumer).

AIRPORTS

Both major and regional airports are plentiful in Florida so you can usually pick one quite close to your destination and often choose from a couple of nearby options. If you're destined for the north side of Miami-Dade County (metro Miami), or are renting a car at the airport, consider flying into Fort Lauderdale–Hollywood International; it's much easier to use than Miami International, and often—if not always—cheaper. The airports are only 40 minutes apart by car.

■TIP➔Long layovers don't have to be only about sitting around or shopping. These days they can be about burning off vacation calories. Check out ⊕ www.airportgyms. com for lists of health clubs that are in or near many U.S. and Canadian airports. There are several participating gyms within 15 minutes of Florida's major airports. All offer a $8–$12 day pass. Miami International has a gym in the airport.

Airport Information Daytona Beach International Airport (DAB) (☎386/248–8069 ⊕www.volusia.org/airport). **Fort Lauderdale–Hollywood International (FLL)** (☎954/359–6100 ⊕www.broward.org/airport). **Jacksonville International**

I) (☎904/741-4902 ⊕www.jaa.
Miami International Airport (MIA)
(☎305/876-7000 ⊕www.miami-airport.com).
Orlando International (MCO) (☎407/825-
2001 ⊕www.orlandoairports.net). Palm
Beach International (PBI) (☎561/471-7420
⊕www.pbia.org). Sarasota Bradenton International Airport (SRQ) (☎941/359-2777
⊕www.srq-airport.com). Southwest Florida
International Airport (FMY) (☎239/590-
4800 ⊕www.flylcpa.com). St. Peters-
burg-Clearwater International Airport
(PIE) (☎727/453-7800 ⊕www.fly2pie.com).
Tampa International (TPA) (☎813/870-8700
⊕www.tampaairport.com).

GROUND TRANSPORTATION

SuperShuttle has service to and from
Miami International, Palm Beach International, and Tampa International airports.
Downtown Miami to Miami International Airport is typically $15 and takes
30 minutes. Downtown Miami to Palm
Beach International Airport is typically
$92 and takes 1½ hours. Downtown St.
Pete to Tampa International Airport is
approximately $20; the shuttle will pick
you up three hours before your scheduled
departure. There is no shared-shuttle service from downtown Tampa to Tampa
International Airport, but SuperShuttle
can book you with their car-service operators: Exclusive, which costs $92 from
downtown to the airport; or ExecuCar,
which runs approximately $55 from
downtown to the airport. It is best to
book your reservations with SuperShuttle
at least two days in advance. They will
pick you up from a hotel, office, or residence. There are hubs inside the airports
where you can obtain SuperShuttle tickets to take you from the airport to your
desired local destination.

Taxis are available at Miami International's arrival zone; flat rates vary by the zone
you will be traveling to, but run between
$19 and $52 in the immediate Miami
area—the flat rate to Miami Beach is $32.
Yellow Cab taxis from Orlando Interna-

tional to downtown Orlando run approx-
imately $35. Yellow Cab and United
Cab have service to and from downtown
Tampa and have a flat rate of $22.

FLIGHTS

Airline Contacts Air Canada (☎888/247-
2262 ⊕www.aircanada.com). **Alaska Airlines** (☎800/252-7522 ⊕www.alaskaair.
com). **American Airlines** (☎800/433-7300
⊕www.aa.com). **ATA** (☎800/435-9282
or 317/282-8308 ⊕www.ata.com). **Continental Airlines** (☎800/523-3273 for U.S.
and Mexico reservations, 800/231-0856 for
international reservations ⊕www.continental.
com). **Delta Airlines** (☎800/221-1212 for
U.S. reservations, 800/241-4141 for international reservations ⊕www.delta.com).
jetBlue (☎800/538-2583 ⊕www.jetblue.
com). **Northwest Airlines** (☎800/225-2525
⊕www.nwa.com). **Southwest Airlines**
(☎800/435-9792 ⊕www.southwest.
com). **Spirit Airlines** (☎800/772-7117 or
586/791-7300 ⊕www.spiritair.com). **United
Airlines** (☎800/864-8331 for U.S. reservations, 800/538-2929 for international reservations ⊕www.united.com). **USAirways**
(☎800/428-4322 for U.S. and Canada reservations, 800/622-1015 for international reservations ⊕www.usairways.com).

Smaller Airlines AirTran (☎800/247-8726
⊕www.airtran.com) to Miami, Fort Lauderdale, Fort Myers, Jacksonville, Orlando, Sarasota, Tampa, and West Palm Beach. **jetBlue**
(☎800/538-2583 ⊕www.jetblue.com) to
Tampa, Fort Lauderdale, Sarasota, Fort Myers,
West Palm Beach, and Orlando. **Midwest Airlines** (☎800/452-2022 ⊕www.midwestair-
lines.com) to Fort Lauderdale, Fort Myers,
Orlando, and Tampa. **Southwest Airlines**
(☎800/435-9792 ⊕www.southwest.com)
to Fort Lauderdale, Fort Myers, Jacksonville,
Orlando, Tampa, and West Palm Beach.

▌ BY BUS

Greyhound passes through practically
every major city in Florida. For schedules
and fares, contact your local Greyhound
Information Center.

Using a major credit card you can purchase Greyhound tickets online or by using the carrier's toll-free phone numbers. You can also purchase tickets—using cash, traveler's checks, or major credit cards—at any Greyhound terminal where tickets are sold or through one of the many independent agents representing Greyhound. A complete state-by-state list of agents is available at the Greyhound Web site.

Bus Information Greyhound Lines (☎800/231-2222 or 800/229-9424 ⊕www.greyhound.com).

BY CAR

Three major interstates lead to Florida. Interstate 95 begins in Maine, runs south through the Mid-Atlantic states, and enters Florida just north of Jacksonville. It continues south past Daytona Beach, the Space Coast, Vero Beach, Palm Beach, and Fort Lauderdale, ending in Miami.

Interstate 75 begins in Michigan at the Canadian border and runs south through Ohio, Kentucky, Tennessee, and Georgia, then moves south through the center of the state before veering west into Tampa. It follows the west coast south to Naples, then crosses the state through the northern section of the Everglades, and ends in Fort Lauderdale.

California and most southern states are connected to Florida by Interstate 10, which moves east from Los Angeles through Arizona, New Mexico, Texas, Louisiana, Mississippi, and Alabama; it enters Florida at Pensacola and runs straight across the northern part of the state, ending in Jacksonville.

ROAD CONDITIONS

Florida has its share of traffic problems. Downtown areas of such major cities as Miami, Orlando, and Tampa can be extremely congested during rush hours, usually 7 to 9 [am] and 3:30 to 6 [pm] on weekdays. When you drive the interstate

system in Florida, try to plan your trip so that you are not entering, leaving, or passing through a large city during rush hour, when traffic can slow to 10 mph for 10 mi or more. In addition, snowbirds usually rent in Florida for a month at a time, which means they all arrive on the first of the month and leave on the 31st. Believe it or not, from November to March, when the end and beginning of a month occur on a weekend, north–south routes like Interstate 75 and Interstate 95 almost come to a standstill during daylight hours. It's best to avoid traveling on these days if possible.

ROADSIDE EMERGENCIES

If you need emergency assistance while traveling on roads in Florida, dial 911 or *FHP from your cell phone.

Emergency Services Florida Highway Patrol (☎911 or *FHP ⊕www.dot.state.fl.us); their Web site provides real-time traffic information—including areas congested with construction or accidents.

RULES OF THE ROAD

Speed limits are 60 mph on state highways, 30 mph within city limits and residential areas, and 70 mph on interstates and Florida's Turnpike. Be alert for signs announcing exceptions.

In Florida, you must strap a child six or younger into a child-restraint device: children aged through three years must be in a separate carrier or child seat, and children four through six can be secured in a separate carrier, integrated child seat, or by a seat belt. The driver will be held responsible for passengers under the age of 16 who are not wearing seat belts. All front-seat passengers are required to wear seat belts.

Florida's Alcohol/Controlled Substance DUI Law is one of the toughest in the United States. A blood alcohol level of .08 or higher can have serious repercussions even for the first-time offender.

ON THE GROUND

■ BUSINESS SERVICES & FACILITIES

There are FedEx Kinko's all over Florida. To find the most convenient Kinko's, their Web site lists locations via ZIP code or call their toll-free number. Many hotels in Florida cater to business conventions. Call the local convention and visitors bureaus listed in the Essentials sections in each chapter.

Contacts FedEx Kinko's (☎800/254–6567 ⊕www.kinkos.com).

■ COMMUNICATIONS

INTERNET

Wi-Fi is widely available in Florida's high-end hotels and even B&Bs. Most hotels have at least an Internet room in their business-service center or in-room data ports in guest rooms. Wi-Fi is usually accessible in certain hot spots of the hotel, such as the main floor or in the lobby. In-room data ports generally cost $10 for 24 hours of use. Some hotels charge you by 15-minute increments (fees vary by hotel) to use the Internet in the business-service center, whereas other hotels offer this as a complimentary service. Many U.S. cities are instituting Wi-Fi hot spots in downtown areas.

Contacts Cybercafes (⊕www.cybercafes. com) lists more than 4,000 Internet cafés worldwide.

■ EATING OUT

An antismoking amendment endorsed in 2002 by Florida voters bans smoking statewide in most enclosed indoor workplaces, including restaurants. Exemptions are permitted for stand-alone bars where food takes a backseat to the libations.

A cautionary word: raw oysters have been identified as a potential problem for people with chronic illness of the liver, stomach, or blood, or who have immune disorders. Since 1993 all Florida restaurants serving raw oysters have been required to post a notice in plain view of all patrons, warning of the risks associated with consuming them.

The restaurants we list are the cream of the crop in each price category. Properties indicated by ✕☐ are lodging establishments whose restaurant warrants a special trip.

CATEGORY	COST
¢	under $10
$	$10–$15
$$	$15–$20
$$$	$20–$30
$$$$	over $30

All prices are per person for a main course at dinner.

FLORIBBEAN FOOD

A trip to the Tampa area or South Florida is incomplete without a taste of Cuban food. The cuisine is heavy, with pork dishes like *lechon asado,* served in garlic-based sauces. The two most typical dishes are *arroz con frijoles* (the staple side dish of rice and black beans) and *arroz con pollo* (chicken in sticky yellow rice). Key West is a mecca for lovers of key lime pie (the best is found here) and conch fritters, another local favorite. Stone crab claws, another South Florida delicacy, can be savored from November through May.

MEALS & MEALTIMES

Unless otherwise noted, the restaurants listed in this guide are open daily for lunch and dinner.

PAYING

For guidelines on tipping see Tipping below.

Most restaurants in Florida accept credit cards, with the exception of some smaller mom-and-pop establishments.

RESERVATIONS & DRESS

Regardless of where you are, it's a good idea to make a reservation if you can. In some places (Hong Kong, for example), it's expected. We mention them specifically only when reservations are essential (there's no other way you'll ever get a table) or when they are not accepted. For popular restaurants, book as far ahead as you can (often 30 days), and reconfirm as soon as you arrive. (Large parties should always call ahead to check the reservations policy.) We mention dress only when men are required to wear a jacket or a jacket and tie.

Online reservation services make it easy to book a table before you even leave home. OpenTable covers most states, including 20 major cities, and has limited listings in Canada, Mexico, the United Kingdom, and elsewhere. DinnerBroker has restaurants throughout the United States as well as a few in Canada.

Contacts **OpenTable** (⊕ www.opentable.com).
DinnerBroker (⊕ www.dinnerbroker.com).

WINES, BEER & SPIRITS

Beer and wine are usually available in Florida's restaurants, whether you're dining first class or at a beachside bistro. A few chain restaurants in the major cities are also microbreweries and have a variety of premise-made beers that change with the season. Liquor is generally available at fine-dining establishments only.

▌ HEALTH

SPECIFIC ISSUES IN FLORIDA

If you are unaccustomed to strong subtropical sun, you run a risk of sunburn and heat prostration, even in winter. So hit the beach or play tennis, golf, or another outdoor sport before 10 or after 3. If you must be out at midday, limit strenuous exercise, drink plenty of liq-

uids, and wear a hat. If you begin to feel faint, get out of the sun immediately and sip water slowly. Even on overcast days, ultraviolet rays shine through the haze, so use a sunscreen with an SPF of at least 15, and have children wear a waterproof SPF 30 or higher.

While you're frolicking on the beach, steer clear of what look like blue bubbles on the sand. These are Portuguese men-of-war, and their tentacles can cause an allergic reaction. Also be careful of other large jellyfish, some of which can sting.

If you walk across a grassy area on the way to the beach, you'll probably encounter sand spurs. They are quite tiny, light brown, and remarkably prickly. You'll feel them before you see them; if you get stuck with one, just pull it out.

▌ HOURS OF OPERATION

Many museums in Florida are closed Monday, but offer extended hours on another weekday and are usually open on weekends. Some museums reserve a day of the week for free admission. Popular visitor attractions are usually open daily, with the exception of Thanksgiving and Christmas Day.

Most pharmacies are open seven days a week, but some close early on weekends. Many Wal-Mart stores and CVS and Walgreens pharmacies offer 24-hour pharmacy services.

FOR INTERNATIONAL TRAVELERS

CURRENCY

The dollar is the basic unit of U.S. currency. It has 100 cents. Coins are the penny (1¢); the nickel (5¢), dime (10¢), quarter (25¢), half-dollar (50¢), and the very rare golden $1 coin and even rarer silver $1. Bills are denominated $1, $5, $10, $20, $50, and $100, all mostly green and identical in size; designs and background tints vary. You may come across a $2 bill, but the chances are slim.

CUSTOMS

Information U.S. Customs and Border Protection (⊕ www.cbp.gov).

DRIVING

Driving in the United States is on the right. Speed limits are posted in miles per hour (usually between 55 mph and 70 mph). Watch for lower limits in small towns and on back roads (usually 30 mph to 40 mph). Most states require front-seat passengers to wear seat belts; many states require children to sit in the back seat and to wear seat belts. In major cities rush hour is between 7 and 10 AM; afternoon rush hour is between 4 and 7 PM. To encourage carpooling, some freeways have special lanes, ordinarily marked with a diamond, for high-occupancy vehicles (HOV)—cars carrying two people or more.

Highways are well paved. Interstates—limited-access, multilane highways designated with an "I–" before the number—are fastest. Interstates with three-digit numbers circle urban areas, which may also have other limited-access expressways, freeways, and parkways. Tolls may be levied on limited-access highways. U.S. and state highways aren't necessarily limited-access, but may have several lanes.

ELECTRICITY

The U.S. standard is AC, 110 volts/60 cycles. Plugs have two flat pins set parallel to each other.

EMBASSIES

Contacts Australia (☎ 202/797–3000 ⊕ www.austemb.org).

Canada (☎ 202/682–1740 ⊕ www.canadianembassy.org).

United Kingdom (☎ 202/588–7800 ⊕ www.britainusa.com).

EMERGENCIES

For police, fire, or ambulance, dial 911 (0 in rural areas).

HOLIDAYS

New Year's Day (Jan. 1); Martin Luther King Day (3rd Mon. in Jan.); Presidents' Day (3rd Mon. in Feb.); Memorial Day (last Mon. in May); Independence Day (July 4); Labor Day (1st Mon. in Sept.); Columbus Day (2nd Mon. in Oct.); Thanksgiving Day (4th Thurs. in Nov.); Christmas Eve and Christmas Day (Dec. 24 and 25); and New Year's Eve (Dec. 31).

MAIL

You can buy stamps and aerograms and send letters and parcels in post offices. Stamp-dispensing machines can occasionally be found in airports, bus and train stations, and convenience stores. U.S. mail boxes are dark blue steel bins; pickup schedules are posted on the bin. Parcels weighing more than a pound must be mailed at a post office or at a private mailing center.

Within the United States a first-class letter weighing 1 ounce or less costs 39¢; each additional ounce costs 24¢. Postcards cost 24¢. A 1-ounce airmail letter to most countries costs 84¢, an airmail postcard costs 75¢; a 1-ounce letter to Canada or Mexico costs 63¢, a postcard 55¢.

To receive mail on the road, have it sent c/o General Delivery at your destination's main post office (use the correct five-digit ZIP code). You must pick up mail in person within 30 days, with a driver's license or passport for identification.

Contacts DHL (☎ *800/225–5345* ⊕ *www.dhl.com*).
Federal Express (☎ *800/463–3339* ⊕ *www.fedex.com*).

Mail Boxes, Etc./The UPS Store (☎ *800/789–4623* ⊕ *www.mbe.com*).

United States Postal Service (⊕ *www.usps.com*).

PASSPORTS & VISAS

Visitor visas aren't necessary for citizens of Australia, Canada, the United Kingdom, or most citizens of European Union countries coming for tourism and staying for fewer than 90 days. If you require a visa, the cost is $100, and waiting time can be substantial, depending on where you live. Apply for a visa at the U.S. consulate in your place of residence; check the U.S. State Department's special Visa Web site for further information.

VISA INFORMATION

Destination USA (⊕ *www.unitedstatesvisas. gov*).

PHONES

Numbers consist of a three-digit area code and a seven-digit local number. Within many local calling areas you dial only the seven digits; in others you dial "1" first and all 10 digits—just as you would for calls between area-code regions. The same is true for calls to numbers prefixed by "800," "888," "866," and "877"—all toll-free. For calls to numbers prefixed by "900" you must pay—usually dearly.

In New York City, there are three area codes: "212," "646," and "917." Although it's not long distance, "1" plus the area code is necessary to call here.

For international calls, dial "011" followed by the country code and the local number. For help, dial "0" and ask for an overseas operator. Most phone books list country codes and U.S. area codes. The country code for Australia is 61, for New Zealand 64, for the United

Kingdom 44. Calling Canada is the same as calling within the United States, whose country code, by the way, is 1.

For operator assistance, dial "0." For directory assistance, call 555–1212 or occasionally 411 (free at many public phones). You can reverse long-distance charges by calling "collect"; dial "0" instead of "1" before the 10-digit number.

Instructions are generally posted on pay phones. Usually you insert coins in a slot (usually 25¢–50¢ for local calls) and wait for a steady tone before dialing. On long-distance calls the operator tells you how much to insert; prepaid phone cards, widely available in various denominations, can be used from any phone. Follow the directions to activate the card (there's usually an access number, then an activation code), then dial your number.

CELL PHONES

The United States has several GSM (Global System for Mobile Communications) networks, so multiband mobiles from most countries (except for Japan) work here. Unfortunately, it's almost impossible to buy a pay-as-you-go mobile SIM card in the U.S.—which allows you to avoid roaming charges—without also buying a phone. That said, cell phones with pay-as-you-go plans are available for well under $100. The cheapest ones with decent national coverage are the GoPhone from Cingular and Virgin Mobile, which only offers pay-as-you-go service.

Contacts Cingular (☎ *888/333–6651* ⊕ *www.cingular.com*).

Virgin Mobile (☎ *No phone* ⊕ *www. virginmobileusa.com*).

▌ MONEY

Prices throughout this guide are given for adults. Substantially reduced fees are almost always available for children, students, and senior citizens.

ITEM	AVERAGE COST
Cup of Coffee	$2
Glass of Wine	$8
Glass of Beer	$5
Sandwich	$6
Museum Admission	$15

CREDIT CARDS

Throughout this guide, the following abbreviations are used: **AE**, American Express; **D**, Discover; **DC**, Diners Club; **MC**, MasterCard; and **V**, Visa.

It's a good idea to inform your credit-card company before you travel, especially if you're going abroad and don't travel internationally very often. Otherwise, the credit-card company might put a hold on your card owing to unusual activity—not a good thing halfway through your trip. Record all your credit-card numbers—as well as the phone numbers to call if your cards are lost or stolen—in a safe place, so you're prepared should something go wrong. Both MasterCard and Visa have general numbers you can call (collect if you're abroad) if your card is lost, but you're better off calling the number of your issuing bank, since MasterCard and Visa usually just transfer you to your bank; your bank's number is usually printed on your card.

Reporting Lost Cards American Express (☎800/992-3404 in U.S. or 336/393-1111 collect from abroad ⊕www.americanexpress. com). **Diners Club** (☎800/234-6377 in U.S. or 303/799-1504 collect from abroad ⊕www. dinersclub.com). **Discover** (☎800/347-2683 in U.S. or 801/902-3100 collect from abroad ⊕www.discovercard.com). **MasterCard** (☎800/622-7747 in U.S. or 636/722-7111 collect from abroad ⊕www.mastercard.com).

Visa (☎800/847-2911 in U.S. or 410/581-9994 collect from abroad ⊕www.visa.com).

TRAVELER'S CHECKS & CARDS

Some consider this the currency of the cave man, and it's true that fewer establishments accept traveler's checks these days. Nevertheless, they're a cheap and secure way to carry extra money, particularly on trips to urban areas. Both Citibank (under the Visa brand) and American Express issue traveler's checks in the United States, but AmEx is better known and more widely accepted; you can also avoid hefty surcharges by cashing AmEx checks at AmEx offices. Whatever you do, keep track of all the serial numbers in case the checks are lost or stolen.

It is not necessary to carry traveler's checks in Florida, because there are endless ATMs and bank branches in all but the most remote areas.

American Express now offers a stored-value card called a Travelers Cheque Card, which you can use wherever American Express credit cards are accepted, including ATMs. The card can carry a minimum of $300 and a maximum of $2,700, and it's a very safe way to carry your funds. Although you can get replacement funds in 24 hours if your card is lost or stolen, it doesn't really strike us as a very good deal. In addition to a high initial cost ($14.95 to set up the card, plus $5 each time you "reload"), you still have to pay a 2% fee for each purchase in a foreign currency (similar to that of any credit card). Further, each time you use the card in an ATM you pay a transaction fee of $2.50 on top of the 2% transaction fee for the conversion—add it all up and it can be considerably more than you would pay when simply using your own ATM card. Regular traveler's checks are just as secure and cost less.

Contacts American Express (☎888/412-6945 in U.S., 801/945-9450 collect outside the

J.S. to add value or speak to customer service (⊕www.americanexpress.com).

▌ SAFETY

Stepped-up policing of thieves who prey on tourists in rental cars has helped address what was a serious issue in the early 1990s. Still, visitors should be especially wary when driving in strange neighborhoods and leaving the airport, especially in the Miami area. Don't assume that valuables are safe in your hotel room; use in-room safes or the hotel's safety deposit boxes. Try to use ATMs only during the day or in brightly lighted, well-traveled locales.

▌TIP→**Distribute your cash, credit cards, IDs, and other valuables between a deep front pocket, an inside jacket or vest pocket, and a hidden money pouch. Don't reach for the money pouch once you're in public.**

BEACH SAFETY

Before swimming, make sure there's no undertow. Rip currents, caused when the tide rushes out through a narrow break in the water, can overpower even the strongest swimmer. If you do get caught in one, resist the urge to swim straight back to shore—you'll tire before you make it. Instead, stay calm. Swim parallel to the shoreline until you are outside the current's pull, then work your way in to shore.

▌ TAXES

Florida's sales tax is 6% or higher depending on the county, and local sales and tourist taxes can raise what you pay considerably, especially for certain items, such as lodging. Miami hoteliers, for example, collect roughly 12.5% for city and resort taxes. It's best to ask about additional costs up front, to avoid a rude awakening.

▌ TIME

The western portion of the Panhandle is in the central time zone, but the rest of Florida is in the eastern time zone.

▌ TIPPING

Whether they carry bags, open doors, deliver food, or clean rooms, hospitality employees work to receive a portion of your travel budget. In deciding how much to give, base your tip on what the service is and how well it's performed.

In transit, tip an airport valet $1 to $3 per bag, a taxi driver 15% to 20% of the fare.

For hotel staff, recommended amounts are $1 to $3 per bag for a bellhop, $1 to $2 per night per guest for chambermaids, $5 to $10 for special concierge service, $1 to $3 for a doorman who hails a cab or parks a car, 15% of the green fee for a caddy, 15% to 20% of the bill for a massage, and 15% of a room-service bill (bear in mind that sometimes 15% to 18% is automatically added to room-service bills, so don't add it twice).

In a restaurant, give 15% to 20% of your bill before tax to the server, 5% to 10% to the maître d', 15% to a bartender, and 15% of the wine bill for a wine steward who makes a special effort in selecting and serving wine.

INDEX

A

A. E. "Bean" Backus Gallery, 278
Acqualina 🖾, 391–392
Adams Key, 517
Adventura, 391–393
Adventure Island, 601–602
Adventure Landing and Shipwreck Island Water Park, 95
African-American Research Library and Cultural Center, 295, 312
Ah-Tha-Thi-Ki Museum, 317
Air Force Armament Museum, 42
Air travel, 661, 665–666
Everglades, 540–541
Florida Keys, 502
Fort Lauderdale and Broward County, 335–336
Lower Gulf Coast, 591–592
Miami and Miami Beach, 420–422
Northeast Florida, 148–149
Palm Beach and the Treasure Coast, 284–285
Panhandle, 73–74
Tampa Bay area, 648
Walt Disney World and Orlando, 225–226
Alan Shepard Park, 133
Alexander Brest Museum, 81–83
Alexander Springs, 142
Alfred Maclay Gardens State Park, 68
Alice's Key West Restaurant ✕, 486–487
Alison Fahrer Environmental Education Center, 448
Alligators, 16
Ambrosia House 🖾, 490
Amelia Island, 100–104
Amelia Island Historic District, 100
Amelia Island Plantation 🖾, 102–103
American Police Hall of Fame and Museum, 127
Amimoto Japanese Restaurant ✕, 559
Anastasia State Park, 106
Anglin's Fishing Pier, 320, 322
Anheuser-Busch Jacksonville Brewery, 82

Animal Kingdom Lodge 🖾, 202
Ann Norton Sculpture Gardens, 244
Anna Maria Bayfront Park, 634
Anna Maria Island, 632, 634
Anne's Beach, 449
Antique Row (West Palm Beach), 250
Apalachicola, 59–62
Apalachicola National Forest, 72
Apartment and house rentals, 659
Apollo Beach, 123
Appleton Museum of Art, 142
Aquariums
Florida Keys, 481
Miami, 366–367
Panhandle, 43
Tampa Bay area, 597, 620, 625, 632, 637–638
Archie Carr National Wildlife Refuge, 283
Architectural Antiques (shop), 412
Armani's ✕, 602
Art and Culture Center of Hollywood, 327
Art Deco District Welcome Center, 344
Art galleries and museums. ⇨ See Museums and galleries
Arthur R. Marshall-Loxahatchee National Wildlife Refugee, 257
Artisans in the Dining Room ✕, 580
Artist Point ✕, 191–192
Arts on Douglas, 122
ArtSouth, 522
Aruba Beach Café ✕, 320
Atlantic, The 🖾, 309
Atlantic Center for the Arts, 122
Audubon House and Gardens, 478
Audubon's Center for Birds of Prey, 181
Auto racing
Everglades, 524
Miami and Miami Beach, 402
Northeast Florida, 121, 148

Palm Beach and Treasure Coast, 270
Walt Disney World and Orlando, 221
Azul ✕, 373–374

B

Babcock Wilderness Adventures, 559
Baby's Coffee ✕, 472
Bahia Honda Key, 468–469
Bahia Honda State Park, 468
Bailey-Matthews Shell Museum, 564–565
Bal Harbour, 388–391
Bal Harbour Shops, 410
Barefoot Beach Preserve, 575
Barnacle Historic State Park, 358
Barracuda Grill ✕, 464
Base (shop), 413
Baseball
Fort Lauderdale and Broward County, 314
Lower Gulf Coast, 555
Miami and Miami Beach, 402–403
Northeast Florida, 92, 138
Palm Beach and the Treasure Coast, 272, 277, 282
Tampa Bay area, 608–609, 619, 622, 624, 635, 645
Basilica Cathedral of St. Augustine, 106
Basketball, 221, 403
Bass Museum of Art, 344, 346
Bayside Tours, 613
BayWalk (St. Petersburg), 612
Bb's ✕, 85–86
Beaches, 16
Florida Keys, 447, 448, 449, 461, 463, 478, 481, 484, 485
Fort Lauderdale and Broward County, 293, 298–300, 327–328, 332
Lower Gulf Coast, 564, 565–566, 574–575, 579, 580, 587–588
Miami and Miami Beach, 402, 403–405
Northeast Florida, 94–95, 101, 109, 118, 122–123, 127–128, 129, 133, 138
Palm Beach and the Treasure Coast, 255, 257, 259, 260, 266, 270, 271, 277, 282
Panhandle, 40–41, 49, 55

safety tips, 293, 673
Tampa Bay area, 613, 614, 620, 625, 632, 634, 638, 646
Bed and breakfasts, 659–660
Beech Street Grill ✕, 101–102
Bell Tower Shops, 556
Bellasera ⊡, 582
Bern's Steak House ✕, 603
Bert's Bar & Grill ✕, 557
Best Western Pelican Beach ⊡, 309–310
Bethesda-by-the-Sea, 232
Bha! Bha! ✕, 581
Big Cypress National Preserve, 539–540
Big Cypress Seminole Reservation, 317
Big Fish ✕, 351
Big Kahuna's Lost Paradise, 45–46
Big Pine Key, 469–472
Big Pine Key Fishing Lodge ⊡, 471
Big Pink ✕, 370
Bijou Café ✕, 639
Biking
Everglades, 529
Florida Keys, 444, 466, 471, 498, 573
Fort Lauderdale and Broward County, 314, 335
Lower Gulf Coast, 555, 560, 562, 569, 573, 576, 585–586, 590–591
Miami and Miami Beach, 405, 422
Northeast Florida, 99, 114, 133, 136
Palm Beach and the Treasure Coast, 241, 262, 269
Panhandle, 44
Tampa Bay area, 614, 622, 635, 645, 647
Bill Baggs Cape Florida State Park, 365, 404
Billie Swamp Safari, 317
Biltmore Hotel ⊡, 361–362, 396
Birding, 16, 575
Biscayne National Park, 514–517
Biscayne National Underwater Park, Inc., 515
Bistro Aix ✕, 85
Bistro de Paris ✕, 187
Bistro 41 ✕, 552
Black Tulip Restaurant ✕, 132
Blind Pass Beach, 646
Blowing Rocks Preserve, 273

Blue Door at the Delano ✕, 370
Blue Moon Fish Company ✕, 307
Blue Spring State Park, 139
Bluewater Bay Resort ⊡, 47
BoardWalk Inn and Villas ⊡, 200–201
Boat travel
Everglades, 541
Florida Keys, 503
Fort Lauderdale and Broward County, 336
Lower Gulf Coast, 592
Northeast Florida, 149
Boating
Everglades, 524, 529, 532, 539, 586
Florida Keys, 454–455, 466
Fort Lauderdale and Broward County, 331
Lower Gulf Coast, 569, 576
Miami and Miami Beach, 405–406
Northeast Florida, 100, 131, 140
Palm Beach and the Treasure Coast, 266
Panhandle, 63
Walt Disney World and Orlando, 181
Boca Bistro ✕, 561–562
Boca Chita Key, 516
Boca Grande, 561–562
Boca Raton, 262–266
Boca Raton Museum of Art, 263
Boca Raton Resort & Club ⊡, 264–265
Bonefish Grill ✕, 195
Bonita Springs, 574–577
Bonita Springs Public Beach, 574–575
Bonnet House, 299
Books & Books, Inc. (shop), 413
Bowman's Beach, 565–566
Boynton Beach, 257–258
Boynton Beach Oceanfront Park, 257
Bradenton, 632–636
Brazilian Court ⊡, 239–240
Breakers, The ⊡, 232, 240
Brevard Community College Planetarium and Observatory, 131
Brevard Museum of History & Science, 131
Brevard Zoo, 137–138

Brickell Avenue Bridge (Miami), 351–352
BridgeWalk, a landmark resort ⊡, 635
Broadwalk (Hollywood), 327
Broadway Palm Dinner Theater, 554–555
Brokaw-McDougall House, 67
Brooks ✕, 325
Broward County. ⇨ *See* Fort Lauderdale and Broward County
Broward County Main Library, 295
Brownes & Co. (shop), 412
Bus travel, 666–667
Everglades, 541
Florida Keys, 503–504
Fort Lauderdale and Broward County, 336
Lower Gulf Coast, 592
Miami and Miami Beach, 422
Northeast Florida, 149
Palm Beach and the Treasure Coast, 285
Panhandle, 74
Tampa Bay area, 648–649
Busch Gardens, 601
Business hours, 159, 161, 669
Business services, 668
Butterfly World, 317
By Word of Mouth ✕, 304

C

C. B. Harvey Rest Beach, 484
Cabbage Key, 563
Cabins at Grayton Beach State Park ⊡, 50
Cadet Hotel ⊡, 387
Café, A Mostly Vegetarian Place ✕, 487
Café Boulud ✕, 236
Café Chardonnay ✕, 269
Café Marquesa ✕, 486
Café Prima Pasta ✕, 367
Café Solé ✕, 488
Cafe Maxx ✕, 322
Cafe Thirty-A ✕, 52
Caladesi Island State Park, 623–624
California Grill ✕, 191
Calusa Nature Center and Planetarium, 551
Cameo (dance club), 400–401
Camping
Everglades, 516–517, 528–529, 535, 538–539, 540
Florida Keys, 443, 458

Fort Lauderdale and Broward County, 310–311
Northeast Florida, 129
Walt Disney World and Orlando, 200
Canaveral National Seashore, 123, 127
Canoeing
Everglades, 515, 529, 539
Lower Gulf Coast, 562, 570, 573, 576–577
Northeast Florida, 142
Palm Beach and the Treasure Coast, 272, 284
Panhandle, 38–39, 58, 72
Tampa Bay area, 609, 614
Cape Canaveral, 129–130
Cape Coral, 556–558
Cape Florida Lighthouse, 365
Capital Grille ✕, 374
Cap's Place ✕, 324
Captiva Beach, 566
Captiva Island, 565–570
Car rentals, 660–662, 663, 664
Everglades, 541–542
Florida Keys, 504–505
Lower Gulf Coast, 592
Miami and Miami Beach, 422–423
Palm Beach and the Treasure Coast, 285
Panhandle, 75
Car travel, 667, 670
Everglades, 541–542
Florida Keys, 504–505
Fort Lauderdale and Broward County, 336–337
Lower Gulf Coast, 592
Miami and Miami Beach, 422–423
Northeast Florida, 149–150
Palm Beach and the Treasure Coast, 285
Panhandle, 74
Tampa Bay area, 649
Walt Disney World and Orlando, 226
Caribbean Beach Resort ⌧, 201
Carlin Park, 271
Carol Castle, 521–522
Casa Monica Hotel ⌧, 111
Casa Morada ⌧, 451
Casa Tina ✕, 623
Casa Tua ✕, 371
Casablanca Cafe ✕, 300–301

Casablanca Inn Bed & Breakfast on the Bay ⌧, 111–112
Casements, 116
Cason Cottage, 259
Caspersen Beach, 646
Castillo de San Marcos National Monument, 106
Casita de la Verdad ⌧, 607
Catalina Hotel & Beach Club ⌧, 385
Cedar Key, 630–631
Cedar Key Historical Society Museum, 630
Celebration, 182
Celebration Hotel ⌧, 212
Centennial Park, 600
Centro Ybor, 600
Champions Gate Golf Club, 222
Charcuterie Too ✕, 295
Charles Hosmer Morse Museum of American Art, 181
Charlotte Harbor Historical Center, 559
Chautauqua Winery, 65
Chef Jean-Pierre Cooking School, 313
Chez Jean-Pierre ✕, 238
Children's activities
Everglades, 518, 521–522, 528, 530–531, 532, 534, 537
Florida Keys, 436, 440, 443, 448, 449, 450–451, 459
Fort Lauderdale and Broward County, 309–310, 327, 328, 333, 334
Lower Gulf Coast, 551–552, 553–554, 556, 559, 563, 564–565, 566, 567, 568, 570–571, 572–573, 574, 575–576, 577, 579–580, 582, 583–584, 587–588, 590
Miami and Miami Beach, 352, 358, 365–366, 402–405, 408–409, 419
Northeast Florida, 83–85, 92, 95, 118, 125–126, 131, 137–138
Palm Beach and the Treasure Coast, 245, 246, 247, 257, 263, 264, 273, 278, 279, 281
Panhandle, 33–34, 42–43, 45–46, 54–55, 69
Tampa Bay area, 597, 600–602, 611, 617, 636–638
Walt Disney World and Orlando, 178, 180, 187–188, 189, 191, 193, 200, 209–210

Children's Museum of Tampa, 600
Children's Science Explorium, 264
Chispa ✕, 376
Chops City Grill ✕, 581
Churches
Miami and Miami Beach, 362
Northeast Florida, 100–101, 106, 108
Palm Beach and the Treasure Coast, 232
Panhandle, 59
Tampa Bay area, 624
Cinderella's Royal Table ✕, 184, 186
Cioppino ✕, 375
Circa 39 ⌧, 390–391
Circle Drive (DeFuniak Springs), 65
Cirque du Soleil, 219
City Cemetry (Key West), 478
City Gate (St. Augustine), 106
Clam Pass Beach Park, 579
Clearwater, 619–623
Clearwater Beach, 620
Clearwater Marine Aquarium, 620
Clewiston Museum, 251
Climate, 9
Coastal Islands, 560–573
Cocoa, 130–133
Cocoa Beach, 133–137
Cocoa Beach Pier, 133
Cocoa Village, 130
Coconut Grove, 354, 358–359, 375, 394–395
Coconut Grove Farmers Market, 416–417
CocoWalk, 358
Collier County Museum, 580
Collier Inn & Cottages ⌧, 562–563
Collier-Seminole State Park, 533
Colonial Spanish Quarter (St. Augustine), 106
Colony Beach & Tennis Resort ⌧, 641–642
Colony Hotel, 259
Columbia (St. Augustine) ✕, 110
Columbia (Tampa) ✕, 604
Comedy Warehouse, 218
Conch Key, 459
Consign of the Times (shop), 415
Convoy Point, 515

Coral Castle of Florida, 417–418

Coral Gables, 359–363, 375–377, 396

Coral Gables Congregational Church, 362

Coral Gables Merrick House and Gardens, 362

Corkscrew Swamp Sanctuary, 575

Cornell Museum of Art & History, 259

Coronado Springs Resort ⌕, 201–202

Cortez Beach, 634

Court House Cultural Center, 274

Crackers, 446

Crandon Park and Gardens, 365, 404–405

Credit cards, 8, 672

Crest Theatre, 259

Crow's Nest Marina Restaurant & Tavern ✕, 647

Crystal River, 629–630

Crystal River National Wildlife Refuge, 629

Cuban Memorial Boulevard (Miami), 354

Cuisine, 15

Cummer Museum of Art and Gardens, 82–83

Currency, 670

Currie Park, 244

Curry Hammock State Park, 461

Customs, 670

Cypress, a Bed & Breakfast Inn ⌕, 642

D

Dagney Johnson Key Largo Hammocks Botanical State Park, 434

Dania Beach, 332–334

Dante Fascell Visitor Center, 515

Davie, 334–335

Daytona and Space Coast, 116–148

Daytona Beach, 117–122

Daytona Lagoon, 117–118

Daytona USA, 118

De Léon Springs State Park, 141

De Soto National Memorial, 632

Deerfield Beach, 325–326

Deerfield Island Park, 325

Deering Estate at Cutler, 418

DeFuniak Springs, 64–65

DeLand, 139–140

DeLand Gallery of Art, 139

DeLand Museum of Art, 139

Delano Hotel ⌕, 377, 380

Delnor-Wiggins Pass State Park, 577, 579

Delray Beach, 258–262

Delray Beach Municipal Beach, 260

Destin, 45–48

Devil's Millhopper State Geological Site, 145

Discounts and deals, 659, 662, 664

Discovery Cove, 174–175

Disney-MGM Studios, 161, 189–190

Disney's Animal Kingdom, 161, 202–203

Disney's Wide World of Sports, 221

Disney Water Parks, 161

Dixie Crossroads ✕, 128

Dog Bar (shop), 416

Dog Beach, 478

Dog racing

Fort Lauderdale and Broward County, 331

Lower Gulf Coast, 577

Northeast Florida, 93, 121

Palm Beach and the Treasure Coast, 241

Panhandle, 39, 58

Tampa Bay area, 609, 619, 645

Dolphin Connection at Hawk's Cay Resort, 460

Dolphin Cove, 460

Dolphin Landings Tours, 613–614

Dolphin Research Center, 459, 460, 461

Dolphins Plus, Inc., 460

Don CeSar Beach Resort, a Loews Hotel ⌕, 616–617

Don Vicente de Ybor Historic Inn ⌕, 607

Downtown Disney, 203–204, 206–207, 209–211

Downtown Miami, 348–352, 373–374, 393–394

Downtown Orlando and environs, 180–181, 195–196, 216–217

Downtown Tallahassee Historic Trail, 67

Drop Anchor Resort & Marina ⌕, 453

Dubois Home and Park, 271

Duck Key, 459

Dunedin, 623–624

Dwyer's Pub, 555

E

East Martello Tower, 484–485

Eastwood Golf Club, 555

Eco-Discovery Center, 480

Echo Global Farm & Nursery, 556–557

Eden Gardens State Park, 49

Eden House ⌕, 493

Edgewater Beach Resort ⌕, 56

Edison & Ford Winter Estates, 548, 551

Eglin Air Force Base, 42

Egmont Key, 613–614

El Credito Cigar Factory, 354

El Solano, 235

Electricity, 670

11 Maple Street ✕, 276

Elizabeth Pointe Lodge ⌕, 103

Elliott Key, 516–517

Elliott Museum, 276

El Toro Taco ✕, 522

Embassies, 670

Emergencies, 670

Everglades, 542

Florida Keys, 505

Lower Gulf Coast, 593

Miami and Miami Beach, 426–427

Northeast Florida, 150

Palm Beach and the Treasure Coast, 286

Panhandle, 75

Tampa Bay area, 650

Walt Disney World and Orlando, 227

Emeril's ✕, 192

Englewood Beach, 646

Environmental Learning Center, 280

Eō Inn and Urban Spa ⌕, 216–217

Epcot, 161, 186–189, 200–202, 204, 206

Ernest F. Coe Visitor Center, 518

Ernest Hemingway Home & Museum, 480

Española Way (Miami), 346

Essex House ⌕, 384

Estero, 574–577

Estero Island, 570–573

European Street Cafe ✕, 88

Euphemia Haye ✕, 639
Everglades, *12–13, 511–544*
*children's activities, 518,
521–522, 528, 530–531, 532,
534, 537*
emergencies, 542
*hotels, 513, 516–517, 523,
525–527, 534–535, 537–539*
itinerary recommendations, 520
media, 542
price categories, 513
*restaurants, 512–513, 522–523,
524–525, 533–534, 536–537*
shopping, 524, 527–528, 535
*sports and the outdoors, 515,
524, 529, 535, 539*
tours, 532, 542–544
transportation, 540–542
visitor information, 544
Everglades Alligator Farm,
362
Everglades City, *535–539*
Everglades Gator Park, *530*
Everglades National Park,
517–539
Everglades Safari Park, *530*
Everglades Wonder Gardens,
574

F

Fairchild Tropical Garden, *362*
Fairmont Turnberry Isle Resort
& Club ⚏, *392*
Fakahatchee Strand Preserve
State Park, *533*
Falling Waters State Park, *65*
Farmers' Market Restaurant
✕, *525*
Fernandina Beach, *100–104*
Festivals and seasonal events,
21–26
Fish House, The ✕, *436, 438*
Fish Out of Water ✕, *49*
Fisher Island Hotel & Resort
⚏, *380*
Fishing, *664–665*
Everglades, 529
*Florida Keys, 444, 455,
466–467, 471, 499*
*Fort Lauderdale and Broward
County, 314, 318, 320, 322,
323, 326, 331*
*Lower Gulf Coast, 555, 560,
561, 570, 573, 586, 591*
*Northeast Florida, 115,
136–137, 140, 142*
*Palm Beach and the Treasure
Coast, 253, 256, 258, 269,
279, 284*

Panhandle, 39, 44, 47
*Tampa Bay area, 609, 614, 645,
647*
Flagler College, *106*
Flagler Memorial Presbyterian
Church, *108*
Flamingo, *528–529*
Flamingo Gardens and Wray
Botanical College, *334*
Flamingo Lodge, Marina &
Outpost Resort, *529*
Flamingo Visitor Center, *528*
Florida Aquarium, *597*
Florida Botanical Gardens, *620*
Florida Caverns State Park, *66*
Florida City, *524–528*
Florida Holocaust Museum,
612
Florida International Museum,
611–612
Florida Keys, *12, 430–509*
*beaches, 447, 448, 449, 461,
463, 478, 481, 484, 485*
*children's activities, 436, 440,
443, 448, 449, 450–451, 459*
emergencies, 505
*hotels, 432, 439–443, 451–453,
458, 459, 461–462, 465–466,
468–469, 470–471, 473–474,
490–497, 506*
itinerary recommendations, 435
media, 505–506
*nightlife and the arts, 443–444,
453–454, 497–498*
price categories, 432
*restaurants, 432, 436, 438–439,
449–451, 457–458, 461, 463,
464–465, 470, 472–473,
485–489*
*shopping, 445–446, 456–457,
499–502*
*sports and the outdoors,
444–445, 454–456, 460,
466–467, 469, 471–472,
474–475, 498–499*
tours, 506–509
transportation, 502–505
visitor information, 509
Florida Keys Wild Bird Center,
436
Florida Marlins, *402–403*
Florida Museum of Natural
History, *145*
Florida Oceanographic Coastal
Center, *276*
Florida Panther National
Wildlife Refuge, *532–533*
Florida Repertory Theater,
555

Florida State Archives and
Library, *67*
Football, *93, 121, 407, 609*
Fort Barrancas, *35*
Fort Clinch State Park, *101*
Fort De Soto Park, *613*
Fort George Island, *100*
Fort Lauderdale and Broward
County, *11, 289–338*
*beaches, 293, 298–300,
327–328, 332*
*children's activities, 309–310,
327, 328, 333, 334*
*hotels, 291, 308–310, 317–318,
320–323, 325–326, 329–330*
*itinerary recommendations,
292*
*nightlife and the arts, 311–313,
330, 334–335*
price categories, 291
*restaurants, 291, 295, 300–308,
320, 322, 324, 325, 328–329,
332–333, 334*
safety tips, 293
*shopping, 314–315, 316, 319,
324, 333–334*
*sports and the outdoors, 314,
318–319, 320, 322, 323–324,
326, 331–332, 333, 335*
tours, 337
transportation, 301, 335–337
visitor information, 337–338
Fort Lauderdale Antique Car
Museum, *295–296*
Fort Lauderdale Beachfront,
300
Fort Myers and environs, *548,
551–560*
Fort Myers Beach, *570–573*
Fort Pickens, *41*
Fort Pierce, *278–280*
Fort Pierce Inlet State
Recreation Area, *279*
Fort Pierce State Park, *278*
Fort Walton Beach, *42–45*
Fort Wilderness Resort
Campground ⚏, *200*
Fort Zachary Taylor State Park,
480
Fountain of Youth National
Archaeological Park, *108*
Four Seasons Hotel Miami ⚏,
393
Four Seasons Resort Palm
Beach ⚏, *240–241*
Friendship TrailBridge, *611*
Fruit & Spice Park, *521*
FSU Ringling Center for the
Cultural Arts, *636–637*

G

G. WIZ Museum, 637
Gainesville, 145–148
Gamble Plantation Historic
    State Park, 634
Gardens Hotel, The ⚏, 490
Garlit's Museum of Drag
    Racing, 143
Gasparilla Inn ⚏, 562
Gasparilla Island (Boca
    Grande), 561–562
Gasparilla Island State Park
    and Boca Grande Lighthouse
    Museum, 561
Gatorland, 178
Gaylord Palms Resort ⚏, 212
Gene's Steak House ✕, 119
George Adderly House, 463
Germain Arena, 577
Gilbert's House of Refuge
    Museum, 276
Gillespie Museum, 139
Gold Coast Railroad Museum,
    418
Golf
Florida Keys, 467, 499
Fort Lauderdale and Broward
    County, 314, 318–319, 323,
    326, 331–332
Lower Gulf Coast, 555–556,
    558, 560, 570, 573, 586
Miami and Miami Beach,
    407–408
Northeast Florida, 93, 110, 115,
    121, 138, 144
Palm Beach and the Treasure
    Coast, 242, 250, 253, 258,
    266, 270, 273, 277, 282
Panhandle, 39, 44–45, 47, 58
Tampa Bay area, 609–610, 619,
    622, 624, 627, 630, 635–636,
    645, 647
Walt Disney World and
    Orlando, 221–222
Government advisories, 653
Governors Inn ⚏, 70
Grand Floridian Resort & Spa
    ⚏, 198
Grandview Gardens Bed &
    Breakfast ⚏, 248
Grassy Key, 459, 461–462
Grayton Beach, 48–51
Grayton Beach State Park, 49
Great Explorations, 611
Great Florida Birding Trail, 575
Green Meadows Farm, 178
Grosvenor Resort ⚏, 207
Grove Inn Country Guesthouse
    ⚏, 523

Guided tours, 663–664
Gulf Coast, 41–63. ⇨ Also
    Lower Gulf Coast;
    Panhandle
Gulf Coast Museum of Art, 620
Gulf Coast Visitor Center, 536
Gulf Islands National Seashore,
    40–41
Gulf Stream, 258
Gulf World, 54–55
Gulfarium, 43
Gulfside Park, 564
Gumbo Limbo Nature Center,
    263

H

Halifax Historical Museum, 118
Hampton Inn ⚏, 526–527
Harry P. Leu Gardens, 180
Harry S. Truman Little White
    House Museum, 480–481
Havana Harry's ✕, 376
Hawk's Cay Resort ⚏, 459
Health, 669
Heathcote Botanical Gardens,
    278
Hemingway, Ernest, 480, 482
Henry Morrison Flagler
    Museum, 235
Heritage Center and Indian
    River Citrus Museum, 280
Heritage Village, 620
Higgs Beach-Astro Park, 481
High Noon Beach Resort ⚏,
    321–322
Hillsboro Light, 324
Hilton Cocoa Beach Oceanfront
    ⚏, 135
Hilton Daytona Beach
    Oceanfront Resort ⚏, 120
Historic Bok Sanctuary, 178,
    180
Historic Downtown Stuart, 274
Historic Pensacola Village, 31,
    33
Historic Seaport at Key West
    Bight, 481
Historical Museum of Southern
    Florida, 352
Hobe Sound National Wildlife
    Refuge, 273
Hobe Sound Nature Center,
    273
Hockey, 93
Holiday Park, 317
Holidays, 670
Hollywood, 327–332
Hollywood North Beach Park,
    327–328

Hollywood Seminole Gaming,
    328
Holocaust Memorial, 346
Home exchanges, 660
Homestead, 518, 521–524
Homestead Bayfront Park, 521
Homestead-Miami Speedway,
    402
Homosassa Springs, 628–629
Homosassa Springs Wildlife
    State Park, 628
Horse racing, 323, 332, 610
Horseback riding, 104, 142
Hotel, The ⚏, 383
Hotel St. Michel ⚏, 396
Hotel Victor ⚏, 380–381
Hotels, 657, 660
Everglades, 513, 516–517, 523,
    525–527, 534–535, 537–539
Florida Keys, 432, 439–443,
    451–453, 458, 459, 461–462,
    465–466, 468–469, 470–471,
    473–474, 490–497, 506
Fort Lauderdale and Broward
    County, 291, 308–310,
    317–318, 320–323, 325–326,
    329–330
Lower Gulf Coast, 547–548,
    553–554, 557–558, 559–560,
    562–563, 567–569, 572–573,
    576, 582–585, 589–590
Miami and Miami Beach,
    377–396
Northeast Florida, 79, 88–91,
    96–98, 102–104, 111–114,
    117, 119–120, 124, 128–129,
    130, 134–136, 140, 143–144,
    145, 146–147
Palm Beach and the Treasure
    Coast, 230, 239–241,
    248–249, 252, 254, 256, 258,
    261, 264–265, 267, 269, 272,
    275, 277, 279, 281, 283–284
Panhandle, 29, 37–38, 43–44,
    46–47, 50, 52–53, 56–57,
    60–62, 63, 65, 70–71, 72–73
price categories, 30, 79, 197,
    231, 291, 377, 432, 513, 548,
    596, 657
Tampa Bay area, 596, 605–607,
    616–618, 621–622, 624, 627,
    628–630, 631, 635, 640–643,
    647
Walt Disney World and
    Orlando, 157, 197–217
House of Blues, 219
Howard Park Beach, 625
Hugh Taylor Birch State
    Recreation Area, 300

Hutchinson Island (Jensen Beach), *275–277*
Hyatt Coconut Point Resort & Spa ⚏, *576*
Hyatt Regency Bonaventure Conference Center Hotel & Spa ⚏, *318*
Hyatt Regency Grand Cypress Resort ⚏, *209*
Hyatt Regency Pier Sixty-Six ⚏, *308*
Hy-Vang Vietnamese Cuisine ✕, *375*

I

Ice hockey, *577, 610*
Ice-skating, *324, 556, 577*
IGFA Fishing Hall of Fame and Museum, *332*
Imaginarium Hands-On Museum, *551*
Indian Key Historic State Park, *448–449*
Indian Temple Mound Museum, *42–43*
In-line skating, *408*
Inn at Cocoa Beach ⚏, *135–136*
Inn at Oak Street, The ⚏, *90*
Insurance, *654–656*
International Drive Area (Orlando), *193–194, 213–216*
International Swimming Hall of Fame Museum and Aquatic Complex, *300*
International travelers, tips for, *670–671*
Internet, *668*
Islamorada, *446–457*
Islamorada County Park, *448*
Islamorada Founder's Park, *447*
Islands of Adventure, *170–171*
Itinerary recommendations, *18–20*
Ivey House ⚏, *538*

J

J. N. "Ding" Darling National Wildlife Refuge, *565*
Jacksonville, *79–104*
Jacksonville Landing, *83*
Jacksonville Zoo and Gardens, *83*
Jacobs Aquatic Center, *436*
Jai alai, *144, 279, 333*
Jazid (music club), *402*
Jensen Beach, *275–277*

Jetty Park Campgrounds, *129*
Jiko ✕, *190*
John and Mable Ringling Museum of Art, *636–637*
John C. Beasley Wayside Park, *42*
John D. MacArthur Beach State Park, *270*
John Gorrie Museum State Park, *59*
John Pennekamp Coral Reef State Park ⚏, *434, 443*
John U. Lloyd Beach State Recreation Area, *332*
Jonathan Dickinson State Park, *273–274*
Jungle Drums (shop), *570*
Juniper Springs, *142*
Jupiter, *271–273*
Jupiter Inlet Lighthouse, *271*
Jupiter Island and Hobe Sound, *273–274*
JW Marriott Orlando Grande Lakes ⚏, *214*

K

Kampong, The, *358*
Karpeles Manuscript Library Museum, *83*
Kathryn Abbey Hanna Park, *99*
Kayaking
Everglades, *529, 539*
Lower Gulf Coast, *562, 570*
Northeast Florida, *104, 137*
Palm Beach and the Treasure Coast, *284*
Panhandle, *38–39*
Tampa Bay area, *645*
Kennedy Space Center Visitor Complex, *125–126*
Key Biscayne, *363–366, 375, 395–396*
Key Largo, *433–446*
Key West, *475–502*
Key West Aquarium, *481*
Key West Museum of Art and History, *481*
Kids Kampus, *83–84*
King Center for the Performing Arts, *138*
Kingsley Plantation, *100*
Kissimmee, *178, 180, 211–213*
Kona Kai Resort ⚏, *439–440*
Kona Skatepark, *84*
Konger Tarpon Springs Aquarium, *625*
Koreshan State Historic Site, *574*

L

La Crepe en Haut ✕, *117*
La Tre ✕, *264*
Lago Mar Resort & Club ⚏, *310*
Lake Jackson Mounds Archaeological State Park, *68*
Lake Okeechobee, *250–253*
Lake Woodruff National Wildlife Refuge, *141*
Lake Worth, *253–255*
Lake Worth Municipal Park, *253*
Lantana, *255–256*
Lanatana Public Beach, *255*
LaPlaya Beach & Golf Resort ⚏, *583*
Largo Lodge ⚏, *442*
Last Flight Out (shop), *501*
Lauderdale-by-the-Sea, *320–322*
Lawrence E. Will Museum, *251*
Layton Nature Trail, *457*
Le Coq au Vin ✕, *195–196*
Lee's Crab Trap and Crab Trap II ✕, *634*
Leigh Ann's (More Than Just A) Coffee House ✕, *463*
Les Chefs de France ✕, *187*
Lido Key, *636*
Lighthouse Beach, *564*
Lighthouse Museum, *483*
Lighthouse Point, *324*
Lighthouses
Florida Keys, *483*
Fort Lauderdale and Broward County, *324*
Lower Gulf Coast, *561, 564*
Miami and Miami Beach, *365*
Northeast Florida, *109*
Palm Beach and Treasure Coast, *271*
Panhandle, *72*
Lightner Museum, *108*
Lignumvitae Key Botanical State Park, *449*
Lincoln Road Antique and Collectibles Market, *417*
Lincoln Road Mall, *345–347, 411–412*
Lion Country Safari, *245*
Little Havana (Miami), *352–354, 374–375*
Little Palm Island Resort & Spa ⚏, *473*
Little Saigon ✕, *196*
Little Torch Key, *472–475*
Lodge & Club, The ⚏, *96–97*

Loews Miami Beach Hotel ⊞, *381*

Loggerhead Park Marine Life Center of Juno Beach, *271*

Long Key, *457–458*

Long Key State Park, *457*

Long Key Viaduct, *458*

Longboat Key, *636*

L'Originale Alfredo di Roma Ristorante ✕, *188*

Lovers Key Beach Club & Resort ⊞, *572*

Lovers Key State Park, *571*

Lowdermilk Park, *580*

Lower Gulf Coast, *13, 546–593*
  beaches, *564, 565–566, 574–575, 579, 580, 587–588*
  children's activities, *551–552, 553–554, 556, 559, 563, 564–565, 566, 567, 568, 570–571, 572–573, 574, 575–576, 577, 579–580, 582, 583–584, 587–588, 590*
  emergencies, *593*
  hotels, *547–548, 553–554, 557–558, 559–560, 562–563, 567–569, 572–573, 576, 582–585, 589–590*
  itinerary recommendations, *549*
  nightlife and the arts, *554–555, 585*
  price categories, *548*
  restaurants, *547, 552–553, 557, 559, 561–562, 566–567, 571–572, 575–576, 580–582, 588–589*
  shopping, *556, 558, 570, 577, 586–587*
  sports and the outdoors, *555–556, 558, 560, 561, 563, 569–570, 573, 575, 576–577, 585–586, 590–591*
  transportation, *591–592*
  visitor information, *593*

Lower Keys, *467–475*

Lowry Park Zoo, *600–601*

Loxahatchee River Historical Museum, *271*

Luggage, *654*

Lynn Hall Memorial Park, *570–571*

Lyric Theatre, *274*

M

Magic Kingdom, *161, 186, 198–200*

Magnolia Grill ✕, *59–60*

Mail, *670–671*

Main Beach (Amelia Island), *101*

Main Park Road (Everglades National Park), *517–518*

Main Public Library (Miami), *352*

Maitland, *181*

Maltz Jupiter Theatre, *271–272*

Manalapan, *255*

Manasota Beach, *646*

Manatee County Beach, *634*

Manatee Park, *551–552*

Manatee Village Historical Park, *632*

Manatees, *16*

Mandarin Oriental, Miami ⊞, *393*

Mangia Mangia ✕, *488–489*

Mango Inn ⊞, *254*

Mango Tree Restaurant ✕, *134*

Mar-a-Lago, *235*

Marathon, *462–467*

Marchand's Grill ✕, *614*

Marco Beach Ocean Resort ⊞, *589–590*

Marco Island, *587–591*

Marco Island Historical Society Museum, *588*

Marco Island Marriott Resort, Golf Club & Spa ⊞, *590*

Margulies Collection at the Warehouse, *352*

Marie Selby Botanical Gardens, *637*

Marina Café ✕, *46*

Maritime & Yachting Museum, *274*

Marjorie Kinnan Rawlings State Historic Site, *144–145*

Marjory Stoneman Douglas Biscayne Nature Center, *365*

Marker 88 ✕, *449*

Mark's Las Olas ✕, *304–305*

Marquesa Hotel ⊞, *495*

Marriott Bay Point Resort Village ⊞, *57*

Matthew's ✕, *85*

Mayfair in the Grove, *358*

Mayport, *99–100*

McGregor Boulevard (Fort Myers), *548*

McKee Botanical Garden, *280*

McLarty Treasure Museum, *283*

Meal plans, *8, 157*

Media
  Everglades, *542*
  Florida Keys, *505–506*

Miami and Miami Beach, *427*

Palm Beach and the Treasure Coast, *286*

Tampa Bay area, *650*

Meginnis-Monroe House, *67*

Mel Fisher Maritime Heritage Society Museum, *483*

Mel Fisher's Treasure Museum, *282*

Melbourne, *137–138*

Merlin Guesthouse ⊞, *493–494*

Mermaid & the Alligator ⊞, *492*

Merritt Island National Wildlife Refuge, *128*

Metrozoo, *363, 418–419*

MIA Jewels (shop), *414*

Miami and Miami Beach, *12, 340–428*
  beaches, *402, 403–405*
  children's activities, *352, 358, 365–366, 402–405, 408–409, 419*
  e-mail service, *426*
  emergencies, *426–427*
  hotels, *377–396*
  itinerary recommendations, *341*
  media, *427*
  nightlife and the arts, *351, 396–402*
  price categories, *366, 377*
  restaurants, *346, 347, 351, 354, 366–377*
  shopping, *409–417*
  sports and outdoors, *402–409*
  tours, *427–428*
  transportation, *420–426*
  visitor information, *428*
  weather, *9*

Miami Art Museum, *352*

Miami Children's Museum, *347*

Miami-Dade Cultural Center, *352*

Miami Design District, *411*

Miami Dolphins, *407*

Miami Lakes, *391–393*

Miami Museum of Science and Space Transit Planetarium, *358*

Miami River Inn ⊞, *394*

Miami Seaquarium, *365–366*

Miami Twice (shop), *415*

Micanopy, *144–145*

Miccosukee Indian Village, *531*

Miccosukee Restaurant ✕, *534*

Middle Keys, *458–467*

Mille Saparé ✕, *552*

Miniature golf, *335, 622–623*

Miracle Mile, *363*

Miramar Outlets complex, *577*

Mise en Place ✕, *603*

Mission of Nombre de Dios, *108*

Mizner Park, *266*

Molly's Trolleys, *243*

Money matters, *156, 159, 174, 670, 672*

Monkey Jungle, *419*

Moorings, The 🖾, *452*

Morada Bay ✕, *459*

Morikami Museum and Japanese Garden, *259*

Morrison, Samuel F., *312*

Mote Marine Aquarium, *637–638*

Mounts Botanical Gardens, *246*

Municipal Complex (Lake Okeechobee), *251*

Museum of Art (Fort Lauderdale), *296*

Museum of Arts and Sciences (Daytona Beach), *118*

Museum of Contemporary Art Jacksonville, *84*

Museum of Discovery and Science/Blockbuster IMAX Theater, *296*

Museum of Fine Arts (St. Petersburg), *612*

Museum of Florida History, *67*

Museum of Historic St. Augustine Government House, *108*

Museum of Lifestyle & Fashion History, *2590*

Museum of Science and History, *84–85*

Museum of Science and Industry (MOSI), *602*

Museum of the Everglades, *536*

Museum of the Man in the Sea, *54*

Museums and galleries
Everglades, 515, 518, 521–522, 528, 531–532, 536
Florida Keys, 463, 478, 480–481, 483, 484–485
Fort Lauderdale and Broward County, 295–296, 298, 300, 317, 327, 332, 334
Lower Gulf Coast, 548, 551, 562, 564–565, 579, 580, 588
Miami and Miami Beach, 344, 346, 347, 348, 352, 358, 359, 362, 418, 420

Northeast Florida, 81–83, 84–85, 106, 108, 109, 110, 116, 117, 118, 122, 126–127, 131, 139, 142, 143, 145
Palm Beach and the Treasure Coast, 235–236, 244, 247, 251, 257, 259, 263, 264, 267, 271, 274, 276, 278, 280, 282, 283
Panhandle, 31, 33–34, 35, 42–43, 54, 59, 67, 69
Tampa Bay area, 600, 602, 611–613, 620, 624–625, 630, 632, 636–637
Walt Disney World and Orlando, 180–181

Museums and Nature Center of Crane Point Hammock, *463*

Myakka River State Park, *638*

N

NACT-Everglades Rentals & Eco Adventures, *539*

Nancy Forrester's Secret Garden, *483*

Naples and environs, *573–591*

Naples Botanical Garden, *580*

Naples Grande Resort & Club 🖾, *583–584*

Naples Museum of Art, *579*

Naples Nature Center, *579–580*

Naples Philharmonic Center for the Arts, *585*

Naples Zoo, *579*

National and state parks
Everglades, 514–540
Florida Keys, 434, 447–449, 457, 461, 468, 469, 480
Fort Lauderdale and Broward County, 300, 332
Lower Gulf Coast, 565, 571, 574, 577, 579
Miami and Miami Beach, 358, 365, 403–404
Northeast Florida, 101, 106, 108, 116, 123, 127, 128, 139, 141, 142, 144–145
Palm Beach and the Treasure Coast, 257, 270, 273–274, 278, 279, 283
Panhandle, 40–41, 49, 55, 59, 62, 65, 66, 68, 69, 72
state park pass, 64
Tampa Bay area, 600, 613–614, 623–624, 628, 629, 632, 634, 638
Walt Disney World and Orlando, 181

National Croquet Center, *246*

National Hotel, The 🖾, *383–284*

National Key Deer Refuge, *469*

National Museum of Naval Aviation, *35*

Natural Bridge Battlefield State Park, *72*

Nature Coast, *627–631*

Navy SEAL Museum, *278*

Nemo ✕, *370–371*

New Capitol (Tallahassee), *67–68*

New Smyrna Beach, *122–124*

New Town (Key West), *484–485*

New World Inn 🖾, *37–38*

Nickelodeon Family Suites by Holiday Inn 🖾, *209–210*

Nightlife and the arts
Florida Keys, 443–444, 453–454, 497–498
Fort Lauderdale and Broward County, 311–313, 330, 334–335
Lower Gulf Coast, 554–555, 585
Miami and Miami Beach, 351, 396–402
Northeast Florida, 91–92, 99, 114, 120–121, 124, 132, 136, 147
Palm Beach and the Treasure Coast, 241, 249, 254, 256, 261–262, 265, 270, 281–282
Panhandle, 38, 44, 47, 50, 53, 58, 71
Tampa Bay area, 607–608, 618–619, 622, 644–645, 647
Walt Disney World and Orlando, 217–220

95 Cordova ✕, *110*

Nokomis Beach, *646*

Norman's (Coral Gables) ✕, *376*

Norman's (Orlando) ✕, *194*

North Captiva Island Club Resort, *563*

North Fort Myers, *556–558*

North Hill Preservation District (Pensacola), *34*

North Jetty Park, *646*

Northeast Florida, *10, 77–151*
beaches, 94–95, 101, 109, 118, 122–123, 127–128, 129, 133, 138
children's activities, 83–85, 92, 95, 118, 125–126, 131, 137–138

emergencies, *150*
hotels, *79, 88–91, 96–98, 102–104, 111–114, 117, 119–120, 124, 128–129, 130, 134–136, 140, 143–144, 145, 146–147*
itinerary recommendations, *78*
nightlife and arts, *91–92, 99, 114, 120–121, 124, 132, 136, 147*
price categories, *79*
restaurants, *79, 85–88, 95–96, 101–102, 110–111, 117, 118–119, 123–124, 128, 129–130, 132, 134, 139–140, 141, 143, 146*
shopping, *94, 104, 115, 122, 124, 132–133, 137*
sports and outdoors, *84, 92–94, 99, 104, 114–115, 121, 130, 133, 136–137, 138, 140, 142, 144, 148*
tours, *150–151*
transportation, *100, 148–150*
visitor information, *151*
Norton Museum of Art, *244*

O

Oasis Visitor Center, *531–532*
Observation Tower, *536*
Ocala, *142–144*
Ocala National Forest, *142*
Ocean Drive, *404*
Ocean Key Resort 🏨, *495*
Ocean Surf 🏨, *390*
Ochopee Post Office, *532*
Okeeheelee Nature Center, *246*
Old Capitol (Tallahassee), *68*
Old Floresta, *263*
Old Fort Lauderdale Village & Museum, *296*
Old Rickenbacker Causeway Bridge, *366*
Old School Bakery ✕, *260–261*
Old School Square Cultural Arts Center, *29*
Old Seven Mile Bridge, *467*
Old Town (Key West), *477–484*
Olde Marco Island Inn ✕, *588*
Oldest House, *108*
Oldest Wooden Schoolhouse, *109*
Oleta River State Park, *403–404*
Omni Jacksonville Hotel 🏨, *90–91*
Opal Beach Day Use Area, *41*

Orlando. ⇨ *See* Walt Disney World and Orlando
Orlando Magic, *221*
Orlando Science Center, *180–181*
Ormond Beach, *116–117*
Ormond Memorial Art Museum and Gardens, *117*
Osteria del Teatro ✕, *371*
Outdoor markets, *416–417*
Outdoor Resorts 🏨, *538–539*
Oxygen Lounge, *401*
Oyster House Restaurant ✕, *537*

P

Pacific Time ✕, *372*
Packages, *662–663*
Packing tips, *654*
Palafax Historic District (Pensacola), *34*
Palm Beach and the Treasure Coast, *10, 229–287*
beaches, *255, 257, 259, 260, 266, 270, 271, 277, 282*
children's activities, *245, 246, 247, 257, 263, 264, 273, 278, 279, 281*
emergencies, *286*
hotels, *230, 239–241, 248–249, 252, 254, 256, 258, 261, 264–265, 267, 269, 272, 275, 277, 279, 281, 283–284*
itinerary recommendations, *234*
media, *286*
nightlife and the arts, *241, 249, 254, 256, 261–262, 265, 270, 281–282*
price categories, *231*
restaurants, *230, 236–239, 247–248, 252, 253–254, 255–256, 257–258, 260–261, 264, 267, 269–270, 272, 274–275, 276–277, 279, 280–281, 283*
shopping, *242, 250, 262, 266, 270, 275, 282*
sports and the outdoors, *241–242, 246, 250, 253, 255, 256, 258, 262, 266, 269, 270, 272–273, 274, 275, 277, 279, 282, 284*
tours, *286–287*
transportation, *243, 284–286*
visitor information, *287*
Palm Beach Gardens, *269–271*
Palm Beach Maritime Museum, *267*

Palm Beach Photographic Centre, *259*
Palm Beach Shores, *267, 269*
Palm Beach Zoo at Dreher Park, *246*
Palm Cottage, *580*
Palms South Beach, The 🏨, *390*
Panama City, *9*
Panama City Beach, *53–58*
Pandora's Steakhouse and Lounge ✕, *43*
Panhandle, *10, 28–75*
beaches, *40–41, 49, 55*
children's activities, *33–34, 42–43, 45–46, 54–55, 69*
emergencies, *75*
hotels, *29, 37–38, 43–44, 46–47, 50, 52–53, 56–57, 60–62, 63, 65, 70–71, 72–73*
itinerary recommendations, *33*
nightlife and the arts, *38, 44, 47, 50, 53, 58, 71*
price categories, *30*
restaurants, *29, 36–37, 43, 46, 49–50, 51–52, 55–56, 59–60, 62–63, 65, 69–70, 72–73*
shopping, *39–40, 45, 50–51, 53, 58, 62*
sports and outdoor activities, *38–39, 44–45, 47–48, 50, 53, 58, 63, 72*
transportation, *73–75*
visitor information, *75*
Paradise Beach, *138*
Parmer's Resort 🏨, *474*
Parrot Jungle Island, *347–348*
Pascal's on Ponce ✕, *376*
Pass-A-Grille Beach, *613*
Passports and visas, *671*
Paynes Prairie State Preserve, *144*
Peabody Orlando 🏨, *213–214*
Peanut Island, *267*
Pearl (bar), *398*
Pelican Island National Wildlife Refuge, *283*
Pensacola, *31–40*
Pensacola Bay and environs, *30–41*
Pensacola Beach, *40–41*
Pensacola Beach Gulf Pier, *41*
Pensacola Museum of Art, *34*
Pensacola Naval Air Station, *34–35, 36*
Pensacola Visitor Information Center, *31*

Perricone's Marketplace and Café ✕, *351*
PerriHouse Bed & Breakfast Inn ▥, *210–211*
Philly Junction ✕, *553*
Phipps Ocean Park, *235*
Pierre's ✕, *449–450*
Pigeon Key, *463–464*
Pine Jog Environmental Education Center, *246*
Pinewood Cultural Park, *620*
Pirate Soul Museum, *483*
Pisces ✕, *489*
Pit Bar-B-Q ✕, *534*
Plantation Key, *447*
Playalinda Beach, *127–128*
Plaza de la Constitución (St. Augustine), *109*
Polo, *255, 266*
Pompano Beach, *322–324*
Ponce de Léon Historical Park and Peace River Wildlife Center, *558–559*
Ponte Vedra Inn & Club ▥, *97*
Popular House/Key West Bed & Breakfast ▥, *492*
Porcher House, *131*
Price categories
dining, 30, 79, 183, 231, 291, 366, 432, 513, 548, 596, 668
Everglades, 513
Florida Keys, 432
Fort Lauderdale and Broward County, 291
lodging, 30, 79, 197, 231, 291, 377, 432, 513, 548, 596, 657
Lower Gulf Coast, 548
Miami and Miami Beach, 366, 377
Northeast Florida, 79
Palm Beach and the Treasure Coast, 231
Panhandle, 30
Tampa Bay area, 596
Walt Disney World and Orlando, 183, 197
Prime Outlets Orlando, *224*
Punta Gorda, *558–560*

Q

Quiet Waters Park, *325*
Quincy, *72*

R

Racquetball, *610*
Radisson Resort Parkway ▥, *212–213*
Ragtime Tavern & Seafood Grill ✕, *96*

Ramrod Key, *472*
Raney House, *59*
Raymond F. Kravis Center for the Performing Arts, *249*
Redland Fruit & Spice Park, *419*
Redland Hotel ▥, *523*
Redwoods Restaurant ✕, *614*
Regatta (shop), *587*
Renaissance Resort at World Golf Village ▥, *112–113*
Renaissance Vinoy Resort and Golf Club ▥, *617*
Restaurant Akershus ✕, *189*
Restaurant Medure ✕, *95*
Restaurants, *668–669*
Everglades, 512–513, 522–523, 524–525, 533–534, 536–537
Florida Keys, 432, 436, 438–439, 449–451, 457–458, 461, 463, 464–465, 470, 472–473, 485–489
Fort Lauderdale and Broward County, 291, 295, 300–308, 320, 322, 324, 325, 328–329, 332–333, 334
Lower Gulf Coast, 547, 552–553, 557, 559, 561–562, 566–567, 571–572, 575–576, 580–582, 588–589
Miami and Miami Beach, 346, 347, 351, 354, 366–377
Northeast Florida, 79, 85–88, 95–96, 101–102, 110–111, 117, 118–119, 123–124, 128, 129–130, 132, 134, 139–140, 141, 143, 146
Palm Beach and the Treasure Coast, 230, 236–239, 247–248, 252, 253–254, 255–256, 257–258, 260–261, 264, 267, 269–270, 272, 274–275, 276–277, 279, 280–281, 283
Panhandle, 29, 36–37, 43, 46, 49–50, 51–52, 55–56, 59–60, 62–63, 65, 69–70, 72–73
price categories, 30, 79, 183, 231, 291, 366, 432, 513, 548, 596, 668
Tampa Bay area, 596, 602–605, 614–616, 620–621, 623, 624, 628, 629, 631, 634, 638–640, 647
Walt Disney World and Orlando, 182–197
Richard Petty Driving Experience, *221*

Ringling Circus Museum, *636–637*
Ritz-Carlton, Amelia Island ▥, *102*
Ritz-Carlton Golf Resort ▥, *584*
Ritz-Carlton, Key Biscayne ▥, *395–396*
Ritz-Carlton, Naples ▥, *584*
Ritz-Carlton Orlando Grande Lakes ▥, *214*
Ritz-Carlton, Palm Beach ▥, *256*
Ritz-Carlton Sarasota ▥, *641*
Ritz-Carlton South Beach ▥, *381–383*
Riverside Children's Theatre, *281*
Riverview Hotel and Spa ▥, *124*
Riverwalk (Fort Lauderdale), *296*
Riverwalk (Tampa), *597*
Robbie's Marina, *449*
Robert and Mary Montgomery Armory Arts Center, *244*
Robert Is Here (shop), *527–528*
Rod and Gun Club ✕, *536–537*
Rodeo, *335*
Roller coasters, *333*
Ron Jon Surf Shop, *137*
Rookery Bay Environmental Learning Center, *587*
Rose Bar at the Delano, *399*
Rosemary Beach, *51–53*
Rosita's Restaurante ✕, *525*
Royal Pacific Resort ▥, *208*
Royal Palm Visitor Center, *518*
Rubell Family Collection, *352*
Rumrunners ✕, *557*

S

Sabal Palm House ▥, *254*
Saddlebrook Resort Tampa ▥, *605–606*
Safety tips, *293, 529, 673*
Sagamore ▥, *384*
Sailboat Bend, *296*
Sailing, *405–406, 556, 591*
St. Andrews State Park, *55*
St. Augustine, *106–115*
St. Augustine Alligator Farm Zoological Park, *109–110*
St. Augustine Beach, *109*
St. Augustine Lighthouse & Museum, *109*
St. George Island, *62–63*

St. George Island State Park, 62

St. John's County Visitor Information Center, 109

St. Johns River Ferry, 100

St. Lucie County Historical Museum, 278

St. Lucie Marine Station, 279

St. Marks National Wildlife Refuge and Lighthouse, 72

St. Nicholas Greek Orthodox Cathedral, 624

St. Peter's Episcopal Church, 100–101

St. Petersburg, 611–619

St. Petersburg Museum of History, 612

Sale e Pepe ✕, 588–589

Salt ✕, 101

Salt Springs, 142

Salt Water Cowboy's ✕, 110–111

Salute Ristorante Sul Mare ✕, 488

Salvador Dali Museum, 613

San Carlos Institute, 483

Sand Key Park, 620

Sand Lake Road, 194–195

Sandestin Golf and Beach Resort ☶, 46

Sanford L. Ziff Jewish Museum of Florida, 348

Sanibel/Captiva Conservation Foundation, 565

Sanibel Harbour Resort & Spa ☶, 553–554

Sanibel Historical Village and Museum, 564

Sanibel Island, 564–570

San Luis Archaeological and Historic Site, 69

Sarasota, 636–646

Sarasota Bay Explorers, 637–638

Sarasota Classic Car Museum, 637

Sarasota Jungle Gardens, 637

Satellite Beach, 138

Savannas Recreation Area, 278

Sawgrass Recreation Park, 317

Scenic A1A, 319–326

Scenic Boat Tour, 181

Schnebly Redland's Winery, 521

Schoolhouse Children's Museum, 257

Scooter rentals, 424

Scuba diving
Everglades, 515
Florida Keys, 444–445, 455–456, 467, 472, 474–475, 499
Fort Lauderdale and Broward County, 314, 326
Miami and Miami Beach, 408–409
Palm Beach and Treasure Coast, 266, 279
Panhandle, 45, 48, 58

Sea Dog Charters, 467

Sea turtles, 16, 268

Seagate Beach, 259

Seaside, 51–53

Seaside Cottage Rental Agency ☶, 52

Seasons 52 ✕, 194

Seaworld, 174–175

Sebastian, 282–284

Sebastian Inlet State Recreation Area, 283

Seminole Hard Rock Hotel & Casino, 602

Seminole Native Village, 328

Senzatempo (shop), 412

Seven Fish ✕, 489

Seven Mile Bridge, 467

7 Mile Grill ✕, 464–465

Seven Sisters Inn ☶, 144

Seville Square Historic District (Pensacola), 31

Shark Valley, 517, 530–531

Shark Valley Tram Tours, 535

Shell Island, 55

Shipwreck Island, 54

Shopping
Everglades, 524, 527–528, 535
Florida Keys, 445–446, 456–457, 499–502
Fort Lauderdale and Broward County, 314–315, 316, 319, 324, 333–334
Lower Gulf Coast, 556, 558, 570, 577, 586–587
Miami and Miami Beach, 409–417
Northeast Florida, 94, 104, 115, 122, 124, 132–133, 137
Palm Beach and the Treasure Coast, 242, 250, 262, 266, 270, 275, 282
Panhandle, 39–40, 45, 50–51, 53, 58, 62
Tampa Bay area, 610, 619, 636, 645–646, 648
Walt Disney World and Orlando, 222–225

Shores Resort & Spa, The ☶, 119–120

Shula's on the Beach ✕, 300

Sidney Fischer Park, 133

Siesta Beach, 638

Siesta Key, 636

Silver Springs Wild Waters, 143

Silvia Tcherassi (shop), 414

Simonton Street Beach, 484

SkyBar at the Shore Club, 399

Skydiving, 94, 140

Smallwood Store, 536

Smathers Beach, 485

Smyrna Dunes Park, 122

Snorkeling
Everglades, 515
Florida Keys, 444–445, 455–456, 467, 472, 474–475, 499
Fort Lauderdale and Broward County, 314
Miami and Miami Beach, 408–409
Palm Beach and Treasure Coast, 266

Society of the Four Arts, 235–236

Sombrero Beach, 463

South Beach (Key West), 484

South Beach (Miami and Miami Beach), 342–348, 367, 370–372, 377, 380–388

South Beach Scooters (shop), 416

South Broward, 326–335

South Dade, 417–420

South Florida Museum and Parker Manatee Aquarium, 632

South Florida Science Museum, 247

South Lido Park, 638

South Seas Island Resort ☶, 568

Southeast Museum of Photography, 118

Southernmost Hotel & Resorts ☶, 496–497

Southwest Florida Museum of History, 551

Southwest Florida Yachts, 556

Sovereign ✕, 146

Space Coast, 116–148

Spanish River Grill ✕, 123

Sponge Factory, 624–625

Sponges, 624–625, 626

Sports and the outdoors, 14–15
Everglades, 515, 524, 529, 535, 539
Florida Keys, 444–445, 454–456, 460, 466–467, 469, 471–472, 474–475, 498–499
Fort Lauderdale and Broward County, 314, 318–319, 320, 322, 323–324, 326, 331–332, 333, 335
Lower Gulf Coast, 555–556, 558, 560, 561, 563, 569–570, 573, 575, 576–577, 585–586, 590–591
Miami and Miami Beach, 402–409
Northeast Florida, 84, 92–94, 99, 104, 114–115, 121, 130, 133, 136–137, 138, 140, 142, 144, 148
Palm Beach and the Treasure Coast, 241–242, 246, 250, 253, 255, 256, 258, 262, 266, 269, 270, 272–273, 274, 275, 277, 279, 282, 284
Panhandle, 38–39, 44–45, 47–48, 50, 53, 58, 63, 72
Tampa Bay area, 608–610, 614, 619, 622–623, 624, 627, 630, 635–636, 645, 647
Walt Disney World and Orlando, 220–222
Sterling Casino Lines, 129
Stranahan House, 296, 298
Stuart, 274–275
Stuart Heritage Museum, 274
Suite 225 ✕, 255
Sun Splash Family Waterpark, 556
Suncoast Seabird Sanctuary, 619–620
Sundial Beach & Golf Resort 🏨, 568
Sundowners ✕, 436
Sundy House ✕🏨, 261
Sunken Gardens, 611
Sun-N-Fun Lagoon, 579
Sunny Isles, 391–393
Sunset Beach, 625
Sunset Key 🏨, 496
Surfing, 137
Symbols, 8

T

T. T. Wentworth Jr. Florida State Museum, 33–34
Ta-boó ✕, 239
Tallahassee, 66–73

Tallahassee Museum, 69
Talula ✕, 371
Tamara's Cafe Floridita ✕, 60
Tamiami Trail, 530–535
Tampa, 597–610
Tampa Bay area, 13, 595–651
beaches, 613, 614, 620, 625, 632, 634, 638, 646
children's activities, 597, 600–602, 611, 617, 636–638
emergencies, 650
hotels, 596, 605–607, 616–618, 621–622, 624, 627, 628–630, 631, 635, 640–643, 647
itinerary recommendations, 599
media, 650
nightlife and the arts, 607–608, 618–619, 622, 644–645, 647
price categories, 596
restaurants, 596, 602–605, 614–616, 620–621, 623, 624, 628, 629, 631, 634, 638–640, 647
shopping, 610, 619, 636, 645–646, 648
sports and the outdoors, 608–610, 614, 619, 622–623, 624, 627, 630, 635–636, 645, 647
tours, 613–614, 650
transportation, 648–649
visitor information, 651
Tampa Museum of Art, 600
Tarpon Bay Beach, 564
Tarpon Bay Explorers, 570
Tarpon Springs, 624–627
Tavernier, 436
Taxes, 673
Taxis
Florida Keys, 505
Fort Lauderdale and Broward County, 301, 337
Miami and Miami Beach, 424–425
Palm Beach and the Treasure Coast, 285
Walt Disney World and Orlando, 226–227
Tchoup Chop ✕, 193
Ted Peter's Famous Smoked Fish ✕, 616
Telephones, 671
Tennis
Florida Keys, 456
Fort Lauderdale and Broward County, 314
Lower Gulf Coast, 558, 570, 586

Northeast Florida, 94, 115
Palm Beach and the Treasure Coast, 262
Panhandle, 39, 45, 58
Tampa Bay area, 610, 623
Theater of the Sea, 448
32 East ✕, 260
Tiburón Golf Club, 586
Tides, The 🏨, 382–383
Tigertail Beach, 587–588
Timing the visit, 9
Timo ✕, 367
Tipping, 673
Titusville, 125–129
Tobacco Road (bar), 351, 399, 402
Tomoka State Park, 116
Town Hall Museum (Boca Raton), 263
Townhouse 🏨, 384–385
Traders Store & Cafe ✕, 566
Train travel
Fort Lauderdale and Broward County, 337
Miami and Miami Beach, 425–426
Northeast Florida, 150
Palm Beach and the Treasure Coast, 285–286
Panhandle, 75
Tampa Bay area, 649
Travel agents, 656–657
Travel times, 665
Traveler's checks and cards, 672–673
Travelodge Monaco Beach Resort 🏨, 392–393
Treasure Coast. ⇨ See Palm Beach and the Treasure Coast
Treasure Island, 613
Triay House, 106
Trinity Episcopal Church, 59
Trolley travel, 243
Turner Beach, 566
Turtle Beach, 638
Tuscan Steak ✕, 371
Twister Airboat Rides, 131
2 East El Camino Real, 263

U

Union Bank Building, 68
United States Astronaut Hall of Fame, 126–127
Universal Citywalk, 171
Universal Orlando, 170–171, 174, 192–193, 207–208, 219, 223
Universal Studios, 170

Upper Keys, *433–458*
Upper Matecumbe Key, *448*
Useppa Island, *562–563*

V

Vacation packages, *662–663*
Valiant Air Command Warbird
 Air Museum, *127*
Venetian Pool, *363, 408*
Venice, *646–648*
Veranda, The ✕, *552*
Vero Beach, *280–282*
Victoria and Albert's ✕, *191*
Vilano Beach, *109*
Villa Paradiso , *387–288*
Village of Merrick Park, *410*
Virginia Key, *363–366*
Visas, *671*
Visitor information, *653*
 Everglades, 544
 Florida Keys, 509
 *Fort Lauderdale and Broward
  County, 337–338*
 Lower Gulf Coast, 593
 Miami and Miami Beach, 428
 Northeast Florida, 151
 *Palm Beach and the Treasure
  Coast, 287*
 Panhandle, 75
 Tampa Bay area, 651
 *Walt Disney World and
  Orlando, 170, 174, 227*
Vizcaya Museum & Gardens,
 359

W

Wakulla Springs State Park, *69*
Walt Disney World and
 Orlando, *10–11, 153–227*
 *admission fees, 156, 171, 174,
  175*
 business hours, 159, 161
 *children's activities, 178, 180,
  187–188, 189, 191, 193, 200,
  209–210*
 emergencies, 227
 hotels, 157, 197–217

 itinerary recommendations, 153
 meal plans, 157
 money matters, 156, 159, 174
 nightlife and the arts, 217–220
 parking, 170, 174, 175
 price categories, 183, 197
 restaurants, 182–197
 shopping, 222–225
 sports and outdoors, 220–222
 tickets, 156–157
 time-saving tips, 154–155
 tours, 181
 transportation, 159, 225–227
 *visitor information, 170, 174,
  227*
 weather, 9
Walt Disney World Dolphin ,
 204, 206
Walton-DeFuniak Public
 Library, *64*
Water sports, *14*
 Florida Keys, 445, 456, 472
 Northeast Florida, 115, 121
 Tampa Bay area, 647
WaterColor Inn , *50*
Waterside Shops, *587*
Waterskiing, *262*
Weather, *9*
Web sites, *653, 656, 658,
 663*
Weeki Wachee Springs, *627*
Wekiwa Springs State Park,
 181
West Palm Beach, *243–250*
West Lake Park, *328*
West Martello Tower, *485*
West Miami-Dade, *394*
Westin Diplomat Resort & Spa
 , *330*
Westin Innisbrook Golf Resort
 , *625, 627*
Whale's Rib ✕, *325*
Wilderness Lodge ,
 199–200
William T. Kirby Nature Center,
 270–271
Windley Key, *447*

Windley Key Fossil Reef
 Geological State Park,
 447–448
Wings Over Miami, *420*
Winter Park, *181, 196–197,
 217*
Wolfgang Puck ✕, *191*
Wolfsonian-Florida
 International University, *348*
Wooten's Airboat Tours, *532*
World Erotic Art Museum
 (WEAM), *348*
World Golf Hall of Fame, *110*
World of Disney (shop), *223*
Worth Avenue (Palm Beach),
 236, 242
Wynwood Art District (Miami),
 352

X

Ximenez-Fatio House, *109*

Y

Yacht and Beach Club Resorts
 , *201*
Ybor City, *600*
Ybor City Museum State Park,
 600
Young at Art Children's
 Museum, *334*
Yulee Sugar Mill Ruins Historic
 State Park, *628*

Z

Zoo, The, *35*
Zoos
 Lower Gulf Coast, 579
 *Miami and Miami Beach, 363,
  418–419*
 *Northeast Florida, 35, 83,
  109–110, 137–138*
 *Palm Beach and the Treasure
  Coast, 245, 246*
 Tampa Bay area, 600–601
 *Walt Disney World and
  Orlando, 178*

PHOTO CREDITS

Cover Photo (Florida Keys): Susan Findlay/Masterfile. 10, *Richard Cummins/viestiphoto.com.* 11 (left), *Ace Stock Limited/Alamy.* 11 (right), *Jeff Greenberg/age fotostock.* 12, *Joe Viesti/viestiphoto.com.* 13 (left), *culliganphoto/Alamy.* 13 (right), *Sylvain Grandadam/age fotostock.* 14–15, *Jeff Greenberg/age fotostock.* 16, 17 (left), *Jeff Greenberg/age fotostock.* 17 (right), *Richard Cummins/viestiphoto.com.* 23 (left), *Stuart Pearce/World Pictures/age fotostock.* 23 (right), *J.D. Heaton/Picture Finders/age fotostock.* 25 (left), *Visit Florida.* 25 (right), *Jeff Greenberg/age fotostock.* 26, *Fritz Poelking/age fotostock.*

ABOUT OUR WRITERS

Diane Bair and Pamela Wright, who updated the Keys chapter, have perfected the quick getaway. The pair write for *Cooking Light, FamilyFun,* the *Miami Herald,* and other publications, including Fodor's *Miami & Miami Beach* and *Boston.*

Suzy Buckley is Lifestyle Editor at South Beach–based *Ocean Drive Magazine* and a frequent contributor for magazines including *Town & Country, Departures, Lucky, New York Post,* and *New York Magazine.* She has also appeared on Discovery's *Life's a Trip* and Bravo's *First Class All the Way.*

After being hired sight unseen by a South Florida newspaper, Fort Lauderdale updater and freelance travel writer Lynne Helm arrived from the Midwest anticipating a couple years of palm-fringed fun. More than 25 years later, she's still enamored of Florida's sun-drenched charms.

Jennie Hess is a travel and feature writer based in Orlando. Formerly a publicist for Walt Disney World Resort, Jennie still enjoys exploring the kingdom and gathering theme-park details faster than Pooh can sniff out honey. She gets us the scoop on Disney, plus insights gleaned from her family.

Snowbird Susan MacCallum-Whitcomb spends as much time as possible in the Sunshine State. Little wonder: winters in her Nova Scotian hometown can be *looong.* Having already worked on Fodor's Bermuda, Boston and Budapest guides, she jumped at the chance to update the front matter for *Florida 2008.*

Alicia Mandigo, our Walt Disney World shopping updater, is a freelance broadcast journalist and writer. Though technically a transplant, she considers herself a Central Florida native. Alicia worked at Epcot while she was in college, and she still considers it the best job she's ever had.

Gary McKechnie, who reported on the Panhandle and parts of Orlando, knows *a lot* about his native Florida having worked as a Walt Disney World ferryboat pilot, Jungle Cruise skipper, steam-train conductor, and double-decker bus driver. He is author of *Great American Motorcycle Tours.*

Kristin Milavec is a former Fodor's editor who has traveled extensively but calls Sarasota home. She has also managed the production of several art-history books and a Pulitzer prize–winning war story covering Srebrenica, Bosnia. Kristin updated our Essentials chapter.

A Yankee by birth, Northeast writer Kerry Speckman moved to Jacksonville in the early 1980s and has been basking in the sun and Southern hospitality ever since. She's a contributing writer for *Jacksonville* magazine and freelance travel writer.

Orlando restaurant, hotel, and sports updater Rowland Stiteler has served as editor and dining critic of *Orlando* and *Central Florida* magazines. During the past 10 years he's researched more than 500 Florida hotels and restaurants for travel publications and the resort industry.

For 12 years, Palm Beach/Treasure Coast writer Mary Thurwachter has written about Florida travel, including *The Palm Beach Post's* popular Bed, Breakfast & Beyond and INNside Scoop features. She's cased all sorts of Florida joints, from the Panhandle to the Keys.

Homegrown Floridians Jim and Cynthia Tunstall grew up in the Tampa Bay area and have spent much of their lives tasting the state's treasures. Today, they live with their flock of critters in a radar blip called Lecanto. They added their very personal touch to our Tampa/St. Petersburg chapter.

From her home of more than 25 years on Sanibel Island, Everglades and Lower Gulf Coast writer Chelle Koster Walton has written and contributed to 10 guidebooks—two of which won Lowell Thomas Awards—and written articles for *USA Today, National Geographic Traveler,* and other print and electronic media.